THE OXFORD HANDBOOK OF

AMERICAN ELECTIONS AND POLITICAL BEHAVIOR

THE
OXFORD
HANDBOOKS
OF
AMERICAN
POLITICS

GENERAL EDITOR: GEORGE C. EDWARDS III

The Oxford Handbooks of American Politics is a set of reference books offering authoritative and engaging critical overviews of the state of scholarship on American politics.

Each volume focuses on a particular aspect of the field. The project is under the General Editorship of George C. Edwards III, and distinguished specialists in their respective fields edit each volume. The *Handbooks* aim not just to report on the discipline, but also to shape it as scholars critically assess the current state of scholarship on a topic and propose directions in which it needs to move. The series is an indispensable reference for anyone working in American politics.

THE OXFORD HANDBOOK OF

AMERICAN ELECTIONS AND POLITICAL BEHAVIOR

Edited by

JAN E. LEIGHLEY

OXFORD

UNIVERSITY PRESS

OXFORD

UNIVERSITY PRESS

Great Clarendon Street, Oxford OX2 6DP
United Kingdom

Oxford University Press is a department of the University of Oxford.
It furthers the University's objective of excellence in research, scholarship,
and education by publishing worldwide. Oxford is a registered trade mark of
Oxford University Press in the UK and in certain other countries

British Library Cataloguing in Publication Data
Data available

Library of Congress Cataloging in Publication Data
Data available

ISBN 978-0-19-960451-7

Contents

PART IV VOTE CHOICE

PART V INTERESTS, SELF- AND OTHERWISE

PART VI ELECTIONS OTHER THAN PRESIDENTIAL

PART VII ELITES AND INSTITUTIONS

PART VIII REFLECTIONS

LIST OF FIGURES

List of Tables

Abbreviations

ANES	American National Election Studies
CPS	Current Population Surveys
DRE	Direct recording electronic voting equipment
EDR	Election day registration
FEC	Federal Election Commission
FTF	Face-to-face
GDP	Gross domestic product
IEM	Iowa Electronic Markets
NES	National Election Studies
NHIS	National Health Interview Survey
NSF	National Science Foundation
NVRA	National Voting Rights Act
PAC	Political action committee
RDD	Random-digit dialing
RDS	Respondent-driven sampling
SES	Socioeconomic Status
VRA	Voting Rights Act

About the Contributors

Paul R. Abramson, Professor of Political Science at Michigan State University.

T. K. Ahn, Associate Professor, Department of Public Administration, Korea University.

John H. Aldrich, Pfizer–Pratt University Professor of Political Science at Duke University.

R. Michael Alvarez, Professor of Political Science, California Institute of Technology.

Maria Armoudian, Commissioner on the Environment at the City of Los Angeles Environmental Affairs Commission.

Lonna Rae Atkeson, Professor and Regents' Lecturer, University of New Mexico, Department of Political Science.

Larry M. Bartels, Donald E. Stokes Professor of Public and International Affairs and Director of the Center for the Study of Democratic Politics at Princeton University.

Shaun Bowler, Professor of Political Science, UC Riverside.

Robert D. Brown, Professor, Department of Political Science, University of Mississippi.

Thomas L. Brunell, Professor of Political Science at the University of Texas, Dallas.

Barry C. Burden, Professor of Political Science, University of Wisconsin-Madison.

Matthew K. Buttice, Ph.D. candidate in the Political Science Department at the University of California, Davis.

Ann N. Crigler, Professor of Political Science, University of Southern California.

Tiffany C. Davenport, doctoral student in Political Science at Yale University.

Todd Donovan, Professor of Political Science, Western Washington University.

Mark N. Franklin, Stein Rokkan Professor of Comparative Politics, European University Institute, Florence; Reitemeyer Professor Emeritus of International Politics, Trinity College Connecticut.

Peter L. Francia, Associate Professor of Political Science, East Carolina University.

Kim L. Fridkin, Professor of Political Science, School of Politics and Global Studies, Arizona State University.

John A. Garcia, Professor in the School of Government and Public Policy at the University of Arizona.

Alan S. Gerber, Charles C. and Dorathea S. Dilley Professor of Political Science at Yale University.

Daniel Gillion, Assistant Professor of Political Science, University of Pennsylvania.

Kenneth M. Goldstein, Professor of Political Science, University of Wisconsin-Madison.

John C. Green, Distinguished Professor of Political Science and Director of the Bliss Institute at the University of Akron, Ohio.

Donald P. Green, A. Whitney Griswold Professor of Political Science at Yale University.

John D. Griffin, Associate Professor in the Department of Political Science at the University of Notre Dame.

Bernard Grofman, Jack W. Peltason Endowed Chair of Political Science, University of California, Irvine.

Thad E. Hall, Associate Professor of Political Science, University of Utah.

Fredrick Harris, Professor of Political Science and Director of the Center on African-American Politics and Society at Columbia University.

Kim Quaile Hill, Cullen-McFadden Professor of Political Science, Texas A&M University.

D. Sunshine Hillygus, Associate Professor of Political Science, Duke University.

Thomas Holbrook, Wilder Crane Professor of Government, Department of Political Science, University of Wisconsin-Milwaukee.

Matthew Holleque, Graduate Student in Political Science at the University of Wisconsin-Madison.

Robert Huckfeldt, Distinguished Professor of Political Science University of California, Davis.

Patricia A. Hurley, Professor of Political Science and Associate Dean of Liberal Arts, Texas A&M University.

William G. Jacoby, Professor, Department of Political Science, Michigan State University and Director, ICPSR Summer Program in Quantitative Methods of Social Research, University of Michigan.

Jane Junn, Professor of Political Science, University of Southern California.

Patrick J. Kenney, Professor of Political Science, Director School of Politics and Global Studies, Arizona State University.

Jon A. Krosnick, Frederic O. Glover Professor in Humanities and Social Sciences and Professor of Communication, Political Science, and Psychology, Stanford University.

Laura Langer, Associate Professor, School of Government and Public Policy, University of Arizona.

Meghan Leonard, Ph.D. candidate, School of Government and Public Policy, University of Arizona.

Jan E. Leighley, Professor of Political Science at the University of Arizona.

Suzanna Linn, Professor of Political Science at Pennsylvania State University.

Arthur Lupia, Hal R. Varian Collegiate Professor of Political Science and Research Professor, Institute for Social Research, University of Michigan.

Melissa J. Marschall, Associate Professor, Department of Political Science, Rice University.

Michael D. Martinez, Professor of Political Science, University of Florida.

Alexander K. Mayer, Ph.D. candidate in Political Science at the University of California, Davis.

Michael P. McDonald, Associate Professor, George Mason University.

Marco A. Morales, Ph.D. candidate, Wilf Family Department of Politics, New York University.

Karen Mossberger, Professor, Department of Public Administration, University of Illinois at Chicago.

Jonathan Nagler, Professor of Politics, Wilf Family Department of Politics, New York University.

Barbara Norrander, Professor, School of Government and Public Policy, University of Arizona.

Josh Pasek, Ph.D. candidate, Department of Communication, Stanford University.

Andrea Polk, Ph.D. candidate, School of Government and Public Policy, University of Arizona.

Lynda W. Powell, Professor of Political Science, University of Rochester.

David W. Rohde, Ernestine Friedl Professor of Political Science and Director of the Political Institutions and Public Choice Program at Duke University.

John B. Ryan, Assistant Professor, Florida State University, Department of Political Science.

Kira Sanbonmatsu, Associate Professor of Political Science and Senior Scholar at the Center for American Women and Politics, Eagleton Institute of Politics, Rutgers University.

Robert M. Stein, Lena Gohlman Fox Professor of Political Science, Rice University.

Walter J. Stone, Professor in the Political Science Department at the University of California, Davis.

Caroline J. Tolbert, Professor, Department of Political Science, University of Iowa.

Greg Vonnahme, Assistant Professor, Department of Political Science, University of Alabama.

Till Weber, Ph.D. Researcher, European University Institute, Florence.

Amber Wichowsky, Ph.D. candidate in Political Science, University of Wisconsin-Madison.

Clyde Wilcox, Professor of Government, Georgetown University.

PART I

INTRODUCTION

CHAPTER 1

....

INTRODUCTION

....

JAN E. LEIGHLEY

THE study of American elections and political behavior has been at the core of our understanding of the vitality (or frailty) of American democracy for decades. Prior to the use of nationally representative public opinion surveys in the late 1940s and 1950s, a handful of scholars relied primarily on aggregate-level analyses, quasi-experimental designs, and intensive case studies to assess what and how citizens thought about politics, made political choices, and otherwise engaged in the rituals and mechanisms of American politics. Most of what we knew about electoral behavior indicated that the electoral foundations of our democracy were alive and well, functioning as expected in many respects.

Fifty years later, scholars have significantly expanded the theoretical approaches and analytical tools used to study American elections and political behavior. Importantly, these innovations have not only been used to revisit old questions, but have also led to addressing new ones. This accumulated knowledge is the focus of this volume.

My hope for the *Handbook* was to offer a set of thoughtful essays assessing the intellectual developments and challenges in the field of American elections and political behavior. Beyond those broad overviews, I also hoped for incisive commentary and creative proposals of the scholarly work that lies ahead, identifying those questions—new and old—that merit our attention. I believe that the scholars who accepted this charge have handsomely met these expectations. As you read these chapters, their arguments, analyses, and proposed research agendas should engage you to think more fully, and perhaps differently, about the study of American elections and political behavior.

ORGANIZATION

The chapters that follow are intended to cover a wide range of original research on American elections and political behavior. Rather than thinking of them as a comprehensive set of topics, however, one should think of them as broadly representative of the past several decades in the study of electoral behavior. There are undoubtedly missed opportunities here, the result of limited pages, time constraints, and necessary choices about what represents the key issues in studying American elections and political behavior.

The organization of the volume, as well as the particular chapter topics, were guided by two observations. First, that the study of American elections and political behavior, though diverse, nonetheless reflects both the advances and challenges of seeking to understand the political world through empirical scientific approaches. Since the 1950s, we have accumulated a huge body of literature, one that has both expanded and deepened our knowledge, but also one that has exposed new, unanswered questions. This is the nature of scientific inquiry, however, and the topics addressed in this volume represent—individually and in combination—the key intellectual contours of these scientific developments.

Second, independent of these scholarly approaches, the realities of American elections and political behavior have changed over the past fifty years. Many ballots are now cast prior to election day and new types of elections and voting technology have potentially challenged the very meaning of campaigns and voting. We have an increasingly diverse and mobile electorate, as well as a growing set of technology-based channels for citizens and elected officials to use in communicating with each other. Assessing the field would thus be incomplete if we did not consider the extent to which we have, intellectually speaking, "kept up" with these "real world" changes. Documenting these changes in election practices and political behaviors and understanding their consequences are also especially important for policymakers and practitioners. To the extent that we fully address these issues, our research becomes more relevant.

Reflecting the scientific nature of our work, then, the volume begins with a section on issues in research design, primarily highlighting the varied approaches that mark the field today. Chapters focusing on the perennial issue of question-wording and survey design, and the challenges of new technologies for survey research design, remind us that even our standard approaches need to be constantly evaluated and improved. Other chapters focus on laboratory and field experiments, along with formal modeling. As many of these authors note, unlike decades past, the variety of methods with which scholars are working today allow us to make stronger inferences about the causal relationships we are typically most interested in.

Following this section, the volume shifts to the more "substantive" topics of political participation, vote choice, and interests in American electoral politics, addressing the key questions that have occupied scholars of American political behavior over the past several decades. Who participates? In what ways? How do citizens decide who to vote for? What issues, interests, and identities matter—and under what circumstances? What influence do campaigns have on citizens' choices? These chapters convey much of the central core of our scholarship on American elections, and are key to understanding electoral behavior, both past and present.

However, most of these studies focus almost exclusively on behavior and choice in presidential elections. And so Part VI of the volume highlights non-presidential elections. As many of these authors argue, looking beyond presidential elections provides scholars the opportunity to assess the extent to which different institutional and political contexts influence citizens' political behavior, but also the extent to which the findings of studies focusing exclusively on presidential elections can be generalized beyond those particular elections. Importantly, this change of venue also requires asking some new, and very interesting, questions.

The next section, "Elites and Institutions," is perhaps the most striking example of how we as a field have moved our scientific knowledge forward over the past several decades. Over the last two decades the theoretical import of elites and institutions to understanding electoral behavior has increased dramatically. The general argument is that we cannot understand the behavior of the mass public fully without incorporating the actions, resources, and strategies of political elites such as candidates, elected officials, groups or parties. (Doing so from a comparative perspective—getting outside the American "box"—is yet another way of doing so.) Authors of chapters in this section provide strong and persuasive evidence that electoral behavior in any form reflects the incentives and capabilities of citizen and elites alike.

The volume concludes with three chapters that provide overviews and critical analyses of the study of individuals, elections, and representation. Though these three concluding chapters are somewhat varied in their approaches, they each nonetheless underscore the centrality of American elections to American democracy: to the extent that elections allow the interests and preferences of individuals to be clearly conveyed to candidates competing for office, we are one step closer to the democratic ideal that those who are in positions of power will exercise it on behalf of those they represent.

And that is really why we care, is it not? We study American elections and political behavior because we know they matter for the nature of democracy and representation. Decades ago, the adoption of more systematic, scientific modes of research, along with a greater reliance on quantitative methods, led some to argue that this intellectual shift would lead scholars to focus on irrelevant and unimportant questions. I would argue that the essays in this volume elegantly refutes this claim. Instead, our increasing methodological sophistication, motivated by broader theoretical concerns, has collectively spoken clearly and loudly to fundamental issues of representation and democracy. Certainly there is more to be done. But what we know now on these important matters is in stunning contrast to what we knew several decades ago. I hope that reading these chapters will convince you on this point as well.

PART II

RESEARCH DESIGN

THE STATE OF SURVEY RESEARCH AS A RESEARCH TOOL IN AMERICAN POLITICS

LONNA RAE ATKESON

SURVEY research is one of the most common types of quantitative research methodologies in the social sciences. It is a straightforward primary data collection technique that usually involves the selection of a sample of respondents from a population of interest and solicits their responses to standardized questionnaires. It dates back to the 1930s (Elinson 1992) and was primarily conducted through the mail or personal visits to households. However, the administering of the survey instrument can come in multiple formats or modes and over the past eighty years the number of modes available has increased. The expansion of survey modes and the use of mixed-mode surveys, especially over the last decade, is, in part, due to the prohibitive costs associated with face-to-face (FTF) interviewing, the introduction of new technology (the web, Interactive Voice Response (IVR), the Personal computer, fax machines, cell phones, etc.), and the interaction of technology with population demographics. These changes, along with rapidly declining response rates and new theoretical interpretations of the survey environment, have created a critical moment in the field of survey research. The field is exploding with new opportunities for theory advancement and methodological innovation.

Methodologically survey research has offered a rich source of data for scholars, journalists, market-researchers, government agencies, and others to understand the preferences, opinions, and motivations of the American electorate. Prior to the Second World War and the behavioral revolution in political science, survey research was primarily the purview of marketing firms (Gallup, Roper, and Crossley). But a heavy reliance on self-administered surveys in the Second World War, especially the *Studies in Social Psychology in World War II: The American Soldier* (Stouffer et al. 1949), which lent its name to the later *American Voter* (Campbell et al. 1960), led to it becoming a primary research technique within the discipline.

OVERVIEW AND APPLICATION

Today, it is a widely used tool to study many different kinds of questions in political science and across many subfields. However, for the study of voting, public opinion, and more broadly political participation and engagement, the survey research methodology is the dominant methodology applied to answer primary questions about individual-level political behavior. These questions include voter decision-making, political participation, political change, the influence of campaigns and major events in shaping public opinion, individual political knowledge, comprehension of the political world, and the importance of social context and social dynamics in influencing public opinion and political participation. Fundamental to these questions are normative issues about the functioning of democracy, how political elites respond to and are influenced by elections and public opinion, and issues of representation. Without survey research methods it would be nearly impossible to understand the public and its role and value in democratic governing (although see Ginsberg 1986 and Herbst 1993).

Survey research is, therefore, important because it offers a systematic way to examine fundamental questions about society and democracy by connecting the citizen to government. In a recent article, Brady (2000, 48) convincingly argues that survey research is a particularly powerful empirical method because of its range of applicability, linkage to theory, conceptual richness, capacity for confirming theories about politics, and policy relevance.

For example, the American National Election Studies (ANES), planned around presidential and midterm elections since 1952, has provided cross-sectional, panel, and time series data for over sixty years. For some theoretical questions simple cross-sections suffice, but for others, particularly when issues of causality are difficult, short-term panels over the campaign period or longer-term panels in which the same respondents are interviewed repeatedly are necessary. The ANES database provides rich descriptive and comparative data in a single election context and over time yielding a variety of ways to test theories and learn about the social world.

Although the method of survey research often relies on correlational studies to evaluate theories, other methods are also used. Propensity matching is one such innovative new tool potentially available to survey researchers to determine causality. Panel data also allows for the use of quasi-experimental designs (Campbell and Stanley 1963) to determine how attitudes or behaviors change after an event or crisis. Researchers also have added rich contextual data, such as candidate advertising data, candidate expenditures, congressional voting records, or GIS data, to survey respondents to gain variance across different electoral contexts.

Another innovative tool is the use of experiments embedded in surveys. Survey experiments allow researchers to randomly distribute respondents to treatment and control conditions, thus manipulating the survey environment to determine how various stimuli alter the decision-making process. By comparing respondents from the control and treatment conditions the researcher can determine the causal relationship under question. Researchers often "frame" a particular characteristic or thought to determine whether it influences an attitude, opinion, or behavior. For example, in experiments on the role of gender and race in influencing voter choice in low information contests, McDermott (1998) uses hypothetical male, female, and black candidates to examine her question. Other scholars focus on attitudes, but the underlying method is the same: alter the survey content for some respondents relative to others and compare their opinions (Hurwitz and Peffley 1997; Sniderman and Piazza 1993). For example, Sniderman and Piazza (1993) examine how priming white respondents to think about affirmative action influences their attitudes about blacks.

Although these studies have shown some impressive effects from framing of survey questions, it is unclear whether framing experiments have long lasting effects on people's core attitudes (Druckman and Nelson 2003; Gaines, Kuklinski, and Quirk 2007; Luskin, Fishkin, and Jowell 2002). Nevertheless, the strengths of these designs in determining causal mechanisms and in internal validity are extremely valuable and political behavior studies will continue to be strengthened by future advancements in survey experimental methodology.

The Changing Nature of Survey Research

Twenty-five years ago, survey research had achieved a broad consensus on technique and methodology. Perfected sampling techniques for both FTF and telephone surveys allowed a small subset of respondents to represent large populations. Although FTF interviews seemed best suited to very long surveys, and to governmental surveys, where very high response rates were expected, telephone surveys were, because of higher costs and efficiency, by far the most commonly used interview technique.

As the new millennium approached, survey response rates began to rapidly decline across all formats due, in part, to significant changes in technology (De Leeuw and De Heer 2002). For example, Curtin, Presser, and Singer (2005) examined how response rates changed over two periods using the University of Michigan's Survey of Consumer Attitudes and Behavior, which has been administered monthly using RDD designs beginning in 1978. From 1979 to 1996 they showed a steady .75 percent drop in response rate annually. But, with the advent of caller-ID, the response rate has plummeted to 1.5 percent annually since 1996. The overall change was from 72 percent to 48 percent over the entire period.

Rapid changes in communication have created a problem for survey researchers because they present serious challenges to the previous paradigm. For example, the advent and growth in popularity of the cell phone and VOIP (voice over internet) has led to larger numbers of people terminating their traditional landlines. The most recent report by the National Health Interview Survey (NHIS) suggests that nearly 17.5 percent of US households or 36 million adults no longer have landline telephones and, instead, rely on cell phones (Blumberg and Luke 2008). When less than 5 percent of the US population did not have landlines, coverage error resulting from their automatic exclusion was insignificant. But now, with one in six adults without landlines and that number growing significantly every six months, the problem is far greater. And, we know that cell-phone-only households are not equally represented throughout the population, ensuring a biased sample. Younger adults, Southerners, non-whites, renters, and poorer adults were much more likely than older adults, non-Southerners, whites, homeowners, and wealthier adults to live in cell-phone-only homes (Blumberg and Luke 2008).

Given survey researchers' huge reliance on and comfort with RDD designs, these changes in telephone use along with increases in refusal rates are highly problematic. Coverage issues lead to potential problems of inference as potential respondents are often not contacted because they are not available using traditional methodologies or once contacted they refuse, also frustrating researchers. These non-respondents are a serious concern to the survey research community, and especially to scholars who want to understand, explain, and predict political events, as many academic studies rely on RDD designs to address their questions. The primary method for solving problems between survey samples and populations of interest is to weight the survey across several demographic dimensions, especially sex, age, and race. This, however, is not necessarily a panacea because the method assumes that those respondents who are in the sample are representative of the larger underrepresented population, which may not be a valid assumption.

The conventional wisdom, of course, is that response rates *per se* are a signal of the quality of the survey and its representativeness. Under this view, low response rates lead to non-response bias, which leads to problems of representation and inference. Low response rates make many academics skeptical.

Non-response error is a valid concern. Significant differences between respondents and non-respondents on a sample statistic like the mean can lead to problems in survey inference. Intuitively it seems obvious, and conventional wisdom assumes, that non-response error is a function of response rate. This is based on the theoretical notion that non-respondents differ from respondents in systematic ways (Groves and Couper 1998) and that those from whom we never get responses should resemble those from whom it is difficult to get responses. Therefore, as the response rate increases a more diverse group of respondents, who are more similar to the perpetual non-responders, are included in the survey, enhancing the sample's representativeness. However, non-response error is not necessarily a function of the response rate, but is a function of the response rate interacting with the characteristics of the non-respondent (Curtin, Presser, and Singer 2000). Thus, if survey topic salience, for example, leads to differences in response patterns then non-response error becomes a problem (Groves, Singer, and Corning 2000). But when does response rate become an issue, if at all? Does a 50 percent response rate suggest a better quality survey then one at 30 percent or 15 percent? If so, what should that threshold be?

Response rates, however, appear not to be the core of the problem. Evidence is increasingly being presented suggesting that response rate is not a good measure of representativeness (Atkeson et al. 2008; Curtin, Presser, and Singer 2000; Groves and Peytcheva 2008; Groves, Presser, and Dipko 2004; Keeter et al. 2000; Merkle and Edelman 2002; Pew Research Center for the People and the Press 2004). In several studies now, tests of representativeness have showed little difference between high and low response rates. For example, Keeter et al. (2000), using identical questionnaires and the same survey firm, paid for two RDD studies. The first study was a typical academic study, taking eight weeks and allowing for extended callbacks and attempts to locate individuals in the sample. The second study used a more standard commercial approach of five days. The first study yielded a response rate of 60.6 percent, the second 36 percent. Analysis showed there were few differences across survey items: only fourteen out of ninety-one questions were statistically different. Half of these were on demographic questions, raising an initial red flag, but further examination showed that the quick survey yielded a sample that was closer to Current Population Surveys (CPS) demographic characteristics than the longer and more academically rigorous one, suggesting that response rates had little effect on survey quality. Thus, the larger question for survey researchers is in understanding non-response bias more than response rates, and more theory and empirical tests in this area are needed.

In addition, the implications of these findings are of particular importance for research. Techniques used to increase response rates such as refusal conversion and repeated callbacks are extremely costly. If, instead, those resources were used to acquire more interviews, sampling error would decline, while non-response error (which is not necessarily affected by response rates) would not change. Such a resource allocation decision would also produce larger subgroups for analysis (the size of which is often a serious problem), which would be very useful to scholarly research.

ALTERNATIVES TO TRADITIONAL SURVEY RESEARCH MODES: THE GROWTH OF INTERNET AND MIXED-MODE SURVEYS, AND NON-PROBABILITY SAMPLES

Internet Surveys

At the same time that in-person interviewing costs were increasing, making FTF survey prohibitive, and demographic and technological changes were making telephone surveys questionable, the prevalence of PCs and the advance of the Internet created a new survey venue. Internet surveying offers a wide-range of possibilities to the researcher that alternative and more traditional methods of interviewing do not and at a small percentage of the price of those costlier methods. Specifically, the Internet is an interactive and complex media that allows the respondent to view video and audio material and react to that material in real time. It also allows for extended discussion groups, essentially virtual focus groups, from which to obtain qualitative data, which is already in electronic format and essentially ready for analysis.

Internet surveys offer a number of advantages to researchers. For example, similar to Computer Assisted Telephone Interviewing (CATI), Internet surveys offer extensive branching abilities and opportunities to do question validity tests using split halves. Data collection is often very quick in these settings and it is easy to determine when a reminder needs to be provided to non-respondents. Because people tend to begin the survey immediately when it hits their inbox, survey responses surge almost immediately upon receipt of the request and decline shortly thereafter, providing clear time frames for sending out a reminder to non-respondents (Atkeson and Tafoya 2008).

The advantage of a quick turnaround time of web surveys allows researchers to collect data during or immediately following an event. Programming web surveys has become very easy with many menu-driven programs (Opinio, Survey Monkey, PHP Surveyor, etc.) allowing each scholar to theoretically engage in survey research from their desktops. This format is particularly useful in capturing attitudes and emotions when they are being formed and in response to specific tragedies, crises, or important political moments in time. Data, of course, is already in electronic form from this method and as such offers a cost-effective and quick turnaround time from response to analysis. Response latency can also be monitored and recorded for future analysis, offering advantages for public opinion researchers who use response time as a key to understanding attitude information and intensity.

Internet surveys also offer other advantages, especially to the respondent. Like other self-administered surveys, Internet surveys provide greater flexibility to the respondent. Because the questionnaire is answered in the privacy of the respondent's home or office, it can be completed whenever the respondent wants and over an extended period of time. Software tools can allow respondents to "save" their data and "return" to the survey later. Reminders can also be sent to respondents, encouraging them to begin, or return to, the survey by simply clicking on a link embedded in an email or typing in a URL to a web browser.

Comparisons with other data collection modes also suggest additional strengths for Internet or Computer-Assisted Self-Interviewing (CASI). Previous research, for example, shows that computer interviewing resulted in fewer completion mistakes and fewer unanswered items, compared to paper-and-pencil respondents (Kiesler and Sproull 1986). Internet designs reduce socially desirable answers compared to interviewer-assisted designs (Chang and Krosnick 2003a, 2003b; Fricker et al. 2005). Other research on data quality across survey modes suggests that FTF research has less satisficing and fewer socially desirable responses[1] than telephone interviews and that telephone respondents are less cooperative and less interested than FTF respondents (Holbrook, Green, and Krosnick 2003). Taken together, the data suggest that in many ways FTF surveys provide the best data quality on a variety of dimensions, followed by the computer-assisted or Internet survey, followed by pencil-and-paper survey, which is followed by telephone surveys. More carefully constructed research designs, however, are needed to identify the strengths and weaknesses of each mode relative to one another and when modes can and cannot be combined.

---

[1] On these concepts, see Krosnick and Pasek, this volume, pp. 31–2.

Internet surveys also have drawbacks. Using a computer interface to capture interviews may create a bias in respondents. Literacy is key among them. Less literate respondents are less likely to have a computer and less likely to participate. In addition, respondents need familiarity or comfort with the tools required to participate including a computer, keyboard, a mouse, and how to navigate within the survey window browser (see Dillman 2002).

This leads to perhaps the most important drawback, which is sampling and weighting. Commercial firms participating in this new technology rely on different methods to create their samples. Some firms (e.g. Knowledge Networks) use traditional probability-based RDD sampling to recruit their respondents and then provide them with the hardware, if necessary, to be an ongoing respondent. One potential problem with this method is that the low response rates associated with telephone interviews are compounded by those who are reached, but then refuse to participate in the web panel. However, their very low response rates appear to produce demographically representative samples of US residents (Krosnick and Chang 2001). Other firms (e.g. Polimetrix) build a large list of volunteers from which to sample, producing non-probability samples.

Perhaps the strongest endorsement of probability based web survey as the technology of the future comes from the ANES, which decided to use this methodology for the ANES 2008–09 panel (in addition to the traditional FTF pre-post election panel). The research design is very ambitious, involving six ANES panel waves and fifteen "secondary" panel waves that do not include questions on politics, to reduce panel attrition. The sample is based on an RDD design for identifying respondents, but then respondents will actually answer surveys over the Internet.

Mixed-mode Designs

One way of dealing with the problems of representativeness of Internet samples is to utilize mixed-mode designs (Dillman 2002). Mixed-mode designs combine different modes of interviewing including phone, mail, Internet, and/or FTF to create a representative sample. Mixed-mode designs can also mix contact method with different survey modes. So, for example, a respondent may be contacted by phone and then sent a mail survey to complete. The basic idea in mixed-mode designs is that different modes of surveying reach different types of individuals and therefore provide many mode options for survey response to increase response rates and the overall representativeness and hence quality of the survey data. Although mixed-mode designs have become more popular outside of the United States (De Leeuw 2005), they are beginning to be used by the United States Government and by academics (Atkeson and Saunders

2007; Rosen and Gomes 2004). The increasing costs of survey research and the declining response rates make mixed-mode surveys attractive across both dimensions because these surveys tend to reduce costs and produce higher response rates.

It is unclear what the potential pitfalls are of a mixed-mode design because little data has been collected to assess their strengths and weaknesses. One primary concern is that different modes might lead to different response patterns, leading to serious questions about data quality and its comparability. This is true even when the question wording is identical for both cross-sectional designs and panel design. In the first case, the question is: do respondents who answer the same questions across different survey modes result in the same distribution of responses? In the second case, the question is: can questions be compared across the same respondent over time when the data were collected using different survey modes?

A series of academic articles suggest that mode of response may influence data quality (de Leeuw and Van Der Zowen 1988; Dillman et al. 1996; Fowler, Roman, and Di 1998). If we imagine that the survey process is similar to a conversation (Schwarz 1996), then the context provided by the survey, either through the interviewer or through the presentation of questions and answer scales, may affect question interpretation and response. If such is the case, then it may be problematic to combine different modes into one variable to obtain an aggregate representation of the cross-section or panel. Indeed, when mode changes over time it could make changes seen in panel data unreliable and therefore make inferences from the data impossible. One example where this is a problem is in the 2000 ANES (Bowers and Ensley 2003), in which respondents were interviewed in person, over the phone, or a combination of both.

Other possibilities for problems associated with survey mode may be due to social desirability, question order, interviewer presence or absence, primacy or recency effects, or the visual layout of questions (Christian and Dillman 2004; Fowler, Roman, and Di 1998; Schuman 1992; Schuman and Presser 1981; Smyth et al. 2006; Sudman, Bradburn, and Schwarz 1996; Tourangeau, Couper, and Conrad 2004). Social desirability, for example, suggests that one cue for survey response is the perceived expectations of those around the respondent during the interview, especially the telephone or FTF survey where an interviewer is involved in the survey conversation. In these cases, the pressure of the interviewing situation leads respondents to answer questions in socially desirable ways. For example, this potential problem is seen consistently in ANES studies where large numbers of respondents indicate they voted, when in fact they did not (Abelson, Loftus, and Greenwald 1992; Silver, Anderson, and Abramson 1986; Traugott and Katosh 1979). But the fact that respondents have spent literally multiple hours with an interviewer in their own home over more than one occasion and talking almost exclusively about politics leads respondents to give the socially desirable response (Presser 1990). Similarly, research on over reporting for the winner suggests the same problem (Atkeson 1999; Wright 1990, 1993).

Given these cross-mode concerns, paying attention to these mode effects is important to researchers' analysis and conclusions. This suggests an important line of future research, which explores the limits of mixed-mode designs. For example, given the similarities in survey environment, mail and Internet mixed-mode design may allow for combining responses, but combining Internet and phone survey data may be more problematic given the significant differences in survey format.

Non-probability Samples

Non-probability Internet Samples

The difficulties involved in traditional survey design and sampling are well known. Chief among them are the skyrocketing costs associated with contacting difficult-to-reach respondents, and for RDD designs the changing nature of the population that researchers have access to through this method. Because of the difficulties and the new opportunities provided by new communication technologies many scholars and researchers are considering the value of non-probability samples in their research. Because many of these are Internet samples, they have many desirable strengths, as discussed above, but they are also fundamentally different because they do not purport to come from a random sample of the population of interest. Instead, they are volunteer samples. Self-selection potentially creates problems for surveys because of response error. Simply put, self-selected individuals are not necessarily going to look like the potential electorate or other populations of interest.

The methods used to recruit respondents vary across firms, but, in general, commercial firms create large access panels of potential respondents. Panel members are recruited through Internet advertisements, the purchase of electronic mailing lists, recommendations by friends, phone surveys, mail surveys, etc (Barrens et al. 2003). Samples are then generated from panel members, based upon population characteristics, and contacted for survey participation. Periodic tests of sample adequacy use parallel FTF surveys and phone surveys to estimate propensity scores for participation mode (Terhanian 2008). Weighting is applied after survey completion to make the sample representative of the population. For example, Harris interactive uses post stratification weights to adjust their sample to the population based upon the CPS. This method is also used for RDD designs and is common in Internet survey studies.

Many firms are engaging in this new methodology including YouGov (which owns a portion of Polimetrix), Harris Interactive, Zogby Interactive, and others. For political scientists, the firm Polimetrix, founded by political scientist Douglas

Rivers, is an important emerging player in this new methodology. In 2006 and 2008, Polimetrix sponsored various Cooperative Election Studies (CES) in which university teams opt in to the Polimetrix pre- and post-election surveys for a $15,000 fee (Vavreck and Rivers 2008). Each team receives data from 1,000 respondents who were asked common content questions and unique content questions provided by the university team. The Polimetrix policy is to embargo the data for one year before it is made available to the larger research community.

Polimetrix uses a unique mechanism called sample matching for sample selection and weighting (Vavreck and Rivers 2008). Sample matching begins by creating a sampling frame that is stratified across a variety of dimensions such as race, age, gender, region, and party registration and then a sample is drawn. But, of course, these individuals are not reachable because Polimetrix has no personal information about these respondents to contact them. Instead these individuals are matched with members of their access panel who are then invited to participate in the survey. Weight adjustments for non-response can then be made after the fact.

There is a vigorous debate about these non-probability sampling methodologies and whether they, in the end, can be used to make inferences about populations or are primarily an experimental tool. Non-probability samples have always been used in experimental studies where internal validity is maximized at the expense of external validity and have gained acceptance in political science as a viable and useful method (see Sears 1986). But, today, researchers want to consider the viability of non-probability samples in making inferences to populations. On the one hand, Douglas Rivers argues that in essence traditional RDD designs are non-probability samples because so many people are impossible to contact and many respondents once contacted choose not to participate (Rivers n.d.). Thus, RDD designs may be equivalent to volunteer Internet sampling. On the other hand, there are those who feel uncomfortable for many reasons with a method that is not fundamentally based on probability sampling. They tend to argue that since response rates are not a good signal of survey quality, there is no theoretical reason to be disturbed by low response rates, but argue that selection bias in non-probability opt-in studies leads to samples that are distinct from respondents who would result from a probability-based design.

Typical of studies in their infancy, recent research suggests there may be cause for alarm or joy. In Malhortra and Krnosick's comparison (2007) of two ANES FTF probability samples with non-probability samples from YouGov and Harris Interactive, they found striking differences between survey modes. These results appear to be, in part, due to the opt-in sample members being overly interested in politics relative to sample members in the probability FTF design. Across sixteen points of comparison Malhorta and Krosnick (2007, 311) found that the FTF data collection method was more accurate 88 percent of the time. Sanders et al. (2007), however, in an examination of the 2005 British Election Study find just the reverse. They found that the British Election Study, which uses FTF interviewing, compared favorably to the YouGov study, which uses a sampling method similar to Harris Interactive. In Polimetrix's own analysis of their 2006 CCES Study, they found some similarities and some differences between their study and other national data sets (Hill et al. 2007). In particular, they found that their respondents were more knowledgeable about politics, stronger partisans, and have more item constraint than those respondents in face-to-face interviews, but demographically the Polimetrix bias seems very similar to the RDD sampling method.

Other Non-probability Samples: Snow Ball Sampling or Respondent-Driven Sampling

Recently, another additional sampling method has been characterized that offers new opportunities for survey research in political science. It is a variation on snowball sampling (Coleman 1958) referred to as respondent-driven sampling (RDS) (Heckathorn 1997, 2002). Recent advances in RDS allows this method to make inferences to the population of interest (Salganik and Heckathorn 2004). This method is appropriate when researchers do not have a sampling frame and the target population is considered rare and difficult to reach (Salganik and Heckathorn 2004). As a methodology in political behavior, this technique could be applied to the study of social movements, political activists, or perhaps other sub-populations that would be difficult to reach using traditional survey methods. For example, this methodology was used to survey American men in Canada who immigrated to avoid the Vietnam War draft (Hagan 2001). It may also be useful in studying populations of displaced persons such as Katrina victims or victims of civil war in other nations. Furthermore, RDS could use any survey mode, depending on what was best to reach the population of interest.

Previously, hard-to-find populations were often unreachable except by the use of snowball sampling, which relies on chain-referral sampling. Studies of social networks (see Huckfeldt and Kuklinski 1995; Mutz and Martin 2001) provide examples of scholarly work using this type of methodology to address political science questions. In these studies, the researcher relies on the social network of existing members of the sample, instead of a sampling frame. Although these methods do an excellent job of reaching hidden populations, they are also problematic. The primary problem is that when they are used to reach hidden populations, as opposed to studies of the influence of social networks, it becomes difficult, if not impossible, to make inferences beyond the sample to the population of interest (Eland-Goosensen et al. 1997; Erickson 1979, Kalton and Anderson 1986; Welch 1975). This is true because all members of the population do not have the same probability of selection, making the sample a non-probability or convenience sample.

New advances in this methodology, however, make it possible for chain-referral samples to produce unbiased estimates about hidden populations (though see Wejnert and Heckathorn 2008 and Lee 2009). Though this new methodology has not been applied in political science, it has been successfully used in sociology (Hagan 2001; Heckathorn and Jeffries 2001) and public health research (Magnani et al. 2005; Semann, Lauby, and Liebman 2002). The basic premise behind RDS is not to estimate directly to the population as in a traditional sample, but indirectly by making estimates about the social network first and then from the social networks making estimates about the population (Salganik and Heckathorn 2004).

To obtain comprehensive coverage of the target population, so that each individual has a non-zero chance of being selected, it is necessary to have between four and seven waves of referrals. This is based on the principle of "six degrees of separation" (Dodds, Muhamad, and Watts 2003; Travers and Milgram 1969; Watts and Strogatz 1998), which indicates that the distance between individuals is on average quite short. Heckathorn (1997, 2002) has shown that this property of networks means that as the sample expands from wave to wave it eventually reaches equilibrium, such that the demographic characteristics such as age, race, and gender resemble the underlying population of interest. This prevents the bias of homophily (that respondent referrals are similar to the referrers). The sample is then weighted by network relationships (Heckathorn 2006) and provides unbiased population estimates (Salganik and Heckathorn 2004).

THE FUTURE OF SURVEY RESEARCH

Survey research will continue to be a valuable source of data for scholars in political science. The survey environment, however, is rapidly changing, providing new, alternative, and sometimes cheaper methods to obtain the necessary data to test and advance our theories. It has also created new opportunities for methodological advancement in the field of survey research and therefore many new questions in the field of survey methodology to ask and answer. It is important for the academic community, especially political scientists, to play an important role in its growth and development. Therefore, it is important for the academic community to carefully consider the different survey methods used and their strengths and weaknesses. For example, different designs may offer different strengths for certain populations or questions over others. Therefore, as academics and/or practitioners, we need to be careful as we adapt and adopt these new survey opportunities. We need to think theoretically about what survey design (traditional, mixed-mode, non-probability, RDS) offers the most advantages in terms of our population of interest and question, and how the choices we make influence the answers we get and the inferences we make. Although we need to have a very critical eye—the academy by nature is very conservative—we also need to be open to change and opportunity in this dynamic and rapidly evolving research methodology.

REFERENCES

ABELSON, R. P., LOFTUS, E. F., and GREENWALD, A. G. 1992. Attempts to Improve the Accuracy of Self-Reports of Voting. In *Questions about Questions*, ed. J. M. Tanur. New York: Russell Sage Foundation.

ATKESON, L. R. 1999. "Sure, I voted for the Winner!" Over Report of the Primary Vote for the Party Nominee in the American National Election Studies. *Political Behavior*, 21/3: 197–215.

—— and SAUNDERS, K. L. 2007. Voter Confidence: A Local Matter? *PS: Political Science & Politics*, 40: 655–60.

—— and TAFOYA, L. 2008. Surveying Political Activists: An Examination of the Effectiveness of a Mixed Mode Survey Design. *Journal of Elections, Public Opinion and Parties*, 18/4: 367–86.

—— BRYANT, L. A., ZILBERMAN, L., ADAMS, A. N., and SAUNDERS, K. L. 2008. Data Quality in Mixed Mode (Internet and Mail) General Elesction Surveys. Unpublished manuscript, University of New Mexico.

BARRENS, R. B., BOHARA, A. K., JENKINS-SMITH, H., SILVA, C., and WEIMER, D. L. 2003. The Advent of Internet Surveys for Political Research: A Comparison of Telephone and Internet Samples. *Political Analysis*, 11/1: 1–11.

BLUMBERG, S. J. and LUKE, J. V. 2008. Wireless Substitution: Early Release of Estimates From the National Health Interview Survey, July-December 2007. <http://www.cdc.gov/nchs/data/nhis/earlyrelease/wireless200812.htm>.

BOWERS, J. and ENSLEY, M. J. 2003. Issues in Analyzing Data from the Dual-Mode 2000 American National Election Study. NES Technical Report Series (Document nes010751), available at <http://www.electionstudies.org/resources/papers/technical_reports.htm>.

BRADY, H. E. 2000. Contributions of Survey Research to Political Science. *PS: Political Science and Politics* 33 (1): 47–57.

CAMPBELL, A., CONVERSE, P., MILLER, W., and STOKES, D. 1960. *The American Voter*. Chicago: The University of Chicago Press.

CAMPBELL, D. T. and STANLEY, J. C. 1963. *Experimental and Quasi-Experimental Designs for Research*. Boston: Houghton Miffin.

CHANG, L.-C. and KROSNICK, J. A. 2003a. RDD Telephone vs. Internet Survey Methodology: Comparing Sample Representativeness and Response Quality. Unpublished manuscript, under review.

—— —— 2003b. Comparing Oral Interviewing with Self-Administered Computerized Questionnaires: An Experiment. Unpublished manuscript, Ohio State University.

CHRISTIAN, L. and DILLMAN, D. 2004. The Influence of Graphical and Symbolic Language Manipulations on Responses to Self-Administered Questions. *Public Opinion Quarterly*, 68/1: 57–80.

COLEMAN, J. S. 1958. Relational Analysis: The Study of Social Organization with Survey Methods. *Human Organization*, 17: 28–36.

CURTIN, R., PRESSER, S., and SINGER, E. 2000. The Effects of Response Rate Changes on the Index of Consumer Sentiment. *Public Opinion Quarterly*, 64: 413–28.

—— —— —— 2005. Changes in Telephone Survey Nonresponse Over the Past Quarter Century. *Public Opinion Quarterly*, 69: 87–98.

DE LEEUW, E. 2005. To Mix or Not to Mix: Data Collection Modes in Surveys. *Journal of Official Statistics*, 21: 233–55.

—— and DE HEER, W. 2002. Trends in Household Survey Nonresponse: A Longitudinal and International Comparison. In *Survey Nonresponse* ed. R. M. Groves, D. A. Dillman, J. L. Eltinge, and R. J. A. Little. New York: John Wiley & Sons Inc.

—— and VAN DER ZOUWEN, J. 1988. Data Quality in Telephone and Face to Face Surveys: A Comparative Meta-Analysis. In *Telephone Survey Methodology*, ed. R. Groves, P. P. Bimer, L. Lyberg, I. T. Massey, W. L. Nicholls, and J. Waksberg. New York: John Wiley & Sons.

DILLMAN, D. A. 2002. *Mail and Internet Surveys: The Tailored Design Method*, 2nd edn. New York: Wiley.

—— SANGSTER, R., TARNAI, J., and ROCKWOOD, T. 1996. Understanding Differences in People's Answers to Telephone and Mail Surveys. In *Directions for Evaluations Series: Advances in Survey Research*, ed. M. T. Braverman and J. K. Slater. San Francisco: Jossey-Bass.

DODDS, P. S., MUHAMAD, R., and WATTS, D. J. 2003. An Experimental Study of Search in Global Social Networks. *Science* 301: 827–9.

DRUCKMAN, J. N. and NELSON, K. R. 2003. Framing and Deliberation: How Citizens' Conversations Limit Elite Influence. *American Journal of Political Science*, 47: 729–45.

ELAND-GOOSENSEN, M., VAN DE GOOR, L., VOLLEMANS, E., HENDRIKS, V., and GARRETSEN, H. 1997. Snowball Sampling Applied to Opiate Addicts Outside the Treatment System. *Addiction Research*, 5/4: 317–30.

ELINSON, J. 1992. Methodology Issues. In *A Meeting Place: The History of the American Association for Public Opinion Research*, ed. P. B. Sheatesley and W. J. Mitofsky. U.S.A: AAPOR.

ERICKSON, B. H. 1979. Some Problems of Inference from Chain Data. *Sociological Methodology*, 10: 276–302.

FOWLER, F. J., JR., ROMAN, A. M., and DI, Z. X. 1998. Mode Effects in a Survey of Medicare Prostate Surgery Patients. *Public Opinion Quarterly*, 62: 29–46.

FRICKER, S., GALESIC, M., TOURANEGEAU, R., and YAN, T. 2005. An Experimental Comparison of Web and Telephone Surveys. *Public Opinion Quarterly*, 3(Fall): 370–92.

GINSBERG, B. 1986. *The Captive Public*. New York: Basic Books.

GAINES, B. J., KUKLINSKI, J. H., and QUIRK, P. J. 2007. The Logic of the Survey Experiment Examined. *Political Analysis*, 15: 1–20.

GROVES, R. M. and COUPER, M. P. 1998. *Nonresponse in Household Interview Surveys*. New York: Wiley.

—— and PEYTCHEVA, E. 2008. The Impact of Nonresponse Rates on Nonresponse Bias: A Meta Analysis. *Public Opinion Quarterly*, 72/2: 167–89.

—— PRESSER, S., and DIPKO, S., 2004. The Role of Topic Interest in Survey Participation Decisions. *Public Opinion Quarterly*, 68: 2–31.

—— SINGER, E., and CORNING, A. 2000. Leverage Salience Theory of Survey Participation: Description and an Illustration. *Public Opinion Quarterly*, 64: 299–308.

HAGAN, J. 2001. *Northern Passage: American Vietnam War Resisters in Canada.* Cambridge, Mass.: Harvard University Press.

HECKATHORN, D. D. 1997. Respondent-Driven Sampling: A New Approach to the Study of Hidden Populations. *Social Problems,* 44/2: 174–99.

—— 2002. Respondent-Driven Sampling II: Deriving Valid Population Estimates from Chain-Referral Samples of Hidden Populations. *Social Problems,* 49/1: 11–34.

—— and JEFFRIES, J. 2001. Finding the Beat: Using Respondent-Driven Sampling to Study Jazz Musicians. In *Changing the Beat: A Study of the Worklife of Jazz Musicians, Volume 3: Respondent-Driven Sampling: Survey Results by the Research Center for Arts and Culture,* Research Division Report 42. Washington, DC: National Endowment for the Arts.

—— 2006. Respondent Driven Sampling. <http://www.respondentdrivensampling.org/>, accessed January 23, 2006.

HERBST, S. 1993. *Numbered Voices.* Chicago: University of Chicago Press.

HILL, S. J., LO, J., VAVRECK, L., and ZALLER, J. 2007. The Opt-in Internet Panel: Survey Mode, Sampling Methodology and the Implications for Political Research. CCES Working Paper 07-05 available at <http://web.mit.edu/polisci/portl/cces/papers.html>.

HOLBROOK, A. L., GREEN, M. C., and KROSNICK, J. A. 2003. Telephone Versus Face-to-face Interviewing of National Probability Samples with Long Questionnaires. *Public Opinion Quarterly,* 67: 79–125.

HUCKFELDT, R. and KUKLINSKI, J. H. 1995. *Citizens, Politics, and Social Communication: Information and Influence in an Election Campaign.* Cambridge: Cambridge University Press.

HURWITZ, J. and PEFFLEY, M. 1997. Public Perception of Race and Crime: The Role of Racial Stereotypes. *American Journal of Political Science,* 41: 375–401.

KALTON, G. and ANDERSON, D. W. 1986. Sampling Rare Populations. *Journal of the Royal Statistical Society Series A (General),* 149/1: 65–82.

KEETER, S., MILLER, C., KOHUT, A., GROVES, R. M., and PRESSER, S. 2000. Consequences of Reducing Nonresponse in a National Telephone Survey. *Public Opinion Quarterly,* 64: 125–48.

KIESLER, S. and SPROULL, L. S. 1986. Response Effects in the Electronic Survey. *Public Opinion Quarterly,* 50: 402–13.

KROSNICK, J. A. and CHANG, L.-C. 2001. A Comparison of Random Digit Dialing Telephone Survey Methodology with Internet Survey Methodology as Implemented by Knowledge Networks and Harris Interactive. Unpublished manuscript, Ohio State University. Available at <http://communication.stanford.edu/faculty/krosnick.html>.

LEE, S. 2009. Understanding Respondent Driven Sampling from a Total Survey Error Perspective. *Survey Practice,* August: http://surveypractice.org/.

LUSKIN, R. C., FISHKIN, J. S., and JOWELL, R. 2002. Considered Opinions: Deliberative Polling in Britain. *British Journal of Political Science,* 32: 455–87.

MAGNANI, R., SABIN, K., SAIDEL, T., and HECKATHORN, D. 2005. Review of Sampling Hard-to-Reach and Hidden Populations for HIV Surveillance. *AIDS,* 19: 567–72.

MALHORTRA, N. and KROSNICK, J. A. 2007. The Effect of Survey Mode and Sampling on Inferences about Political Attitudes and Behavior: Comparing the 2000 and 2004 ANES to Internet Surveys with Nonprobability Samples. *Political Analysis,* 15: 286–323.

McDERMOTT, M. L. 1998. Race and Gender Cues in Low-Information Elections. *Political Research Quarterly,* 51/4: 895–918.

MERKLE, D. M. and EDELMAN, M. 2002. Nonresponse in Exit Polls: A Comprehensive Analysis. In *Survey Nonresponse*, ed. R. M. Groves, D. A. Dillman, J. L. Eltinge, and R. J. A. Little. New York: John Wiley & Sons Inc.

MUTZ, D. C. and MARTIN, P. S. 2001. Facilitating Communication Across Lines of Political Difference: The Role of Mass Media. *American Political Science Review*, 95/1: 97–114.

THE PEW RESEARCH CENTER FOR THE PEOPLE AND THE PRESS. 2004. Polls Face Growing Resistance, But Still Representative: Survey Experiment Shows. <http://people-press.org/reports/display.php3?ReportID=211>.

PRESSER, S. 1990. Can Context Changes Reduce Vote Overreporting? *Public Opinion Quarterly*, 54: 586–93.

RIVERS, D. N.d. Sample Matching: Representative Sampling from Internet Panels. Available at <http://www.polimetrix.com/documents/Polimetrix_Sampling.pdf>.

ROSEN, R. and GOMES, T. 2004. Converting CES Reporters from TDE to Web Data Collection. Paper presented at the Joint Statistical Meetings, Toronto, Canada.

SANDERS, D., CLARKE, H. D., STEWART, M. C., and WHITELY, P. 2007. Does Mode Matter for Modeling Political Choice? Evidence from the 2005 British Election Study. *Political Analysis*, 15: 257–86.

SALGANIK, M. J. and HECKATHORN, D. D. 2004. Sampling and Estimation in Hidden Populations Using Respondent-Driven Sampling. *Sociological Methodology*, 5: 193–239.

SCHUMAN, H. 1992. Context Effects: State of the Past/State of the Art. In *Context Effects in Social Psychological Research*, ed. N. Schwarz and S. Sudman. New York: Springer-Verlag.

—— and PRESSER, S. 1981. *Questions and Answers in Attitude Survey: Experiments on Question Form, Wording and Context*. New York: Academic Press.

SCHWARZ, N. 1996. *Cognition and Communication: Judgmental Biases, Research Methods, and the Logic of Conversation*. Mahwah, N.J.: Lawrence Erlbaum.

SEARS, D. O. 1986. College Sophomores in the Laboratory: Influences of a Narrow Database on Social Psychology's View of Human Nature. *Journal of Personality and Social Psychology*, 51 (September): 515–30.

SEMANN, S., LAUBY, J., and LIEBMAN, J. 2002. Street and Network Sampling in Evaluation Studies of HIV Risk-Reduction Interventions. *AIDS Reviews*, 4: 213–23.

SILVER, B. D., ANDERSON, B. A., and ABRAMSON, P. R. 1986. Who Overreports Voting? *American Political Science Review*, 80: 613–24.

SMYTH, J. D., DILLMAN, D., CHRISTIAN, L. M., and STERN, M. J. 2006. Effects of Using Visual Design Principles to Group Response Options in Web Surveys. *International Journal of Internet Science*, 1: 6–16.

SNIDERMAN, P. M. and PIAZZA, T. 1993. *The Scar of Race*. Cambridge, Mass.: Bellknap Press.

STOUFFER, S. A., SUCHMAN, E. A., DeVINNEY, L. C., STAR, S. A., and WILLIAMS, JR., R. M. 1949. *Studies in Social Psychology in World War II: The American Soldier*, Volume 1: *Adjustment During Army Life*. Princeton, N.J.: Princeton University Press.

SUDMAN, S., BRADBURN, N. M., and SCHWARZ, N. 1996. *Thinking about Answers*. San Francisco: Josey-Bass.

TERHANIAN, G. 2008. Changing Times, Changing Modes: The Future of Public Opinion Polling. *Journal of Elections, Public Opinion and Parties*, 18/4: 331–42.

TOURANGEAU, R., COUPER, M. P., and CONRAD, F. 2004. Spacing, Position, and Order: Interpretive Heuristics for Visual Features of Survey Questions. *Public Opinion Quarterly*, 68/3: 368–93.

TRAUGOTT, M. W. and KATOSH, J. P. 1979. Response Validity in Surveys of Voting Behavior. *Public Opinion Quarterly*, 43: 359–77.

TRAVERS, J. and MILGRAM, S. 1969. An Experimental Study of the Small World Problem. *Sociometry*, 32: 425–43.

VAVRECK, L. and RIVERS, D. The 2006 Cooperative Congressional Election Study. *Journal of Elections, Public Opinion and Parties*, 18/4: 355–66.

WATTS, D. J. and STROGATZ, S. H. 1998. Collective Dynamics of "Small-World" Networks. *Nature*, 393/2: 237–45.

WEJNERT, C. and HECKATHORN, D. D. 2008. Web-Based Network Sampling: Efficiency and Efficacy of Respondent-Driven Sampling for Online Research. *Sociological Methods and Research*, 37(1): 105–34.

WRIGHT, G. C. 1990. Misreports of Vote Choice in the NES Senate Election Study. *Legislative Studies Quarterly*, 15: 543–64.

—— 1993. Errors in Measuring Vote Choice in the National Election Studies, 1952–88. *American Journal of Political Science*, 37/1: 291–316.

CHAPTER 3

....

OPTIMIZING SURVEY QUESTIONNAIRE DESIGN IN POLITICAL SCIENCE

INSIGHTS FROM PSYCHOLOGY

JOSH PASEK

JON A. KROSNICK

....

QUESTIONNAIRES have long been a primary means of gathering data on political beliefs, attitudes, and behavior (F. H. Allport 1940; G. W. Allport 1929; Campbell et al. 1060; Dahl 1961; Lazarsfeld and Rosenberg 1949–1950; Merriam 1926; Woodward and Roper 1950). Many of the most frequently studied and important measurements made to understand mass political action have been done with questions in the American National Election Studies (ANES) surveys and other such data collection enterprises. Although in principle, it might seem desirable to observe political behavior directly rather than relying on people's descriptions of it, questionnaire-based measurement offers tremendous efficiencies and conveniences for researchers over direct observational efforts. Furthermore, many of the most important explanatory variables thought to drive political behavior are subjective phenomena that can only be measured via people's descriptions of their own thoughts. Internal political efficacy, political party identification, attitudes toward social groups, trust in government, preferences among government policy options on specific issues, presidential approval, and many more such variables reside in citizens' heads, so we must seek their help by asking them to describe those constructs for us.

A quick glance at ANES questionnaires might lead an observer to think that the design of self-report questions need follow no rules governing item format, because formats have differed tremendously from item to item. Thus, it might appear that just about any question format is as effective as any other format for producing valid and reliable measurements. But in fact, this is not true. Nearly a century's worth of survey design research suggests that some question formats are optimal, whereas others are suboptimal.

In this chapter, we offer a summary of this literature's suggestions. In doing so, we point researchers toward question formats that appear to yield the highest measurement reliability and validity. Using the American National Election Studies as a starting point, the chapter illuminates general principles of good questionnaire design, desirable choices to make when designing new questions, biases in some question formats and ways to avoid them, and strategies for reporting survey results. Finally, the chapter offers a discussion of strategies for measuring voter turnout in particular, as a case study that poses special challenges. We hope that the tools we present will help scholars to design effective questionnaires and utilize self-reports so that the data gathered are useful and the conclusions drawn are justified.

THE QUESTIONS WE HAVE ASKED

Many hundreds of questions have been asked of respondents in the ANES surveys, usually more than an hour's worth in one sitting, either before or after a national election. Many of these items asked respondents to place themselves on rating scales, but the length of these scales varies considerably. For example, some have 101 points, such as the feeling thermometers:

Feeling Thermometer. I'd like to get your feelings toward some of our political leaders and other people who are in the news these days. I'll read the name of a person and I'd like you to rate that person using something we call the feeling thermometer. The feeling thermometer can rate people from 0 to 100 degrees. Ratings between 50 degrees and 100 degrees mean that you feel favorable and warm toward the person. Ratings between 0 degrees and 50 degrees mean that you don't feel favorable toward the person. Rating the person at the midpoint, the 50 degree mark, means you don't feel particularly warm or cold toward the person. If we come to a person whose name you don't recognize, you don't need to rate that person. Just tell me and we'll move on to the next one.[1]

Other ratings scales have offered just seven points, such as the ideology question:

Liberal–conservative Ideology. We hear a lot of talk these days about liberals and conservatives. When it comes to politics, do you usually think of yourself as extremely liberal, liberal, slightly liberal; moderate or middle of the road, slightly conservative, conservative, extremely conservative, or haven't you thought much about this?

Still others have just five points:

Attention to Local News about the Campaign. How much attention do you pay to news on local news shows about the campaign for President—a great deal, quite a bit, some, very little, or none?

Or three points:

Interest in the Campaigns. Some people don't pay much attention to political campaigns. How about you? Would you say that you have been very much interested, somewhat interested or not much interested in the political campaigns so far this year?

Or just two:

Internal efficacy. Please tell me how much you agree or disagree with these statements about the government: "Sometimes politics and government seem so complicated that a person like me can't really understand what's going on."

Whereas the internal efficacy measure above offers generic response choices ("agree" and "disagree"), which could be used to measure a wide array of constructs, other items offer construct-specific response alternatives (meaning that the construct being measured is explicitly mentioned in each answer choice), such as:

Issue Importance. How important is this issue to you personally? Not at all important, not too important, somewhat important, very important, or extremely important? (ANES 2004)

Some rating scales have had verbal labels and no numbers on all the points, as in the above measure of issue importance, whereas other rating scales have numbered points with verbal labels on just a few, as in this case:

---

[1] All the question wordings displayed are from the 2004 ANES.

Defense Spending. Some people believe that we should spend much less money for defense. Suppose these people are at one end of the scale, at point number 1. Others feel that defense spending should be greatly increased. Suppose these people are at the other end, at point 7. And, of course, some other people have opinions somewhere in between at points 2, 3, 4, 5 or 6. Where would you place yourself on this scale, or haven't you thought much about this?

In contrast to all of the above closed-ended questions, some other questions are asked in open-ended formats:

Candidate Likes–dislikes. Is there anything in particular about Vice President Al Gore that might make you want to vote for him?

Most Important Problems. What do you think are the most important problems facing this country?

Political Knowledge. Now we have a set of questions concerning various public figures. We want to see how much information about them gets out to the public from television, newspapers and the like. What job or political office does Dick Cheney now hold?

Some questions offered respondents opportunities to say they did not have an opinion on an issue, as in the ideology question above ("or haven't you thought much about this?"). But many questions measuring similar constructs did not offer that option, such as:

U.S. Strength in the World. Turning to some other types of issues facing the country. During the past year, would you say that the United States' position in the world has grown weaker, stayed about the same, or has it grown stronger?

Variations in question design are not, in themselves, problematic. Indeed, one cannot expect to gather meaningful data on a variety of issues simply by altering a single word in a "perfect," generic question. To that end, some design decisions in the ANES represent the conscious choices of researchers based on pre-testing and the literature on best practices in questionnaire design. In many cases, however, differences between question wordings are due instead to the intuitions and expectations of researchers, a desire to retain consistent questions for time-series analyses, or researchers preferring the ease of using an existent question rather than designing and pre-testing a novel one.

All of these motivations are understandable, but there may be a better way to go about questionnaire design to yield better questions. Poorly designed questions can produce (1) momentary confusion among respondents, (2) more widespread frustration, and (3) compromises in reliability, or (4) systematic biases in measurement or analysis results. Designing optimal measurement tools in surveys sometimes requires expenditure of more resources (by asking longer questions or more questions to measure a single construct), but many measurements can be made optimal simply by changing wording without increasing a researcher's costs. Doing so requires understanding the principles of optimal design, which we review next.

BASIC DESIGN PRINCIPLES

Good questionnaires are easy to administer, yield reliable data, and accurately measure the constructs for which the survey was designed. When rapid administration and acquiring reliable data conflict, however, we lean toward placing priority on acquiring accurate data. An important way to enhance measurement accuracy is to ask questions that respondents can easily interpret and answer and that are interpreted similarly by different respondents. It is also important to ask questions in ways that motivate respondents to provide accurate answers instead of answering sloppily or intentionally inaccurately. How can we maximize respondent motivation to provide accurate self-reports while minimizing the difficulty of doing so? Two general principles underlie most of the challenges that researchers face in this regard. They involve (1) understanding the distinction between "optimizing" and "satisficing," and (2) accounting for the conversational norms and conventions that shape the survey response process. We describe these theoretical perspectives next.

Optimizing and Satisficing

Imagine the ideal survey respondent, whom we'll call an optimizer. Such an individual goes through four stages in answering each survey question (though not necessarily strictly sequentially). First, the optimizer reads or listens to the question and attempts to discern the question's intent (e.g., "the researcher wants to know how often I watch television programs about politics"). Second, the optimizer searches his or her memory for information useful to answer the question (e.g., "I guess I usually watch television news on Monday and Wednesday nights for about an hour at a time, and there's almost always some political news covered"). Third, the optimizer evaluates the available information and integrates that information into a summary judgment (e.g., "I watch two hours of television about politics per week"). Finally, the optimizer answers the question by translating the summary judgment onto the response alternatives (e.g. by choosing "between 1 and 4 hours per week") (Cannell et al. 1981; Krosnick 1991; Schwarz and Strack 1985; Tourangeau and Rasinski 1988; Turner and Martin 1984).

Given the substantial effort required to execute all the steps of optimizing when answering every question in a long questionnaire, it is easy to imagine that not every respondent implements all of the steps fully for every question (Krosnick 1999; Krosnick and Fabrigar in press). Indeed, more and more research indicates that some individuals sometimes answer questions using only the most readily available information, or, worse, look for cues in the question that point toward easy-to-select answers and choose them so as to do as little thinking as possible

(Krosnick 1999). The act of abridging the search for information or skipping it altogether is termed "survey satisficing" and appears to pose a major challenge to researchers (Krosnick 1991, 1999). When respondents satisfice, they give researchers answers that are at best loosely related to the construct of interest and may sometimes be completely unrelated to it.

Research on survey satisficing has revealed a consistent pattern of who satisfices and when. Respondents are likely to satisfice when the task of answering a particular question optimally is difficult, when the respondent lacks the skills needed to answer optimally, or when he or she is unmotivated (Krosnick 1991; Krosnick and Alwin 1987). Hence, satisficers are individuals who have limited cognitive skills, fail to see sufficient value in a survey, find a question confusing, or have simply been worn down by a barrage of preceding questions (Krosnick 1999; Krosnick, Narayan, and Smith 1996; McClendon 1986, 1991; Narayan and Krosnick 1996). These individuals tend to be less educated and are lower in "need for cognition" than non-satisficers (Anand, Krosnick, Mulligan, Smith, Green, and Bizer 2005; Narayan and Krosnick 1996). Importantly, they do not represent a random subset of the population, and they tend to satisfice in systematic, rather than stochastic, ways. Hence, to ignore satisficers is to introduce potentially problematic bias in survey results.

No research has yet identified a surefire way to prevent respondents from satisficing, but a number of techniques for designing questions and putting them together into questionnaires seem to reduce the extent to which respondents satisfice (Krosnick 1999). Questions, therefore, should be designed to minimize the incentives to satisfice and maximize the efficiency of the survey for optimizers.

Conversational Norms and Conventions

In most interpersonal interactions, participants expect a conversant to follow certain conversational standards. When people violate these conversational norms and rules, confusion and misunderstandings often ensue. From this perspective, a variety of researchers have attempted to identify the expectations that conversants bring to conversations, so any potentially misleading expectations can be overcome. In his seminal work *Logic and Conversation*, Grice (1975) proposed a set of rules that speakers usually follow and listeners usually assume that speakers follow: that they should be truthful, meaningfully informative, relevant, and to the point. This perspective highlights a critical point that survey researchers often ignore: respondents enter all conversations with expectations, and when researchers violate those expectations (which they often do unwittingly), measurement accuracy can be compromised (Lipari 2000; Schuman and Ludwig 1983; Schwarz 1996).

Krosnick, Li, and Lehman (1990) illustrated the impact of conversational norms. They found the order in which information was presented in a survey question could substantially change how respondents answered. In everyday conversations, when people list a series of pieces of information leading to a conclusion, they tend to present that whey think of as the most important information last. When Krosnick et al.'s respondents were given information and were asked to make decisions with that information, the respondents placed more weight on the information that was presented last because they presumed the questioner ascribed most importance to that information. In another study, Holbrook et al. (2000) presented response options to survey questions in either a normal ("are you *for* or *against* X?") or unusual ("are you *against* or *for* X?") order. Respondents whose question used the normal ordering were quicker to respond to the questions and answered more validly. Thus, breaking rules of conversation manipulates and compromises the quality of answers.

Implications

Taken together, these theoretical perspectives suggest that survey designers should follow three basic rules. Surveys should:

(1) be designed to make questions as easy as possible for optimizers to answer,
(2) take steps to discourage satisficing, and
(3) be sure not to violate conversational conventions without explicitly saying so, to avoid confusion and misunderstandings.

The specifics of how to accomplish these three goals are not always obvious. Cognitive pre-testing (which involves having respondents restate questions in their own words and think aloud while answering questions, to highlight misunderstandings that need to be prevented) is always a good idea (Willis 2004), but many of the specific decisions that researchers must make when designing questions can be guided by the findings of past studies on survey methodology. The literature in these areas, reviewed below, provides useful and frequently counter-intuitive advice.

DESIGNING OPTIMAL SURVEY QUESTIONS

Open-ended Questions or Closed Questions?

In the 1930s and 1940s, when modern survey research was born, a debate emerged as to whether researchers should ask open-ended questions or should ask respondents to select among a set of offered response choices (J. M. Converse 1984). Each method had apparent benefits. Open-ended questions could capture the sentiments of individuals on an issue with tones of nuance and without the possibility that offered answer choices colored respondent selections. Closed questions seemed easier to administer and to analyze, and more of them could be asked in a similar amount of time (Lazarsfeld 1944). Perhaps more out of convenience than merit, closed questions eclipsed open-ended ones in contemporary survey research. For example, in surveys done by major news media outlets, open-ended questions constituted a high of 33 percent of questions in 1936 and dropped to 8 percent of questions by 1972 (T. Smith 1987).

The administrative ease of closed questions, however, comes with a distinct cost. Respondents tend to select among offered answer choices rather than selecting "other, specify" when the latter would be optimal to answer a question with nominal response options (Belson and Duncan 1962; Bishop et al. 1988; Lindzey and Guest 1951; Oppenheim 1966; Presser 1990b). If every potential option is offered by such a question, then this concern is irrelevant. For most questions, however, offering every possible answer choice is not practical. And when some options are omitted, respondents who would have selected them choose among the offered options instead, thereby changing the distribution of responses as compared to what would have been obtained if a complete list had been offered (Belson and Duncan 1962). Therefore, an open-ended format would be preferable in this sort of situation.

Open-ended questions also discourage satisficing. When respondents are given a closed question, they might settle for choosing an appropriate-sounding answer. But open-ended questions demand that individuals generate an answer on their own and do not point respondents toward any particular response, thus inspiring more thought and consideration. Furthermore, many closed questions require respondents to answer an open-ended question in their minds first (e.g., "what is the most important problem facing the country?") and then to select the answer choice that best matches that answer. Skipping the latter, matching step will make the respondent's task easier and thereby encourage optimizing when answering this and subsequent questions.

Closed questions can also present particular problems when seeking numbers. Schwarz et al. (1985) manipulated response alternatives for a question gauging amount of television watching and found striking effects. When "more than 2½ hours" was the highest category offered, only 16 percent of individuals reported watching that much television. But when five response categories broke up "more than 2½ hours" into five sub-ranges, nearly 40 percent of respondents placed themselves in one of those categories. This appears to occur because whatever range is in the middle of the set of offered ranges is perceived to be typical or normal by respondents, and this implicit message sent by the response alternatives alters people's reports (Schwarz 1995). Open-ended questions seeking numbers do not suffer from this potential problem.

The higher validity of open-ended questions does not mean that every question should be open-ended. Open-ended questions take longer to answer (Wason 1961) and must be systematically coded by researchers. When the full spectrum of possible nomial responses is known, closed questions are an especially appealing approach. But when the full spectrum of answers is not know, or when a numeric quantity is sought (e.g., "during the last month, how many times did you talk to someone about the election?"), open-ended questions are preferable. Before asking a closed question seeking nominal answers, however, researchers should pre-test an open-ended version of the question on the population of interest, to be sure the offered list of response alternatives is comprehensive.

Rating Questions or Ranking Questions?

Rating scale questions are very common in surveys (e.g., the "feeling thermometer" and "issue importance" questions above). Such questions are useful because they place respondents on the continua of interest to researchers and are readily suited to statistical analysis. Furthermore, rating multiple items of a given type can permit comparisons of evaluations across items (McIntyre and Ryans 1977; Moore 1975; Munson and McIntyre 1979).

Researchers are sometimes interested in obtaining a rank order of objects from respondents (e.g., rank these candidates from most desirable to least desirable). In such situations, asking respondents to rank-order the objects is an obvious measurement option, but it is quite time-consuming (Munson and McIntyre 1979). Therefore, it is tempting to ask respondents instead to rate the objects individually and to derive a rank order from the ratings.

Unfortunately, though, rating questions sometimes entail a major challenge: when asked to rate a set of objects on the same scale, respondents sometimes fail to differentiate their ratings, thus clouding analytic results (McCarty and Shrum 2000). This appears to occur because some respondents choose to satisfice by non-differentiating: drawing a straight line down the battery of rating questions. For example, in one study with thirteen rating scales, 42 percent of individuals evaluated nine or more of the objects identically (Krosnick and Alwin 1988). And such non-differentiation is most likely to occur under the conditions that foster satisficing (see Krosnick 1999).

If giving objects identical ratings is appropriate, rating scales would be desirable. But when researchers are interested in understanding how respondents rank-order objects when forced to do so, satisficing-induced non-differentiation in ratings yields misleading data (Alwin and Krosnick 1985). Fortunately, respondents can be asked to rank objects instead. Although ranking questions take more time, rankings acquire responses that are less distorted by satisficing and are more reliable and valid than ratings (Alwin and Krosnick 1985; Krosnick and Alwin 1988; Miethe 1985; Reynolds and Jolly 1980). Thus, ranking questions are preferable for assessing rank orders of objects.

Rating Scale Points

Although the "feeling thermometer" measure has been used in numerous American National Election Study surveys, it has obvious drawbacks: the meanings of the many scale points are not clear and uniformly interpreted by respondents. Only nine of the points have been labeled with words on the show-card handed to respondents, and a huge proportion of respondents choose one of those nine points (Weisberg and Miller 1979). And subjective differences in interpreting response alternatives may mean that one person's 80 is equivalent to another's 65 (Wilcox, Sigelman, and Cook 1989). Therefore, this very long and ambiguous rating scale introduces considerable error into analysis.

Although 101 points is far too many for a meaningful scale, providing only two or three response choices for a rating scale can make it impossible for respondents to provide evaluations at a sufficiently refined level to communicate their perceptions (Alwin 1992). Too few response alternatives can provide a particular challenge for optimizers who attempt to map complex opinions onto limited answer choices. A large body of research has gone into assessing the most effective number of options to offer respondents (Alwin 1992; Alwin and Krosnick 1985; Cox 1980; Lissitz and Green 1975; Lodge and Tursky 1979; Matell and Jacoby 1972; Ramsay 1973; Schuman and Presser 1981). Ratings tend to be more reliable and valid when five points are offered for unipolar dimensions (e.g., "not at all important" to "extremely important"; Lissitz and Green 1975) and seven points for bipolar dimensions (e.g., "Dislike a great deal" to "like a great deal" Green and Rao 1970).

Another drawback of the "feeling thermometer" scale is its numerical scale point labels. Labels are meant to improve respondent interpretation of scale points, but the meanings of most of the numerically labeled scale points are unclear. It is therefore preferable to put verbal labels on all rating scale points to clarify their intended meanings, which increases the reliability and validity of ratings (Krosnick and Berent 1993). Providing numeric labels in addition to the verbal labels increases respondents' cognitive burden but does not increase data quality and in fact can mislead respondents about the intended meanings of the scale points (e.g., Schwarz et al. 1991). Verbal labels with meanings that are not equally spaced from one another can cause respondent confusion (Klockars and

Yamagishi 1988), so the selected verbal labels should have equally spaced meanings (Hofmans et al. 2007; Schwarz, Grayson, and Knauper 1998; Wallsten et al. 1986).

"Don't Know" Options and Attitude Strength

Although some questionnaire designers advise that opinion questions offer respondents the opportunity to say they do not have an opinion at all (e.g., Vaillancourt 1973), others do not advise including "don't know" or "no opinion" response options (Krosnick et al. 2002). And most major survey research firms have routinely trained their interviewers to probe respondents when they say "don't know" to encourage them to offer a substantive answer instead. The former advice is sometimes justified by claims that respondents may sometimes be unfamiliar with the issue in question or may not have enough information about it to form a legitimate opinion (e.g., P. Converse 1964). Other supportive evidence has shown that people sometimes offer opinions about extremely obscure or fictitious issues, thus suggesting that they are manufacturing non-attitudes instead of confessing ignorance (e.g., Bishop, Tuchfarber, and Oldendick 1986; Hawkins and Coney 1981; Schwarz 1996).

In contrast, advice to avoid offering "don't know" options is justified by the notion that such options can encourage satisficing (Krosnick 1991). Consistent with this argument, when answering political knowledge quiz questions, respondents who are encouraged to guess after initially saying "don't know" tend to give the correct answer at better-than-chance rates (Mondak and Davis 2001). Similarly, candidate preferences predict actual votes better when researchers discourage "don't know" responses (Krosnick et al. 2002; Visser et al. 2000). Thus, discouraging "don't know" responses collects more valid data than does encouraging such responses. And respondents who truly are completely unfamiliar with the topic of a question will say so when probed, and that answer can be accepted at that time, thus avoiding collecting measurements of non-existent "opinions." Thus, because many people who initially say "don't know" do indeed have a substantive opinion, researchers are best served by discouraging these responses in surveys.

Converse (1964) did have an important insight, though. Not all people who express an opinion hold that view equally strongly, based upon equal amounts of information and thought. Instead, attitudes vary in their strength. A strong attitude is very difficult to change and has powerful impact on a person's thinking and action. A weak attitude is easy to change and has little impact on anything. To understand the role that attitudes play in governing a person's political behavior, it is valuable to understand the strength of those attitudes. Offering a "don't know" option is not a good way to identify weak attitudes. Instead, it is best to ask follow-up questions intended to diagnose the strength of an opinion after it has been reported (see Krosnick and Abelson 1992).

Acquiescence Response Bias

In everyday conversations, norms of social conduct dictate that people should strive to be agreeable (Brown and Levinson 1987). In surveys when researchers ask questions, they mean to invite all possible responses, even when asking respondents whether they agree or disagree with a statement offered by a question. "Likert scales" is the label often used to describe the agree–disagree scales that are used in many surveys these days. Such scales are appreciated by both designers and respondents because they speed up the interview process. Unfortunately, though, respondents are biased toward agreement. Some 10–20 percent of respondents tend to agree with both a statement and its opposite (e.g., Schuman and Presser 1981). This tendency toward agreeing is known as acquiescence response bias and may occur for a variety of reasons. First, conversational conventions dictate that people should be agreeable and polite (Bass 1956; Campbell et al. 1960). Second, people tend to defer to individuals of higher authority (a position they assume the researcher holds) (Carr 1971; Lenski and Leggett 1960). Additionally, a person inclined to satisfice is more likely to agree with a statement than to disagree (Krosnick 1991).

Whatever the cause, acquiescence presents a major challenge for researchers. Consider, for example, the ANES question measuring internal efficacy. If certain respondents are more likely to agree with any statement regardless of its content, then these individuals will appear to believe that government and politics are too complicated to understand, even if that is not their view. And any correlations between this question and other questions could be due to associations with the individual's actual internal efficacy or his or her tendency to acquiesce (Wright 1975).

Agree–disagree rating scales are extremely popular in social science research, and researchers rarely take steps to minimize the impact of acquiescence on research findings. One such step is to balance batteries of questions, such that affirmative answers indicate a high level of the construct for half the items and a low level of the construct for the other half, thus placing acquiescers at the midpoint of the final score's continuum (Bass 1956; Cloud and Vaughan 1970). Unfortunately, this approach simply moves acquiescers from the agree of a rating scale (where they don't necessarily belong) to the midpoint of the final score's continuum (where they also don't necessarily belong).

A more effective solution becomes apparent when we recognize first that answering an agree–disagree question is more cognitively demanding than answering a question that offers construct-specific response alternatives. This is so because in order to answer most agree–disagree questions (e.g., "Sometimes politics is so complicated that I can't understand it"), the respondent must answer a construct-specific version of it in his or her own mind ("How often is politics so complicated that I can't understand it?") and then translate the answer onto the agree–disagree response continuum. And in this translation process, a person might produce an answer that maps onto the underlying construct in a way the researcher would not anticipate. For example, a person might disagree with the statement, "Sometimes politics is so complicated that I can't understand it," either because politics is never that complicated or because politics is always that complicated. Thus, the agree–disagree continuum would not be monotonically related to the construct of interest. For all these reasons, it is preferable simply to ask questions with construct-specific response alternatives.

Yes/No questions and True/False questions are also subject to acquiescence response bias (Fritzley and Lee 2003; Schuman and Presser 1981). In these cases, a simple fix involves changing the question so that it explicitly offers all possible views. For example, instead of asking "Do you think abortion should be legal?" one can ask "Do you think abortion should or should not be legal?"

Response Order Effects

Another form of satisficing is choosing the first plausible response option one considers, which produces what are called response order effects (Krosnick 1991, 1999; Krosnick and Alwin 1987). Two types of response order effects are primacy effects and recency effects. Primacy effects occur when respondents are inclined to select response options presented near the beginning of a list (Belson 1966). Recency effects occur when respondents are inclined to select options presented at the end of a list (Kalton, Collins, and Brook 1978). When categorical (non-rating scale) response options are presented visually, primacy effects predominate. When categorical response options are presented orally, recency effects predominate. When rating scales are presented, primacy effects predominate in both the visual and oral modes. Response order effects are most likely to occur under the conditions that foster satisficing (Holbrook et al. 2007).

One type of question that can minimize response order effects is the seemingly open-ended question (SOEQ). SOEQs separate the question from the response alternatives with a short pause to encourage individuals to optimize. Instead of asking, "If the election were held today, would you vote for Candidate A or Candidate B?," response order effects can be reduced by asking, "If the election were held today, whom would you vote for? Would you vote for Candidate A or Candidate B?" The pause after the question and before the answer choices encourages respondents to contemplate, as if when answering an open-ended question, and then offers the list of the possible answers to respondents (Holbrook et al. 2007). By rotating response order or using SOEQs, researchers can prevent the order of the response options from coloring results.

Response order effects do not only happen in surveys. They occur in elections as well. In a series of natural experiments, Brook and Upton (1974), Krosnick and Miller (1998), Koppell and Steen (2004), and others found consistent patterns indicating that a few voters choose the first name on the ballot, giving that candidate an advantage of about 3 percent on average. Some elections are decided by less than 3 percent of the vote, so name order can alter an election outcome. When telephone survey questions mirror the name order on the ballot, those surveys are likely to manifest a recency effect, which would run in the direction opposite to what would be expected in the voting booth, thus creating error in predicting the election outcome. Many survey firms rotate candidate name order to control for potential effects, but this will maximize forecast accuracy only in states, such as Ohio, that rotate candidate name order in voting booths.

Question Order Effects

In 1948, a survey asked Americans whether Communist news reporters should be allowed in the United States and found that the majority (63 percent) said "no." Yet in another survey, an identical question found 73 percent of Americans believed that Communist reporters should be allowed. This discrepancy turned out to be attributable to the impact of the question that preceded the target question in the latter survey. In an experiment, a majority of Americans said "yes" only when the item immediately followed a question about whether American reporters should be allowed in Russia. Wanting to appear consistent and attuned to the norm of even-handedness after hearing the initial question, respondents were more willing to allow Communist reporters into the US (Schuman and Presser 1981).

A variety of other types of question order effects have been identified. *Subtraction* occurs when two nested concepts are presented in sequence (e.g., George W. Bush and the Republican Party) as items for evaluation. When a question about the Republican Party follows a question about George W. Bush, respondents assume that the questioner does not want them to include their opinion of Bush in their evaluations of the GOP (Schuman, Presser, and Ludwig 1981). *Perceptual contrast* occurs when one rating follows another, and the second rating is made in contrast to the first one. For example, respondents who dislike George Bush may be inclined to offer a more favorable rating of John McCain when a question about McCain follows Bush than when the question about McCain is asked first (Schwarz and Bless 1992; Schwarz and Strack 1991). And *priming* occurs when questions earlier in the survey increase the salience of certain attitudes or beliefs in the mind of the respondent (e.g., preceding questions about abortion may make respondents more likely to evaluate George W. Bush based on his abortion views) (Kalton et al. 1978). Also, asking questions later in a long survey enhances the likelihood that respondents will satisfice (Krosnick 1999).

Unfortunately, it is impossible to prevent question order effects. Rotating the order of questions across respondents might seem sensible, but doing so may cause topics of questions that seem to jump around in ways that don't seem obviously sensible and tax respondents' memories (Silver and Krosnick 1991). And rotating question order will not make question order effects disappear. Therefore, the best researchers can do is to use past research on question order effects as a basis for being attentive to possible question order effects in a new questionnaire.

Attitude Recall

It would be very helpful to researchers if respondents could remember the opinions they held at various times in the past and describe them accurately in surveys. Unfortunately, this is rarely true. People usually have no recollection of how they thought about things at previous times. When asked, they will happily guess, and their guesses are strongly biased—people tend to assume they always believed what they believe today (Goethals and Reckman 1973; Roberts 1985). Consequently, attitude recall questions can produce wildly inaccurate results (T. Smith 1984). Because of the enormous amount of error associated with these questions, they cannot be used for statistical analyses. Instead, attitude change must be assessed prospectively. Only by measuring attitudes at multiple time points is it possible to gain an accurate understanding of attitude change.

The Danger of Asking "Why?"

Social science spends much of its time determining causality. Instead of running dozens of statistical studies and spending millions of dollars, it might seem much more efficient simply to ask people to describe the reasons for their thoughts and actions (Lazarsfeld 1935). Unfortunately, respondents rarely know why they think and act as they do (Nisbett and Wilson 1977; E. R. Smith and Miller 1978; Wilson and Dunn 2004; Wilson and Nisbett 1978). People are willing to guess when asked, but their guesses are rarely informed by any genuine self-insight and are usually no more accurate than would be guesses about why someone else thought or acted as they did. Consequently, it is best not to ask people to explain why they think or act in particular ways.

Social Desirability

Some observers of questionnaire data are skeptical of their value because they suspect that respondents may sometimes intentionally lie in order to appear more socially admirable, thus manifesting what is called social desirability response bias. Many observers have attributed discrepancies between survey reports of voter turnout and official government turnout figures to intentional lying by survey respondents (Belli, Traugott, and Beckmann 2001; Silver, Anderson, and Abramson 1986). Rather than appearing not to fulfill their civic duty, some respondents who did not vote in an election are thought to claim that they did so. Similar claims have been made about reports of illegal drug use and racial stereotyping (Evans, Hansen, and Mittelmark 1977; Sigall and Page 1971).

A range of techniques have been developed to assess the scope of social desirability effects and to reduce the likelihood that people's answers are distorted by social norms. These methods either assure respondents that their answers will be kept confidential or seek to convince respondents that the researcher can detect lies—making it pointless not to tell the truth (see Krosnick 1999). Interestingly, although these techniques have often revealed evidence of social desirability response bias, the amount of distortion is generally small. Even for voting, where social desirability initially seemed likely to occur, researchers have sometimes found lower voting rates when people can report secretly but no large universal effect (Abelson, Loftus, and Greenwald 1992; Duff et al. 2007; Holbrook and Krosnick in press; Presser 1990a). Even after eliminating for social desirability response bias, surveyed turnout rates are above those reported in government records.

A number of other errors are likely to contribute to overestimation of voter turnout. First, official turnout records contain errors, and those errors are more likely to be omissions of individuals who did vote than inclusions of individuals who did not vote (Presser, Traugott, and Traugott 1990). Second, many individuals who could have voted but did not fall outside of survey sampling frames (Clausen 1968–1969; McDonald 2003; McDonald and Popkin 2001). Third, individuals who choose not to participate in a political survey are less likely to vote than individuals who do participate (Burden 2000; Clausen 1968–1969). Fourth, individuals who were surveyed just before an election may be made more likely to vote as the result of the interview experience (Kraut and McConahay 1973; Traugott and Katosh 1979).

Surveys like the ANES could overestimate turnout partially because follow-up surveys are conducted with individuals who had already been interviewed (Clausen 1968–1969). All of these factors may explain why survey results do not match published voter turnout figures.

Another reason for apparent overestimation of turnout by surveys may be acquiescence, because answering "yes" to a question about voting usually indicates having done so (Abelson, Loftus, and Greenwald 1992). Second, respondents who usually vote may not recall that, in a specific instance, they failed to do so (Belli, Traugott, and Beckmann 2001; Belli, Traugott, and Rosenstone 1994; Belli et al. 1999). Each of these alternate proposals has gotten some empirical support. So although social desirability may be operating, especially in telephone interviews, it probably accounts for only a small portion of the overestimation of turnout rates.

Question Wording

Although much of questionnaire design should be considered a science rather than an art, the process of selecting words for a question is thought to be artistic and intuitive. A question's effectiveness can easily be undermined by long, awkward wording that taps multiple constructs. Despite the obvious value of pithy, easy-to-understand queries, questionnaire designers sometimes offer tome-worthy introductions. One obvious example is the preamble for the "feeling thermometer." When tempted to use such a long and complicated introduction, researchers should strive for brevity.

Choices of words for questions are worth agonizing over, because even very small changes can produce sizable differences in responses. In one study, for instance, 73 percent of respondents said they strongly or somewhat "favored" policies on average, whereas only 45 percent strongly or somewhat "supported" the same policies (Krosnick 1989). Many studies have produced findings showing that differences in word choice can change individuals' responses remarkably (e.g., Rugg 1941). But this does not mean that respondents are arbitrary or fickle. The choice of a particular word or phrase can change the perceived meaning of a question in sensible ways and therefore change the judgment that is reported. Therefore, researchers should be very careful to select words tapping the exact construct they mean to measure.

Conclusion

Numerous studies of question construction suggest a roadmap of best practices. Systematic biases caused by satisficing and the violation of conversational conventions can distort responses, and researchers have both the opportunity and ability to minimize those errors. These problems therefore are mostly those of design. That is, they can generally be blamed on the researcher, not on the respondent. And fortunately, intentional lying by respondents appears to be very rare and preventable by using creative techniques to assure anonymity. So again, accuracy is attainable.

The American National Election Study questionnaires include a smorgasbord of some good and many suboptimal questions. Despite these shortcomings, those survey questions nonetheless offer a window into political attitudes and behaviors that would be impossible to achieve through any other research design. Nonetheless, scholars designing their own surveys should not presume that previously written questions are the best ones to use. Applying best practices in questionnaire design will yield more accurate data and more accurate substantive findings about the nature and origins of mass political behavior.

REFERENCES

ABELSON, R. P., LOFTUS, E., and GREENWALD, A. G. 1992. Attempts to Improve the Accuracy of Self-Reports of Voting. In *Questions About Questions: Inquiries into the Cognitive Bases of Surveys*, ed. J. M. Tanur. New York: Russell Sage Foundation.

ALLPORT, F. H. 1940. Polls and the Science of Public Opinion. *Public Opinion Quarterly*, 4/2: 249–57.

ALLPORT, G. W. 1929. The Composition of Political Attitudes. *American Journal of Sociology*, 35/2: 220–38.

ALWIN, D. F. 1992. Information Transmission in the Survey Interview: Number of Response Categories and the Reliability of Attitude Measurement. *Sociological Methodology*, 22: 83–118.

—— and KROSNICK, J. A. 1985. The Measurement of Values in Surveys: A Comparison of Ratings and Rankings. *Public Opinion Quarterly*, 49/4: 535–52.

AMERICAN NATIONAL ELECTION STUDIES 2004. The 2004 National Election Study [code-book]. Ann Arbor, MI: University of Michigan, Center for Political Studies (producer and distributor). <http://www.electionstudies.org>.

ANAND, S., KROSNICK, J. A., MULLIGAN, K., SMITH, W., GREEN, M., and BIZER, G. 2005. Effects of Respondent Motivation and Task Difficulty on Nondifferentiation in Ratings: A Test of Satisficing Theory Predictions. Paper presented at the American Association for Public Opinion Research Annual Meeting, Miami, Florida.

BASS, B. M. 1956. Development and evaluation of a scale for measuring social acquiescence. *Journal of Abnormal and Social Psychology*, 53/3: 296–9.

BELLI, R. F., TRAUGOTT, M. W., and BECKMANN, M. N. 2001. What Leads to Voting Overreports? Contrasts of Overreporters to Validated Voters and Admitted Nonvoters in the American National Election Studies. *Journal of Official Statistics*, 17/4: 479–98.

BELLI, R. F., TRAUGOTT, S., and ROSENSTONE, S. J. 1994. Reducing Over-Reporting of Voter Turnout: An Experiment Using a "Source Monitoring" Framework. In *NES Technical Reports*.

—— Traugott, M. W., Young, M., and McGonagle, K. A. 1999. Reducing Vote Over-reporting in Surveys: Social Desirability, Memory Failure, and Source Monitoring. *Public Opinion Quarterly*, 63/1: 90–108.

Belson, W. A. 1966. The Effects of Reversing the Presentation Order of Verbal Rating Scales. *Journal of Advertising Research*, 6: 30–7.

—— and Duncan, J. A. 1962. A Comparison of the Check-List and The Open Response Questioning Systems. *Applied Statistics*, 11/2: 120–32.

Bishop, G. F., Hippler, H.-J., Schwarz, N., and Strack, F. 1988. A Comparison of Response Effects in Self-Administered and Telephone Surveys. In *Telephone Survey Methodology*, ed. R. M. Groves, P. P. Biemer, L. E. Lyberg, J. T. Massey, W. L. Nocholls II, and J. Waksberg. New York: Wiley.

—— Tuchfarber, A. J., and Oldendick, R. W. 1986. Opinions on Fictitious Issues: The Pressure to Answer Survey Questions. *Public Opinion Quarterly*, 50/2: 240–50.

Brook, D. and Upton, G. J. G. 1974. Biases in Local Government Elections Due to Position on the Ballot Paper. *Applied Statistics*, 23/3: 414–19.

Brown, P. and Levinson, S. C. 1987. *Politeness: Some Universals in Language Usage*. New York: Cambridge University Press.

Burden, B. C. 2000. Voter Turnout and the National Election Studies. *Political Analysis*, 8/4: 389–98.

Campbell, A., Converse, P. E., Miller, W. E., and Stokes, D. 1960. *The American Voter: Unabridged Edition*. New York: Wiley.

Cannell, C. F., Miller, P. V., and Oskenberg, L. 1981. Research on Interviewing Techniques. *Sociological Methodology*, 12: 389–437.

Carr, L. G. 1971. The Srole Items and Acquiescence. *American Sociological Review*, 36/2: 287–93.

Clausen, A. R. 1968–1969. Response Validity: Vote Report. *Public Opinion Quarterly*, 32/4: 588–606.

Cloud, J. and Vaughan, G. M. 1970. Using Balanced Scales to Control Acquiescence. *Sociometry*, 33/2: 193–202.

Converse, J. M. 1984. Strong Arguments and Weak Evidence: the Open/Closed Questioning Controversy of the 1940s. *Public Opinion Quarterly*, 48/1: 267–82.

Converse, P. E. 1964. The Nature of Belief Systems in Mass Publics. In *Ideology and Discontent*, ed. D. Apter. New York: Free Press.

Cox, E. P., III. 1980. The Optimal Number of Response Alternatives for a Scale: A Review. *Journal of Marketing Research*, 17/4: 407–22.

Dahl, R. A. 1961. The Behavioral Approach in Political Science: Epitaph for a Monument to a Successful Protest. *American Political Science Review*, 55/4: 763–72.

Duff, B., Hanmer, M. J., Park, W.-H., and White, I. K. 2007. Good Excuses: Understanding Who Votes With An Improved Turnout Question. *Public Opinion Quarterly*, 71/1: 67–90.

Evans, R. I., Hansen, W. B., and Mittelmark, M. B. 1977. Increasing the Validity of Self-Reports of Smoking Behavior in Children. *Journal of Applied Psychology*, 62/4: 521–3.

Fritzley, V. H. and Lee, K. 2003. Do Young Children Always Say Yes to Yes–No Questions? A Metadevelopmental Study of the Affirmation Bias. *Child Development*, 74/5: 1297–313.

Goethals, G. R. and Reckman, R. F. 1973. Perception of Consistency in Attitudes. *Journal of Experimental Social Psychology*, 9: 491–501.

GREEN, P. E. and RAO, V. R. 1970. Rating Scales and Information Recovery. How Many Scales and Response Categories to Use? *Journal of Marketing*, 34/3: 33–9.

GRICE, H. P. 1975. Logic and Conversation. In *Syntax and Semantics*, Volume 3, *Speech Acts*, ed. P. Cole and J. L. Morgan. New York: Academic Press.

HAWKINS, D. I. and CONEY, K. A. 1981. Uninformed Response Error in Survey Research. *Journal of Marketing Research*, 18/3: 370–4.

HOFMANS, J., THEUNS, P., BAEKELANDT, S., MAIRESSE, O., SCHILLEWAERT, N., and COOLS, W. 2007. Bias and Changes in Perceived Intensity of Verbal Qualifiers Effected by Scale Orientation. *Survey Research Methods*, 1/2: 97–108.

HOLBROOK, A. L. and KROSNICK, J. A. In Press. Social Desirability Bias in Voter Turnout Reports: Tests Using the Item Count Technique. *Public Opinion Quarterly.*

—— —— CARSON, R. T, and MITCHELL, R. C. 2000. Violating Conversational Conventions Disrupts Cognitive Processing of Attitude Questions. *Journal of Experimental Social Psychology*, 36: 465–94.

—— —— MOORE, D., and TOURANGEAU, R. 2007. Response Order Effects in Dichotomous Categorical Questions Presented Orally: The Impact of Question and Respondent Attributes. *Public Opinion Quarterly*, 71/3: 325–48.

KALTON, G., COLLINS, M. and BROOK, L. 1978. Experiments in Wording Opinion Questions. *Applied Statistics*, 27/2: 149–61.

KLOCKARS, A. J. and YAMAGISHI, M. 1988. The Influence of Labels and Positions in Rating Scales. *Journal of Educational Measurement*, 25/2: 85–96.

KOPPELL, J. G. S. and STEEN, J. A. 2004. The Effects of Ballot Position on Election Outcomes. *Journal of Politics*, 66/1: 267–81.

KRAUT, R. E. and McCONAHAY, J. B. 1973. How Being Interviewed Affects Voting: An Experiment. *Public Opinion Quarterly*, 37/3: 398–406.

KROSNICK, J. A. 1989. Question Wording and Reports of Survey Results: The Case of Louis Harris and Aetna Life and Casualty. *Public Opinion Quarterly*, 53: 107–13.

—— 1991. Response Strategies for Coping with the Cognitive Demands of Attitude Measures in Surveys. *Applied Cognitive Psychology*, 5: 213–36.

—— 1999. Maximizing Questionnaire Quality. In *Measures of Political Attitudes*, ed J. P. Robinson, P. R. Shauer, and L. S. Wrightsman. New York: Academic Press.

—— 1999. Survey Research. *Annual Review of Psychology*, 50: 537–67.

—— and ABELSON, R. P. (1992). The Case for Measuring Attitude Strength in Surveys. In *Questions About Questions: Inquiries into the Cognitive Bases of Surveys*, ed. J. M. Tanur. New York: Russell Sage Foundation.

—— and ALWIN, D. F. 1987. An Evaluation of a Cognitive Theory of Response-Order Effects in Survey Measurement. *Public Opinion Quarterly*, 51/2: 201–19.

—— ——.1988. A Test of the Form-Resistant Correlation Hypothesis: Ratings, Rankings, and the Measurement of Values. *Public Opinion Quarterly*, 52/4: 526–38.

—— and BERENT, M. K. 1993. Comparisons of Party Identification and Policy Preferences: The Impact of Survey Question Format. *American Journal of Political Science*, 37/3: 941–64.

—— and FABRIGAR, L. R. In press. *The Handbook of Questionnaire Design*. New York: Oxford University Press.

—— LI, F., and LEHMAN, D. R. 1990. Conversational Conventions, Order of Information Acquisition, and the Effect of Base Rates and Individuating Information on Social Judgments. *Journal of Personality and Social Psychology*, 59: 1140–52.

——— and MILLER, J. M. 1998. "The Impact of Candidate Name Order on Election Outcomes." *Public Opinion Quarterly* 62/3: 291–330.

——— NARAYAN, S., and SMITH, W. R. 1996. Satisficing in Surveys: Initial Evidence. *New Directions for Program Evaluation*, 70: 29–44.

——— HOLBROOK, A. L, BERENT, M. K., CARSON, R. T, HANEMANN W. M., KOPP, R. J., MITCHELL, R. C., PRESSER, S., RUUD, P. A., SMITH, V. K., MOODY, W. R., GREEN, M. C., and CONAWAY, M. 2002. The Impact of "No Opinion" Response Options on Data Quality: Non-Attitude Reduction or an Invitation to Satisfice? *Public Opinion Quarterly*, 66: 371–403.

LAZARSFELD, P. F. 1935. The Art of Asking *Why*: Three Principles Underlying the Formulation of Questionnaires. *National Marketing Review*, 1: 32–43.

——— 1944. The Controversy Over Detailed Interviews—An Offer for Negotiation. *Public Opinion Quarterly*, 8/1: 38–60.

——— and ROSENBERG, M. 1949–1950. The Contribution of the Regional Poll to Political Understanding. *Public Opinion Quarterly*, 13/4: 569–86.

LENSKI, G. E. and LEGGETT, J. C. 1960. Caste, Class, and Deference in the Research Interview. *American Journal of Sociology*, 65/5: 463–7.

LINDZEY, G. E. and GUEST, L. 1951. To Repeat—Check Lists Can Be Dangerous. *Public Opinion Quarterly*, 15/2: 355–8.

LIPARI, L. 2000. Toward a Discourse Approach to Polling. *Discourse Studies*, 2/2: 187–215.

LISSITZ, R. W. and GREEN, S. B. 1975. Effect of the Number of Scale Points on Reliability: A Monte Carlo Approach. *Journal of Applied Psychology*, 60/1: 10–3.

LODGE, M. and TURSKY, B. 1979. Comparisons between Category and Magnitude Scaling of Political Opinion Employing SRC/CPS Items. *American Political Science Review*, 73/1: 50–66.

MATELL, M. S. and JACOBY, J. 1972. Is There an Optimal Number of Alternatives for Likert-scale Items? Effects of Testing Time and Scale Properties. *Journal of Applied Psychology*, 56/6: 506–9.

McCARTY, J. A. and SHRUM, L. J. 2000. The Measurement of Personal Values in Survey Research. *Public Opinion Quarterly*, 64/3: 271–98.

McCLENDON, M. J. 1986. Response-Order Effects for Dichotomous Questions. *Social Science Quarterly*, 67: 205–11.

——— 1991. Acquiescence and Recency Response-Order Effects in Interview Surveys. *Sociological Methods & Research*, 20/1: 60–103.

McDONALD, M. P. 2003. On the Overreport Bias of the National Election Study Turnout Rate. *Political Analysis*, 11: 180–6.

——— and POPKIN, S. L. 2001. The Myth of the Vanishing Voter. *American Political Science Review*, 95/4: 963–74.

McINTYRE, S. H. and RYANS, A. B. 1977. Time and Accuracy Measures for Alternative Multidimensional Scaling Data Collection Methods: Some Additional Results. *Journal of Marketing Research*, 14/4: 607–10.

MERRIAM, C. E. 1926. Progress in Political Research. *American Political Science Review*, 20/1: 1–13.

MIETHE, T. D. 1985. Validity and Reliability of Value Measurements. *Journal of Psychology*, 119/5: 441–53.

MONDAK, J. J. and DAVIS, B. C. 2001. Asked and Answered: Knowledge Levels When We Will Not Take "Don't Know" for an Answer. *Political Behavior*, 23/3: 199–222.

MOORE, M. 1975. Rating Versus Ranking in the Rokeach Value Survey: An Israeli Comparison. *European Journal of Social Psychology*, 5/3: 405–8.

MUNSON, J. M. and McINTYRE, S. H. 1979. Developing Practical Procedures for the Measurement of Personal Values in Cross-Cultural Marketing. *Journal of Marketing Research*, 16/1: 48–52.

NARAYAN, S. and KROSNICK, J. A. 1996. Education Moderates Some Response Effects in Attitude Measurement. *Public Opinion Quarterly*, 60/1: 58–88.

NISBETT, R. E. and WILSON, T. D. 1977. Telling More Than We Can Know: Verbal Reports on Mental Processes. *Psychological Review*, 84/3: 231–59.

OPPENHEIM, A. N. 1966. *Questionnaire Design and Attitude Measurement*. New York: Basic Books.

PAYNE, S. L. 1951. *The Art of Asking Questions*. Princeton, N.J.: Princeton University Press.

PRESSER, S. 1990a. Can Changes in Context Reduce Vote Overreporting in Surveys? *Public Opinion Quarterly*, 54/4: 586–93.

—— 1990b. Measurement Issues in the Study of Social Change. *Social Forces*, 68/3: 856–68.

—— TRAUGOTT, M. W., and TRAUGOTT, S. 1990. Vote "Over" Reporting in Surveys: The Records or the Respondents? In *International Conference on Measurement Errors*. Tucson, Ariz.

RAMSAY, J. O. 1973. The Effect of Number of Categories in Rating Scales on Precision of Estimation of Scale Values. *Psychometrika*, 38/4: 513–32.

REYNOLDS, T. J. and JOLLY, J. P. 1980. Measuring Personal Values: An Evaluation of Alternative Methods. *Journal of Marketing Research*, 17/4: 531–6.

ROBERTS, J. V. 1985. The Attitude-Memory Relationship After 40 Years: A Meta-analysis of the Literature. *Basic and Applied Social Psychology*, 6/3: 221–41.

RUGG, D. 1941. Experiments in Wording Questions: II. *Public Opinion Quarterly*, 5/1: 91–2.

SCHAEFFER, N. C. and BRADBURN, N. M. 1989. Respondent Behavior in Magnitude Estimation. *Journal of the American Statistical Association*, 84 (406): 402–13.

SCHUMAN, H. and LUDWIG, J. 1983. The Norm of Even-Handedness in Surveys as in Life. *American Sociological Review*, 48/1: 112–20.

—— and PRESSER, S. 1981. *Questions and Answers in Attitude Surveys*. New York: Academic Press.

—— —— and LUDWIG, J. 1981. Context Effects on Survey Responses to Questions About Abortion. *Public Opinion Quarterly*, 45/2: 216–23.

SCHWARZ, N. 1995. What Respondents Learn from Questionnaires: The Survey Interview and the Logic of Conversation. *International Statistical Review*, 63/2: 153–68.

—— 1996. *Cognition and Communication: Judgmental Biases, Research Methods and the Logic of Conversation*. Hillsdale, N.J.: Erlbaum.

—— and BLESS, H. 1992. Scandals and the Public's Trust in Politicians: Assimilation and Contrast Effects. *Personality and Social Psychology Bulletin*, 18/5: 574–9.

—— GRAYSON, C. E, and KNAUPER, B. 1998. Formal Features of Rating Scales and the Interpretation of Question Meaning. *International Journal of Public Opinion Research*, 10/2: 177–83.

—— and STRACK, F. 1985. Cognitive and Affective Processes in Judgments of Subjective Well-Being: A Preliminary Model. In *Economic Psychology*, ed. E. Kirchler and H. Brandstatter. Linz, Austria: R. Tauner.

———— 1991. Context Effects in Attitude Surveys: Applying Cognitive Theory to Social Research. *European Review of Social Psychology*, 2: 31–50.

——— HIPPLER, H.-J., DEUTSCH, B., and STRACK, F. 1985. Response Scales: Effects of Category Range on Reported Behavior and Comparative Judgments. *Public Opinion Quarterly*, 49/3: 388–95.

——— KNAUPER, B, HIPPLER, H.-J., NOELLE-NEUMANN, E., and CLARK, L. 1991. Rating Scales: Numeric Values May Change the Meaning of Scale Labels. *Public Opinion Quarterly*, 55/4: 570–82.

SIGALL, H. and PAGE, R. 1971. Current Stereotypes: A Little Fading, A Little Faking. *Journal of Personality and Social Psychology*, 18/2: 247–55.

SILVER, B. D., ANDERSON, B. A., and ABRAMSON, P. R. 1986. Who Overreports Voting? *American Political Science Review*, 80/2: 613–24.

SILVER, M. D. and KROSNICK, J. A. 1991. Optimizing Survey Measurement Accuracy by Matching Question Design to Respondent Memory Organization. In *Federal Committee on Statistical Methodology Conference*. NTIS: PB2002-100103. <http://www.fcsm.gov/01papers/Krosnick.pdf>.

SMITH, E. R. and MILLER, F. D. 1978. Limits on Perception of Cognitive Processes: A Reply to Nisbett and Wilson. *Psychological Review*, 85/4: 355–62.

SMITH, T. W. 1984. Recalling Attitudes: An Analysis of Retrospective Questions on the 1982 GSS. *Public Opinion Quarterly*, 48/3: 639–49.

——— 1987. The Art of Asking Questions, 1936–1985. *Public Opinion Quarterly*, 51/2: S95–108.

TOURANGEAU, R. and RASINSKI, K. A. 1988. Cognitive Processes Underlying Context Effects in Attitude Measurement. *Psychological Bulletin*, 103/3: 299–314.

TRAUGOTT, M. W. and KATOSH, J. P. 1979. Response Validity in Surveys of Voting Behavior. *Public Opinion Quarterly*, 43/3: 359–77.

TURNER, C. F. and MARTIN, E. 1984. *Surveying Subjective Phenomena 1*. New York: Russell Sage Foundation.

VAILLANCOURT, P. M. 1973. Stability of Children's Survey Responses. *Public Opinion Quarterly*, 37/3: 373–87.

VISSER, P. S., KROSNICK, J. A., MARQUETTE, J. F., and CURTIN, M. F. 2000. Improving Election Forcasting: Allocation of Undecided Respondents, Identification of Likely Voters, and Response Order Effects. In *Election Polls, the News Media, and Democracy*, ed. P. Lavarakas and M. W. Traugott. New York: Chatham House.

WALLSTEN, T. S., BUDESCU, D. V., RAPOPORT, A., ZWICK, R., and FORSYTH, B. 1986. Measuring the Vague Meanings of Probability Terms. *Journal of Experimental Psychology: General*, 115/4: 348–65.

WASON, P. C. 1961. Response to affirmative and negative binary statements. *British Journal of Psychology*, 52: 133–42.

WEISBERG, H. F. and MILLER, A. H. 1979. *Evaluation of the Feeling Thermometer: A Report to the National Election Study Board Based on Data from the 1979 Pilot Survey*. ANES Pilot Study Report No. nes002241.

WILCOX, C., SIGELMAN, L., and COOK, E. 1989. Some Like It Hot: Individual Differences in Responses to Group Feeling Thermometers. *Public Opinion Quarterly*, 53/2: 246–57.

WILLIS, G. B. 2004. *Cognitive Interviewing: A Tool for Improving Questionnaire Design*. Thousand Oaks, CA: Sage Publications.

WILSON, T. D. and DUNN, E. W. 2004. Self-Knowledge: It's Limits, Value, and Potential for Improvement. *Annual Review of Psychology*, 55: 493–518.

—— and NISBETT, R. E. 1978. The Accuracy of Verbal Reports About the Effects of Stimuli on Evaluations and Behavior. *Social Psychology*, 41/2: 118–131.

WOODWARD, J. L. and ROPER, E. 1950. Political Activity of American Citizens. *American Political Science Review*, 44/4: 872–85.

WRIGHT, J. D. 1975. Does Acquiescence Bias the "Index of Political Efficacy?" *Public Opinion Quarterly*, 39/2: 219–26.

CHAPTER 4

··

LABORATORY EXPERIMENTS IN AMERICAN POLITICAL BEHAVIOR

··

KIM L. FRIDKIN

PATRICK J. KENNEY

EXPERIMENTAL research in political science has a relatively short history, but the presence and influence of political science experiments have grown significantly over the past few decades (e.g., McDermott 2002; McGraw and Hoekstra 1994). A recent article by Druckman, Green, Kuklinski, and Lupia (2006), published in the centennial edition of the *American Political Science Review*, examined the number of randomized experiments published over the journal's first 100 years. The number, fifty-seven in total, has grown sharply in the last few years. The first experiment published in the *American Political Science Review* was Eldersveld's (1956) examination of the impact of mail and personal contact on turnout in the 1953 and 1954 local elections in Ann Arbor, Michigan. A smattering of articles utilizing experimental methods appeared in the next few decades. However, by the 1980s, a steady stream of experimental articles was being published in the *American*

Political Science Review. And, more than half of the fifty-seven experimental articles appearing in the *APSR* were published after 1992 (Druckman et al., 2006).

Political science experiments can take many forms, including laboratory experiments, field experiments, and survey experiments. In this chapter, we focus on laboratory experiments. We begin with a short discussion of the virtues and limitations of experimental research. However, much of the debate concerning whether experiments are an appropriate technique for the study of politics has long since been resolved. What remains are discussions concerning when it is necessary or best to use an experimental approach and what can be learned from such experiments? Consequently, in this chapter, we turn our discussion primarily towards summarizing the contributions and advances derived from experiments in American political behavior. We contend that in certain key areas of inquiry, theoretical explanations of enduring puzzles could not be corroborated without turning to experiments. Answers to important and interesting questions have begun to take shape in the wake of experimental evidence. The focus of this chapter, then, is less on the defense of the experimental method and more on the contributions experiments have made to diverse debates in the field of American political behavior. We focus our discussion on three areas within American political behavior: the role of stereotypes in campaigns, impression formation, and the influence of the media.[1]

WHY EXPERIMENTS?

Experiments, unlike any other method, can provide authoritative answers to causal questions. The use of experiments allows researchers to draw conclusions about causality because they "intrude upon nature" (Kinder and Palfrey 1993, 6). In other words, the experimentalist exerts control over the experimental setting by modifying conditions in systematic ways, varying only one factor at a time. In addition, the random assignment of subjects to stimulus and control conditions holds constant all potentially confounding forces. These two advantages of experiments—control over the stimulus and random assignment of subjects—provide the analytical leverage necessary to make causal inferences. As Kinder and Palfrey (1993, 6) point out, "it is the feature of intervention, and the control that such intervention brings, that distinguishes experimental research from other systematic empirical methods."

---

[1] Experiments have been conducted in divergent areas of political science, including international relations, committee decision-making, jury behavior, bargaining, and markets.

The virtues of experiments are plentiful. First, and foremost, because of the control inherent in experimentation, experiments are superior to all other methods at sorting out cause and effect relationships. For example, in an experiment, we can determine if watching a particular political advertisement influences citizens' assessments of the candidate targeted in the commercial. With other methods, such as a survey, we can only measure covariation between exposure to a political advertisement and subsequent evaluations of the targeted candidate.

Second, with experiments, researchers can untangle complex phenomena, to sort out the details of the underlying process. For example, experiments help us understand how campaign information affects citizens' impressions of candidates. Unraveling the diverse elements that contribute to people's evaluations of candidates is only feasible in the laboratory when the experimentalist can isolate and interact various factors likely to affect people's views of candidates.

Third, experiments are often relatively simple and economical to execute. A single researcher, for example, can design and implement an experiment with a relatively limited budget. Finally, when experiments are properly designed, the data analysis is clear-cut, allowing researchers to present their findings in a straightforward and easy-to-comprehend manner.

Experiments, of course, have limitations. And these limitations are primarily derived from an experiment's strongest assets: the ability to control the nature and timing of the stimulus, while simultaneously holding constant all rival explanations. In particular, in political science, the experimental setting is artificial, limiting the external validity and generalizability of the experimental results. We discuss this problem in more detail in the conclusion. In addition, experiments are often conducted with students as subjects, raising questions about whether the results can be generalized to more diverse populations. This is a particularly serious issue in political science because the college-age population has little in common with the typical American citizens to whom we want to generalize. Also, many experiments, especially laboratory tests, rely on a very small number of subjects, making inferences to millions of voters potentially problematic. Although these weaknesses are well documented and researchers typically take precautions to offset these limitations, one needs to keep these shortcomings front and center when assessing the contributions of experiments.

We turn now to several topics where experimental designs have advanced our knowledge about particular political phenomena. In selecting the specific experiments to include in our chapter, we considered two criteria: we selected experiments that moved the literature forward in significant ways; and we chose experiments where researchers went to extraordinary lengths to develop interesting stimuli while simultaneously striving to enhance external validation. Our selections, then, are exemplars and are not intended to represent an exhaustive review of the literature.

STEREOTYPES

Free elections are a singular characteristic of democracies and an important question for political scientists is how citizens evaluate political candidates. With the tools of survey research, we have identified several factors influencing people's view of candidates, including party identification, ideology, issues, and personality traits (e.g., Campbell et al. 1960; Miller and Shanks 1996). In one of our sister disciplines, social psychology, scholars examine factors influencing individuals' evaluations of people more generally. According to this research, stereotypes powerfully influence people's views of others. Stereotypes are energy-saving devices that serve the important cognitive function of simplifying information-processing (e.g., Macrae and Bodenhausen 2001). Stereotypes provide a "theme" around which the perceiver organizes incoming information (Bodenhausen 1988).

Given the strength and importance of stereotypes in social psychology, it was an easy leap for political scientists to ask: do stereotypes influence citizens' attitudes about politicians and political candidates? However, survey methodology could not be used to identify the impact of stereotypes in politics since people are unlikely to admit to adhering to "politically incorrect" stereotypes and people do not always know when they are employing stereotypes. Political scientists, therefore, turned to the psychologist's preferred method of inquiry, laboratory experiments, to study the impact of stereotypes in political campaigns. Researchers examined the impact of several different types of stereotypes, including gender stereotypes, racial stereotypes, and stereotypes about gays and lesbians (e.g., Golebiowska 2001; Huddy and Terkildsen 1993; Terkildsen 1993).

Virginia Sapiro (1981–1982) is one of the first political scientists to explore the role of political stereotypes with an experimental design. Sapiro wanted to explore reasons for women's lack of success in the electoral arena. To explore people's attitudes toward women candidates, Sapiro relied on an experiment elegant in its simplicity. Sapiro presented subjects in introductory political science classes with a short portion of a speech entered into the *Congressional Record* by US Senator Howard Baker. Sapiro selected the speech because it was topical, but it also presented few specific policy proposals and offered no explicit partisan or ideological positions. When subjects were given the speech, they were informed it came from a campaign speech delivered by a candidate for the US House of Representatives.

Sapiro distributed two different forms to the subjects: one identified the candidate giving the speech as John Leeds; the other identified the candidate as Joan Leeds. After reading the speech, subjects were given a series of questions asking for their evaluations of the speech and the candidate. The experimental stimulus, then, was the gender identification of the candidate for the US House of Representatives. Nothing else varied in the two conditions.

In this experiment, subjects did not know Sapiro was investigating the impact of gender stereotypes in the political arena. In fact, Sapiro offered a cover story at the start of the experiment: subjects were informed the study was about people's reactions to political speeches. Therefore, subjects could not deliver the "socially desirable" answers since they did not know what the "desirable" answer might be. Furthermore, the experiment, by presenting identical candidates, and manipulating only the gender of the candidate, insured that the two candidates were identical in every other way (e.g., experience, qualifications, and political positions). In the real world, when examining people's reactions to actual men and women candidates, it is difficult to parcel out the impact of the gender of the candidate from factors that may covary with gender, such as political background, policy priorities, personal characteristics, and political experience.

Sapiro's experimental results showed that gender mattered. In particular, subjects rated Joan Leeds as better at dealing with education and health issues and as more likely to maintain honesty in government, whereas subjects viewed John Leeds as significantly more competent at dealing with military and farm issues. Sapiro's experimental method has been replicated a number of times by researchers exploring different aspects of gender stereotypes in politics such as gender stereotypes and level of office (e.g., Huddy and Terkildsen 1993), gender stereotypes and media coverage (e.g., Kahn 1996), gender stereotypes and negative campaigning (e.g., Gordon, Shafie, and Crigler 2003).

Racial stereotypes, like gender stereotypes, have been the subject of experimental examination in political science (e.g., Mendelberg 2001; Valentino, Hutchings, and White 2002). Terkildsen (1993), in a study published in the *American Journal of Political Science*, explored the impact of race on white voters' views of black candidates. Terkildsen examined whether white voters discriminate against African American candidates, based solely on their race. She looked also at whether whites who are less racially tolerant are more negative toward African American candidates, compared to more racially tolerant whites. To examine these questions, subjects in the experiment were provided with campaign materials for one of three "real" candidates running for governor in a nearby state. The campaign packet contained excerpts from realistic-looking newspaper articles describing the candidate's experience, personal characteristics, and policy stances. A professionally altered photograph of a male candidate was attached to the campaign materials. In one condition, the photograph was of a white male, in the second condition, a light-skinned African American male was pictured, and a dark-skinned African American male was featured in the third condition.

Care was taken in altering the photograph to make sure that only race—and not physical attractiveness—was altered. In particular, the original photograph was of a light-skinned black male. For the white and dark-skinned color conditions, the photograph was "minimally transformed—skin color changes and subtle modifications in hair, lips, and cheeks were made by a professional graphic designer" using a computer graphics design program (Terkildsen 1993, 1040).

Subjects were recruited from jury pool members from the Jefferson County, Kentucky court system and were randomly assigned to one of the three experimental conditions. Subjects read the campaign materials and were asked to judge the candidate on a number of dimensions, including feeling thermometer ratings and vote choice. After evaluating the candidate, subjects were asked additional questions, including an assessment of their racial attitudes.

Results of the experiment confirmed that white voters discriminated against African American candidates. In particular, white subjects gave the white candidate significantly higher scores on the vote choice and feeling thermometer scale, compared to African American candidates. Racial prejudice mattered as well. Racially prejudiced respondents expressed more negative attitudes about African American candidates than less prejudiced voters. Terkildsen also found that the skin color of the African Americans mattered for certain white voters, with racially intolerant whites evaluating dark-skinned black candidates less favorably than light-skinned black candidates.

In summary, these experiments confirmed theoretical expectations emanating from social psychology that individuals employ gender and racial stereotypes when evaluating politics and forming impressions of candidates and politicians.

INFORMATION PROCESSING

Understanding, explaining, and even predicting how potential voters develop views about candidates has been a central focus of political science since the advent of survey research. During campaigns, the constant onslaught of information emanating from the campaigns and from the news media interacts with individuals' political predispositions (e.g., party attachment, ideological beliefs) to ultimately affect evaluations of the competing candidates. How do citizens process this immense load of information? How does this information shape citizens' beliefs and behaviors about candidates? Survey-based researchers could not determine precisely how incoming information alters people's views of political contestants. Consequently, scholars turned to experimental designs. In particular, political psychologists began to explore the mechanisms by which people process information about candidates.

Milton Lodge, Kathleen M. McGraw, and Patrick Stroh (1989), drawing on findings from social psychology, examined whether voters use an "on-line" or a "memory-based" process for interpreting incoming information. In the on-line processing model, campaign information shapes and alters citizens' evaluations of candidates, but only at the moment citizens hear, see, or read the campaign information. Therefore, only the overall impressions of the candidates remain in memory, while the underlying information is forgotten. In the memory-based models, people can recall the underlying information and will use this information when updating impressions of candidates during a campaign.

To examine the on-line versus memory-based models of information processing, Lodge and his colleagues devised a complex experimental design to determine if citizens used "on-line processing" to develop impressions of candidates. The experiment, based on a sample of 422 adults from Long Island, New York, contained six stages. In stage one, subjects read a five-page campaign brochure about a fictitious congressman named Williams Troy. Subjects were randomly assigned to one of four experimental conditions where each group was presented with forty policy statements attributed to Williams; but, at the same time, researchers varied positive and negative endorsements of Williams as well as varying whether subjects were asked to evaluate or form an overall impression of Williams.

In stage two, subjects were given a distracter task for five minutes. In stage three, subjects were asked to develop an overall impression of Williams. In stage four, the subjects were asked to recall Williams's policy statements. In stage five, subjects were shown the policy statements and they were asked if they recognized Williams's positions. In the final stage, subjects were asked to characterize the policy statements on a scale ranging from characteristic of the Republican Party to characteristic of the Democratic Party.

With this design, the researchers could examine the nature of the information stored in subjects' memory and how this information shaped evaluations of Williams. Lodge et al. found that "on-line" evaluations were a much stronger predictor of candidate impressions than information drawn from memory. The researchers concluded that potential voters do not typically rely on specific issues stored in memory.

Rather, the evidence suggests an "on-line counter" activated when information was initially encountered, retrieved, and used to render an evaluation. The results of Lodge et al.'s experiment were consistent with the "cognitive miser" conclusions of social psychologists. And, the findings resonated with Fiorina's (1981) notion that voters keep a "running tally" in their heads about political events and candidates. However, the empirical evidence was derived from one experiment employing a single fictitious candidate. Subsequent experimental findings advanced the literature by examining rival candidates in a more realistic campaign environment (e.g., Rahn, Aldrich, and Borgida 1994).

Lodge, Steenbergen, and Brau (1995) devised a more realistic experiment to examine how citizens process information about competing candidates at multiple points in time, similar to an ongoing political campaign. The experiment, drawing on a non-student sample of 356 subjects, took place in several stages. In the first stage, subjects read a one-page facsimile of a campaign fact sheet presenting the party affiliation, seven issue positions, and nine personal attributes of two hypothetical congressional candidates. The format of the fact sheet was modeled on how candidates are summarily compared in local newspapers.

After reading the candidate fact sheet, half of the subjects (selected randomly) were thanked and dismissed. The remaining subjects received a series of about fifty questions designed to prod them into thinking more about the candidates and their issue stands. These subjects were asked to evaluate the two candidates on a five-point scale that ranged from "very positive" to "very negative," to list their likes and dislikes of each candidate, to make trait assessments, and to make a vote choice. This manipulation was intended to generate a deeper level of information processing, which should bolster memory-based evaluations.

In the next stage of the experiment, the "delay" period, subjects were recontacted once randomly across thirty-one days. During the recontact, subjects were asked to give their evaluations of the two candidates on a five-point scale, ranging from "very positive" to "very negative." After providing an evaluation of each candidate, subjects were asked if there was anything positive or negative they could remember about each candidate,

Several findings emerge from the Lodge et al. (1995) study. First, subjects' recall of information from memory was poor and was related to the subjects' level of sophistication and to when the subjects were recontacted during the thirty-one-day period. The candidates' messages influenced citizens' evaluations of candidates when the information was first encountered, but did not appear to play any role in shaping evaluations at a later point in time. Lodge et al. (1995, 321) concluded, "the campaign raises issues that mobilize issue opinions that voters subsequently integrate, along with other factors like party identification, into a running affective tally for each candidate. In this process, recollections do not play a decisive role, short of the requisite that the on-line tally be recalled."

The theoretical simplicity and experimental evidence regarding on-line processing sped its appeal and incorporation into the standard literature on how citizens use information during political campaigns. However, not all political scientists were convinced. For example, David Redlawsk designed an experiment, published in *The Journal of Politics* in 2001, to test the supremacy of on-line processing. Redlawsk, instead of focusing on a two-candidate race, examined a multi-candidate contest, mirroring a presidential nomination campaign. In Redlawsk's experiment, information was not only dynamic, but came from several different sources. He introduced 102 subjects to a technique borrowed from psychology where subjects watched an "information board" with bits and streams of information presented in columns and rows. Subjects selected the type of information they would like to read and researchers recorded and "traced" the process by which subjects acquired information. At the end of the experiment, subjects were told they needed to vote for one candidate.

Redlawsk was interested in demonstrating that citizens do not rely exclusively on on-line processing, but will employ "memory-based" information when deciding which candidate to support. Redlawsk's key manipulation was his instructions to the experimental subjects. One group of subjects, randomly selected, was told to select information that they would need in order to vote for one candidate at the end of the experiment. The second group of subjects was told, "once you have voted for your preferred candidate, you will be asked to justify your choice. . . . In addition, you will be asked to list everything you can remember about the candidates in the primary election. So, you should do your best to remember everything you can as you look at each piece of information."

With this experimental manipulation, Redlawsk was able to document that subjects in the "memory-based" condition could remember more of the campaign information and could recall this information at the time they were making a choice between competing candidates, compared to the "on-line processing" group. Redlawsk concluded that models regarding impression formation and candidate evaluation need to be more inclusive, recognizing that citizens employ a range of information-processing techniques when taking in campaign information and forming impressions of rival candidates.

As these studies illustrate, the experimental method was vital in advancing our understanding of how citizens incorporate and process information during contemporary campaigns.

THE INFLUENCE OF THE MEDIA

The first Congress in 1789 solidified the role of the press in America's democracy by crafting and passing the First Amendment. Almost immediately, debates emerged about the press's influence on the actions of the government, on the behavior of politicians, and on the attitudes and actions of citizens. Over the last 200 years, the pervasiveness of the mass media has grown dramatically. Today, people are bombarded with political information instantaneously, around the clock, and from multiple media. The idea that the news media does not shape citizens' attitudes about politics runs counter to common sense. However, measuring the impact of the news media has proven to be a difficult undertaking.

Early survey research (e.g., Lazarsfeld, Berelson, and Gaudet 1944) found that the news media largely reinforced people's predisposition about political candidates. This "minimal effects" finding was largely reinforced by subsequent researchers examining the impact of both television and newspapers on people's preferences (e.g., Patterson and McClure 1976). Cohen (1963) pushed scholars to worry less about trying to document whether the news media told people *what to think*, and to focus on the news media's ability to tell people *what to think about*. The first empirical study of agenda-setting, a cross-sectional comparison of survey data with news coverage patterns, uncovered covariation between media attention and people's perception of the most important issues facing the nation (McCombs and Shaw 1972). However, subsequent cross-sectional studies yielded inconsistent results (e.g., Erbring, Goldenberg, and Miller 1980). Longitudinal studies examining the connection between survey data and media coverage patterns suggested modest to moderate agenda-setting effects (MacKuen 1981).

Real progress on documenting the agenda-setting power of the news media would not come, in any definitive way, until Iyengar, Peters, and Kinder's (1982) experimental demonstration of "not-so-minimal consequences of television news programs." The researchers systematically manipulated the attention that network news programs devoted to national problems by unobtrusively inserting actual stories about a particular problem into news broadcasts that were shown to subjects (see also Iyengar and Kinder 1987).

In designing their study, the researchers took great pains to increase the realism of the study. First, instead of relying on undergraduates for subjects, Iyengar and his colleagues recruited adults from New Haven, Connecticut by advertising in the local newspapers. Second, the researchers relied on sophisticated video equipment that permitted the cutting, adding, and rearranging of news stories so subjects would not know that the broadcasts had been altered. Third, Iyengar et al. tried to increase the realism of the experimental experience by arranging a setting that was casual and encouraging subjects to watch the news as they did at home.

In both of the experiments, subjects came to a location on the Yale University campus to take part in "a study of television newscasts." On the first day, subjects completed a questionnaire that covered a wide range of political topics, including the importance of various national problems. For the next four days, subjects came back to the experimental location, and viewed a videotape of the preceding evening network newscast which had been altered to provide more coverage of certain national problems (unbeknownst to subjects). On the final day of the experiment (twenty-four hours after the last broadcast), subjects completed a post-test questionnaire.

In the first experiment, experimental subjects saw several stories focusing on weaknesses in the US military preparedness, while the control subjects saw newscasts with no defense-related stories. In the second experiment, three problems were examined, requiring three conditions: one group of subjects viewed newscasts questioning US military preparedness, a second group watched a newscast emphasizing problems facing the environment, and a third group watched stories focusing on inflation. Iyengar, Peters, and Kinder uncovered clear evidence for agenda-setting: subjects who saw newscasts emphasizing a certain issue came to believe that issue was more important. In addition, the experiment demonstrated that certain people, those with less political information, were more susceptible to agenda-setting by the news media.

In this same set of experiments, Iyengar, Peters, and Kinder explored the idea that the press can "prime" the criteria citizens use to evaluate politicians. According to the authors, priming is accomplished because the news media, by emphasizing certain issues, alters the criteria citizens use to evaluate political figures. Iyengar and his colleagues found convincing evidence for priming. For example, when newscasts focused on a particular issue, like the environment, subjects who viewed these broadcasts were more likely to think about the president's ability to deal with the environment when developing overall evaluations of the president. The experimental work by Iyengar et al. initiated a lively and important debate regarding the news media's ability to "prime" citizens' considerations when evaluating elected officials and political candidates (e.g., Iyengar and Simon 1993; Krosnick and Brannon 1993; Miller and Krosnick 2000).

At approximately the same time that researchers were documenting the agenda-setting and priming effects of the news media, researchers began employing experiments to demonstrate that the news media, by "framing" issues, influence people's understanding of these issues (e.g., Druckman 2001; Iyengar 1991). Nelson, Clawson, and Oxley (1997) examined how alternative media frames regarding a Klu Klux Klan rally influenced people's level of political tolerance. As the authors explained, the debate over tolerance for hate groups produces a conflict over two competing values: the right to free speech and assembly versus the preservations of public order. Nelson et al. contended that an individual's level of tolerance is not only influenced by the individual's personal characteristics (e.g., education), but is influenced by contextual factors, such as the news media's framing of a political event or controversy.

To examine whether media framing of an issue influenced tolerance levels, Nelson and his colleagues conducted two experiments. In the first experiment, 222 undergraduate students were exposed to a news story about a KKK rally which was presented with either a free speech frame or a public order frame. Subjects began the experiment by watching one of two different seven-minute videotapes compiled of stories from recent local television news broadcasts. Each tape began with five minutes of "control" stories, including a story about a local science museum, two human interest stories, and one commercial.

After the commercial, the story about the KKK rally was shown. Two versions of the story were presented to the different experimental conditions. Both versions of the story focused on the same event: a speech and rally by the KKK on the steps of the Ross County Courthouse in Chillicothe, Ohio. Each story included a reporter on location and a video of KKK speakers, crowd scenes, and interviews. Although there was a great deal of similarity in the two stories, they represented two alternative frames: a free speech frame and a public order frame. The free speech frame emphasized the right of KKK members to speak to the public and the right of others to hear what the KKK had to say. The second story highlighted disturbances that occurred during the rally and included images of police officers in riot gear.

When subjects were done watching the videotape, they were asked a series of questions, for example, "Do you support or oppose allowing members of the Ku Klux Klan to hold public rallies in our city?" "Do you support or oppose allowing members of the Ku Klux Klan to make a speech in our city?" The results of the experiment suggested that the framing of the story mattered. People exposed to the free speech frame were significantly more tolerant than subjects exposed to the public order frame.

In the first experiment, the researchers relied on actual news stories when presenting alternative frames to subjects in the experiment. In the second experiment, Nelson and his colleagues constructed artificial but realistic stories and embedded these stories in an "electronic newspaper-style format." In this experiment, the authors were able to make sure that the only things varying in the two stories were the frame of the story. The headline, picture, and quotes within the body of the article determined each story's frame. The photograph accompanying the free speech frame showed the US Constitution, while the photograph accompanying the public order frame showed police containing a riot. In addition, a fictional law professor was quoted in the free speech frame as stressing the importance of free speech, while the same professor explained, in the public order frame, that public safety must be the top priority. All other aspects of the story were held constant.

In the second experiment, seventy-one undergraduates participated in the study. Subjects were randomly assigned to either the free speech or public order condition. After reading the news story, subjects completed a questionnaire that included tolerance measures. As in the first experiment, people who were exposed to the free speech frame were significantly more tolerant than people exposed to the public order frame.

As evidence mounted regarding the power of agenda setting, priming, and framing, researchers began exploring a larger array of "media effects." For example, an emerging and important question is whether negative advertising influences people's likelihood of participating in elections. Ansolabehere et al. (1994) were among the first political scientists to examine this question. Ansolabehere et al. developed a realistic experimental design for assessing the effects of advertising tone on turnout. The experiments took place during ongoing political campaigns (the 1990 California gubernatorial race, the 1992 California Senate races, and the 1993 Los Angeles mayoral race). The experimental manipulation, a political advertisement that was professionally produced, looked like an advertisement from the actual political campaigns. The "treatment" advertisement was inserted into the first commercial break midway through a fifteen-minute newscast shown to subjects.

The advertisements developed and used in the experiment were identical in all respects, except for the tone of the advertisement. In the experiment conducted during the 1992 California Senate primary, for example, viewers watched a thirty-second advertisement that either promoted or attacked the candidate on the general trait of "integrity." The visual elements in the advertisements and the announcer were held constant, thereby limiting differences between the conditions to differences in the tone of the advertisement. Ansolabehere et al.'s experimental design enabled the researchers to establish a much tighter degree of control over the tone of campaign advertising than had been possible in previous experimental studies (e.g., Garramone 1985; Pfau and Kenski 1990). Compared to survey research, the experiment offered a great deal more leverage on the causal connection between tone of advertisement and turnout. In survey research, for example, researchers often need to measure exposure to positive and negative advertisements by asking respondents to recall the advertisements they have seen during the campaign (e.g., Wattenberg and Brians 1999). However, recall data is problematic since respondents are likely to remember the most influential advertisements, while forgetting commercials that were less powerful.

Ansolabehere et al. also relied on a non-student sample to increase the generalizability of their findings. In particular, they recruited subjects by including advertisements placed in local newspapers, distributing flyers in shopping malls and other public venues, and posting announcements in employer newsletters.

To measure turnout, subjects in all the experimental conditions completed a post-test questionnaire measuring their opinions on a wide range of issues, including a series of questions regarding their participation and interest in the ongoing campaign. In analyzing the causal relationship between advertising tone and turnout, Ansolabehere et al. pooled each of the separate campaign experiments together (e.g., the gubernatorial study, the various senatorial studies, and the mayoral study) into a single dataset. The findings of the experiment showed that exposure to negative (as opposed to positive) advertising depressed intention to vote by 5 percent.

As these examples illustrate, the experimental methodology has enabled researchers to convincingly show that the media influence how citizens view politics in a number of distinct ways.

CONCLUSION

The goal of this chapter was to illustrate that experimental research is not only a valuable tool in the discipline of political science, but it is the only tool available to probe certain questions and puzzles. We intentionally isolated and discussed literatures that were important in the field of political behavior, but could not easily progress without findings from experiments. In addition, we chose studies that employed innovative experimental designs, where researchers went to great lengths to include non-student samples and to enhance the external validity in other ways (e.g., increasing the realism of the experimental stimuli).

At this point in time, it is unimaginable that we would be teaching or doing research in the general field of American political behavior without recognizing the results of classic experimental work. And these experiments, in many instances, have changed our understanding of how people react to the political world. For example, in the late 1970s and early 1980s, political scientists believed that the media had only "minimal effects" on the way citizens viewed politics and politicians. This belief was established and reinforced by years of survey research. But, almost overnight, in the mid-1980s, experimental evidence upended the "minimal effects" paradigm. Now, it is routine to argue in class or in research articles that the media's influence on citizens' attitudes is complex, multifaceted, and probably growing.

Although experiments are a useful tool for political scientists, we are mindful of the limitations of experimental designs. The problem of external validity, always dutifully noted by scholars employing experimental designs, is severe, especially when studying the beliefs and behaviors of citizens. So severe, in fact, that some scholars have a difficult time accepting results emanating from experiments. In an effort to mollify concerns raised by non-experimentalists, researchers try to enhance external validity with more heterogeneous, non-student samples and by trying to increase the authenticity of the experimental setting. However, it is unlikely that people's experience in the experimental laboratory actually approximates their experience in the real world, like seeing a political advertisement while watching CNN or reading a newspaper at the kitchen table.

One problem centers on trying to replicate the attention busy citizens dedicate to politics. We know from mountains of survey data that politics is not a high priority for most people most of the time (e.g., Delli Carpini and Keeter 1996). A large percentage of the American public is inherently and chronically uninterested in politics. In addition, even those citizens who find politics relevant and interesting are often distracted and frequently overwhelmed by the problems and concerns associated with the grind of daily life. The experimental setting intentionally focuses the attention of subjects on a political stimulus. Outside of catastrophic and overwhelming political events (e.g., 9/11 or launching a war in Iraq), citizens' attention is rarely fixed on a political topic like it is in an experimental setting.

A second problem, related to the first, is that many citizens do not hold carefully constructed or informed attitudes about politics or politicians. However, when asked about a topic, individuals are likely to reveal an attitude on the spot. This attitude may or may not truly exist and it may or may not guide or inform behavior. As Converse (1964) noted more than forty years ago, citizens may create an attitude simply because they are asked for their opinion. Or, citizens may have a true and stable attitude that guides their behavior. The quandary, then, is identifying a "true attitude" versus a "non-attitude." This problem is not unique to experiments but plagues survey researchers as well. However, the problem may be especially acute in experiments where subjects have agreed to leave their homes and come to a laboratory setting. These individuals, in many cases, have been specifically recruited for the experiment and, more often than not, they are being paid for their time and efforts. Experimental subjects, then, are highly likely to cooperate with researchers by dutifully answering questions before and after the presentation of the experimental stimulus.

A third problem with experiments is that for reasons of internal validity, experiments only vary one stimulus at a time. That is, experimentalists aim one message at subjects, while holding all else constant. But, in contrast, in the age of information, citizens going about their daily lives receive a barrage of political messages from different sources almost simultaneously. It is extremely unlikely that citizens living in the twenty-first century are exposed to a single message at a time. Indeed, in the contemporary United States, especially during political campaigns, the political world is filled with numerous competing messages all vying for the attention of citizens.

One way to combat the problem of external validity is to employ multiple datasets when addressing a research question. We have two suggestions; neither is new and both have been used before. The first suggestion is to make use of existing data sources (e.g., existing surveys or aggregate data) to supplement the findings from the experiments, even if they provide nothing more than "side" information. An excellent example comes from the work of Ansolabehere et al. (1994) reviewed earlier in this chapter. Although their experiments demonstrated that negative campaign information affects the attitudes and behavior of potential voters, the authors went one step further to validate their findings. They examined aggregate turnout data from the thirty-two senatorial campaigns from 1992 and content-analyzed newspaper data to determine the "tone" of the various US Senate campaigns. The aggregate data, supplemented with the content analysis, supported the experimental findings (i.e., negative campaign messages discourage people from voting.)

A second approach is to develop a research design relying on alternative methods addressing the same research question from the outset. Fridkin et al.'s (2007) study of the final 2004 presidential debate provides an example. The researchers examined how a presidential debate and subsequent news coverage shaped people's attitudes about the candidates in real time. They employed a six-group experimental design with subjects from the greater metropolitan Phoenix area and simultaneously commissioned a survey study of Phoenix residents that was in the field immediately after the final 2004 debate and stayed in the field for the next twenty-four hours. They also content-analyzed the news coverage that the people in Phoenix were likely to be exposed to in the twenty-four hours after the debate. This triangulation approach, three complementary datasets aimed at the same research question, allowed the researchers to control for the campaign setting because the research components were "in the field" at the same time. The researchers found strong debate and media effects, corroborated by the experiment and the survey data.

Experiments have unique benefits that make them an invaluable tool in the study of political behavior. In particular, the ability of experiments to isolate causal factors has greatly improved our understanding of how people process political information, how stereotypes affect political impressions, and how media messages influence people's attitudes about politics. In utilizing and interpreting the findings of experimental research, students of politics need to fully appreciate both the strengths and weaknesses of the experimental method.

References

ANSOLABEHERE, S., IYENGAR, S., SIMON, A., and VALENTINO, N. 1994. Does Attack Advertising Demobilize the Electorate? *The American Political Science Review*, 88: 829–38.

BODENHAUSEN, G. V. 1988. Stereotypic Biases in Social Decision Making and Memory: Testing Process Models of Stereotype Use. *Journal of Personality and Social Psychology*, 55: 726–37.

CAMPBELL, A., CONVERSE, P. E., MILLER, W. E., and STOKES, D. (1960). *The American Voter*. New York: Wiley.

COHEN, B. 1963. *The Press and Foreign Policy*. Princeton, N. J.: Princeton University Press.

CONVERSE, P. E. 1964 The Nature of Belief Systems in Mass Publics. In *Ideology and Discontent*, ed. David Apter. New York: Free Press.

DELLI CARPINI, M. X. and KEETER, S. 1996. *What Americans Know About Politics and Why It Matters*. New Haven, Conn.: Yale University Press.

DRUCKMAN, J. N. 2001. On the Limits of Framing Effects. *Journal of Politics*, 63: 1041–66.

—— GREEN, D. P., KUKLINSKI, J. H., and LUPIA, A. 2006. The Growth and Development of Experimental Research in Political Science. *American Political Science Review*, 100: 109.

ELDERSVELD, S. J. 1956. Experimental Propaganda Techniques and Voting Behavior. *American Political Science Review*, 50: 154–65.

ERBRING, L., GOLDENBERG, E. N., and MILLER, A. H., 1980. Front-Page News and Real-World Cues: A New Look at Agenda Setting by the Media. *American Journal of Political Science*, 24: 16–49.

FIORINA, M. P. 1981. *Retrospective Voting in American National Elections*. New Haven, Conn.: Yale University Press.

FRIDKIN, K. L., KENNEY, P. J., GERSHON, S. A., SHAFER, K., and WOODALL, G. S., 2007. Capturing the Power of a Campaign Event: The 2004 Presidential Debate in Tempe. *The Journal of Politics*, 69: 770–84.

GARRAMONE, G. M. 1985. Effects of Negative Political Advertising: The Roles of Sponsor and Rebuttal. *Journal of Broadcasting and Electronic Media*, 29: 147–59.

GOLEBIOWSKA, E. A. 2001. Group Stereotypes and Political Evaluation. *American Politics Research*, 29: 535–65.

GORDON, A., SHAFIE, D. M., and CRIGLER, A. N. 2003. Is Negative Advertising Effective for Female Candidates? An Experiment in Voters' Uses of Gender Stereotypes. *The Harvard International Journal of Press/Politics*, 8: 35–53.

HUDDY, L. and TERKILDSEN, N. 1993. Gender Stereotypes and the Perception of Male and Female candidates. *American Journal of Political Science*, 37: 119–47.

IYENGAR, S. 1991. *Is Anyone Responsible?: How Television Frames Political Issues*. Chicago: University of Chicago Press.

—— and KINDER, D. R. 1987. *News that Matters: Television and American Opinion*. Chicago: University of Chicago Press.

—— PETERS, M. D., and KINDER, D. R. 1982. Experimental Demonstrations Of the "Not-So-Minimal" Consequences of Television News Programs. *The American Political Science Review*, 76: 848–58.

—— and SIMON, A. 1993. News Coverage of the Gulf Crisis and Public Opinion A Study of Agenda-Setting, Priming, and Framing. *Communication Research*, 20: 365–83.

KAHN, K. F. 1996. *The Political Consequences of Being a Woman*. New York: Columbia University Press.

KINDER, D. R. and PALFREY, T. R. 1993. On Behalf of an Experimental Political Science. In *Experimental Foundations of Political Science*, ed. D. R. Kinder and T. R. Palfrey. Ann Arbor: University of Michigan, 1–42.

KROSNICK, J. A. and BRANNON, L. A. 1993. The Impact of the Gulf War on the Ingredients of Presidential Evaluations: Multidimensional Effects of Political Involvement. *American Political Science Review*, 87: 963–75.

LAZARSFELD, P., BERELSON, B., and GAUDET, H. 1944. *The People's Choice*. New York: Columbia University Press.

LODGE, M., McGRAW, K. M., and STROH, P. 1989. An Impression-Driven Candidate Evaluation. *American Political Science Review*, 83: 399–419.

—— STEENBERGEN, M. R., and BRAU, S. 1995. The Responsive Voter: Campaign Information and the Dynamics of Candidate Evaluation. *American Political Science Review*, 89: 309–26.

MacKUEN, M. B. 1981. Social Communication and the Mass Policy Agenda. In *More than News: Media Power in Public Affairs*, ed. M. B. MacKuen and S. L. Coombs. Beverly Hills: Sage Publications.

MACRAE, C. N. and BODENHAUSEN, G. 2001. Social Cognition: Categorical Person Perception. *British Journal of Psychology*, 92/1: 239–55.

MENDELBERG, T. 2001. *The Race Card: Campaign Strategy, Implicit Messages, and the Norm of Equality*. Princeton, N. J.: Princeton University Press.

McCOMBS, M. E. and SHAW, D. L. 1972. The Agenda Setting Function of the Mass Media. *Public Opinion Quarterly*, 36: 176–87.

McDERMOTT, R. 2002. Experimental Methods in Political Science. *Annual Review of Political Science*, 5: 31–61.

McGRAW, K. and HOEKSTRA, V. 1994. Experimentation in Political Science: Historical Trends and Future Directions. *Research in Micropolitics*, 4: 3–29.

MILLER, J. M. and KROSNICK, J. A. 2000. News Media Impact on the Ingredients of Presidential Evaluations: Politically Knowledgeable Citizens are Guided by a Trusted Source. *American Journal of Political Science*, 44: 301–15.

MILLER, W. E. and SHANKS, J. M. 1996. *The New American Voter*. Cambridge, Mass.: Harvard University Press.

MORTON, R. B. and WILLIAMS, K. C. 2008. Experimentation in Political Science. To appear in *The Oxford Handbook of Political Methodology*, ed. J. Box-Stennensmeier, D. Collier, and H. Brady. Oxford: Oxford University Press.

NELSON, T. H., CLAWSON, R. A., and OXLEY, Z. M. 1997. Media Framing of a Civil Liberties Conflict and its Effect on Tolerance. *American Political Science Review*, 91: 567–83.

PATTERSON, T. E. and McCLURE, R. D. 1976. *The Unseeing Eye: The Myth of Television Power in National Elections*. New York: G. P. Putnam.

PFAU, M. and KENSKI, H. C. 1990. *Attack Politics: Strategy and Defense*. New York: Praeger.

RAHN, W. M., ALDRICH, J. H., and BORGIDA, E. 1994. Individual and Contextual Variations in Political Candidate Appraisal. *American Political Science Review*, 88: 193–9.

REDLAWSK, D. P. 2001. You Must Remember This: A Test of the On-line Model of Voting. *Journal of Politics*, 63: 29–58.

SAPIRO, V. 1981–1982. If U.S. Senator Baker were a Woman: An Experimental Study of Candidate Images. *Political Psychology*, 3: 161–83.

TERKILDSEN, N. 1993. When White Voters Evaluate Black Candidates: The Processing Implications of Candidate Skin Color, Prejudice, and Self-Monitoring. *American Journal of Political Science*, 37: 1032–53.

VALENTINO, N. A., HUTCHINGS, V. L., WHITE, I. K. 2002. Cues That Matter: How Political Ads Prime Racial Attitudes during Campaigns. *The American Political Science Review*, 96: 75–90.

WATTENBERG, M. P. and BRIANS, C. L. 1999. Negative Campaign Advertising: Demobilizer or Mobilizer? *The American Political Science Review*, 93: 891–9.

....

CHAPTER 5

FIELD EXPERIMENTS AND THE STUDY OF POLITICAL BEHAVIOR

....

TIFFANY C. DAVENPORT

ALAN S. GERBER

DONALD P. GREEN

EXPERIMENTS are studies in which the units of observation—people, locations, organizations—are randomly assigned to different interventions. The purpose of an experiment is to isolate the causal influence of these interventions. In political science, the term "field experiment" refers to experiments that take place in real-world settings. Field experimentation attempts to approximate the conditions under which a causal process occurs, the aim being to enhance the external validity, or applicability, of experimental findings. Four criteria are often used to assess the degree to which field experiments approximate real-world conditions: whether the stimulus used in the study resembles the stimuli of interest in the political world, whether the participants resemble the actors who ordinarily encounter these stimuli, whether the context within which subjects receive the stimulus resembles the political context of interest, and whether the outcome measures resemble the actual political outcomes of theoretical or practical interest.

Political science field experiments take many forms. For example, Miller and Krosnick (2004) collaborated with an interest group in order to test the effectiveness of alternative fundraising appeals. The treatments were fundraising letters; the experiment was unobtrusive in the sense that recipients of the fundraising appeals were unaware that an experiment was being conducted; and the outcomes were financial donations. Similarly, Bergan (2009) teamed up with a grassroots lobbying organization in order to test whether constituents' email to state representatives influences roll call voting. The lobbying organization allowed Bergan to extract a random control group from its list of targeted legislators; otherwise, its lobbying campaign was conducted in the usual way, and outcomes were assessed based on the legislators' floor votes.

Not all field experiments are as realistic and unobtrusive as these examples. Sometimes the interventions that are deployed in the field are designed by researchers rather than by practitioners. For example, Gosnell (1927) and Eldersveld (1956) fashioned their own get-out-the-vote campaigns in order to test whether they would cause registered voters to cast ballots. Sometimes treatments are administered and outcomes are measured in a way that notifies participants that they are being studied, as in Paluck's (2009) experimental investigation of radio's effects on inter-group attitudes in Rwanda. Her study enlisted groups of Rwandan villagers to listen to recordings of radio programs on a monthly basis for a period of one year.

The distinction between field experiments and other types of experiments hinges on the causal question that the researcher has in mind. To the researcher who seeks to understand how college students behave when presented with dilemmas involving the distribution of small sums of money, laboratory experiments in which undergraduates vie for monetary payoffs may be regarded as field experiments. On the other hand, if one seeks to understand how members of the general public respond to political communication, the external validity of lab studies involving undergraduates has been questioned (Sears 1986), and similar objections have been levied against the artificial ways in which outcomes are often measured in the lab (Aronson, Wilson, and Brewer 1998). These kinds of external validity concerns may one day subside if research demonstrates that lab studies involving undergraduates consistently produce results that are corroborated by experimental studies outside the lab; for now, the degree of correspondence remains an open question.

The same may be said of survey experiments. By varying question wording and order, survey experiments may provide important insights into the factors that shape survey response, and they may also shed light on decisions that closely resemble survey responses, such as voting in elections (Glaser 2006) and approval of presidential performance in the wake of a foreign policy confrontation (Tomz 2007). Whether survey experiments provide externally valid insights about the effects of exposure to media messages or other campaign influences, however, remains unclear. What constitutes a field experiment therefore depends on how "the field" is defined. Early agricultural experiments were called field experiments because they were literally conducted in fields. But if the question were how to maximize agricultural productivity of greenhouses, the appropriate field experiment might be conducted indoors.

Studies classified as "natural experiments" or "quasi-experiments" are related to field experiments in that they enable researchers to gauge the causal influence of real-world interventions. Although usage varies, the term "natural experiment" typically denotes randomized experiments where the treatments are assigned by government agencies or non-academic entities. For example, the Vietnam Draft Lottery (Angrist 1990), the random assignment of defendants to judges (Green and Winik 2010; Waldfogel 1994), the random audit of local municipalities (Ferraz and Finan 2008), the assignment of students to schools by means of school choice lotteries (Hastings et al. 2007), and state-run Powerball lotteries (Doherty, Gerber, and Green 2006) are a few examples where randomization procedures were employed by non-researchers, setting the stage for an experimental analysis.

Related are "quasi-experiments" (Cook and Campbell 1979) in which near-random processes cause places, groups, or individuals to receive different treatments. Scholars have used seemingly arbitrary breaks in jurisdiction (Huber and Gordon 2004), geography (Huber and Arceneaux 2007; Krasno and Green 2008), representation rules (Pettersson-Lidbom 2004), and election thresholds (Lee 2007) to identify a wide array of different parameters. Huber and Arceneaux (2007), for example, use the arbitrary shapes of television markets and the incidental exposure of voters in non-battleground states to presidential advertisements in order to test whether these ads shape voters' preferences. Pettersson-Lidbom (2004) tests whether the number of municipal representatives affects the amount of government spending by seizing on the fact that certain Scandinavian countries require the number of local representatives to change with population size according to a rigid schedule. By looking at towns on either side of these population thresholds, Pettersson-Lidbom is able to test whether budgets shift as otherwise similar towns experience a shift in representation. Because quasi-experiments do not involve random assignment, the causal inferences they support are subject to greater uncertainty (Gerber et al. 2009). Nevertheless, we review field, natural, and quasi-experiments together because they all reflect a style of analysis that places emphasis on generating secure causal inferences through carefully constructed comparisons of groups receiving different treatments.

This chapter provides an overview of field experiments and their contribution to the study of political behavior. We begin by briefly summarizing the history of field experimentation in political science and neighboring disciplines. We then review a series of important and interrelated research literatures examining the effects of political campaigns, political communication, and political socialization. Our review suggests that the advent of field experimentation represents a significant departure from what had been a field dominated by survey and lab research. The net effect of this development has been to focus new attention on causal inference and to challenge key claims that had heretofore rested on observational or laboratory data.

History and Revival of Field Experimentation

The history of field experimentation may be traced to early attempts to conduct controlled interventions in the context of political campaigns. An early example of such work was Harold Gosnell's (1927) study of voter registration and turnout in Chicago prior to the 1924 and 1925 elections. Gosnell divided neighborhoods into blocks, assigning certain blocks to the treatment condition of his experiment, which consisted of a letter urging adults to register to vote. Tabulating the registration and voting rates in his treatment and control group, Gosnell found his intervention produced a small increase in voting in 1924 but a large increase in voting in the mayoral election of 1925. In 1935 George Hartmann conducted a controlled experiment in which he distributed 10,000 leaflets bearing either "rational" or "emotional" appeals for the Socialist party. Examining ballot returns, Hartmann (1936–37) found Socialist voting to be somewhat more common in wards that received emotional leaflets.

These early studies might be characterized as controlled field experiments, as distinct from randomized field experiments. Although Gosnell and Hartmann determined which blocks or wards were to receive their solicitations, they did not assign observations to treatment and control conditions on a random basis. As the statistical insights of Fisher (1935) took root in social science, experimentation became synonymous with randomized experimentation. For example, Hovland, Lumsdaine, and Sheffield (1949), working in the Experimental Section of the Research Division of the War Department during the Second World War, conducted a series of randomized experiments examining the effectiveness of various training films designed to indoctrinate Army personnel. Eldersveld's (1956) classic study of voter mobilization in the Ann Arbor elections of 1953 and 1954 built randomization into the basic design of the Gosnell study. Assigning voters to receive phone calls, mail, or personal contact prior to election day, Eldersveld examined the marginal effects of different types of appeals, both separately and in combination with one another.

Although Eldersveld's research was admired, the research methodology that it introduced did not catch on in political science. New developments in data analysis, sampling theory, and computing seemed to make non-experimental research more promising and experimentation less necessary. Surveys offered an inexpensive means by which to gather information from nationally representative samples; they could inquire whether the respondent had been contacted by parties or campaigns; indeed, they could examine the psychological mechanisms that might explain why canvassing leads to higher rates of political participation. Moreover, survey data could be mined again and again by researchers interested in an array of different questions, not just the causal question that animated a particular experiment. Surveys seemed not only superior as instruments of measurement and description, but also as vehicles for causal analysis.

Overshadowed by survey-based investigations, field experimentation had trouble taking root as a method for studying mass political behavior. The *Handbook of Political Science* devoted a chapter to "Experimentation and Simulation" (Brody and Brownstein 1975). Although the authors praised field experiments, they could point to few examples. In Donald Kinder and Thomas Palfrey's edited volume *Experimental Foundations of Political Science* (1993), only one of the twenty research essays may be considered a field experiment, Cover and Brumberg (1982). No field experiments were published in leading political science journals during the 1990s.

The turning point in field experimentation may be traced to economics, which saw during the 1980s and 1990s increasing debate about the accuracy of inferences derived from observational research. In a memorable essay, Lalonde (1986) argued that regression models—even technically sophisticated ones—may fail to extract accurate parameter estimates from survey data. LaLonde's demonstration involved comparing survey results to estimates generated by randomized field experiments. The exercise provided an unusually clear demonstration of the biases of non-experimental methods. Especially disconcerting was the fact that observational estimates remained inaccurate even when state-of-the-art statistical methods, such as propensity score matching or Heckman selection models, were used to correct for threats of bias (Glazerman, Levy, and Myers 2003). In short, despite the growing sophistication of statistical techniques, they remain unable to reliably address the threat of bias, and they remain unable to properly quantify the uncertainty of the estimates they generate.

Growing skepticism about the accuracy of conclusions rooted in observational research helped pave the way for a series of ambitious randomized experiments in a variety of social science disciplines. Criminologists launched a series of remarkable studies to assess the deterrent effects of arresting perpetrators of domestic violence (Sherman and Berk 1984) or police raids of drug distribution centers (Sherman and Rogan 1995). Sociologists and economists collaborated to study the effects of randomly moving residents of economically depressed housing projects to nearby neighborhoods with lower poverty and crime rates (Kling, Liebman, and Katz 2007). Economists working in developing countries introduced field experimentation on a grand scale to study the effectiveness of anti-poverty measures ranging from public health interventions to schooling to loans (Banerjee and Duflo 2006; Kremer 2003). The net effect was a rapidly expanding network of scholars working in different substantive areas but using similar methodological tools.

Amid these intellectual currents, field experimentation resurfaced in political science. Gerber and Green (2000) conducted a randomized experiment in New Haven, Connecticut in 1998, testing the extent to which door-to-door canvassing, calls from a commercial phone bank, and direct mail increased voter turnout. The study was in many ways reminiscent of earlier work by Eldersveld (1956) but differed in two important respects. First, the scale of the Gerber and Green (2000) study was approximately one hundred times larger than Eldersveld's. The number of observations in the New Haven study for the first time enabled researchers to gauge reliably the relative effectiveness and cost-efficiency of different get-out-the-vote tactics. Second, Gerber and Green took advantage of statistical advances that had occurred in the decades since the publication of Eldersveld's path-breaking study. Their statistical analysis addressed the problems that arise in field experiments where some of those who are assigned to receive phone calls or visits turn out to be unreachable. Whereas Eldersveld and other scholars classified the unreachable subjects together with the control group, Gerber and Green preserved the original randomly assigned categories and showed how they could be used to estimate properly the effects of the phone calls and visits. This study sparked interest in field experimentation, and during the next decade dozens of articles employing field experimentation appeared in political science journals and edited volumes. The next section considers the ways in which field experimental studies shaped the research in political behavior.

The Effects of Political Campaigns and Political Communication

Before the recent advent of field experimentation, the literature on campaign effects consisted of three main lines of research. The first relied on surveys conducted over the course of a political campaign or series of political campaigns. Many of the most influential studies of public opinion and voting behavior draw on surveys that measured respondents' choices and the kinds of environmental influences that may have shaped them. For example, Rosenstone and Hansen (1993) used a series of American National Election Studies to demonstrate that voter mobilization efforts conducted by political parties and campaigns increase voter turnout. Regression analysis indicated that, controlling for other factors that may influence turnout, those who report having been called or visited by campaign workers are more likely to report having voted. The problem with this type of analysis is that it is prone to bias. Campaigns do not target voters at random. Rather, they tend to target frequent voters. Thus, even if campaign contact had no causal effect on turnout, a regression analysis might indicate that those who were contacted by campaigns tend to vote at higher rates. The threat of bias is compounded by survey error. Survey respondents are notoriously inaccurate in their reports of campaign exposure, and there appears to be a tendency for self-reported voters to exaggerate the amount of campaign contact to which they are exposed. Similar problems afflict efforts to estimate the persuasive effects of campaign messages or communication within one's social network.

The second line of research on campaigns grew out of the work of Jacobson (1978), who pioneered the study of campaign spending and its effects on congressional election outcomes. In contrast to the survey-based studies mentioned above, Jacobson's approach involved assembling a database in which each House or Senate election comprised an observation. The independent variables of central interest in his analysis were expenditures by challengers and incumbents; by estimating the translation of money into votes, Jacobson's analysis addressed policy debates about campaign finance reform while at the same time speaking to the broader social science question of how voters form preferences about candidates. This line of research, however, became deadlocked over the question of whether reliable inferences could be drawn. Green and Krasno (1988), Levitt (1994), and Erikson and Palfrey (1998) each advanced critiques suggesting that regression analysis could be biased if the amount that candidates spend is a marker for unobserved factors that affect election outcomes. Incumbents, for example, may raise and spend more money when faced with a talented and well-connected challenger. If incumbents in general spend more when unmeasured factors make them more vulnerable, the analyst might underestimate the causal influence of incumbent spending on the incumbent's vote share. Each of the aforementioned authors advances a different statistical approach for grappling with this issue, but each model imposes its own set of assumptions. This literature came to a standstill when it became clear that different assumptions generated contradictory results: some authors found challenger spending to be influential; some found challenger and incumbent spending to be influential; and some found neither to be influential.

The third line of research uses laboratory experiments to assess the influence of campaign communications. Laboratory settings permit the researcher to randomly assign different kinds of campaign stimuli. Because randomly assigned campaign exposure is statistically independent of factors that might affect vote choice or behavior, laboratory experiments overcome one of the key impediments preventing survey researchers from drawing sound inferences about the causal influence of commercials and other forms of communication. Laboratory studies such as Ansolabehere and Iyengar (1995), Brader (2006), Iyengar, Peters, and Kinder (1982), Mendelberg (1997), and Mutz (1998) are outstanding examples of research that demonstrated the causal influence that televised news and commercials could have on public opinion and voting behavior. The limitations of lab research have to do with the extent to which results from the lab can be generalized to real world settings. Often, the subjects in laboratory experiments are drawn from the ranks of undergraduate classrooms; subjects are presented with the experimental communication in an unusual context (often a simulated living room on a college campus); and outcomes measures are survey responses gathered shortly after the stimulus is presented to the subject. These concerns raise the question of what laboratory results suggest about the effectiveness of an actual advertising campaign, in which the general population may be exposed to ads days before an election takes place.

Field experimental studies have brought a new level of precision to the study of campaign communication. In contrast to survey research, which typically categorizes campaign activity in very broad terms ("Did anyone from one of the political parties call you up or come around and talk to you about the campaign?"), experimental control enables the research to know what the communication was, who delivered it, and when. More importantly, the campaign intervention is randomly assigned and therefore unrelated to attributes that might predict the receiver's political attitudes and behavior. Although this virtue is also applicable to lab work, most field experiments have the advantage of measuring outcomes in an unobtrusive fashion so that participants remain unaware of the connection between the intervention and the outcome. When surveys are used to assess the effectiveness of campaigns, they are conducted so that neither the treatment nor control group is aware of the connection between the survey and the experimental intervention.

Interpersonal influence is another topic of broad concern to students of political behavior that has in recent years seen renewed use of experimental methods. Building on the earlier socialization studies of Jennings and Niemi (1974, 1981), Huckfeldt and Sprague (1987, 1995) pioneered the survey-based investigation of how friends and family members influence each other's political views. Their methodological approach was to survey respondents and people with whom these respondents discussed politics, a methodology that rapidly spread to other studies of interpersonal influence (Mutz 1998). Huckfeldt and Sprague found that the correlation between discussion-mates' political views persisted even after controlling for their background characteristics. These authors inferred that discussion itself caused the transmission of political views. However, the discussions themselves were neither observed nor randomly manipulated. Field experimental studies that have taken the Huckfeldt and Sprague findings as their point of departure have sought to test whether the correlation observed in these surveys reflects the causal influence of interpersonal communication *per se*, as opposed to unmeasured similarities between discussion-mates.

What has been learned through field experimental investigation? Let us preface the answer by defining what we mean by learning. We take a Bayesian perspective and envision a learning process by which prior beliefs about causal parameters are updated in the wake of new findings in order to form posterior beliefs (see Gerber, Green, and Kaplan 2004). These beliefs may be described as distributions, so that at any point in time a researcher's beliefs may be characterized in terms of their location and dispersion. The mean of this distribution indicates what the researcher takes to be the expected value of the causal parameter; the wider the dispersion of these beliefs, the greater the researcher's uncertainty about the causal parameter. From this vantage point, learning is a matter of reducing uncertainty. Even if the mean of the prior and posterior distribution remains unchanged in the wake of new data, the narrowing of the distribution indicates that learning has occurred. Thus, we must be careful not to disparage experimental results as merely "telling us what we already know" if they substantially reduce our uncertainty.

Collective Action

With that in mind, the field experimental literature has shed light on four important propositions about the effects of campaigns on voting behavior and candidate choice. The first concerns collective action. The basic theoretical insight from formal analysis of collective action problems is this: pursuit of a collective goal will falter in situations where individuals can enjoy a collective outcome without incurring the private costs of bringing it about. In the context of an election, for example, a voter may strongly prefer to see a Republican presidential candidate elected; however, the chances of influencing the outcome are infinitesimal, and the success of the GOP candidate can be enjoyed regardless of whether the voter cast a ballot. Thus, the voter abstains rather than expend time and effort to cast a ballot. Unless people find voting intrinsically rewarding, only a small portion of the electorate casts ballots or, for that matter, engages in any kind of collective political action (Olson 1965).

From this theoretical vantage point, voter mobilization campaigns are predicted to influence voter turnout when they change the benefit–cost ratio. Merely imploring strangers to vote should have little effect on whether they cast ballots. And yet it does. Door-to-door canvassing has a powerful effect on voter turnout (Gerber and Green 2000; Green, Gerber, and Nickerson 2003; Michelson 2005). One interpretation is that mobilization by canvassers imparts information to voters about when and where to cast ballots. But contrary to this hypothesis, reminders to vote by professional phone banks on average have little effect on turnout (Gerber and Green 2005; Green and Gerber 2008; McNulty 2005; but see Nickerson 2007). The overall pattern of results is inconsistent with the standard logic of collective action insofar as turnout is stimulated by factors having nothing to do with the direct personal costs and benefits of casting a ballot.

Source Credibility and Persuasion

The persuasive influence of credible sources is a second major proposition that field experiments address. The extensive laboratory and survey literature on persuasion has long suggested that people readily take cues from trusted individuals and groups (Lupia 2000; Petty and Wegener 1998), particularly in the context of low-salience elections in which information about the candidates is scarce. This proposition has recently been tested in various field contexts using campaign messages from party leaders and issue-advocacy groups. The results suggest that such communications have a surprisingly limited role in shaping vote choice (Arceneaux and Kolodny 2009). Perhaps the most striking result comes from a field experiment in which the popular Republican governor of a solidly Republican state recorded phone messages directed at Republican voters targeted by the campaign as the governor's likely supporters. The messages endorsed a sitting Supreme Court justice who had been appointed by the governor, urging Republicans to vote for him in the upcoming GOP primary on the basis of his record as a "true conservative." The experimental results, however, suggested that these messages had minimal effects on both vote choice and voter turnout (Gerber et al. 2007a). Field experimental results, in other words, seem to underscore the difficulty of changing voters' minds through direct appeals, whereas studies conducted in laboratory settings and eliciting immediate survey responses from participants tend to find much stronger interactions between messages and credibility (Iyengar and Valentino 2000; Yoon, Pinkleton, and Ko 2005). The more muted effects observed in field experiments are consistent with the observation that aggregate public opinion seldom shows marked and enduring shifts in the wake of persuasive communications (Gaines, Kuklinski, and Quirk 2007).

The Effects of Campaign Spending on Election Outcomes

The first article to draw the link between field experimentation and the literature on campaign finance was Gerber (2004), which attempted to gauge the cost-per-vote from experiments and compare it to the cost-per-vote implied by previous observational studies. Gerber's own experiments looked at the cost-effectiveness of partisan direct mail in congressional, state legislative, and mayoral contests, using voter turnout records to assess mobilization effects and post-election surveys to measure persuasive effects on vote choice. Although these studies were limited to direct mail, they were conducted with both Democratic and Republican candidates and both incumbents and challengers. These studies suggest that campaign spending is much more effective for challengers than incumbents, consistent with the original claims of Jacobson (1978).

Why do challengers enjoy greater marginal returns from their campaign spending? One long-standing hypothesis (Mann and Wolfinger 1980) is that challengers suffer from low name recognition, and voters are reluctant to vote for candidates whose names they cannot recognize. Through campaign expenditures, challengers can make rapid gains in name recognition, but incumbents cannot. The name-recognition hypothesis has a number of testable implications, one being that publicizing the names of both incumbents and challengers in lowsalience elections has the net effect of benefiting challengers. Panagopoulos and Green (2008) tested this proposition using a series of radio advertisements. In randomly selected cities and towns where mayoral contests were being conducted in 2005 and 2006, Panagopoulos and Green placed radio advertisements that encouraged voter participation in the upcoming elections and mentioned the names of the leading candidates (without endorsing any of them). In both years, they found that towns in which these ads aired gave higher vote percentages to mayoral challengers. Like the Gerber (2004) findings, the Panagopoulos and Green (2008) results merit further experimentation, for it would be interesting to know how much of the effectiveness of campaign communication on behalf of challengers is due to augmented name recognition and how much is due to other factors, such as communicating the challenger's qualifications, policy stances, or endorsements. Nevertheless, field experiments can be credited with breathing new life into important research literatures.

Interpersonal Influence

The experimental study of interpersonal influence dates back to the 1950s, when Katz (1957) studied the diffusion of rumors. In recent years, research has used three experimental paradigms. The first was pioneered by Sacerdote (2001), who studied the effects of randomly assigned college roommates on grades and other academic outcomes. This line of research was extended to the effects of randomly assigned racial contact or racial priming cues on racial policy attitudes (Newswanger 1996; Valentino, Traugott, and Hutchings 2002; Van Laar et al. 2005). Nickerson (2004) extended this analysis still further, looking at the transmission of political attitudes among randomly-assigned roommates and suitemates. Nickerson's findings challenge both the conclusions and methodology of the Huckfeldt and

Sprague studies. The roommate study finds little or no transmission of political orientations or policy opinions, except for those topics that are especially salient to undergraduates, such as legalization of marijuana or the statutory drinking age. Nickerson also shows that the statistical analysis used by Huckfeldt and Sprague, when applied to the experimental roommate data, severely exaggerates the interpersonal transmission of attitudes.

A second line of interpersonal influence research was also pioneered by Nickerson, this time in the context of voter mobilization. Nickerson (2008), in what probably ranks as the most elegant experimental design used to date, studied the effects of a canvassing campaign in which canvassers alternated between a get-out-the-vote script and a please-recycle script. In both cases, canvassers targeted two-voter households and communicated their script to the first person who came to the door. In keeping with prior turnout experiments, Nickerson finds that the get-out-the-vote script raised turnout substantially (those who came to the door and were treated with the voter mobilization script were approximately 9 percentage-points more likely to vote than those who came to the door and were encouraged to recycle). More importantly, Nickerson finds that the untreated voter in the households who were assigned to the voter mobilization script were substantially more likely to vote than their counterparts in the households assigned to the recycle condition. This result implies that those who heard the get-out-the-vote appeal somehow transmitted its influence to their housemate.

A third approach to the study of social influence is to communicate varying messages, each representing somewhat different social psychological forces. One such study is Gerber, Green, and Larimer's (2008) study of the role of social pressure on voting. Gerber et al. test the hypothesis that the likelihood of voting increases when people are reminded of the norm of voting and convinced that others are monitoring whether they comply with this norm. Their experiment consists of five randomly assigned groups, a control group comprising 100,000 households and four treatment groups of 20,000 households apiece, each of which received one mailing. The first treatment group received mail encouraging them to vote on the grounds that voting is a civic duty. The next treatment group was encouraged to vote using a similar appeal but was further informed that researchers were monitoring whether they voted for academic purposes. This treatment was designed to measure the Hawthorne effect of openly studying a person's turnout. More social pressure was exerted in the third treatment group, which encouraged recipients to do their civic duty and vote but also presented household members with official records of whether they had voted in two prior elections. The treatment exerting maximal social pressure presented not only the household's official voting records but also the voting records of several neighbors. In the last two conditions, recipients were told that they would receive a follow-up mailing indicating whether they (and their neighbors) voted. The results show a steady and dramatic increase in the effectiveness of each treatment as social pressure increases. The maximal social pressure condition raised turnout from 29.7 percent in the control group to 37.8 percent in the treatment group, an effect that rivals the effect of contact with a door-to-door canvasser. The finding that a single mailing can have explosive effects suggests the importance of surveillance to the enforcement of norms. The implication is that social pressure to conform to norms is one of the factors sustaining collective action.

PROSPECTS AND LIMITATIONS OF FIELD EXPERIMENTAL RESEARCH

The recent turn toward experiments and quasi-experiments reflects a growing sense among students of political behavior that the field had begun to reach the limits of what could be learned from observational research. Although observational studies supplied crucial descriptive information about the contours of public opinion, rates of political participation, subgroup differences, and changes over time, they meet with increasing skepticism from a social science community that has grown wary of inferences premised on untestable assumptions.

This pessimistic assessment of observational research methods has met resistance from those who believe that sophisticated statistical methods can resuscitate observational research. In recent years, scholars in economics (Dehejia and Wahba 1999) and political science (Imai 2005) have contended that methods such as propensity score matching enable observational researchers to closely approximate experimental results, thus sidestepping the practical and ethical challenges of experimentation. This argument set in motion a surge of observational research employing matching on topics such as the effects of deliberation on opinion change (Barabas 2004). However, the claim that matching provides reliable estimates of causal effects has drawn criticism outside of political science (Glazerman, Levy, and Myers 2003) and, increasingly, within it (Gerber and Green 2005). For example, Arceneaux, Gerber, and Green (2006) demonstrate that matching grossly misestimates the mobilizing effects of non-partisan phone calls on voter turnout. Their field experiment involving over one million registered voters showed these calls to have negligible effects on voter turnout; reanalyzing the same data using matching suggested that the calls profoundly increased turnout.

This finding and others like it do not demonstrate that all matching exercises are doomed to fail, but they do call attention to a fundamental problem that besets all observational studies, even those that rely on sophisticated statistical techniques: it is extremely difficult to assess *ex ante* the adequacy of an observational study's key assumptions. A researcher can argue forcefully that a statistical technique eliminates bias only to find one's conclusions upended by an experiment. As Gerber, Green, and Kaplan (2004) demonstrate, it is the *threat* of bias that fundamentally alters the statistical precision of an observational study. The nominal standard errors that are reported by statistical software packages ignore altogether this source of uncertainty. Indeed, even if the sample sizes of an observational study were infinite, the uncertainty associated with its conclusions would not be reduced to zero because there remains uncertainty about whether unmeasured differences between those who received different treatments invalidate the conclusions. In sum, the advantages of experiments are not easily approximated via observational research and statistical technique.

The principal argument for observational research is that it enables scholars to study a broad class of causal questions, not just those that are amenable to experimental manipulation. The question is how to balance the magnitude of the research question against the difficulty of extracting reliable answers. One approach is to look for quasi-experiments that speak more convincingly to broad-ranging questions than a conventional observational study. Gentzkow's (2006) study of television's consequences for electoral participation is an outstanding example of this style of research. Taking advantage of the stop-and-start way in which broadcast licenses were granted over time, Gentzkow shows that as broadcast television entered different geographic areas, it caused a decline in radio and newspaper consumption, which in turn produced a decline in voter turnout that was especially pronounced in off-year elections. Another approach is to conduct more ambitious field experiments. The scale and scope of field experimentation continues to grow. Until recently, it would have been un-thinkable to experimentally manipulate a set of competing parties' campaign appeals (Wantchekon 2003) or millions of dollars in television ads aired on behalf of an incumbent governor (Gerber et al. 2007b) or a nationwide campaign to hold legislators accountable to their constituents (Humphreys and Weinstein 2007).

One way to make field experiments more ambitious is to sharpen their theoretical focus. For example, research in social psychology has long argued that people conform to the views and behaviors of others, an argument of special relevance given recent interest in deliberative democracy (Fishkin 1997). The pressures of conformity could induce members of a minority to succumb to opinions expressed by a majority, regardless of the merit of those opinions (Mendelberg 2002). By randomly assigning individuals to discussion groups, Farrar et al. (2009) tested whether people assigned to more conservative or liberal discussion groups emerged with more conservative or liberal views and found that they did not. Findings such as these serve two functions. They speak to long-standing propositions about political behavior in the context of small groups and present a challenge to laboratory experiments on conformity that have tended to rely on undergraduate subjects and have largely focused on non-political decisions. A wide array of core propositions from social and cognitive psychology awaits experimental testing in political settings.

Another unexplored opportunity for field experimental research is the interaction between political elites and the mass public. Consider, for example, the domain of constituency service, which is said to bolster the incumbent's "personal vote" (Cain, Ferejohn, and Fiorina 1987). Apart from one relatively small field experiment looking at the effectiveness of franked mail (Cover and Brumberg 1982), scholars have not seized on opportunities to evaluate the impact of various facets of interaction between elected officials and their constituents. The number and timing of trips to the home district, actions on behalf of constituents who raise questions or request assistance, and initiatives designed to raise the visibility of a political issue all represent experimentally manipulable interventions that speak to the general question of whether constituents notice and reward legislative effort. Conversely, from the standpoint of the constituent one could evaluate the relationship between the attributes of those who request assistance or information from government officials and the nature of their response. Just as experiments are used to gauge discrimination by employers against those with putatively African American names (Bertrand and Mullainathan 2004), they could be used to assess whether constituents with different ethnic, age, class, gender, or partisan attributes receive different treatment.

The history of science suggests that significant advances often occur in the wake of new measurement technologies, such as the telescope or microscope. The experimental method represents this type of generative technology in the social sciences. Druckman et al. (2006) document the steep rise in experimental methods since the 1970s and the recent advent of field experimentation, noting the important substantive contributions that have been made during a relatively short period of time. But the benefits of the experimental method extend well beyond the specific research conducted to date. Experimental design forces researchers to state their hypotheses with greater clarity and often allows them to analyze the results more simply and transparently. Experimental procedures enable all researchers, not just those with a flair for statistical analysis, to draw unbiased inferences from data. And experiments conducted in the field draw the social scientist into the world of practitioners, where questions of cause and effect are of both immediate and scientific significance. Just as the challenges of civil engineering informed physics, the rigorous study of political interventions informs political science by providing a reliable empirical foundation from which theoretical propositions can be derived.

REFERENCES

ANGRIST, J. D. 1990. Lifetime Earnings and the Vietnam Era Draft Lottery: Evidence from Social Security Administrative Records. *The American Economic Review*, 80/3: 313–36.

ANSOLABEHERE, S. and IYENGAR, S. 1995. *Going Negative: How Attack Ads Shrink and Polarize the Electorate.* New York: Free Press.

ARCENEAUX, K., GERBER, A. S., and GREEN, D. P. 2006. Comparing Experimental and Matching Methods using a Large-Scale Voter Mobilization Experiment. *Political Analysis*, 14: 1–36.

—— and KOLODNY, R. 2009. Educating the Least Informed: Group Endorsements in a Grassroots Campaign. *American Journal of Political Science*, 54/3.

ARONSON, E., WILSON, T. D., and BREWER, M. B. 1998. Experimentation in Social Psychology. In *The Handbook of Social Psychology*, ed. D. T. Gilbert, S. T. Fiske, and G. Lindzey. Boston: McGraw-Hill.

BANERJEE, A. and DUFLO, E. 2006. Addressing Absence. *Journal of Economic Perspectives*, 20/1: 117–32.

BARABAS, J. 2004. How Deliberation Affects Policy Opinions. *American Political Science Review*, 98/4: 687–701.

BERGAN, D. 2007. Does Grassroots Lobbying Work?: A Field Experiment Measuring the Effects of an e-Mail Lobbying Campaign on Legislative Behavior. *American Politics Research*, 37/2: 327–52.

BERTRAND, M. and MULLAINATHAN, S. 2004. Are Emily and Greg More Employable than Lakisha and Jamal? A Field Experiment on Labor Market Discrimination. *The American Economic Review*, 94/4: 991–1013.

BRADER, T. 2006. *Campaigning for Hearts and Minds: How Emotional Appeals in Political Ads Work.* Chicago: University of Chicago Press.

BRODY, R. and BROWNSTEIN, C. 1975. Experimentation and Simulation. In *Handbook of Political Science*, volume 7, ed. F. Greenstein and N. Polsby. Reading, Mass.: Addison-Wesley.

CAIN, B., FEREJOHN, J., and FIORINA, M. 1987. *The Personal Vote: Constituency Service and Electoral Independence.* Cambridge, Mass.: Harvard University Press.

COOK, T. D. and CAMPBELL, D. T. 1979. *Quasi-Experimentation: Design and Analysis Issues for Field Settings.* Boston: Houghton-Mifflin.

COVER, A. D. and BRUMBERG, B. S. 1982. Baby Books and Ballots: The Impact of Congressional Mail on Constituent Opinion. *American Political Science Review*, 76: 347–59.

DEHEJIA, R. and WAHBA, S. 1999. Causal Effects in Nonexperimental Studies: Reevaluating the Evaluation of Training Programs. *Journal of the American Statistical Association*, 94: 1053–62.

DOHERTY, D. J., GERBER, A. S., and GREEN, D. P. 2006. Personal Income and Attitudes toward Redistribution: A Study of Lottery Winners. *Political Psychology*, 27/3: 441–58.

DRUCKMAN, J. N., GREEN, D. P., KUKLINSKI, J. H., and LUPIA, A. 2006. The Growth and Development of Experimental Research in Political Science. *American Political Science Review*, 100: 627–35.

ELDERSVELD, S. J. 1956. Experimental Propaganda Techniques and Voting Behavior. *American Political Science Review*, 50: 154–65.

ERIKSON, R. S. and PALFREY, T. R. 1998. Campaign Spending and Incumbency: An Alternative Simultaneous Equations Approach. *The Journal of Politics* 60/2: 355–73.

FARRAR, C., GREEN, D. P., GREEN, J. E., NICKERSON, D., and SHEWFELT, S. 2009. Does Discussion Group Composition Affect Policy Preferences? Results from Three Randomized Experiments. *Political Psychology*, 30/4: 615–47.

FERRAZ, C. and FINAN, F. 2008. Exposing Corrupt Politicians: The Effect of Brazil's Publicly Released Audits on Electoral Outcomes. *Quarterly Journal of Economics*, 123/2: 703–45.

FISHER, R. 1935. *Design of Experiments.* New York: Hafner Publishing.

FISHKIN, J. S. 1997. *The Voice of the People.* New Haven, Conn.: Yale University Press.

GAINES, B. J., KUKLINSKI, J. H., and QUIRK, P. J. 2007. The Logic of the Survey Experiment Reexamined. *Political Analysis*, 15: 1–20.

GENTZKOW, M. 2006. Television and Voter Turnout. *The Quarterly Journal of Economics*, 121/3: 931–72.

GERBER, A. S. 2004. Does Campaign Spending Work? Field Experiments Provide Evidence and Suggest New Theory. *American Behavioral Scientist*, 47/5: 541–74.

—— and GREEN, D. P. 2000. The Effects of Canvassing, Direct Mail, and Telephone Contact on Voter Turnout: A Field Experiment. *American Political Science Review*, 94: 653–63.

—— —— 2005. Do Phone Calls Increase Turnout? An Update. *The Annals of the American Academy of Political and Social Science*, 601: 142–54.

—— —— and KAPLAN, E. H. 2004. The Illusion of Learning from Observational Research. In *Problems and Methods in the Study of Politics*, ed. I. Shapiro, R. Smith, and T. Massoud. New York: Cambridge University Press.

—— —— and LARIMER, C. W. 2008. Social Pressure and Voter Turnout: Evidence from a Large-Scale Field Experiment. *American Political Science Review*, 102/1: 33–48.

—— GIMPEL, J. G., GREEN, D. P., and SHAW, D. R. 2007a. Do Robotic Calls from Credible Sources Influence Voter Turnout or Vote Choice? Evidence from a Randomized Field Experiment. Unpublished manuscript, Institution for Social and Policy Studies, Yale University.

—— —— —— —— 2007b. The Influence of Television and Radio Advertising on Candidate Evaluations: Results from a Large Scale Randomized Experiment. Presented at the Annual Meeting of the Midwest Political Science Association, Chicago, Ill.

GLASER, J. M. 2006. Public Support for Political Compromise on a Volatile Racial Issue: Insight from the Survey Experiment. *Political Psychology*, 27/3: 423–39.

GLAZERMAN, S., LEVY, D. M., and MYERS, D. 2003. Nonexperimental Versus Experimental Estimates of Earnings Impacts. *The Annals of the American Academy of Political and Social Science*, 589/1: 63–93.

GOSNELL, H. F. 1927. *Getting-out-the-vote: An Experiment in the Stimulation of Voting.* Chicago: University of Chicago Press.

GREEN, D. P. and GERBER, A. S. 2008. *Get Out The Vote: How to Increase Voter Turnout*, 2nd edn. Washington, D.C.: Brookings Institution Press.

—— and KRASNO, J. S. 1988. Salvation for the Spendthrift Incumbent: Reestimating the Effects of Campaign Spending in House Elections. *American Journal of Political Science*, 32: 884–907.

—— and LEONG, Y. Y., KERN, H. L., GERBER, A. S., and LARIMER, C. W. 2009. Testing the Accuracy of Regression Discontinuity Analysis Using Experimental Benchmarks. *Political Analysis*, 17.

—— and NICKERSON, D. W. 2003. Getting Out the Vote in Local Elections: Results from Six Door-to-Door Canvassing Experiments. *Journal of Politics*, 65/4: 1083–96.

—— and WINIK, D. 2010. Using Random Judge Assignments to Estimate the Effects of Incarceration and Probation on Recidivism among Drug Offenders. *Criminology*, 48.

HARTMANN, G. W. 1936–1937. Field Experiment on the Comparative Effectiveness of "Emotional" and "Rational" Political Leaflets in Determining Election Results. *Journal of Abnormal Psychology*, 31: 99–114.

HASTINGS, J. S., KANE, T. J., STAIGER, D. O., and WEINSTEIN, J. M. 2007. The Effect of Randomized School Admissions on Voter Participation. *Journal of Public Economics*, 91/5–6: 915–37.

HOVLAND, C. I., LUMSDAINE, A. A., and SHEFELD, F. D. 1949. *Experiments on Mass Communication*. Princeton, N.J.: Princeton University Press.

HUBER, G. A. and ARCENEAUX, K. 2007. Identifying the Persuasive Effects of Presidential Advertising. *American Journal of Political Science*, 4: 957–77.

—— and GORDON, S. C. 2004. Accountability and Coercion: Is Justice Blind When It Runs for Office? *The American Journal of Political Science*, 48: 247–63.

HUCKFELDT, R. and SPRAGUE, J. 1987. Networks in Context: The Social Flow of Political Information. *The American Political Science Review*, 81/4: 1197–216.

—— —— 1995. *Citizens, Politics, and Social Communication: Information and Influence in an Election Campaign*. New York: Cambridge University Press.

HUMPHREYS, M. and WEINSTEIN, J. M. 2007. Policing Politicians: Citizen Empowerment and Political Accountability in Africa. Presented at the annual meeting of the American Political Science Association, Chicago, Ill.

IMAI, K. 2005. Do Get-Out-the-Vote Calls Reduce Turnout? The Importance of Statistical Methods for Field Experiments. *American Political Science Review*, 99/2: 283–300.

IYENGAR, S., PETERS, M. D., and KINDER, D. R. 1982. Experimental Demonstrations of the "Not-So-Minimal" Consequences of Television News Programs. *The American Political Science Review*, 76/4: 848–58.

—— and VALENTINO, N. A. 2000. Who Says What? Source Credibility as a Mediator of Campaign Advertising. In *Elements of Reason: Cognition, Choice, and the Bounds of Rationality*, ed. A. Lupia, M. D. McCubbins, and S. L. Popkin. Cambridge: Cambridge University Press.

JACOBSON, G. C. 1978. The Effects of Campaign Spending in Congressional Elections. *The American Political Science Review*, 72/2: 469–91.

JENNINGS, M. K. and NIEMI, R. G. 1974. *The Political Character of Adolescence: The Influence of Families and Schools*. Princeton, N.J.: Princeton University Press.

—— —— 1981. *Generations and Politics: A Panel Study of Young Adults and Their Parents*. Princeton, N.J.: Princeton University Press.

KATZ, E. 1957. The Two-Step Flow of Communication: An Up-To-Date Report on an Hypothesis. *The Public Opinion Quarterly*, 21/1: 61–78.

KINDER, D. R. and PALFREY, T. R. 1993. *Experimental Foundations of Political Science*. Ann Arbor: University of Michigan Press.

KLING, J. R., LIEBMAN, J. B., and KATZ, L. F. 2007. Experimental Analysis of Neighborhood Effects. *Econometrica*, 75/1: 83–119.

KRASNO, J. S. and D. P. GREEN. 2008. Do Televised Presidential Ads Increase Voter Turnout? Evidence from a Natural Experiment. *Journal of Politics*, 70/1: 245–61.

KREMER, M. 2003. The Contribution of Recent Innovations in Data Collection to Development Economics, Randomized Evaluations of Educational Programs in Developing Countries: Some Lessons. *The American Economic Review*, 93/2: 102–6.

LALONDE, R. J. 1986. Evaluating the Econometric Evaluations of Training Programs with Experimental Data. *American Economic Review*, 76: 604–20.

LEE, D. S. 2007. Randomized Experiments from Non-Random Selection in U.S. House Elections. *Journal of Econometrics*, 142: 675–97.

LEVITT, S. D. 1994. Using Repeat Challengers to Estimate the Effect of Campaign Spending on Election Outcomes in the U.S. House. *The Journal of Political Economy*, 102/4: 777–98.

LUPIA, A. 2000. Who Can Persuade Whom?: Implications from the Nexus of Psychology and Rational Choice Theory. In *Political Psychology*, ed. J. H. Kuklinski. New York: Cambridge University Press.

MANN, T. and WOLFINGER, R. 1980. Candidates and Parties in Congressional Elections. *American Political Science Review*, 74: 617–32.

McNULTY, J. E. 2005. Phone-Based GOTV—What's on the Line? Field Experiments with Varied Partisan Components, 2002–2003. In "The Science of Voter Mobilization," special ed. D. P. Green and A. S. Gerber, *The Annals of the American Academy of Political and Social Science*, 601: 41–65.

MENDELBERG, T. 1997. Executing Hortons: Racial Crime in the 1988 Presidential Campaign. *The Public Opinion Quarterly*, 61/1: 134–57.

—— 2002. The Deliberative Citizen: Theory and Evidence. *Political Decision Making, Deliberation, and Participation*, 6: 151–93.

MICHELSON, M. R. 2005. Meeting the Challenge of Latino Voter Mobilization. In "The Science of Voter Mobilization." special ed. D. P. Green and A. S. Gerber, *The Annals of the American Academy of Political and Social Science* 601: 85–101.

MILLER, J. M. and KROSNICK, J. A. 2004. Threat as a Motivator of Political Activism: A Field Experiment. *Political Psychology*, 25/4: 507–23.

MUTZ, D. C. 1998. *Impersonal Influence: How Perceptions of Mass Collectives Affect Political Attitudes*. New York: Cambridge University Press.

NEWSWANGER, J. F. 1996. The Relationship between White Racial Identity Attitudes and the Experience of Having a Black College Roommate. *Journal of College Student Development*, 37/5: 536–42.

NICKERSON, D. W. 2004. *Measuring Interpersonal Influence*. Ph.D. dissertation, Department of Political Science, Yale University.

—— 2007. Quality is Job One: Professional and Volunteer Voter Mobilization Calls. *American Journal of Political Science*, 51/2: 269–82.

—— 2008. Is Voting Contagious? Evidence from Two Field Experiments. *American Political Science Review*, 102/1: 49–57.

OLSON, M. 1965. *The Logic of Collective Action: Public Goods and the Theory of Groups*. Cambridge, Mass.: Harvard University Press.

PALUCK, E. L. 2009. Reducing Intergroup Prejudice and Conflict Using the Media: A Field Experiment in Rwanda. *Journal of Personality and Social Psychology*, 96: 574–87.

PANAGOPOULOS, C. and GREEN, D. P. 2008. Field Experiments Testing the Impact of Radio Advertisements on Electoral Competition. *American Journal of Political Science*, 52/1: 156–68.

Pettersson-Lidbom, P. 2004. Does the Size of the Legislature Affect the Size of Government? Evidence from Two Natural Experiments. Unpublished manuscript, Department of Economics, Stockholm University.

Petty, R. E. and Wegener, D. T. 1998. Attitude Change: Multiple Roles for Persuasion Variables. In *Handbook of Social Psychology*, 4th edn., volume 2, ed. D. T. Gilbert, S. T. Fiske, and G. Lindzey. New York: McGraw-Hill.

Rosenstone, S. J. and Hansen, J. M. 1993. *Mobilization, Participation, and Democracy in America*. New York: MacMillan Press.

Sacerdote, B. 2001. Peer Effects with Random Assignment: Results for Dartmouth Roommates. *Quarterly Journal of Economics*, 116/2: 681–704.

Sears, D. O. 1986. College Sophomores in the Laboratory: Influences of a Narrow Database on Social-Psychology View of Human Nature. *Journal of Personality and Social Psychology*, 51/3: 515–30.

Sherman, L. W. and Berk, R. A. 1984. The Specific Deterrent Effects of Arrest for Domestic Assault. *American Sociological Review*, 49: 261–72.

—— and Rogan, D. P. 1995. Deterrent Effects of Police Raids on Crack Houses: A Randomized, Controlled Experiment. *Justice Quarterly*, 12/4: 755–81.

Tomz, M. 2007. Domestic Audience Costs in International Relations: An Experimental Approach. *International Organization*, 61: 821–40.

Valentino, N. A., Traugott, M. W., and Hutchings, V. L. 2002. Group Cues and Ideological Constraint: A Replication of Political Advertising Effects Studies in the Lab and in the Field. *Political Communication*, 19: 29–48.

Van Laar, C., Levin, S., Sinclair, S., and Sidanius, J. 2005. The Effect of University Roommate Contact on Ethnic Attitudes and Behavior. *Journal of Experimental Social Psychology*, 41/4: 329–45.

Waldfogel, J. 1994. Does Conviction Have a Persistent Effect on Income and Employment? *International Review of Law and Economics*, 14: 103–19.

Wantchekon, L. 2003. Clientelism and Voting Behavior. Evidence from a Field Experiment in Benin. *World Politics*, 55/3: 399–422.

Yoon, K., Pinkleton, B., and Ko, W. 2005. Effects of Negative Political Advertising on Voting Intention: An Exploration of the Roles of Involvement and Source Credibility in the Development of Voter Cynicism. *Journal of Marketing Communications*, 11/2: 95–112.

···

CHAPTER 6

FORMAL MODELING, STRATEGIC BEHAVIOR, AND THE STUDY OF AMERICAN ELECTIONS

···

JOHN H. ALDRICH

ARTHUR LUPIA

In research on voting behavior in American elections, many scholars use statistical or quantitative methods. Each of these methods can help scholars derive causal and descriptive inferences from available data. The continuing success of such work has generated increasingly ambitious research agendas. But growing ambitions can bring new challenges, particularly when they widen the gap between the questions that scholars raise and the inferences that are possible to derive from available data. For example, scholars may want to understand implications of important counterfactuals (e.g., what if there had been more female candidates over the years) or ask whether a particular psychological process played a role in voting decisions.

To address these and many more cases where a gap separates research questions and available data, scholars must make assumptions about how what they can observe relates to what they cannot observe. Such assumptions can be stated explicitly or implicitly. They can be stated precisely or vaguely. But no scholar can escape the fact that deriving inferences about things that one cannot observe from things that one can observe requires assumptions to be made.

Political scientists explore many methods for deriving desired causal inferences in such circumstances. One such method is formal modeling. A formal modeler's inferential process is simple to describe. Formal modelers first make assumptions about voters and candidates. They then use logic (usually in a mathematical form) to differentiate conclusions about voting behavior that are consistent with these assumptions from conclusions that are inconsistent.

Most formal models of voting behavior today use non-cooperative game theory. In a non-cooperative model, a scholar assumes that actors such as voters, candidates, or interest group members have varying preferences and information levels. Modelers typically assume that these actors encounter one another in a well-specified institutional setting. They then examine whether particular strategic adaptations by these actors are logically consistent with the model's assumptions.

An important attribute of formal models is that they allow scholars to analyze, with precision and transparency, complex conditional relationships between multiple variables. As such, scholars can use formal models to evaluate the conditions under which various kinds of causal relationships are logically consistent with clearly stated assumptions about actors and institutions. The distinguishing characteristic of formal models is their ability to facilitate constructive and precise conversations about what-is-related-to-what in the domain of electoral choice.

In this chapter, we explore contributions of formal modeling to the study of American elections and voting behavior. Formal modelers have examined many aspects of voting behavior. Rather than provide a cursory review of a long list of findings, however, we will focus on two topics (strategic voting and voter competence) for which formal models have challenged how many people think about key aspects of voting behavior. Using these examples, we will attempt to elucidate the broader potential contributions of the method to the study of voting behavior.

At present, the use of formal modeling to study voting behavior is controversial. While no one contends that an explicit statement of assumptions and attention to logical consistency are anything other than good components of scientific practice, controversy comes from the content of the assumptions themselves. The political opinions and behaviors of the general public are often thought not to conform very closely to the assumptions found in many formal models. Even formal modelers, who can point to how their methods have transformed scholarly understanding of how the US Congress works, may believe that their methods are better suited to the study of elite behavior. In this view of formal modeling, elite politics are suitable for examination because they:

- involve situations that regularly recur;
- occur in well defined institutional settings;
- and involve decisions that are important to the actors being studied.

Most members of Congress (MCs) are asked to vote on legislation on a regular basis, for example. The rules under which MCs make many decisions are exceedingly well defined. Of course, MCs care a great deal about being reelected, and they devote substantial time and effort to achieving that goal. The Congress, therefore, appears to provide an ideal setting for models to clarify causes and consequences of strategic behavior.

For voters, the situation is often different. While people may care about an election outcome, voting is not their profession. The actions available to voters are limited both in number (cast a single vote for McCain or Obama) and in time (elections are held infrequently). Moreover, it is unlikely that any voter can affect the outcome of the election by herself. So even if the election of one candidate over the other will have a substantial effect on a voter's daily life, the actions available to a single voter will not have much, if any, direct effect on that outcome.

Some therefore conclude that formal modeling should be used only to explain elite behavior. Still, if voters have motives and if we can offer a set of assumptions that constitutes a suitable analogy for what voters want, know, and believe, then we can use logic to clarify conditions under which they will, and will not, take particular actions. Indeed, there exist many formal models that predict complex and subtle patterns in voting behavior—patterns that were not well known in advance of the modeling work but have since been supported empirically by survey, experimental, and case study data.

Yet, many models contain unrealistic assumptions. This is true because models are not reality. They are simplifications of reality. As such, they will contain assumptions that correspond uneasily with reality. But what is true about the non-reality of models *is also true about every other commonly used scientific means of trying to draw generalizable inferences about voting behavior from available data.* Every time that a case study, election survey, experiment, or other observational database is used as a basis for generalization, the observations themselves are simplifications of a larger reality. So the fact that formal models simplify reality does not distinguish them from other commonly used methods. What distinguishes formal models is that their assumptions are usually stated with greater clarity and the relationships between their conclusions and assumptions are usually evaluated with greater logical transparency.

In this chapter, we focus on two topical areas for which formal models have been used to explain complex, subtle, and important patterns of behavior that other theories did not explain well. In these domains, models advanced substantive debates about why voters act as they do and what meanings one can draw from electoral outcomes. They are also areas in which controversies over the content of key assumptions influenced model development in ways that helped modelers offer new explanations of voting behavior.

The first area is *strategic voting*. The research question is, "Under what conditions do voters choose a candidate or party other than the one they prefer most?" A key decision for scholars is whether voters should be modeled as *expected utility maximizers*. We therefore focus our discussion on the extent to which observed patterns of behavior are consistent with formal models that posit voters as expected utility maximizers.

The second area is *voter competence*. Here, the research question is, "Under what conditions can incompletely informed voters use the statements of others (e.g., speeches, endorsements, or advertisements) to cast the same votes they would have cast if they knew more?" A key decision for scholars working in this area is how to represent processes of communication and learning. We focus our discussion of this topic on how the precision of formal modeling can clarify what voters learn from others.

After reviewing these two areas, we conclude this chapter with a brief discussion of the likely role of formal modeling in future voting behavior scholarship. In so doing, we offer examples of current scholarly pursuits whose precision and validity could be improved by greater clarity about assumptions and logical transparency in inference.

MODELS OF STRATEGIC VOTING AND UTILITY MAXIMIZATION ASSUMPTIONS

Duverger's Law is that a plurality rule election system favors the sustenance of two major political parties, and no more, regardless of the distribution of preferences in a society. Duverger's Law, like Boyle's Law, is an empirical regularity that was originally observed but not theoretically explained (Riker 1982). Duverger was not the first to observe the regularity but he is credited with the Law because he was the first to pursue a theoretical explanation. He developed a two-part account based on "mechanical" and "psychological" effects. The mechanical component is the way that single-member districts translate votes into seats, ordinarily exaggerating the lead of the party that receives the most votes. The psychological aspect is a basic account of why voters might refuse to support attractive candidates (or parties) who (that) have no chance of winning in favor of less preferred candidates who can defeat even less desirable choices. Consider, for example, the thought processes of people who preferred Green Party candidate Ralph Nader in 2000. How did they respond to the many attempts to shape their voting behavior?

That Duverger's "psychological" effect has become so closely associated with formal modeling was not inevitable. Duverger (1986) himself denied that his was a choice-theoretic explanation, but the contemporary understanding of strategic voting is deeply and broadly informed by work in formal modeling rather than more psychological examinations.

Formal modelers were the first (and so far the only) scholars to derive the Law with conceptual clarity and logical precision. Palfrey (1989) did so first, followed by a variety of others—such as Feddersen (1992) and then Cox (1997), who provided many additional important advances in this area (see also Greenberg and Shepsle 1987; Shepsle 1991).

The implications of these results for American politics are deep. For example, Cox (1997) derived the general $m+1$ rule, which is that if, in plurality types of systems, there are to be m candidates selected from a district, there are no more than $m+1$ viable contenders in equilibrium. The empirical implication is that America's two-party system is not inherently a result of its political culture as much as it is a result of America's adoption of single-member districts to elect legislatures. Indeed, if the US were to move to more multi-member districts, it is possible that more than two major parties could be sustained even in a plurality system (see Rapoport and Stone 2005 for empirical examination).

In the rest of this section, we will describe a series of hypotheses pertaining to strategic voting that were derived from formal models and then evaluated empirically. We will start with basic hypotheses and move to more complex and less obvious findings. We begin with Niou (2001) and Niou and Kselman (n.d.), who have clarified when voters in American elections are most likely to vote strategically. They show that everyone who most prefers one of the two most popular candidates should vote for that candidate. Only those backing the third strongest candidate *should at least consider* voting for their second-most preferred candidate. This prediction engenders a testable hypothesis—all voting for someone other than a voter's most preferred candidate should be for voters who favor the third most popular candidate. The Niou–Kselman hypothesis has been tested in numerous electoral settings. Alvarez and Nagler (1998, 2000) and Alvarez, Boehmke, and Nagler (2006) provide estimation strategies for multi-party and candidate contests, with applications outside the US. Abramson et al. (forthcoming) compare the US, Britain, the Netherlands, and Israel.

Abramson, Aldrich, and Rohde (e.g., 2003) present the relevant data for US presidential elections. There was a "significant" third-party candidate in 1968, 1980, 1992, 1996, and 2000, where significant is defined by receiving enough support to make empirical analysis of American National Election Studies (ANES) surveys feasible. The hypothesis is evaluated by comparing reported candidate preference to reported vote. On average over 96 percent of those who most preferred a major party candidate voted for him but only six in ten of those who most preferred a third-party or independent candidate did the same. In the 2000 ANES, for example, 15 percent rated Nader as their most preferred candidate, but only 3 percent voted for him. Such patterns are strongly consistent with the Niou–Kselman hypothesis.

Other research agendas focus on whether the assumption that voters are expected utility maximizers is consistent with relevant observations. This focus is relevant, because formal models of strategic voting typically assume that voters combine their preferences, as considered above, with information about the probabilities of various outcomes. Voters are assumed to act as if they have well-formed expectations and to be skilled at probabilistic reasoning. When the number of candidates or parties from which voters can choose is small, the assumption that voters have such preferences and skills is not heroic. Still, Kahneman and Tversky (1979; and Tversky and Kahneman 1974) and others who study the behavioral psychology of decision-making have been critical of this modeling practice. Thus, it is important to see if voters judge probabilities relevant to strategic voting in ways that would correspond to their ability to act as if they maximize expected utility.

There is good evidence in support of the proposition that voters act as if they maximized expected utility. In many cases around the world, voters understand which candidates do, and do not, have a chance of winning (in addition to citations below, see Blais and Bodet 2006; Blais, Young, and Turcotte 2005; Blais et al. 2006). In what follows, we will focus on the applicability of the models to circumstances where such evidence exists.

The benefit of voting strategically depends on the voter's beliefs about the consequence of doing so. With probability assessments necessary to form expected utility calculations, such maximizing voters will be particularly concerned about whether the election is close. *Are real voters good judges of "closeness"?* To answer this question, we return to the Abramson et al. data. Every third candidate in their dataset actually trailed both major party nominees in the polls. In 1992, Perot briefly was in a near three-way tie for first place in the polls. However, this was in May and early June, and he dropped out of the election well before the first ANES survey. As a result, we cannot use his contest to study what would happen if a non-major-party candidate were one of the two most likely candidates to win or were at least tied for second place.

In 1968, however, American Independence Party candidate George Wallace not only got very close to Democrat Hubert Humphrey's standing in the Gallup Poll in September, but he actually was strongly competitive for electoral votes in a number of states—winning several. This scenario raises an "institutional" issue. The Electoral College allocates electoral votes by state. It is at least a testable question as to whether voters consider how close the election is in their state.

Aldrich (1976) looked at ANES responses to 100-point "electability" scales, asking about the candidates' chances in the nation and separately in the respondent's home state. He found that a voter's view of the candidate's chances in their state was more strongly correlated with turnout than was their view of the race's closeness considered at the national level. Second, the above logic of strategic voting leads us to expect voters who preferred Wallace to be more likely to vote for him if they perceived the race in their state to be close. This would be in contrast to voters who preferred Wallace but perceived him as far behind. The expectation is that these voters would "defect" to their second-most preferred candidate. There are very few cases of respondents who met these criteria in the 1968 ANES survey, so the test is not particularly powerful, but Bensel and Sanders (1979) found exactly the predicted pattern—defections from Wallace by supporters were high in states where he was not running well, and low where he was close or actually winning.

These examples show that voters can judge "closeness" in ways that are consistent with the capacity to base decisions on expected utility maximization. Since the correlations between this assumption and observational data were far from inevitable *ex ante*, the evidence in favor of a voters-as-expected-utility-maximizers proposition merits attention. But these examples are based on inexact measures of voter probability assessments. A stronger test would use more detailed probabilities.

Abramson et. al. (1992) contains such a test. They used ANES data from a rolling cross-section during the 1988 presidential primary season. Those surveys contained 100-point measures of preferences (candidate "feeling thermometers") and 100-point measures of probabilities (candidate "viability"—referring to the nomination—and "electability"—referring to the general election—ratings) and hence permitted a more direct test of the expected utility formulation. Previous studies had found that activists (such as those who attend state caucuses and conventions) appeared to act in a manner consistent with expected utility maximization. Stone and Abramowitz (1983), for example, found that convention delegates considered both candidate preference and probabilities of winning in determining for whom they voted. Abramson et al., expanded the focus to primary voters. Their models fit the expected patterns exactly, with good fits for both parties, and with estimations and corrections for possible endogeneity (that is, that voters prefer winning candidates because they are winning or that they see their favorite candidate as a stronger choice than others). The full set of hypotheses is even a closer rendition of support for the proposition that many voters act as if they were expected utility maximizers and the proposition that, as such, they can and do engage in strategic voting.

Some models make even more refined assumptions about voters. Cox (1997), for example, assumes that voters choose amongst candidates as if they apply the Bayesian perfect equilibrium solution to their decisions. In other words, voters have well-formulated prior beliefs about the likelihood of different outcomes and find a way to reconcile their choices with their expectations about what others will do. If this notion sounds implausible on its face, consider the fact that this representation of voter decision-making also has strong empirical support. Cox presents a substantial body of evidence, much of it testing a variety of precise and non-obvious hypotheses, that electoral choices do, in fact, conform closely to patterns that would emerge if voters were employing Bayesian perfect equilibrium strategies.

So far, we have focused on a few assumptions pertinent to strategic voting—notably preferences and expectations. A third set of considerations is the voter's perception of party positions. Many models include the simple, but strong, assumption that there is a true policy position in a policy space for each party and that voters act as though they see each position accurately. There has long been reason to doubt that this assumption is always true. Levine (2007) examined whether voters would vote strategically if their perceptions were variable. His data are experimental and mimic the Nader–Gore–Bush formulation, although he correctly chose not to give the candidates in his experiments real names. His key idea is that the set of candidates affects the perceived locations of the candidates. For example, in a contest featuring just Gore and Bush, people would locate the candidates differently than if a Nader-like candidate were also in the race. That is just what he found. In particular, the Gore-like candidate was perceived more moderately when the contest also included an extremist on his left. Moreover, Levine found that regardless of the origin of the perceptions, people act on what they observe. Thus, while the Gore-like candidate lost votes to the candidate to his left, he gained votes from the Bush-like candidate on his right, because people saw him as more moderate in the presence of Nader. Of course, this is only one of many possible variants of perceptual effects that might shape the nature of decision-making based on expected utility maximization.

Having evaluated the plausibility of important assumptions underlying formal models of strategic voting, we close this section by examining implications of using this approach in attempts to understand strategic voting. For example, if voters are strategic, would campaigns choose different strategies than they would if they believed that strategic voting would not occur? Merolla (2003) examined the Nader–Gore–Bush race in 2000. Nader was certain to draw the great majority of his support from erstwhile Gore supporters. If Nader supporters were in a state in which he was less competitive, but the race between Gore and Bush was close, Gore would have incentives to campaign vigorously against those voting for Nader. That is, the Gore campaign would have an incentive to persuade Nader voters to vote strategically. The great body of formal-model-based evidence, such as that described above, suggests that such an argument from a candidate in Gore's circumstances would be understood and acted upon by at least some voters.

Merolla (2003) compared circumstances that were ripe for strategic appeals for tactical voting to circumstances where such appeals were not effective (e.g., North

Carolina, at the extreme, where voters were barred even from writing in Nader's name). She examined campaign ads to examine whether, in the more favorable states, Gore and Nader did offer point–counterpoint ad-claims for tactical voting, while in the less favorable states for such appeals, they did not. Her findings starkly and strongly support this claim. We do not know at this point if voters are more likely to vote strategically when campaigns suggest they do than when they do not so suggest, and we do not know the mechanism by which such appeals (if appealing) actually work. But this pattern of ad buys is very strong evidence in favor of the hypothesis that presidential campaigns incorporate the logic of strategic voting into their own campaign decisions.

In sum, while the realism of assumptions in formal models of strategic voting can be questioned, formal models of voting predict specific patterns of behavior that are otherwise hard to explain. Perhaps the most important part of this set of findings is the development of a chain of evidence, from the stark and straightforward to the subtle and unexpected, from the simple observation of voting contrary to one's simple preferences to the interactive strategies of candidates to affect the probabilistic and preferential calculations of voters. There appears to be logic to strategic voting in American elections. Formal models have provided a basis for discovering it.

Strategic Communication and Voter Competence

Communication is an important part of any political campaign. In elections where the number of voters is high, campaigns are largely carried out through mass communication media. For presidential and other high-profile elections, the Internet and television are the primary means by which candidates communicate to voters.

Whatever the communicative medium, candidates have decisions to make about what to say and how to say it. Voters, in turn, must decide when and whether to pay attention to election-related information. When they do pay attention, they must also decide what and whom to believe.

The conventional wisdom about election-oriented political communication is that candidates and their handlers seek to manipulate a gullible public and that the public makes inferior decisions as a result (see, e.g., Converse 1964). Game-theoretic studies of political communication have focused on such situations and have raised important challenges to the conventional wisdom. Formal models now clarify conditions under which the kinds of political communication described above do—and do not—lead voters to make inferior decisions.

In this section, we will review two examples of such work. In each case, formal models clarify whether claims about the manipulability of voters are—or are not—consistent with clearly stated assumptions about voters' and candidates' incentives and knowledge. Their authors have also used experiments to evaluate key attributes of the models.

McKelvey and Ordeshook (1986, 1990) offered an early game-theoretic treatment of political communication and its effect on voters. The papers focus on a spatial voting model in which two candidates compete for votes by taking policy positions on a one-dimensional policy space. Voters have spatial preferences, which is to say that they have an "ideal point" that represents the policy outcome they most prefer. A voter in these models obtains higher utility when the candidate whose policy preference is closest to their ideal point is elected.

If the game were one of complete information, the outcome would be that both candidates adopt the median voter's ideal point as their policy preference and the median voter's ideal point becomes the policy outcome. The focal research question for McKelvey and Ordeshook was how such outcomes change when voters know less. To address these questions, McKelvey and Ordeshook develop a model with informed and uninformed voters. Informed voters know the policy positions of two candidates. Uninformed voters do not, but they can observe poll results or interest group endorsements. McKelvey and Ordeshook examine when such uninformed voters can use the polls and endorsements to cast the same votes they would have cast if completely informed.

In the model's equilibrium, voters make inferences about candidate locations by using poll results to learn about how informed voters are voting. Uninformed voters come to correctly infer the candidates' positions from insights such as "if that many voters are voting for the [rightist candidate], he can't be *too* liberal." McKelvey and Ordeshook prove that the greater is the percentage of informed voters represented in such polls, the quicker uninformed voters come to the correct conclusion about which candidate is closest to their interests.

McKelvey and Ordeshook evaluated key aspects of their theoretical work experimentally. As Palfrey (2007, 923; caveat in brackets inserted by us) reports,

Perhaps the most striking experiment... used a single policy dimension, but candidates had no information about voters and only a few of the voters in the experiments knew where the candidates located. The key information transmission devices explored were polls and interest group endorsements. In a theoretical model of information aggregation, adapted from the rational expectations theory of markets, they proved that this information alone [along with the assumption that voters know approximately where they stand relative to the rest of the electorate on a left–right scale] is sufficient to reveal enough to voters that even uninformed voters behave optimally—i.e., as if they were fully informed.

Of course, uninformed voters in the McKelvey–Ordeshook model do not cast informed votes in all circumstances. The caveat inserted into the Palfrey quote reminds us of additional assumptions that contribute to the stated result. However, it is important to remember that the conventional wisdom at the time was that uninformed voters could seldom, if ever, cast competent votes—where competence refers to whether or not a voter casts the same vote that she would have cast if she possessed full information about all matters in the model that are pertinent to her choice (e.g., candidate policy positions). The breadth of conditions under which McKelvey and Ordeshook proved that (a) *uninformed voters vote competently* and (b) *election outcomes are identical to what they would have been if all voters were informed* prompted a reconsideration of the conditions under which limited information made voters incompetent.

Lupia and McCubbins (1998) pursue these conditions further. Their work differs from McKelvey and Ordeshook in that it examines multiple ways in which voters can be uninformed and examines the dynamics of political communication more deeply by integrating insights from the social psychological study of persuasion. By using formal models to attack this question, Lupia and McCubbins were able to analyze the effect of many psychological and incentive-related variables simultaneously. In so doing they could clarify how beliefs and communicative rules combine to affect voter competence. Their approach specified conditional relationships pertinent to questions of competence and persuasion in ways that the dominant approach to studying the topic—survey-based analyses—had not.

The starting point for Lupia and McCubbins is that citizens must make decisions about things that they cannot experience directly. For voters, the task is to choose candidates whose future actions in office cannot be experienced in advance of the election. Relying on others for information in such circumstances can be an efficient way to acquire knowledge. However, many people who provide political information (e.g., campaign organizations) do so out of self-interest, and some may have an incentive to mislead. For voters who rely on others for information, competence depends on how they choose whom to believe. If they believe people who provide accurate information and ignore people who do otherwise, they are more likely to be competent.

A key rhetorical move in the development of the Lupia–McCubbins model is to follow empirical scholars of voting behavior and public opinion who linked this question to the social psychological study of *persuasion*. O'Keefe (1990, 17) defines persuasion as "a successful intentional effort at influencing another's mental state through communication in a circumstance in which the persuadee has some measure of freedom." Seen in this way, the outcomes of many political interactions hinge on *who* can persuade *whom*. Social psychologists have generated important data on the successes and failures of persuasive attempts (see, e.g., McGuire 1985, Petty and Cacioppo 1986).

While psychological studies distinguish factors that can be antecedents of persuasion from factors that cannot, they are typically formulated in a way that limits their applicability to questions of voting behavior. The typical social psychological study of persuasion is a laboratory experiment that examines how a single variation in a single factor corresponds to a single attribute of persuasiveness. Such studies are not well equipped for answering broader questions about the conditions under which some attributes will be more important than others in affecting the persuasive power of a particular presentation. In a formal model, it is possible to conduct an analysis of the conditions under which a range of factors have differential and conditional effects on whether persuasion occurs. Lupia and McCubbins do just that, examining the logical consequences of mixing a range of assumptions about beliefs and incentives to generate precise conclusions about the conditions under which (a) one person can persuade another and (b) persuasive attempts make voters competent.

Their findings demonstate that the knowledge threshhold for voting competently is lower than the normative and survey-based literatures at the time had conjectured. Instead of being required to have detailed information about the utility consequences of all electoral alternatives, it can be sufficient for the voter to know enough to make good choices about whom to believe. So when information about endorsers is easier to acquire than information about policies, voters who appear to be uninformed can cast the same votes they would have cast if they knew more.

Their findings also challenge the psychologically based literature on persuasion. Many studies in this domain find that a particular speaker-attribute causes persuasion (e.g., a speaker's ideology, partisanship, race, gender, or likability). The work as a whole does not provide a mechanism for sorting these findings by the conditions under which particular attributes are most powerful. The formal theoretic treatment makes progress on both counts. For example, Lupia and McCubbins show that any attribute causes persuasion *only if it informs a receiver's perceptions of a speaker's knowledge or interests*. Otherwise, the attribute cannot affect persuasion, even if it actually affects the speaker's choice of words. The models also clarify how environmental, contextual, or institutional variables (such as those that make certain kinds of statements costly for a speaker to utter) make learning from others easy in some cases and difficult in others. At the extreme, there exist conditions under which the context in which a person makes a statement is such an effective substitute for detailed information about the speaker, that the voter can use the contextual information to make effective choices about which claims to believe.

These models reveal conditions under which incompletely informed voters can use simple cues to make the same choices they would have made if they knew more. In a series of exit polls, laboratory experiments, and survey experiments (many of which are described in Lupia and McCubbins 1998), they and other scholars have demonstrated that voters—if they are in the right circumstances—can emulate well-informed voting behavior. In sum, there appears to be logic to how uninformed voters use information. Formal models have provided a basis for discovering it.

A Constructive Future

American elections and voting behavior are studied in many ways. Circumstances often dictate which methods will be most effective. While nature sometimes provides all the observations needed to draw an empirically reliable inference about *how* people vote—such as in cases where you can observe how someone voted or see an actual voting record—it is more often the case that nature's raw materials are insufficient for answering the most interesting questions (such as *why* people voted as they did). One way to try to answer these questions is to recreate the situations where the choices occur (e.g., simulations and experiments). After these observations are manufactured, they can be compared and, if the experiments are well designed, strong inferences about causality can be drawn.

In other cases, nature does not provide the observations we want and it is impossible or infeasible to create them in a lab. This circumstance occurs, for example, when asking whether a particular behavior or outcome occurs under a large number of conditions. In these cases, the key to greater knowledge is to effectively use what we can observe to draw credible conclusions about what we cannot observe. These are circumstances where the importation of transparent and replicable applications of formal logic can be particularly helpful.

As scholars move forward in their attempts to explain American elections and voting behavior, it can be useful to think about the roles that formal modeling can play. One place where formal modeling can fuel greater understanding is in the study of how various aspects of context affect voting behavior. Institutional attributes are one set of contextual variables that have drawn substantial attention from formal modelers. And yet, the empirical literature on voting behavior has evolved with limited attention to institutions. The chasm between research on institutions and research on political behavior hampers our discipline's ability to explain when institutions can change beliefs. Formal models can clarify complex interactions between cognitive endowments and institutional attributes. Indeed, it was this kind of circumstance that led us to focus on strategic voting and communication. And it is instructive that these two cases involve interactions between voters and candidates or parties. Many approaches to the study of voting behavior are weak on such interactions, whereas formal modeling permits them to be examined with great specificity.

Another venue in which formal modeling can be valuable is in studies that pursue psychological explanations of behavior. Models can help scholars determine whether claims being made about citizen psychology *must be true* given a set of clearly stated assumptions, or whether the claim is possibly true given those foundations. Inquiries about how cognitive and emotional factors interact with incentive effects of institutions can fuel insight about important political implications of common psychological phenomena (see, e.g., Lupia and Menning 2009).

Such endeavors would mark a stark improvement over some research practices that are common today. Consider, for example, many survey-based attempts to make inferences about aspects of "political psychology." It is not unusual to see scholars take variables from an existing survey, give these variables names that appear to relate to psychological concepts, place these variables into a linear regression model with other demographic variables, and then claim to make a valid discovery about psychological underpinnings of voting behavior. Our critique of this work is not that it is illegitimate on its face. Rather, our critique is that it is frequently lacking in its introspection about what assumptions would have to be true for the conclusion to be true. When plugging such a variable into a linear regression model, for example, scholars are making implicit assumptions about the range of relationships that the presumed psychological phenomenon and voting behavior can have. Such assumptions include the relationship being linear and the psychological effect on voting being independent of other individual-level or contextual variables (see, e.g., the critique of Bartels 2005 in Lupia et al. 2007). In short, much work done in "political psychology" is not sufficiently introspective about the properties of, and relationships between, key psychological and contextual variables.

A formal modeling approach can counter this trend. If scholars working in this field state their assumptions with greater precision and clarity and offer transparent derivations of conclusions from these assumptions, the scholarship could provide more valid and reliable conclusions about voting behavior. Formal models provide a rigorous means for converting knowledge from fields such as social or cognitive psychology into more effective research designs and stronger conclusions about why voters act as they do.

References

ABRAMSON, P. R., ALDRICH, J. H, and ROHDE, D. W. 2003. *Change and Continuity in the 2000 and 2002 Elections*. Washington, D.C.: CQ Press, 2003.

—— —— PAOLINO, P., and ROHDE, D. W. 1992. "Sophisticated" Voting in the 1988 Presidential Primaries. *American Political Science Review*, 86/1: 55–69.

—— —— BLAIS, A., DIAMOND, M., DISKIN, A., INDRIDASON, I. H., LEE, D., and LEVINE, R. Forthcoming. Comparing Strategic Voting under FPTP and PR. *Comparative Political Studies* (2010).

ALDRICH, J. H. 1976. Some Problems in Testing Two Rational Models of Participation. *American Journal of Political Science*, 20/4: 713–33.

ALVAREZ, R. M., BOEHMKE, F. J., and NAGLER, J. 2006. Strategic Voting in British Elections. *Electoral Studies*, 25: 1–19.

—— and NAGLER, J. 1998. When Politics and Models Collide: Estimating Models of Multi-Party Elections. *American Journal of Political Science*, 42: 55–96.

—— —— 2000. A New Approach for Modeling Strategic Voting in Multiparty Elections. *British Journal of Political Science*, 30: 57–75.

BARTELS, L. M. 2005. Homer Gets a Tax Cut: Inequality and Public Policy in the American Mind. *Perspectives on Politics*, 3/1: 15–32.

BENSEL, R. F. and SANDERS, M. E. 1979. The Effect of Electoral Rules on Voting Behavior: The Electoral College and Shift Voting. *Public Choice*, 34/1: 69–86.

BLAIS, A. and BODET, M. A. 2006. How Do Voters Form Expectations About the Parties' Chances of Winning the Election? *Social Science Quarterly*, 87: 477–93.

—— YOUNG, R., and TURCOTTE, M. Direct or Indirect? Assessing Two Approaches to the Measurement of Strategic Voting. *Electoral Studies*, 24: 163–76.

—— ALDRICH, J., INDRIDASON, I., and LEVINE, R. 2006. Do Voters Care about Government Coalitions? *Party Politics* 12: 691–705.

CONVERSE, P. E. 1964. The Nature of Belief Systems in Mass Publics. In *Ideology and Discontent*, ed. D. E. Apter. New York: The Free Press of Glencoe, 1964.

COX, G. W. 1997. *Making Votes Count: Strategic Coordination in the World's Electoral Systems*. New York: Cambridge University Press.

DUVERGER, M. 1986. Duverger's Law 40 Years Later. In *Electoral Laws and Their Political Consequences*, ed. B. Grofman and A. Lijphart. New York: Agathon Press.

FEDDERSEN, T. J. 1992. A Voting Model Implying Duverger's Law and Positive Turnout. *American Journal of Political Science*, 36/4: 938–62.

GREENBERG, J. and SHEPSLE, K. A. 1987. The Effects of Electoral Rewards in Multiparty Competition with Entry. *American Political Science Review*, 81/3: 525–38.

KAHNEMAN, D. and TVERSKY, A. 1979. Prospect Theory: An Analysis of Decisions under Risk. *Econometrica*, 47: 313–27.

LEVINE, R. 2007. Third Parties Can Change Perceptions of Major Party Candidates. Unpublished manuscript, <http://works.bepress.com/renan/12>.

LUPIA, A. and MCCUBBINS, M. D. 1998. *The Democratic Dilemma: Can Citizens Learn What They Need to Know?* New York: Cambridge University Press.

—— and MENNING, J. O. 2009. When Can Politicians Scare Citizens Into Supporting Bad Policies? *American Journal of Political Science*, 53/1: 90–106.

—— LEVINE, A. S., MENNING, J. O., and SIN, G. 2007. Were Bush Tax Cut Supporters "Simply Ignorant?" A Second Look at Conservatives and Liberals in "Homer Gets a Tax Cut." *Perspectives on Politics*, 5/4: 761–72.

MCGUIRE, W. J. 1985. Attitudes and Attitude Change. In Gardner Lindzey, and Elliot Aronson (eds.), *Handbook of Social Psychology*, ed. G. Lindzey and E. Aronson, 3rd edn., volume 2. New York: Random House.

McKELVEY, R. D. and ORDESHOOK, P. C. 1986. Elections with Limited Information: A Fulfilled Expectations Model Using Contemporaneous Poll and Endorsement Data as Information Sources. *Journal of Economic Theory*, 36: 55–85.

—— —— 1990. A Decade of Experimental Research on Spatial Models of Elections and Committees. In *Government, Democracy, and Social Choice*, ed. M. J. Hinich and J. Enelow. New York: Cambridge University Press.

MEROLLA, J. L. 2003. Too Close for Comfort: Elite Cues and Strategic Voting in Multi-candidate Elections. Ph.D. thesis, Duke University.

NIOU, E. 2001. Strategic Voting under Plurality and Runoff Rules. *Journal of Theoretical Politics*, 13/2: 209–27.

—— and KSELMAN, D. n.d. Strategic Voting in Plurality Elections. Unpublished manuscript, Duke University.

O'KEEFE, D. J. 1990. *Persuasion: Theory and Research*. Newbury Park, Calif: Sage Publications.

PALFREY, T. R. 1989. A Mathematical Proof of Duverger's Law. In *Models of Strategic Choice in Politics*, ed. P. C. Ordeshook. Ann Arbor: University of Michigan Press.

—— 2007. Laboratory Experiments. In *The Oxford Handbook of Political Economy*, ed. B. R. Weingast and D. Wittman. New York: Oxford University Press.

PETTY, R. E. and CACIOPPO, J. T. 1986. *Communication and Persuasion: Central and Peripheral Routes to Attitude Change*. New York: Springer-Verlag.

RAPOPORT, R. and STONE, W. J. 2005. *Three's a Crowd: The Dynamic of Third Parties, Ross Perot, and Republican Resurgence*. Ann Arbor: University of Michigan Press.

RIKER, W. H. 1982. The Two-Party System and Duverger's Law: An Essay on the History of Political Science. *American Political Science Review*, 76/4: 753–66.

SHEPSLE, K. A. 1991. *Models of Multiparty Electoral Competition*. London: Harwood Press.

STONE, W. J. and ABRAMOWITZ, A. I. 1983. Winning May Not Be Everything, But It's More than We Thought: Presidential Party Activists in 1980. *American Political Science Review*, 77/4: 945–56.

TVERSKY, A. and KAHNEMAN, D. 1974. Judgment under Uncertainty: Heuristics and Biases. *Science*, 185: 1124–31.

PART III

PARTICIPATION

WHY IS AMERICAN TURNOUT SO LOW, AND WHY SHOULD WE CARE?

MICHAEL D. MARTINEZ

THE vast literature on voter turnout in the United States addresses a variety of theoretical perspectives with a range of methodological tools, but students often return to three basic questions: Why is American voter turnout so low? Why is American voter turnout declining? And does low turnout really matter? While normative issues are often implicit, and occasionally explicit, these questions are empirical and require that we examine American voter participation with both comparative and longitudinal perspectives. Understanding why US turnout is lower than turnout in other democracies requires an appreciation of how social and institutional forces shape voter participation across political systems, and understanding the decline demands some appreciation of how American society and institutions have evolved over time. In turn, if participation is more than just its own reward, we would expect to see differences in politics or policy across time or space that correspond to variations in voter turnout. Scholars have continually returned to these questions in various formulations.

WHY IS AMERICAN TURNOUT SO LOW?

One of the most noticeable aspects of turnout in US elections is that it is typically low, at least in comparison to electoral participation in most other advanced democracies. Occasionally, politicians, commentators, and professors will bemoan the fact that even in the most hotly contested and high-profile American elections, turnout barely exceeds half of the voting age population, while three-quarters of eligible Britons or Germans routinely participate in their national elections, and turnout rates are in a few countries are even higher. While low turnout rates are not exclusively an American phenomenon (thanks to Switzerland and a couple of emerging democracies in Eastern Europe), US turnout rates remain near the low end of all established democracies. (Franklin 2002). Pundits who note the embarrassing comparisons often place much of the blame squarely on the American people's lack of political responsibility and interest. However, comparative survey evidence suggests that Americans are at least as politically interested as citizens in most other democracies, and that interest is manifest in other forms of political action. Americans have relatively high rates of petitioning, campaign activity, communal activity, and lawful protesting (Dalton 2008; Powell 1986), so it seems unlikely that political sloth accounts for most of the difference in turnout rates between Americans and citizens in other democracies. It is possible that American society has more of a caste system of political participation than other democracies do, with a smaller proportion of people participating in multiple venues and a larger proportion of people completely removed from politics, but that seems unlikely.

As Mark Franklin and Till Weber point out in Chapter 35 of this volume, comparative analysis across democracies helps us to understand the effects of various features of the American political system on voter turnout. That research has shown that for the most part, comparatively low turnout in US elections is *not* the result of demographic and attitudinal differences between Americans and citizens of other democracies. When compared to Western Europeans in the 1970s, Americans on average had stronger partisanships, higher political efficacy, more political interest, more frequent discussions about politics (including attempts to persuade others how to vote), higher levels of formal education, more people in white collar jobs (Powell 1986), and greater devotion to religion (Wald 1987), all of which are associated with higher rates of voter turnout. Americans' relative youth explained a small fraction of the difference between aggregate US and European turnout, but the effect of age distribution is swamped by other demographic factors that should lead to higher turnout in the United States (Powell 1986). Moreover, the total effects of individual-level characteristics that might account for differences in turnout across democracies are dwarfed by country-level effects. In short, "it matters whether one is rich or poor, educated or uneducated, interested in politics or not; but none of these things matters nearly as much as whether one is an Australian or an American" (Franklin 2002, 150).

If low turnout in the United States cannot be explained by distinctive character-istics of the American people, the bigger culprits are likely the several institutional differences between the United States and other democracies. In his comparative analyses of turnout, Franklin (2002) notes that the United States and Switzerland have distinctively low levels of "electoral salience," which can be understood as the theoretical effect that a single vote is likely to have on the direction of effective public policy. In other words, "electoral salience" is the institutional component of the PB term (the benefit of having one candidate in office over his or her opponent multiplied by the probability that an individual vote will bring about that differ-ence) in the classic "calculus of voting" (Riker and Ordeshook 1968), and several aspects of the American electoral and constitutional system dampen it. First, most elections in the United States are conducted under the "first past the post" electoral system, allocating seats of power only to candidates who secure plurality support in their elections (Powell 1980). Due to low levels of partisan competition within many states and electoral districts, supporters of both the majority party and the minority party have less incentive to invest in the costs of voting or in the cost of mobilizing others to vote. Serious competition in US House elections is also limited as the two major parties battle for control of the House in a few key districts around the country, while incumbents use their resources increasingly effectively to ward off serious challenges (Jacobson 2004). In contrast, proportional representa-tion and transferable vote systems (commonly but not universally used outside the United States) do more to ensure that parties, interest groups, and candidates will always have a greater incentive to mobilize supporters wherever they are found, creating a greater proportionality of seats to votes (Blais 2000; Jackman 1987), and giving supporters of minority parties in particular a greater sense that their vote might matter in electing a sympathetic member to the legislature (Blais 2000). Even in US presidential elections, campaigns usually concentrate their efforts in mobi-lizing voters in a few "battleground" states, and millions of potential voters in "safe Republican" or "safe Democratic" states might reasonably conclude that their individual votes are unlikely to make any difference in the outcome of the presi-dential election. As a result, voter turnout in presidential elections is higher in "battleground states" than in non-battleground states, but most Americans live outside the zone of competition (Gimpel, Kaufmann, and Pearson-Merkowitz 2007; Hill and McKee 2005; Shaw 2006).

A second aspect of "electoral salience" stems from the constitutional system itself. As powerful as the US president is in absolute terms, he shares authority with an independently elected Congress and an insulated judiciary. In such a system of separated powers, voters might find it difficult to clearly attribute responsibility for either successful or failed policies, as Congress, the President, and state govern-ments could plausibly claim credit for successes or divert blame for failures to one another, powerful organized interests, or the courts (Franklin 2004, 98–104). This is especially true in eras of divided government, which may produce significant legislation (Mayhew 2005) but still make it more difficult for the voter to decide who deserves electoral rewards or punishments. Multiple elections give Americans electoral control over more offices (Wolfinger 1994), but they fragment power so much that no one election is decisive. Moreover, separation of powers systems are also more open to influence from interest groups and interest litigants, which in turn may reduce the perception among potential voters that elections can effectively change the direction of public policy. When faced with a president of one party and Congressional majorities of the other party (and perhaps governors of both parties from different states) claiming credit and casting blame, and with the significant influence of moneyed interest groups and unelected judges, some citizens apparently either cannot decide who in government deserves reward or punishment, or believe that the unelected and elected veto-players will limit the effectiveness of elections as institutions of policy change. That notion is supported by time-series evidence that the effect of divided government on national turnout in US elections is cumulative (Franklin and Hirczy de Miño 1998), and cross-national correlational evidence that turnout is higher when elections for the lower house are more decisive (Blais 2000, 26–29; Jackman 1987).

Another aspect of electoral salience is the degree to which the party system represents the significant cleavages in society. When social class is the only significant cleavage in a democracy, parties align their positions on government services and redistribution questions to appeal to their class bases, and voters can clearly see the policy differences between the parties and cast their votes for candidates that best represent their real or perceived interests. However, politics is a messy sport, and it is messier in the United States where class consciousness is relatively weak and where other issues are often salient. As the two major US parties have taken more or less well-defined positions on social issues such as abortion and gay rights, the class bases of both parties have expanded. Republicans appeal to both a financial class and voters with strong moralist values, and Democrats appeal to both the working class and voters with more secular orientations. As a result, the party system's linkages to both the class and religious cleavages are relatively weak, which often leaves gay bankers, Bible-toting laborers, and other socially cross-pressured citizens in a quandary. Many resolve that dilemma by prioritizing either moralist or fiscal policy, but some citizens remain undecided right up through election day. Powell (1986; see also Powell 1980) estimated that the relatively weak party–group linkage in the United States accounted for most of the difference between American turnout and the average turnout in other democracies in the 1970s, and the social cleavages have eroded in the United States (and other democracies) since that time (Abramson, Aldrich, and Rohde 2007; Dalton 2006).

While some institutional factors that contribute to relatively low turnout in the United States are "baked into" the American constitutional system and political process, one aspect of the legal context that has been susceptible to efforts of reformers is the voter registration system in the United States. Voter registration in many democracies is "automatic" in the sense that the electorate is identified by permanent police list, a permanent voter list updated with other government records (such as drivers' licenses and naturalization), or by an enumeration of eligible electors prior to each election. In contrast, voter registration in the United States (as well as in France and other democracies) is voluntary, and in most instances before the mid-1980s, the registration process had to be initiated by the prospective voter at least a month in advance of the election.

As Robert Brown notes in Chapter 10 of this volume, research on how the legal context shapes turnout *within* the United States is built on Wolfinger and Rosenstone's (1980) finding that variations in state registration laws (closing dates, regular and evening or weekend hours for registration, and absentee registration) were correlated with voter turnout rates in the states. The 1993 National Voter Registration Act mandated that states without election day registration offer registration at other public agencies, so that driver's license offices, welfare agencies, and military recruiting stations now offer citizens the opportunity to register to vote in one trip. Most of the evidence from the American states shows that more facilitative registration procedures do promote voter registration, especially among the young and those with enough education to stimulate some political awareness and interest, but not so much as to make them political junkies (Brians and Grofman 2001; Brown, this volume, Chapter 10; Highton 2004; Highton and Wolfinger 1998). Yet, Brown also highlights research that shows that the effects of NVRA and other registration reforms are contingent on the political context. These findings might begin to explain the gap between studies within the US that show significant effects of registration laws on turnout and the weight of the comparative cross-national evidence that suggests that automatic registration itself is not a consistent stimulus to voting when controlling for other institutional differences between the United States and other democracies (Franklin 2002, 159–60).

Other laws and administrative procedures also modestly affect the probability of voting among people who are registered to vote. Turnout is higher (especially among young people and the least educated) in states in which election officials mail each registrant a sample ballot and information about the location of his or her polling place, and where polls are open for longer periods (Wolfinger, Highton, and Mullin 2005). States that have made voting more convenient for registrants through vote-by-mail, early voting, early in-person voting, "no excuse" absentee voting, electronic voting, and voting by fax, generally have slightly higher turnout rates, usually ranging from 2 to 4 percent (Gronke et al. 2008). But to the extent that convenience has any discernible effect on *who* votes, it appears to stimulate participation among people who are already the most likely to vote based on strength of preference (Dyck and Gimpel 2005; Stein and Vonnahme, Chapter 11 in this volume), exacerbating rather than ameliorating socioeconomic biases in turnout (Berinsky 2005).

Governments can offer incentives to vote, in the form of either positive or negative sanctions. A few democracies do impose light (and occasionally, heavy) civil fines for not voting, and although voting is not universal in those countries, compulsory voting does significantly boost voter turnout (Franklin 2002; Lijphart 1997; Powell 1980). Between 1968 and the 1990s, US states were actually more likely to impose weightier legal obligations on voters than on non-voters, in the form of jury duty. However, in response to concerns that many people declined to register to vote in order to avoid the possibility of jury duty, many states have begun to use driver's license lists for their jury pools. (Knack 1993; Knack 2000; Oliver and Wolfinger 1999)

The US lag in turnout is probably less than meets the eye, as many comparative analyses of turnout are based on slightly different measures. In most democracies, turnout is reported as the proportion of the registered or enumerated population that casts votes, based on the premise that the registration or enumeration proce-dure is nearly universally successful in identifying the eligible voters in the elector-ate, an assumption that may not always be tenable (Black 2005). In the United States, where voter registration is voluntary, turnout is routinely reported as the proportion of the voting-age population that casts votes. This measure is also problematic in that its denominator excludes thousands of eligible voters (overseas Americans who are eligible to vote by virtue of their citizenship) and, more importantly for comparative analyses, it includes millions of people who are not legally eligible to vote in the United States (mostly non-citizens, but also felons and ex-felons in states that have varying degrees of "civil death" penalties for felony convictions) (McDonald and Popkin 2001). Substituting estimates of the voting-eligible population for the voting-age population in comparative analyses of turn-out might account for a substantial fraction of the difference between American turnout and that in other democracies. To be sure, there are normative issues that should be considered (such as whether democratic states should disenfranchise felons), but every democracy currently excludes non-citizens from voting in na-tional elections, so at the very least they should be excluded from our comparisons.

WHY DID TURNOUT DECLINE IN THE US (OR DID IT)?

Michael McDonald's historical perspective (Chapter 8 in this volume) provides a useful reminder that voter turnout has fluctuated dramatically over the course of US history, mostly in response to electoral needs of political elites. A substantial body of research is based on observations about trends in voter turnout beginning in the mid-twentieth century, but, as McDonald points out, voter participation in this period is both considerably lower than during the Party Machine Era (1828–1896) and notably higher than participation during the Founding Era (1789–1824). Nevertheless, Richard Brody's (1978) simple puzzle still shapes much of the research on turnout in the United States. Brody observed that, from the 1950s to the 1970s, registration requirements (particularly the residency requirements) were relaxed in many states, and at the same time, educational attainment was steadily increasing. Turnout did increase markedly in the South (where prior to the 1965 Voting Rights Act, adult blacks were included in the voting-age population denominator but systematically excluded from the ballot box by literacy tests, poll taxes, obstruction, and intimidation), but outside the South, turnout crested in 1960 and then started a steady decline through 1976 (and ultimately bottoming out in 1996). In an era when registration was becoming easier and more people had access to education and higher-status occupations, Americans were becoming less interested, less concerned about electoral outcomes, less efficacious about the electoral process, and less likely to vote. Why?

Party identification was about to reach its nadir when Brody posed his puzzle, and many wondered whether the decline in turnout was associated with the dealignment in the electorate. Not surprisingly, attitudes toward the parties had some impact on turnout, though Teixeira (1992) suggested that overall the effect was rather modest due to a rather stable trend in the number of "pure independents" and an increase in the proportion of people who saw differences between the two parties. So, much of the decrease was left to explain.

The expansion of educational opportunities may have been the most significant post-war change in the social tapestry of the United States (which as Brody and others noted, should have bolstered turnout), but other social changes that were underway in the latter part of the twentieth century apparently contributed to the decline in turnout. As a whole, the American electorate become younger in the 1970s (after the adoption of the Twenty-sixth Amendment in 1971), less married, and less likely to attend church. The declines in marriage and churchgoing are symptomatic of a general decline in social connectedness (Putnam 1995), and (together with age) account for a significant part of the decline in turnout from 1960 to 1988. Teixiera (1992) finds that the largest impact on the decline in turnout is from the decline in newspaper reading, political interest, and efficacy. But because these motivational variables are so close to the "tip of the funnel" of causality of turnout, the total effects of social connectedness and the decline of partisanship (including indirect effects through political motivation) may be even larger than they appear in Teixeira's estimates.

In addition to the changes in the social and partisan landscapes, changes in mobilization patterns also accounted for a portion of the change in turnout. The decline in voter turnout from the 1960s to the 1980s coincided with a shift by parties and candidates from reaching out to voters individually, in small groups, or in coffee klatches (retail politics) to communicating to voters through the ubiquitous but expensive medium of television (wholesale politics). Controlling for other factors that should have boosted turnout (easing voter registration laws and the increase in education) and other factors that contributed to its decline (a younger voting-age population, as well as weakened social involvement, political efficacy, and partisanship), Rosenstone and Hansen (1993, 214–19) estimate the decrease in voter contacting accounts for about half of the decline in turnout between the 1960s and 1980s. This research is complemented by large-scale field-experimental research that shows significant effects of personal contacting, and substantially smaller effects of more impersonal contacting (telephone and mail) on the likelihood of voting (Gerber and Green 2000; Green and Gerber 2004; Green, Gerber, and Nickerson 2003).

Kenneth Goldstein and Matthew Holleque (Chapter 30 in this volume) remind us that much of the research on mobilization is focused on the medium of contacting (with a special emphasis on canvassing voters), and they urge more attention to how message content affects voter participation. There are suggestions in the literature that messages matter, but no consensus yet on the magnitude, or even in some cases the direction of those effects. In non-partisan canvassing experiments, the effects of message content pale in comparison to the main effects of contact itself (Gerber and Green 2000, 658), but those experimental manipulations may miss the full range of message intensity and substance that might affect voter participation. Some research does suggest that a shift in the content of paid media, in the form of increased "attack advertising" on television (see Ansolabehere and Iyengar 1995; Ansolabehere et al. 1994), has contributed to the demobilization of the American electorate by lowering efficacy and increasing cynicism among viewers, but critics dispute their evidence and argue that deleterious effects of attack ads on efficacy are offset by the increased provision of political information (Brooks and Geer 2007; Finkel and Geer 1998; Geer 2006). Changes in unpaid media messages, in the form of "interpretive" news (Patterson 2002), may also account for some of the decline, though proponents of this notion have not yet provided estimates of *how much* of the decline might be attributable to those sources.

Changes in social institutions affect mobilization patterns, as well. As labor unions in the United States and elsewhere have both weakened and become less representative of the proletariat and more representative of the burgeoning "new middle class" or "salatariat" (Dalton 2008, 145–50), their decreased capacity to mobilize generally and to mobilize the working class specifically accounts for about 3.5 percent of the low- and middle-income groups' drop in turnout between 1964 and 2000, and about 2.5 percent of the upper-income drop (Leighley and Nagler 2007).

Of course, the decline in turnout from the 1970s onward is not as dramatic as was first observed. As alluded to earlier, McDonald and Popkin (2001) showed that the populations of disenfranchised felons and, especially, ineligible non-citizens increased dramatically in the United States beginning in the 1970s. When ineligible adults are excluded from the denominator (and eligible overseas citizens are included), the hemorrhaging of turnout appears to have been mostly abated after 1972. There are peaks (1992) and valleys (1996), but no clear monotonic trend in turnout from 1972 to 1996. McDonald and Popkin's correction does not completely solve Brody's original puzzle (as turnout of the voting-eligible population did decline between 1960 and 1972), but it does reduce the amount of decline that requires explanation.

More recent trends in turnout in the United States pose a new question. Turnout in Clinton's reelection in 1996 reached a local minimum (VEP rate of 51.7 percent), bumped up in 2000 (54.2 percent), surged in 2004 (to 60.1 percent), and increased again in 2008 (to an estimated 61.2 percent) (McDonald 2008). We need to begin to assess whether the explanations of the turnout decline in the post-war era help us to understand the increase in voter participation in the last three presidential elections. I doubt that there have been significant upticks in social involvement, but the number of battleground states increased in 2008. Has contacting also increased in those states, or are potential voters simply more aware of the competitiveness of the national (and state) races and, post-Florida 2000, sensitive to the potential importance of a handful of votes?

Does it Matter if Turnout is High or Low?

It is not uncommon to read pundits laments' that relatively low American turnout (either historically or comparatively) is an indicator of the low or declining health of our political system, though the resultant conditions that we might expect to see in such a sick patient are rarely articulated in the popular media. If, as Austin Ranney (1983) argued, "non-voting is not a social disease," what are the important political consequences of varying levels of turnout?

The intellectual ancestry of much of the work cited in this chapter traces directly back to *Who Votes?*, where Raymond Wolfinger and Steven Rosenstone (1980) laid the foundation for much of the research that has examined differences in rates of voting among men and women, young and old, rich and poor, and black, white, and brown. Their chapter on the effects of state registration laws on turnout was a keystone in shaping arguments in support of registration reforms at both the state and national levels. Wolfinger has also been a strong voice on Capitol Hill, speaking in support of both successful attempts to liberalize registration laws (such as the 1993 National Voter Registration Act), as well as other attempts to simplify re-registration among the residentially mobile through use of the Postal Service change of address cards (Squire, Wolfinger, and Glass 1987). Throughout this line of research, Wolfinger and his colleagues have been astute enough politically to know that major reform efforts were unlikely to succeed if any of the major players in the debate had an ox that was likely to be gored by higher levels of turnout that would result from liberalized registration laws. Again and again, Wolfinger's (and later Highton's) analyses would show that the reforms were politically possible, precisely because the most likely beneficiaries of such reform efforts (mostly young people and the residentially mobile) did not have a partisan tilt that was substantially different than that in the existing electorate (Highton 2004; Highton and Wolfinger 2001; Wolfinger and Rosenstone 1980, 80–8). Those arguments should (and to Wolfinger's credit, probably did) help mollify Republican legislators who otherwise might have presumed the conventional wisdom that higher turnout would ultimately work against their party's interests. But then the question becomes, if turnout doesn't have a significant (or even predictable) partisan consequence, why bother? Why should Democratic legislators choose to invest their limited time and political capital on legislation that would ease voter registration, instead of on proposals in other policy areas that would more directly affect their constituents' welfare, security, and political rights and freedoms? For that matter, why should we, as citizens or as members of the scholarly community, care whether turnout is high or low? What difference does it make? Are there communal benefits to societies where turnout is high, beyond whatever aggregated sense of satisfaction millions of people might derive from having participated in the political process?

One of the ways to assess the consequences of the level of participation is to examine its relationship to the bias in participation. Bias reflects a state when the active participants are descriptively *unrepresentative* of the population of potential participants. By definition, bias is zero when all potential actors participate, and in general, class-based measures of participation bias tend to be negatively, but imperfectly, correlated with the rate of participation. Thus, when turnout is relatively high, bias tends to be relatively low (Mahler 2008, 176–8; Rosenstone and Hansen 1993, 228–48), and modes of political activity that have lower participation rates than voting, such as running for office, contributing money, and working in campaigns, evidence even higher education and income bias than does turnout (Rosenstone and Hansen 1993, 240–1).

Moreover, in cross-national comparisons, correlations between measures of class and turnout tend to be higher in the United States than in sister democracies with higher levels of turnout (Dalton 2008, 59–65; Ginsberg 1982), suggesting again that class bias is inversely related to the level of turnout. Concern about whose ox is gored closely follows from concerns about the declining rates of turnout, and Burnham (1980; see also Piven and Cloward 1988) argued that the late–twentieth-century decline in turnout reflects a continuation of the demobilization of the working class. However, it appears that turnout rates were declining among all socioeconomic classes in the 1970s and 1980s, so that the income-turnout bias in the 1988 presidential election was not all that different than it was in the 1972 election (Leighley and Nagler 1992; Teixeira 1992). The relationship between turnout level and bias over time is negative, but it is also imperfect, suggesting that factors other than turnout rate can substantially affect turnout bias.

While the active electorate's accent has a distinct upper-middle-class tinge (in comparison to that of habitual non-voters), the policy preferences of voters and non-voters appear to be remarkably similar on a wide range of issue areas, including moralist (abortion, gay rights), foreign policy (interventionism), and racial issues (Bennett and Resnick 1990; Gant and Lyons 1993). Abstainers are also not much different than voters on their attitudes toward the political system; in other words, few abstainers *and* voters have high levels of trust in the political system, but not many in either group are itching for revolutionary change either. Voters are slightly less supportive of redistributive policies than are non-voters, which in part reflects the class differences in the compositions of the two groups. But, it is also true that those slight differences persist when controlling for socioeconomic status. In other words, less-educated voters are more conservative on issues directly involving the welfare state than less-educated non-voters are. Whether those differences are attributable to selective mobilization or socialization remains an open question.

Quite naturally, the evidence of class-based bias in turnout leads to the "conventional wisdom" that higher turnout should tend to help the parties on the left that represent the interests of the working class. In the United States, practitioners and pundits commonly assume that any effective reform measures that would increase turnout generally would work to the Democrats' advantage. Implicitly invoking the Columbia school's perspective that people act politically as they are socially, this perspective is based on the assumption that higher turnout would result from the mobilization of a significant fraction of the population of non-voters, which is disproportionately less educated, lower income, working class, and ergo, should have a greater propensity to support Democratic candidates. DeNardo's (1980) alternative perspective, roughly based on the Michigan model of voter behavior, suggests that higher-stimulus elections would include strong short-term forces that would generate higher turnout *and* spur more partisan defections. According to this logic, the partisan effects of higher turnout should be context-dependent, and generally work to the benefit of the minority party. Thus, in areas where Democrats are the majority party, the pool of potential Democratic defectors (who would vote Republican) is larger than the pool of potential Republican defectors (who would vote Democratic). Empirical research has either regressed aggregate votes on turnout across states and time (Erikson 1995; Nagel and McNulty 1996, 2000; Radcliff 1994) or simulated the likely partisan choices of actual non-voters under varying levels of turnout (Citrin, Schickler, and Sides 2003; Martinez and Gill 2005). While there has been some support for the conventional wisdom

(Gomez, Hansford, and Krause 2007; Radcliff 1994; Tucker and Vedlitz 1986), most findings point to partisan turnout effects that are either variable (Citrin, Schickler, and Sides 2003) or contingent on the partisan make-up of the state (Nagel and McNulty 1996, 2000) or the strength of the class–party linkage (Martinez and Gill 2005).

Notwithstanding the mixed findings in research on the effects of turnout on election outcomes, the known effects of turnout on policy outputs seem to be clearer. On the whole, states that have higher working-class turnout also tend to have more generous welfare policies (Hill and Leighley 1992) and less regressive tax policies (Martinez 1997). Economists who have investigated this question from a cross-national perspective have also concluded that higher levels of turnout, reflecting greater working-class mobilization, encourages more government inter-vention in the economy, which in turn, results in lower rates of economic growth (Mueller and Stratmann 2003).

Another approach that has started to answer the "so what" question has been to focus on the process of representation. Higher levels of turnout may indicate to a policymaker that more constituents are paying attention, and thus engender a greater degree of responsiveness to all interests. Research that has pursued this line has shown that descriptive representation of minority populations is higher in cities with higher levels of turnout (Hajnal and Trounstine 2005), congressional policy responsiveness to voters is higher than it is to non-voters (Griffin and Newman 2005), and counties with higher levels of turnout exact a modestly larger share of pork from the federal government, other things being equal (Martin 2003). Some may view more pork in the federal budget as a tragedy of the commons, but these findings do suggest that higher levels of turnout can shape patterns of representation. As Patricia Hurley and Kim Quaile Hill argue (in Chapter 38 of this volume), the mechanisms that provide for this enhanced representation for voters are not altogether fully understood nor well integrated into the literature on representation theory.

The focus on communal benefits of higher turnout (via enhanced representation or other forms) could also provide a partial answer to a long-standing paradox. From a rational choice perspective, the real puzzle is that turnout is as *high* as it is. In the classic calculus of voting (Riker and Ordeshook 1968), an individual's probability of voting should be negatively related to C, the costs of voting (includ-ing the time and effort required to register, acquire useful information about the candidates to make a decision, and actually cast a vote), and should be positively related to B, the differential benefit of having one party elected over the other, multiplied by P, the probability that an individual's vote will affect the outcome of the election. By and large, turnout is higher among individuals who bear lower costs (such as less restrictive registration laws) when they see more than "a dime's worth of difference" between the candidates and when the election is expected to be close. The paradox arises from the non-zero cost of voting and the infinitesimal value of P, reflecting the likelihood that any single vote will determine the outcome of a presidential, gubernatorial, congressional, legislative, mayoral, or referendum election, which is virtually nil. According to most interpretations of rational choice theory, every voter has an incentive to abstain, because each person should recognize that his or her preferred candidate(s) will almost certainly win (or lose) with or without his or her vote.

But, "unfortunately for the theory, many people do vote" (Blais 2000, 2). Beginning with Riker and Ordeshook's inclusion of a D (citizen duty) term in the individual calculus, rational theorists have suggested a variety of ways to account for the fact that people do indeed vote (reviewed in Blais 2000, 2–14; Fiorina 1990), notably including the rationality of groups in mobilizing blocs of voters (Morton 1991) and individual aspiration levels and feedback mechanisms that affect future decisions to vote (Bendor, Diermeier, and Ting 2003). None of these "patches" are remotely satisfactory to critics of rational choice theory, who view consumptive benefits in the D term and psychological devaluations of the C term as proof that rational choice can be saved only by the inclusion of irrational terms (Green and Shapiro 1994, 47–71). However, empirical findings that representation is enhanced under conditions of higher turnout suggest that D can be viewed not just as an individual consumptive benefit (i.e., the personal satisfaction from voting), but also as a public good that is provided when large numbers of people either learn that they are better off cooperating than shirking (see Axelrod 2006) or are compelled to vote (Lijphart 1997). Thus, an individual vote both marginally affects the probability of electing a preferred candidate, as well as contributing to the collective good of better representation regardless of who is elected to govern.

CONCLUSION

As the behavioral revolution in political science began several decades ago, contras warned that the emphasis on new analytical tools would shift our attention away from theoretically meaningful and normatively important concepts, such as justice, toward more easily quantifiable concepts. Voter turnout was perhaps the prototype among the latter: turnout is easily countable, and relatively inexpensive data would provide large numbers of cases amenable to powerful statistical techniques. Early critics and their Perestroikan descendants largely accepted the premise that we would be able to successfully model voter turnout and other easily measured concepts, but wondered whether we will have stripped "politics" out of the question in the process. While critics could no doubt point to particular studies in support of such a position, my reading of the field as a whole is that we have retained a healthy respect for the theoretical and normative underpinnings of popular participation in democratic settings. We have asked, and should continue to ask, how American institutions shape attitudes, opportunities, and incentives to vote (Leighley 1995), as well as whether and under what conditions voter turnout in the United States is biased, both in comparison to other democracies and compared to other forms of political participation (Verba, Schlozman, and Brady 1995).

It may also be instructive for us to begin to examine the attitudes, opportunities, and incentives of elites who shape the environment of electoral participation. A couple of years ago, I served as an academic consultant to my city's Charter Review Commission, and I heard some conscientious and dedicated public servants lament the low participation and voter turnout in our municipal elections. They clearly wanted more public involvement in local government, and looked to me for advice on how to stimulate voter participation in local elections. When I suggested that the most certain way to increase turnout rates would be to move the city election from a spring ballot to a fall ballot, concurrent with either the presidential or gubernatorial election, the same conscientious and dedicated leaders suddenly expressed concern about whether important issues on the city's agenda would be buried (or distorted) amidst the noise of national or statewide campaigns. I have no doubt about either the sincerity of their desire for more participation or about their concern for the quality of information that might get through to city voters in a fall election. But that exchange illustrates the conflicting incentives felt by elites, who shape the environment in which Americans vote. Election officials and candidates may value higher voter turnout in the abstract, but not to the exclusion of other political concerns and motivations.

REFERENCES

ABRAMSON, P. R., ALDRICH, J. H., and ROHDE, D. W. 2007. *Change and Continuity in the 2004 and 2006 Elections*. Washington, D.C.: CQ Press.

ANSOLABEHERE, S. and IYENGAR, S. 1995. *Going Negative: How Attack Ads Shrink and Polarize the Electorate*. New York: Free Press.

────── SIMON, A., and VALENTINO, N. 1994. Does Attack Advertising Demobilize the Electorate? *American Political Science Review*, 88: 829–38.

AXELROD, R. M. 2006. *The Evolution of Cooperation*. New York: Basic Books.

BENDOR, J., DIERMEIER, D., and TING, M. 2003. A Behavioral Model of Turnout. *American Political Science Review*, 97: 261–80.

BENNETT, S. E. and RESNICK, D. 1990. The Implications of Nonvoting for Democracy in the United States. *American Journal of Political Science*, 34: 771–802.

BERINSKY, A. J. 2005. The Perverse Consequences of Electoral Reform in the United States. *American Politics Research*, 33: 471–91.

BLACK, J. H. 2005. From Enumeration to the National Register of Electors: An Account and an Evaluation. In *Strengthening Canadian Democracy*, ed. P. Howe, R. Johnston, and A. Blais. Montreal: Institute for Research on Public Policy.

BLAIS, A. 2000. *To Vote or Not to Vote: The Merits and Limits of Rational Choice Theory.* Pittsburgh: University of Pittsburgh Press.

BRIANS, C. L. and GROFMAN, B. 2001. Election Day Registration's Effect on U.S. Voter Turnout. *Social Science Quarterly*, 82: 170–83.

BRODY, R. 1978. The Puzzle of Political Participation in America. In *The New American Political System*, ed. Anthony King. Washington, D.C.: AEI.

BROOKS, D. J. and GEER, J. G. 2007. Beyond Negativity: The Effects of Incivility on the Electorate. *American Journal of Political Science*, 51: 1–16.

BURNHAM, W. D. 1980. The Appearance and Disappearance of the American Voter. In *Electoral Participation: A Comparative Analysis*, ed. Richard Rose. Beverly Hills: Sage.

CITRIN, J., SCHICKLER, E., and SIDES, J. 2003. What If Everyone Voted? Simulating the Impact of Increased Turnout in Senate Elections. *American Journal of Political Science*, 47: 75–90.

DALTON, R. J. 2006. *Citizen Politics: Public Opinion and Political Participation in Advanced Industrial Democracies.* New York: CQ Press.

—— 2008. *Citizen Politics: Public Opinion and Political Participation in Advanced Industrial Democracies.* New York: CQ Press.

DENARDO, J. 1980. Turnout and the Vote—the Joke's on the Democrats. *American Political Science Review*, 74: 406–20.

DYCK, J. J. and GIMPEL, J. G. 2005. Distance, Turnout, and the Convenience of Voting. *Social Science Quarterly*, 86: 531–48.

ERIKSON, R. S. 1995. State Turnout and Presidential Voting. *American Politics Quarterly*, 23: 387–96.

FINKEL, S. E. and GEER, J. G. 1998. A Spot Check: Casting Doubt on the Demobilizing Effect of Attack Advertising. *American Journal of Political Science*, 42: 573–95.

FIORINA, M. P. 1990. Information and Rationality in Elections. In *Information and Democratic Processes*, ed. J. A. Ferejohn and J. H. Kuklinski. Urbana: University of Illinois Press.

FRANKLIN, M. N. 2002. The Dynamics of Electoral Participation. in *Comparing Democracies 2: New Challenges in the Study of Elections and Voting*, ed. L. LeDuc, R. G. Niemi, and P. Norris. London/Thousand Oaks: Sage.

—— 2004. *Voter Turnout and the Dynamics of Electoral Competition in Established Democracies since 1945.* Cambridge/New York: Cambridge University Press.

—— and HIRCZY DE MIÑO, W. P. 1998. Separated Powers, Divided Government, and Turnout in U.S. Presidential Elections. *American Journal of Political Science*, 42: 316–26.

GANT, M. M. and LYONS, W. 1993. Democratic Theory, Nonvoting, and Public Policy: The 1972–1988 Presidential Elections. *American Politics Quarterly*, 21: 185–204.

GEER, J. G. 2006. *In Defense of Negativity: Attack Ads in Presidential Campaigns.* Chicago: University of Chicago Press.

GERBER, A. S. and GREEN, D. P. 2000. The Effects of Canvassing, Telephone Calls, and Direct Mail on Voter Turnout: A Field Experiment. *American Political Science Review*, 94: 653–63.

GIMPEL, J. G., KAUFMANN, K. M., and PEARSON-MERKOWITZ, S. 2007. Battleground States Versus Blackout States: The Behavioral Implications of Modern Presidential Campaigns. *Journal of Politics*, 69: 786–97.

GINSBERG, B. 1982. *Consequences of Consent: Elections, Citizen Control, and Popular Acqui-escence*. New York: Random House.

GOMEZ, B. T., HANSFORD, T. G., and KRAUSE, G. A. 2007. The Republicans Should Pray for Rain: Weather, Turnout, and Voting in U.S. Presidential Elections. *Journal of Politics*, 69: 649–63.

GREEN, D. P. and GERBER, A. S. 2004. *Get out the Vote! How to Increase Voter Turnout*. Washington, D.C.: Brookings Institution Press.

—— —— and NICKERSON, D. W. 2003. Getting out the Vote in Local Elections: Results from Six Door-to-Door Canvassing Experiments. *Journal of Politics*, 65: 1083–96.

—— and SHAPIRO, I. 1994. *Pathologies of Rational Choice Theory: A Critique of Applications in Political Science*. New Haven, Conn.: Yale University Press.

GRIFFIN, J. D. and NEWMAN, B. 2005. Are Voters Better Represented? *Journal of Politics*, 67: 1206–27.

GRONKE, P., GALANES-ROSENBAUM, E., MILLER, P. A., and TOFFEY, D. 2008. Convenience Voting. *Annual Review of Political Science*, 11: 437–55.

HAJNAL, Z. and TROUNSTINE, J. 2005. Where Turnout Matters: The Consequences of Uneven Turnout in City Politics. *Journal of Politics*, 67: 515–35.

HIGHTON, B. 2004. Voter Registration and Turnout in the United States. *Perspectives on Politics*, 2: 507–16.

—— and WOLFINGER, R. E. 1998. Estimating the Effects of the National Voter Registration Act of 1993. *Political Behavior*, 20: 79–104.

—— —— 2001. The Political Implications of Higher Turnout. *British Journal of Political Science*, 31: 179–92.

HILL, D. and McKEE, S. C. 2005. The Electoral College, Mobilization, and Turnout in the 2000 Presidential Election. *American Politics Research*, 33: 700–25.

HILL, K. Q. and LEIGHLEY, J. E. 1992. The Policy Consequences of Class Bias in State Electorates. *American Journal of Political Science*, 36: 351–65.

JACKMAN, R. W. 1987. Political Institutions and Voter Turnout in the Industrial Democracies. *American Political Science Review*, 81: 405–23.

JACOBSON, G. C. 2004. *The Politics of Congressional Elections*. New York: Pearson Longman.

KNACK, S. 1993. The Voter Participation Effects of Selecting Jurors from Registration Lists. *Journal of Law and Economics*, 36: 99–114.

—— 2000. Deterring Voter Registration through Juror Selection Practices: Evidence from Survey Data. *Public Choice*, 103: 49–62.

LEIGHLEY, J. E. 1995. Attitudes, Opportunities and Incentives—a Field Essay on Political Participation. *Political Research Quarterly*, 48: 181–209.

—— and NAGLER, J. 1992. Socioeconomic Bias in Turnout 1964–1988: The Voters Remain the Same. *American Political Science Review*, 86: 725–36.

—— —— 2007. Unions, Voter Turnout, and Class Bias in the U.S. Electorate, 1964–2004. *Journal of Politics*, 69: 430–41.

LIJPHART, A. 1997. Unequal Participation: Democracy's Unresolved Dilemma. *American Political Science Review*, 91: 1–14.

MAHLER, V. A. 2008. Electoral Turnout and Income Redistribution by the State: A Cross-National Analysis of the Developed Democracies. *European Journal of Political Research*, 47: 161–83.

MARTIN, P. S. 2003. Voting's Rewards: Voter Turnout, Attentive Publics, and Congressional Allocation of Federal Money. *American Journal of Political Science*, 47: 110–27.

MARTINEZ, M. D. 1997. Don't Tax You, Don't Tax Me, Tax the Fella Behind the Tree: Partisan and Turnout Effects on Tax Policy. *Social Science Quarterly*, 78: 895–906.

—— and GILL, J. 2005. The Effects of Turnout on Partisan Outcomes in U.S. Presidential Elections, 1960–2000. *Journal of Politics*, 67: 1248–74.

MAYHEW, D. R. 2005. *Divided We Govern: Party Control, Lawmaking, and Investigations, 1946–2002.* New Haven, Conn.: Yale University Press.

McDONALD, M. P. 2008. United States Election Project. <http://elections.gmu.edu/> (Accessed 12 November 2008.)

—— and POPKIN, S. L. 2001. The Myth of the Vanishing Voter. *American Political Science Review*, 95: 963–74.

MORTON, R. B. 1991. Groups in Rational Turnout Models. *American Journal of Political Science*, 35: 758–76.

MUELLER, D. C. and STRATMANN, T. 2003. The Economic Effects of Democratic Participation. *Journal of Public Economics*, 87: 2129–55.

NAGEL, J. H. and McNULTY, J. E. 1996. Partisan Effects of Voter Turnout in Senatorial and Gubernatorial Elections. *American Political Science Review*, 90: 780–93.

—— —— 2000. Partisan Effects of Voter Turnout in Presidential Elections. *American Politics Quarterly*, 28: 408–29.

OLIVER, J. E. and WOLFINGER, R. E. 1999. Jury Aversion and Voter Registration. *American Political Science Review*, 93: 147–52.

PATTERSON, T. E. 2002. *The Vanishing Voter: Public Involvement in an Age of Uncertainty.* New York: Alfred A. Knopf.

PIVEN, F. F. and CLOWARD, R. A. 1988. *Why Americans Don't Vote.* New York: Pantheon Books.

POWELL, G. B., Jr. 1980. Voting Turnout in Thirty Democracies: Partisan, Legal, and Socio-Economic Influences. In *Electoral Participation: A Comparative Analysis*, ed. R. Rose. Beverly Hills, Calif.: Sage.

—— 1986. American Turnout in Comparative Perspective. *American Political Science Review*, 80: 17–44.

PUTNAM, R. D. 1995. Tuning in, Tuning Out: The Strange Disappearance of Social Capital in America. *PS—Political Science & Politics* 28: 664–83.

RADCLIFF, B. 1994. Turnout and the Democratic Vote. *American Politics Quarterly*, 22: 259–76.

RANNEY, A. 1983. Non-Voting Is Not a Social Disease. *Public Opinion*, 6: 16–19.

RIKER, W. and ORDESHOOK, P. 1968. A Theory of the Calculus of Voting. *American Political Science Review*, 62: 25–42.

ROSENSTONE, S. J. and HANSEN, J. M. 1993. *Mobilization, Participation, and Democracy in America.* New York: Macmillan Publishing Company.

SHAW, D. R. 2006. *The Race to 270: The Electoral College and the Campaign Strategies of 2000 and 2004.* Chicago: University of Chicago Press.

SQUIRE, P., WOLFINGER, R. E., and GLASS, D. P. 1987. Residential Mobility and Voter Turnout. *American Political Science Review* 81: 45–66.

TEIXEIRA, R. A. 1992. *The Disappearing American Voter.* Washington, D.C.: Brookings.

TUCKER, H. J. and VEDLITZ, A. 1986. Controversy: Does Heavy Turnout Help Democrats in Presidential Elections? *American Political Science Review*, 80: 1291–304.

VERBA, S., SCHLOZMAN, K. L., and BRADY, H. E. 1995. *Voice and Equality: Civic Voluntarism in American Politics.* Cambridge, Mass.: Harvard University Press.

WALD, K. D. 1987. *Religion and Politics in the United States.* New York: St. Martin's Press.

WOLFINGER, R. E. 1994. The Rational Citizen Faces Election Day or What Rational Choice Theorists Don't Tell You About American Elections. In *Elections at Home and Abroad: Essays in Honor of Warren E. Miller*, ed. M. K. Jennings and T. E. Mann. Ann Arbor: University of Michigan Press.

—— HIGHTON, B., and MULLIN, M. 2005. How Postregistration Laws Affect the Turnout of Citizens Registered to Vote. *State Politics and Policy Quarterly*, 5: 1–23.

—— and ROSENSTONE., S. J. 1980. *Who Votes?* New Haven, Conn.: Yale University Press.

CHAPTER 8

....

AMERICAN VOTER TURNOUT IN HISTORICAL PERSPECTIVE

....

MICHAEL P. MCDONALD

In absolute terms, a record number of people voted in the last American presidential election, a statement that is generally true even without referencing a specific year. In contemporary elections, the number of voters may experience a short-term decrease due to election-specific factors such as the relative competitiveness of a presidential election before resuming its inexorable upward trend in the next election. The accuracy of the statement rests on the assumption that the number of voters continues to increase along with the United States' population, so it is more appropriate to discuss voter turnout in terms of rates, which exhibit meaningful variation over time, rather than total numbers. However, the statement is also true because historical battles over disfranchising laws that restrict the electorate's size have largely been settled in favor of expansion to near-universal eligibility for all citizens of voting age, with exception for lingering issues such as felon voting rights. What remain are legacy procedural barriers that impose costs that motivated voters must overcome. To understand voter turnout rates in historical perspective, we must therefore understand context: the pool of eligible voters, the voting procedures, and the political circumstances surrounding the elections in a given period.

Alexander Keyssar (2000) has written perhaps the most definitive historical narrative of the expansion and contraction of the American electorate. As he relates, the most contentious constitutional convention debates among the Founding Fathers included the voting qualifications in national elections. Those that desired expanded suffrage framed the debate in terms of rights, while those that wanted to restrict the franchise framed the debate in terms of privileges. Unable to resolve their differences, they crafted a compromise in Article I, Section 4 of the United States constitution that delegated congressional authority over the regulation of congressional elections to the state legislatures, a decision that would have profound consequences for voting rights and turnout rates in subsequent years. (Note, as originally conceived state legislatures selected US senators and were under no obligation to hold direct elections for members of the Electoral College.)

At first blush, the franchise appears to have expanded to encompass ever more Americans. While most colonial states restricted by varying degrees voting to resident white males or freemen who had not been convicted of a felony or infamous crime, the constitutional convention debate largely centered on property requirements or poll taxes, required at the time by all states. Property requirements faded in the early nineteenth century and poll taxes were later outlawed by the Twenty-fourth Amendment in 1964. Suffrage was extended to all African Americans by the Fifteenth Amendment in 1870, to women by the Nineteenth Amendment in 1920, and to persons aged 18 and older by the Twenty-sixth Amendment in 1971. This enfranchising trend is notable in that it was largely driven by federal constitution amendments to override state variation; and as Keyssar notes, these seminal moments often followed contributions by affected groups during a preceding major war.

Countervailing this trend have been periods when the franchise was restricted. In the mid-nineteenth century, states began restricting voting to citizens as a means to curtail the immigrant support base of urban Northern political machines (prior to this, states encouraged non-citizens to vote as a means to socialize immigrants to their new country). The franchise was also limited through less direct means, such as voter registration and literacy or understanding tests. These 'innovations' would later be imported into the Southern states as a means to effectively disfranchise uneducated African Americans and Whites during the Jim Crow era following the passage of the Fifteenth Amendment and the end of Southern Reconstruction. Nearly a century would pass before these demobilizing restrictions were lifted by the 1965 Voting Rights Act and other contemporary policies.

Today the franchise is extended to all American citizens age eighteen and older and who—depending on state law—have not committed a felony or been deemed mentally incompetent. All states except North Dakota require voter registration, though variation among states' registration laws continues to interest voting scholars, particularly such policy innovations as election day registration (see Brown, this volume, Chapter 10). Voting in America is a personal choice, and increasingly, scholars and policy-makers are drawn to reforming voting mechanics to make voting more convenient and thereby raise participation rates (see Stein and Vonnahme, this volume, Chapter 11).

Four Eras in American Participation

Turnout rates from 1789 to 2006 among the voting-eligible population in presidential and congressional elections are provided in Figure 8.1, and in presidential elections for Southern and non-Southern states in Figure 8.2 (Stanley and Niemi 2006: 12–15). These turnout rates should be considered our best estimates, as measurement error enters into both the numerator and denominator of the rate equation. The numerator is the highest of the total number of votes cast for president, governor, or Congress; it is surprisingly not the total number of ballots cast, which may include blank or spoiled ballots, simply because historically few states reported this number and even today a few still do not report it. The denominator for these rates, the eligible population, is difficult to pinpoint even for contemporary elections (McDonald and Popkin 2001), but even more so for historical elections (Burnham 1965, 1986).

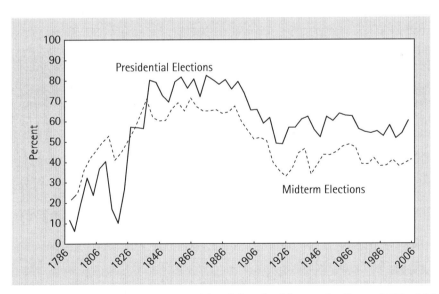

Figure 8.1 Voter turnout rates, presidential and midterm elections, 1789–2006

Source: Stanley and Niemi (2006).

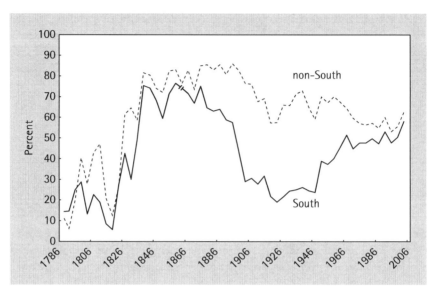

Figure 8.2 Voter turnout rates, presidential elections, South and non–South, 1789–2004

Source: Stanley and Niemi (2006); broken line indicates no Southern presidential votes in 1864.

The problem of calculating accurate turnout rates arises on two accounts. First, there has been historically much variation in state voter eligibility laws on issues such as property requirements and poll taxes, among many others detailed by Keyssar (2000). Second, estimating the size of affected populations can be near-impossible when little or no accurate census data were collected. As one example, until 1908 Wisconsin extended voting to non-citizens who stated an intention to become citizens; estimating this population requires "speculative" (Burnham 1965, 9) census data on the number of non-citizens *and* assumptions about how many of these people intended to become citizens. The numbers presented in the figures should thus be considered estimates, even for contemporary elections.

For expositional purposes, I classify American voter participation into four periods: The Founding Era (1789–1824), The Party Machine Era (1828–1896), The Segregation Era (1900–1948), and The Nationalization Era (1952–present). There is no bright line dividing these eras. America's decentralized election administration system allows policy innovations affecting turnout rates to be adopted piecemeal by the states. Even major national events such as suffrage expansion through national constitutional amendments are often presaged by similar adoptions among trendsetting states. There are no real national elections, either, since congressional elections are held on a district-by-district or state-by-state basis, including presidential elections which are filtered through the Electoral College. Party competition—which can energize an electorate—within states and regions may fluctuate gradually over time, rather than as a discontinuous change between two elections. Much of this rich variation is necessarily lost in constructing the short historical narrative of American voter turnout rates that follows.

THE FOUNDING ERA: 1789–1824

The Founding Era witnessed the lowest voter turnout rates in American history. A contributing factor to these low turnout rates is measurement error: they are based on the white male voting-age population and are undoubtedly related to an inability to properly modify the denominator for various disfranchising laws of the period. Even so, these early low national turnout rates make sense from what we know about politics and culture of the time. Elections were difficult to participate in and of low salience for most voters.

Elections were not conveniently held at nearby polling locations for many rural persons. Voters often had to travel long distances, sometimes without the benefit of roads, to cast their ballots at places designated by state and local governments. As Virginia Representative Chilton, arguing in opposition to establishing a single uniform day to hold federal elections, stated, "frequently . . . all the votes were not polled in one day" because Virginia is "mountainous and interconnected by large streams of water" that in times of inclement weather impeded travel (*Congressional Globe* 1844, 15). When they arrived, persons would vote by one of two methods: *viva voce* (by public spoken affirmation of a voter's choice), or by ballots, which in those days referred to color-coded beans or handwritten pieces of paper dropped into a receptacle. Voting among frontiersmen was likely an event planned along with other necessary errands, and could easily be passed up in favor of other pressing needs. It thus could be possible to favor mercantile interests by holding elections at an "inconvenient distance"—in the words of *Federalist* No. 61 author Alexander Hamilton—exclusively in large cities far removed from agrarian interests.

Many frontiersmen would not have made time to vote simply because they did not meet property eligibility requirements. Reform agitation came from militiamen who participated in the American Revolution and War of 1812, who counted among their ranks a growing population of "mechanics" in the cities (Keyssar 2000, 34–5), and frontiersmen in Appalachia and westward, where inadequate record-keeping made property qualifications difficult to implement and enforce (Kousser 1984). Of course, those with the franchise held political power, so reform could only happen by their leave, which they granted so as to, in an uncertain and violent world, "enhance their own security and help preserve their way of life, by assuring such men would continue to serve in the army and the militias" (Keyssar 2000, 37). Yet, dismantling of property requirements could be highly contentious, the most notorious example being the 1834 "Dorr war" armed insurrection to protest Rhode Island's $134 property requirement (Kousser 1984). Indeed, the argument that the franchise should be extended only to competent persons—property being an indicator of competence—remained persuasive, and such principles persisted in pauper and felon exclusionary laws (Steinfeld 1989).

Electoral competition for national office was limited during this period, which contributed to low turnout rates. George Washington ran unopposed in 1789 and 1792; the 6.3 percent turnout rate in 1792 estimated by Burnham is the lowest in the nation's history for any federal election. As two-party competition between the Federalists and Democratic-Republicans developed following Washington's retirement, turnout rates began to climb for presidential elections, reaching 40.4 percent in 1812. They then plunged again to the low double digits following the disintegration of the Federalist Party and the ensuing one-party Era of Good Feeling that lasted until 1824.

An interesting feature of this early period is that turnout in congressional elections was uniformly higher than presidential elections. The Framers of the Constitution believed that Congress would be the most powerful branch of government and designed the constitution to limit its power. During this period, the United States operated almost as a parliamentary democracy whereby national congressional leaders selected their party's presidential candidates. Likewise, many state and local government offices were filled by appointment rather than by election (Keyssar 2000, 40). However, an increasing number of offices were elected, including holding popular votes for members to the Electoral College instead of direct appointment by state legislatures. The political order—at least at the federal level—unraveled following the contentious four-way presidential election of 1824. Because no presidential candidate won an Electoral College majority, Congress was empowered to elect John Quincy Adams, son of John Adams, over General Andrew Jackson, a hero of the war of 1812 and winner of a popular vote plurality. In 1828, Andrew Jackson would parlay outrage over his 'stolen' election to win the presidency by building a mass campaign organization based out of the frontier states to challenge the Washington insiders of his day.

The end of the Founding Era marks America's transition from a small, elite ruling class to an enlarging middle-class electorate. Politicians such as Aaron Burr, who successfully executed political-machine-style voter mobilization efforts for the New York state legislative elections of 1800 (Lawson 2007), and Andrew Jackson tapped into these voters' potential by building mass political parties organized to mobilize their supporters and thereby secure government control and the resulting privileges. An emerging competitive electoral environment at the end of the era was a motivating stimulus for Jackson's Democratic Party to continue enfranchising trends (Keyssar 2000, 39–40). Yet, pathways to expand the electorate did not travel through the national government during this era; instead, they traced territory unique to a state's politics to arrive at similar destinations.

THE PARTY MACHINE ERA: 1828–96

The enlargement of the electorate to a mass scale soon gave rise to the era of strong political machines, which were efficiently organized from the local level up and designed to deliver votes—often including those of recent immigrants—in exchange for patronage and other preferment. During the Party Machine Era, turnout rates rose to historical highs of around eighty percent and persisted at these high levels until the beginning of the twentieth century. While these political machines are often associated with urban politics, rural interests also formed machine organizations capable of mobilizing their electorates (e.g., Converse 1974; Kernell and McDonald 1999).

This period is characterized by fierce party competition, nationally and within states (Burnham 1965). The irreconcilable policy debates facing the nation eventually erupted in Civil War in 1861. At issue was the increasing encroachment of the national government into state policy areas, particularly with regards to slavery. The growth of these controversies signaled that the federal government's power was waxing relative to the states. Indeed, the heightened party competition increased incentives for political machines to mobilize their supporters so that they could control governments, policymaking, and the distribution of patronage.

This period also saw the first major expansion of the electorate through formal amendment of the national constitution. Following the Civil War, the victorious North imposed concessions on the South, including the Fifteenth Amendment which granted voting rights to all persons of color and former slaves. In the period of Southern Reconstruction (1863–1877) following the Civil War, the Republican North vigorously enforced the Fifteenth Amendment as it fostered the election of Republican African American officeholders in many Southern states and thereby served as a means to ensure Republican control of the southern state and national governments, particularly important since state legislatures still appointed US senators. With racial tensions high and rough parity in the numbers of African American and White voters, Southern voting was elevated and racially polarized (Key 1949). Following Reconstruction, ascendant Southern Whites embarked on a violent pogrom to intimidate African Americans from voting that eventually made it possible to cement disfranchising "Jim Crow" laws into state constitutions that cleverly did not specifically refer to race, so as to conform to the Fifteenth Amendment (Kousser 1999).

The ability of political parties to monitor voting was an important gear in their machinery. In 1799, Pennsylvania became the first state to ostensibly streamline the voting process by permitting parties to print ballots, which they would do so on brightly colored paper to distribute at polling places to their supporters. Parties could then reward or punish voters based on which party ballot they were seen dropping into a ballot box. "Money, or 'soap,' as it was called, with increasing frequency was used to carry elections after the Civil War" (Evans 1917, 11); this money could offset poll taxes, and where pauper laws were linked to timely tax payments, parties would even shoulder supporters' unpaid taxes (Keyssar 2000, 130). With such direct financial gains to be realized by voting, it is not surprising that people would be highly motivated to vote. Burnham (1965, 22) describes the latter half of this period as "intensely party-oriented voting participation," not just in terms of high levels of turnout, but also low levels of split-ticket voting and roll-off, which would logically be lower when parties enforced straight-party voting through party-printed ballots.

If political machines had such control and influence over voters, it is possible that they exerted similar control of the counting of ballots (Converse 1972, 1974). A portion of the high turnout rates of the nineteenth century is likely related to election rigging, although we cannot know how much, and as Burnham (1986) argues, stories of "vote early, vote often," while sometimes valid, were often exaggerated. We know that voter registration laws enacted near the close of the machine era ostensibly designed to limit fraud were related to lower turnout rates (Burnham 1974), although political considerations entered when these laws were not applied evenly across urban and rural areas (Keyssar 2000, 151–9).

A positive view of voter turnout in the Party Machine Era is that it serves as an indicator of the important role political parties played in organizing American society. In the absence of television and other modern diversions politics was a central component of American culture, as demonstrated by high levels of political participation, and further served a role of assimilating and socially supporting the significant influx of immigrants. Yet, political machines were rife with corruption, and in this light high voter turnout rates are a manifestation of political machines' abuse of power. Election reforms at the end of the machine period certainly had their intended effect: turnout rates dropped precipitously as machines were systematically dismantled and voting became a costly activity.

THE SEGREGATION ERA: 1900–48

The Segregation Era is characterized not just by segregationist policies in the South that effectively disfranchised African Americans, though that was a major factor in the abysmally low Southern turnout rates during this era. Outside the South, a by-product of the Progressive election reforms was a segregation of the electorate into those who chose to participate and those who did not or could not shoulder the burdens these reforms imposed. Finally, the country was politically segregated following the realigning election of 1896 such that party competition waned nationally and within states (Burnham 1965), most notably, the rise of one-party Democratic dominance of the South (Key 1949).

The Progressive reform movement starting in the late nineteenth century implemented policies to dismantle the political machines' power structures, such as civil service to rid the country of patronage, voter registration laws to curtail legendary vote fraud, and the secret ballot to purge direct political influence on voter's choices. By 1920, participation plummeted to under 50 percent, and has never since returned to such high levels as during the heyday of machine politics. Undoubtedly, breaking the political machines' mobilization engines reduced turnout. We cannot know how much of a role political party mobilization efforts played in the nineteenth century, but we do know these activities are related to higher turnout rates in contemporary elections (see Gerber, Green, and Davenport, this volume, Chapter 5).

While voter registration laws were rationalized as a means of reducing vote fraud, they impose direct voting costs that contemporary voting behavior studies find reduce voting propensities (e.g., Erickson 1981; Timpone 1998). Massachusetts first enacted voter registration in 1801, but such laws were "uncommon before the Civil War" and it was "between the 1870s and World War I" that the majority of states adopted voter registration (Keyssar 2000, 151–2). In comparison to modest modern registration requirements, these registration laws could be quite onerous in frequency (e.g., every election), length of time in advance of the election (e.g., three months), and opportunities to register (e.g., registration was open for only four days). As Keyssar (2000, 153) writes, "To no one's surprise, these reforms depressed voter turnout" (see also Burnham 1974). These laws often mandated lengthy residency qualifications of up to six months, which, when accompanied by difficult registration requirements, all but assured that persons who had recently moved would be unable to vote. Furthermore, they were sometimes accompanied by procedures that made it difficult for persons who found their way on to 'suspect lists' to verify their voting eligibility.

Secret ballot laws were also targeted to dismantle the political machine's ability to monitor how people voted, but had further negative spillover effects on turnout. Massachusetts was the first state to adopt the secret ballot in 1888, modeled on the 1856 Australian ballot, and was quickly followed by most states, with all but a handful adopting the reform prior to the First World War (Rusk 1970). For uneducated voters, the secret ballot "served as a *de facto* literacy test, since illiterates were not allowed assistance in voting" (Kousser 1999, 34). Some states attempted to address this "problem" through party-strip ballot designs that required checking but a single box to vote for all party-endorsed candidates, with party emblems to help guide illiterate voters (Rusk 1970). It is not surprising, then, that Southern states were attracted to the secret ballot as a means to disfranchise former slaves, who had not received any formal education. An offensive 1892 Arkansas campaign song celebrated the disfranchising effect:

> The Australian Ballot works like a charm,
> It makes them think and scratch,
> And when a Negro gets a ballot
> He has certainly got his match.
> (Quoted in Graves 1967, 212–13).

The secret ballot was among the many disfranchising tools available to Southern Whites to restrict African American suffrage, which often swept up poor, uneducated Whites. A more direct method was the literacy or understanding test, which was first adopted in the Northeast in the 1850s to restrict immigrant voting since most native-born persons were literate. Yet, outside the Northeast and South, their adoption was often contentious; for example, heavily Hispanic New Mexico wrote a non-discriminatory language suffrage clause into its first state constitution (Keyssar 2000, 143). Literacy tests were particularly attractive for Southerners since they could administer the tests in a discriminatory fashion, and were sometimes accompanied by 'grandfather clauses' that exempted persons whose grandfathers had voted, which would not include former slaves.

In state after state, once African Americans were intimidated through violence from participating in elections, constitutional conventions were held to institute poll taxes, registration laws with lengthy residency requirements, literacy tests, secret ballots (and their kin, multiple-ballot laws that required voters to drop ballots into the correct box), and even felony disfranchisement laws that together disproportionately affected African Americans (Kousser 1999). As one delegate to the Virginia constitutional convention of 1901–2 stated, "The great underlying principle of the Convention movement . . . was the elimination of the negro from politics in this State" (quoted in Keyssar 2000, 112). And they were successful: Southern turnout was already in decline following the end of Reconstruction, by 1904 less than 30 percent of eligible Southerners cast a presidential ballot, and Southern turnout would remain at these low levels until 1952. African American voter registration rates in Southern states dropped even more precipitously (Kousser 1999).

While turnout rates were abysmally low in Southern general elections, they were actually higher in primaries (Key 1949). As Whites and the Southern Democratic Party strangled competition in general elections, meaningful elections occurred in primaries. To ensure that Whites would not inadvertently split their votes among multiple candidates in a general election, some Southern states went as far as to hold 'White primaries' to select a single White candidate to run in the general election. In the first chipping away at the Jim Crow system, the American Civil Liberties Union successfully challenged the law before the US Supreme Court in the 1944 case, *Smith* v. *Allwright*. This case would presage greater federal intervention in dismantling the discriminatory Jim Crow laws, and also increasingly setting national standards for suffrage and election administration.

While the "Solid South" emerged as a bastion of Democratic Party strength, political coalitions across the entire country fundamentally changed following the election of 1896 (Key 1955; Burnham 1965). Democrats selected Populist William Jennings Bryan as their nominee, realigning the major party coalitions along an agrarian–urban divide. The results were decisive, but in favor of the Republican Party. Following the 1896 realigning election, the distribution of party support in American politics split roughly into regions, thereby reducing party competition at the presidential level across states (although pockets of competition persisted in states like Ohio; see Burnham 1965, 17) and at the congressional level (Franklin 2004, 110). In some Republican-dominated Northeastern states, competition was further eroded by the evisceration of the Democratic urban political machines.

A bright spot during this period was the national extension of women's suffrage through the Nineteenth Amendment, ratified in 1920, following women's contribution to the domestic wartime effort during The First World War. Unfortunately, this expansion of the electorate was concurrent with the 1920 and 1924 presidential elections, two of the lowest turnout elections of the twentieth century, which led some to conclude that this—at the time—relatively uneducated segment of the population depressed turnout rates (Merriam and Gosnell 1924). Still, the negative effect may not have been all that great and today women vote at marginally higher rates than men; as Burnham (1965) notes, it is difficult to disentangle the introduction of women's suffrage from the overall downward trend in turnout that started in 1870.

The Segregation Era marks a period of retrenchment in voter turnout. Without political machines to mobilize the electorate, voting rates dropped as voting costs previously born by the political parties' organizations were shifted to individuals. Indeed, elaborate hoops were often placed in the way with the intention to reduce participation, particularly in the Southern states and Northern cities. Yet, it is also during this period that the last major segment of the population, women, were officially granted suffrage. Voting barriers were thus transformed into procedures that were not overtly targeted at a particular group. In theory, every American citizen now had a right to vote, and an issue that had deeply divided the Founding Fathers was laid to rest. Once voting was framed as a right rather than a privilege, it would only be a matter of time before the more procedural barriers preventing the exercise of this right would be torn down.

THE NATIONALIZATION ERA (1952–PRESENT)

The present Nationalization Era is characterized by nationalization in two ways. First, the sectional differences in turnout rates starkly visible in the Segregation Era have dissipated as party competition has been restored within regions. Second, the federal government has taken an increasing role in defining suffrage and overseeing election administration. More than at any time in the nation's history, contemporary federal elections are a national contest rather than organized and contested first at a local level.

The 1948 presidential election of Harry Truman, along with the Democratic Party first adopting civil rights in their platform marked the resurgence of the Republican Party in the South (Campbell 1977). The increase of inter-party competition sparked greater participation in the region. Indeed, contemporary students of politics are often surprised to learn that the "Solid South" refers to Democratic Party dominance of this region, as opposed to seeming Republican dominance in current federal elections. Party competition remains, though. Southern Republicans have been successful at the federal level, while Democratic state parties have proven surprisingly resilient in state elections.

The shifting allegiance of the South from solid Democratic to Republican dominance in federal elections lies in part with the non-Southern wing of the Democratic Party championing African American rights. Joined by liberal congressional Republicans, these Democrats enacted the 1964 Civil Rights Act and the 1965 Voting Rights Act (VRA). The Voting Rights Act effectively enforced the Fifteenth Amendment nearly a hundred years after it had been ratified by empowering the federal government to monitor elections and register African Americans in so-called 'covered jurisdictions' with a history of electoral discrimination (Kousser 1999). To prevent further chicanery, the federal government was required to approve any changes in election administration in these jurisdictions. Current legal and scholarly work focuses on the significant constraint such oversight imposes on redistricting, but the oversight includes seemingly mundane procedures that affect turnout such as selective placement of polling places (Haspel and Knotts 2005; Gimpel and Dyck 2005). Often further overlooked is that the VRA reduced other voting barriers by abolishing literacy and understanding tests and reducing residency requirements and registration deadlines to a maximum of thirty days.

The Voting Rights Act is among many federal initiatives designed to provide national uniformity of election administration and reduce voter registration barriers. Concurrent with the VRA was the adoption in 1964 of the Twenty-Fourth Amendment, which outlawed poll taxes. In 1971, the Twenty-Sixth Amendment established the minimum voting age as 18, which brought the rest of the country in line with the handful of states that granted voting rights to persons aged under 21. The National

Voter Registration Act of 1993 (NVRA), or so-called "motor voter," mandated that voter registration forms be made available at driver's license offices and public assistance agencies. Despite proponents' expectations, the increased participation effect of "motor voter" appears to be modest (Knack 1995), perhaps because those who register through an NVRA agency do not have a clear intention to vote. NVRA also established national standards for maintainance of voter registration records, such as setting minimal standards on how to remove voters from lists, and included provisions that permit movers within local election jurisdictions to transfer their voter registration with them.

Further interest in improving election administration arose in the wake of the problems exposed in the 2000 presidential election. The US Supreme Court decision *Bush* v. *Gore* had the immediate effect of stopping a Florida recount that established George W. Bush as the winner, but the ruling had a long-term effect as well, prompting states to develop statewide uniform voting procedures. The federal government provided money to upgrade poorly performing voting equipment, such as the notorious punch-card ballots, through the Help America Vote Act of 2002 (HAVA). HAVA also mandated establishment of statewide electronic voter registration lists and provided a uniform system of provisional balloting to help resolve voter registration problems arising at the polls.

Experimentation continues among the states, as it has throughout the country's history, and variation in state and local election administrative procedures has created a vibrant subfield in American politics. In 1973, Minnesota adopted election day registration, which permits new voters and those transferring their registration to register and vote at their polling place. Voting-behavior scholars (e.g., Mitchell and Wlezien 1995; Highton 1997) have consistently found a positive turnout effect from the policy that harks back to the no-registration days of the Founding Era. As of 2008, eleven states have adopted election day registration for general elections (this includes North Dakota, which never adopted voter registration, and Connecticut and Rhode Island, which permit election day registration for votes cast for presidential electors only). Other states have reduced their registration period to less than the thirty days permitted by the Voting Rights Act, which also has appreciable positive turnout effects (Wolfinger and Rosenstone 1980). Some states have adopted statewide portable voter registration, too, exceeding the NVRA requirements requiring registration transfers within local jurisdictions, which has a measurable positive turnout impact for recent movers (McDonald 2008). Other states are experimenting with early voting, no-fault absentee balloting, and even all-mail elections (see Stein and Vonnahme, this volume, Chapter 11).

Another historical holdover—felon disfranchisement laws—continues in a patchwork of state laws (McDonald 2002; Uggen and Manza 2002). A small number of states grant the franchise even to felons in prison, a greater number have some form of post-correctional provision that may pose a permanent burden, while most fall in between by disfranchising felons at various points within the judicial system. Recently, governors in states with post-correctional provisions, such as Florida and Virginia, have restored voting rights to large blocks of permanently disfranchised felons, and a few states have relaxed their felon disfranchisement laws (The Sentencing Project 2008).

The overwhelming voting trend during the Nationalization Era has been a tearing down of walls, not building them. During this era, variation in procedures designed to restrict access to the polling booth has been replaced with variation in procedures to increase access. Through federal legislation or constitutional amendment, this era has witnessed the demise of literacy tests, poll taxes, and excessively long registration deadlines and residency requirements; and the rise of voting by eighteen-year-olds, "motor voter," provisional balloting, and uniform standards for the management and residency transfer of voter registration. In their place, states and localities are experimenting with all-mail elections, election day registration, and central voting precincts, among many other policy innovations. Entering the twenty-first century, more than at any other time in the history of the country, voting is considered a fundamental right for all citizens, to be protected and extended, rather than a privilege restricted to the few.

THE NEXT VOTING ERA

The Nationalization Era poses a conundrum for voting behavior scholars. New policies enacted during this period should, all things being equal, have lowered voting costs and thereby increased voter turnout. Furthermore, education levels, which are correlated with voting (Wolfinger and Rosenstone 1980), also increased. In the South, turnout did rise, yet similar benefits did not accrue elsewhere. We are left then with a puzzle first posed by Brody (1978): why has turnout not increased nationally when the underlying inputs have favored it? A small part of the answer lies with the most recent expansion of the electorate. The Twenty-Sixth Amendment effectively extended the franchise to persons aged 18–21, a group whose participation is significantly lower than other age categories; thus, turnout rates among eligible voters dropped a little over a percentage point starting in 1972 (McDonald and Popkin 2001). Yet, this falls far short of solving the puzzle.

Brody's puzzle has developed into a major subfield within political science. We know more about voting behavior in the current Nationalization Era than in any other due to the advent of public opinion polling. The American National Election Study (ANES) is perhaps the most analyzed election survey by voting-behavior scholars because of its wide range and consistent questioning on a number of attitudinal and behavioral questions that are known to be related to voting.

Although the first ANES was conducted in 1948, it was a pilot study with questionable validity; the first reliable survey was conducted in 1952. The coverage of the ANES has thus greatly influenced the questions that voting-behavior scholars have asked because 1952 was the first of four sequentially high-turnout-rate presidential elections from 1952 to 1964. In 1968, turnout rates began a long-term "decline," a perception that was reinforced by the introduction of low-turnout youths in 1972 and the curious decision by scholars to calculate turnout rates for the voting-age population.

The framing of voter turnout as in decline led many scholars to seek explanations for "the most important, most familiar, most analyzed, and most conjectured trend in recent American political history" (Rosenstone and Hansen 1993, 57). Scholars posited many theories: the introduction of cable television that permits voters to tune out political programming (Baum and Kernell 1999), negative campaign advertising that disgusts voters (Ansolabehere and Iyengar 1995), generational replacement of high-propensity New Deal with apathetic Vietnam Era voters (Miller and Shanks 1996), and a general decay of civic society (Putnam 2000), among many others. Book titles lamented "disappearing" (Teixeira 1992) and "vanishing" voters (Patterson 2002).

Some of these theories may validly explain variation in political behavior during the Nationalization Era; however, the apparent ongoing post-1972 decline is an artifact of measurement error (McDonald and Popkin 2001). Starting in 1972, the United States experienced a significant influx of legal and illegal immigration that when properly accounted for reveals no ongoing decline in voter turnout rates. Walter Dean Burnham, who deserves praise for his meticulous work, might well have identified this trend earlier as he carefully adjusted historical turnout rates for ineligible populations, had he not experienced a publishing hiatus from 1987 to 2007 (Burnham 1987; 2007).

When examined over the long term (from 1908 to 2006), national turnout rates among eligible voters have fluctuated within a trading range of a little over ten percentage points. The 2004 presidential election broke the 60 percent mark for the first time since 1968, demonstrating that higher turnout levels are still possible in current elections. A longer study of turnout variation may prove enlightening as to why turnout may apparently be resurging. Yet, reframing the question of turnout variation to consider the long view still requires an answer to Brody's question, since it merely demonstrates that national turnout is not in decline, but neither has it increased appreciably. Voting scholars will likely continue to find addressing this hanging question a fertile ground for research.

History teaches that there are three paths that will eventually lead from the current situation in a way that will affect turnout rates. The first path would restructure the country's electoral competition, which is known to be associated with turnout (e.g., Burnham 1965; Cox and Munger 1989). Turnout rates suffer when presidential campaigns target their limited resources into highly competitive "battleground" states and largely ignore others (Hill 2006) and when congressional campaigns narrow their focus to a scattering of competitive US House seats (Franklin 2004, 110). A major realignment of the party's electoral coalitions may produce new, geographically based party coalitions, and turnout will shift as party competition wanes or waxes within states and districts. The geography-based nature of the American electoral system may also contribute to the nation's lower turnout compared to other developed democracies that use proportional representation electoral systems (Franklin 2004). Voters in proportional representation systems are offered more political parties to choose from and their votes are more proportionally translated into seats (Duverger 1959). While adopting an alternative electoral system may be too radical for policy makers, states are experimenting with methods to increase competition in legislative elections through campaign finance, term limit, and redistricting reforms (McDonald and Samples 2006). Another reform gaining momentum is scrapping the Electoral College in favor of a national direct popular vote.

A second pathway that the parties sought in previous eras to change the electoral balance—and affecting turnout as a consequence—was increasing or decreasing the electorate's size in their favor. For example, Andrew Jackson rose to power on the strength of expanding the electorate and Southern Democrats sought to cement their power in the late 1800s through contraction. Since the franchise for most citizens aged 18 and older is now hardwired into the US constitution, formally enfranchising or disfranchising large segments of the population is not a viable option to change the electorate's size. Yet, both parties today are interested in expanding and mobilizing their bases, particularly through peer-to-peer mobilization contact reminiscent of the bottom-up political machine organizations of the nineteenth century.

A third pathway would change the costs of voting through procedures. The two political parties have adopted different positions on proposed election administration policies that are rooted in academic research explaining why voters participate. The Democrats generally favor means to expand the electorate by enacting policies that lower voting costs, such as election day registration, since they believe that people who choose not to participate tend to be disadvantaged populations who cannot bear voting costs, and favor their economically liberal policies. They charge that Republicans favor contracting the electorate by imposing additional burdens on these at-risk populations, such as aggressive purging of voter registration rolls, which may force people to re-register, or requiring government-issued photo identification, which can be difficult for at-risk populations to attain. Republicans argue that voter registration purges and photo identification requirements impose minimal costs and are necessary to prevent vote fraud, similar to the stated intent of rigorous identification requirements at the close of the Political Machine Era (Keyssar 2000, 138), and charge that Democrats want to impose procedures, such as election day registration, that make it easier to commit vote fraud. Indeed, the debate is often framed in similar terms to those that divided the Founding Fathers: Democrats characterize voting as a fundamental right that must be protected and extended, while Republicans speak of voting as a privilege that should be granted to people capable of meeting minimal standards imposed to safeguard the election process.

Academic research reflects the state of current politics. Little research is being conducted on changing the composition of the electorate since nearly all citizens of voting age are now eligible to vote, except for felons (Uggen and Manza 2002). An active area of research is how procedural changes affect voter turnout, from how people are registered to when and how they cast their ballots (see Brown, this volume, Chapter 10; Stein and Vonnahme, this volume, Chapter 11). State and local variability in laws and procedures will likely prove fertile ground in the near future for research among these voting scholars. Another active line of research investigates incentives for persons to vote, particularly how campaigns can mobilize their supporters (see Davenport, Gerber, and Green, this volume, Chapter 5). Academics are often criticized for observing the world from afar in their ivory tower. Not so for voting scholars. Many are actively engaged with election administrators and political campaigns in studying and developing experiments to test novel procedures and mobilization methods to increase voter turnout.

REFERENCES

ANSOLABEHERE, S. and IYENGAR, S. 1995. *Going Negative: How Political Advertisements Shrink and Polarize the Electorate*. New York: Simon & Schuster.

BAUM, M. and KERNELL, S. 1999. Has Cable Ended the Golden Age of Presidential Television? *The American Political Science Review*, 93/1: 99–114.

BRODY, R. 1978. The Puzzle of Political Participation in America. In *The New American Political System*, ed. A. King. Washington, D.C.: American Enterprise Institute.

BURNHAM, W. D. 1965. The Changing Shape of the American Political Universe. *The American Political Science Review*, 59/1: 7–28.

—— 1974. Theory and Voting Research: Some Reflections on Converse's "Change in the American Electorate." *The American Political Science Review*, 68/3: 1002–23.

—— 1986. Those High Nineteenth-Century American Voting Turnouts: Fact or Fiction? *Journal of Interdisciplinary History*, 16/4: 613–44.

—— 1987. 'The Turnout Problem' in *Elections American Style*, ed. A. J. Reichley, The Brookings Institution, Washington, DC.

—— 2007. Triumphs and Travails in the Study of American Voting Participation Rates, 1788–2006. *The Journal of the Historical Society*, 7/4: 505–09.

CAMPBELL, B. A. 1977. Change in the Southern Electorate. *American Journal of Political Science*, 21/1: 37–64.

CONVERSE, P. E. 1972. Change in the American Electorate. In *The Human Meaning of Social Change*, ed. A. Campbell and P. E. Converse. New York: Russell Sage Foundation.

CONVERSE, P. E. 1974. Comment on Burnham's "Theory and Voting Research." *The American Political Science Review*, 68/3: 1024–7.

CONGRESSIONAL GLOBE. 1844, vol. 14, no. 1.

COX, G. W. and MUNGER, M. C. 1989. Closeness, Expenditures, and Turnout in the 1982 U.S. House Elections. *The American Political Science Review*, 83/1: 217–31.

DUVERGER, M. 1959. *Political Parties: Their Organization and Activity in the Modern State, Second English Revised Edition*. London: Methuen and Company.

ERIKSON, R. S. 1981. Why Do People Vote? Because They are Registered. *American Politics Quarterly*, 9/3: 259–76.

EVANS, E. C. 1917. *A History of the Australian Ballot System in the United States*. Chicago, Ill.: University of Chicago Press.

FRANKLIN, M. N. 2004. *Voter Turnout and the Dynamics of Electoral Competition in Established Democracies since 1945*. Cambridge: Cambridge University Press.

HASPEL, M. and KNOTTS, H. G. 2005. Location, Location, Location: Precinct Placement and the Costs of Voting. *The Journal of Politics*, 67/2: 560–73.

GIMPEL, J. and DYCK, J. J. 2005. Distance, Turnout and the Convenience of Voting. *Social Science Quarterly*, 86/3: 531–48.

GRAVES, J. W. 1967. Negro Disfranchisement in Arkansas. *Arkansas Historical Quarterly*, 26 (Autumn): 199–225.

HIGHTON, B. 1997. Easy Registration and Voter Turnout. *The Journal of Politics*, 59/2: 565–75.

HILL, D. L. 2006. *American Voter Turnout: An Institutional Perspective*. Boulder, Colo.: Westview Press.

KERNELL, S. and MCDONALD, M. P. 1999. Congress and America's Political Development: Political Strategy and the Transformation of the Post Office from Patronage to Service. *American Journal of Political Science*, 43/3: 792–811.

KEY, V. O. 1949. *Southern Politics in State and Nation*. New York: Alfred A. Knopf Publishers.

—— 1955. A Theory of Critical Elections. *The Journal of Politics*, 17/1: 3–18.

KEYSSAR, A. 2000. *The Right to Vote: The Contested History of Democracy in the United States*. New York: Basic Books.

KNACK, S. 1995. Does "Motor Voter" Work? Evidence from State-Level Data. *The Journal of Politics*, 57/3: 796–811.

KOUSSER, J. M. 1984. Suffrage. In *Encyclopedia of American Political History*, ed. J. P. Greene. New York: Charles Scribner's Sons.

—— 1999. *Colorblind Injustice: Minority Voting Rights and the Undoing of the Second Reconstruction*. Chapel Hill, N.C.: University of North Carolina Press.

LAWSON, E. J. 2007. *A Magnificent Catastrophe: The Tumultuous Election of 1800, America's First Presidential Campaign*. New York: Free Press.

MCDONALD, M. P. 2002. The Turnout Rate Among Eligible Voters for U.S. States, 1980–2000. *State Politics and Policy Quarterly*, 2/2: 199–212.

—— 2008. Portable Voter Registration. *Political Behavior*, 20/4: 491–501.

—— and POPKIN, S. 2001. The Myth of the Vanishing Voter. *American Political Science Review*, 95/4: 963–74.

—— and SAMPLES, J. 2006. *The Marketplace of Democracy: Electoral Competition and American Politics*. Washington, D.C.: Brookings Press.

MILLER, W. E. and SHANKS, J. M. 1996. *The New American Voter*. New York: Harvard University Press.

MITCHELL, G. E. and WLEZIEN, C. 1995. The Impact of Legal Constraints on Voter Registration, Turnout, and the Composition of the American Electorate. *Political Behavior*, 17/2: 179–202.

MERRIAM, C. E. and GOSNELL, H. F. 1924. *Non-Voting*. Chicago, Ill.: University of Chicago Press.

PATTERSON, T. 2002. *The Vanishing Voter: Public Involvement in an Age of Uncertainty*. New York: Alfred A. Knopf Publishers.

PUTNAM, R. 2000. *Bowling Alone: The Collapse and Revival of American Community*. New York: Simon & Schuster.

ROSENSTONE, S. J. and HANSEN, J. M. 1993. *Mobilization, Participation, and Democracy in America*. New York: Macmillian Publishing Company.

RUSK, J. G. 1970. The Effect of the Australian Ballot Reform on Split Ticket Voting, 1876–1908. *American Political Science Review*, 64/4: 1220–38.

STANLEY, H. W. and NIEMI, R. G. 2006. *Vital Statistics on American Politics 2005–2006*. Washington, D.C.: Congressional Quarterly Press.

STEINFELD, R. J. 1989. Property and Suffrage in the Early American Republic. *Stanford Law Review*, 41/2: 335–72.

TEIXEIRA, R. 1992. *The Disappearing American Voter*. Washington, D.C.: The Brookings Institution.

THE SENTENCING PROJECT. 2008. Felony Disfranchisement Laws in the United States. Washington, D.C.: The Sentencing Project.

TIMPONE, R. J. 1998. Structure, Behavior, and Voter Turnout in the United States. *The American Political Science Review*, 92/1: 145–58.

UGGEN, C. and MANZA, J. 2002. Democratic Contraction? The Political Consequences of Felon Disenfranchisement in the United States. *American Sociological Review*, 67/6: 777–803.

WOLFINGER, R. E. and ROSENSTONE, S. 1980. *Who Votes?* New Haven, Conn.: Yale University Press.

CHAPTER 9

EXPANDING THE POSSIBILITIES

RECONCEPTUALIZING POLITICAL PARTICIPATION AS A TOOLBOX

FREDRICK HARRIS

DANIEL GILLION

THE preoccupation with voting or electoral-oriented political activities in the study of American political behavior has narrowed the scope and the study of political participation. A thick line of demarcation has been traditionally drawn between political activities that reflect conventional channels of decision-making and governance and those activities that are considered to be outside the boundaries of legitimate and "rational" political discourse. Admittedly, the focus on voting and electoral-oriented participation has been more of a problem for students of American politics than comparative politics, a field that analyzes revolutions, violent rebellions, reform movements, and political cultures in which citizens employ a variety of political tactics beyond voting and electoral activities (Piven and Cloward 1977; Scott 1992; Skocpol 1979; Tarrow 1998).

It is not that non-electoral activities have not been part of the landscape of American politics, for the United States in various periods of its history has witnessed rebellions, reform movements, and other modes of contentious politics (Gaventa 1989; Goldberg 1990; McAdam, Tarrow, and Tilly 2001). Rather, the study of unconventional participation has been ceded to sociology while scholars of American politics have focused, almost exclusively, on conventional participation (Conway 2000; Verba and Nie 1972; Verba, Schlozman, and Brady 1995). Besides research on particular moments of contentious politics in the subfield of American political development, the examination of a broad conception of participation that incorporates both conventional and "unconventional" participation is absent from the way political behaviorists approach and conceptualize participation.

In this chapter we call for a reconceptualization of the way participation has traditionally been studied. We call for the incorporation of perspectives on both conventional and so-called unconventional tactics into a toolbox theory of participation in which individuals employ a variety and a combination of partici-patory acts to achieve desired political and social goals. We argue that individuals, particularly those from marginal groups who have less access to governmental actors and other institutional decision-makers, will choose actions that are selected less for their acceptability in the political culture than for their perceived effective-ness in obtaining desired political goals.

But before we consider this alternative perspective, we would first like to review how political scientists and sociologists have conceptualized political activism. The study of political activism in both disciplines has skewed the way scholars have commonly thought about political participation in general and the participa-tion of marginal groups in particular. We suggest that perspectives on activism from political science and sociology, though limited in their own conception of activism, offer an opportunity to expand the scope of research on activism by combining theoretical insights from both disciplines.

DIFFERENT FRAMEWORKS, DIFFERENT TOOLS

The sharpest distinction separating the body of research on political activism by political scientists and sociologists is the characterization of activism as conventional or unconventional, or as some studies describe the differences, institutionalized versus non-institutionalized behavior (Conway 2000; Verba and Nie 1972). In the widely held and normatively driven definition of participation in political science, conventional participation involves activities that are "accepted as appropriate by the dominant political culture," such as voting or contacting a public official about a problem, while unconventional acts, such as marching in a public demonstration or participating in a consumer boycott, are perceived in the literature as "inappropriate" political behavior (Conway 2000). By unconventional political behavior we are not strictly defining these actions as unusual, uncommon, or inappropriate modes of political action, though they are rarely used in comparison with other actions. Unconventional political participation, as used in this chapter, can also be referred to as non-institutional, extra-institutional, non-electoral, or simply political protest. The syntax is unimportant. The title "unconventional" attempts to convey that these forms of political action are unrelated to the electoral process. Similar to Barnes and Kaase (1979, 84), we view conventional political participation as modes of political behavior that are directly or indirectly related to the electoral process.

Students of political participation have viewed conventional activities in a linear fashion, where political acts like voting stand on one end of a wide spectrum of participatory acts while modes of action that demand more in time and resources such as campaigning for a political candidate or contacting a public official stand on the other end. Additionally, unconventional political action is viewed dichotomously, divided between non-violent behavior such as participating in a consumer boycott and violent behavior such as riots (Conway 2000, 40). Students of political participation have used an array of socioeconomic and psychological frameworks to analyze participation, including the impact of human capital, values, beliefs, attitudes, social context, legal constraints, and rational decision-making (Conway 2000; Leighley 2001; Verba and Nie 1972; Verba, Schlozman, and Brady 1995). However, these perspectives have been used to explain conventional participation rather than non-conventional modes of political action, since conventional and non-conventional activities are rarely studied alongside each other. Consequently, studies on political participation have not yielded much scholarship on the dynamics of unconventional participation and how unconventional acts may interact, if at all, with conventional modes of political engagement. Unlike the scholarship on conventional participation, we know little about which individuals or groups are likely to engage in unconventional activities, how legal factors might either constrain or expand protest activities, or how political socialization might foster beliefs in the legitimacy or illegitimacy of unconventional activities. Extra-institutionalized or protest activities are simply not given the same attention or theoretical rigor as so-called conventional political action in the study of American politics.

In addition to the lack of sufficient attention to unconventional participation, students of political participation have also skewed perspectives on activism by only considering activities that are directed toward governmental decision-makers rather than to activities that may be directed against other institutions or authorities.

In their landmark study *Participation in America*, Sidney Verba and Norman Nie define political participation as "activities by private citizens that are more or less directly aimed at influencing the selection of governmental personnel and/or the actions of the state" (Verba and Nie 1972, 2). Writing during the decline of the civil rights movement and the emergence of the women's movement and other movements for social change, Verba and Nie observed that "the importance of [protest] tactics has grown in recent years, at least for particular groups and particular interests" (1972, 3), but not enough to include them as activities that were a part of the scholars' broader conception of political participation.

This absence becomes especially problematic when considering the political activism of marginal groups who often rely on extra-institutionalized tactics and strategies to pursue desired goals. Some argue that sustained political activism is so rare in American life that this might account for the lack of attention to the subject. As one observer notes: "Committed, full-time political activists are relatively unusual in American politics, and, perhaps, for that reason, they are rarely analyzed closely or systematically by political scientists" (Teske 1997). Thus, it is difficult to know how rare protest activism in American life has been or currently is since survey data on extra-institutionalized modes of engagement have not been regularly included in opinion surveys gauging American political behavior. Consider the American National Election Study, a survey of American political attitudes and behavior that has been conducted for every presidential year since 1948. Respondents have been asked a battery of questions regarding their participation, specifically whether they persuaded others to vote for a candidate, attended meetings or rallies in behalf of electoral campaigns, did any work in behalf of a candidate, wore a button or adorned a car sticker in support of a candidate, contributed money to a campaign, followed or paid attention to the election, or voted or planned to vote in an upcoming election. Though it is understandable that there would be an emphasis on electoral activities, these activities are thought to constitute the universe of political activities in a campaign year. Only in 1976 did the American National Election Study ask respondents had they participated in some protest activities (See Conway, appendix, 209–15).

This means that for the protest years of the 1960s and 1970s a major survey of American political life failed to capture other important, alternative modes of political engagement, again making it difficult for students of political participation to trace the rise, decline, or stability of extra-institutionalized modes of participation over time or analyze their relationship to electoral politics in a given year.

More recent research has revealed that protest activities are more common in American life than students of political participation have previously acknowledged. Robert Putnam shows, for instance, that while protest activism has been "graying" since the early 1970s, with middle-aged and older Americans becoming more active in protest actions, these activities are not considered as alternatives to conventional politics but as part of an array of political activities (Putnam 2000, 165). Using the Roper Social and Trends survey, which has asked questions on participation in protest demonstrations for every year since the mid-1970s, Putnam reports that for Americans between the ages of 30 and 59 participation in demonstrations increased from 12 percent then to nearly 20 percent in the mid-1990s. For Americans over 59 their rate of engagement has doubled from about 5 percent in the mid-1970s to 10 percent in the mid-1990s (ibid.). These trends indicate that Americans who came of age during the 1960s and 1970s may have been socialized into seeing protest activities as legitimate forms of political action, a finding that suggests the broadening of political acts since the 1960s.

The trend toward protest activism has also been confirmed by Sidney Verba, Kay Lehman Schlozman, and Henry Brady (1995) in their work on civic participation. Although nearly three-quarters of the respondents in their Citizen Participation Survey reported that they voted in the last presidential election (71 percent) and about a quarter reported that they gave money to a political campaign (24 percent), only slightly more respondents engaged in campaign work (8 percent) than participated in a protest activity (6 percent). This finding suggests that participation in protest activities is just as common as participation in campaign activities in American political life. Though there have been attempts to incorporate unconventional acts of participation into studies on participation (Brady, Verba, and Schlozman 1995; Burns, Schlozman, and Verba 1997; Schlozman, Verba, and Brady 1995; Wong, Lien, and Conway 2005), most of these works have examined only one act of unconventional activism or viewed a particular measure of unconventional participation as a stand-in for all forms of unconventional participation (Verba et al. 1993).

Similarly, Inglehart and Catterberg (2002) find the number of individuals engaging in unconventional acts of political participation in the US has risen in the last twenty-five years. Analyzing the time period between 1974 and 2000, Inglehart and Catterberg found that the percentage of individuals engaging in a demonstration and the percentage of those who have engaged in a boycott have each increased by 9 points. Demonstrations increased from 12 percent to 21 percent and boycotts shifted from 16 percent to 25 percent. In addition, the percentage of individuals who have taken part in an unofficial strike has increased by 4 points, shifting from 2 to 6 percent, and the percentage of individuals who have participated in more aggressive forms of protest such as occupying a building increased by 2 points, moving from 2 to 4 percent. The overall result is a steady increase in the percentage of individuals who engage in unconventional political behavior. The increase in the percentage of individuals who engage in unconventional political behavior suggests that some of these unconventional activities are becoming incorporated into "normal" politics in the United States.

The body of research in the social movement literature has also confirmed this trend (McCarthy and McPhail 1998; Meyer and Tarrow 1998). And some works have discovered a strong link between unconventional political participation and policy outcomes (Burstein 1979, 1998; Burstein and Freudenburg 1978; Lohmann 1993). For instance, McAdam and Su (1982) found that citizens' engagement in anti-war protest substantially influenced congressional roll-call votes on war-related issues during the Vietnam era, from 1965 to 1973. The authors showed that unconventional political action that involved violence increased the probability of a pro-peace vote in Congress, while political action that involved a large number of demonstrators increased the pace of congressional responsiveness.

The impact of unconventional action on policy and shifts, though small, in the proportion of individuals employing unconventional acts suggest that scholars of political participation are beginning to recognize the multidimensionality of participation beyond electoral politics. Indeed, while protest acts may have been considered unconventional a generation ago, many have become routine acts in contemporary American political life. Activists on both the left and the right have employed various protest tactics to express their political preferences and goals. In the past decades these activities have included pro-life activists blocking abortion clinics to express their opposition to the legalization of abortion, Catholic parishioners demonstrating in front of churches to register outrage over revelations of sexual abuse by priests, anti-World Trade Organization (WTO) protesters violently targeting corporate institutions to express their concern over globalization, and anti-War protesters holding mass rallies across the country in opposition to war in Iraq and Afghanistan.

SOCIAL MOVEMENT PERSPECTIVES ON ACTIVISM

While students of political participation have been mostly silent on extra-institutionalized activism, students of social movements have developed a wealth of research on protest-oriented political action. Indeed, the study of social movements is often about how marginal groups in society struggle to affect social change. In an introductory text on collective behavior, Gary Marx and Doug McAdam define social movements as "organized efforts to promote or resist change in society that rely, at least in part, on noninstitutionalized forms of political action" (Marx and McAdam 1994). Thus, the very nature of social movements, as forces that are engaged in extra-institutionalized activities, provide important insights into the dynamics of political activism, but like scholars of American political behavior, the study of activism is skewed toward one sphere of activism.

Social movement scholars have provided mostly macro-level frameworks in explaining the rise and decline of mass-level activism. Research in the field has shed light on how preexisting social and communication networks influence movement formation, how the internal structure of organizations and institutions of insurgents promote and constrain action, how open or closed the political system is to protest, and how movement actors coordinate the actions of insurgents by framing group interests and goals (McAdam 1982; McAdam, Tarrow, and Tilly 2001; Morris 1993; Piven and Cloward 1977; Tarrow 1998).

Presumably, these macro-level factors also influence institutionalized politics. However, rarely do students of social movements consider the influence of macro-level social and economic forces on institutionalized participation (for an exception in the field of political participation see Harris, Sinclair-Chapman, and McKenzie 2006) nor the interaction of institutionalized and non-institutionalized activism in their analysis of social movements. In the study of social movements institutionalized politics is considered anathema to the life of movements; movement leaders and organizations that engage in electoral politics or lobbying political elites are thought to be co-opted by mainstream actors or movements and become incorporated into "normal" politics (Piven and Cloward 1977). These perceptions of movements are understandable since such movements usually emerge from groups that are shut out of the decision-making processes of government institutions and authorities. However, these perceptions are based on an underestimation of how movements often rely on conventional forms of politics in their quest for social change (McAdam 1982).

Another limitation of social movement perspectives on activism is that since movements are episodic and hard to sustain over time, it is difficult to know whether activism associated with social movements mirrors everyday forms of political activism. What are we to make of actors who use protest tactics but are not part of a movement? Like students of political participation, social movement scholars too often see political activism as an either/or proposition in which actors are either engaged in institutionalized politics or engaged in movement-related activities. Again, this perspective on activism has skewed perceptions of what constitutes political activism. As Doug McAdam, Sidney Tarrow, and Charles Tilly (2001, 6) argue in their work on contentious forms of politics, "the study of politics has too long reified the boundary between official, prescribed politics and politics by other means." As a consequence, "analysts have neglected or misunderstood both the parallels and the interactions between the two" spheres of action.

Consequently, there has been a disciplinary divide between the way that political scientists and sociologists study protest and conventional political behavior, with political scientists who study American politics narrowing their research to just conventional political action and sociologists solely analyzing unconventional political behavior. Though both study political action, they have been doing so by analyzing activism with separate toolboxes (and with different tools) while actors can and have combined tools as part of their repertoire of participatory acts. Combining conventional and unconventional political tools together allows for a more holistic understanding of political behavior and introduces an innovative conceptualization of political action as a toolbox.

PARTICIPATION AS A TOOLBOX

In some ways the separation of conventional and non-conventional participation in the analysis of activism (particularly non-violent forms of unconventional participation) is a false dichotomy. Setting aside disciplinary boundaries that have driven the analysis of activism to develop in different ways, we believe that our toolbox theory of participation can begin to merge the study of political participation, a collaboration that takes into account the rich theoretical developments from electoral-representational participation, and social movement studies. Using our toolbox metaphor, scholars of political participation and social movements assume that individuals have two boxes, not one, at their disposal: one box filled with conventional tools for participation and the other with the tools to deploy unconventional political acts. To the contrary, we see individuals using a variety of tools from one toolbox filled with tools used to employ activism outside the circumscribed boundaries of the electoral-representative system and within the system. From a toolbox perspective, there is the possibility that individuals are engaged as voters and boycotters, as political campaigners and demonstrators.

A citizen engaging in political behavior is very similar to a carpenter selecting a specific instrument from her toolbox to accomplish a particular task. A carpenter assesses the job that he must complete, decides on the most appropriate tool to accomplish this task, and then applies this tool until the chore is complete. If the particular tool that the carpenter is currently using is unsuccessful at accomplishing the task at hand, she then reassesses the situation and uses another tool to achieve the goal. This process is almost identical to an individual engaging in politics. A citizen assesses the political preferences she wants to implement in government, decides on the most effective political action that will garner the preferred governmental or societal response, and then deploys this form of political behavior within a group or by themselves.

The spectrum of activity is not continuous, as participation theorists might suggest; nor do these tools of activism reflect shifts back and forth between conventional and unconventional activities, as movement theorists would assume.

Actors do not decide to choose a political act, one-by-one, down a continuum from voting on one end to political violence on the other until a specific action produces a desired outcome. Instead we see various tactics as part of a toolbox where actors, especially actors from marginal communities, have available to them a repertoire of tactics that can be deployed to address their immediate and long-term interests and concerns. Samuel Barnes and Max Kaase in their book *Political Action* (1979) were among the few political scientists to recognize that institutionalized and non-institutionalized activities operated jointly as part of a "political action repertory." The authors developed a topology of political action that assigned respondents to categories of political action based on degrees of engagement—no participation, only conventional participation, various mixes of institutionalized action and support for protest, and exclusive support for protest activism (1979, 137–201).

Instead of placing individuals into categories of action, where individuals collectively fit some participation profile, we consider each individual to have his or her own toolbox that includes institutionalized and extra-institutionalized tactics. Potential actors have the option of choosing from a repertoire of tactics that may elicit a desired response from decision-makers. While everyone has the same type and number of tools available to them actors vary in the amount of access they have to decision-makers as well as the number of material resources they have available to them to exercise particular tools. Thus, for individuals with greater access and resources (skills, money, time, status) they are more likely to employ tools that reflect their privileged position in society.

Actors might need particular skills, knowledge, and material resources to deploy particular tools, while other tools are easy to employ. Just as hammers and screwdrivers are tools that require no special training or knowledge, wearing a campaign button and boycotting a product, tactics that respectively require individuals to express preference for a candidate or to refuse to purchase an item, can be viewed as part of the normal course of political activism. However, as the theorists of electoral participation and social movements show, marginal groups have fewer resources to engage in the political process than privileged groups, a condition that we argue would affect the deployment of different tools by different groups in society.

The greater the access to decision-makers the more likely tools will be linked to institutionalized modes of action while less access—such as marginal individuals and groups tend to have less of—will lead actors to employ extra-institutionalized tools of action. Thus, privileged actors are likely to initially select institutionalized tools, such as campaign contributions to decision-makers or reaching decision-makers through social networks, to elicit a desired outcome. However, an individual's or group's access to decision-makers may vary from issue to issue. Actors might have influence in one domain but not in another, which would alter the choice of tactics as situations and targets change. If a particular tool or a set of tools fails to produce a desired outcome or if access to decision-makers is blocked or denied, privileged actors will expand their action repertoire to include extra-institutionalized tools of engagement, thereby adjusting their tools to fit new circumstances. Like privileged groups, marginal groups will also adjust to new situations by selecting different tactics. But marginal groups are disadvantaged from the start since they lack access to decision-makers and have fewer material resources than privileged groups and individuals. Therefore, they are more likely to select widely from their toolbox, choosing a mix of tactics to elicit desired responses from decision-makers.

Just as they affect conventional participation and the dynamics of social movements, resources, mobilization, opportunities, institutions, and perceived effectiveness may also influence the deployment of an individual's political tools (McAdam 1982; Rosenstone and Hansen 1993). As resource mobilization theory and the SES model of political participation attest, material resources facilitate individual and collective action. Additionally, institutions and organizations dictate the use of political tools because they can directly mobilize or provide selective incentives for individuals to engage in particular modes of action. Churches as institutions, for instance, can influence the participation choice of congregants by encouraging worshipers to engage in specific forms of civic activities. Workplaces can facilitate strikes and/or contributions to political campaigns. Institutional context matters in facilitating which tactical tools individuals select.

The expansion or contraction of political opportunities for engagement, while difficult to detect, also influences the selection of political tools. An opportunity is perceived as an opening to have interests acted upon, and is characterized by new situations such as divisions among political elites or shifts in public opinion regarding a particular policy. Social movement scholars have examined these opportunities as protest cycles or waves (Tarrow 1998). These opportunities, however, are not restricted to unconventional modes of political action, but are also reflected in opportunities for engagement in conventional modes of political behavior (Rosenstone and Hansen 1993). When opportunities are perceived, citizens select the most appropriate political tool to capitalize on them, whether it is conventional or unconventional.

Perhaps the most understudied explanation of how citizens decide which mode of activism to choose is the perception that individuals and groups have of the effectiveness of specific political actions. The effectiveness of a political action can be assessed by the responses of government, media, and public opinion. The political tools that garner the greatest level of responsiveness depend upon the target of the action. For example, more direct and possibly violent political tools might be appropriate for garnering media attention and informing the public of an issue than writing a public official about a problem.

In sum, a toolbox framework of political participation accomplishes three things. First, it unifies approaches from political science and sociology as a way to expand our understanding of political participation. This unification, in turn, suggests that we conceive political behavior as being part of a mix of activities ranging from conventional modes of political behavior to unconventional modes of political action. Thinking of participation as part of a toolbox separates political action into discrete and individual forms of behavior that citizens select as part of a repertoire of participatory acts. Second, a toolbox theory addresses how individuals select among their political tools by adopting already established perspectives on resources, mobilization, and opportunities. Third, a toolbox theory looks to understand shifts in engagement through both a macro- and micro-level approach.

This is accomplished by addressing the way that individuals have selected to engage in political behavior at a micro-level over time, while also understanding these individual shifts in behavior at the macro-level that are influenced by cycles in the political environment. In the end, this interdisciplinary approach offers a more holistic understanding of political behavior.

TACTICAL REPERTOIRES OF MARGINAL GROUPS

The political activities of marginal groups have been described in various ways— "community politics," "grassroots politics," "protest politics," or "disruptive politics," to name a few definitions. These descriptions reflect the practice of both conventional and non-conventional forms of political action in the everyday struggle of marginal communities. Those at the margins of social and political life are less likely to make sharp distinctions about whether their political activities constitute insider or outsider strategies or tactics than are scholars of participation and social movements.

Since marginal groups are less likely to have access to decision-makers and are more skeptical of government institutions and authority, the choice of political tactics marginal groups employ might reflect what some analysts have referred to as the "politics of survival." Here, the selection of tactics and strategies of marginal groups reflects the immediate needs of people in crisis. In a profile of black women activists in Boston's black communities, Cheryl Townsend Gilkes (2001) illustrates the variety of activities working-class women employ to assist people in need. In noting the schedule of one activist, Gilkes' observation highlights the everyday forms of activism in marginal communities. This particular activist juggled a variety of activities, including "getting a group of adolescent males assigned to early morning jobs, going to court as a character witness for a teenager, meeting with a board of directors in another part of the city, and coordinating a public demonstration against the same board of directors before leaving for the meeting" (2001, 19).

Carol Hardy-Fanta (1993), in her analysis of Latina women activists in Boston, also demonstrates how various activities are connected to the politics of survival. When asking one activist the question "what is political?," Hardy-Fanta received this response: "Survival is politics. Struggling with DSS [Department of Social Services] to keep your kids, the landlord about your rent, keeping your kids safe from drugs, dealing with the trash and abandoned cars—it's everyday politics—trying to keep control" (1993, 45). Recognizing the male-dominated world of electoral politics in her community, this activist also highlighted the behind-the-scenes contributions of women to institutionalized politics, a form of activism that might be missed when only considering formal modes of engagement. This activist notes, "for all the men who worked on the (electoral) scene there were women who made it possible. You saw women who pooled the kids, took care of each other's kids so someone could vote or work on a campaign" (ibid.).

Insights from research on social movements provide a lens to explore how marginal groups can coordinate tactics from their member's toolboxes during episodes of collective action. When actors are mobilized into employing particular tactics they do not abandon their toolboxes. They merely intensify their uses of particular tools, such as engaging in campaign activities during an election or disruptive tactics during a movement campaign. However, actors still retain the ability to shift tactics to fit new situations. Although particular tools might become hegemonic during intense episodes of collective action the predominance of those tactics will contract back into a mix of tactics as activism settles into everyday forms of participation.

Moving Forward to a Research Agenda that Incorporates a Toolbox Framework of Political Behavior

The conception of a toolbox theory of political behavior has practical implications for how scholars analyze and study political behavior. A toolbox framework of political behavior can be incorporated into a new research agenda by asking innovative questions, as well as through the data collection process and methodological approaches.

Questions and Theory Building

A toolbox framework first provides an alternative to the type of questions that scholars pose about political behavior. Future research should not hinge around the overarching question of "what leads to higher levels of political participation?" but rather it should move the literature forward by asking "what leads to a citizen's engagement of x versus their engagement in y?" This question can be especially insightful for addressing differences in engagement between racial and ethnic minorities and majorities. Research has shown that minorities are less likely to engage in overall political participation than majorities (Verba, Schlozman, and Brady 1995). Focusing on just unconventional political behavior, however, reveals that minorities are actually more engaged in the political process than majorities (McVeigh and Smith 1999). A toolbox framework of political behavior can begin to resolve these conflicting results by asking "what are the factors that lead a higher percentage of minorities than majorities to use their unconventional political tools?" as well as "what are the factors that lead a higher percentage of majorities over minorities to use their conventional political tools?"

Naturally, these questions will alter the way scholars formulate theories. Scholars have shown that political mistrust and efficacy (Shingles 1981), group consciousness (Dawson 1994), group identity (Hero 1992; Lien, Conway, and Wong, 2004), marital status (Strate et al. 1989; Timpone 1998), length of residence (Highton and Wolfinger 2001), home ownership (Uhlaner, Cain, and Kiewiet 1989), and education and income (Almond and Verba 1963; Milbrath 1965; Verba and Nie 1972; Verba, Schlozman, and Brady 1995; Verba et al. 1993) all influence an individual's level of engagement. As one can discern from this very extensive list, numerous factors influence an individual's likelihood to engage in politics. While all of these factors could have a sweeping impact on overall levels of engagement, a toolbox framework for studying political behavior would seek to tailor these theories to a specific political action.

Data and Methods

If scholars wish to study political action as a toolbox, then data on the various modes of political action must be collected. In turn, this would mean expanding the list of questions on political engagement that major surveys ask. Participation in demonstrations, marches, boycotts, buycotts, internet petitions, and political blogging, are among the many forms of political behavior that should be routinely asked about on the American National Election Survey (ANES), General Social Survey (GSS), and the World Values Survey (WVS).

After tailoring the theory and data to account for differences among political actions, the statistical analysis should follow suit and account for disparities across the different modes of political behavior. Viewing political behavior as a toolbox forces scholars to analyze the individual characteristics of each mode of political action. If political actions are theorized to exhibit differences in terms of the information they provide us on an individual's likelihood to participate, should not the analysis reflect these differences? It should, but often does not. Implementing a toolbox theory of political behavior requires that scholars incorporate an empirical analysis that differentiates citizens' political actions.

Analyzing the dependent variable of political behavior through Item Response Theory (IRT) or Rasch models is a good starting point for the field to begin to incorporate a methodological technique that distinguishes among the various modes of political action. Political scientists have used item response theory to analyze roll-call data (Clinton, Jackman, and Rivers 2004; Poole and Rosenthal 1985), measure legislative significance and accomplishment (Clinton and Lapinski 2006), scale political knowledge (Carpini and Keeter 1993; Jerit, Barabas, and Bolsen 2006; Mondak 2001), and interpret tolerance of ethnic minorities in a comparative setting (Weldon 2006). While IRT or Rasch models might be unfamiliar to students of political participation, these models are widely used in the field of psychometrics, the study of educational and psychological measurements, to understand an individual's latent ability. IRT models are able to discern a student's latent propensity to perform well on a standardized test by placing weights on various questions on an exam (Linden and Hambleton 1997). This weighting scheme can be helpful for political scientists in distinguishing among political actions.

If we conceptualize political engagement as a list of actions that you can do (similar to answering a question correctly on an exam) or not (similar to answering a question incorrectly on an exam), then weights can be placed on various modes of political behavior in a citizen's toolbox and IRT can be helpful in assessing an individual's latent ability to engage in politics. Here the theory of an individual selecting to engage in political behavior parallels the underlining functional form of the statistical model.

There are several benefits to this new research agenda. First, over time, citizens have changed the way that they engage in the political process. Scholarship should keep pace with these changes. The benefit of expanding the data on political behavior is the potential result that might reshape our understanding of political participation. Recent work by Dalton (2007) has already shown that an analysis of rarely collected political actions, such as web-based or non-traditional behavior, reveals that a younger generation is, contrary to expectations, actively engaged in the political arena. New insight into political behavior, similar to Dalton's recent work, is facilitated by exploring additional modes of political actions. By collecting information on unconventional political behavior, scholars have access to an encompassing list of political actions that reflect the actual range of alternatives citizens have to voice their political preferences.

Second, this new research agenda strengthens our understanding of political engagement by narrowing theories of political participation to specific modes of behavior. This increased level of specificity will uncover many of the small nuances that distinguish engagement in one mode of political action over another.

Third, a new methodological approach that stems from a new research agenda allows us to better map theory to analysis and to possibly revisit previous results. If there are differences among the various forms of political actions, then methodological approaches suggested in this new research agenda will account for these disparities. Moreover, the benefit of a new statistical approach allows us to make claims about weighting schemes on a dependent variable of political participation that are not created in a controversial subjective manner, but rather through an unbiased data-driven approach. With a new weighting scheme placed on various modes of political participation, previous results in the participation literature can be evaluated and more rigorous theories can emerge. In applying a toolbox theory of political behavior we both broaden our understanding of citizens' behavior by expanding the various modes of political action that we study, and at the same time provide a more detailed analysis by distinguishing between political actions.

CONCLUSION

We have addressed the state of political participation, and called for a rethinking in the way scholars study and conceptualize political and civic behavior. Political scientists have added much in terms of our understanding of citizens' engagement in conventional modes of political action that revolve around electoral politics. Nevertheless, given the increase in the percentage of individuals engaging in unconventional political action and the effectiveness of these activities, it appears that studies in American politics have offered an incomplete understanding of political behavior. Similarly, students of social movements have only offered a partial understanding of participation. While studies that stem from theories of social movements have contributed to our understanding of collective behavior, we know little about the individual choice to engage in these extra-institutional acts. Both students of voting or electoral-oriented political activities and students of social movements have examined political behavior, but through two different approaches. Each is inadequate to offer an understanding of political behavior that examines the complete array of specific political options an individual can employ.

We have attempted to reconcile these two approaches to studying political behavior by offering a toolbox understanding of participation. Through this unified approach individuals select the most appropriate political tool to accomplish their political or societal goals. From a toolbox perspective, there is the possibility that individuals are engaged as voters and boycotters, as political campaigners and demonstrators rather than as actors in two different sets of participatory worlds. It is an interdisciplinary approach that attempts to change the way scholars approach the study of participation. This call for change should be expected. Citizens continuously adjust and modify the manner in which they express their political grievances or preferences to government. Academic scholars must keep pace with these alterations in this ever-changing world. This includes not only changing the way we perceive reality, but also how we study it.

References

ALMOND, G. and VERBA, S. 1963. *Civic Culture.* Princeton, N.J.: Princeton University Press.

BARNES, S. and KAASE, M. 1979. *Political Action: Mass Participation in Five Western Democracies.* Beverly Hills, Calif.: Sage.

BRADY, H., VERBA, S., and SCHLOZMAN, K. 1995. Beyond SES: A Resource Model of Political Participation. *American Political Science Review,* 89/2: 271–94.

BURNS, N., SCHLOZMAN, K., and VERBA, S. 1997. The Public Consequences of Private Inequality. *American Political Science Review,* 91/2: 373–89.

BURSTEIN, P. 1979. Public Opinion, Demonstration, and the Passage of Anti-discrimination Legislation. *Public Opinion Quarterly,* 43: 157–72.

—— 1998. Bringing the Public Back In: Should Sociologists Consider the Impact of Public Opinion on Public Policy? *Social Forces,* 77/1: 27–62.

—— and FREUDENBURG, W. 1978. Changing Public Policy. *American Journal of Sociology,* 84/1: 199–22.

CARPINI, M. X. D. and KEETER, S. 1993. Measuring Political Knowledge: Putting First Things First. *American Journal of Political Science,* 37/4: 1179–1206.

CLINTON, J., JACKMAN, S., and RIVERS, D.. 2004. The Statistical Analysis of Roll Call Data. *American Political Science Review,* 98/2: 355–70.

CLINTON, J. D. and LAPINSKI, J. S. 2006. Measuring Legislative Accomplishment, 1877–1994. *American Journal of Political Science,* 50/1: 232–49.

CONWAY, M. 2000. *Political Participation in the United States.* Washington, D.C.: Congressional Quarterly Press.

DALTON, R. 2007. *The Good Citizen: How Young People are Transforming American Politics.* Washington, D.C.: CQ Press.

GAVENTA, J. 1989. *Power and Powerlessness: Quiescence and Rebellion in an Appalachian Valley.* Urbana, Ill.: University of Illinois Press.

GILKES, C. 2001. *If It Wasn't for the Women: Black Women's Experience and Womanist Culture in Church and Community.* New York: Orbis Books.

GOLDBERG, R. A. 1990. *Grassroots Resistance: Social Movements in Twentieth Century America.* Prospects Heights, Ill.: Wayland Press.

HARDY-FANTA, C. 1993. *Latina Politics, Latino Politics: Gender, Culture, and Political Participation in Boston.* Philadelphia, Pa: Temple University Press.

HARRIS, F., SINCLAIR-CHAPMAN, V., and MCKENZIE, B. 2006. *Countervailing Forces in African-American Civic Activism, 1973–1994.* New York: Cambridge University Press.

HERO, R. 1992. *Latinos and the U.S. Political System: Two-Tiered Pluralism.* Philadelphia, Pa.: Temple University Press.

HIGHTON, B. and WOLFINGER, R. E. 2001. The First Seven Years of the Political Life Cycle. *American Journal of Political Science*, 45: 202–09.

INGLEHART, R. and CATTERBERG, G. 2002. Trends in Political Action: The Development Trend and the Post-Honeymoon. *Sage* 43/3–5: 300–18.

JENNIFER J., BARABAS, J., and BOLSEN, T. 2006. Citizens, Knowledge, and the Information Environment. *American Journal of Political Science*, 50/2: 266–82.

LEIGHLEY, J. 2001. *Strength in Numbers? The Political Mobilization of Racial and Ethnic Minorities*. Princeton, N.J.: Princeton University Press.

LIEN, P.-T., CONWAY, M., and WONG, J. 2004. *The Politics of Asian Americans: Diversity and Community*. New York: Routledge.

LINDEN, W. van der and HAMBLETON, R. 1997. *Handbook of Modern Item Response Theory*. New York: Springer.

LOHMANN, S. 1993. A Signaling Model of Informative and Manipulative Political Action. *American Political Science Review*, 87/2: 319–33.

MARX, G. and MCADAM, D. 1994. *Collective Behavior and Social Movements: Process and Structure*. Englewood Cliffs, N.J.: Prentice Hall.

MCADAM, D. 1982. *Political Process and the Development of Black Insurgency, 1930–1970*. Chicago, Ill.: University of Chicago Press.

—— and SU, Y. 2002. The War at Home: Anti-War Protests and Congressional Voting, 1965–73. *American Sociological Review*, 67: 696–721.

—— TARROW, S., and TILLY, C. 2001. *Dynamics of Contention*. Cambridge: Cambridge University Press.

MCCARTHY, J. and MCPHAIL, C. 1998. The Institutionalization of Protest in the United States. In *The Social Movement Society: Contentious Politics for a New Century*, ed. D. Meyer and S. Tarrow. New York: Rowman and Littlefield.

MCVEIGH, R. and SMITH, C. 1999. Who Protests in America: An Analysis of Three Political Alternatives—Inaction, Institutionalized Politics, or Protest. *Sociological Forum*, 14/4: 685–702.

MEYER, D. and TARROW, S. 1998. *The Social Movement Society: Contentious Politics for a New Century*. Lanham, Md: Rowman and Littlefield.

MILBRATH, L. 1965. *Political Participation*. Chicago, Ill.: Rand McNally.

MONDAK, J. 2001. Developing Valid Knowledge Scales. *American Journal of Political Science*, 45/1: 224–38.

MORRIS, A. D. 1993. Birmingham Confrontation Reconsidered: An Analysis of the Dynamics and Tactics of Mobilization. *American Sociological Review*, 58: 621–36.

PIVEN, F. and CLOWARD, R. 1977. *Poor People's Movements: Why They Succeed, How They Fail*. New York: Pantheon.

POOLE, K. T. and ROSENTHAL, H. 1985. A Spatial Model for Legislative Roll Call Analysis. *The American Political Science Review*, 29/2: 357–84.

PUTNAM, R. 2000. *Bowling Alone: The Collapse and Revival of the American Community*. New York: Simon and Schuster.

ROSENSTONE, S. and HANSEN, J. 1993. *Mobilization, Participation, and Democracy in America*. New York: Macmillan Publishing Company.

SCHLOZMAN, K., VERBA, S., and BRADY, H. 1995. Participation's Not a Paradox: The View from American Activists. *British Journal of Political Science*, 25/1: 1–36.

SCOTT, J. C. 1992. *Domination and the Arts of Resistance: Hidden Transcripts*. New Haven, Conn.: Yale University Press.

SHINGLES, R. 1981. Black Consciousness and Political Participation. *American Political Science Review*, 75/1: 76–91.

SKOCPOL, T. 1979. *States and Social Revolutions: A Comparative Analysis of France, Russia and China*. London: Cambridge University Press.

STRATE, J. M., PARRISH, C. J, ELDER, C. D., and FORD, C. 1989. Life Span Civic Development and Voting Participation. *American Political Science Review*, 83/2: 443–64.

TARROW, S. 1998. *Power in Movement: Social Movements and Contentious Politics*. Cambridge: Cambridge University Press.

TESKE, N. 1997. *Political Activists in America: The Identity Construction Model of Political Participation*. Cambridge: Cambridge University Press.

TIMPONE, R. J. 1998. Ties That Bind: Measurement, Demographics, and Social Connectedness. *Political Behavior*, 20/1: 53–77.

UHLANER, C., CAIN, B. E., and KIEWIET, R. 1989. Political Participation of Ethnic Minorities in the 1980s. *Political Behavior*, 11/3: 195–231.

VERBA, S. and NIE, N. 1972. *Participation in America: Political Democracy and Social Equality*. New York, NY: Harper and Row.

—— SCHLOZMAN, K., and BRADY, H. 1995. *Voice and Equality: Civic Voluntarism in American Democracy*. Cambridge, Mass.: Harvard University Press.

—— —— —— and NIE, N. 1993. Race, Ethnicity and Political Resources: Participation in the United States. *British Journal of Political Science*, 23/4: 453–97.

WELDON, S. 2006. The Institutional Context of Tolerance for Ethnic Minorities: A Comparative, Multilevel Analysis of Western Europe. *American Journal of Political Science*, 50/2: 331–49.

WONG, J., LIEN, P.-T., and CONWAY, M. M. 2005. Group Based Resources and Political Participation among Asian Americans. *American Politics Research*, 33/4: 545–76.

CHAPTER 10

VOTER REGISTRATION

TURNOUT, REPRESENTATION, AND REFORM

ROBERT D. BROWN

THE requirement that citizens register to vote constitutes the principal legal mechanism for regulating most citizens' access to the voting booth.[1] Initiated as a mechanism to combat fraudulent voting and manage the administration of elections, the registration requirement has evolved into an institution commonly seen as both an impediment to voting in the United States (e.g., Kelly, Ayres, and Bowen 1967; Kim, Petrocik, and Enokson 1975; Piven and Cloward 1988; Wolfinger and Rosenstone 1980), and as an important contributor to lower participation rates in the US relative to other countries (Powell 1986).[2] In addition, voter registration has been hypothesized to affect the composition of the electorate, with the

---

[1] In most states, this means that citizens must register from between ten and thirty days prior to the election to be eligible to vote. The exceptions to this are Idaho, Maine, Minnesota, New Hampshire, Wisconsin, and Wyoming, which have election-day registration provisions, and North Dakota, which does not require registration.

[2] Residency requirements—requirements that a citizen have residence in the state in which they are voting for a minimum specified period of time—are an additional and related restriction currently

registration hurdle seemingly more burdensome for those of lower income and educational attainment (Piven and Cloward 1988; Wolfinger and Rosenstone 1980). Thus a primary concern with the lower levels of turnout generated by voter registration requirements is that those who actually do vote may not be representative of the electorate as a whole (Jackson, Brown, and Wright 1998; Piven and Cloward 1988; Rosenstone and Hansen 1993; Teixeira 1992). These concerns are important, and speak to the heart of what constitutes a healthy democracy. On election day in a healthy electoral system, citizens are motivated to go to the polls, and high levels of voter turnout generate an electorate representative of the overall citizenry. To the degree that these goals are not met, we must examine factors that might work against their success.

It is not surprising, therefore, that the requirement to register before voting has spurred numerous efforts at electoral reform. Accordingly, scholars have worked to understand the impact of registration on participation, as well as examining the impacts of registration reform. In this chapter I examine the most prominent themes in this research. In addition, I will discuss an important limitation in the work on voter registration: research on voter registration has focused primarily on voter registration as a determinant of political behavior, to the detriment of our understanding the actual behavior of registering itself. Finally, I offer some concluding observations on how addressing this limitation may provide insight into an important paradox in the voter registration and participation literatures: how it is possible that registration laws have become significantly liberalized over the years, yet with relatively little payoff in terms of voter turnout and increased representativeness of those who vote?

Scholarship examining voter registration has proceeded along several broad and related themes. First and foremost is the impact of the registration requirement on voter turnout, a question that has received the lion's share of research in this area (e.g., Brians and Grofman 1999; Erikson 1981; Kelly, Ayres, and Bowen 1967; Kim, Petrocik, and Enokson 1975; Nagler 1991; Patterson and Caldeira 1983; Piven and Cloward 1988; Powell 1986; Squire, Wolfinger, and Glass 1987; Teixeira 1992; Wolfinger and Rosenstone 1980). Stated simply, registration raises the cost of voting. By asking citizens to be aware of registration deadlines, locate their registration office, and take time from work to go there, often up to thirty days prior to the actual election, registration laws create an additional barrier to participation that many citizens either cannot or choose not to overcome.[3]

---

in place in most states. This requirement is particularly onerous for people who move frequently, and thus must register again after establishing residency (Squire, Wolfinger, and Glass 1987).

[3] There is significant state-level variation in terms of in-person registration closing date. Currently the longest registration deadline prior to the election is thirty days, and exists in Alaska, Arkansas, Hawaii, Louisiana, Michigan, Mississippi, Montana, Ohio, Pennsylvania, Rhode Island, South Carolina, Tennessee, Texas, Washington, and D.C. The remainder of the states break down as follows: twenty-nine days (Arizona, Colorado, Florida, Indiana, Kentucky, New Jersey, Virginia), twenty-eight days (Georgia, Illinois, Missouri, New Mexico), twenty-five days (New York, North Carolina,

Yet while there is little debate regarding the negative impact of registration on turnout, the question quickly becomes more nuanced, and evolves into a second dominant theme: the degree to which certain segments of the population are differentially affected by the registration hurdle (e.g., Jackson, Brown, and Wright 1998; Mitchell and Wlezien 1995; Nagler 1991; Rosenstone and Hansen 1993; Wolfinger and Rosenstone 1980). Some even go so far as to propose that registration laws are purposively maintained to produce these specific outcomes regarding the composition of the electorate (Piven and Cloward 1988). Whether by design or not, the possibility that registration requirements result in non-representative electorates has the potential for significant policy effects (e.g., Avery and Peffley 2005; Hill and Leighley 1992).

Finally, a third strain of work examines the impacts of reforms designed to reduce the impact of this institutional barrier to voting. From allowing for election-day registration, to mail registration, to national "motor voter" legislation, a sizeable body of work has emerged to evaluate the effectiveness of efforts to reduce the potential costs on voting imposed by registration (e.g., Brown and Wedeking 2006; Fenster 1994; Fitzgerald 2005; Franklin and Grier 1997; Highton 1997; Highton and Wolfinger 1998; Hill 2003; Knack 1995; Martinez and Hill 1999; Mitchell and Wlezien 1995; Rhine 1995). Recent research may be bringing the issue full circle, with some studies finding a minimal impact of easing registration requirements on voter turnout, and consequently questioning whether it is institutional or motivational factors that are the true impediment to participation in the United States (e.g., Brown and Wedeking 2006; Highton 1997; Martinez and Hill 1999; Mitchell and Wlezien 1995; Timpone 1998).

THE IMPACT OF REGISTRATION ON
VOTER TURNOUT

....

Research linking registration to turnout represents a significant segment of the work examining voter registration and its impacts. Drawn broadly from a rational choice perspective, where rational voters at least subconsciously weigh the costs and benefits of participation (Downs 1957), registration is portrayed as a contextual element in the political environment, one that presents a bureaucratic hurdle that

---

Oklahoma), twenty-one days (Maryland, Nevada, Oregon, West Virginia), 20 days (Delaware, Massachusetts, Utah), fifteen days (California, Kansas, South Dakota), fourteen days (Connecticut), eleven days (Nebraska), ten days (Alabama, Iowa), eight days (Vermont). Idaho, Maine, Minnesota, New Hampshire, Wisconsin, and Wyoming allow for election-day registration, and North Dakota does not require registration.

citizens must clear before they can vote. Until recent passage of national "motor voter" legislation, registration generally meant a trip to the county courthouse, often several weeks prior to the election. These deadlines are often not well publicized, and may occur well before the real heat of a particular campaign. As such, political motivations to participate are often lacking when registration deadlines occur. While certainly not an overwhelming burden, it is not difficult to see how the politically unmotivated might choose not to negotiate this additional element of the electoral process. It also seems plausible that the registration requirement might work most prominently against the poorer and less educated segments of society, who may find these additional costs to participation more difficult to overcome.

Stated most plainly by Erikson (1981) when he asks and answers the question "Why do people vote? Because they are registered," a large volume of literature exists to document the registration–turnout relationship.[4] Initial work by Wolfinger and Rosenstone (1980) remains important roughly thirty years after its publication, with the authors finding that early deadlines for registration represent significant impediments to turnout. Specifically, Wolfinger and Rosenstone document a roughly 9 percent decline in voter turnout associated with asking potential voters to take on the additional burden of registering.

Subsequent work followed up on these initial findings, adding both depth and conviction to how political scientists and advocates view the relationship between registration and turnout. Squire, Wolfinger, and Glass (1987) posited that the impact of registration on voting is likely to be felt most keenly by people who have recently moved, finding that the requirement to re-register after a change in residence represents an important barrier to voting. Highton (2000) provides greater support for this relationship by controlling for an important counter-hypothesis: that lower turnout among those who move stems from the breakdown of community ties that encourage participation. While social disruption is certainly associated with moving to a new community, the need to re-register presents a much greater burden in terms of voting.

The negative relationship between registration requirements and turnout also holds across electoral contexts. At the congressional level, registration closing dates have been found to be important factors in turnout in off-year elections (Gilliam 1985). From a comparative perspective, Powell (1986) found that the United States has much more stringent registration requirements than most other Western democracies. The result is that in spite of relatively favorable levels of citizen attitudes related to participation, US registration laws reduced turnout by up to 14 percent relative to other countries.

---

[4] The relationship is robust to either the individual or aggregate (generally comparing US state participation rates) level of analysis.

Finally, more recent work speaks to the robustness of the registration–turnout relationship. Teixeira (1992), in his comprehensive analysis of voter turnout decline, estimates that reducing registration barriers will increase turnout by 8 percent—roughly equivalent to Wolfinger and Rosenstone (1980). Mitchell and Wlezien (1995) take a broader approach than most studies, and examine the impact of not only registration closing date, but several other indicators of registration as a barrier to voting (residency requirements, precinct registration, mail registration, regular registration hours, extended registration, and purging of the registration rolls).[5] While their results differ in some areas, the overall results indicate that greater liberalization of registration laws would increase turnout by approximately 8 percentage points, very similar to that found by Wolfinger and Rosenstone.[6]

The negative relationship between voter registration and voter turnout is arguably one of the most definitive in American political behavior. Regulating access to the voting booth via registration represents an additional roadblock in the voting process that a sizeable portion of the citizenry either chooses not to manage or finds too difficult to negotiate. The impact of registration on voter turnout is robust, occurring across electoral contexts and providing a systematic impediment to voting over time. It is possible to argue, however, that aside from normative concerns regarding the importance of high levels of voter turnout, the negative impact of registration on turnout may be of little practical consequence. If those that actually do vote mirror those that do not in terms of social class, ethnicity, education, and attitudes, then the mechanism of elections for the transmission of political wants and needs is presumably unaffected.

VOTER REGISTRATION AND THE REPRESENTATIVENESS OF THE ELECTORATE

While documenting the nature and strength of the relationship between registration and turnout, researchers have been simultaneously examining its qualitative impacts on the electorate. If voter registration reduces turnout, does it do so selectively, with certain segments of the population finding this hurdle more difficult to overcome? Of course, such a possibility seems eminently plausible. To

---

[5] Purging of registration rolls refers to state practices of periodically removing voters from their lists of registered voters if they have not voted for a specified period of time.

[6] For example, Mitchell and Wlezien find purging laws to be more important, especially with regard to suppressing registration.

the degree that the need to register increases the costs of participation, it seems reasonable to argue that these costs will be felt differentially across the electorate.

The normative implications of such a possibility are enormous. If registration laws create a larger burden for some segments of the population than others, and thus serve as a source of systematic bias in the electorate, then fundamental notions of equal access and representation become compromised.

Studies looking at changes in national turnout levels and participatory bias across time provide support for the linkage between the level of overall participation and the composition of the electorate. Examining electoral participation rates in the 1952–1988 American National Election Studies (ANES) Rosenstone and Hansen (1993, 241–3) find that, in terms of both education and income levels, "when many citizens turn out to vote, they are more representative than when fewer people vote." Teixeira (1992) presents complementary evidence, drawn from both the ANES series and presidential-year November *Current Population Surveys*, finding that biases in income, education, and especially age worsened as turnout declined from 1960 to 1988.

Moreover, there is reason to believe that class bias in electorates is related to public policy outputs. Piven and Cloward (1988) argue that socioeconomic bias in turnout has profound negative implications for the scope and generosity of welfare policy. Hill and Leighley (1992) draw directly from Piven and Cloward, and find upper-class bias in the active electorate in all states, along with substantial variation across the states. In linking class bias to four separate indicators of welfare effort, the authors find strong policy consequences of class bias, with lower welfare effort associated with lower representation of the poor in the active electorate. Interestingly, Hill and Leighley find only a modest relationship between turnout levels and class bias, thereby leaving open the question of whether turnout (and by extension, forces that influence turnout) are the driving force behind the class bias–policy linkage.[7] Avery and Peffley (2005) extend Hill and Leighley's approach into the post welfare reform period, finding that upper-class bias has an impact on the stringency of welfare eligibility rules in the Temporary Assistance for Needy Families program.

Yet while there is evidence indicating that differences between the potential and active electorates exist, and that these differences have real policy implications, the degree to which these concerns are generated by voter registration requirements is subject to debate. Piven and Cloward (1988, 2000) advance the argument quite forcefully, claiming that registration requirements serve as an important structuring force on the composition of the electorate. Piven and Cloward argue that biases in the active electorate (largely against those of lower SES) are largely the result of

---

[7] Leighley and Nagler (1992) find that while class bias (measured in terms of income) exists, it did not increase (or decrease) between 1964 and 1988.

institutional factors (especially voter registration procedures) that create a burden that is more difficult for these demographic groups to overcome.

Piven and Cloward's work has been criticized for being too long on advocacy and too short on empirical evidence,[8] yet the basic premise of their thesis is reflected in a great deal of scholarly effort. Initial work focused on the impact of registration across education levels, with Wolfinger and Rosenstone finding that registration laws impose a larger hurdle for the less educated.[9] Subsequent work by Nagler (1991), however, contradicts these findings regarding the differential effect of registration by education level, showing them to be a methodological artifact.[10]

Hill and Leighley (1994, 1996) expand the focus beyond education, and find that while registration is related to turnout, it has no impact on class representation in the electorate. While easier registration requirements boost turnout, they do not do so differentially across social classes. Mitchell and Wlezien (1995) expand on Wolfinger and Rosenstone's analyses, but find largely similar results. While liberalizing registration laws[11] may serve to increase turnout, the authors also note that these increases do little to change the composition of the electorate in terms of its demographic bias. Work by Highton (1997) examining individual participation in states with "easy" registration shows similar results.

Yet despite research indicating that the composition of the electorate would see little change with the liberalization of registration laws, additional work continues to document that turnout and the composition of the voting electorate are strongly related to levels of registration. Brown, Jackson, and Wright (1999) examine these relationships by focusing on the indirect influence of registration laws as they work through state registration rates. The authors find that registration closing date influences registration rates across the states, and the degree of registration has a significant impact on the social composition of the electorate. Jackson, Brown, and Wright (1998) take a broader look at the composition of the electorate, assessing the impact of registration laws on education, income, and age representativeness. Jackson et al. conclude that registration provides an important structuring influence on the composition of active voters. A restrictive registration environment and resulting levels of depressed registration translate into low turnout, and, consequently, less representative active electorates. In

---

[8] For example, see book reviews by: Abramson (1989), Leighley (2001), and Polsby (1988), as well as Bennett (1990).

[9] At the same time, however, the authors conclude that while registration may affect these groups more prominently, an electorate expanded by the implementation of more liberal registration laws would not differ markedly from the present electorate.

[10] See Huang and Shields (2000), who offer additional insight on the methodological issues here, and who confirm Nagler's findings.

[11] Specific measures include: extended registration hours, less frequent purging of registration rolls, and reduced closing dates prior to registration.

contrast, high levels of registration facilitate heavier turnout, producing more representative voting (Jackson, Brown, and Wright 1998). More recently, Avery and Peffley (2005) draw from this work, and link registration to class bias in turnout, which, in turn, influences greater liberalism in welfare (TANF) eligibility requirements.

VOTER REGISTRATION REFORM

Up to this point, I have examined two of the three major threads in research analyzing voter registration laws: the impact of registration on turnout and the resulting implications for the composition of the active electorate. Research clearly documents a negative link between restrictive registration and turnout. At the individual level, the need to register does indeed present a hurdle to voting. In the aggregate, states with higher rates of registration also tend to have higher participation rates. The evidence for the impact of registration on the composition of the electorate, while perhaps less clear and more indirect, is still sufficient enough to generate concern over the role played by voter registration here as well. It is hardly surprising, then, that numerous reforms have been enacted with an eye toward reducing the perceived negative impacts of voter registration requirements.

A significant body of research has emerged to evaluate the impacts of these reforms. These studies have ranged from those that examine single reforms such as election-day registration (Brians and Grofman 1999; Calvert and Gilchrist 1993; Fenster 1994; Francia and Herrnson 2004; Highton 1997; Knack 2001), to those that try to parse out the specific impacts of several concurrent reforms, such as election-day registration, mail-in registration, extended registration hours, and purging of registration rolls (Fitzgerald 2005; Knack 1995; Mitchell and Wlezien 1995; Rhine 1996; Teixeira 1992).

As noted by Highton (2004), the logic behind election-day registration (EDR) is quite straightforward: to the degree that registration presents costs to participation, we might expect potential voters to be more willing to incur this cost as election day nears and campaigns are better able to direct attention toward the potential offsetting benefits of voting. Examinations of EDR indicate the reform shows some promise. Fenster (1994), for example, estimates that a nationwide EDR law would lead to a modest 5 percent increase in turnout. Rhine (1996), however, estimates a larger potential increase of between 10 and 14 percentage points. Highton and

Wolfinger also estimate a substantial (roughly 9 percent) turnout increase if EDR were to be implemented nationwide. Others, however, match Fenster's estimate of more modest results (Brians and Grofman 1999, 2001; Fitzgerald 2005; Highton 1997; Knack 2001; Mitchell and Wlezien 1995), and the general consensus suggests that full implementation of EDR, while helpful, offers no panacea for the registration–turnout issue.

With regard to the composition of the electorate, examinations of election-day registration indicate less reason to be optimistic. While Knack and White (2000) offer the most reason to be hopeful, even their results are less than overwhelming. On the one hand, they find substantial improvement in the equality of representation across age groups and by mobility status. Importantly, however, similar improvements were not found for income and education. This lack of improvement in representation of lower income and education is the predominant finding of research into EDR and the composition of the electorate (Highton 1997; Mitchell and Wlezien 1995).[12] These results lead Highton (1997) to offer an important summary observation—that we must look past registration requirements to understand the nature of socioeconomic bias in the electorate.[13]

A similar story can be told for the impact of other reforms. Knack (1995) finds mixed evidence that mail-in registration boosts turnout, whereas Rhine (1996) and Fitzgerald (2005) find no effect. Similarly, both Knack and Rhine find little support for liberal registration-roll purging. On a more positive note, Mitchell and Wlezien (1995) find that less frequent purging and extended registration office hours increase turnout. Yet at the same time, Mitchell and Wlezien find little evidence that wholesale reforms in these areas will have much impact on the composition of the active electorate.

The results noted above are instructive, and point us in an important direction—toward a recognition that old precepts about the impact of registration on turnout need revision. Registration and turnout do not appear to be synonymous after all. Reform after reform has been implemented under the notion that if we simply reduce the registration barrier greater participation will result. Yet while reforms have followed this dictum, and registration has become significantly easier over time, the impacts of these changes on turnout and the composition of the electorate have been only modest at best.

---

[12] Contrary to expectations, Brians and Grofman find the largest impact of EDR to be on middle-class voters.

[13] In addition, Highton finds that turnout among the registered (in those states that require registration) is substantially higher than turnout in states with no registration (North Dakota) or EDR. This suggests that factors other than institutional registration requirements are also related to turnout, and by extension, bias in the electorate.

Voter Registration Reform and the National Voter Registration Act

This conclusion is solidified when we examine the effect of the National Voter Registration Act (NVRA). Arguably the nation's most significant effort at registration reform since the Voting Rights Act, NVRA is a comprehensive, national attempt to ease registration burdens by requiring states to allow citizens the opportunity to register as part of the more common routines of their lives.[14] NVRA targeted several barriers to registration commonly cited in the literature (general difficulty in registering, residential mobility, education, income, purging of voter rolls for non-voting, etc.) and received the name "motor voter" because of its signature reform: the ability of citizens to register when they are renewing their driver's license.[15] As such, NVRA represents a comprehensive effort to eliminate the costs associated with voter registration.

A substantial body of work has emerged to assess NVRA's impacts on voter turnout and the composition of the electorate. The implications of this work are important. NVRA was designed to attack precisely those registration hurdles that are commonly seen as exerting the most influence on both voting and bias in the electorate. If NVRA is successful at ameliorating the negative participation effects commonly attributed to registration, then we should expect voter turnout to increase and the active electorate to be more representative. If this comprehensive reform is not successful, then we are left to wonder about the utility of targeting registration as a means of achieving these goals.

Studies conducted prior to NVRA offered reason to be optimistic that a national program would have an impact. Knack (1995) examined states that had implemented "motor voter" programs prior to full implementation of NVRA and estimated that a nationwide implementation would significantly increase registration, with a sizeable increase in turnout to follow.[16] Additionally, Highton and Wolfinger (1998) indicated that the "motor voter" and purging aspects of state programs are likely to be the most important upon national implementation, and that they should have their strongest effect among the young and mobile segments of the potential electorate.

---

[14] NVRA was passed in 1993 and fully implemented in 1996, and was partly the result of advocacy work by Piven and Cloward. Piven and Cloward formed the Human SERVE (Human Service Employees Voter Registration and Education). See Moss (1993) and Piven and Cloward (1985) for more on this organization, and its formation and goals.

[15] NVRA requires states to provide several avenues for registration. These include: (1) "motor voter" registration, or voter registration at the same time as driver's license renewal; (2) mail-in registration—voter registration by mail; (3) agency-based voter registration—the ability to register at public assistance offices; (4) limits on purging of voter registration rolls.

[16] Franklin and Grier (1997) echo these findings, and further note little reason to suspect a partisan advantage by this potential increase in participation.

Studies examining NVRA after its full implementation, however, tend to be rather mixed with regard to its impacts on turnout and bias in the electorate. Knack (1999) notes a significant drop in turnout occurring in 1996, the first full year of NVRA implementation, but also shows that this turnout decline would likely have been even greater had NVRA not been in effect. At the same time, however, Knack finds little evidence of improvements in demographic biases in the composition of the electorate. Martinez and Hill (1999) find evidence of registration increases associated with NVRA, but nothing to indicate that this increased registration translated into increases in turnout (or slower decline in turnout). Moreover, Martinez and Hill find NVRA to have actually *increased* class and racial inequality in state electorates.

Subsequent work by Hill (2003), however, suggests that after several elections the results may be more promising. Specifically, Hill finds a positive impact on the composition of the registered, with greater representation of lower-education and lower-income citizens. This, of course, is to be expected, but a positive sign nonetheless. The real evidence of NVRA's impact is if these increases in representation among registrants translate into a more representative voting electorate, and here, Hill finds some support for this possibility, particularly with regard to education.[17] Still, Hill suggests caution in interpreting these results, finding that while increased equity in registration has occurred, there is substantial "slippage" in terms of how this translates into similar increases among the voting electorate (Hill 2003, 714).

Brown and Wedeking (2006) examine the impact of NVRA on registration, turnout, and the composition of the electorate across the 1980–2004 period. Their results mirror those of Hill with regard to the effect of NVRA on registration—NVRA reforms have clearly had a positive and significant impact on registration rates in the states. Yet while Brown and Wedeking find effects for registration, their analyses show that subsequent turnout effects have not materialized.[18]

To explain these disparate findings, Brown and Wedeking model the impact of registration on turnout directly, finding that this familiar linkage has changed with implementation of NVRA. While registration still exerts a strong impact on turnout, the linkage is attenuated in the elections following full implementation of NVRA. This is important, as NVRA was premised on the stable, positive relationship between registration and turnout. Subsequent analyses tie this result to a second effect of NVRA—an increase in lower-class (income) representativeness among the registered. These increases are related to actual decreases in turnout

---

[17] Hill notes that similar findings with regard to income and age are harder to attribute to NVRA because of the effect of competing reforms.

[18] Similarly, Avery and Peffley (2005) find no impact of "motor voter" provisions on reducing class bias.

among the registered.[19] As intended, NVRA increased registration among groups that previously found it more difficult to register—those in lower-income and -education categories. But in doing so, NVRA appears to have increased the pool of citizens that while *qualified* to participate on election day, are also the *least inclined* to do so.

TAKING STOCK

Examinations of the three principal areas of voter registration research leave us with a puzzle. Studies indicate that registration laws influence turnout, and that this impact is more keenly felt by some segments of the population than others. Registration laws, in turn, may affect the composition of the electorate, creating an upper-class bias among those who vote. This upper-class bias has consequences for policy-making in the states. Yet the impact of registration reforms designed to mitigate these effects seems to have worked only minimally at best. While election-day registration, mail-in registration, NVRA, and other reforms may hold promise, it seems fair to characterize the overall impact of these efforts as largely marginal. Moreover, it is even possible that by increasing the relative number of lower-income registrants, reforms have produced a registrant pool that is actually less likely to vote. In the end, we are left to contend with the following question: if registration laws are indeed the culprit behind low voter participation, then why, after decades of electoral reform targeted at precisely this issue, does voter turnout in the United States continue to be so low?

In attempting to negotiate this paradox, we are left with several observations. First and perhaps foremost, advocates of electoral reform need to (finally) recognize what political scientists have suspected for some time now: that voter registration is more than a hurdle to voting. It is, in fact, a political act, one that precedes voting and one that is also, perhaps, subject to different influences than voting. To assume that simply lowering this hurdle will automatically result in increased participation ignores what we know about the importance of political interest and other factors motivating voter participation (e.g., Brady, Verba, and Schlozman 1995; Highton 2004; Rosenstone and Hansen 2002). Having the motivation to engage in political activity matters, and simply making it easier to register does nothing to provide this motivation (Brown and Wedeking 2006; Highton 2004; Hill 2003; Knack 1995; Martinez and Hill 1999; Mitchell and Wlezien 1995).

---

[19] Brown and Wedeking also examine changes in education equality, but find no impact of these changes on turnout.

Political scientists, however, are not completely free from criticism on this point. We too, tend to fall into the trap of thinking registration is merely a necessary evil to voting. Most of the research examined in this chapter is based on the premise that registration and voting are largely synonymous, and that once registration occurs, voting will follow. The research on registration reform reviewed here suggests quite strongly that this is not the case. It is not that we do not know better. Indeed, one of the most instructive things about recent studies of registration reform (particularly NVRA) is that they are virtually unanimous in their sense of caution regarding the ability of registration reform, by itself, to facilitate increased participation.

At the very least, we are guilty of not knowing enough about this important component of the most fundamental political act in which citizens can engage. Indeed, one of the great ironies of the voter registration literature is how little of it actually looks at registration as a political behavior to be explained. Examinations of registration focus almost solely on registration as an explanatory variable.[20] We know that registration impacts whether people turn out to vote. We have evidence indicating that, through these turnout effects, registration influences the degree of socioeconomic, age, and perhaps racial bias in the electorate. Yet we have significantly less information on what actually influences registration in the first place.

Participation as a Two-Step Process

One principal reason for this shortcoming is the tendency for examinations of registration and turnout to treat these two separate activities as largely indistinct. This is true in spite of the fact that we have long recognized that voter participation is a two-step process, where prospective voters must engage in this first behavior (registration) if they are to engage in the second (voting).[21] This is not a trivial distinction. Indeed, while registration may well be the more difficult of the two steps (Rosenstone and Hansen 2002; Wolfinger and Rosenstone1980), it is nonetheless separate from voting and should be treated as such in our examinations of political behavior. A better understanding of what drives registration as an act of participation that is distinct from voting may lend insight into what motivates individuals to register, in addition to guiding reforms designed to facilitate the linkage between registration and turnout. This may be particularly true for those at

[20] In the comparative state politics literature, for example, almost all studies of voter turnout routinely employ registration closing date as a standard, largely throwaway, control variable. Yet even this is a theoretical misspecification of the use of registration in turnout models. Analytically, registration closing date has no direct impact on voter turnout. To the degree that closing date influences turnout it can only do so indirectly through its direct impact on registration itself.

[21] Kelley, Ayres, and Bowen (1967) and Erikson (1981) are among the more prominent earlier studies that make this distinction between registration and turnout.

whom most recent electoral reforms have been aimed—those new registrants who showed little evidence of engaging in the political process prior to (and after) sweeping registration reform.

Recent work has begun to address this issue, employing modeling strategies that explicitly recognize participation as a two-step process, and the results are instructive (Brown and Wedeking 2006; Hill 2003; Jackson 1996; Jackson, Brown, and Wright 1998; Mitchell and Wlezien 1995; Timpone 1998). Jackson (1996) notes the importance of separating registration and turnout analytically because factors that are normally assumed to influence turnout may actually be at work through registration. His findings indicate that this is the case, with important individual characteristics (e.g., education, residential stability, partisan intensity) working at the first stage of participation, and election-specific influences having little impact on registration. Once registered, however, campaign stimuli can motivate people to the polls. Timpone (1998) finds similar results in what is perhaps the most comprehensive analysis of this type, separating the two processes via a selection bias model that allows for the examination of the structural relationships between registration and turnout. Timpone shows that two factors long considered to be mainstays of the voter turnout literature (partisan intensity and political efficacy) are significant influences on registration but not turnout.[22] Turnout, in contrast, results more from short term, campaign-specific forces. These results are important. By documenting different influences at different stages of the participation process, we may in fact be separating out necessary and sufficient conditions for participation. Residential stability, partisan intensity, and a sense of investment in the political system may well be necessary conditions for political participation, and thus it is not surprising that they are found to be strong influences on registration, the first stage of the process.

The importance of long-term forces acting on registration rather than turnout is confirmed at the state level by Brown, Jackson, and Wright (1999) when they find that a liberal political context influences registration rather than turnout, and that this influence is greatest among the poor.[23] Like Jackson (1996) and Timpone (1998), Brown et al. confirm that higher registration translates into greater turnout, but in doing so they highlight the importance of moving beyond registration laws in our consideration of what constitutes a political environment that is conducive to registration. Rather than just institutional barriers, Brown et al. focus on an additional long-term component of the state electoral environment—the ideological tenor set by the states' party elites. Without feeling that they have a stake in the system that may be responsive to their needs, many citizens apparently see little

---

[22] Political efficacy is characterized in the Timpone analysis as a belief about the responsiveness of the system.

[23] See Hill and Leighley (1994, 1996) for additional work on the importance of liberal party elites as part of an electoral context that stimulates participation.

reason to participate. Brown et al. find that a liberal political context promotes turnout, but that it does so by facilitating registration, especially among the poor.

Taken together, the work considering participation as a two-stage process is highly informative for discussions of the impact of registration on turnout. That the effects of these more long-term components of the political environment (partisan intensity, political efficacy, ideological environment) are concentrated at the first stage of participation is instructive, as it suggests that potential reforms focusing on registration as merely an institutional barrier are inherently limited. Unless a much larger hurdle is overcome—that of feeling invested in the political system—simply making it easier to register misses the underlying issue (Brady, Verba, and Schlozman 1995).

CONCLUSION

I began the previous section by chastising advocates and political scientists alike for the lack of work treating voter registration as a political behavior to be explained—a behavior separate from that of turnout. I conclude by noting their most important similarity. Both registration and turnout are behaviors that people are not likely to undertake unless they find some motivation to do so. These motivations may be different at each stage of the enterprise, but motivation is necessary nonetheless. For some voters the importance of contributing to the democratic process may serve as sufficient motivation for both registration and turnout. For most, it seems that additional influences are necessary.

Future research efforts by political scientists can be helpful in providing greater understanding of these significant challenges, as the state of the work on voter registration points to several different areas that may prove fruitful for future research. I see two particularly important avenues: further research into the motivations for participation, and research into those factors that help individuals once they are registered, especially those that have been newly registered by recent reforms.

The wave of registration reform that culminated with NVRA has created a pool of new registrants that present an important opportunity for political scientists as we seek greater understanding of what motivates individuals to participate. There is significant concern about whether these newly registered citizens possess the requisite sense of investment in the political system to translate these increases in registration into voting. Further work on the political attitudes of this cohort of new registrants, and how they may differ from those registered prior to the wave of reform, should provide interesting insight into the motivations necessary to translate increased registration into voting.

Relatedly, I see possibilities in examining post-registration efforts to bring these new registrants to the polls. Now that the barriers have fallen, how do we stimulate voting? Some work of this type is already being done. Wolfinger, Highton, and Mullin (2005), for example, examine the impact of policies designed to reduce post-registration costs and make it easier for registered citizens to vote. Wolfinger et al. find that several state policies (e.g., a longer voting day, mailing each registrant a sample ballot and the location of their polling place) have an impact on turnout, and that these impacts are strongest among younger and less educated registrants. Francia and Herrnson (2004) have taken a different approach and examined motivational factors working in conjunction with election-day registration. In their analysis of state legislative races, Francia and Herrnson conclude that EDR works when there are campaign efforts (e.g., get-out-the-vote drives) that help heighten citizen interest close to the election. Similarly, Gerber and Green (2000) note the importance of face-to-face political mobilization (personal canvassing) in getting registrants to the polls.

While these studies help answer some questions, others remain. On the one hand, they suggest that individuals registered via active efforts are more likely to vote than those registered via passive programs, such as NVRA. Further research needs to explore this distinction more directly. What remains to be seen is what happens to these new registrants when the mobilization forces of specific campaigns are gone. How important are the individual, campaign-specific organizations in translating registration into voting? Is there a roll-off effect, with these registrants less likely to vote in subsequent elections once the mobilizing impact of specific issues and candidates are no longer at work? Are the future voting habits of these registrants likely to differ from those registered through passive registration efforts such as NVRA? While adequate data are not yet available, the registration and campaign activities of the recent Obama presidential campaign should prove fruitful in examining each of these areas.

In addition, I see research possibilities in the potential activities of the political parties. No doubt the mobilization activities described above represent recognition by the parties that NVRA has created a larger pool of registered voters that they cannot afford to ignore. Examinations of how the parties react to and compete for these registered non-voters should provide fruitful ground for researchers as we continue to seek to understand the relationship between registration, turnout, and the subsequent composition of the electorate.

These possibilities also point to where advocates may look for additional reforms. Those concerned with low voter participation would do well to move away, and vigorously so, from a preoccupation with voter registration laws as simply an institutional hurdle to voting. Work examining the impact of NVRA may be most instructive here. The body of research on NVRA highlights an important aspect of registration reform. As numerous analyses have noted, even if motor voter increased registration and reduced the equality gap (in terms of income or education) among those that are registered, it provides no impetus for these newly registered actually to head to the polls on election day. This is because reforms such as NVRA are passive when it comes to the recruitment of potential voters. Voters are not asked to engage in any political activity and thus motivation is not an issue. Rather, registration simply occurs during the course of other activities—activities that are no doubt considered more important by the individual at the time. Yet to follow through with the next political act—voting—requires passive citizens to become active. Absent the motivation to engage in politics in the first place, reforms that rely solely on treating registration as an institutional barrier appear destined for disappointment.

This is not to say that increased registration is not important for producing increased turnout and more representative electorates. Rather, it is a vital component. But the question becomes how do we avoid the "slippage" that occurs when newly registered voters decline to take advantage of this status on election day. The answer is to look beyond a strict focus on institutional barriers to registration. Simply making registration easier does not provide citizens with a reason to vote. As Hill (2003) notes, it merely opens the door to the electoral process, but does nothing to lead them through.

This suggests that future reform efforts need to shift the focus away from registration and toward fostering attitudes and attachments to the political system that motivate citizens to want to engage in politics. No doubt, this is a far more difficult task. But as Wattenberg (2002) notes, "most of the people who want to vote will manage to register." When citizens find politics that appeals to their interests—where they perceive politics as relevant to their lives—they will participate, regardless of the institutional barriers that might stand in their way.

References

Abramson, P. R. 1989. Review of *Why Americans Don't Vote* by Francis Fox Piven and Richard A. Cloward. *Public Choice*, 62: 299–300.

Avery, J. M. and Peffley, M. 2005. Voter Registration Requirements, Voter Turnout, and Welfare Eligibility Policy: Class Bias Matters. *State Politics and Policy Quarterly*, 5: 47–87.

Bennett, S. E. 1990. The Uses and Abuses of Registration and Turnout Data: An Analysis of Piven and Cloward's Studies of Nonvoting in America. *Political Science and Politics*, 23: 166–71.

Brady, H. E, Verba, S., and Schlozman, K. L. 1995. Beyond SES: A Resource Model of Political Participation. *American Political Science Review*, 89: 271–94.

Brians, C. L. and Grofman, B. 1999. When Registration Barriers Fall, Who Votes? An Empirical Test of a Rational Choice Model. *Public Choice*, 99: 161–76.

———— 2001. Election Day Registration's Effect on U.S. Voter Turnout. *Social Science Quarterly*, 82: 170–83.

BROWN, R. D., JACKSON, R. A., and WRIGHT, G. C. 1999. Registration, Turnout, and State Party Systems. *Political Research Quarterly*, 52: 463–79.

—— and WEDEKING, J. 2006. People Who Have Their Tickets But Do Not Use Them: "Motor Voter," Registration, and Turnout Revisited. *American Politics Research*, 34: 479–504.

CALVERT, J. W. and GILCHRIST, J. 1993. Suppose They Held an Election and Almost Everybody Came! *PS: Political Science and Politics*, 26: 695–700.

DOWNS, A. 1957. *An Economic Theory of Democracy*. New York: Harper and Row.

ERIKSON, R. S. 1981. Why Do People Vote? Because They Are Registered. *American Politics Quarterly*, 9: 259–76.

FENSTER, M. J. 1994. The Impact of Allowing Day of Registration Voting on Turnout in U.S. Elections from 1960 to 1992. *American Politics Quarterly*, 22: 74–87.

FITZGERALD, M. 2005. Greater Convenience But Not Greater Turnout: The Impact of Alternative Voting Methods on Electoral Participation in the United States. *American Politics Research*, 33: 842–67.

FRANCIA, P. L. and HERRNSON, P. 2004. The Synergistic Effect of Campaign Effort and Election Reform on Voter Turnout in State Legislative Elections. *State Politics and Policy Quarterly*, 4: 74–93.

FRANKLIN, D. P. and GRIER, E. E. 1997. Effects of Motor Voter Legislation: Voter Turnout, Registration, and Partisan Advantage in the 1992 Presidential Election. *American Politics Quarterly*, 25: 104–17.

GERBER, A. S. and GREEN, D. P. 2000. The Effects of Canvassing, Telephone Calls, and Direct Mail on Voter Turnout: A Field Experiment. *American Political Science Review*, 94: 653–63.

GILLIAM, F. D. 1985. Influences on Voter Turnout for U.S. House Elections in Non-Presidential Years. *Legislative Studies Quarterly*, 10: 339–51.

HIGHTON, B. 1997. Easy Registration and Voter Turnout. *Journal of Politics*, 59: 565–75.

—— 2000. Residential Mobility, Community Mobility, and Electoral Participation. *Political Behavior*, 22: 109–20.

—— 2004. Voter Registration and Turnout in the United States. *Perspectives on Politics*, 2: 507–15.

—— and WOLFINGER, R. E. 1998. Estimating the Effects of the National Voter Registration Act of 1993. *Political Behavior* 20: 79–104.

HILL, D. 2003. A Two-Step Approach to Assessing Composition Effects of the National Voter Registration Act. *Electoral Studies*, 22: 703–20.

HILL, K. Q. and LEIGHLEY, J. E. 1992. The Policy Consequences of Class Bias in State Electorates. *American Journal of Political Science*, 36: 351–65.

———— 1994. Mobilizing Institutions and Class Representation in U.S. State Electorates. *Political Research Quarterly*, 47: 137–50.

———— 1996. Political Parties and Class Mobilization in Contemporary United States Elections. *American Journal of Political Science*, 40: 787–804.

HUANG, C. and SHIELDS, T. G. 2000. Interpretation of Interaction Effects in Logit and Probit Analyses: Reconsidering the Relationship Between Registration Laws, Education, and Voter Turnout. *American Politics Quarterly*, 28: 80–95.

JACKSON, R. A. 1996. A Reassessment of Voter Mobilization. *Political Research Quarterly*, 49: 441–9.

—— BROWN, R. D., and WRIGHT, G. C. 1998. Registration, Turnout, and the Electoral Representativeness of U.S. State Electorates. *American Politics Quarterly*, 26: 259–87.

KELLEY, S., Jr., AYRES, R. E., and BOWEN, W. G. 1967. Registration and Voting: Putting First Things First. *American Political Science Review*, 61: 359–79.

KIM, J.-O., PETROCIK, J. R., and ENOKSON, S. N. 1975. Voter Turnout Among the American States: Systemic and Individual Components. *American Political Science Review*, 69: 107–31.

KNACK, S. 1995. Does Motor Voter Work? Evidence From State-Level Data. *Journal of Politics*, 57: 796–811.

—— 1999. Drivers Wanted: Motor Voter and the Election of 1996. *PS: Political Science and Politics*, 32: 237–43.

—— 2001. Election Day Registration: The Second Wave. *American Politics Research*, 29: 65–78.

—— and WHITE, J. 2000. Election-Day Registration and Turnout Inequality. *Political Behavior*, 22: 29–44.

LEIGHLEY, J. 2001. Review of *Why Americans Still Don't Vote and Why Politicians Want it That Way* by Francis Fox Piven and Richard A. Cloward. *Public Opinion Quarterly*, 65: 610–12.

—— and NAGLER, J. 1992. Socioeconomic Bias in Turnout 1964–1988: The Voters Remain the Same. *American Political Science Review*, 86: 725–36.

MARTINEZ, M. D. and HILL, D. 1999. Did Motor Voter Work? *American Politics Quarterly*, 27: 296–315.

MITCHELL, G. E. and WLEZIEN, C. 1995. The Impact of Legal Constraints on Voter Registration, Turnout, and the Composition of the Electorate. *Political Behavior*, 17: 179–202.

MOSS, J. 1993. Motor Voter: From Movement to Legislation. *Social Policy* (Winter): 21–31.

NAGLER, J. 1991. The Effect of Registration Laws and Education on U.S. Voter Turnout. *American Political Science Review*, 85: 1393–405.

PATTERSON, S. C. and CALDEIRA, G. A. 1983. Getting Out the Vote: Participation in Gubernatorial Elections. *American Political Science Review*, 77: 675–89.

PIVEN, F. F. and CLOWARD, R. A. 1985. Prospects for Voter Registration Reform: A Report on the Experiences of the Human SERVE Campaign. *Political Science*, 18: 582–93.

—— —— 1988. *Why Americans Don't Vote*. New York: Pantheon Books.

—— —— 2000. *Why Americans Don't Vote: And Why Politicians Want it That Way*. Boston: Beacon Press.

POLSBY, N. W. 1988. Review of *Why Americans Don't Vote* by Francis Fox Piven and Richard A. Cloward. *Contemporary Sociology*, 17: 784–5.

POWELL, G. B. 1986. American Voter Turnout in Comparative Perspective. *American Political Science Review*, 80: 17–44.

RHINE, S. L. 1995. Registration Reform and Turnout Change in the American States. *American Politics Quarterly*, 23: 409–26.

—— 1996. An Analysis of the Impact of Registration Factors On Turnout in 1992. *Political Behavior*, 18: 171–85.

ROSENSTONE, S. J. and HANSEN, J. M. 1993. *Mobilization, Participation, and Democracy in America*. New York: Macmillan.

——— ——— 2002. *Mobilization, Participation, and Democracy in America.* New York: Long-man.

Squire, P., Wolnger, R. E., and Glass, D. P. 1987. Residential Mobility and Voter Turnout. *American Political Science Review,* 81: 45–66.

Teixeira, R. A. 1992. *The Disappearing American Voter.* Washington, D.C.: Brookings Institution.

Timpone, R. J. 1998. Structure, Behavior, and Voter Turnout in the United States. *American Political Science Review,* 92: 145–58.

Verba, S. and Nie, N. H. 1972. *Participation in America: Political Democracy and Social Equality.* New York: Harper & Row.

Wattenberg, M. P. 2002. *Where Have all the Voters Gone?* Cambridge, Mass: Harvard University Press.

Wolfinger, R. E., Highton, B., and Mullin, M. 2005. How Postregistration Laws Affect the Turnout of Citizens Registered to Vote. *State Politics and Policy Quarterly,* 5: 1–23.

—— and Rosenstone, S. J. 1980. *Who Votes?* New Haven, Conn.: Yale University Press.

CHAPTER 11

....

EARLY, ABSENTEE, AND MAIL-IN VOTING

....

ROBERT M. STEIN

GREG VONNAHME

WHEN do we vote and does it matter that we all don't vote together? As of 2007 voters in thirty-one states were able to vote in person up to three weeks before election day (*Electionline* 2007). In all fifty states mail-in absentee voting is available with few if any restrictions on who can exercise this electoral option. As a result, approximately one-fifth of all votes cast in the 2004 presidential election were cast before election day (2004 Current Population Survey), and the proportion of votes cast before election day ranges from a low of less than 5 percent in ten states to over 40 percent in eight states (Gronke et al. 2007). These significant changes in how and when voters may cast their ballots raise critical questions regarding their consequences for democratic politics in the US. Does the opportunity to vote prior to election day increase voter turnout? Do individuals who cast their ballots before election day differ from individuals who vote on election day? Do the determinants of vote choice differ depending on when individuals cast their ballots? How have public officials, the public, and the press responded to these new opportunities to vote?

Our review of literature pertaining to these questions focuses on what we know and what we do not know about voting early. We refer to absentee voting, mail-in voting, and in-person early voting generally as "early voting," although these three types of early voting are procedurally distinctive. We do this in part because systematic studies of one type of early voting compared to others typically produce similar results. We conclude the chapter by identifying what we believe might be a fruitful research agenda on early voting, as well as the methodological challenges that scholars will likely confront.

A BRIEF HISTORY OF EARLY VOTING

Opportunities to vote before election day are not new to the American electoral process. Voters have long had the opportunity to vote before election day by casting an absentee ballot, normally by mail (see Bensel 2004). In the past, states limited this form of early voting to individuals who were unable for reasons of travel or disability to vote on election day at a voting place in their voting jurisdiction. The significant rise in number of votes cast before election day begins with the adoption of in-person early voting in Texas in 1988.

In-person early voting differs from absentee voting in that voters may ballot at one or more satellite voting locations, and cast a vote in person without offering an excuse for not being able to vote on election day (Gronke and Toffey 2008; Stein and Garcia-Monet 1997). Satellite voting locations vary by state, and may include government facilities as well as non-traditional locations such as grocery stores, shopping malls, schools, libraries, and other locations. Early voting generally is conducted on the same voting equipment used on election day, as opposed to vote by mail, which is conducted on paper ballots. The time period for early voting varies from state to state, but most often it is available during a period of ten to fourteen days before the election, generally ending on the Friday or Saturday immediately preceding the election. More than half the states (thirty-one), offer some sort of in-person early voting including early in-person and mail-in absentee voting (*Electionline* 2007).

An important feature of in-person or satellite early voting is that a voter can ballot at any of a number of early voting places within the voting jurisdiction, usually a county. Because voters are not required to ballot at their residential precinct they are given a ballot appropriate to their residential location. This condition allows election administrators significant discretion in locating polling places at larger venues more centrally located to where voters work, shop, recreate, and travel. The larger venues also afford election administrators greater efficiencies in the use of their poll workers and polling equipment. These characteristics of in-person early voting are thought to make voting more convenient and increase voter participation.

Absentee voting or "vote by mail" continues, with twenty-nine states allowing no-excuse absentee voting by mail. Another twenty-one states (and the District of Columbia) require an excuse to vote absentee by mail (*Electionline* 2007). Oregon conducts all of its elections by mail.[1]

Early voting is not limited to the US. Gronke, Galanes-Rosenbaum, and Miller (2008) report that 46 percent of the democratic nations allow voters to cast ballots before the designated national election day (see EPIC 2004). Alternative forms of voting seem to be popular with voters, as reported by Southwell and Burchett (1997) and as can be seen with the increasing number of individuals using alternative methods of voting (Gronke, Galanes-Rosenbaum, and Miller 2007).

EARLY VOTING AND VOTER PARTICIPATION

The empirical expectation is that voter turnout will be higher in states with relaxed absentee voting and in-person early voting, *ceteris paribus*, than in states without these options for early voting. Who is most advantaged by the increased opportunities to ballot before election day is not obvious. Presumably the costs of voting (e.g., time) are a greater obstacle to those who are least able to bear these costs, i.e., the poor, uneducated, and politically disinterested. Conversely, we might expect that those who are best able to bear the costs of voting are also best positioned to take advantage of the added convenience of early voting opportunities.

In this way, convenience voting reforms such as early voting, relaxed absentee voting, and mail-in ballots are thought to lower the costs of voting and thereby increase turnout. By expanding opportunities to vote, the link between voting reforms and the costs of voting seem clear. However, the link between the costs of voting and levels of participation as suggested by the Downs (1957) model of turnout might be more problematic as it under-predicts levels of turnout (Fiorina 1990). This is potentially problematic for research on election reforms that primarily rely on the connection between the costs of voting and levels of voter turnout.

However, recent refinements to the Downsian model of turnout suggest rates that are consistent with observed levels of turnout (Bendor, Collins, and Kumar

---

[1] Washington and Colorado allow all-mail balloting in non-federal elections as requested by county election officials.

2006; Bendor, Diermeier, and Ting 2003; Fowler 2006). Specifically, these models argue that while voters are responsive to the costs and benefits of voting they do not necessarily have full information about those costs. Rather, voters are argued to learn about the costs and benefits of voting over time such that they condition their present and future behavior on their past experiences. In that way, an individual who has had better past experiences voting is more likely to vote in future elections than an individual who has had less positive experiences.

Theoretical models that incorporate a learning mechanism have suggested rates of turnout that are consistent with observed aggregate levels of turnout (Bendor, Collins, and Kumar 2006; Bendor, Diermeier, and Ting 2003). Others have specified different learning mechanisms which also produce predictions that are consistent with observed levels of turnout at the individual and aggregate levels (Fowler 2006). Empirical work on how voting is habit-forming additionally seems to suggest that individuals may rely on a learning mechanism for determining the likely costs and benefits of voting when deciding whether or not to vote (Gerber, Green, and Shachar 2003; Plutzer 2002).

These theoretical refinements to the Downsian model of turnout seem to have at least three important implications for the study of election reforms. The first is that it helps to establish a stronger theoretical rationale for the effects of election reforms on turnout. Second, it suggests that election reforms might have a greater long-term effect such that the full effect might not be immediately realized. And third, we might additionally expect voters to settle into a particular mode of voting. That is, theoretical models might suggest that voting is not only habit-forming generally, but voters might also stay with a particular mode of voting (e.g., early, absentee) across elections.

Liberalized voting by mail (Berinsky, Burns, and Traugott 2001) and in-person early voting (Gronke, Galanes-Rosenbaum, and Miller 2007; Karp and Banducci 2000, 2001; Kousser and Mullin 2007; Neeley and Richardson 2001; Stein 1998; Stein and Garcia-Monet 1997) were found to have an insignificant or marginal effect on increasing the likelihood an individual will vote. Neeley and Richardson report "that early voting merely conveniences those who would have voted anyway" (2001, 381). Stein (1998) reports that voter turnout among resource-poor voters does not benefit from the adoption of in-person early voting. More importantly, early voters are disproportionately likely to have voted in the past (Hanmer and Traugott 2004; Southwell and Burchett 2000). Southwell and Burchett offer a dissent from this finding, for voting by mail. Studying voter turnout in forty-eight Oregon elections, "all-mail elections increased registered voter turnout by 10% over the expected turnout in a traditional polling place election" (2000, 76)—although others have reported the effect of vote by mail in Oregon to be about 4.7 percent (Gronke, Galanes-Rosenbaum, and Miller 2007).

The effects of vote-by-mail might also vary by the type of election. While studies have found that the effects of vote-by-mail are generally not substantial, Magleby

(1987) reports that mail ballots in local elections led to an increase in turnout of around 19 percent in San Diego, California and Portland, Oregon. Analyzing data from Oregon between 1986 and 2000, Karp and Banducci (2000) also report variation in the effects of mail-in ballots by the type of election as local elections show the greatest effect, with an increase of 26.5 percent, while midterm elections actually show a decrease of 2.9 percent. These findings suggest that vote-by-mail might have the greatest effect for less salient and less publicized elections. That vote-by-mail might be particularly effective at increasing turnout in local elections is consistent with findings also reported by Hamilton (1988).

Others have also reported varying effects of vote-by-mail. Using a unique opportunity to study the effects of vote-by-mail, Kousser and Mullin (2007) also report that vote-by-mail seems to increase turnout in local elections but not national elections. Kousser and Mullin analyze data on California elections, wherein precincts with less than 250 people use mail-in ballots while larger precincts use traditional polling locations in the same election. This might provide greater control for potentially confounding variables and more reliable estimates of the causal effect of vote-by-mail on turnout.[2] Kousser and Mullin report that vote by mail seems to decrease turnout by around 2 percent in national general elections and increases turnout by about 7.6 percent in local elections.

Berinsky, Burns, and Traugott find that "contrary to the expectations of many reformers VBM [voting by mail] advantages the resource-rich by keeping them in the electorate and VBM does little to change the behavior of the resource-poor" (2001, 178). Simply put, electoral reforms have only been used by those who otherwise would have been most likely to vote without them. Berinsky, Burns, and Traugott (2001), Karp and Banducci (2000, 2001), Southwell (2000), Southwell and Burchett (2000), and Stein (1998) find that early voters are more likely to have strong partisan and ideological preferences, to be more attentive and interested in politics, wealthier, and older. Curiously, early voters are not significantly different than election-day voters on most socio-demographic variables, including race/ethnicity and education. Most importantly, scholars have failed to identify a significant partisan or candidate bias between early and election-day voters.

Convenience is more influential to the infrequent voter's decision to vote. For the frequent voter convenience influences when they vote (election day or before). Since non-habitual voters are less likely to vote, early or on election day, convenience may have a significant and positive effect on their decision to vote, before or on election day. The extant literature provides supports for this position. As discussed, the literature (Berinsky 2005; Berinsky, Burns, and Traugott 2001; Stein 1998) shows that early voters are significantly more partisan, ideological, interested in politics, and more likely to have voted in past elections. Most importantly, early

---

[2] Kousser and Mullin also use a matching procedure to further account for imbalances in the data.

voters are more likely than election-day voters to make their vote choice before election day. We suspect this is the reason why convenience voting before election day (i.e., in-person early voting, mail-in ballots, and mail-in absentee voting) does not entice infrequent voters to ballot before election day.

One reason why early voting has not significantly increased voter participation may be the absence of an effective means and agent for implementing early voting. Those who administer and conduct elections, county-level election administrators, have little incentive and fewer resources with which to harness early voting opportunities into increased voter participation. The more likely agents for converting early voting opportunities into voter turnout are political parties and their contesting candidates. Political parties and candidates have an incentive to employ early voting as part of their electoral campaigns if these actions enhance their chances of winning election. There is empirical evidence to support this hypothesis.

Examining absentee voting in California and Iowa, Patterson and Caldeira (1985) provide systematic evidence for the varying effects of electoral reforms on voter turnout. Consistent with other literature on electoral reforms, they find that the proportion of votes cast by mail is correlated with the demographic characteristics associated with election-day balloting (e.g., age, income, and urban residence). Similar relationships between absentee voting and demographic characteristics have been reported by others but age seems to be the most consistent, with conflicting findings for race, income, education, and partisanship (Barreto et al. 2006; Dubin and Kaslow 1996). The most striking finding, however, was that the correlates of absentee voting *varied across elections and between states*. More specifically, Patterson and Caldeira report that "the state in which one party mounted a substantial effort had a higher rate of absentee voting" (1985, 785). This finding suggests that the effect early voting may have on voter turnout is dependent on a mediating condition, the campaign activities of political candidates and parties.

The cumulative evidence to date suggests that early voting has made voting more convenient for engaged and frequent voters while doing little to enhance the likelihood that infrequent voters will ballot before election day. There is, however, some evidence that several attributes of early voting, (e.g., being able to vote at any voting place in the jurisdiction, larger number of voting machines, parking, voting places that are centrally located to where voters work, shop, and recreate, and more qualified poll workers) are more stimulative of election-day voting among infrequent voters. This of course suggests that the turnout effect of early voting is wasted on early voters but has a significant and positive effect on the likelihood that infrequent voters will ballot on election day. We return to this finding and its implications for new research later in the chapter.

EARLY VOTING AND CONDUCT
OF POLITICAL CAMPAIGNS

There is both anecdotal and empirical evidence that early voting has significantly changed the way candidates and parties conduct their campaigns. One Republican pollster aptly described the effect: "You need to divide the electorate into two groups. Run one campaign at early voters and another at Election Day voters" (Nordlinger 2003). Supportive of this assessment is the rise in the number of votes cast before election day. Common to all campaigns are efforts to bring voters to the polls on election day. These get out the vote (GOTV) activities are expensive in terms of both labor and capital. Before the adoption of early voting GOTV activities were concentrated on the weekend before election day. Every day of early voting, however, is an occasion for GOTV activities, significantly increasing campaign costs. One Democratic consultant estimated that early voting has increased the cost of campaigns by 25 percent (Nordlinger 2003).

Surveying county party chairs in Texas, Leighley (2001) and Stein, Leighley, and Owens (2003) confirm that both parties took significant steps to mobilize their supporters through early voting opportunities in their respective counties. Moreover, the incidence with which leaders in each party have used early voting to mobilize their base has increased over time. Leighley's 1995 survey of county party chairs found that 42 percent of county party chairs reported using early voting as part of their campaign strategies to mobilize partisan supporters (i.e., provide voters with transportation to the polls during early voting). Democratic county chairs (55 percent) were significantly more likely to report using early voting as part of their campaign strategies than their Republican counterparts (32 percent).

Stein et al. (2003) find that when Democratic mobilization activities are matched with significant opportunities to vote early (i.e., a great number of sites and days of early voting) there is a significant increase in the likelihood that partisan supporters will ballot. Moreover, Texas Democrats were rewarded at the ballot box in 1992 when their mobilization efforts were matched with greater opportunities to vote at non-traditional voting places including convenience stores and shopping malls (Stein and Garcia-Monet 1997). These findings are consistent with and partially explain the weak relationship between early voting and voter turnout, especially among infrequent voters. In addition to significant opportunities to vote early at places where voters are likely to be located, there must also be a partisan effort to use early voting to mobilize likely party supporters before early voting will have a positive effect on turnout. Here, however, the beneficiaries of early voting are both strong partisans and likely voters.

As discussed earlier, Patterson and Calderia (1985) also suggest that absentee voting and its impact on turnout and performance are sensitive to partisan efforts to mobilize mail-in voters. Absentee voting increases when political parties identify likely absentee voters among their supporters and work to turn out these persons for absentee voting. Absent any effort on the part of political parties to mobilize absentee voting among their partisan supporters, the effect of mail-in balloting on voter turnout is expected to be negligible.

Oliver's (1996) multi-state study of absentee voting tests Patterson and Caldeira's partisan mobilization hypothesis of absentee voting. Oliver finds that in states where absentee voting requirements are most liberal and where political parties invest time and resources to mobilize absentee voters, "the levels of absentee voting rise and the characteristics of absentee voters change" (1996, 510). The most important by-product of absentee voting and liberalized absentee voting "has come from the greater mobilizing campaigns of the Republican party" (1996, 511). Curiously, Democratic candidates do not benefit from increased liberalization of absentee voting and Democratic efforts to mobilize absentee voting. This might suggest that Democratic candidates confront a different set of obstacles when mobilizing their supporters, leading Democrats to rely on early voting and other electoral reforms when mobilizing their partisans.

Together, the findings of Leighley, Stein et al., Patterson and Caldeira, and Oliver suggest that the relationship between electoral reform, social-demographic factors (i.e., target populations of voters), and electoral participation may be mediated by partisan campaign activity. Candidates and their parties are expected to know who their supporters are, the likelihood that they will ballot in an election, the costs of mobilizing these supporters, and the probable impact voter mobilization will have on the outcome of an election. These findings suggest that parties and candidates have an important role in catalyzing the effects of election reforms.

EARLY VOTING, DISTRIBUTION OF POLITICAL INFORMATION, AND THE DETERMINANTS OF VOTE CHOICE

To what extent do voters who ballot early miss late-breaking campaign activities that could be decisive to their candidate choices? To what extent are early voters simply individuals who have made their vote choices early; strong partisans uninfluenced by campaign messages and political news; inattentive to political news?

Using data on California similar to the Kousser and Mullin (2007) study, Meredith and Malhotra (2008) examine the effects of mail-in ballots on the information that individuals have to make their vote choice. Specifically, they analyze votes cast for presidential candidates in California's primary election in 2008, focusing on John Edwards, Fred Thompson, and Rudy Guiliani. They focus on these candidates because they withdrew from the race prior to election day. Meredith and Malhotra (2008) report results which suggest that a number of voters missed important information by voting by mail. Specifically they estimate that between 40 and 50 percent of Edwards voters and 20–30 percent of Guiliani and Thompson voters would have voted differently had they not voted by mail (Meredith and Malhotra 2008, 18).

As discussed above, Stein (1998), Neeley and Richardson (2001), and Berinsky. Burns, and Traugott (2001) report that early voters are significantly more interested in and attentive to politics than election-day voters. This finding has led several researchers to hypothesize that the determinants of vote choice might significantly vary by when a voter casts their ballot. More specifically, Stein, Leighley, and Owens (2003) hypothesize that early voters will rely more on their partisan affiliation and ideological preferences than election-day voters when choosing among contending candidates. The candidate choices of early voters pre-date the active period of a political campaign. Though early voters are highly attentive to and knowledgeable about politics, candidate issue positions, and candidate traits, Stein et al. hypothesize that these factors are not as influential as partisanship in the choices of early voters. Like the strong partisans and ideologues they are, early voters believe their party's nominees share their own values and issue positions. The adage "I am Democrat (Republican) don't confuse me with the facts," is an apt description of how early voters choose their candidates.[3]

In contrast, Stein et al. reason that election-day voters rely more on candidate evaluations and less on partisan affiliation and ideology when choosing between contending candidates. Even among strong partisans, the expectation is that party affiliation of election-day voters will exert less influence on their vote choices than other attitudes and beliefs. Unlike early voters, election-day voters are less likely to rely only on their partisan affiliation in making their electoral choices. Election-day voters may also be less attentive and knowledgeable about politics than early voters, as indicated in previous research, and rely more on their limited information about the candidates and issues when making their vote decision. There is some evidence that practitioners of political campaigns believe in the veracity of these hypotheses. One Republican campaign consultant offered the following description of how early voting influences his campaign strategy. "By concentrating on solidifying the base early, I can bank these [early] voters and concentrate on debating issues of concern to swing voters at the end [of the election]" (Nordlinger 2003, 3).

---

[3] This observation is not intended to be a disparaging comment on partisan voting. As Downs (1957) has demonstrated, a reliance on party identification as a cue for voting is rational, efficient, and highly effective (i.e., choosing a candidate closest to the voter's own preferences).

Stein et al. (2003) report modest but statistically significant support for their hypotheses. Studying the 2002 Texas gubernatorial and senatorial elections, the authors find that party identification and ideology have greater impacts on early voters than on election-day voters' choices among contesting gubernatorial candidates. The same finding, however, does not hold for voting in the 2002 Texas senatorial election. These findings are at best suggestive of what researchers might find as the number of ballots cast before election day increases. If campaigns influence how electoral rules are implemented, we might expect that in time candidates and their parties follow the advice of one consultant and differentiate their campaign messages between early and election-day voters. Given the recent adoption of early voting in many states, it may take longer than a few election cycles before we observe this effect.

Lessons Learned from Early Voting and New Election Reforms

One of the most significant disappointments with these reforms is that the balance of evidence suggests a general failure to significantly increase voter participation, especially among those least likely to vote. In spite of this consensus finding, there are significant lessons from the experience of early voting that can inform how we organize and conduct elections in ways that may also stimulate participation among infrequent voters. New research suggests that effects of early voting may be related to the location of voting places as well as the number of days before election day voters are allowed to cast their ballot.

What would happen if infrequent voters were afforded the convenience of early voting on election day? Accessible parking, short waiting lines to vote, and an abundance of election-day workers to assist voters with balloting on electronic voting machines might be a strong incentive for infrequent voters to vote on election day. Again, there is supporting empirical evidence to suggest that the corresponding costs of voting have a significant negative impact on the likelihood of voting.

Gimpel and Schuknecht (2003) find that the geographic accessibility of polling places has a significant and independent effect on the likelihood that individuals will vote: "even after controlling for variables that account for the motivation, information and resource levels of local precinct populations, we find that accessibility does make a significant difference to turnout" (2003, 471). Dyck and Gimpel (2005) extend this same finding for election-day voting to the likelihood that individuals will cast an absentee ballot by mail, or vote at an in-person early-voting polling place.

Haspel and Knotts (2005) report that voting is extremely sensitive to distance between the voter's residence and polling place. They find "small differences in distance from the polls can have a significant impact on voter turnout" (2005, 560). Moreover, Haspel and Knotts find that turnout increases after moving a voter's polling place closer to their residence. The authors explain that "it appears that the gain in turnout that accrues from splitting precincts outweighs the loss due to any confusion over the location of the polling place" (2005, 569), in part because distance from the new polling place was reduced.

Brady and McNulty's (2004) study of Los Angeles County's precinct consolidation in 2003 confirms Haspel and Knotts finding. "The change in polling place location has two effects: a transportation effect resulting from the change in distance to the polling place and a disruption effect resulting from the information required to find a new polling place" (Brady and Mcnulty 2004, 40). These two effects are roughly equal for the voter who had experienced an increase of one mile between their home and voting place.

Stein and Garcia-Monet (1997) similarly find that the incidence of early voting is sensitive to the location of early-voting polling places. The proportion of votes cast early was significantly greater at non-traditional locations (e.g., grocery and convenience stores, shopping malls, and mobile voting places) than traditional locations like government buildings and schools. The logic underlying this finding is simple; voters are more likely to frequent stores and other commercial locations than schools and government facilities.

Together these findings suggest that the convenience and accessibility of a voter's election-day voting place is a significant incentive to voting. If this assessment is true, could election-day balloting be organized and administered to enhance voter turnout especially among infrequent voters? The popularity of early voting (Southwell and Burchett 2000) and other forms of convenience voting (i.e., voting by mail) suggests that many voters prefer the ease afforded by early voting, i.e., accessible voting locations, short lines, and assistance in using new or unfamiliar voting technologies. There is some reason to believe that voter turnout might marginally increase if we imported these "conveniences" to election-day balloting, especially for infrequent voters.

A recent innovation adopted in Colorado, Indiana, and Texas involves replacing traditional precinct-based voting places with election-day vote centers. Election-day vote centers are non-precinct-based locations for voting on election day. The sites are fewer in number than precinct-based voting stations, centrally located to major population centers (rather than distributed among many residential locations), and rely on county-wide voter registration databases accessed by electronic voting machines. Voters in the county are provided ballots appropriate to their specific voting jurisdiction. Of course this mode of balloting is what early voters are afforded before election day. It is thought (Stein and Vonnahme 2008) that the use of voting centers on election day will increase voter turnout by reducing the cost and/or inconvenience associated with voting at traditional precinct locations for election-day voters. Unlike those who vote early, election-day voters are less partisan, ideological, and interested in politics. Consequently they may be more susceptible to the convenience of election-day vote centers.

Conceptually, there are two features of vote centers that separate them from precinct-based polling locations that might also be useful in understanding how early voting affects voter turnout. The first characteristic is whether the polling sites are open to all voters in the county or exclusive to a certain precinct (or combined precincts). The second is centralization, where polling locations are larger and more centrally located. Previous research argues that there may be a number of theoretical connections between these characteristics and voter turn-out. There is also some empirical evidence which suggests that vote centers might increase turnout, particularly among less engaged voters (Stein and Vonnahme 2008).

DIRECTIONS FOR FUTURE RESEARCH

There are a number of possible directions for future research. As mentioned above, future research on election reforms might pick up from more basic research on models of voter turnout. Specifically, behavioral models of turnout that incorporate a learning mechanism into Downs's classical model of turnout not only provide a stronger theoretical basis for the immediate effect of election reforms on turnout but might also suggest other effects.

Specifically, if voters are thought to learn about the costs and benefits of voting over time, the full effect of election reforms might not be realized when the reform is first implemented. Rather, it might take several elections for voters to gain information about the ease of voting with convenience voting reforms. This raises at least two additional questions. The first is how long it would take to realize the full effect of reform, which would be affected by how many individuals initially consider alternative modes of voting. The second is how quickly the learning process is thought to take place.

Theoretical models of turnout might also suggest that voters will stick with a particular mode of voting. If a voter finds a particular mode of voting very convenient, the voter might tend to stay with it across elections. Previous empirical research suggests that voting is habit-forming (Gerber, Green, and Shachar 2003; Plutzer 2002) but insofar as voting encompasses a number of specific modes of voting we might further consider whether voters tend to stay with a particular method across elections.

At least two other areas of recent research might have interesting implications for the study of election reforms. We have seen how voters who cast their ballot on or before election day might differ. Research on how personality traits affect one's likelihood of voting might suggest additional differences between early and election-day voters. That is, previous research has found that an individual's willingness to delay benefits affects their likelihood of voting, such that individuals who are less likely to discount future benefits relative to current costs are more likely to vote (Fowler and Kam 2007). Temporal discounting of benefits might be magnified for early voting, which increases the gap between when a voter incurs the costs of voting (even if reduced) and when the benefits are realized. If early voters have especially low rates of discounting, they might also make their vote choices on the basis of different issues, or be more willing to tolerate short-term costs for better long-term policies.

There has also been research on the social influences of voting that might have important implications for the study of election reforms. Previous research suggests that individuals do not vote in isolation from one another, but rather influence one another in a positive way such that if one associates with voters, one is more likely to vote, while having associates that are non-voters makes one less likely to participate (Fowler 2005; Nickerson 2008). This has at least two important implications for the study of voter turnout. First, it might create methodological challenges for the study of election reforms which might implicitly assume that the reforms affect individuals separately (Rubin 2006). Second, social influence on voting suggests that we might experience turnout (or abstention) cascades (Fowler 2005). That is, certain contexts might be ripe for a turnout cascade such that if a small number of abstainers can be converted to voters it could lead to a dramatic increase in turnout through social influence. Applied to election reforms, it suggests that an election reform with a relatively modest direct impact could have a larger indirect effect (Vonnahme 2008). This raises the possibility that we might see a differentiated effect of election reforms, which might work well in a particular area but have less effect in another.[4]

The information voters obtain about candidates and their campaigns comes from the candidates via the news media. If, as suggested, early voting accelerates the pace and the duration of a campaign and varies the messages delivered to voters, this should be reflected in the news media's coverage of campaigns. We might expect that news coverage in states with early voting will differ, *ceteris paribus*, from news coverage in non-early-voting states. For example, if candidates in early-voting

---

[4] This type of process might also explain the substantially larger effects of vote-by-mail in local elections than for national elections.

states initiate GOTV activities earlier than in non-early-voting states, we should observe a greater volume of political news coverage earlier in the campaign cycle in early-voting states than in non-early-voting states. The difference in news coverage might extend to the content of political reporting and reflect the earlier emphasis on partisan and ideological appeals candidates make in early-voting rather than non-early-voting states (Dunaway 2007).

One of the expected outcomes of early voting (Rosenfield 1994 report) was a significant saving in the administrative cost of conducting elections. Research on the costs of election administration is scant and even more so for alternative methods of voting. A 1994 study by the Federal Election Commission on the costs of early voting in Texas reported that early voting was substantially more expensive per vote than election-day voting. Vote-by-mail is also expected to reduce the costs of election administration and there is some evidence of cost reductions for local elections (Hamilton 1988). It would be interesting to know whether early voting in its various forms helps or hinders efforts to obtain efficiency gains in the operation of elections, particularly in the wake of the *Help America Vote Act*. Potential effects on the costs of election administration might also contribute to our understanding of how these reforms spread.

Conducting research on alternative modes of voting, especially their effect on voter participation, faces several methodological challenges and problems. First, there is a paucity of reliable survey data on how voters ballot. The standard sources for voter studies include the American National Election Study (ANES) and Current Population Survey (CPS). The ANES produces a sample of approximately 1,500 that is not representative of the states with different voting opportunities. Consequently the sample of voters who report voting early, absentee, or by mail is neither random nor sufficiently large enough to conduct analysis of early voting as either an endogenous or exogenous variable. The sample of persons interviewed for the CPS is sufficiently large (N=50,000) to cover all fifty states and produce a sample representative of states with different methods of voting. Unfortunately, few other questions are asked of respondents that might be useful for the purposes of explaining voter participation, including partisan affiliation.

A significant limitation with survey data on voter participation is the tendency for respondents to over-report participation (Bernstein, Chadha, and Montjoy 2001; Cassel and Sigelman 2001; Katosh and Traugott 1981; Sigelman 1982; Silver, Abramson, and Anderson 1986). Though over-reporting may be less problematic for predicting vote choice (Cassel and Sigelman 2001) it seems to be problematic for researchers studying vote turnout and modes of balloting.

Ideally we would test our theories of early voting and its impact on voter turnout with reliable and valid measures of voter participation and mode of participation. Furthermore, tests of the efficacy of early voting and other modes of balloting designed to increase voter turnout would be tested with longitudinal/ panel designs in which the same voter can be observed over time and across different elections.

Annotated archival voting histories, available from county clerks and election officials, provide researchers with some of the needed precision for studying early voting and voter participation. Archival voting records provide precision on the key dependent variable: whether and when (how often) an individual voted. Of course, voter mobility may introduce significant obstacles to tracking a voter over time. This obstacle to maintaining longitudinal voting histories may be short-lived. The *Help America Vote Act* requires that all states have voter registration databases that are interoperable between jurisdictions within their states by 2008. Interoperability between states is under way, increasing the likelihood we can obtain reliable longitudinal voting histories in the near future.[5]

Recent methodological innovations in political science research might also improve research on the effects of early voting and related methods of voting. Matching methods (or data pre-processing) might allow us to better understand the effects of the reform by allowing for more reliable estimates of the causal effects of the reforms from observational data. Matching has been shown to be particularly useful for studies that attempt to establish a causal relationship between two factors, such as early voting and turnout (Morgan and Winship 2007). The advantages of matching are that the statistical results are less sensitive to model specification than are regression estimates alone and the results from matching analyses have been closer to experimental benchmarks (Ho et al. 2007). Matching methods have been useful in many areas of scientific research and have recently been used in political science studies (Rubin 2006).

While matching is a useful way of making adjustments for control variables, a persistent problem in studies of the effects of electoral reforms is control variables that we do not observe. Voting is a complex decision and it is difficult (or impossible) to control for every important factor. To supplement matching methods, which allow us to better account for observed variables, scholars can also use formal sensitivity analyses to assess how unobserved variables could affect the results (Gastwirth, Krieger, and Rosenbaum 1998; Imbens 2003; Rosenbaum 1989). While this approach has not been widely used in studies of electoral reforms it provides a useful way to assess the robustness of the results from a particular research design.

More generally, the future study of election reforms might benefit from additional research questions, advances in data collection, developments in the analysis of observational studies for causal inference, and basic theoretical and empirical

---

[5] Four midwestern states have agreed to share voter registration data across their states. See <http://www.sos.mo.gov/elections/2005-12-11_MO-KS-IA-NE-MemorandumOfUnderstanding. pdf>.

research on models of turnout. By building from these areas of research the study of election reforms might not only contribute to a larger body of research on voter turnout but also provide more and better information about the effects of election reforms in particular.

REFERENCES

BARRETO, M., STREB, M., MARKS, M., and GUERRA, F. 2006. Do Absentee Voters Differ from Polling Place Voters? *Public Opinion Quarterly*, 70/2: 224–34.

BENDOR, J., COLLINS, N., and KUMAR, S. 2006. Voting with a Whole Lot of People: Analytical Results for a Behavioral Model of Turnout. Presented at the 64th Annual Meeting of the Midwest Political Science Association, Chicago, Ill., April 20–23.

—— DIERMEIER, D., and TING, M. 2003. A Behavioral Model of Turnout. *American Political Science Review*, 97/2: 261–80.

BENSEL, R. 2004. *The American Ballot Box in the Mid-Nineteenth Century*. Cambridge: Cambridge University Press.

BERNSTEIN, R., CHADHA, A., and MONTJOY, R. 2001. Overreporting Voting: Why It Happens and Why It Matters. *Public Opinion Quarterly*, 65/1: 22–44.

BERINSKY, A. 2005. The Perverse Consequences of Electoral Reform in the United States, *American Politics Research*, 33/3: 471–91.

—— BURNS, N., and TRAUGOTT, M. 2001. Who Votes by Mail? A Dynamic Model of the Individual-Level Consequences of Vote-By-Mail Systems. *Public Opinion Quarterly*, 65/2: 178–97.

BRADY, H. and McNULTY, J. 2004. The Costs of Voting: Evidence from a Natural Experiment. Paper prepared for the 2004 Annual Meeting of the Society for Political Methodology, Stanford University, July 29–31.

CASSEL, C. and SIGELMAN, L. 2001. Misreporters in Candidate Choice Models. *Political Research Quarterly*, 54/3: 643–55.

DOWNS, A. 1957. *An Economic Theory of Democracy*. New York: Harper & Brothers.

DUBIN, J. and KASLOW, G. 1996. Comparing Absentee and Precinct Voters: A View Over Time. *Political Behavior*, 18/4: 369–92.

DUNAWAY, J. 2007. What Makes the News? The Institutional Determinants of the Political News Agenda. Ph.D. Dissertation, Rice University.

DYCK, J. and GIMPEL, J. 2005. Distance, Turnout and the Convenience of Voting. *Social Science Quarterly*, 86/3: 531–48.

ELECTIONLINE 2009. <http://www.pewcenteronthestates.org/uploadedFiles/Primary.EV.Calendar.pdf>

FIORINA, M. 1990. Information and Rationality in Elections. In *Information and Democratic Processes*, ed. J. Ferejohn and J. Kuklinski. Chicago: University of Chicago Press.

FOWLER, J. 2005. Turnout in a Small World. In *Social Logic of Politics*, ed. A. Zuckerman. Philadelphia, Pa.: Temple University Press.

—— 2006. Habitual Voting and Behavioral Turnout. *Journal of Politics*, 68/2: 335–44.

FOWLER, J. and KAM, C. D. 2007. Beyond the Self: Altruism, Social Identity, and Political Participation. *Journal of Politics*, 61: 813–27.

GASTWIRTH, J., KRIEGER, A., and ROSENBAUM, P. 1998. Dual and Simultaneous Sensitivity Analysis for Matched Pairs. *Biometrika*, 85/4: 907–20.

GERBER, A., GREEN, D., and SHACHAR, R. 2003. Voting May be Habit-Forming: Evidence from a Randomized Field-Experiment. *American Journal of Political Science*, 47/3: 540–50.

GIMPEL, J. and SCHUKNECHT, J. 2003. Political Participation and the Accessibility of the Ballot Box. *Political Geography*, 22/4: 471–88.

GRONKE, P., GALANES-ROSENBAUM, E., and MILLER, P. 2007. Early Voting and Turnout. *PS: Political Science and Politics*, 40: 639–45.

—— —— —— 2008. Convenience Voting. *Annual Review of Political Science*, 11: 437–55.

—— and TOFFEY, D. K. 2008. The Psychological and Institutional Determinants of Early Voting. *Journal of Social Issues*, 64/3: 503–24.

HAMILTON, R. 1988. American All-Mail Balloting: A Decade's Experience. *Public Administration Review*, 48/5: 860–6.

HANMER, M. and TRAUGOTT, M. 2004. The Impact of Voting by Mail on Voter Behavior. *American Politics Research*, 32/4: 375–405.

HASPEL, M. and KNOTTS, H. G. 2005. Location, Location, Location: Precinct Placement and the Costs of Voting. *Journal of Politics*, 67/2: 560–73.

HO, D., IMAI, K., KING, G., and STUART, E. 2007. Matching as Non-parametric Pre-processing for Reducing Model Dependence in Parametric Causal Inferences. *Political Analysis*, 15/3: 199–236.

IMBENS, G. 2003. Sensitivity to Exogeneity Assumptions in Program Evaluation. *American Economic Review*, 93/2: 126–32.

KARP, J. A. and BANDUCCI, S. A., 2000. Going Postal: How All-Mail Elections Influence Turnout. *Political Behavior*, 22/3: 223–39.

—— —— 2001. Absentee Voting, Mobilization, and Participation. *American Politics Research*, 29/2: 183–95.

KATOSH, J. and TRAUGOTT, M. 1981. The Consequences of Validated and Self-Reported Voting Measures. *Public Opinion Quarterly*, 45/4: 519–35.

KOUSSER, T. and MULLIN, M. 2007. Does Voting by Mail Increase Participation? Using Matching to Analyze a Natural Experiment. *Political Analysis*, 15/4: 428–45.

LEIGHLEY, J. E. 1995. Attitudes, Opportunities, and Incentives: A Field Essay on Political Participation. *Political Research Quarterly*, 48/1: 181–209.

—— 2001. *Strength in Numbers? The Political Mobilization of Racial and Ethnic Minorities.* Princeton, N.J.: Princeton University Press.

MAGLEBY, D. 1987. Participation in Mail Ballot Elections. *Western Political Quarterly*, 40/1: 79–91.

MEREDITH, M. and MALHOTRA, N. 2008. Can October Surprise? A Natural Experiment Assessing Late Campaign Effects. SSRN Working Papers Series, October 20, 2008.

MORGAN, S. and WINSHIP, C. 2007. *Counterfactuals and Causal Inference: Methods and Principles for Social Research.* Cambridge: Cambridge University Press.

NEELEY, G. and RICHARDSON, L. 2001. Who is Early Voting? An Individual Level Examination. *Social Science Journal*, 38/3: 381–92.

NICKERSON, D. 2008. Is Voting Contagious? Evidence from two Field experiments. *American Journal of Political Science*, 102: 49–57.

NORDLINGER, G. 2003. Early Voting: How its changing campaign strategies, timing and costs. *Campaigns & Elections*. <http://www.findarticles.com/cf_0/m2519/7_24 /105657646/p1/article.jhtml>

OLIVER, J. E. 1996. Who Votes at Home? The Influence of State Law and Party Activity on Absentee Voting and Overall Turnout. *American Journal of Political Science*, 40/2: 498–513.

PATTERSON, S. C. and CALDEIRA, G. 1985. Mailing in the Vote: Correlates and Consequences of Absentee Voting. *American Journal of Political Science*, 29: 766–88.

PLUTZER, E. 2002. Becoming a Habitual Voter: Inertia, Resources, and Growth in Young Adulthood. *American Political Science Review*, 96/1: 41–56.

RHINE, S. 1996. An Analysis of the Impact of Registration Factors on Turnout in 1992. *Political Behavior*, 18/2: 171–85.

ROSENBAUM, P. 1989. On Permutation Tests for Hidden Biases in Observational Studies: An Application of Holley's Inequality to the Savage Lattice. *Annals of Statistics*, 17/2: 643–53.

ROSENELD, M. 1994. *Innovations in Election Administration: Early Voting.* Washington, D.C.: National Clearinghouse on Election Administration, Federal Election Commission.

RUBIN, D. 2006. *Matched Sampling for Causal Effects.* Cambridge: Cambridge University Press.

SIGELMAN, L. 1982. The Nonvoting Voter in Voting Research. *American Journal of Political Science*, 26/1: 47–56.

SILVER, B., ABRAMSON, P., and ANDERSON, B. 1986. The Presence of Others and Overreporting of Voting in American National Elections. *Public Opinion Quarterly*, 50/2: 228–39.

SOUTHWELL, P. and BURCHETT, J. 1997. Survey of Vote-by-Mail Senate Election in the State of Oregon. *PS: Political Science and Politics*, 30/1: 53–7.

—— —— 2000. The Effect of All-Mail Elections on Voter Turnout. *American Politics Quarterly*, 29/1: 72–80.

STEIN, R. 1998. Early Voting. *Public Opinion Quarterly*, 62/1: 57–70.

—— LEIGHLEY, J., and OWENS, C. 2003. Electoral Reform, Party Mobilization and Voter Turnout. Paper presented at the 61st Annual Meeting of the Midwest Political Science Association, Chicago, Ill., April 3–6.

—— and GARCIA-MONET, P. 1997. Voting Early, But Not Often. *Social Science Quarterly*, 78: 657–77.

—— and VONNAHME, G. 2008. Engaging the Unengaged Voter: Vote Centers and Voter Turnout. *Journal of Politics*, 2: 487–97.

VONNAHME, G. 2008. Helping America Vote? The Institutional Design of Elections and Recent Reforms. Ph.D. Dissertation, Rice University.

CHAPTER 12

....

DIGITAL DEMOCRACY

HOW POLITICS ONLINE IS CHANGING ELECTORAL PARTICIPATION

....

KAREN MOSSBERGER

CAROLINE J. TOLBERT

THE explosive growth in online communication for organizing politics in the past decade is most apparent during elections, and use of the internet to seek information about elections has clearly expanded over time. While only 4 percent of the population went online for election information in 1996, 46 percent reported looking at information online or discussing politics online in 2008 (see also Pew Internet and American Life Project 2008; Smith and Rainie 2008). A 2008 national opinion survey of registered voters conducted before and after the Super Tuesday primaries found 14 percent of Americans had watched a campaign video on YouTube, 24 percent had read a political blog online and 32 percent had sent or received political email.[1] In light of the fact that only a little more than half of

---

[1] The national random digit dialed telephone survey was conducted over a two-week period pre- and post-February 5 (Super Tuesday); it included responses from registered voters in forty states

Americans vote in presidential elections, citizen involvement in electoral activities online is remarkably high.

A fundamental advantage that the internet has over traditional information media is its interactivity. Online participation related to elections includes discussing issues or mobilizing supporters through individual email and listservs, posting comments in chatrooms or on blogs, contributing online, creating videos, campaigning on social networking sites, and organizing for face-to-face meetings on sites such as meetup.com. The 2008 election emphasized the fresh vigor of digital technology in campaigns. While not unprecedented—after all, Howard Dean made significant use of the internet in 2004—Democratic presidential candidates built comprehensive internet strategies in 2008 that did more than just duplicate offline efforts. Candidates used sophisticated websites and listservs to teach voters about the primaries and caucuses and the voting process, and to enlist their help with mobilization online and offline. This perhaps demystified the process for those who had not been engaged before, and online strategies appear to have been particularly effective in mobilizing participation by the young in the 2008 primaries and caucuses (McDonald 2008).

This chapter examines evidence and debates over the effects of the internet on how, and how much, citizens participate. Our focus is on the knowledge and involvement of individual citizens rather than the activities of parties, candidates (Bimber and Davis 2003), interest groups, or social movements.[2] We are especially interested in how online participation influences "offline" participation, the nature of participation, and political representation more generally. A key consideration is how internet use for information or participation differs from alternatives "offline," and whether citizens' use of the internet actually causes, or merely reflects, changes in civic engagement and participation.

Political participation, as measured by voting, has been in decline or flat for most of the past three decades (see McDonald and Popkin 2001). Explanations for this are varied, including lower trust and confidence in government (Donovan and Bowler 2003), failures of the party system (Blais 2006; Donovan and Bowler 2003; Schattschneider 1960), and a diminishing stock of social capital that motivates political participation (Levi and Stoker 2000; Nye, Zelikow, and King 1997; Putnam 2000). One view of the internet is that it has the potential to reverse these trends, making information-gathering, discussion, communication, and

---

(respondents from states that had already voted were omitted, as were Alaska and Hawaii) and yielded a sample of 1,285 registered voters. The Hawkeye Poll was conducted by the University of Iowa with a response rate of 19 percent.

[2] Changes in elite use of the internet are just as notable: during the 2008 primaries, televised debates included questions for the candidates posed by viewers through videos submitted on YouTube; John McCain had a presence on Facebook (Heffernan 2008); text messages became new campaign tools; and online donations reached new levels in Barack Obama's campaign (Mann 2008).

mobilization easier and participatory opportunities more accessible (Barber 1997; Bimber 2003; Budge 1996; Grossman 1995; Krueger 2002; Norris 2001; Rheingold 1993; Tolbert and McNeal 2003). Greater access to government online has also been portrayed as a remedy for declining trust and confidence in government (Fountain 2001; Tolbert and Mossberger 2006; Welch, Hinnant, and Moon 2005; West 2004). Critics, however, have argued that online information can lead to greater "cyberbalkanization," reducing discourse across competing viewpoints and the possibility of democratic deliberation (Sunstein 2001); that participation online diminishes traditional social capital (Putnam 2000); and that online politics magnifies inequalities between the rich and the poor, the educated and the uneducated (Katz and Rice 2002; Mossberger, Tolbert, and Stansbury 2003; Norris 2001).

The Effect Of The Internet on Voting and Participation Offline

Political participation requires motivation (interest), capacity (knowledge), and mobilization (Verba, Schlozman, and Brady 1995, 3). Because the internet contrasts with other media in information content and with traditional modes of discussion and mobilization, we argue that the internet has the potential to transform participation in several important ways. First, as Krueger (2002, 2006) has noted, the internet has the ability to engage individuals who otherwise would not be involved in politics, and this pattern is most evident among younger individuals. Second, the internet allows for interaction between users, promoting political interest and mobilization as well as the information-gathering and political knowledge fostered by all forms of media. And, third, politics online enables some new types of participation by making them easier. As a result, we believe that the internet enlarges the politically active population in general, and not only among the young (the effect that is often emphasized). We now turn to examining the evidence for each of these claims.

An accumulating body of research demonstrates a positive association between internet use and voter turnout (Bimber 2003; Graf and Darr 2004), campaign contributions (Bimber 2001, 2003; Graf and Darr 2004; Kenski and Stroud 2006), attendance at campaign meetings or volunteering for a campaign (Kenski and Stroud 2006), engagement in community activities (Shah et al. 2005), and citizen-initiated contact with government (Bimber 1999; Thomas and Streib 2003).

Yet we need to ask whether those who are online are merely individuals who are more politically involved apart from the internet, or whether using the internet truly has a causal effect of increasing participation in other ways. To assess whether internet use exercises any independent effect, we must account for the fact that some of the same factors that lead to greater participation also lead to greater internet use. Education, for example, is related to both political participation and internet use, and if we do not take this into account we could overestimate the effects of technology on political involvement.

One approach to doing this is offered by Mossberger, Tolbert, and McNeal (2008), who use two-stage models, for example, to predict internet use and participation as separate but interrelated activities. They find that participating in online activities significantly increases the likelihood of voting. This is true even when we consider the use of traditional media, such as newspapers and television, and the effects are visible across two presidential elections (2000 and 2004). This suggests that in comparison with other media, the internet has some unique characteristics that enhance participation.

INCREASED PARTICIPATION AMONG THE YOUNG

In addition to attracting some previously inactive individuals, digital democracy has had a mobilizing effect among young people in particular. Politics on the internet differs from voting and many other forms of political participation insofar as young people are more likely to participate (Bimber 2003; DiGennaro and Dutton 2006; Gibson, Lusoli, and Ward 2005; Krueger 2002, 2006; Mossberger, Tolbert, and McNeal 2008; Muhlberger 2003). This is evident comparing parallel activities, such as online discussion and offline discussion (Best and Krueger 2005; 2006; Muhlberger 2003). Traditionally, young people are among those least likely to participate in politics (Campbell et al. 1960; Wolfinger and Rosenstone 1980). The greater presence of young people in internet politics should increase voter turnout among youth according to the research, and in fact recent elections show a surge of interest among the young. If these trends are sustained, they may result in higher overall levels of political interest and activity in the future and less bias in the electorate.

Figure 12.1 shows the percentage of Americans engaged in politics online during the 2008 primaries and caucuses, using the 2008 national opinion data discussed above. Online activities include whether the respondent (1) reads political news online, (2) has visited a candidate website, (3) has sent or received political email, (4) has read a political blog online, and/or (5) has donated money to a candidate online.

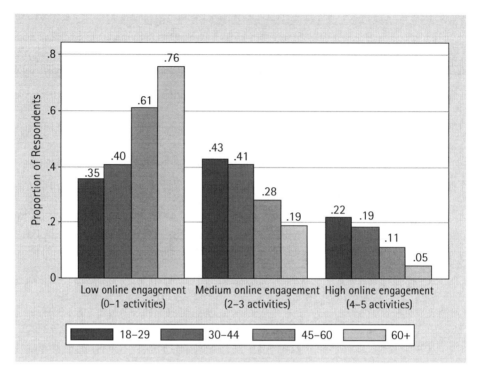

Figure 12.1 Level of online participation by age group in 2008 caucuses and primaries

Note: Online activities include whether the respondent (1) reads political news online, (2) has visited a candidate website, (3) has sent or received political email, (4) has read a political blog online, and/or (5) has donated money to a candidate online.

Source: Super Tuesday National Iowa Hawkeye Poll, 2008.

As shown in Figure 12.1, the young (age 18–29) are significantly more likely to be engaged in presidential electoral activities online than middle aged and older respondents. Of the young (age 18–29), 22 percent were highly involved in the presidential nomination online (reported doing four or five activities), another 43 percent were moderately active online (two or three activities), and only 35 percent were either not engaged in the nomination online or had only low engagement (one activity). Thus, 65 percent of young people in our sample of registered voters were moderately or highly active in the presidential nomination online.

In comparison, of those in the oldest age group (60+), only 5 percent were very active online, another 19 percent were moderately active online and most (76 percent) were either not involved politically online or only slightly so (one activity). These data provide strong evidence that the young may benefit the most from campaigning and mobilization online in presidential nomination contests.

THE INTERNET AS A SOURCE OF INFORMATION: KNOWLEDGE AND INTEREST

Heightened knowledge and interest associated with online information sources may explain the findings connecting internet use to voting and other forms of participation. Mossberger, Tolbert, and McNeal (2008) found that the use of online news in 2000 and 2004 was related to increased political knowledge, controlling for factors such as the use of other media. This effect was most pronounced among younger internet users. Use of online news was also consistently associated with greater political interest in the 2000, 2002, and 2004 elections.

Theoretically, it is important to consider what explains the distinctively "positive" effect of online news as compared to more traditional forms of news delivery. We have identified five possible explanations.

First, *information is easier to obtain.* Information online is convenient and always available for those who have regular access to the internet at home or, increasingly, through mobile devices including internet-enabled phones and laptops. Some surveys show that nearly half of those who use online news and political information cite its convenience (Pew Internet and American Life Project 2004). Finding specific information is simplified by search engines, links, and search functions within web pages.

Second, *online news may "accidentally" mobilize individuals* who are online for other reasons. As a result, politics finds the individual, rather than the other way around. Doris Graber (1988) has referred to the "accidental" mobilization of the electorate through the election news and convention coverage that many Americans were exposed to by default when there were only a few television networks. Markus Prior (2005) argues that greater media choice through both cable television and the internet has led to wider disparities in participation based on content preference. In other words, the politically interested enjoy better access to information, but others avoid political information entirely in favor of entertainment.

Some research shows, however, that frequent internet use is related to greater political participation among those who are only modestly interested in politics. Frequent internet users are more likely than others to participate in political activities online. Gains in participation are most noticeable among those who claim only moderate levels of political interest (Mossberger, Tolbert, and Bowen 2007). The internet may have its own version of accidental mobilization, for those who are greeted by headlines, newslinks, and political ads when they open their email or search online. Internet users also receive messages with political content through listservs, social networking sites, and email forwarded by friends. Exposure to politics without a concerted information search may be one reason that frequent internet use activates the mildly interested.

Third, *the flexibility of the internet has allowed candidates to micro-target campaign ads* to "persuadable voters," or cross-pressured partisans who hold different views than their parties on specific salient policy issues (Hillygus and Shields 2008). Topics for micro-targeting include so-called wedge issues that individual voters may feel strongly about such as gay marriage, abortion, and the Iraq war. Exposure to these micro-ads has been found to influence voter choice of presidential candidates.

Fourth, *the internet shares qualities of print media that promote knowledge as well as the visual aspects of television that promote interest and engagement* (Neuman, Just, and Crigler 1992). Online news covers events and issues with the same immediacy as television, but with the in-depth treatment that is typical of newspapers. The multi-media capacity of the internet allows information to be presented in varied ways, but websites still rely heavily upon written information. Reading facilitates greater recall of information, which in turn encourages the acquisition of political knowledge (Healy and McNamara 1996; Kyllonen and Christal 1990). The internet blends more detailed treatment of topics with the visual and emotive appeal of streaming videos.

And, fifth, *online sources are more diverse than those found in the traditional media*, and this may influence participation through its effects on political knowledge and interest. While online news is dominated by mainstream outlets available in other modes (such as websites sponsored by television networks and major newspapers in the US) (Margolis and Resnick 2000), the web is still populated by a wide range of information sources for those who are inclined to dig deeper or at least to search a few key words. The internet has reduced the impact of distance, making foreign media easily available. Citizens can access information directly from the websites of political candidates or from political blogs, whether known or unknown.

One-third of those who get their political information online believe that other information media are inadequate in comparison (Pew Internet and American Life Project 2004). Indeed, with the diversity of information sources online, internet users may seek information that is more meaningful for their purposes, or that generates higher levels of interest on their part.[3]

The internet enables new forms of expressive participation through the creation of content on blogs, videos, and websites (Dalton 2006; Stolle and Micheletti 2005). This expressive capacity of the technology could be expected to produce increased

---

[3] The democratization of information online, however, also introduces substantial variation in the quality of information. Multiple perspectives are allowed to compete, as John Stuart Mills advocated. But, in the marketplace of ideas, hate speech, unsubstantiated rumors, and outdated information rival the thoughtful, original, and civically oriented voices. Informed participation in the online environment requires even more attention to "information literacy," or the ability to find, evaluate, and apply information, because of its variability. Greater access to information emphasizes the need for critical thinking among citizens.

citizen involvement. Although writing a blog is an obviously creative activity, 67 percent of those who follow blogs say that they consider reading them an expression of their political beliefs (Graf 2006).

These online participatory acts also occur within an environment that is less geographically bound. The internet facilitates participation that is potentially broad, with looser connections between participants than more traditional networks of co-workers or neighbors (Castells 1997; Wuthnow 1998). The breadth of networks is encouraged by the low marginal costs of sending information or appeals through hyperlinked websites and blogs as well as email. While this may promote more extensive organizing efforts, it also encourages forms of participation that are low-intensity and sporadic (Stolle and Micheletti 2005), possibly attracting individuals with only moderate political interest. Participation online may be broader, but also less intense and characterized by easy entry and exit (Stolle and Micheletti 2005; Bimber 2003). The forwarding of an email to a friend or the posting of a brief comment on a local newspaper website are individual acts without commitment to sustained activity or to organizational membership.

Is the Internet Undermining Participation, or Changing It?

Critics of internet politics focus on both changes in information and communication. A common thread in their predictions is the loss of community as it has traditionally been conceived. This loss is due to greater fragmentation of the polity through less shared information or less face-to-face interaction.

Selective Information and Limited Discourse

The diversity of information sources online makes it feasible for internet users to be selective about the opinions and sources they consult, especially with search tools that allow them to limit the range of options that they examine. Sunstein (2001) has decried the balkanization of information online, making it possible for internet users to access only websites representing their own ideological positions. The end result, he predicts, is the impoverishment of political discussion that takes into account competing viewpoints.

While it is true that the internet facilitates ideologically oriented information-gathering, it is not clear that this leads to diminished understanding of other points of view. Approximately 8 percent of internet users in 2004 stated that they used the internet to find information that reflected their own values, indicating that this narrowing of information is a factor for a small percentage of internet users. This is considerably lower than the near-majority who use the internet for convenience (Pew Internet and American Life Project 2004).

Other evidence indicates that the internet can encourage knowledge of a wider range of positions. Horrigan, Garrett, and Resnick (2004) report that internet users enjoy greater exposure to diverse political arguments, including those that challenge their own opinions. If Margolis and Resnick (2000) are correct that existing newspaper chains and television networks dominate the news on the web, then it seems that internet use is not likely to so radically alter the perspectives to which the majority of internet users are exposed.

Social Capital and Trust

Other scholars argue that online communication weakens the interpersonal trust and social capital necessary for civic engagement. Influential models of political participation have emphasized face-to-face interaction for discussion and mobilization and place-based notions of participation (Pateman 1970; Putnam 2000). One critique of digital democracy is that the internet lacks the non-verbal cues of face-to-face interaction that generate social trust (Putnam 2000). Early studies portray frequent internet users as socially isolated (Nie and Erbring 2000) or less likely to volunteer, trust, or spend time with one another (Putnam 2000, 479).

Much empirical work raises doubts about these negative impacts of online participation. One analysis of national survey data indicates that those who spend time interacting frequently with people whom they know only online do in fact develop generalized social trust (Best and Krueger 2006). Shah et al. (2005) discover that online information-seeking and messaging about political and civic issues leads to greater community voluntarism.

Trust and Confidence in Government

Putnam and others have emphasized interpersonal trust as a basis for participation, but trust in government may have a greater effect. Studies have indicated some encouraging effects for e-government and citizen attitudes toward government. Survey research shows that those who have visited government websites have more positive attitudes toward government, although the findings on trust in government are mixed. West (2004) found that e-government users had more positive attitudes toward government, but that there were no significant increases in trust in government. Two other studies have used two-stage models to control for possible differences in e-government users that could explain more positive attitudes. Both concluded that e-government does indeed increase trust in government. One study (Tolbert and Mossberger 2006) found improved trust only for local governments, although more positive attitudes were apparent among e-government users at all levels. Using different data, Welch, Hinnant, and Moon (2005) found greater trust to be significant overall.

Some former skeptics conclude that changes in technology and its more widespread use have now produced positive outcomes for participation (Kraut et al. 1998; Kraut et al. 2002). There is a greater consensus among scholars about the positive effects of the internet for voting and other forms of participation (see Bimber 2003; Graf and Darr 2004; Kenski and Stroud 2006; Krueger 2002, 2003).

New Networks and Forms of Participation: Can They Extend Democracy?

The early research likely exaggerated negative effects for online interaction, ignoring the probability that individuals maintain relationships in their communities as well as online. Still, some differences in online networks and relationships are in fact emerging, with their own strengths and weaknesses. Exclusively online networks likely do not foster strong ties (Bargh and McKenna 2004; Best and Krueger 2006), or what Putnam (2000) has called bonding social capital. But, the internet does make possible networks of participation that are not otherwise feasible because of geographic distance (Wellman 1997). Broader networks can benefit participation. Weak ties have advantages for the acquisition of new information or new perspectives, because they increase the sources of information and the heterogeneity of the network (Chadwick 2006, 105; Granovetter 1973). Beyond these weak ties are what Haythornthwaite (2002, 389) has called "latent ties" that can be activated online. Participants may forward emails to personal or organizational networks, communicating beyond the original group of participants. In this way, the internet reduces costs of mobilization and the problems of collective action (Lupia and Sin 2003).

The breadth of networks encouraged by the low marginal costs of sending information or appeals over the internet promotes more extensive organizing efforts, but also encourages forms of participation that are low-intensity and sporadic, such as forwarding emails or donating online (Stolle and Micheletti 2005), possibly attracting individuals with only moderate political interest. Bimber (2003) has shown that some interest groups are responding in this internet-enabled climate by making it possible for individuals to support a specific issue or campaign through a website without making a commitment to membership in the organization as a whole.

Participation online can also be more individualistic and expressive, through the creation of content on blogs, videos, and websites. Dalton (2006) argues that participation is not declining, but actually changing to include more expressive norms of citizenship other than voting. The internet plays one part in these trends, according to Dalton.

What this suggests to us is that democratic participation derives different benefits from online participation and face-to-face interaction. A healthy polity will contain multiple ways of participating, as well as multiple sources of information that are easily accessed. The internet has the potential for narrowing political debate, but that has not yet been apparent and is certainly not determined by a technology that also makes awareness of varied information sources possible. The debate over the effects of the internet has a tendency to overstate the effects of technology (Norris 2001). While the internet may excel at building weak ties rather than strong ties, the internet is far from the only form of interaction between citizens that exists. Consideration of opposing positions and deliberative discussion is influenced by the actions of political parties and many other factors—not just the internet. As Krueger (2002, 2006) argues, the internet has the potential to extend political participation and mobilization, but only if disparities in technology access and use are addressed.

DIGITAL INEQUALITY, PARTICIPATION, AND REPRESENTATION

At the same time that technology has facilitated participation among the young and some other frequent internet users, online participation replicates and in some cases deepens existing inequalities. More specifically, the internet requires different skills than political participation offline. Best and Krueger (2005) found that civic skills such as writing letters, chairing meetings, making presentations, and participating in group decisions outside of political settings accounted for higher levels of offline political participation, whereas these skills are not statistically significant for online participation. Rather, internet access and skills are critical for online participation.

While internet use has increased exponentially over the past decade, it is certainly not universal, for more than one-quarter of the population did not use the internet at all in 2008 (Pew Internet and American Life Project 2008). Digital citizenship, or the ability to participate in society online, requires regular access to technology, skills such as information literacy, and basic technical competence. Frequent use, skill, and literacy are particularly important for political participation online. As experience and frequency of use increase, internet users are more likely to engage in politics online or visit a government website, among other activities (Howard, Rainie, and Jones 2001). Frequent use, experience, and education contribute to the deepening of activities online, including a higher likelihood of political engagement (DiMaggio and Celeste 2004). Only about two-thirds of internet users report going online on a daily basis, and many less-frequent users lack internet connections at home (Pew Internet and American Life Project 2008). Low-income individuals and minorities are more likely to rely on public access sites such as libraries, or on infrequent access at the homes of friends or relatives (Mossberger, Kaplan, and Gilbert 2008; Mossberger, Tolbert, and McNeal 2008).

Persistent Inequalities in Technology Access and Skill

Those who are disadvantaged in internet participation are older individuals who are offline, less-educated and poor Americans, and poor minorities most of all. Age and education exercise the most influence on information technology use, but disparities based on income, race, and ethnicity are also statistically significant, and have not faded over time (Fairlie 2004; Fox and Livingston 2007; Mossberger, Tolbert, and McNeal 2008). Living in high-poverty communities decreases the likelihood of technology use for individuals of all backgrounds, and accounts for the persistent differences between African Americans and whites in technology use (Mossberger, Tolbert, and Gilbert 2006).[4]

Place matters for rural communities, too. Studies examining broadband use have found that rural residents are disadvantaged by a lack of broadband availability in less populated areas (Ayres and Williams 2003; Horrigan 2004; US Department of Commerce 2004). Broadband use is important for full connectivity, as campaign websites and news sites (among many others) use complex and interactive graphics, video streaming, and other features that require higher speeds to download. High-speed connections are associated with more frequent use and more diverse uses online (Horrigan 2004; Mossberger, Tolbert, and McNeal 2008).

Will time simply close these gaps? It is likely that new wireless technologies will eventually increase access to broadband in rural areas. Age gaps are decreasing over time, as have gender inequalities (at least measured in terms of access and frequency of use). But while internet use has increased among all groups, significant gaps

---

[4] The authors use multi-level models to control for individual-level and zip-code-level factors.

persist. Even among young people aged 16–32, less educated individuals, African Americans, and Latinos are significantly less likely to be digital citizens or daily internet users (Mossberger, Tolbert, and McNeal 2008).

Educational Disparities Matter for Online Participation

The challenge for online participation goes beyond internet access. Variation in literacy and basic educational competencies can be expected to affect politics online even more than activities on the internet that require less reading and background knowledge. Education has repeatedly appeared in studies as a critical factor in attention to politics on the internet, just as it is strongly associated with voting and other forms of offline participation (Alvarez and Hall 2004; Best and Krueger 2005; Bimber 2003, 218; 2006; Muhlberger 2003). Online politics effectively magnifies the effect of education on participation. The significance of community-level poverty for technology use likely reflects unequal educational opportunities in the United States, where the quality of education varies considerably by the race and class composition of communities (Orfield and Lee 2005). As politics moves increasingly online, it becomes more urgent for public policy to address both technology and educational disparities in terms of their effects on participation. Communities as well as individuals will suffer in terms of representation and political voice.

FUTURE RESEARCH ON TECHNOLOGY
AND ELECTIONS

....

With rapidly evolving uses of technology, there is great potential and substantial need for further research, especially research drawing on experimental designs, panel studies, social network analysis, and other methods to tease out causal mechanisms. The extant evidence tells us more about relationships between internet use and voting than *how* online politics affects the decision to vote (or candidate choice, for that matter).

To better understand the processes underlying participation we will need more methods that control for endogeneity, or differences that distinguish those who participate online from other citizens. To understand how the internet itself changes participation, we need experiments (online, in the laboratory, and natural experiments offered by changes in public policy). Longitudinal surveys (i.e., panel studies), are needed to track young adults now engaged online to find out how internet use matters for political participation over time—over a decade or more. The literature about the differences in networks and participation online strongly suggests the need for more social network analysis, including studies of the density of online social networks compared to other political networks. New methods such as these can open doors for a richer and more fine-grained understanding of online political engagement.

Existing theories of participation will likely inform our causal understanding of these processes, but given the multifaceted dimensions of the internet, we do not yet know which mechanisms apply. If technology use increases knowledge, interest, and discussion—in what ways does this occur? Does accidental mobilization explain the engagement of the modestly interested, or is it some other factor, such as the richer content online, or mobilization through listservs, online videos, or social networking sites? Does online information improve citizen knowledge on ballot measures, especially in states where there is a plethora of initiatives or referenda? Most studies have focused on high-profile elections at the national level. What role does online information play in less visible but often critical state or local elections?

While existing theories are a good starting point, they may be insufficient. We need to ask whether digital media change what we already know about the influence of information, discourse, and mobilization. Are they fundamentally changing participation, or enabling multiple ways to participate? Because technology makes it possible for citizens to have direct access to the views of politicians, interest groups, and parties, how does this affect trust in government and in political institutions? Are there new communities being built online—for example through social networking sites—that are capable of mobilizing participation? Blogs are a relatively new medium, but they have the potential for combining information with rich discourse. To what extent is this developing, and how does this matter for political engagement and participation?

What are the long-term effects of digital democracy, including whether technology will change the size and composition of the electorate? Will young people increase their participation on a long-term basis, and will there be any sustained increases in voting and electoral participation overall? Will disparities widen among those who are engaged and those who are not—particularly along racial, ethnic, and class lines? While current trends suggest some outcomes, many of these questions can only be answered over time. They should remain at the top of the research agenda, however, because they are fundamental questions for American democracy.

Increasing Participation in the Digital Age

Even with the excitement surrounding the 2008 elections, national turnout was a little under 62 percent (United States Election Project 2008), and voter turnout in US presidential elections has hovered between 55 and 60 percent of the electorate during the past few decades. In congressional elections, turnout is under 40 percent of the electorate. The US has far from full or universal participation. In the twenty-first century, information technology is reshaping political participation offline and online. Technology is mobilizing the young, and it is creating a style of online participation that can be sporadic and less intense, but this may also facilitate the involvement of some who would otherwise be on the sidelines.

Online news and information hold out the possibility that citizens are accessing richer, more in-depth, and more diverse sources of information. Some evidence indicates that the information capacity of the internet contributes to political knowledge, interest, and offline discussion, as well as the probability of voting. Frequent internet use increases the likelihood of participating in political activities online, especially among those who have moderate levels of political interest.

New modes of participation may be evolving alongside traditional forms. The internet facilitates mobilization that has the potential to be very broad and less tied to place. Such broad mobilization often features low-cost participation through email, listservs, social networking, blogs, or donations. Yet, it is not a foregone conclusion that participation in the internet age needs to be limited to such low-intensity activities, for research shows that online participation often supplements or increases the probability of activity offline.

As Schattschneider (1960) argued, expanding the scope of conflict is critical for engaging more Americans in politics. The internet may be one such mechanism for expanding the scope of political conflict, reducing the costs of being informed and engaged in politics. Yet, at the same time that technology promises to engage more young people and to make government more open and accessible, it compounds the educational and income disparities that already influence political participation. Without addressing this unequal capacity for digital citizenship, the internet threatens greater political inequality, mobilizing and engaging some while further marginalizing others. The policy challenge is to address this inequality and fully exploit the potential of the internet for promoting civic knowledge and democratic voice.

References

ALVAREZ, R. M. and HALL, T. E. 2004. *Point, Click and Vote: The Future of Internet Voting*. Washington, D.C.: Brookings Institution Press.

AYRES, R. U. and WILLIAMS, E. 2003. The Digital Economy: Where Do We Stand? *Technological Forecasting and Social Change*, 71/4: 315–39.

BARBER, B. 1997. The New Telecommunications Technology: Endless Frontier or the End of Democracy. *Constellations*, 4/2: 208–28.

BARGH, J. A. and McKENNA, K. Y. A. 2004. The Internet and Social Life. *Annual Review of Psychology*, 55: 573–90.

BEST, S. and KRUEGER, B. 2005. Analyzing the Representativeness of Internet Political Participation. *Political Behavior*, 27/2: 183–216.

—— —— 2006. Online Interactions and Social Capital: Distinguishing Between New and Existing Ties. *Social Science Computer Review*, 24: 395–410.

BIMBER, B. 1999. The Internet and Citizen Communication with Government: Does the Medium Matter? *Political Communication*, 16/4: 409–28.

—— 2001. Information and Political Engagement in America: The Search for Effects of Information Technology at the Individual Level. *Political Research Quarterly*, 54: 53–67.

—— 2003. *Information and American Democracy: Technology in the Evolution of Political Power.* Cambridge: Cambridge University Press.

—— and DAVIS, R. 2003. *Campaigning Online: The Internet in U.S. Elections.* Oxford: Oxford University Press.

BLAIS, ANDRE. 2006. What Affects Voter Turnout? *Annual Review of Political Science* 9: 111–25.

BUDGE, I. 1996. *The New Challenge of Direct Democracy.* Cambridge: Blackwell Publishers.

CAMPBELL, A., CONVERSE, P. E., MILLER, W. E., and STOKES, D. E. 1960. *The American Voter.* Chicago: University of Chicago Press.

CASTELLS, M. 1997. *The Rise of the Network Society: The Information Age: Economy, Society, and Culture.* Oxford: Blackwell.

CHADWICK, A. 2006. *Internet Politics: States, Citizens, and New Communication Technologies.* Oxford: Oxford University Press.

DALTON, R. J. 2006. Citizenship Norms and Political Participation in America: The Good News is . . . the Bad News is Wrong. <http://www.georgetown.edu/centers/cdacs> (accessed August 22, 2007).

DiGENNARO, C. and DUTTON, W. 2006. The Internet and the Public: Online and Offline Political Participation in the United Kingdom. *Parliamentary Affairs*, 59/2: 299–313.

DiMAGGIO, P. and CELESTE, C. 2004. Technological Careers: Adoption, Deepening, and Dropping Out in a Panel of Internet Users. <http://www.russellsage.org/publications/workingpapers> (accessed February 15, 2006).

DONOVAN, T. and BOWLER, S. 2003. *Reforming the Republic: Democratic Institutions for the New America.* Upper Saddle River, N.J.: Pearson Prentice Hall.

FAIRLIE, R. 2004. Race and the Digital Divide. *Contributions of Economic Analysis and Policy*, 3/1: 1–35. Available at <http://www.bepress.com/bejeap> (accessed September 10, 2007).

FOUNTAIN, J. E. 2001. *Building the Virtual State: Information Technology and Institutional Change.* Washington, D.C.: Brookings Institution.

FOX, S. and LIVINGSTON, G. 2007, Hispanics with Lower Levels of Education and English Proficiency Remain Largely Disconnected from the Internet. Washington, D.C.: Pew Internet and American Life Project/Pew Hispanic Center. <www.pewinternet.org> (accessed April 3, 2007).

GIBSON, R. K., LUSOLI, W., and WARD, S. 2005. Online Participation in the UK: Testing a "Contextualized" Model of Internet Effects. *British Journal of Politics & International Relations*, 7/4: 561–83.

GRABER, D. A. 1988. *Processing the News: How People Tame the Information Tide*, 2nd edn. New York: Longman.

GRAF, J. 2006. The Audience for Political Blogs: New Research on Blog Readership. <www.ipdi.org> (accessed August 20, 2007).

GRAF, J. and DARR, C. 2004. Political Influentials Online in the 2004 Presidential Election. <http://www.ipdi.org> (accessed December 7, 2006).

GRANOVETTER, M. S. 1973. The Strength of Weak Ties. *American Journal of Sociology*, 78/6: 1360–80.

GROSSMAN, L. K. 1995. *The Electronic Commonwealth*. New York: Penguin.

HAYTHORNTHWAITE, C. 2002. Strong, Weak, and Latent Ties and the Impact of New Media. *Information Society*, 18/5: 385–401.

HEALY, A. and MCNAMARA, D. 1996. Verbal Learning and Memory: Does the Modal Model Still Work? *Annual Review of Psychology*, 47: 143–72.

HEFFERNAN, V. 2008. Facebook Politics? *New York Times Magazine*, September 12, 2008. <http://www.newyorktimes.com> (accessed October 8, 2008).

HILLYGUS, S. and SHIELDS, T. 2008. *The Persuadable Voter: Wedge Issues in Presidential Campaigns*. Princeton, N.J.: Princeton University Press.

HORRIGAN, J. 2004. Broadband Penetration on the Upswing. Washington, D.C.: Pew Internet and American Life Project. <http://www.pewinternet.org> (accessed December 7, 2006).

—— GARRETT, K., and RESNICK, P. 2004. The Internet and Democratic Debate: Wired Americans Hear More Points of View About Candidates and Key Issues Than Other Citizens; They Are Not Using the Internet to Screen Out Ideas with Which They Disagree. <http://www.pewinternet.org> (accessed December 7, 2006).

HOWARD, P., RAINIE, L., and JONES, S. 2001. Days and Nights on the Internet: The Impact of a Diffusing Technology. *American Behavioral Scientist*, 45/3: 383–404.

KATZ, J. E. and RICE, R. E. 2002. *Social Consequences of Internet Use: Access, Involvement, and Interaction*. Cambridge, MA: MIT Press.

KENSKI, K. and STROUD, N. J. 2006. Connections Between Internet Use and Political Efficacy, Knowledge, and Participation. *Journal of Broadcasting & Electronic Media*, 50/2: 173–92.

KRAUT, R., KIESLER, S., BONEVA, B., CUMMINGS, J., HELGESON, V., and CRAWFORD, A. 2002. Internet Paradox Revisited. *Journal of Social Issues*, 58/1: 49–74.

—— LUNDMARK, V., PATTERSON, M., KIESLER, S., MUKOPADHYAY, T., and SHERLIS, W. 1998. Internet Paradox: A Social Technology that Reduces Social Involvement and Psychological Well-Being? *American Psychologist*, 53/9: 1017–31.

KRUEGER, B. S. 2002. Assessing the Potential of Internet Political Participation in the United States. *American Politics Research*, 30: 476–98.

KRUEGER, B. S. 2006. A Comparison of Conventional and Internet Political Mobilization. *American Politics Research*, 34/6: 759–76.

KYLLONEN, P. and CHRISTAL, R. 1990. Reasoning Ability is (Little More Than) Working-Memory Capacity? *Intelligence*, 14: 389–433.

LEVI, M. and STOKER, L. 2000. Political Trust and Trustworthiness. *Annual Review of Political Science*, 3: 475–507.

LUPIA, A. and SIN, G. 2003. Which Public Goods Are Endangered? How Evolving Communication Technologies Affect "The Logic of Collective Action." *Public Choice*, 117: 315–31.

MANN, T. E. 2008. Money in the 2008 Elections. Brookings Institution. <http://www.brookings.edu/opinions/2008/0701_publicfinance_mann.aspx>.

MARGOLIS, M. and RESNICK, D. 2000. *Politics as Usual: The Cyberspace "Revolution."* Thousand Oaks, Calif.: Sage.

McDonald, M. 2008. United States Election Project. <http://elections.gmu.edu/voter_turnout.htm> (accessed January 3, 2009).

—— and Popkin, S. 2001. The Myth of the Vanishing Voter. *American Political Science Review*, 95: 963–74.

Mossberger, K., Kaplan D., and Gilbert, M. 2008. Going Online Without Easy Access: A Tale of Three Cities. *Journal of Urban Affairs*, 30/5: 469–88.

—— Tolbert, C., and Bowen, D. 2007. Who is Mobilized by the Internet? Online and Offline Political Participation. Presented at the 3rd Karlstad Seminar on Studying Political Action, Karlstad University, Sweden, October 18–20, 2007.

—— —— and M. Gilbert. 2006. Race, Place and Information Technology. *Urban Affairs Review* 41/5: 583–620.

—— —— and McNeal, R. 2008. *Digital Citizenship: The Internet, Society, and Participation.* Cambridge, Mass.: MIT Press.

—— —— and Stansbury, M. 2003. *Virtual Inequality: Beyond the Digital Divide.* Washington, D.C.: Georgetown University Press.

Muhlberger, P. 2003. Political Values, Political Attitudes, and Attitude Polarization in Internet Discussion. *Communications*, 2: 107.

Neuman, W. R., Just, M. R., Crigler, A. N. 1992. *Common Knowledge: News and the Construction of Political Meaning.* Chicago: University of Chicago Press.

Nie, N. and Erbring, L. 2000. *Internet and Society: A Preliminary Report.* Stanford, Calif.: Stanford Institute for the Qualitative Study of Society, Stanford University.

Norris, P. 2001. *Digital Divide: Civic Engagement, Information Poverty, and the Internet Worldwide.* New York: Cambridge University Press.

Nye, J. S., Jr., Zelikow, P. D., and King, D. C. (eds.) 1997. *Why People Don't Trust Government.* Cambridge, Mass.: Harvard University Press.

Orfield, G. and Lee, C. 2005. Why Segregation Matters: Poverty and Educational Inequality. Cambridge, Mass.: Civil Rights Project, Harvard University. <http://www.civilrightsproject.harvard.edu> (accessed December 10, 2006).

Pateman, C. 1970. *Participation and Democratic Theory.* New York: Cambridge University Press.

Pew Internet and American Life Project 2008. Tracking Survey, May 2008. <http://www.pewinternet.org> (accessed December 29, 2008).

—— 2004. The 2004 Postelection Survey. <http://www.pewinternet.org> (accessed December 29, 2008).

Prior, M. 2005. News vs. Entertainment: How Increasing Media Choice Widens Gaps in Political Knowledge and Turnout. *American Journal of Political Science*, 49/3: 577–92.

Putnam, R. 2000. *Bowling Alone: The Collapse and Revival of American Community.* New York: Simon & Schuster.

Rheingold, H. 1993. *The Virtual Community: Homesteading on the Electronic Frontier.* Reading, Mass.: Addison-Wesley.

Schattschneider, E. E. 1960. *The Semi-Sovereign People.* New York: Holt, Rinehart and Winston.

Shah, D., Cho, V., Eveland, J., William, P., and Kwak, N. 2005. Information and Expression in a Digital Age: Modeling Internet Effects on Civic Participation. *Communication Research*, 32/5: 531–65.

SMITH, A. and RAINIE, L. 2008. The Internet and the 2008 Election. <http://www. pewinternet.org> (accessed October 26, 2008).

STOLLE, D. and MICHELETTI, M. 2005. *The Expansion of Political Action Repertoires: Theoretical Reflections on Results from the Nike Email Exchange Internet Campaign.* Washington, D.C.: American Political Science Association.

SUNSTEIN, C. 2001. *Republic.com.* Princeton, N.J.: Princeton University Press.

THOMAS, J. and STREIB, G. 2003. The New Face of Government: Citizen-Initiated Contacts in the Era of E-Government. *Journal of Public Administration Theory and Research*, 13/1: 83–102.

TOLBERT, C. and MCNEAL, R. 2003. Unraveling the Effects of the Internet on Political Participation. *Political Research Quarterly*, 56/2: 175–85.

—— and MOSSBERGER, K. 2006. The Effects of E-Government on Trust and Confidence in Government. *Public Administration Review*, 66/3: 354–69.

UNITED STATES ELECTIONS PROJECT 2008. 2008 General Election Turnout Rates. <http:// elections.gmu.edu/Turnout_2008G.html> (accessed January 3, 2009).

US DEPARTMENT OF COMMERCE 2004. Economics and Statistics Administration and National Telecommunications and Information Administration. *A Nation Online: Entering the Broadband Age.* <http://www.ntia.doc.gov/reports/anol/NationOnlineBroadband04. htm> (accessed February 26, 2005).

VERBA, S., SCHLOZMAN, K., and BRADY, H. 1995. *Voice and Equality: Civic Voluntarism in American Politics.* Cambridge, Mass.: Harvard University Press.

WELCH, E. W., HINNANT, C., and MOON, M. J. 2005. Linking Citizen Satisfaction with E-government with Trust in Government. *Journal of Public Administration Research and Theory*, 15/1: 271–91.

WELLMAN, B. 1997. An Electronic Group is Virtually a Social Network. In *Cultures of the Internet*, ed. S. Keiser. Mahwah, N.J.: Lawrence Erlbaum.

WEST, D. M. 2004. E-government and the Transformation of Service Delivery and Citizen Attitudes. *Public Administration Review*, 64/1: 15–27.

WOLFINGER, R. and ROSENSTONE, S. J. 1980. *Who Votes?* New Haven, Conn.: Yale University Press.

WUTHNOW, R. 1998. *Loose Connections: Joining Together in America's Fragmented Communities.* Cambridge, Mass.: Harvard University Press.

CHAPTER 13

VOTING TECHNOLOGY

R. MICHAEL ALVAREZ
THAD E. HALL

VOTING technology and procedures have changed dramatically since the first American elections in 1788, when voters either expressed their preferences aloud and in person or voted using paper ballots listing slates of candidates (Keyssar 2000; Saltman 2006). Since 1788, there has been an evolution of voting technologies, starting with the move to paper ballots printed by the political parties and then to the Australian ballot. Mechanical (lever) voting machines were developed in the early 1900s. In the 1960s there was a movement toward computerized tabulation of paper ballots, first using punch cards and then using optical-scanning technology. In the last fifteen years direct recording electronic voting equipment (DREs) has been developed (Alvarez and Hall 2008; Saltman 2006). Although the two are not often connected, voting technology can have direct effects on the winners and losers of elections.

Prior to the US 2000 presidential election, there were few studies of voting technologies and their effects on voter behavior and election outcomes. The primary exceptions were the few studies that looked at the effects of the introduction of new voting technologies on voter participation (Fraser 1985; Mather 1964, 1986; Montgomery 1985; Thomas 1968; White 1960). Another line of research prior to the 2000 presidential election examined the potential correlations between voting systems and technologies and "ballot roll-off" (e.g., Walker 1966). Since the 2000 election, a growing and vibrant research literature has sprung up, in which social scientists, computer scientists, and representatives from other scientific disciplines studied many important issues associated with voting technologies. In this chapter we summarize a number of these avenues of new research and conclude with our suggestions for how this new area of research can be improved.

A BRIEF HISTORY OF VOTING TECHNOLOGY

There are three broad periods in American history that characterize the technology and methods Americans have used to cast votes. From the 1700s to late 1800s, voting was centered on the use of partisan paper ballots. From the late 1800s to the 1960s there was a transition to non-partisan paper ballots and lever voting machines. Today, we are in a period centered on the use of electronic voting and ballot-counting technologies.

In this first period, voters cast votes using either a paper ballot that was printed by one of the political parties or by voice voting. Both techniques were used well into the post-Civil War era.[1] These ballots did not offer voters a choice of candidates; instead, a voter obtained a partisan paper ballot—from a party official, a friend, or the newspaper—that listed only the candidates of one party. The voter took that ballot into a polling place on Election Day and dropped it into the ballot box, after being identified as an eligible voter. Political parties often made these ballots large and colorful so that party officials could monitor who cast ballots in support of the party.[2]

Some voters, especially in the South, used the oral tradition of casting votes aloud. In such places, the eligible males in the locality would gather before an election judge on election day and, when their name was called, state verbally which candidate they supported. In Virginia, voters cast a vote by signing the poll book next to the name of their preferred candidate. The oral tradition explicitly linked a voter to his vote. Although this system allowed for complete election auditability, there was no secret ballot.

Without a secret ballot, party officials could easily influence the voting process. Some party officials purchased votes with drinks or small items and then monitored voters as they cast their ballot. Voters could also be threatened with the loss

---

[1] Bensel (2004, 54–7) notes that voice voting existed in a handful of states through the Civil War period and its immediate aftermath; the last state to use voice voting was Kentucky, which ended the practice in 1891.

[2] For examples of ballots from this period in California, see Goodrich (2004), and her website of historical ballots (<http://vote.caltech.edu/ballots/huntington>, last touched May 11, 2005).

of jobs or physical harm if they did not vote "correctly." Vote-buying and coercion schemes were easy and efficient to conduct because of the public nature of balloting.[3] Such schemes influenced turnout; it is estimated that the mobilization that resulted from this process substantially increased turnout compared to turnout with secret ballots.

At the turn of the twentieth century, in order to combat coercion, elections transitioned to multi-candidate "Australian" secret ballots. Candidates were listed on a single ballot and voters could choose among candidates for each race. Some voters took a paper ballot into a booth, marked it secretly, and deposited it in a box without revealing their votes. In many large urban areas, voters used mechanical vote casting and recording "voting machines," often called lever machines. A voter votes on a lever machine by standing in front of a machine with a large set of small levers with candidate names (or ballot measure descriptions) next to each lever. Each vote choice is recorded mechanically, typically using physical counters that aggregated votes like the mileage counter in a car. Lever machines were adopted as a tool for combating ballot-box stuffing in some jurisdictions.

Progressive reforms that accompanied the move to the Australian ballot made ballots considerably longer. Voters began electing more representatives to state and local offices and voting on referenda, initiatives, and other ballot measures. Longer ballots and an increase in the number of voters increased ballot-counting time. These issues, and improved technology, led to the introduction of electronic ballot tabulation and DRE voting technologies. The first electronic voting systems were introduced in the 1960s, using punch-card ballots and electronic tabulation. Counties either adopted "Votomatic" punch cards, which use a thin computer card with columns and rows of very small, pre-punched rectangles or "Datavote" punch cards, which list the names of candidates or ballot measures directly on the card and use a hole-punch handle to punch a rectangular hole in the card.[4] Later, optical scan technology, which works by filling an oval or connecting two arrows with a pen, and then electronically scanning the ballot for marks, were developed.

Since the passage of the Help America Vote Act of 2002, state and local governments have been debating whether to transition to DREs. And in recent years some states have moved from DRE technologies to optical scan. DRE technologies have produced security concerns and questions about the ability of election officials to audit elections.

---

[3] Much has been written about fraud and paper ballots (e.g., Bensel 2004).

[4] For an example of this type of punch card ballot, see <http://vote.caltech.edu/media/documents/ballotfront.pdf> and <http://vote.caltech.edu/media/ballotback.pdf>.

VOTING TECHNOLOGY AND VOTER CONFIDENCE

···

A key issue with voting technologies is whether voters are confident that a given technology is effective in counting votes. A growing body of research examines voter confidence in the election process, especially related to voting technology (Atkeson and Saunders 2007; Alvarez and Hall 2008). Research by Alvarez, Hall, and Llewellyn (2007, 2008a, 2008b) considered the overall confidence voters have that ballots will be counted accurately and the factors that influence this level of confidence. After the 2004 election, Alvarez, Hall, and Llewellyn (2007, 2008a) found that 55 percent of adult registered, likely voters were very confident and 20 percent were somewhat confident that their votes were counted as intended in the 2004 election; 12 percent were "not too confident" and 10 percent were "not at all confident." The least confident voters were by-mail absentee voters and the most confident voters used optical scan technologies.

Alvarez, Hall, and Llewellyn (2007) found that political, socio-demographic, and informational factors affected confidence. After the 2004 elections, Republicans were significantly more confident than Democratic or Independent voters; this is likely the result of Democrats losing the previous two presidential elections. Likewise, black voters were significantly less confident than white voters that their ballots would be counted accurately. Finally, voters who were familiar with DREs and had used the technology were as confident as optical scan voters that their ballots would be counted accurately. However, voters with negative assessments of DREs were less confident that their ballot would be counted accurately. Interestingly, absentee voters were the least confident. As more states move to convenience voting—especially relaxed absentee voting—this question of confidence among absentee voters is very important.

A panel study of voters in the 2006 election by Alvarez, Hall, and Llewellyn (2008b) found differences in the factors that influence voter confidence that their vote *will be* counted accurately before the election and whether their vote *was* counted accurately after the election. Before the 2006 election, Democrats and Independents were less confident than Republicans and men and higher-income individuals were more confident. After the election, confidence was driven by voting for the winner; individuals who voted for parties and candidates who won, and those who live in jurisdictions where the dominant political party reflects the individual's political preferences, were more likely to be confident. Democrats, having won a national election in 2006, were more confident after the 2006 election than they had been either before or after the 2004 election or prior to the 2006 election.

RESIDUAL VOTES AND ROLL-OFF

··

After the 2000 election, researchers examined which voting technologies captured votes most accurately, using the concept of the residual vote. The residual vote is the difference between the number of votes counted in a specific race relative to the total number of ballots cast in the election (Caltech/MIT Voting Technology Project (VTP) 2001; Alvarez, Ansolabehere, and Stewart 2005; Ansolabehere and Stewart 2005; Hamner and Traugott 2004). The residual vote is typically caused by an individual over- or under-voting in a specific race. The VTP (2001) found that the presidential residual vote rate for punch-card voting systems was 2.5 percent, 2.3 percent for DRE systems, 1.8 percent for paper ballots, and 1.5 percent for both optical scanning and lever machines. Allowing voters to scan their ballot for errors reduces residual votes; for example, precinct-based optical scanning likely leads to fewer mistakes, measured using residual votes, by voters (Alvarez, Sinclair, and Wilson 2004). Between 1988 and 2004, the residual vote rates declined for all voting technologies except paper ballots. Declines were dramatic for optical scan and DREs during this period (Alvarez and Hall 2008).

Several academic studies have found differences in residual votes across voting technologies and raised concerns about voting rights violations (Alvarez, Sinclair, and Wilson 2004; Buchler, Jarvis, and McNulty 2004; Brady et al. 2001; Sinclair and Alvarez 2004; Tomz and Van Houweling 2003; see also Ansolabehere 2002). These studies documented that punch-card voting systems were often used in localities with high minority populations and that, compared with white voters, minority voters were more likely to over- and under-vote on punch-card voting systems (especially Votomatic punch cards). Since 1988, the use of optical scan and DRE machines has increased rapidly at the cost of paper ballots and lever machines.[5] After the 2000 election, there was a rapid movement to acquire either optical scan voting systems or DRE technologies.

Several studies have identified associations between residual votes and certain types of voting equipment. Tomz and Van Houweling (2003) identified a 4–percentage-point gap between residual vote rates in high-percentage white and black precincts that used punch cards and a 6-point gap in precincts that used optical scan balloting. The gap in precincts using DREs was 0.3 percent. The residual vote gap in optical scan precinct was lowered in some precincts by the use of in-precinct vote tabulators that provide voters information about ballot errors. However, Knack and Kropf (2003) found that precinct-count optical-scan voting systems minimized racial gaps in the 1996 general elections. Racial bias is a very important issue, as studies conducted after 2000 in several states all found a

---

[5] These data originated from Election Data Services, Inc., but have been updated by Delia Grigg and Charles Stewart (Grigg 2005).

strong relationship between high percentages of rejected ballots and high percentages of black voters in a precinct or jurisdiction (Alvarez, Sinclair, and Wilson 2004; Brady et al. 2001; Bullock and Hood 2002; Herron and Sekhon 2003). Kimball and Kropf (2005) examined paper-based ballots and found that some designs (for example, the "connect-the-arrow" style) led to more unrecorded votes.

Stewart (2006) examined changes in residual voting between the 2000 and 2004 elections and identified four types of equipment changes: moves from punch card to DRE, from optical scan to DRE, from lever machine to DRE, and from punch card to optical scan. Many jurisdictions used the same voting technology in both elections and there was a decline in residual votes of 0.61 percent from 2000 to 2004 in these jurisdictions, suggesting that general reforms and more educated voters reduced residual votes. Larger reductions in residual vote rates occurred in localities that changed voting technology. Switching from punch cards to optical scan reduced residual vote rates by 1.12 percentage points; moving from punch cards to DREs reduced the rate by 1.46 percentage points; moving from optical scan to DREs reduced the rate by 1.26 percentage points; and moving from lever machines to DREs reduced the rate by 0.80 percentage points.

Closely related to the problem of residual votes is ballot roll-off. Ballot roll-off occurs when voters skip races toward the end of the ballot, either intentionally or accidentally. Studies of ballot roll-off initially explained this phenomenon by studying ballot length and the salience of races on the ballot (e.g., Bullock and Dunn 1996; Darcy and Schneider 1989; Walker 1966). There is also evidence that fatigue and salience interact on long ballots (Bullock and Dunn 1996). More recent studies have considered the role of voting technology on ballot roll-off, since DRE technologies might reduce fatigue and encourage voters to cast a more complete ballot. A study of DREs and ballot roll-off in Franklin County, Ohio, found that "electronic voting machines sharply decrease aggregate roll-off, even after controlling for socio-demographic variables" (Nichols and Strizek 1995, 311). The declines were dramatic: 9 percentage points in county-level races, 12 percentage points in state and lower court races, and 19 percentage points in unopposed races. A study of ballot roll-off in Pasco County, Florida, also found that ballot roll-off declined when the county transitioned to DREs (Herron and Lewis 2006). When Pasco County used Votomatic punch cards, there was a strong correlation between roll-off and precinct demographics. No such correlation existed with the use of DREs: it reduced roll-off for all voters. Recently, Kimball and Kropf (2008) examined residual vote rates on ballot measures and how voting technologies might affect residual votes. One intriguing result is that residual vote rates on ballot measures are higher for voting technologies that use so-called "full-face" ballots. More research on the relationship between voting technology, residual votes, and roll-off is necessary so that steps, like voter education and better voting technologies, can be taken to minimize residual votes in future elections.

ELECTION AUDITING AND
ELECTORAL MANIPULATION

Two additional research questions about voting technology are auditing elections and the potential for electoral manipulation. Election auditing has become an important issue in voting-technology policy discussions. The available survey data on voter confidence suggests that voter confidence may be improved if voters think that the election can be audited (Alvarez, Hall, and Llewellyn 2008a). The key questions with election audits are how to conduct them and how to ensure that audit results can be used to improve the election process.

Despite the interest of policy-makers in election audits—for example, post-election ballot audits have figured prominently in legislation under debate in Congress—social scientists have only recently begun to pay attention to this issue. The handful of studies that exist have focused on the discrepancies that arise in post-election audits or recounts. Comparisons of the deviations between original ballot count and subsequent recount have found that these deviations are small in magnitude.[6] Currently research is ongoing in Michigan, New Mexico, and Utah and we are optimistic that these studies will develop new data and methods for studying post-election ballot recounts and audits.

However, these studies have focused narrowly on the deviations observed between two different methods of counting ballots. There are many other aspects of election administration where principles of auditing should be used; these present new research opportunities for social scientists and students of public administration. For example, there have not been many studies auditing voter registration databases, especially the relatively new statewide voter registration databases now required in most states by the Help America Vote Act.[7] Nor have there been performance-based audits of other aspects of election administration, such as chains of custody of election materials and ballots (Alvarez and Hall 2008).

One of the primary motivations for conducting post-election ballot recounts and audits is to detect irregularities and to investigate potential election fraud. Studying election fraud is difficult, although social scientists have periodically investigated allegations of election fraud.[8] More recently, social scientists have begun to develop methods of "election forensics," including qualitative election observation (Hyde 2008; Simpser 2008), the quantitative analysis of historical election data to attempt to detect irregularities (Alvarez and Katz 2008), analyses

---

[6] See Alvarez, Katz, and Hill (2005); Ansolabehere and Reeves (2004); Hansen (2003); Herron and Wand (2007).

[7] See McDonald (2007) for an interesting step in this direction.

[8] Fabrice Lehoucq (2003) has summarized the historical and comparative literature on election fraud.

of cross-sectional and cross-election data (Myagkov, Ordeshook, and Shaikin 2008), post-election recounts (Herron and Wand 2007), and the development of novel statistics for finding oddities in elections data (Mebane 2008). Election forensics, and the analysis of the relationship of election irregularities and voting technology, is an area where social science will make important policy and substantive contributions in the near future (Alvarez, Hall, and Hyde 2008).

THE USABILITY OF VOTING SYSTEMS

Different voting technologies have different usability issues. We consider five usability issues here, starting with ballot complexity. Neimi and Herrnson (2003) summarize the literature on ballot complexity in the United States and identify variations in ballot forms. Ballots were of great interest to political scientists in the early 1900s, especially the length of the ballot (Allen 1906; Beard 1909; Ludington 1911) but many of the issues that existed then still exist today. Neimi and Herrnson find much variation in how ballots look and are structured across states.[9] For example, several states provide symbols for parties on their ballots but only Louisiana and Utah use the traditional Democratic (donkey) and Republican (elephant) party symbols. They also found variations in ballot instructions, with terms like "vote for one" and "vote once" often used interchangeably, even when the usage is confusing. The ways in which candidates are identified—with nicknames, place of residence, and occupation—vary by state as well.

Some states have straight ticket voting, where voters can choose to vote for all of the candidates of one party for part of the ballot. All straight-party voting states allow voters to opt out either entirely or partly (casting a party slate ballot but then excluding some number of races from the straight party total). States also vary in how they handle write-in candidates; write-in candidates may have to qualify to be an official candidate and the rules governing when their votes count vary widely.

A second issue is that voting technology can facilitate split-ticket voting. Rusk (1970) found that the transition to the Australian ballot in twenty-three states from 1876 to 1908 led to an increase in split-ticket voting, compared to voting without the secret ballot. When voters were given a ballot that listed all candidates and were given the opportunity to vote for any candidate of any party across all races on a ballot, some voters began to select candidates from different political parties for different offices on the ballot. In Rusk's analysis, split-ticket voting doubled, on average, in the first election after the Australian ballot was introduced in states.

---

[9] See Goodrich (2004) for historical examples of other ballot designs in history.

Third, there can be ballot order effects, where candidates who are listed first may receive a marginally, but statistically significant, larger numbers of votes. Previous research identified by Miller and Krosnik (1998) found mixed results related to ballot order effects. In their own analysis of Ohio's three largest counties, Miller and Krosnik found modest ballot order effects. More recently, Koppell and Steen (2004) examined precinct-level Democratic primary election data from New York City in 1998 and found significant ballot order effects, especially for down-ballot races, such as city council. However, other studies find mixed evidence for significant and consistent ballot order effects (Alvarez, Hasen, and Sinclair 2006; Ho and Imai 2008; Sinclair 2006). Election officials have adopted many techniques to address this problem, including producing multiple "types" of ballots, where the candidate names in a specific race in a jurisdiction are either randomly ordered or the list is rotated on the ballot in different state legislative districts to alleviate these potential problems (Bain and Hecock 1957; Harris 1934; Merriam and Overacker 1928). However, even with ballot rotation it is likely that one candidate will be listed first more than another.

The 2003 California recall election revealed a fourth issue: vertical proximity effects. In this election, the last in California involving the use of pre-scored punchcard voting devices, research conducted by Sled (2003) and Alvarez et al. (2004) found a "vertical proximity" effect (also called an "adjacency effect"). This effect occurs when candidates that are next to a prominent candidate on the ballot (e.g., George Schwartzman, who was next to Arnold Schwarzenegger) receive a statistically higher number of votes than would otherwise be expected. The impact of the vertical proximity effect is dramatic because it takes votes away from one candidate and gives the vote to another, typically less prominent, candidate. In 2003, vertical proximity effects were statistically greater in California counties that used punch cards.

Finally, there are usability studies examining specific voting technologies. For example, Roth (1998) found that mechanical voting machines are difficult for many voters to use. To appreciate the usability problems of lever machines, especially "full-face" voting machines that present the entire ballot to the voter, it is helpful to remember that these full-face machines can be the size of a large refrigerator. The size of these mechanical voting machines means that voters with physical handicaps or visual impairments have problems using these machines and that individuals who are shorter than the voting machine may have significant difficulties.[10]

Recently, Herrnson et al. (2008a) studied the usability of a number of DRE machines and produced results that point to a number of ways in which their usability can be improved. Specifically, they found that voters have different experiences based on the specific brand of voting equipment that they use.

---

[10] Susan King Roth examined the usability of these machines in depth and found that being short or having physical dexterity issues resulted in many voting errors. See Roth (1998).

Although voters can typically navigate the voting machines used today without problem, they do find certain features difficult or annoying. Voters also evaluate various voting machines differently in regards to ease of use, comfort, overall satisfaction, and ability to correct mistakes. There are also features, like write-in voting, that caused more difficulties with certain types of voting equipment. Herrnson et al. (2008b) also found important differences in the experiences that voters had using standard office-block ballot designs and straight-party voting designs. The straight-party feature caused more problems for voters than did the standard office block.

The seminal work on the usability pathologies in voting technologies is Saltman's 1988 study of computerized vote-tallying systems that noted a series of "vulnerabilities" of the Votomatic and Datavote punch-card systems that presaged the events in November 2000 in Florida. When he considered the Votomatic system, which has pre-scored punch cards, Saltman identified several problems, including a lack of candidate information on the punch card, the need to turn all of the pages in the vote recorder, the issue of having to align the ballot correctly in the voting machine, and the possible malicious alteration of the instructions. When he considered the Datavote system, Saltman identified several vulnerabilities, including the possible need for the voter to cast votes on multiple voting cards and the difficulties on the part of the local election officials in tracking and processing multiple cards for a single voter. Reading Saltman's work, it is clear that the problems associated with punch-card voting systems had been well documented and were well known within the election community long before the 2000 election.

CONVENIENCE VOTING AND NEW TECHNOLOGIES

Political scientists have long recognized that the act of voting is costly, and that as the benefits of voting may be slight, voter turnout should be slight in many situations (Downs 1957; Riker and Ordeshook 1968). Research in the United States has typically focused on one of the most significant costs associated with voting: becoming and staying a registered voter (e.g., Nagler 1991; Rosenstone and Wolfinger 1978; Wolfinger and Rosenstone 1980). Although reforms in the United States have made the voter registration process easier, many states and localities have tried to make the act of voting easier and more convenient. These reforms include the liberalization of voting by mail procedures (Hamner and Traugott 2004; Karp and Banducci 2000; Oliver 1996), the development of so-called "voting centers" (Stein and Vonnahme 2008), early voting (Stein 1998), and other initiatives that seek to make the act of voting easier for certain populations that find the current process costly (Alvarez, Hall, and Roberts 2007). However, many of these efforts have merely made it easier for traditional voters to vote and appear not to have made voting easier for the disenfranchised (Berinsky 2005).

One frequently discussed but controversial convenience voting approach is remote internet voting (Alvarez and Hall 2004). Originally widely discussed during the dot.com revolution and widely debated in the post-2000 Florida environment, remote internet voting has seen only limited deployment in the United States. These limited deployments focus on primary elections or overseas voters (Alvarez and Hall 2004, 2008; Alvarez and Nagler 2001; Prevost and Schaffner 2008). The use of remote internet voting has been explored outside the United States, including a series of field trials in the United Kingdom, use in a number of Swiss cantons, and use in Estonia. In general, Internet voting has had similar effects to those of enhanced absentee voting: the results tend to increase voting among those who are already likely to vote (Alvarez and Hall 2004, 2008; Trechsel and Mendez 2005). However, because Estonia is the only nation to have conducted repeated internet voting elections where all voters were eligible to vote online, it is too early to say what the impact of this technology will be on turnout and participation. Data from the 2007 Estonian election showed that internet voting did grow in use from its first use in 2005 and is especially popular among younger voters. The internet voters also participate in politics differently compared to the traditional polling place voters (Trechsel et al. 2007).

VOTING TECHNOLOGY AND ELECTION OUTCOMES

Research has recently looked at how different voting technologies, especially DREs, might advantage certain parties or candidates and influence the outcomes of elections. A critical issue is whether some voting technologies are more prone to manipulation and election fraud (Moretti and Card 2007; Herron and Wand 2007; Stewart 2006). For example, recent work examined the race for Florida's 13th congressional district in 2006 and the various voting technologies used in that election, how those ballots were formatted and displayed for voters, and whether the technologies used influenced the casting of ballots (e.g., Frisina et al. 2008). Others have considered whether the adoption of different voting technologies might affect votes (e.g., Moretti and Card 2007).

Although this research is relatively recent, it is clear that voting technologies might influence election outcomes. Research in this area is complicated by the fact that state laws differ dramatically in what ballot designs they allow, voting systems differ regarding how information is presented to voters, and how voters can correct mistakes (2008b). If specific characteristics of voting technologies interact with the odds that certain segments of the electorate make mistakes, and these segments of the electorate are likely to have common partisan, ideological, or other interests, then voting technologies may affect election outcomes in less direct ways (Alvarez, Hall, and Llewellyn 2008b; Sinclair and Alvarez 2004; Tomz and Van Houweling, 2003). Similar to the research discussed earlier on usability, differences in how information is displayed to voters might affect the cues that voters use to find and select their choices (Herron, Mebane, and Wand 2008; Katz et al. 2008). Such problems might be especially pronounced in multi-party elections, which may place greater informational burdens on voters (Katz et al. 2008; Reynolds and Steenbergen 2006).

Much of the evidence to date for how voting technologies affect election outcomes is conflicting and inconclusive (Moretti and Card 2007; Frisina et al. 2008; Herron, Mebane, and Wand 2008; Herron and Wand 2007; Katz et al. 2008). Most studies have focused on the American case (thus ignoring the potentially greater problems that might arise in multi-party settings) and have relied upon observational data. We see great promise in laboratory studies and on field experiments in non-American situations (e.g., Katz et al. 2008), as ways to study how voting technologies might affect election outcomes.

CONCLUSION: IMPROVING THE STUDY OF VOTING TECHNOLOGY

The study of voting technologies and their effects on political behavior and election outcomes is still in the early stages of becoming a new subfield—and perhaps it is on the verge of becoming a new multidisciplinary academic endeavor (Alvarez and Antonsson 2007). Much as the study of political behavior has benefited from interdisciplinary work conducted by economists, psychologists, sociologists, and political scientists, the study of voting technology also benefits from interdisciplinary work by political scientists, management scholars, engineers, computer scientists, and psychologists. Research prior to 2000 provided some foundations for the new study of voting technologies, and social scientists have quickly moved to apply existing theories to many of the new research questions that have arisen since that important presidential election. This type of collaborative research has the benefit of pushing the research agenda to include questions where the dependent variable is not just turnout or vote choice. Questions of efficiency and equity are also important to the administrators who run elections and the legislators who establish the legal framework in which decisions about voting technologies and ballot rules are made.

One pressing issue is for the research community to work with election officials to obtain better observational data on election administration and election outcomes, to get that data measured at the lowest possible level of aggregation, and to get access to that data in a timely manner (within days after an election). The poor quality of observational data on election administration was noted early on by the Caltech/MIT Voting Technology Project in their 2001 study and was reinforced in a research article on data quality from three of the principals in the VTP (Alvarez, Ansolabehere, and Stewart 2005). At the time that we write this chapter, the US Election Assistance Commission is engaged in a variety of efforts to facilitate the provision of high-quality data from low levels of aggregation in the United States, and other entities involved in the study of election administration have embarked on similar projects.

Hand-in-hand with access to better observational data is the need for the development and use of better methods for studying this data. One concern is that many of the institutional or policy-driven "treatments" in observational data are not randomly assigned and inferences drawn from the analysis of such data might be incorrect unless efforts are undertaken to transform the observational data into a form that better replicates a randomized experiment (e.g., Morgan and Winship 2007; Rosenbaum 2002). Some of the most recent research on voting technologies has recognized these potential issues, for example, in the study of ballot design effects (Ho and Imai 2008; Sinclair 2006) and the effect of voting technology on residual votes (e.g., Bailey 2007; Sekhon 2004). Scholars also need to be cognizant of the natural experiments that occur when legal or technological changes occur and should use these opportunities to gain leverage on key research questions. Better exposition of the use of these techniques for the study of observational data in the election administration setting is needed.

The use of new techniques for studying observational data, however, should not be seen as a substitute for the use of actual randomized laboratory or field experiments. There has been an explosion of interest in the social sciences in the development and use of laboratory experiments (e.g., Morton 1999) and randomized field experiments (e.g., Gerber and Green 2000; also see Davenport, Gerber, and Green, this volume, Chapter 5). There have been few attempts to use randomized experiments to study many of the questions we have discussed earlier in this chapter but those attempts have generated some intriguing and important results (e.g., Katz et al. 2008). Working in collaboration with election officials, researchers need to seek out additional opportunities to implement randomized field experiments that can help answer many of the remaining questions regarding how voting technology affects political behavior and election outcomes.

Researchers also need to exploit the variance that exists in both space and time. Cross-sectional and time-series studies of how voting technology affects political behavior have yielded important results in our understanding of residual votes (Ansolabehere 2002; Bailey 2007) but the analytic importance of taking advantage of the variance that exists in technologies, procedures, and behavioral outcomes across space and time has not been exploited as well as it can be. In particular, there has been little research on voting technology in multi-party and multi-candidate settings (Katz et al. 2008). One key research agenda scholars should pursue is to examine many of the key research questions we have identified previously—including voter trust in the voting system, residual vote rates, election auditing, and usability—and apply them to multi-party and multi-candidate elections in other nations. In addition, scholars should study emerging voting technologies, such as internet voting and mobile phone "M-voting," that are emerging in Europe. These new technologies raise questions that are directly analogous to the debate currently ongoing regarding electronic voting in the United States.

Finally, researchers need to focus on heterogeneity. For example, in the American setting, issues associated with equal protection and other federal and state laws mean that it is important to study the behavior of subpopulations of the electorate such as racial and linguistic minorities and those with disabilities. Observational and experimental studies in the American context need to study the complex interactions between voting technology, political behavior, and many of the descriptive characteristics of voters. Other important variables to consider are familiarity and use of computers and other forms of technology, gender, education, and socioeconomic status.

REFERENCES

ALLEN, P. L. 1906. Ballot Laws and Their Workings. *Political Science Quarterly*, 21/1: 38–58.

ALVAREZ, R. M., ANSOLABEHERE, S., and STEWART III, C. 2005. Studying Elections: Data Quality and Pitfalls in Measuring of Effects of Voting Technologies. *Policy Studies Journal*, 15–24.

—— and ANTONSSON, E. K. 2007. Bridging Science, Technology and Politics in Election Systems. *The Bridge*, 37/2: 6–10.

—— and HALL, T. E. 2008. *Electronic Elections: The Perils and Promises of Digital Democracy*. Princeton, N.J.: Princeton University Press.

—— —— 2004. *Point, Click and Vote: The Future of Internet Voting*. Washington, D.C.: Brookings Institution Press.

—— —— and HYDE, S. D. (eds.) 2008. *Election Fraud: Detecting and Deterring Electoral Manipulation*. Washington, D.C.: Brookings Institution Press.

—— —— and LLEWELLYN, M. 2007. On American Voter Confidence. *University of Arkansas at Little Rock Law Review*.

—— —— —— 2008a. Are Americans Confident Their Ballots Are Counted? *Journal of Politics*, 70/3: 754–66.

—— —— —— 2008b. The Winner's Effect: Voter Confidence Before and After the 2006 Elections. Unpublished manuscript, Caltech.

—— —— and ROBERTS, B. 2007. Military Voting and the Law: Procedural and Technological Solutions to the Ballot Transit Problem. *Fordham Urban Law Review*, 34/3: 935–96.

ALVAREZ, R. M., HASEN, R., and SINCLAIR, B. 2006. How Much is Enough? The Ballot
Order Effect and the Use of Social Science Research in Election Law Disputes. *Election
Law Journal*, 5/1: 40–56

—— and KATZ, J. N. 2008. The Case of the 2002 General Election. In *Election
Fraud: Detecting and Deterring Electoral Manipulation*, ed. R. M. Alvarez, T. E. Hall,
and S. D. Hyde. Washington, D.C.: Brookings Institution Press.

—— —— and HILL, S. A. 2005. Machines Versus Humans: The Counting and Recounting
of Pre-Scored Punchcard Ballots. Caltech/MIT Voting Technology Project Working
Paper.

—— and NAGLER, J. 2001. *Loyola of Los Angeles Law Review*, 34/3: 1115–53.

—— SINCLAIR, D. E. B., and WILSON, C. 2004. Counting Ballots and the 2000 Election:
What Went Wrong? In *Rethinking the Vote*, ed. A. Crigler et al. New York: Oxford
University Press.

—— GOODRICH, M., HALL, T. E., KIEWIET, D.R., and SLED, S. M. 2004. The Complexity of
the California Recall Election. *PS: Political Science and Politics*, 37/1: 23–6.

ANSOLABEHERE, S. 2002. Voting Machines, Race and Equal Protection. *Election Law
Journal*, 1/1: 61–70.

—— and REEVES, A. 2004. Using Recounts to Measure the Accuracy of Vote Tabulations:
Evidence from New Hampshire Elections, 1946–2002. Caltech/MIT Voting Technology
Project Working Paper.

—— and STEWART III, C.. 2005. Residual Votes Attributable to Technology. *Journal of
Politics*, 67/2: 365–89.

ATKESON, L. R. and SAUNDERS, K. L. 2007. The Effect of Election Administration on Voter
Confidence: A Local Matter. *P.S: Political Science and Politics*, 40: 655–60.

BAILEY, D. R. G. 2007. Essays on Causal Inference and Political Representation. Ph.D.
Thesis, California Institute of Technology.

BAIN, H. M., JR. and HECOCK, D. S. 1957. *Ballot Position and Voter's Choice*. Detroit: Wayne
University Press.

BEARD, C. A. 1909. The Ballot's Burden. *Political Science Quarterly*, 24/4: 589–614.

BENSEL, R. F. 2004. *The American Ballot Box in the Mid-Nineteenth Century*. New York:
Cambridge University Press.

BERINSKY, A. 2005. The Perverse Consequences of Electoral Reform in the United States.
American Politics Research, 33/3: 471–91.

BRADY, H. E., BUCHLER, J., JARVIS, M., and McNULTY, J. 2001. Counting All the Votes: The
Performance of Voting Technology in the United States. Unpublished manuscript,
University of California, Berkeley.

BUCHLER, J., JARVIS, M., and McNULTY, J. 2004. Punch Card Technology and the Racial
Gap in Residual Votes. *Perspectives on Politics*, 2: 517–24.

BULLOCK III, C. S. and DUNN, R. E. 1996. Election Roll-Off: A Test of Three Explanations.
Urban Affairs Review, 32/1: 71–86.

—— and HOOD III, M. V. 2002. One Person—No Vote; One Vote; Two Votes: Voting
Methods, Ballot Types, and Undervote Frequency in the 2000 Presidential Election. *Social
Science Quarterly*, 83/4: 981–93.

CALTECH/MIT VOTING TECHNOLOGY PROJECT 2001. *Voting: What Is, What Could Be.*

DARCY, R. and SCHNEIDER, A. 1989. Confusing Ballots, Roll-Off, and the Black Vote. *Western Political Quarterly*, 42/3: 347–64.

DOWNS, A. 1957. *An Economic Theory of Democracy*. New York: Harper & Brothers.

FRASER, J. L. 1985. The Effects of Voting Systems on Voter Participation: Punch Card Voting Systems in Ohio. Ph.D. Dissertation, Ohio State University.

FRISINA, L., HERRON, M. C., HONAKER, J., and LEWIS, J. B. 2008. Ballot Formats, Touchscreens, and Undervotes: A Study of the 2006 Midterm Elections in Florida. *Election Law Journal*, 7/1: 25–47.

GERBER, A. S. and GREEN, D. P. 2000. The Effects of Canvassing, Telephone Calls, and Direct Mail on Voter Turnout: A Field Experiment. *American Political Science Review*, 94/3: 653–63.

GOODRICH, M. 2004. 19th Century Ballot Reform in California: A Study of the Huntington Library's Political Ephemera Collection. Caltech/MIT Voting Technology Project Working Paper.

GRIGG, D. 2005. Measuring the Effect of Voting Technology on Residual Votes. California Institute of Technology Working Paper.

HAMNER, M. J. and TRAUGOTT, M. W. 2004. The Impact of Voting by Mail on Voter Behavior. *American Politics Research*, 32/4: 375–405.

HANSEN, B. E. 2003. Recounts from Undervotes: Evidence from the 2000 Presidential Election. *Journal of the American Statistical Association*, 98/462: 292–8.

HARRIS, J. P. 1934. *Election Administration in the United States*. Washington, D.C.: The Brookings Institution.

HERRNSON, P. S., NIEMI, R. G., HAMNER, M. J., FRANCIA, P. L., BEDERSON, B. B., CONRAD, F. G., and TRAUGOTT, M. W. 2008a. Voters' Evaluations of Electronic Voting Systems. *American Politics Research*, 36/4: 580–611.

———— ———— BEDERSON, B. B., CONRAD, F. G., and TRAUGOTT, M. W. 2008b. *Voting Technology: The Not-So-Simple Task of Casting a Ballot*. Washington, D.C.: Brookings Institution Press.

HERRON, M. and LEWIS, J. B. 2006. From Punchcards to Touchscreens: Some Evidence from Pasco County, Florida on the Effects of Changing Voting Technology. Dartmouth University Working Paper.

—— MEBANE, W. R., JR., and WAND, J. N. 2008. Voting Technology and the 2008 New Hampshire Primary. Working Paper, University of Michigan.

—— and SEKHON, J. 2003. Overvoting and Representation: An Examination of Overvoted Presidential Ballots in Broward and Miami-Dade Counties. *Electoral Studies*, 22/1: 21–47.

—— and WAND, J. 2007. Assessing Partisan Bias in Voting Technology: The Case of the 2004 New Hampshire Recount. *Electoral Studies*, 26/2: 247–61.

HO, D. E. and IMAI, K. 2008. The Impact of Partisan Electoral Regulation: Ballot Effects from the California Alphabet Lottery, 1978–2002. *Public Opinion Quarterly*.

HYDE, S. D. 2008. How International Election Observers Detect and Deter Fraud. In *Election Fraud: Detecting and Deterring Electoral Manipulation*, ed. R. M. Alvarez, T. E. Hall, and S. D. Hyde. Washington, D.C.: Brookings Institution Press.

KARP, J. A. and BANDUCCI, S. A. 2000. Going Postal: How All-Mail Elections Influence Turnout. *Political Behavior*, 22/3: 223–39.

KEYSSAR, A. 2000. *The Right to Vote: The Contested History of Democracy in the United States*. New York: Basic Books.

KIMBALL, D. C. and KROPF, M. 2005. Ballot Design and Unrecorded Votes on Paper-Based Ballots. *Public Opinion Quarterly*, 69/4: 508–29.

—— —— 2008. Voting Technology, Ballot Measures, and Residual Votes. *American Politics Research*, 36/4: 479–509.

KNACK, S. and KROPF, M. 2003. Invalidated Ballots in the 1996 Presidential Election: A County-Lever Analysis. *Journal of Politics*, 65/3: 881–97.

KOPPELL, J. and STEEN, J. A. 2004. The Effects of Ballot Positions on Election Outcomes. *Journal of Politics*, 66/1: 267–81.

LEHOUCQ, F. 2003. Election Fraud: Causes, Types, and Consequences. *Annual Review of Political Science*, 6: 233–56.

LUDINGTON, A. 1911. Short Ballot Movement. *American Political Science Review*, 5/1: 79–83.

MATHER, G. B. 1964. Effects of the Use of Voting Machines on Total Votes Cast: Iowa—1920–1960. Institute of Public Affairs: University of Iowa, Iowa City.

—— 1986. Lost Votes: Effects of Methods of Voting on Voter Participation, Iowa, 1920–1984. Institute of Public Affairs, Division of Continuing Education: University of Iowa, Iowa City.

McDONALD, M. P. 2007. The True Electorate: A Cross-Validation of Voter Registration Files and Election Survey Demographics. *Public Opinion Quarterly*, 71/4: 588–602.

MEBANE, W. R., Jr. 2008. Election Forensics: The Second-Digit Benford's Law Test and Recent American Presidential Elections. In *Election Fraud: Detecting and Deterring Electoral Manipulation*, ed. R. M. Alvarez, T. E. Hall, and S. D. Hyde. Washington, D.C.: Brookings Institution Press.

MERRIAM, C. E. and OVERACKER, L. 1928. *Primary Elections*. Chicago: University of Chicago Press.

MILLER, J. E. and KROSNICK, J. A. 1998. The Impact of Candidate Name Order on Election Outcomes. *Public Opinion Quarterly*, 51/2: 201–19.

MONTGOMERY, M. J. 1985. Voting Systems and Disenfranchisement. *Election Politics*, 2: 16–19.

MORETTI, E. and CARD, D. 2007. Does Voting Technology Affect Election Outcomes? Touch-screen Voting and the 2004 Presidential Election. *The Review of Economics and Statistics*, 89/4: 660–73.

MORGAN, S. L. and WINSHIP, C. 2007. *Counterfactuals and Causal Inference: Methods and Principles for Social Research*. Cambridge: Cambridge University Press.

MORTON, R. B. 1999. *Methods and Models: A Guide to the Empirical Analysis of Formal Models in Political Science*. New York: Cambridge University Press.

MYAGKOV, M., ORDESHOOK, P. C., and SHAIKIN, D. 2008. On the Trail of Fraud: Estimating the Flow of Votes between Russia's Elections. In *Election Fraud: Detecting and Deterring Electoral Manipulation*, ed. R. M. Alvarez, T. E. Hall, and S. D. Hyde. Washington, D.C.: Brookings Institution Press.

NAGLER, J. 1991. The Effect of Registration Laws and Education on US Voter Turnout. *American Political Science Review*, 85/4: 1393–405.

NICHOLS, S. M. and STRIZEK, G. A. 1995. Electronic Voting Machines and Ballot Roll-Off. *American Politics Quarterly*, 23/3: 300–18.

NEIMI, R. G. and HERRNSON, P. S. 2003. Beyond the Butterfly: The Complexity of U.S. Ballots. *Perspectives on Politics*, 1/2: 317–26.

OLIVER, J. E. 1996. Who Votes at Home? The Influence of State Law and Party Activity on Absentee Voting and Overall Turnout. *American Journal of Political Science*, 40/2: 498–513.

PREVOST, A. K. and SCHAFFNER, B. F. 2008. Digital Divide or Just Another Absentee Ballot? *American Politics Research*, 36/4: 510–29.

REYNOLDS, A. and STEENBERGEN, M. 2006. How the World Votes: The Political Consequences of Ballot Design, Innovation and Manipulation. *Electoral Studies*, 25: 570–98.

RIKER, W. and ORDESHOOK, P. C. 1968. A Theory of the Calculus of Voting. *American Political Science Review*, 62 (March): 25–42.

ROSENBAUM, P. R. 2002. *Observational Studies*, 2nd edn. New York: Springer.

ROSENSTONE, S. J. and WOLFINGER, R. E. 1978. The Effects of Registration Laws on Voter Turnout. *American Political Science Review*, 72/1: 22–45.

ROTH, S. K. 1998. Disenfranchised by Design: Voting Systems and the Election Process. *Information Design Journal*, 9/1: 1–8.

RUSK, J. G. 1970. The Effect of the Australian Ballot Reform on Split Ticket Voting: 1876–1908. *American Political Science Review*, 64/4: 1220–38.

SALTMAN, R. 1988. Accuracy, Integrity, and Security in Computerized Vote-Tallying. NBS Special Publication 500–158, Institute for Computer Sciences and Technology, National Bureau of Standards.

—— 2006. *The History and Politics of Voting Technology*. New York: Palgrave MacMillan.

SEKHON, J. S. 2004. The 2004 Florida Optical Voting Machine Controversy: A Causal Analysis Using Matching. Unpublished manuscript.

SLED, S. 2003. Vertical Proximity Effects in the California Recall Election. Caltech/MIT Voting Technology Project Working Paper, Pasadena, Calif.

STEIN, R. 1998. Early Voting. *Public Opinion Quarterly*, 62/1: 57–70.

SIMPSER, A. Unintended Consequences of Election Monitoring. In *Election Fraud: Detecting and Deterring Electoral Manipulation*, ed. R. M. Alvarez, T. E. Hall, and S. D. Hyde. Washington, D.C.: Brookings Institution Press.

SINCLAIR, B. 2006. Matching and the Multi-valued Treatment Problem: An Application to the Estimation of the Ballot Order Effect. Unpublished manuscript, University of Chicago.

SINCLAIR, D. E. "Betsy" and ALVAREZ, R. M. 2004. Who Overvotes, Who Undervotes, Using Punch cards? Evidence from Los Angeles County. *Political Research Quarterly*, 57/1: 15–26.

STEIN, R. and VONNAHME, G. 2008. Engaging the Unengaged Voter: Vote Centers and Voter Turnout. *Journal of Politics*, 70: 487–97.

STEWART III, C. 2006. Changes in the Residual Vote Rates Between 2000 and 2004. *Election Law Journal*, 5/2: 158–69.

THOMAS, N. C. 1968. Voting Machines and Voter Participation in Four Michigan Constitutional Revision Referenda. *Western Political Quarterly*, 21/3: 409–19.

TOMZ, M. and VAN HOUWELING, R. 2003. How Does Voting Equipment Affect the Racial Gap in Voided Ballots. *American Journal of Political Science*, 47/1: 46–60.

TRECHSEL, A. H. and MENDEZ, F. (eds.) 2005. *The European Union and E-voting: Addressing the European Parliament's Internet Voting Challenge*. London: Routledge.

—— SCHWERDT, G., BREUER, F., ALVAREZ, M., and HALL, T. 2007. Report for the Council of Europe, Internet Voting in the March 2007 Parliamentary Elections in Estonia. Strasbourg: Council of Europe.

WALKER, J. L. 1966. Ballot Forms and Voter Fatigue: An Analysis of the Office Block and Party Column Ballots. *Midwest Journal of Political Science*, 10/4: 448–63.

WHITE, J. P. 1960. Voting Machines and the 1958 Defeat of Constitutional Revision in Michigan. Institute of Public Administration at the University of Michigan, Papers in Public Administration, No. 35.

WOLFINGER, R. and ROSENSTONE, S. 1980. *Who Votes?* New Haven, Conn.: Yale University Press.

PART IV

....

VOTE CHOICE

....

CHAPTER 14

....

THE STUDY OF ELECTORAL BEHAVIOR

....

LARRY M. BARTELS

THE scholarly study of electoral behavior has a long and vibrant history. My aim here is to provide a selective summary of that history, focusing on developments that seem to me to have been especially important in shaping the current contours of the field. Since new preoccupations and insights have usually emerged as responses to salient past successes and failures, the organization of my survey is largely (though not entirely) chronological.

I have, of course, ignored many important contributions and elided many relevant details. That is inevitable, given limitations of space and of my own expertise.[1] Fortunately, much of what is missing here is handsomely addressed in other chapters of this volume. In any event, my hope is that the range of scholarship touched upon in the following pages will provide some sense of the richness and significance of what has been accomplished by scholars of electoral behavior over the past seventy years, while also inspiring the scholars who chart the mainstream of electoral research in the future to tackle some of the many fundamental issues that remain unresolved.

[1] A longer version of this chapter is posted at <http://www.princeton.edu/~bartels/electoralbehavior.pdf>. I am grateful to Christopher Achen, Tali Mendelberg, and Lynn Vavreck for helpful comments and discussion.

THE COLUMBIA STUDIES

The modern history of academic voting research began in 1940 at Columbia University, where a team of social scientists assembled by Paul Lazarsfeld pioneered the application of survey research to the study of electoral behavior. As occasionally happens with major innovations, this pioneering effort seems even in the light of subsequent advances to have been remarkably sophisticated. Lazarsfeld and his colleagues surveyed 600 prospective voters in a single community (Erie County, Ohio) as many as seven times over the course of the 1940 presidential campaign, mixing new and repeated questions in each successive interview, and adding fresh cross-sections to serve as baselines for assessing the effects of repeated interviewing on the respondents in the main panel.

The results of the 1940 Columbia study were published in *The People's Choice: How the Voter Makes Up His Mind in a Presidential Campaign* (Lazarsfeld, Berelson, and Gaudet 1944). A second panel study conducted by the Columbia team in Elmira, New York, in 1948 provided the basis for an even more influential book, *Voting: A Study of Opinion Formation in a Presidential Campaign* (Berelson, Lazarsfeld, and Mcphee 1954). Together, these two volumes defined a set of questions and research methods that have had a variety of profound effects on subsequent work in the field.

Lazarsfeld's panel studies were carefully designed to measure changes in individual vote intentions over the course of a presidential campaign. This focus reflects the intellectual roots of the project in market research on consumer behavior and wartime analyses of the effects of propaganda. Indeed, Lazarsfeld seems all along to have viewed "the psychology of choice" as his real subject matter, and turned to the study of presidential campaigns only when foundation support was not forthcoming for a panel analysis of consumer behavior (Rossi 1959, 15–16).

Given their interests and study design, the Columbia researchers must have been surprised by what they found. Their careful measurement of media content turned out to be of little use in accounting for voters' choices, most of which seemed to be based upon strong "brand loyalties" rooted in religion and social class and reinforced by face-to-face interactions with like-minded acquaintances. Their lavish panel design revealed a good deal of reinforcement of preexisting political predispositions, but rather little outright conversion. Thus, by the time of their 1948 study, Lazarsfeld and his colleagues were downplaying the role of the parties and the mass media and elaborating their analysis of interpersonal influence by measuring respondents' perceptions of the political views of their families, friends, and co-workers, emphasizing the homogeneity of these social networks and their tendency to produce increasing political conformity over the course of the campaign.

To their credit, the Columbia researchers did not cling to their preconceptions about the nature of electoral choice. Rather, they concluded (Berelson et al. 1954, 310–11) that

the usual analogy between the voting "decision" and the more or less carefully calculated decisions of consumers or businessmen or courts... may be quite incorrect. For many voters political preferences may better be considered analogous to cultural tastes—in music, literature, recreational activities, dress, ethics, speech, social behavior.... Both have their origin in ethnic, sectional, class, and family traditions. Both exhibit stability and resistance to change for individuals but flexibility and adjustment over generations for the society as a whole. Both seem to be matters of sentiment and disposition rather than "reasoned preferences." While both are responsive to changed conditions and unusual stimuli, they are relatively invulnerable to direct argumentation and vulnerable to indirect social influences. Both are characterized more by faith than by conviction and by wishful expectation rather than careful prediction of consequences.

Thus, a team led by one of the great sociologists of his era succeeded, almost despite themselves, in producing a classic study of the sociology of electoral behavior.

If *Voting* was a richer work of *sociology* than *The People's Choice*, it was also noticeably richer in its specifically *political* aspects. Lazarsfeld and his colleagues focused more attention on the role of political issues, stressing the frequency with which respondents ignored or misperceived their favorite candidates' issue stands when these were in conflict with the respondents' own views. They also demonstrated in considerable detail the extent to which Truman's late surge represented the "reactivation" of latent Democratic loyalties as the salience of traditional class issues came to the fore over the course of the fall campaign. Finally, a concluding chapter by Berelson on "Democratic Practice and Democratic Theory" provided a much-noted—and vigorously criticized—interpretation of the implications of the authors' findings for political theory.[2] Perhaps not surprisingly, these specifically political aspects of the Columbia studies are the ones that have turned out to have the most influence on subsequent voting research.

---

[2] According to Berelson, the Elmira data revealed that campaigns involve "little true discussion" and "more talk than debate," that "for large numbers of people motivation is weak if not almost absent," and that "the voter falls short" of the democratic expectation that he "be well informed about political affairs" (Berelson et al. 1954, 308). "If the democratic system depended solely on the qualifications of the individual voter," he concluded (311), "then it seems remarkable that democracies have survived through the centuries." But in fact, he argued (and this is the point that has been most vociferously challenged by democratic theorists) that "Lack of interest by some people is not without its benefits.... The apathetic segment of America probably has helped to hold the system together and cushioned the shock of disagreement, adjustment, and change" (314, 322).

THE "MICHIGAN MODEL"

The work of Lazarsfeld and his Columbia colleagues demonstrated the rich potential of election surveys as data for understanding campaigns and elections. The next, and even more important, advance in election studies emerged in the following decade at the University of Michigan.

Like their counterparts at Columbia, the Michigan scholars did not set out to study electoral politics. Angus Campbell and Robert Kahn conducted a national survey of foreign policy attitudes in October 1948, and "at the end of these interviews, in order to determine the degree of political interest of the respondents and their general political orientations," they asked respondents whether and how they planned to vote in the upcoming presidential election. After the election— and stimulated by the much-publicized failure of the Gallup Poll to foretell Harry Truman's come-from-behind victory—they reinterviewed the same respondents in order to "analyze the crystallization of the vote," to "record the personal, attitudinal, and demographic characteristics of voters and non-voters, Republicans and Democrats," and to "assess the influence of various psychological, sociological, and political factors on the determination of the vote" (Campbell and Kahn 1952, 3). They could hardly have imagined that this would be the beginning of one of the longest-running research projects in the history of academic social science.

Over the course of the subsequent decade the Michigan election studies became increasingly institutionalized, with national surveys conducted in 1952, 1954, 1956, and 1958 and analyzed by a growing interdisciplinary team, including three young scholars who would turn out to be the central figures in the Michigan school—Warren Miller, Philip Converse, and Donald Stokes. Together, they would make the great leap forward, intellectually and organizationally, that produced the most important landmark in the whole canon of electoral research, *The American Voter* (Campbell et al. 1960).

The primary data for *The American Voter* came from Michigan surveys conducted in connection with the 1952 and 1956 presidential elections. These surveys followed the same basic design that had been improvised in 1948, with respondents interviewed during the fall campaign and then reinterviewed after the election. Unlike the earlier Columbia studies, the Michigan election studies were based upon national survey samples. Thus, they were well suited not only to develop and test theories of voting behavior, but also to provide an historical record of the considerations shaping the outcomes of specific national elections.

Theory and historical description were brilliantly meshed in the most striking finding of *The American Voter*—that Eisenhower's landslide victories did little to disturb the long-standing loyalties of a plurality of American voters to the Democratic Party. This finding emphasized the political significance of the authors' fundamental distinction between long-term and short-term forces. On one hand,

"Few factors are of greater importance for our national elections than the lasting attachments of tens of millions of Americans to one of the parties. These loyalties establish a basic division of electoral strength within which the competition of particular campaigns takes place" (Campbell et al. 1960, 121). On the other hand, "it is *not* true that attitudes toward the several elements of politics are only reflections of party loyalty or group memberships or of other factors that may lead to perceptual distortion.... attitudes toward the objects of politics, varying through time, can explain short-term fluctuations in partisan division of the vote, whereas party loyalties and social characteristics, which are relatively inert through time, account but poorly for these shifts" (Campbell et al. 1960, 65).

By building their account upon an analysis of political *attitudes* of greater or lesser durability, the authors of *The American Voter* clearly hoped to provide an explanatory framework capable of encompassing both impressive partisan stability and shifting election outcomes, including "deviating" elections like those that swept Eisenhower into office. Thus, while acknowledging the important sense in which the political landscape of the 1950s reflected the impact of partisan loyalties traceable to the New Deal or even the Civil War era, they also focused close attention on the short-term variations in perceptions and concerns that differentiated the electorates of 1952 and 1956. For example, they noted the relative paucity and partisan balance of references to prosperity and depression in 1956 by comparison with 1952, and the significant increase in unfavorable personal references to the Democratic candidate, Adlai Stevenson (Campbell et al. 1960, 46, 55). Their systematic weighing of six distinct "attitudinal forces" on the outcome of each election (attitudes toward Stevenson, Eisenhower, relevant social groups, the parties as managers of government, domestic issues, and foreign policy) emphasized the "paramount importance" of Eisenhower's popular appeal in accounting for his landslide victory in 1956 (Campbell et al. 1960, 524–8).

In light of subsequent misreadings, it seems worth emphasizing that the partisan loyalties of *The American Voter* were portrayed as relatively stable, but by no means unchanging: "When we examine the evidence on the manner in which party attachment develops and changes during the lifetime of the individual citizen, we find a picture characterized more by stability than by change—not by rigid, immutable fixation on one party rather than the other, but by a persistent adherence and a resistance to contrary influence" (Campbell et al. 1960, 146). This pattern of "persistent adherence" and "resistance to contrary influence," inferred on the basis of retrospective reports in the cross-sectional surveys of the 1950s, has been handsomely confirmed in subsequent studies based upon more direct measurement in repeated interviews with the same individuals over periods of several years (Converse and Markus 1979; Green, Palmquist, and Schickler 2002) and cross-generational comparisons of parents and their children (Jennings and Niemi 1981).

The other major contribution of *The American Voter* was to reiterate and elaborate the finding of the Columbia studies that political information, engagement, and ideological reasoning were far less widespread in the public than most political commentators seemed to imagine. The Michigan data suggested that "many people know the existence of few if any of the major issues of policy," and that "major shifts of electoral strength reflect the changing association of parties and candidates with general societal goals rather than the detail of legislative or administrative action" (Campbell et al. 1960, 170, 546).

The American Voter portrayed an electorate whose orientations toward politics were strongly influenced by partisan loyalties developed early in life, whose votes in specific elections reflected the overlaying of short-term forces such as Eisenhower's personal popularity upon these long-term influences, and whose familiarity with and attachment to abstract ideologies and policy agendas was remarkably limited. In the subsequent half century, every major element of this portrait has been subjected to energetic criticism and painstaking reevaluation using new data, theories, and research methods. In my view, at least, none of the scores and hundreds of resulting scholarly books and articles has succeeded in making a significant dent in the central findings of what has come to be called the "Michigan model" of electoral studies. While elaborations and modifications in detail have been plentiful and productive, more ambitious revisionists have invariably turned out either to be attacking a caricature of the original argument, or to be even more time-bound in their perspectives than the original authors acknowledged themselves to be, or to be simply wrong about the facts. By the standards of empirical social science, *The American Voter* has been a work of remarkable influence and staying power.

A CHANGING AMERICAN VOTER?

The American Voter was the acknowledged foundation for the entire field of voting research in the decade following its publication. Scholars of voting behavior increasingly relied on the Michigan data and methods, and many of them made pilgrimages to Ann Arbor to learn from the masters, either as graduate students or in summer classes and workshops. Meanwhile, the subsequent statements of the Michigan team (Butler and Stokes 1969; Campbell et al. 1966; Converse 1964) became important scholarly works in their own right, continuing to shape the burgeoning field.

Outside the ivory tower, however, history was afoot in America. The civil rights movement, urban unrest, and war in Vietnam seemed to be superseding the issues of the New Deal era, precipitating a collapse of the rather staid and stable electoral system portrayed in *The American Voter*. In a political world rocked by the defection of the "Solid South" from the Democratic ranks and the fracturing of the putative majority party in 1968 and 1972, what good was a theoretical framework in which "normal" voting behavior was traced to partisan loyalties arising from the Great Depression or the Civil War?

Revisionists argued that political issues had come to play a much larger role than in the 1950s, superseding party identification as the central element in shaping voting behavior. Even more impressively, revisionists argued that the very structure of political thinking had changed significantly since the 1950s, as evidenced by a marked increase in the ideological consistency of mass political attitudes from the low levels described in *The American Voter* or (even more elaborately and persuasively) in Converse's (1964) landmark essay on "The Nature of Belief Systems in Mass Publics." These revisionist claims received their most extensive and influential statement in Nie, Verba, and Petrocik's (1976) *The Changing American Voter.*

Before long, however, the thesis of increased attitude consistency was subjected to a forceful methodological critique by Bishop, Oldendick, and Tuchfarber (1978a; 1978b), Brunk (1978), and Sullivan, Piereson, and Marcus (1978). These critics noted that the average correlation among distinct issue positions jumped suspiciously between 1960 and 1964, rather than rising gradually in response to the political events of the 1960s more generally—and that this suspicious jump corresponded with a significant change in the format of some of the relevant issue items. Experimental surveys in which the old and new item formats were presented to comparable samples of respondents produced patterns of correlations across issues among the respondents who answered the new-style questions closely resembling those reported by Nie, Verba, and Petrocik (1976) for the 1964–1972 period, while the pattern of correlations among the respondents who answered the old-style questions resembled the pattern reported by Nie, Verba, and Petrocik (1976) for 1952–1960. The obvious inference was that much of the increased ideological "coherence" reported in *The Changing American Voter* was attributable to the changes in question wording rather than to any fundamental transformation in the structure of political attitudes.

Meanwhile, data from a major new panel survey conducted by the Michigan team in 1972, 1974, and 1976 made it possible to measure the *stability* of these attitudes by comparison with the corresponding attitudes in the 1950s. The result was another significant blow to the revisionist thesis. Despite the intervention of the Watergate scandal and the resignation and subsequent pardoning of Richard Nixon, partisan attachments were just as stable in the 1970s as they had been in the 1950s. Meanwhile, the stability of issue preferences was no greater in the 1970s than in the 1950s. Thus, as Converse and Markus (1979, 45) put it, "there has been scarcely any change in the comparative continuity of party and issue positioning between the two eras, despite manifold reasons to expect not only change, but change of major proportions."

In this respect as well, then, careful analysis seemed to reveal more continuity than change in the nature of political attitudes between the 1950s and the 1970s. Despite the manifest importance of the intervening political developments, the deviations from the "Michigan model" seemed to be a good deal more limited in scope and magnitude than the more dramatic revisionist claims had implied. Nevertheless, the revisionists seem to me to have made two significant contributions to the study of voting behavior. First, they put the interaction between citizens and political elites more firmly on the scholarly agenda. Key's (1966, 2) metaphor of the electoral process as an "echo chamber" in which "the people's verdict can be no more than a selective reflection from among the alternatives and outlooks presented to them" was taken up not only as a likely explanation for changing patterns of voting behavior, but also as a spur to innovative research on elite behavior and its electoral implications (Page 1978).

Second, the revisionists and their critics together directed greater attention to issues of measurement. From the viewpoint of continuity, the fact that new survey questions produced stronger results than the old questions they replaced was a vexing complication; but from the viewpoint of mapping the "issue space" of contemporary American politics it represented an important step forward. As the Michigan surveys have continued through the decades—recast since the 1970s as National Election Studies and supported by the National Science Foundation as a collective scientific resource—changes in survey content have often had the same dual character. Having been sensitized to both the power and the pitfalls of new survey instrumentation, scholars of voting behavior have been better equipped to exploit the power of subsequent innovations while minimizing the corresponding pitfalls.

Spatial Models, Retrospective Voting, and Rational Choice

The intensifying interest in "issue voting" in the electoral research of the late 1960s and 1970s was reinforced by theoretical ferment inspired by the emerging "rational choice" paradigm, which applied the hypothesis of utility maximization developed in economics to political decision-making. Rational choice theory also played an important role in the incorporation of the empirical insights of Stokes (1963), Kramer (1971), and others regarding the electoral significance of "perceptions and appraisals of policy and performance" (Key 1966, 150) into the mainstream of voting research under the rubric of "retrospective voting" (Fiorina 1981). In each of these instances, as is often the case with successful theories, rational choice theory reorganized existing knowledge, stimulated new discoveries, and raised new questions for scholars of electoral behavior.

The most influential single work in the rational choice tradition was Anthony Downs's (1957) book, *An Economic Theory of Democracy*. Perhaps due to its unconventional analytical style, Downs's work had little immediate impact upon political scientists. It was not reviewed in the *American Political Science Review* until 1963, and was not published in paperback until 1965. Nevertheless, Stanley Kelley, Jr., was prophetic in suggesting, in his foreword to the paperback edition, that Downs's work would eventually be "recognized as the starting point of a highly important development in the study of politics."[3]

Downs's first and most important contribution was to introduce spatial models of electoral competition to the field of political science. Indeed, for the first two decades following its original publication, the influence of *An Economic Theory of Democracy* seems to have rested almost entirely upon a single chapter describing "The Statics and Dynamics of Party Ideologies." This chapter laid out the now-familiar model in which voters are arrayed along a unidimensional ideological continuum, parties choose policies corresponding to points on that continuum, and voters choose parties on the basis of ideological proximity. Downs argued, as one implication of this model, that the competing parties in a two-party system should "converge rapidly upon the center" of the distribution of voters if most voters were themselves relatively moderate (Downs 1957, 118).[4]

In an important sense, this aspect of Downs's work merely formalized a line of reasoning that was already familiar to political scientists (for example, from Schattschneider 1942, ch. 4). Nevertheless, the formalization was enormously fruitful. In addition to spawning a considerable theoretical literature on various aspects of what has come to be called the "median voter theorem" (for example, Black 1958; Calvert 1985; Enelow and Hinich 1984), Downs's work changed the way political issues and "issue voting" figured in empirical studies of voting behavior. For example, the National Election Studies (NES) surveys began in 1968 to ask respondents to place themselves, candidates, and parties on seven-point issue scales

---

[3] This intellectual trajectory is nicely captured in Wattenberg's (1991, 17–20) analysis of citations for the period 1966–1987. In the late 1960s, Wattenberg found, *An Economic Theory of Democracy* was cited about half as often as *The American Voter*; but by the late 1980s it was cited about twice as often.

[4] Downs (1957, 117–32) argued more generally that the distribution of voters along the ideological continuum would have significant implications for the nature of the party system, with two ideologically distinct parties arising if the distribution of voters was bimodal, multi-party systems arising if the distribution of voters was multi-modal, new parties arising when expansions of the electorate significantly altered the distribution of voters, and so on. This aspect of Downs's argument is logically less compelling (depending crucially upon the assumed willingness of voters to abstain if no party is sufficiently close to them on the ideological continuum—a willingness rationalized in turn on the grounds that uncertain voters would be sufficiently "future oriented" to resist supporting a slightly better party in the current election in hopes of supporting a much better party in a future election), and has had less impact on subsequent theoretical and empirical research.

reminiscent of Downs's ideological continuum, and relative distances between voters' positions and candidates' positions began to appear as explanatory variables in statistical models of electoral choice (for example, Enelow and Hinich 1984, ch. 9; Erikson and Romero 1990; Markus and Converse 1979; Page and Jones 1979).

Another key strand of Downs's influence on the field of voting behavior stemmed from his observation that "for a great many citizens in a democracy, rational behavior excludes any investment whatever in political information *per se*," since their individual choices have "almost no chance of influencing the outcome" of an election (Downs 1957, 245). This facet of Downs's book seems to have attracted relatively little attention or interest in the first two decades following its publication, but it has been increasingly influential in recent years.

Fiorina (1981) used Downs's insight as theoretical support for his own emphasis upon the electoral significance of retrospective evaluations of the incumbent party's performance in office. Even uninformed citizens, he reasoned (Fiorina 1981, 5), "typically have one comparatively hard bit of data: they know what life has been like during the incumbent's administration." Thus, the less they know about the details of policies and platforms, the more likely it seems that they will rely upon "retrospective voting as a cost-cutting element" in arriving at a vote choice (Fiorina 1981, 6).

Fiorina documented the importance of retrospective voting by including variables tapping voters' evaluations of economic conditions, foreign policy, presidential performance, and other politically relevant conditions in models of voting behavior which also included such traditional explanatory variables as party identification and issue positions. He concluded that "the effects of retrospective evaluations on the vote are pervasive, though often indirect" through their impact on partisan loyalties or expectations regarding future performance (Fiorina 1981, 175).[5] This work provided further empirical support for Key's (1966, 150) claim that "voters, or at least a large number of them, are moved by their perceptions and appraisals of policy and performance"—and thus that elections provide an important form of *post hoc* political accountability. It also helped to integrate vibrant strands of research on presidential approval (Mueller 1973) and economic voting (Kramer 1971) into the narrower survey-based literature on individual voting behavior.

---

[5] Fiorina (1981, 80) usefully distinguished between "simple" retrospective evaluations (based upon "more or less direct experiences or impressions of political events and conditions") and "mediated" retrospective evaluations (involving assessments of political figures or institutions, such as government economic performance). In a subsidiary analysis, he established that the latter "are not purely artifacts of personal bias," but also reflect "the impact of political reality" (Fiorina 1981, 129). Nevertheless, the role of retrospective evaluations in models of voting behavior remains highly problematic. While complexities regarding the causal status of issue preferences and partisan loyalties have received a great deal of scholarly attention, parallel complexities regarding the causal status of retrospective evaluations are often overlooked.

Burgeoning interest in retrospective voting represented one response to the challenge of low-information rationality in the realm of electoral politics. In the early 1990s a spate of books and articles examined how prospective voters use "information shortcuts" (Popkin 1991) to make reasoned electoral choices in the absence of detailed knowledge about policies and platforms. For example, Lupia (1994) showed that voters in a California insurance referendum used the position of insurance companies as a cue in formulating their own preferences regarding a complicated menu of alternative proposals. Meanwhile, Page and Shapiro's (1992) portrayal of *The Rational Public* stressed what Converse (1990) referred to as the "miracle of aggregation"—the tendency for random "error" at the individual level to cancel out in a large electorate. However, subsequent research has suggested that neither cues nor aggregation are likely to be fully effective substitutes for a better-informed electorate (Bartels 1996; Fournier 2006; Lau and Redlawsk 2006), and that even supposedly straightforward retrospective voting is significantly skewed by systematic errors such as myopia and misattribution of responsibility for good or bad times (Achen and Bartels 2002, 2004; Bartels 2008, ch. 4). These findings suggest that much remains to be learned about the nature and extent of "rationality" in electoral behavior.

THE SEARCH FOR CAUSAL ORDER IN THE ELECTORAL UNIVERSE

The theoretical account of voting behavior offered in *The American Voter* drew heavily upon the metaphor of a "funnel of causality," in which proximate influences on voting behavior were themselves subject to explanation, at least in principle, in terms of temporally and causally prior forces (Campbell et al. 1960, 24–37). Thus, for example, personal evaluations of the parties' current presidential candidates might be explained, in part, in terms of more general partisan loyalties which existed before the candidates themselves emerged as salient objects of political consciousness.

The "funnel of causality" provided a convenient framework within which to pursue both a comprehensive program of electoral accounting (by "concentrating on a cross section of measurements at a point close to the dependent behavior") and a more selective strategy of explanation in depth (by "rang[ing] freely in time back through the funnel" in search of historical, social, or institutional antecedents of proximate electorally relevant attitudes). Electoral change could be incorporated in this framework through the "political translation" of external, non-political factors into politically relevant considerations, as when voters brought their assessments of the Great Depression in the 1930s or Eisenhower's military career in the 1940s to bear upon their vote choices in the 1950s (Campbell et al. 1960, 33, 25, 29–32).

By the mid-1960s, methodological advances filtering through political science in the wake of the behavioral revolution were beginning to transform the "funnel of causality" from a conceptual framework into a more concrete causal model with potentially testable statistical implications. Goldberg (1966) examined a variety of alternative multi-equation models relating parental influences, sociological characteristics, party identification, and partisan attitudes to vote choices. Whereas Goldberg's analysis was limited to *recursive* causal models (in keeping with the logic of the "funnel of causality"), scholars in the subsequent decade began to take seriously the possibility of *reciprocal* influences among the various antecedents of electoral behavior. For example, Brody and Page (1972; Page and Brody 1972) cautioned against taking the correlation between perceived issue proximity and vote choices as *prima facie* evidence of "issue voting," on the grounds that perceived issue proximity might reflect psychological projection of voters' own issue positions onto their preferred candidates (harking back to the analyses of Berelson et al. 1954), or persuasion of voters on specific issues by candidates preferred on other grounds, rather than (or in addition to) the impact of issue voting in the usual sense.

Jackson (1975) published the first analysis of voting behavior based upon an explicit non-recursive causal model. He concluded that "party identifications are highly influenced by people's evaluations of what policies each party advocates relative to their own preferences," and that "party affiliations have little direct influence on the voting decision except for people who see little or no difference" between the parties' issue positions (Jackson 1975, 176). This was a major challenge to the theoretical status of party identification in the "Michigan model," and a methodological challenge to more conventional statistical analyses that ignored the possibility of reciprocal influences among the various antecedents of voting behavior.

How would these challenges be resolved? Scholars could hardly be blamed for hoping that more sophisticated methodology would rapidly lead to a new substantive consensus. Alas, things did not prove to be quite that simple. Indeed, the next notable development in the search for causal order in voting behavior seems in retrospect to have crystallized the qualms of many scholars about the fruitfulness of the whole "causal modeling" program: the back-to-back publication in the same issue of the *American Political Science Review* of articles by Markus and Converse (1979) and Page and Jones (1979) reporting alternative simultaneous equation models relating party identifications, issue preferences, candidate evaluations, and vote choices.

Despite various differences in model specification, at the heart of each of these analyses was an equation in which overall candidate evaluations (as measured by the difference in "feeling thermometer" scores for the two competing candidates) were related to three major causal factors: party identification, comparative issue positions, and evaluations of the candidates' personal qualities. Unfortunately, the structural similarities between the two analyses were not sufficient to produce similar conclusions. The discrepancies between the two sets of results were most stark in the case of party identification—the variable at the heart of the "Michigan model," and the primary target of revisionist critics for a decade or more:

- Markus and Converse (1979, 1064) reported that party identification was the strongest influence on evaluations of the candidates' personalities; Page and Jones (1979, 1082) treated party identification and personality evaluations as totally unrelated, except insofar as exogenous personality evaluations influenced overall candidate evaluations, which in turn influenced party attachments.

- Markus and Converse (1979, 1059) did not allow for any contemporaneous effect of issue stands on party identification, but allowed party identification to influence issue stands indirectly; Page and Jones (1979, 1083) modeled both direct and indirect links between party attachments and comparative policy distances, and estimated much stronger effects of policy distances on partisanship than of partisanship on policy distances.

- Markus and Converse (1979, 1066) estimated a substantial direct effect of party identification on voting behavior—over and above its effect on candidate evaluations; Page and Jones (1979) did not allow for any direct effect of party identification on the vote.

- Markus and Converse (1979, 1069) concluded that partisan predispositions "make repeated inputs of substantial magnitude throughout the process" of electoral choice; Page and Jones (1979, 1088) concluded that "the effect of partisanship on the vote varies considerably across elections," adding that "when party loyalties do enter in, they do not function purely as fixed determinants of the vote; those loyalties can themselves be affected by attitudes toward the current candidates."

What was one to make of these seemingly contradictory findings? If two teams of highly competent analysts asking essentially similar questions of the same data could come to such different conclusions, it seemed clear that the results of causal analysis must depend at least as much on the analysts' theoretical preconceptions and corresponding statistical assumptions as on the behavior of voters. Nor was one set of assumptions clearly more reasonable than the other; indeed, critics of either analysis could easily point to restrictive assumptions that seemed to strain plausibility. Pending stronger theory or better data—or both—the search for causal order in voting behavior seemed to have reached an unhappy dead end.

Out of Their Heads and Into the World

The apparent failure of causal modeling to answer fundamental questions about voting behavior produced a variety of disparate reactions. Some electoral analysts have continued to pursue the quest for causal order using models and methods clearly recognizable as successors of those used by Markus and Converse and Page and Jones. For example, Goren (2005) used panel data and structural equation models to examine the impact of partisanship on supposedly fundamental "core values" like equal opportunity and moral tolerance. Other analysts have side-stepped the knottiest complexities of causal modeling by reviving the assumption of recursive causation embodied in the "funnel of causality" posited by the authors of *The American Voter*. For example, Miller and Shanks (1982, 1996) developed an elaborate recursive model arraying most of the important factors identified in previous studies of voting behavior in seven distinct causal stages. By assuming that factors assigned to each of these stages could influence those in later stages, but not vice versa, Miller and Shanks produced a detailed accounting of direct and indirect effects of each factor on the vote.

Lewis-Beck et al. (2008) undertook a much more literal replication of *The American Voter*, not only applying the basic analytical framework of the earlier work but replicating dozens of specific tables and figures using data from the 2004 NES survey. While acknowledging that "Methods for analyzing data have developed considerably over the past half-century" and that "the funnel model has not always been treated well in the subsequent literature," the authors argued that "the attitudinal model in *The American Voter*... is no less correct than the alternatives" (Lewis-Beck et al. 2008, 15, 26, 28).

Notwithstanding this nostalgic look backward, few scholars of electoral behavior have been content merely to recycle the theories and methods of the past. However, equally few have been content to hope that new theories and statistical wizardry might untangle the causal complexities that emerged in the 1960s and 1970s. Instead, the most common impulse among electoral analysts of the past quarter-century has been to change the subject. Rather than building ever more complex and comprehensive models of individual voting behavior, they have focused on more tractable questions.

As a result, contemporary voting research has become increasingly eclectic and opportunistic. Scholars have relied on a broader array of relevant data, including not only the succession of National Election Studies surveys initiated by the authors of *The American Voter* but also a variety of other large and small surveys and laboratory experiments. Even more importantly, they have been increasingly inventive in getting outside the heads of survey respondents and into the broader political world, supplementing individual-level data on attitudes and perceptions with systematic measurement of variations in the political context of electoral behavior. This emphasis on exploiting contextual variation has provided invaluable causal leverage for analyses of voting behavior.

Congressional elections have provided obvious opportunities for exploring the impact of political contexts on voting behavior. The incorporation of considerable new congressional content in NES surveys beginning in 1978 facilitated more detailed analyses of how members' activities in Washington and in their districts contributed to their electoral security (Cain, Ferejohn, and Fiorina 1987). Franklin (1991) used survey data from the National Election Studies' fifty-state Senate Election Study to analyze the impact of candidates' campaigns on the clarity of prospective voters' perceptions of senators' issue positions. Kahn and Kenney (1999) merged the same survey data with detailed content analysis of ads and news to investigate how campaigns affect voting behavior in Senate elections. They found that more intense campaigns caused voters to rely more heavily on partisanship, issues, and presidential approval than in low-key races.

Even at the presidential level, leverage for contextual analysis has been greatly augmented by the growing length of the NES time series, which now encompasses more than a half century of American political history. For example, Markus (1988) exploited temporal variation in national economic conditions to effect a merger between aggregate-level and survey analyses of economic voting. By pooling survey data from eight presidential elections, he was able to assess the sensitivity of voters to both national economic conditions (which vary across election years) and individual economic circumstances (which vary both across and within surveys).

Vavreck (2009) used the NES time series to explore another aspect of economic voting—the extent to which candidates' strategic decisions to emphasize or deemphasize economic issues alter voting behavior. She argued that incumbent party candidates in prosperous election years and challengers in slow-growth years should and usually do focus primarily on the economy, while candidates disadvantaged by economic conditions should and usually do run "insurgent" campaigns emphasizing other, more advantageous issues. By merging survey data with detailed content analysis of campaign ads, speeches, and news coverage, Vavreck found that candidates who pursue strategies consistent with their political circumstances are more successful in shaping the campaign agenda to their advantage. More broadly, Gilens, Vavreck, and Cohen (2007) showed that the shifting focus of voters' likes and dislikes of presidential candidates over the past half-century mirrors the shifting content of campaign advertising—and that the policy content of ads has produced a more policy-focused electorate, despite significant declines in the reach and policy content of campaign news coverage.

On a much shorter time-scale, analysts have also exploited temporal variation within campaigns to shed light on the electoral impact of a variety of political events, including primary election outcomes (Bartels 1988), debates (Johnston et al. 1992), and campaign advertising (Johnston, Hagen, and Jamieson 2004). Johnston, Hagen, and Jamieson effectively exploited both temporal variation (over the last four months of the 2000 campaign) and cross-sectional variation (contrasting "battleground" states with those in which little campaigning occurred). Matching survey responses from the 2000 National Annenberg Election Survey with detailed data on advertising patterns in specific media markets, Johnston, Hagen, and Jamieson tracked prospective voters' responses to changes in the volume and content of campaign ads as well as to news coverage and other aspects of the national campaign. Their analysis suggested that George W. Bush's razor-thin victory hinged on the fact that "at the end, critically, the ad signal became decisively unbalanced" in his favor in the battleground states (Johnston, Hagen, and Jamieson 2004, 13).

Hill et al. (2008) elaborated Johnston, Hagen, and Jamieson's analysis by focusing closer attention on the rate at which advertising effects decayed. Their results supported Johnston, Hagen, and Jamieson's account of the electoral impact of Bush's late advertising surge: most of the effect of any given ad on vote intentions evaporated within one week, and "Only the most politically aware voters exhibited . . . long-term effects" (Hill et al. 2008, 24). In a separate paper (Hill et al. 2007), the same authors found even shorter half-lives for advertising effects in a variety of state-level and congressional races, reinforcing the impression that voters can be powerfully swayed by television advertising in the days just before an election.

Scholars have not only *exploited* variation in electoral contexts but also *created* contextual variation through experimental manipulation. For example, Ansolabehere and Iyengar (1995) measured the responsiveness of experimental subjects to positive and negative campaign advertisements, while Mendelberg (2001) compared the effectiveness of implicit and explicit racial appeals using both experiments and observational analyses focusing on the "Willie Horton" incident in the 1988 presidential campaign.

In recent years, laboratory experiments have increasingly been supplemented by large-scale field experiments. Much of this work has focused on assessing the effectiveness of get-out-the-vote efforts (Green and Gerber 2008). However, in the early stages of a 2006 gubernatorial campaign in Texas some $2 million of advertising was randomly deployed across eighteen of the state's twenty media markets, allowing for an unusually straightforward and powerful test of the impact of advertising on evolving candidate evaluations and vote intentions (Gerber et al. 2007). This large-scale experiment revealed strong effects of television advertising, but those effects were even more ephemeral than in Hill et al.'s (2007, 2008) analyses of non-experimental data: a major ad buy producing a 7 percent shift in vote intentions one day later but no discernible effect two days later. As Gerber et al. (2007, 26) put it, this "pattern of abrupt change and equilibration" in vote intentions in response to campaign advertising "appears to be inconsistent with a model of rational learning."

ELECTIONS AND THE POLITICAL ORDER

The final sentence of *The American Voter* called attention to "the influence relations binding the electoral process to the other means of decision in the political system" (Campbell et al. 1960, 558). The title of the same authors' subsequent collection of essays, *Elections and the Political Order*, signaled a continuing interest in the relationship between electoral behavior and the broader workings of government. The pieces collected in that volume included survey-based interpretations of specific elections, historical analyses of the dynamics of party competition, and a path-breaking analysis of political representation, among other contributions. Subsequent analysts have made significant headway along each of these lines. Nevertheless, the aspiration of situating the study of electoral behavior firmly within a more general understanding of American politics seems to me, five decades later, to remain largely unfulfilled.

Scholarly interpretations of election outcomes continue to be produced with some regularity, but they have continued to be stymied by the difficulty of generating convincing estimates of the impact of specific issues, candidates, and campaign events. Indeed, it is probably no coincidence that the most detailed and ambitious works of electoral interpretation since the 1970s have been based either on recursive causal models (Miller and Shanks 1982, 1996) or on tabulations of the reasons offered by voters themselves for supporting one candidate or the other (Kelley 1983). While both of these approaches have significant limitations, both also have the substantial virtue of facilitating straightforward accounting of the potentially distinct bases of individual and collective electoral choice—a crucial prerequisite for illuminating the broader political implications of voting behavior.

Another notable blind spot is the interrelationship between electoral behavior and the party system. Much of the best scholarship in the latter realm has focused on "critical elections" and "realignments" predating the era of detailed survey data (Burnham 1970; Key 1955, 1959; Sundquist 1983). While Mayhew (2002) has cataloged the empirical limitations of this historical genre, we have yet to develop a compelling alternative account of how the interaction of party elites and masses defines what elections are about at any given time. Carmines and Stimson's (1989) analysis of the racial realignment of the 1960s as a process of "issue evolution" provides an illuminating start in that direction, and Adams's (1997) application of the same framework to the evolving role of abortion in the party system of the 1970s and 1980s underscores its utility. In both cases, the authors found strong evidence that changing views among partisan elites preceded and contributed to partisan change in the mass electorate. But how and why party elites take the sides they do on issues like these, how their choices are shaped by correct or incorrect beliefs about the likely responses of supporters and opponents, and how "evolution" with respect to any one issue spurs or depends upon other changes in the political and social bases of party coalitions are all topics deserving much more sustained scholarly attention.

Finally, and perhaps most importantly, scholars of electoral politics have much more to learn about when, how, and to what extent election outcomes shape the course of public policy. At a very general level, political scientists recognize—even if many ordinary Americans do not—that elections have significant consequences. Since the 1970s, the ideological gulf in voting behavior between Democratic and Republican members of Congress has widened considerably (McCarty, Poole, and Rosenthal 2006; Poole and Rosenthal 1997). Democratic and Republican senators representing the same states typically differ more in their voting behavior than senators of the same party representing the most liberal and most conservative states in the country, while Democratic and Republican presidents have historically presided over vastly disparate economic fortunes for middle-class and poor people (Bartels 2008). However, despite having observed these impressive partisan contrasts, we are far from having a detailed understanding of the policy consequences of election outcomes.

The most ambitious attempt by contemporary scholars to integrate analyses of public opinion, electoral behavior, party politics, and public policy is Robert Erikson, Michael MacKuen, and James Stimson's (2002) volume, *The Macro Polity*. Building on a series of related studies of "public mood," presidential approval, "macropartisanship," and dynamic representation, Erikson, MacKuen, and Stimson developed an impressively comprehensive "system model" in which the broad policy choices of elected officials both reflect and help to shape broad currents of public opinion. Although the authors of *The Macro Polity* stressed the direct responsiveness of governmental policy to shifts in public sentiment, their findings imply that the policy changes that would be produced by shifting from the most liberal public mood on record to the most conservative public mood on record are dwarfed by the changes produced when a typical Democrat replaces a typical Republican in the White House (Erikson, Mackuen, and Stimson 2002, ch. 8).

These partisan disparities in policy cast considerable doubt on the political relevance of the median voter theorem developed by Anthony Downs (1957), Duncan Black (1958), and their successors. They also cast considerable light on the political consequences of electoral politics in the contemporary American setting. Elections matter, and thus so does electoral behavior. But if election outcomes largely drive policy, what drives election outcomes?

Erikson, MacKuen, and Stimson's analyses of election outcomes focused on "rational retrospections" based on the state of the economy, judgments of ideological proximity, and shifting partisan loyalties and presidential approval reflecting these and other factors. However, much of the impressive statistical performance of their regression models turns out to be attributable to "transient macropartisan-ship"—shifts in partisan sentiment over the course of the election year that are "volatile and essentially uncorrelated with the other variables of the model.... These otherwise unaccounted-for causes explain a considerable share of the out-come" (Erikson, Mackuen, and Stimson 2002, 272). If the future course of public policy is powerfully shaped by "volatile" and "unaccounted-for causes" of election outcomes, is the macro polity really such a well-oiled democratic machine? This is one point at which broad integrative analysis will have to build upon a more detailed understanding of electoral behavior.

For that to happen, scholars of electoral behavior will have to pursue their work while also keeping the big picture clearly in view. In the opening paragraph of the preface to his magisterial survey of *Public Opinion and American Democracy*, V. O. Key, Jr. complained that the sociologists and social psychologists who had taken up the study of public opinion and elections since the 1940s had produced "a large body of research findings...whose relevance for the workings of the governmental system is not always apparent" (Key 1961, vii). Too much current work is equally vulnerable to that criticism. However, the best contemporary work, like Erikson, MacKuen, and Stimson's, reminds us that that need not be the case.

Although Key didn't say so, a compelling model of what a *political* science of electoral behavior might look like was provided by his own classic study of *Southern Politics in State and Nation* (Key 1949). Writing in the dark ages before extensive survey research and powerful computing technology, Key drew upon detailed observation, over 500 interviews with politicians and political observers, and rudimentary analysis of aggregate voting patterns to produce a masterful portrait of a political order in which electoral behavior meshed seamlessly with party politics, political culture, and the prevailing realities of economic and racial hierarchy. No reader of Key's book, then or now, would be likely to question the relevance of electoral behavior for the workings of the governmental system he portrayed—or the potential relevance of electoral behavior for undoing it.

Of course, there is no reason for scholars in the twenty-first century to limit themselves to data and methods of the sort available to Key in the 1940s. With respect to style and technique, the best future work in the field is likely to resemble *The Macro Polity* much more than it does *Southern Politics*. Nevertheless, the people who produce it could do much worse than to draw inspiration from the breadth, depth, and political sophistication of Key's analysis. That sort of broad-ening and deepening seems essential if future scholars of electoral behavior are to achieve the degree of intellectual influence and political relevance aspired to—and sometimes attained—by such past masters as Converse, Lazarsfeld, Miller, Stokes, and Key himself.

References

ACHEN, C. H. and BARTELS, L. M. 2002. Blind Retrospection: Electoral Responses to Drought, Flu, and Shark Attacks. Paper presented at the Annual Meeting of the American Political Science Association.

—— —— 2004. Musical Chairs: Pocketbook Voting and the Limits of Democratic Accountability. Paper presented at the Annual Meeting of the American Political Science Association.

ADAMS, G. D. 1997. Abortion: Evidence of an Issue Evolution. *American Journal of Political Science*, 41: 718–37.

ANSOLABEHERE, S. and IYENGAR, S. 1995. *Going Negative: How Attack Ads Shrink and Polarize the Electorate*. New York: Free Press.

BARTELS, L. M. 1988. *Presidential Primaries and the Dynamics of Public Choice*. Princeton, N.J.: Princeton University Press.

—— 1996. Uninformed Votes: Information Effects in Presidential Elections. *American Journal of Political Science*, 40: 194–230.

—— 2008. *Unequal Democracy: The Political Economy of the New Gilded Age*. New York and Princeton, N.J.: Russell Sage Foundation and Princeton University Press.

BERELSON, B. R., LAZARSFELD, P. F., and McPHEE, W. N. 1954. *Voting: A Study of Opinion Formation in a Presidential Campaign*. Chicago: University of Chicago Press.

BISHOP, G. F., OLDENDICK, R. W., and TUCHFARBER, A. J. 1978a. Change in the Structure of American Political Attitudes: The Nagging Question of Question Wording. *American Journal of Political Science*, 22: 250–69.

—— —— —— 1978b. Effects of Question Wording and Format on Political Attitude Consistency. *Public Opinion Quarterly*, 38: 81–92.

BLACK, D. 1958. *Theory of Committees and Elections*. Cambridge: Cambridge University Press.

BRODY, R. A. and PAGE, B. I. 1972. The Assessment of Policy Voting. *American Political Science Review*, 66: 450–8.

BRUNK, G. G. 1978. The 1964 Attitude Consistency Leap Reconsidered. *Political Methodology*, 5: 347–59.

BURNHAM, W. D. 1970. *Critical Elections and the Mainsprings of American Politics*. New York: W. W. Norton.

BUTLER, D. and STOKES, D. 1969. *Political Change in Britain: Forces Shaping Electoral Choice*. New York: St. Martin's Press.

CAIN, B., FEREJOHN, J., and FIORINA, M. 1987. *The Personal Vote: Constituency Service and Electoral Independence*. Cambridge, Mass.: Harvard University Press.

CALVERT, R. L. 1985. Robustness of the Multidimensional Voting Model: Candidate Motivations, Uncertainty, and Convergence. *American Journal of Political Science*, 29: 69–95.

CAMPBELL, A. and KAHN, R. L. 1952. *The People Elect a President*. Ann Arbor, Mich.: Survey Research Center, Institute for Social Research, University of Michigan.

—— CONVERSE, P. E., MILLER, W. E., and STOKES, D. E. 1960. *The American Voter*. New York: John Wiley & Sons.

—— —— —— —— 1966. *Elections and the Political Order*. New York: John Wiley and Sons.

CARMINES, E. G. and STIMSON, J. A. 1989. *Issue Evolution: Race and the Transformation of American Politics*. Princeton, N.J.: Princeton University Press.

CONVERSE, P. E. 1964. The Nature of Belief Systems in Mass Publics. In *Ideology and Discontent*, ed. D. E. Apter. Glencoe, Ill.: Free Press.

—— 1990. Popular Representation and the Distribution of Information. In *Information and Democratic Processes*, ed. J. A. Ferejohn and J. H. Kuklinski. Urbana: University of Illinois Press.

—— and MARKUS, G. B. 1979. Plus ça change . . . : The New CPS Election Study Panel. *American Political Science Review*, 73: 32–49.

DOWNS, A. 1957. *An Economic Theory of Democracy*. New York: Harper & Row.

ENELOW, J. M. and HINICH, M. J. 1984. *The Spatial Theory of Voting: An Introduction*. New York: Cambridge University Press.

ERIKSON, R. S., MACKUEN, M. B, and STIMSON, J. A. 2002. *The Macro Polity*. New York: Cambridge University Press.

—— and ROMERO, D. W. 1990. Candidate Equilibrium and the Behavioral Model of the Vote. *American Political Science Review*, 84: 1103–26.

FIORINA, M. P. 1981. *Retrospective Voting in American National Elections*. New Haven, Conn.: Yale University Press.

FOURNIER, P. 2006. The Impact of Campaigns on Discrepancies, Errors, and Biases in Voting Behavior. In *Capturing Campaign Effects*, ed. H. E. Brady and R. Johnston. Ann Arbor: University of Michigan Press.

FRANKLIN, C. H. 1991. Eschewing Obfuscation? Campaigns and the Perception of U.S. Senate Incumbents. *American Political Science Review*, 85: 1193–214.

GERBER, A., GIMPEL, J. G., GREEN, D. P., and SHAW, D. R. 2007. The Influence of Television and Radio Advertising on Candidate Evaluations: Results from a Large Scale Randomized Experiment. Paper presented at the Annual Meeting of the Midwest Political Science Association.

GILENS, M., VAVRECK, L., and COHEN, M. 2007. The Mass Media and the Public's Assessments of Presidential Candidates, 1952–2000. *Journal of Politics*, 69: 1160–75.

GOLDBERG, A. S. 1966. Discerning A Causal Pattern Among Data on Voting Behavior. *American Political Science Review*, 60: 913–22.

GOREN, P. 2005. Party Identification and Core Political Values. *American Journal of Political Science*, 49: 881–96.

GREEN, D. P. and GERBER, A. S. 2008. *Get Out the Vote: How to Increase Voter Turnout*, 2nd edn. Washington, D.C.: Brookings Institution Press.

—— PALMQUIST, B., and SCHICKLER, E. 2002. *Partisan Hearts and Minds: Political Parties and the Social Identity of Voters*. New Haven, Conn.: Yale University Press.

HILL, S. J., LO, J., VAVRECK, L., and ZALLER, J. 2007. The Duration of Advertising Effects in Political Campaigns. Paper presented at the Annual Meeting of the American Political Science Association.

—— —— —— —— 2008. The Duration of Advertising Effects in the 2000 Presidential Campaign. Paper presented at the Annual Meeting of the Midwest Political Science Association.

JACKSON, J. E. 1975. Issues, Party Choices, and Presidential Votes. *American Journal of Political Science*, 19: 161–85.

JENNINGS, M. K. and NIEMI, R. G. 1981. *Generations and Politics: A Panel Study of Young Adults and Their Parents*. Princeton, N.J.: Princeton University Press.

JOHNSTON, R., BLAIS, A., BRADY, H. E., and CRÊTE, J. 1992. *Letting the People Decide: Dynamics of a Canadian Election.* Montreal: McGill-Queen's University Press.

—— HAGEN, M. G., and JAMIESON, K. H. 2004. *The 2000 Presidential Election and the Foundations of Party Politics.* New York: Cambridge University Press.

KAHN, K. F. and KENNEY, P. J. 1999. *The Spectacle of U.S. Senate Campaigns.* Princeton, N.J.: Princeton University Press.

KELLEY, S., Jr. 1983. *Interpreting Elections.* Princeton, N.J.: Princeton University Press.

KEY, V. O., Jr. 1949. *Southern Politics in State and Nation.* New York: Alfred A. Knopf.

—— 1955. A Theory of Critical Elections. *Journal of Politics,* 17: 3–18.

—— 1959. Secular Realignment and the Party System. *Journal of Politics,* 21: 198–210.

—— 1961. *Public Opinion and American Democracy.* New York: Alfred A. Knopf.

—— (with the assistance of M. C. Cummings, Jr.) 1966. *The Responsible Electorate: Rationality in Presidential Voting, 1936–1960.* New York: Vintage.

KRAMER, G. H. 1971. Short-term Fluctuations in U.S. Voting Behavior, 1896–1964. *American Political Science Review,* 65: 131–43.

LAU, R. R. and REDLAWSK, D. P. 2006. *How Voters Decide: Information Processing during Election Campaigns.* New York: Cambridge University Press.

LAZARSFELD, P. F., BERELSON, B., and GAUDET, H. 1944. *The People's Choice: How the Voter Makes Up His Mind in a Presidential Campaign.* New York: Columbia University Press.

LEWIS-BECK, M. S., JACOBY, W. G., NORPOTH, H., and WEISBERG, H. F. 2008. *The American Voter Revisited.* Ann Arbor: University of Michigan Press.

LUPIA, A. 1994. Short Cuts versus Encyclopedias: Information and Voting Behavior in California Insurance Reform Elections. *American Political Science Review,* 88: 63–76.

MARKUS, G. B. 1988. The Impact of Personal and National Economic Conditions on the Presidential Vote: A Pooled Cross-Sectional Analysis. *American Journal of Political Science,* 32: 137–54.

—— and CONVERSE, P. E. 1979. A Dynamic Simultaneous Equation Model of Electoral Choice. *American Political Science Review,* 73: 1055–70.

MAYHEW, D. R. 2002. *Electoral Realignments: A Critique of an American Genre.* New Haven, Conn.: Yale University Press.

MCCARTY, N., POOLE, K. T., and ROSENTHAL, H. 2006. *Polarized America: The Dance of Ideology and Unequal Riches.* Cambridge, Mass.: MIT Press.

MENDELBERG, T. 2001. *The Race Card: Campaign Strategy, Implicit Messages, and the Norm of Equality.* Princeton, N.J.: Princeton University Press.

MILLER, W. E. and SHANKS, J. M. 1982. Policy Directions and Presidential Leadership: Alternative Interpretations of the 1980 Presidential Election. *British Journal of Political Science,* 12: 299–356.

—— —— 1996. *The New American Voter.* Cambridge, Mass.: Harvard University Press.

MUELLER, J. 1973. *War, Presidents and Public Opinion.* New York: Wiley.

NIE, N. H., VERBA, S., and PETROCIK, J. R. 1976. *The Changing American Voter.* Cambridge, Mass.: Harvard University Press.

PAGE, B. I. 1978. *Choices and Echoes in Presidential Elections: Rational Man and Electoral Democracy.* Chicago: University of Chicago Press.

—— and BRODY, R. A. 1972. Policy Voting and the Electoral Process: The Vietnam Issue. *American Political Science Review,* 66: 979–95.

—— and JONES, C. C. 1979. Reciprocal Effects of Policy Preferences, Party Loyalties and the Vote. *American Political Science Review,* 73: 1071–89.

—— and SHAPIRO, R. Y. 1992. *The Rational Public: Fifty Years of Trends in Americans' Policy Preferences*. Chicago: University of Chicago Press.

POOLE, K. T. and ROSENTHAL, H. 1997. *Congress: A Political-Economic History of Roll Call Voting*. New York: Oxford University Press.

POPKIN, S. L. 1991. *The Reasoning Voter: Communication and Persuasion in Presidential Campaigns*. Chicago: University of Chicago Press.

ROSSI, P. H. 1959. Four Landmarks in Voting Research. In *American Voting Behavior*, ed. E. Burdick and A. J. Brodbeck. Glencoe, Ill.: The Free Press.

SCHATTSCHNEIDER, E. E. 1942. *Party Government*. New York: Holt, Rinehart and Winston.

STOKES, D. E. 1963. Spatial Models of Party Competition. *American Political Science Review*, 57: 368–77. Reprinted in Campbell et al. (1966).

SULLIVAN, J. L., PIERESON, J. E., and MARCUS, G. E. 1978. Ideological Constraint in the Mass Public: A Methodological Critique and Some New Findings. *American Journal of Political Science*, 22: 233–49.

SUNDQUIST, J. L. 1983. *Dynamics of the Party System: Alignment and Realignment of Political Parties in the United States*, revised edn. Washington, D.C.: The Brookings Institution.

VAVRECK, L. 2009. *The Message Matters: The Economy and Presidential Campaigns*. Princeton, N.J.: Princeton University Press.

WATTENBERG, M. P. 1991. *The Rise of Candidate-Centered Politics: Presidential Elections of the 1980s*. Cambridge, Mass.: Harvard University Press.

CHAPTER 15

···

THE AMERICAN VOTER

···

WILLIAM G. JACOBY

Upon first consideration, any attempt to provide a comprehensive description of voting choice in the American electorate might seem to be a very daunting task. Just about any life experience can become politically relevant under appropriate circumstances and, in so doing, affect a person's choices in the voting booth. But these potentially limitless social and psychological influences rarely have a direct effect on electoral decisions. Instead, their effects are usually indirect, and "filtered" through a set of factors which are relatively close to the voting act itself.

Ever since the appearance of *The American Voter*, there has been a general consensus among political scientists that three variables stand out as the most critical proximal influences on voting: personal attachments to political parties; individual reactions to public policy controversies; and evaluations of the candidates' personal characteristics. Other variables may come to the forefront under particular circumstances, such as ideological orientations or judgments about recent governmental performance. But the combination of party, issue, and candidate factors appear to retain ongoing importance as "the iron triangle" of explanatory concepts for understanding voting behavior (Achen 1992).

Party Identification

Party identification does not imply a formal organizational membership or even any degree of overt activity in support of a political party. Instead, it is simply an individual's sense of personal attachment to the party label. In other words, party identification exists entirely as a psychological state, "in the heads" of citizens. Most behavioral manifestations of partisan activity (e.g., preferring the issue stands from one party rather than the other, consistently voting for candidates from one party, etc.) are considered to be conceptually distinct phenomena.

Given the psychological nature of this variable, party identification is almost always ascertained by simply asking individual citizens what they consider themselves to be. The precise question wording varies from one survey organization to the next,[1] but it is generally assumed that party identifications can be represented as a unidimensional, bipolar continuum, with Democratic identifiers at one end, self-professed independents in the center, and Republican identifiers at the other end (Campbell et al. 1960, ch. 6).

The theoretical importance of party identification stems from its temporal stability and broad influence across a range of other political beliefs, attitudes, and behavior. Partisan attachments develop very early in life, as one of the first results of the political socialization process (Jennings and Niemi 1974). And, for most people, these attachments do not change very much across the entire life-cycle (Jennings and Markus 1984). Once formed, partisan loyalties are believed to act as a "perceptual screen," which helps individuals to evaluate incoming information about the political world, formulate attitudes, and determine subsequent behaviors in an efficient manner (Miller 1976). Stimuli associated with one's own party—primarily candidates and policy stands—are viewed more favorably, while those from the other party are regarded more negatively. The clarity and intensity of such connections are mediated by the strength of individual partisan attachments. This, in turn, generates predictable relationships between the party identification continuum and a wide variety of other variables, such as individual issue attitudes, retrospective evaluations of economic conditions, assessments of governmental performance, and beliefs about presidential candidates' personal traits.

---

[1] The Center for Political Studies' American National Election Studies (ANES) measure party identification through a set of questions which have remained virtually unchanged since the early 1950s. Respondents are first asked, "Generally speaking, do you usually think of yourself as a REPUBLICAN, a DEMOCRAT, an INDEPENDENT, or what?" Those who answer that they think of themselves as Republicans or Democrats are next asked, "Would you call yourself a STRONG [Democrat/Republican] or a NOT VERY STRONG [Democrat/Republican]?" People who consider themselves independents are asked, "Do you think of yourself as CLOSER to the Republican Party or to the Democratic party?" The various combinations of responses to these questions are combined to create a single variable, with seven categories.

The fact that these latter variables are, themselves, colored by partisan loyalties implies that party identification has multiple impacts on the vote. On the one hand, it can have a direct influence by providing a readily available cue for deciding between candidates (i.e., voters can simply choose the candidate from their own party). On the other hand, this type of immediate impact may be superfluous, if party identification has already "biased" a voter in favor of the past performance manifested by, the issue stands articulated by, and the candidates nominated by, one party rather than the other.

Party identification is also important for another reason: partisan attachments help to integrate individuals into the political world. In this manner, they promote interest, involvement, and overt participation in election campaigns and other political activities (Verba and Nie 1972). This stands in contrast to some traditional views, which hold that political independence is more desirable according to standards of good citizenship, because such a position avoids preconceived biases and enables more complete evaluation of the evidence pertaining to voting choices. Nevertheless, the empirical evidence has repeatedly shown that strong partisans are more likely to exhibit the characteristics of the "good citizen" (e.g., attention to public affairs, well-formed policy attitudes, active political participation, and voter turnout) than are self-professed independents (especially those who do not lean toward either party).

There is a broad consensus among political scientists about the importance of party identification for understanding political behavior. Nevertheless, the theoretical status of this concept has been questioned repeatedly over the sixty years since its first appearance in the research literature. For example, some analysts have questioned the temporal stability and long-term nature of party identification. Much of the evidence about familial transmission of partisanship and its longevity across the life-cycle is derived from self-reports of parents' partisan loyalties and previous personal orientations. As such, they are almost certainly susceptible to rationalization processes which make individual beliefs and attitudes appear to be more consistent than they really are.

Direct information about the persistence of party identification is relatively rare, due to the lack of long-term panel studies of public opinion. And those studies which do exist have generated somewhat disparate conclusions. On the one hand, one well-known dataset which tracks party identification across several decades shows that people who came of political age during the late 1960s exhibit quite a bit of instability in their party affiliations over the subsequent years (Franklin 1984; Lewis-Beck et al. 2008, ch. 7; Niemi and Jennings 1991). On the other hand, several other famous panel studies of political attitudes reveal a great deal of continuity in party identifications over time periods of forty to fifty years (Alwin, Cohen, and Newcomb 1991; Sears and Funk 1999). A number of shorter-term panel studies have also repeatedly shown much higher levels of stability in party identification than in many other political attitudes (e.g., Converse 1970; Converse and Markus 1979; Krosnick 1991).

Questions have also been raised about the nature of political independence. Many independent leaners—that is, those individuals who call themselves independents, but then admit that they lean toward either the Democratic or Republican parties—are more partisan in their behavior than are weak party identifiers, creating "intransitivities" in the usual monotonic relationship between partisan strength and political involvement (Petrocik 1974). Based on this evidence, some analysts argue that independent leaners are hidden partisans who should be combined with weak party identifiers (Keith et al. 1992). Others maintain that the initial identification as independent is the important characteristic, and they should be kept separate from admitted partisans of any degree (Miller 1991). The questions about these two categories remain largely unresolved, but the differences between independent leaners and weak partisans are definitely less pronounced than are the differences between weak and strong party identifiers.

It is also not entirely clear that party identification really has the pervasive influence on attitudes and behavior that is often attributed to it. Instead, partisan ties may be the result of issue attitudes, such that an individual affiliates with the party that espouses the issue positions that he or she prefers (e.g., Franklin and Jackson 1983; Jackson 1975; Page and Jones 1979). Alternatively, party identification may reflect previous voting behavior, with individuals who chose Democratic candidates in previous elections calling themselves Democrats, and vice versa for Republicans (Markus and Converse 1979). An individual's partisanship also could be a manifestation of previous experiences with life and social conditions under the leadership of the respective parties (Fiorina 1981).

Few scholars truly believe that party identification is a completely "unmoving mover" of other attitudes and behavior. In fact, not even Campbell, Converse, Miller, and Stokes—the researchers who basically created the modern concept of party identification—held such an extreme position. Nevertheless, the predominant view still maintains that the causal flow emanating from partisan ties is more pronounced than any immediate influences upon it from the external political environment. For example, Sears and his colleagues emphasize that party identification is a symbolic political orientation which usually exerts a stronger influence on other political orientations than factors stemming from immediate self-interest (Sears 1993; Sears and Funk 1990). And, the work of Paul Sniderman and his colleagues indicates that party identification is a useful heuristic device facilitating a variety of political decisions, including vote choices (Sniderman, Brody, and Tetlock 1991). In summary, the theoretical underpinings may be somewhat different, but modern understandings about the importance of individual partisan attachments are remarkably similar to those that were laid out in *The American Voter* nearly fifty years ago.

ISSUE ATTITUDES

....

The empirical evidence reported over the past few decades presents a highly varied, and not entirely optimistic, picture of the degree to which citizens take issues into account when making their voting decisions. Larry Bartels' contribution to this volume (Chapter 14) provides an excellent account of the varied interpretations and scholarly controversies that have emerged over the years in the voluminous literature on issue voting. But an important question remains: why have political scientists reported so many disparate conclusions about citizens' capacities or willingness to use policy controversies as the basis of their electoral decisions?

At least part of the answer lies in the differing strategies that have been employed to measure issue voting. The authors of *The American Voter* used a particularly straightforward approach. Their survey questions elicited attitudes on an issue by simply asking people whether and how strongly they agreed or disagreed with a statement describing a single policy position.[2] Responses were usually recorded on a five-point scale, ranging from "agree strongly," through a neutral midpoint, to "disagree strongly."

The first change to occur was a seemingly minor modification to the format of the survey questions used to measure opinions on issues. This was a "filter" which allowed respondents to opt out of answering the question if they had not thought very much about the issue; adopted by the University of Michigan's Survey Research Center in 1964, it has been used by the NES ever since. The purpose of the new question format is to identify and remove people who do not possess opinions on a given issue.[3] So, it seems to produce a more accurate representation of the opinion distribution on an issue than questions which do not include such a filter. But the "new" format creates problems for comparisons over time, precisely because questions on earlier surveys in the 1950s and 1960 did not include such a filter (e.g., Bishop 2005).

A second change in the measurement of mass issue orientations is the use of bipolar scales. As mentioned earlier, the original issue questions from *The American Voter* had respondents agree or disagree with a single policy position. A new format, originally developed in 1968 and put into common use in the NES in 1972,

---

[2] For example, the interview schedule for the 1956 National Election Study measured opinions about employment policy by asking people whether they agreed or disagreed with the statement, "The government in Washington ought to see to it that everybody who wants to work can find a job."

[3] For example, the 1964 National Election Study used the following question to measure opinions about guaranteed employment: "In general, some people feel that the government in Washington should see to it that every person has a job and a good standard of living. Others think the government should just let each person get ahead on his own. Have you been interested enough in this to favor one side over the other?" Respondents who said they were interested enough to have an opinion were next asked what they believed the government should do. Respondents who said they had no interest were not questioned further about this issue.

presents survey respondents with two opposing issue positions, along with a numerical scale running between them (usually including seven numbered positions). Each respondent places him or herself along the scale at a position corresponding to his or her relative feelings about the two issue statements at either end.[4]

The seven-point issue scales also make it very easy for survey respondents to place other stimuli along the continuum representing an issue conflict. And this leads to a third important innovation in the study of issue voting: measuring citizens' beliefs about the party and candidate positions on the same set of issues for which their own opinions were measured. This information is generally used to calculate "issue proximity," defined as the absolute difference between the individual's own position on a given issue and that person's perception of a candidate's (or party's) position on the same issue. Given such proximities for all candidates competing in an election, voters are expected to choose the candidate whose issue stands are most proximal to their own across the entire set of issues being debated in the election campaign.

Issue proximities are widely accepted within the political science research community, and they have appeared in many empirical analyses of voting behavior. However, there may be some problematic elements in their use as analytic tools. For example, some scholars have questioned the interpretation and reliability of the numerical scales used to locate the individual citizens, candidates, and parties (Aldrich and McKelvey 1977; Krosnick 1991; Lodge and Tursky 1979). Another potential problem involves rationalization processes in which a person might "project" his or her own position onto a candidate that is preferred for other reasons, while simultaneously projecting the opposing issue stand onto the non-preferred candidate. Such problems certainly should not be ignored. Fortunately, however, the seven-point scales do seem to provide adequate empirical representations of issue beliefs and attitudes (Aldrich et al. 1982; Jacoby 1996). And, even though rationalization processes undoubtedly occur frequently, the magnitude of their impact appears to be rather limited (Feldman and Conover 1983; Markus and Converse 1979; Martinez 1988).

A fourth modification in the analysis of issue voting incorporates variability in the salience of different issues to individual citizens. Some critics argued that many empirical analyses underestimate the extent of issue-based political action because public opinion surveys confront people with issues that are simply not important

---

[4] For example, the National Election Studies now uses the following question to measure opinions about guaranteed jobs: "Some people feel the government in Washington should see to it that every person has a job and a good standard of living. Suppose these people are at one end of a scale, at point 1. Others think the government should just let each person get ahead on their own. Suppose these people are at the other end, at point 7. And, of course, some other people have opinions somewhere in between, at points 2, 3, 4, 5, or 6. Where would you place YOURSELF on this scale, or haven't you thought much about this?"

to them (e.g. Repass 1971). When asked about issues that are personally salient to them, individuals often show higher levels of awareness, and a greater propensity to translate their policy preference on that issue into a vote choice (e.g., Krosnick 1988). For this reason, a number of researchers have added measures of personal salience to the issues that they include in models of electoral behavior. While this seems like a very reasonable step, it has produced only mixed results. Some studies report that feelings of personal importance have strong mediating effects on the degree to which issues affect subsequent political behavior (Krosnick 1990; Rabinowitz, Prothro, and Jacoby 1982), while others find that individual-level issue salience adds very little to the predictive power of voting models (Markus and Converse 1979; Niemi and Bartels 1985).

In a fifth innovation, serious questions have been raised about the general process through which issue stands are incorporated into voting choices. The research literature since the 1950s has been dominated clearly by the "proximity model" described earlier, in which voters choose the candidate that falls closest to their own position along the relevant dimensions of issue conflict. This representation of issue voting is appealing on both intuitive and theoretical grounds (Downs 1957). However, its empirical support is surprisingly weak. Specifically, candidates and parties generally adopt relatively extreme issue positions, rather than the moderate policies that should win them maximal voting support (Budge, Crewe, and Farlie 1976; Rabinowitz 1978). One possibility is that political elites are acting irrationally, by adopting positions that provide them with suboptimal returns. However, this seems very unlikely, given that candidates and parties have clear motivations and relatively high levels of expertise (Jacobs and Shapiro 2000; Page 1978). Therefore, it is more likely that the proximity model, itself, is problematic as a representation of voter choice.

As an alternative model, Rabinowitz and Macdonald (1989) have proposed a "directional theory" of issue voting. According to this perspective, citizens maintain diffuse issue preferences, corresponding to a preferred *direction* of policy activity (e.g., more or less governmental intervention in some area of society) rather than a specific and crystallized policy position. People vote for the candidate who articulates the clearest stand in the direction that they prefer. The latter tend to be relatively extreme in content, rather than the centrist positions which should dominate electoral competition when citizens act on the basis of proximity considerations. There is currently a great deal of disagreement about the relative merits of the directional and proximity theories of issue voting (e.g., Macdonald, Rabinowitz, and Listhaug 1998; Westholm 1997). Both of these models seem to be useful for predicting voter choice on the basis of issue stands. However, the directional model does have some advantages in clarifying the ways that voters, candidates, and parties interact with each other in democratic electoral systems. In summary, it appears that American voters do generally cast their ballots in a manner that is consistent with their issue orientations, even though the exact processes through which they arrive at their voting decisions remain a bit unclear and open to some questions from researchers (Lewis-Beck et al. 2008; Macdonald, Rabinowitz, and Brasher 2003).

CANDIDATE EVALUATIONS

Popular assessments of presidential candidates were clearly one of the major elements driving the shift in scholarly attention from earlier, sociological models of the vote (e.g., Berelson, Lazarsfeld, and McPhee 1954) to more attitude-based conceptions of electoral choice (e.g., Campbell, Gurin, and Miller 1954). The latter were explicitly conceived to be more responsive to changes in the external political environment. Attitudes toward the personal characteristics of the Democratic and Republican candidates comprised two of the six partisan attitudes which acted as direct influences on the vote in Campbell et al.'s "funnel of causality" model. Taking a somewhat longer-term perspective, Stokes (1966) extended this idea and suggested that the electorate's changing reactions to new candidates contributed very heavily to the dynamic aspects of American electoral behavior.

While political scientists clearly recognized the relevance of candidate evaluations, scholarly interpretations of this variable's importance often were not very positive. For example, *The American Voter* seemed to suggest that mass belief systems dominated by ideas about the candidates' backgrounds and personalities are inherently less sophisticated than those which are organized along ideological, group-based, or policy-oriented lines (Campbell et al. 1960, ch. 10; Converse 1964). And, some researchers characterized personality-based voting as irrational, idiosyncratic, and incapable of contributing to popular control over government and policy (e.g., Page 1978; Patterson 1980). But there were several lines of research which took a different perspective, and generated a view that assessments of the candidates do provide reasonable and rational foundations for individual electoral decisions.

One long-standing line of work has examined the judgmental criteria that citizens use when they evaluate presidential candidates. The basic objective has been to provide empirical estimates of the "mental map" that citizens bring to bear upon the political world. Political actors, such as presidential candidates, the parties, and other visible public figures are shown as points within a geometric space. The axes of the space correspond to the evaluative dimensions that people rely on to construct their overall perceptions of those political actors. The locations of the points are determined by the political actors' positions along the relevant dimensions. Similar candidates (or parties) will be represented by points that are located close to each other within the space, while dissimilar candidates will have points that are more distant from each other. It is this latter feature which facilitates empirical estimation: multidimensional scaling methods are used to work from empirical data on perceived similarities between the candidates in order to generate the spatial point configuration.

A key feature of the multidimensional scaling approach is that the underlying dimensions are not specified in advance by the researcher. Instead, they are estimated from the data. This means that the spatial configuration and the dimensions of the space should conform closely to the way the electorate really does perceive the candidates and other actors. Although the technical details vary from one study to the next, such spatial models have been used a number of times over the years, by several different researchers, to study the ways the electorate looks at presidential candidates (e.g., Enelow and Hinich 1984; Jacoby 1986, 2004; Rabinowitz 1978; Weisberg and Rusk 1970).

The results obtained in the multidimensional scaling studies are remarkably consistent over the years, despite what appear to be enormous differences in the specific electoral contexts under investigation. Generally, public perceptions of the candidates within any given election campaign period are based upon two evaluative dimensions. From the 1960s on through the first presidential elections of the twenty-first century, one of these dimensions has always corresponded closely to a general liberal–conservative continuum. However, the second dimension has changed over time: During the 1960s and 1970s, it represented either partisanship or specific issues that were salient in particular elections. From 1980 on, the second dimension has tapped valence judgments corresponding to mass perceptions of candidate credibility or electability. What caused this change? While it is impossible to provide a definitive answer to that question, the changing structure of mass candidate perceptions is probably due to a combination of evolving campaign practices (i.e., the long pre-nomination campaign which places greater emphasis on the "horserace" elements of the contest) and the heightened polarization of American politics which has muted ideological distinctions within the parties and increased the ideological differences between them (Bartels 1988; Hetherington 2001; McCarty, Poole, and Rosenthal 2006).

For present purposes, the specific content of the spatial models is probably less important than the fact that such models can be used to provide excellent representations of the ways that citizens look at, and think about, presidential candidates. That would not be the case if people employed idiosyncratic criteria to evaluate political stimuli. Instead, the electorate does seem to be capable of differentiating candidates according to their substantive appeals and their positions within the political environment.

In another long-standing and broad line of work, scholars have looked more closely at the ways citizens think about the personal characteristics of presidential candidates. Information-processing models of public opinion suggest that people think about stimuli in the world around them on the basis of organized cognitive structures, or "schemata" (e.g., Lau and Sears 1986). In the case of presidential candidates, the predominant schemata underlying public assessments are organized according to partisan, issue, and personality criteria (Hamill, Lodge, and Blake 1985). Political science research prior to the mid-1980s had focused on the first two of these, while tending to regard the latter as irrational and idiosyncratic (as explained above). But a number of researchers began to question that negative interpretation.

For example, Miller, Wattenberg, and Malanchuk (1986) examined the content of survey respondents' answers to open-ended questions asking what they liked and disliked about the presidential candidates. They found that comments about the candidates' personal characteristics are usually more common than statements about parties, social groups, or issue stands. Furthermore, political sophistication is positively related to the likelihood that an individual will judge the candidates on the basis of personality traits. They conclude: "Rather than a concern with appearance, candidate assessments actually concentrate on instrumental concerns about the manner in which a candidate would conduct governmental affairs" (page 536).

At about the same time, several analysts focused on citizens' judgments about candidates' specific personality traits. The electorate's evaluations of presidential candidates appear to be generated on the basis of processes that are remarkably similar to those that guide everyday interpersonal interactions (e.g. Kinder and Fiske 1986). And these evaluations are structured along dimensional lines that seem to be appropriate for judging potential political office-holders, such as competence, integrity, and leadership (e.g. Kinder 1986).

Rahn et al. (1990) develop a general model of candidate appraisal, which fully recognizes the rather unique aspects of candidate judgments. On the one hand, they agree with other researchers that a large part of the evaluation process is carried out using the same psychological routines that people employ habitually, in their everyday lives. But Rahn et al. also point out that a presidential election involves extraordinary considerations which do not arise commonly in other contexts. Therefore, judgments about certain characteristics—particularly, leadership and competence—usually play a more pronounced role in forming each citizen's generalized affective response toward each candidate.

Perhaps the most unique aspect of personality judgments is that they are readily accessible to everyone, regardless of political sophistication or political involvement. This feature sets these kinds of evaluations apart from partisanship and issue orientations which are, respectively, more important determinants of electoral choices for party identifiers and relatively sophisticated strata within the electorate. Instead, Rahn et al. argue that candidate personality assessments have a more uniform influence throughout the mass public for two reasons: first, everyone has a great deal of experience developing judgments about other people, and this is easily "translated" to the political context of voter decision-making; second, citizens tend to pick up consistent, reinforcing, and almost redundant cues from the media and other external sources. It does not require a great deal of political expertise to assimilate this information and apply it to subsequent judgments (e.g., voting choices).

In summary, the scholarly consensus now maintains a fairly positive view of candidate evaluations. Feelings about the candidates comprise a very reasonable heuristic device for cutting through the complexities that abound in any election campaign. The broad accessibility of these judgments to citizens at all levels of political sophistication, combined with the simple fact that American elections require choices between candidates (and not parties or issues), means that candidate traits are an especially potent influence on electoral decisions.

CONCLUSIONS

Perhaps the most telling feature from the vast amount of research that has been conducted on American voting behavior is the remarkable continuity in the findings. This is not to say that there have been uniform results over the years. Differences in the external political environment, conceptualizations of central variables, and methodological approaches have all contributed to varying results from empirical analyses and differing interpretations of the ways that individual voters reach their electoral decisions. But there does seem to be remarkable agreement about which factors are relevant and the general sequence through which they come into play as influences on vote choice.

Does this mean that there is nothing more to be learned about American voting behavior? Of course not! Each new election raises the possibility that unanticipated factors will emerge as variables that have to be incorporated into models of individual voting choice. And existing approaches could be modified in several ways that might provide new insights and significant refinements to theoretical understandings of the electoral choice.

One general direction would be to recognize the potential for heterogeneity within the electorate, and incorporate individual differences in the "mixtures" of factors that citizens use to reach their decisions. This is definitely not a new idea (e.g., Rivers 1988). For example, we have already considered varying issue salience as a source of differences across voters. Other possible sources of variability include socioeconomic status (e.g., Manza and Brooks 1999) and racial identity (e.g., Tate 1993). Undoubtedly, the most widely-recognized bases for individual differences are political sophistication and knowledge (Knight 1985; Sniderman, Brody, and Tetlock 1991; Zaller 1992). But questions remain about the precise meaning and operationalization of these concepts, as well as the extent to which they really do enhance the quality of voters' decisions (Gilens 2001; Kuklinski et al. 2000, 2001; Lau and Redlawsk 2001).

A second line of innovation aims to reincorporate campaigns into the study of voting behavior (e.g., Johnston, Hagen, and Jamieson 2004). Political scientists have definitely not *ignored* this factor in previous work (e.g., Holbrook 1996). But, even though some research shows that individual beliefs and attitudes are responsive to campaign-related events (e.g., Markus 1982), other analysts still maintain that they have minimal effects on voters' eventual decisions (Finkel 1993). More recent work, relying on new data sources and innovative methodologies, suggests that the relevant processes are much more complicated, and not amenable to simple interpretations about whether or not campaigns have any impact on voters (e.g., Gelman and King 1993; Hillygus and Jackman 2003; Lau and Redlawsk 2006).

A third direction would be to develop models which span multiple elections. Political scientists have always recognized that the decision-making calculus employed by individual voters is affected by the external environment confronting the electorate (e.g., Nie, Verba, and Petrocik 1979). Indeed, *The American Voter*, along with the line of subsequent work that it generated, emphasized the importance of election-specific "short-term forces" which could either reinforce or cut across citizens' long-term predispositions (Converse 1966; Petrocik 1989). Aggregated from the individual to the societal level, this conceptualization led to an influential typology which differentiated among elections according to the degree to which these short- and long-term forces dominated the final outcome (Campbell 1966).

Even so, virtually all scholars continue to treat specific elections as discrete and largely independent events. But methodological innovations probably guarantee that this will change in the near future. As political scientists develop greater understanding of statistical techniques for handling multi-level data (e.g., Steenbergen and Jones 2002), attention will undoubtedly focus on models which nest individual behavior within electoral contexts. The great advantage of such an approach is that it will be possible to obtain specific estimates of the ways that features of elections impinge on the factors that citizens bring to bear on their own decisions.

Along with the preceding kinds of innovations, progress will certainly continue to be made along the pathways of "normal science," through improvements in the measurement of central concepts and refinements in model specification. But it appears highly unlikely that the near future will see any major change in the general understandings the scholars use to account for the ways that most citizens make their electoral decisions. As the authors of *The American Voter Revisited* say

(Lewis-Beck et al. 2008, 428), evolving elements of American politics, substantive theories, and methodological approaches "do not alter the overarching conclusion that *The American Voter's* paradigm for explanation of individual political behavior remains compelling."

REFERENCES

ACHEN, C. H. 1992. Social Psychology, Demographic Variables, and Linear Regression: Breaking the Iron Triangle in Voting Research. *Political Behavior*, 14: 195–211.

ALDRICH, J. H. and MCELVEY, R. D. 1977. A Method of Scaling with Applications to the 1968 and 1972 Presidential Elections. *American Political Science Review*, 71: 111–30.

—— NIEMI, R. G., RABINOWITZ, G., and ROHDE, D. W. 1982. The Measurement of Public Opinion about Public Policy: A Report on Some New Issue Question Formats. *American Journal of Political Science*, 26: 391–414.

ALWIN, D. F., COHEN, R. L., and NEWCOMB, T. M. 1991. *Political Attitudes over the Life Span: The Bennington Women after Fifty Years*. Madison: University of Wisconsin Press.

BARTELS, L. M. 1988. *Presidential Primaries and the Dynamics of Public Choice*. Princeton, N.J.: Princeton University Press.

BERELSON, B. R., LAZARSFELD, and P. F., MCPHEE, W. N. 1954. *Voting: A Study of Opinion Formation in a Presidential Campaign*. Chicago: University of Chicago Press.

BISHOP, G. F. 2005. *The Illusion of Public Opinion: Fact and Artifact in American Public Opinion Polls*. Lanham, Md.: Rowman and Littlefield.

BUDGE, I., CREWE, I., and FARLIE, D. (eds.) 1976. *Party Identification and Beyond: Representations of Voting and Party Competition*. New York: John Wiley.

CAMPBELL, A. 1966. A Classification of the Presidential Elections. In *Elections and the Political Order*, ed. A. Campbell, P. E. Converse, W. E. Miller, and D. E. Stokes. New York: Wiley.

—— CONVERSE, P. E., MILLER, W. E., and STOKES, D. E. 1960. *The American Voter*. New York: John Wiley.

—— GURIN, G., and MILLER, W. E. 1954. *The Voter Decides*. Evanston, Ill.: Row, Peterson.

CONVERSE, P. E. 1964. The Nature of Belief Systems in Mass Publics. In *Ideology and Discontent*, ed. D. E. Apter. New York: Free Press.

—— 1966. The Concept of the "Normal Vote." In *Elections and the Political Order*, ed. A. Campbell, P. E. Converse, W. E. Miller, and D. E. Stokes. New York: Wiley.

—— 1970. Attitudes and Nonattitudes: Continuation of a Dialogue. In *The Quantitative Analysis of Social Problems*, ed. E. R. Tufte. Reading, Mass.: Addison-Wesley.

—— and MARKUS, G. B. 1979. Plus ça Change...: The New CPS Election Study Panel. *American Political Science Review*, 73:2–49.

DOWNS, A. 1957. *An Economic Theory of Democracy*. New York: Harper and Row.

ENELOW, J. M. and HINICH, M. J. 1984. *The Spatial Theory of Voting: An Introduction*. Cambridge: Cambridge University Press.

FELDMAN, S. and CONOVER, P. J. 1983. Candidates, Issues, and Voters: The Role of Inference in Political Perception. *Journal of Politics*, 45: 810–39.

FINKEL, S. E. 1993. Reexamining the "Minimal Effects" Model in Recent Presidential Campaigns. *Journal of Politics*, 55: 1–21.

FIORINA, M. P. 1981. *Retrospective Voting in American National Elections*. New Haven: Yale University Press.

FRANKLIN, C. H. 1984. Issue Preferences, Socialization, and the Evolution of Party Identification. *American Journal of Political Science*, 28: 459–78.

—— and JACKSON, J. E. 1983. The Dynamics of Party Identification. *American Political Science Review*, 77: 957–73.

GELMAN, A. and KING, G. 1993. Why are American Presidential Election Polls so Variable When Votes are So Predictable? *British Journal of Political Science*, 23: 409–51.

GILENS, M. 2001. Political Ignorance and Collective Policy Preferences. *American Political Science Review*, 95: 379–96.

HAMILL, R., LODGE, M., and BLAKE, F. 1985. The Breadth, Depth, and Utility of Class, Partisan, and Ideological Schemata. *American Journal of Political Science*, 29: 850–70.

HETHERINGTON, M. J. 2001. Resurgent Mass Partisanship: The Role of Elite Polarization. *American Political Science Review*, 95: 619–32.

HILLYGUS, D. S. and JACKMAN, S. 2003. Voter Decision Making in Election 2000. *American Journal of Political Science*, 47: 583–96.

HOLBROOK, T. M. 1996. *Do Campaigns Matter?* Thousand Oaks, Calif.: Sage.

JACKSON, J. E. 1975. Issues, Party Choice, and Presidential Votes. *American Journal of Political Science*, 19: 161–85.

JACOBS, L. R. and SHAPIRO, R. Y. 2000. *Politicians Don't Pander: Political Manipulation and the Loss of Democratic Responsiveness*. Chicago: University of Chicago Press.

JACOBY, W. G. 1986. Levels of Conceptualization and Reliance on the Liberal–Conservative Continuum. *Journal of Politics*, 48: 423–32.

—— 1996. Testing the Effects of Paired Issue Statements on the Seven-Point Issue Scales. *Political Analysis*, Vol. 5 (1993–1994). Ann Arbor: University of Michigan Press.

—— 2004. Ideology in the 2000 Election: A Study in Ambivalence. In *Models of Voting in Presidential Elections: The 2000 Election*, ed. H. F. Weisberg and C. Wilcox. Stanford, Calif.: Stanford University Press.

JENNINGS, M. K. and MARKUS, G. B. 1984. Partisan Orientations over the Long Haul: Results from the Three-Wave Political Socialization Study. *American Political Science Review*, 78: 1000–18.

—— and NIEMI, R. 1974. *The Political Character of Adolescence: The Influence of Families and Schools*. Princeton, N. J.: Princeton University Press.

JOHNSTON, R., HAGEN, M. G., and JAMIESON, K. H. 2004. *The 2000 Presidential Election and the Foundations of Party Politics*. Cambridge: Cambridge University Press.

KEITH, B. E., MAGLEBY, D. B., NELSON, C. J., ORR, E., WESTLYE, M. C., and WOLNGER, R. E. 1992. *The Myth of the Independent Voter*. Berkeley, Calif., and Los Angeles, Calif.: University of California Press.

KINDER, D. R. 1986. Presidential Character Revisited. In *Political Cognition*, ed. R. R. Lau and D. O. Sears. Hillsdale, N.J.: Lawrence Erlbaum.

—— and FISKE, S. T. 1986. Presidents in the Public Mind. In *Political Psychology*, ed. M. Hermann. San Francisco: Jossey-Bass.

KNIGHT, K. K. 1985. Ideology in the 1980 Election: Ideological Sophistication Does Matter *Journal of Politics*, 47: 828–53.

KROSNICK, J. A. 1988. Attitude Importance and Attitude Change. *Journal of Experimental Social Psychology*, 24: 240–55.

—— 1990. Government Policy and Citizen Passion: A Study of Issue Publics in Contemporary America. *Political Behavior*, 12: 59–92.

—— 1991. The Stability of Political Preferences: Comparisons of Symbolic and Nonsymbolic Attitudes. *American Journal of Political Science*, 35: 547–76.

KUKLINSKI, J. H., QUIRK, P. J., JERIT, J., SCHWEIDER, D., and RICH, R. F. 2000. Misinformation and the Currency of Democratic Citizenship. *Journal of Politics*, 62: 790–816.

—— —— —— RICH, R. F. 2001. The Political Environment and Citizen Decision Making: Information, Motivation, and Policy Tradeoffs. *American Journal of Political Science*, 45: 410–24.

LAU, R. R. and REDLAWSK, D. P. 2001. Advantages and Disadvantages of Cognitive Heuristics in Political Decision Making. *American Journal of Political Science*, 45: 951–71.

—— —— 2006. *How Voters Decide: Information Processing During Election Campaigns*. Cambridge: Cambridge University Press.

—— and SEARS, D. O. (eds.) 1986. *Political Cognition*. Hillsdale, N.J.: Lawrence Erlbaum.

LEWIS-BECK, M. S., JACOBY, W. G., NORPOTH, H., and WEISBERG, H. F. 2008. *The American Voter Revisited*. Ann Arbor, Mich.: University of Michigan Press.

LODGE, M. and TURSKY, B. 1979. Comparisons between Category and Magnitude Scaling of Political Opinion Employing SRC/CPS Items. *American Political Science Review*, 73: 50–66.

MACDONALD, S. E., RABINOWITZ, G.M, and BRASHER, H. 2003. Policy Issues and Electoral Democracy. In *Electoral Democracy*, ed. M. B. MacKuen and G. Rabinowitz. Ann Arbor: University of Michigan Press.

—— —— and LISTHAUG, O. 1998. On Attempting to Rehabilitate the Proximity Model: Sometimes the Patient Just Can't Be Helped. *Journal of Politics*, 60: 653–90.

MANZA, J. and BROOKS, C. 1999. *Social Cleavages and Political Change*. Oxford: Oxford University Press.

MARKUS, G. B. 1982. Political Attitudes during an Election Year: A Report on the 1980 NES Panel Study. *American Political Science Review*, 76: 538–60.

—— and CONVERSE, P. E. 1979. A Dynamic Simultaneous Equation Model of Electoral Choice. *American Political Science Review*, 73: 1055–70.

MARTINEZ, M. D. 1988. Political Involvement and the Projection Process. *Political Behavior*, 10: 151–67.

MCCARTY, N., POOLE, K. T., and ROSENTHAL, H. 2006. *Polarized America: The Dance of Ideology and Unequal Riches*. Cambridge, Mass.: MIT Press.

MILLER, A. H., WATTENBERG, M. P., and MALANCHUK, O. 1986. Schematic Assessments of Presidential Candidates. *American Political Science Review*, 80: 521–40.

MILLER, W. E. 1976. The Cross-National Use of Party Identification as a Stimulus to Political Inquiry. In *Party Identification and Beyond*, ed. I. Budge, I. Crewe, and D. Farlie. New York: Wiley.

—— 1991. Party Identification, Realignment, and Party Voting: Back to Basics. *American Political Science Review*, 85: 557–68.

NIE, N. H., VERBA, S., and PETROCIK, J. R. 1979. *The Changing American Voter*, rev. edn. Cambridge, Mass.: Harvard University Press.

NIEMI, R. G. and BARTELS, L. M. 1985. New Measures of Issue Salience: An Evaluation. *Journal of Politics*, 47: 1212–20.

—— and JENNINGS, M. K. 1991. Issues and Inheritance in the Formation of Party Identification. *American Journal of Political Science*, 35: 970–88.

PAGE, B. I. 1978. *Choices and Echoes in Presidential Elections*. Chicago: University of Chicago Press.

—— and JONES, C. 1979. Reciprocal Effects of Policy Preferences, Party Loyalties, and the Vote. *American Political Science Review*, 73: 1071–89.

PATTERSON, T. E. 1980. *The Mass Media Election: How Americans Choose Their President.* New York: Praeger.

PETROCIK, J. R. 1974. An Analysis of the Intransitivities in the Index of Party Identification. *Political Methodology*, 1: 31–47.

—— 1989. An Expected Party Vote: New Data for an Old Concept. *American Journal of Political Science*, 33: 44–66.

RABINOWITZ, G. 1978. On the Nature of Political Issues: Insights from a Spatial Analysis. *American Journal of Political Science*, 22: 793–817.

—— and MACDONALD, S. E. 1989. A Directional Theory of Issue Voting. *American Political Science Review*, 83: 93–121.

—— PROTHRO, J. W., and JACOBY, W. G. 1982. Salience as a Factor in the Impact of Issues on Candidate Evaluation. *Journal of Politics*, 44: 41–63.

RAHN, W., ALDRICH, J., BORGIDA, E., and SULLIVAN, J. L. 1990. A Social-Cognitive Model of Candidate Appraisal. In *Information and Democratic Processes*, ed. J. Ferejohn and J. Kuklinski. Urbana, Ill.: University of Illlinois Press.

REPASS, D. E. 1971. Issue Salience and Party Choice. *American Political Science Review*, 65: 389–400.

RIVERS, D. 1988. Heterogeneity in Models of Electoral Choice. *American Journal of Political Science*, 32: 737–57.

SEARS, D. O. 1993. Symbolic Politics: A Socio-Psychological Theory. In *Explorations in Political Psychology*, ed. S. Iyengar and W. J. McGuire. Durham, N.C.: Duke University Press.

—— and FUNK, C. L. 1990. Self-Interest in Americans' Political Opinions. In *Beyond Self-Interest*, ed. J. J. Mansbridge. Chicago: University of Chicago Press.

—— —— 1999. Evidence of the Long-Term Persistence of Adults' Political Predispositions. *Journal of Politics*, 61: 1–28.

SNIDERMAN, P. M., BRODY, R. A., and TETLOCK, P. E. 1991. *Reasoning and Choice: Explorations in Political Psychology*. New York: Cambridge University Press.

STEENBERGEN, M. R. and JONES, B. S. 2002. Modeling Multilevel Data Structures. *American Journal of Political Science*, 46: 218–37.

STOKES, D. E. 1966. Some Dynamic Elements of Contests for the Presidency. *American Political Science Review*, 60: 19–28.

TATE, K. 1993. *From Protest to Politics: The New Black Voters in American Elections.* Cambridge, Mass.: Harvard University Press.

VERBA, S. and NIE, N. H. 1972. *Participation in America*. New York: Harper and Row.

WEISBERG, H. F. and RUSK, J. G. 1970. Dimensions of Candidate Evaluation. *American Political Science Review*, 64: 1167–85.

WESTHOLM, A. 1997. Distance versus Direction: The Illusory Defeat of the Proximity Theory of Electoral Choice. *American Political Science Review*, 91: 865–83.

ZALLER, J. R. 1992. *The Nature and Origins of Mass Opinion*. New York: Cambridge University Press.

CHAPTER 16

....

POLITICS, EXPERTISE, AND INTERDEPENDENCE WITHIN ELECTORATES

....

T. K. AHN

ROBERT HUCKFELDT

ALEXANDER K. MAYER

JOHN B. RYAN

THIS chapter reconsiders the role of politically expert citizens as primary movers within a democratic political process characterized by patterns of interdependence among citizens. The concept of political expertise is normally restricted to political elites and elite decision making—to the politicians, consultants, bureaucrats, and handlers who populate the corridors of power. While important efforts have certainly been made at introducing the role of expertise into discussions of grassroots politics among the citizens populating the corridors of everyday life, these efforts have been notable for their failure to penetrate the dominant, enduring vision of democratic politics held among political scientists.

This failure is especially striking in view of early efforts in political science and sociology that focused attention on differentiated levels of political capacity among citizens via "opinion leaders" and a "two-step flow" of communication. The earliest two-step model was a simplified rendering in which some people (the opinion leaders) paid attention to politics and the media, while other individuals (virtually everyone else) took their information and guidance from these opinion leaders (Lazarsfeld, Berelson, and Gaudet 1948). This early model was vulnerable to criticisms of political elitism—that it underestimated the capacity of individual citizens consigned to the role of followers. It was also vulnerable to criticisms that it oversimplified communication processes in which leaders and followers were tied together in complex horizontal as well as vertical networks of relationships where, for example, leaders and followers change roles depending on the particular subject matter. These problems were addressed in later, more sophisticated treatments of opinion leaders and the two-step flow (Berelson, Lazarsfeld, and McPhee 1954; Katz 1957; Katz and Lazarsfeld 1955; Weimann 1982, 1991). Nevertheless, expertise and the role of expert individuals have been slow to penetrate research on voting, public opinion, political communication, and political participation.

This lack of penetration is primarily the consequence of a historical reluctance to consider citizens as interdependent actors in politics. The primary historical model of a voter in the empirical literature is a socially disembodied individual whose decisions, judgments, and voting choices are based on individually held preferences, opinions, beliefs, attitudes, and identifications. This atomistic model is probably best seen as an unintentional by-product of particular observational strategies that have been dominant in political research—most notably randomized sample surveys of large populations that divorce individuals from their social and political environments (Huckfeldt and Sprague 1993, 1995). While relatively few students of politics would advocate an atomistic model on its intellectual merits, traditional methods of data collection have resulted in a *de facto* adherence to a model that separates and isolates one citizen from another in a way that is both theoretically unsatisfying and empirically inadequate.

The welcome news is that rapidly accelerating progress has taken place in alternative modes of data collection and analysis regarding communication among interdependent individuals. These alternatives include contextual studies, network studies, and experimental studies that intentionally locate one citizen relative to other citizens in both time and space, and they generate new opportunities to revisit opinion leaders and political expertise in the context of horizontal and vertical networks creating n-step flows of communication and persuasion (for discussions see: Huckfeldt and Sprague 1993; Huckfeldt 2007a, 2009). The moment has arrived, in short, to reconsider and extend the earliest conceptions of communication, expertise, and interdependence within democratic electorates.

THE CIVIC CAPACITY OF VOTERS
AND ELECTORATES

The failure of political expertise to gain traction as a useful concept in the study of political communication is particularly striking in view of our discipline's historic investment in the study of political knowledge, awareness, and belief systems among citizens (Converse 1964; Delli Carpini and Keeter 1993, 1996; Gilens 2001; Kuklinski et al. 2000; Zaller 1992). This body of work, which is typically based on large-scale national surveys and normally focused on individual determinants and consequences of knowledge and beliefs, has demonstrated levels of political competence that are typically disappointing. As Sniderman suggests (1993), shocked disbelief and opposition to the earliest work ultimately gave way to a new stream of research that takes low levels of civic capacity as a given, turning instead to several important and derivative questions. If voters are so naive, how are they able to make decisions that often seem well informed (Lodge and Steenbergen with Brau 1995; Sniderman, Brody, and Tetlock 1991)? And how do aggregate electorates manage to perform in a manner that appears to respond to the political environment in meaningful ways (Erikson, MacKuen, and Stimson 2002; Page and Shapiro 1992; Sniderman 2000)?

Within this context, a renewed emphasis on communication networks is potentially relevant to the distribution and diffusion of political expertise among interdependent citizens, as well as to individual and aggregate decision making. The selection of informants, and hence the construction of networks, not only responds to the preferences of potential discussants, but also to their potential for being informative (Downs 1957). The presence or absence of bias on the part of potential informants does not necessarily reduce their information potential (Calvert 1985a), and empirical studies show that the construction of communication networks responds directly to the expertise of potential discussants. Discussion occurs more frequently with individuals who possess higher levels of interest and knowledge about politics, and it is only modestly depressed by disagreement (Huckfeldt 2001; Huckfeldt and Mendez 2008; also see Anderson and Paskeviciute 2005, 2006).

Our argument is that typically low levels of individually held knowledge are neither surprising nor necessarily troublesome, and they are best placed in a somewhat larger context. First, citizenship involves more than political knowledge, expertise, and voting. The fabric of democratic politics depends on a range of talents and contributions, supplied both through markets as well as through voluntary communal efforts, and thus passionate citizenship is not simply the residue of individuals who are able and willing to read the *New York Times*. If time spent consuming and analyzing information on current affairs comes at the expense of these other commitments—coaching little league baseball, organizing the girl scout troop, or volunteering at the local library—it may very well be a bad bargain for the more complex and variegated fabric of democratic politics (Berelson, Lazarsfeld, and McPhee 1954, ch. 14).

Moreover, if individuals do not enjoy consuming information on politics—if they do not place intrinsic value on political information—why would we be surprised that the level of political expertise within populations is heterogeneous? Viewed from the vantage point of even the most myopic form of individual rationality, political information consumption is not irrational for everyone (Downs 1957; Fiorina 1990). Some people enjoy politics more than others, and it is entirely reasonable that these people spend more time on political matters. Fortunately, the consumption of political information makes perfectly good sense *both* among those who enjoy politics and public affairs *and* among those who value it instrumentally.

What is the solution to the problem of heterogeneous levels of political expertise within populations? Alternatively, is this heterogeneity a problem? This chapter argues that the problem—to the extent it is a problem—is mitigated through the patterns of interdependence realized in the form of complex networks of political communication. The implication of this argument is that, by ignoring the relationship between interdependent citizens and varying levels of political expertise, we underestimate the capacity of citizens in the aggregate, as well as misspecifying models of political judgment and decision. None of this means that interdependent citizens necessarily produce beneficial outcomes. Rather, by ignoring individual interdependence within electorates, we run the risk of fundamentally misunderstanding not only the nature of citizenship, but also the potential strengths and weaknesses of democratic politics.

Expertise Versus Knowledge

What is the difference between knowledge and expertise? Knowledge involves an individual's ability to access relevant political information from long-term memory (Lodge and Taber 2000). In contrast, we define expertise in terms of political choices informed by subjectively defined interests, and hence the ability of an individual to act in accord with her own view of the world. Some citizens are politically knowledgeable and hence likely to be expert, and many of these individuals further enhance their expertise based on communication with others. Some citizens possess modest or negligible amounts of political knowledge, but their judgments are informed through various mechanisms, including political discussion (Green, Palmquist, and Schickler 2002; Lodge et al. 1995; MacKuen and Marcus

2001; Marcus, Neuman, and MacKuen 2000; Sniderman et al. 1991). Still other citizens base their choices directly on the knowledge and expertise held by others— *they act as though they are expert by imitating the choices of others in their environments* (Boyd and Richerson 1985; Fowler and Smirnov 2005). While such imitation may not produce optimal choices, it is a particularly effective strategy for individuals who are unwilling or unable to invest in the individually based acquisition of information but are able to imitate the choices of others who provide appropriate guidance.

These distinctions are important because political communication need not enhance knowledge in order to enhance expertise within the electorate. Indeed, Ryan (2008) shows that individuals do not necessarily become more knowledgeable simply by discussing politics with knowledgeable discussion partners, and there is no evidence to suggest that people automatically weigh the advice of politically knowledgeable informants more heavily when arriving at their own political judgments and choices (Huckfeldt and Sprague 1995). Moreover, an interesting set of studies on "correct" voting (see Lau and Redlawsk's 1997 definition) produce mixed consequences for the effects that arise due to communication with experts (Richey 2007; Sohkey and McClurg 2008).

These observations raise a series of questions related to the selection criteria that individuals employ to construct political communication networks, the contextually based supply of experts as a constraint on these selection mechanisms, and the capacity of expert citizens to influence the communication process. Is the expertise of a potential informant relevant to the construction of communication networks? Under what circumstances is expert advice influential, credible, or worthwhile? What are the circumstances and consequences of political communication beyond the boundaries of proximate groups—the conditions giving rise to networks that bridge the divides between groups? What are the implications of these various mechanisms of communication and interdependence for politics in the aggregate?

Our response to these questions is framed around three propositions. First, the messages conveyed through political communication networks are neither persistently nor inevitably homogeneous, and the extent of diversity varies systematically as a consequence of individual and contextual factors. Second, networks are constructed by individual choices and opportunities for interaction that accumulate to form and reshape patterns of communication, but these choices respond to the availability of potential discussants and their levels of expertise. Third, varying levels of diversity, combined with the importance of expertise, carry complex dynamical implications for the diffusion of information, the self-educating properties of electorates, and patterns of influence within aggregate populations.

Persistence of Network Diversity

The study of political diversity within communication networks is inspired by the mismatch between long-standing theory and observation. In their classic study of the 1948 election, Berelson, Lazarsfeld, and McPhee (1954, ch. 7) argue that social interaction produces agreement and homogeneity within small groups. In his analysis of diversity, Abelson (1964, 1979) identifies a seemingly inexorable tendency toward homogeneity within formal models of communication. This same tendency is found in agent-based simulations of communication and diffusion (Axelrod 1997a), where the preservation of heterogeneity and disagreement is frequently rendered problematic (Johnson 1999; Johnson and Huckfeldt 2005).

More than twenty-five years of research demonstrate the importance of clustered political preferences within political communication networks, but the same evidence also points toward persistent levels of residual disagreement, even within the smallest and most closely held social groups (Huckfeldt, Johnson, and Sprague 2004; Huckfeldt and Sprague 1995; Huckfeldt et al. 1998). For example, a network name generator was employed in the 2000 National Election Study in which respondents were asked to provide the first names of people with whom they were most likely to discuss "government, elections, and politics." Approximately 40 percent of those supporting a major party candidate (Bush or Gore) named at least one discussant who supported the opposite party's candidate, and less than half the respondents perceived that all the discussants they had named supported their own preferred candidate (Huckfeldt, Mendez, and Osborn 2004). Similar patterns of preference heterogeneity within networks are demonstrated across time and space within the United States (Huckfeldt, Johnson and Sprague 2004; Huckfeldt and Sprague 1995; Huckfeldt et al. 1998), as well as in cross national comparisons (Huckfeldt, Ikeda, and Pappi 2005).

Why is preference heterogeneity important to expertise among citizens? If citizens avoid divergent preferences, the potential for persuasive communication is reduced. This was demonstrated early and convincingly in the work of William McPhee's (1963) vote simulator: disagreement gives rise to continued information search and hence the potential for "influence" in the broadest sense of the term (see also Taber and Lodge 2006). That is, influence occurs not only when individuals are persuaded to change their preferences in response to divergent information, but also when individuals must "counter-argue"—either socially or internally. Contrary messages are influential if they force individuals to rethink their own preferences, even if their initial commitments to those preferences are sustained.

Network Endogeneity and Diverse Preferences

Individuals exercise choice in the construction of communication networks, but choice is constrained by supply, and the supply of discussion partners looms particularly large with respect to network composition. The supply of potential discussants is, in turn, a stochastic function of proximate populations—families, work places, places of worship, sports clubs. Moreover, individuals have multiple preferences in the construction of communication networks, and politics is only one among a long list of preferential criteria—sparkling personalities, trustworthiness, a hatred for the Yankees, and so on. Finally, extended information searches are personally and socially expensive, and hence individuals will typically build networks of association that reflect the contexts within which they reside, regardless of their own political preferences (Brown 1981; Greer 1961). In short, clustered preferences within networks arise in large part as a consequence of environmentally imposed supply, quite independently of individual control over associational patterns, in circumstances where proximate populations are sorted by characteristics correlated with political preference (Buttice, Huckfeldt, and Ryan 2008; Huckfeldt 1983).

As we have seen in the context of the 2000 National Election Study, many individuals experience political heterogeneity within their political communication networks. This does not necessarily mean, however, that individuals are unable to exercise control over the content of information transmitted through their communication networks (Finifter 1974; MacKuen 1990). This control is potentially exercised in at least two different ways: by creating specialized networks of political communication—either contained within or separate from their larger and more generalized networks of association—or, alternatively, by avoiding political discussion with individuals in non-specialized communication networks who hold disagreeable viewpoints.

The first explanation, network specialization, can be assessed using the experimentally manipulated name generator employed in the 1996 Indianapolis–St. Louis study. One random half sample of the main respondents was asked to provide the names of people with whom they discussed "government, elections, and politics," while the other half sample was asked to provide the names of people with whom they discussed "important matters." If people construct specialized networks of political communication that serve to shield them from political disagreement, we should expect to see higher levels of homogeneity within political discussion networks, but this expectation is not sustained. Indeed, there is very little difference in the levels of disagreement between the political networks and the important matters networks (Huckfeldt and Mendez 2008). Hence, the evidence suggests that people do not construct specialized networks of political communication in an effort to avoid disagreement, even though specialization becomes more relevant with respect to issues of political expertise.

Finally, people might also manage disagreement with associates who hold contrary political viewpoints by reducing the frequency of political discussion, thereby reducing the frequency of disagreement. The Indianapolis–St. Louis study is useful for these purposes because it includes a snowball survey with discussants named by the main respondents, and this snowball survey provides the opportunity to estimate a simultaneous model of political disagreement frequency and political discussion frequency within political communication networks (Huckfeldt and Mendez 2008). This model shows that individuals *do* censure their patterns of political communication to avoid political disagreement (Mackuen 1990)—the frequency of disagreement retards the frequency of discussion.

At the same time, while disagreement produces negative feedback that dampens political discussion frequency, politically engaged citizens cannot resist discussing politics! That is, political engagement produces political discussion, and higher frequencies of political discussion yield higher frequencies of political disagreement, even though disagreement attenuates discussion frequency. As a consequence, dyadic relationships are characterized by a dynamic equilibrium in which discussion and disagreement coexist at levels that are influenced by the levels of political interest and engagement of the participants in the dyad (Huckfeldt and Mendez 2008). Thus, patterns of political communication and disagreement are endogenous to the individual preferences and choices of these participants, *but this endogeneity does not produce a world without disagreement.* Among those who care about politics and are exposed to heterogeneous preferences, the experience of political disagreement is likely to be a fact of life.

Autoregressive Influence and Limits on Persuasion

Why does disagreement fail to be resolved by persuasion—why do we not see the *creation* of uniformity within these networks of communication? This is a particularly important question because a range of sophisticated modeling efforts appear to suggest that such a persuasion dynamic is nearly irresistible within large populations (Abelson 1964, 1979; Axelrod 1997a, 1997b; Huckfeldt, Johnson, and Sprague 2004, 2005; Johnson and Huckfeldt 2005). The perhaps counter-intuitive answer to this question is that complex patterns of communication and influence are, in fact, self limiting within the context of diverse preferences, and hence interdependence can be seen to sustain heterogeneity!

If disagreement within a dyad leads to a process of counter-argument in which the views of other discussants are taken into account, then the influence of communication within any particular dyad is conditioned on communication within all other dyads. In other words, not only is the formation of an individual's preference autoregressive with respect to the distribution of preferences in an individual's communication network (Marsden and Friedkin 1994), but the influence within a particular dyad is autoregressive with respect to the flow of information within the participants' other dyads (Huckfeldt, Johnson, and Sprague 2004). As a consequence, the influence of a contrary message is attenuated by the dominant messages within networks, and heterogeneity is thus sustained.

It may be helpful to provide an example. Mutz and Mondak (2006) provide a compelling account of the fact that individuals are more likely to encounter political disagreement in the workplace (also see Baybeck and Huckfeldt 2002). Within that context, suppose that Sidney and Lisa are co-workers, and that Sidney is imbedded in a family full of Republicans, while Lisa is imbedded in a family of Democrats. For a variety of reasons—workplace proximity, shared interests, and so on—Lisa and Sidney regularly communicate about a range of topics, including politics. Neither of them is likely to be convinced by the other to change their political stripes for the simple reason that both still reside within an informational environment dominated by their respective families. And hence one might argue that agreement as well as disagreement are both socially sustained through complex patterns of social interaction and communication (Huckfeldt, Johnson, and Sprague 2004).

In short, political heterogeneity within networks is a necessary but insufficient condition for political change due to persuasive communication driven by expert opinion. Disagreement provides the occasion for influence, but if expert opinion is not weighted more heavily within the communication process, diversity would not translate into the diffusion of expertise. This weighting does not occur because individuals genuflect with respect to citizens with higher levels of expertise. Rather, the weighting process occurs because the views of expert citizens are disproportionately represented within the process of political communication.

EXPERT CITIZENS AND POLITICAL COMMUNICATION

One of the enduring innovations of the political economy literature on citizenship is to take information costs seriously in the analysis of political communication and expertise. Within this context, Downs (1957, 229) argues that political discussion minimizes the information costs of political engagement. Sensible people search out *well informed* associates who possess *compatible* political orientations, and hence citizens become efficiently informed—both individually and collectively.

Calvert (1985a) also focuses on the utility of socially communicated information, but he argues that information is more useful if it is acquired from someone with a well-identified bias, independent of the recipient's own bias. In contrast, Lupia and McCubbins (1998) and Boudreau (2009) argue that information from a source with whom you disagree is only useful if the source is compelled to tell the truth— either through sanctions or some other means for verifying the information. These issues become still more complex because, even if citizens do communicate with others based on perceived levels of political expertise, they might respond to divergent opinions by overestimating the expertise of those with whom they agree and underestimating it among those with whom they disagree (Lodge and Taber 2000; Lord, Ross, and Lepper 1979).

Observational studies of information flows within communication networks suggest that the distribution of expertise plays an important role in affecting patterns of political communication (Huckfeldt 2001). First, citizen judgments regarding the political expertise of others are based in reality, driven primarily by *actual levels of expertise defined in terms of knowledge and interest on the part of potential discussants*. The capacity of individuals to render meaningful judgments regarding the expertise of various informants is quite striking. People are not lost in a cloud of misperception when they engage in social communication about politics, and neither is the information they obtain simply a mirror of their own preferences. Perceived expertise is driven primarily by the characteristics of the discussant being perceived—*not* the respondent who is doing the perceiving.

Second, citizens communicate about politics more frequently with those whom they judge to be politically expert, quite independently of agreement or disagreement. People talk more with those who know more! Hence, one of the reasons that "democracy works" might be that citizens rely on "horizontal networks of relations" for meaningful political engagement (Mondak and Gearing 1998; Putnam 1993), thereby reducing information costs and enhancing democratic efficiency. At the same time, there is no evidence to suggest that people weight discussants' opinions by perceived discussant expertise in forming their own judgments (Huckfeldt and Sprague 1995). Rather, they weight a discussant's opinion by the extent to which other discussants hold the same opinion (Huckfeldt, Johnson, and Sprague 2004).

The point is not that individuals listen more respectfully to experts, but rather that they listen to experts more frequently. Expert opinion tends to dominate the air time within political communication networks. Indeed, an alternative explanation for higher reported frequencies of discussion with experts is not that citizens seek out expert opinion, but rather that experts simply spend more time talking about politics! In this way we might even say that expert opinion is *self-weighted* within communication networks (Huckfeldt 2001).

INDIVIDUAL, AGGREGATE, AND
DYNAMIC IMPLICATIONS

Traditional models suggest that social communication insulates individuals from events in the external political environment. Individual citizens are imbedded within homogeneous groupings of like-minded individuals, and politics is reinterpreted relative to dominant views in the group. Hence, political information is filtered, conformity encouraged, and group boundaries reinforced. (Berelson et al. 1954). The problem is that the persistence of diversity, coupled with the centrality of political experts within communication networks, calls into question this sort of determinate outcome (McPhee 1963).

A number of efforts have pursued the proximate, individual-level implications of homogeneous versus heterogeneous communication networks. While a consensus has not been reached, a diverse set of findings are generating progress in the identification of important underlying issues. Mutz's results (2002a, 2006) suggest that individuals residing in politically heterogeneous networks are less likely to participate and more likely to make decisions closer to the election. Huckfeldt, Mendez, and Osborn (2004) show modestly negative effects of heterogeneity on political interest but no effects on turnout. They also demonstrate higher levels of ambivalence and lower levels of partisanship among those located in heterogeneous networks. Fowler (2005) shows that one individual in a homogeneous network deciding to vote could lead to a turnout cascade, while McClurg (2006) finds that the most important social determinant of turnout is not heterogeneity but rather expertise—people in expert networks are more likely to turn out. Based on his empirical analysis, Kotler-Berkowitz (2005, 167) argues that "networks made up of a diverse set of friends expose people to various nonredundant opportunities and requests for political participation." Both Gibson (1992; also 2001) and Mutz (2002b) show that individuals in heterogeneous networks are more likely to be politically tolerant.[1]

The various aggregate and dynamic implications of heterogeneous networks for democratic politics and political communication are quite profound. The survival of disagreement within networks of political communication, in combination with the important effects on communication that arise due to the distribution of expertise, lead to a reconsideration of the mechanisms of political interdependence among citizens, the diffusion of expertise within networks, and the aggregate implications of political interdependence among citizens. Indeed, the theory of the consequences of social communication for the dynamics of an election campaign might be transformed fundamentally. Rather than serving as a source of

---

[1] For an interesting effort to reconcile findings see Gimpel, Lay, and Schuknecht (2003).

insulation from the external political environment, social communication might even serve to magnify the consequences of the external environment by connecting individuals to extensive and far-reaching networks of political information (Barabási 2002; Watts 1999).

The intersection of these phenomena—the survival of disagreement, the self-educating capacities of electorates, and the resulting dynamic consequences of interdependent individuals—forces a reassessment of the models and mechanisms of communication among citizens (Barber 1984; Fishkin 1991; Mendelberg 2002). It also points toward particular observational strategies for collecting relevant information on these problems. In particular, it is not enough to collect information on individuals, although information on individuals is of course central to progress in understanding political communication patterns. Rather, individuals are understood within the context of communication and interaction—within the groups where they are located. Hence, an observational strategy is needed which provides the opportunity to move back and forth, both theoretically and observationally, between individuals and groups.

OBSERVING INTERDEPENDENCE AND DENSITY DEPENDENCE

A great deal of what we know about political communication networks among citizens is based on a series of election studies in the United States, Japan, Germany, Russia, and South Africa (for examples, see Gibson 1992, 2001; Huckfeldt, Ikeda, and Pappi 2005; Huckfeldt, Johnson, and Sprague 2004; Huckfeldt and Sprague 1995; Huckfeldt et al. 1998). These studies are built around a network name generator in which survey respondents are asked to provide the first names and various characteristics of the people in their communication networks, and a number of these studies also include snowball surveys with interviews of the discussants thus identified by the respondents to the main survey. Moreover, the interviews with the main respondents are typically indexed on a particular spatial locale—a neighborhood, a city, a state, a nation. In some instances, the initial interviews with main respondents are sufficiently clustered to use aggregated survey data for contextual measures at intermediate levels of aggregation (Huckfeldt and Sprague 1992). These observational procedures offer a great many opportunities to address a range of important questions from the standpoint of interdependence among citizens. They not only provide information on individuals, but on the relationships among individuals, and how these relationships are configured by, and imbedded within, larger environments.

While these observational procedures sustain important research programs, there are limits on any set of observational procedures—limits that confront any effort aimed at understanding a dynamic process based on *post hoc* observational data. As we have seen, observational studies of networks, contexts, and political communication effects are plagued by a series of endogeneity issues (Achen 1986; Achen and Shively 1995; Huckfeldt 2007b; Huckfeldt and Mendez 2008). Progress has been made on these problems through the use of experiments imbedded within surveys, through the use of structural models, through quasi-experiments and field experiments, and through conventional methods of inferential reasoning. Ultimately, however, continued progress is likely to be accelerated through the development of new and complementary research strategies that depend on laboratory-based experimental studies.

EXPERIMENTAL STRATEGIES

The use of experimental research strategies based in laboratory settings is nothing new to studies of political communication, and a great deal of progress has been accomplished (Boudreau, Coulson, and McCubbins 2008; Druckman and Nelson 2003; Lupia and McCubbins 1998).[2] Our own work pursues an experimental framework based on a Downsian spatial model of political preference and competition. Such a spatial model offers several advantages. First, it allows the explicit modeling of heterogeneous political preferences among citizens, as well as among candidates in an election. Correspondingly, it becomes possible to address the "distance" between any pair of citizens or candidates on a continuum. Second, uncertainty in politics and the level of political expertise can be directly incorporated within analyses (see Baron 1994; Budge 1994; Calvert 1985b; Shepsle 1972, to name a few). Third, the level of political expertise can be represented in various ways, including the amount of information voters have acquired. Finally, and just as important, the level of expertise can be conveniently endogenized by assigning variable information costs among the voters.

An experimental framework built on spatial models provides the opportunity to address a growing literature on communication among agents with heterogeneous preferences (Crawford 1998; Crawford and Sobel 1982). This literature has inspired

---

[2] While laboratory experiments are advantageous because of their increased internal validity, survey experiments and even quasi-experiments have provided important insights into when interpersonal influence is more likely (e.g., Huckfeldt and Mendez 2008; Mondak 1995; Parker, Parker, and McCann 2008). Significant progress has also occurred through the construction of field experiments (Nickerson 2008).

a focus on "cheap talk" within political science (Austen-Smith 1990; Austen-Smith and Banks 1996; Coughlan 2000; Farrell and Rabin 1996; Feddersen and Pesendorfer 1998), and it has inspired an effort to link game-theoretic models of communication to enduring issues regarding political deliberation (Hafer and Landa 2007; Johnson 1993). The fundamental issue underlying this "cheap talk" communication literature is whether individuals with diverging preferences can communicate effectively via non-costly signals, i.e., cheap talk. Thus, by allowing subjects to communicate with each other in an experimental framework built on a spatial model of political competition, we combine several lines of research—psychological and sociological, as well as game-theoretic research on cheap talk.

Such an experimental framework combines the advantages of small-group dynamics with network representations of communication in the context of an experimental design (Ahn, Huckfeldt, and Ryan 2006; Ahn et al. 2008; Ostrom et al. 1992; Verba 1961). One version of the experiment involves two groups of seven subjects who communicate with one another via networked computers within a quasi-electoral context. Subjects choose between two "candidates," neither of whom are real human subjects. Rather, these candidates are represented as fixed positions on a one-dimensional policy space, but the candidate positions are unknown to the subjects. The policy space varies from 1 to 7, and each subject has an integer position that remains constant across the rounds in an experimental session. The candidate positions are reset at each round, and all subjects are accurately informed that Candidate A's position always lies in the interval between 1 and 6 inclusive, while Candidate B's position always lies in the interval between 2 and 7 inclusive.

The subjects are rewarded with a cash incentive if the candidate closest to them wins the election, and thus they are motivated to obtain information in two different ways. First they have an opportunity to make private investments in the acquisition of information, followed by an opportunity to request information from other subjects. Private investments in information vary across subjects because the cost of information is experimentally manipulated. Information taken from other members of the same group is free, but a cost is imposed for information that is acquired from subjects lying beyond the boundaries of the subject's own group. Privately purchased information is unbiased but noisy, while socially communicated information is noisy and potentially biased because informants need not provide accurate information.

In selecting an informant, subjects know the individual preferences of the other subjects, as well as the amount of information purchased by each subject. A potential dilemma faces the subjects regarding the relative weights to place on preference proximity and expertise in the selection of an informant. No dilemma exists for subjects who have the opportunity to select expert informants with preferences close to their own. The joint distribution of preferences and expertise levels is manipulated across experimental sessions, however, and thus some subjects must choose between an expert informant with divergent preferences versus an inexpert discussant with shared preferences.

This framework allows us to pursue a series of important issues related to the centrality of informants within networks (Freeman 1979)—issues which lie beyond the reach of even the most innovative observational studies. Who are the experts, and are the advantages of expertise over-rated? What are the most important (behavioral) criteria for selecting informants—informant expertise or shared preferences between the recipient and the prospective informant? Is the advice of experts useful when their viewpoints diverge from those of the recipients? Does "cheap talk" hold political consequence for the recipients—do the recipients take it seriously and how do they assess the veracity of messages? What are the effects of group boundaries for the aggregate flow of political information and for patterns of bias in aggregate opinion distributions?

The experimental results consistently show that subjects pay more attention to expertise than shared preferences in selecting an informant. The importance of expertise persists even though informants regularly introduce their own biases into the communicated messages, particularly when they provide information to subjects with divergent preferences. While subjects pay attention to "cheap talk," they also employ various heuristic devices in assessing the value of information that conflicts with their own prior assessments of the candidates (Ahn, Huckfeldt, and Ryan 2006).

The costs of communication beyond a subject's own group carry important consequences. In particular, experimentally manipulating the distributions of preferences and information levels within and between the two seven-member groups generates direct effects on information flows between and within the groups. First, identical distributions of expertise within groups diminish the rates of communication between groups. Second, when expertise is distributed identically within groups but preference distributions are skewed across groups, political communication is more likely to occur among subjects with corresponding preferences—political communication is polarized along lines of political preference. Third, when political expertise is concentrated within a particular political group, that group is likely to play a dominant role in the patterns of communication. Such a group supplies a disproportionate share of socially communicated information, and with that information comes attendant biases reflecting the political preferences of the group. Hence correlations between expertise levels and preferences across groups create biases in the aggregate distribution of information.

These efforts provide an inevitably abstract rendering of the circumstances under which most people communicate about politics with one another. For most individuals, the acquisition of political information does not generate any substantial and foreseeable short-term payoff. Moreover, people often lack well-informed preferences, as well as information regarding implications of well-formed preferences for their votes. In even more situations, they lack information regarding the specific preferences of others and the implications of these preferences for their own political well-being. In contrast, while our subjects are certainly not omniscient, they possess a great deal of information to employ in evaluating advice taken from others, in deciding upon the messages to send to others, and in arriving at a vote choice.

Does this lack of realism compromise the utility of our analysis for providing insights regarding political communication? To the contrary, this abstraction is inspired by past research (Huckfeldt, Johnson, and Sprague 2004; Huckfeldt and Sprague 1995), and it provides the opportunity to carry out a contingent, counterfactual line of reasoning with respect to the political communication process. If people knew with certainty the preferences and expertise of potential informants, what would be the consequences for patterns of political communication? Indeed, the experimental results complement and extend the accumulated behavioral record. These analyses are thus revealing, not only with respect to the abstract experimental model, but also with respect to the real-life consequences for information and communication among citizens in democratic politics (Ahn, Huckfeldt, and Ryan 2007a, 2007b; Ahn et al. 2008).

IMPLICATIONS AND CONCLUSIONS

While information costs constitute an impediment to participation for many individuals, these costs are highly variable across individuals. As Wolfinger and Rosenstone (1980) suggest, information costs are lower among those individuals for whom the acquisition and processing of information is easier—typically individuals with higher levels of education. And as Fiorina (1990) argues, many individuals may find information about politics to be intrinsically rewarding— they read about the Democrats and Republicans with the enthusiasm of a basketball fan reading about the Lakers and Celtics. For these people, information costs are in fact negative, and staying informed thus becomes a self-reinforcing behavior.

Hence, we should not be surprised to see the division of labor in the communication of political information suggested by Berelson and his colleagues (1954) so long ago. Individuals with high information costs will intentionally or unintentionally rely on individuals with minimal (or negative) information costs. The resulting patterns of communication may indeed produce an electorate that makes surprisingly expert choices—at least relative to the low mean levels of political awareness among individuals within the electorate (Converse 1964; Delli Carpini and Keeter 1996; Erikson, MacKuen, and Stimson 2002; Page and Shapiro

1992; Zaller 1992). In this way, civic capacity in the aggregate benefits from the diffusion of expert opinion within and throughout networks of political communication.

At the same time, political communication is not an antiseptic exercise in civic education. It involves people with opinions and interests who are not only learning from one another but also persuading one another. The accumulated record, based on surveys and experiments, suggests that the process tends to be driven by knowledge and expertise. That is, the process is skewed in favor of politically engaged participants with more information—the very individuals identified by Lodge and Taber (2000) as being most opinionated and most likely to demonstrate motivated reasoning.

To the extent that the distribution of political expertise within the electorate is correlated with the distributions of particular interests and preferences, the process we have described carries important partisan consequences. Hence it becomes important to take interdependence seriously in the study of democratic politics. Progress in such an undertaking requires, in turn, a continuing effort to design and implement novel ways of both locating and observing individuals within the social settings where they obtain political information and make political choices.

References

ABELSON, R. P. 1964. Mathematical Models of the Distribution of Attributes Under Controversy. In *Contributions to Mathematical Psychology*, ed. N. Fredriksen and H. Gulliksen. New York: Holt, Rinehart, and Winston.

—— 1979. Social Clusters and Opinion Clusters. In *Perspectives on Social Network Research*, ed. P. W. Holland and S. Leinhardt. New York: Academic Press.

ACHEN, C. H. 1986. *The Statistical Analysis of Quasi-Experiments.* Berkeley: The University of California Press.

—— and SHIVELY, W. P. 1995. *Cross Level Inference.* Chicago: University of Chicago Press.

AHN, T. K., HUCKFELDT, R., and RYAN, J. B. 2006. Information Costs, Information Sources and the Implications for Democratic Politics. Paper presented at the annual meeting of the American Political Science Association, Philadelphia.

—— —— —— 2007a. Political Expertise, Shared Biases, and Patterns of Political Communication. Paper presented at the annual meeting of the Midwest Political Science Association, Chicago.

—— —— —— 2007b. Political Judgment, Informational Asymmetries, and Influence among Citizens. Paper presented at the annual meeting of the Midwest Political Science Association, Chicago.

—— —— MAYER, A. K., and RYAN, J. B. 2008. Political Experts and the Collective Enhancement of Civic Capacity. Paper presented at the annual meeting of the Midwest Political Science Association, Chicago.

ANDERSON, C. J. and PASKEVICIUTE, A. 2005. Macro-Politics and Micro-Behavior: Mainstream Politics and the Frequency of Political Discussion in Contemporary Democracies. In *The Social Logic of Politics*, ed. A. S. Zuckerman. Philadelphia: Temple University Press.

—— —— 2006. How Linguistic and Ethnic Heterogeneity Influences the Prospects for Civil Society. *Journal of Politics*, 68: 783–802.

AUSTEN-SMITH, D. 1990. Information Transmission in Debate. *American Journal of Political Science*, 34: 124–52.

—— and BANKS, J. 1996. Information Aggregation, Rationality, and the Condorcet Jury Theorem. *American Political Science Review*, 90/1: 34–45.

AXELROD, R. 1997a. The Dissemination of Culture: A Model with Local Convergence and Global Polarization. *Journal of Conflict Resolution*, 41: 203–26.

—— 1997b. *The Complexity of Cooperation: Agent-Based Models of Competition and Collaboration*. Princeton, N.J.: Princeton University Press.

BARABÁSI, A.-L. 2002. *Linked: The New Science of Networks*. Cambridge, Mass.: Perseus.

BARBER, B. 1984. *Strong Democracy: Participatory Politics for a New Age*. Berkeley, Calif.: University of California Press.

BARON, D. P. 1994. Electoral Competition with Informed and Uniformed Voters. *American Political Science Review*, 88/1: 33–47.

BAYBECK, B. and HUCKFELDT, R. 2002. Urban Contexts, Spatially Dispersed Networks, and the Diffusion of Political Information. *Political Geography*, 21: 195–220.

BERELSON, B. R., LAZARSFELD, P. F., and MCPHEE, W. N. 1954. *Voting: A Study of Opinion Formation in a Presidential Election*. Chicago: University of Chicago Press.

BOUDREAU, C. 2009. Closing the Gap: When Do Cues Eliminate Differences Between Sophisticated and Unsophisticated Citizens? *Journal of Politics*, 71(3): 1–13.

—— COULSON, S., and MCCUBBINS, M. 2008. The Effect of Institutions on Behavior and Brain Activity: Insights from EEG and Timed-Response Experiments. Paper presented at the annual meeting of the Midwest Political Science Association, Chicago.

BOYD, R. and RICHERSON, P. J. 1985. *Culture and the Evolutionary Process*. Chicago: The University of Chicago Press.

BROWN, T. A. 1981. On Contextual Change and Partisan Attributes. *British Journal of Political Science*, 11: 427–47.

BUDGE, I. 1994. A New Spatial Theory of Party Competition: Uncertainty, Ideology and Policy Equilibria Viewed Comparatively and Temporally. *British Journal of Political Science*, 24/4: 443–67.

BUTTICE, M., HUCKFELDT, R., and RYAN, J. B. 2008. Political Polarization and Communication Networks in the 2006 Congressional Elections. In *Fault Lines: Why the Republicans Lost Congress*, ed. J. J. Mondak and D.-G. Mitchell. New York: Routledge.

CALVERT, R. L. 1985a. The Value of Biased Information: A Rational Choice Model of Political Advice. *Journal of Politics*, 47: 530–55.

—— 1985b. Robustness of the Multidimensional Voting Model: Candidate Motivations, Uncertainty, and Convergence. *American Journal of Political Science*, 29: 69–95.

CONVERSE, P. E. 1964. The Nature of Belief Systems in Mass Publics. In *Ideology and Discontent*, ed. D. E. Apter. New York: Free Press.

COUGHLAN, P. J. 2000. In Defense of Unanimous Jury Verdicts: Mistrials, Communication and Strategic Voting. *American Political Science Review*, 94: 375–93.

CRAWFORD, V. 1998. A Survey of Experiments on Communication via Cheap Talk. *Journal of Economic Theory*, 78: 286–98.

CRAWFORD, V. and SOBEL, J. 1982. Strategic Information Transmission. *Econometrica*, 50/6: 1431–51.

DELLI CARPINI, M. X., and KEETER, S. 1993. Measuring Political Knowledge: Putting First Things First. *American Journal of Political Science*, 37: 1179–206.

——— 1996. *What Americans Know about Politics and Why It Matters*. New Haven, Conn.: Yale University Press.

DOWNS, A. 1957. *An Economic Theory of Democracy*. New York: Harper and Row.

DRUCKMAN, J. N. and NELSON, K. R. 2003. Framing and Deliberation: How Citizens' Conversations Limit Elite Influence. *American Journal of Political Science*, 47: 728–44.

ERIKSON, R. S., MacKUEN, M. B, and STIMSON, J. A. 2002. *The Macro Polity*. New York: Cambridge University Press.

FARRELL, J. and RABIN, M. 1996. Cheap Talk. *Journal of Economic Perspectives*, 10: 103–18.

FEDDERSEN, T. and PESENDORFER, W. 1998. Convicting the Innocent: The Inferiority of Unanimous Jury Verdicts under Strategic Voting. *American Political Science Review*, 92/1: 23–35.

FINIFTER, A. 1974. The Friendship Group as a Protective Environment for Political Deviants. *American Political Science Review*, 68: 607–25.

FIORINA, M. P. 1990. Information and Rationality in Elections. In *Information and Democratic Processes*, ed. J. A. Ferejohn and J. H. Kuklinski. Urbana: University of Illinois Press.

FISHKIN, J. S. 1991. *Democracy and Deliberation: New Directions for Democratic Reform*. New Haven, Conn.: Yale University Press.

FOWLER, J. H. 2005. Turnout in a Small World. In *Social Logic of Politics*, ed. A. Zuckerman. New York: Temple University Press.

—— and SMIRNOV, O. 2005. Dynamic Parties and Social Turnout: An Agent Based Model. *American Journal of Sociology*, 110: 1070–94.

FREEMAN, L. C. 1979. Centrality in Social Networks: Conceptual Clarification. *Social Networks*, 1: 215–39.

GIBSON, J. L. 1992. The Political Consequences of Intolerance: Cultural Conformity and Political Freedom. *American Political Science Review*, 86: 338–56.

—— 2001. Social Networks, Civil Society and the Prospects for Consolidating Russia's Democratic Transition. *American Journal of Political Science*, 45: 51–69.

GILENS, M. 2001. Political Ignorance and Collective Policy Preferences. *American Political Science Review*, 95: 379–96.

GIMPEL, J. G., LAY, J. C., and SCHUKNECHT, J. E. 2003. *Cultivating Democracy*. Washington, D. C.: Brookings Institution Press.

GREEN, D., PALMQUIST, B., and SCHICKLER, E. 2002. *Partisan Hearts and Minds: Political Parties and the Social Identities of Voters*. New Haven, Conn.: Yale University Press.

GREER, S. 1961. Catholic Voters and the Democratic Party. *The Public Opinion Quarterly*, 25: 611–25.

HAFER, C. and LANDA, D. 2007. Deliberation as Self-Discovery and Institutions for Political Speech. *Journal of Theoretical Politics*, 19/3: 329–60.

HUCKFELDT, R. 1983. Social Contexts, Social Networks, and Urban Neighborhoods: Environmental Constraints on Friendship Choice. *The American Journal of Sociology*, 89: 651–69.

—— 2001. The Social Communication of Political Expertise. *American Journal of Political Science*, 45: 425–38.

—— 2007a. Information, Persuasion, and Political Communication Networks. In *Oxford Handbook of Political Behavior*, ed. R. Dalton and H.-D. Klingemann. Oxford: Oxford University Press.

—— 2007b. Unanimity, Discord, and the Communication of Public Opinion. *American Journal of Political,* 51: 978–95.

—— 2009. Citizenship in Democratic Politics: Density Dependence and the Micro-Macro Divide. In *Comparative Politics: Rationality, Culture, and Structure*, ed. M. Lichbach and A. Zuckerman, 2nd edn. New York: Cambridge University Press.

—— IKEDA, K., and PAPPI, F. U. 2005. Patterns of Disagreement in Democratic Politics: Comparing Germany, Japan, and the United States. *American Journal of Political Science*, 49: 497–514.

HUCKFELDT, ROBERT, JOHNSON, P. E., and SPRAGUE, J. 2004. *Political Disagreement: The Survival of Diverse Opinions within Communication Networks.* New York: Cambridge University Press.

—— —— —— 2005. Individuals, Dyads and Networks: Autoregressive Patterns of Political Influence. In *The Social Logic of Politics: Personal Networks as Contexts for Political Behavior*, ed. A. S. Zuckerman. Philadelphia, Pa.: Temple University Press.

—— and MENDEZ, J. M. 2008. Moths, Flames, and Political Engagement: Managing Disagreement within Communication Networks. *Journal of Politics*, 70: 83–96.

—— —— and OSBORN, T. 2004. Disagreement, Ambivalence and Engagement: The Political Consequences of Heterogeneous Networks. *Political Psychology*, 26: 65–96.

—— and SPRAGUE, J. 1992. Political Parties and Electoral Mobilization: Political Structure, Social Structure, and the Party Canvass. *American Political Science Review*, 86: 70–86.

—— —— 1993. Citizens, Contexts, and Politics. In *Political Science: The State of the Discipline II*, ed. A.W. Finifter. Washington, D.C.: American Political Science Association.

—— —— 1995. *Citizens, Politics, and Social Communication: Information and Influence in an Election Campaign.* New York: Cambridge University Press.

—— BECK, P. A., DALTON, R. J., LEVINE, J., and MORGAN, W. 1998. Ambiguity, Distorted Messages, and Nested Environmental Effects on Political Communication. *Journal of Politics*, 60: 996–1030.

JOHNSON, J. 1993. Is Talk Really Cheap? Prompting Conversation Between Critical Theory and Rational Choice. *American Political Science Review*, 87: 74–86.

JOHNSON, P. E. 1999. Simulation Modeling in Political Science. *American Behavioral Scientist*, 42: 1509–30.

—— and HUCKFELDT, R. 2005. Agent-Based Explanations for the Survival of Disagreement in Social Networks. In *The Social Logic of Politics: Personal Networks as Contexts for Political Behavior*, ed. A. S. Zuckerman. Philadelphia, Pa.: Temple University Press.

KATZ, E. 1957. The Two Step Flow of Communication: An Up-to-Date Report on an Hypothesis. *Public Opinion Quarterly*, 21: 67–81.

—— and LAZARSFELD, P. F. 1955. *Personal Influence: The Part Played by People in the Flow of Mass Communications.* New York: Free Press.

KOTLER-BERKOWITZ, L. 2005. Friends and Politics: Linking Diverse Friendship Networks to Political Participation. In *The Social Logic of Politics*, ed. A. S. Zuckerman. Philadelphia, Pa.: Temple University Press.

KUKLINSKI, J. H., QUIRK, P. J., JERIT, J., SCHWIEDER, D., and RICH, R. F. 2000. Misinformation and the Currency of Democratic Citizenship. *The Journal of Politics*, 62/3: 790–816.

LAU, R. R. and REDLAWSK, D. P. 1997. Voting Correctly. *American Political Science Review*, 91: 585–98.

LAZARSFELD, P. F., BERELSON, B., and GAUDET, H. 1948. *The People's Choice: How a Voter Makes Up His Mind in a Presidential Campaign*. New York: Columbia University Press.

LODGE, M., STEENBERGEN, M., and BRAU, S. 1995. The Responsive Voter: Campaign Information and the Dynamics of Candidate Evaluation. *American Political Science Review*, 89: 309–26.

—— and TABER, C. 2000. Three Steps Toward a Theory of Motivated Political Reasoning. In *Elements of Reason: Cognition, Choice, and the Bounds of Rationality*, ed. A. Lupia, M. D. McCubbins, and S. L. Popkin. New York: Cambridge University Press.

LORD, C. G., ROSS, L., and LEPPER, M. R. 1979. Biased Assimilation and Attitude Polarization: The Effects of Prior Theories on Subsequently Considered Evidence. *Journal of Personality and Social Psychology*, 37: 2098–109.

LUPIA, A. and McCUBBINS, M. D. 1998. *The Democratic Dilemma: Can Citizens Learn What They Need To Know?* New York: Cambridge University Press.

MACKUEN, M. B. 1990. Speaking of Politics: Individual Conversational Choice, Public Opinion and the Prospects for Deliberative Democracy. In *Information and Democratic Processes*, ed. J. A. Ferejohn, J. H. Kuklinski. Urbana: University of Illinois Press.

—— and MARCUS, G. E. 2001. Emotions and Politics: The Dynamic Functions of Emotionality. In *Citizens and Politics: Perspectives from Political Psychology*, ed. J. H. Kuklinski. New York: Cambridge University Press.

MARCUS, G. E., NEUMAN, W. R., and MACKUEN, M. 2000. *Affective Intelligence and Political Judgment*. Chicago: University of Chicago Press.

MARSDEN, P. V. and FRIEDKIN, N. E. 1994. Network Studies of Social Influence. In *Advances in Social Network Analysis*, ed. S. Wasserman and J. Galaskiewicz. Thousand Oaks, Calif.: Sage Publications.

McCLURG, S. D. 2006. The Electoral Relevance of Political Talk: Examining Disagreement and Expertise Effects in Social Networks on Political Participation. *American Journal of Political Science*, 50: 737–54.

MCHEE, W. N. 1963. *Formal Theories of Mass Behavior*. New York: Free Press.

MENDELBERG, T. 2002. The Deliberative Citizen: Theory and Evidence. In *Political Decision-Making, Deliberation and Participation: Research in Micropolitics*, ed. M. Delli Carpini, L. Huddy, and R. Y. Shapiro, Vol. 6. Greenwich, Conn.: JAI Press.

MONDAK, J. J. 1995. Media Exposure and Political Discussion in U.S. Elections. *The Journal of Politics*, 57: 62–85.

—— and GEARING, A. F. 1998. Civic Engagement in a Post-Communist State. *Political Psychology*, 19: 615–37.

MUTZ, D. 2002a. The Consequences of Cross-Cutting Networks for Political Participation. *American Journal of Political Science*, 46: 838–55.

—— 2002b. Cross-Cutting Social Networks: Testing Democratic Theory in Practice. *American Political Science Review*, 96: 111–26.

—— 2006. *Hearing the Other Side: Deliberative versus Participatory Democracy*. New York: Cambridge University Press.

—— and MONDAK, J. J. 2006. The Workplace as a Context for Cross-Cutting Political Discourse. *Journal of Politics*, 1: 140–55.

NICKERSON, D. 2008. Is Voting Contagious? Evidence from Two Field Experiments. *American Political Science Review* 102: 49–57.

OSTROM, E., WALKER, J., and GARDNER, R. 1992. Covenants With and Without a Sword: Self-Governance is Possible. *American Political Science Review*, 86: 404–17.

PAGE, B. I. and SHAPIRO, R. Y. 1992. *The Rational Public: Fifty Years of Trends in Americans' Policy Preferences*. Chicago: University of Chicago Press.

PARKER, S. L., PARKER, G. R., and McCANN, J. A. 2008. Opinion Taking in Friendship Networks. *American Journal of Political Science*, 52: 412–20.

PUTNAM, R. D., with LENARDI, R., and NANETTI, R. Y. 1993. *Making Democracy Work: Civic Traditions in Modern Italy*. Princeton, N.J.: Princeton University Press.

RICHEY, S. 2007. The Social Basis of Voting Correctly. Paper presented at the annual meeting of the American Political Science Association, Chicago.

RYAN, J. B. 2008. The Effects of Network Expertise and Biases on Objective Evaluations and Vote Choice. Working paper, The University of California, Davis.

SHEPSLE, K. A. 1972. The Strategy of Ambiguity: Uncertainty and Electoral Competition. *American Political Science Review*, 66: 555–68.

SNIDERMAN, P. M. 1993. The New Look in Public Opinion Research. In *Political Science: The State of the Discipline II*, ed. A.W. Finifter. Washington, D.C.: American Political Science Association.

—— 2000. Taking Sides: A Fixed Choice Theory of Political Reasoning. In *Elements of Reason: Cognition, Choice, and the Bounds of Rationality*, ed. A. Lupia, M. D. McCubbins, and S. L. Popkin. New York: Cambridge University Press.

—— BRODY, R. A., and TETLOCK, P. E. 1991. *Reasoning and Choice: Explorations in Political Psychology*. New York: Cambridge University Press.

SOKHEY, A. E. and McCLURG, S. D. 2008. Social Networks and Correct Voting. Paper presented at the annual meeting of the Midwest Political Science Association, Chicago.

TABER, C. and LODGE, M. 2006. Motivated Skepticism in the Evaluation of Political Beliefs. *American Journal of Political Science*, 50: 755–69.

VERBA, S. 1961. *Small Groups and Political Behavior*. Princeton, N.J.: Princeton University Press.

WATTS, D. J. 1999. Networks, Dynamics and the Small World Phenomenon. *American Journal of Sociology*, 105: 493–527.

WEIMANN, G. 1982. On the Importance of Marginality: One More Step into the Two-Step Flow of Communication. *American Sociological Review*, 47/6: 764–73.

—— 1991. The Influentials: Back to the Concept of Opinion Leaders? *Public Opinion Quarterly*, 55: 267–79.

WOLNGER, R. E. and ROSENSTONE, S. J. 1980. *Who Votes?* New Haven, Conn.: Yale University Press.

ZALLER, J. R. 1992. *The Nature and Origins of Mass Opinion*. New York: Cambridge University Press.

CHAPTER 17

....

CONSTRUCTING THE VOTE

MEDIA EFFECTS IN A CONSTRUCTIONIST MODEL

....

MARIA ARMOUDIAN
ANN N. CRIGLER

NON-TRADITIONAL news media outlets and the apparent frequency with which national candidates are engaging them signify one of the developing dynamics in the relationship between media, candidates, and the public which are altering media's effects on campaigns and vote choice. The roles and significance of late-night comedian David Letterman, ABC's *The View*, a program hosted by Barbara Walters and four female panelists, and internet music videos (such as Obama Girl's "Crush on Obama," viewed by five million people) in the 2008 presidential election underscore the variety of media outlets and strategies that now distinguish presidential campaigns in the US.

Yet the media have always played a role in American elections and political decision making. Because citizens generally do not have direct access to politics and policy making, they rely—either directly or indirectly—on some form of media to derive information from which they can make political decisions (Lippmann 1922; Patterson 1980). Rather than seeing the "real" campaigns and candidates, they see the "media's version" of them (Patterson 1980, 9). But in today's media environment, voters have many more options from which to draw information and can participate to a greater extent in the construction of political meaning.

In this chapter, we examine the changing nature of the media's power to influence electoral decision making, reviewing the vast research on the effects of media content, including agenda-setting, priming, persuasion, learning, and the influence of visual and emotional cues on information seeking and opinion formation. Media effects—especially in today's dynamic media environment—are a complex interaction among many players who influence one another and collectively contribute to the construction of messages, meanings, and outcomes in the electoral process (Gamson 1988). In this process, campaigns struggle to shape discourse while the public attends irregularly, interpreting messages by drawing on their own experiences and other "pictures in their heads" (Lippmann 1922).

With today's increasingly complex media environment, media effects are best understood from a constructionist approach. The emergence of powerful new political actors in both entertainment and the internet has blurred the traditional lines that once existed between consumer and producer and between news and entertainment. Campaigns, bloggers, home video producers, comedians, and "soft news" programmers each contribute to the barrage of messages that are ultimately considered in making voting decisions. These new media fill in the gaps left by traditional news and allow ordinary citizens to engage more in campaigns through email, blogs, YouTube, text messaging, social networking sites such as Facebook and MySpace, and other new media.

MEDIA CONTENT: GATE-KEEPING, POLITICAL CONTENT, AND FRAMING

For many years, traditional news media, including newspapers, television, and radio, have functioned as "gate-keepers," controlling information and persons entering the public sphere (Bennett 2007; Bennett and Klockner 1998; Graber 2006). Over time, they increasingly cover fewer candidates, voices, and issues—mostly large, personal, or conflict-ridden issues—making it difficult for most individuals or important issues to be heard (Bennett 2007; Clark 1968; Just et al. 2008; Stephens and Mindich 2005). Their content is often superficial, narrow, stereotypical, and propaganda-laden, with little relevant context or explanatory value—ultimately inadequate for participatory democracy (Bagdikian 2000; Bennett 2007; McChesney 1999; Page 1987). Instead, traditional news media, particularly television, predominantly utilize frames and narratives such as the "horse-race" or larger meta-narratives, conveyed through image and sound "bites" (Adatto 1990; Bucy and Grabe 2007; Farnsworth and Lichter 2007; Hallin 1991; Kovach and Rosenstiel 2001; Patterson 1980).

Frames are conceptual tools that are used to convey and evaluate information. They function stealthily, highlighting some types of information, diminishing and excluding others, and activating the audience's schemas (Entman 1993, 2007; Gamson 1988; Neuman, Just, and Crigler 1992; Van Gorp 2007). Within a particular cultural milieu, a "shared repertoire of frames" becomes the foundation from which individuals construct meaning (Van Gorp 2007, 61). However, frames inherently bias information, limit understanding of substantive issues, and can reduce events, policies, and people to unidimensional, categorical portrayals (Capella and Jamieson 1997; Entman 2007).

Although the media structure the overall framing of issues, all political actors use frames to shape information, prompt people's considerations and agendas, and influence opinion (Callaghan and Schnell 2001; Entman 2007). The media's most frequent campaign reporting frame is the "game" frame, which features campaign strategy, polls, and other signals to predict winners (Atkin and Gaudino 1984; Craig 2000; Entman 1996; Kovach and Rosenstiel 2001; Patterson 1993, 2002, 2005). This frame relegates the meaning of campaigns to daily sporting contests (Capella and Jamieson 1997; Craig 2000).

Frames sometimes meld into larger "meta-narratives," which can reduce candidates to caricatures. Once formed, meta-narratives are difficult to shed, despite inaccuracies. For example, Vice President Al Gore, once portrayed as a serial exaggerator, could not shake this narrative, even after the theme was debunked (Scott 2003). Indeed, the media caricatured the entire 2000 presidential campaign as Pinocchio (Gore) versus Dumbo (Bush) until after 9/11, when President Bush's image was transformed into one of a capable leader (Jamieson and Waldman 2002).

Because the news media attempt to reduce an entire world to short messages and stories, they inevitably generate bias. Bias can take several forms, including omissions, distortions of facts, or privileging some information or persons over others (Bennett 2007; Entman 2007). The media also bias their content through the use of audio-visuals and by generating a perception of viability among certain candidates (Jamieson 1992). And while bias can spring from partisanship or ideology, much bias results from the media's structural elements—the economics of traditional media, journalistic routines, and the commonly understood definition of "news"(Hamilton 2004; Hofstetter 1976; McManus 1994).

Both the public and conservative elites assert that news media are biased against them (Domke, Watts, et al. 1999; Eveland and Shah 2003; Watts et al. 1999), not surprisingly since perceptions of bias depend on the perspective one brings to the media. And although the media sometimes slightly favor one of the major parties (Lichter 2001; Lowry and Shidler 1995), overall, scholarship has found little partisan bias related to the major parties (D'Alessio and Allen 2000; Domke et al. 1997; Hofstetter 1976; Just et al. 1996; Patterson 1980; Patterson and McClure

1976).[1] Traditional news media's "moderate," "status quo" ideology guides their coverage (Gans 1980), thereby ignoring and disadvantaging third-party or lesser-known candidates (Lichter and Smith 1996).

News media privilege perceived winners over perceived losers—often based on polling results, whether expectations are met, and the candidate's ability to raise money (Bartels 1985; Bennett 2007; Brady and Johnston 1987; Jamieson 2006). However, they also "stick needles" into political leaders (Patterson 2002, 68–72), especially the perceived frontrunner, as evidenced, for example, by Dean's 2004 downfall (Lichter and Lichter 2004) and Clinton's in 2008. These practices create "self-fulfilling prophecies" that prematurely eliminate worthy candidates (Graber 2006, 220–1).

When covering candidates, television media focus on candidates' personal qualities, images, and character traits (Druckman 2004; Just et al. 1996; Keeter 1987; Leubsdorf 1976; Nimmo and Savage 1976; Wattenberg 1991). Although focusing on personal qualities limits deeper political meanings (Bennett 2007; Bennett and Klockner 1998), the candidate's character is also used as a heuristic for broader understanding (Crigler 1998; Just et al. 1996; Lau and Redlawsk 2006). With the struggle to control coverage, politicians have turned to professional image consultants, but the media can reinvent candidates' images (Jamieson 1992, 2006; Miller and Gronbeck 1994; Nimmo 1976) with "Svengalian" or king-making power (Graber 2006; Jamieson 1992, 9).

Bias also results from the media's structure: the market emphasis, the definition of "news," and the training and rewards structure and routines for journalists (Bagdikian 2000; Bennett 2007; Cook 1998; Gitlin 1980; Glasser 2005; Patterson 2005). The market influences content, as most traditional media outlets are owned by publically traded entities that need to attract audiences and profits, which guide their choices for content (Bagdikian 2000; Bennett 2007; Compaine and Gomery 2000; Croteau and Hoynes 2001; Hamilton 2004, 2005; McManus 1994; Picard 2005). This market orientation also influences the definition of "news," which has been called "novelty without change" (Phillips 1976). "News" includes drama, crisis, scandal, and the "violation of values" (Bennett 2007; Entman 1996; Farnsworth and Lichter 2007; Gans 1980, 40; Kerbel 2000). And because "news" tends to be event-centered, it omits important content, contexts, and trends (Bennett 2007; Entman 1996; Iyengar 1991; Iyengar and Kinder 1987).

Journalists are trained and rewarded in this orientation towards "news," and often protect their jobs by self-censoring (Croteau and Hoynes 2001; Glasser and Gunther 2005) or by "sticking with the pack" (Crouse 1974, 20) to report either scandal-based stories (Farnsworth and Lichter 2007) or "inoffensive and inconclusive" material (Crouse 1974, 20). In their routines, journalists rely largely on the

---

[1] Currently, however, news media are again becoming more ideologically polarized, thereby losing some of their "moderate," "objective" standards (Rainie, Cornfield, and Horrigan 2005).

same sources (speeches, polls, "beats," "pool report(s)," "daily handout(s)," and communications professionals seeking publicity), which lead them to believe "the same rumors," subscribe "to the same theories" and write "the same stories" (Bennett 2007; Bennett and Klockner 1998; Bennett and Manheim 2001; Cook 1998; Crouse 1974, 8; Entman 2005; Kerbel 1998).

Although these gate-keepers play the largest role in shaping the news media's content, media personnel, campaign personnel, and the public collectively contribute to the messages that are conveyed. Culture and perceptions of the public's tastes contribute to what the media choose to feature and emphasize (Entman 1996). And although traditional media still rely on candidates for information, with the growing political content on the internet, talk shows, and entertainment media, the nature of media content is changing. Collectively, these programs provide more access, information, and considerations for voters than were previously available.

THE NEW DYNAMICS OF CONTENT: INTERNET, TALK SHOWS, AND ENTERTAINMENT MEDIA

The internet and expanded sources of political information such as soft news and entertainment programs are making the construction of political messages and meaning more dynamic and participatory. As these new media add elements of interactivity and levity, they appeal to broader segments of the American population than traditional campaign messages.

The internet is interactive, collaborative, and gives voice to oppositional political views that are often overlooked by mainstream media (Bimber and Davis 2003; Chadwick 2006; Mayer 2008). Prior to the internet, information was generally filtered through traditional media's opinion-leaders. Now, however, with direct channels and greater media choices (Bimber and Davis 2003; Prior 2007), information flows more directly, reducing yesterday's opinion leaders' roles to those of opinion reinforcement (Bennett and Manheim 2006). Further, with blogs, websites, podcasts, social networking sites, YouTube, and email lists, many ordinary citizens, who were historically relegated to a consumer role, now play dual roles, simultaneously consumer and purveyor of information and opinion.

Traditional news's gate-keeping role has diminished. Web politicos, without the same journalistic norms, have broken important stories and persisted in their coverage for longer than traditional news outlets (Williams and Delli Carpini 2004). Traditional news media sometimes follow the lead of these new media outlets. This occurred with the fall of Senate Majority Leader Trent Lott, the Lewinsky "scandal," and the Virginia senatorial race of 2006 (Graf 2008; Scott

2003; Williams and Delli Carpini 2004). This phenomenon has a double-edged sword. Because anyone can post content onto the internet, it lacks the fact-checking standards that traditional news media have utilized.

The internet has also changed the flow and reach of political information, directly connecting people to each other and to campaigns, dispersing power (Devine 2008; Mayer 2008; Patterson 2007; Williams and Tedesco 2006). Candidates and political organizations bypass traditional media and use their own websites, email, and other emerging technologies to manage their images, organize and recruit volunteers, raise funds, and communicate directly with constituents (Bimber and Davis 2003; Graf 2008; Howard 2005; Schneider and Foot 2006; Trippi 2004; A. P. Williams and Tedesko 2006; Williams et al. 2005). Digital communications extend the reach of political campaigns across space and time, continuously "breaking" stories and allowing citizens to access and interact with information conveniently (Hamilton 2005; Kovach and Rosenstiel 1999; Mayer 2008). The change in information flow is evidenced by surging internet audiences and declining broadcast and newspaper audiences, with the latter's web versions gaining ground (Patterson 2007). By 2003, more than 60 percent of Americans were on the internet (Klotz 2004; Rainie, Cornfield, and Horrigan 2005). During the 2004 campaign, 40 percent of Americans used the internet for political purposes, a 50 percent jump since the 2000 campaign (Rainie et al. 2005). Many use online political information to track key events such as Super Tuesday primary elections (Tewksbury 2006). The often decried socioeconomic "digital divide" is shrinking as access increases (Bimber 2003; Klotz 2004; Norris 2001).

Historically, news and entertainment were clearly divided by both timeslots and content, but those barriers have been blurred, particularly with late-night comedy such as Jon Stewart's *The Daily Show*, the *Colbert Report* (Baym 2005; Delli Carpini and Williams 2001) and talk shows like *The View*. This proliferation of entertainment and soft news programs featuring politics further challenges the traditional media's gate-keeping and framing powers (Jones 2005). For example, news elites could not control either the information flow or the new frames that developed during the Lewinsky "scandal" (Owen 2000; Williams and Delli Carpini 2004). In this case, the entertainment-related frames separated President Clinton's personal foibles from his performance as president while prompting discussion of deeper issues, such as morality (Owen 2000; Williams and Delli Carpini 2004; Zaller 2001).

Appearing on talk shows and entertainment programs also helps candidates relate to voters personally and add emotional dimensions that become critical to voters' candidate evaluations. Comedians also lampoon political blunders and inconsistencies, accentuating candidates' foibles. Comedienne Tina Fey's satirical skits as Republican vice presidential nominee Sarah Palin on *Saturday Night Live*, for example, highlighted Palin's inexperience and colloquialisms.

FROM CONTENT TO EFFECTS: THE
CONSTRUCTIONIST APPROACH

While most of the political communication literature has focused on measuring the size and conditions of the media's direct effects on consumers, these new developments lend themselves well to approaching media effects from a constructionist perspective. This perspective argues that socioeconomic conditions, institutions, culture, and emotions all shape the activities and communications of content providers, campaigns, and audiences.

Institutionally, for example, new media developments are generating greater competition for both breaking stories and gaining audience share. Traditional news media, once opinion leaders, are losing power to other players, including entertainment media outlets and the campaigns themselves, which frequently bypass traditional media through direct engagement with voters via emails, websites, text messaging, and by appearing more frequently on entertainment and soft news programs. Traditional news media, however, are adapting to the changing environment by adding their own interactive web counterparts, changing journalistic standards and featuring more entertainment-oriented content and fewer politically substantive stories.

In the competition for audience share, media outlets feature material that attracts and appeals to the masses. Media personnel draw upon their own emotions and cultural bearings to select and frame material, including current social conditions that are deemed important. The media and campaign strategists use symbols, drawn from shared culture and history, and affective framing to provoke particular emotions, such as fear, empathy, or anger, about particular issues and candidates. The 2008 presidential election, for example, often mentioned the candidates' race and gender and their significance in light of American history.

The way in which content is constructed—its tone, framing, source of information, and amount of coverage—impacts how voters interpret and integrate material into their understandings (Belt, Crigler, and Just 2007; Sheafer 2007; Wolak 2006). Changing frames, for example, often changes beliefs and opinions about the information within the frames (Nelson and Oxley 1999; Nelson, Oxley, and Clawson 1997; Rhee 1997). Similarly, simpler or more concrete issues are integrated more easily (Watt, Mazza, and Snyder 1993; Wolak 2006; Yagade and Dozier 1990).

The inclusion of particular images, music, color, and stories further impacts meaning and absorption of information, as these elements arouse emotions and associated thoughts and opinions (Crigler, Just, and Neuman 1994; Domke, Perlmutter, and Spratt 2002; Graber 1990, 2001; Neuman et al. 1992). Visuals, for example, can enhance learning if they are personalized or contribute useful components to verbal messages (Graber 1990, 2001). Images convey important information non-verbally. Contextual settings, for example, lead viewers to process candidates according to social phenomena while close-ups have them process candidates by personal attributes (Bucy and Newhagen 1999). Close-ups also emphasize facial features, which shape judgments about politicians (Lanzetta et al. 1985). Even slight alterations in facial features can change viewers' perceptions of candidate characteristics, such as trustworthiness (Keating, Randall, and Kendrick 1999), and can impact candidates' favorability. This content interacts with both the larger contextual factors and the audience's own past experiences, dispositions, and knowledge to construct political meanings.

Emotions guide construction of political meaning: They drive the pursuit and absorption of new information, organize political judgment, enhance recall, and, at times, lead voters to discount relevant information (Cassino and Lodge 2007, 102; Redlawsk, Civettini, and Lau 2007; Taber and Lodge 2006). Certain emotions, such as fear and anxiety, heighten attention and cause deeper processing and therefore enhance the media's agenda-setting and learning effects (Cassino and Lodge 2007; Graber 2007; MacLeod and Mathews 1988; Marcus and MacKuen 1993; Marcus, Neuman, and MacKuen 2000; Matsaganis and Payne 2005). Voters also rely heavily on emotional judgments about candidates when casting their votes.

Voters' prior knowledge, experiences, predispositions, and trust in particular media all inform their absorption and interpretation of media content. People with prior knowledge, for example, absorb and retain more information and generally benefit more from all media, including political advertisements (Craig, Kane, and Gainous 2005; Neuman 1986; Neuman, Just, and Crigler 1992; Valentino, Hutchings, and Williams 2004). Less sophisticated voters often ignore or "fend off" political information (Kim, Scheufele, and Shanahan 2005; Neuman 1986, 156; Price and Zaller 1993). Voters choose sources of political information according to existing political predispositions and often resist considerable media information (Mutz and Martin 2001; Neuman 1986; Pew 2005; Taber and Lodge 2006), particularly if it contradicts their established beliefs (Westin 2007).

Some voters, however, seek and recall negative information about preferred candidates in order to counter-argue in their candidates' favor (Meffert et al. 2007). Similarly, voters who trust media or a particular source of information more readily integrate featured information. These voters also consume more media, which enhances this process (Druckman 2001; Groendyk and Valentino 2002; Miller and Krosnick 2000; Tsfati 2003; Wanta and Hu 1994).

Ultimately, voters construct their opinions and vote choice by melding select information obtained from the media with their existing beliefs and knowledge (Neuman et al. 1992; Perloff 1998; Zaller 2006). Within this ongoing construction, the media influence opinion formation through agenda setting, priming, offering information from which to learn about candidates and issues, or persuading. However, rather than occurring as unidirectional media effects, these "effects" result from an interaction among media, campaigns, and voters.

The media often drive the public's political agenda and their concerns by making certain issues, candidates, and their characteristics salient (Iyengar 1991; Iyengar and Kinder 1987; Iyengar, Peters, and Kinder 1982; Kiousis and McCombs 2001; MacKuen and Coombs 1981; McCombs 2004; McCombs and Shaw 1972), even when these concerns do not correlate with real-world phenomena. For some issues, such as crime, television news coverage is a more effective agenda-setter than actually experiencing crime and works even when the coverage does not make people more fearful (Gross and Aday 2003). Similarly, voters' considerations about candidate characteristics tend to reflect those featured in the media and polls (Kiousis, Bantimaroudis, and Ban 1999; Kiousis and McCombs 2004). For example, a *Los Angeles Times* poll about George W. Bush's "stubbornness" increased salience for Bush's "stubbornness" (Hardy and Jamieson 2005).

The media also influence a second level of agenda-setting through "frame-setting," affective framing, opinion development, socialization, and behavior (Coleman and Banning 2006; Golan and Wanta 2001; Hester and Gibson 2003; Iyengar 1991; Jamieson and Waldman 2002; Kim, Scheufele, and Shanahan 2002; Kiousis, McDevitt, and Wu 2005; Roberts 1992; Weaver 2007). Consumers often adopt media framing of issues and candidates, particularly when the media use "advocacy frames" (Aday 2006), and even when they are conveyed non-verbally (Coleman and Banning 2006). Media frames and content can affect people's opinion strength, political dispositions, ranking of issues, and group affiliations (Kiousis et al. 2005; Shaw et al. 2001).

Closely related to agenda-setting is priming, which pertains to establishing or changing criteria with which people make political evaluations (Iyengar and Kinder 1987). Because people form opinions largely based upon information that "happens to come to mind" (Kinder 1998, 178), news and campaign media prime issues, attributes, emotions, and identity (Belt et al. 2007; Druckman 2004; Iyengar and Kinder 1987; Iyengar, Peters, and Kinder 1982; Sheafer 2007). Voters tend to make political evaluations based on material and frames to which they are exposed (Domke, Shah, and Wackman 1998; Gross 2008; Iyengar et al. 1982; Weaver 1991; Wells 1998). For example, when exposed to particular issues, such as national defense or economics, voters prioritize those issues and evaluate presidents accordingly (Iyengar et al. 1982). When exposed to candidate characteristics and endorsements, they cast votes based on these criteria (Kinder 1998). Similarly, when media use "ethical or moral" framing, voters tend to evaluate candidates and issues using ethical and moral considerations (Domke et al. 1998).

The media also prime emotions and identity-based thinking. For example, using "racialized" visuals, narratives, or issues can prime stereotypical racial attitudes in political evaluations and constrain opinions on certain "race-coded" issues such as welfare, affirmative action, and crime policy (Domke 2001; Domke, Mccoy, and Torres 1999; Gilens 1999; Valentino, Hutchings, and White 2002), particularly for less-educated voters (Huber and Lapinski 2006). In contrast, counter-stereotypical cues reduce racial thinking (Valentino et al. 2002).

Campaigns intentionally prime opinion, affect, and identity by focusing on particular issues and frames intended to redirect attention, present the debate in a particular way or evoke particular emotions or identity that might mobilize specific voting blocs (Belt, Crigler, and Just 2007; Brader 2006; Druckman 2004; Druckman, Jacobs, and Ostermeier 2004; Jacobs and Shapiro 1994; Kelleher and Wolak 2006; Mendelberg 2002; Schaffner 2005). For example, because women tend to vote Democratic when women's issues are prominent, campaigns strategically feature or avoid women's issues, depending on the "gender gap" effect on their candidate (Schaffner 2005). This priming, alongside media's different treatment of male and female candidates, ostensibly creates a "women's vote" (Kahn and Goldenberg 1991).

Similarly, in contests featuring minority candidates, racial priming is done by both the media and campaigns. To gain support, some candidates prime race by claiming racial authenticity (Caliendo and McIlwain 2006). In the reverse, subtle references to a candidate's race are also used to mobilize conservative whites (Mendelberg 2002; Reeves 1997). These differences highlight the active construction of the campaign: campaigns and journalists choose material while audience members attend to and interpret this material differently based on their own experiences, emotions, cultures, and histories.

Entertainment programs also prime issues and candidate attributes, which contribute to the construction of political attitudes (Delli Carpini and Williams 1998; Holbrook and Hill 2005). Frequent viewers of crime dramas, for example, believe crime is the most important issue, affecting their judgments about politicians (Holbrook and Hill 2005). By reframing issues, entertainment programs change the contexts or understanding about issues and can alter opinions on some subjects (Strange and Leung 1999), such as the death penalty, but not for others, such as gay marriage (Holbrook and Hill 2005; Slater, Rouner, and Long 2006; Strange and Leung 1999). Late-night comedy primes candidate attributes and traits, particularly those that are caricatured, and are particularly effective for the least politically knowledgeable (Baum 2005; Moy, Xenos, and Hess 2006; Young 2006).

Considerable debate has arisen about whether the media persuade or simply reinforce existing proclivities (Finkel 1993; Weaver 1996; Zaller 1999). Nevertheless, because elections are decided by a small percentage of the population, even minimal persuasive effects can substantially impact election outcomes (Emery 1976).

The media can be directly or indirectly persuasive. Because voting decisions are often dependent on information accumulated about candidates from the media (Hagen et al. 2000), greater coverage of campaigns enhances the media's persuasiveness, particularly for daily newspaper readers (Kahn and Kenney 2002). On the aggregate level, when non-partisan sources cover candidates and their personal attributes, the candidates become more salient to the public, which increases their poll standing (Son and Weaver 2005). Generally, high levels of media exposure are linked to support for incumbents (Shields, Goidel, and Tadlock 1995).

Moreover, newspaper endorsements (Kahn and Kenney 2002), the editorial slant of news (Druckman and Parkin 2005), political advertising (Franz and Ridout 2007; Huber and Arseneaux 2007), and favorable news coverage can all persuade (Shaw 1999; Shaw and Roberts 2000). Because voters are situated within a larger social context, however, other influences, such as interpersonal communications and candidate contact, may either be more influential than mass media or mitigate the media's persuasive powers (Beck et al. 2002; Mendelsohn 1996; Pfau et al. 1995; Vavreck 2001).

One-sided communications, such as conservative talk radio, are particularly persuasive (Barker 1999; Barker and Lawrence 2006; Pfau et al. 1997), rivaling interpersonal communication (Pfau et al. 1995), although that influence may be in decline (Bennett 2002). Many studies find that listening to talk-show host Rush Limbaugh accounts for "significant changes" in voting behavior (Barker 1999).[2] Although Limbaugh listeners tend to vote Republican (Barker 1999), exposure to Limbaugh is related to candidate preferences even among Democrats. During the 2000 primary election, for example, listening to Limbaugh was strongly associated with a preference for George W. Bush among Republicans and Bill Bradley among Democrats (Barker and Lawrence 2006). This latter study also illustrates how voters' different backgrounds interact with the same messages to arrive at different conclusions.

Citizens construct political knowledge from many sources of election information (Kim et al. 2005), including campaign events, news and entertainment media, debates, political advertising, and polls (Benoit and Hanson 2004; Meyer and Potter 1998; Popkin 1991; Shaw 1999; Weaver 1996). However, they can also become misinformed when inaccurate or distorted information is presented (Jackson and Jamieson 2007; Jamieson 1992).

People learn through the development of a composite framework, not by remembering disparate facts (Graber 2001; Neuman 1986; Neuman, Just, and Crigler 1992). Through the "barrage" of campaign messages, voters extract and compile information to "construct" candidates (Neuman et al. 1992). Thus, more consumption of news media leads to better developed understandings, which result in greater knowledge about both issues and candidate positions (Kim et al. 2005; Price and Zaller 1993). The media help citizens learn about select issues, candidates' character traits (Weaver 1996), and opposing viewpoints (Mutz 2007), but not as much about candidates' issue positions (Weaver 1996).

---

[2] One study has found no "Limbaugh effect" (Jones 1998).

The media's impact on learning can be cumulative, complementary (Holbert 2005), or indirect, because most people are exposed to different media and communicate with one another (Neuman et al. 1992). Generally, voters focus their learning of electoral information during elections in order to cope with massive amounts of information (Graber 1988).

Entertainment programs have become an important source of political information (Baum 2003, 2007; Delli Carpini and Williams 2001; Jones 2005), particularly for young people (Hollander 2005), who routinely rely on late-night television shows such as Comedy Central's *Daily Show* for political information. Television and filmmakers regularly embed social and political issues into their product and stories (Baum 2007; Brodie et al. 2001). And because entertainment media reach larger audiences than news media, political information in entertainment programs is more widely accessed, which helps narrow the knowledge gap (Baum 2003, 2007; Delli Carpini and Williams 1998; Graber 2006; Holbrook and Hill 2005; Poindexter 1980) and integrate politics and culture (Jones 2005).

For most television audiences who do not regularly seek political information through traditional channels, "soft news," delivered via drama, comedy, and other entertainment forms, becomes a means for political elites to communicate and for the less politically attentive to learn about politics (Baum 2003, 2007; Poindexter 1980). As discussed in this chapter's introduction, candidates now routinely join talk-show hosts and late-night comics. Some, such as Senator John Edwards and California Governor Arnold Schwarzenegger, chose entertainment programs to announce their candidacies (Baum 2005; Delli Carpini and Williams 2001; Jones 2005).

Many talk shows, however, teach voters very little (Weaver 1996). Even when controlling for amount of exposure, partisanship, ideology, political interest, education, age, and income, frequent listeners of conservative talk radio are less knowledgeable and more misinformed about political facts than listeners of radio programs like National Public Radio (Hofstetter et al. 1999). This is true despite greater interest in politics and more avid reading of newspapers. Listeners of Rush Limbaugh are also more likely to discount "substantive election explanations" than other media consumers (Hall and Capella 2002).

The Internet and Political Engagement

The internet facilitates the construction of political messages and meanings by different participants. Recent studies indicate that internet access fosters political discussion and stimulates civic participation and the probability of voting (Tolbert and Mcneal 2003). More than 60 million Americans either created or forwarded original political content (Rainie and Horrigan 2007). Internet use also corresponds with financial contributions (Bimber 2001).

The Web connects people who would otherwise not cross paths, allows for collaboration, offers venues for non-mainstream political voices (Foot and Schneider 2002; Grossman 2007; Mayer 2008), and enables large, even global campaigns to develop (Chadwick 2006; Dartnell 2006; Keck and Sikkink 1998). This is reflected in organizations such as MoveOn.org and Meetup.com (Devine 2008; Williams and Tedesco 2006). But ordinary citizens also embark on their own efforts. For example, activists designed NaderTrader.com, a website allowing safe states and swing states to trade votes in order to prevent a Bush election while simultaneously ensuring that candidate Ralph Nader received the requisite 5 percent of votes for federal funding (Chadwick 2006; Howard 2006; Klotz 2004). Some 30,000 people signed on to swap votes (Howard 2006).

Conclusion and Future Directions for Research

As a review of the literature shows, scholarship in political communication has focused largely on identifying and measuring the media's direct effects, how big those effects might be, and the conditions under which its effects occur. But with the changing media environment, we increasingly see that media content and political meaning are constructed in complex, interactive relationships between content providers, politicians, and the public. Political content and meaning are shaped by institutional, cultural, and emotional factors.

News and entertainment media provide political information, which is a fragment of reality, using standard "cookie-cutter" frames that naturally generate bias. While traditional news media play a strong role in providing political information, institutional changes are fundamentally altering the dynamics of campaign communication. Today's media, especially with the internet and political entertainment programs, provide more diverse information and frames, and new opportunities to interact, create, share, collaborate, and participate in politics. This allows a more interactive process of content creation and dissemination. In this process, traditional news media are losing their dominance over information production and delivery. Candidates bypass traditional media by frequenting entertainment and soft news programs and by connecting directly with voters via the internet, text messaging, and other online activity. In order to maintain audience share, traditional news outlets are acquiring new media outlets, adopting new formats, and increasing entertainment-oriented content. These developments highlight the changing norms of journalism.

Campaign messages are strongly guided by culture and emotion. Media personnel rely upon their own cultural backgrounds and emotions to select and frame material. Similarly, campaigns design and frame their messages to appeal to voters through language and symbols that elicit particular emotional responses. For example, coverage of the 2008 presidential election utilized race and gender frames more than age frames. These frames capitalized on voters' identities and emotions, shaping the construction of political meanings and yielding different reactions.

Some voters increasingly choose media sources that reinforce existing proclivities and shut out other information, ultimately creating deeper divisions without shared common ground. Others will integrate different perspectives, emotional cues, and conflicting messages to yield more numerous considerations.

Emotions are a key dimension influencing elections. Emotions guide the audience's pursuit of information, comprehension, and interpretation of media messages. The literature suggests that voters rely upon emotional judgments about candidates. Studies show that candidates and media activate and interact with consumers' emotions through affective framing and priming, both verbally and non-verbally.

With new developments in the media environment and growing evidence of audience participation in the construction of political meaning, it is important for future research to address how institutions, culture, and emotions interact with media and campaigns to impact opinion formation and vote choice. Institutionally, for example, research can focus on whether new media developments exacerbate the trend toward fewer substantive political stories. With greater competition, increased avenues for information, and greater participation by the public, research should also reexamine the changing roles of media outlets as gate-keepers or watchdogs, and resultant changes in power relationships. As different media outlets emerge, it is also important to understand which will be deemed credible and capable of agenda-setting. Another avenue for research pertains to candidates' ability to use new media to bypass traditional media outlets, and the consequences of this.

Also ripe for additional research in a constructionist approach is the role different contexts play in shaping media content to impact learning, priming, persuasion, and opinion formation. In the US, for example, scholars could conduct comparisons that reach across regions, cultures and languages to discern the emergence of media messages and their meanings from shared cultural norms, their propagation through symbols, narratives, and codes, and their impact on vote choice. The study of non-English-language media during campaigns would also be revealing. This work has commenced, but more is needed.

The emotional component of campaign communications is a key dimension that influences elections. Emotions are important at many levels, including content production, audience interactions with candidates, and interpretation of media messages. The literature suggests that voters rely upon emotional judgments about candidates. And studies show that candidates and media activate and interact with consumers' emotions through affective framing and priming, through both verbal and non-verbal messages. Further research should explore voters' emotional appraisals of candidates and issues and their affective responses to non-verbal communications, including candidates' facial expressions, body posture, and the use of images, music, and color, and how these resonate with voters in different cultural settings.

Pursuing these avenues of research requires multiple methods to capture the dynamics of campaign communications. This will help scholars capture a greater sense of the ongoing construction of political information, political meaning, and the formation of voter preferences.

The media play an important and evolving role in American elections. But their impact is not unidirectional. Neither are they all-powerful. Through the use of digital media, candidates, their consultants, and the public increasingly share in the construction of campaign messages and meaning. What this portends for American elections and for the media is unclear. If the effects of the media on vote choice are to be understood, it is incumbent upon researchers to examine the entire field of actors and the context in which they operate.

REFERENCES

ADATTO, K. 1990. *Sound Bite Democracy.* Cambridge, Mass.: John F. Kennedy School of Government, Joan Shorenstein Center on the Press, Politics and Public Policy, Harvard University.

ADAY, S. 2006. The Framesetting Effects of News: an Experimental Test of Advocacy Versus Objectivist Frames. *Journalism & Mass Communication Quarterly,* 83/4: 767–84.

ATKIN, C. K. and GAUDINO, J. 1984. The Impact of Polling on the Mass Media. *The ANNALS of the American Academy of Political and Social Science,* 472/1: 119–28.

BAGDIKIAN, B. H. 2000. *The Media Monopoly.* Boston: Beacon Press.

BARKER, D. C. 1999. Rushed Decisions: Political Talk Radio and Vote Choice, 1994–1996. *The Journal of Politics,* 61: 527–39.

—— and LAWRENCE, A. B. 2006. Media Favoritism and Presidential Nominations: Reviving the Direct Effects Model. *Political Communication,* 23/1: 41–59.

BARTELS, L. M. 1985. Expectations and Preferences in Presidential Nominating Campaigns. *American Political Science Review,* 79/3: 804–15.

BAUM, M. A. 2003. Soft News and Political Knowledge: Evidence of Absence or Absence of Evidence? *Political Communication,* 20/2: 173–90.

—— 2005. Talking the Vote: Why Presidential Candidates Hit the Talk Show Circuit. *American Journal of Political Science,* 49/2: 213–34.

—— 2007. How Soft News Brings Policy Issues to the Inattentive Public. In *Media Power in Politics*, 5th edn., ed. D. A. Graber. Washington, D.C.: CQ Press.

BAYM, G. 2005. The Daily Show: Discursive Integration and the Reinvention of Political Journalism. *Political Communication*, 22: 259–76.

BECK, P. A., DALTON, R., GREENE, S., and HUCKFELDT, R. 2002. The Social Calculus of Voting: Interpersonal, Media and Organizational Influences on Presidential Choices. *American Political Science Review*, 96/1: 57–73.

BELT, T. L., CRIGLER, A. N., and JUST, M. R. 2007. Affective Priming in the 1996 Presidential Campaign. Presented at the annual meeting of the American Political Science Association.

BENNET, S. E. 2002. Predicting Americans' Exposure to Political Talk Radio in 1996, 1998, and 2000. *The Harvard International Journal of Press/Politics*, 7/1: 9–22.

BENNETT, W. L. 2007. *News: The Politics of Illusion*, 6th edn. New York: Pearson Education, Inc.

—— and KLOCKNER, J. D. 1998. The Psychology of Mass-Mediated Publics. In *The Psychology of Political Communication*, ed. A. N. Crigler. Ann Arbor: University of Michigan Press.

—— and MANHEIM, J. B. 2001. The Big Spin: Strategic Communication and the Transformation of Pluralist Democracy. In *Mediated Politics: Communication in the Future of Democracy*, ed. W. L. Bennett and R. M. Entman. Cambridge: Cambridge University Press.

—— —— —— 2006. The One-Step Flow of Communication. *The ANNALS of the American Academy of Political and Social Science*, 608/1: 213–32.

BENOIT, W. L. and HANSEN, G. J. 2004. Presidential Debate Watching, Issue Knowledge, Character Evaluation, and Vote Choice. *Human Communication Research*, 30/1: 121–44.

BIMBER, B. 2001. Information and Political Engagement in America: The Search for Effects of Information Technology at the Individual Level. *Political Research Quarterly*, 54/1: 53–67.

—— 2003. *Information and American Democracy: Technology in the Evolution of Political Power*. New York: Cambridge University Press.

—— and DAVIS, R. 2003. *Campaigning Online: The Internet in U.S. Elections*. Oxford: Oxford University Press.

BRADER, T. 2006. *Campaigning for Hearts and Minds: How Emotional Appeals in Political Ads Work*. Chicago: University of Chicago Press.

BRADY, H. E. and JOHNSTON, R. 1987. What's the Primary Message: Horse Race or Issue Journalism? in *Media and Momentum: The New Hampshire Primary and Nominating Politics*, ed. G. R. Orren and N. W. Polsby. Chatham, N.J.: Chatham House.

BRODIE, M., FOEHR, U., RIDEOUT, V., BAER, N., MILLER, C., FLOURNOY, R., and ALTMAN, D. 2001. Communicating Health Information Through the Entertainment Media. *Health Affairs*, 20/1: 192–9.

BUCY, E. P. and GRABE, M. E. 2007. Taking Television Seriously: a Sound and Image Bite Analysis of Presidential Campaign Coverage, 1992–2004. *Journal of Communication*, 57: 652–75.

—— and NEWHAGEN, J. E. 1999. The Micro- and Macrodrama of Politics on Television: Effects of Media Format on Candidate Evaluations. *Journal of Broadcasting & Electronic Media*, 43/2: 193–210.

CALIENDO, S. and McILWAIN, C. 2006. Minority Candidates, Media Framing, and Racial Cues in the 2004 Election. *The Harvard International Journal of Press/Politics*, 11/4: 45–69.

CALLAGHAN, K. and SCHNELL, F. 2001. Assessing the Democratic Debate: How the News Media Frame Elite Policy Discourse. *Political Communication*, 18/2: 183–212.

CAPELLA, J. N. and JAMIESON, K. H. 1997. *Spiral of Cynicism: The Press and the Public Good.* New York: Oxford University Press.

CASSINO, D. and LODGE, M. 2007. The Primacy of Affect in Political Evaluations. From *The Affect Effect*, ed. W. R. Neuman, G. E. Marcus, A. N. Crigler, and M. Mackuen. Chicago: University of Chicago Press.

CHADWICK, A. 2006. *Internet Politics: States, Citizens and New Communication Technologies.* Oxford: Oxford University Press.

CLARK, W. C. 1968. The Impact of Mass Communications in America. *The ANNALS of the American Academy of Political and Social Science*, 378/1: 68–74.

COLEMAN, R. and BANNING, S. 2006. Network TV News' Affective Framing of the Presidential Candidates: Evidence for a Second-Level Agenda-Setting Effect Through Visual Framing. *Journalism & Mass Communication Quarterly*, 83/2: 313–28.

COMPAINE, B. M. and GOMERY, D. 2000. *Who Owns the Media? Competition and Concentration in the Mass Media Industry.* Mahwah, N.J.: Lawrence Erlbaum Associates.

COOK, T. 1998a. *Governing with the News: The News Media as a Political Institution.* Chicago: University of Chicago Press.

—— 1998b. The Negotiation of Newsworthiness. In *The Psychology of Political Communication*, ed. A. N. Crigler. Ann Arbor: University of Michigan Press.

CRAIG, R. 2000. Expectations and Elections: How Television Defines Campaign News. *Critical Studies in Media Communication*, 17/1: 28.

CRAIG, S. C., KANE, J. G., and GAINOUS, J. 2005. Issue-Related Learning in a Gubernatorial Campaign: A Panel Study. *Political Communication*, 22/4: 483–503.

CRIGLER, A. N. 1998. Making Sense of Politics: Constructing Political Messages and Meanings. In *The Psychology of Political Communication*, ed. A. N. Crigler. Ann Arbor: University of Michigan Press.

—— JUST, M., and NEUMAN, W. R. 1994. Interpreting Visual Versus Audio Messages in Television News. *Journal of Communication*, 44/4: 132–49.

CROTEAU, D. and HOYNES, W. 2001. *The Business of Media: Corporate Media and the Public Interest.* Thousand Oaks, Calif.: Pine Forge Press.

CROUSE, T. 1974. *The Boys on the Bus.* New York: Ballantine Books.

D'ALESSIO, D. and ALLEN, M. 2000. Media Bias in Presidential Elections: A Meta-Analysis. *Journal of Communication*, 50/4: 133–57.

DARTNELL, M. Y. 2006. *Insurgency Online: Web Activism and Global Conflict.* Toronto: University of Toronto Press.

DELLI CARPINI, M. X. and WILLIAMS, B. A. 1998. Constructing Public Opinion: The Uses of Fictional and Nonfictional Television in Conversations about the Environment. In *The Psychology of Political Communication*, ed. A. N. Crigler. Ann Arbor: University of Michigan Press.

—— —— —— 2001. Let Us Infotain You: Politics in the New Media Environment. In *Mediated Politics: Communication in the Future of Democracy*, ed. W. L. Bennett and R. M. Entman. Cambridge: Cambridge University Press.

DEVINE, T. 2008. Paid Media: In an Era of Revolutionary Change. In *Campaigns on the Cutting Edge*, ed. R. J. Semiatin. Washington, D.C.: CQ Press.

DOMKE, D. 2001. Racial Cues and Political Ideology: An Experiment of Associative Priming. *Communication Research,* 28/6: 772–801.

—— MCCOY, K., and TORRES, M. 1999. News Media, Racial Perceptions, and Political Cognition. *Communication Research,* 26/5: 570–607.

—— PERLMUTTER, D., and SPRATT, M. 2002. The Primes of Our Times? An Explanation of the "Power" of Visual Images. *Journalism Quarterly,* 3/2: 131–59.

—— SHAH, D. V., and WACKMAN, D. B. 1998. Media Priming Effects: Accessibility, Association, and Activation. *International Journal of Public Opinion Research,* 10/1: 51–74.

—— FAN, D. P., FIBISON, M., SHAH, D. V., SMITH, S. S., and WATTS, M. D. 1997. News Media, Candidates and Issues, and Public Opinion in the 1996 Presidential Campaign. *Journalism and Mass Communication Quarterly,* 74/4: 18–37.

—— WATTS, M. D., SHAH, D. V., and FAN, D. 1999. The Politics of Conservative Elites and the "Liberal Media" Argument. *Journal of Comunication,* 49: 35–58.

DRUCKMAN, J. N. 2001. On the Limits of Framing Effects: Who Can Frame? *The Journal of Politics,* 63/4: 1041–66.

—— 2004. Priming the Vote: Campaign Effects in a U.S. Senate Election. *Political Psychology,* 25/4: 577–94.

—— JACOBS, L. R., and OSTERMEIER, E. 2004. Candidate Strategies to Prime Issues and Image. *The Journal of Politics,* 66/4: 1180–202.

—— and PARKIN, M. 2005. The Impact of Media Bias: How Editorial Slant Affects Voters. *The Journal of Politics,* 67/4: 1030–49.

EMERY, E. 1976. Changing Role of the Mass Media in American. *The ANNALS of the American Academy of Political and Social Science,* 427/1: 84–94.

ENTMAN, R. 1993. Framing: Toward Clarification of a Fractured Paradigm. *Journal of Communication,* 43/4: 51–8.

—— 1996. Reporting Environmental Policy Debate: The Real Media Biases. *Harvard International Journal of Press/Politics,* 1/3: 77–92.

—— 2005. The Nature and Sources of News. In *The Press,* ed. G. Overholser and K. H. Jamieson. Oxford: Oxford University Press.

—— 2007. Framing Bias: Media in the Distribution of Power. *Journal of Communication,* 57/1: 163–73.

EVELAND, W. P. and SHAH, D. V. 2003. The Impact of Individual and Interpersonal Factors on Perceived News Media Bias. *Political Psychology,* 24/1: 101–17.

FARNSWORTH, S. J. and LICHTER, S. R. 2007. *The Nightly News Nightmare: Television's Coverage of US Presidential Election, 1988–2004,* 2nd edn. Oxford: Rowman & Littlefield Publishers, Inc.

FINKEL, S. 1993. Re-Examining the "Minimal Effects" Model in Recent Presidential Campaigns. *Journal of Politics,* 55: 1–21.

FOOT, K. A. and SCHNEIDER, S. M. 2002. Online Action in Campaign 2000: An Exploratory Analysis of the U.S. Political Web Sphere. *Journal of Broadcasting & Electronic Media,* 46/2: 222–44.

FRANZ, M. and RIDOUT, T. 2007. Does Political Advertising Persuade? *Political Behavior,* 29/4: 465–91.

GAMSON, W. A. 1988. The 1987 Distinguished Lecture: A Constructionist Approach to Mass Media and Public Opinion. *Symbolic Interaction,* 11/2: 161–74.

GANS, H. 1980. *Deciding What's News: A Study of CBS Evening News, NBC Nightly News, Newsweek and* Time. New York: Vintage Books.

GILENS, M. 1999. *Why Americans Hate Welfare: Race, Media and the Politics of Antipoverty Policy.* Chicago: University of Chicago Press.

GITLIN, T. 1980. *The Whole World is Watching.* Berkeley: University of California Press.

GLASSER, T. L. 2005. Structure and Nature of the American Press. In *The Press*, ed. G. Overholser and K. H. Jamieson. New York: Oxford University Press.

—— and GUNTHER, M. 2005. The Legacy of Autonomy in American Journalism. In *The Press*, ed. G. Overholser and K. H. Jamieson. New York: Oxford University Press.

GOLAN, G. and WANTA, W. 2001. Second-Level Agenda Setting in the New Hampshire Primary: a Comparison of Coverage in Three Newspapers and Public Perceptions of Candidates. *Journalism and Mass Communication Quarterly*, 78/2: 247–59.

GRABER, D. 1988. *Processing the News: How People Tame the Information Tide*, 2nd edn. New York: Longman.

—— 1990. Seeing Is Remembering: How Visuals Contribute to Learning from Television News. *Journal of Communication*, 40/3: 134–55.

—— 2001. *Processing Politics: Learning from Television in the Internet Age.* Chicago: University of Chicago Press.

—— 2006. *Mass Media & American Politics*, 6th edn. Washington, D.C.: CQ Press.

—— 2007. The Road to Public Surveillance: Breeching Attention Thresholds. In *The Affect Effect: Dynamics of Emotion in Political Thinking and Behavior*, ed. W. R. Neuman, G. E. Marcus, A. N. Crigler, and M. MacKuen. Chicago: University of Chicago Press.

GRAF, J. 2008. New Media—The Cutting Edge of Campaign Communications. In *Campaigns on the Cutting Edge*, ed. R. J. Semiatin. Washington, D.C.: CQ Press.

GROENDYK, E. Q. and VALENTINO, N. A. 2002. Of Dark Clouds and Silver Linings: Effects of Exposure to Issue Versus Candidate Advertising on Persuasion, Information Retention and Issue Salience. *Communication Abstracts*, 25/6: 295–319.

GROSS, K. 2008. Framing Persuasive Appeals: Episodic and Thematic Framing, Emotional Responses, and Policy Opinion. *Political Psychology*, 29/2: 169–92.

—— and ADAY, S. 2003. The Scary World in Your Living Room and Neighborhood: Using Local Broadcast News, Neighborhood Crime Rates, and Personal Experience to Test Agenda Setting and Cultivation. *Journal of Communication*, 53/3: 411–26.

GROSSMAN, L. 2007. Person of the Year: You. *Time* Magazine, December 25–January 1, 2008.

HAGEN, M. G., JOHNSTON, R., JAMIESON, K. H., DUTWIN, D., and KENSKI, K. 2000. Dynamics of the 2000 Republican Primaries. *The ANNALS of the American Academy of Political and Social Science*, 572/1: 33–49.

HALL, A. and CAPELLA, J. N. 2002. The Impact of Political Talk Radio Exposure on Attributions About the Outcome of the 1996 U.S. Presidential Election. *Journal of Communication*, 52/2: 332–50.

HALLIN, D. C. 1991. *Sound Bite News: Television Coverage of Elections, 1968–1988.* Washington, D.C.: Woodrow Wilson International Center for Scholars.

HAMILTON, J. T. 2004. *All the News That's Fit to Sell: How the Market Transforms Information into News.* Princeton, N.J.: Princeton University Press.

—— 2005. The Market and the Media. In *The Press*, ed. G. Overholser and K. H. Jamieson. Oxford: Oxford University Press.

HARDY, B. W. and JAMIESON, K. H. 2005. Can a Poll Affect Perception of Candidate Traits? *Public Opinion Quarterly* 69/5: 625–743.

HESTER, J. B. and GIBSON, R. 2003. The Economy and Second Level Agenda Setting: a Time-Series Analysis of Economic News and Public Opinion About the Economy. *Journal and Mass Communication Quarterly*, 80/1: 73–90.

HOFSTETTER, C. R. 1976. *Bias in the News: Network Television Coverage of the 1972 Election Campaign*. Columbus: Ohio State University Press.

—— BARKER, D., SMITH, J. T., ZARI, G. M., and INGRASSIA, T. A. 1999. Information, Misinformation on Political Talk Radio. *Political Research Quarterly*, 52: 353–69.

HOLBERT, R. L. 2005. Intramedia Mediation: The Cumulative and Complementary Effects of News Media Use. *Political Communication*, 22/4: 447–61.

HOLBROOK, A. and HILL, T. G. 2005. Agenda-Setting and Priming in Prime Time Television: Crime Dramas as Political Cues. *Political Communication*, 22/3: 277–95.

HOLLANDER, B. A. 2005. Late-Night Learning: Do Entertainment Programs Increase Political Campaign Knowledge for Young Viewers? *Journal of Broadcasting & Electronic Media*, 49/4: 402–15.

HOWARD, P. N. 2005. Deep Democracy, Thin Citizenship: the Impact of Digital Media in Political Campaign Strategy. *The ANNALS of the American Academy of Political and Social Science*, 597/1: 153–70.

—— 2006. *New Media Campaigns and the Managed Citizen*. New York: Cambridge University Press.

HUBER, G. A. and ARCENEAUX, K. 2007. Identifying the Persuasive Effects of Presidential Advertising. *American Journal of Political Science*, 51/4: 957–97.

—— and LAPINSKI, J. S. 2006. The "Race Card" Revisited: Assessing Racial Priming in Policy Contests. *American Journal of Political Science*, 50/2: 421–40.

IYENGAR, S. 1991. *Is Anyone Responsible? How Television Frames Political Issues*. Chicago: University of Chicago Press.

—— and KINDER, D. R. 1987. *News that Matters: Television and American Public Opinion*. Chicago: University of Chicago Press.

—— PETERS, M., and KINDER, D. 1982. Experimental Demonstrations of the "Not so Minimal" Consequences of TV News Programs. *American Political Science Review*, 76: 848–58.

JACKSON, B. and JAMIESON, K. H. 2007. *Unspun: Finding Facts in a World of Disinformation*. New York: Random House, Inc.

JACOBS, L. R. and SHAPIRO, R. Y. 1994. Issues, Candidate Image and Priming: The Use of Private Polls in Kennedy's 1960 Presidential Campaign. *American Political Science Review*, 88/3: 527–40.

JAMIESON, K. H. 1992. *Dirty Politics: Deception, Distraction and Democracy*. New York: Oxford University Press.

—— 2006. *Electing the President*. Philadelphia: University of Pennsylvania Press.

—— and WALDMAN, P. 2002. *The Press Effect: Politicians, Journalists and the Stories that Shape the Political World*. New York: Oxford University Press.

JONES, D. A. 1998. Political Talk Radio: the Limbaugh Effect on Primary Voters. *Political Communication*, 15/3: 367.

JONES, J. P. 2005. *Entertaining Politics: New Political Television and Civic Culture*. Lanham, Md.: Rowman and Littlefield.

JUST, M., COOK, T. E., ALGER, D. E., and CRIGLER, A. N. 1996. *Crosstalk: Citizens, Candidates and the Media in a Presidential Campaign*. Chicago: University of Chicago Press.

JUST, M. R., TODD, B., and CRIGLER, A. N. 2008. New Media, Old Media . . . The Same Old Story. Paper presented to the Annual Meeting of the American Political Science Association, Boston, MA.

KAHN, K. F. and GOLDENBERG, E. N. 1991. The Media: Obstacle or Ally of Feminists? *The ANNALS of the American Academy of Political and Social Science*, 515/1: 104–13.

—— and KENNEY, P. J. 2002. The Slant of the News: How Editorial Endorsements Influence Campaign Coverage and Citizens' Views of Candidates. *American Political Science Review*, 96/2: 381–94.

KEATING, C. F., RANDALL, D., and KENDRICK, T. 1999. Presidential Physiognomies: Altered Images, Altered Perceptions. *Political Psychology*, 20: 593–610.

KECK, M. E. and SIKKINK, K. 1998. *Activists Beyond Boarders*. Ithaca, N.Y.: Cornell University Press.

KEETER, S. 1987. The Illusion of Intimacy: Television and the role of Candidate Personal Qualities in Voter Choice. *Public Opinion Quarterly*, 51/3: 344–58.

KELLEHER, C. A. and WOLAK, J. 2006. Priming Presidential Approval: The Conditionality of Issue Effects. *Journal of Political Behavior*, 28/3: 193–210.

KERBEL, M. R. 1998. *Edited for Television: CNN, ABC and American Presidential Elections*. Boulder, Colo.: Westview Press.

—— 2000. *If it Bleeds, It Leads: An Anatomy of Television News*. Boulder, Colo.: Westview Press.

KIM, S.-H., SCHEUFELE, D. A., and SHANAHAN, J. 2002. Think about it This Way: Attribute Agenda-Setting Function of the Press and the Public's Evaluation of a Local Issue. *Journalism & Mass Communication Quarterly*, 79/1: 7–25.

—— —— —— 2005. Who Cares About the Issues? Issue Voting and the Role of News Media During the 2000 U.S. Presidential Election. *Journal of Communication*, 55/1: 103–21.

KINDER, D. R. 1998. Communication and Opinion. *Annual Review of Political Science*, 1: 167–97.

KIOUSIS, S., BANTIMAROUDIS, P., and BAN, H. 1999. Candidate Image Attributes. *Communication Research*, 26/4: 414–28.

—— and MCCOMBS, M. 2001. Political Figures During the 1996 Presidential Election. *American Behavioral Scientist*, 44/12: 2048–67.

—— —— 2004. Agenda-Setting Effects and Attitude Strength. *Communication Research*, 31/1: 36–57.

—— MCDEVITT, M., and WU, X. 2005. The Genesis of Civil Awareness: Agenda Setting in Political Socialization. *Journal of Communication*, 55/4: 756–74.

KLOTZ, R. J. 2004. *The Politics of Internet Communication*. Oxford: Rowman and Littlefield Publishers, Inc.

KOVACH, B. and ROSENSTIEL, T. 1999. *Warp Speed: America in the Age of Mixed Media*. New York: Century Foundation Press.

—— and ROSENSTIEL, T. 2001. Campaign Lite: Why Reporters Won't Tell Us What We Need to Know. *The Washington Monthly*, January 1.

LANZETTA, J., SULLIVAN, D., MASTERS, R., and MCHUGO, G. 1985. Emotional and Cognitive Responses to Televised Images of Political Leaders. In *Mass Media and Political Thought*, ed. S. Kraus and R. Perlof. Newbury Park, Calif.: Sage Publications.

LAU, R. R. and REDLAWSK, D. P. 2006. *How Voters Decide: Information Processing During Election Campaigns*. New York: Cambridge University Press.

LEUBSDORF, C. P. 1976. The Reporter and the Presidential Candidate. *The ANNALS of the American Academy of Political and Social Science*, 427/1: 1–11.

LICHTER, R. S. 2001. A Plague on Both Parties: Substance and Fairness in TV Election News. *Harvard International Journal of Press/Politics*, 6/3: 8–30.

—— and LICHTER, L. S. 2004. Campaign 2004—the Primaries: TV News Coverage of the Democratic Primaries. *Media Monitor*, 18/1.

—— and SMITH, T. 1996. Why Elections are Bad News: Media and Candidate Discourse in the 1996 Presidential Primaries. *Harvard International Journal of Press/Politics*, 1/4: 15-35.

LIPPMANN, W. 1922. *Public Opinion*. New York: The Free Press.

LOWRY, D. T. and SHIDLER, J. A. 1995. The Sound Bites, the Biters and the Bitten: A Two-Campaign Test of the Presidential Primaries. *Journalism & Mass Communication Quarterly*, 72/1: 33–44.

MACUEN, M. B. and COOMBS, S. L. 1981. *More Than News: Media Power in Public Affairs*. Beverly Hills, Calif.: Sage Publications.

MACLEOD, C. and MATHEWS, A. 1988. Anxiety and the Allocation of Attention to Threat. *Quarterly Journal of Experimental Psychology*, 38: 659–70.

MARCUS, G. E. and MACUEN, M. B. 1993. Anxiety, Enthusiasm, and the Vote: The Emotional Underpinnings of Learning and Involvement During Presidential Campaigns. *American Political Science Review*, 87: 672–85.

—— NEUMAN, W. R., and MACUEN, M. 2000. *Affective Intelligence and Political Judgment*. Chicago: University of Chicago Press.

MATSAGANIS, M. D. and PAYNE, J. G. 2005. Agenda Setting in a Culture of Fear. *American Behavioral Scientist*, 49: 379–92.

MAYER, J. D. 2008. Campaign Press Coverage—At the Speed of Light. From *Campaigns on the Cutting Edge*, ed. R. J. Semiatin. Washington, D.C.: CQ Press.

MCCHESNEY, R. 1999. *Rich Media, Poor Democracy*. Chicago: University of Illinois Press.

MCCOMBS, M. 2004. *Setting the Agenda: The Mass Media and Public Opinion*. Cambridge: Polity Press.

—— and SHAW, D. L. 1972. The Agenda-Setting Function of Mass Media. *The Public Opinion Quarterly*, 36/2: 176–87.

MCMANUS, J. 1994. *Market Driven Journalism: Let the Citizen Beware?* Thousand Oaks, Calif.: Sage Publications.

MEFFERT, M. F., CHUNG, S., JOINER, A. J., WAKS, L., and GARST, J. 2007. The Effects of Negativity and Motivated Information Processing During a Political Campaign. *Journal of Communication*, 56: 27–51.

MENDELBERG, T. 2002. The Race Card: Campaign Strategy, Implicit Messages and the Norm of Equality. Princeton, N.J.: Princeton University Press.

MENDELSOHN, M. 1996. The Media and Interpersonal Communications: The Priming of Issues, Leaders and Party Identification. *The Journal of Politics*, 58/1: 112–25.

MEYER, P. and POTTER, D. 1998. Polling Effects: Pre-election Polls and Issue Knowledge in the 1996 U.S. Presidential Election. *Harvard International Journal of Press/Politics*, 3/4: 35–43.

MILLER, A. and GRONBECK, B. 1994. *Presidential Campaigns and American Self-Images*. Boulder, Colo.: Westview Press.

MILLER, J. M. and KROSNICK, J. A. 2000. News Media Impact on the Ingredients of Presidential Evaluations: Politically Knowledgeable Citizens Are Guided by a Trusted Source. *American Journal of Political Science*, 44/2: 301–15.

MOY, P., XENOS, M. A., and HESS, V. K. 2006. Priming Effects of Late-Night Comedy. *International Journal of Public Opinion Research*, 18/2: 198–210.

MUTZ, D. C. 2007. Effects of "In-Your-Face" Television Discourse on Perceptions of a Legitimate Opposition. *American Political Science Review*, 101/4: 621–35.

—— and MARTIN, P. S. 2001. Facilitating Communication Across Lines of Political Differences: The Role of Mass Media. *American Political Science Review*, 95/1: 97–114.

NELSON, T. E. and OXLEY, Z. M. 1999. Issue Framing Effects on Belief Importance and Opinion. *The Journal of Politics*, 61/4: 1040–67.

—— —— and CLAWSON, R. A. 1997. Toward a Psychology of Framing Effects. *Political Behavior*, 19/3: 221–46.

NEUMAN, W. R. 1986. *The Paradox of Mass Politics: Knowledge and Opinion in the American Electorate*. Cambridge and London: Harvard University Press.

—— JUST, M. R., and CRIGLER, A. N. 1992. *Common Knowledge: News and the Construction of Political Meaning*. Chicago: University of Chicago Press.

NIMMO, D. 1976. Political Image Makers and the Mass Media. *The ANNALS of the American Academy of Political and Social Science*, 427/1: 33–44.

—— and SAVAGE, R. L. 1976. *Candidates and Their Images: Concepts, Methods and Findings*. Pacific Palisades, Calif.: Goodyear.

NORRIS, P. 2001. *Digital Divide: Civic Engagement, Information Poverty and the Internet Worldwide*. Cambridge: Cambridge University Press.

OWEN, D. 2000. Popular Politics and the Clinton/Lewinsky Affair: the Implications for Leadership. *Political Psychology*, 21/1: 161–77.

PAGE, B. I. 1987. *Who Deliberates? Mass Media in Modern Democracy*. Chicago: University of Chicago Press.

PATTERSON, T. E. 1980. *The Mass Media Election: How Americans Choose Their President*. New York: Praeger Publishers.

—— 1993. *Out of Order*. New York: Alfred A. Knopf.

—— 2002. *The Vanishing Voter: Public Involvement in an Age of Uncertainty*. New York: Alfred A. Knopf.

—— 2005. Of Polls, Mountains: U.S. Journalists and Their Use of Election Surveys. *Public Opinion Quarterly*, 69/5 (Special Issue 2005): 716–24.

—— 2007. *Creative Destruction: An Exploratory Look at News on the Internet*. A Report from the Joan Shorenstein Center on the Press, Politics and Public Policy. John F. Kennedy School of Government, Harvard University.

—— and McCLURE, R. D. 1976. *The Unseeing Eye: The Myth of Television Power in National Elections*. New York: Putnam.

PERLOFF, R. M. 1998. *Political Communication: Politics, Press, and Public in America*. Mahwah, N.J.: Lawrence Erlbaum Associates.

PEW CENTER FOR THE PEOPLE AND THE PRESS 2005. *Trends, 2005*.

PFAU, M., DIEDRICH, T., LARSON, K. M., and VAN WINKLE, K. M. 1995. Influence of Communication Modalities on Voters' Perceptions of Candidates During Presidential Primary Campaigns. *Journal of Communication*, 45/1: 122–33.

—— KENDALL, K., REICHERT, T., HELLWEG, S., LEE, W., TUSING, K., and PROSISE, T. 1997. Influence of Communication During the Distant Phase of the 1996 Republican Presidential Primary Campaign. *Journal of Communication*, 47/4: 6–26.

PHILLIPS, E. B. 1976. What is News? Novelty without Change. *Journal of Communication*, 26/4: 87–92.

PICARD, R. G. 2005. Money, Media and the Public Interest. In *The Press*, ed. G. Overholser and K. H. Jamieson. Oxford: Oxford University Press.

POINDEXTER, P. M. 1980. Non-News Viewers. *Journal of Communication*, 30: 58–65.

POPKIN, S. 1991. *The Reasoning Voter*. Chicago: University of Chicago Press.

PRICE, V. and ZALLER, J. 1993. Who Gets the News? Alternative Measures of News Reception and Their Implications for Research. *Public Opinion Quarterly*, 57/2: 133–64.

PRIOR, M. 2007. *Post-Broadcast Democracy: How Media Choice Increases Inequality in Political Involvement and Polarizes Elections*. Cambridge: Cambridge University Press.

RAINIE, L., CORNELD, M., and HORRIGAN, J. 2005. *The Internet and Campaign 2004*. Pew Internet and American Life Project, March 6.

—— and HORRIGAN, J. 2007. *Election 2006 Online*. Pew Internet and American Life Project, January 17.

REDLAWSK, D. P., CIVETTINI, A. J. W., and LAU, R. R. 2007. Affective Intelligence and Voting: Information Processing and Learning in a Campaign. In *The Affect Effect*, ed. W. R. Neuman, G. E. Marcus, A. N. Crigler, and M. Mackuen. Chicago: University of Chicago Press.

REEVES, K. 1997. *Voting Hopes or Fears?* New York: Oxford University Press.

RHEE, J. W. 1997. Strategy and Issue Frames in Election Campaign Coverage: a Social Cognitive Account of Framing Effects. *Journal of Communication*, 47/3: 26–48.

ROBERTS, M. S. 1992. Predicting Voting Behavior Via the Agenda-Setting Tradition. *Journalism Quarterly*, 69/4: 878–92.

SCHAFFNER, B. F. 2005. Priming Gender: Campaigning on Women's Issues in U.S. Senate Elections. *American Journal of Political Science*, 49/4: 803–17.

SCHNEIDER, S. M. and FOOT, K. A. 2006. Web Campaigning by U.S. Presidential Primary Candidates in 2000 and 2004. In *The Internet Election: Perspectives on the Web in Campaign 2004*, ed. A. P. Williams and J. C. Tedesco. Lanham, Md.: Rowan & Littlefield Publishers, Inc.

SCOTT, E. for Alex ONES. 2003. Al Gore and the 'Embellishment' Issue: Press Coverage of the Gore Presidential Campaign. (Case Program No. C15-02-1679.0). Kennedy School of Government Case Program. Retrieved from <http://www.ksg.harvard.edu/presspol/Research_Publications/Case_Studies/1679_0.pdf>.

SHAW, D. R. 1999. The Impact of News Media Favorability and Candidate Events in Presidential Campaigns. *Political Communication*, 16/2: 183–383.

—— and B. E. Roberts. 2000. Campaign Events, the Media and the Prospects of Victory: the 1992 and 1996 US Presidential Elections. *British Journal of Political Science*, 30/2: 259–89.

SHAW, D. L., MCCOMBS, M., WEAVER, D. H., and HAMM, B. J. 2001. Individuals, Groups, and Agenda Melding: a Theory of Social Dissonance. *International Journal of Public Opinion Research*, 11/1: 2–24.

SHEAFER, T. 2007. How to Evaluate It: The Role of Story-Evaluative Tone in Agenda Setting and Priming. *Journal of Communication*, 57/1: 21–39.

SHIELDS, T. G., GOIDEL, R. K., and TADLOCK, B. 1995. The Net Impact of Media Exposure on Individual Voting Decisions in U.S. Senate and House Elections. *Legislative Studies Quarterly*, 20/3: 415–30.

SLATER, M. D., ROUNER, D., and LONG, M. 2006. Television Dramas and Support for Controversial Public Policies: Effects and Mechanisms. *Journal of Communication*, 56: 235–52.

SON, Y. J. and WEAVER, D. H. 2005. Another Look At What Moves Public Opinion: Media Agenda Setting and Polls in the 2000 U.S. Election. *International Journal of Public Opinion*, 18/2: 174–97.

STEPHENS, M. and MINDICH, D. T. Z. 2005. The Press and the Politics of Representation. In *The Press*, ed. G. Overholser and K. H. Jamieson. Oxford: Oxford University Press.

STRANGE, J. J. and LEUNG, C. C. 1999. How Anecdotal Accounts in News and in Fiction Can Influence Judgments of a Social Problem's Urgency, Causes, and Cures. *Personality & Social Psychology Bulletin*, 25/4: 436.

TABER, C. and LODGE, M. 2006. The Motivated Construction of Political Judgments. In *Citizens and Politics: Perspectives from Political Psychology*, ed. J. Kuklinski. London: Cambridge University Press.

TEWKSBURY, D. 2006. Exposure to the Newer Media in a Presidential Primary Campaign. *Political Communication*, 23/3: 313–32.

TOLBERT, C. J. and MCNEAL, R. S. 2003. Unraveling the Effects of the Internet on Political Participation? *Political Research Quarterly*, 56/2: 175–85.

TRIPPI, J. 2004. *The Revolution Will Not Be Televised: Democracy, the Internet and the Overthrow of Everything*. New York: Regan Books.

TSFATI, Y. 2003. Does Audience Skepticism of the Media Matter in Agenda Setting? *Journal of Broadcasting and International Media*, 47/2: 157–76.

VALENTINO, N.A., HUTCHINGS, V. L., and WHITE, I. K. 2002. Cues That Matter: How Political Ads Prime Racial Attitudes During Campaigns. *American Political Science Review*, 96/1: 75–90.

——— and WILLIAMS, D. 2004. The Impact of Political Advertising on Knowledge, Internet Information Seeking, and Candidate Preference. *Journal of Communication*, 54/2: 337–54.

VAN GORP, B. 2007. The Constructionist Approach to Framing: Bringing Culture Back. *Journal of Communication*, 57/1: 60–78.

VAVRECK, L. 2001. Voter Uncertainty and Candidate Contact: New Influences on Voting Behavior." In *New Agendas: Communication and U.S. Elections*, ed. R. Hart and D. Shaw. New York: Rowman and Littlefied.

WANTA, W. and HU, Y.-W. 1994. The Effects of Credibility, Reliance, and Exposure on Media Agenda-Setting: a Path Analysis Model. *Journalism Quarterly*, 71/1: 90–8.

WATT, J. H., MAZZA, M., and SNYDER, L. 1993. Agenda-Setting Effects of Television News Coverage and the Effects Decay Curve. *Communication Research*, 20: 408–35.

WATTENBERG, M. 1991. *The Rise of Candidate-Centered Politics*. Cambridge, Mass.: Harvard University Press.

WATTS, M. D., DOMKE, D., SHAH, D. V., and FAN, D. P. 1999. Elite Cues and Media Bias in Presidential Campaigns: Explaining Public Perception of a Liberal Press. *Communication Research*, 26/2: 144–75.

WEAVER, D. H. 1991. Issue Salience and Public Opinion: Are There Consequences of Agenda-Setting? *International Journal of Public Opinion Research*, 3: 53–68.

—— 1996. What Voters Learn From Media. *The ANNALS of the American Academy of Political and Social Science*, 546/1: 34–47.

—— 2007. Thoughts on Agenda Setting, Framing, and Priming. *Journal of Communication*, 57/1: 142–7.

WELLS, W. D. 1998. Advertising Effectiveness and Indirect Effects of Advertisement. *Communication Abstracts*, 21/4: 47–63.

WESTIN, D. 2007. *The Political Brain: The Role of Emotion in Deciding the Fate of the Nation.* New York: Public Affairs Books.

WILLIAMS, A. P. and TEDESCO, J. C. 2006. *The Internet Election: Perspectives on the Web in Campaign 2004.* Lanham, Md.: Rowan & Littlefield Publishers, Inc.

—— TRAMMELL, K. D., POSTELNICU, M., LANDREVILLE, K. D., and MARTIN, J. D. 2005. Blogging and Hyperlinking: Use of the Web to Enhance Viability During the 2004 U.S. Campaign. *Journalism Studies,* 6/2: 177–86.

WILLIAMS, B. A. and DELLI CARPINI, M. X. 2004. Monica and Bill All the Time and Everywhere. *American Behavioral Scientist,* 47/9: 1208–30.

WOLAK, J. 2006. The Consequences of Presidential Battleground Strategies for Citizen Engagement. *Political Research Quarterly,* 59/3: 353–61.

YAGADE, A. and DOZIER, D. M. 1990. The Media Agenda-Setting Effect of Concrete Versus Abstract Issues. *Journalism Quarterly,* 67/1: 3–10.

YOUNG, D. G. 2006. Late-Night Comedy and the Salience of the Candidates' Caricatured Traits in the 2000 Election. *Mass Communication & Society,* 9/3: 339–66.

ZALLER, J. 1992. *The Nature and Origins of Mass Opinion.* Cambridge and New York: Cambridge University Press.

—— 1999. The Myth of Massive Media Impact Revived: New Support for a Discredited Idea. In *Political Persuasion and Attitude Change,* ed. D. C. Mutz, P. M. Sniderman, and R. A. Brody. Ann Arbor: University of Michigan Press.

—— 2001. Monica Lewinsky and the Mainsprings of American Politics. In *Mediated Politics: Communication in the Future of Democracy,* ed. W. L. Bennett and R. M. Entman. Cambridge: Cambridge University Press.

—— 2006. *The Nature and Origins of Mass Opinion.* Cambridge and New York: Cambridge University Press.

CHAPTER 18

....

CAMPAIGN EFFECTS ON VOTE CHOICE

....

D. SUNSHINE HILLYGUS

WE can perhaps best sum up recent research on campaign effects with the adage, "We've come a long way, baby." Just a short decade ago, political campaigns research would typically begin by describing an academic conventional wisdom of minimal effects.[1] As Thomas Holbrook described this once-prevailing scholarly view: "the voting decision largely is a product of long-standing predispositions (party identification) and retrospective evaluations of the performance of the parties. There is little room here for the campaigns to change minds or influence behavior" (Holbrook 1996, 10). In the last decade or so, dozens of studies have since offered compelling evidence that campaigns can and do have a measurable influence on the beliefs, attitudes, and behaviors of the voting public. Whether looking at the effects of television advertisements (Huber and Arceneaux 2007; Johnston, Hagen, and Jamieson 2004; Shaw 2006), campaign events (Hillygus and Jackman 2003; Holbrook 1996), candidate endorsements (Lau and Redlawsk 2001), or personal canvassing (Gerber and Green 2000), scholars have found that campaign efforts can have a significant impact on voters' turnout and candidate choice

---

[1] This perspective really only applies to presidential campaigns. There has long been evidence that campaign efforts in lower-level elections can have considerable influence on electoral behavior (e.g., Carsey 2000; Jacobson 1983; Kahn and Kenney 1999).

decisions. We can safely say there is no longer a scholarly consensus of minimal effects.

In truth, a case could be made that there never was such a consensus in the first place—the "conventional wisdom" may have just been an oversimplification of the existing empirical research on the topic. Recent studies now conclude that campaigns matter in part because of a shift in thinking about what constitutes a meaningful campaign effect. Early research defined campaign effects very narrowly, as they were evaluating the potential for campaign propaganda to persuade individuals to vote against their political interests. In a context in which Hitler had risen to power amidst an unprecedented propaganda campaign and an Orson Welles radio broadcast of *The War of the Worlds* had created mass panic, Paul Lazarsfeld and his colleagues were concerned that campaigns could manipulate the public. Instead, these early studies found that most people did not change their minds over the course of the campaign, and those who did were doing so in a way consistent with their predispositions (Berelson, Lazarsfeld, and McPhee 1954; Lazarsfeld, Berelson, and Gaudet 1944).[2] This conclusion was later bolstered by research showing that vote choice was predictable by long-term characteristics about an individual, especially party attachments, group identities, and retrospective evaluations (A. Campbell et al. 1960).

More recent research, in contrast, has expanded focus beyond evaluation of persuasive effects to consider a wider range of indirect campaign effects, including learning, priming, and mobilization. Yet, it is worth pointing out that the early campaign research—the so-called minimal effects body of research— often recognized and documented many of these same indirect campaign effects. The Columbia school studies, for instance, offered some of the first evidence that campaigns can change the relative weight of some vote considerations more than others, a priming effect: "What the political campaign did, so to speak, was not to form new opinions but to raise old opinions over the thresholds of awareness and decision. Political campaigns are important primarily because they *activate* latent predispositions" (Lazarsfeld et al. 1944, 74).

In *The Changing American Voter*, Nie, Verba, and Petrocik (1976) argued that the campaign environment contributed to greater levels of issue awareness and issue voting in the electorate—a campaign learning effect. They conclude that "the political behavior of the electorate is not determined solely by psychological and sociological forces, but also by the issues of the day and by the way in which candidates present those issues" (319). And Kramer (1970) argued that campaigns work not by changing minds, but by increasing the number of party supporters in the electorate, a mobilization effect. By further documenting these indirect effects,

---

[2] It is worth pointing out that roughly 40 percent of respondents did change their mind in some way, perhaps illustrating the importance of context and expectations in the interpretation of results.

recent research has built on and expanded this classic research rather than directly refuting it.

The task of this chapter, however, is not only to document how far this literature has come, but also to suggest where it should go. It seems clear that the effects of campaigns are more constrained than often presented in the media, although it is also clear that we are a long way from fully understanding campaign effects, especially campaign persuasion. But rather than continuing the "do campaigns matter" debate, the field would most benefit from the development of a more comprehensive theory of campaign dynamics that helps to shed light on the conditions under which campaign information can shape voter behavior. In other words, scholars should move beyond trying to estimate *the* effect of campaigns, and instead should study for whom, when, and in what ways campaigns matter.

THE "MINIMAL EFFECTS" PERSPECTIVE

The "minimal effects" hypothesis dates to the early voting studies of the 1940s, but decades of political behavior research since then implicitly advanced the perspective by ignoring political campaigns in models of vote behavior. After accounting for such long-term forces as party identification, sociological, and demographic characteristics, campaigns simply had little room for making much of a difference. With the development of forecasting models, political scientists were able to predict aggregate election outcomes using just a few fundamental variables such as presidential approval and economic conditions (e.g., Rosenstone 1983), again ignoring campaign factors.

A variety of theoretical explanations have been offered to explain the conclusion that campaigns are little more than "sound and fury signifying nothing."[3] One explanation is that presidential campaigns have a small net effect on electoral outcomes because the candidates are typically balanced with respect to skill and money. Thus, the opposing campaigns neutralize each other, and the aggregate effect is near zero (Finkel 1993). Others contend that any dynamics during the campaign are predictable (e.g., partisans are activated), so there is no need to consider campaign variables in the empirical models (J. E. Campbell 2000). Finally, some have suggested that it is unnecessary to focus research on campaigns because the effectiveness or success of campaigns themselves depend on non-campaign factors such as the economy or presidential approval (Fiorina and Pcherson 2002).

---

[3] See Holbrook (1996), Iyengar (2001), or Shaw (1999) for more thorough discussion of the minimal effects perspective.

In other words, presidential candidates will always run optimal campaigns, subject to the constraints of existing social and economic conditions.

In response, campaign scholars have pointed out that predictable outcomes and campaign effects are not mutually exclusive. So, election outcomes are predictable because the campaign provides voters with the information that helps them to vote in line with their predispositions (Gelman and King 1993). Moreover, because elections play out near the 50-yard line in the US two-party system, it is not that surprising that forecasting models can get close to the right answer since the popular vote is rarely lopsided at the national level.

Scholars interested in the effect of campaigns on individual-level voter behavior have countered the minimal effects hypothesis with new data and better methods. But they also have shifted to better documenting *indirect* campaign effects, such as learning, priming, and mobilization. Since other chapters in this volume are focused on turnout and mobilization, I outline below the state of research regarding the influence of campaigns on vote choice (rather than turnout), including campaign effects due to citizen learning, campaign priming, and, more directly, voter persuasion.

LEARNING

Despite the common lament that contemporary campaigns focus only on the horse-race, sound bites, and scandal, there is now a large body of evidence showing that the information-rich environment of a political campaign increases voters' knowledge of the candidates and issues. As the campaign progresses, voters reduce their uncertainty about the candidates' policy positions and ideology (Alvarez 1998; Bartels 1993; Franklin 1991; Popkin 1991). Although there are many different sources of information in the campaign that can educate voters, research has shown learning specifically associated with presidential debates (Chaffee 1978; Holbrook 1999), news coverage (Johnston, Hagen, and Jamieson 2004), television advertising (Johnston et al. 2004; Ridout et al. 2004), and interpersonal discussions (Beck et al. 2002).

One unresolved debate in this literature concerns the particular source of campaign information that produces the greatest learning effects. Some argue that television advertising has greater informational value (Brians and Wattenberg 1996; Mondak 1995; Patterson and McClure 1976), while others find more learning effects from news coverage (Chaffee and Zhao 1995). Unfortunately, the methodological difficulty of measuring and isolating the impact of each source has limited our ability to identify the "best" source of political information. And just as pedagogical research finds that different people learn best from different teaching styles, so too might we expect variation in the most effective information sources.

This debate also generally fails to consider the nature and influence of the new media. There has been an explosion in the number of sources of political information available—on the internet, cable TV, and so on—which undoubtedly complicates the study of campaign learning effects. In *Post-Broadcast Democracy* (2007), Markus Prior makes a compelling case that the expansion of media choice has exacerbated the knowledge gap in the electorate. The information age enables political junkies to follow the political world more closely than ever before, but it also allows others to avoid it altogether. In the 1960s and 1970s, the public had little choice but to watch the network news if they wanted to watch television at dinnertime; today, the viewing options are endless. As a consequence, a large portion of the electorate is actually less informed even as general education levels have risen and the volume and scope of available political information has expanded.

A related debate is whether the electorate can learn from entertainment or "soft" news programs, like *David Letterman* or *The Daily Show* (Baum 2003; Moy, Xenos, and Hess 2004; Niven, Lichter, and Amundson 2003; Prior 2003). A recent Pew survey finds comedian John Stewart to be the most admired "journalist" among young people (and tied for fourth among all respondents), suggesting this is an especially consequential topic.[4] More generally, the fragmentation of the contemporary information environment raises interesting questions about how characteristics of information source (e.g., mode, bias, quality, etc.) might shape campaign learning.

It is important to understand campaign learning effects not only because the normative ideal assumes campaigns serve a civic education function in American democracy, but also because campaign learning directly shapes how voters make up their minds (Popkin 1991).[5] By providing much-needed information about the candidates, campaigns help voters to make an "enlightened" vote decision— a decision that more closely reflects the voters' fundamental predispositions (Gelman and King 1993). And because voters are generally risk averse, campaign learning helps to decrease the incumbency advantage (Alvarez 1998; Bartels 1993; Brady and Johnston 1987; Holbrook 1999) and increase issue voting (Kahn and Kenney 1999).

---

[4] Pew Research Center for the People and the Press, "Today's Journalists Less Prominent," March 8, 2007. Available at: <http://people-press.org/reports/display.php3?ReportID=309>.

[5] There is also a long-standing debate about how voters process information they receive, whether memory-based or online (Lodge, McGraw, and Stroh 1989; Zaller 1992).

PRIMING

Another body of research has shown that the campaigns affect vote choice through priming—changing the weight voters attach to different considerations (Iyengar and Kinder 1987). By calling attention to some matters and ignoring others, the campaign can shape the standards by which candidates are evaluated (Druckman 2004; Johnston et al. 1992). For example, Lazarsfeld and his colleagues argued that Truman was able to win the 1948 election by increasing the salience of New Deal issues, which benefited the Democrats. Evidence of priming effects has been found in experimental and observation studies alike, making it one of the rare findings that cross methodological divisions in the field (Iyengar and Kinder 1987; Johnston et al. 1992; Krosnick and Kinder 1990; Mendelberg 2001).[6]

Research has found a wide variety of considerations activated by the campaign, including party identification (Berelson, Lazarsfeld, and McPhee 1954), ideology (Gelman and King 1993), economic evaluations (Vavreck 2009), policy issues (Johnston et al. 1992), race (Mendelberg 2001), gender (Kahn and Goldenberg 1991), candidate images (Druckman, Jacobs, and Ostermeier 2004), and emotion (Brader 2006). Still unclear, however, is which particular considerations are most susceptible to campaign activation and exactly how voters manage the relationship between these various considerations. It has long been thought that campaigns were especially likely to activate party attachments (Berelson, Lazarsfeld, and McPhee 1954; McClurg and Holbrook 2005). According to this perspective, campaigns largely served to bring home wayward partisans by reinforcing partisan attachments and reminding voters why they affiliate with the party (Berelson et al. 1954; Finkel 1993; Kramer 1970). As James Campbell puts it, "Campaigns remind Democrats why they are Democrats rather than Republican and remind Republicans why they are Republicans rather than Democrats" (J. E. Campbell 2001, 13). But other research finds ideology or issues more likely to be activated than partisanship (Bartels 2006; Gelman and King 1993; Hillygus and Shields 2008).

The existing literature is also unclear about the cognitive process by which priming works (Peterson 2004). It is typically assumed that priming makes some information more accessible in the memory (Iyengar and Kinder 1987; Valentino, Hutchings, and White 2002). According to this view, individuals call upon "top of the head" considerations in making decisions (Zaller 1992), so the frequency and recency of exposure to particular stimuli determines the likelihood it is used in the vote decision. Yet, there are other possible ways for considerations to be brought to the foreground of an individual's decision making. We know, for instance, that people who see particular issues as important (those in "issue publics") are more

---

[6] Lenz (2009) argues that some of the observed priming evidence actually reflects rationalization, in which a voter changes his or her attitude to match that of her preferred candidate.

likely to use those issues in their voting decision irrespective of campaign attention to the issue (Converse 1964; Krosnick 1990). It seems possible, then, that the campaign might also be able to increase the intensity, certainty, importance, or relevance of a given consideration. If so, characteristics of the campaign message beyond just frequency or recency might also shape how it influences the electorate.

PERSUASION

In justifying the focus on indirect effects like learning and priming, research too often simply concedes that campaigns have minimal persuasive effects. Yet, persuasion is arguably the campaign effect that deserves the greatest scholarly attention. Persuasion, after all, is the primary motivation of candidates' campaign efforts—they want to convince more voters to support them than their opponent. But the study of campaign persuasion has been hampered by the lack of scholarly consensus on the definition of a persuasive effect, and how best to operationalize and measure it.

Some scholars define persuasion as any campaign-induced changes in the attitudes or considerations that underlie the vote decision. For instance, Adam Simon (2002) looks for evidence that a television advertisement about the death penalty changes the voters' position on the issue. Although revising an individual's policy attitudes is certainly one type of persuasion, campaign communications are fundamentally directed toward influencing the public's vote decision rather than their underlying predispositions. It is important to recognize that the campaign need not manipulate a voter or change her underlying predispositions for it to influence her vote choice. For instance, the wayward partisan who returns home in response to the party conventions might be considered evidence of campaign persuasion. So, too, is the voter who moves from being undecided to making a candidate choice because of information learned during the campaign. Campaigns do not typically get individuals to vote against their predispositions, but they do help voters sort through diverse and conflicting predispositions, shaping which ones voters bring to bear in selecting a preferred candidate (Hillygus and Shields 2008). This means, then, that learning and priming could be the mechanisms by which individuals might change their vote choice (persuasion). In other words, the lines between the standard typology of campaign effects are quite blurry.

Although some scholars have found null persuasion effects (e.g., J. E. Campbell 2000; Cardy 2005; Finkel 1993), there is a growing body of evidence that campaigns can change voters' minds. The persuasion effects have been linked to specific campaign events, such as conventions and debates (J. E. Campbell, Cherry, and

Wink 1992; Geer 1988; Hillygus and Jackman 2003; Holbrook 1996). Others have found that television advertising can shape individual vote choice (Brader 2006; Valentino, Hutchings, and Williams 2004) and aggregate vote share (Althaus, Nardulli, and Shaw 2002; Huber and Arceneaux 2007; Shaw 1999). Using market-level ad-tracking data to evaluate advertising's impact on individual vote choice in the 2000 election, for instance, Johnston, Hagen, and Jamieson (2004) find that ads increased the probability of supporting Bush. Research has also found a persuasive effect from direct mail (Gerber, Green, and Green 2003), personal canvassing, and phone calls (Arceneaux 2007).

Despite these advances, we are still a long way from fully understanding who is persuadable, under what conditions, and why.

MEASUREMENT AND ANALYSIS OF CAMPAIGN EFFECTS

Too often, the literature on campaign effects feels a bit like a "back and forth" of competing empirical models and methodological approaches rather than a coherent body of research that is steadily advancing our understanding of political campaigns. For instance, Gerber, Green, and Kaplan (2004) dismiss most of the existing evidence of campaign effects on methodological grounds. To be sure, no methodological approach is immune to criticism. Lab experiments, panel surveys, rolling cross-sections, field experiments, and qualitative interviews all have their own strengths and weaknesses (and can be implemented well or poorly). As a discipline, it is important that we do not dismiss out of hand one approach or another; rather, we should insist that all scholars be transparent in the methods that they use and cognizant of the limitations for their design.

In many respects, the way campaign data have been collected and analyzed has had a profound effect on our conclusions regarding the influence of campaigns on the electorate. Our research questions about campaigns—as well as the answers—have shifted as social science research methods have developed and evolved. The early Columbia school studies relied on detailed panel data of respondents in a single community, which allowed for an examination of individual-level dynamics in the campaign but were not generalizable beyond the one community. Such a format was conducive to looking for evidence of campaign persuasion since individual-level changes in candidate choice could be tracked over the course of the campaign.

But as social science survey methodology progressed, the discipline moved towards studies that were representative of the entire population but were largely inadequate for directly linking campaign efforts with voter behavior. The cross-sectional surveys (and two-wave National Election Study) that dominated the study of political behavior for much of the twentieth century encouraged focus on the correlates of the final vote decision rather than the dynamics of the process. So our theories of voting behavior focused on the long-term attributes measured in the surveys—things like party identification, ideology, and the like. As others have discussed in more detail, such data have many limitations for evaluating the influence of campaigns on voter behavior (e.g., Iyengar 2001).

Experimental design emerged as one alternative for evaluating campaign effects (Ansolabehere, Iyengar, and Simon 1999; Lau and Redlawsk 2006; Lupia and Philpot 2005; Mendelberg 2001), but some have discounted such evidence because it was not clear the effects would hold outside the laboratory. Innovations in field experiments and survey experiments have allowed for cleaner assessments of voter exposure to and reaction to campaign activities. Recent field experiments, in which campaign treatments are randomly assigned in an actual campaign setting, offer greater control over the causal effects of a campaign treatment without the concerns of an artificial laboratory experiment, but this method too has limits to generalizability (Brady, Johnston, and Sides 2006).[7]

The recent evidence of campaign effects largely reflects the availability of better data and more sophisticated research designs. Improvements in the data available both about campaign activities and voter behavior have allowed scholars to more closely and carefully examine the link between the two.[8] On the campaign side, it has become much easier to find and collect information about the campaign efforts being used to try to influence voters. Because of advances in computing and information-sharing technology, as well as the innovative data collection efforts of various scholars, it is now easier to get quantifiable data about a wide range of campaign activities, including television advertising (e.g., Goldstein and Freedman 2002), campaign visits (e.g., Shaw 2006), and political mail (e.g., Magleby, Monson, and Patterson 2006). There have also been a number of important changes in the data available about individual voters as well. There are now a number of alternatives to the ANES surveys, many with large enough sample sizes to identify even small campaign effects (e.g., Hillygus and Jackman 2003; Johnston, Hagen, and Jamieson 2004). To the extent that campaign scholars have been constrained in the questions they ask by the available data, these new sources of data (as well as more sophisticated analytical approaches) mean a richer campaign research agenda is now possible.

---

[7] Although most field experiments have focused on non-partisan get-out-the-vote efforts (Gerber and Green 2000; Green, Gerber, and Nickerson 2003), more recent experiments have also attempted to measure the effects of persuasive messages (Arceneaux 2007; Gerber, Green, and Green 2003; Nickerson 2005).

[8] For a more thorough discussion of data advances see Brady, Johnston, and Sides (2006).

TOWARD A NEW STUDY OF CAMPAIGN EFFECTS

As a field of study, though, it remains unfortunate that our research questions have been more often dictated by data rather than theoretical expectations. A clearer understanding of campaign effects not only requires richer data, it also requires a theoretical recognition that campaign dynamics reflect an interaction between voters and candidates. Recognizing this link and taking into account the interest, abilities, and incentives of the relevant actors in a political campaign should help us in developing broader theoretical expectations about when, why, how, and for whom campaigns matter.

In particular, for the field to move beyond the basic documentation that "campaigns matter" toward a more thorough and comprehensive understanding of how and when campaign information influences vote choice, we need to step back to consider the reciprocal flow of influence between candidates and voters in a political campaign.[9] And we should start with clearer expectations about the decision-making process of both candidates and voters in a political campaign. This perspective highlights the fact that there is no *one* campaign effect. Rather, for any campaign effect—especially persuasion—we should expect that it may be larger or smaller depending on characteristics of the campaign information and characteristics of the respondent. In other words, variation both in voter decision making and in candidate strategy should shape our expectations about observable campaign effects.

HETEROGENEITY IN VOTER DECISION MAKING

Although the early research on voter decision making often described it as a static decision linked to socio-demographic characteristics (Berelson et al. 1954), party loyalties (A. Campbell et al. 1960), or material interests (Downs 1957), research today recognizes that these perspectives offer too simplistic a view of how voters make up their minds. Rather, we should think of voter decision making as a dynamic process in which voters have a set of predispositions—existing beliefs, attitudes, interests, and attachments—and they are charged with the task of matching those predispositions with a candidate selection. And for some individuals, campaign information helps to connect those predispositions with

---

[9] A handful of recent works are notable exceptions: Carsey (2000), Hillygus and Shields (2008), Shaw (2006), and Vavreck (2009).

vote choice. It seems clear that heterogeneity in voter decision making (Leighley 2004; Peterson 2005; Rivers 1988; Zaller 1992) should influence our expectations about how voters will respond to campaign information. Unfortunately, there is no consensus in the literature as to how various voter characteristics shape campaign responsiveness.

Since John Zaller's seminal work, *The Nature and Origins of Mass Opinion* (1992), scholars have often looked at variation in responsiveness to campaign information based on political sophistication or knowledge, but there is no consistency in the expectations or findings about how it shapes responsiveness. Some argue that the least sophisticated respondents should be most persuaded by campaign information because they are least equipped to resist persuasive appeals (Freedman, Franz, and Goldstein 2004; Zaller 2004). Others argue that the most sophisticated are more likely to be persuaded because they are better able to understand and remember persuasive messages (Hillygus 2007; Krosnick and Brannon 1993). And Zaller (1992) and Converse (1964), of course, argue that those with mid-levels of sophistication are most likely to change their mind in response to new information.

Research on priming effects has reached similarly mixed conclusions, with some finding stronger priming effects among the less politically sophisticated (Iyengar et al. 1984; Krosnick and Kinder 1990), others finding stronger priming effects among the most sophisticated (Miller and Krosnick 2000), and still others finding no relationship between priming and sophistication (Iyengar and Kinder 1987).

A parallel debate is active in the campaign learning literature. Some argue that the campaign serves to bring the unsophisticated up to speed with the sophisticated so that they are able to make informed and rational decisions (Fournier 2006; Freedman, Franz, and Goldstein 2004; Norris and Sanders 2003; Popkin 1991; Valentino, Hutchings, and Williams 2004). Others find that campaign learning is most pronounced among the most sophisticated respondents, so that the campaign serves to widen the knowledge gap in the electorate (Craig, Kane, and Gainous 2005; Holbrook 2002; Tichenor, Donohue, and Olien 1975). It seems likely that the way in which political sophistication matters for voter responsiveness might depend on a variety of factors, including campaign context (e.g., competitiveness of race), the complexity of the message, the mode of the message, the timing of the message during the campaign, among others.

Strength of partisanship is another characteristic that is thought to influence receptivity to campaign information. Again, however, the theoretical expectations are underdeveloped and the empirical findings inconsistent. Some scholars contend that political independents will be most influenced by the campaign because they are less likely to be committed to one side or the other and less inclined to resist campaign information (Kaid 1997; Zaller 1996). But others emphasize that partisan activation is the primary dynamic of the campaign, implying that partisans should be most susceptible to campaign effects (Gerber and Green 2004; Holbrook and McClurg 2005). Again, future research could shed light on the conditions under which one group or the other might be more responsive to particular campaign efforts. We might expect, for instance, that some messages or activities are more likely to resonate with independents and others with partisans.

Beyond partisanship and sophistication, though, there may be many other sources of voter variability that could mediate campaign responsiveness, including the strength of existing predispositions (Krosnick and Petty 1995), the relationship between competing predispositions (Alavarez and Brehm 2002; Basinger and Lavine 2005; Hillygus and Shields 2008), or voter personality (Forehand, Gastil, and Smith 2004). Rather than trying to classify one group of individuals as persuadable or not, a research agenda that focuses on the conditions under which campaigns can influence vote choice will ultimately provide a better understanding of why particular individuals do or do not change their minds. And, in the end, we might very well conclude that *all* voters are potentially persuadable under the right set of conditions. Harry Daudt reached this conclusion in his classic study:

> Is it perhaps so that everyone is a potential floater? ... Saying that all enfranchised persons are potential floaters is not the same as saying whether persons actually float and, if so, how many of them. This will depend on the political problems, the ways the political parties propose dealing with them and the voters' reactions to these proposals. Consistent voting behavior on the part of persons or groupings may, then, imply that they are satisfied with the way in which their party approaches the political problems. (Daudt 1961, 160–1)

Heterogeneity in Campaign Messages

In addition to individual-level variation in the way voters process campaign information, there is also variation in the particular campaign messages they receive. If different voters are receiving different messages, it complicates estimation of campaign effects. Previous research has focused on how variation in campaign exposure reflected characteristics of the individual voter—especially levels of political interest, knowledge, or motivation (Zaller 1992). Yet, in today's campaigns there is considerable variation in the messages that individuals received because of the strategic decisions of the candidates. Thus the volume and content of campaign messages will differ across geographic areas, communication modes, and different households.

We know, for instance, that campaign efforts vary across states and media markets, with candidates focusing their attention and money in the most competitive states. In the 2004 presidential contest, thirty-three states received no television advertising dollars from the presidential campaigns or the national parties, while battleground states received on average more than $8 million, and Florida alone received $36 million.[10] Scholars have leveraged this variability to study campaign effects, most commonly by comparing voter behavior across battleground and non-battleground locations (Holbrook and McClurg 2005; Just et al. 1996; Shaw 1999, 2006). In a recent article, Greg Huber and Kevin Arceneaux (2007) use a clever research design that takes advantage of the fact that media markets overlap state boundaries, enabling them to isolate the effects of television advertisements and demonstrating notable persuasion effects.

Beyond geography, though, there are many other sources of variation in the campaign efforts of the candidates. Once again, the literature offers no consensus about who is receiving what campaign messages. Goldstein and Ridout (2002) argue that campaign efforts have increasingly been targeted to previous voters and strong party loyalists. Holbrook and McClurg (2005, 689) similarly conclude that "core party voters are more likely to receive and respond to campaign information." Others, however, contend that campaign efforts are primarily targeted to swing voters and independents (Downs 1957; Hillygus and Shields 2008; Shaw 2006). Thus, in resolving the previously mentioned debate about which of these groups is most persuadable, we should take into account who is actually receiving campaign messages. There can be no campaign effect if the voter does not receive the campaign message.

To the extent scholars have considered variation in campaign exposure, it has typically focused on differences in volume—campaign spending, gross point ratings, the amount of campaign coverage. Much less is known about the nature and influence of campaign content (see Ken Goldstein and Matthew Holleque's chapter in this volume). Is it consequential, for instance, not only that Bush ran more ads than Kerry in Ohio in 2004, but also that those ads focused primarily on issues of national security? In other words, how does the message matter? Some scholars have hypothesized that individuals are more susceptible to messages on issues that are personally important to them (Hutchings 2003; Krosnick 1990), but there has been little empirical evidence testing this expectation.

Others argue that messages that reinforce existing stereotypes about a candidate's affiliated party should be more persuasive (Iyengar and Valentino 2000; Petrocik 1996; Riker 1986). According to this perspective, Democrats should focus on the issues on which their party has a strong performance record—education, health care, and social security, while Republicans should focus on the

---

[10] Estimates based on numbers reported in Shaw (2006).

issues they "own"—taxes, national security, crime. Yet, recent research has challenged the idea that candidates are actually following such a strategy (Kaplan, Park, and Ridout 2006; Sides 2006). And, of course, the content of the message is not likely to be static, it will likely change as the candidates react to each other, polls, media, and the broader environment—another source of variation that has rarely been accounted for in academic research.[11]

It is also the case that campaign messages have grown more complex and fragmented with changes in the information environment. New computing and statistical technologies have made it possible for candidates and parties to narrowly target messages to specific groups of voters based on information about those voters (Jacobs and Shapiro 2005). The political parties have built enormous databases with information about every registered voter in the United States, and they use this information to determine who should be targeted with what messages. The cornerstone of these databases is voter registration files, including a voter's name, home address, vote history (in most states), party affiliation, phone number, date of birth, and other information. By matching polling data and consumer information to these voter files, candidates can personalize campaign messages to different voters. In the 2004 presidential election, for instance, the candidates took positions on some seventy-five different issues in political mail sent, with very different messages sent to different voters (Hillygus and Shields 2008). The fragmentation of the content of campaign messages makes it difficult for scholars to measure who is being targeted with what messages. Yet, this variation in messages undoubtedly affects the patterns of campaign responsiveness we observe in the campaign. For instance, personalized messages might well increase effectiveness compared to generic TV appeals.

Ultimately, the great variation in candidate strategy and voter decision making should be viewed as both an opportunity and challenge for campaign scholars. Inevitably, we will confront issues of measurement and statistical estimation in trying to assess the impact of heterogeneous campaign efforts on a heterogeneous electorate. But these empirical challenges should not prevent us from acknowledging and examining how this variation in both sets of actors shapes when and how campaigns affect vote choice. Whereas the field once trumpeted every new piece of empirical evidence that "campaigns matter," it is no longer enough for scholars to simply look for new and better ways to document that campaigns matter. The task of future research is to move beyond this stale research agenda to more fully examine the nature of the interaction between candidates and voters (as well as parties, interest groups, and the media) in political campaigns.

---

[11] Notable exceptions include Carsey (2000) and Lau and Pomper (2004).

REFERENCES

ALTHAUS, S. L., NARDULLI, P., and SHAW, D. 2002. Candidate Appearances in Presidential Elections, 1972–2000. *Political Communication*, 19/1: 49–72.

ALVAREZ, R. M. 1998. *Information and Elections*. Ann Arbor: University of Michigan Press.

—— and BREHM, J. 2002. *Hard Choices, Easy Answers: Values, Information, and American Public Opinion*. Princeton, N.J.: Princeton University Press.

ANSOLABEHERE, S., IYENGAR, S., and SIMON, A. 1999. Replicating Experiments Using Aggregate and Survey Data. *American Political Science Review*, 93: 901–10.

ARCENEAUX, K. 2007. I'm Asking for Your Support: The Effects of Personally Delivered Campaign Messages on Voting Decisions and Opinion Formation. *Quarterly Journal of Political Science*, 2/1: 43–65.

BARTELS, L. M. 1993. Messages Received: The Political Impact of Media Exposure. *American Political Science Review*, 87: 267–85.

—— 2006. Priming and Persuasion in Presidential Campaigns. In *Capturing Campaign Effects*, ed. Henry E. Brady and Richard Johnston. Ann Arbor: University of Michigan Press.

BASINGER, S. and LAVINE, H. 2005. Ambivalence, Information, and Electoral Choice. *American Political Science Review*, 99: 169–84.

BAUM, M. 2003. *Soft News Goes to War: Public Opinion and American Foreign Policy in the New Media Age*. Princeton, N.J.: Princeton University Press.

BECK, P. A., DALTON, R., GREENE, S., and HUCKFELDT, R. 2002. The Social Calculus of Voting: Interpersonal, Media, and Organizational Influences on Presidential Choices. *American Political Science Review*, 96/1: 57–73.

BERELSON, B. R., LAZARSFELD, P. F., and MCHEE, W. N. 1954. *Voting: A Study of Opinion Formation in a Presidential Campaign*. Chicago: University of Chicago Press.

BRADER, T. 2006. *Campaigning for Hearts and Minds: How Emotional Appeals in Political Ads Work*. Chicago: University of Chicago Press.

BRADY, H. E. and JOHNSTON, R. 1987. What's the Primary Message? Horse Race or Issue Journalism? in *Media and Momentum: The New Hampshire Primary and Nomination Politics*, ed. N. W. Polsby and G. R. Orren. Chatham, N.J.: Chatham House.

—— —— and SIDES, J. 2006. The Study of Political Campaigns. In *Capturing Campaign Effects*, ed. H. E. Brady and R. Johnston. Ann Arbor: University of Michigan Press.

BRIANS, C. L. and WATTENBERG, M. P. 1996. Campaign Issue Knowledge and Salience: Comparing Reception from TV Commercials, TV News and Newspapers. *American Journal of Political Science*, 40: 172–93.

CAMPBELL, A., CONVERSE, P. E., MILLER, W. E., and STOKES, D. E. 1960. *The American Voter*. Chicago: University of Chicago Press.

CAMPBELL, J. E. 2000. *The American Campaign: U.S. Presidential Campaigns and the National Vote*. College Station, Tex.: Texas A&M University Press.

—— 2001. Presidential Election Campaigns and Partisanship. In *American Political Parties: Decline or Resurgence*, ed. J. E. Cohen, R. Fleischer, and P. Kantor. Washington, D.C.: CQ Press.

—— L. L. Cherry, and K. A. Wink. 1992. The Convention Bump. *American Politics Research*, 20: 287–307.

CARDY, E. A. 2005. An Experimental Field Study of the GOTV and Persuasion Effects of Partisan Direct Mail and Phone Calls. In *The Science of Voter Mobilization*, ed. D. P. Green and A. S. Gerber, Special Edition of *The Annals of the American Academy of Political and Social Science*, 601: 28–40.

Carsey, T. 2000. *Campaign Dynamics: The Race for Governor*. Ann Arbor: University of Michigan Press.

Chaffee, S. H. 1978. Presidential Debates: Are they Helpful to Voters? *Communication Monographs*, 45: 330–46.

—— and Zhao, X. 1995. Campaign Advertisements Versus Television News as Sources of Political Issue Information. *Public Opinion Quarterly*, 59: 41–65.

Converse, P. 1964. The Nature of Belief Systems in Mass Publics. In *Ideology and Discontent*, ed. D. Apter. New York: Free Press.

Craig, S., Kane, J., and Gainous, J. 2005. Issue-Related Learning in a Gubernatorial Campaign: A Panel Study. *Political Communication*, 22/4: 483–503.

Daudt, H. 1961. *Floating Voters and the Floating Vote: A Critical Analysis of. American and English Election Studies*. Leiden, Holland: H. E. Stenfert.

Downs, A. 1957. *An Economic Theory of Democracy*. New York: Harper & Row.

Druckman, J. 2004. Priming the Vote: Campaign Effects in a US Senate Election. *Political Psychology*, 25: 577–94.

—— Jacobs, L. R., and Ostermeier, E. 2004. Candidate Strategies to Prime Issues and Image. *Journal of Politics*, 66/4: 1180–1202.

Finkel, S. 1993. Reexamining the "Minimal Effects" Model in Recent Presidential Elections. *Journal of Politics*, 55/1: 1–21.

Fiorina, M. and Peterson, P. 2002. *The New American Democracy*. 2nd edn. New York: Longman Press.

Forehand, M., Gastil, J., and Smith, M. A. 2004. Endorsements as Voting Cues: Heuristic and Systematic Processing in Initiative Elections. *Journal of Applied Social Psychology*, 34: 2215–31.

Fournier, P. 2006. The Impact of Campaigns on Discrepancies, Errors, and Biases in Voting Behavior. In *Capturing Campaign Effects*, ed. H. E. Brady and R. Johnston. Ann Arbor: University of Michigan Press.

Franklin, C. 1991. Eschewing Obfuscation? Campaigns and the Perception of US Senate Incumbents. *American Political Science Review*, 85: 1193–214.

Freedman, P., Franz, M., and Goldstein, K. 2004. Campaign Advertising and Democratic Citizenship. *American Journal of Political Science*, 48: 723–41.

Geer, J. G. 1988. The Effects of Presidential Debates on the Electorate's Preferences for Candidates. *American Politics Research*, 16: 486–501.

Gelman, A. and King, G. 1993. Why are American Presidential Election Campaign Polls So Variable When Votes Are So Predictable? *British Journal of Political Science*, 23: 409–51.

Gerber, A. S. and Green, D. P. 2000. The Effects of Canvassing, Telephone Calls, and Direct Mail on Voter Turnout: A Field Experiment. *American Political Science Review*, 94: 653–63.

—— —— 2004. *Get Out the Vote! How to Increase Voter Turnout*. Washington, D.C.: Brookings Institution Press.

—— —— and Green, M. N. 2003. The Effects of Partisan Direct Mail on Voter Turnout. *Electoral Studies*, 22: 563–79.

—— —— and Kaplan, E. H. 2004. The Illusion of Learning from Observational Research. In *Problems and Methods in the Study of Politics*, ed. I. Shapiro, R. Smith, and T. Massoud. New York: Cambridge University Press.

GOLDSTEIN, K. and FREEDMAN, P. 2002. Lessons Learned: Campaign Advertising in the 2000 Elections. *Political Communication*, 19/1: 5–28.

—— and RIDOUT, T. N. 2002. The Politics of Participation: Mobilization and Turnout over Time. *Political Behavior*, 24: 3–29.

GREEN, D. P., GERBER, A. S., and NICKERSON, D. W. 2003. Getting Out the Vote in Local Elections: Results from Six Door-to-Door Canvassing Experiments. *Journal of Politics*, 65/4: 1083–96.

HILLYGUS, D. S. 2007. The Dynamics of Voter Decision Making among Minor-party Supporters: The 2000 U.S. Presidential Election. *British Journal of Political Science*, 37: 225–44.

—— and JACKMAN, S. 2003. Voter Decision Making in Election 2000: Campaign Effects, Partisan Activation, and the Clinton Legacy. *American Journal of Political Science*, 47: 583–96.

—— and SHIELDS, T. 2008. *The Persuadable Voter: Wedge Issues in Presidential Campaigns.* Princeton, N.J.: Princeton University Press.

HOLBROOK, T. M. 1996. *Do Campaigns Matter?* Thousand Oaks, Calif.: Sage.

—— 1999. Political Learning from Presidential Debates. *Political Behavior*, 21: 67–98.

—— 2002. Presidential Campaigns and the Knowledge Gap. *Political Communication*, 19: 437–54.

—— and McCLURG, S. 2005. Presidential Campaigns and the Mobilization of Core Supporters. *American Journal of Political Science*, 49: 689–703.

HUBER, G. and ARCENEAUX, K. 2007. Identifying the Persuasive Effects of Presidential Advertising. *American Journal of Political Science*, 4: 957–77.

HUTCHINGS, V. 2003. *Public Opinion and Democratic Accountability: How Citizens Learn about Politics.* Princeton, N.J.: Princeton University Press.

IYENGAR, S. 2001. The Method is the Message: The Current State of Political Communication Research. *Political Communication*, 18/2: 225–9.

—— and KINDER, D. R. 1987. *News That Matters.* Chicago: University of Chicago Press.

—— and VALENTINO, N. A. 2000. Who Says What? Source Credibility as a Mediator of Campaign Advertising. In *Elements of Reason*, ed. A. Lupia, M. D. McCubbins, and S. L. Popkin. Cambridge: Cambridge University Press.

—— KINDER, D. R., PETERS, M. D., and KROSNICK, J. A. 1984. The Evening News and Presidential Evaluations. *Journal of Personality and Social Psychology*, 46: 778–87.

JACOBS, L. and SHAPIRO, R. 2005. Polling Politics, Media, and Electoral Campaigns. *Public Opinion Quarterly*, 69: 635–41.

JACOBSON, G. C. 1983. *The Politics of Congressional Elections*, 6th edn. New York: Little, Brown, and Company.

JOHNSTON, R., HAGEN, M. G., and JAMIESON, K. H. 2004. *The 2000 Presidential Election and the Foundations of Party Politics.* Cambridge: Cambridge University Press.

—— BLAIS, A., BRADY, H. E., and CRETE, J. 1992. *Letting the People Decide: Dynamics of a Canadian Election.* Stanford: Stanford University Press.

JUST, M., CRIGLER, A. N., ALGER, D. E., and COOK, T. E. 1996. *Crosstalk: Citizens, Candidates, and the Media in a Presidential Campaign.* Chicago: The University of Chicago Press.

KAHN, K. F. and GOLDENBERG, E. N. 1991. Women Candidates in the News: AN Examination of Gender Differences in U.S. Senate Campaign Coverage. *Public Opinion Quarterly*, 55: 180–99.

—— and KENNEY, P. 1999. *The Spectacle of U.S. Senate Campaigns.* Princeton, N.J.: Princeton University Press.

KAID, L. L. 1997. Effects of the Television Spots on Images of Dole and Clinton. *American Behavioral Scientist*, 40/8: 1085–94.

KAPLAN, N., PARK, D., and RIDOUT, T. 2006. Dialogue in American Political Campaigns? An Examination of Issue Convergence in Candidate Television Advertising. *American Journal of Political Science*, 50: 724–36.

KRAMER, G. 1970. The Effects of Precinct-level Canvassing on Voter Behavior. *Public Opinion Quarterly*, 34: 560–72.

KROSNICK, J. A. 1990. Government Policy and Citizen Passion: A Study of Issue Publics in Contemporary America. *Political Behavior*, 12: 59–92.

—— and BRANNON, L. A. 1993. The Impact of the Gulf war on the Ingredients of Presidential Evaluations: Multidimensional Effects of Political Involvement. *American Political Science Review*, 87: 963–75.

—— and KINDER, D. R. 1990. Altering the Foundations of Support for the President Through Priming. *American Political Science Review*, 84: 497–512.

—— and PETTY, R. E. (eds.) 1995. *Attitude Strength: Antecedents and Consequences*. Malwah, N.J.: Lawrence Erlbaum Associates.

LAU, R. R. and POMPER, G. M. 2004. *Negative Campaigning: An Analysis of U.S. Senate Elections*. Lanham, Md.: Rowman & Littlefield.

—— and REDLAWSK, D. P. 2001. Advantages and Disadvantages of Cognitive Heuristics in Political Decision Making. *American Journal of Political Science*, 45/4: 951–71.

—— —— 2006. *How Voters Decide: Information Processing During Election Campaigns*. New York: Cambridge University Press.

LAZARSFELD, P., BERELSON, B., and GAUDET, H. 1944. *The People's Choice: How the Voter Makes Up His Mind in a Presidential Campaign*. New York: Duell, Sloan and Pearce.

LEIGHLEY, J. E. 2004. *Mass Media and Politics: A Social Science Perspective*. New York: Houghton Mifflin Company.

LENZ, G. S. 2009. Learning and Opinion Change, Not Priming: Reconsidering the Evidence for the Priming Hypothesis. *American Journal of Political Science*, 53/4 (forthcoming).

LODGE, M., McGRAW, K., and STROH, P. 1989. An Impression-Driven Model of Candidate Evaluation. *American Political Science Review*, 87: 399–419.

LUPIA, A. and PHILPOT, T. S. 2005. Views from Inside the Net: How Websites Affect Young Adults' Political Interest. *Journal of Politics*, 67/4: 1122–42.

MAGLEBY, D. B., MONSON, J. Q., and PATTERSON, K. D. 2006. *Dancing Without Partners: How Candidates, Parties, And Interest Groups Interact in the Presidential Campaign*. Rowman & Littlefield Publishers, Inc.

McCLURG, S. and HOLBROOK, T. H. 2005. Presidential Campaigns and the Mobilization of Core Supporters. *American Journal of Political Science*, 49: 689–703.

MENDELBERG, T. 2001. *The Race Card: Campaign Strategy, Implicit Messages, and the Norm of Equality*. Princeton, N.J.: Princeton University Press.

MILLER, J. M. and KROSNICK, J. A. 2000. News Media Impact on the Ingredients of Presidential Evaluations: Politically Knowledgeable Citizens are Guided by a Trusted Source. *American Journal Political Science*, 44/2: 301–15.

MONDAK, J. J. 1995. Newspapers and Political Awareness. *American Journal of Political Science*, 39/2: 513–27.

MOY, P., XENOS, M. A., and HESS, V. K. 2004. Priming Effects of Late-Night Comedy. *International Journal of Public Opinion Research*, 18: 198–210.

NICKERSON, D. 2005. Partisan Mobilization Using Volunteer Phone Banks and Door Hangers. *The Annals of the American Academy of Political and Social Science*, 601: 10–27.

NIE, N., VERBA, S., and PETROCIK, J. R. 1976. *The Changing American Voter*. Cambridge, Mass.: Harvard University Press.

NIVEN, D., LICHTER, S. R., and AMUNDSON, D. 2003. The Political Content of Late Night Comedy. *The Harvard International Journal of Press/Politics*, 8: 118–33.

NORRIS, P. and SANDERS, D. 2003. Message or Medium? Campaign Learning During the 2001 British General Election. *Political Communication*, 20: 233–62.

PATTERSON, T. E. and McCLURE, R. D. 1976. *The Unseeing Eye: The Myth of Television Power in National Politics*. New York: G.P. Putman's Sons.

PETERSON, D. A. M. 2004. Certainty or Accessibility: Attitude Strength in Candidate Evaluations. *American Journal of Political Science*, 48/3: 513–20.

—— 2005. Heterogeneity and Certainty in Candidate Evaluations. *Political Behavior*, 27/1: 1–24.

PETROCIK, J. R. 1996. Issue Ownership in Presidential Elections, with a 1980 Case Study. *American Journal of Political Science*, 40: 825–50.

POPKIN, S. L. 1991. *The Reasoning Voter: Communication and Persuasion in Presidential Campaigns*. Chicago: University of Chicago Press.

PRIOR, M. 2003. Any Good News in Soft News? The Impact of Soft News Preference on Political Knowledge. *Political Communication*, 20/2: 149–71.

—— 2007. *Post Broadcast Democracy*. Cambridge: Cambridge University Press.

RIDOUT, T. N., SHAH, D. V., GOLDSTEIN, K. M., and FRANZ, M. M. 2004. Evaluating Measures of Campaign Advertising Exposure on Political Learning. *Political Behavior*, 26: 201–25.

RIKER, W. 1986. *The Art of Political Manipulation*. New Haven, Conn.: Yale University Press.

RIVERS, D. 1988. Heterogeneity in Models of Electoral Choice. *American Journal of Political Science*, 32: 737–57.

ROSENSTONE, S. 1983. *Forecasting Presidential Elections*. New Haven, Conn.: Yale University Press.

SHAW, D. R. 1999. The Effect of TV Ads and Candidate Appearances on Statewide Presidential Votes, 1988–1996. *American Political Science Review*, 93: 345–61.

—— 2006. *The Race to 270: The Electoral College and the Campaign Strategies of 2000 and 2004*. Chicago: University of Chicago Press.

SIDES, J. 2006. The Origins of Campaign Agendas. *British Journal of Political Science*, 36: 407–36.

SIMON, A. 2002. *The Winning Message: Candidate Behavior, Campaign Discourse, and Democracy*. Cambridge: Cambridge University Press.

TICHENOR, P. J., DONOHUE, G. A., and OLIEN, C. N. 1975. Mass Media and the Knowledge Gap. *Communication Research*, 2: 3–23.

VALENTINO, N. A., HUTCHINGS, V. L., and WHITE, I. K. 2002. Cues that Matter: How Political Ads Prime Racial Attitudes During Campaigns. *American Political Science Review*, 96: 75–90.

—— —— and WILLIAMS, D. 2004. The Impact of Political Advertising on Knowledge, Internet Information Seeking, and Candidate Preference. *Journal of Communication*, 337–54.

VAVRECK, L. 2009. *The Message Matters*. Princeton, N.J.: Princeton University Press.

ZALLER, J. R. 1992. *The Nature and Origins of Mass Opinion.* Cambridge: Cambridge University Press.

—— 1996. The Myth of Massive Media Impact Revived: New Support for a Discredited Idea. In *Political Persuasion and Attitude Change*, ed. D. Mutz, R. Brody, and P. Sniderman. Ann Arbor: University of Michigan Press.

—— 2004. Floating Voters in the U.S. Presidential Election, 1948–2000. In *Studies in Public Opinion: Attitudes, Nonattitudes, Measurement Error, and Change*, ed. W. E. Saris and P. M. Sniderman. Princeton, N.J.: Princeton University Press.

CHAPTER 19

··

FORECASTING US PRESIDENTIAL ELECTIONS[1]

··

THOMAS HOLBROOK

Never make predictions, especially about the future
Attributed to Casey Stengel[2]

We should have gotten our brains beat
Karl Rove, following the 2000 election[3]

As suggested by Casey Stengel's admonition and Karl Rove's observation on the 2000 presidential race, predicting the future can be a difficult and perhaps surprising enterprise. As one who has proffered very public and occasionally very wrong forecasts of presidential election outcomes, I can also attest to the fact that predicting is not always for the faint of heart.[4] Yet occasional misfires by a couple of election forecasting models do not render the entire enterprise of no use. In fact, given the lead time with which most forecasts are made, along with the limited

---

[1] This chapter was written in the spring and summer of 2008, well before the outcome of the presidential election was known.

[2] http://thinkexist.com/quotation/never_make_predictions-especially_about_the/154388.html

[3] Berke (2001).

[4] See Lewis-Beck (2005) for an example of the type of "citizen response" forecasters were exposed to during and after the 2000 campaign.

number of predictors used (see below), the vast majority of academic forecasting models are surprisingly accurate.

In this chapter I provide an assessment of the current state of presidential election forecasting models. Although congressional election models are also quite prevalent (see Abramowitz 2002, 2006; Bardwell and Lewis-Beck 2004; Erikson and Bafumi 2002; Klarner and Buchanan 2006a, 2006b; Lewis-Beck and Rice 1992), and while the history and evolution of academic election forecasting is interesting and instructive (see Campbell and Lewis-Beck 2008; Lewis-Beck 2005; Lewis-Beck and Rice 1984, 1992), I direct my attention to presidential forecasting models from the last three election cycles. I begin the chapter with a look "under the hood" and discuss the specifics of the most widely known models from the 2004 election; I then consider the predictions made by these models and evaluate the determinants of forecasting accuracy from 1996 to 2004; next, I examine lessons learned from the 2000 campaign; finally, I examine alternatives to the dominant aggregate-national forecasting models: electronic markets, citizen forecasts, and state-level forecasting models.

Election forecasters have encountered some level of criticism over both method and (lack of) theory (Beck 1992; Colomer 2007; Greene 1993; Tetlock 2005). Campbell (1993, 2008a, 2008b) provides a spirited defense of the forecasting enterprise, pointing out that the forecasting community has generally been very responsive to methodological criticisms and that most models are based on a particular theoretical framework: retrospective voting (Fiorina 1981). Indeed, the charge that forecasting models are void of theory strikes me as particularly ludicrous. Given that most models (below) are based on the assumption that the electorate rewards the incumbent party for good times and punishes it for bad times, it would appear that forecasters are on fairly solid footing. Having said this, I do think that forecasters are subject to criticism regarding their selection of indicators of important theoretical concepts. In the end, as Campbell (2008b) points out, the goal of forecasting models is not to generate or test grand theories but to predict election outcomes. Nevertheless, it seems to me that one way to have both interesting and accurate forecasting models is to base them on theoretically plausible assumptions about the electorate, which is the case for most models discussed in the next section.

THE FORECASTING MODELS, 2004

Perhaps the best way to get a sense of what constitutes contemporary forecasting models is to examine a group of models developed and made public prior to the 2004 presidential election. Table 19.1 summarizes many of the key aspects of nine

Table 19.1 A summary of presidential forecasting models, 2004

Author	Economic Variables	Political Variables	Trial-Heat Variables	# Obs.	Predicted Vote Bush	Error
Abramowitz	GDP Change (first 2 qtrs. of election year)	Approval Time for Change		1948–2000 14 obs.	53.7%	2.4
Campbell	GDP Growth (2nd qtr)		Early Sept. Poll	1948–2000 14 obs.	53.8%	2.5
Fair (October)	GDP Growth (first 3 qtrs. of election yr) Inflation GoodNews (# qtrs. with growth > 3.2%)	President's Party Incumbency Time for Change War		1916–2000 22 obs.	57.5%	6.3
Holbrook	Personal Finances, adjusted for Economic news	Approval Time for Change		1956–2000 12 obs.	56.1%	4.9
Lewis-Beck and Tien	GNP Growth (4th to 2nd qtr. of elect. yr)	Approval Incumbency		1952–2000 13 obs.	49.9%	−1.3

Author	Variables	Model	Predictors / Notes	Period / obs	Result	
	GNP Growth (x) Incumbent Job Growth	Time for Change		1956–2000 12 obs.	57.6%	6.4
Lockerbie	Prospective Personal Finances (1st qtr)					
Norpoth		Primary Support		1912–2000 23 obs.	54.7%	3.5
		Partisan Baseline				
Wlezien and Erikson	Leading Economic Indicators (LEI) Growth: through 13th qtr of sitting President's term	Approval	August Trial Heat Polls (only in 2nd model)	1952–2000 13 obs.	52.9%	1.7
					51.7% (model 2)	0.5
Cuzán and Bundrick	GDP Growth (first 3 qtrs.)	Incumbency		1916–2000 22 obs.	51.1%	.14
	Inflation	Time for change				
	All News (Fair's Good News not adjusted for war years)					

different models developed by forecasters who have proffered their prognostications for the past several presidential elections.[5] All of the models are popular vote models and focus on predicting the two-party division of the national votes. While there is much overlap among the forecasting models, there is also considerable diversity. One overriding characteristic of the models—alluded to above—is that most of them are retrospective in nature; that is, most of them incorporate measures of economic or presidential performance and assume an electorate that rewards presidents for good outcomes and punishes presidents for bad outcomes. Indeed, four of the nine models include a measure of presidential approval, and eight out of the nine incorporate at least one measure of economic performance. Another predictor held in common by five of the nine models is some form of Abramowitz's (1988) "time for change" variable, which indicates whether or not the incumbent party has held the White House for at least two consecutive terms. Somewhat less common are measures of trial-heat poll results (two models) and controls for whether or not the incumbent president is running (three models). The one model that stands out from the others is Norpoth's (2004), which does not share any variables in common with the other models. Instead Norpoth's forecast is based on how well the candidates fared in their party's New Hampshire primary, lagged presidential election results, and a partisan baseline.

Table 19.1 also shows some variation in how far in advance of the election the independent variables are measured, as well as the number of elections upon which the forecasts are made. In terms of timing, the Fair and Cuzán and Bundrick models measure gross domestic product (GDP) growth over the first three quarters, meaning that their data are measured through the end of September and are not available until late October. At the other extreme, Norpoth stands out again, with his independent variables measured by late January. Most of the variation in the number of data points used across the models is a function of whether or not the model includes survey-based measures, such as presidential approval, economic perceptions, or trial-heat polls, most of which are not available for elections prior to 1948, at the earliest. Those that do not use such measures (Fair, Cuzán and Bundrick, and Norpoth) incorporate data from many more elections than those that do.

---

[5] With the exception of the Fair (2004) and Cuzán and Bundrick (2005) models, all others were presented at a roundtable discussion at the 2004 meeting of the American Political Science Association and published in the pre-election issue of *PS: Political Science and Politics* (Abramowitz 2004; Campbell 2004; Holbrook 2004; Lewis-Beck and Tien 2004; Lockerbie 2004; Norpoth 2004; Wlezien and Erikson 2004).

Finally, there is also appreciable variation in the accuracy of the predictions generated by the forecasting models. The most accurate forecasts in 2004 were Cuzán and Bundrick and Wlezien and Erikson, off by .14 and .5 percentage points, respectively; and the least accurate predictions were generated by Fair and Lockerbie, off by 6.3 and 6.4 percentage points, respectively. Overall, the average absolute error for the 2004 models was 2.96 percentage points.

FORECASTING ACCURACY, 1996–2004

Figure 19.1 provides a broader descriptive look at forecasting accuracy from the 1996, 2000, and 2004 presidential elections. The top panel of the figure displays the absolute error in the forecasts, and the bottom panel displays the real value of the error. Several interesting findings are revealed here. First, there is considerable variation in forecasting accuracy both within and across elections: the average absolute error and variation in absolute error were greatest in 2000 and lowest in 1996. The bottom panel reveals another interesting pattern regarding the direction of error: in all three election cycles, the vast majority of the predictions (twenty-five out of twenty-eight) *overestimated* the expected vote of the incumbent party. One possibility here is that there is some sort of systematic bias in the models that leads to erroneously positive expectations for the incumbent party. The source of this bias remains a mystery and is something about which forecasters should be aware. One other finding that is not apparent from these data is that the models do a very good job of calling the popular vote winner: in twenty-seven of twenty-eight cases the forecasting models predicted the correct winner of the two-party vote.[6] Even in 2000, when the average error was relatively high, every model called the popular vote for Gore. This may seem like a minor point, since presidential elections are won with electoral votes, but in all fairness forecasting models do focus on predicting the outcome of the two-party popular vote.

---

[6] Lewis-Beck and Tien's 2004 model predicted a Bush vote share of 49.9 percent of the two-party vote.

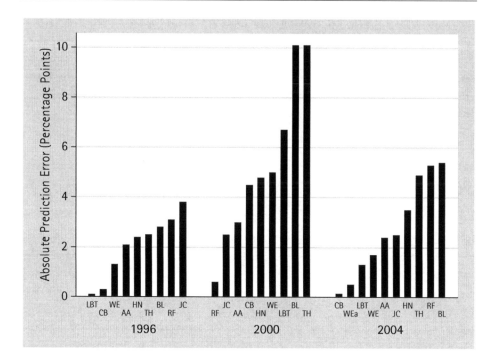

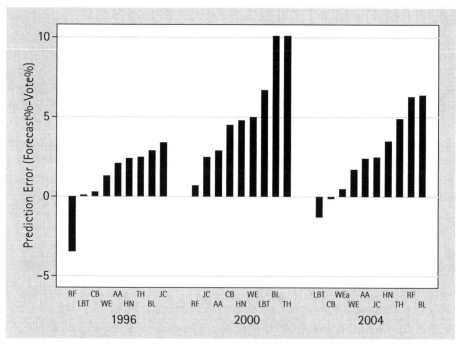

Figure 19.1 Forecasting accuracy in US presidential elections, 1996–2004

Note: AA=Alan Abramowitz; BL= Brad Lockerbie; CB=Cuzán and Bundrick; HN=Helmut Norpoth; JC=Jim
Campbell; LBT=Lewis-Beck and Tien; RF=Ray Fair; TH=Tom Holbrook; WE(a)=Wlezien and Erikson

WHAT MAKES FOR A GOOD MODEL?

The data in Figure 19.1 also show that there is no single model that is always the "best" model. Given the above description of the error rates in 2004 (Table 19.1), one might be tempted to conclude that the Cuzán and Bundrick and Wlezien and Erikson models are the "best" models, while the Fair and Lockerbie models are the "worst." However, this requires us to pin everything on only the most recent election when we know the models show different levels of accuracy in other elections. For instance, in the difficult-to-call election of 2000, Fair's model came within seven-tenths of a percentage point of the actual vote while Cuzán and Bundrick and Wlezien and Erikson missed by 4.5 and 5 percentage points, respectively. The point here is that judging models based on single elections is hardly a sound strategy for understanding what constitutes a good forecasting model.

Lewis-Beck (1985, 2005) argues that accuracy, parsimony, reproducibility, and lead time (with more weight assigned to lead time) should all be taken into account when evaluating a model. I have no problem with this, in principle, as these are all important characteristics. However, Campbell (2008b) argues that Lewis-Beck's indicator of quality is imperfect, primarily because rearranging the same components and assigning more weight to accuracy than lead time produces very different results. For instance, using Lewis-Beck's conceptualization, Campbell's 2004 forecast is ranked sixth (out of seven forecasts), whereas assigning more weight to accuracy than to lead time vaults Campbell's forecast to first among the seven models. Again, though, I would argue that the larger problem is not how you arrange the components but the fact that we are evaluating forecasting models on the basis of single election outcomes.

One alternative to focusing on which single model is "best" is to instead turn to an analysis of the types of model characteristics that lead, on average, to greater accuracy in predictions. In other words, given the variation in forecasting accuracy, why are some models more accurate than others? This is the task to which I now turn. However, in order to avoid the pitfalls of relying on results from just one election I examine accuracy across the last three elections.

DETERMINANTS OF ACCURACY

In order to assess the determinants of forecasting accuracy I use the absolute errors in forecasting presidential elections from 1996 to 2004 (presented in the top panel of Figure 19.1) as a dependent variable and then model that error as a function of model characteristics that are expected to provide a good statistical account of it. Although this analysis is somewhat limited due to the number of forecasts, and also because of the general similarities among models, there is enough variation both in error and model characteristics that a plausible model can be developed and evaluated. In addition, it should be pointed out that while some of the models retained the same characteristics across all three elections, many of them incorporated modest changes from year to year.

Lead time. It is important to consider lead time because models based on data measured more proximate to the election should generally be the most accurate, as they are more likely to capture the actual conditions surrounding the election. There is appreciable variation in lead time, ranging from the Fair and Cuzán and Bundrick October models, which include a measure of GDP growth in the first three quarters (measured in September), to Norpoth's 2004 model which relies on the outcome of the New Hampshire primary, measured in January. Here, the Fair and Cuzán and Bundrick models are given a score of 2 on lead time since the latest time of measurement for their model occurred two calendar months prior to the election, and Norpoth's 2004 model is given a value of 10, since his latest measurement was ten months prior to the election. The median lead time (time of last measurement) across all twenty-eight estimates is 3.5 and the mean is 3.96.

Retrospective Elements. As previously mentioned, most of the models are retrospective in nature, including, in some combination, measures of the economy, presidential approval, and "time for change." In order to assess the importance of these variables for forecasting accuracy, I include separate dichotomous indicators for whether the models included a measure of presidential approval or a measure for time for change.[7] Across all three election cycles 46 percent of the models included a measure of presidential approval and 54 percent included a "time for change" measure.

Data Points. Theoretically, models based on more data should involve less error, since they incorporate a wider range of electoral experiences and the impact of single elections is minimized. Once again, there is considerable variation in sample size, ranging from ten observations for Lockerbie's 1996 model to twenty-three observations for Norpoth's 2004 model. The mean and median numbers of observations (sample size) across all three years are 15.2 and 13 observations, respectively.

Year of Election. Of course, the number of observations available for analysis increases naturally with each election cycle. Because of this, and also to control for year-specific factors not captured in the models, I also add dummy variables for 1996 and 2000.

---

[7] Norpoth's 2000 and 2004 models are the only ones that did not include a measure of the economy, so adding a control for the presence of an economic variable would be equivalent to a control for Norpoth.

Table 19.2 Determinants of error in forecasting models, 1996–2004

	b	s.e.	t-score	$p \leq$ (one-tailed)
Lead Time	0.423	0.201	2.11	0.024
Time for Change	1.568	0.836	1.88	0.038
Approval	−1.548	1.036	−1.49	0.075
Sample Size	−0.225	0.119	−1.89	0.037
1996	−1.045	1.021	−1.02	0.159
2000	1.957	0.993	1.97	0.031
Constant	4.734	2.475	1.91	0.035
N=28				
S.E. = 2.15				
Adj. R^2=.346				

Note: Variables described in text

Table 19.2 presents the findings from the forecasting accuracy model.[8] Here we see that some of the expectations were borne out and some not. The slope for lead time suggests that for every additional month prior to the election that a model's last measurement was taken, error can be expected to increase by .42 percentage points. This means, for instance, that models using data measured in June can be expected, all else held constant, to have 1.3 points more error than models whose last measurement is in September. According to Lewis-Beck (2005) one of the virtues of a good forecasting model is greater lead time. The evidence presented here shows that this emphasis on lead time must be balanced against a very real cost in forecasting accuracy.

The results also illustrate the virtue of basing forecasts on as many observations of past electoral behavior as possible. For every additional data point used in the models, forecasting error declined by .23 percentage points. One could argue that this coefficient does little more than distinguish those models that rely on survey-based measures, such as presidential approval and trial-heat polls—which are limited to data from 1948 (at the earliest) onward—from the models that rely on aggregate economic and political data (Fair, Norpoth, and Cuzán and Bundrick). However, three points undermine this argument. First, the model also includes a control variable for whether the forecast was based on a measure of presidential approval, so this distinction is already adequately captured. Second, when the variable for number of observations was dropped in favor of a dichotomous

---

[8] Given the left-censored nature of the dependent variable (absolute errors cannot be less than zero) I also ran the model presented in Table 19.2 as a tobit model. The results of the two specifications were very similar, except that the tobit model produced coefficients with slightly higher t-scores.

variable distinguishing between the two groups of models, the coefficient was slightly less significant (t=-1.82) and the model fit declined slightly (adjusted R^2=.335). Finally, it is hard to argue that more data is not a good thing.

The evidence for the role of retrospective variables is a bit mixed. On the one hand, if one were willing to stretch the bounds of the traditional limits on statistical significance (as one might do with such a small sample), there appears to be a significant influence from presidential approval. The error from models that include a measure of approval is, on average, 1.53 points lower than models that do not control for approval. On the other hand, models that include some form of the "time for change" variable, on average, have about 1.59 percentage points greater error than other models. This finding is a bit at odds with expectations and suggests that the focus on incumbency-oriented effects does not always lead to less error, or perhaps that the "time for change" concept does not fit as squarely within the retrospective framework.

To reiterate, the purpose of this analysis is not to declare one model as "best" but rather to highlight the characteristics of models that generally lead to less forecasting error. Based on these results, models that have a relatively short lead time, include presidential approval, maximize the number of observations from past elections, and do not include a measure of "time for change" typically generate less error in election forecasts.

LESSONS FROM 2000

The analysis above reinforces the exceptional nature of the 2000 presidential election. At least in recent history it stands out as the most difficult election—on average and across models—to predict; and although the data in Figure 19.1 illustrate that the 2000 election was more a disaster for some forecasters (me, for instance) than for others, the average error was large enough that it seems reasonable to be open to lessons from the 2000 experience. Two general explanations have been offered for the discrepancy between results and prediction: one that focuses on campaign strategies and another that focuses on the role of incumbency. I, along with others (Campbell 2001; Holbrook 2001; Wlezien 2001), have argued that at least part of the explanation rests with Al Gore's failure to embrace the Clinton–Gore record and reinforce retrospective voting. At the same time, a case can be made that the retrospective cue may generally be weaker when the president himself is not on the ticket (Campbell 2001; Lewis-Beck and Tien 2001; Nadeau and Lewis-Beck, 2001). Indeed, Campbell (2001, 2008a) argues in favor of only giving half weight to presidential performance variables when the vice president rather

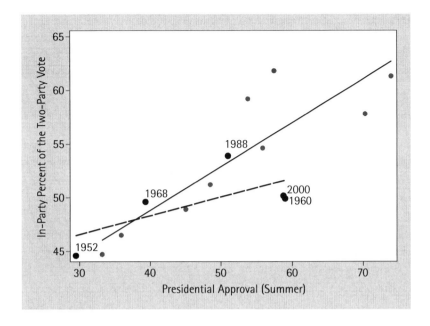

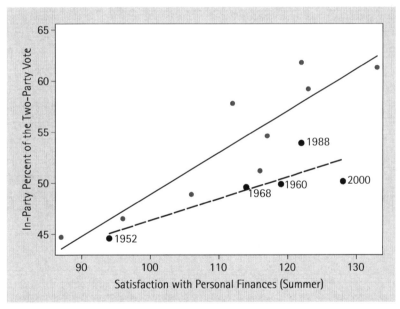

Figure 19.2 The effects of presidential approval and personal finances on support for the incumbent party, 1952–2004

than president is representing the incumbent administration. My own view is that Campbell's general idea is right but that there is no strong reason for assuming the half weight is the right factor. This issue takes on more importance as the 2008 election—an election in which neither the president nor vice president will be on the ticket—draws near. This election represents the first since 1952 in which the race can truly be considered an open race, with no representative from the incumbent administration.

Rather than assuming the in-party candidate gets only half blame (or credit) for presidential performance when the president is not running, it is probably better to let the data decide the appropriate weighting. As a means of assessing the importance of controlling for incumbency, I test a simple forecasting model, based on my own work, that controls for whether the contests involve an incumbent president or not. I use two variables as predictors of the incumbent party share of the two-party vote from 1952 to 2004: the average rate of presidential approval and the average level of consumer satisfaction[9] in the summer before the presidential election.

Following the logic articulated above, the expectation is that the relationship between presidential approval, personal finances, and the vote should be weaker in non-incumbent years than in years when the incumbent is running. The potential for these asymmetric effects is shown in Figure 19.2 where the top panel shows the plot of the relationship between presidential approval (summer) and the percentage vote for the incumbent presidential party. Election years with no incumbent running are highlighted with year labels and regression prediction lines are generated separately for incumbent (solid) and open seat (dashed) contests. At first glance, there appears to be a meaningful difference in the impact of approval on vote shares, with approval translating more readily into votes in incumbent contests than in open contests. One reservation that must be acknowledged however is that much of this difference seems to be driven by the 1960 and 2000 elections. Indeed, the 1952, 1968, and 1988 elections do not appear to follow a distinct pattern. But still, the 1960 and 2000 elections constitute 40 percent of the open-seat contests and can, therefore, hardly be dismissed as oddball, or atypical.

The second panel of Figure 19.2 illustrates the same pattern for the relationship between personal finances and vote shares. Here, we see a more clearly different pattern among the open-seat contests, where there is an appreciably shallower slope (taking into account the interaction) than in the incumbent contests. Again,

---

[9] The measure of aggregated personal finances is taken from the monthly survey of consumers (University of Michigan) and is measured as 100 plus the difference between the percentage saying they are better off financially than a year ago, and the percentage saying they are worse off financially. The measure of presidential approval is taken from the Gallup Poll and is the percentage responding "approve" when asked, "Do you approve or disapprove of the way [president's name] is handling his job as president?" Both measures are averaged across June, July, and August. For 1952, there was no summer measure of personal finances, so the value from May was used.

Table 19.3 The conditioning effect of incumbents on retrospective elements of a forecasting model

	b	T	b	t	B	t
Personal Finances	0.41	6.06				
Personal Finances*Open Seat	−0.20	−1.58				
Approval			0.41	5.00		
Approval*Open Seat			−0.23	−1.58		
National Conditions					0.42	6.42
National Conditions*Open Seat					−0.23	−1.98
Open Seat	17.18	1.20	8.85	1.18	14.34	1.57
Constant	7.90	1.03	32.56	7.37	21.20	4.09
N		14		14		14
Adj. R²		0.78		0.70		0.80
S.E.		2.72		3.19		2.62
Prob. F>		.002		.0003		.0002

Note: Variables described in text

this scatter-plot suggests a somewhat lower level of accountability for the incumbent party in years in which the president is not on the ticket.

These visual suggestions are put to the test in Table 19.3, which displays the results of a regression analysis in which the independent variables are interacted with a dichotomous variable scored 0 for incumbent contests and 1 for open-seat contests. If there is really less accountability during open-seat contests, the interaction slope should be negative. The first two models present the slopes and t-scores for the approval and personal finance equations run separately. In both cases we see a reduction in accountability by roughly the same proportion: the slopes for both approval and personal finances are cut just about in half in open-seat contests. And, while the interaction slopes are only marginally significant, it might be good to exercise a bit of latitude in interpreting significance, given the small number of cases, as well as the relatively high level of collinearity (tolerances range from .01 to .06).

The third model is a combined model in which both approval and personal finances are transformed so that each observation is expressed as a percentage of its highest value in the data set, and then averaged together to provide a measure of national conditions that reflects both presidential approval and satisfaction with personal finances. Once again, we see that the impact of the personal finances and presidential approval is much greater in incumbent races than in open-seat contests. In this case, the interaction coefficient is safely within the standard limits of statistical significance.

These results fit quite nicely with Campbell's contention that forecasting models need to account for incumbency when using "accountability" variables. It also reflects the same sentiment found in Nadeau and Lewis-Beck's (2001) individual-level work, which found that voters generally assigned less blame or credit to the incumbent party during open-seat contests. At the same time, these results should probably be regarded with some level of caution, as they are based on a single forecasting model, with a limited number of observations. Indeed, when the same analysis is done substituting second-quarter GDP growth for perceptions of personal finances, there is no incumbency effect. This may suggest that conditional effects from incumbency are more likely when using survey-based measures such as presidential approval and perceived personal finances, though this analysis is too limited to make that determination. The bottom line is that forecasters should check to see if the reward–punishment aspects of their models are sensitive to the conditioning influence of incumbency.

POLITICAL MARKETS

Electronic political markets represent an important alternative to traditional forecasting models and are also viewed as an alternative to trial-heat polls. These markets operate similarly to the standard stock markets, with investors able to buy and sell shares of certain political outcomes rather than publicly traded companies. The "granddaddy" of the political markets (modern markets,[10] at any rate) is the Iowa Electronic Markets (IEM), created by a group of faculty at the University of Iowa prior to the 1988 election. Although many other markets have sprung up in the meantime, including those that predict outcomes in sports, current events, and entertainment,[11] the IEM remains the standard for political markets and is the focus of this discussion.

The mechanism for translating market activity into an election forecast is fairly straightforward. Investors buy candidate shares (units) and the payoff for those shares is equal to the percentage of the final vote won by the candidate. If an investor thinks a candidate is likely to win with 55 percent of the vote, she has an

---

[10] See Strumpf and Rohde (2004).

[11] See Wolfers and Zitewitz (2004) for a nice discussion regarding the multiple political and other markets.

incentive to buy that candidate's units when they are available at less than 55 cents per unit and to sell when they cost more than 55 cents per unit. The market aggregates traders' expectations to produce a market price that ends up reflecting the expected (among market participants) percentage of the vote the candidate will receive in the election. Wolfers and Zitzewitz describe the predictive power of electronic markets as deriving "from the fact that they provide incentives for *truthful revelation*, they provide incentives for research and *information discovery*, and the market provides an algorithm for *aggregating opinions*" (2004, 121).

One of the central claims of market proponents is that the market estimates are actually better predictors of vote shares than the results of trial-heat polls (Berg, Nelson, and Rietz 2008). And indeed, when comparing the accuracy of the market estimates of candidate vote shares with trial-heat polls, the markets do dominate. However, Erikson and Wlezien (2008) point out that this comparison is based on a naive treatment of trial-heat polls. What Erikson and Wlezien suggest is that rather than using the level of candidate support from trial-heat polls on day *t* as our estimate of the eventual election outcome, we should be *projecting* the expected election-day level of candidate support based on the historical relationship between polls on day *t* and the election-day results. Erikson and Wlezien are able to generate these estimates based on data from their "poll of polls" (Wlezien and Erikson 2002), in which they calculate a weighted daily average of all trial-heat polls from 1952 to 2004, from as far out as 200 days prior to the election. These daily estimates are then used to generate election-day predictions from daily observations of poll results, based on the historical trends in the data. Erikson and Wlezien's analysis of poll projections shows the polls dominating the 1988 and 1992 contests, edging out market predictions in 2004, and losing to market projections in 1996 and 2000. Erikson and Wlezien go on to show that when the winner-take-all market projections are compared to poll-based projections, the polls dominate in every election cycle.

As I see it, there are several points to take away based on the work of Erikson and Wlezien (2008) and Berg et al. (2008). First, election predictions drawn from the vote-share market are generally very close to the eventual outcome, especially as the election draws near. Second, it's not clearly the case that these predictions "dominate" the polls, especially if poll-based projections are used rather than simple poll-based vote shares.[12] Third, one important point that should not be lost is that trial-heat polls are expressions of vote intention, not of the respondents' perceptions of the expected vote share for each of the candidates. So, at some very real level, a comparison of raw trial-heat numbers to investors' expectations of the eventual outcome is not a fair fight. Finally, although the poll projections generally offer a higher level of accuracy, one of the chief advantages of the vote-share market is that

[12] However, it strikes me that the most valid comparison for the poll projections is the vote-share market and not the winner-take-all market.

market prices can be translated directly into expected vote shares without much effort. By comparison, the poll projections require Erikson and Wlezien's "poll of polls"-based daily regression slopes to translate the trial-heat results into expected vote totals. This advantage in ease-of-use makes the market a more accessible and, probably, preferred source for interested consumers of "horse-race" information.

Still, I wonder if "forecast" is the appropriate term for translating market shares into expected election outcomes. After all, the traditional understanding of forecasting, and the approach used by the models discussed earlier (Table 19.1), is that the historical relationship between predictor variables (measured prior to the election) and past election outcomes is used to forecast future outcomes. While one of the attractive features of the vote-share market is that the prices translate directly into expected outcomes, a behavioral model that estimates the relationship between market prices and actual outcomes, similar to traditional forecasting models, might eventually provide even better predictions. For instance, à la Erikson and Wlezien, instead of simply using something like the average market share price during, say, the last two weeks of the campaign as our estimate of the eventual outcome, it might be more interesting to ask what the expected outcome is based on the historical relationship between market prices during the last two weeks and the outcome on election day.

Unfortunately, the IEM has only been in existence since 1988 and there are only five data observations for any given pre-election time period from which to develop such a behavioral model, so it is a bit risky to bet too much on estimates generated

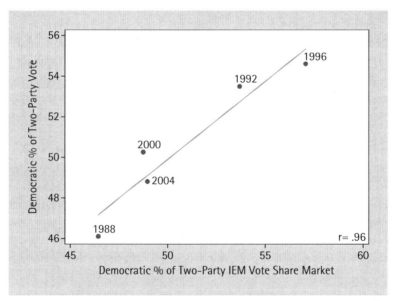

Figure 19.3 The linear relationship between the IEM vote share market (last two weeks of the campaign) and election outcomes, 1988–2004

from such a model. Figure 19.3, which plots the relationship between the IEM vote-share prices during the last two weeks of the campaign and actual election results, demonstrates the potential for a behavioral model that translates vote-share prices into vote projections in a manner similar to Erikson and Wlezien's projections using poll-based vote shares. There is a very strong relationship between the vote-share market and election outcomes, one that follows a predictable, linear pattern. Again, there are probably too few observations to get a reliable sense of the predictive power of the relationship, but when a regression slope is estimated using observations from 1988 to 2000 and used to generate an out-of-sample prediction of the 2004 election,[13] the prediction error is .4 percentage points, whereas the error based on a direct translation of the market share price from the last two weeks of the 2004 campaign is 1.17 percentage points.

CITIZEN FORECASTS

One of the explanations for the relative accuracy of the IEM vote-share market is that the market provides incentives for investors to gather information and weigh it objectively. One question this raises is whether investors are really better at predicting election outcomes than non-investors. Do investors out-perform casual observers? Put another way, and borrowing from Lewis-Beck and Skalaban (1989) and Lewis-Beck and Tien (1999), do investors out-perform "citizen forecasters"?

Lewis-Beck and Skalaban (1989) and Lewis-Beck and Tien (1999) demonstrate that, in aggregate, the American public is pretty good at picking the winners of US presidential elections. Lewis-Beck and colleagues are not able to use citizen-based estimates of the actual vote *share* for each candidate, but they are able to use a survey question from the pre-election wave (September through election day) of the National Election Study (NES) that asks respondents, "Who do you think will be elected President in November?" Aggregated responses to this question show an uncanny ability on the part of the general public to sniff out the likely winner, as shown in Figure 19.4. Here we see a strong, positive, linear relationship (r = .87) between citizen forecasts in the last two weeks of the campaign and actual election outcomes; and if the criterion is simply whether the citizen forecasts called the correct winner, they were only off the mark in 1976, 1980, and 2000. Since two of these elections (1976 and 2000) saw razor-thin margins of victory, this is a strong record during this period.

---

[13] Vote = 12.0 +.76X; N=4; r²=.91

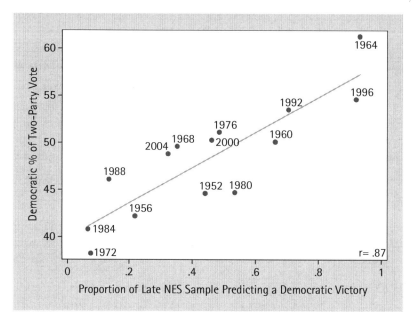

Figure 19.4 Citizen forecasts (last two weeks of campaign) and election outcomes, 1952–2004

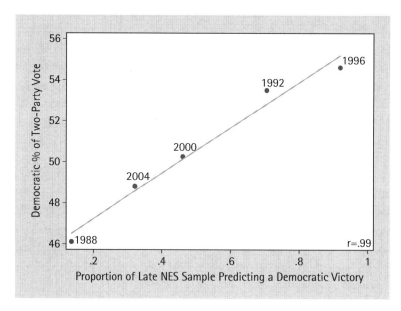

Figure 19.5 Citizen forecasts (last two weeks of campaign) and election outcomes, 1988–2004

But how do citizen forecasts in the last two weeks of the campaign stack up to those made by investors? A direct comparison based on Figures 19.3 and 19.4 is unfair since Figure 19.4 encompasses a longer time period and we don't know what the investor predictions would have been for the years 1952–1984. Instead, the best way to compare the two groups is to look at the relationship between citizen forecasts and votes for the same years (1988–2004) covered in Figure 19.3; these data are provided in Figure 19.5. From these data we can say that during the time period when both IEM- and NES-based citizen forecasts have been available, both sources of prediction track very closely with the actual vote received, and the relationship between citizen forecasts and actual votes is actually a bit stronger. So, again, the question is, do we need complex voting markets to generate accurate predictions of election outcomes? The evidence presented here suggests that surveys of the general public's sense of the likely election outcome may be just as useful.

STATE-LEVEL MODELS

All of the preceding discussion has focused on forecasting mechanisms for predicting the *national* vote. But while the popular vote winner generally wins the election, American presidential elections are determined by winning a majority of the electoral votes, which are parceled out among the states. Given this feature of the American electoral system, it is somewhat surprising that more attention has not been given to forecasting state-level presidential election outcomes. This is not to say that this area has been completely neglected. Indeed, a number of scholars (Campbell 1992; Campbell, Ali, and Jalazai 2006; Desart and Holbrook 2003; Holbrook and Desart 1999; Rosenstone 1983; Soumbatiants, Chappell, and Johnson 2006) have assembled state-level forecasting models that have yielded impressive results.

In this section, I focus on those state-level models that utilize trial-heat polls to forecast election outcomes. This approach, used by Desart (2005), Desart and Holbrook (2003), Holbrook and Desart (1999), and Soumbatiants, Chappell, and Johnson (2006), has yielded impressive results and should assume a more prominent position in forecasts, as state-level polls grow in abundance.[14] The Holbrook and DeSart and the Soumbatiants et al. models are similar in spirit (trial-heat polls predict election outcomes) but different in implementation. Soumbatiants et al.

---

[14] This points to the one limitation in using state-level trial-heat polls: the polls themselves have only become plentiful in the last few election cycles, and the earliest usable data for all states is the 1988 election cycle.

(2006) use slopes based on state-level trial-heat polls from one day and fifteen days prior to elections, from 1988 to 2000, to generate predicted outcomes for the 2004 presidential election. In addition to providing point estimates, they also use simulation techniques to generate estimates of the probability of alternative state-level outcomes, as well as the probability of Electoral College outcomes. Using this methodology, Soumbatiants et al. are able to predict 86 percent of the 2004 state outcomes correctly from fifteen days out and 88 percent correctly from one day out.

The Holbrook and DeSart model predicts the Democratic share of the two-party popular vote in the states as a function of the Democratic vote in the previous two elections, and the statewide Democratic share of the two-party vote in trial-heat polls averaged across all publicly available polls taken in September. Using data from 1992–2000 to forecast the 2004 state outcomes generates correct predictions in forty-seven (94 percent) of the fifty states; and, on average, the out-of-sample projections from 1992–2004 estimated 93 percent of the state outcomes correctly (Desart 2005). Although the lagged vote variable makes an important contribution to the model, the real power comes from the September poll average. In the 130 instances from 1992–2004 when one of the candidates had a lead in the September state-poll average outside the margin of error, the leading candidate went on to win 126 times (96.9 percent). If the margin of error is ignored and projections are based simply on which candidate is ahead in the September poll average, the September polls themselves predict 87.5 percent of all outcomes correctly.[15]

Even just these few examples of state-level forecasting models demonstrate that they offer an interesting and, I think, underutilized alternative to the standard national-aggregate model. Whether based mostly on aggregated state characteristics, similar to Campbell and colleagues, or taking advantage of state-level polling, similar to Soumbatiants et al. and Holbrook and DeSart, state-level models can generate highly accurate forecasts that, through aggregation, can also be used to generate predictions of the national outcome.

CONCLUSION

A number of recommendations flow directly from the analysis of forecasting models presented in this chapter. First, it is not terribly useful to declare one model or approach the "winner" based on accuracy in a single election period.

---

[15] Calculated with data presented in Holbrook and Desart (1999), Desart and Holbrook (2003), and Desart (2005).

Instead, it makes a good deal more sense to evaluate model characteristics that generally lead to greater accuracy across election cycles. Second, while we should not pin too much on single elections, we should not be closed off to learning from them. One lesson from the 2000 election that shows some promise is the idea of incorporating the conditioning effect of incumbency into forecasting models. The analysis presented here suggests just such a conditioning influence on the effects of presidential approval and perceived economic conditions. Finally, the dominant approach to forecasting presidential elections is to use national, longitudinal models, such as those presented in Table 19.1. While these models have been relatively successful over the past three election cycles, a number of interesting alternatives also exist, including electronic markets, "citizen" forecasts, and state-level forecasting models. Among these, the state-level models represent the closest kin to the dominant approach and (although they have already shown great success) also represent an area where much more work can be done—work that will hopefully help us better understand and forecast US presidential elections.

But I think it would also be fruitful to consider other innovations, not directly touched on in this chapter. One possibility is to consider differential weighting of forecasting data to assign more emphasis to recent elections than to those in the relatively distant past. This would seem to be most important for models such as those used by Fair, Norpoth, and Cuzán and Bundrick, whose models include data from elections from the early twentieth century. Intuition suggests that the relationships in the model have evolved over time and that more weight assigned to recent elections could improve accuracy.

Another strategy that I think could bear fruit is to focus on more of a meta-analytic approach to forecasting. With each passing election cycle there is an increasing number of forecasts and approaches to forecasting, almost all of which are on sound theoretical ground, and most of which have an established track record. One interesting approach is to not pin everything on a single model or single approach, but instead to take advantage of the collective wisdom of the forecasting community and consider something like meta-forecasting. This "combining" approach is advocated by Armstrong (2001) and is applied to election forecasting at PollyVote (http://www.forecastingprinciples.com/PollyVote/). Although combining does not have much of a track record in election forecasts, it did provide an accurate prediction of the 2004 presidential election (Cuzán, Armstrong, and Jones 2005) and has improved the accuracy of prediction in other domains (Armstrong 2001). This approach warrants monitoring in the next couple of election cycles in order to get a sense of its advantages and disadvantages relative to traditional models.

UPDATE: THE 2008 FORECASTS

The 2008 election provides an opportunity to update and evaluate many of the points made in this chapter. As in the past, most models are set up to predict the expected level of support (usually share of the two-party vote) for the incumbent party candidate, so the reference point here is McCain's 46.6 percent of the two-party popular vote and his 173 Electoral College votes. Nine forecasters published eleven pre-election predictions[16] in the October issue of *PS: Political Science and Politics* (Campbell 2008a), ranging from predictions of a narrow McCain victory to an Obama blowout. The average absolute error of the predictions (with Ray Fair's model added to the mix as the twelfth forecast) was 2.86 percentage points, making 2008 a better year than either 2000 (5.26 points) or 2004 (2.96 points). Similar to the data presented earlier, there was a tendency to over-predict the incumbent party's vote share, though the pattern was not as strong as in the past (seven of twelve models over-predicted McCain's vote share). The accuracy of the incumbency interaction model developed in this chapter was slightly better than the average model, missing the actual vote by just 2.3 points. Also similar to previous years, nearly every model (ten of twelve) predicted the correct winner of the popular vote. Alternatives to the national econometric models also fared well: the average IEM vote-share market during the last two weeks of the campaign predicted McCain would get 45.6 percent of the two-party vote, just one point less than he received, and the market's prediction on the day before the election was 46.9 percent for McCain. State-level models were also fairly accurate: DeSart and Holbrook's September poll model predicted 48.2 percent of the national (two-party) popular vote and 202 electoral votes for McCain, whereas their October model did somewhat better, predicting 46.1 percent of the popular vote and 189 electoral votes for McCain; and Klarner's (2008) state-level model nearly called the national popular vote on the nose, predicting 47 percent of the two-party vote for McCain, and also predicted 192 electoral votes for McCain.

In sum, from a forecasting perspective, the 2008 election outcome was business as usual. Some models were more accurate than others, as is always the case, but the average error was somewhat lower than in the past two elections cycles.

REFERENCES

ABRAMOWITZ, A. I. 1988. An Improved Model for Predicting Presidential Election Outcomes. *PS: Political Science and Politics*, 21: 843–7.

---

[16] Some forecasters provide two separate predictions. In these cases I include both predictions.

—— 2002. Who Will Win in November: Using the Generic Ballot Question to Forecast the Outcome of the 2002 Midterm Election. Symposium on midterm elections, <www.apsanet.org/~elections/archives.html>.

—— 2004. When Good Forecasts Go Bad: The Time-for-Change Model and the 2004 Presidential Election. *PS: Political Science & Politics*, 37: 745–6.

ABRAMOWITZ, A. I. 2006. National Conditions, Strategic Politicians, and U.S. Congressional Elections: Using the Generic Vote to Forecast the 2006 House and Senate Elections. *PS: Political Science & Politics*, 39: 863–9.

ARMSTRONG, J. S. 2001. Combining Forecasts. In *Principles of Forecasting: A Handbook for Researchers and Practitioners*, ed. J. S. Armstrong. Norwell, Mass.: Kluwer Academic Publishers.

BARDWELL, K. and LEWIS-BECK, M. S. 2004. State-level Forecasts of U.S. Senate Elections. *PS: Political Science & Politics*, 37: 821–6.

BECK, N. 1992. Forecasting the 1992 Presidential Election: The Message is in the confidence Interval. *The Public Perspective*, 3(6, September/October).

BERG, J. E., NELSON, F. D., and RIETZ, T. A. 2008. Prediction Market Accuracy in the Long Run. *International Journal of Forecasting*, 24: 285–300.

BERKE, R. L. 2001. Gore and Bush Strategists Analyze Their Campaigns. *New York Times*, 12 February 2001. Accessed online at <http://query.nytimes.com/gst/fullpage.html?res=9B03E0DA1131F931A25751C0A9679C8B63&sec=&spon=>.

CAMPBELL, J. E. 1992. Forecasting the Presidential Vote in the States. *American Journal of Political Science*, 36: 386–407.

—— 1993. Weather Forecasters Should Be So Accurate: A Response to "Forewarned Before Forecast." *PS: Political Science & Politics*, 28: 165–6.

—— 2001. The Referendum that Didn't Happen: The Forecasts of the 2000 Presidential Election. *PS: Political Science & Politics*, 34: 33–8.

—— 2004. Forecasting the Presidential Vote in 2004: Placing Preference Polls in Context. *PS: Political Science & Politics*, 37: 763–7.

—— 2008a. Editor's Introduction: Forecasting the 2008 National Elections *PS: Political Science & Politics*, 41/4 (October 2008): 679–81.

—— 2008b. Evaluating U.S. Presidential Election Forecasts and Forecasting Equations. *International Journal of Forecasting*, 24: 259–71.

—— ALI, S., and JALALZAI, F. 2006. Forecasting the Presidential Vote in the States, 1945–2004: An Update, Revision, and Extension of a State-level Presidential Forecasting Model. *Journal of Political Marketing*, 5: 33–57.

—— and LEWIS-BECK, M. S. 2008. U.S. Presidential Election Forecasting: An Introduction. *International Journal of Forecasting*, 24: 189–92.

COLOMER, J. M. 2007. What Other Sciences Look Like. *European Political Science*, 6: 134–42.

CUZÁN, A. G., ARMSTRONG, J. S., and JONES, R. 2005. Combining Methods to Forecast the 2004 Presidential Election. Presented at the Southern Political Science Association, New Orleans, January 6, 2005.

—— and BUNDRICK, C. M. 2005. Deconstructing the 2004 Presidential Election Forecasts: The Fiscal Model and the Campbell Collection Compared. *PS: Political Science and Politics*, 38: 255–62.

DESART, J. A. 2005. Forecasting the 2004 Presidential Election with State Trial-Heat Polls. Paper presented at the annual meeting of the Midwest Political Science Association, Chicago, Ill., April 7–10.

DESART, J. A. and HOLBROOK, T. M. 2003. Statewide Trial-Heat Polls and the 2000 Presidential Election: A Forecast Model. *Social Science Quarterly*, 84: 561–73.

ERIKSON, R. S. and BAFUMI, J. 2002. Generic Polls, Late Balancing Acts, and Midterm Outcomes: Lessons from History for 2002. Symposium on midterm elections, <www.apsanet.org/~elections/archives.html>.

—— and WLEZIEN, C. 2008 Are Political Markets Really Superior to Polls as Election Predictors? *Public Opinion Quarterly*, 72: 190–215.

FAIR, R. 2004. Presidential Vote Equation—October 20, 2004. <http://fairmodel.econ.yale.edu/vote2004/vot1004.htm.>

FIORINA, M. P. 1981. *Retrospective Voting in American National Elections*. New Haven, Conn.: Yale University Press.

GREENE, J. P. 1993. Forewarned Before Forecast: Presidential Election Forecasting Models and the 1992 Election. *PS: Political Science & Politics*, 26: 17–21.

HOLBROOK, T. M. 2001. Forecasting with Mixed Economic Signals: A Cautionary Tale. *PS: Political Science & Politics*, 34: 39–44.

—— 2004. Good News for Bush? Economic News, Personal Finances, and the 2004 Presidential Election. *PS: Political Science & Politics*, 37: 759–61.

—— and DESART, J. A. 1999. Using State Polls to Forecast Presidential Election Outcomes in the American States. *International Journal of Forecasting*, 15: 137–42.

KLARNER, C. 2008. Forecasting the 2008 U.S. House, Senate and Presidential Elections at the District and State Level. *PS: Political Science & Politics*, 41: 723–8.

—— and BUCHANAN, S. 2006a. Forecasting the 2006 elections for the U. S. House of Representatives. *PS: Political Science & Politics*, 39: 857–61.

—— —— 2006b. Forecasting the 2006 Elections for the United States Senate. *PS: Political Science & Politics*, 39: 849–55.

LEWIS-BECK, M. S. 1985. Election Forecasts in 1984: How accurate were they? *PS: Political Science & Politics*, 18: 53–62.

—— 2005. Election Forecasting: Principles and Practice. *British Journal of Politics & International Relations*, 7: 145–64.

—— and RICE, T. W. 1984. Forecasting U.S. House Elections. *Legislative Studies Quarterly*, 9: 475–86.

—— —— 1992. *Forecasting Elections*. Washington, D.C.: CQ Press.

—— and SKALABAN, A. 1989. Citizen Forecasting: Can Voters See into the Future? *British Journal of Political Science*, 19: 146–53.

—— and TIEN, C. 1999. Voters as Forecasters: A Micromodel of Election Prediction. *International Journal of Forecasting*, 15: 175–84.

—— —— 2001. Modeling the Future: Lessons from the Gore Forecast. *PS: Political Science & Politics*, 34: 21–3.

—— and TIEN, S. 2004. Jobs and the Job of President: A Forecast for 2004. *PS: Political Science & Politics*, 37: 753–8.

LOCKERBIE, B. 2004. A Look to the Future: Forecasting the 2004 Presidential Election. *PS: Political Science & Politics*, 37: 741–3.

NADEAU, R. and LEWIS-BECK, M. S. 2001. National Economic Voting in U.S. Presidential Elections. *Journal of Politics*, 63: 159–81.

NORPOTH, H. 2004. From Primary to General Election: A Forecast of the Presidential Vote. *PS: Political Science & Politics*, 37: 737–40.

ROSENSTONE, S. J. 1983. *Forecasting Presidential Elections.* New Haven, Conn.: Yale University Press.

SOUMBATIANTS, S., CHAPPELL, H. W., JR., and JOHNSON, E. 2006. Using State Polls to Forecast U.S. Presidential Election Outcomes. *Public Choice*, 127: 207–23.

STRUMPF, K. F. and RHODE, P. 2004. Historical Presidential Betting Markets. *Journal of Economic Perspectives*, 18: 127–42.

TETLOCK, P. E. 2005. *Expert Political Judgment: How Good Is It? How Can We Know It?* Princeton, N.J.: Princeton University Press.

WLEZIEN, C. 2001. On Forecasting the Presidential Vote. *PS: Political Science and Politics*, 34: 24–31.

—— and ERIKSON, R. S. 2002. The Timeline of Presidential Election Campaigns. *Journal of Politics*, 64: 969–93.

—— —— 2004. The Fundamentals, the Polls, and the Presidential Vote. *PS: Political Science & Politics*, 37: 747–51.

WOLFERS, J. and ZITZEWITZ, E. 2004. Prediction Markets. *Journal of Economic Perspectives*, 18: 107–26.

PART V

INTERESTS, SELF- AND OTHERWISE

CHAPTER 20

ECONOMICS, ELECTIONS, AND VOTING BEHAVIOR

SUZANNA LINN

JONATHAN NAGLER

MARCO A. MORALES

POLITICAL scientists have agreed for over thirty years that the state of the economy affects elections. But, explaining how and why the economy affects elections has turned out to be difficult. Downs (1957) and Key (1966) argued that voters should look at the economy in making voting decisions. Downs argued that voters would vote for the candidate likely to deliver the best economic performance. And Key argued that voters see elections as referenda, punishing incumbents if they presided over poor economic times. But it is Kramer's seminal 1971 article that first demonstrated a robust empirical link between economic performance and election outcomes. Kramer demonstrated that between the period 1896 and 1964 there was a positive correlation between improvements in real income and the incumbent party's share of the two-party congressional vote. This empirical finding essentially begins the scholarly industry that we review in this chapter. Note that there is little dispute about Kramer's finding (though in fact an error in one of the data series led to a future correction of the findings): no one disputes that over the period in question, economic prosperity was associated with higher vote-shares for the incumbent party; and no one doubts that this relationship extends beyond the period Kramer analyzed (which is now dated by thirty years).

However, hundreds of articles have been written since, attempting to do everything from better specify what we mean by "the incumbent party" to better identify the individual-level calculations leading to the aggregate phenomena that Kramer (1971) observed. Kramer was not attemping to examine the motivations of voters. He assumed that voters would punish or reward the incumbent party for the state of the economy, and that this should lead to the aggregate phenomena he observed. However, since then scholars have come up with many alternative explanations for what Kramer observed. And, scholars have developed an interest in considering whether or not the explanatory variables Kramer used were the "right" variables, or simply proxies that were highly correlated with the underlying variables driving his result.

The first refinement of the basic Kramer work to be developed was research analyzing whether voters were actually looking at the state of the *aggregate* economy in voting, or whether they were examining their own *personal* economic situation. At the aggregate level, these could be observationally equivalent. If we observe that voters reward the incumbent when the mean of real disposable income goes up, they could be doing this because they learned that real disposable income was up nationwide and they are rewarding the incumbent for this nationwide prosperity; or because an increase in real disposable income could imply—if it is distributed reasonably uniformly, an assumption we return to later—that most voters had an increase in their own personal income and they are rewarding the incumbent for that. Kiewiet and Kinder (1981; Kiewiet 1983) examined this question in detail, and introduced the notions of "pocketbook voting" versus "sociotropic voting" into the literature.

And whereas Kramer implicitly assumed that voters would vote "retrospectively," punishing or rewarding the incumbent as suggested by Key, scholars since have wondered whether voters are looking backwards or forwards in time. A naive model would suggest that since any forecast the voter has of the future must be based on the past, there is really no difference between these two perspectives. However, much ink has been spilled on the question.

Further questioning the reasoning of voters has been a line in the literature questioning how sophisticated voters are. Whereas in the simplest retrospective voting model the voters simply decide whether or not the performance of the incumbent in office, as measured by the performance of the macro economy, meets some pre-defined standard, more sophisticated models can require the voters to evaluate policy choices made by incumbents, and to make a more nuanced decision regarding attribution. Recall that in Kramer's model, he relied on the notion of "an incumbent" government. But in the United States there may not be one party so obviously responsible, as in cases of divided government.

Yet another way that voters could reveal sophistication is to have preferences over economic policies, *or* over economic outcomes if they believe they have a choice. Exploring voter decision making, and presidential approval, Hibbs, Rivers, and Vasilatos (1982) allowed voters to behave as if they saw a Phillips-curve tradeoff between unemployment and inflation. Another mode of sophistication for voters would be to condition their vote-choice on preferred policy tool, knowing the penchant of the political parties. Thus voters in a recession might prefer the Democratic party, thinking it would be more likely to pursue expansionist fiscal and monetary policy than the Republican party. And voters seeing high inflation might prefer the Republican party if they believed that a Republican government would fight inflation more aggressively than a Democratic one. This is considered in the literature on rational partisans.

Along with allowing voters to prefer different policies, a relatively unexamined area of voter sophistication in the literature is the idea that voters look at measures of the economy between the level of aggregation of the individual (i.e., "pocketbook") and the national macro-economy (i.e., "sociotropic"). If economic growth is distributed evenly across the population, all voters prefer the candidate offering the most growth and preferring the candidate who would raise growth the most is the same as preferring the candidate who would maximize one's own income. But if voters observe that some parties provide unequally distributed growth, then some voters may prefer a party providing a lower aggregate growth-rate, but one in which they receive a larger share of the growth. We take up this question in two sections on groups and economic voting. And in times when there is variation across region in economic performance, voters may also look at regional economic performance rather than national economic performance. We consider this as well below.

Finally, concerns about the endogeneity of economic evaluations have arisen in the context of models that rely on subjective perceptions of the economy. When voters are asked to evaluate the economy, party identification and intended vote choice may drive economic evaluations as voters favorable to the incumbent could see the economy through "rose-colored glasses," and voters opposed to the incumbent may see the economy as half-empty rather than half-full. If economic perceptions are in fact affected by respondents' vote choice, then inferences of economic perceptions causing vote choice based on cross-sectional models are obviously suspect. Recent research has confronted this issue head on, and we discuss this in the section on endogeneity.

In what follows we discuss each of these issues with particular attention to classic and recent work on economic voting at both the individual level and in the aggregate. We start with the question of whether voters care most about the state of their own personal finances or whether they weigh national conditions most heavily in their voting calculus—the question of pocketbook versus sociotropic voting. We then consider the additional questions raised above. We end with a discussion of the directions research on economic voting is heading.

POCKETBOOK VERSUS SOCIOTROPIC VOTING

The first major attempt to understand the mechanism causing the observed relationship between the state of the economy and voting was the attempt to discover whether voters were paying attention to the aggregate economy, or to their own pocketbook. The belief was that these were observationally equivalent at the aggregate level. If an improving aggregate economy meant that most individuals were seeing improvement in their personal finances, then we would observe a correlation between aggregate economic circumstances and the vote across time whether individuals were voting on their personal finances or on the state of the aggregate economy. And the work at the aggregate level had been very much motivated by the idea that persons were looking at their personal finances (in a rational Downsian manner, looking for the candidate who would increase their own utility, or in this case, personal fortune).

In highly influential works Kiewiet (1983) and Kinder and Kiewiet (1981) analyzed individual survey data to determine whether individuals were motivated by personal or national economic circumstances. Kinder and Kiewiet were explicit that they were *not* looking to distinguish self-interested motivation versus altruistic motivation. They argue that a voter may view the incumbent's handling of the national economy as an "indicator of the incumbent's ability to promote (eventually) their own economic welfare." And Kiewiet and Rivers (1984, 381) point out the theoretical limitations of using one's own pocketbook: "suppose a distant relative dies, leaving a substantial inheritance. Does the lucky recipient attribute his or her good fortune to whoever happens to be in the White House at that moment?" In other words, how well the national economy does might be a better predictor of an individual's future well-being than the individual's own recent economic performance. Kinder and Kiewiet look at a variety of questions respondents were asked about both personal finances and the national economy. They report that it is *not* the case that respondents' national evaluations are simply functions of their personal experience. In fact they note that the correlation between such responses across individuals is quite low.[1]

Kiewiet (1983) examined responses to National Election Study questions on pocketbook evaluations versus evaluations of the national economy. He found that for presidential elections, national evaluations won the race of the variables. They were generally significant in models of vote choice, while pocketbook evaluations were not generally significant.

---

[1] They report median correlations across the sets of questions of .09, .02, and .03 for 1972, 1974, and 1976, respectively (p. 139).

RETROSPECTIVE VERSUS
PROSPECTIVE VOTING

When we assess the influence of economic assessments on the vote, we must not only consider whether pocketbook or national conditions weigh most heavily in the vote calculus, but we must also consider whether voters assess the past or look forward and gauge the future. Here we ask: do voters vote retrospectively, assessing past economic performance, or do they vote prospectively, basing votes on expectations of the future?

The time horizon relevant to voters has important implications both for the sophistication of voters and the interpretation of election outcomes. In the earliest work, Downs speculated voters assess their expectations about *future* (economic) performance and vote for the party giving them the greatest expected utility. In contrast, Key argued voters punish or reward the incumbent party based on *past* economic performance. In his major work on retrospective voting, Fiorina (1981) adopted Key's perspective. Downs requires of voters that they assess future *policies*, Fiorina that they assess past *outcomes*. Underlying each theory, then, is a distinct understanding both of what elections require of voters and also what elections mean. In the case of prospective voting, voters are relatively sophisticated as they must have expectations of future performance of the economy under the policy positions of the different parties. Votes cast reflect on the best direction for the future. Elections in effect become mandates for the party in power. Under retrospective voting, much less sophistication is required of voters, they need only reflect on the past performance of the parties, the outcomes. Elections in the retrospective case are then referenda on party performance. Overall, as we shall see, the evidence is mixed, suggesting some role for both retrospective and prospective evaluations. Voters are often portrayed as relatively sophisticated, especially in the aggregate, but they do not neglect the role of past economic conditions.

The early empirical work on economic voting was based on aggregate data, and implicitly followed Key, testing whether recent objective economic conditions drove election outcomes. Kramer (1971) showed that voters use economic performance over the last year to guide their vote choice, voting for the incumbent party when times are good and against it when times are bad. He showed that congressional elections respond in particular to national income over the last year. In the immediate aftermath of Kramer's work, empirical analyses of economic voting continued to rely on aggregate-level time-series data. Tufte (1975) demonstrated that midterm elections were referenda on the performance of the economy under the incumbent president's party; Meltzer and Vellrath (1975) and Fair (1978) extended the analysis to presidential elections; and Bloom and Price (1975) showed that the effects of economic downturns hurt incumbents while the symmetric effect was absent. Models of presidential approval relying on aggregate economic data also showed strong economic effects in parallel (see Hibbs 1987, Kernell 1978, Mueller 1970). Thus evidence of economic voting based on aggregate-level data over time has been quite strong for over thirty years.

But this work did not compare the roles of retrospections and prospections of the state of the economy. Prospections were absent from the analysis. Analysis that directly compares the relative role of the past and the future in the economic voting calculus soon followed. This work had to come to grips with two other questions. First, should tests of the time frame of voters' horizons be assessed with respect to national or pocketbook considerations? Second, should tests involve objective economic conditions or should they be based on subjective evaluations of the economy? Data and design considerations led to distinct answers to these questions. At the individual level, analysis focused on subjective evaluations, particularly of personal economic conditions. But as Kramer (1983) pointed out, objective conditions presented two problems. First, measures of personal objective income are composed of a mix of government-and non-government-induced income, making it impossible to know the effect of government-induced income, the only portion of income that should matter in economic voting. Second, national economic conditions are constant within an election, making assessment of their effects impossible in the context of a single election. The effect of these two concerns was a focus on subjective evaluations of economic conditions. Pocketbook evaluations were the primary means to assess retrospective evaluations, especially in the early work, but sociotropic evaluations also played some role in later work. At the same time, aggregate analyses began to consider subjective economic evaluations, generally both personal and sociotropic.

The first individual-level analysis of the time frame of economic voting considered comparisons of the effects of retrospective and prospective pocketbook evaluations. A number of scholars looked at individual congressional elections with mixed findings. Using the 1978 National Election Study, Kuklinksi and West (1981) found that retrospective evaluations explained neither Senate nor House votes. Prospective evaluations contributed significantly (both statistically and substantively) to the Senate model, but not the House model, of the vote. Also looking at congressional elections, Abramowitz (1985) showed that results of the House elections of 1974, 1978, and 1982 responded more to prospective than retrospective evaluations. Lockerbie (1992) echoed this result in his analysis of retrospective and prospective pocketbook evaluations in each House election from 1956 to 1988.[2] Accounting for the potential endogeneity of economic evaluations in a path model, Lockerbie finds that both retrospections and prospections matter.

---

[2] No single measure of either retrospections or prospections is available in the NES for the full period and to make matters worse, sometimes attribution is to parties, sometimes not, making pooling the data impossible.

Scholars focused on presidential elections similarly found mixed results. Miller and Wattenberg (1985) analyzed a series of presidential elections from 1952 to 1980 and found that retrospections were much more commonly significant and substantively important than were prospective evaluations, especially in races with incumbents (incumbents were much more likely to be evaluated retrospectively). In open-seat races elections were more Downsian: prospective evaluations proved more important. Lewis-Beck (1988a) found that vote choice is a function of both retrospective and prospective evaluations in the 1984 presidential election.

Individual-level analysis focusing on pocketbook evaluations is best characterized as mixed, with findings varying across elections and branches of government. These findings are perhaps unsurprising given that sociotropic evaluations have been shown to be more important than pocketbook evaluations in work comparing the two. Lewis-Beck (1988b) examined the effects of both pocketbook and sociotropic evaluations using a unique survey by the Survey of Consumer Attitudes and Behavior (SCAB). In both January and July of 1984, SCAB asked not only the usual battery of economic questions, but also asked political questions to a panel of respondents. This unique panel allowed him to model current vote choice for the president and congressional candidate as a function of retrospective and prospective evaluations (both pocketbook and sociotropic) and also partisanship in the previous time period such that evaluations today are treated as exogenous to partisanship in the previous time period. He found that both retrospective and prospective evaluations (personal and sociotropic) influence current general evaluations of government economic performance in equal amounts. General economic evaluations in turn influence the vote. Once sociotropic evaluations are included in the mix, the single analysis of Lewis-Beck seems to suggest that retrospective and pocketbook evaluations are both important to general economic assessments and ultimately vote choice. But at the individual level, we are left with no clear answer as to the relative importance of retrospective and prospective evaluations.

While early aggregate work traced votes and presidential approval to retrospective conditions, recent aggregate-level analysis has focused on subjective evaluations and explicitly looked at the relative roles of retrospective and prospective evaluations, generally also assessing whether pocketbook or sociotropic evaluations carry the day. In their seminal piece, Mackuen, Erikson, and Stimson (1992) examined presidential approval as a function of four aggregate measures of economic assessments: (1) mean perceptions of current family finances, *personal retrospections*, (2) mean perceptions of current business conditions, *business retrospections*, (3) mean perceptions of next year's family finances, *personal expectations*, and (4) mean long-term *business expectations*, all measured from the Survey of Consumer Attitudes and Behavior from 1954:3 to 1988:2. When all four measures were included in the same regression, business expectations won the race to explain approval. The other three indicators were not even collectively significant. "Clearly, the reason presidential approval responds to the economy is that presidential approval responds to economic expectations" (603). They found, in turn, that economic expectations are a function of leading indicators, which are themselves a function of what people have heard in the news about the economy. They concluded that people use the past to judge perhaps, but more importantly, they behave as if following rational expectations, using any available information they have about the future to make their evaluations of the president as well.

There is some consensus that prospective evaluations matter and do so more than retrospections, but debate remains over the role of retrospective evaluations. Clarke and Stewart (1994) take issue with MacKuen, Erikson and Stimson's (MES) (1992) analysis and findings, arguing that many of the key variables in their work are non-stationary and that presidential approval is cointegrated with long-term business expectations (five-year). Reestimating the MES model as an error correction model over the period 1954:2–1992:2, they found that both business expectations *and* business retrospections have significant short-run effects on presidential approval and that business expectations also have a long-term effect on presidential approval. Retrospective evaluations are not wholly irrelevant in this story, but an important component of evaluations of the president.

Nadeau and Lewis-Beck (2001) compared retrospective and prospective voting using an alternative measure of prospective evaluations. Like Clarke and Stewart, they found an important role for retrospective evaluations. Arguing that voters weigh different aspects of the economy differently, they built a national business index (NBI) to measure retrospective evaluations and an economic future index (EFI) to measure expectations.[3] When NBI and EFI were both in the model, each was significant, with retrospective assessments having a slightly larger effect than prospective assessments. Moreover, Nadeau and Lewis-Beck interacted elections in which no incumbent ran with each NBI and EFI and found (1) significant positive direct effects for each NBI and EFI; (2) retrospective economic voting was weaker when no incumbent was running; and (3) prospective economic voting was stronger when no incumbent was running. In the end the voter looks fairly sophisticated. Economic voting is almost entirely retrospective when an incumbent is running and there is a record to evaluate. When there is no incumbent, the electorate is more forward-looking. However, these results are based on pooling the NES from 1956 to 1996, and estimating individual-level models with the economic variables—NBI and EFI—entered as year-specific terms. Thus Nadeau and Lewis-Beck are inferring statistical significance with approximately 13,000 observations,

---

[3] NBI is built from the following question: "Would you say that at the present time business conditions are better or worse than a year ago?" The authors assign a score of 1 for better, -1 for worse, and 0 for same. Calculate the percentage in each category and subtract the percentage worse from better. EFI is built in the same way from the following future-oriented question: "Now turning to business conditions as a whole—do you think that during the next 12 months we'll have good times financially, or bad times financially?"

when in fact they have eleven distinct cases of their economic variable varying. It is hard to imagine that the results would reach traditional levels of statistical significance with either clustering to correct the standard errors, or with multi-level modeling.

Are economic votes cast retrospectively or prospectively? Individual-level analysis is mixed. Concerns about the endogeneity of economic evaluations and the focus on pocketbook voting at the individual level cloud our conclusions. The evidence at the aggregate level for prospective voting, especially national-level prospective voting, seems to dominate that for retrospective voting, but retrospective evaluations appear to be relevant as well. Voters appear to be Downsian, looking to the future, but grounding assessments in retrospective evaluations: both prospective and retrospective evaluations matter to the voter. Elections appear to be both mandates for the future and referenda on the past.

DIVIDED GOVERNMENT AND ECONOMIC VOTING

Divided government raises an important question for students of economic voting. Who do voters hold accountable for the state of the economy when control of government is divided? How do they cast an economic vote? The authority for economic policy making is shared by both Congress and the president. So who gets credit when the economy is strong and blame when it is weak if each branch of government is controlled by a different party? Interestingly this question received attention only following on the heels of cross-national work on government accountability and transparency. Powell and Whitten (1993), Anderson (2000), Royed, Leyden, and Borrelli (2000), Nadeau Nienni, and Yoshinaka (2002), and others argued that "Voters' economic assessments have stronger effects on government support when it is clear who the target is, when the target is sizable, and when voters have only a limited number of viable alternatives to throw their support to" (Anderson 2000, 168). The implication is that divided government should reduce economic voting because the target of economic responsibility is less clear to voters.

Norpoth (2001) looked explicitly at the role divided government plays in economic voting in the US. He began by asking which party voters hold accountable for their economic evaluations when government is divided. Following Powell and Whitten, Norpoth predicted that there will be less economic voting with divided government and suggested four plausible hypotheses regarding voter behavior: (1) voters cannot decide who to hold accountable so no economic votes are cast, the *hung jury hypothesis*, (2) economic voting at the presidential level reflects on the president's party, while economic voting at the congressional level reflects on the party controlling Congress, the *split decision hypothesis*, (3) all blame or credit goes to the president's party in both presidential and congressional elections, the *president liable hypothesis*, and (4) all blame or credit goes to the congressional party in both presidential and congressional elections, the *Congress liable hypothesis*. Norpoth used exit-poll data in the elections of 1992 and 1996 and found that economic evaluations work in the direction of the presidential party for both presidential and House vote. The *president liable hypothesis* received overwhelming support. Norpoth did not, however, consider any elections that feature unified control and thus cannot compare the degree of economic voting under the two types of regimes.

In contrast to Norpoth's evidence that all economic voting reflects on the president's party, Rudolph and Grant (2002) and Rudolph (2003b) proposed a theory of "attribution moderation" in which economic voting is conditional on holding the president (in presidential elections) or Congress (in congressional elections) responsible for the state of the economy. By this theory we would find support for the president liable hypothesis only if voters hold the president accountable for economic conditions under divided government. Yet there is reason to expect that attribution moderation would occur under divided government as the question who to blame or credit for economic conditions rises front and center. To test this theory, the authors used survey data from 1998 and 2000 in which respondents were asked who they hold most responsible for the state of the economy. They found that economic voting at the presidential (congressional) level was stronger when voters hold the president (Congress) responsible for the state of the economy. To the extent that divided government obscures control, economic evaluations are likely to be of less importance when casting a vote than they are under unified control.

Rudolph (2003a) also looked at the consequences of divided control of government at the state level. What happens when the governor and state legislature are held by different parties? Who do citizens hold responsible for fiscal policy and how does it effect economic voting? The patterns here repeat those at the national level, with those attributing responsibility to the governor more likely to cast an economic vote for the governor. Further, as his authority in the budgetary process grows, they are even more likely to cast their economic votes for the governor.

Divided government has the potential to make economic voting harder by obscuring the responsibility for economic outcomes. In terms of the comparative work, the target for economic voting becomes less clear. And yet Norpoth found that Americans tend to hold the president accountable for economic conditions even under divided government. But, as Rudolph's work shows, not everyone will blame or credit the president's party. Some will hold Congress responsible, others the president. One thing appears to be clear. Divided government can complicate the voter's decision calculus for at least a portion of the electorate.

HETEROGENEOUS PREFERENCES: GROUPS
AND ECONOMIC VOTING

Groups matter in politics. But often what places one in a group also determines one's preference, or in some cases, one's preference can place one in a group. For instance, Hibbs et al. (1982) compares the preferences of Republicans and Democrats over different economic policies. Yet it is those preferences that caused respondents to become Republicans or Democrats. Linn and Nagler (2005) compare the preferences of people in the bottom and top quintile. But it is not their membership in a "group" that generates the preference in the Linn and Nagler story, rather it is objective circumstance that leads to the preference, and leads to being measured as part of a "group." In this section we consider groups of people only so far as those groups consist of people with shared preferences, in the section following we take a broader view of groups.

Hibbs and Vasilatos (1982), Hibbs et al. (1982), and Linn and Nagler (2005) note that voters do not have homogeneous preferences. This is, after all, the basis of all politics. If all voters had the same preferences, we would be describing a homogeneous society that does not exist. Hibbs noted that voters have different unemployment versus inflation tradeoffs. In Hibbs's world left-voters, who are presumably lower-income, would prefer less unemployment even at the cost of more inflation; whereas right-voters, who are presumably higher-income, would prefer lower inflation, even at the cost of higher unemployment. This description of the world is not simply more nuanced than saying that "all voters prefer more growth to less" (since *ceteris paribus*, it is difficult to imagine that that would not be true), but it describes fundamental economic conflict. Linn and Nagler do not specify particular tradeoffs as Hibbs does with inflation versus unemployment, but rather consider that voters might prefer less growth for the *aggregate* economy, if they were to receive a larger *share* of that growth. Linn and Nagler move between individual-based preferences to group characteristics in arguing that voters are likely to view their share of growth as easiest to measure by a characteristic such as place in the income distribution. Thus Linn and Nagler postulate that voters will look at the growth rate of their income-quintile as a way to simultaneously measure aggregate growth, and their share of it. The intuition is straightforward: if the aggregate economy grows 3 percent, but an individual sits in the bottom income quintile that shows no growth in disposable per-capita income, then it seems foolish to reward the incumbent for such a performance. But this view of "group" aggregation is arbitrary in some ways. Obviously where one sits in the income distribution matters. Tax policy varies based on one's level of income. But a voter could also look at other ways that the effects of economic growth vary across citizens in deciding how good a job the incumbent has done. At the specific policy level, union workers might choose to punish an incumbent who signed a trade agreement they felt lowered wages in their industry, even if the agreement provided an overall boost to GDP. Or, citizens in a state doing poorly might simply observe that their region is doing badly, and see no reason to reward the incumbent for prosperity happening in other parts of the country.

Aggregate analyses of economic evaluations or incumbent party support based on groups in the electorate show that groups respond differently to economic conditions. Hibbs, Rivers, and Vasilatos (1982) found that Republicans are more sensitive to inflation than Democrats and Independents while Democrats show greater sensitivity to unemployment and real income when evaluating the president. Among different segments of the labor force, they find that greater sensitivity to inflation exists among those outside the labor force (retirees), while unemployment and real income sensitivity is greatest among blue-collar workers. Linn and Nagler (2005) examine income groups and find no difference in the responsiveness of poorer or wealthier Americans to economic performance.

Other scholars have looked at membership in groups, and identification with groups, as mediating entities between pocketbook voting and sociotropic voting. We turn next to that.

GROUPS

Mutz and Mondak (1997, 285) note that "In studies of American political behavior it is axiomatic that groups matter." There are many reasons to expect that groups may matter or, put differently, that voters may respond heterogeneously to economic performance based on group identification or membership. Information may be filtered and interpreted through the perspective of a group (Campbell et al. 1960); group membership may result in different objective interests (as we discussed above; see Hibbs 1982a, Hibbs and Vasilatos 1982, Linn and Nagler 2005) or different information sources (Krause 1997); people may be encouraged to think in terms of politically relevant groups based on race, gender, class, or incomes (Mutz and Mondak 1997). Groups may also matter because group evaluations are either or both more personally relevant than national evaluations and more politically relevant than personal circumstances (Glasgow 2005, Mutz and Mondak 1997).

There is an observational equivalence between group membership providing shared preferences leading to common behavior among group members, and group membership providing a social identification with the group and an interest in the membership of the overall group leading to common behavior. In other words, we can't tell if someone who is black is paying attention to the economic well-being of blacks because they view it as a measure of how well the government is treating them, or if they are paying attention to the economic well-being of blacks because they care about blacks. This is precisely the identification problem with sociotropic voting. A sociotropic voter could be altruistic, or they could simply view the state of the national economy as a measure of incumbent economic competence—a competence likely to affect their *own* economic well-being in the future.

Group evaluations are typically found to be distinct from both pocketbook and sociotropic evaluations (Conover 1985; Kinder, Adams, and Gronke 1989; Kinder, Rosenstone, and Hansen 1983; Mutz and Mondak 1997). Conover (1985) and Kinder, Rosenstone, and Hansen (1983) find an independent effect for group evaluations on presidential vote choice.

Krause (1997), in an analysis of education/information groups, finds that as voters' level of education declines economic expectations rely more heavily on retrospective evaluations while more educated voters draw on more information, particularly media coverage of the economy, to shape their expectations. Welch and Hibbing (1992) consider gender, and claim to show that men are more likely to be economic voters than women, at least in part because women see themselves as accountable for their own economic situations. Welch and Foster (1992) show that black voters consider the change in economic fortunes of blacks, as well as the change in national economic conditions, when voting.

SUBNATIONAL ECONOMIC CONDITIONS AND ECONOMIC VOTING

While we are able to cite a preponderance of evidence to show that a relationship exists between national economic conditions and presidential election outcomes, there has been much less research on whether economic conditions at the subnational (i.e., state or county) level affect vote shares in a presidential election. This is a sensible question as there is substantial variation of economic conditions—and electoral results—across states.

The few available pieces looking into this matter have documented a relationship between subnational economic conditions and vote shares for presidential candidates at the subnational level. Wright (1974) shows that changes in state-level per capita income were a strong predictor of state-level vote shares for the Democratic candidate in the 1936 and 1940 elections, and Abrams (1980) finds similar results for the incumbent running for reelection in the 1956 and 1972 elections. In contrast,

Meltzer and Vellrath (1975) find weak evidence for effects of per capita income on vote shares at the state level for the 1960–1972 elections, but provide strong evidence that higher state-level unemployment and inflation help Democratic candidates. Peltzman (1990) looks at presidential elections between 1950 and 1988 and finds that increases in state-level personal income and reductions in state-level inflation rates increase the vote shares for the incumbent party. For the 1992 election, Blackley and Shepard (1994) and Abrams and Butkiewicz (1995) find that increases in state-level per capita personal income increased Bush's vote shares, but higher unemployment increased Clinton's vote shares at the state level. The 2004 election was analyzed with county-level data by Lacombe and Shaughnessy (2007), who show that per capita personal income and unemployment rates at the county level are good predictors of vote shares for Bush at the county level.

Evidence suggests that per capita income at the state and county level is a good and consistent predictor of electoral outcomes at the state and county levels. But while results are not as clear regarding inflation and unemployment, it must be noted that econometric specifications vary across analyses, making some of these comparisons difficult. It might also be the case that specific conditions lead to different effects of economic variables across elections. But this matter is hard to settle without more detailed research.

Few attempts have been made to determine whether national or subnational economic conditions matter most in determining electoral outcome. Strumpf and Phillippe (1999) compare the effects of state-level and national economic conditions in vote shares at the state level, while Eisenberg and Ketcham (2004) take a fuller approach and compare county-level, state-level, and national economic conditions on vote shares at the county level. They both find that subnational economic conditions are related to the vote shares obtained by each party at the subnational level, but they confirm that national economic conditions have much stronger effects. In particular, both studies suggest that: (1) national per capita income growth and unemployment rates have robust effects on electoral outcomes at the state and county level; (2) state-level per capita income growth and inflation rates determine vote shares at the state and county level; and (3) only county-level per capita income growth influences vote shares at the county level.

ENDOGENEITY OF ECONOMIC PERCEPTIONS

A strain of the literature on economic voting that has existed since at least the 1990s has argued that estimates of the impact of economic perceptions, and thus of economic conditions, on voting have been vastly exaggerated because economic perceptions are themselves influenced by the respondents' vote choice. The argument is straightforward. A typical cross-sectional model puts economic perceptions on the right-hand side, assuming such perceptions are exogenous explanatory variables, and finds that such perceptions are significantly related to vote choice. But, if the causality is backwards, if in fact the economic perceptions are caused by the vote choice, then the inference that economic perceptions, or economic conditions, affect vote choice would be invalidated. So if voters who intend to vote for the incumbent rationalize their response to the economic perception question by stating that the economy has been good, then we could mistakenly infer that economic perceptions influence vote choice when no such relationship exists.

The critique of the cross-sectional individual-level voting models is obviously troubling. And it is difficult to resolve with cross-sectional data. Inference in cross-sectional data does generally depend upon assumptions of the direction of causality. There are (at least) four strategies to resolve the issue. First, one can attempt to gain leverage with panel data. Second, one can look for a "slower-moving" measure of political preferences (i.e., partisanship) to attempt to anchor the economic perceptions. Third, one can move away from the cross-sectional individual-level data to look at changes in real economic conditions over time and how they affect vote choice. Fourth, one can find less aggregated real economic measures that differ in the cross-section and would allow for cross-sectional analysis of the impact of economic conditions on vote choice.

As early as the 1960s, the idea that perceptions of the state of the world are influenced by partisanship via a "perceptual screen" had been advanced (Campbell et al. 1960). Perceptions of the state of the economy are no exception. While not concerned with endogeneity in economic evaluations, but with the origins of economic evaluations, Conover, Feldman, and Knight's (1987) widely cited analyses find evidence that (sociotropic) prospective evaluations might be influenced by partisanship in the United States, but no relationship was uncovered between retrospective (sociotropic) evaluations and partisanship (Conover and Feldman 1986).

These findings have been qualified lately by Evans and Andersen (2006), who introduce new evidence suggesting that economic evaluations might be endogenous to partisanship. They show that partisanship influences retrospective economic evaluations, although its impact is stronger on sociotropic than pocketbook evaluations in Britain. They claim that their analysis proves that the effects of partisanship on economic evaluations are stronger than those of economic evaluations on partisanship. Lewis-Beck (2006) severely criticizes their analysis, arguing that the measure of government-approval that Evans and Anderson use is non-standard, and closer to a measure of partisanship. The question they use is "Please choose a phrase from this card to say how you feel about the Conservative Party. Strongly against (1); Against (2); Neither in favor nor against (3); In favor (4); Strongly in favor (5)." Lewis-Beck is correct that this is *not* a question of "approval of the *job* the party is doing." This should set the stage for several attempts at replication with alternative measures of approval.

The endogeneity of partisanship to economic evaluations is relevant so long as we are concerned with modeling these evaluations. But for purposes of economic voting, our more pressing concern would be to assess whether economic evaluations are endogenous to vote choice as this would bias our estimates of the impact of perceived economic conditions on vote choice.

Wlezien, Franklin, and Twiggs (1997) were the first to claim that individuals would tend to give better assessments for the candidates they support. That is, vote choice would shape economic evaluations. Their empirical analysis in Britain, France, Italy, and Germany found mixed evidence. They found that vote choice predicted prospective evaluations in Britain, France, and Germany; but that it predicted retrospective evaluations only in France.

Prospective evaluations are of course clouded by uncertainty over which party will be in office after a coming election. Ladner and Wlezien (2007) argue that individuals who think their most preferred party will win the election would be more likely to have a more positive evaluation about the future state of the economy than those individuals who think their most preferred party will not win. They find evidence to support their claim in the United States and Britain.

On the other end of this argument, Anderson, Mendes, and Tverdova (2004) argue that individuals improve their assessment about the future state of the economy if they voted for the party that actually won the election, while those who voted for the losing party will tend to worsen their assessment. They present evidence to support their claim from Britain.[4]

Lewis-Beck, Nadeau, and Elias (2008) try to addres the question of endogeneity of economic perceptions with a combination of panel data and the use of allegedly exogenous instruments for economic perceptions. But the panel nature of the data seems only to be used to address potential endogeneity of party identification. They actually address potential endogeneity of economic perceptions by using respondents' perceptions of their personal finances as an instrument for respondents' perceptions of national economic conditions in an instrumental variables setup. Their instrumental variables result for the impact of perception of national economic conditions on vote choice is indistinguishable from their OLS estimate of the impact of perception of national economic conditions on the vote.

---

[4] Glasgow and Weber (2005), while investigating a related issue in Germany—whether individuals think that a victory by their preferred candidate will improve their well-being—find evidence that they explicitly argue supports the findings of Anderson et al. (2004).

WHAT NEXT

....

While political scientists know a lot about economic voting, as the discussion above reveals, there is much we still do not know. The weight of evidence from all sorts of data makes clear that voters reward incumbents for good times, and punish them for bad times. We know this from data over time comparing election outcomes to measures of the macro-economy. And we know it from individual-level data in cross-sections comparing perceptions of the economy to individual vote choice.

But we do not have good ideas of what necessarily constitutes "good times" or "bad times". Hibbs (2000) exhaustively tests competing economic measures to show that real disposable per capita income is the best aggregate economic measure for predicting incumbent vote-share. But we do not have a good idea of what the baseline is against which voters measure changes in real disposable per capita income (or any other aggregate economic measure). Declining real income would surely be bad times. But how much of an increase in real income is required for voters to reward the incumbent? And, is there any reason to believe that this number is fixed over time? Voters conditioned to think that 3 percent growth in real disposable per capita income is normal in the 1980s may be willing to adjust to 2 percent growth in the 2010s. We simply do not know the answer to this. And in the absence of examining alternative economic performance and voter reaction in parallel universes, we may never know the answer to this.[5]

Finally, we return to what has been recognized as a crucial question in the economic voting literature for at least thirty years, but has yet to receive a satisfactory answer: what aspect of the economy are voters looking at in deciding whether to reward or punish the incumbent? Sociotropic concerns seem to have decisively won out over pocketbook measures. But there are many economic measures in between the level of an individual voter's bank account, and an aggregate measure of the macro economy such as GDP or real disposable per capita income. As two of us have written elsewhere, voters might choose to consider the distribution of changes in economic performance. Rewarding an incumbent for an increase in income that has gone entirely to members of a different part of the economic stratum might make little sense. If real disposable per capita income goes up 3 percent, but 95 percent of the increase goes to the top 1 percent of the income distribution—why should voters in the bottom 99 percent of the income distribution reward the incumbent? We are studying voters, not stockholders. And unlike stockholders, not all voters are simply interested in maximizing the value of their shares. Politics is about conflict and voters are a heterogeneous bunch with varied

---

[5] This of course suggests we should ask a more precise question.

preferences. *Ceteris paribus*, they all prefer more economic growth to less. But that is rarely the choice offered.

Further considering heterogeneity in voters, we think that some voters probably pay more attention than other voters to things such as the stock market or federal deficits. Research going forward should be paying attention to what forms voters' economic perceptions. And that research will have to acknowledge the heterogeneity of voters. In addition, research needs to consider what measures of the economy voters *should* consider. For a voter in the bottom of the income distribution: what aggregate measures are the most reliable indicators of how they are likely to fare in the future?

Some areas of the impact of the economy on vote choice remain surprisingly under-researched. We know something about the impact of media coverage of the economy on economic perceptions. But it is obviously an area where more research would be helpful. Can we really predict the impact on the vote for the incumbent given a 2 percent increase in real disposable per capita income, or does it depend upon what the media say? Research on the impact of the media generally would suggest that by talking about the economy the media could get voters to put more emphasis on the economy, but that the media could not tell the voters how to think about the economy. But De Boef and Kellstedt (2004) find that the amount and tenor of news coverage of the economy drives aggregate perceptions along with an independent effect for objective economic indicators. However, more work is needed. Voters have both local and general sources of information about the economy. They can observe how their peers or friends and family are doing economically. But they depend on a range of government statistics, and the media bringing those statistics to them, to learn about the macro-economy. Again, we note the heterogeneity of voters here. There is obviously a set of financially tuned-in voters who will know the state of the economy whether the media emphasizes it or not. However, many voters are more passive about seeking information on the economy, and will not know of economic change unless it is reported via mainstream media.

Another area of research obviously suggested by reviewing the existing literature is into the potential endogeneity of economic perceptions as reported in surveys. Existing work on this topic is thoroughly inconclusive. We are not optimistic that this will be solved by a search for a valid instrument. As the congressional campaigns field has spent thirty years searching for valid instruments for campaign spending, we do not see political scientists finding some variable that influences economic perceptions, but does *not* also influence vote choice. But obviously the genie is out of the bottle on the question of whether such perceptions are endogenous. So this is clearly an area where research is needed if we are to have faith in cross-sectional models of voting.

And there remains a normative cloud over the whole concept of economic voting. If the government is disproportionately rewarded or punished for something it has relatively little control over, then it suggests that voters are behaving suboptimally and failing to exercise enough control over policy decisions that *are* completely in the hands of the levers of government.

REFERENCES

ABRAMOWITZ, A. 1985. Economic Conditions, Presidential Popularity, and Voting Behavior in Midterm Congressional Elections. *The Journal of Politics*, 47/1: 31–43.

ABRAMS, B. A. 1980. The Influence of State-Level Economic Conditions on Presidential Elections. *Public Choice*, 35/5: 623–31. <http://www.springerlink.com/content/p196n1853027p452/>.

——— and BUTKIEWICZ, J. L. 1995. The Influence of State-Level Economic Conditions on the 1992 U.S. Presidential Election. *Public Choice*, 85/1–2: 1–10. <http://www.springerlink.com/content/j01624358u7180t5/>.

ANDERSON, C. 2000. Economic Voting and Political Context: A Comparative Perspective. *Electoral Studies*, 19/2–3: 151–70.

——— MENDES, S., and TVERDOVA, Y. 2004. Endogenous Economic Voting: Evidence from the 1997 British Election. *Electoral Studies*, 23/4: 683–708.

BLACKLEY, P. R. and SHEPARD, E. M. 1994. A Statistical Analysis of the Effect of State-Level Economic Conditions on the 1992 Presidential Election. *Public Finance Review*, 22/3: 366–82.<http://pfr.sagepub.com/cgi/content/abstract/22/3/366>.

BLOOM, H. S. and PRICE, H. D. 1975. Vote Response to Short-Run Economic Conditions: The Asymmetric Effect of Prosperity and Recession. *American Political Science Review*, 69/4: 1240–54.

CAMPBELL, A., CONVERSE, P. E., MILLER, W. E., and STOKES, D. E. 1960. *The American Voter*, unabridged edn. Chicago, Ill.: University of Chicago Press.

CLARKE, H. D. and STEWART, M. C. 1994. Prospections, Retrospections, and Rationality: The "Bankers" Model of Presidential Approval Reconsidered. *American Journal of Political Science*, 38/4: 1104–23.

CONOVER, P. J. 1985. The Impact of Group Economic Interests on Political Evaluations. *American Politics Research*, 13/2: 139–66. <http://apr.sagepub.com/cgi/content/abstract/13/2/139>.

——— and FELDMAN, S. 1986. Emotional Reactions to the Economy: I'm Mad as Hell and I'm Not Going to Take It Anymore." *American Journal of Political Science*, 30/1: 50–78. <http://www.jstor.org/stable/2111294>.

——— ——— and KNIGHT, K. 1987. The Personal and Political Underpinnings of Economic Forecasts. *American Journal of Political Science*, 31: 559–83.

DE BOEF, S. and KELLSTEDT, P. M. 2004. The Political (and Economic) Origins of Consumer Confidence. *American Journal of Political Science*, 48/4: 633–49.

DOWNS, A. 1957. *An Economic Theory of Democracy*. New York: Harper-Collins.

EISENBER, D. and KETCHAM, J. 2004. Economic Voting in U.S. Presidential Elections: Who Blames Whom for What. *Topics in Economic Analysis & Policy*, 4/1. Article 19.

EVANS, G. and ANDERSEN, R. 2006. The Political Conditioning of Economic Perceptions. *Journal of Politics*, 68/1: 194–207.

FAIR, R. C. 1978. The Effect of Economic Events on Votes for President. *The Review of Economics and Statistics*, 60/2: 159–73.

FIORINA, M. P. 1981. *Retrospective Voting in American National Elections*. New Haven, Conn.: Yale University Press.

GLASGOW, G. 2005. Evidence of Group-Based Economic Voting: Nafta and Union Households in the 1992 US Presidential Election. *Political Research Quarterly*, 58/3: 427–34.

—— and WEBER, R. A. 2005. Is There a Relationship Between Election Outcomes and Perceptions of Personal Economic Well-Being? A Test Using Post-Election Economic Expectations. *Electoral Studies* 24/4: 582–601.

HIBBS, D. A. 1987. *The American Political Economy: Macroeconomics and Electoral Politics*. Cambridge, Mass.: Harvard University Press.

—— 2000. Bread and Peace Voting in US Presidential Elections. *Public Choice* 104/1–2: 149–80.

—— RIVERS, D., and VASILATOS, N. The Dynamics of Political Support for American Presidents Among Occupational and Partisan Groups. *American Journal of Political Science*, 26/2: 312–32.

—— and VASILATOS, N. 1982. Economic Outcomes and Political Support for British Governments Among Occupational Classes: A Dynamic Analysis. *American Political Science Review*, 76/2: 259–79. <http: www.jstor.org/stable/1961107>.

KERNELL, S. 1978. Explaining Presidential Popularity. How Ad Hoc Theorizing, Misplaced Emphasis, and Insufficient Care in Measuring One's Variables Refuted Common Sense and Led Conventional Wisdom Down the Path of Anomalies. *American Political Science Review*, 72/2: 506–22. <http://www.jstor.org/stable/1954107>.

KEY, V. O. 1966. *The Responsible Electorate: Rationality in Presidential Voting 1936–1960*. Cambridge, Mass: Harvard University Press.

KIEWIET, D. R. 1983. *Macroeconomics and Micropolitics: The Electoral Effects of Economic Issues*. Chicago, Ill.: University of Chicago Press.

—— and RIVERS, R. D. 1984. A Retrospective on Retrospective Voting. *Political Behavior*, 6/4: 369–93.

KINDER, D. R., ADAMS, G. S., and GRONKE, P. W. 1989. Economics and Politics in the 1984 American Presidential Election. *American Journal of Political Science*, 33/2: 491–515.

—— and KIEWIET, D. R. 1981. Sociotropic Politics: The American Case. *British Journal of Political Science*, 11/2: 129–61.

—— ROSENSTONE, S. J., and HANSEN, J. M. 1983. Group Economic Well Being and Political Choice: Pilot Study Report to the 1984 NES Planning Committee and NES Board. *American National Election Study Pilot Report*. Ann Arbor, Mich.

KRAMER, G. H. 1971. Short-Term Fluctuations in U.S. Voting Behavior: 1896–1964. *American Political Science Review*, 65/1: 131–43.

—— 1983. The Ecological Fallacy Revisited: Aggregate- Versus Individual-Level Findings on Economics and Elections, and Sociotropic Voting. *American Political Science Review*, 77/1: 92–111.

KRAUSE, G. A. 1997. Voters, Information Heterogeneity, and the Dynamics of Aggregate Economic Expectations. *American Journal of Political Science*, 41/4: 1170–200.

KUKLINSKI, J. H. and WEST, D. M. 1981. Economic Expectations and Voting-Behavior in United-States House and Senate Elections. *American Political Science Review*, 75/2: 436–47.

LACOMBE, D. J. and SHAUGHNESSY, T. M. 2007. Accounting for Spatial Error Correlation in the 2004 Presidential Popular Vote. *Public Finance Review*, 35/4: 480–99. <http://pfr.sagepub.com/cgi/content/abstract/35/4/480>.

LADNER, M. and WLEZIEN, C. 2007. Partisan Preferences, Electoral Prospects, and Economic Expectations. *Comparative Political Studies*, 40/5: 571–96.

LEWIS-BECK, M. S. 1998a. *Economics and Elections*. Ann Arbor, Mich.: University of Michigan Press.

—— 1988b. Economics and the American Voter: Past, Present, Future. *Political Behavior*, 10/1: 5–21.

—— 2006. Does Economics Still Matter? Econometrics and the Vote. *Journal of Politics*, 68/1: 208–12.

—— NADEAU, R., and ELIAS, A. 2008. Economics, Party, and the Vote: Causality Issues and Panel Data. *American Journal of Political Science*, 52/1: 84–95.

LINN, S. and NAGLER, J 2005. Do Voters Really Care Who Gets What? Economic Growth, Economic Distribution, and Presidential Popularity. Paper presented at the Annual Meeting of the Midwest Political Science Association, April 2005, Chicago, Ill.

LOCKERBIE, B. 1992. Prospective Voting in Presidential Elections, 1956–1988. *American Politics Quarterly*, 20/3: 308–25.

MACKUEN, M. B., ERIKSON, R. S., and STIMSON, J. A. 1992. Peasants or Bankers? The American Electorate and the U.S. Economy. *American Political Science Review*, 86/3: 597–611.

MELTZER, A. H. and VELLRATH, M. 1975. Effects of Economic-Policies on Votes for Presidency—Some Evidence from Recent Elections. *Journal of Law & Economics*, 18/3: 781–98.

MILLER, A. H. and WATTENBERG, M. P. 1985. Throwing the Rascals Out—Policy and Performance Evaluations of Presidential-Candidates, 1952–1980. *American Political Science Review*, 79/2: 359–72.

MUELLER, J. E. 1970. Presidential Popularity from Truman to Johnson. *American Political Science Review*, 64/1: 18–34. <http://www.jstor.org/stable/1955610.>

MUTZ, D. C. and MONDAK, J. J. 1997. Dimensions of Sociotropic Behavior: Group-Based Judgments of Fairness and Well-Being. *American Journal of Political Science*, 41/1: 284–308.

NADEAU, R. and LEWIS-BECK, M. S. 2001. National Economic Voting in US Presidential Elections. *Journal of Politics*, 63/1: 159–81.

—— NIEMI, R. G., and YOSHINAKA, A. 2002. A Cross-National Analysis of Economic Voting: Taking Account of the Political Context Across Time and Nations. *Electoral Studies*, 21/3: 403–23.

NORPOTH, H. 2001. Divided Government and Economic Voting. *Journal of Politics*, 63/2: 414–35.

PELTZMAN, S. 1990. How Efficient Is the Voting Market? *Journal of Law and Economics*, 33/1: 27–63. <http://www.jstor.org/stable/725510>.

POWELL, G. B. and WHITTEN, G. D. 1993. A Cross-National Analysis of Economic Voting—Taking Account of the Political Context. *American Journal of Political Science*, 37/2: 391–414.

ROVED, T. J. LEYDEN, K. M., and BORRELLI, S. A. 2000. Is "Clarity of Responsibility" Important for Economic Voting? Revisiting Powell and Whitten's Hypothesis. *British Journal of Political Science*, 30/4: 669–85.

RUDOLPH, T. J. 2003a. Institutional Context and the Assignment of Political Responsibility. *Journal of Politics*, 65/1: 190–215.

—— 2003b. Who's Responsible for the Economy? The Formation and Consequences of Responsibility Attributions. *American Journal of Political Science*, 47/4: 698–713.

—— and GRANT, J. T. 2002. An Attributional Model of Economic Voting: Evidence from the 2000 Presidential Election. *Political Research Quarterly*, 55/4: 805–23.

STRUMPF, K. S. and PHILLIPPE, J. R. 1999. Estimating Presidential Elections: The Importance of State Fixed Effects and the Role of National Versus Local Information. *Economics & Politics*, 11/1: 33–50.

TUFTE, E. R. 1975. Determinants of the Outcomes of Midterm Congressional Elections. *American Political Science Review*, 69/3: 812–26.

WELCH, S. and FOSTER, L. S. 1992. The Impact of Economic Conditions on the Voting Behavior of Blacks. *Western Political Quarterly*, 45/1: 221–36.

—— and HIBBING, J. 1992. Financial Conditions, Gender, and Voting in American National Elections. *Journal of Politics*, 54/1: 197–213.

WLEZIEN, C. FRANKLIN, M., and TWIGGS, D. 1997. Economic Perceptions and Vote Choice: Disentangling the Endogeneity. *Political Behavior*, 19/1: 7–17.

WRIGHT, G. 1974. The Political Economy of New Deal Spending: An Econometric Analysis. *The Review of Economics and Statistics*, 56/1: 30–8. <http://www.jstor.org/stable/1927524>.

....

CHAPTER 21

LATINOS AND POLITICAL BEHAVIOR

DEFINING COMMUNITY TO EXAMINE CRITICAL COMPLEXITIES

....

JOHN A. GARCIA

FOR over two decades, social demographers and journalists have chronicled Latinos' significant population growth, documenting it as one of America's fastest growing populations. Yet, a more systematic examination of the "public life" of this diverse aggregation is a more recent phenomenon. This chapter identifies central questions regarding the political behaviors of Latinos and the continuing challenges to exploring and understanding this population. In doing so, this chapter goes beyond an inventory and assessment of the extant research and offers a discussion of key issues and questions that warrant more complex approaches and theories (Fraga et al. 2006).

My underlying theoretical concern focuses on the nature of community among persons of Spanish origin and its public consequences (i.e., transformation of community inter-connections to public expressions). What are the components, attributes, experiences, and dispositions of the social category that is generally referred to as Hispanic or Latino? What are the structural and societal forces that can facilitate or impede the maintenance and development of this group distinctiveness and viability? With such a large and diverse aggregation of persons from different countries of origin and different range of experiences in the US, what are the bases for functioning as a community of interests with cultural similarities? To whatever degree a Latino community may exist, what difference does it make politically to themselves and to the larger political system and institutions?

Importantly, this discussion of Latino political behavior underscores how social science research has more systematically included contextual and institutional factors as determinants of both individual and group political behavior (Hritzuk and Park 2000). Thus, the intersection of individual experiences and attributes in conjunction with contextual elements provides a more interactive and full understanding of the dynamics of political behavior.

THE MEXICAN AMERICAN EXPERIENCE

Earlier studies of this population took the form of examining the Mexican-origin community in the Southwestern US, a community defined by a change in political boundaries as a result of the war with Mexico and the Treaty of Guadalupe Hidalgo (Gómez-Quiñones 1990). National origin, language, cultural traditions and practices, and a newly acquired political status as American residents/citizens served to characterize this population; while continued linkages with their country of origin, a more informal border demarcation, and their economic niches also persisted (Barrera 1979), to characterize their economic and political statuses in American society. Themes of survival, resistance, acquiescence, empowerment, and adaptations were among the descriptions and models from which to characterize the political behavior of Mexican-Americans (Gutierrez and Hirsch 1973, 1974).

For the most part, the political behaviors of Latinos were represented by the actions and attitudes of the Mexican origin community until the mid-1980s. Initially, the cultural influences of one's country of origin and the "civic culture" of Mexico served to define the participatory orientations and behaviors of the Mexican-origin citizens. Yet, current research on Latino political behavior has challenged the pervasiveness of cultural determinants. These studies describe an active organizational life assisting Mexican-Americans' adaptation to life in the US, especially at the local level (Gómez-Quiñones 1990; Barrera 1979).

Alternative explanations for Mexican-American political behavior were the impact of structural and contextual factors (e.g., economic subjugation,

intimidation, segregated and/or inferior schools, residential segregation, and limited access to societal institutions) which impeded full participation. The presence
of these barriers also result in Mexican-Americans reporting lower levels of
political efficacy and trust, and higher levels of political cynicism and alienation
(Hero et al. 2000).

BUILDING COMMUNITY: NATIONAL ORIGIN AND PAN-ETHNICITY

The concepts of *social identity* (Tajfel 1982) and *situational identity* (Padilla 1985)
developed by social psychologists and sociologists offer important theoretical
insight into thinking about how Latinos think about themselves as a group. Studies
of pan-ethnicity (Espiritu 1992; Omni and Winant 1994) have incorporated the
notion of inter-group *social identities* (Tajfel 1982), which is the result of an
individual's cognitive process developing group attachments, as well as social
structures that create and perpetuate these social categories (Jones-Correa and
Leal 1996). In general, these categorizations have taken the form of class, race,
gender, and ethnicity. In the case of the latter, ethnicity had been rooted in ancestry,
national origin, and culture. According to social identity theory, the bases for
affinity and association as a "social category" of persons are represented by
primordial factors—i.e. familial and ancestral.

Situational identity[1] is, in contrast, a more purposeful, socially constructed,
selection of group association (Padilla 1985) chosen by individuals in an effort to
broaden the parameters of traditional group boundaries, expand group size and
prospective resources, and increase group visibility to the larger society. The
interplay of context and group characteristics can best be illustrated by Padilla's
work (1985) in Chicago. In the 1970s and 1980s, there was a mix of Latino subgroups
residing in a highly politically structured city. Given their relatively small and
diverse groupings, the creation of a "Latino-ness" was a conscious effort by
different Latino activists to enhance the political capital of Chicago's Latino communities. It was a situation, for political or economic or legally related matters, in
which the use of a pan-ethnic identity served a utilitarian function of portraying a
larger and more politically unified group (Garcia-Bedolla 2005).

---

[1] The concept of situational identity refers to adoption of a group identity (pan ethnic, in this
case) that is more strategic and purposeful than necessarily a personal internalization of this group
identity.

Social scientists have recognized the development of pan-ethnicity and have concentrated their energies in two primary directions. The behavioral dimension reflects the development of identifying and associating as a community which recognizes common interests and produces collective expressions in the public sphere. Factors such as language use (i.e., English vs. Spanish or bilingualism), nativity, generational status from one's country of origin, social mobility, and levels of perceived discrimination are among the range of contributing factors (Jensen et al. 2006; Portes and McCleod 1996).

The second dimension is the linkage of pan-ethnic identification with political ramifications (Sanchez 2006; Stokes 2003). That is, does this sense of community only serve an individual for adaptive purposes (i.e. information regarding employment, residential locations, maneuvering economic transactions, etc.) as well as a social anchor and sense of self-esteem? Or does a sense of community highlight social and political standing—facilitate the aggregation of collective resources and formation of organizational structures with leadership to seek redress and policy responses for group needs and concerns (Ramakrishnan 2005)? This latter dimension addresses the primacy of pan-ethnic identifications as a cognitive affect; then tests the contribution of the measure(s) to specific political orientations and behaviors (e.g., voter registration and turnout, campaign related activities, mobilization, organizational involvement, etc.).

The extant research on pan-ethnicity has linked demography, socioeconomic status, and cultural dimensions, and contextual factors. Other factors associated with pan-ethnicity have been lower levels of assimilation, poorer English-language skills, lower levels of self-esteem, and lower socioeconomic status. Work by Masuoka (2006) gives a slightly different composition of pertinent factors for pan-ethnicity: higher levels of educational attainment, being male, being foreign-born, being civically engaged, and higher levels of perceived discrimination toward Latinos. Also, the greater the likelihood that the Latino is structurally and culturally isolated, the more likely he/she is to maintain a culturally based identity—usually in national origin terms. Work by Tafoya (2004) associates the Latino identifiers as having lighter skin color, more likely to be English speakers, and having longer residence in the US. The composition and settlement patterns of Latinos in particular locales and the framing of group affiliation by leaders and organizations also affect the presence of a pan-ethnic identification. The dynamics of "place matters" is suggested as paralleling the concept of political culture. That is, a "cultural" milieu has been created that enhances this sense of solidarity as a pan-ethnic and connects its members to public life. Again, the theme of the importance of context and social structures has become a critical component in the understanding of Latino political behavior (Bullock and Hood 2006).

In addition, works have examined the extent of assimilation among Latinos in terms of their social identity(ies). For example, the work by Itzigsohn and Dore-Cabral (2000) has focused upon Dominicans who migrate to the US. Many share a sense of marginality and social distance from the American mainstream. As a result, their adaptive identity takes the form of pan-ethnicity rather than an exclusively American identity. Work on nationality that focuses upon identifying oneself as being American as an indication of integration has being challenged (Desipio 2002; Fraga and Segura 2006). That is, individuals identifying themselves as Latinos and/or Hispanics are expressing a form of American national identity (Garcia 2006). While the persistence of cultural and emotive ties to one's country of origin is present among Latinos, this phenomenon is not unique to this group, both historically and contemporarily (Citrin et al. 2001; Schildkraut 2003).

What have been examined less systematically are possible behavioral indicators of pan-ethnicity. For example, racially and ethnically diverse sets of networks (e.g., social and/or familial ties outside of one's national origin group, the racial/ethnic composition of one's neighborhood, inter-marriage, etc.) might dilute a sense of pan-ethnicity or reinforce "Latino-ness." Additional research directed toward the extent of these interactions, their political content and substance of such exchanges, and the saliency of this community for collective action remains under-researched.

Any discussion of Latino pan-ethnicity necessarily leads one to consider how Latinos' social identities are associated with their integration into American society. Recent contributions by social scientists, particularly minority scholars, have developed and operationalized the concept of multiple identities that are both complementary as well as situationally impacted. That is, individuals develop a variety of social identities that are salient within specific contexts and purposes. Multiple identities can be useful to sort out the importance and relevance of national-origin primacy on certain occasions; the salience of pan-ethnicity with political behaviors or policy domains; or the diminished relevance of ethnicity in other circumstances. Jones-Correa and Leal (1996) found that pan-ethnicity served as a secondary identity in relation to one's national origin. At that time, the concept of pan-ethnicity was viewed as part of multiple social identities with some hierarchical order or situationally triggered. More recent works, such as Barvosa-Carter (1999), have developed further the concept of multiple identities as both interrelated and complementary.

ADDING RACE TO THE LATINO COMMUNITY "EQUATION"

The description of persons of Spanish origin as Latinos or Hispanics has created a social category that acts like ethnicity (i.e., characterized by national origin or ancestral ties). Yet, more recently, the "categorization" of Latinos has raised questions as to whether they "should" be considered an ethnic group, a racial group—or some combination. This issue is partly the result of Spanish-origin persons' responses to race and heritage questions on governmental and social science surveys. In most governmental surveys/censuses, almost one-half of the Spanish-origin respondents will respond by indicating "some other race" (Barreto 2002; Falconi and Mazotti 2008). Over 95 percent of the persons who indicate "some other race" are Latinos.

Adding to the conceptual confusion, the 2000 Census allowed individuals to indicate more than one race. Whereas less than 2.5 percent of all Americans indicated more than one race, over 6.5 percent of Latinos did so (Amaro and Zambrano 2001). These response patterns have raised issues about whether Latinos see themselves as an ethnic or a racial group (Landale and Oropesa 2002).

So the basic question is: are Latinos a marginalized ethnic group or a racialized minority (similar to African Americans)? Recent research has taken two major directions toward answering this question. The first is reconceptualizing the concept of race, which is typically linked to notions of skin color and other phenotypical characteristics, and institutionally, with slavery and formal legal status as property; and later as "second-class citizens." Ethnicity continues to be defined by criteria such as ancestral origins, language, and other cultural practices and traditions. Official governmental statistical agencies conceptualize and measure race and ethnicity separately, indicating these are distinct concepts, which is not necessarily correct.

For example, a special supplement to the May 1995 Current Population Survey included a battery of questions to explore notions of race, ethnicity, and national origin. A significant percentage of the respondents regarded race and ethnicity as interchangeable. Still, others made some distinctions; but it was based upon a diverse set of factors. One conclusion for the concept of race, particularly, is that there is no uniform or universal operating definition or meaning. Researchers who examine race do so in the context of social constructions (Nicholson, Pantoja, and Segura 2005).

Consistent with this, evidence suggests that Latinos who identify as African Americans behave very differently from Latinos who identify themselves as white. Contemporary research has also examined the extent and sources of racial identification among "ethnically" identified Latinos. This "sorting out" of the bases of community for Latinos has identified a variety of contextual factors, and has reformulated concepts that have been used in understanding individual and group political behavior. The research is in its infancy, but still suggests the potential for broadening the notion of minority group status by examining the political manifestations of the intersection of race and ethnicity (Tafoya 2004).

Related measures of racial identification take into account not only phenotypical traits, but cognitive affinities to the social construct of race (Park and Park 1999; Rodriguez 1992). The linkage of race and social status is documented by sociologists and economists, who show racial disparities in earnings, economic status, educational attainment, and job mobility. Phenotypically, specific measures of shades of skin tone also differentiate persons in these areas. That is, darker-skinned Latinos have lower levels of educational attainment and earnings (Bohara and Davila 1992; Telles and Murguia 1990). For Latinos, the added aspect of an accent also results in differential treatment.

Another focus in exploring race might be the cognitive realm of group affinity and affiliation. Contributing factors would include social networks with other racial group members, residence in primary non-Latino neighborhoods, inter-racial marriages, and incorporation of other groups' cultural expressions and practices. These types of interactions are placed in the context of racial milieus. Stokes (2006), for example, found that the presence of racial identification among Latinos results in greater support for co-ethnics. Much of this research has been directed toward differentiating Latinos with a racial identification vs. those with an ethnic one.

The other aspect of dealing with race and its interface with Latinos is extending the bifurcation of race in the US beyond black and white (Park and Park 1999). Racial categories are defined by variations of skin tone and indigenous "features." In Latin America, racial classification schemes are not bifurcated, but contain a wider range of categories or distinctions. In part, social class is highly interrelated with racial categories. Using other countries' racial classification systems may in part explain Latinos' identification within the US schema. On the other hand, a sense of "otherness" in which Latinos will not place themselves into the traditional US racial categories, may signify seeing themselves as a distinctive race *or* something "other than black or white."

LATINO POLITICAL BEHAVIOR AND DEMOGRAPHIC FACTORS

At the core of political behavior research is the utilization of socio-demographic variables (SES) to explain behavioral patterns. Consistently, SES (i.e., education, occupation, and income) is a foundational component of any form of political behavior (Marschall 2001). Yet, the predictive capability of SES has been less powerful for Latinos. Only educational attainment has proven to be a significant predictor of Latino electoral and organizational activities. Gains in educational attainment are associated with greater probabilities of registration, and voting, as well as proclivity to be engaged in organizational activities (Arvizu and Garcia 1996; Garcia 2003; Hero and Campbell 1996). The variables of income and

occupational status have been less fruitful. Yet, there are relatively limited explanations as to why these two variables have less instructive effects. Some of the
explanations focus upon the relatively limited degree of variations along occupational and income levels; while others suggest that controls for generational status
and establishing income thresholds reduce those differences (Lien 1994). Other
demographic variables used in political behavioral research have been gender, age,
and homeowner status (Garcia and Sanchez 2004).

Another important factor identified as influential for Latino political behavior is
group consciousness (Garcia and Sanchez 2004), which serves a variety of functions—attenuates awareness of the group's status and structural disparities, group
attitudes to the role and responsiveness of political institutions, activation for
political mobilization, and awareness of and support for co-ethnic candidates
(Sanchez 2006; Stokes 2003; Stokes-Brown 2006). National-origin and pan-ethnic
group consciousness has varied effects, including higher levels of political awareness, activism, and electoral support for co-ethnics (Sanchez 2006).

ADDING LATINO-SPECIFIC DEMOGRAPHICS

Beyond the use of "conventional" socio-demographic variables, examination
of Latino political behavior benefits by the expansion of other background characteristics representing elements of being Latino in the US. The elements are
nativity, language use, generational status, and transnationalism. The prevalence
of Latino migration to the US raises the role of nativity as a key status and sets of
experiences and structural relationships due to foreign-born and immigrant status
(Garcia and Sanchez 2004). Differentiating Latinos by their nativity provides a
variable which incorporates a multiplicity of factors and experiences.

Importantly, nativity—reflected by factors such as language use, length of time
in the US, transnationalism, and generational status—captures more than merely
an ascriptive status. That is, a nominal measure of nativity can be viewed as
a limited surrogate for socialization experiences and formal structural relationships
and standing in the American socio-political system (Aparicio 2006; Oboler 2006).
More systematic attention has been directed recently toward the foreign-born
segment in terms of both their political attitudes and engagements, especially
mobilization and organizational involvement (de la Garza and Yetim 2003;
Ramakrishnan 2005; Wenzel 2006; Wong 2006).

In the case of language use, English proficiency and bilingualism generally
represent Latinos' access to political information as well as knowledge about the
American political system and processes; whereas primarily Spanish language

might suggest greater societal isolation. Thus, the English abilities of Latinos enable them to access conventional political resources and interact with, and participate in, political institutions and actors.

Johnson et al. (2003) demonstrate that the amount of political information available to Latinos is an indicator of access to community resources and not impedance for political participation. The growth of Spanish-language media and political parties' overtures to Latinos in Spanish and/or bilingual messages have facilitated access to political information apart from the traditional English mass media sources. As a consequence, acquiring knowledge and information is not constrained by limited or non-existent English-language abilities. The challenge becomes uncovering and understanding the processes involved in the communication processes, and how they differ by language use (Jones-Correa 1998).

Familiarity with the US political system is related to one's length of time in America and one's age at immigration. Longer "exposure" assists the individual to maneuver and learn the machinations of American society and its prevailing practices. By integrating the age at immigration in lieu of the total length of time in the US, one can introduce the socialization process that can occur. Coming to America at a young age would result in participation in the US educational system, earlier exposure to the American cultural milieu, and enhanced English language skills. As a result, the confluence of the "immigration" experience includes not only foreign-born status, but language use and abilities, and length of time here, as well as age on arrival.

The concept of generational distance from that immigration status is also pertinent. That is, once settled in America, second-generation Latinos are now native-born as well as subsequent generations. The application of concepts of assimilation and acculturation reflects the extent of attitudinal and behavioral changes that can come about growing up in the US as one's home country (Junn 1999). For example, Hill and Moreno (1996) found that second-generation Cubans depart from their parents ideologically and, to some degree, partisan-wise, while retaining similar policy views toward Cuba. Wenzel (2006) examined the extent of acculturation among Latinos in relation to trust in federal and local governments. He found that the more acculturated had greater degrees of trust in local government than the federal government. Similarly, Michelson (2003) corroborated the "corrosive effects of acculturation" among Latinos with greater levels of acculturation.

Sociologically, Latinos who are second-generation or beyond evidenced some upward mobility, higher rates of exogamy, living in more residentially diverse areas, and lesser attachment to their ancestral countries. Parenti (1967) and Wolfinger (1965) had posited the impact of immigrant assimilation would result in Americanization and the declining significance of one's ethnicity. The assumptions are that the second generation and beyond will exhibit higher levels of political engagement and be less affected by ethnic factors. Thus the manifestation and effects of persistent ethnicity (in national origin and/or pan-ethnicity terms) was expected to diminish across the Latino generations. Yet, much of the extant research indicates that Latino ethnicity via group consciousness, and social identity and networks, continue to influence Latino political behavior. The impact is especially evident in relation to bloc voting, support for co-ethnic candidates, voter turnout, and response to ethnic mobilization (see, for example, Barretto, Ramírez, and Woods 2005; Michelson 2006; Michelson and Pallares 2001). The importance of context is reflected by research by Barretto, Segura, and Woods (2004) which finds that Latinos residing in majority–minority districts feel more empowered and have higher turnout than their non-Hispanic counterparts. This pattern is more pronounced when there are overlapping majority–minority districts (e.g., state and federal political jurisdictions) (Gay 2001).

Initiative politics in California provides another example of how "external" developments mobilize the Latino community and accentuate a sense of group identity. Newton (2000) shows that a heightened sense of cultural markers such as Spanish use and ancestral pride served to increase interest in the Proposition 187 initiative and promote group solidarity. Similarly, Segura, Falcon, and Pachon (1996) found that as a consequence of Proposition 187, Latinos shifted toward the Democratic Party, became more interested in politics, and viewed issues through an ethnic filter (see also Pantoja and Gershon 2006; Pantoja, Ramírez, and Segura 2002). The intensified activism of Latinos was greater for those in California than for Latinos in other states, which may illustrate further the role of context affecting political behavior.

Another element that affects Latino political behavior is the concept of transnationalism. Transnationalism involves individuals who engage in social networks in their respective communities of origin as well as in their receiving communities. Their connection lies with institutionalized structures that are engaged in familial and collective objectives. The nature of international migration has taken a broader global reality. The flow of immigrants does not result in the severance of their ties to their countries of origin and local regions. Ongoing networks and exchanges occur; formal organizations are created to facilitate exchanges and provide mechanisms for activities; and transnationalism assists the adaptation and investment by immigrants in both their countries of origin and of residence (Jones-Correa 1998). Previous research has looked at continued ties to one's mother country as impeding the political integration of immigrants in the host society and slowing development of attachment and affinity. The dynamics of globalism allow immigrants to maintain regular contacts with families and hometowns with the assistance of modern technology.

The extent of contact is driven by economic obligations and other commitments to family members and local communities. The forms of transnational behaviors include remittances, regular returns, organizational affiliation with hometown associations, dual citizenship (Escobar 2004), and continued political engagement in their countries of origin. For example, since the 1980s expatriates have been involved in lobbying their legislative bodies for policies recognizing their interests regarding property rights and privileges and suffrage (Jones-Correa 2001). Latino expatriates have secured policies that allow for dual citizenship so that rights are enhanced rather than limited. In Columbia, the federal legislature has a representative that speaks for "countrymen" living abroad, as well as electing representatives from their home districts. Countries like Mexico, the Dominican Republic, and Ecuador allow their nationals to vote in their elections, even though they reside elsewhere. In addition, the Mexican government has a "cabinet level" agency to deal with its citizens living abroad. Institutions are responsive to their expatriates' interests, in part to the significant economic impact they have, as well as their organized efforts.

These patterns challenge existing notions about immigrants' maintained connections with their countries of origin. As immigrants invest and acquire equity in their communities of residence, there is a net effect on both communities. Recent studies have demonstrated that Latinos engaged in transnational activities are accumulating social capital; and they are more engaged than other immigrants in their residing communities (Garcia 2008; Segura 2007). Their activities within hometown associations and their political interests and engagement in their country's politics have carry-over effects in terms of skills, informational levels, networks, and participatory orientations. For example, Klesner (2003) ties in the accumulation of social capital, using involvement in non-political organizations, as having a positive effect on social trust and higher levels of political engagement. Similarly, Segura (2007) and Garcia (2008) examine the various dimensions of transnationalism and find that political engagement in the US is enhanced among Latino transnationals. These dynamics require some rethinking or reframing of the notion of citizenship and/or membership in a political community as transnationalism reflects a multiplicity of memberships rather than a singular one.

A major theme of this chapter is a challenge to researchers to view Latinos with greater complexity, and expand the full range of their political behaviors. This would involve more complex framework(s). The area of transnationalism is a good example of broadening the notions of what it means to have multiple attachments and connections to several political systems. While some previous research has portrayed this linkage as divided loyalties or a hierarchical order of allegiance, the reality of these relationships would indicate a more complex nexus of situationally activated ties.

LATINOS, NATURALIZATION, AND POLITICAL BEHAVIORS

The most significant form of political expression among Latino immigrants has been the act of naturalization. Historically, rates of naturalization for people of Mexican origin have been at the lower end of all immigrants (Desipio 2002; Garcia 1981).

Overall, almost one-half of permanent residents naturalize; whereas the percentage for those of Mexican origin was closer to 25–30 percent. More recently (post-1995), the naturalization rate has increased significantly. To a great extent, the rise of anti-immigrant initiatives and propositions has not only mobilized and politicized Latinos, but stimulated more legal nationals to seek naturalization (Pantoja et al. 2002). For the most part, the naturalization decision has focused upon the extent of assimilation, upward social mobility, and attachment to the US as predictors for new citizens (Desipio 1996a; Pantoja et al. 2002). Variables such as English-language proficiency, length of time in the US, higher educational attainment and social status, and a positive view of the opportunity structures in America have been key factors influencing individuals' decisions to naturalize (Desipio 1996a; Garcia 1981).

Overall, rates of registration and turnout between all naturalized and native-born citizens indicate lower rates among the naturalized. For the Mexican-origin naturalized citizens, their registration and turnout rates are higher; but when one controls for socioeconomic status, the advantage disappears (Bass and Casper 1999). The act of naturalization is viewed as an indicator of political incorporation (Citrin and Green 1990; Citrin et al. 2001). Yet, Desipio (1996b) points out that it is a first step in the incorporation process as naturalized citizens are less likely to vote or be engaged in organizational activities than their native counterparts.

More recent studies (Barretto 2005) have taken into account the anti-immigrant activities, with naturalized citizens feeling voting is more efficacious, holding stronger beliefs about democratic ideals, and having higher participatory levels than their native-born counterparts. This is another example of contextual factors related to electoral participation and patterns among Latino naturalized and native-born citizens. These contextual factors and national moods/opinions and institutional practices affect the naturalization decision, beyond individual-based characteristics.

Nativity affects other political behaviors and attitudes, especially with immigrants and naturalized citizens, and specifically in the case of attitudes toward immigration policy. Surveys by the Pew Hispanic Center (2007; Suro 2005) indicate that if one characterizes immigration reform proposals as being restrictive/punitive (e.g., close off the border, more border personnel and physical barriers, deportations, etc.) vs. more immigrant-friendly proposals (e.g., guestworker programs, pathways to legalization, access to higher education for undocumented students, etc.), then Latinos are more supportive of "immigrant-friendly" policy proposals. While there are some limited variations based on nativity status (i.e., foreign-born slightly more supportive), attitudes toward immigrants' contributions (i.e., positive attitudes = more supportive) are affected more by levels of acculturation (i.e., less acculturated = more supportive), and group consciousness (i.e., more supportive) than nativity status.

A sense of a community under siege has activated Latinos across most socio-demographic statuses, irrespective of legal status, generational status, and regional location (Lopez 2008). The rising negative climate directed toward undocumented immigrants (especially Latinos) has resulted in more negative encounters with a variety of institutions and discriminatory behavior. It is important not to limit our consideration of these consequences to electoral activities. Yet with another round of national elections, including an open presidential "seat," the heightened attention on immigration as a major issue and the negative "consequences" that Latinos share and experience will pose the quadrennial query of their likely electoral impact, as well as how voter choice is affected by candidates' stances on immigration policies.

But given variations of generational status, language use, and nativity, many different but similar national-origin groups, and variability of experiences with US institutions and processes, the manifestation of political behaviors need not be confined to only the act of registering and voting. Demographically, the Latino base as a proportion of the American electorate will continue to increase due to its youthful population. One important question is how Latinos are mobilized in this new electoral era. It is no surprise that recently more attention has been directed toward mobilization of Latinos (Leighley 2001). The focus of who is targeted and being asked, characteristics of the person contacting, identifying networks and mobilizing cues (Rosenstone and Hanson 1993) has been a starting point for the examination of Latino political mobilization.

Again, the theme of adding complexities re-enters this research area as the impact of context, structural relations, and public opinion not only affects political behaviors, but serves to activate political engagement. The challenge is to integrate the ascriptive and achieved characteristics of Latinos, as well as their socio-political context (i.e., networks, interactions, events, and external factors) and political structures and processes (Gerber, Morton, and Rietz 1998; Lublin 1999; Segura and Bowler 2006). There have been recent efforts by Latino-based community organizations to activate more Latino prospective registrants with face-to-face contact, and utilization of co-ethnics to be the "mobilizing" actors. This area of political behavior needs to incorporate the relevant dimensions of "being Latino" as well as contextual factors. While I have not devoted any direct attention to the "rules of the game" and electoral systems (Garcia 2003; Grofman, Handley, and Niemi 1992), it is clear that voter registration systems, types of election systems, and partisan efforts figure in the political behavior equation.

LATINOS AND POLITICAL BEHAVIOR: ADDITIONAL CONSIDERATIONS AND DIRECTIONS

Our discussion of Latinos and political behavior has focused on "elements" of the Latino population, their experiences in the US, and distinctions as a racialized and/or ethnic minority. The challenge has been to extend the conventional approaches to Latinos to include consideration of the salient characteristics, statuses, and experiences that shape their political orientations, evaluations, and ways of thinking and acting politically. I would make three suggestions toward the further examination of Latino political behavior. The first would be a more extensive examination of Latino political behavior beyond electoral behaviors. While the growth of the Latino electorate and their electoral impact is quite salient, other domains of political behavior are equally compelling to examine. Organizational affiliations and policy orientations both serve to direct civic engagement as well as the Latinos' manifest demands and expectations of the American political system. How does a national and/or pan-ethnic identification affect group consciousness, political orientations such as efficacy and trust, mobilization linkages with leaders and organizations, and greater civic engagement?

Second, the scope of relevant political actors must include both the native and foreign-born segments of this community. Particularly, the foreign-born bring forth a diverse range of political orientations and political involvements from their countries of origin; and they maintain political connections through transnational interactions. The rise in naturalization rates among Latino immigrants and active political expression by immigrants cause a reevaluation of a group previously viewed as apolitical and disconnected as a burgeoning group that is expressive with a nexus of personal and structural sets of relationships. For the native-born segments, the lower degree of explanatory power of socioeconomic status for political behavior directs researchers to conceptualize and measure indicators of the Latino experiences as precursors of participatory activities.

Finally, the third emphasized research direction to pursue is the inclusion of contextual factors that impact individual political behaviors. Clearly, there is a growing body of behaviorally oriented research that takes into consideration (via model specification and methodological approaches) the effects of both individual attributes and the socioeconomic and political factors in one's personal milieu. For example, levels of political representation, geographic composition of one's area, racial/ethnic mix of one's neighborhoods, "public opinion climate," organizational densities, etc. serve as both the backdrop and impetus for political engagement. Overall political behavior is a complex set of relationships that involves structural, organizational, situational, and personal dimensions in which attempts to examine and understand these phenomena require more confrontation of these complexities and attempts to "capture" them analytically.

References

AMARO, H. and ZAMBRANO, R. E. 2001. Criollo, Mestizo, Mulato, LatiNegro, Indigena, White, or Black? The U.S. Hispanic/Latino Population and Multiple Responses in the 2000 Census. *American Journal of Public Health*, 90/11: 1724–7.

Aparicio, A. 2006. *Dominican-Americans and the Politics of Empowerment.* Gainesville: University of Florida Press.

Arvizu, J. and Garcia, F. C. 1996. Latino Voting Participation: Explaining and Differentiating Latino Voting Turnout. *Hispanic Journal of Behavioral Sciences,* 18/2: 104–28.

Barrera, M. 1979. *Race and Class in the Southwest: a Theory of Racial Inequality.* South Bend, Ind.: University of Notre Dame.

Barreto, M. A. 2002. National Origin (Mis)identification Among Latinos in the 2000 Census: The Growth of the "Other Hispanic or Latino" Category. *Harvard Journal of Hispanic Policy,* 15: 39–63.

—— 2005. Latino Immigrants at the Polls: Foreign Born Latino Turnout in the 2002 Election. *Political Research Quarterly,* 58: 79–86.

—— Ramírez, R., and Woods, N. D. 2005. "Are Naturalized Voters Driving the California Latino Electorate? Measuring the Effect of IRCA Citizens on Latino Voting." *Social Science Quarterly,* 86 /4: 792–811.

—— Segura, G., and Woods, N. 2004. The Mobilizing Effects of Majority–Minority Districts on Latino Turnout. *American Political Science Review,* 98/1: 65–75.

Barvosa-Carter, E. 1999. Multiple Identity and Coalition Building: How Identity Differences Within us Enable Radical Alliances among Us. *Contemporary Justice Review,* 2/2: 111–26.

Bass, L. and Casper, L. M. 1999. Are There Differences in Voting Behavior Between Naturalized and Native-born Americans? Population Division Working Papers, U.S. Census Bureau (March).

Bohara, A. K. and Davila, A. 1992. A Reassessment of the Phenotypic Discrimination and Income Differences among Mexican Americans. *Social Science Quarterly,* 73/1: 114–19.

Bullock, C. and Hood, M. V. III. 2006. A Mile-Wide Gap: The Evolution of Hispanic Political Emergence in the Deep South. *Social Science Quarterly,* 87/1: 1117–35.

Citrin, J., Reingold, B., and Green, D. 1990. American Identity and the Politics of Ethnic Change. *Journal of Politics,* 52/4: 1124–54.

—— Sears, D. O., Muste, C., and Wong, C. 2001. Multiculturalism in American Public Opinion. *British Journal of Political Science,* 31/2: 247–75.

de la Garza, R. O. and Yetim, M. 2003. The Impact of Ethnicity and Socialization on Definitions of Democracy: The Case of Mexican Americans and Mexicans. *Mexican Studies/Estudios Mexicanos,* 19/1: 81–104.

Desipio, L. 1996a. *Counting on the Latino Vote: Latinos as a New Electorate.* Charlottesville: University Press of Virginia.

—— 1996b. Making Citizens or Good Citizens? Naturalization as a Predictor of Organizational and Electoral Behavior among Latino Immigrants. *Hispanic Journal of Behavioral Sciences,* 18/2: 194–213.

—— 2002. Immigrant Organizing, Civic Outcomes: Civic Engagement, Political Activity, National Attachment, and Identity in Latino Immigrant Communities. Center for the Study of Democracy Paper 02-08.

Escobar, C. 2004. Dual Citizenship and Political Participation: Migrants in the Interplay of United States and Colombian Politics. *Latino Studies,* 2/1: 45–69.

Espiritu, Y. L. 1992. *Asian American Pan-ethnicity: Bridging Institutions and Identities.* Philadelphia, Pa.: Temple University Press.

Falconi, J. L. and Mazzotti, J. A. (eds.) 2008. *The Other Latinos.* David Rockefeller Center for Latin American Studies.

Fraga, L. R. and Segura, G. M. 2006. Culture Clash? Contesting Notions of American Identity and the Effects of Latin American Immigration. *Perspectives on Politics*, 4/2: 279–87.

Fraga, L. R., Garcia, J., Hero, R., Jones-Correa, M., Martinez-Ebers, V., and Segura, G. 2006. Su Casa *Es* Nuestra Casa: Latino Politics Research and the Development of American Political Science. *American Political Science Review*, 100/4: 515–22.

Garcia, J. A. 1981. Political Integration of Mexican Immigrants: Explorations into the Naturalization Process. *International Migration Review* (Winter).

—— 2003. *Latino Politics in America: Community, Culture, and Interests*. Lanham, Md.: Rowman & Littlefield Publishers, Inc.

—— —— 2006. Ethnicity and Nationalism: Explorations of US National Identities Among Latin Immigrants and Bases for National Incorporation. Paper presented at the Political Demography: Ethnic, National and Regional Dimensions Conference, September 29–30, London School of Economics.

—— —— 2008. Latino Immigrants: Transnationalism and Patterns of Multiple Citizenship Patterns. In *Latinos, Transnationalism and Immigration*, ed. D. Leal. New York: Palgrave Macmillan.

—— and Sanchez, G. 2004. Electoral Politics. In *Latino Americans and Participation of Latinos*, ed. S. Navarro and A. Mejia. Santa Barbara: ABC-CLIO.

Garcia-Bedolla, L. 2005. *Fluid Borders: Latino Power, Identity, and Politics in Los Angeles*. Berkeley: University of California Press.

Gay, C. 2001. The Effect of Minority Districts and Minority Representation on Political Participation in California. Public Policy Institute of California.

Gerber, E. R., Morton, R., and Rietz, T. A. 1998. Minority Representation in Multimember Districts. *American Political Science Review*, 92/1: 127–44.

Gómez-Quiñones, J. 1990. *Chicano Politics: Realities and Promise*. Albuquerque: University of New Mexico Press.

Grofman, B., Handley, L., and Niemi, R. 1992. *Minority Representation and the Quest for Voting Equality*. New York: Cambridge University Press.

Gutierrez, A. and Hirsch, H. 1973. The Militant Challenge and the American Ethos: Chicanos and Mexican Americans. *Social Science Quarterly*, 53/4: 830–45.

—— —— 1974. Political Maturation and Political Awareness: The Case of Crystal City Chicanos. *Aztlán*, 5/1–2 (Spring/Fall).

Hero, R. and Campbell, A. 1996. Understanding Latino Political Participation: Exploring the Evidence from the Latino National Political Survey. *Hispanic Journal of Behavioral Sciences*, 18/2: 129–41.

—— Garcia, F. C., Garcia, J., and Pachon, H. 2000. Latino Participation, Partisanship, and Office Holding. *PS: Political Science and Politics*, 33/3: 529–34.

Hill, K. and Moreno, D. 1996. Second Generation Cubans. *Hispanic Journal of Behavioral Sciences*, 18/2: 175–93.

Hritzuk, N. and Park, D. K. 2000. The Question of Latino Participation: From an SES to a Social Structural Explanation. *Social Sciences Quarterly*, 81/1: 151–66.

Itzigsohn, J. and Dore-Cabral, C. 2000. Competing Identities? Race, Ethnicity and Panethnicity Among Dominicans in the United States. *Sociological Forum*, 15/2: 225–40.

Jensen, L., Cohen, J., Toribio, J. A., Dejong, G., and Rodriquez, L. 2006. Ethnic Identities, Language, Economic Outcomes among Dominicans in a New Destination. *Social Science Quarterly*, 87/1: 1088–99.

JOHNSON, M., STEIN, R. M., and WRINKLE, R. 2003. Language Choice, Residential Stability, and Voting among Latino Americans. *Social Science Quarterly*, 84/2: 412–24.

JONES-CORREA, M. 1998. *Between Two Nations: The Political Predicament of Latinos in New York City*. Ithaca, N.Y.: Cornell University Press.

—— 2001. Under Two Flags: Dual Nationality in Latin America and Its Consequences for Naturalization in the United States. *International Migration Review*, 35/4: 997–1029.

—— and LEAL, D. L. 1996. Becoming "Hispanic": Secondary Pan-ethnic Identification among Latin American-Origin Populations in the United States. *Hispanic Journal of Behavioral Sciences*, 18/2: 214–54.

JUNN, J. 1999. Participation in Liberal Democracy: The Political Assimilation of Immigrants and Ethnic Minorities in the United States. *American Behavioral Scientist*, 42/9: 1417–38.

KLESNER, J. 2003. Political Attitudes, Social Capital and Political Participation: The United States and Mexico Compared. *Mexican Studies/Estudios Mexicanos*, 19/1: 29–63.

LANDALE, N. S. and OROPESA, R. S. 2002. White, Black, or Puerto Rican? Racial Self-identification Among Mainland and Island Puerto Ricans. *Social Forces*, 81/1: 231–54.

LEIGHLEY, J. E. 2001. *Strength in Numbers: The Political Mobilization of Racial and Ethnic Minorities*. Princeton, N.J.: Princeton University Press.

LIEN, P.-T. 1994. Ethnicity and Political Participation: A Comparison between Asian and Mexican Americans. *Political Behavior*, 16/2: 237–64.

LOPEZ, M. 2008. 2008 Survey of Latinos: Hispanics See Their Situation in U.S. Deteriorating; Oppose Key Immigration enforcement Measures. Pew Hispanic Center, Washington D.C.

LUBLIN, D. 1999. *The Paradox of Representation: Racial Gerrymandering and Minority Interests in Congress*. Princeton, N.J.: Princeton University Press.

MARSCHALL, M. J. 2001. Does the Shoe Fit? Testing Models of Participation for African-American and Latino Involvement in Local Politics. *Urban Affairs Review*, 37/2: 227–48.

MASUOKA, N. 2006. Together They Become One: Examining the Predictors of Group Consciousness among Asian Americans and Latinos. *Social Science Quarterly*, 87/1: 993–1011.

MICHELSON, M. R. 2003. The Corrosive Effect of Acculturation: How Mexican Americans Lose Political Trust. *Social Science Quarterly*, 84: 918–33.

—— 2006. Mobilizing the Latino Vote: Some Experimental Results. *Social Science Quarterly*, 87/1: 1188–206.

—— and PALLARES, A. 2001. The Politicization of Chicago Mexican Americans: Naturalization, the Vote, and Perceptions of Discrimination. *Aztlán*, 26/2: 63–86.

NEWTON, L. 2000. Why Some Latinos Supported Proposition 187: Testing Economic Threat and Cultural Identity Hypotheses. *Social Sciences Quarterly*, 81/1: 180–93.

NICHOLSON, S. P., PANTOJA, A. D., and SEGURA, G. M. 2005. Race Matters: Latino Racial Identities and Political Beliefs. Institute of Governmental Studies, Paper WP2005-47, <http://repositories.cdlib.org/igs/WP2005-47>.

OBOLER, S. 2006. *Latinos and Citizenship: The Dilemma of Belonging*. New York: Palgrave Macmillan.

OMNI, M. and WINANT, H. 1994. *Racial Formation in the United States: From the 1960s to the 1990s*. New York: Routledge.

PADILLA, F. M. 1985. *Latino Ethnic Consciousness: The Case of Mexican Americans and Puerto Ricans in Chicago*. Notre Dame, Ind.: University of Notre Dame Press.

PANTOJA, A. and GERSHON, S. A. 2006. Political Orientations and Naturalization among Latino and Latina Immigrants. *Social Science Quarterly*, 87/1: 1171–87.

PANTOJA, A., RAMIREZ, R., and SEGURA, G. 2002. Citizens by Choice, Voters by Necessity: Patterns in Political Mobilization by Naturalized Latinos. *Political Research Quarterly*, 54/4: 729–50.

PARENTI, M. 1967. Ethnic Politics and the Persistence of Ethnic Identification. *The American Political Science Review*, 61/3: 717–26.

PARK, E. J. W. and PARK, J. S. W. 1999. A New American Dilemma? Asian Americans and Latinos in Race Theorizing. *Journal of Asian American Studies*, 2/3: 289–309.

PEW HISPANIC CENTER 2007. 2007 National Survey of Latinos: As Illegal Immigration Issue Heats Up, Hispanics Feel a Chill. Washington D.C., December.

PORTES, A. and MACLEOD, D. 1996. What Shall I Call Myself? Hispanic Identity Formation in the Second Generation. *Ethnic and Racial Studies*, 19/3: 523–47.

RAMAKRISHNAN, S. K. 2005. *Democracy in Immigrant America: Changing Demographics and Political Participation*. Stanford, Calif.: Stanford University Press.

RODRIGUEZ, C. E. 1992. Race, Culture, and Latino "Otherness" in the 1980 Census. *Social Science Quarterly*, 73/4: 930–7.

ROSENSTONE, S. J. and HANSEN, J. M. 1993. *Mobilization, Participation, and Democracy in America*. New York: Macmillan Pub. Co.

SANCHEZ, G. R. 2006. The Role of Group Consciousness in Political Participation among Latinos in the United States. *American Politics Research*, 34: 427–50.

SCHILDKRAUT, D. J. 2003. American Identity and Attitudes toward Official-English Policies. *Political Psychology*, 24/3: 469–500.

SEGURA, G. 2007. "Transnational Linkages, Generational Change, and Latino Political Engagement" Chicago, IL; Paper presented at the annual meeting of the Midwest Political Science Association.

—— and BOWLER, S. (eds.) 2006. *Diversity in Democracy: Minority Representation in the United States*. Charlottesville: University of Virginia Press.

—— FALCON, D., and PACHON, H. 1996. Dynamics of Latino Partisanship in California: Immigration, Issue Salience, and Their Implications. *Harvard Journal of Hispanic Policy*, 10: 62–80.

STOKES, A. K. 2003. Latino Group Consciousness and Political Participation. *American Politics Research*, 31: 361–78.

—— [STOKES-BROWN] 2006. Racial Identity and Latino Vote Choice. *American Politics Research*, 34: 627–52.

SURO, R. 2005. *Hispanics and the 2004 Election*. Washington, D.C.: Pew Hispanic Center.

TAJFEL, H. 1982. *Social Identity and Inter-Group Behavior*. Cambridge: Cambridge University Press.

TAFOYA, S. 2004. Shades of Belonging: Latinos and Racial Identity. Pew Hispanic Center Report. Available at <http://www.pewhispanic.org>.

TELLES, E. E. and MURGUIA, E. 1990. Phenotypic Discrimination and Income Differences among Mexican Americans. *Social Science Quarterly*, 71/4: 682–96.

WENZEL, J. P. 2006. Acculturation Effects on Trust in National and Local Government among Mexican Americans. *Social Science Quarterly*, 87/1: 1073–87.

WOLNGER, R. 1965. The Development and Persistence of Ethnic Voting. *The American Political Science Review*, 59/4: 896–908.

WONG, J. 2000. 2006. *Democracy's Promise: Immigrants and American Civic Institutions*. Ann Arbor: University of Michigan Press.

CHAPTER 22

....

ORGANIZING AMERICAN POLITICS, ORGANIZING GENDER*

KIRA SANBONMATSU

Do you think that people who are voting on the basis of gender solidarity ought to be allowed to vote in a perfect world? Of course they shouldn't be allowed to vote on those grounds. That's moronic. I'm sorry, I [could] get bounced off the air for saying it. But it's true.... I'm merely saying the obvious, that you shouldn't vote for her [Hillary Clinton] because she's a woman.

Tucker Carlson, October 15, 2007[1]

The 2008 presidential campaign featured a prominent role for both candidate and voter gender. US Senator Hillary Clinton, the frontrunner for most of the Democratic primary, made a concerted appeal to women voters and campaigned on the

* I thank Kelly Dittmar for research assistance. I thank Susan Carroll, Kathleen Dolan, Timothy Frye and Janet Leighley for comments.
[1] Transcript from *Tucker Carlson*. <http://www.msnbc.msn.com/id/21322580/> (accessed December 3, 2007).

potential of becoming the country's first female president. Clinton's pollster Mark Penn predicted that she would attract a large number of Republican women voters in the general election. The other Democratic primary candidates disputed the idea that Clinton was the natural choice of women voters, though polls revealed that more women than men supported her. Some critics denigrated Clinton's appeals to gender solidarity and argued that voters should not base their decision on a candidate's gender, while others argued that Clinton's failure to attract more women voters was a problem for her campaign.

To what extent do men and women behave differently in politics? When does gender organize American political behavior? These are familiar questions about the role of gender in elections. But the 2008 case—which featured the most competitive presidential bid by a woman in US history—was unusual in many respects. The election reminds us of how much we do not yet know about how gender organizes American politics. For example, pre-election polls failed to anticipate Clinton's success in the New Hampshire primary and the unprecedented gender gap that fueled her victory.

I consider gender to organize American politics when there is evidence of gender difference at either the individual or aggregate level, although a focus on difference is not the only way that gender could be said to organize politics.[2] It would be a mistake to assume that the absence of gender difference at the individual level means that gender is unrelated to political behavior; as Nancy Burns (2007, 105–6) has argued, gender can be more difficult to observe at the individual level than at the aggregate level because gender is constructed at the aggregate level.[3]

I focus this review chapter on gender differences in mass behavior and candidacy. Past studies have yielded sufficient evidence of gender differences in political behavior that we can think beyond the commonly asked question "Do men and women behave differently?" to ask broader, over time, and aggregate-level questions about *when* men and women behave differently.[4] Questions to orient

---

[2] Due to space limitations, I am not able to review the entire literature. I focus in this chapter on candidate and voter gender, although gender roles, gender-linked traits, and gender-related issues can also shape behavior and elections (see Duerst-Lahti 2002; Sanbonmatsu 2002; Winter 2005; Wolbrecht 2000). In addition, although I focus on gender difference as a gap between men and women, gender can organize behavior if men and women reach the vote decision differently (see Carroll and Zerilli 1993; Klein 1984; Sapiro and Conover 1997). The reader should bear in mind the pitfalls that accompany an emphasis on difference (see Reingold 2000).

[3] See Burns (2002) and Achen (1992) on the limitations of learning about gender from the gender coefficient in a multivariate model. On how individual and aggregate analysis can be linked, see Burns (2007).

[4] I do not mean to imply that we should expect an unchanging or universal relationship between gender and politics. As Karen Beckwith notes, "male and female, as categories of 'sex,' do not lead inexorably to any particular practices or meanings and, hence, do not directly embody politics or political practice" (2005, 130). If interests are endogenous to politics, then the relationship of gender to politics is likely to be a dynamic one. Instead of a fixed relationship between gender and American

future scholarship, then, are: when does gender organize American politics? Under what conditions does gender structure political behavior and elections? And why? Behavior scholarship has already become more attentive to these questions about context, as I discuss in the coming pages.

At the end of the chapter, I argue that we also need to ask: when does American politics organize gender? Past research has treated gender as a social difference that originates outside and prior to politics, asking whether this social difference matters in the political sphere. We typically assume the existence of two social groups—men and women—and ask whether the two groups behave similarly or differently in politics. This approach regards gender as a characteristic that individuals possess. However, we can view gender as a set of social relationships and practices that are partially created within the political sphere. We can treat gender as a political category rather than, or in addition to, a social category. By political category I mean that the category of gender is at least partially created and reproduced by politics.

Thinking about gender in this way—as a category that can be shaped by politics rather than as a purely social category with consequences for politics—suggests a somewhat different research agenda than that typically pursued by behavior scholars.[5] Scholars can ask whether elections help *create* gender as a category in addition to asking whether the social category of gender is cued in politics. Political behavior and elections themselves may shape beliefs about gender, instructing society about what men and women are like, as well as what they should be like (Carroll 1999, 2006a; Duerst-Lahti 2006). Politics may help define gender, imbuing the category of gender with particular meanings. Thus, perhaps American politics helps make men and women groups.

Organizing American Politics: Gender Differences in Political Behavior

Perhaps the most common theoretical foundation underlying research on gender and behavior is the idea that gender differences in interests may lead to gender differences in voting behavior. Virginia Sapiro (1981) argues that women have

---

politics, we should expect time-bound and conditional gender effects precisely because the meaning and nature of gender as a social category is contested and changes over time and its salience changes as well (Carroll and Zerilli 1993). At the same time, we would not expect complete randomness to how gender is related to political behavior that would prevent us from building general theories.

[5] Scholarship on the role of politics in constructing gender has largely taken place in literatures other than elections (e.g., Gordon 1990; Leonard and Tronto 2007; Ritter 2006). For example, recent gender scholarship on institutions argues that gender is created and reproduced within institutions (Acker 1992; Duerst-Lahti 2002; Hawkesworth 2003; Kenney 1996; Rosenthal 2002; Smooth 2001).

unique interests originating in their shared social position that require political representation. For example, men and women are likely to have different interests because of different domestic responsibilities, relationships to children and child care, types of jobs, and resources. Indeed, public opinion studies find that women tend to be more liberal on "compassion" issues such as helping the poor and spending on social welfare, more liberal on racial issues, and more hesitant to use force abroad (Seltzer, Newman, and Leighton 1997; Shapiro and Mahajan 1986). Women tend to be more supportive of an activist role for government, to be more religious than men, more opposed to capital punishment, and more supportive of gun control. Men and women often hold similar views on gender-related issues, but those issues are usually more important to women.

Since women won the right to vote in 1920, observers and scholars have scoured election results for evidence of a women's voting bloc—a bloc feared by some suffrage opponents and anticipated by some suffragists. Indeed, the threat of a women's vote assisted the congressional lobbying efforts of women's organizations in the 1920s (Mueller 1988). Yet, a women's voting bloc failed to emerge and women's collective influence declined as a result. It would not be until the 1980 presidential election that the existence of a gap became widely known and became a "generalized political resource" for women's influence (Mueller 1988, 18). Between 1980 and 2004 the gender gap in presidential elections ranged from 4 to 11 points (Carroll 2006b). In 2004, for example, 48 percent of women and 55 percent of men voted for George W. Bush. The effect of gender persists in multivariate analysis after taking demographic factors into account (Huddy, Cassesse, and Lizotte 2008).

A gap in partisan identification can explain much of the presidential voting gender gap (Kaufmann and Petrocik 1999; Kenski 1988). Women had been somewhat more likely than men to prefer the Republican party in the 1950s (A. Campbell et al. 1960; Kaufmann and Petrocik 1999; Norris 2003). Since the 1960s women have largely remained Democratic while men have been more likely to shift to the Republican party (Kaufmann and Petrocik 1999; Kenski 1988; Wirls 1986). Women voters are also less likely to identify as independents (Norrander 1997).

Gender gaps are often larger in races featuring Democratic women candidates than in races with Democratic men, while races featuring Republican women candidates have yielded smaller gaps than races with Republican men (Carroll 2006b; Seltzer, Newman, and Leighton 1997). Individual-level analysis also reveals that women vote for women, though the results depend on the year, level of office, and party (Brians 2005; Dolan 2004; Plutzer and Zipp 1996). Meanwhile, African–American female voters are the strongest supporters of African–American female candidates (Philpot and Walton 2007).

It is common to emphasize gender difference (Epstein 1988), but the magnitude of gender differences should not be overstated (Sears and Huddy 1990; Seltzer, Newman, and Leighton 1997). Gender is not usually viewed as an important factor in American politics whereas the centrality of race is widely recognized (Burns 2007; Ritter 2008). One reason that the category of gender is believed to be less important than race is that women as a group do not exhibit the same level of group-based voting behavior as African–Americans (Seltzer, Newman, and Leighton 1997; Tate 1994). Racial inequality is also more visible because of racial segregation whereas gender hierarchies, which cumulate over time, are often less visible (Burns 2005; 2007, 106–7). In addition, women and men are larger groups than racial and ethnic minorities. In general, women as a group tend to exhibit less group consciousness than other groups such as African–Americans (Burns, Schlozman, and Verba 2001; Gurin 1985).

Analyzing gender in isolation suggests that there is a common essence to being a woman. Yet gender intersects with other identities such as race and class (Spelman 1988). A singular focus on gender will be inadequate to capture the relationship between gender and politics if gender, race, and ethnicity are mutually constitutive (Hancock 2007; Hardy-Fanta 2006; Smooth 2006; Weldon 2006). Instead of viewing women as a cohesive group, it may be more accurate to recognize that women are politically fragmented (Sears and Huddy 1990). Both men and women can be categorized by factors other than gender, such as race/ethnicity, religion, occupation, partisanship, and ideology.

One possible explanation for why we do not observe more or larger gender gaps is that such gaps are conditional. Women arguably need to be aware of their interests as women in order to act on them (Miller et al. 1981; Sapiro 1981). Philip Paolino (1995) argues that salient events may explain why women seek group representation.

More persistent than the voting behavior gap is the gender gap in political participation (Andersen 1975; Andersen and Cook 1985; Beckwith 1986; Burns, Schlozman, and Verba 2001; Welch 1977). Women are less likely to be affiliated with a political organization, contact a government official, work informally in the community, and give money to politics, and women give less money to politics than men (Burns, Schlozman, and Verba 2001). Women tend to be less interested in and knowledgeable about politics than men (Delli Carpini and Keeter 1996; Verba, Burns, and Schlozman 1997)[6] and tend to participate on somewhat different issues (Burns, Schlozman, and Verba 2001; Goss and Skocpol 2006).

The participation gap is not large, however. Nancy Burns, Kay Lehman Schlozman, and Sidney Verba (2001, 2) find on an eight-point scale of participatory acts that women participate on average in .31 of a political act less than men. In some areas of political participation, no significant gender gap is evident (Burns, Schlozman, and Verba 2001). The gender gap also tends to be smaller than other gaps, such as racial

---

[6] However, the gender gap in political knowledge may partly be an artifact of the survey response. See Mondak and Anderson (2004). Men and women also specialize in their political knowledge (Burns, Schlozman, and Verba 2001; Delli Carpini and Keeter 1993).

or ethnic differences (Verba, Schlozman, and Brady 1995). In addition, the participation gender gap has reversed direction in one case: since 1980 women's voter turnout has exceeded that of men (CAWP 2004; Kenski 1988).

In sum, the existence of gender differences depends on what aspect of behavior is examined, at what point in time, and whether men and women are compared at the individual or aggregate level. Gender differences are often small or nonexistent, which would seem to suggest that gender is not a central dividing line in American politics. Yet gender differences in political behavior are too common and persistent to ignore (Sapiro and Conover 1997).

THE POLITICAL ORIGINS OF GENDER DIFFERENCES IN POLITICAL BEHAVIOR

Studies have generally assumed that gender differences in politics have a social basis. But gender differences in political behavior may have political origins in addition to—or instead of—social origins. For example, the exclusion of women from the vote by law meant that gender defined the electorate. Male suffrage created a second gender difference in political behavior: because women did not have the vote, they pioneered a new form of political participation in interest group politics (Clemens 1997; Cott 1987; Skocpol 1992). Women's success in obtaining the vote did not end the association of gender with political activity; instead, politics continues to convey messages to voters about the appropriate relationship between political participation and gender. In this section, I focus on mobilization studies that identify politics as a source of gender differences in political behavior.

The presence of women candidates and officeholders is expected to close the traditional gender gap in political engagement and participation by mobilizing women voters. Kathleen Dolan summarizes the logic: "The signals of openness, legitimacy, and identity sent by the presence of women candidates can, in turn, stimulate activity and engagement on the part of those members of the public heartened by an increasingly democratic and representative candidate pool" (2006, 688). Women are expected to respond to the presence of women candidates, but a narrowing of the gender gap could result from a decline in men's engagement or participation (Hansen 1997). Indeed, Burns, Schlozman, and Verba (2001) find that the gap in psychological engagement with politics closed with the presence of women candidates or elected officials. Other studies reach more ambiguous conclusions, however (Dolan 2006; Lawless 2004). The symbolic effect of women elites appears to be conditional rather than fixed (Atkeson 2003; D. E. Campbell and Wolbrecht 2006; Dolan 2006; Hansen 1997; Sapiro and Conover 1997).

Political elites and parties may consciously seek to mobilize voters on a gender basis, which may explain why the gender gap varies over time and place. The decisions of women candidates to emphasize their gender and appeal to women voters is one example of a gender-based mobilization strategy. But a gender strategy is not solely the province of women candidates. The potential to mobilize voters on the basis of gender exists in any election. As McConnaughy has recently argued, behavior scholarship could move beyond a goal of explaining specific elections to think about systematic processes and model "how long-run gendered political processes unfold over time at both the macro and micro levels" (2007, 383). Similarly, Nancy Burns (2007, 105) argues for the study of "when social and political contexts can make gender relevant" by using "a research design centered on comparison across contexts—different states, different years, different electoral campaigns." Burns asks if there are "'electoral temptations' of gender" that are similar to the use of race in elections, and calls for "an explicitly political model of citizen mobilization and demobilization around gender" (Burns 2007, 117).[7]

Scholars are already beginning to turn their attention to politics in order to understand when gender is related to political behavior (Box-Steffensmeier, De-Boef, and Lin 2004; Kaufmann 2002). Gender gaps in vote choice are conditional and at least partly a function of campaigns, rather than an inevitable consequence of gender differences in interests (Ondercin and Bernstein 2007). Brian F. Schaffner (2005) finds that Senate campaigns that feature women's issues affect the vote choices of women but not men.

Few studies have investigated when and why elites choose to use gender as a basis for mobilization. In her study of women's enfranchisement, Anna L. Harvey (1998) argues that because parties sought to mobilize women first—before women's organizations—it would be several decades before another opportunity would emerge for women's organizations to direct women's electoral loyalties. Schaffner (2005) finds that candidate decisions about when to campaign on women's issues and target women voters are related to state public opinion and past electoral gender gaps.

Though elites may seek to induce political behavior structured on gender lines, they may also seek to prevent it. Early in the twentieth century, for example, male party leaders insisted on party loyalty and discouraged party women from forging a gender-based solidarity (Freeman 2000). Thus, elites may denigrate the idea of gender-based politics. Moreover, elite decisions about mobilizing men and women may depend on their beliefs and strategic decisions about mobilization on other bases, such as class and race (McConnaughy 2004; Ritter 2008). The decision to *not* mobilize on the basis of gender would seem to be as important as the decision *to* mobilize on gender.

---

[7] See also McConnaughy (2007, 381).

GENDER DIFFERENCES: CANDIDACY AND OFFICEHOLDING

Even larger than the gender gaps in participation and mass behavior are gaps in candidacy and officeholding. Upon winning the right to vote, women did not automatically have the right to hold office in all places (Andersen 1996). Indeed, relatively few women sought or held office in the early part of the twentieth century. The number of women candidates and elected officials grew slowly over subsequent decades. But increases over time in women's representation have not been inevitable; as Susan J. Carroll (2004, 396) has argued, "there is no invisible hand at work to insure that more women will seek and be elected to office with each subsequent election."

Women's officeholding is at its zenith today. Yet women remain underrepresented compared to their presence in the population. Women today hold 17 percent of congressional seats and men 83 percent; women hold 24 percent of state legislative seats and men 76 percent (CAWP 2009b, 2009c). In the history of the US Congress, only 2 percent of legislators have been women.[8] A woman has never been president or vice-president. Only thirty women have ever served as governor (CAWP 2009a). The gender imbalance in officeholding reflects a gender imbalance in candidacy (Lawless and Pearson 2008; Sanbonmatsu 2006c).

Today, women are no longer believed to be disqualified for office simply because of gender. In the 1930s, only 33 percent of the public expressed willingness to vote for a woman for president compared to today's polls revealing that an overwhelming majority is willing to support a woman ("Clinton vs. Obama?" 2007; Jones and Moore 2003). Moreover, election results demonstrate that women are no longer at an automatic disadvantage and are advantaged in some cases (Burrell 1994; Clark et al. 1984; Darcy and Schramm 1977; Lawless and Pearson 2008; Seltzer, Newman, and Leighton 1997).

It would be premature to conclude that gender is completely unrelated to electoral success, however. For example, women congressional candidates tend to face more primary competition than men (Lawless and Pearson 2008; Palmer and Simon 2006). Women candidates appear to be more sensitive to strategic considerations—perhaps because they anticipate gender discrimination (Fulton et al. 2006; Pearson and McGhee 2004). Meanwhile, women Democratic members of Congress tend to represent more liberal, urban, racially diverse, and wealthier districts than men Democrats, and Republican women represent more liberal and more electorally marginal districts than their male counterparts (Evans 2005; Palmer and Simon 2006). We also know that women state legislators are not randomly distributed across the United States.

---

[8] <http://www.cawp.rutgers.edu/Facts2.html>, accessed January 8, 2008.

For example, in Colorado, the state with the highest level of women's representation, women are 38 percent of the legislature; the state with the lowest level, 10 percent, is South Carolina (CAWP 2009b).

In order to explain the gender gap in officeholding, much attention has focused on the scarcity of women candidates (Burrell 1994; Dolan 2008). Women are underrepresented in the supply of candidates, or the social eligibility pool. Women have been less likely to be in the occupations from which men have tended to launch their political careers, such as law and business (Darcy, Welch, and Clark 1994). For much of the twentieth century, women ran for office who were housewives or widows of officeholders, or who had backgrounds in female-dominated occupations (Carroll and Strimling 1983; Gertzog 1995; Kirkpatrick 1974). Women continue to come from a more diverse set of occupations than men, although the paths that men and women take to public office have converged in recent decades (Burrell 1994; Dolan and Ford 1997; Gertzog 1995, 2002; Sanbonmatsu 2006b; Thomas 1994).

The Political Origins of Gender Differences in Candidacy and Officeholding

Much scholarly attention has focused on the social factors that contribute to women's descriptive underrepresentation, including voter attitudes, the presence of women in the social eligibility pool, and the willingness of women to seek office. But political factors also explain the gender distribution of officeholders and candidates. Incumbency represents an institutional hurdle to women's representation because most incumbents are men and incumbents are highly likely to win reelection (Burrell 1994; Carroll 1994; Darcy, Welch, and Clark 1994; Fox 2006). Elections with a greater number of open seats—such as the 1992 so-called "Year of the Woman"—are known to provide opportunities for newcomers such as women. And women fare better in states where legislators are elected from multi-member rather than single-member districts (Carroll 1994; Darcy, Hadley, and Kirksey 1997; Darcy, Welch, and Clark 1994; Diamond 1977; Norrander and Wilcox 1998; Rule 1981, 1990; Werner 1968).

In addition, the mere fact of women's descriptive underrepresentation can communicate to voters and women potential candidates that officeholding may not be appropriate for women.[9] Men and women also seek different types of elective office. Some types of offices are "feminine," or more in keeping with

---

[9] See McDonagh (2002) on the effect of welfare state policies on women's election to national office.

women's traditional areas of expertise and others are more "masculine" and more likely to be held by a man, such as the presidency (Duerst-Lahti 2006; Fox and Oxley 2003).

Political sources of the gender imbalance in officeholding can also be found in some studies of recruitment. If parties do not believe that women can win, or if women party leaders—who are more likely to know women potential candidates—are scarce, then parties will be less likely to recruit women (Niven 1998; Sanbonmatsu 2006a, 2006d; but see Burrell 1994; Caul and Tate 2002; Darcy, Welch, and Clark 1994). Lawless and Fox (2005) find that women potential candidates are less likely to receive the suggestion to run and that they tend to underestimate their qualifications for office.

Thus, recent behavior scholarship has looked to politics in order to understand when gender differences occur, finding that various actors can politicize gender and induce gender-based behavior. Meanwhile, the presence—or absence—of women in politics conveys information to agents of recruitment, voters, and women potential candidates about the appropriateness of women's officeholding and the viability of women candidates. These studies identify political conditions—rather than social conditions alone—that can create gender gaps in political behavior and elections.

ORGANIZING GENDER

The relationship of gender to politics may be even more complex. Future research should consider the possibility that American politics can organize gender—and not just that gender can organize American politics. American politics may help create—rather than merely cue—gender. In this section, I suggest new areas for research with two brief examples.

The conventional wisdom is that as more women run for and are elected to office, the public should become more accepting of women in politics and elect more women. Because most politicians are men, voters usually picture a man when they picture a politician. Therefore, a rise in the presence of women in office and in different types of offices—perhaps offices that were not previously held by women—is expected to change voter expectations about what a typical politician looks like.

But the gender imbalance among politicians may convey a wider meaning—beyond beliefs about politicians. The gender gap in candidacy may contribute to public beliefs about the leadership ability and personality traits of men and women *in society,* thereby helping to construct gender (Eagly 1987).[10] As Jane Mansbridge (1999, 649) explains:

the presence or absence in the ruling assembly . . . of a proportional number of individuals carrying the group's ascriptive characteristics shapes the social meaning of those characteristics in a way that affects most bearers of those characteristics in the polity. . . . Low percentages of Black and women representatives, for example, create the meaning that Blacks and women cannot rule, or are not suitable for rule.

According to Mansbridge, then, observing a preponderance of men in elective office may convey the social message that women as a group are not able to rule. Women's underrepresentation in politics may instruct the public about the characteristics of men and women in society, and not just the characteristics of men and women in politics.

If true, one implication is that there may be more inertia in the underrepresentation of women than we previously thought. Even if there are gains for women in elective office, if an overall gender gap in officeholding persists, social beliefs about men and women may not change; the gender imbalance in officeholding may continue to "teach" society that men as a group are more likely to have the skills necessary for politics. The persistence of social beliefs about differences in the nature of men and women is likely to continue to reproduce the gender gap in officeholding. The public could come to believe that *some* women have the right traits for public office while continuing to believe that women in general are less likely to have those traits than men.

Such a dynamic might help explain the persistence of the belief that men are more emotionally suited for politics than women (Sanbonmatsu 2002). It might also help explain the persistence of differences across the American states in women's officeholding. We typically assume that social beliefs about women's roles explain cross-state variation in women's officeholding. But perhaps the level of women's representation in a state instructs the public about women's abilities and nature.

These types of questions point to the need for research on what the public learns about men and women in society from the gender distribution of candidates and officeholders. Scholars could investigate this question empirically with experimental, panel, or longitudinal analysis in order to tease out the causal relationship between women's descriptive representation and social beliefs.

---

[10] Eagly (1987) argues that social meaning is conveyed by the social division of labor in which men are more likely to work outside the home than women. The public infers that men and women are pursuing the social roles most conducive to their respective traits, with women more communal and men more agentic. She explains: "The distribution of the sexes into specific social roles indirectly supports stereotypic sex differences because this distribution is an important source of people's expectations about female and male characteristics" (1987, 31).

Politics can also organize gender through elite messages. We have already seen that elites' strategic choices about mobilization are related to the presence or absence of gender gaps in political participation. In addition, elite messages and mobilization strategies may influence voters' beliefs about gender and the existence of gender-based interests. If social beliefs about men and women are shaped by elite mobilization strategies, then those strategies may have more extensive and longer lasting effects than we originally thought. For example, we ordinarily consider gender to be exogenous to campaigns. However, if campaigns help to create the social meaning of gender, campaigns may have longer-lasting effects on the electorate—beyond the existence of gender differences within one election cycle. Likewise, the decisions of elites to *not* mobilize along gender lines may help to empty the category of gender—making it less likely that voters perceive men and women to be social groups with distinct interests.

These questions suggest the need for research on the content and effect of elite messages in order to determine if elections are creating and reproducing gender as a category. How do candidates view the electorate? Do elites seek to mobilize women or men on the basis of gender? On the basis of motherhood or fatherhood? Do they seek to mobilize women as a disadvantaged group? Do these messages and mobilization strategies affect the public's beliefs about men and women?

These questions about the construction of gender call for theoretical and empirical innovation. They also suggest that there is more endogeneity in the relationship between gender and politics than we originally thought. For example, any group-based response of women to women candidates may arise because of women's historic underrepresentation in American politics, rather than from a feeling of solidarity or identification that originates prior to or outside of politics. In sum, there is much to be gained by examining how and when politics organizes gender.

CONCLUSION

The role of gender in shaping political behavior is perhaps most obvious when we observe gender gaps at the aggregate level. Scholars have made considerable progress in identifying the ways that gender organizes American politics. We know that political factors can help explain when gender as a social category becomes relevant to elections and behavior. The gender composition of government institutions and the gender-based strategies of elites are important features of the political context in which voters and candidates act.

But politics may be more than a mere background factor influencing when gender becomes relevant. American elections and political behavior may give meaning to gender itself. Thinking about how politics constructs gender goes beyond the research agenda of studying the politicization of gender. Future research should consider whether politics is creating and reproducing gender rather than merely cueing it.

References

ACHEN, C. H. 1992. Social Psychology, Demographic Variables, and Linear Regression: Breaking the Iron Triangle in Voting Research. *Political Behavior*, 14/3: 195–211.

ACKER, J. 1992. Gendered Institutions: From Sex Roles to Gendered Institutions. *Contemporary Society*, 21: 565–9.

ANDERSEN, K. 1975. Working Women and Political Participation, 1952–1972. *American Journal of Political Science*, 19: 439–53.

—— 1996. *After Suffrage: Women in Partisan and Electoral Politics before the New Deal.* Chicago: University of Chicago Press.

—— and COOK, E. A. 1985. Women, Work, and Political Attitudes. *American Journal of Political Science*, 29: 606–25.

ATKESON, L. R. 2003. Not All Cues are Created Equal: The Conditional Impact of Female Candidates on Political Engagement. *Journal of Politics*, 65: 1040–61.

BECKWITH, K. 1986. *American Women and Political Participation: The Impacts of Work, Generation, and Feminism.* New York: Greenwood Press.

—— 2005. A Common Language of Gender? *Politics & Gender*, 1: 128–37.

BOX-STEFFENSMEIER, J. M., DEBOEF, S., and LIN, T.-M. 2004. The Dynamics of the Partisan Gender Gap. *American Political Science Review*, 98: 515–28.

BRIANS, C. L. 2005. Voting for Women? Gender and Party Bias in Voting for Female Candidates. *American Politics Research*, 33: 357–75.

BURNS, N. 2002. Gender: Public Opinion and Political Action. In *Political Science: The State of the Discipline*, ed. I. Katznelson and H. V. Milner. New York: W.W. Norton and Co.

—— 2005. Finding Gender. *Politics & Gender*, 1: 137–41.

—— 2007. Gender in the Aggregate, Gender in the Individual, Gender and Political Action. *Politics & Gender*, 3: 104–24.

—— SCHLOZMAN, K. L., and VERBA, S. 2001. *The Private Roots of Public Action: Gender, Equality, and Political Participation.* Cambridge, Mass.: Harvard University Press.

BURRELL, B. C. 1994. *A Woman's Place Is in the House: Campaigning for Congress in the Feminist Era.* Ann Arbor: University of Michigan Press.

CAMPBELL, A., CONVERSE, P. E., MILLER, W. E., and STOKES, D. E. 1960. *The American Voter.* New York: Wiley.

CAMPBELL, D. E. and WOLBRECHT, C. 2006. See Jane Run: Women Politicians as Role Models for Adolescents. *Journal of Politics*, 68: 233–47.

CARROLL, S. J. 1994. *Women as Candidates in American Politics*, 2nd edn. Bloomington, Ind.: Indiana University Press.

CARROLL, S. J. 1999. The Disempowerment of the Gender Gap: Soccer Moms and the 1996 Elections. *P.S.: Political Science and Politics*, 32: 7–11.

—— 2004. Women in State Government: Historical Overview and Current Trends. In *The Book of the States 2004*. Lexington, Ky.: Council of State Governments.

—— 2006a. Moms Who Swing, or Why the Promise of the Gender Gap Remains Unfulfilled. *Politics & Gender*, 2: 362–74.

—— 2006b. Voting Choices: Meet You at the Gender Gap. In *Gender and Elections: Shaping the Future of American Politics*, ed. S. J. Carroll and R. L. Fox. New York: Cambridge University Press.

—— and STRIMLING, W. S. 1983. *Women's Routes to Elective Office: A Comparison with Men's*. Center for the American Woman and Politics, Eagleton Institute of Politics. New Brunswick, N.J.: Rutgers University.

—— and ZERILLI, L. M. G. 1993. Feminist Challenges to Political Science. In *Political Science: The State of the Discipline II*, ed. A. W. Finifter. Washington, D.C.: American Political Science Association.

CAUL, M. and TATE, K. 2002. Thinner Ranks: Women as Candidates and California's Blanket Primary. In *Voting at the Political Fault Line: California's Experiment with the Blanket Primary*, ed. B. E. Cain and E. R. Gerber. Berkeley: University of California Press.

CAWP (CENTER FOR AMERICAN WOMEN AND POLITICS). 2004. Sex Differences in Voter Turnout. Fact sheet. National Information Bank on Women in Public Office, Eagleton Institute of Politics. New Brunswick, N.J.: Rutgers University.

—— 2009a. Statewide Elective Executive Women 2009. Fact sheet. National Information Bank on Women in Public Office, Eagleton Institute of Politics. New Brunswick, N.J.: Rutgers University.

—— 2009b. "Women in State Legislatures 2009." Fact sheet. National Information Bank on Women in Public Office, Eagleton Institute of Politics. New Brunswick, N.J.: Rutgers University.

—— 2009c. Women in the U.S. Congress 2009. Fact sheet. National Information Bank on Women in Public Office, Eagleton Institute of Politics. New Brunswick, N.J.: Rutgers University.

CLARK, J., DARCY, R., WELCH, S., and AMBROSIUS, M. 1984. Women as Legislative Candidates in Six States. In *Political Women: Current Roles in State and Local Government*, ed. J. A. Flammang. Beverly Hills, Calif.: Sage Publications.

CLEMENS, E. S. 1997. *The People's Lobby: Organizational Innovation and the Rise of Interest Group Politics in the United States, 1890–1925*. Chicago: University of Chicago Press.

"Clinton vs. Obama?" 2007. Press release. January 22, 2007. CBS News. <http://www.cbsnews.com/htdocs/pdf/012207_dems_poll.pdf>

COTT, N. F. 1987. *The Grounding of Modern Feminism*. New Haven, Conn.: Yale University Press.

DARCY R., HADLEY, C. D., and KIRKSEY, J. F. 1997. Election Systems and the Representation of Black Women in American State Legislatures. In *Women Transforming Politics: An Alternative Reader*, ed. C. J. Cohen, K. B. Jones, and J. C. Tronto. New York: New York University Press.

—— and SCHRAMM, S. S. 1977. When Women Run Against Men. *Public Opinion Quarterly*, 41: 1–12.

—— WELCH, S., and CLARK, J. 1994. *Women, Elections, and Representation*, 2nd edn. Lincoln: University of Nebraska Press.

DELLI CARPINI, M. X. and KEETER, S. 1993. Measuring Political Knowledge: Putting First Things First. *American Journal of Political Science*, 37: 1179–206.

——— ——— 1996. *What Americans Know About Politics and Why it Matters*. New Haven, Conn.: Yale University Press.

DIAMOND, I. 1977. *Sex Roles in the State House*. New Haven, Conn.: Yale University Press.

DOLAN, K. 2004. *Voting for Women: How the Public Evaluates Women Candidates*. Boulder, Colo.: Westview Press.

——— 2006. Symbolic Mobilization? The Impact of Candidate Sex in American Elections. *American Politics Research*, 34: 687–704.

——— 2008. Women as Candidates in American Politics: The Continuing Impact of Sex and Gender. In *Political Women and American Democracy*, ed. C. Wolbrecht, K. Beckwith, and L. Baldez. Cambridge: Cambridge University Press.

——— and FORD, L. E. 1997. Change and Continuity among Women State Legislators: Evidence from Three Decades. *Political Research Quarterly*, 50: 137–51.

DUERST-LAHTI, G. 2002. Knowing Congress as a Gendered Institution. In *Women Transforming Congress*, ed. C. S. Rosenthal. Norman, Okla.: University of Oklahoma Press.

——— 2006. Presidential Elections: Gendered Space and the Case of 2004. In *Gender and Elections: Shaping the Future of American Politics*, ed. S. J. Carroll and R. L. Fox. New York: Cambridge University Press.

EAGLY, A. H. 1987. *Sex Differences in Social Behavior: A Social-Role Interpretation*. Hillsdale, N.J.: Lawrence Erlbaum Associates.

EPSTEIN, C. F. 1988. *Deceptive Distinctions: Sex, Gender, and the Social Order*. New Haven, Conn.: Yale University Press.

EVANS, J. J. 2005. *Women, Partisanship, and the Congress*. New York: Palgrave MacMillan.

FOX, R. L. 2006. Congressional Elections: Where Are We on the Road to Gender Parity? In *Gender and Elections: Shaping the Future of American Politics*. ed. S. J. Carroll and R. L. Fox. New York: Cambridge University Press.

——— and OXLEY, Z. M. 2003. Gender Stereotyping in State Executive Elections: Candidate Selection and Success. *Journal of Politics*, 65: 833–50.

FREEMAN, J. 2000. *A Room at a Time: How Women Entered Party Politics*. Lanham, Md.: Rowman and Littlefield.

FULTON, S. A., MAESTAS, C. D., MAISEL, L. S., and STONE, W. J. 2006. The Sense of a Woman: Gender, Ambition, and the Decision to Run for Congress. *American Journal of Political Science*, 59: 235–48.

GERTZOG, I. N. 1995. *Congressional Women: Their Recruitment, Integration, and Behavior*, 2nd edn. Westport, Conn.: Praeger.

——— 2002. Women's Changing Pathways to the U.S. House of Representatives: Widows, Elites, and Strategic Politicians. In *Women Transforming Congress*, ed. C. S. Rosenthal. Norman, Okla.: University of Oklahoma Press.

GORDON, L. 1990. The New Feminist Scholarship on the Welfare State. In *Women, the State, and Welfare*, ed. L. Gordon. Madison: University of Wisconsin Press.

GOSS, K. and SKOCPOL, T. 2006. Changing Agendas: The Impact of Feminism on American Politics. In *Gender and Social Capital*, ed. B. O'Neill and E. Gidengil. New York: Routledge.

GURIN, P. 1985. Women's Gender Consciousness. *Public Opinion Quarterly*, 49/2: 143–63.

HANCOCK, A.-M. 2007. When Multiplication Doesn't Equal Quick Addition: Examining Intersectionality as a Research Paradigm. *Perspectives on Politics*, 5: 63–79.

HANSEN, S. 1997. Talking About Politics: Gender and Contextual Effects on Political Proselytizing. *Journal of Politics*, 59: 73–103.

HARDY-FANTA, C. (ed.) 2006. *Intersectionality and Politics: Research on Gender, Race, and Political Representation in the United States.* New York: Haworth Press.

HARVEY, A. L. 1998. *Votes Without Leverage: Women in American Electoral Politics, 1920–1970.* Cambridge: Cambridge University Press.

HAWKESWORTH, M. 2003. Congressional Enactments of Race-Gender: Toward a Theory of Raced-Gendered Institutions. *American Political Science Review*, 97: 529–50.

HUDDY, L, CASSESE E., and LIZOTTE, M.-K. 2008. Sources of Political Unity and Disunity among Women: Placing the Gender Gap in Perspective. In *Voting the Gender Gap*, ed. L. D. Whitaker. Champaign, Ill.: University of Illinois Press.

JONES, J. M. and MOORE, D. W. 2003. Generational Differences in Support for a Woman President. <http://www.gallup.com/poll/8656/Generational-Differences-Support-Woman-President.aspx> (accessed January 8, 2008).

KAUFMANN, K. M. 2002. Culture Wars, Secular Realignment, and the Gender Gap in Party Identification. *Political Behavior*, 24: 283–307.

—— and PETROCIK, J. 1999. The Changing Politics of American Men: Understanding the Sources of the Gender Gap. *American Journal of Political Science*, 43: 864–87.

KENNEY, S. J. 1996. New Research on Gendered Political Institutions. *Political Research Quarterly*, 49: 445–66.

KENSKI, H. C. 1988. The Gender Factor in a Changing Electorate. In *The Politics of the Gender Gap: The Social Construction of Political Influence*, ed. C. Mueller. Newbury Park, Calif.: Sage.

KIRKPATRICK, J. J. 1974. *Political Woman.* New York: Basic Books.

KLEIN, E. 1984. *Gender Politics.* Cambridge: Harvard University Press.

LAWLESS, J. L. 2004. Politics of Presence? Congresswomen and Symbolic Representation. *Political Research Quarterly*, 57: 81–99.

—— and FOX, R. L. 2005. *It Takes a Candidate: Why Women Don't Run for Office.* Cambridge: Cambridge University Press.

—— and PEARSON, K. 2008. The Primary Reason Women's Underrepresentation? Reevaluating the Conventional Wisdom. *Journal of Politics*, 70: 67–82.

LEONARD, S. T. and TRONTO, J. C. 2007. The Genders of Citizenship. *American Political Science Review*, 101: 33–46.

MANSBRIDGE, J. 1999. Should Blacks Represent Blacks and Women Represent Women? A Contingent "Yes." *Journal of Politics*, 61: 628–57.

McCONNAUGHY, C. M. 2004. The Politics of Suffrage Extension in the American States: Party, Race, and the Pursuit of Women's Voting Rights. Ph.D. Dissertation, University of Michigan.

—— 2007. Seeing Gender over the Short and Long Haul. *Politics & Gender*, 3: 378–86.

McDONAGH, E. 2002. Political Citizenship and Democratization: The Gender Paradox. *American Political Science Review*, 96: 535–52.

MILLER, A. H., GURIN, P., GURIN, G., and MALANCHUK, O. 1981. Group Consciousness and Political Participation. *American Journal of Political Science*, 25: 494–511.

MONDAK, J. J. and ANDERSON, M. R. 2004. The Knowledge Gap: A Reexamination of Gender-Based Differences in Political Knowledge. *Journal of Politics*, 66: 492–512.

MUELLER, C. 1988. The Empowerment of Women: Polling and the Women's Voting Bloc. In *The Politics of the Gender Gap: The Social Construction of Political Influence*, ed. C. Mueller. Newbury Park, Calif.: Sage.

NIVEN, D. 1998. *The Missing Majority: The Recruitment of Women as State Legislative Candidates*. Westport, Conn.: Praeger.

NORRANDER, B. 1997. The Independence Gap and the Gender Gap. *Public Opinion Quarterly*, 61: 464–76.

—— and WILCOX, C. 1998. The Geography of Gender Power: Women in State Legislatures. In *Women and Elective Office: Past, Present, & Future*, ed. S. Thomas and C. Wilcox. New York: Oxford University Press.

NORRIS, P. 2003. The Gender Gap: Old Challenges, New Approaches. In *Women and American Politics: New Questions, New Directions*, ed. S. J. Carroll. New York: Oxford University Press.

ONDERCIN, H. L. and BERNSTEIN, J. L. 2007. Context Matters: The Influence of State and Campaign Factors on the Gender Gap in Senate Elections, 1988–2000. *Politics & Gender*, 3: 33–53.

PALMER, B. and SIMON, D. 2006. *Breaking the Political Glass Ceiling: Women and Congressional Elections*. New York: Routledge.

PAOLINO, P. 1995. Group-Salient Issues and Group Representation: Support for Women Candidates in the 1992 Senate Elections. *American Journal of Political Science*, 39: 294–313.

PEARSON, K. and MCGHEE, E. 2004. Strategic Differences: The Gender Dynamics of Congressional Candidacies, 1982–2002. Paper presented at the American Political Science Association Annual meetings, Chicago.

PHILPOT, T. S. and WALTON, H., Jr. 2007. One of Our Own: Black Female Candidates and the Voters Who Support Them. *American Journal of Political Science*, 51: 49–62.

PLUTZER, E. and ZIPP, J. F. 1996. Identity Politics, Partisanship, and Voting for Women Candidates. *Public Opinion Quarterly*, 60: 30–57.

REINGOLD, B. 2000. *Representing Women: Sex, Gender, and Legislative Behavior in Arizona and California*. Chapel Hill, N.C.: University of North Carolina Press.

RITTER, G. 2006. *The Constitution as Social Design: Gender and Civic Membership in the American Constitutional Order*. Stanford, Calif.: Stanford University Press.

—— 2008. Gender as a Category of Political Analysis in American Political Development. In *Political Women and American Democracy*, ed. C. Wolbrecht, K. Beckwith, and L. Baldez. Cambridge: Cambridge University Press.

ROSENTHAL, C. S, (ed.) 2002. *Women Transforming Congress*. Norman, Okla.: University of Oklahoma Press.

RULE, W. 1981. Why Women Don't Run: The Critical Contextual Factors in Women's Legislative Recruitment. *Western Political Quarterly*, 34: 60–77.

—— 1990. Why More Women Are State Legislators: A Research Note. *Western Political Quarterly*, 43: 437–48.

SANBONMATSU, K. 2002. *Democrats, Republicans, and the Politics of Women's Place*. Ann Arbor: University of Michigan Press.

—— 2006a. Do Parties Know that "Women Win"? Party Leader Beliefs about Women's Electoral Chances. *Politics & Gender*, 2: 431–50.

—— 2006b. Gender Pools and Puzzles: Charting a "Women's Path" to the Legislature. *Politics & Gender*, 2: 387–400.

—— 2006c. State Elections: Where Do Women Run? Where Do Women Win? In *Gender and Elections: Shaping the Future of American Politics*, ed. S. J. Carroll and R. L. Fox. New York: Cambridge University Press.

SANBONMATSU, K. 2006d. *Where Women Run: Gender and Party in the American States*. Ann Arbor, Mich.: University of Michigan Press.

SAPIRO, V. 1981. Research Frontier Essay: When Are Interests Interesting? The Problem of Political Representation of Women. *American Political Science Review*, 75: 701–16.

—— and CONOVER, P. 1997. The Variable Gender Basis of Electoral Politics: Gender and Context in the 1992 US Election. *British Journal of Political Science*, 27: 497–523.

SCHAFFNER, B. F. 2005. Priming Gender: Campaigning on Women's Issues in U.S. Senate Elections. *American Journal of Political Science*, 49: 803–17.

SEARS, D. O. and HUDDY, L. 1990. On the Origins of Political Disunity Among Women. In *Women, Politics, and Change*, ed. P. Gurin and L. A. Tilly. New York: Russell Sage Foundation.

SELTZER, R. A., NEWMAN, J., and LEIGHTON, M. V. 1997. *Sex as a Political Variable: Women as Candidates & Voters in U.S. Elections*. Boulder, Colo: Lynne Rienner.

SHAPIRO, R. Y. and MAHAJAN, H. 1986. Gender Differences in Policy Preferences: A Summary of Trends From the 1960s to the 1980s. *Public Opinion Quarterly*, 50: 42–61.

SKOCPOL, T. 1992. *Protecting Soldiers and Mothers: The Political Origins of Social Policy in the United States*. Cambridge, Mass.: Harvard University Press.

SMOOTH, W. G. 2001. African American Women State Legislators: The Impact of Gender and Race on Legislative Influence. Ph.D. Dissertation, University of Maryland at College Park.

—— 2006. Intersectionality In Electoral Politics: A Mess Worth Making. *Politics & Gender*, 2: 400–14.

SPELMAN, E. V. 1988. *Inessential Woman: Problems of Exclusion in Feminist Thought*. Boston, Mass.: Beacon Press.

TATE, K. 1994. *From Protest to Politics: The New Black Voters in American Elections*, enlarged edn. Cambridge, Mass.: Harvard University Press.

THOMAS, S. 1994. *How Women Legislate*. New York: Oxford University Press.

VERBA, S., BURNS, N., and SCHLOZMAN, K. L. 1997. Knowing and Caring about Politics: Gender and Political Engagement. *Journal of Politics*, 59: 1051–72.

—— SCHLOZMAN, K. L., and BRADY, H. E. 1995. *Voice and Equality: Civic Voluntarism in American Politics*. Cambridge, Mass.: Harvard University Press.

WELCH, S. 1977. Women as Political Animals? A Test of Some Explanations for Male–Female Political Participation Differences. *American Journal of Political Science*, 21: 711–30.

WELDON, S. L. 2006. The Structure of Intersectionality: A Comparative Politics of Gender. *Politics & Gender*, 2: 235–48.

WERNER, E. E. 1968. Women in the State Legislatures. *Western Political Quarterly*, 19/1: 40–50.

WINTER, N. J. G. 2005. Framing Gender: Political Rhetoric, Gender Schemas, and Public Opinion on U.S. Health Care Reform. *Politics & Gender*, 1/3: 453–80.

WIRLS, D. 1986. Reinterpreting the Gender Gap. *Public Opinion Quarterly*, 50: 316–30.

WOLBRECHT, C. 2000. *The Politics of Women's Rights: Parties, Positions, and Change*. Princeton, N.J.: Princeton University Press.

CHAPTER 23

GAUGING THE GOD GAP

RELIGION AND VOTING IN US PRESIDENTIAL ELECTIONS

JOHN C. GREEN

EARLY in the 2004 presidential campaign, journalists discovered the impact of worship attendance on the presidential vote. As one story put it:

Want to know how Americans will vote next Election Day? Watch what they do the weekend before . . . If they attend religious services regularly, they probably will vote Republican by a 2-1 margin. If they never go, they likely will vote Democratic by a 2-1 margin.

(Thomma 2003)

This pattern was eventually dubbed the "God gap" and entered the political lexicon alongside the gender gap and the generation gap (Olson and Green 2008a). Indeed, coverage of the 2008 presidential election featured a fascination with the fate of the God gap, which changed only modestly (Pew Forum 2008).

Like many such terms, the God gap has its limitations—for example, more than nine of ten Americans regularly tell pollsters they believe in God, so general theistic belief is not likely to produce much of a gap in presidential voting. But the term also captures an important reality, namely, that worship attendance, along with other aspects of religion, matters at the ballot box, and it matters more in contemporary politics than in the past. This temporal feature is of special note, revealing that the political impact of worship attendance is not static but changeable (Olson and Green 2008b).

Over the last three decades, scholars have developed useful accounts of the role of religion in American politics (see Leege and Kellstedt 1993; Wald, Silverman, and Fridy 2005; Wald and Wilcox 2006) and these accounts can help in gauging the causes of the God gap. Worship attendance is typically understood as a measure of religious commitment (Kellstedt et al. 1996) and three strands of the literature identify a key factor that help explain the electoral impact of religious commitment: faith-based communal context, faith-based attitudes, and faith-based personal connections. These factors are not mutually exclusive and may often be complementary. On a practical note, worship attendance is among the most common religious practices in the American public, and as a consequence, it is regularly included in a wide variety of surveys. Worship attendance is thus a widely available measure of religiosity that can be used to address a variety of research questions.

Attendance Gaps and the Presidential Vote in 2004

The God gap is based largely on the association of worship attendance with presidential voting, and following the voting behavior literature, it can be thought of as a source of at least two "attendance" gaps: a "vote gap" in the candidate choice among voters and a "turnout gap" between voters and non-voters. It was the former that led to the discovery of the God gap, but the latter was implicit in the discovery. The relevance of these attendance gaps can be easily illustrated for the 2004 presidential election.

In terms of the vote gap, the 2004 National Election Pool (NEP) found a 28-percentage-point difference in the Republican vote of respondents who reported attending worship more than once a week (65 percent for Bush) and those who reported never attending worship (37 percent for Bush). Meanwhile, the 2004 National Survey of Religion and Politics (NSRP) found a 39-point vote gap by attendance and the 2004 National Election Study (NES) showed a 12-point gap. By way of comparison, the gender gap in vote choice was 8 percentage points in the 2004 NEP and 7 percentage points in the 2004 NES (with men casting more Republican votes than women).

In terms of the turnout gap, the 2004 NES found a 15-point difference in reported turnout between respondents that claimed to attend the most (87 percent) and least frequently (72 percent). And the 2004 NSRP found a 12-point turnout gap between the most and least frequent worship attenders. By way of comparison, gender produced a 3-point turnout gap in the 2004 NES and a 1-point gap in the 2004 NSRP (with men reporting lower turnout than women).

These differences in the size of the attendance gaps arise from factors inherent in survey research, such as sampling error, samples surveyed, and question wording. Some of the variation in the question wording reflects attempts to improve the accuracy of the reported worship attendance.[1] In fact, the accuracy of such measures has generated controversy. Some scholars argue that survey respondents regularly over-report their attendance at worship services (Hadaway, Marler, and Chaves 1993, 1998). Social desirability is the main culprit and in a fashion reminiscent of other socially approved behaviors, such as voter turnout (as can be seen in the reported NES turnout in the previous paragraph). Plausible non-survey evidence supports this argument, and moreover, attendance questions worded so as to minimize social desirability effects tend to produce lower levels of reported attendance (Wald, Kellstedt, and Leege 1993).

However, other observers have argued that survey estimates of worship attendance are reasonably accurate within the context of survey research, noting a great deal of consistency in such estimates in numerous surveys over many years (see Newport 2006a and 2006b). Reported worship attendance appears to have reached a high point in the 1950s and 1960s, and after a decline in the 1970s, has remained remarkably stable (Green and Dionne 2008; Smidt et al. 2008, 44–8). Indeed, even some advocates of the over-reporting of worship attendance agree that survey estimates of worship attendance have changed little over the last two decades, despite many other changes in American religion (Presser and Chaves 2007).

This debate suggests worship attendance estimates in top-line survey results should be interpreted with caution. However, this problem does not change the underlying relationship between reported worship attendance and reported voting: the attendance gaps appear in nearly all contemporary surveys, including those with different samples and differently worded attendance questions (as illustrated above). It also appears that the attendance gaps are not simply a product of other demographic factors related to voting behavior, such as income, education, age, or gender. Multivariate analyses of vote choice and turnout find that worship attendance has an independent impact when other demographic factors are controlled (Green and Olson 2008; Layman 1997; Timpone 1998).

---

[1] The NEP used a single five-point attendance scale, while the NSRP used a single six-point scale and the NES used a multipart measure of attendance.

Attendance Gaps and the Presidential Vote, 1952–2004

The attendance gaps appear to have increased in size toward the end of the twentieth century. Figure 23.1 shows the vote and turnout gaps from 1952 to 2004 using the NES Cumulative File. Because of wording changes in the attendance questions, the figure reports the gaps as the difference in the Republican portion of the two-party vote and the level of turnout between "regular" and "less regular" worship attenders; the percentage of regular worship attenders is plotted as a point of reference.[2]

The vote gap has a clear pattern in Figure 23.1 (solid line), rising substantially over the period. In the 1950s and 1960s, the vote gap was very modest and often negative (meaning that regular attenders on balance voted Democratic), but in 1972, it moved dramatically in a positive direction (with regular attenders voting on balance Republican). After 1972, the vote gap remained positive but fluctuated in

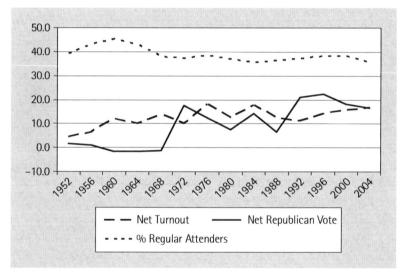

Figure 23.1 The attendance gaps, 1952–2004. Vote choice and turnout by regular worship attenders

Source: NES Cumulative File, 1952–2004

[2] From 1952 to 1968, NES asked a four-point attendance question; from 1970 to 1988 it asked a six-part question; and from 1990 on, a multipart question was asked. This series was combined to produce a dichotomous measure of "regular" and "less regular" attenders; see Fiorina et al. (2005) for a similar treatment of these items.

size. The 1990s witnessed another surge in the vote gap before it declined in 2000 and 2004, essentially returning to the 1972 level.

The turnout gap (dashed line in Figure 23.1) was positive throughout the entire period (meaning that regular worship attenders had higher turnout) and also increased over time. In the 1950s and 1960s, the turnout gap was larger than the vote gap, and although it fell below the vote gap in 1972, it regained the upper hand until 1988. Beginning in 1992, the turnout gap was again smaller than the vote gap, but began a steady increase, so that by 2004 the turnout and vote gaps were essentially equal in size.

These patterns over time suggest that while worship attendance always had an effect on turnout, its effect on vote choice changed circa 1972. This suggestion is supported by the general stability of the frequency of worship attendance since 1952 (the dotted line in Figure 23.1). Thus the expansion of the attendance gaps is unlikely to have been caused by changes in the overall level of reported attendance: rather, they appear to have been contingent on political factors. The flux of presidential politics is no doubt central to these contingencies (Kohut et al. 2000; Layman 2001; Leege et al. 2002). However, three strands of the literature help explain how worship attendance can be politicized: through religious traditions, religious beliefs, and religious engagement.

ATTENDANCE GAPS AND RELIGIOUS TRADITIONS

One strand of the literature sees worship attendance as a source of exposure to the political ethos of a particular religious community. After all, worship attendance typically occurs in a particular place and the characteristics of the place could influence the politics of attenders, directly or indirectly. The starkest version of this perspective draws an analogy to drug therapy, where a religious community is a particular "treatment" employed and worship attendance is the "dosage" administered (Kellstedt et al. 1996; Mockabee, Monson, and Grant 2001). More frequent attenders are likely to be exposed to a larger "dose" of a religious "treatment" than their less observant co-religionists, thus generating the attendance gaps.

Here the basic insight is that faith-based communal contexts can help politicized worship attendance. Drawing on the contextual effects literature (Huckfeldt, Plutzer, and Sprague 1993), scholars have studied in a variety of faith-based communal contexts, including local congregations (Wald, Owen, and Hill 1988), personal friendship networks (Gilbert 1993), and religious traditions (Jelen 1992; Kellstedt and Green 1993). Religious tradition has received the most attention in studies of presidential voting, largely because this broad measure is most useful in national surveys.

Defined in part by denominational affiliation, ethnicity, and race (see Green 2007, ch. 2), religious traditions provided the primary linkage between faith and the presidential vote throughout American history. Indeed, American party coalitions have been in part alliances of religious traditions, with some identifying with the Democrats, others with first the Whigs and then the Republicans, and still others more divided between the major parties and/or less interested in party politics (for a good summary of the historical literature see McCormick 1974). The major party coalitions of the New Deal era are good examples of these patterns, with the Democratic coalition including Catholics, Jews, Evangelical and Black Protestants, while the Republican coalition was made up of various kinds of white Mainline Protestants (Kellstedt et al. 2007). Religious traditions have continued to be part of party coalitions in the late twentieth and early twenty-first centuries (see Espinosa 2008 for a detailed look at religious traditions and contemporary presidential politics).

In terms of the vote gap, this perspective suggests that frequent attenders would be most likely to apply the partisanship of their religious tradition to their presidential vote choice, with some traditions tending to vote Republican and others tending to vote Democratic. And in terms of the turnout gap, frequent attenders would be most likely to reflect the partisan intensity of their religious tradition, with the members of the most partisan religious traditions more likely to cast ballots than others. In both cases, less frequent attenders would be less likely to display these patterns.

There is certainly strong evidence that religious tradition influences presidential voting (see Wilson 2007 and Campbell 2007 for recent evidence). The "affiliation" gap in vote choice is often larger than the difference in vote choice between the most and least frequent worship attenders—for instance, in the 2004 NEP, the difference in the Bush vote between Evangelical Protestants and Jews was over 50 percentage points, almost twice as large as the difference in the Bush vote between the most and least frequent attenders. There is also some evidence that the attendance gaps reinforced the partisan profile of religious traditions (especially before 1972) and that the attendance gaps vary in size by religious traditions and across elections (Green 2007). But by the end of the twentieth century, frequent attenders voted more Republican and more often than their less observant co-religionists in nearly all religious traditions (Kohut et al. 2000). This pattern suggests that communal context is not the only factor at work in the attendance gaps.

ATTENDANCE GAPS AND RELIGIOUS BELIEFS

Another strand of the literature sees worship attendance as associated with particular faith-based attitudes that are relevant to politics. After all, worship attendance is mandated by the religious beliefs in the largest religious communities in the

United States and such beliefs could influence the politics of attenders, either directly or indirectly. A stark example of this perspective posits a sharp divide between individuals who accept traditional moral authority, based in the revealed will of God, and individuals who accept less traditional forms of moral authority, based in human knowledge and experience (Himmelfarb 2001). Frequent worship attenders would be more likely to hold such faith-based attitudes than the less observant, thus generating the attendance gaps.

The basic insight of this strand of the literature is that faith-based attitudes can help politicize worship attendance. Drawing on the public opinion literature, scholars have investigated a range of such attitudes, including specific religious doctrines (Kellstedt and Smidt 1993), pre-policy values (Baker 2005), and issue positions (Norrander and Wilcox 2002). Some religious beliefs, such as views of the Bible and belief in God, have received considerable attention in studies of the presidential vote, largely because of their wide availability in surveys. A variety of values and issue positions thought to be related to religious beliefs have been investigated as well (Layman and Green 2005).

Beginning in the 1970s, scholars noted a major change in American faith-based politics, with religious beliefs and practices exercising influence on presidential voting apart from religious tradition. Commonly known as the "restructuring" of American religion (Wuthnow 1988), this change was associated with the rise of the "culture wars" in national politics (Hunter 1991). One effect of these new patterns was to alter the religious components of the major party coalitions: more traditional elements of the Democratic constituencies (such as Evangelical Protestants and Catholics) moved toward the GOP, while less traditional elements of the Republican coalition (such as Mainline Protestants) moved in a Democratic direction. These trends continued into the twenty-first century (Guth et al. 2006b).

In terms of the vote gap, this perspective suggests that frequent worship attenders would favor Republican presidential candidates because of their traditional attitudes, while the less observant would favor the Democrat candidates because of less traditional attitudes. The expectation is less clear with regard to the turnout gap. Such traditional attitudes might motivate a higher level of voting, but the absence of such attitudes is unlikely to discourage voting. In fact, the relationship could be just the opposite: traditional attitudes could discourage turnout due to a focus on otherworldly concerns, while less traditional attitudes could encourage such worldly activities (Wuthnow 1973).

There is considerable evidence that traditional religious beliefs influence the presidential vote and that worship attendance is highly correlated with such beliefs (Green 2007, 61; Green et al. 2007). Much of the evidence on vote gap fits well with this perspective, including the Republican bias of attenders across religious traditions in 2004 and the growth in the vote gap since 1972. However, traditional beliefs are not strongly associated with turnout, especially when other variables are taken into account. These patterns suggest that still other factors are at work in the attendance gaps.

ATTENDANCE GAPS AND RELIGIOUS ENGAGEMENT

Yet another strand of the literature sees worship attendance as a locus of personal connections among co-religionists that encourage political activity. After all, worship attendance typically occurs in an institutional setting that offers numerous opportunities for engagement with fellow adherents and this engagement can help politicize attenders, directly or indirectly. A stark version of this perspective imagines that such results are by-products of religious engagement that spills over into political life (see Djupe and Gilbert 2008; Peterson 1992).

This perspective resembles the effects of faith-based communal context but without the emphasis on a particular religious tradition; it also resembles the effects of faith-based attitudes but without the emphasis on particular faith-based attitudes. Instead, this approach sees religious engagement as a social expression of faith found in many, if not all, religious traditions, and also associated with a variety of beliefs and related attitudes (see Smidt et al. 2008). In any event, frequent worship attenders would be more likely to experience higher levels of such connections than the less observant, thus generating the attendance gaps.

The basic insight of this strand of the literature is that religious engagement is a source of faith-based personal connections that can help politicize worship attendance. The literatures on social capital (Putnam 2000, ch. 4), political participation (Verba, Schlozman, and Brady 1995, ch. 11), and group identity (Calhoun-Brown 1996; Jamal 2005; Jones-Correa and Leal 2001) have found a strong association between worship attendance and a wide variety of personal connections. As a consequence of these connections, individuals acquire social trust, civic skills, and/or strong group identities, all of which can foster civic engagement, including political activity (Cassel 1999; Djupe and Grant 2001; Wuthnow 1999). However, students of voting behavior have been most interested in instrumental efforts to capitalize on the faith-based personal connections of potential voters (Kohut et al. 2000, chs. 5, 6).

Presidential campaigns have long sought to mobilize bias and participation among religiously engaged citizens, especially those closely allied with their political parties, and these efforts have often been aided by allies within these religious communities (Reichley 1985). Perhaps the best known are the activities of Christian Right groups, such as the Moral Majority and Christian Coalition, to register and turn out Evangelical Protestant voters on behalf of Republican candidates (Wilcox and Larson 2006). However, such electoral activities have hardly been limited to the right: religious liberals and progressives have a long history of similar efforts, especially among Mainline Protestants (Wuthnow and Evans 2002) and Catholics (Steinfels 2004), while minority religious communities, such as Black Protestants (Harris 1999) and Jews (Maisel and Forman 2001) have developed special styles of politics. Such organized efforts to mobilize religiously engaged voters have been aided by a wide range of less formal campaign contacts within religious communities, including messages from the clergy and discussion among the laity (Djupe and Neiheisel 2008). In the 2004 presidential campaign, a wide range of religious groups were active in these regards across religious traditions (Green 2007, ch. 7).

In terms of the vote gap, this perspective suggests that frequent attenders with the most net campaign contacts by or on behalf of the Republican candidate would be most likely to vote Republican, while those with the most net campaign contacts by or on behalf of the Democratic candidate would be most likely to vote Democratic. In terms of the turnout gap, frequent attenders would be the most likely to cast a ballot due to higher volume of such contacts. In both cases, the less observant would be less likely to exhibit these patterns because of fewer contacts of all kinds.

There is evidence that faith-based campaign contacts influence presidential voting, with the strongest support coming from special surveys that asked about a full range of contacts in the context of a presidential campaign (Guth et al. 1998, 2002, 2006a). These studies found that the net political bias of faith-based contacts was associated with the vote gap and that the volume of contacts was associated with the turnout gap. Additional studies point to the sources of these contacts among the religiously engaged, including the parish clergy (Guth et al. 1997), religious activists (Guth et al. 1994), and party elites (Layman 2001) as well as evidence that the laity is aware of, and responds to, such contacts (Welch et al. 1993). This evidence also fits with the fact that the turnout gap was positive back into the 1950s.

Decomposing the Attendance Gaps, 2004

Figures 23.2 and 23.3 illustrate the relative importance of the key factors identified by the three strands of literature to help account for the vote and turnout gaps. These figures are the product of very simple models of vote choice and turnout using the 2004 NRSP (Pew Forum 2004). Each of the attendance gaps is modeled as the result of standard demographic variables and four religion measures: religious tradition (to measure faith-based communal context), belief in God (to measure faith-based attitudes), reported campaign contacts (to measure one kind of faith-based personal connection), and of course, worship attendance.[3]

Figure 23.2 plots the Republican presidential vote by worship attendance under four conditions. The first graph (solid line) controls for other demographic factors (by setting all the demographic variables at their mean scores). The Republican vote continues to rise from the least to the most frequent attenders, showing that standard demographic controls do not eliminate the vote gap (as mentioned previously); these demographic controls appear in all the succeeding graphs. The second graph in Figure 23.2 (dashed line) removes the impact of reported campaign contacts on the vote gap (by setting the value of the contact variable at zero), measured as the net political bias of reported campaign contacts. As one can see,

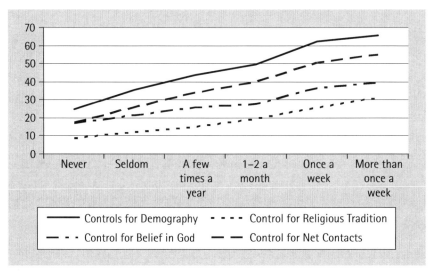

Figure 23.2 Decomposing the vote gap, 2004. Probability of Republican vote by worship attendance

Source: Fourth National Survey of Religion and Politics, 2004 (N=1660)

---

[3] Both models used binary logistic regression. For the vote gap model, GOP presidential vote coded as 1 and the Democratic vote as 0; for the turnout gap model, casting a ballot was coded as 1 and no vote as 0. All of the independent variables were coded to range between 0 and 1. Both models included income, education, gender, age, region, and marital status measured in a standard fashion. In both models, religious tradition was measured in the standard fashion but coded from the most Democratic tradition (black Protestants) to the most Republican (white Evangelical Protestants). In both models, belief in God was a five-point composite measure ranging from no belief in God to certain belief in a personal God. Faith-based contacts were based on a battery of nine kinds of contacts, including messages from the clergy, talk among the laity, and contacts from faith-based religious groups on the right and left. For the vote gap model, this battery was coded from reported net Democratic to net Republican contacts, and for the turnout gap model, these contacts were summed. The vote gap model predicted 70 percent of the cases correctly and the turnout gap predicted 75 percent of the cases correctly. Further details are available from the author.

the level of Republican vote drops—but it drops across every level of attendance, so that the vote gap persists once the impact of the political bias of the campaign contacts is taken into account.

The third graph in Figure 23.2 (dotted and dashed line) removes the impact of belief in God on vote choice (by setting its value at zero), a measure that ranges from no belief in God to certain belief in a personal God. Here, too, the level of Republican vote drops—but it also drops across every level of attendance. Thus the vote gap remains even when the effect of belief in God is taken into account. The fourth and final graph (dotted line) removes the impact of religious tradition on the vote gap (also by setting its value at zero); the religious traditions are coded in order of partisanship, reflecting the notion that worship attendance exposes individuals to the partisan context of these religious communities. And as before, the Republican vote drops across the levels of attendance—and the vote gap persists even when the effects of communal context are taken into account.

Figure 23.2 reveals that measures of faith-based communal context, faith-based attitudes, and faith-based connections were each associated with the impact of worship attendance on the 2004 presidential vote (in this order). Interestingly, these three factors do not completely eliminate the vote gap in these data when their effects are combined—worship attendance continues to exercise an independent effect on the vote gap. This result could reflect the limitations of the simple models estimated,[4] but it could also reveal a residual impact of the turnout gap on the vote gap.

Figure 23.3 plots the level of reported turnout by worship attendance under three conditions. As in Figure 23.2, the first graph (solid line) controls for other demographic factors (by setting all these variables at their mean scores). Here, too, standard demographic controls do not eliminate the turnout gap (also as noted previously). The second graph in Figure 23.3 (dotted line) removes the impact of religious tradition (by setting its value at zero). As with the vote gap, this graph reduces the level of turnout across the levels of attendance, but the turnout gap remains. The third and final graph removes the impact of campaign contacts (by setting its value at zero), measured here by the total number of contacts reported. This graph essentially eliminates the turnout gap, producing a nearly constant prediction of turnout across the frequency of worship attendance. Interestingly, belief in God was not related to turnout in this model (and hence no graph is shown). Thus in these data, the effect of faith-based contacts has the most important influence on the impact of attendance on the vote, followed by the effects of faith-based communal context.

---

[4] As one would expect, including political attitudes in these simple models improves their overall power. However, the inclusion of attitudes does not alter the basic results reported here, although it does obscure the relationship between worship attendance and the other religious variables.

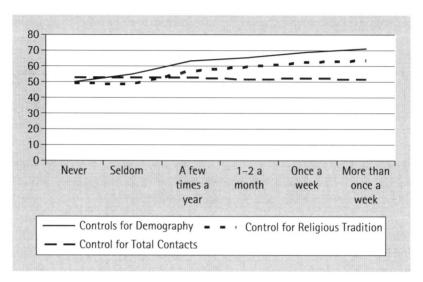

Figure 23.3 Decomposing the turnout gap, 2004. Probability of voting by worship attendance

Source: Fourth National Survey of Religion and Politics, 2004 (N=1660)

GAUGING THE GOD GAP

The God gap discovered by journalists in 2004 captures an important feature of contemporary politics: the impact of worship attendance on presidential voting both in terms of vote choice and turnout. Despite measurement problems common in survey research, the attendance gaps appear to be real, more important than in the past, and independent of basic demography. The attendance gaps are not, however, independent of other religious factors. In part, the vote and turnout gaps reflect the impact of the faith-based communal context of attenders, where the political ethos of religious traditions helps politicize attendance. And in part the vote gap (but not the turnout gap) reflects the impact of faith-based attitudes of attenders, where traditional beliefs help politicize worship attendance (including belief in God—revealing that journalistic intuition was not entirely off the mark when coining the "God gap" terminology). Finally, the vote and especially the turnout gaps reflect the faith-based personal connections of attenders, with campaign contacts helping to politicize worship attendance.

What are the implications of these findings for future research? First, frequency of worship attendance is a good general measure of religiosity. Religion is a complex phenomenon and worship attendance is a useful measure for simplifying its impact. Thus it can be used with confidence in a wide variety of models when controls for religiosity are called for, including models of vote choice, turnout, and electorally relevant attitudes or activities. Put another way, the God gap is a useful gauge in assessing the findings of the literature.

The God gap also suggests new avenues of future research on religion and politics. For example, there is a need for a fuller exploration of the faith-based communal contexts that can help politicize worship attendance. Case studies of congregations are needed to fully understand the local variation in religious contexts, even within the same denomination. Such studies could be conducted with survey methodologies, but there is much to be gained from other approaches, such as participant-observer, interviews, and ethnographic studies. Along these lines, studies of denominations, as a whole or in organizational units, and para-church organizations are needed as well. On this score, there is much work to be done because of the vast number and variety of denominations in the United States. It is worth understanding the ethos of these faith-based communal contexts in their own right, but such knowledge can help improve survey research as well.

Another area for future research is religious beliefs. Overall, most surveys of the mass public have asked only a few belief questions, and most of these have been general measures with the potential to reach across religious traditions. A good example is standard items on the authority of religious scriptures, most typically asked about the "Bible." These items are quite useful in studying voting behavior, but do not begin to cover the full range of general religious beliefs in the American public. In addition, many denominations have their own particular beliefs that may matter politically, allowing researchers to better understand their special brands of political action. And religious beliefs are not the only faith-based attitudes that can matter in elections. Additional research is needed into how and when such beliefs are associated with values and issue positions that are directly relevant to electoral choice. As with faith-based communal contexts, it is worth knowing more about faith-based attitudes for its own sake, but such knowledge can improve survey research and studies of voting behavior as well.

More research is also needed on faith-based religious engagement. An inventory of the many kinds of faith-based connections is in order. How are they distributed across religious traditions and how are they related to religious beliefs? How do the different kinds of personal connections relate to political choices, and further-more, how do these kinds of connections fit together? Do some combine in a reinforcing manner to impact the vote or do some kinds cancel each other out? How do candidates and religious activists understand religious engagement and how is this knowledge worked into their campaign strategies and tactics? All of these questions are worth answering in any event, but they could also improve survey research and studies of voting behavior.

REFERENCES

BAKER, W. 2005. *America's Crisis of Values*. Princeton, N.J.: Princeton University Press.

CALHOUN-BROWN, A. 1996. African American Churches and Political Mobilization: The Psychological Impact of Organizational Resources. *Journal of Politics*, 58: 935–53.

CAMPBELL, D. E. (ed.) 2007. *A Matter of Faith: Religion in the 2004 Presidential Election*. Washington, D.C.: Brookings Institution Press.

CASSEL, C. A. 1999. Voluntary Associations, Churches, and Social Participation Theories of Turnout. *Social Science Quarterly*, 80: 504–17.

DJUPE, P. A. and GILBERT, C. 2008. Politics and Church: By-Product or Central Mission? *Journal for the Scientific Study of Religion*, 47: 45–62.

—— and GRANT, J. T. 2001. Religious Institutions and Political Participation. *Journal for the Scientific Study of Religion*, 40: 303–14.

—— and NEIHEISEL, J. R. 2008. Christian Right Horticulture: Grassroots Support in a Republican Primary Campaign. *Politics and Religion*, 1: 55–85.

ESPINOSA, G. (ed.) 2008. *Religion, Race and the American Presidency*. Lanham, Md.: Rowman & Littlefield.

FIORINA, M., with ABRAMS, S. J., and POPE, J. C. 2005. *Culture War? The Myth of a Polarized America*. New York: Pearson Longman.

GILBERT, C. P. 1993. *The Impact of Churches on Political Behavior: An Empirical Study*. Westport, Conn.: Greenwood.

GREEN, J. C. 2007. *The Faith Factor: How Religion Influences the Vote*. Westport, Conn.: Praeger Press.

GREEN, J. C. and DIONNE, E. J. 2008. Religion and American Politics: More Secular, More Evangelical or Both? In *Red, Blue & Purple American: The Future of Election Demographics*, ed. R. Teixeira. Washington, D.C.: Brookings Institution Press.

—— and OLSON, L. R. 2008. "Gapology" and the 2004 Presidential Vote. In *Beyond Red State and Blue State*, ed. L. R. Olson and J. C. Green. Upper Saddle River, N.J.: Prentice Hall.

—— KELLSTEDT, L. A., SMIDT, C. E., and GUTH, J. L. 2007. How the Faithful Voted: Religious Communities and the Presidential Vote. In *A Matter of Faith: Religion in the 2004 Presidential Election*, ed. D. E. Campbell. Washington, D.C.: Brookings Institution Press.

GUTH, J. L., GREEN, J. C., KELLSTEDT, L., and SMIDT, C. E. 1994. Onward Christian Soldiers: Religious Interest Group Activists. In *Interest Group Politics*, 4th edn., ed. A. Cigler and B. Loomis. Washington, D.C.: CQ Press.

—— —— SMIDT, C. E., KELLSTEDT, L. A., and POLOMA, M. 1997. *The Bully Pulpit: The Politics of Protestant Clergy*. Lawrence, Kans.: University Press of Kansas.

—— KELLSTEDT, L. A., SMIDT, C. E., and GREEN, J. C. 1998. Thunder on the Right? Religious Interest Group Mobilization in the 1996 Election. In *Interest Group Politics*, 5th edn., ed. A. J. Cigler and B. A. Loomis. Washington, D.C.: CQ Press.

—— —— GREEN, J. C., and SMIDT, C. E. 2002. A Distant Thunder? Religious Mobilization in the 2000 Elections. In *Interest Group Politics*, 6th edn., ed. A. J. Cigler and B. A. Loomis. Washington, D.C.: CQ Press.

—— —— —— —— 2006a. Getting the Spirit? Religious and Partisan Mobilization in the 2004 Elections. In *Interest Group Politics*, 7th edn., ed. A. J. Cigler and B. A. Loomis. Washington, D.C.: CQ Press.

—— —— SMIDT, C. E., and GREEN, J. C. 2006b. Religious Influences in the 2004 Presidential Election. *Presidential Studies Quarterly*, 36: 223–42.

HADAWAY, C. K., MARLER, P. L., and CHAVES, M. 1993. What the Polls Don't Show: A Closer Look at U.S. Church Attendance. *American Sociological Review*, 58: 741–52.

—— —— —— 1998. Over-reporting Church Attendance in America: Evidence that Demands the Same Verdict. *American Sociological Review*, 63: 122–30.

HARRIS, F. C. 1999. *Something Within: Religion in African-American Political Activism*. Oxford: Oxford University Press.

HIMMELFARB, G. 2001. *One Nation, Two Cultures*. New York: Vintage Books.

HUCKFELDT, R., PLUTZER, E., and SPRAGUE, J. 1993. Alternative Contexts for Political Behavior: Churches, Neighborhoods, and Individuals. *Journal of Politics*, 55: 365–81.

HUNTER, J. 1991. *Culture Wars: The Struggle to Define America*. New York: Basic Books.

JAMAL, A. 2005. The Political Participation and Engagement of Muslim Americans: Mosque Involvement and Group Consciousness. *American Politics Quarterly*, 33: 521–44.

JELEN, T. G. 1992. Political Christianity: A Contextual Analysis. *American Journal of Political Science*, 36: 692–714.

JONES-CORREA, M. A. and LEAL, D. L. 2001. Political Participation: Does Religion Matter? *Political Research Quarterly*, 54: 751–70.

KELLSTEDT, L. A. and GREEN, J. C. 1993. Knowing God's Many People: Denominational Preference and Political Behavior. In *Rediscovering the Religious Factor in American Politics*, ed. D. C. Leege and L. A. Kellstedt. Armonk, N.Y.: M.E. Sharpe.

—— and SMIDT, C. E. 1993. Doctrinal Beliefs and Political Behavior: Views of the Bible. In *Rediscovering the Religious Factor in American Politics*, ed. D. C. Leege and L. A. Kellstedt. Armonk, N.Y.: M.E. Sharpe.

—— GREEN, J. C., GUTH, J. L., and SMIDT, C. E. 1996. Grasping the Essentials: The Social Embodiment of Religion and Political Behavior. In *Religion and the Culture Wars*, ed. J. C. Green, J. L. Guth, C. E. Smidt, and L. A. Kellstedt. Lanham, Md.: Rowman & Littlefield.

—— —— —— —— 2007. Faith Transformed: Religion and American Politics from FDR to George W. Bush. In *Religion and American Politics: From the Colonial Period to the Present*, 2nd edn., ed. M. A. Noll and L. E. Harlow. Oxford: Oxford University Press.

KOHUT, A., GREEN, J. C., KEETER, S., and TOTH, R. 2000. *The Diminishing Divide: Religion's Changing Role in American Politics*. Washington, D.C.: Brookings Institution Press.

LAYMAN, G. C. 1997. Religion and Political Behavior in the United States: The Impact of Beliefs, Affiliation, and Commitment from 1980 to 1994. *Public Opinion Quarterly*, 61: 288–316.

—— 2001. *The Great Divide: Religious and Cultural Conflict in American Party Politics*. New York: Columbia University Press.

—— and GREEN, J. C. 2005. Wars and Rumors of Wars: The Contexts of Cultural Conflict in American Political Behavior. *British Journal of Political Science*, 36: 61–89.

LEEGE, D. C. and KELLSTEDT, L. A. (ed.) 1993. *Rediscovering the Religious Factor in American Politics*. Armonk, N.Y.: M.E. Sharpe.

—— WALD, K. D., MUELLER, P. D., and KRUEGER, B. S. 2002. *The Politics of Cultural Differences: Social Change and Voter Mobilization Strategies in the Post-New Deal Period*. Princeton, N.J.: Princeton University Press.

MAISEL, L. S. and FORMAN, I. 2001. *Jews in American Politics*. Lanham, Md.: Rowman & Littlefield.

McCormick, R. L. 1974. Ethno-Cultural Interpretations of Nineteen-Century American Voting Behavior. *Political Science Quarterly*, 89: 351–77.

Mockabee, S. T., Monson, J. Q., and Grant, J. T. 2001. Measuring Religious Commitment among Protestants and Catholics: A New Approach. *Journal for the Scientific Study of Religion*, 40:675–90.

Newport, F. 2006a. Estimating Americans Worship Behavior Part I. <http://poll.gallup.com/content/default.aspx?ci=20701&pg=1> (accessed August 2006).

—— 2006b. Estimating Americans Worship Behavior Part II. <http://poll.gallup.com/content/default.aspx?ci=20701&pg=1> (accessed August 2006).

Norrander, B. and Wilcox, C. (eds.) 2002. *Understanding Public Opinion*. Washington, D.C.: CQ Press.

Olson, L. R. and Green, J. C. (eds.) 2008a. *Beyond Red State and Blue State: Electoral Gaps in the Twenty-First Century American Electorate*. Upper Saddle River, N.J.: Prentice Hall.

—— —— 2008b. The Worship Attendance Gap. In *Beyond Red and Blue State*, ed. L. R. Olson and J. C. Green. Upper Saddle River, N.J.: Prentice Hall.

Peterson, S. A. 1992. Church Participation and Political Participation: The Spillover Effect. *American Politics Quarterly*, 20: 123–39.

Pew Forum on Religion and Public Life. 2004. Religion and the 2004 Election: A Post-Election Analysis. <http://pewforum.org/docs/?DocID=64> (accessed November 2008).

—— 2008. How the Faithful Voted. <http://pewforum.org/docs/?DocID=367#1> (accessed November 2008).

Presser, S. and Chaves, M. 2007. Is Religious Service Attendance Declining? *Journal for the Scientific Study of Religion*, 46: 417–23.

Putnam, R. D. 2000. *Bowling Alone: The Collapse and Revival of American Community*. New York: Simon and Schuster.

Reichley, A. J. 1985. *Religion in American Public Life*. Washington, D.C.: Brookings Institution Press.

Smidt, C. E., den Dulk, K. R., Penning, J. M., Monsma, S. V., and Koopman, D. L. 2008. *Pews, Prayers, and Participation: Religion & Civic Responsibility in America*. Washington, D.C.: Georgetown University Press.

Steinfels, P. 2004. *A People Adrift: The Crisis of the Roman Catholic Church in America*. New York: Simon and Schuster.

Thomma, S. 2003. Americans' Religious Practices Serve As Gauge of Political Choice. *Philadelphia Inquirer*, December 2.

Timpone, R. J. 1998. Structure, Behavior, and Voter Turnout in the United States. *American Political Science Review*, 92: 145–98.

Verba, S., Schlozman, K. L., and Brady, H. E. 1995. *Voice and Equality: Civic Voluntarism in American Politics*. Cambridge, Mass.: Harvard University Press.

Wald, K. D., Kellstedt, L. A., and Leege, D. C. 1993. Church Involvement and Political Behavior. In *Rediscovering the Impact of Religion on Political Behavior*, ed. D. C. Leege and L. A. Kellstedt. Armonk, N.Y.: M.E. Sharpe.

—— Owen, D. E., and Hill, S. S., Jr. 1988. Churches as Political Communities. *American Political Science Review*, 82: 531–48.

—— Silverman, A. L., and Fridy, K. S. 2005. Making Sense of Religion in Political Life. *Annual Review of Political Science*, 8: 121–43.

—— and Wilcox, C. 2006. Getting Religion: Has Political Science Rediscovered the Faith Factor? *American Political Science Review*, 100: 523–29.

WELCH, M. D., LEEGE, D. C., WALD, K. D., and KELLSTEDT, L. A. 1993. Are the Sheep Hearing the Shepherds? Cue Perception, Congregational Response, and Political Communication Processes. In *Rediscovering the Impact of Religion on Political Behavior*, ed. D. C. Leege and L. A. Kellstedt. Armonk, N.Y.: M.E. Sharpe.

WILCOX, C. and LARSON, C. 2006. *Onward Christian Soldiers? The Religious Right in American Politics*, 3rd edn. Boulder, Colo.: Westview.

WILSON, J. M. 2007. *From Pews to Polling Places: Faith and Politics in the American Mosaic*. Washington, D.C.: Georgetown University Press.

WUTHNOW, R. 1973. Religious Commitment and Conservatism: In Quest of an Elusive Relationship. In *Religion in Sociological Perspective*, ed. C. Y. Glock. Belmont, Calif.: Wadsworth.

—— 1988. *The Restructuring of American Religion*. Princeton, N.J.: Princeton University Press.

—— 1999. Mobilizing Civic Engagement: The Changing Impact of Religious Involvement. In *Civic Engagement in American Democracy*, ed. T. Skocpol and M. Fiorina. Washington, D.C.: Brookings Institution Press/Russell Sage Foundation.

—— and EVANS, J. H. (eds.) 2002. *The Quiet Hand of God: Faith-based Activism and the Public Role of Mainline Protestantism*. Berkeley, Calif.: University of California Press.

PART VI

ELECTIONS OTHER THAN PRESIDENTIAL

....

CHAPTER 24

LOCAL AND NATIONAL FORCES IN CONGRESSIONAL ELECTIONS

....

BARRY C. BURDEN
AMBER WICHOWSKY

RESEARCHERS have gleaned important insights about voter decision making, the role of partisanship, and the impact of campaign activity based primarily on analyses of presidential elections. The scholarly community often assumes that these findings hold for other elections as well. But there are good reasons to believe that presidential elections are in fact unique. We contend that congressional elections deserve special attention because they are the only American elections that can be characterized as both national and local, often at the same time.

Before turning to this theme, we would highlight the other ways in which congressional and presidential elections differ. Although scholars do not think about them in this way, House and Senate elections are actually more representa-tive of the typical US electoral contest. In contrast to presidential elections, races for Congress feature smaller constituencies, are more frequent, are lower salience, are much less competitive, provide less information to voters, are not supported by public funding, use simpler nomination methods, and tend to be more about incumbency than partisanship. As a result of these differences, the standard findings from the presidential election literature are not always useful for understanding congressional elections.

Congressional elections are ideal environments for gaining leverage on questions not easily answered by a single-minded focus on presidential contests. The sheer number of House elections provides an abundance of data. Moreover, the heterogeneity of congressional elections means that these data are especially informative. The great diversity of district characteristics, campaign intensities, and voter attentiveness means that the relative influence of these factors may be observed more clearly.

LOCAL AND NATIONAL

The most compelling feature of congressional elections is the tension between local and national forces. In the 1970s the major works on Congress were focused on legislators as district servants who looked out for their own fortunes rather than the national interest. In the 1980s this evolved into a focus on estimating the rising incumbency advantage, again highlighting the degree to which incumbents could insulate themselves from national forces. Yet this time period was marked by several congressional cycles that were dominated by national factors. Among others, the 1974, 1980, 1992, 1994, and 2006 elections saw massive change due to forces operating beyond the district. Precisely why some election years appear to be little more than a collection of local elections while other years look like national referendums remains unclear.

There are things to be learned from the study of elections at any level, but it is only in congressional elections that the competing influences of local concerns and national sentiments collide. This stems from the design of Congress as an institution. The Congress is a decentralized body with relatively weak parties and a fair amount of autonomy for its members. Each legislator presides over the equivalent of a small firm designed to meet the electoral and policy needs of its boss (Salisbury and Shepsle 1981). Strengthened by the seniority norm, legislators' committee assignments give them access to the policy-making process, benefits for their constituents, and campaign donors. At the same time, the Congress must also act collectively. A bill does not become law unless party and committee leaders shepherd the legislation through both chambers and negotiate with the president. Legislators use party discipline and hierarchical leadership to curb their temptations to focus on parochial district concerns to the exclusion of national policy needs (Cox and McCubbins 2007). In periods of divided government the Congress acts as the opposition to the presidency; under unified government the Congress often "carries water" for the administration.

In short, the wavering of congressional elections between local and national matters is a direct result of the institution's wavering between a national body of policy makers and a collection of local representatives. The tension Congress faces results in cycles of centralization and decentralization of power (Dodd 1977), which in turn shape how candidates and voters view elections. Understanding the institution thus goes a long way toward understanding the elections of its members.

A CANDIDATE-CENTERED TRADITION

The central unit of analysis in the study of congressional elections has been the candidate. The variation in candidates makes the election in one district different from another held in an adjacent district, and the set of elections held one cycle different from those just two years later. The candidate focus sets congressional elections in stark contrast to presidential elections where voters' party allegiances and views about issues and incumbent performance are central.

From this vantage point the modern study of congressional elections quickly became fixated on incumbency. Scholars took note when incumbents' victory margins increased from the mid-1960s to the late 1980s (Cain, Ferejohn, and Fiorina 1987; Erikson 1971; Ferejohn 1977; Mayhew 1974). Beginning with Mayhew's observation that "marginal" districts were on the wane, researchers focused their attention on understanding and estimating the incumbency advantage.[1] Researchers employed simple calculations such as the "retirement slump" (the decline in a party's vote share after an incumbent retires) and the "sophomore surge" (the increase in vote share between a representative's first election and his reelection) (Alford and Brady 1993). Inadequacies in this measure led others to develop regression-based estimates (e.g., Gelman and King 1990). These estimates indicated that incumbency was worth only a percentage point or two of the vote until the immediate post-war era, but then increased steadily from the 1950s until the late 1980s; it reached a maximum of more than 10 points and has more recently receded somewhat (Ansolabehere, Snyder, and Stewart 2000; Gelman and Huang 2008).

---

[1] The earliest estimates by Erikson (1971) actually pre-date Mayhew's "vanishing marginals" analysis.

Why did the incumbency advantage rise and fall when it did? This question is of great interest because it also hints at the causes of incumbency advantage. The search for answers continues, but we are able to rule out some possible explanations.

Careful empirical studies indicate that the advantage rose as the ability to scare off strong challengers grew (Cox and Katz 1996; Levitt and Wolfram 1997). Yet evidence that the quality of challengers also mattered in late nineteenth- and early twentieth-century elections warns us that the rise of incumbency cannot be solely attributed to the growing importance of challenger quality (Carson and Engstrom 2005; Carson, Engstrom, and Roberts 2007) and debate remains as to what mechanisms allowed incumbents to become more successful at deterring the most threatening challengers.

The "casework hypothesis" contends that constituent service is primarily responsible for incumbency reelection. Fiorina (1977) argues that the willingness of legislators to become non-partisan "errand boys" in the 1960s aided in their reelection. The empirical evidence, however, is sometimes favorable (Serra and Moon 1994) but often not (Bond, Covington, and Fleisher 1985; Johannes and McAdams 1981).

There is better evidence that the dispersion of network television contributed to the rise of the incumbency advantage (Prior 2006). The spread and expansion of cable television in the 1980s and 1990s might have also contributed to its decline. Incumbents tend to be safer when television media markets do not line up neatly with district or state lines since fragmented markets are more difficult for challengers to navigate (J. E. Campbell, Alford, and Henry 1984; Levy and Squire 2000; Stewart and Reynolds 1990).

One might suspect then that campaign funding has fostered the growing power of incumbency, particularly since television became the medium that made money so useful. Yet the evidence on whether campaign war chests actually deter challengers is quite mixed, with some support (Box-Steffensmeier 1996; Carson 2003) but also some contrary findings (Goodliffe 2001; Krasno and Green 1988). Despite methodological disagreements, most researchers agree that challenger spending has more impact on the vote than does incumbent spending (Gerber 1998; Green and Krasno 1988; Jacobson 1978, 1990). Of course, incumbents typically raise more money than challengers (Herrnson 2008; Jacobson 2004), so one must account for both the levels of funds available to candidates and the effects of those funds on challenger deterrence, turnout, and vote choice.

Another popular explanation for incumbency's rise was that incumbents benefited from gerrymandered districts (Tufte 1973). Surprisingly, little empirical evidence was found to support the claim that incumbents were safer after redistricting (Bullock 1975; Cover 1977; Ferejohn 1977). Cox and Katz (2002) argue that in the aftermath of the Supreme Court redistricting decisions in the late 1960s incumbents and challengers were better able to coordinate their respective exit and entry decisions, with incumbents running against quality challengers at considerably lower rates. Others, however, find little evidence that redistricting is to blame for decreasing competition (Abramowitz, Alexander, and Gunning 2006; Oppenheimer 2005).

Scholars should entertain the possibility that the heavy focus on incumbency simply has been overblown. Recent work shows that nearly equivalent incumbency advantages exist for presidents (Weisberg 2001) and statewide office holders (Ansolabehere and Snyder 2002), neither of whom benefit from the trappings of legislative office. And although incumbents' vote margins did in fact increase in the 1960s, so did vote swings. As a result, incumbents might be "no safer" even though they are reelected with larger vote shares (Jacobson 1987). Reelection rates are also misleading indicators since they are calculated only among those seeking reelection. In fact, legislators who fear losing their seats due to scandal, health, redistricting, or policy disagreements with their constituents retire strategically (Groseclose and Krehbiel 1994; Hall and Van Houweling 1995; Hetherington, Larson, and Globetti 2003), which has the effect of inflating reelection rates. Some would not view an incumbent's head start of five or ten points as making her invincible.

It also appears that the nature of the incumbency advantage has changed over time. Between the 1970s and 2000s the number of members representing districts that also supported the presidential candidate from their parties increased, a trend that is not completely accounted for by partisan realignment in the South (Abramowitz, Alexander, and Gunning 2006). As a result, the portion of the incumbency advantage due to personal characteristics and resources has declined, while that resulting from the underlying partisan composition of the district has increased (Oppenheimer 2005). Recasting incumbency as a modest rather than dominant force in congressional elections opens the door again for national tides to compete with local considerations.

COATTAILS AND MIDTERMS

Perhaps the most obvious way in which national variables affect district races is the phenomenon of presidential "coattails," which bring into office a disproportionate number of the winning presidential candidate's co-partisans.[2] Incumbents' vote

[2] As in so many areas of congressional elections scholarship, these patterns are more likely to hold in House elections than in Senate elections. There is lively discussion of the differences and similarities between these two based on the 1988–1992 Senate Election Studies (Abramowitz and Segal 1992; Gronke 2000; Krasno 1994; Lee and Oppenheimer 1999).

shares might have grown, but one study suggests that coattail effects remained constant between 1952 and 1980 (Born 1984). Yet another finds that the effect declined significantly beginning in 1968 as the correspondence between the presidential and congressional vote weakened (Calvert and Ferejohn 1983). Analyses conducted at the height of the incumbency advantage reveal that a party gains three House seats for every point increase in the presidential nominee's vote share (J. E. Campbell 1986).

On the other side of the coin is the phenomenon of midterm loss. Midterm elections have the potential to reveal a great deal about the relative impacts of national and local forces. Aside from two recent elections (1998 and 2002) and one during the New Deal (1934), the president's party has lost House seats (and often Senate seats) in every midterm since the Civil War. This remarkable regularity is not as easily explained as it might seem. Although the size of the loss does in fact correspond to the public's evaluations of the president, the economy, and other aspects of national performance (Tufte 1975), the simple fact that the president's party almost always loses seats cannot be attributed to changes in national forces since some presidents are well regarded at midterm. The consistency of the loss has led to conjecture about "negative voting" (Kernell 1977) and the notion of a "presidential penalty" or "balancing" of the president's ideology (Alesina and Rosenthal 1995; Erikson 1988; Fiorina 1996), although these ideas are challenged empirically (Born 1990; Burden and Kimball 2002). The regularity of coattails and midterm loss suggests persistent tendencies in voters and elites rather than responsiveness to either national or local forces.

The classic theory integrating these two phenomena is that of "surge and decline." As formulated by A. Campbell (1960), the winning presidential candidate draws a "surge" of support for his party down the ballot. This is due mostly to the higher turnout of persuadable independents. Two years later voter turnout "declines" and these peripheral voters mostly abstain and the results conform more closely to the "normal vote." A revised version of the theory focuses on abstention by supporters of the loser in a presidential election (J. E. Campbell 1997). From this viewpoint, the decline of turnout in the midterm is more likely to hurt the president's party, which was overrepresented in the previous election.

Although "surge and decline" remains a popular explanation for the differences between presidential year and midterm elections, the evidence is frequently inconsistent with the theory. For example, changes in vote choice are more important drivers than changes in turnout (Born 1990; Burden and Kimball 2002; Mebane and Sekhon 2002).[3] Moreover, the standard deviation of the national congressional vote is actually larger in midterm than in presidential years (Erikson 1988; Jacobson and Kernell 1983). As attractive as the theory might be, more evidence is needed for it to

---

[3] In addition, there is the puzzle that Democrats fare worse in midterms than do Republicans, even after "surge and decline" variables have been considered (Coleman 1997).

be regarded as the definitive explanation of how national and local forces see-saw in importance between presidential and midterm elections.

Setting these specific theories aside for the moment, researchers have uncovered strong effects of national conditions on aggregate congressional election outcomes. Kramer (1971) and Tufte (1975) launched something of a cottage industry when they demonstrated the consistent relationships between changes in midterm House seats and national variables such as presidential approval and economic performance. This spawned a series of forecasting models that demonstrated the great responsiveness of congressional elections to national influences (e.g., Lewis-Beck and Rice 1984, 1992). But individual-level studies relying on survey data found little relationship between personal economic evaluations and congressional voting patterns (Kinder and Kiewiet 1979; Mann and Wolfinger 1980). There is little dispute today that macroeconomic variables influence congressional election outcomes in the aggregate (Erikson, Mackuen, and Stimson 2002; cf. Erikson 1990), but the inconsistent behavior of individual voters still raises questions.[4] One review of the literature documents just how sensitive our findings are to the choice of economic indicator (Ragsdale 1994), suggesting that more theoretical development is required to make sense of the mixed findings.

CHALLENGER EMERGENCE

It appeared by the early 1980s that two simultaneous but contradictory plot lines were emerging about the meaning of congressional elections. To one camp they were mainly about the reelection of well-funded and well-liked incumbents, without much consideration for policy or government performance. To the other camp they were orderly aggregations of larger forces that could be predicted quite readily on the basis of national performance, particularly that of the economy and the president.

The "strategic politicians" theory offered by Jacobson and Kernell (1983) seemed to solve this contradiction. In their theory it is the career decisions made by candidates and donors that make congressional elections responsive to national conditions. The reading of aggregate tea leaves—mainly in the form of presidential approval ratings and economic indicators—drives decisions by the best candidates about when they will seek election. Voters, on the other hand, are mainly choosing

---

[4] Radcliff (1988) is among those arguing the macroeconomy had a decreasing effect on congressional voting patterns due to the rise of incumbency as an insulating force (see also Alesina and Rosenthal 1989). And while collective economic judgments were found to affect congressional voting (Kinder and Kiewiet 1981), it is not clear why individuals voted by their pocketbook in presidential but not congressional elections (Erikson 1990).

among local candidates without regard for national factors. As a result, it appears as though voters are reacting to national conditions even though they are not, a clever solution that has guided a great deal of research (Bianco 1984; Bond, Covington, and Fleisher 1985; Carson and Roberts 2005; Stone, Maisel, and Maestas 2004).

Subsequent work by Jacobson (1989, 2004) focused on the emergence of "quality" challengers, defined as those who have held previous elective office. Consistent with the theory, he found that parties field more quality challengers when national conditions were favorable, and that more quality challengers in a party translates into a larger number of seats won. By focusing on candidates' decisions as the key intervening variable, the theory of "strategic politicians" thus appears to solve the national-versus-local divide. It also nicely accounts for other phenomena, namely the midterm loss and presidential coattails, all in one theoretical package.

As satisfying as this solution is, it has been criticized. In terms of measurement, researchers complain that measures of candidate quality that improve on Jacobson's dichotomous indicator sometimes question the original theory (Canon 1990; Krasno and Green 1988; Squire 1992). In addition, several studies find evidence that candidate decisions are not in fact the critical moving parts connecting national conditions and voter decision making (Basinger and Ensley 2007; Born 1986). Theoretically, Erikson (1990) wonders how candidate choices can become self-fulfilling if not based on real conditions rather than just elite expectations.

Research on the factors behind candidate emergence indicates that district partisanship and the party of the incumbent—both local factors—are quite important (Stone and Maisel 2003; cf. Stone, Maisel, and Maestas 2004). One study finds that Senate challengers make decisions based more on how many other potential quality challengers are in the pool rather than the incumbent's vulnerability (Adams and Squire 1997) while another finds incumbent vote totals to be the most important deterrent (Krasno and Green 1988). In both accounts local rather than national conditions are more important to the candidate calculus. If challenger decisions are indeed the keys to understanding congressional elections, clearly more research is needed to understand how deterrence and strategic decisions operate.

A CLOSER LOOK AT CONGRESSIONAL ELECTION VOTERS

Aside from consideration of district partisanship, noticeably absent in much of the literature is any notion of the voter. In one of the first examinations of congressional voters, Stokes and Miller (1962) concluded that partisanship was the strongest predictor and that over half the voters did not know either House candidate in their district or what party held the majority of House seats. This traditional view of voters was reinforced by later work demonstrating that congressional outcomes were responsive to national economic conditions and presidential approval.

Part of the reason for such a limited view of voters was a paucity of data. That changed in 1978 when the American National Election Studies (ANES) included new questions about public perceptions of congressional candidates and incumbents and changed its sampling units from counties to congressional districts. Examining these new data, a more nuanced picture of the congressional voter emerged (Abramowitz 1980; Hinckley 1980; Mann and Wolfinger 1980). While few voters were able to recall candidates' names, many more were able to recognize them, an act that most clearly mirrored what voters actually experienced at the polls (Mann 1978). Voters had much more contact with and, consequently, greater awareness of the incumbent than the challenger. But while candidate evaluations proved to be strong predictors of vote choice (Hinckley 1980), the content of those evaluations generally lacked ideological or issue considerations (Mann and Wolfinger 1980). This would appear to leave little room for national conditions to affect congressional elections unless voters evaluate the incumbent at least partially in terms of economic, presidential, or congressional performance.

Under some conditions voters appear responsive to the political environment, electoral context, and strategies of congressional candidates. Not surprisingly, research finds voters are more likely to turn out in congressional elections when they are closely contested (Caldeira, Patterson, and Markko 1985). As in other elections, voters are more likely to be mobilized in competitive districts and it is those elite activities and investments that stimulate turnout (Cox and Munger 1989; Huckfeldt et al. 2007). Competitiveness may be driven by either local or national factors, but it is often national elite decisions that result in higher levels of mobilization.

Campaign dynamics also matter. What voters know about incumbents and challengers is shaped by candidates' campaign strategies (Coleman and Manna 2000; Franklin 1991; Franz et al. 2007). Journalists use fundraising to guide their coverage of candidates (Westlye 1991). While conventional wisdom holds that congressional elections are about incumbency and partisanship, and not issues, the effects of issues on vote choice appear to be dependent upon the salience of those issues in the campaign (Abramowitz 1985) and the competitiveness of the race (Kahn and Kenney 1999). There is also evidence that the ideological positioning of candidates affects who votes (Plane and Gershtenson 2004).[5]

---

[5] These findings, however, come from research on Senate elections in two midterm years. It is unclear whether such patterns hold up in House elections.

As we might suspect, issues and ideology play a greater role in Senate elections than House elections. Senate elections are more visible elections, are more likely to pit quality candidates against one another, and are more inhospitable to the cultivation of "home style" relationships with constituents (Jacobson and Wolfinger 1989; Krasno 1994; Miller 1990; Wright and Berkman 1986). On the other hand, Gronke (2000) suggests that House and Senate elections have become more similar.[6]

Studies of the congressional voter largely focus on what voters know and the cues they rely on when casting a vote. Jacobson (2004) argues that how national conditions are handled by congressional candidates makes more of a difference now than in the past and notes that such responses vary among candidates, between parties, and across election years. As discussed above, studies of candidate emergence provide one way to assess when and how national conditions matter. But we should also consider this question from the voter's perspective. Brady, D'Onofrio, and Fiorina (2000) suggest that voters now have access to more policy information, and that this may explain why congressional elections have become more nationalized. Whether this is indeed the case, and whether in turn it means that elites are now better at nationalizing elections, remains to be seen.

SCANDAL

Scandals can also shake up what are perceived to be fairly prosaic elections. To date, scant research has been done in this area. Peters and Welch's (1980) study examined the effect of charges of scandal on members' electoral prospects and found that it decreased their vote shares by between six and eleven percentage points. Using the strategic politicians framework, Jacobson and Dimock (1994) found that the bank overdraft scandal in 1992 contributed to the unusually high turnover of House seats in that election. While corruption charges appear to only marginally influence whether a member of the House decided to retire, an incumbent facing a corruption charge is about nine times more likely to lose in the general election than an incumbent not charged (Welch and Hibbing 1997). Scandals also appear to impact candidate quality (Canon 1990) and may even have more of an effect on electoral outcomes than most of the standard variables such as campaign spending and incumbency (Herrnson 2008).

---

[6] For additional research on Senate elections see Abramowitz and Segal (1992), Kahn and Kenney (1999), and Westlye (1991).

The textbook version taught in most introductory American politics courses is that while voters may hold the institution in low esteem, most are quite pleased with their own member of Congress (Fenno 1978). Yet it appears that under certain conditions incumbents find it difficult to escape public disapproval of Congress and the president. The 1974 midterms are a dramatic example in which disgust with the Watergate scandal led to a wave of new Democratic freshmen. Even though it was a presidential election year, the influx of 110 new representatives in 1992 was due in large part to the House bank scandal (Jacobson and Dimock 1994). Despite only modest variation in disapproval of Congress since the 1970s, public reaction against the majority party appears to have defined the 1994 (Hibbing and Tiritilli 2000), 1998 (Abramowitz 2001) and 2006 (Abramson, Aldrich, and Rohde 2007; Grose and Oppenheimer 2007) midterm elections. In retrospect it is surprising how little attention scholars have given to scandal. Importantly, the perception of widespread scandal appears to have the ability to transform a mundane election cycle into a national referendum by connecting candidates of the same party or institution.

RESEARCH IMPLICATIONS

As we have documented, the congressional elections literature wavers between small technical debates (such as how to measure candidate quality, how to estimate the incumbency advantage properly, and how to get around the endogeneity of spending and election outcomes, to name only a few) and grand issues of democratic representation. Integrating the "big" and "small" issues has been a challenge, particularly when theory about congressional elections is viewed by some as underdeveloped (Ragsdale 1994). How are we to make sense of the myriad factors that influence congressional elections? Congressional elections are unique in that both the local and national vie for attention. We could safely conclude that both sets of factors matter, a statement that is undoubtedly true but also unsatisfactory. We would prefer to push researchers to identify the conditions under which congressional elections are either mainly local or national affairs.

One way to gain leverage on the question of "what matters when" is to consider how the local–national balance varies along three dimensions. First, researchers should understand variance *over time*: why elections are more nationalized in some years than others. The factors relevant to variance over time include things such as public mood and congressional approval. Moreover, we would hope to identify factors that separate national elections that revolve around discontent toward Congress from national elections that are referendums on the president, the

majority party, or national indicators such as economic performance. Other than
studies tracking the incumbency advantage over time, we are dismayed at how
few projects seek to understand how the impacts of standard variables have
fluctuated longitudinally.

Second, researchers should explain differences *across districts*: why candidate
choices and election outcomes have national roots in one district but local origins
in another, even in the same election year. Here the salient variables are such things
as district demographics, scandals, and competitiveness. Scholars will want to
delve further into the career calculations of candidates and identify the precise
tea leaves they read when deciding to run or retire.

Third, we need to understand variation *among voters*: why some voters rely on
candidate characteristics and incumbency service as cues while others focus on
partisanship or national indicators. Indeed, one might push to understand why the
same voter views one election year as a local choice and the next election as a
barometer of national conditions. Work by Petrocik and Desposato (2004) on
short-term forces and incumbency is an exemplar of this approach. Under this
framework scholars could assess how well our theories of voting behavior hold up
in congressional elections defined by local concerns compared to those where the
outcomes were driven by national partisan tides.

Additionally, scholars could inspect systematic variations in the national-local
tension by identifying the conditions that separate the two and examining them
across our three dimensions: time, districts, and voters. For example, one "national" marker is the issue environment, whether the dominant issues of the day are
positional or valence. Over time, scholars could look at how the issue environment
expands and contracts to gain insight into whether and how local–national tensions have evolved. Scholars could also examine how the local–national balance
varies across districts and whether there are significant differences in how candidates connect their campaigns to national conditions.[7] It may or may not be the
case that standard variables such as candidate quality or incumbency explain such
differences. Alternatively, we might look at the open-ended survey responses of
"peripheral" voters to test the hypothesis that congressional elections have become
more nationalized. Indeed, the question of nationalization presents a bit of a
chicken-and-egg dilemma: whether a congressional election is "nationalized" is
predicated on what the candidates do, but whether candidates raise national
themes is also dependent upon the issues motivating voters in the first place.

While each of these dimensions—over time, across districts, and among
voters—says something about our long-standing theories of congressional elections, existing theories may be more or less relevant under different conditions,
such as unified or divided government. Our careful reading of the literature also

---

[7] The point that candidates might vary in how they handle national conditions is noted by
Jacobson (2004).

reveals that standard models in fact receive mixed support empirically. Ideas such as "surge and decline," "incumbency advantage," and "strategic politicians" are powerful explanations, but they also need to be improved if we are to accommodate data that challenge those theories. One possibility is to probe the contexts of elections more carefully to understand the situations in which voters find themselves. For example, when public discontent appeared before the 1994 and 2006 elections, it was clear who voters should blame since the same party controlled both the presidency and the Congress. In contrast, the winds of change in 1992 were more targeted at incumbents rather than politicians from a particular party, yet both elections are viewed as "national." The presence of unified or divided government and the public perception of a scandalous environment both seem to be key factors that drive decisions by parties, candidates, and voters.

Although we do not think a grand unified theory of congressional elections is possible, the growing sources of data on voters, candidates, and the campaign environment provide rich opportunities to develop middle-range theories examining systematic variations in the national–local divide. We believe congressional elections offer great possibilities, not only for assessing the quality of democratic representation in the US but also for scholars who wish to understand how voters make decisions and identify the conditions under which local races develop into national mandates.

REFERENCES

ABRAMOWITZ, A. I. 1980. A Comparison of Voting for US Senator and Representative in 1978. *American Political Science Review*, 74: 633–40.

—— 1985. Economic Conditions, Presidential Popularity, and Voting Behavior in Midterm Congressional Elections. *Journal of Politics*, 47: 31–43.

—— 2001. It's Monica, Stupid. The Impeachment Controversy and the 1998 Midterm Election. *Legislative Studies Quarterly*, 26: 211–26.

—— ALEXANDER, B., and GUNNING, M. 2006. Incumbency, Redistricting, and the Decline of Competition in U.S. House Elections. *Journal of Politics*, 68: 75–88.

—— and SEGAL, J. A. 1992. *Senate Elections*. Ann Arbor, Mich.: University of Michigan Press.

ABRAMSON, P. R., ALDRICH, J. H., and ROHDE, D. W. 2007. *Change and Continuity in the 2004 and 2006 Elections*. Washington, D.C.: CQ Press.

ADAMS, G. D. and SQUIRE, P. 1997. Incumbent Vulnerability and Challenger Emergence in Senate Elections. *Political Behavior*, 19: 97–111.

ALESINA, A. and ROSENTHAL, H. 1989. Partisan Cycles in Congressional Elections and the Macroeconomy. *American Political Science Review*, 83: 373–98.

—— —— 1995. *Partisan Politics, Divided Government, and the Economy*. New York: Cambridge University Press.

ALFORD, J. R. and BRADY, D. W. 1993. Personal and Partisan Advantages in U.S. Congressional Elections, 1846–1990. In *Congress Reconsidered*, 5th edn., ed. L. C. Dodd and B. I. Oppenheimer. Washington, D.C.: CQ Press.

ANSOLABEHERE, S. and SNYDER, J. M. 2002. The Incumbency Advantage in U.S. Elections: An Analysis of State and Federal Offices, 1942–2000. *Election Law Journal*, 1: 315–38.

—————— and STEWART, C., III. 2000. Old Voters, New Voters, and the Personal Vote: Using Redistricting to Measure the Incumbency Advantage. *American Journal of Political Science*, 44: 14–34.

BASINGER, S. J. and ENSLEY, M. J. 2007. Candidates, Campaigns, or Partisan Conditions? Reevaluating Strategic-Politicians Theory. *Legislative Studies Quarterly*, 32: 361–94.

BIANCO, W. T. 1984. Strategic Decision on Candidacy in U.S. Congressional Districts. *Legislative Studies Quarterly*, 9: 351–64.

BOND, J. R., COVINGTON, C., and FLEISHER, R. 1985. Explaining Challenger Quality in Congressional Elections. *Journal of Politics*, 47: 510–29.

BORN, R. 1984. Reassessing the Decline of Presidential Coattails: U.S. House Elections from 1952–80. *Journal of Politics*, 46: 60–79.

—— 1986. Strategic Politicians and Unresponsive Voters. *American Political Science Review*, 80: 559–612.

—— 1990. Surge and Decline, Negative Voting, and the Midterm Loss Phenomenon: A Simultaneous Choice Analysis. *American Journal of Political Science*, 34: 615–45.

BOX-STEFFENSMEIER, J. M. 1996. A Dynamic Analysis of the Role of War Chests in Campaign Strategy. *American Journal of Political Science*, 40: 352–71.

BRADY, D. W., D'ONOFRIO, R., and FIORINA, M. P. 2000. The Nationalization of Electoral Forces Revisited. In *Continuity and Changes in House Elections*, ed. D. W. Brady, J. F. Cogan, and M. P. Fiorina. Stanford, Calif.: Stanford University Press.

BULLOCK, C. S. 1975. Redistricting and Congressional Stability, 1962–72. *Journal of Politics*, 37: 569–75.

BURDEN, B. C. and KIMBALL, D. C. 2002. *Why Americans Split Their Tickets: Campaigns, Competition, and Divided Government*. Ann Arbor, Mich.: University of Michigan Press.

CAIN, B., FEREJOHN, J., and FIORINA, M. 1987. *The Personal Vote*. Cambridge, Mass.: Harvard University Press.

CALDEIRA, G. A., PATTERSON, S. C., and MARKKO, G. A. 1985. The Mobilization of Voters in Congressional Elections. *Journal of Politics*, 47: 490–509.

CALVERT, R. L. and FEREJOHN, J. A. 1983. Coattail Voting in Recent Presidential Elections. *American Political Science Review*, 77: 407–19.

CAMPBELL, A. 1960. Surge and Decline: A Study of Electoral Change. *Public Opinion Quarterly*, 24: 397–418.

CAMPBELL, J. E. 1986. Predicting Seat Gains from Presidential Coattails. *American Journal of Political Science*, 30: 165–83.

—— 1997. *The Presidential Pulse of Congressional Elections*. Lexington, Ky.: University of Kentucky Press.

—— ALFORD, J. R., and HENRY, K. 1984. Television Markets and Congressional Elections. *Legislative Studies Quarterly*, 9: 665–78.

CANON, D. T. 1990. *Actors, Athletes, and Astronauts*. Chicago, Ill.: University of Chicago Press.

CARSON, J. L. 2003. Strategic Interaction and Candidate Competition in U.S. House Elections: Empirical Applications of Probit and Strategic Probit Models. *Political Analysis*, 11: 368–80.

—— and ENGSTROM, E. J. 2005. Assessing the Electoral Connection: Evidence from the Early United States. *American Journal of Political Science*, 49: 746–57.

—— and ROBERTS, J. M. 2005. Strategic Politicians and U.S. House Elections, 1874–1914. *Journal of Politics*, 67: 474–96.

—— —— 2007. Candidate Quality, the Personal Vote, and the Incumbency Advantage in Congress. *American Political Science Review*, 101: 289–301.

COLEMAN, J. J. 1997. The Importance of Being Republican: Forecasting Party Fortunes in House Midterm Elections. *Journal of Politics*, 59: 497–519.

—— and MANNA, P. F. 2000. Congressional Campaign Spending and the Quality of Democracy. *Journal of Politics*, 62: 757–89.

COVER, A. D. 1977. One Good Term Deserves Another: The Advantage of Incumbency in Congressional Elections. *American Journal of Political Science*, 21: 523–41.

COX, G. W. and KATZ, J. N. 1996. Why Did the Incumbency Advantage in U.S. House Elections Grow? *American Journal of Political Science*, 40: 478–97.

—— —— 2002. *Elbridge Gerry's Salamander: The Electoral Consequences of the Reapportionment Revolution*. New York: Cambridge University Press.

—— and MCCUBBINS, M. D. 2007. *Legislative Leviathan: Party Government in the House*, 2nd edn. New York: Cambridge University Press.

—— and MUNGER, M. C. 1989. Closeness, Expenditures, and Turnout in the 1982 U.S. House Elections. *American Political Science Review*, 83: 217–31.

DODD, L. C. 1977. Congress and the Quest for Power. In *Congress Reconsidered*, ed. L. C. Dodd and B. I. Oppenheimer. New York: Praeger.

ERIKSON, R. S. 1971. The Advantage of Incumbency in Congressional Elections. *Polity*, 3: 395–405.

—— 1988. The Puzzle of Midterm Loss. *Journal of Politics*, 50: 1011–29.

—— 1990. Economic Conditions and the Congressional Vote: A Review of the Macrolevel Evidence. *American Journal of Political Science*, 34: 373–99.

—— MACKUEN, M., and STIMSON, J. A. 2002. *The Macro Polity*. New York: Cambridge University Press.

FENNO, R. F. 1978. *Home Style: House Members in Their Districts*. Boston, Mass.: Little, Brown.

FEREJOHN, J. A. 1977. On the Decline of Competition in Congressional Elections. *American Political Science Review*, 71: 166–76.

FIORINA, M. P. 1977. The Case of the Vanishing Marginals: The Bureaucracy Did It. *American Political Science Review*, 71: 177–81.

—— 1996. *Divided Government*, 2nd edn. Needham Heights, Mass.: Allyn & Bacon.

FRANKLIN, C. H. 1991. Eschewing Obfuscation? Campaigns and the Perception of U.S. Senate Incumbents. *American Political Science Review*, 85: 1193–214.

FRANZ, M. M., FREEDMAN, P. B., GOLDSTEIN, K. M., and RIDOUT, T. N. 2007. *Campaign Advertising and American Democracy*. Philadelphia, Pa.: Temple University Press.

GELMAN, A. and HUANG, Z. 2008. Estimating Incumbency Advantage and Its Variation, as an Example of a Before/After Study. *Journal of the American Statistical Association*, 103: 437–46.

—— and KING, G. 1990. Estimating Incumbency Advantage without Bias. *American Journal of Political Science*, 34: 1142–64.

GERBER, A. 1998. Estimating the Effect of Campaign Spending on Senate Election Outcomes Using Instrumental Variables. *American Political Science Review*, 92: 401–11.

GOODLIFFE, J. 2001. The Effect of War Chests on Challenger Entry in U.S. House Elections. *American Journal of Political Science*, 45: 830–44.

GREEN, D. P. and KRASNO, J. S. 1988. Salvation for the Spendthrift Incumbent: Reestimating the Effects of Campaign Spending in House Elections. *American Journal of Political Science*, 32: 884–907.

GRONKE, P. 2000. *The Electorate, the Campaign, and the Office: A Unified Approach to Senate and House Elections*. Ann Arbor, Mich.: University of Michigan Press.

GROSE, C. R. and OPPENHEIMER, B. I. 2007. The Iraq War, Partisanship, and Candidate Attributes: Variation in Partisan Swing in the 2006 U.S. House Elections. *Legislative Studies Quarterly*, 32: 531–57.

GROSECLOSE, T. and KREHBIEL, K. 1994. Golden Parachutes, Rubber Checks, and Strategic Retirements form the 102nd House. *American Journal of Political Science*, 38: 75–99.

HALL, R. L. and VAN HOUWELING, R. P. 1995. Avarice and Ambition in Congress: Representatives' Decisions to Run or Retire from the U.S. House. *American Political Science Review*, 89: 121–36.

HERRNSON, P. S. 2008. *Congressional Elections: Campaigning at Home and in Washington*. Washington, D.C.: CQ Press.

HETHERINGTON, M. J., LARSON, B., and GLOBETTI, S. 2003. The Redistricting Cycle and Strategic Candidate Decisions in U.S. House Races. *Journal of Politics*, 65: 122–34.

HIBBING, J. R. and TIRITILLI, E. 2000. Public Disapproval of Congress Can Be Dangerous to Majority Party Candidates: The Case of 1994. In *Continuity and Change in House Elections*, ed. D. W. Brady, J. F. Cogan, and M. P. Fiorina. Stanford, Calif.: Stanford University Press.

HINCKLEY, B. 1980. The American Voter in Congressional Elections. *American Political Science Review*, 74: 641–50.

HUCKFELDT, R., CARMINES, E. G., MONDAK, J. J., and ZEEMERING, E. 2007. Information, Activation, and Electoral Competition in the 2002 Congressional Elections. *Journal of Politics*, 69: 798–812.

JACOBSON, G. C. 1978. The Effects of Campaign Spending in Congressional Elections. *American Political Science Review*, 72: 469–91.

——1987. The Marginals Never Vanished: Incumbency and Competition in Elections to the U.S. House of Representatives, 1952–82. *American Journal of Political Science*, 31: 126–41.

——1989. Strategic Politicians and the Dynamics of U.S House Elections, 1946–86. *American Political Science Review*, 83: 773–93.

——1990. The Effects of Campaign Spending in House Elections: New Evidence for Old Arguments. *American Journal of Political Science*, 34: 334–62.

——2004. *The Politics of Congressional Elections*, 6th edn. New York: Longman.

——and DIMOCK, M. A. 1994. Checking Out: The Effects of Bank Overdrafts on the 1992 House Elections. *American Journal of Political Science*, 38: 601–24.

——and KERNELL, S. 1983. *Strategy and Choice in Congressional Elections*, 2nd edn. New Haven, Conn.: Yale University Press.

——and WOLFINGER, R. E. 1989. Information and Voting in California Senate Elections. *Legislative Studies Quarterly*, 14: 509–29.

JOHANNES, J. R. and McADAMS, J. C. 1981. The Congressional Incumbency Effect: Is It Casework, Policy Compatibility, or Something Else? An Examination of the 1978 Election. *American Journal of Political Science*, 25: 512–42.

KAHN, K. F. and KENNEY, P. J. 1999. *The Spectacle of U.S. Senate Campaigns*. Princeton, N.J.: Princeton University Press.

KERNELL, S. 1977. Presidential Popularity and Negative Voting: An Alternative Explanation of the Midterm Congressional Decline of the President's Party. *American Political Science Review*, 71: 44–66.

KINDER, D. R. and KIEWIET, D. R. 1979. Economic Discontent and Political Behavior: The Role of Personal Grievances and Collective Economic Judgments in Congressional Voting. *American Journal of Political Science*, 23: 495–527.

—— —— 1981. Sociotropic Politics: The American Case. *British Journal of Political Science*, 11: 129–61.

KRAMER, G. H. 1971. Short-Term Fluctuations in U.S. Voting Behavior, 1896–1964. *American Political Science Review*, 65: 131–43.

KRASNO, J. 1994. *Challengers, Competition, and Reelection: Comparing Senate and House Elections*. New Haven, Conn.: Yale University Press.

—— and GREEN, D. 1988. Preempting Quality Challengers in House Elections. *Journal of Politics*, 50: 920–36.

LEE, F. C. and OPPENHEIMER, B. I. 1999. *Sizing Up the Senate: The Unequal Consequences of Equal Representation*. Chicago, Ill: University of Chicago Press.

LEVITT, S. D. and WOLFRAM, C. D. 1997. Decomposing the Sources of Incumbency Advantage in the U.S. House. *Legislative Studies Quarterly*, 22: 45–60.

LEVY, D. and SQUIRE, P. 2000. Television Markets and the Competitiveness of U.S. House Elections. *Legislative Studies Quarterly*, 25: 313–25.

LEWIS-BECK, M. S. and RICE, T. W. 1984. Forecasting U.S. House Elections. *Legislative Studies Quarterly*, 9: 475–86.

—— —— 1992. *Forecasting Elections*. Washington, D.C.: CQ Press.

MANN, T. E. 1978. *Unsafe at Any Margin: Interpreting Congressional Elections*. Washington, D.C.: AEI Press.

—— and WOLFINGER, R. E. 1980. Candidates and Parties in Congressional Elections. *American Political Science Review*, 74: 617–32.

MAYHEW, D. R. 1974. Congressional Elections: The Case of the Vanishing Marginals. *Polity*, 6: 295–317.

MEBANE, W. R., JR. and SEKHON, J. S. 2002. Coordination and Policy Moderation at Midterm. *American Political Science Review*, 96: 141–57.

MILLER, A. H. 1990. Public Judgments of Senate and House Candidates. *Legislative Studies Quarterly*, 15: 525–42.

OPPENHEIMER, B I. 2005. Deep Red and Blue Congressional Districts: The Causes and Consequences of Declining Party Competitiveness. In *Congress Reconsidered*, 8th edn., ed. L. C. Dodd and B. I. Oppenheimer. Washington, D.C.: CQ Press.

PETERS, J. G. and WELCH, S. 1980. The Effects of Charges of Corruption on Voting Behavior in Congressional Elections. *American Political Science Review*, 74: 697–708.

PETROCIK, J. R. and DESPOSATO, S. W. 2004. Incumbency and Short-Term Influences on Voters. *Political Research Quarterly*, 57: 363–73.

PLANE, D. L. and GERSHTENSON, J. 2004. Candidates' Ideological Locations, Abstention, and Turnout in U.S. Senate Midterm Elections. *Political Behavior*, 26: 69–93.

PRIOR, M. 2006. The Incumbent in the Living Room: The Rise of Television and the Incumbency Advantage in U.S. House Elections. *Journal of Politics*, 68: 657–73.

RADCLIFF, B. 1988. Solving a Puzzle: Aggregate Analysis and Economic Voting Revisited. *Journal of Politics*, 50: 440–55.

RAGSDALE, L. 1994. Old Approaches and New Challenges in Legislative Election Research. *Legislative Studies Quarterly*, 19: 537–82.

SALISBURY, R. H. and SHEPSLE, K. A. 1981. U.S. Congressman as Enterprise. *Legislative Studies Quarterly*, 6: 559–76.

SERRA, G. and MOON, D. 1994. Casework, Issue Positions, and Voting in Congressional Elections: A District Analysis. *Journal of Politics*, 56: 200–13.

SQUIRE, P. 1992. Challenger Quality and Voting Behavior in U.S. Senate Elections. *Legislative Studies Quarterly*, 17: 247–63.

STEWART, C., III. and REYNOLDS, M. 1990. Television Markets and U.S. Senate Elections. *Legislative Studies Quarterly*, 15: 495–523.

STOKES, D. E. and MILLER, W. E. 1962. Party Government and the Saliency of Congress. *Public Opinion Quarterly*, 26: 531–46.

STONE, W. J. and MAISEL, L. S. 2003. The Not-so-Simple Calculus of Winning: Potential U.S. House Candidates' Nomination and General Election Prospects. *Journal of Politics*, 65: 951–77.

—— and MAESTAS, C. D. 2004. Quality Counts: Extending the Strategic Politician Model of Incumbent Deterrence. *American Journal of Political Science*, 48: 479–95.

TUFTE, E. R. 1973. The Relationship between Seats and Votes in Two-Party Systems. *American Political Science Review*, 67: 540–54.

—— 1975. Determinants of the Outcomes of Midterm Congressional Elections. *American Political Science Review*, 69: 812–26.

WEISBERG, H. F. 2001. Partisanship and Incumbency in Presidential Elections. *Political Behavior*, 24: 339–60.

WELCH, S. and HIBBING, J. R. 1997. The Effects of Charges of Corruption on Voting Behavior in Congressional Elections, 1982–1990. *Journal of Politics*, 59: 226–39.

WESTLYE, M. C. 1991. *Senate Elections and Campaign Intensity*. Baltimore, Md.: Johns Hopkins University Press.

WRIGHT, G. C., Jr. and BERKMAN, M. B. 1986. Candidates and Policy in United States Senate Elections. *American Political Science Review*, 80: 567–88.

CHAPTER 25

THE STUDY OF LOCAL ELECTIONS IN AMERICAN POLITICS

MELISSA J. MARSCHALL

GIVEN the large number of cases and considerable institutional and contextual variation across and within local governments, one might assume that the study of local elections is an area already well harvested by participation scholars. The truth, however, is that this is a relatively unexplored area of inquiry. In fact, to say that a field of study on local elections exists would be a bit of an overstatement. Not only is the literature rather small and not particularly cohesive, but the data collection and methods of analysis are also somewhat primitive, particularly when compared to research on state and federal elections. While on the one hand this means that there are many unanswered and even unexplored questions, it also means that the possibilities for future research are practically limitless.

Before examining what we know, don't know, and should know about local elections in American politics, there are two preliminary questions that need to be addressed. First, why the dearth of scholarly attention when it comes to local elections? Second, what is meant by "local" and what are some of the features that distinguish local jurisdictions from their state and national counterparts? The initial sections of this chapter address these questions, outlining four explanations for why participation and urban politics scholars have largely ignored local elections and emphasizing the themes of volume and variation in describing the landscape of local government and local elections. This discussion points to a set of conceptual and empirical challenges that make the application of conventional models of electoral behavior to the local level less straightforward and relevant. In particular, the prevalence of non-partisan elections at the local level makes the standard vote-choice model (the probability of, or percentage voting Democrat, Republican, or other) mostly moot, therefore forcing students of local elections to focus on alternative outcomes.

What are these alternative outcomes? Two of the most widely studied include turnout and voting for minority candidates.[1] Thus, in addressing the question of what we know and don't know about local elections, I focus on research and findings in these two areas. And, since nearly all of this research examines these outcomes exclusively in the context of municipalities and school districts, this chapter will have very little to say about other local elections, namely those for counties or special districts. In my review of the research, I pay particular attention to the data and methods of analysis employed in these studies in order to not only emphasize other things that we should know, but to also identify important data sources that future studies might further exploit. In the final section of this chapter I elaborate on this point and sketch out several directions for future research.

Why the Paucity of Scholarly Research on Local Elections?

For a variety of reasons, research on political behavior at the local level has focused less on electoral behavior—voting, campaigning, contributing—and more on what might be considered non-traditional forms of behavior such as contacting government officials, joining groups, attending meetings, and volunteering. While the most prominent studies tend to view these forms of involvement as mere stepping-stones to electoral participation (Leighley 1996; Verba, Schlozman, and Brady 1995), local politics scholars have treated them more centrally, as ends in themselves. One reason has to do with the broader view of citizen engagement taken by these scholars. For example, research on "coproduction" includes the policy implementation stage of politics in its conceptualization of citizen participation, focusing exclusively on questions of how and why citizens participate in activities associated with the provision of public goods (Marschall 2004; Sharp 1980).

---

[1] A third is voting for incumbents, though there is considerably less research here (but see Krebs 1998; Oliver and Ha 2007).

Similarly, the literature on citizen contacting of government officials examines how citizens respond politically when they are dissatisfied with local governance and/or the quality of local services (Lyons, Lowery, and DeHoog 1992). In short, research on local political behavior has been more occupied with participatory acts associated with the provision and quality of local public services than with electoral behaviors.

A second reason that non-electoral forms of participation are featured more prominently in political behavior research at the local level is because Americans participate in various local organizations at a much higher rate than they do in local elections or campaigns (Verba et al. 1995) and because political scientists have taken greater interest in these forms of engagement, particularly in recent decades. Indeed, the popularity of concepts such as social capital and civic capacity has spawned considerable research and scholarly debate concerning their purported decline, role in economic and political development, and sources and sustainability. Consequently, scholarly inquiry into civic involvement has occupied a prominent place in the discipline and may have overshadowed interest in and research on local electoral behavior.

Third, low rates of voter turnout in local elections reduce the saliency of local elections and contribute to the lack of attention given to these elections by participation scholars. And finally, the absence of readily available, centralized data is also an important factor in the dearth of research on local election. As Caren (2007) notes, while many European countries have central depositories for all subnational elections, this is not the case in the United States. Instead, data are typically collected by local jurisdictions and only occasionally by states or state associations (such as state school board associations). Scholars interested in studying local elections must therefore invest considerable time and energy piecing together data from myriad sources that are often unorganized and limited in temporal coverage.

THE LANDSCAPE OF LOCAL GOVERNMENTS AND ELECTIONS IN THE US

While the foregoing discussion helps us understand the relative inattention paid to elections in the field of local participation, it does not explain why scholarship has focused almost exclusively on municipal and school district elections or why turnout and voting for minority candidates have been the most popularly studied phenomena. By reviewing the basic contours of local government and local elections, this section offers some insights into these questions, while also providing a more general description of how and why these elections are distinctive.

The Varied Forms and Functions of Local Government

Volume is perhaps the most distinguishing characteristic of local governments. Of the 87,576 governmental units enumerated in 2002, 87,525 (99.9 percent) were local governments (US Census Bureau 2002). A second distinguishing characteristic is the considerable variation in the form and function of local governments. While there are two primary forms, general- and special-purpose, these can be further classified (see Table 25.1).

General-purpose governments include counties, municipalities, and towns/ townships and numbered nearly 39,000 in 2002. In general, variation in the size and function of each of the three types of general-purpose governments is considerable both across and within states.

Counties make up the smallest share (7.8 percent) of general-purpose governments with only 3,034 (US Census Bureau 2002). Though the small number is largely due to the fact that counties cover the largest land area, the total absence of counties in two states (Connecticut and Rhode Island) and partial absence of county governments in other states are also contributing factors. As arms of their states, counties traditionally performed more uniform and limited, state-mandated duties (e.g., property assessment, record keeping, and elections). Over time, however, they have added new responsibilities, including child welfare, consumer protection, and water quality to name just a few. Municipal and town/township governments make up the lion's share of general-purpose governments with 19,429 (49.9 percent) and 16,504 (42.4 percent) respectively (US Census Bureau 2002). These governments are distinguished primarily by the historical circumstances surrounding their incorporation. Although in some states they have similar powers and functions, more typically the governmental services they provide vary widely.

Table 25.1 Number of local governments by type, 1952–2002

	2002	1992	1982	1972	1962	1952
General Purpose (All)	38,967	38,978	38,851	38,552	38,184	37,061
County	3,034	3,043	3,041	3,044	3,043	3,052
Municipal	19,429	19,279	19,076	18,517	17,997	16,807
Town/Township	16,504	16,656	16,734	16,991	17,144	17,202
Special Purpose (All)	48,558	45,977	42,929	39,666	53,001	79,695
School District	13,506	14,422	14,851	15,781	34,678	67,355
Special District	35,052	31,555	28,078	23,885	18,323	12,340
Total Local Governments	87,525	84,955	81,780	78,218	91,185	116,756

Source: US Census Bureau (2002)

At the other end of the spectrum are special-purpose governments, which include two types: school districts and special districts. These exist as separate entities with substantial administrative and fiscal independence from general-purpose local governments, and in most cases (93 percent) provide a single service such as education, water, or mosquito abatement. Special-purpose governments accounted for more than half (55 percent) of all governments in 2002; however, their numbers have decreased substantially over time, from nearly 80,000 in 1952 to 48,558 in 2002. This decline is explained by the school district consolidation movement in education (Berry 2005), but has been tempered by the proliferation of special districts over roughly the same period.

Not surprisingly the volume of local governments in the U.S. means that there is an enormous number (nearly half a million in 1992) of public officials who hold positions in these governments. Indeed, nearly all elected officials in the U.S. (96.2 percent) represent local rather than state or federal jurisdictions. What kind of positions do these officials occupy and how do they make their way into office?

The Offices and Officials of Local Government

Like the form and function of local governments, there is considerable variation in the number and type of local government officials. As Table 25.2 reports, the majority of local elected officials come from municipal and town/township governments (27 and 26 percent respectively), followed by school and special district governments (18 and 17 percent respectively), and finally county governments (12 percent) (US Census Bureau 1995). While municipal, town/township, and school district governments elect on average about the same number of officials

Table 25.2 Distribution of local officials by government type and office, 1992

	All Govts	Cnty	Municipal	Town Twnshp	School Dist	Special Dist
Total local elected officials	493,830	58,818	135,531	126,958	88,434	84,089
Officials per government	5.81	19.33	7.03	7.62	6.13	2.66
% all local elected officials	100	12	27	26	18	17
% in legislatures	70	29	79	41	95	98
% in other bodies	9	18	3	20	4.7	n/a
% in exec/admin/judicial positions	21	52	18	39	0.3	n/a

Source: US Census Bureau (1995)

per government (between 6.13 and 7.62), counties and special districts stand out for their relatively large (19.33) and small (2.66) number of elected officials per government. For counties this is explained by the sizeable number of "row offices" (executive, administrative, and judicial positions), most of which are elective, whereas for special districts the small number is due to the fact that nearly half of all officials in these governments are appointed rather than elected (US Census Bureau 1995).

While the sizeable number of non-legislative elective offices and appointed officials may help explain why the election of county and special district officials has been so little studied, they are features that distinguish local governments from their state and federal counterparts more generally. Indeed, appointed officials can be found across every type of local government in the US. For example, roughly 10 percent of all school board members are appointed rather than elected,[2] and although less common, other officials, including city councilors, town supervisors, and county commissioners are sometimes appointed. Furthermore, a much large number of elected officials (roughly 30 percent) serve in non-legislative offices at the local level than at the state or national level (see Table 25.2). These officers act in concert with the county, city, or town legislative body to provide services and represent an extremely diverse set of offices, ranging from sheriff and tax collector to prothonotary and drain commissioner.

The Timing and Methods of Local Elections

There are several important distinctions to be made regarding how and when local governments elect their officials. For starters, at no other level of government is the timing of elections so varied. Indeed, the term "off-cycle" would be irrelevant were it not for local governments. Although comprehensive and comparable data on the timing of local elections are not available, existing data indicate that a very large number of local governments hold elections at times other than state or federal contests. The 2001 ICMA survey of municipal governments showed only 22.6 percent of cities held elections exclusively in even years; 77.4 percent held elections in only odd or in both odd and even years (ICMA 2002).[3] A survey of school board members found 34.7 percent of school board elections were always held off-cycle, whereas 46.5 percent were always held on-cycle (Hess 2002).[4]

---

[2] These are typically in "dependent" school districts, which are classified as agencies of other governments. In 2002 there were 1,508 dependent school districts.

[3] Based on data for 4,244 (54 percent) of the 7,867 municipalities with populations over 2,500.

[4] Based on a survey of 2,000 school boards with 827 respondents, yielding a 41 percent response rate.

The methods by which local governments elect officials are also quite varied. Unlike Congressional elections and most state legislative elections, many local council and board elections are multi-member (at-large) rather than single-member (district/ward). In fact, survey data suggest that the majority of both city council and school board members (66 and 57 percent respectively) are elected at-large (AL) rather than by single-member districts (SMD) (Hess 2002; ICMA 2002). Further, modified AL systems such as cumulative and limited voting are used to elect school board and city council members in a number of small- and medium-sized jurisdictions in several Southern and Southwestern states (Brockington et al. 1998), as well as some larger cities such as Philadelphia, Hartford, and Washington, D.C.

A final notable feature of local elections is the prevalence of non-partisan elections. Under this institutional arrangement, a candidate's party designation is absent from the ballot and may be proscribed in campaigning as well. With the exception of the unicameral and non-partisan Nebraska state legislature, non-partisanship is wholly absent from state and national elections. On the other hand, non-partisanship is the rule in local elections, reportedly applying to 77 percent of municipalities and 89 percent of school boards in 2001 (Hess 2002; ICMA 2002).

As noted in the introductory section of this chapter, the prevalence of non-partisan elections at the local level largely explains why electoral outcomes other than vote choice must be examined. However, election timing and selection methods provide clues as to why scholars have focused on turnout and minority representation rather than other outcomes. Specifically, because these electoral structures significantly alter the costs and benefits of voting, they have important implications for who turns out to vote and for how these votes are translated into legislative seats. As we will see in the next section, the geographic concentration of minorities, particularly African Americans, makes the question of selection methods especially important in the study of minority representation in local legislatures.

RESEARCH ON LOCAL ELECTIONS

Research on local elections and local electoral behavior can be divided into two main types: (1) macro-level studies that treat the local jurisdiction (almost always the city or school district) as the unit of analysis, and (2) micro-level studies that treat the individual as the unit of analysis. In the latter case, the most typical approach has been the single-city study, though occasionally individual-level analyses from multiple cities are employed. A third (uncommon) approach combines data from both levels so hypotheses about individuals and political jurisdictions can be simultaneously tested. As I will argue in the concluding section of this chapter, this third approach holds substantial promise for future research.

Most of what we know about local elections focuses on two primary outcomes: turnout and voting for minority candidates. With regard to turnout, research has focused on three broad sets of explanatory factors: (1) electoral and other institutional arrangements; (2) candidate characteristics (primarily racial/ethnic features, but sometimes incumbency status as well); (3) the local context. When it comes to the election of minority candidates, studies have investigated two primary research questions:

(1) How do electoral institutions affect the proportional representation of African Americans and to a lesser extent Latinos on city councils and local school boards?

(2) What is the nature and extent of bi-racial or "rainbow" coalitions (versus racial voting) in mayoral and local legislative elections?

In the next two sections, I review this research, paying particular attention to data sources and methods.

Turnout in Local Elections

The bulk of the research on turnout in local elections has focused on how Progressive Era reforms, at least implicitly designed to limit turnout, have fared. According to conventional wisdom, corrupt and inefficient party machines capitalized on socioeconomic cleavages in the population, playing on class antagonisms and racial and religious differences (Lineberry & Fowler 1967, 701), to promote what came to be known as a "private-regarding" ethos—the advancement of individual needs and personal loyalties over community interests (Banfield and Wilson 1963). "Good-government" reformers, on the other hand, promoted a "public-regarding" ethos and sought to remove the influence of party machines from local politics by instituting sweeping electoral and governance reforms that included the manager and commission forms, at-large, non-partisan, and off-cycle elections.[5]

Municipal Forms of Government

Two of the earliest studies investigating the effects of Progressive Era reforms on voter turnout focused on municipal forms of government. Alford and Lee (1968) examined elections from the early 1960s in all cities with a population over 25,000 (N = 282), whereas Karnig and Walter (1983) employed a longitudinal design to examine

---

[5] Others include the recall, referendum and initiative, Australian ballot, and civil service commission.

elections in 310 cities between 1930 and 1975. Both studies found that turnout in cities employing the council–manager form was significantly lower than in cities with the mayor–council or commission form.[6] This was consistent with research on reformed governments, which argued that the narrowed political sphere and transferral of many political functions of government to professional administrators under the council–manager form made government less responsive to elections, thereby reducing voters' incentives to participate (Lineberry and Fowler 1967). More recent studies confirm this. Analyzing 350 California cities, Hajnal and Lewis (2003) find turnout rates 6 percentage points lower in council–manager than mayor–council cities. Similarly, Caren's (2007) analysis of 332 elections in thirty-eight cities between 1979 and 2003 shows a 7.5 percentage point difference in turnout between council–manager and mayor–council cities (see also Bridges 1997). Finally, treating municipal forms as a categorical rather than binary variable, Wood (2002) finds average turnout declined 2.93 percentage points for each form of government (from most political to most administrative) in mayoral elections between 1993 and 2000.[7]

Non-partisan Elections

Although the reform of municipal governance structures was a critical component of the Progressive movement, the centerpiece was the non-partisan election. Designed to remove party cues from the voting calculus, the non-partisan election caused voters to seek alternative information about candidates and ultimately increased the costs of voting. While this presumably depressed voter turnout in general, the effect was expected to be particularly strong for low-income, immigrant, and non-white voters.

Interestingly, findings investigating the effects of non-partisan elections on turnout in municipal elections has been somewhat mixed. Early studies using correlation analysis and a limited set of control variables found that non-partisanship was associated with reductions of 7 and 9 percentage points in council–manager and mayor–council cities respectively (Alford and Lee 1968), and that cities adopting non-partisan elections had greater declines in voter turnout than cities retaining partisan elections (Karnig and Walter 1983). More recent research employing regression techniques has found no effect of non-partisanship (Caren 2007; Lublin and Tate 1995; Wood 2002; but see Schaffner, Streb, and Wright 2001).

Off-cycle Elections

Similar to the non-partisan election, off-cycle (or non-concurrent) elections are expected to decrease voter turnout by increasing the costs of voting. Unlike

---

[6] Both studies controlled for partisanship.

[7] His sample included fifty-seven cities with populations between 25,000 and one million.

findings on non-partisan elections, however, research has consistently found strong negative effects of off-cycle elections on voter turnout. Hajnal, Lewis, and Louch's (2002) study of council and mayoral elections in 350 California cities finds off-cycle elections have the largest (negative) impact on voter turnout and are associated with a 36 percent lower turnout rate than elections held during presidential contests (p. 36).[8] Wood (2002) and Caren (2007) also found election timing attenuated turnout more than any other structural feature, by 28 and 31 percentage points respectively.

Electoral Systems

There are two arguments in the literature regarding how at-large (AL) elections affect turnout (Bullock 1990; Heilig and Mundt 1984). The first suggests that turnout will be lower in AL races because voters feel less connected to politics compared to single member districts (SMD). Because AL councils and boards represent jurisdiction-wide rather than neighborhood interests, they presumably engender lower levels of interest and efficacy, which translate into lower turnout rates. The alternative explanation is that AL elections have higher voter turnout rates because they are almost guaranteed to be more competitive. Specifically, AL elections require only one candidate more than the number of seats in order to be competitive, whereas in SMDs, incumbency may discourage all competitors (Heilig and Mundt 1984, 76).

The effect of electoral systems on turnout has received almost no empirical examination, and the few studies that have been done are limited due to very small (and unrepresentative) samples (Bullock 1990; Heilig and Mundt 1984). While Hajnal et al. (2002) analyze a larger number of cities and elections, the small number of cases with SMDs (17 of 421) suggest caution in interpreting the negative relationship they find between SMDs and turnout. Finally, Bowler, Brockington, and Donovan (2001) take a slightly different approach, focusing not on SMD systems but rather cumulative voting (CV). Based on a matched sample design of twenty-one municipalities employing CV systems they find that CV cities had turnout rates 4–5 percentage points higher than cities using plurality elections (p. 912).

Candidate Characteristics

A second area of inquiry on turnout in local elections focuses on the effects of candidates' racial/ethnic characteristics. Although theories developed to explain these effects can be applied at any level, it is at the local level, where the incidence of minority candidates and prevalence of minority elected officials are greatest, that

---

[8] For registered voters; among adult residents turnout was 23 percent lower.

they are most fruitfully tested. At the most basic level, researchers have investigated whether the presence of minority candidates (typically in mayoral elections) leads to higher voter turnout. The answer has overwhelmingly been yes. For example, examining elections in twenty-six major cities from 1969 to 1991, Lublin and Tate (1995) find turnout rates roughly 4 percentage points higher in mayoral elections with black candidates,[9] and Caren (n.d., 24) finds elections involving white candidates in opposition to minority candidates have higher turnout than elections where all candidates are of the same race. Finally, looking at black challenger and black incumbent elections,[10] Hajnal (2007, 45) finds turnout in half of the black challenger elections reached or exceeded record levels in these cities and on average exceeded the national average by 10 percentage points.

Not surprisingly, scholars have also been interested in *who* is turning out at higher levels in these elections. The most popular hypothesis posits that co-ethnics are largely responsible for higher turnout rates and is based on the argument that the presence of a minority candidate on the ballot heightens group pride and loyalty, stimulates interest, and ultimately leads to greater voter turnout among co-ethnics (Tate 1991). To date, this hypothesis has been examined almost exclusively via case study research, and the evidence produced by these studies has been supportive. Average turnout among blacks in cities such as Los Angeles, Cleveland, Atlanta (Gilliam and Kaufmann 1998), Denver (Kaufmann 2003), Dade County (Hill, Moreno, and Cue 2001), Chicago, and Philadelphia (Munoz and Henry 1986) has been higher when black candidates are present. The same pattern has obtained for Latino mayoral candidates (Barreto 2007; Barreto, Villarreal, and Woods 2005; Kaufmann 2003).

A second hypothesis posits that whites drive elevated turnout in elections with minority candidates and is based on racial prejudice and social dominance theories, which argue that whites' perceptions that qualified minority candidates threaten their political hegemony and the established racial hierarchy lead them to turn out at higher rates in order to vote against minorities (Hajnal 2007). Case study evidence overwhelmingly supports this hypothesis as well. In addition, though not disaggregated by race, findings from several multi-city, longitudinal studies suggest higher turnout among both whites and co-ethnics (Caren n.d; Hajnal 2007; Lublin and Tate 1995).

Finally, based on insights from two competing theories, a third hypothesis focusing explicitly on minority incumbents proposes that in these elections turnout among whites will either be unaffected or attenuated. According to Hajnal's (2007) information theory, because whites learn that black political leadership

---

[9] Cities had populations over 100,000.

[10] His sample includes twenty-six cities with populations over 100,000; challenger elections were those where a black candidate was first elected mayor and faced a white challenger in his first reelection bid.

generally does not harm their interests, uncertainty and fear about black empow-erment disappears once blacks have been elected to office and whites resume more normal turnout levels. In contrast, the intergroup competition theory predicts that as the losing or "out-group," whites will turn out at lower rates than they did when they were in power (Gilliam and Kaufmann 1998). Though findings have been used to support both theories, the lack of turnout data by race makes it impossible to discern whether and how white turnout has changed across these elections (Hajnal 2007; Lublin and Tate 1995). Furthermore, limitations in the method employed to infer racial turnout make findings based on such analytic models only provisional.

Local Context

The literature on turnout also considers how contextual factors influence individ-ual political decisions, including voter turnout. Although much of this literature has been theoretical and normative in scope, a handful of recent studies attempt to empirically examine hypotheses regarding how features of the local context influ-ence voter turnout.

One such aspect of the local context is size, specifically whether and how city size influences the participatory culture of local places or individuals' decisions regard-ing their political behavior. On the one hand, a negative relationship between size and turnout has been posited based on arguments that: (1) psychological attach-ments, loyalty, and shared values are more prevalent in smaller jurisdictions, (2) smaller governments are associated with lower costs and more direct benefits, and (3) smaller jurisdictions provide more opportunities for participation. On the other hand, a positive relationship has been posited based on the claim that larger communities are more likely to address issues compelling to voters.

Interestingly, tests of these hypotheses found no effect whatsoever of city size. Oliver (1999, 2000) examined self-reports of participation in local elections for roughly 2,400 survey respondents in 800 municipalities and found that while city size was significantly and negatively associated with interest in local politics, it did not have a significant effect on turnout in local elections.[11] Examining actual voter turnout in city council elections in 466 municipalities, Kelleher and Lowery (2004) found city size an insignificant predictor of turnout across all of their models (see also Caren 2007, n.d.).

Although a second body of work has examined how socioeconomic context affects political behavior, voter turnout has featured less prominently than other forms of participation. Studies looking specifically at voter turnout have focused on city-level measures of socioeconomic status (SES) and emphasized competition,

---

[11] Based on the American Citizen Participation Study (Verba et al. 1995).

interest, and capacity as the key mechanisms driving contextual effects. While most of these studies have posited a positive relationship between city SES and turnout (Caren 2007, n.d.; Kelleher and Lowery 2004), Oliver (1999) proposed a non-linear relationship, expecting turnout to be highest in middle-income cities and lower in both high- and low-income cities. According to his argument, in middle-income cities not only are social needs and pressures to participate present, but also competition and thus interest in local politics and elections are likely to be most intense. Empirical tests have consistently found a positive relationship between city SES and turnout, and whereas Oliver finds support that economic heterogeneity drives turnout in local elections, his evidence does not confirm the non-linear relationship.

Local Elections and Minority Representation

The second major area of inquiry in local elections examines the incidence of minority elected officials, most typically African Americans and Latinos. Given that the majority of black and Latino elected officials hold local rather than state or federal offices, this focus clearly makes sense. Indeed, in 2006 approximately 80 percent of elected officials of color served on municipal councils or school boards (Hardy-Fanta et al. 2007).

Because of the historically larger size of the black population and the long-standing disenfranchisement of African Americans, research is more developed with regard to black than Latino representation in local politics. And, whereas both groups have made significant gains in local officeholding over time (see Figures 25.1 and 25.2), these gains have been stronger for blacks, particularly at the municipal level.[12] Indeed, studies have consistently found Latinos less proportionally represented in local legislatures than blacks (Meier et al. 2005; Zax 1990).

Unlike research on voter turnout, which has focused almost exclusively on mayoral elections, research on minority representation is most developed in the area of local legislatures—both city councils and school boards. As I outline below, the question of how electoral arrangements condition the relationship between the size of the minority population and the proportional representation of minorities on local legislatures has occupied a central place in this literature.

---

[12] The drop in the number of Latino elected officials in 1995 is due to a change in reporting by NALEO (National Association of Latino Elected Officials). Whereas previously annual rosters included officials who had served at any time during the year, in 1995 rosters began including only officials who were in office as of January.

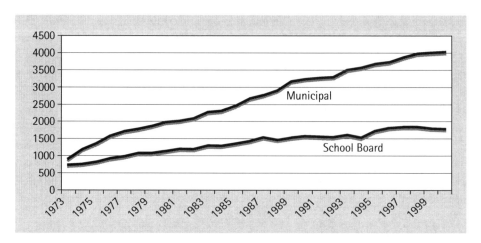

Figure 25.1 Total blacks elected to municipal and school board offices, 1973–2000

Source: Joint Center for Political and Economic Studies

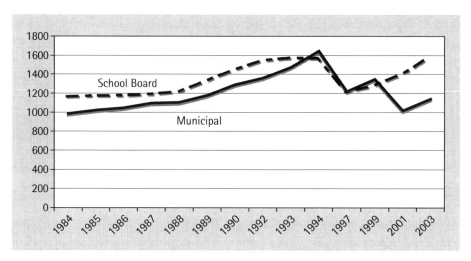

Figure 25.2 Total Latinos elected to municipal and school board offices, 1984–2003

Source: National Association of Latino Elected and Appointed Officials (various years)

Electoral Arrangements and Proportional Representation in Local Legislatures

A wave of early studies using data from the 1970s and bivariate statistical tests largely showed that blacks were more proportionally represented under SMDs and mixed arrangements compared to AL systems. Further, black proportional representation estimates tended to be higher for boards than councils. While this finding suggested blacks achieved more equitable representation on school boards than on city councils, it was inconsistent with descriptive evidence (see Figure 25.1) and survey data (Hess 2002; ICMA, various years). With regard to Latinos, early studies found that Latinos were significantly more underrepresented on boards and councils compared to blacks, and that electoral systems mattered much less (MacManus 1978; Taebel 1978). The lower level of residential segregation among Latinos was offered as an explanation for why SMD arrangements provided at best a marginal improvement in Latino representation in local legislatures.

Findings from a second wave of studies, relying on new measures of representation, larger samples, and more recent data, show increases in black representation in all but one place: councils using SMD systems. Cities electing council members via AL arrangements and school districts employing SMD systems registered particularly strong increases in black representation. Although the size of the black population again had stronger effects on black board than council representation, the difference across electoral methods was greater for boards than councils, unlike earlier findings. For Latinos, findings were more mixed. Though several studies found no difference between SMD and AL arrangements (Fraga, Meier, and England 1986; Rocha 2007; Welch 1990; Zax 1990), others found AL systems significantly more detrimental to Latino representation than SMD systems (Alozie and Manganaro 1993; Leal, Martinez-Ebers, and Meier 2004; Meier et al. 2005).

Discrepancies in the empirical evidence across time and legislative arena raise questions about the extent and locus of minority gains in representation. For starters, none of these studies examined school boards and councils simultaneously, and none analyzed a consistent sample of jurisdictions. A recent study by Marschall, Shah, and Ruhil (2010) overcomes these limitations by utilizing panel data for a constant sample of boards and councils from 1980 to 2000. In marked contrast to previous research, they find descriptive differences between councils and school boards mostly illusory, stemming from differences in sampling and measurement rather than shifts in representational patterns, and electoral structures, particularly SMD arrangements, equally, if not more important now than in previous decades.

Racial/Ethnic Voting, Cross-over Voting, and Rainbow Coalitions

A second major area of study with regard to minority representation in local politics focuses on who votes for minority candidates and, more specifically, which groups are pivotal in the electoral success of minority candidates. Not surprisingly, the accumulated evidence demonstrates that the voting strength of the minority population is the most reliable predictor of minority representation in both local legislatures and the mayor's office (e.g., Murray and Vedlitz 1978). Findings from numerous case studies show that racial voting is widespread. For example, analyzing the 1981 municipal elections in Atlanta, Bullock and Campbell (1984) found that while race was not the sole determinant of vote choice, racially motivated voting dominated in mayoral contests, with approximately 90 percent of each race voting for their racial candidate. Similarly, in the 1989 and 1993 New York mayoral elections, 91 percent and 95 percent of blacks voted for Dinkins and roughly-three quarters of white voters, many who crossed party lines, voted for Republican candidate Rudy Giuliani (Kaufmann 2003). As for Latinos, Hill, Moreno, and Cue (2001) find the presence of Cuban American candidates is associated with heightened ethnic politics in Miami, and Barreto (2007) finds the Latino population always voted overwhelmingly in favor of the Latino candidate in mayoral elections in Los Angeles, Denver, San Francisco, New York, and Houston, whereas non-Latinos never did.

While racial/ethnic voting may be the norm, it explains only part of the success of minority candidates in local elections. This is not only because blacks and Latinos constitute the majority in only a small fraction of local jurisdictions, but also because most cities and school districts employ AL electoral systems. Under these conditions, minority candidates typically must seek electoral support beyond their own racial/ethnic group. In fact, this is true even in electoral contests where blacks or Latinos constitute the majority, since these often involve incumbents and challengers of the same race. Thus, a key research question in this literature asks which segments of the electorate minority candidates seek to mobilize and with whom they seek to build electoral coalitions.

The tendency in the literature has been to assume that black and Latino candidates will either attempt to form "rainbow" coalitions with one another or seek primarily Anglo "cross-over" voters, particularly those with more liberal political views and/or high levels of educational attainment. Browning et al. (1985) popularized the rainbow coalition thesis, particularly for Latinos, in their analysis of minority incorporation in ten California cities. High-profile cases of black candidates relying on black–Latino coalitions for their electoral success suggest that rainbow coalition might work at least some of the time for blacks as well. The question, however, is when?

Though this question has motivated numerous case studies over the past several decades, the lack of systematic evidence and rigorous analytic methods has made it difficult to draw conclusions from this body of work. Recently, several studies involving large-N samples have shed new empirical light on this question. Although this research has found no support for rainbow coalitions when it comes to black mayoralties and black council representation (Marschall and Ruhil 2006; Marschall et al. 2007), in the context of school boards, studies have found black candidates fare better in districts with larger Latino populations, whereas Latino candidates do worse in districts with larger African American populations (Marschall 2005; Marschall et al. 2007; Rocha 2007; but see Meier and Stewart 1991, who find the opposite pattern).

Is there an asymmetrical relationship between rainbow coalitions and black versus Latino success in school board elections? Why do black school-board candidates benefit from larger Latino populations, whereas council and mayoral candidates do not? Clearly additional research is needed to address these and other questions. However, work by McClain (1993) suggests that socioeconomic and political competition between Latinos and blacks manifests itself in ways that could leave blacks feeling more threatened by Latino gains in representation, which might in turn explain why blacks do not support Latino candidates.

In fact, a number of scholars have questioned the viability of rainbow coalitions, suggesting that racial polarization in many major cities makes black–Latino coalitions implausible (Sonenshein 1986). Others have applied the "power thesis," which suggests that social distance between groups determines whether they forge coalitions with one another, to explain why Latino–Anglo coalitions are more likely than Latino–black coalitions (Meier and Stewart 1991; Rocha 2007). Although this thesis has not typically been applied to black–Anglo coalitions, Rocha (2007) develops a "revised power thesis" that predicts increasing Anglo support of blacks in places with rapidly growing Latino immigrant populations, based on the argument that perceived social distance between Anglos and blacks is narrowed in this setting. While case-study literature is replete with examples of black mayors winning office with the help of liberal white supporters, it is not clear what mechanism is driving these voters.

An alternative to the power thesis is Hajnal's (2007) information model, which posits that white cross-over voting is more likely after whites have experienced black political leadership because they learn that their interests are generally not harmed by black empowerment. Looking strictly at cases with black incumbent mayors, Hajnal finds that white voters are more likely to support black candidates when they run as incumbents rather than challengers, and that whites pay increasing attention to non-racial factors like candidate quality and the economy in black incumbent elections.

While the information model provides compelling evidence to explain white voting behavior after blacks have overcome the representational hurdle, it does not explain how whites behave in elections without black incumbents. Evidence is less encouraging on this score. Marschall and Ruhil (2006) for example, find no evidence that the size of the liberal white population increases the likelihood of observing black mayors. And, in the context of council and school-board contests, they find it not only decreases the electoral prospects of black candidates, but is also most acute in locations with both a history of past black political incorporation and large black populations, suggesting that traditional explanations focusing on prejudice and racial threat may be more accurate than the information model (Marschall et al. 2010).

CONCLUSIONS AND FUTURE DIRECTIONS

As noted at the outset of this chapter, students of both local politics and political behavior have largely overlooked the study of local elections. Moreover, most research on local elections is based on case studies and, apart from the research on minority representation in local legislatures, a handful of studies that employ samples of less than 100 jurisdictions. Although the body of case-study research offers considerable insights about specific electoral contests and proves indispensable when it comes to theory- and hypothesis-building, the inferences that can be drawn from this work regarding voter turnout or voting for minority candidates in local elections are limited.

On the other hand, the vast majority of larger-N studies employing research designs appropriate for testing causal hypotheses rely on aggregate-level data and samples of large cities and thus are limited in both generalizability and the questions they address. Most of what we do know involves the role of institutional arrangements and, to a lesser extent, features of the local context. In particular, evidence rather unequivocally demonstrates that off-cycle elections severely depress turnout and AL systems hinder the success of especially blacks in local legislative contests. However, we don't know whether these relationships obtain in smaller municipalities and school districts, or counties and special districts more generally, since almost no studies of these jurisdictions exist. Furthermore, considerable work still needs to be done in systematically analyzing the effects of other electoral and governing arrangements, including term limits, the initiative, and the referendum to name a few, across jurisdictions and also time.

While the huge volume of local governments and considerable variation in their forms, functions, and electoral arrangements make aggregate-level studies of local elections an extremely fruitful area of inquiry, the absence of institutionalized, ongoing data collection poses a substantial impediment to this area of inquiry and represents perhaps the most pressing priority. Given the scope of such data collection, it may be achievable only through collaborative efforts among academics, national associations, and governmental agencies.

A pressing need for aggregate-level data also exists when it comes to studies seeking to explain the decision calculus of voters in local elections, for without such data it is impossible to test or control for the effects of context, governing arrangements, and other time/location-specific factors (e.g., race riots, crime, local economy) that presumably factor into vote choice. However, here individual-level data are also essential since nearly all theories of voting behavior are based on micro-level theories. Unfortunately, because almost no dataset combines a sufficient number of both individuals and jurisdictions, most studies have relied on aggregate-level data that suffer not only from ecological inference problems, but also limitations in their capacity to operationalize key explanatory variables.

Models of cross-over voting/rainbow coalitions are a case in point since they have not included measures tapping which groups (or neighborhoods) candidates seek to mobilize, whether candidates pursue colorblind or deracialized campaigns, or whether voters' racial attitudes make them amenable to voting for candidates of different racial/ethnic backgrounds. In my work I have argued that the local context, including the relative size, resources, and degree of political incorporation of different racial/ethnic groups, influences whether and with whom minority candidates seek to build electoral coalitions. These contextual factors in turn interact with candidate characteristics and campaign dynamics in critical, complicated, and as yet untested ways, to affect voters' decision calculi. Future research must employ cross-level datasets with a richer set of explanatory variables in order to examine these relationships and begin building the empirical foundation for further theory development. At present, the literature does a reasonable job explaining *post hoc* which groups supported minority candidates in specific elections, but is very far from predicting when and where minority candidates succeed (except where their racial/ethnic group constitutes a majority), let alone when and where they will emerge as serious challengers.

REFERENCES

ALFORD, R. and LEE, E. 1968. Voting Turnout in American Cities. *American Political Science Review*, 62/3: 796–813.

ALOZIE, N. O. and MANGANARO, L. L. 1993. Black and Hispanic Council Representation: Does Council Size Matter? *Urban Affairs Review*, 29/2: 276–98.

BANFIELD, E. C. and WILSON, J. Q. 1963. *City Politics*. Cambridge, Mass.: Harvard University Press and the MIT Press.

BARRETO, M. A. 2007. Si Se Puede! Latino Candidates and the Mobilization of Latino Voters. *American Political Science Review*, 101/3: 425–41.

——— VILLARREAL, M., and WOODS, N. D. 2005. Metropolitan Latino Political Behavior: Voter Turnout and Candidate Preference in Los Angeles. *Urban Affairs Review*, 27/1: 71–91.

BERRY, C. R. 2005. School District Consolidation and Student Outcomes: Does Size Matter? In *Besieged: School Boards and the Future of Education Politics*, ed. W. G. Howell. Washington, D.C.: Brookings Institution.

BOWLER, S., BROCKINGTON, D., and DONOVAN, T. 2001. Election Systems and Voter Turnout: Experiments in the United States. *The Journal of Politics*, 63/3: 902–15.

BRIDGES, Amy. 1997. *Morning Glories: Municipal Reform in the Southwest*. Princeton, N.J.: Princeton University Press.

BROCKINGTON, D., DONOVAN, T., BOWLER, S., and BRISCHETTO, R. 1998. Minority Representation under Cumulative and Limited Voting. *Journal of Politics*, 60/4: 1108–25.

BROWNING, R. P., MARSHALL, D. R., and TABB, D. H. 1985. *Protest is Not Enough: The Struggle of Blacks and Hispanics for Equality in Urban Politics.* Berkeley: University of California Press.

BULLOCK, C. S. III. 1990. Turnout in Municipal Elections. *Policy Studies Journal,* 9/3: 539–49.

—— and CAMPBELL, B. A. 1984. Racist or Racial Voting in the 1981 Atlanta Municipal Elections. *Urban Affairs Quarterly,* 20: 149–64.

CAREN, N. 2007. Big City, Big Turnout? Electoral Participation in American Cities. *Journal of Urban Affairs,* 29/1: 31–46.

—— N.d. The Salience of Social Cleavages in Political Participation: Race, Ethnicity and Voter Turnout. Working Paper, University of North Carolina, Chapel Hill.

FRAGA, L. R., MEIER, K. J., and ENGLAND, R. E. 1986. Hispanic Americans and Educational Policy: Limits to Equal Access. *Journal of Politics,* 48: 850–76.

GILLIAM, F. D. and KAUFMANN, K. M. 1998. Is There an Empowerment Life Cycle? Long-Term Lack Empowerment and Its Influence on Voter Participation. *Urban Affairs Review,* 33/6: 741–66.

HAJNAL, Z. 2007. *Changing White Attitudes Toward Black Politial Leadership.* New York: Cambridge University Press.

—— and LEWIS, P. 2003. Municipal Institutions and Voter Turnout in Local Elections. *Urban Affairs Review,* 38/5: 645–68.

—— —— and LOUCH, H. 2002. *Municipal Elections in California: Turnout, Timing, and Competition.* San Francisco: Public Policy Institute of California.

HARDY-FANTA, C., LIEN, P., SIERRA, C. M., and PINDERHUGHES, D. 2007. A New Look at Paths to Poitical Office: Moving Women of Color from the Margins to the Center. Paper presented at the Annual Political Science Association Conference.

HEILIG, P. and MUNDT, R. J. 1984. *Your Voice at City Hall: The Politics, Procedures and Policies of District Representation.* Albany, N.Y.: SUNY Press.

HESS, F. 2002. *School Boards at the Dawn of the 21st Century: Conditions and Challenges of District Governance.* Alexandria, Va.: National School Board Association.

HILL, K. A., MORENO, D. V., and CUE, L. 2001. Racial and Partisan Voting in a Tri-Ethnic City: The 1996 Dade County Mayoral Election. *Journal of Urban Affairs,* 23/3–4: 291–307.

INTERNATIONAL CITY/COUNTY MANAGEMENT ASSOCIATION (ICMA). 2002. *Municipal Form of Government, 2001.* Washington, D.C.: ICMA.

KARNIG, A. and WALTER, O. 1983. Decline in Municipal Voter Turnout: A Function of Changing Structure. *American Politics Quarterly,* 11/4: 491–505.

KAUFMANN, K. 2003. Black and Latino Voters in Denver: Responses to Each Other's Political Leadership. *Political Science Quarterly,* Spring: 107–26.

KELLEHER, C. and LOWERY, D. 2004. Political Participation and Metropolitan Institutional Contexts. *Urban Affairs Review,* 39/6: 720–57.

KREBS, T. B. 1998. The Determinants of Candidates' Vote Share and Advantages of Incumbency in City Council Elections. *American Journal of Political Science,* 42: 921–35.

LEAL, D. L., MARTINEZ-EBERS, V., and MEIER, K. J. 2004. The Politics of Latino Education: The Biases of At-Large Elections. *The Journal of Politics,* 66/4: 1224–44.

LEIGHLEY, J. 1996. Group Membership and the Mobilization of Political Participation. *Journal of Politics,* 58/2: 447–63.

LINEBERRY, R. and FOWLER, E. P. 1967. Reformism and Public Policies in American Cities. *American Political Science Review,* 41/3: 701–16.

LUBLIN, D. I. and TATE, K. 1995. Racial Group Competition in Urban Elections. In *Classifying by Race*, ed. P. E. Peterson. Princeton, N.J.: Princeton University Press.

LYONS, W. E., LOWERY, D., and DeHOOG, R. H. 1992. *The Politics of Dissatisfaction*. Armonk, N.Y.: M.E. Sharpe.

MacMANUS, S. A. 1978. City Council Election Procedures and Minority Representation: Are they Related? *Social Science Quarterly*, 59: 153–61.

MARSCHALL, M. 2004. Citizen Participation and the Neighborhood Context: A New Look at the Coproduction of Local Public Goods. *Political Research Quarterly*, 57/2: 231–44.

—— 2005. Minority Incorporation and Local School Boards. In *School Boards Besieged*, ed. W. Howell. Washington, D.C.: Brookings Institution.

—— and RUHIL, A. 2006. The Pomp of Power: Black Mayoralties in Urban America. *Social Science Quarterly*, 87/4: 828–50.

—— SHAH, P., and RUHIL, A. 2010. The New Racial Calculus: Electoral Institutions and Black Representation in Local Legislatures. *Amercian Journal of Political Science*, 54/1.

McCLAIN, P. D. 1993. The Changing Dynamics of Urban Politics: Black and Hispanic Municipal Employment. *Journal of Politics*, 55: 399–414.

MEIER, K. J. and STEWART, J., JR. 1991. Cooperation and Conflict in Multiracial School Districts. *Journal of Politics*, 53: 1123–33.

—— JUENKE, E. G., WRINKLE, R. D., and POLINARD, J. L. 2005. Structural Choices and Representational Biases: The Post-Election Color of Representation. *American Journal of Political Science*, 49: 758–68.

MUNOZ, C., JR. and HENRY, C. 1986. Rainbow Coalitions in Four Big Cities: San Antonio, Denver, Chicago and Philadelphia. *PS*, 19/3: 598–609.

MURRAY, R. and VEDLITZ, A. 1978. Racial Voting Patterns in the South: An Analysis of Major Elections from 1960–1977 in Five Cities. *American Academy of Political and Social Science Annals*, 439: 29–39.

OLIVER, J. E. 1999. The Effects of Metropolitan Economic Segregation on Local Civic Participation. *American Journal of Political Science*, 43: 186–212.

—— 2000. City Size and Civic Involvement in Metropolitan America. *American Political Science Review*, 94: 361–73.

—— and HA, S. E. 2007. Vote Choice in Suburban Elections. *American Political Science Review*, 101: 393–408.

ROCHA, R. 2007. Black-Brown Coalitions in Local School Board Elections. *Political Research Quarterly*, 60/2: 315–27.

SCHAFFNER, B. F., STREB, M., and WRIGHT, G. 2001. Teams Without Uniforms: The Nonpartisan Ballot in State and Local Elections. *Political Research Quarterly*, 54: 7–30.

SHARP, E. 1980. Toward a New Understanding of Urban Services and Citizen Participation: The Coproduction Concept. *Midwest Review of Public Administration*, 14/2: 105–18.

SONENSHEIN, R. 1986. Biracial Coalition Politics in Los Angeles. *PS*, 19: 582–90.

TAEBEL, D. 1978. Minority Representation on City Councils: The Impact of Structure on Blacks and Hispanics. *Social Science Quarterly*, 59: 142–52.

TATE, K. 1991. Black Political Representation in the 1984 and 1988 Presidential Elections. *American Political Science Review*, 85/4: 1159–76.

US CENSUS BUREAU 1995. *1992 Census of Governments*, Volume 1, Number 2: *Popularly Elected Officials GC92(1)–2*. Washington, D.C.: U.S. Government Printing Office.

—— 2002. *2002 Census of Governments*, Volume 1, Number 1: *Government Organization, GC02(1)-1*. Washington, D.C.: U.S. Government Printing Office.

VERBA, S., SCHLOZMAN, K. L., and BRADY, H. E. 1995. *Voice and Equality: Civic Voluntarism in American Politics*. Cambridge, Mass.: Harvard University Press.

WELCH, S. 1990. The Impact of At-Large Elections on the Representation of Blacks and Hispanics. *Journal of Politics*, 52/4: 1050–76.

WOOD, C. 2002. Voter Turnout in City Elections. *Urban Affairs Review*, 38/2: 209–31.

ZAX, J. S. 1990. Election Methods and Black and Hispanic City Council Membership. *Social Science Quarterly*, 71: 339–55.

CHAPTER 26

STUDYING STATE JUDICIAL RACES IN A TRANSFORMED ELECTORAL ENVIRONMENT

LAURA LANGER

MEGHAN LEONARD

ANDREA POLK

ALMOST thirty years ago, one of the most prominent scholars of judicial elections summarized these races as follows: "what is most obviously interesting about judicial elections . . . is that they seem to be very uninteresting. They are typically placid affairs of low salience, involving men usually obscure to the general public" (Dubois 1984, 396). Prior to the 1990s, low levels of voter awareness and scant information about judicial candidates fostered a characterization of these elections as unimportant in the democratic process (Dubois 1984). Indeed, many of the discussions about judicial elections in the 1980s and early 1990s were led by legal practitioners and politicians, and a significant part of the focus was on judicial reform. Very few systematic evaluations of the influences on and consequences of electoral races for judicial seats existed in the literature because adjectives such as uninteresting, unimportant, uncontested were all too commonly used to describe these elections. Fast-forward to the new millennium and the landscape for judicial elections could not have undergone a more radical change.

Much of this change can be attributed to the newly pervasive role of money and media in these races, combined with a diminished role for federal government, which fueled the emergence of state high courts as more critical players in the policy arena. Many examples highlight this significant growth. Between 1993 and 2006, the median amount of campaign funds raised by a judicial candidate increased by almost 90 percent (from about $130,000 to about $250,000).[1] While these figures reflect a dramatic increase in the flow of money in judicial elections, some state high court races exceeded millions of dollars in states where judges are chosen on partisan ballots. In her report on money in judicial races, Nina Totenberg notes that the 2006 race for chief justice in Alabama cost more than $6.2 million.[2] Even in non-partisan races, where the party affiliation of the candidate is not identified on the ballot, state high court races attracted significantly more dollars in 2006 compared to 1996. The most expensive non-partisan race in 2006 was in Georgia where the cost of winning a seat on the state's highest court was just over $1.3 million (National Institute on Money in State Politics); yet in 1996, the winning candidate for a seat on Ohio's Supreme Court spent only $483,302. According to the "Justice at Stake" Campaign, an organization that follows the increasing role of money in judicial elections, this increased spending does not seem to be an aberration. Reports showed that by the fall of 2008 candidates raised $29.4 million, which was almost identical to the amount raised by candidates at the same time in 2006.[3]

Not only has the cost of judicial elections grown significantly over the past three decades, but the structure of campaigns has also undergone a serious transformation. For example, in 2000, television advertisements for judicial candidates ran in just four of the eighteen states with contested elections (22 percent). This is compared to the year 2006, where television ads were utilized in 91 percent of the eleven states with contested elections. Alabama ($6.3 million), Georgia ($2.8m), and Ohio ($2.1m) spent the largest amount of money on television ads in 2006; however, interest groups alone spent over $2.7 million for television ads in the races for seats on the Washington Supreme Court. Perhaps most convincing of the changing nature of the electoral environment in judicial races is that in the year 2000 there were 22,646 television ads in total compared to the total of 121,646 ads

[1] Nina Totenberg. Report: Spending on Judicial Elections Soaring. National Public Radio, May 18, 2007.

[2] Ibid.

[3] Justice at Stake Campaign Press Release, November 5, 2008: "2008 Supreme Court Elections: More Money, More Nastiness."

televised in 2006. Justice At Stake estimated $17 million was spent on television advertising in the 2008 judicial races.[4]

As this electoral environment changed, so did the state of scholarly research on judicial elections. Academics began questioning characterizations of judicial elections as unimportant and non-competitive and instead examined these judicial elections from the perspective of legislative races (Hall 2001a, 2001b). The conceptual lens from which students of judicial behavior have embraced judicial electoral phenomena paved the way for significant advances in this field. The 1990s thus ushered in a new challenge for scholars of judicial politics, which was to better understand the role of state court elections in a democratic society and compare these phenomena with extant scholarly literature on congressional and gubernatorial elections. A call for systematic evaluation of judicial elections and campaigns was heightened in the year 2000, as these, once considered low-information, low-salience events, became increasingly consequential and sparked intense political discussion. Scholarly attention to judicial elections and campaigns has been rekindled and a revised characterization of these elections has emerged from the literature.

Has this revised characterization of judicial elections advanced our understanding of state judicial politics and elections in general? How has the scholarly community evaluated the progress made in studying state judicial elections and campaigns and the influence of these elections on judicial behavior over the last two decades? In this chapter, we address these important questions by reviewing the impressive body of scholarship on state judicial campaigns and elections from 1988 to 2008 and evaluate the extent to which this literature has forwarded general theories of elections and judicial behavior. In so doing, we highlight the major substantive and analytical contributions of this scholarly work through a survey and categorization of the extant research in the subfield of state judicial campaigns and elections over the past twenty years. In many ways, our chapter is similar to field essays; however, we depart from the traditional approach in two ways. First, we focus on a subsection of literature on judicial politics—state court elections and campaigns. Second, we do not attempt to discuss every study conducted in this area of study, nor do we provide a detailed account of scholarly publications on this topic. Rather, we summarize some of the major trends in the existing scholarship and suggest which scholarly directions have advanced our understanding of judicial elections and campaigns, which debates are unresolved, and which lines of inquiry prompted new discoveries and suggested important avenues for future inquiry.

Our survey of this subfield considers research on topics related to state judicial elections and campaigns published in the profession's top journals from 1988 to 2008. The journal list includes the *American Political Science Review*, the

---

[4] Justice at Stake Press Release Nov 5, 2008.

American Journal of Political Science, the *Journal of Politics,* the *Western Political Quarterly/Political Research Quarterly, American Politics Research,* and *Social Science Quarterly.* These journals represent the top national and regional general journals in the political science profession. The competition to get published in one of these journals spans the entire spectrum of political science questions—not just inquiries about law and courts, elections, or general state politics. Given that some specialty journals on law and courts and state politics have become increasingly influential and more widely read we also include the following journals in our survey of the subfield: *State Politics and Policy Quarterly, Justice System Journal,* and *Judicature.*[5] Of course, any selection of journals is somewhat arbitrary, but articles in these journals appeal to more than just specialists in the subfield of state judicial elections and campaigns and thus presumably allow us to make a broader-based conclusion about the state of this subfield in the larger profession of political science. We do so also by making our definition of what constitutes state judicial elections and campaigns deliberately broad. Admittedly, we thus include articles that others may consider outside the parameters of traditional election studies. However, we contend that doing so underscores instances where greater unification in theory and methodology, better cooperation in data collection and sharing, and more examination of multi-state, multi-branch studies, can not only advance research in this subfield but also scholarly inquiries on political and mass behavior vis-à-vis elections and campaigns more broadly.

Using our definition of state judicial elections and campaigns, our search identifies seventy articles published in the nine academic journals surveyed for the 1988 to 2008 time period. Figure 26.1 illustrates the number of articles published in each year of our literature review for both general and specialty journals. The average number of publications per year for top general journals is 1.5 publications whereas the average per year for specialty journals is 3.2.

The distribution of publications by journal is displayed in Figure 26.2. As the figure shows, the most frequent venue for state judicial election research is in the specialized journal, *Judicature.* The *Journal of Politics* published the second most articles and the *Justice System Journal* published the third most.

We also grouped the publications by substantive area in judicial elections as illustrated in Figure 26.3. Specifically, we identified the primary research question in each publication and created groups along similar lines of inquiry. Our purpose was to help compare and contrast this body of scholarship with election studies in other subfields. As such, we did not develop our categories based on the dependent variable or a given independent variable. Thus, for example, we do not include all studies that have included a variable for elected or appointed judges in the analysis;

---

[5] We also considered *Law and Society Review* as well as the *Journal of Law, Economics, and Organization;* however, there were no relevant articles in these publications during our time frame on state court elections and campaigns.

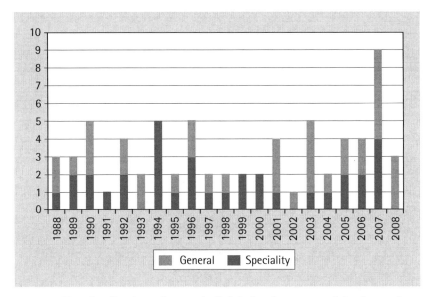

Figure 26.1 The distribution of state judicial election research by journal type per year

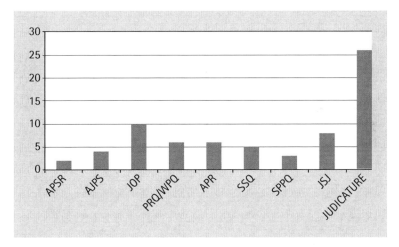

Figure 26.2 The distribution of state judicial election research by journal

however, if the primary research question posed in the study was whether elected versus appointed judges behave differently, we included it in our category called Elections and Judicial Behavior. Using this scheme, we found over 27 percent of scholarly inquiries focused on electoral competition and winning office. Whether elected versus appointed courts influence the composition of the bench along with

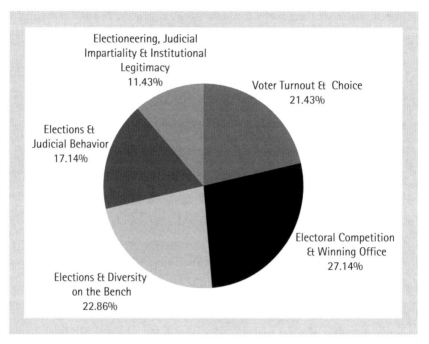

Figure 26.3 The distribution of state judicial election research by primary question

publications on voter turnout and voter choice were the second and third largest categories, respectively. The consequences of electioneering activities and judicial impartiality and legitimacy is an area of research where we see the most promise in terms of theoretical and empirical gains to be made. Not surprisingly this category had the fewest published studies, which is in large part because scholarly attention to this area has only recently begun as necessary data become available.

EXISTING SCHOLARSHIP ON STATE COURT ELECTIONS AND CAMPAIGNS: AN OVERVIEW OF THE PAST TWENTY YEARS

Scholars have developed a substantially rich and methodologically advanced literature covering a wide array of questions about judicial elections and campaigns. Among some of the most persistent questions studied by scholars across these two decades have been:

- Who votes in judicial elections and for whom? (i.e., "Voter Turnout and Vote Choice")
- Are these elections competitive and who wins? ("Electoral Competition and Winning Office")
- Does method of selection influence who gets on the bench? ("Elections and Diversity on the Bench")
- Do elected judges vote differently than appointed judges? ("Elected Judges' Voting Behavior")

More recently, scholarly focus has shifted to questions about when campaigning for office influences a judge's voting behavior and calls into question her legitimacy ("Electioneering Activities and Impartiality on the Bench"). While many of these studies embrace a comparative approach that considers multiple, if not all, states in the analysis, a good majority of scholarly work in this area consists of single-state studies. Despite the contributions of this work, we still have holes in our knowledge because many questions about state court elections and campaigns have yet to be examined in any systematic way. For example, political pundits and various organizations contend that partisan elections combined with an absence of laws regulating campaign spending and disclosure are the primary reason for large amounts of money infiltrating judicial elections.[6] Yet our review of the literature reveals that scholarly systematic examination of these conjectures remains relatively absent. In the sections that follow, we begin our review of the literature and offer our take on the state of research on judicial campaigns and elections.

Voter Turnout and Vote Choice

A primary conclusion drawn from the relatively few early scholarly publications in peer reviewed journals is that voters in judicial contests were largely uninformed (Adamany and Dubois 1976; Johnson, Shaefer, and McKnight 1978; Ladinsky and Silver 1967) and, as a result, there were lower levels of voter participation in judicial contests compared to turnout for major executive and legislative races (Adamany and Dubois 1976; Dubois 1979, 1980). Another conclusion drawn from this earlier work on judicial elections was that these races were not recruiting high quality judges and that electoral accountability of these judges was absent because voters were uninformed and non-responsive to national election cues (Dubois 1979, 1980).

 The political milieu for judicial elections was vastly different in the 1970s and 1980s compared to the 1990s and even more change has occurred since the year 2000. First, very few judicial races were considered competitive prior to the 1990s,

---

[6] Justice at Stake Campaign Press Release, October 11, 2007: "Five States to Watch in 2008." Available online at <http://www.faircourts.org>.

due to low saliency of these races along with low turnout levels. Uninformed voters who voted for state court judges often voted to retain the current judge/justice or did not vote. Lovrich, Pierce, and Sheldon (1989), like those before them, examined the idea of uninformed voters by using survey data from Spokane County, Washington (1984 on-year primary and 1983 off-year primary) to compare registered voters with non-voters with respect to knowledge of the courts and public affairs. Lovrich et al. conclude that voters who were politically knowledgeable about local government were more likely to vote in judicial elections, regardless of national electoral cues.

Hojnacki and Baum (1992a) were among the first to document changes in the character of judicial elections as a result of large-scale campaigns, more media attention, and more policy discussions. These authors examined five contests for Ohio Supreme Court in 1986 and 1988 that reflected these changes. Using post-election telephone surveys in 1986 and 1988, voters were asked their reasons for election choices. Their findings suggest that although the Ohio Supreme Court elections were more visible to voters than "typical" judicial elections, they still only provided voters with a moderate amount of information to base their vote on. Thus, the traditional pattern of judicial voting has persisted despite bigger campaigns.

Among the most comprehensive studies of voters in judicial elections is Hall's 2007 study of ballot roll-off in 654 state high court elections in thirty-eight states from 1980 to 2000. Hall finds that voters respond to important cues such as incumbency and competition, and that the type of judicial election (i.e., partisan, non-partisan, retention) significantly influences participation rates. Partisan elections seem to stimulate participation and improve voter accuracy about justices' preferences. Hall's study demonstrates that factors that influence participation in state high court elections are comparable to those that influence voter turnout in other offices (see also Hall 2001b). In this area, scholars have probed deeper to look at demographics of those who vote, consequences of roll-off, and the linkages judicial election provides between the judiciary and the electorate. Recent scholarship along these lines of inquiry has broadened our understanding of judicial elections and provided valuable comparisons and contrasts with other state and national elections.

These races, once deemed unimportant and races of low visibility, are now conceptualized as more salient elections, much more consequential than once suspected. Further, the trend in this body of literature shows that voters make informed decisions about their candidate choices, which is also different from how participation in judicial elections was originally depicted (Hall 2001a; Hall and Bonneau 2006). Hall and Bonneau (2006) found that judicial elections operate in much the same way as legislative elections: these races have an incumbency advantage, strategic challengers, and informed vote choices. This new conceptualization based on more systematic examination of judicial elections has allowed scholars to explore more completely the intricacies of judicial contests and thereby contribute to a broader knowledge of political behavior. The documented increased saliency of these contests further permits scholarly inquiry on how campaigns alter information levels in elections and the effect of changing contextual cues on voting behavior.

Over the past decade, an increase in scholarly attention has been focused on the role of money in judicial campaigns and elections. Bonneau (2007) finds that money plays an important role, especially in the low-information, low-salience judicial election, because it allows justices running for office to give voters information. An important insight gained by recent scholarship is that campaign expenditures are generally more beneficial for non-incumbents about whom the voters have no prior information (e.g., Bonneau 2005a). One of the main components of the incumbency advantage in congressional elections is name recognition. If judicial elections are low-information and low-salience elections then voters do not generally know either the incumbent or challenger, thus reducing this incumbency advantage in these elections. Bonneau (2005a) posits that the degree of incumbency advantage is likely to depend on how effective a campaign the challenger runs. Studies of differences in judicial campaigning across states and elections also provide significant variance to test the role of campaigning and their outcomes in specialized elections (e.g., Bonneau 2004). More generally, studies of judicial elections provide a natural experiment for examining the role of partisanship on vote choice. Partisan and non-partisan contests allow researchers to probe the emphasis of behavioral cues in salient vote-choice settings (Klein and Baum 2001), while studies of judicial elections provide a valuable way to understand political behavior by examining the importance of information, election saliency, and partisan cues to the American electorate.

Electoral Competition and Winning Office

An old adage in congressional elections is that incumbents never lose (e.g., Jacobson 1997), which has also become a generally accepted notion in state legislative races (e.g., Cassie and Breaux 1998; Jewell and Cassie 1998). While incumbency advantage is now considered a primary tenet held by students of legislative elections, systematic examinations of incumbency effects, and the presence or absence of electoral competition more generally, were less prevalent in the area of judicial elections. For starters, scientific scrutiny of competition in judicial races seemed somewhat misleading, because judges were presumed to be independent and apolitical. As reformers' petitions for judicial independence became increasingly louder and the notion that some methods of selection insured greater judicial independence from electoral pressures was forwarded more as fact than speculation, scholarly attention began to focus on whether there were scientific differences across partisan, non-partisan, or retention elections, and in particular, the degree to which judicial races were competitive (Hall 2001a, 2001b). As such, students of judicial elections embraced the wealth of knowledge gained from studies of congressional and state legislative races, and embarked on more comprehensive, scientific lines of inquiry that evaluated electoral competition in judicial elections across both time and space. Hall's (2001a) pioneering study of state high court elections demonstrated that the degree of electoral competition in these judicial races was remarkably similar to the level of competition faced by members of the US House and in fact, justices had a higher defeat rate (Hall 2001a, 319).

More recent studies of state high court elections have also documented electoral competition in judicial races. Bonneau (2005a), for example, finds that in most election cycles from 1990 through 2000, the percentage of incumbent defeats in state supreme court elections was higher than for other state or federal offices. He also observed higher defeat rates in states with partisan, rather than non-partisan, elections. Bonneau's (2005b) examination of campaign spending in partisan and non-partisan elections for state high courts also demonstrates that judicial campaigns resemble in many ways legislative races (see also Bonneau 2007). The presence of quality challengers in judicial elections is one reason these races have become more visible and more competitive. Increased scholarly attention thus focused on when and why quality challengers emerged and the impact quality challengers had on the electoral success of incumbents in state high court elections.

This scholarship has highlighted some important parallels to congressional races. First and similar to many House and some Senate elections, incumbents on state high courts often do not draw strong challengers (e.g., Hall 2001a). Another important parallel as observed by Hall (2001b) and Bonneau and Hall (2003) is that judicial and congressional challengers are strategic in that they run when the chance of winning is highest (e.g., open-seat races); non-quality challengers run for congressional offices when conditions are favorable for them, or unfavorable for a quality challenger (e.g., Banks and Kiewiet 1989). As is the case with congressional elections (e.g., Adams and Squire 1997; Banks and Kiewiet 1989), scholars studying judicial elections also find that the political environment, economic conditions, and partisan tides all affect the decision of a challenger to run for office (Hall 2001b; Bonneau and Hall 2003). Further, if an incumbent was involved in a close election in their previous contest, they are more likely to be seen as politically vulnerable, and consequently more likely to draw a challenger. Bonneau and Hall (2003) conclude that competition in state court elections is very predictable from factors such as the characteristics of the individual incumbent as well as state-level indicators and the institutional context. When predicting quality challengers, they find the political competition in the state to be less important than indicators of incumbent vulnerability. If an incumbent is a new appointee or if their previous election was close, quality challengers are more likely to emerge.

Also similar to congressional elections, Bonneau (2005a) finds that incumbent defeats can be predicted by the characteristics of the campaign (e.g., spending ratio), the characteristics of the incumbent, and the political context of the state. Like studies that have established that quality challengers fare better in elections in congressional contests (e.g., Abramowitz 1991; Jacobson 1989, 1990; Squire 1989), scholarly research on judicial elections documents a similar phenomenon. For example, Hall and Bonneau (2006) use a two-stage model, where the first stage considers if the election is contested and the second, the percentage of the vote the incumbent received. Challenger quality is measured as a dichotomous variable equal to 1 if the challenger held a position on a trial court or an appellate court. Their research indicates that voters not only respond to challenger quality, as it reduces the incumbent's vote share, but that voters differentiate between challenger types. Appellate court experience is more important than trial court experience. However, in states with no intermediate appellate court, trial court experience is more important. These results indicate that voters make informed decisions. Further, judicial elections are governed by many of the same factors that govern legislative elections.

While many of the conclusions drawn from congressional races are also demonstrated in the work by judicial scholars who have studied state high court elections, there are some important differences. Taken together, Bonneau and Hall (2003) and Hall and Bonneau (2006) find that institutional arrangements and contextual forces, such as the type of the election (partisan versus non-partisan), the size of the constituency (statewide versus district elections), and the salary of the justices, are important factors in predicting the emergence of quality challengers in state high court elections. Another important distinction between judicial elections and other races is that the institutional context of the race, that is when it is partisan and a district-level election, increases the chance of electoral defeat for the incumbent (Bonneau 2005). Open-seat elections are another area where important distinctions have been documented between judicial elections and elections for other offices. Indeed, there are many similarities with open-seat elections in the congressional literature; however, an important departure with these contests is that there is no evidence, at least to date, that open-seat races on state high courts are related to the state's partisan climate (Bonneau 2006, 154). An important distinction between open-seat contests and challenges against incumbents is that prior experience does not seem to influence voters' decision as it does in races with incumbents (Bonneau 2006, 153).

Elections and Diversity on the Bench

For many years, scholarly discussions have focused on the individuals who comprise state courts of last resort and democratic issues such as representation and access. Such compositional studies of these courts have assessed the extent to which method of judicial recruitment, namely elected versus appointed, impacts the representative nature of these courts (e.g., Alozie 1996; Bonneau 2001; Bratton and Spill 2002; Glick and Emmert 1987; Hurwitz and Lanier 2001, 2003; Slotnick 1988).

A primary focus especially in the last decade has been on gender diversity on these state high court benches. Hurwitz and Lanier (2003) emphasized the importance of examining the characteristics of those serving on our nation's appellate courts; though they do not find any links between judicial characteristics and decision making. Nor do they find a relationship between method of selection and gender composition on these high courts (see also Alozie 1996). However, Bratton and Spill (2002) offer some limited evidence that states with appointment systems to select state high court justices are more likely to have a woman serving on that bench than elective systems. Similarly, scholarship that focuses on the chief justices of the state supreme courts has focused on recruitment and its impact on judicial behavior (e.g., Langer et al. 2003).

There are many important reasons to explore the composition of state high courts. For example, Bonneau (2001) argues that judicial characteristics of the justices allow for a link between the effects on decision making and the representativeness of the bench. Although these studies have contributed to a larger political dialogue regarding the democratic nature of the judiciary, Langer and Wilhelm (2005) argue it is necessary to examine whether the ideological tenor of the leaders on state high courts varies systematically across elected versus appointed courts. Despite the amount of attention devoted to the relationship between method of selection and composition of state high courts, debates over whether elected courts are significantly more diverse across gender and race, or whether elected courts are composed of justices with fewer legal qualifications compared to appointed courts, remain unresolved in the literature. As Langer et al. (2003) note, one of the problems with this body of literature is that the focus is on the end part of the selection process—that is who is on the bench, rather than who is a candidate for the bench. Scant attention to the latter is in large part due to limited information about potential nominees in appointment systems and the initial and complete pool of candidates in the pre-election stages of elective systems.

Elected Judges' Voting Behavior

Unlike the legislative and executive branches of government, members of the judiciary are not all elected. As such, scholars have shown an exceptional fascination with method of selection and its relationship to who gets on the bench, as discussed in the previous section. Another question that has received extraordinary attention by judicial scholars is whether judicial selection and retention methods, namely election versus appointment, influences judicial behavior on state high courts. A predominant conclusion in this area of research is that judicial behavior indeed varies across method of judicial selection and retention (see e.g., Brace and Hall 1997; Hall 1992; Pinnello 1995). In particular, scholarly research on this subject provides overwhelming evidence that state high courts are responsive to public opinion when the members of these institutions are elected rather than appointed (e.g., Brace and Hall 1997).

Brace and Hall (1993) and Hall (1992) considered the conditioning effect of selection methods on judicial behavior in death penalty cases. They found that justices behaved differently when faced with the possibility of electoral sanctions or when they had been exposed to the partisan process of recruitment. Hall's earlier work (1987, 1992, 1995) also demonstrated that while voters in judicial elections are generally uninformed, justices nonetheless believe that citizens are aware of some of their decisions. In another important study, Huber and Gordon (2004) find that trial court judges even alter their behavior, by increasing the severity of sentences, as reelection nears. The findings in this study indicate that even in the low information setting of retention elections at ten-year intervals, judges appear to respond to potential electoral consequences.

Combined, this vast body of research has advanced our understanding of the electoral connection between elected judges and their constituents; however, few studies have demonstrated direct linkages between elected state justices and state public opinion. Perhaps the most promising line of research in this area is the study by Brace and Boyea (2008) in which the voting behavior of elected justices on state high courts is tied directly (and indirectly) to public opinion toward the death penalty. Specifically, Brace and Boyea find that "elections and strong public opinion exert a notable and significant direct influence on judge decision making in these [death penalty] cases" (2008, 370). In light of the general conclusions drawn in this area of judicial elections, coupled with increased visibility of high court races, in large part due to highly visible campaigns, and the raised concerns about the impartiality of elected judges, it seems more comprehensive studies of judicial responsiveness across different issues on which the public has expressed opinion pre- and post-election form an important path for students of judicial elections.

Electioneering Activities and Impartiality on the Bench

An important question for any democratic society is whether public trust or approval of an institution affects the degree to which citizens and governmental actors comply with its decisions. What accounts for public trust and approval of government institutions has direct implications on the rule of law. As Gibson et al. note, "[w]ithout institutional legitimacy, courts find it difficult to serve as effective and consequential partners in governance" (Gibson, Caldeira, and Baird 1998, 343). Hence the sources and consequences of public evaluations of government have long occupied scholarly inquiry (e.g., Gibson 1989; Gibson et al. 1998; Hetherington 1998; Hibbing and Theiss-Morse 2001, 2002; Mondak 1993; Tyler 1990). The controversial *Bush* v. *Gore* decision by the United States Supreme Court sparked even more scholarly inquiry about the sources of public confidence in and legitimacy of American courts (e.g., Benesh 2006; Gibson 2008; Gibson, Caldeira, and Spence 2003; Hibbing and Theiss-Morse 2002; Yates and Whitford 2002). One of the most prevalent conclusions to be drawn from this literature is that there is a strong relationship between the public esteem courts enjoy and public compliance with court decisions. Courts lack enforcement power. They do not have the power of the purse nor the sword, which makes these judicial institutions highly dependent on legitimacy afforded to them by the public (Gibson 2008).

Recent scholarship has begun to examine the relationships among elections, campaigning for office, judicial impartiality, and judicial legitimacy. Two studies of judicial elections, for example, offer evidence, albeit limited, that when judges are elected public confidence in state courts suffers (e.g., Benesh 2006; Wenzel, Bowler, and Lanoue 2003). Other research demonstrates that the use of attack ads, which is a relatively new phenomenon in state judicial races, not only contributes to the politicization of these courts, but also undermines court legitimacy (e.g., Gibson 2008, 62). This decrease in confidence has therefore been affected by selection methods, political contexts, and judicial activities, which have altered the public's legalistic view of high courts, especially as judges have engaged in more electioneering activities and solicitation of the media (Gibson 2008; see also Staton 2006).

In addition to studying how the changing nature of judicial campaigns influences judicial legitimacy, students of judicial elections have begun to examine whether money in judicial campaigns buys votes on the bench (e.g., Cann 2007b; McCall and McCall 2007). Campaign money has been shown to be an important contributor to success in judicial elections (e.g., Bonneau 2007). Linking these campaign contributions to favorable outcomes for the attorneys, however, has been problematic. For starters, the presence of a correlation between the contribution and the vote is not causation. It may be the case that liberal (conservative) attorneys are more likely to contribute to liberal (conservative) justices, which increases the chances of the attorney's most preferred candidate winning. If an attorney's candidate wins, there is an increased likelihood that the attorney will win more cases in that court, which may be due to the shared ideology that led the attorney to give money to that candidate initially. An attorney's success rate in court could also be related to a "payback" by the judge for the substantial contributions made to her campaign. Cann's (2007b) two-stage analysis of money and votes on the Georgia Supreme Court tackles these questions. He finds evidence that as the amount of contributions from liberal (conservative) attorneys increases, the probability of the justice voting liberal (conservative) increases. Cann concludes that due to this relationship between money and votes, competitive judicial elections may seriously compromise the independence of the judiciary. Indeed, Cann is among the first to test these linkages with scientific scrutiny; however, the evidence is limited to a single state and single year. It is this line of inquiry where more shared data will help advance our understanding of the role money plays in judicial voting.

Concluding Comments

Over the past decade, an increase in scholarly attention has been focused on the role of money in judicial campaigns and elections. This concentration has offered much insight into the changing nature of judicial elections and the electorate. Once deemed as inconsequential races, judicial contests, especially for seats on state high courts, have become crucial markers of the role money plays in state elections more generally. The increased electioneering by judges has catapulted these races into the national headlines and ushered in a new wave of voters and candidates. The unprecedented amounts of money infiltrating judicial campaigns coupled with extraordinary numbers of television ads has raised scholarly awareness of the unique insights to be gained from studying judicial elections. Indeed, some of the more recent and significant contributions have been made in the area of judicial campaigns and, in particular, the consequences of electioneering activities for electoral success, judicial voting behavior, and a court's legitimacy. We suggest these are the areas where students of judicial elections should continue to probe.

Given the increasingly strained relations between many state legislatures and state high courts, a more complete understanding is needed of a court's institutional legitimacy as perceived not only by the public but also by the other branches. In many ways, state supreme courts have become the scapegoat for governmental problems. These courts of last resort are easy targets because debate over judicial selection and retention in the American states continues, and the shortcomings of each method remain the foci of political discussion (e.g., Hall 2001a). Intense public and political scrutiny of justices on state supreme courts, as well as the method by which they attain office, will continue as long as these courts resolve controversial policy issues. Understanding how the election of judges might undermine a court's legitimacy and thereby detrimentally affect legislative–judicial relations is thus an important avenue for future research.

Equally important for scholarship in this area is that we continue to advance our understanding of the role money plays in judicial voting behavior. Unlike studies on congressional or state legislative elections, state court elections provide a unique opportunity to examine systematically whether a corporation's campaign contributions, for example, alter the outcome of a lawsuit. Whether a judge's vote is for sale is an especially important question in light of the United States Supreme Court's decision to grant certiorari to the case *Caperton v. A.T. Massey Coal Company.* In 2009, the Supreme Court decided that the refusal of Justice Benjamin, of the Supreme Court of Appeals in West Virginia, to recuse himself from an appeal violated the Due Process Clause of the 14th Amendment. The appeal before the West Virginia Court challenged a $50 million jury verdict against Massey Coal Company, whose CEO had spent $3 million in support of Justice Benjamin's campaign for a seat on that bench. The Supreme Court of Appeals for West Virginia overturned the lower court's verdict, which was against Massey Coal Company. Justice Benjamin was part of the 3–2 majority decision in favor of Massey Coal Company. In this new wave of electioneering by judges, the extent to which conflicts of interest raise questions about judicial impropriety is an area of research where many more valuable insights can be made.

Systematic examinations of state court elections and campaigns have advanced the science of politics both theoretically and methodologically and opened new paths of political inquiry about elections across all three branches of government. Despite these tremendous gains, the subfield's movement forward is somewhat disjointed because it is making progress based on empirical findings from single-state studies, multiple-state studies of limited time frame, or multi-state and single-state studies that isolate judicial elections and campaigns from other governmental activities, including other elections. This area of research would benefit from a more unifying theoretical framework that could (1) integrate the broad range of substantive inquiries into state judicial campaigns and elections; (2) reconcile research concerning macro-level outcomes with theories and findings concerning micro-level behavior; (3) utilize the analytical strength of studying elections and campaigns comparatively across types of courts (trial and appellate) within varying institutional contexts and political settings; and (4) capitalize on the unique interactions of state courts with other state governmental actors.

References

ABRAMOWITZ, A. I. 1991. Incumbency, Campaign Spending and the Decline of Competition in U.S. House Elections. *Journal of Politics,* 53: 34–56.
ADAMANY, D. and DUBOIS, P. L. 1976. Electing State Judges. *Wisconsin Law Review,* 731–79.

ADAMS, G. D. and SQUIRE, P. 1997. Incumbent Vulnerability and Challenger Emergence in Senate Elections. *Political Behavior*, 19: 97–111.

ALOZIE, N. O. 1996. Selection Methods and the Recruitment of Women to State Courts of Last Resort. *Social Science Quarterly*, 77/1: 110–26.

ASPIN, L. 1998. Campaigns in Judicial Retention Elections: Do They Make a Difference? *Justice System Journal*, 20: 1–15.

—— 1999. Trends in Judicial Elections, 1964–1998. *Judicature*, 83: 79–81.

—— 2007. Judicial Retention Election Trends: 1964–2006. *Judicature*, 90: 208–13.

—— and HALL, W. K. 1989. Friends and Neighbors Voting in Judicial Retention Elections: a Research Note Comparing Trial and Appellate Court Elections. *Political Research Quarterly*, 42: 587–96.

—— —— 1994. Retention Elections and Judicial Behavior. *Judicature*, 77: 306–15.

—— —— 1996. Campaigning for Retention in Illinois. *Judicature*, 80: 84–7.

BANKS, J. D. and KIEWIET, D. R. 1989. Explaining Patterns of Candidate Competition in Congressional Elections. *American Journal of Political Science*, 33: 997–1015.

BENESH, S. C. 2006. Understanding Public Confidence in American Courts. *Journal of Politics*, 68/3: 697–707.

BONNEAU, C. W. 2001. The Composition of State Supreme Courts 2000. *Judicature*, 85: 26–31.

—— 2004. Patterns of Campaign Spending and Electoral Competition in State Supreme Court Elections. *Justice System Journal*, 25: 21–38.

—— 2005a. Electoral Verdicts: Incumbent Defeats in State Supreme Court Elections. *American Politics Research*, 33: 818–41.

—— 2005b. What Price Justice(s)? Understanding Campaign Spending in State Supreme Court Elections. *State Politics and Policy Quarterly*, 5: 107–25.

—— 2006. Vacancies on the Bench: Open Seat Elections for State Supreme Courts. *Justice System Journal*, 27: 143–59.

—— 2007. The Effects of Campaign Spending in State Supreme Court Elections. *Political Research Quarterly*, 60: 489–99.

—— and HALL, M. G. 2003. Predicting Challengers in State Supreme Court Elections: Context and the Politics of Institutional Design. *Political Research Quarterly*, 56: 337–49.

BRACE, P. and BOYEA, B. 2008. State Public Opinion, the Death Penalty and the Practice of Electing Judges. *American Journal of Political Science*, 52/2: 360–72.

—— and HALL, M. G. 1990. Neo-Institutionalism and Dissent in State Supreme Courts. *The Journal of Politics*, 52: 54–70.

—— —— 1993. Integrated Models of Judicial Dissent. *The Journal of Politics*, 55: 914–35.

—— —— 1997. The Interplay of Preferences, Case Facts, Context, and Rules in the Politics of Judicial Choice. *The Journal of Politics*, 59: 1206–31.

—— LANGER, L., and HALL, M. G. 2000. Measuring the Preferences of State Supreme Court Judges. *The Journal of Politics*, 62: 387–413.

BRATTON, K. A. and SPILL, R. 2002. Existing Diversity and Judicial Selection: The Role of the Appointment Method in Establishing Gender Diversity in State Supreme Courts. *Social Science Quarterly*, 83/2: 504–18.

CANN, D. 2007a. Beyond Accountability and Independence: Judicial Selection and State Court Performance. *Judicature*, 90: 226–32.

—— 2007b. Justice for Sale? Campaign Contributions and Judicial Decisionmaking. *State Politics and Policy Quarterly*, 7: 281–97.

CASSIE, W. E. and BREAUX, D. A. 1998. Expenditures and Election Results. In *Campaign Finance in State Legislative Elections*, ed. J. A. Thompson and G. F. Moncrief. Washington, D.C.: C.Q. Press.

CHEEK, K. and CHAMPAGNE, A. 2000. Money in Texas Supreme Court Elections, 1980–1998. *Judicature*, 84: 20–5.

COMPARATO, S. A. and McCLURG, S. D. 2007. A Neo-Institutional Explanation of State Supreme Court Responses in Search and Seizure Cases. *American Politics Research*, 35: 726–54.

CROLEY, S. P. 1995. The Majoritarian Difficulty: Elected Judiciaries and the Rule of Law. *University of Chicago Law Review*, 62: 689–74.

DUBOIS, P. L. 1979. The Significance of Voting Cues in State Supreme Court Elections. *Law and Society Review*, 13/3: 757–79.

—— 1980. *From Ballot to Bench: Judicial Elections and the Quest for Accountability*. Austin: University of Texas Press.

—— 1984. Voting Cues in Nonpartisan Trial Court Elections: A Multivariate Assessment. *Law & Society Review*, 18: 395–436.

—— 1990. Voter Responses to Court Reform: Merit Selection on the Ballot. *Judicature*, 73: 238–47.

DUDLEY, R. L. 1997. Turnover and Tenure on State High Courts: Does Method of Selection Make a Difference? *Justice System Journal*, 19: 1–16.

EDITOR. 1989. The Voting Rights Act and Judicial Elections: An Update on Current Litigation. *Judicature*, 73: 74–81.

EISENSTEIN, J. 2000. Financing Pennsylvania's Supreme Court Candidates. *Judicature*, 84: 10–19.

ENGSTROM, R. L. 1989. When Blacks Run for Judge: Racial Divisions in the Candidate Preferences of Louisiana Voters. *Judicature*, 73: 87–9.

FELICE, J. D. and KILWEIN, J. C. 1992. Strike One, Strike Two . . . The History of and Prospect for Judicial Reform in Ohio. *Judicature*, 75: 193–200.

GIBSON, J. L. 1989. Understandings of Justice: Institutional Legitimacy, Procedural Justice, and Political Tolerance. *Law and Society Review*, 23/3: 469–96.

—— 2008. Challenges to the Impartiality of State Supreme Courts: Legitimacy Theory and "New-Style" Judicial Campaigns. *American Political Science Review*, 102: 59–75.

—— CALDEIRA, G. A., and BAIRD, V. A. 1998. On the Legitimacy of National High Courts. *The American Political Science Review*, 92/2: 343–58.

—— —— and SPENCE, L. K. 2003. Measuring Attitudes Toward the U.S. Supreme Court. *American Journal of Political Science*, 47/2: 354–67.

GLICK, H. and EMMERT, C. F. 1987. Selection Systems and Judicial Characteristics. *Judicature*, 70: 228–35.

GRAHAM, B. L. 1990a. Do Judicial Selection Systems Matter? A Study of Black Representation on State Courts. *American Politics Research*, 18: 316–36.

—— 1990b. Judicial Recruitment and Racial Diversity on State Courts: An Overview. *Judicature*, 74: 28–34.

GRODIN, J. H. 1988. Developing a Consensus of Constraint: A Judge's Perspective on Judicial Retention Elections. *Southern California Law Review*, 61: 1969–83.

HALL, M. G. 1987. Constituent Influence in State Supreme Courts: Conceptual Notes and a Case Study. *Journal of Politics*, 49: 11–17.

—— 1992. Electoral Politics and Strategic Voting in State Supreme Courts. *The Journal of Politics*, 54: 427–46.

—— 1995. Justices as Representatives: Elections and Judicial Politics in the American States. *American Politics Research*, 23: 485–503.

—— 2001a. State Supreme Courts in American Democracy: Probing the Myths of Judicial Reform. *American Political Science Review*, 95: 315–30.

—— 2001b. Voluntary Retirements from State Supreme Courts: Assessing Democratic Pressures to Relinquish the Bench. *The Journal of Politics*, 63: 1112–40.

—— 2007. Voting in State Supreme Court Elections: Competition and Context as Democratic Incentives. *The Journal of Politics*, 69: 1147–59.

—— and BONNEAU, C. W. 2006. Does Quality Matter? Challengers in State Supreme Court Elections. *American Journal of Political Science*, 50: 20–33.

—— and BRACE, P. 1996. Justices' Responses To Case Facts: An Interactive Model. *American Politics Research*, 24: 237–61.

HAYDEL, J. 1989. Secton 2 of the Voting Rights Act of 1965: A Challenge to State Judicial Election Systems. *Judicature*, 73: 68–73.

HETHERINGTON, M. J. 1998. The Political Relevance of Political Trust. *American Political Science Review*, 92/4: 791–808.

HIBBING, J. R. and THEISS-MORSE, E. 1995. *Congress as Public Enemy: Public Attitudes Toward American Political Institutions*. Cambridge: Cambridge University Press.

—— —— 2001. Process Preferences and American Politics: What the People Want the Government to Be. *American Political Science Review*, 95/1: 145–53.

—— —— 2002. *Stealth Democracy: Americans' Beliefs about How Government Should Work*. Cambridge: Cambridge University Press.

HOJNACKI, M. and BAUM, L. 1992a. "New-Style" Judicial Campaigns and the Voters: Economic Issues and Union Members in Ohio. *Political Research Quarterly*, 45: 921–48.

—— —— 1992b. Choosing Judicial Candidates: How Voters Explain Their Decisions. *Judicature*, 75: 300–9.

HUBER, G. A. and GORDON, S. C. 2004. Accountability and Coercion: Is Justice Blind When it Runs for Office? *American Journal of Political Science*, 48: 247–63.

HURWITZ, M. S. and LANIER, D. N. 2001. Women and Minorities on State and Federal Appellate Benches, 1985 and 1999. *Judicature*, 85: 84–92.

—— —— 2003. Explaining Judicial Diversity: The Differential Ability of Women and Minorities to Attain Seats on State Supreme and Appellate Courts. *State Politics and Policy Quarterly*, 3: 329–52.

JACKSON, D. W. and RIDDLESPERGER, J. W., Jr. 1991. Money and Politics in Judicial Elections: The 1988 Election of Chief Justice of the Texas Supreme Court. *Judicature*, 74: 184–9.

JACOBSON, G. C. 1989. Strategic Politicians and the Dynamics of U.S. House Elections, 1946–86. *American Political Science Review*, 83: 773–93.

—— 1990. The Effects of Campaign Spending in House Elections: New Evidence for Old Arguments. *American Journal of Political Science*, 34: 334–62.

—— 1997. *The Politics of Congressional Elections*. New York: Longman.

JEWELL, M. E. and CASSIE, W. E. 1998. Can The Legislative Campaign Finance System be Reformed? In *Campaign Finance in State Legislative Elections*, ed. J. A. Thompson and G. F. Moncrief. Washington, D.C.: C.Q. Press.

JOHNSON, C. A., SHAEFER, R. C., and McKNIGHT, R. N. 1978. Saliency of Judicial Candidates and Elections. *Social Science Quarterly*, 59: 371.

KIEL, D. L., FUNK, C., and CHAMPAGNE, A. 1994. Two-Party Competition and Trial Court Elections in Texas. *Judicature*, 77: 290–3.

KLEIN, D. and BAUM, L. 2001. Ballot Information and Voting Decisions in Judicial Elections. *Political Research Quarterly*, 54: 709–28.

LADINSKY, J. and SILVER, A. 1967. Popular Democracy and Judicial Independence. *Wisconsin Law Review*, 128.

LANGER, L. and WILHELM, T. 2005. The Ideology of State Supreme Court Justices. *Judicature*, 89: 78–86.

——— McMULLEN, J., RAY, N. P., and STRATTON, D. D. 2003. Recruitment of Chief Justices on State Supreme Courts: A Choice between Institutional and Personal Goals. *The Journal of Politics*, 65: 656–75.

LOVRICH, N. P., PIERCE, J. C., and SHELDON, C. H. 1989. Citizen Knowledge and Voting in Judicial Elections. *Judicature*, 73: 28–33.

——— and SHELDON, C. H. 1994. Is Voting for State Judges a Flight of Vacancy or a Reflection of Policy and Value Preferences? *Justice System Journal*, 16: 57–72.

——— ——— and WASMANN, E. 1988. The Racial Factor in Nonpartisan Judicial Elections: A Research Note. *Political Research Quarterly*, 41: 807–16.

LUSKIN, R. C., et al. 1994. How Minority Judges Fare in Retention Elections. *Judicature*, 77: 316–21.

McCALL, M. M. and McCALL, M. A. 2007. Campaign Contributions, Judicial Decisions, and the Texas Supreme Court: Assessing the Appearance of Impropriety. *Judicature*, 90: 214–25.

McDUFF, R. 1989. The Voting Rights Act and Judicial Elections Litigation: The Plaintiff's Perspective. *Judicature*, 73: 82–4.

MONDAK, J. J. 1993. Institutional Legitimacy and Procedural Justice: Reexamining the Question of Causality. *Law and Society Review*, 27/3: 599–608.

MOOG, R. 1992. Campaign Financing for North Carolina's Appellate Courts. *Judicature*, 76: 68–76.

NASE, J. P. 1997. Election Cycles and the Appointment of State Judges: A National Research Agenda Based on the Pennsylvania Experience. *Justice System Journal*, 19: 37–50.

NICHOLSON, M. A. and NICHOLSON, N. 1994. Funding Judicial Campaigns in Illinois. *Judicature*, 77: 294–9.

PEARSON, W. M. and CASTLE, D. S. 1989. Alternative Judicial Selection Devices: An Analysis of Texas Judges' Attitudes. *Judicature*, 73: 34–9.

PINELLO, D. R. 1995. *The Impact of Judicial Selection Method on State Supreme Court Policy: Innovation, Reaction and Atrophy*. Greenwood Press.

REID, T. V. 1996. PAC Participation in North Carolina Supreme Court Elections. *Judicature*, 80: 21–9.

——— 1999. The Politicization of Retention Elections: Lessons From the Defeat of Justices Lanphier and White. *Judicature*, 83: 68–78.

ROTMANN, D. B. and SCHOTLAND, R. A. 2001. What Makes Judicial Elections Unique? *Loyola of Los Angeles Law Review*, 34: 1369–73.

SALOKAR, R. M. 2007. Endorsements in Judicial Campaigns: The Ethics of Messaging. *Justice System Journal*, 28: 342–57.

—— BERGGREN, D. J., and DePALO, K. A. 2006. The New Politics of Judicial Selection in Florida: Merit Selection Redefined. *Justice System Journal*, 27: 123–42.

SAMPSON, K. M. 1995. Evaluating the Performance of Judges Standing for Retention: An Edited Transcript of a Panel Presentation at the American Judicature Society's 1995 Annual Meeting. *Judicature*, 79: 190–7.

SCHOTLAND, R. A. 2001. Summit on Improving Judicial Selection: Introduction: Personal Views. *Loyola of Los Angeles Law Review*, 34: 1361–7.

—— 2002. Myth, Reality Past and Present, and Judicial Elections. *Indiana Law Review*, 33: 659–67.

—— 2003a. Proposed Legislation on Judicial Election Campaign Finance. *Ohio State Law Journal*, 64: 127–36.

—— 2003b. To the Endangered Species List, Add: Nonpartisan Judicial Elections. *Willamette Law Review*, 39: 1397–423.

—— 2007. Impacts of White. *Drake Law Review*, 55: 625–36.

—— and REED, B. 2002. Judicial Campaign Conduct Committees. *Indiana Law Review*, 35: 781–805.

—— DEBOW, M., BARAN, J., and ENOCH, C. 2002. Judicial Elections and Campaign Finance Reform. *University of Toledo Law Review*, 33: 335–51.

SCRUGGS, A. M., MAZZOLA, J.-C., and ZAUG, M. E. 1995. Recent Voting Rights Act Challenges to Judicial Elections. *Judicature*, 79: 34–41.

SLOTNICK, E. E. 1988. Review Essay on Judicial Recruitment and Selection. *Justice System Journal*, 13: 109–24.

SQUIRE, P. 1989. Competition and Uncontested Seats in U.S. House Elections. *Legislative Studies Quarterly*, 14: 281–95.

STATON, J. K. 2006. Constitutional Review and the Selective Promotion of Case Results. *American Journal of Political Science*, 50/1: 98–112.

STERN, S. 2005. West Virginia Supreme Court Election Shows Effectiveness of Interest Groups. *Judicature*, 89: 38–40.

THIELEMANN, G. S. 1993. Local Advantage in Campaign Financing: Friends, Neighbors, and their Money in Texas Supreme Court Elections. *The Journal of Politics*, 55: 472–8.

THOMAS, C. S., BOYER, M. L., and HREBENAR, R. J. 2003. Interest Groups and State Courts: A New Era and its Challenges. *Judicature*, 87: 135–49.

TRAUT, C. A. and EMMERT, C. F. 1998. Expanding the Integrated Model of Judicial Decision Making: The California Justices and Capital Punishment. *The Journal of Politics*, 60: 1166–80.

TYLER, T. R. 1990. *Why People Obey the Law*. New Haven, Conn.: Yale University Press.

WEBER, R. E. 1989. The Voting Rights Act and Judicial Litigation: The Defendant States' Perspective. *Judicature*, 73: 85–6.

WENZEL, J. P., BOWLER, S., and LANOUE, D. J. 2003. The Sources of Public Confidence in State Courts: Experience and Institutions. *American Politics Research*, 31/2: 191–211.

YATES, J. and WHITFORD, A. B. 2002. The Presidency and the Supreme Court After Bush v. Gore: Implications for Institutional Legitimacy and Effectiveness. *Stanford Law & Policy Review*, 13/1: 101–20.

CHAPTER 27

....

PRIMARY ELECTIONS

....

BARBARA NORRANDER

PRIMARIES provide a more exciting setting than general elections for investigating the effects of campaigns, election rules, media coverage, political elites, and voter decision making. In most presidential elections, partisanship strongly predicts individual voter's support of the Democratic or Republican candidate, and forecasting models, based on the state of the economy and popularity of the incumbent president, accurately predict outcomes months in advance of the election. Congressional elections often are unbalanced contests between semi-known incumbents and unknown (or non-existent) challengers. Neither setting provides an ideal context for investigating the decision-making processes of the voters, the role of the elite (media, interest groups, etc.), or the dynamics of a campaign.

The nomination process involves the decisions of candidates to run, preliminary fundraising and staff organization, the public campaign prior to the primary, and the primary election itself. In presidential nominations, the last two steps are repeated over and over as the contest proceeds from one state to another. Finally, the primary phase is followed by the general election phase, providing sequential elections for both the direct and presidential primaries. These sequential elections bring in two types of electorates (within and across parties), set up a system where prior outcomes influence future outcomes, and ask voters to consider the ability of candidates to win the primary and general elections. The politics of sequential elections are vastly different from those of simultaneous ones (Aldrich 1980; Bartels 1988; Morton and Williams 2001).

The best research on primaries incorporates variations that are found across election years, across parties, across types of contests, or across types of candidates. Not all research on primaries does this. In any field of political behavior, preliminary research often is conducted on one election cycle. Subsequent work also might concentrate on one case to fill in nuances or test alternative theoretical perspectives. However, more research on primary elections needs to stress the comparative components, whether it is by types of candidates, contests, electoral structures, or cross-party differences. As earlier literature reviews exist (Marshall 1986; Norrander 1996), this chapter will concentrate on publications from the last ten years.

VARIATIONS IN CANDIDATE FIELDS

The candidate field for primaries contains diversity in both the strength and number of contenders. Schlesinger's (1966) ambition theory provides a rationale why candidates run, but which candidates run requires more definition. Two pieces (Burden 2002; Steger 2006) focus on the relative strengths of governors versus senators as candidates for the presidential nominations. Yet, we still know little about why specific candidates or governors decide to run while others do not. Even the question of whether or not an incumbent president will be challenged for the nomination remains mostly unanswered with only two (and competing) explanations from Mayer (1996) versus Steger (2003).

The direct primary literature actually does a better job at explaining candidate entry. Traditional literature focused on differences across majority and minority parties, the power of incumbency to deter challengers, and the effects of party endorsements. The congressional and state legislative election literatures continue to debate whether a large war chest deters primary challenges (Goodliffe 2007; Hogan 2001). Recent works on the effects of incumbency to deter competition (Bardwell 2002; Kang, Niemi, and Powell 2003) suggest conditional effects based on the popularity of the incumbent. Finally, Maisel and Stone (2001) find evidence from their Candidate Emergence Study that the primary process in general deters candidates from running. Potential candidates worry about having to win in two different electoral settings and suspect that a primary victory would require either beating an incumbent or another strong candidate.

Other recent additions to the study of candidate entry in direct primaries note that female candidates, including female incumbents, attract more competition in congressional primaries, though women and men win congressional primaries at the same rate (Lawless and Pearson 2008; Palmer and Simon 2006). Still other research on female candidates finds some evidence of their continued placement as sacrificial lambs within the Republican Party for gubernatorial nominations, while Democrats face a pipeline problem in attracting female candidates to compete for their nominations (Stambough and O'Regan 2007).

The number of candidates who enter a primary dictates the dynamics of that contest. Aldrich (1980) argued that a multi-candidate field is more unstable than a two-person contest. In the latter, while equilibrium is possible, it is more likely that one candidate will gain at the other's expense. However, the campaign may stretch across phases when one candidate is advantaged and other times when the alternative candidate leads. A multi-candidate field, Aldrich theorizes, is more unstable, with slight differences in vote totals in early contests able to push one candidate to victory and another to eventual defeat. Using both a formal model and multiple simulations, Cooper and Munger (2000, 337) found "complete unpredictability" in multi-candidate primaries. While the literature is strong on pointing out the differences between two-candidate and multi-candidate races, left unanswered is why some multi-candidate races become two-candidate contests (Democrats, 1984 and 2008), while others maintain the dynamics of a multi-candidate contest.

Scholars of primary elections need to spend more time defining candidate fields and delineating their effects. In the presidential primary literature, Bartels (1988) provided one scenario based on the number and awareness level of the candidates. Mayer's (2004) categorization divides contests according to the emergence of a front-runner. (See Berggren 2007 and McSweeney 2007 for more on variations in frontrunner emergence.) Yet, the candidate field contains significant elements beyond number of candidates, frontrunner strengths, and public awareness of candidates. Many candidate fields have clusters of candidates competing for the same faction within a party, and these factions are not usually ideological in nature. Thus, while spatial models (Aldrich 1980; Kenny and Lotfinia 2005) focus on the ideological alignment of candidates in affecting the outcomes, many of the primary contests are between establishment versus newer or maverick candidates (Shafer 1988), involve jockeying to become the main alternative to the frontrunner (Popkin 1991), include geographic rivalries (e.g., to become the Southern candidate or the candidate preferred by Southern voters), or center on party factions based on values, religion, or specific domestic or foreign policy issues.

VARIATIONS IN CAMPAIGN DYNAMICS

Much of the social science research and journalistic comments about presidential nominations key in on momentum. But momentum is both an ill-defined and over-defined term. It means many things to many people. Momentum as conceptualized by Aldrich (1980) is an increasing (but not inevitable) chance of winning the nomination which results from exceeding expectations in primary outcomes and produces an increase in resources and a gain in accumulated delegates in comparison to other candidates.

Political science research from the 1980s and 1990s pointed to two main actors in momentum: media and voters. The media role in momentum comes through increased, often positive, coverage of a candidate exceeding expectations (Keeter and Zukin 1983; Patterson 1980). Why voters move toward the advantaged candidate has been answered with reference to a number of mechanisms: (1) Bartels (1988) posits strategic voting, cue taking, contagion, and simple support for a winner; (2) Popkin (1991) argues for a coordination game of those dissatisfied with the frontrunner looking for the most viable alternative; (3) Kenney and Rice (1994) describe different processes for those switching preferences among candidates versus those voters who had no firm preferences at the start of the nomination process; while (4) Mutz (1997, 105) employs the notion of consensus cues that lead people to "engage in a process of self-persuasion whereby their own attitudes move in the direction of the arguments that have been primed by others' views." Thus, the momentum literature is theoretically rich, and there are some overlapping ideas, such as variants of cue taking that span theories derived from the rational choice (Popkins 1991) and social psychological (Mutz 1997) perspectives.

The other dynamic element of presidential nomination campaigns is the winnowing of candidates. With a large number of quickly decided contests between 1988 and 2004, the sequential exit of candidates captured more scholarly attention. Empirical models of winnowing use pre-election year resources and results from initial contests across several election cycles to explain candidate withdrawal (Norrander 2006) or model the role of money, media coverage, and competitive standing throughout one nomination contest (Haynes et al. 2004). The importance of cash in determining how long candidates can stay in the race is demonstrated by Hanson (2000). Meanwhile, Strumpf (2002) argues that candidates will remain in the race if upcoming states are those with favorable constituencies. Norrander (2000) examines the end stage of the winnowing process by testing the ability of various measures of the delegate count to predict the withdrawal of the last major challenger to the winning candidate.

Similar to the winnowing literature are the forecasting models (Adkins and Dowdle 2005; Mayer 2004; Steger 2007). All use the same dependent variable— each candidate's share of the aggregate primary vote (i.e., votes cast in all the primaries). Core independent variables are from the invisible primary stage: national standing in the public opinion polls and campaign funds. Models have been tweaked through a number of configurations of campaign funds, and adding in results of Iowa and New Hampshire, candidate types, and candidate endorsements. Both the winnowing and forecasting models need to move beyond analyzing the strengths and weaknesses of each candidate and begin to include measures that relate each candidate to the structure of the candidate field. For example, these models often measure money as the relative amount of money raised. Yet, the competition is different between a frontrunner who raises 50 percent of the total money and faces a second-place candidate who garners 40 percent of the money versus a frontrunner who amasses 50 percent of the total money with the remaining cash distributed almost equally, and in small amounts, among three or four candidates. An important new addition is the research that focuses on the role of party elites in structuring the early strengths of candidates (Cohen, Karol, Noel, and Zaller 2008).

Variations in Campaign Strategies

Paul Henri-Gurian laid a strong base for work on campaign strategies in presidential nomination politics by demonstrating how strategies would differ by different types of candidates (long shots versus established), different goals (maximizing delegates, eliminating rivals, or gaining momentum or media coverage), and variations in electoral rules and nomination calendars (Gurian 1993; Haynes, Gurian, and Nichols 1997). Aldrich (1980) and Brams and Davis (1982) provide additional theoretical predictions for candidate strategies in two-candidate contests. Candidate strategies should vary across all of these dimensions, such that continuing research in these areas should make distinctions by groups of candidates or types of contests.

One of the newer research techniques is to examine candidates' press releases to ascertain their strategies. Several studies look at the content of these press releases and the success of candidates in getting the media to incorporate this content (Miller, Andsager, and Riechert 1998; Tedesco 2001, 2005). Candidates of different strengths, (i.e., frontrunners versus lower-tiered candidates) have different patterns of use for press releases (Haynes, Flowers, and Gurian 2002). Candidate's advertisements also can be keys to campaign strategies. Vavreck (2001), by comparing advertisements in both the general election and primaries, is able to document that candidates make fewer references to parties in advertisements aired during primaries. Open versus closed primary settings do not alter candidate's mentionings of party or ideology in campaign commercials, but candidates in open primaries more frequently refer to issues in attempts to attract support from independents and voters from the opposite party. Kendall (2000) provides a particularly extensive examination of advertisements in presidential nominations stretching from 1912 through 1992.

When candidates will go negative in primary campaigns has several theoretical and empirical works. Negative campaigning is not as prevalent during the primaries as the general election phase. During the invisible primary and initial contest phases, candidates focus more on introducing themselves to a national audience. However, as the field narrows to two or three candidates, campaigns and advertisements become more negative (Haynes and Rhine 1998; Kendall 2000). Candidates aim their negative campaigns at the frontrunner, and frontrunners are unlikely to attack except in response to attacks on themselves (Haynes and Rhine 1998; Skaperdas and Grofman 1995). Using Senate primaries and a content analysis of newspaper coverage, Peterson and Djupe (2005) document temporal, candidate field, and party differences in the amount of negativity.

The effects of candidate advertising during the primary phase are often found to be greater than found during the general election (Just et al. 1996). Candidates are less well known, and partisanship cues do not anchor voter preferences. With more of a blank slate on which to work, the content of candidate advertising strategies appears to be more influential. As a result, candidates are more successful in framing their own images (Kendall 2000; Parmelee 2002). Voter contacting by candidates, whether by mail, phone, or in person, leads to more knowledge and favorability toward the candidate (Vavreck, Spiliotes, and Fowler 2002). Thus, campaign strategies are more varied (across time, candidate types, and electoral settings) and perhaps more effective in primaries rather than general elections.

INFLUENCE OF ELECTORAL RULES

Rules matter. Political scientists have no qualms over that conclusion. Precisely measuring and verifying those effects, however, is not always easy. Primary elections provide scholars with a wealth of rule variation, though conclusions reached are not always consistent. Scholars also are increasingly viewing such electoral rules as endogenous variables, created with specific goals in mind. In this vein, some recent work attempts to explain why states or parties change their nomination rules and what the consequences of those rules changes are. Alternatively, some primary rules, such as run-off primaries in Southern states, remain when the electoral environment changes.

The run-off primary used in Southern states may seem like an historical anachronism. It was the consequence of requiring a majority vote for victory in an era where the Democratic primary victor would automatically win the general election. The question becomes, do the run-off primaries function differently today when the Republican Party is a credible alternative to Democratic candidates? Glaser (2006) finds that run-off primaries still attract more candidates to the primary process, that about one-quarter of the time the victor in the second round is not the winner in the first round, and initially second-place winners do slightly better in the general election. Remarkably, many of the figures Glaser reports are similar to those Key (1949) found at the height of the Jim Crow era. Turnout appears to suffer a greater drop-off between the first and second rounds of the primary in recent decades, but Bullock, Gaddie, and Ferrington (2002) demonstrate that a variety of factors (candidate spending, time lag between primaries, additional run-off elections, open participation rules, and party) can influence the level of turnout in the second round. A lingering concern is whether run-off primaries discriminate against minority or female candidates (Bullock and Maggiotto 2003).

The use of proportional representation rules by the Democratic Party in their presidential nomination system fosters significant debates among journalists and activists as well as scholars. The scholarly literature, however, finds inconsistent effects for these rules. Early work proposed that proportional representation rules would prolong the intraparty contest. Mayer (1996) countered that it was not proportional representation rules but a more divided Democratic Party electorate that led to prolonged races on the Democratic side. Cooper (2002), using computer simulations, finds support for both proportional representation rules and a divided electorate in extending the nomination contest. In support of the party difference thesis, Steger, Hickman, and Yohn (2002) find the Democratic Party to winnow candidates more slowly than the Republican Party throughout the twentieth century, and for the post-reform era attribute these differences to the use of proportional representation rules by the Democratic Party. In contrast, Norrander (2006) finds neither proportional representation rules nor the Democratic Party in general to have candidates remaining in the race for longer periods of time during the post-reform era. One possibility for the discrepancy is that in many recent nomination contests, one candidate quickly becomes the frontrunner and the other candidates drop out, before delegate allocation rules start to matter.

Why states change primary rules has been investigated on a number of fronts. Mayer and Busch (2004) examine historical reasons for states to move their primaries forward, contributing to the frontloading of the nomination calendar. Carmen and Barker (2005) add to the debate the notion that moralistic states, especially those with homogeneous populations, are the most likely to move the dates of their presidential primary forward. Economists Mixon and Hobson (2001) assert an economic benefit (in terms of increased federal grant money) to moving a state's primary forward. Early states also could influence voters in subsequent primaries (Morton and Williams 2001). Switches from caucuses to primaries occurred more often in states controlled by the Democratic Party, with home-state candidates, and where the party's voters were more ideologically similar to the remainder of the state's voters (Meinke, Staton, and Wuhs 2006; Walz and Comer 1999).

ELECTORAL CONNECTIONS:
ARE PRIMARIES DIVISIVE?

Whether primaries can be divisive and harm the party's fortunes in the fall election is a topic explored in both the presidential and direct primary literatures. Recent works search for a mechanism for these divisive primaries, argue that the direction of causality is in the wrong direction, or contend that voter awareness of primary outcomes is too low to matter. Djupe and Peterson (2002) attempt to identify the underlying mechanism and find that it is the negative campaigning associated with divisive primaries that harms the party's fortunes in the fall. Lazarus (2005) argues that weak incumbents draw in challengers, producing divisive primaries. If incumbents survive this primary challenge, they do poorly in the general election as a reflection of their initial weakness. If the challenger wins the primary, these are strong challengers who fare well in the fall election. Romero (2003) is less convinced of the spurious relationship argument, but he too finds differential effects for incumbents (who are harmed by divisive primaries) and open-seat contests (where there is no effect). Hogan (2003) in studying state legislative primaries actually finds divisive primaries to produce higher vote totals in the fall election. He links this to the strategic entry of candidates and the low voter awareness of these primary elections.

Recent research on presidential nominations downplays the divisive primary thesis. Primary battles produce a net gain in mobilizing activists for the fall election, including supporters of losing candidates (Stone, Atkeson, and Rapoport 1992). In addition, Atkeson (1993) demonstrates evaluations of the party's nominee by supporters and those who favored an opponent during the primary converge as the fall election nears. Atkeson (1998) also notes that prior works failed to take account of other factors that can influence the party's fortunes in the fall election such as the state of the economy or evaluations of the incumbent president. Once these other factors are considered, the divisiveness of the primaries no longer affects the party's fate in the general election. Thus, newer research on divisive primaries in both the direct primary and presidential primary fields no longer accepts a simple linkage between primary outcomes and fall election fortunes.

ELECTORAL CONNECTIONS:
CANDIDATE POSITIONING

A second avenue of concern across the primary versus general election continuum is the idea that the primary process inherently select nominees away from the general elections' median voter. A good example of this literature is Brady,

Han, and Pope's (2007) article, which recaps the argument about the tension between policy positions that appeal to the primary median voter versus those that reflect the position of the general election median voter. Their analysis shows representatives cater to the more extreme positions of their primary voters, and thus move the parties in Congress to more ideologically distinct positions. In contrast, Burden (2001) shows House members move slightly in the extreme direction before the primary election and back to a more moderate position before the general election. Other research ties such movement to the influence of primary participation rules (Grofman and Brunell 2001; Kanthak and Morton 2001). Burden (2004) argues for the centrifugal pull of primary electorates in part because he asserts primary voters care more about policy than general election voters. Yet this centrifugal pull can vary depending on the level of competition in the primaries and the general election, any ambiguity in candidate positioning, and alternative strengths of candidates that will draw in supporters for non-policy reasons. Finally, Masket (2007) found an innovative way to test the effects of primary rules on the ideological orientation of elected officials. He uses a natural experiment in primary rule change in California, which during the early part of the twentieth century allowed for candidates to run in both parties' primaries through a system of cross-filing. During this era, partisanship in the state legislature was less pronounced. When cross-filling was banned, partisan divisions increased.

The arguments about the centrifugal pull of primaries on the positions of the party's candidates often contain pictures of an ideological or issue-driven primary voter. Unfortunately, there is little in the way of survey data to confirm or refute such pictures of primary voters, especially for legislative elections. Further, little distinction is made between a model where primary voters are an accurate reflection of the party's median voter, but each party's median voters are distinctive from one another, versus the possibility that primary voters have different positions than their own party's median voter. The presidential primary literature, however, does have some survey data to show that primary voters accurately reflect the issue positions of their non-voting party members, especially in open primaries (Kaufmann, Gimpel, and Hoffman 2003). Smaller electorates are not necessarily more ideologically defined electorates. Primary voters could simply be those with stronger habits of voting, which would be related to demographic factors such as age or education rather than policy positions. Further, Adams and Merrill (2008) demonstrate a number of benefits of primaries, such as voters selecting candidates with good campaign skills, which can outweigh any centrifugal force in policy positions that might exist.

VOTER DECISION MAKING

The recent empirical literature on voter decision making in presidential primaries continues to deemphasize issues and ideology and focuses on candidate qualities, values, group support, electability (Rickershauser and Aldrich 2007), or retrospective voting. Values rather than issues may determine voters' choices in presidential primary elections. Marietta and Barker (2007) define values as centered on normative goals, with dimensions such as libertarianism versus equalitarianism or theism versus humanism. Such values may be tied to some issue positions, but voters may simply respond to candidates who they perceive as sharing their value priorities. Based on a limited local survey, Marietta and Barker found evidence of value orientation reflected in Republican primary preferences in 2000, and in an issue-framing experiment, Barker (2005) found that the values connected to a candidate's issue position could be ascertained by better-educated voters.

Differences in voting behavior may occur across the parties or across different demographic groups. Barker, Lawrence, and Tavits (2006) find that Republican and Democratic voters seek out different qualities in their presidential nominees, with Democrats searching for candidates exhibiting compassion and Republicans searching for candidates with virtue. McMullen and Norrander (2000) find that male and female primary voters search for different qualities in their party nominees. Such candidate quality differences may underlie the gender gaps that occur in primary voting between one-quarter and one-third of the time (with an exception for the 2008 Democratic contest). Racial differences in voter support of candidates also occurred before 2008 and even in contests without African American candidates (Hutchings and Stephens 2008). African American voters appear to be supporting candidates that they perceive will best serve their group interests. Unfortunately, the voting behavior of Latinos has mostly been ignored up to this point, though the 2008 Democratic contests are producing some initial reports (Barreto et al. 2008).

Mayer (2008) provides some of the first across-time analyses of specific types of voting. He finds strong evidence of retrospective voting in presidential primaries. Mayer also examines the influence of partisanship within the presidential primaries over seven election cycles. While a number of scholars dismiss the influence of partisanship in these intraparty contests (Abramson et al. 1992), Mayer notes significant differences in candidate preferences between partisans and independents voting in the same primary. Mayer attributes the influence of partisanship in the primaries to the strength of linkages between various candidates and "partisan symbols and themes" (2008, 193). In examining the influence of ideology over these election cycles, Mayer finds very mixed results. Sometimes the presidential primary contest is characterized by ideological voting (Republicans 1976, Democrats 1980), but at other times there are no differences in candidates' support between liberals, moderates, and conservatives voting in a party's primaries (Democrats 2000, Republican 1992), or ideology only matters for minor candidates (Jackson in 1984, Buchanan in 1996). Linking cross-year analyses of voting behavior to variations in candidate fields may be the best avenue for moving the field forward. The types of candidates from which voters choose should shape the types of factors voters can use to evaluate these candidates.

LOOKING FORWARD: 2008 AND BEYOND

The 2008 presidential nominations at first glance would appear to break from the pattern of recent nominations. On the Republican side, John McCain became the nominee after faltering during the invisible primary, where he lagged behind Rudy Giuliani in the public opinion polls and Mitt Romney in the "money primary." The Democratic contest produced the first sustained intraparty battle since the 1980s. Turnout rose substantially in the Democratic primaries, swelled by an increase among the young, women, and African Americans, while falling on the Republican side. The calendar was more front-loaded than ever before. Nevertheless, the existing political science research on primary elections has much to offer as a baseline for studying 2008, and more importantly for incorporating 2008 into studies that take into account across-time, across-party, or across-candidate-field variations.

The campaign-dynamics models, whether they focus on momentum, candidacy duration, or forecasting, provide a basis for understanding the role of money raised, poll standing, and initial-contest outcomes in explaining nomination outcomes. Some tweaking of the models may improve their ability to incorporate the 2008 results with results from prior years. However, the research field needs to move to a broader explanation of the types of contests in addition to predicting the winning and losing candidates. The most fruitful categorizations would key in on variations in the candidate field: number, frontrunner dominance, competitive strength of other candidates, rivalries, and types of candidates (establishment, maverick, issue advocacy). Models that could predict, or at least explain, why a particular contest fits into one category over another would give us a better grasp of the dynamic elements of the presidential nomination.

Turnout in presidential primaries was frequently investigated at both the aggregate and individual levels in political science research in the 1980s (see Norrander 1996 for a review). At the aggregate level, indicators of exciting races (e.g., more candidates, more campaign spending, and closer national contests) explained higher turnout rates. The 2008 increases on the Democratic side (and decreases on the Republican side) may simply reflect such indicators of an exciting contest. New technology, specifically the internet, certainly plays a role in increasing campaign contributions, and perhaps turnout. Technological innovations often occur in primary campaigns and initial studies have been conducted on the role of the internet (Hindman 2005; Tewksbury 2006). Not to be overlooked is that the internet is following in the wake of candidates using videotapes and 1–800 numbers in the 1980s and 1990s (Parmelee 2002). And as Cohen et al. (2008) report, Franklin Delano Roosevelt sent out phonographic records as part of his campaign to win the Democratic nomination.

The close contest between Obama and Clinton refocuses attention on the rules: rules for delegate distribution, rules for caucuses, and rules for participation (i.e., open versus closed primaries). Once again, these are not new topics among scholars. Lengle and Shafer (1976) detailed the effects of proportional representation versus alternative delegate allocation mechanisms at the beginning of the post-reform era. Other scholars continued the debate over whether proportional representation prolonged Democratic contests or whether the structure of the Democratic electorate mattered more. Cross-over voting has been analyzed across a number of years and across various definitions (see for example Wekkin 1991). The Iowa caucuses have been well studied over the years (Hull 2007; Winebrenner 1998), though few other caucuses have received much attention from scholars (or candidates and the media) in the past. Research on presidential nominations and direct primaries will continue to be exciting because of the diversity across candidate fields, parties, and election years. This diversity only adds to the struggle of social scientists to define the regularities in the political world.

References

ABRAMSON, P. R., ALDRICH, J. H., PAOLINO, P., and ROHDE, D. 1992. "Sophisticated" Voting in the 1988 Presidential Primaries. *American Political Science Review*, 86: 55–69.

ADAMS, J. and MERRILL, S., III 2008. Candidate and Party Strategies in Two-Stage Elections Beginning with a Primary. *American Journal of Political Science*, 52: 344–59.

ADKINS, R. E. and DOWDLE, A. J. 2005. Do Early Birds Get the Worm? Improving Timeliness of Presidential Nomination Forecasts. *Presidential Studies Quarterly*, 35: 646–60.

ALDRICH, J. H. 1980. *Before the Convention: Strategies and Choices in Presidential Nominating Campaigns*. Chicago: University of Chicago Press.

ATKESON, L. R. 1993. Moving Toward Unity: Attitudes in the Nomination and General Election Stages of a Presidential Campaign. *American Politics Quarterly*, 21: 272–89.

—— 1998. Divisive Primaries and General Election Outcomes: Another Look at Presidential Campaigns. *American Journal of Political Science*, 42: 256–71.

BARDWELL, K. 2002. Money and Challenger Emergence in Gubernatorial Primaries. *Political Research Quarterly*, 55: 653–67.

BARKER, D. C. 2005. Values, Frames, and Persuasion in Presidential Nomination Campaigns. *Political Behavior*, 27: 375–94.

—— LAWRENCE, A. B., and TAVITS, M. 2006. Partisanship and the Dynamics of "Candidate Centered Politics" in American Presidential Nominations. *Electoral Studies*, 35: 599–610.

BARRETO, M. A., FRAGA, L. R., MANZANO, S., MARTINEZ-EBERS, V., and SEGURA, G. M. 2008. "Should They Dance with the One Who Brung 'Em?" Latinos and the 2008 Presidential Election. *PS: Political Science & Politics*, 4: 753–60.

BARTELS, L. 1988. *Presidential Primaries and the Dynamics of Public Choice*. Princeton, N.J.: Princeton University Press.

BERGGREN, D. J. 2007. Two Parties, Two Types of Nominees, Two Paths to Winning a Presidential Nomination, 1972–2004. *Presidential Studies Quarterly*, 37: 203–27.

BRADY, D. W., HAN, H., and POPE, J. C. 2007. Primary Elections and Candidate Ideology: Out of Step with the Primary Electorate. *Legislative Studies Quarterly*, 32: 79–105.

BRAMS, S. J. and DAVIS, M. D. 1982. Optimal Resource Allocation in Presidential Primaries. *Mathematical Social Sciences*, 3: 373–88.

BULLOCK, C. S., III, GADDIE, R. K., and FERRINGTON, A. 2002. System Structure, Campaign Stimuli, and Voter Falloff in Runoff Primaries. *Journal of Politics*, 64: 1210–24.

—— and MAGGIOTTO, M. A. 2003. Female Candidate Success in Runoff Primaries. *Women & Politics*, 24: 1–18.

BURDEN, B. C. 2001. The Polarizing Effects of Congressional Primaries. In *Congressional Primaries and the Politics of Representation*, ed. P. F. Galderisi, M. Ezra, and M. Lyons. Lanham, Md.: Rowman & Littlefield.

—— 2002. United State Senators as Presidential Candidates. *Political Science Quarterly*, 117: 81–102.

—— 2004. Candidate Positioning in US Congressional Elections. *British Journal of Political Science*, 34: 211–27.

CARMAN, C. J. and BARKER, D. C. 2005. State Political Culture, Primary Frontloading, and Democratic Voice in Presidential Nominations: 1972–2000. *Electoral Studies*, 24: 665–87.

COHEN, M., KAROL, D., NOEL, H., and ZALLER, J. 2008. *The Party Decides: Presidential Nominations Before and After Reform*. Chicago: University of Chicago Press.

COOPER, A. 2002. The Effective Length of the Presidential Primary Season: The Impact of Delegate Allocation Rules and Voter Preferences. *Journal of Theoretical Politics*, 14: 71–92.

—— and MUNGER, M. C. 2000. The (Un)predictability of Primaries with Many Candidates: Simulation Evidence. *Public Choice*, 103: 337–55.

DJUPE, P. A. and PETERSON, D. A. M. 2002. The Impact of Negative Campaigning: Evidence from the 1998 Senatorial Primaries. *Political Research Quarterly*, 55: 845–60.

GLASER, J. M. 2006. The Primary Runoff as a Remnant of the Old South. *Electoral Studies*, 25: 776–90.

GOODLIFFE, J. 2007. Campaign War Chests and Challenger Quality in Senate Elections. *Legislative Studies Quarterly*, 32: 135–56.

GROFMAN, B. and BRUNELL, T. L. 2001. Explaining the Ideological Differences between the Two U.S. Senators Elected from the Same State: An Institutional Effects Model. In *Congressional Primaries and the Politics of Representation*, ed. P. F. Galderisi, M. Ezra, and M. Lyons. Lanham, Md.: Rowman & Littlefield.

GURIAN, P.-H. 1993. Candidate Behavior in Presidential Nomination Campaigns: A Dynamic Model. *Journal of Politics*, 55: 115–39.

HANSON, G. S. 2000. Out of Cash: U.S. Presidential Pre-Nominations. *Party Politics*, 6: 47–59.

HAYNES, A. A., FLOWERS, J., and GURIAN, P.-H. 2002. Getting the Message Out: Candidate Communication Strategy during the Invisible Primary. *Political Research Quarterly*, 55: 633–52.

—— GURIAN, P.-H., and NICHOLS, S. M. 1997. The Role of Candidate Spending in Presidential Nomination Campaigns. *Journal of Politics*, 59: 213–25.

—— and RHINE, S. L. 1998. Attack Politics in Presidential Nomination Campaigns: An Examination of the Frequency and Determinants of Intermediated Negative Messages Against Opponents. *Political Research Quarterly*, 51: 691–721.

—— GURIAN, P.-H., CRESPIN, M. H., and ZORN, C. 2004. The Calculus of Concession: Media Coverage and the Dynamics of Winnowing in Presidential Nominations. *American Politics Research*, 32: 310–37.

HINDMAN, M. 2005. The Real Lessons of Howard Dean: Reflections on the First Digital Campaign. *Perspectives on Politics*, 3: 121–8.

HOGAN, R. E. 2001. Campaign War Chests and Challenger Emergence in State Legislative Elections. *Political Research Quarterly*, 54: 815–30.

—— 2003. The Effects of Primary Divisiveness on General Election Outcomes in State Legislative Elections. *American Politics Research*, 31: 27–47.

HULL, C. C. 2007. *Grassroots Rules: How the Iowa Caucus Helps Elect American Presidents.* Stanford, Calif.: Stanford University Press.

HUTCHINGS, V. L. and STEPHENS, L. 2008. African American Voters and the Presidential Nomination Process. In *The Making of the Presidential Candidates 2008*, ed. W. G. Mayer. Lanham, Md.: Rowman & Littlefield.

JUST, M. R., CRIGLER, A. N., ALGER, D. E., COOK, T. E., KERN, M., and WEST, D. J. 1996. *Crosstalk: Citizens, Candidates, and the Media in a Presidential Campaign.* Chicago: University of Chicago Press.

KANG, I., NIEMI, R. G., and POWELL, L. W. 2003. Strategic Candidate Decisionmaking and Competition in Gubernatorial Nonincumbent-Party Primaries. *State Politics and Policy Quarterly*, 3: 353–66.

KANTHAK, K. and MORTON, R. 2001. The Effects of Electoral Rules on Congressional Primaries. In *Congressional Primaries and the Politics of Representation*, ed. P. F. Galderisi, M. Ezra, and M. Lyons. Lanham, Md.: Rowman & Littlefield.

KAUFMANN, K. M., GIMPEL, J. G., and HOFFMAN, A. H. 2003. A Promise Fulfilled? Open Primaries and Representation. *Journal of Politics*, 65: 457–76.

KEETER, S. and ZUKIN, C. 1983. *Uninformed Choice: The Failure of the New Presidential Nominating System.* New York: Praeger.

KENDALL, K. E. 2000. *Communication in the Presidential Primaries: Candidates and the Media, 1912–2000.* Westport, Conn.: Praeger.

KENNEY, P. J. and RICE, T. W. 1994. The Psychology of Political Momentum. *Political Research Quarterly*, 47: 923–38.

KENNY, L. W. and LOTNIA, B. 2005. Evidence on the Importance of Spatial Voting Models in Presidential Nominations and Elections. *Public Choice*, 123: 439–62.

KEY, V. O. 1949. *Southern Politics in State and Nation.* New York: A. A. Knopf.

LAWLESS, J. L. and PEARSON, K. 2008. The Primary Reason for Women's Underrepresentation? Reevaluating the Conventional Wisdom. *Journal of Politics*, 70: 67–82.

LAZARUS, J. 2005. Unintended Consequences: Anticipation of General Election Outcomes and Primary Election Divisiveness. *Legislative Studies Quarterly*, 30: 435–61.

LENGLE, J. I. and SHAFER, B. 1976. Primary Rules, Political Power, and Social Change. *American Political Science Review*, 70: 25–40.

MAISEL, L. S. and STONE, W. J. 2001. Primary Elections as a Deterrence to Candidacy for the U.S. House of Representatives. In *Congressional Primaries and the Politics of Representation*, ed. P. F. Galderisi, M. Ezra, and M. Lyons. Lanham, Md.: Rowman & Littlefield.

MARIETTA, M. and BARKER, D. C. 2007. Values and Heuristics: Core Beliefs and Voter Sophistication in the 2000 Republican Nomination Contest. *Journal of Elections, Public Opinion and Parties*, 17: 49–78.

MARSHALL, T. R. 1986. Primaries and Nominations. *Research in Micropolitics*, 1: 189–218.

MASKET, S. E. 2007. It Takes an Outsider: Extralegislative Organization and Partisanship in the California Assembly, 1849–2006. *American Journal of Political Science*, 51: 482–97.

MAYER, W. G. 1996. *The Divided Democrats*. Boulder, Colo.: Westview.

—— 2004. The Basic Dynamics of the Contemporary Nomination Process: An Expanded View. In *The Making of the Presidential Candidates 2004*, ed. W. G. Mayer. Lanham, Md.: Rowman & Littlefield.

—— 2008. Voting in Presidential Primaries: What We Can Learn from Three Decades of Exit Polling. In *The Making of the Presidential Candidates 2008*, ed. W. G. Mayer. Lanham, Md.: Rowman & Littlefield.

—— and BUSCH, A. E. 2004. *The Front-Loading Problem in Presidential Nominations*. Washington, D.C.: Brookings Institution.

McMULLEN, J. L. and NORRANDER, B. 2000. The Gender Gap in Presidential Nominations. In *In Pursuit of the White House, 2000*, ed. W. G. Mayer. Chatham, N.J.: Chatham House.

McSWEENEY, D. 2007. The Front-Runner Falls. *Party Politics*, 13: 109–26.

MEINKE, S. R., STATON, J. K., and WUHS, S. T. 2006. State Delegate Selection Rules for Presidential Nominations, 1972–2000. *Journal of Politics*, 68: 180–93.

MILLER, M. M., ANDSAGER, J. L., and RIECHERT, B. P. 1998. Framing the Candidates in Presidential Primaries: Issues and Images in Press Releases and News Coverage. *Journalism & Mass Communication Quarterly*, 75: 312–24.

MIXON, F. G., JR. and HOBSON, D. L. 2001. Intergovernmental Grants and the Positioning of Presidential Primaries and Caucuses: Empirical Evidence from the 1992, 1996, and 2000 Election Cycles. *Contemporary Economic Policy*, 19: 27–38.

MORTON, R. B. and WILLIAMS, K. C. 2001. *Learning by Voting: Sequential Choices in Presidential Primaries and Other Elections*. Ann Arbor: University of Michigan Press.

MUTZ, D. C. 1997. Mechanisms of Momentum: Does Thinking Make It So? *Journal of Politics*, 59: 104–25.

NORRANDER, B. 1996. Field Essay: Presidential Nomination Politics in the Post-Reform Era. *Political Research Quarterly*, 49: 875–915.

—— 2000. The End Game in Post-Reform Presidential Nominations. *Journal of Politics*, 62: 999–1013.

—— 2006. The Attrition Game: Initial Resources, Initial Contests and the Exit of Candidates During the US Presidential Primary Season. *British Journal of Political Science*, 36: 487–507.

PALMER, B. and SIMON, D. M. 2006. *Breaking the Political Glass Ceiling: Women and Congressional Elections*. New York: Routledge.

PARMELEE, J. 2002. Presidential Primary Videocassettes: How Candidates in the 2000 U.S. Presidential Primary Elections Framed Their Early Campaigns. *Political Communication*, 19: 317–31.

PATTERSON, T. E. 1980. *The Mass Media Election: How Americans Choose Their President*. New York: Praeger.

PETERSON, D. A. and DJUPE, P. A. 2005. When Primary Campaigns Go Negative: The Determinants of Campaign Negativity. *Political Research Quarterly*, 58: 45–54.

POPKIN, S. L. 1991. *The Reasoning Voter: Communication and Persuasion in Presidential Campaigns*. Chicago: University of Chicago Press.

RICKERSHAUSER, J. and ALDRICH, J. H. 2007. "It's the Electability, Stupid" or Maybe Not? Electability, Substance, and Strategic Voting in Presidential Primaries. *Electoral Studies*, 26: 371–80.

ROMERO, D. W. 2003. Divisive Primaries and the House District Vote: A Pooled Analysis. *American Politics Research*, 31: 178–90.

SCHLESINGER, J. A. 1966. *Ambition and Politics: Political Careers in the United States*. Chicago: Ran McNally.

SHAFER, B. E. 1988. *Bifurcated Politics*. Cambridge, Mass.: Harvard University Press.

SKAPERDAS, S. and GROFMAN, B. 1995. Modeling Negative Campaigning. *American Political Science Review*, 89: 49–61.

STAMBOUGH, S. J. and O'REGAN, V. R. 2007. Republican Lambs and the Democratic Pipeline: Partisan Differences in the Nomination of Female Gubernatorial Candidates. *Politics & Gender*, 3: 349–68.

STEGER, W. P. 2003. Presidential Renomination Challenges in the 20th Century. *Presidential Studies Quarterly*, 33: 827–52.

—— 2006. Stepping Stone to the White House or Tombstone on Presidential Ambition: Why Senators Usually Fail When They Run for the White House. *American Review of Politics*, 27: 45–70.

—— 2007. Who Wins Nominations and Why? An Updated Forecast of the Presidential Primary Vote. *Political Research Quarterly*, 60: 91–9.

—— HICKMAN, J., and YOHN, K. 2002. Candidate Competition and Attrition in Presidential Primaries, 1912–2000. *American Politics Research*, 30: 528–54.

STONE, W. J., ATKESON, L. R., and RAPOPORT, R. B. 1992. Turnout On or Turning Off? Mobilization and Demobilization Effects of Participation in Presidential Nomination Campaigns. *American Journal of Political Science*, 36: 665–91.

STRUMPF, K. S. 2002. Strategic Competition in Sequential Election Contests. *Public Choice*, 111: 377–97.

TEDESCO, J. C. 2001. Issues and Strategy Agenda-Setting in the 2000 Presidential Primaries. *American Behavioral Scientist*, 44: 2048–67.

—— 2005. Intercandidate Agenda Setting in the 2004 Democratic Presidential Primary. *American Behavioral Scientist*, 49: 92–113.

TEWKSBURY, D. 2006. Exposure to the New Media in a Presidential Primary Campaign. *Political Communications*, 23: 313–32.

VAVRECK, L. 2001. The Reasoning Voter Meets the Strategic Candidate: Signals and Specificity in Campaign Advertising, 1998. *American Politics Research*, 29: 507–29.

VAVRECK, L., SPILIOTES, C., and FOWLER, L. 2002. The Effects of Retail Politics in the 1996 New Hampshire Primary. *American Journal of Political Science*, 46: 595–610.

WALZ, J. S. and COMER, J. 1999. State Responses to National Democratic Party Reforms. *Political Research Quarterly*, 52: 189–208.

WEKKIN, G. D. 1991. Why Crossover Voters are Not "Mischievous Voters": The Segmented Partisanship Hypothesis. *American Politics Quarterly*, 19: 229–47.

WINEBRENNER, H. 1998. *The Iowa Precinct Caucuses: The Making of a Media Event*, 2nd edn. Ames: Iowa State University Press.

....

CHAPTER 28

DIRECT DEMOCRACY IN THE UNITED STATES

....

SHAUN BOWLER

TODD DONOVAN

OPINIONS about ballot proposition elections—for and against—voiced by academics, journalists, and politicians are often very deeply felt. Unfortunately, those deeply felt opinions often work against making progress in understanding both how direct democracy elections work and the relevance of the study of ballot propositions for voting behavior more generally. It is striking how often discussions of ballot proposition elections see the revisiting of a series of arguments that have been around since the inception of direct democracy, most notably those concerning the abilities of voters to understand ballot propositions.

Our argument here is that other, and more interesting, questions arise from the study of voting on ballot propositions that relate to the variety of voter preferences, how voter opinions are formed, and how voters think about democratic institutions. These latter (less settled) questions have emerged in recent scholarship on direct democracy. We suggest that the answers to these—newer—questions have wider relevance for the study of voting behavior more generally and that grounds for concerns about direct democracy might be found in less familiar territory than the standard critiques which emphasize, and overstate, voter incompetence and the prospects for tyranny of the majority.

DIRECT DEMOCRACY

Roughly half the US states—generally in the West—have some form of direct democracy that allows voters to put policy measures directly on the ballot (the initiative). If enough voters sign a petition in support of a measure then it is placed on the ballot and, if more people vote "yes" than "no" the measure becomes law or, under some conditions, part of the constitutions (see Cronin 1989; Magleby 1984).[1] In most cases, the initiative process was introduced just before the First World War as part of a package of reforms brought about by the Progressive and Populist movements with Socialist support (Lawrence, Bowler, and Donovan, n.d. (a)). Since the first two initiative proposals—one on primary elections, the other on alcohol regulation—appeared on the Oregon ballot in 1904, over two thousand proposals have appeared on ballots across the country and roughly 40 percent of them have passed.

Use of the process has fluctuated over time in a rough 'U' shape: the period from its introduction through to the 1930s saw a flurry of initiative proposals, but use of the process declined from around the time of the Second World War and reached a low point in the 1960s. Beginning in the late 1970s use of the process began to climb again and now ballot propositions are a regular feature of politics in those states with the process. In 2006, 204 ballot propositions went before voters in thirty-seven states, of which 76 were initiatives.

The focus of these propositions is extremely wide, including women's suffrage (Arizona and Oregon in 1912) and Prohibition (Arkansas 1912), through the establishment of a state fair (Colorado 1912) to licensing chiropractors, prohibiting vivisection, and making sure that vaccination not be made a condition of admission to higher education (all three appeared on the California ballot in 1920). Of late, the ballot has seen a similarly wide mix of issues: tax limitation and immigration (both seen in California), treatment of nuclear waste (Oregon and South Dakota 1980), more regulation and taxation of alcohol (Colorado 1982, Ohio 1983) eminent domain (Nevada, Florida, and nine other states in 2006) and the banning of cockfighting (Arizona 1998).

---

[1] Even more states have referendum processes in which some proposals are placed on the ballot for voter approval. The website of the Initiative and Referendum Institute (<http://www.iandrinstitute.org/>) has a great deal of detailed information on the processes and their variations.

One of the features of the initiative process that makes it so important is that it takes agenda-setting power away from the established political processes and institutions and puts it in the hands of citizens. As we know from other studies, citizens are often an unpredictable or at least fickle bunch. Concerns over the fickle, and possibly feckless, public have thus driven a large part of the literature on mass behavior and direct democracy.

Voter Understanding and Ballot Proposition Elections

Ballot propositions can be both long and complex. In November 2006, to take a recent and quite arbitrary example, the text of the thirteen proposals voted on by California took up seventy-five pages of closely packed text in the ballot pamphlet mailed to voters.[2] Not surprisingly, much has been made of the difficulty of the decision facing voters. Voters are notoriously reluctant to spend too much time thinking about the issues, yet the amount and complexity of ballot proposition information may be quite daunting. Not surprisingly, one conclusion to be drawn from this mix of complex decisions coupled with a lack of motivation is that voters are simply not up to the demands of ballot propositions. Couple this challenge with the likely impact of slick advertising campaigns associated with some ballot propositions, and it is plausible to think that voters may be readily led astray in ballot proposition elections.

But a long series of empirical studies have demonstrated that voters can in fact make decisions even in this demanding environment. One influential line of argument (Lupia and McCubbins 1998) has shown that through the use of cues voters can place ballot propositions within their existing ideological framework. The strong implication of this body of work is that voters can vote "correctly," i.e., they are able to identify their own interests and identify whether a YES or NO vote on a ballot proposition is in line with that interest. A related line of argument suggests that voters use heuristics as a reasonable alternative cue, with abstention from voting as another alternative (Bowler and Donovan 1998; Lupia 1994).

What, then, of susceptibility to spending and advertising? Up until recently the conventional wisdom was that it was hard for proponents of a proposition to spend their way to victory (Banducci 1998; Gerber 1999). This finding is consistent with the use of cues and heuristics: voters cannot be readily fooled. More recently

---

[2] For examples of ballot pamphlets themselves see <http://www.sos.ca.gov/elections/elections_i. htm>.

Table 28.1 Official title and summary for two California proposals

Prop 89 November 2006 POLITICAL CAMPAIGNS. PUBLIC FINANCING. CORPORATE TAX INCREASE. CAMPAIGN CONTRIBUTION AND EXPENDITURE LIMITS. INITIATIVE STATUTE.

* Provides that candidates for state elective office meeting certain eligibility requirements, including collection of a specified number of $5.00 contributions from voters, may voluntarily receive public campaign funding from Fair Political Practices Commission, in amounts varying by elective office and election type.
* Increases income tax rate on corporations and financial institutions by 0.2 percent to fund program.
* Imposes new limits on campaign contributions to state-office candidates and campaign committees, and new restrictions on contributions by lobbyists, state contractors.
* Limits certain contributions and expenditures by corporations.

Summary of Legislative Analyst's Estimate of Net State and Local Government Fiscal Impact:
* Increased revenues (primarily from increased taxes on corporations and financial institutions) totaling more than $200 million annually. The funds would be spent on the public financing of political campaigns for state elected officials.
(Flesch reading ease 17.5)

Prop 88 November 2006 EDUCATION FUNDING. REAL PROPERTY PARCEL TAX. INITIATIVE CONSTITUTIONAL AMENDMENT AND STATUTE.

* Provides additional public school funding for kindergarten through grade 12.
* Funded by $50 tax on each real property parcel.
* Exempts certain elderly and disabled homeowners.
* Funds must be used for class size reduction, textbooks, school safety, Academic Success facility grants, and data system to evaluate educational program effectiveness.
* Provides for reimbursement to General Fund to offset anticipated decrease in income tax revenues due to increased deductions attributable to new parcel tax.
* Requires school district audits, penalties for fund misuse.
* Revenue excluded from minimum education funding (Proposition 98) calculations.

Summary of Legislative Analyst's Estimate of Net State and Local Government Fiscal Impact:
* State parcel tax revenue of roughly $450 million annually, allocated to school districts for specified education programs.
(Flesch reading ease 15.2)

Stratmann (2006) has argued that—with appropriate modeling—it is possible to see a positive effect for spending to support a proposal, and one that closely matches that of spending against a proposal. One interpretation of Stratmann's results is that where public opinion does not lean one way or the other there is scope for a campaign to have an effect to generate support for a proposal.[3]

But before getting bogged down too much in the to-ing and fro-ing of academic debates, we should note that this literature as a whole has tended to share the assumptions that voters are in a difficult position on ballot propositions. That is,

---

[3] If spending is modeled as a log function the result broadly holds for pass rates as well.

an implicit assumption of much of this research is that voters have no well-formed preferences over the issues at stake, that the decisions are difficult, and that opinions are open to being swayed by advertising. Although all or some of those assumptions may be true for some propositions, it certainly is not true for all of them.

In fact many propositions are perfectly straightforward even on the face of it. Voters may be asked to extend the death penalty or alter regulations governing abortion. There is nothing terribly "hard" (in the Carmines and Stimson sense of the term) about either of these decisions or, indeed, many others like them on the ballot. Many issues then may well be quite "easy" for voters in that they require "almost no supporting context of factual knowledge, no impressive reasoning ability" (Carmines and Stimson 1989, 11). One variant of this argument is offered by Nicholson (2007), who extends the cue-taking model to show that group benefits figure largely in voter calculations: once voters know that murderers are to be more heavily penalized or that veterans are to be rewarded, then which way to vote becomes much clearer.

One consequence of the literature on cue taking and heuristics is that it can be taken to imply that cue taking is the *only* way voters *can* make decisions on ballot propositions. Yet this is not the case. Many propositions involve quite straightforward (though not "easy") choices that voters are perfectly capable of deciding even without cues or other heuristic devices. Table 28.1 displays the official summaries (ballot language) of two recent proposals. Though voters may only have this text—lacking cues and bleached of context—to rely on, the questions posed nonetheless seem relatively straightforward. In short, although voting on some proposals may well be quite difficult and voting on many proposals may well tax the patience of most voters, it is all too easy to overstate the difficulties voters have in understanding what is going on with a given proposition.

The Relationship between Candidates, Parties, and Voters

A second focus in the literature is on political parties and candidates as cue providers in ballot proposition elections (Branton 2003; Magleby 1984). Recently, attention has shifted to how choices on ballot propositions may prime voters for candidate races (Donovan, Tolbert, and Smith 2008; Nicholson 2005). That is, the decision voters are asked to make on a ballot proposition is not a one-way street of influence from party/candidate cue to voter; instead, that influence can flow the

536 SHAUN BOWLER & TODD DONOVAN

other way, with voters' choices on ballot issues altering their votes in candidate contests.

This is potentially important because it means that it is possible to arrive at an assessment of issue voting that is not endogenous to the candidate contest itself. Issues raised by the candidates and parties may dominate the issue agenda: partisan interests, for example, may raise wedge issues. But it may also be possible for the initiative process to provide an exogenous source of issues for the agenda over which candidates and parties have only limited control (see for example Chavez 1998). Those externally determined issues may then influence voters' views of the candidates. At the very least, a contentious issue raised by the initiative will prompt the question: "where does candidate X stand on this issue?" In this way initiatives can provide sources of priming for candidate campaigns (Donovan et al. 2008; Nicholson 2005).

In addition to helping generate the issue agenda, ballot issues may also generate turnout, particularly in low-stimulus midterm election years (D. Smith and Tolbert 2004; M. A. Smith 2001; Tolbert, Grummel, and Smith 2001). If an election is held in which the contests involve a lackluster candidate race and a contentious ballot proposition then voters may well turn out to vote for the ballot proposition though they would not otherwise turn out to vote for a candidate. Hence turnout in candidate races may well be affected by turnout in proposition contests. One study illustrates that different pools of voters might be affected by ballot measures in different elections, with independents more interested in initiatives (relative to partisans) in a midterm year, and the opposite pattern in a presidential year (Donovan, Tolbert, and Smith 2009). Another shows that initiative campaigns may have a greater effect mobilizing turnout of less educated voters who might otherwise have less interest in politics (Tolbert, Bowen, and Donovan 2009). Of course, the trick for candidate campaigns is for the candidate to be on the same side of the issue as a majority of voters, and to mobilize voters on the majority side who might otherwise not vote.

In the November 2004 election, for example, eleven states had ballot propositions concerning the banning of gay marriage. It was argued that this issue was one which should help Republican presidential candidate George Bush. Even if Bush failed to excite the conservative vote base, the chance to vote against gay marriage could have generated turnout of conservative (pro-Bush) voters who would otherwise have stayed at home.

To date, however, evidence that a specific ballot measure can mobilize turnout in favor of a specific candidate is quite weak (D. Smith, Desantis, and Kassel 2006), although some measures may prime voters to evaluate candidates in terms of the candidates' positions on the issue (Nicholson 2005). However, if an issue that is raised is one firmly and commonly located within the partisan divide, the scope for both priming effects may be muted. If an evangelical Republican voter cared deeply about banning gay marriage, for example, she may likely have supported George Bush over John Kerry notwithstanding any effect of the ballot measure. But for people who might care but not otherwise think of the issue, nor previously see the issue in partisan terms, initiatives may prime them to do so, and affect their vote (Donovan et al. 2008). The scope for these effects, then, may be bigger when the issues involved are important but not part of the current partisan debate.

So far we have considered voting on propositions from the point of view of standard models of voter candidate choice. Because partisanship and candidate choice are so closely bound together, the differences between voters' partisanship and their choices in ballot elections provide a useful analytical approach. One concern, for example, is the degree to which party identification reflects vote intention. Another is the degree to which "independents" are truly independent of party. In either case the theoretical relationship that runs from party identification to voter choice is subject to question and so having a set of elections in which meaningful and consequential decisions are taken and which are not so structured by party gives us some means into asking and answering questions about voter decision making beyond candidate choice. Thus, the study of ballot propositions can advance the study of voting behavior more generally, especially in the areas of framing effects, the dynamics of choice, and questions about how voters reason and about how democratic institutions and processes should function. Ballot proposition elections can also shed light on the issue of public policy responsiveness more broadly. We review each of these points in turn in the following sections.

FRAMING EFFECTS AND THE DYNAMICS OF CHOICE

It is easy to overstate how often new issues arrive on the ballot. Many issues return to the ballot in one form or another again and again. A measure concerning abortion policy, for example, reached the Arkansas ballot in 1986 and another was on the ballot in 1988; a lottery proposal appeared on the ballot there in both 1996 and 2000. Alcohol regulation (Prohibition and counter-Prohibition measures) appeared no fewer than sixteen times on the California ballot between 1914 and 1948. Even less charged issues may reoccur: three proposals relating to daylight savings time were on the Washington state ballot between 1952 and 1960 (there was a fourth appearance—the first one—in 1914). It appeared on the California ballot three times, too, between 1930 and 1949.

Even so, it is possible to see new issues that do not fit terribly easily into existing partisan frameworks arrive at the ballot. These are the ones that allow critics of the process to give another push to the merry-go-round of "direct democracy is much too complicated for voters."

Putting the issue of the complexity of direct democracy elections to one side, what we can say is that relatively new issues or ones that attract bipartisan support or opposition do allow the possibility of studying features of public opinion in a real-world setting that may not be found elsewhere. Two features in particular are those of framing effects and the dynamics of public opinion.

Framing effects can be, as Druckman (2001, 2004) reminds us, quite fragile. In a laboratory setting, question-wording experiments can reveal a shift in opinions of respondents in response, say, to a given cue or given language. But the question remains whether these shifts can occur in the real world of campaigns when voters are subject to cross-cutting pressures. In established candidate-centered or party-centered politics it can be hard to disentangle the effects of a frame as opposed to partisanship. For example, at one time it was possible to see a discussion of AIDS as one between competing "frames": either this was a question of morality or it was a question of public health. A more modern example may be the recent wave of propositions dealing with eminent domain, not an issue that many candidates discuss, but one of concern to some voters. And eminent domain may be seen either as property rights or as a challenge to governing in the public interest.

The framing of ballot proposition issues in various ways can, then, give us some insight into framing effects more generally. For example, the ballot title (of the kind displayed in Table 28.1) may well lead to a favorable or unfavorable view of the proposal in a "judging a book by its cover" sort of way. Filla and Murphy (n.d.), for example, show that titling of a ballot can shift support if it mentions "desirable" populations and/or if it mentions the benefits of a proposal rather than any increase in taxes.

One question stemming from this kind of experimental approach is whether or not voter opinions towards propositions are malleable over the course of a campaign: that is, whether voter opinions switch and switch again. Unfortunately, we have no evidence of the dynamics of opinions on typical American-style ballot propositions (but see Johnston et al. 1996). Importantly, such a study would give insight into opinion formation on new issues.

To date, the evidence has been based on pseudo-panels and cross-sections (e.g., Bowler and Donovan 1994; Branton 2003). That is, in each election cycle there are a number of cross-sectional surveys. It is possible to look at opinion at various times for a given demographic group. For example, if we look at college-educated Anglos over 40 we can see if opinion within that particular group shifts. But absent rolling cross-sectional data (or more extensive panel data), it becomes hard to track opinion change on propositions.

Again, the value of studying this question using ballot propositions is that they may be outside the usual partisan contests or, for want of a better term, "outside party politics" (OPP) propositions. Some of these issues may be new or may involve cross-party coalitions. They therefore allow us to look at opinion formation, if not exactly on a blank slate then close to it. There are two possible kinds of outcome we may see. On the one hand, voter opinion on OPP propositions will be unformed and—consequently—may be readily changed. This would be consistent with the existence of substantive framing and/or campaign effects.

On the other hand, while there may be instability in the early period, once a voter has formed an opinion it may be very hard to change that opinion. And indeed that is what seems to be the case—at least so far as pseudo-panel data are concerned. On many issues voters appear to begin from a "don't know" position and then move to an opinion to which they remain anchored (Bowler and Donovan 1994; but see Magleby 1989). Opinions do not—we think—flicker at the individual level from "yes" to "no" and back again. But absent any detailed data, there is nothing to help establish what the actual pattern looks like, nor which

Table 28.2 Vote shares and propositions on the November 2006 California ballot

Proposition Number	Title	% Yes	% Dems Yes	% GOP Yes
1A	Transportation Funding Protection	77		
1B	Highway Safety/Air Quality/Port Security Bond 2006	61	62	49
1C	Housing/Emergency Shelter Trust Fund 2006	58	64	50
1D	Public Education Facilities Bond 2006	57	66	47
1E	Disaster Preparedness/Flood Prevention Bond 2006	64	59	52
83	Sex Offenders/Residence Restrictions Monitoring	71		
84	Water Qual/Flood/Resource Protection/ Park Bonds	54	58	36
85	Waiting Period/Parental Notification	46	32	66
86	Cigarette Tax Initiative	48	54	37
87	Alternative Energy/Research/Oil Producer Tax	45	54	17
88	Education Funding/Real Property Parcel Tax	23		
89	Political Campaigns/Public Financing/ Corp Tax	26		
90	Govt Acquisition/Regulation of Private Property	48	32	40

Source: Vote totals from the Secretary of State's office; party breakdown is by party registration from Field California Poll 2606.

elements form the set of considerations that allow voters to make a decision and then stick to it.

One other way of illustrating the scope for framing effects on voter decision making is illustrated by results in Table 28.2. These results are again taken from the November 2006 California ballot and cover some of the same proposals mentioned in Table 28.1.

Table 28.2 shows that the vote totals and the level of support by party registration shifts from issue to issue. Although overall vote choices may be, and indeed are, structured by party, these shifting patterns show that some individual voters are also making issue-by-issue choices on these proposals. Two points can be made about these shifting patterns of support, points that will eventually lead us back to the scope for framing effects via a discussion of ideological constraint.

First, it is worth underscoring that partisanship does structure attitudes across a range of ballot proposition issues (see e.g. Branton 2003). We can see this by using the polling data that provide the figures on party breakdown and looking to see if there are party differences in how many of these proposals were supported by Democrats and the left. We can simply add up how many "yes's" the left gave to most of these proposals.[4] If we do this then registered Democrats—on average— supported 3.3 of the 9 measures on which we have survey data. Registered Republicans supported 2.2 of the 9 measures. Or, if we break the numbers down by self-described ideology of liberal, middle-of-the-road, and conservative, the figures for the average number of "yes" votes on the 9 proposals are 4.9, 3.7, and 2.5 respectively.

The degree of consistency that is seen between choices on each issue and partisanship has received a great deal of attention because a demonstration of consistency of choice helps buttress arguments to the effect that voters can, in fact, make sense of ballot propositions (see especially Banducci's 1998 analysis of consistency using voted ballots). Although the statistical techniques involved in showing that connection between the issue and partisanship are generally a lot more sophisticated than this simple counting, the end result is the same: there exists a degree of ideological consistency across a series of measures.

A second point is that there is another way of looking at the deviations from a "party line" on these votes. The demonstration of consistency is only interesting if we see voters as doing little more than flipping coins when they go into the ballot, but when the set of issues being voted on includes—as in this election—abortion, alternative energy, eminent domain, and a series of public spending measures, an assumption of a coin-flipping citizen verges on the insulting. We should expect to see at least some measure of structuring by partisanship and not be surprised by it. What is, perhaps, more interesting, is that we see deviation from the "party line." One way to interpret deviations from a party line is to argue (along Conversian lines) that there is no coherent ideological constraint to mass opinions. But the

---

[4] Counting a No vote on the parental notification measure Proposition 85 as a "left" vote.

deviation from ideological consistency is more interesting than that, and more revealing of the range of political beliefs among the electorate.

Take, for example, the series of nine votes from Table 28.2 and represent them as a preference profile of a string of "yes's" and "no's" (and again reversing that coding on Proposition 85). If we do this we can arrive at a string of nine responses: a vector of "yes's" and "no's" that represent a preference profile for voters on these nine issues. If we do this we see 153 unique preference profiles across the roughly one thousand voters in this survey, the most common profile being a string of "no's," which accounted for about 31 percent of the sample ("no" and "don't know" were lumped together). Another common profile is a string of seven "yes's" which was shared by 3 percent of the sample or 31 people. Even after taking account of these two patterns we are still left with 151 other profiles distributed between roughly 600 people.

What this range of preference profiles tells us is that there is considerable variation in popular preferences on these issues. It also suggests that the expression of policy preferences represented by party is an enormously constraining one: partisanship would seem to reflect a great deal of suppression of the richness of individual policy preferences. Rather than being an expression of consistency, then, partisanship may reflect how multidimensional politics are crunched down into one or two dimensions at the level of voters. One of the consequences that the study of ballot proposition elections may have for political behavior more generally is, then, that they show just how much partisanship may constrain preferences. One, small, illustration of that is given in the last line of Table 28.2, where registered Democrats and registered Republicans do not seem to differ all that much on the question of eminent domain.

Furthermore, and here we return to the broader point of this section, if voter preferences are relatively diverse and it is possible to find bipartisan agreement, then we may well expect to see some scope for framing effects in this important real-world setting. That said, it is not so much the similarity in voter preferences to an underlying ideology or their conformity to a partisan voter profile that may be interesting; rather, it is the differences between voters in preferences that is of interest, since it implies that voters may have a somewhat richer and more complex view of issues than we usually assume in models of democratic citizens.

REASONING ABOUT INSTITUTIONS AND PROCESSES

One of the areas in which the study of direct democracy has wider relevance to voting studies is that of the question of voter attitudes toward democratic institutions and processes themselves. Ballot proposition elections are, generally speaking, quite widely disliked by many journalists and academics (e.g. Broder 2000; Schrag 1998) but are, generally speaking, quite widely liked by voters in the United States and most established democracies (Bowler, Donovan, and Karp 2007).

Voters are not uncritical of the process. Survey data, for example, report California voters supported making it more difficult for voters to approve initiatives, but they showed little support for making it easier for legislators to revise proposals once passed (see Bowler et al. 2001). Surveys also show voters think campaigns are misleading, and have doubts about the quality of laws produced by initiative (see Bowler et al. 2001; Bowler, Donovan, and Karp 2007, for example; and the PPIC surveys from September and October 2005). Notwithstanding these reservations, many polls show that roughly two-thirds to three-quarters of voters express support for the direct initiative process.

There are several questions we note here in relation to the implications of the study of ballot propositions for wider political science themes. First, do voters want a greater say in politics? One of the themes of a series of works by John Hibbing and Elizabeth Theiss-Morse (2001, 2002) is that citizens do not like the process of representative democracy (because they see it as dominated by partisan office-holders), but that they do not desire actual direct democracy. They want "stealth democracy," where experts rather than partisan representatives make decisions, and may support populist reforms as a balance against the power of unpopular representatives. This theme is only one part of their overall argument, but it is one that resonates in part because Hibbing and Theiss-Morse are right: ordinary citizens do share a deep distaste for partisan politics.

Yet survey evidence shows that voters who say they want more opportunities to participate in politics are more likely to agree that use of referendums is a good thing. Although they may have concerns about the role of money and interest groups in direct democracy, they have far greater misgivings about how much representative democracy has been corrupted by "special" interests (Bowler et al. 2007). If legislatures and legislators cannot be trusted to "do the right thing" then one recourse is to direct democracy. This experience with direct democracy thus generates broad, perplexing questions for political science today: does the popularity of direct democracy reflect demands for a "lesser of two evils" minimalist view of politics where initiatives are simply a check on representatives, or does it reflect a desire for a more activist "new politics"? Do people really want a stealth democracy? Is support for direct democracy a function of accurate perceptions about the role of interests in representative democracy, or due to a misunderstanding of how representation functions? Put differently, are voters "wrong" to think that moneyed interests have more influence over their representatives than their fellow voters?

Second, what do attitudes toward direct democracy mean for notions of citizenship? More highly educated individuals typically have the deepest reservations about direct democracy (Bowler et al. 2007). This presents something of a problem to developmental theories of "critical citizens" (Dalton 2004, 2007; Norris 1999). This work argues that cognitive mobilization leads to changes in attitudes toward politics and participation: more cognitively mobilized individuals prefer greater participation. While this argument works well at the generational level to account for changing attitudes towards politics more broadly (and even across societies), the finding that more educated (and hence more cognitively mobilized) voters are less keen on direct democracy is one that runs counter to the general argument.

Another way in which the study of direct democracy is useful to broader concerns (rather than ballot propositions simply being seen as an arena in which broader concerns are tested) is in thinking about policy responsiveness to democratic citizens (Matsusaka 2004). One difficulty in tying, say, the voting record of a member of Congress to district preferences is that appropriate measures are hard to find. It may be possible to single out a few key roll-call votes, but finding opinion data matched to the district may not be available (see, for example, Hurley and Hill, this volume, Chapter 38). The tie of responsiveness and representation between issue at hand and the preferences of voters is inherently hard to measure and is further muddied by partisanship (of the voter or the representative or both). These ties of responsiveness are easier to see at work in the setting of ballot propositions where measures are often more direct.

DIRECT DEMOCRACY AND PUBLIC POLICY

Bad and unrepresentative policy outcomes are frequently cited in discussions of what is wrong with direct democracy. Thoughtful critics of the process suggest that well-financed groups advance their narrow interests via ballot initiatives at the expense of the general public (Broder 2000), and that short-sighted voters approve initiated tax cuts that decimate the state's public sector (Schrag 1998). Others note that successful anti-tax measures such as California's Proposition 13 were crafted and funded by initiative professionals determined to reduce the size of the state's government (D. Smith 1998), and that fiscal initiatives allow voters to express preferences for irresponsible public policy. Anti-tax measures allow voters to demand tax cuts, without any corresponding reduction in public services; or demand "something for nothing" (Sears and Citrin 1982). Other initiatives allow voters to simultaneously approve new spending programs while approving tax cuts. From this perspective, California's recurring fiscal crisis and the scope of its investment in public services are the product of citizen-approved fiscal initiatives. Concerns about the ill effects of direct democracy on policy and governance have led to efforts to reform the citizen initiative process (see Ellis 2002).

There is, however, no consensus from empirical studies that shows initiatives have systematic adverse fiscal effects, or that they produce policies that majorities of voters did not want. Arcenaux (2002), Gerber (1996a), and Lascher, Hagen, and Rochlin (1996) focus on the link between popular preferences and the initiative policy outputs. Gerber (1996b, 1999) and Matsusaka (2004, 2005) argue that the initiative process provides actors external to the legislature the ability to send signals about preferences for policy, and that the threat or use of the initiative thus encourages legislators to set policy closer to the median voter. Tolbert (1998) reports that initiatives also have direct effects on policy by allowing groups to pass popular legislation, such as term limits, that representatives may resist.

Interest in the effects of direct democracy can also reflect political concerns. Some observers of direct democracy on the left decry the impact of direct democracy in shrinking the size of the state sector and state public-welfare sector. Some conservatives see this same pattern as a victory; indeed, some academic observers have supported the use of direct democracy as a tool to institute fiscal discipline (Buchanan and Tullock 1977). One question is whether or not more frequent use of fiscal initiatives is associated with lower state expenditures in key policy areas. Matsusaka's (2004) research suggests that direct democracy did reduce public spending in the last decades of the twentieth century. He suggests that public opinion regarding taxing and spending was generally conservative during this period, and that such opinion may have been better expressed as policy in states where the initiative process was available.

Matsusaka also notes that the effect of initiatives on policy is not inherently conservative. Initiative states spent more in the 1930s than non-initiative states. That may have been a period where opinion was supportive of increased spending, and legislators in initiative states would have been less likely to be out of step with public opinion. Studies less comprehensive than Matsusaka's conclude that the initiative process has not made state policy more representative of state opinion, and that it might actually make policy less representative (Camobreco 1998; Lascher et al. 1996).

For many commentators on the politics of direct democracy in the United States, there was a defining moment when the ill effects of ballot initiatives on public policy became most apparent: that moment came on June 6, 1978, when California voters approved Proposition 13. Popular tax-cutting initiatives then spread to many other direct democracy states and from that time onwards the provision of public services went into a downward spiral. For writers such as Schrag and others such as Daniel Smith (1998) this is not simply a "distributional politics" sort of fight: the damage is to the social contract and even to the very social fabric of the state. Even more thoroughgoing than this critique, however, is the idea that ballot proposition politics are not simply an area in which the haves and have-nots fight and in which the haves win—with generally damaging consequences. Rather, ballot proposition politics continue to make a bad situation worse: their effect is not a "one off" but a downward spiral. Direct democracy has become so much more important in state politics that, for some critics, it challenges the governability of a state (Rosenthal 1998).

Schrag's "new civics" critique broadens the criticism of direct democracy from one in which the objection to direct democracy is more than simple disagreement with policy goals and outputs (e.g., an objection to the level of spending on education). It is an objection to the impact of the initiative on the process of representation. Among journalistic accounts of the effect of direct democracy, David Broder's *Democracy Derailed* (2000) is the one that is most in line both with the new civics critique of direct democracy and with earlier work on the "ungovernability" of modern democratic political systems (Birch 1984; King 1975; Olson 1982, 1986).

One component of this line of argument is that it allows too many demands to be voiced. In consequence, in the short(ish) term, government may not be able to meet these demands and so disappoint its citizens. Longer-term consequences include the declining legitimacy of and regard for democratic institutions (see also Birch 1984; and Dalton 2004). Special interest politics are thus damaging both in the short term and in the long term.

For some, direct democracy simply makes these pathologies even worse.[5] Schrag and others thus identify direct democracy as fostering a downward spiral of short-termism. The tax revolt proposal is emblematic not just of the general critique of direct democracy from the 'new civics' and 'ungovernability' perspectives but often stands as a poster child for everything that is seen to be wrong with direct democracy in general. But what, exactly, is the legacy of that tax revolt?

The answer is not simple. As noted above, Matsusaka's work (2004) suggests that rather than simply advancing specific policies such as Proposition 13, the presence of the initiative process acts to transmit mass preferences broadly into legislative policy outputs. Furthermore, conclusions from empirical research on the initial fiscal effects of Proposition 13-era tax and expenditure limits (TELs) were mixed, and mostly showed such TELs had little effect on state expenditure growth (Joyce and Mullins 1991; Kousser, McCubbins, and Moule n.d.; Lowery 1983; Mullins and Joyce 1996; Poterba and Reuben 1999). Gerber et al. (2001) contend that part of the muted effects of initiatives such as Proposition 13 is that they are not self-implementing, and allow legislators and courts substantial discretion in compliance.

The idea that Proposition 13 was the catalyst for an initiative-fueled tax revolt that started in 1978 may also be overstated. The "revolt" may be seen more narrowly as a reaction to the link between property taxes and rising home values. California voters rejected an initiative proposing an income tax cut in 1980. Since then, voters there and in many other states have also approved initiatives that raised new

---

[5] The Progressives and Populists who introduced direct democracy had a very different idea. They thought direct democracy was a corrective to the abuses of special interest politics.

revenues (cigarette tax, lottery) and required new spending (stem cell research, class size reductions, new health care programs). California voters also approved legislative-referred sales-tax increase (Proposition 172 of 1992). Whatever the legacy of Proposition 13 was (or is), it did not spawn such a large crop of popular tax-cutting initiatives as to crowd out other proposals that raised revenues and spending.

While Proposition 13 may be an important proposal it is not the only one, and developing either a critique or a defense of direct democracy by reference to a single proposition—no matter how important—is of limited value. Direct democracy clearly plays a major role in affecting the state's fiscal priorities, but it works to do much more than simply cut taxes. The broader question thus turns to the link between policy outcomes, citizen preferences, and direct democracy in general.

What do Studies of Policy Making and the Initiative Process Show Us?

How can we assess the overall effects of initiatives on state policy? In very general terms, the literature on the policy outputs of direct democracy is concerned with two broad questions: how do initiatives affect public policy, and how do they affect state fiscal politics in particular? One set of scholars is interested in understanding the general connection between direct democracy, public preferences, and public policy. Their argument is straightforward: direct democracy should mean a more direct connection between popular preferences and policy outputs. Of course, the problem for some observers is that direct democracy may reflect popular preferences all *too* readily. If direct democracy does indeed make policy responsive to popular wishes then policy outputs may be inconsistent, short-term, and narrowly self-interested: voters may pass tax cuts while simultaneously approving spending increases.

A series of studies have examined this issue. Gerber's study of state abortion policies and death penalty laws (1996a), Arcenaux's study of state abortion laws (2002), and the exchange between Matsusaka and Hagen and Lascher et al. (Matsusaka 2001; Hagen, Lascher, and Camobreco 2001; Lascher, Hagen, and Rochlin 1996) are all examples of this kind of work. The difficulty in testing how (or if) ballot initiatives affect state policy lies in how these scholars go about measuring the correspondence between popular preferences and policy outputs. Yet popular preferences for specific policies are not easily measured at the state level. The evidence from this series of studies is somewhat mixed, but some work does suggest that direct democracy increases the likelihood that states have public policies that reflect what citizens in the state want.

DISCUSSION

Substantial academic research on direct democracy has occurred since the 1970s. Much of this work has focused on questions of voter competence and on the relationship between the initiative process and public policy. The two bodies of work are tied together in a critique of direct democracy that might be summarized (and over-simplified) as follows: With deep-pocketed special interests behind them, professional campaign consultants can trick voters into passing policies they don't really want. This, in turn, makes public policy less representative of public opinion than it might otherwise be if the legislative process was not constrained by direct democracy. Matters are made worse by initiative entrepreneurs who feed (and feed off) a distrust of government. The sum effect is to weaken the process of governance in direct democracy states.

Since the 1970s, this critique of direct democracy may have received as much or more attention than the prospects for majority tyranny (but see Chavez 1998; Gamble 1997; Rimmerman, Wald, and Wilcox 2000). Of late, however, more attention has been paid to social policies such as abortion and gay rights. Although social issues that may pit the interests of minorities against majorities remain common (e.g., anti-gay discrimination, gay marriage, immigration), courts appear more ready to reject voter-approved social measures (e.g., *Romer* v. *Evans*) than fiscal measures and government reform measures (Miller 2003).

The overview of research presented here suggests that there is a complex relationship between mass preferences, institutions, and policy. Policy is often seen as a product of the relationship between institutions and mass preferences. Although we know a fair amount about preferences for policies, and about decisions made under various institutional rules, less is known about public preferences for institutions themselves. Nor do we know much about how direct democracy affects institutions. The concept of what a political institution is may be seen differently when we consider that direct democracy might alter how mass preferences are translated into policy as well as whether the institutions themselves are the direct expression of mass preferences.

Studies discussed above suggest that populist democratic practices may alter how preferences are expressed in policy outcomes. Other research suggests direct democracy may also allow preferences to be expressed in political institutions that shape policy. Direct democracy changes the nature of political parties (Bowler and

Donovan 2006), begets term limits (Tolbert 1998), alters primary rules (Lawrence, Bowler, and Donovan, n.d.(b)), and can allow voters to change other "rules of the game."

This last point—on the changing of institutions—suggests some troubling normative consequences of direct democracy. Political institutions (generally understood) have long been seen as ways to limit cycling in popular preferences. This cycling is not ordinarily inherited by institutions because they are "sticky" and subject to change only with great difficulty. The point about direct democracy, however, is that it allows voters to change at least some institutions just about as easily as they may change many policies. It is not, or at least not yet, clear whether opening up the possibility of cycling over institutions is as damaging as it may sound.

REFERENCES

ARCENEAUX, K. 2002. Direct Democracy and the Link between Public Opinion and State Abortion Policy. *State Politics and Policy Quarterly*, 2/4: 372–87.

BANDUCCI, S. 1998. Searching for Ideological Consistency in Direct Legislation Voting. In *Citizens as Legislators: Direct Democracy in the United States*, ed. S. Bowler, T. Donovan, and C. Tolbert. Columbus: Ohio State University Press.

BIRCH, A. H. 1984. Overload, Ungovernability and Delegitimation: The Theories and the British Case. *British Journal of Political Science*, 14/2: 135–60.

BOWLER, S. and DONOVAN, T. 1994. Information and Opinion Change on Ballot Propositions. *Political Behavior*, 16/4: 411–35.

——— 1998. *Demanding Choices*. Ann Arbor, Mich.: University of Michigan Press.

——— 2006. Direct Democracy and Political Parties in America. *Party Politics*, 12/5: 649–69.

——— and KARP, J. 2007. Enraged or Engaged? Preferences for Direct Citizen Participation in Affluent Democracies. *Political Research Quarterly*, 60/3: 351–62.

——— NEIMAN, M., and PEEL, J. 2001. Institutional Threat and Partisan Outcomes: Legislative Candidates' Attitudes toward Direct Democracy. *State Politics and Policy Quarterly*, 1/4: 364–79.

BRANTON, R. 2003. Explaining Individual-Level Voting Behavior on State Ballot Propositions. *Political Research Quarterly*, 56/3: 367–77.

BRODER, D. S. 2000. *Democracy Derailed: Initiative Campaigns and the Power of Money*. New York: Harcourt.

BUCHANAN, J. and TULLOCK, G. 1977. The Expanding Public Sector: Wagner Squared. *Public Choice*, 31 (Fall): 147–50.

CAMOBRECO, J. 1998. Preferences, Fiscal Policies and the Initiative Process. *Journal of Politics*, 60/3: 819.

CARMINES, E. and STIMSON, J. 1989. The Two Faces of Issue Voting. *American Political Science Review*.

CHAVEZ, L. 1998. *The Color Bind: California's Battle to End Affirmative Action.* Berkeley, Calif.: University of California Press.

CRONIN, T. 1989. *Direct Democracy: The Politics of Initiative, Referendum, and Recall.* Cambridge, Mass.: Harvard University Press.

DALTON, R. 2004. *Democratic Challenges, Democratic Choices: The Erosion in Political Support in Advanced Industrial Democracies.* Oxford: Oxford University Press.

—— 2007. *The Good Citizen: How A Younger Generation Is Reshaping American Politics.* Washington, D.C.: Congressional Quarterly Press.

DONOVAN, T., TOLBERT, C., and SMITH, D. 2008. Priming Presidential Votes by Direct Democracy. *Journal of Politics,* 70/4: 1217–31.

—— —— —— 2009. Political Engagement, Mobilization and Direct Democracy. *Public Opinion Quarterly,* 73/1: 98–118.

DRUCKMAN, J. 2001. On the Limits of Framing Effects: Who Can Frame? *Journal of Politics,* 63/4: 1041–66.

—— 2004. Political Preference Formation: Competition, Deliberation and the (Ir)relevance of Framing. *American Political Science Review,* 98/4: 671–86.

ELLIS, R. 2002. *Democratic Delusions: The Initiative Process in America.* Lawrence, Kans.: University Press of Kansas.

FILLA, J. and CHAD, M. N.d. Information Effects in Low Salience Settings. Unpublished manuscript, UC Riverside.

GAMBLE, B. 1997. Putting Civil Rights to a Vote. *American Journal of Political Science,* 41/1: 245–69.

GERBER, E. 1996a. Legislatures, Initiatives, and Representation: The Effects of State Legislative Institutions on Policy. *Political Research Quarterly,* 49/2: 263–86.

—— 1996b. Legislative Response to the Threat of Popular Initiatives. *American Journal of Political Science,* 40/1: 99–128.

—— 1999. *The Populist Paradox: Interest Group Influence and the Promise of Direct Legislation.* Princeton, N.J.: Princeton University Press.

—— LUPIA, A., McCUBBINS, M. D., and KIEWIET, D. R. 2001. *Stealing the Initiative: How State Government Responds to Direct Democracy.* Upper Saddle River, N.J.: Prentice Hall.

HAGEN, M. G., LASCHER, E. L., JR., and CAMOBRECO, J. F. 2001. Response to Matsusaka: Estimating the Effect of Ballot Initiatives on Policy Responsiveness. *Journal of Politics,* 63: 1257–63.

HIBBING, J. and THEISS-MORSE, E. 2001. Process Preferences and American Politics: What the People Want Government to Be. *American Political Science Review,* 95/1: 145–53.

—— —— 2002. *Stealth Democracy.* Cambridge: Cambridge University Press.

JOHNSTON, R., BLAIS, A., GIDENGIL, A., and NEVITTE, N. 1996. *The Challenge of Direct Democracy: The 1992 Canadian Referendum.* Montreal: McGill Queens.

JOYCE, P. and MULLINS, D. 1991. The Changing Fiscal Structure of State and Local Public Sector: The Impact of Tax and Expenditure Limitations. *Public Administration Review,* 51/3: 240–53.

KING, A. 1975. Overload: Problems of Governing in the 1970s. *Political Studies,* 28: 284–96.

KOUSSER, T., McCUBBINS, M. D., and MOULE, E. N.d. Can State Tax and Expenditure Limits Effectively Reduce Spending? Unpublished manuscript, UCSD.

LASCHER, E. L., JR., HAGEN, M. G., and ROCHLIN, S. A. 1996. Gun Behind the Door? Ballot Initiatives, State Policies and Public Opinion. *Journal of Politics,* 58: 760–75.

Lawrence, E., Bowler, S., and Donovan, T. N.d.(a) Adopting Direct Democracy: Testing Competing Explanations of Institutional Change. *American Research Quarterly.* Forthcoming.

——— ——— N.d.(b) Adoption of the Direct Primary. Unpublished manuscript.

Lowery, D. 1983. Limitations on Taxing and Spending: An Assessment of their Effectiveness. *Social Science Quarterly,* 64/2: 247–63.

Lupia, A. 1994. Shortcuts versus Encyclopedias: Information and Voting Behavior in California Insurance Reform Elections. *American Political Science Review,* 88: 63–76.

Lupia, A. and McCubbins, M. 1998. *The Democratic Dilemma: Can Citizens Learn What They Need to Know?* Cambridge: Cambridge University Press.

Magleby, D. B. 1984. *Direct Legislation: Voting on Ballot Propositions in the United States.* Baltimore, Md.: Johns Hopkins University Press.

——— 1989. Opinion formation and Opinion Change on Ballot Proposition Campaigns. In *Manipulating Public Opinion,* ed. M. Margolis and G. Mauser. Pacific Grove, Calif.: Brooks-Cole.

Matsusaka, J. 2001. Problems with a Methodology Used to Test the Responsiveness of Policy to Public Opinion in Initiative States. *Journal of Politics,* 63: 1250–6.

——— 2004. *For the Many or the Few: The Initiative, Public Policy, and American Democracy.* Chicago: University of Chicago Press.

——— 2005. The Eclipse of Legislatures: Direct Democracy in the 21st Century. *Public Choice,* 124/1: 157–77.

Miller, K. 2003. Courts and the Initiative Process. In *The Initiative and Referendum Almanac,* ed. M. D. Waters. Raleigh, N.C.: Carolina Academic Press.

Mullins, D. and Joyce, P. 1996. Tax and Expenditure Limitations and State and Local Finance Structure: An Empirical Assessment. *Public Budgeting and Finance,* 16/1: 75–101.

Nicholson, S. P. 2005. *Voting the Agenda: Candidates, Elections and Ballot Propositions.* Princeton, N.J.: Princeton University Press.

——— 2007. Ballots of Reward and Punishment: Target Group Cues and Electoral Support for Direct Legislation. Paper presented at the Annual Meeting of the Midwest Political Science Association, Chicago, April 12–15.

Norris, P. 1999. *Critical Citizens: Global Support for Democratic Governance.* Oxford: Oxford University Press.

Olson, M. 1982. *Rise and Decline of Nations.* New Haven, Conn.: Yale University Press.

——— 1986. A Theory of the Incentives Facing Political Organizations: Neo-Corporatism and the Hegemonic State. *International Political Science Review / Revue internationale de science politique,* 7/2: 165–89.

Poterba, J. and Reuben, K. 1999. *Fiscal Rules and State Borrowing Costs: Evidence from California and Other States.* San Francisco: Public Policy Institute of California.

Rimmerman, C., Wald, K., and Wilcox, C. 2000. *The Politics of Gay Rights.* Chicago: University of Chicago Press.

Rosenthal, A. 1998. *The Decline of Representative Democracy.* Washington, D.C.: CQ Press.

Schrag, P. 1998. *Paradise Lost: California's Experience, America's Future.* New York: The New Press.

Sears, D. O. and Citrin, J. 1982. *Tax Revolt: Something for Nothing in California.* Cambridge, Mass.: Harvard University Press.

Smith, D. 1998. *Tax Crusaders and the Politics of Direct Democracy.* Routledge.

—— DESANTIS, M., and KASSEL, J. 2006. Same-Sex Marriage Ballot Measures and the 2004 Presidential Election. *State and Local Government Review*, 38/2: 787–91.

—— and TOLBERT, C. J. 2004. *Educated by Initiative: The Effects of Direct Democracy on Citizens and Political Organizations in the American States*. Ann Arbor, Mich.: University of Michigan Press.

SMITH, M. A. 2001. The Contingent Effects of Ballot Initiatives and Candidate Races on Turnout. *American Journal of Political Science*, 45: 700–6.

STRATMANN, T. 2006. Is Spending More Potent For or Against a Proposition? Evidence from Ballot Measures. *American Journal of Political Science*, 50: 788–801.

TOLBERT, C. 1998. Changing Rules for State Legislatures: Direct Democracy and Governance Policy. In *Citizens as Legislators: Direct Democracy in the United States*, ed. S. Bowler, T. Donovan, and C. Tolbert. Columbus: Ohio State University Press.

—— BOWEN, D., and DONOVAN, T. 2009. Initiative Campaigns: Direct Democracy and Voter Mobilization. *American Politics Research*, 37: 155–92.

—— GRUMMEL, J., and SMITH, D. 2001. The Effects of Ballot Initiatives on Voter Turnout in the American States. *American Politics Review*, 29: 625–48.

PART VII

ELITES AND INSTITUTIONS

....

CHAPTER 29

VOTERS IN CONTEXT

THE POLITICS OF CITIZEN BEHAVIOR*

....

WALTER J. STONE
MATTHEW K. BUTTICE

> The role of the people in the political system is determined largely by the conflict system, for it is conflict that involves the people in politics and the nature of conflict determines the nature of the public involvement.
>
> E. E. Schattschneider (1975, 126)

Political scientists have profitably borrowed theoretical perspectives from sociology, psychology, and economics to explain why citizens behave as they do. These theoretical traditions, combined with a strong commitment to the sample survey, have resulted in a sophisticated understanding of voting behavior in national elections. Studies of citizen behavior have done an especially good job of incorporating individual characteristics in their explanations. Impressive gains have been made in our understanding of how the social environment affects citizen behavior,

* The authors would like to thank Cheryl Boudreau and Ronald Rapoport for their helpful comments on a previous draft.

while more work is needed to integrate the explicitly political environment into our research. The relatively low level of attention to the effects of political context is ironic, but understandable. It is ironic because we are, after all, *political* scientists. It is understandable because sample surveys provide individual-level variance and explanations; because the theoretical pedigree of much of our work in economics and social psychology lends itself to methodological individualism; and because of the importance of individualism in the political culture. However, a danger of methodological individualism is that the study of democracy will be reduced to the characteristics, qualifications, and behaviors of individual citizens.

Our starting point is that political behavior is a function of individual character-istics, the political and social contexts in which they are embedded, and interactions between context and individual variables. This point has long been recognized, including in works committed to the individual as the focus of analysis. One of the reasons Anthony Downs' *An Economic Theory of Democracy* is so influential is that spatial models of the sort it pioneered place candidates and parties in the same analytic framework as voters, offering important insights about the relationship between two central actors in a democracy. In a paper that illustrates the value of incorporating the Downsian framework into a study of individual voters, Charles Franklin (1991) concludes: "As we have become adept at studying voters, it is ironic that we have virtually ignored the study of candidates. Yet it is in candidate behavior that politics intrudes into voting behavior. Without the candidates, there is only the psychology of the vote choice and none of the politics."

One of the most important hypotheses from the spatial framework is that parties and candidates in a two-party system will, under certain circumstances, converge toward the preferences of the median voter (cf. D. Black 1958; Downs 1957). The median-voter hypothesis has led to speculation about why the parties and their candidates typically do not converge in the center of the political space. The dominant perspective in this literature is on the behavior of candidates and parties in response to electoral pressures, opportunities, and personal preferences (Adams, Merrill, and Groffman 2005; Enelow and Hinich 1984).

A much less common line of inquiry from the Downsian setup runs the other way: what is the effect of party/candidate positioning on voter behavior? Downs considered the possibility of a "fundamental tension" in his model, arising from parties' pursuit of office in conflict with the voter's interest in the party that promises the most utility. "if any party believes it can increase its chances of gaining office by discouraging voters from being rational, its own rational course is to do so . . . Thus if parties succeed in obscuring their policy decisions in a mist of generalities, and voters are unable to discover what their votes really mean, a rationality crisis develops" (Downs 1957, 138–9).[1] One hypothesis that emerges

---

[1] As Burden (2004, 211) put it: "Because ideology is all that matters [in the spatial model], candidates converge, leading to an election where ideology does not matter."

from this "crisis" is that when parties diverge voters can more easily distinguish between them and vote on their ideological preferences.

The example of how voters respond to party convergence illustrates the potential in the spatial-modeling tradition for thinking about how party and candidate strategic behavior affects voters. However, as noted, the bulk of the modeling and empirical literature builds on the Downsian setup by exploring the effects of voters on candidate and party behavior rather than vice versa. This strikes us as a significant lacuna, especially in the theoretical literature. What Schattschneider called the "nature of conflict" may be critical to understanding citizen behavior once individual differences, interests, and resources are taken into account. Indeed, differences in individual opinions, perceptions, and interests may reflect variation in the political context that results from candidate behavior.

What might a political theory of the citizen look like? The essential point is that citizens do not act as autonomous individuals. Important gains have been made recognizing the interdependence of citizens whose relationship to the political world depends on their interpersonal networks and social contexts (Huckfeldt and Sprague 1992, 1995; Huckfeldt, Johnson, and Sprague 2004; Mutz 2002). Emphasizing the political context suggests that it is not enough to think of citizens as motivated by interests because interests are activated or suppressed by the structure of conflict to which citizens respond. Of particular importance, we argue, are the strategic choices candidates make when they decide to invest in an electoral contest (first and foremost by entering as candidates), when they present their issue positions and priorities, and when they emphasize their personal qualities. Understanding the citizen response to these stimuli requires research designs that map these and other aspects of the political context onto survey studies.

POLITICAL RESEARCH ON THE CITIZEN

Our focus is on studies and hypotheses organized on one dimension by two types of citizen response: *engagement* and *choice*. The second dimension of our concern is defined by the strategic decisions of candidates and others who define the political context. The two aspects of this second dimension are candidate *investment* and *differentials*. The core of our argument is that indicators of contextual variables measuring candidate investment and differentials external to citizen surveys are necessary to test hypotheses fundamental to understanding citizen engagement and choice in politics.

Aspects of the Political Context: Candidate Investment and Differentials

The strategic decisions potential candidates, candidates, party leaders, activists, and contributors make define the political context that shapes voter response. These decisions are "strategic" in that candidates and others are governed by their expectations about success or failure based on how voters and other key actors will react to their decisions and behavior. For example, high-quality candidates run when they expect to win, and refrain from running when they judge their electoral prospects to be poor (Banks and Kiewiet 1989; G. Black 1972; Brace 1984; Jacobson 1989; Jacobson and Kernell 1983; Rohde 1979; Squire 1995).

The first variable of interest in understanding the political context, therefore, is *investment*, the most important of which is made by skilled potential candidates when they decide whether to enter the race. Likewise, activists and professionals must decide whether to invest in a particular campaign by risking such scarce resources as their time, expertise, reputations, and money. These investments depend on the entry decisions of strong candidates. In a two-party system, if one side invests heavily and the other side's investment is minimal or non-existent, the campaign is one-sided with important consequences for how citizens respond (Zaller 1992). As investments equalize, the campaign's intensity grows with increases in visibility and mobilization.[2]

The choices posed by the candidates determine the *differentials* that are the second aspect of the context defined by candidate behavior. One important type of candidate differential is on policy. Candidates may adopt positions at the median voter's ideal point as Downs predicted, or they may be pulled toward the extremes by the preferences of primary constituencies, activists, and others whose preferences are at odds with the general electorate (Aronson and Ordeshook 1978; Baron 1994; Moon 2004). Because candidates often have histories as officeholders and activists, their ability to position themselves strategically may be limited. That may be especially true for incumbents, who have records they must defend. In addition, some models suggest that candidates are "policy seeking" in that their positions reflect sincere preferences on issues as well as strategic calculations (Wittman 1973, 1983).

Candidate valence differentials are defined by non-policy advantages one or the other side might have. The concept of valence issues was first introduced into political science by Donald Stokes (1963, 1992) in his critiques of the spatial model of elections. He defined valence issues as "those that merely involve the linking of the parties with some condition that is positively or negatively valued by the

---

[2] Campaign intensity, a variable often included in studies of citizen response to campaigns (Gronke 2000; Partin 1995; Westlye 1991), results from investment. As skilled candidates, parties, activists, and donors invest more in campaigns, more money is spent, candidates become more visible, media attention increases, and the level of competition grows.

electorate" (Stokes 1963, 373). Political outcomes often turn on which party or candidate is associated with valued outcomes such as integrity in government, peace, and economic prosperity.

Since the publication of Stokes's articles, many have referred to valence as any non-policy advantage enjoyed by one candidate or party over the other. For example, Groseclose (2001, 862) equates a candidate's valence advantage to such factors as "incumbency, greater campaign funds, better name recognition, superior charisma, superior intelligence, and so on."

Rather than the broad definition of valence that includes any non-policy advantage, we limit candidate valence differentials to differences based on outcomes such as a robust economy or to those defined by personal qualities intrinsically valued in candidates by voters, such as personal integrity and competence (Bianco 1994; McCurley and Mondak 1995; Miller 1990; Mondak 1995). Valence differentials based on qualities and outcomes intrinsically favored by voters may affect citizen behavior directly because of differences in candidate skills, qualities, and attributes. In contrast, candidate differentials that reflect differences in investment such as financial resources are not intrinsically valued by voters, although they may be instrumental to winning office. Differences in investment produce citizen response for reasons of visibility, not because they represent qualities voters value in their representatives. They fundamentally reflect differentials based on investment rather than valence, as we define it.

Candidate investments and differentials shape citizen response, but they also interact with one another. For example, candidates and potential candidates who are experienced, competent, and dedicated may be especially reluctant to enter a race unless they are confident of their prospects. Such candidates may also be better able to attract investments both because contributors and activists value these qualities in candidates they support and because these qualities explain which candidates are electable (Stone and Maisel 2003). Another example is in the conditional relationship between candidate valence and position taking. Some studies suggest candidates with a valence advantage take positions closer to the median voter, while others contend that a valence advantage frees candidates to take more extreme positions consistent with their own policy preferences (Adams et al. 2005; Burden 2004; Groseclose 2001; Moon 2004). Disadvantaged candidates on valence or investment grounds may be compelled to take more extreme positions on the issues in order to have a chance of winning (Groseclose 2001; Moon 2004).

Thus, although we can distinguish conceptually between dimensions of the political context that may be relevant for understanding voters' responses,[3] the

---

[3] For an argument that employs different dimensions of the political context but anticipates ours in pointing to the importance of political context for understanding citizen behavior, see Sniderman (2000) and Sniderman and Levendusky (2007).

relationships among contextual factors and the ways they play out in political campaigns are likely to be complex. Valence and policy differentials between candidates and parties may create interesting strategic tradeoffs; investigating how candidate investments and differentials relate to one another should be a high priority.

Political Context and Citizen Engagement

Citizen engagement, including participation, interest, and awareness, is the subject of an enormous literature (Delli Carpini and Keeter 1996; Verba and Nie 1972; Verba, Schlozman, and Brady 1995). As Rosenstone and Hansen (1993) and Jan Leighley (1995) point out, much of this research emphasizes individual-level explanations, especially those related to the SES model, without sufficient attention to the mobilizing force of political campaigns and other aspects of the political context. Writing at about the same time, John Aldrich (1993) sought to reinterpret the "failures" of rational-choice models of voter turnout in light of investment decisions made by strategic politicians, while Leighley (1995) emphasized political context as one leg of her tripartite analysis of the sources of political participation. In keeping with the hypothesis that investments by politicians mobilize citizens to participate, Rosenstone and Hansen (1993, 164–5) demonstrate that citizen contacts increase in close elections at the presidential, gubernatorial, or congressional levels. The hypothesis that competitive elections increase turnout receives widespread support (Blais 2000; Leighley and Nagler 1992; Patterson and Caldeira 1983). Alternative modes of participation such as working for the parties and donating money also increase with the competitiveness of the campaign (Rosenstone and Hansen 1993, 130–1).

Other forms of citizen engagement besides participation are also affected by how competitive the election is. For example, campaign intensity boosts voter awareness of the candidates, as well as voter ability and willingness to express positive or negative affect toward the candidates, especially of the challenger, who is new to the voter (Gronke 2000; Kahn and Kenney 1999). In her study of Senate elections, Kam (2006) demonstrates that intense campaigns increase the amount of "open-mind-ed" and "effortful" thinking by citizens.

Aldrich (1993, 268) states the importance of candidate investment for citizen engagement: "Strategic politicians will invest more heavily in the closest contests, and this investment will be reflected in increasing levels of turnout, even if voters do not consider the closeness of the contest." The link between the competitiveness of an election and investments made by strategic candidates at the heart of Aldrich's argument offers "a richer, highly political, and strategic account of campaigns and elections" (Aldrich 1993, 274). Aldrich drew on the work of Jacobson and Kernell (1983) showing that strategic entry in congressional elections by high-quality candidates both anticipates and shapes voter response. This account recognizes that candidate investment is an important explanatory factor, although competitiveness may also reflect the underlying distribution of citizen preferences.

In addition to the effects of investment on citizen engagement, candidate policy and valence differentials may stimulate voter participation by influencing the "B" term in the calculus of voting (Riker and Ordeshook 1968). A large valence differential results when one candidate is associated with undesirable outcomes such as a recession or high crime rate. Scandal often signals a valence differential in the personal competence or integrity of the candidates. The burden would be to demonstrate that valence effects of whatever sort on citizen engagement are distinct from investment or policy effects.

Political Context and Voting Choice

Voter choice, including such closely allied concepts as candidate affect and relative candidate evaluation, is the second category of citizen response. Voter choice should depend on candidate policy and valence differentials. These hypotheses are well known to all political scientists who study citizen behavior, as are the problems with testing them on individual-level data. However, unlike studies of the effects of candidate investment and competition on citizen engagement, research on choice has not typically relied on external indicators of the independent variables. There are exceptions in studies of candidate differentials on ideology (e.g., Kahn and Kenney 1999; Wright and Berkman 1986; Zaller 2004) and valence studies that link a candidate or party to economic outcomes (Lewis-Beck 1990; Markus 1988; Partin 1995). But we know of no non-experimental studies of the effect of valence differentials based on the personal qualities and skills of the candidates.[4] The typical approach is either to rely on voter perceptions of candidate valence characteristics or issue positions, or, in studies of voting choice, to leave candidate positions implicit and rely on voter positions to motivate choice (Jacobson 2009; Miller and Shanks 1996).

Voting choice may also reflect candidate investments, especially to the extent that investments create differences in candidate visibility. As Fiorina put it in a homage to Stokes and Miller's (1962) seminal article on voting in congressional elections, "to be known at all is to be known favorably" (Fiorina 1989, 22). Strictly speaking, the hypothesis is that visibility *per se* increases support. Problems with

---

[4] In an innovative study of the effects of US House incumbent competence and integrity on voting choice, McCurley and Mondak (1995) incorporate external indicators of incumbent competence and integrity on constituent evaluations and voting choice. But their study lacks comparable data on House challengers, so it cannot measure the valence differential between candidates competing for the same votes.

testing the hypothesis on ordinary survey data abound. Respondent reports of exposure to candidate messages may be contaminated by a tendency to remember contacts by candidates the respondent is otherwise predisposed to support. Even when such biases are controlled, as in experiments where exposure to information about the candidate is manipulated (Cover and Brumberg 1982; Gerber and Green 2000), the exposure itself usually carries a message about the candidate with substantive content about policy positions or valence. Therefore, it can be difficult to separate exposure effects from valence and policy differentials.

In short, much of the literature on citizen response to political context can be reduced to a two-by-two matrix defined by candidate investment and differentials on one dimension, and by citizen engagement and choice on the other. Thinking of it this way suggests several core hypotheses:

(1) *Mobilization hypotheses:*
a. The greater the investment in the campaign by candidates and their surrogates, the higher the level of citizen engagement.
b. The greater the policy and valence differentials of candidates, the higher the level of citizen engagement.

(2) *Voting choice hypotheses:*
a. All else equal, voters support the candidate with an investment advantage.
b. The greater the issue differences between candidates, the stronger the effect of voter issue preferences on choice.
c. Voter choice reflects candidate valence differences.

These hypotheses are not startling or new; all are investigated at considerable length in the literature. We state them, in fact, precisely because they are so fundamental, and because they highlight our argument that context has been unevenly and incompletely incorporated into the study of citizen behavior.

Limitations of a Voter-centered Approach

The study of citizen behavior must not be limited to the citizen. This is best illustrated by reexamining the effects of candidate differentials on voter choice, which are among the most central problems for research on contemporary democracy. Studies that rely on individual perceptions of candidate issue or policy positions or on assessments of candidate traits must contend with perceptual biases and rationalization effects that contaminate estimates of policy and candidate valence differentials. Individuals generally process information with a bias toward maintaining previously held beliefs (Kunda 1987, 1990; Lodge and Taber 2000; Taber and Lodge 2006). Thus, to rely on individual respondents' perceptions of candidate positions on the issues or an ideological scale is to risk hopelessly entangling perception and reality (Bartels 1988; Brody and Page 1972; Conover and Feldman 1986, 1989; Evans and Anderson 2004). Likewise, we want to know whether candidates who are more honest, competent, and dedicated to public service attract votes over competitors low in these qualities, but voter perceptions and the reality of the choices presented them on such valence characteristics are difficult or impossible to sort out (Bartels 2002; Fischle 2000; Lebo and Cassino 2007; McGraw et al. 1996). The ideal is to avoid voter perceptions entirely—to design research that relates voter response to candidate attributes known to the investigator in experimental settings or in field surveys matched to external indicators, rather than as perceived by survey respondents.

The vast "issue voting" literature rests primarily on characteristics of individuals, rather than the choices they are actually presented, and illustrates the benefits of employing explicit measures of the political context, rather than relying on indicators internal to the sample survey. The authors of *The American Voter* specified three conditions for issue voting that have shaped much of the work on the subject (Campbell et al. 1960, 169–70; cf. Converse 1964):

(1) The issue must be cognized in some form.
(2) It must arouse some minimal intensity of feeling.
(3) It must be accompanied by some perception that one party represents the person's own position better than do the other parties.

This way of framing the issue-voting hypothesis places the burden on individual voters by specifying "conditions" that the voter must meet in order for the hypothesis that candidate policy differentials drive voter choice to be accepted. The conditions specified by the authors of *The American Voter* are better considered as related to the mobilization or engagement hypotheses. Thus, for example, voters are more likely to be aware of candidate differentials on the issues when candidates adopt distinct positions. It is possible that voters' issue cognition results from candidate investment; another possibility is that an interaction between candidate investment and differentials is necessary to activate voter awareness. The point is that *both* the opinions and perceptions listed and the phenomenon of interest—voting choice based on candidate differentials—are dependent on unmeasured variables that define the political context (cf. Zaller 1992). Moreover, the tests offered by *The American Voter* and scholars working in that tradition *fail to address hypotheses implied by an expressly political approach to issue voting.* Put another way, missing data on measures of the *American Voter* conditions for issue voting, such as awareness of candidate differences, has political meaning if it reflects respondent reaction to the political context.

A similar point applies to efforts to assess the effects of valence differentials (often framed around candidate traits). In order to test for either valence or issue voting, we must have independent measures of the relevant candidate differentials said to drive the behavior of voters. The notion of valence is based on the idea that everyone values the qualities or outcomes in question, which means that candidate differentials are critical (is one candidate more honest or competent than the other? Is one party responsible for economic malaise?). Studies that rely on perceptions assume that voter response must be memory-based and that perceptions reflect actual valence differentials, both of which are questionable claims. This is what led to Franklin's previously quoted observation that ignoring candidates leaves only the psychology of voting, without the politics.

Hypotheses incorporating individual and political-context variables often specify conditional, or interactive, relationships. This is evident from the original formulation offered by Downs in spelling out his "rationality crisis." When parties converge they make it difficult or impossible for voters to rely on ideology; when they diverge, voters can choose on the basis of these considerations (Abramowitz 1981; Lachat 2007). In an intriguing analysis of variations in the context of presidential elections between 1948 and 2000, John Zaller (2004) shows that valence effects in the form of presidential performance on the economy vary by individual voters' political information levels. Thus, performance on the economy affects voting choice differentially, with low-information voters more sensitive to variation in the performance of the economy than high-information voters. Likewise, parallel effects of candidate policy differences are evident, as information levels in the electorate temper the impact of policy differences (Zaller 2004, 190).

One of the most developed areas of work on context effects examines "campaign effects" in US congressional elections (Brady and Johnston 2006; Hillygus, this volume, Chapter 18). While there is substantial research on candidate investment in the form of spending and experienced challenger entry (Jacobson 2006), it is often difficult to separate such effects from the impact of candidate valence. For example, Kenny and McBurnett (1994) present a nuanced analysis of the interactive effects of individual and context variables, such as interest and candidate spending, on voter choice. However, without explicit measures of candidate valence differentials, we cannot determine whether the effects are due to visibility owing to investment, or if voters are actually picking up on substantive differences between candidates on valence characteristics.

Design Implications and an Example

One way of including explicit measures of the political context that are independent of respondent perception or recall is to turn to laboratory experiments. Fortunately an emerging literature employing experimental techniques in political science is making rapid progress toward addressing many of the issues we have pointed out (Davenport, Gerber, and Green, this volume, Chapter 5; Fridkin and Kenney, this volume, Chapter 4). Work on the effects of media advertising that directly or indirectly addresses citizen response to various ways of defining candidate valence and issue differentials is one example, with respect to both citizen engagement (Ansolabehere and Iyengar 1995; Brader 2005; Brooks and Geer 2007; Clinton and Lapinski 2004; Freedman, Wood, and Lawton 1999; Geer and Geer 2003) and vote choice (Ansolabehere and Iyengar 1995; Brader 2005; Freedman, Wood, and Lawton 1999; Kahn and Geer 1994; Lau and Redlawsk 2006; Schultz and Pancer 1997).

A second approach is to incorporate into survey designs conducted in natural settings independent measures of the political context. Research that captures media exposure and broadcast rates in the markets in which respondents reside is an example (Goldstein and Ridout 2004). We conducted a study of the 2006 US House elections designed to assess the relevance of the political context alongside personal factors. Our approach is to rely on political experts sampled from the same districts from which voter respondents were surveyed. In the month before the 2006 election, we posed questions to 2004 Democratic and Republican national convention delegates and state legislators about the incumbent and the challenger, the district, and the content and conduct of the campaign. Of particular interest to this illustration are questions put to experts about the ideological positions of the Republican and Democratic candidates and valence items designed to measure candidates' personal skills, qualities, and attributes of intrinsic interest to voters.[5] We aggregated individual expert valence ratings and perceptions of the candidates' locations to the district level, which provides estimates of the Democratic and Republican candidates' personal qualities and positions on the left–right scale independent of the perceptions of voters in the same districts.[6]

Our example tests the voting-choice hypotheses, each of which, we have argued, require external indicators of the policy and valence differentials that shape voters' context. As noted, *The American Voter* indicated that one important condition for issue voting is that voters are aware of the differences between the candidates. Voter perception of choice between the candidates is best thought of as a form of awareness or engagement and therefore should reflect the actual difference between the candidates, rather than being treated only as a condition that voters must meet in order to vote on the issues. A number of non-memory-based mechanisms such as online processing and opinion-leading in social networks could explain how

---

[5] The items used to construct a valence index for each candidate asked district experts to rate each candidate's personal integrity; ability to work well with other leaders; competence; grasp of the issues; ability to find solutions to problems; qualifications to hold office; and overall strength as a public servant. These items formed an index distinct from campaign skills (by principal components analysis). For more detail, see Stone et al. (2008).

[6] Prior to computing district means of expert ratings, we adjusted individual expert ratings by the partisan congruity, since there is substantial partisan bias, especially in the valence items. We can partially validate the expert-based measure by comparing placements of incumbents by district experts with NOMINATE and ADA scores, which correlate strongly with the informant measure (.94 in both cases). For additional discussion, see Stone et al. (2008).

Table 29.1 Individual's perception of an ideological choice between candidates

	Perception of Choice
Candidates' Ideological Polarization	0.90* (0.515)
Individual's Political Sophistication	1.82* (0.128)
Individual's Education	0.04* (0.024)
Individual's Party Identification	0.20* (0.086)
Individual's Partisan Extremity	0.17* (0.024)
Individual's Ideological Extremity	0.02 (0.035)
Constant	−0.72* (0.113)
N	10821

Logit coefficient estimates and standard errors clustering on district in parentheses; * p<0.05 one-tailed test

candidate issue differentials influence voter choice without voters being able to report differences between the candidates on a survey.

We begin with voter awareness of an ideological difference between the candidates.[7] In keeping with our argument, awareness of a difference between the candidates should be a function of characteristics of individual respondents and of the political context to which they react. We measure the ideological polarization between the candidates in the district as the difference between informants' placements of the Republican and Democratic candidates. In addition to this aspect of the political context, we have individual characteristics that might affect respondents' perception of whether there was an ideological choice between the candidates in their district, including the political knowledge of the respondent, education, party identification, and ideological extremity. As the results in Table 29.1 show, all of the individual variables save ideological extremity have significant effects on perception of a choice, as does the degree of ideological difference between the two candidates in the district. Independent of these individual-level explanations, in other words, the political reality in the district, as reported by expert district informants, shapes voter perceptions. Figure 29.1 shows the magnitudes of the voter-knowledge and candidate-polarization effects, both of which are substantial.

[7] The mass survey data are from the 2006 CCES common-content study (<http://web.mit.edu/polisci/portl/cces/index.html>). Respondents were asked to place both candidates on a left–right scale. Respondents who said they did not know one or both candidates' locations, or who placed both candidates at the same point, are coded as not recognizing a difference. Respondents who placed the candidates at different points are coded as perceiving a difference; 54% of the sample did not perceive a difference between candidates.

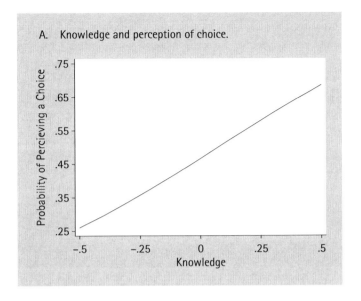

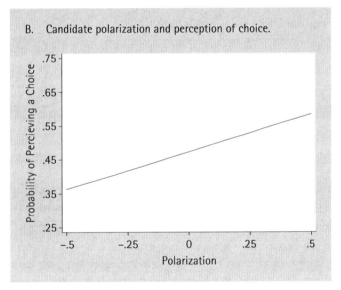

Figure 29.1 The effects of knowledge and candidate polarization on voter perception of a choice between the candidates

The next step is to consider the factors that affected voting choice in 2006. A memory-based or perceptual model of issue voting consistent with the conditions spelled out in *The American Voter* might include the respondent's ideology, whether the respondent perceived a difference between the candidates, and the interaction between perceived choice and ideology. The interaction is suggested by

Table 29.2 Individual traits, contextual characteristics, and vote choice, 2006 House elections

	Vote Republican
Individual-level Effects of Ideology	
Individual's Ideology	2.08*(0.379)
Individual's Perception of Choice	−0.99*(0.349)
Individual's Political Knowledge	−2.37*(0.572)
Ideology X Perception of Choice	2.05*(0.526)
Ideology X Political Knowledge	4.44*(0.921)
Effect of Ideological Polarization between Candidates	
Candidates' Ideological Polarization	−2.00*(1.044)
Ideology X Ideological Polarization	4.08*(1.583)
Effect of Candidate Valence Differential	
Candidates' Character Valence Differential	0.21*(0.073)
Individual-level Controls	
Party Identification	2.60*(0.190)
Presidential Approval	1.20*(0.061)
Familiarity with Republican Candidate	0.46*(0.190)
Familiarity with Democratic Candidate	−0.89*(0.193)
Republican Incumbent	0.39*(0.191)
Constant	−5.07*(0.297)
N	7777

Logit coefficients with standard errors clustering on district in parentheses; * $p<0.05$ one-tailed tests

the expectation that the effect of voter ideology is conditioned on whether the individual perceives a choice between the candidates. We include political knowledge on the grounds that more aware voters should be more likely to rely on complex considerations such as ideology in casting their ballot (Basinger and Lavine 2005). The interactions in the upper section of Table 29.2 indicate that voter ideology has a stronger effect among respondents who perceive a difference between the candidates in their district than it does among those who do not see a difference. Likewise, as voters become more knowledgeable, the impact of ideology on vote choice increases significantly. The effects captured by the interaction coefficients are depicted in Figure 29.2 (A and B).

The individual effects discussed so far are consistent with a standard treatment of issue voting. In addition to capturing differences linked to perceiving a choice and political knowledge, however, we also have an external indicator of candidate difference from the expert survey measuring how polarized the two major-party candidates in the district were. The effect is quite strong, as the significant coefficient for the *Ideology X Ideological Polarization* term in Table 29.2, and the graphic representation in Figure 29.2C indicate. Even apart from the perceptual and

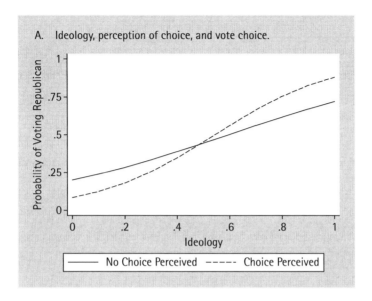

A.   Ideology, perception of choice, and vote choice.

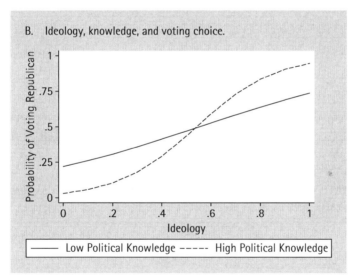

B.   Ideology, knowledge, and voting choice.

Continued

knowledge conditions included in the statistical model, the effect of the candidates' ideology differential on the relationship between voters' ideology and their vote is strong. In fact, the external measure of ideological choice appears to have a stronger effect on the relationship between ideology and vote choice than individuals' own perception of a choice. In districts where the candidates are clearly differentiated in their ideological stands, respondent ideology has a powerful impact on voting choice. In districts where the candidate differential is low, ideology has a much weaker effect on vote choice. Moreover, *the effect of candidate*

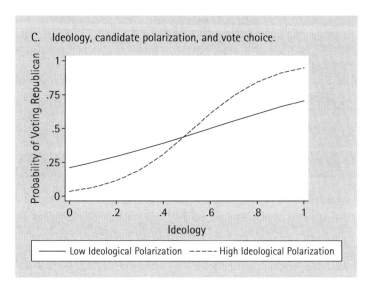

Figure 29.2 Interactions between ideology, polarization, knowledge, and perception of a choice, 2006

polarization is independent of whether the individual voter perceives a difference between the House candidates in his district.

In sum, our analysis supports our contention that the conditions specified in *The American Voter* do not fully address the problem of issue voting because voter awareness about whether there is a difference between the candidates reflects the political context; and because voter awareness of a choice is not a necessary condition for voter ideology to affect choice. Not only does ideology affect voting choice when voters do not see an ideological difference between the candidates, but the degree of difference between the candidates influences the effect of individuals' ideology on vote choice as much or more than voters' perception of candidate differences.

Note in addition to the conditioning effect of candidate differences, the character valence differential also affects voting choice.[8] The estimated difference in probability of voting Republican over the observed range of the candidate valence differential is .42. When the differential most favors the Democratic candidate, the estimated probability of voting Republican is .34; when the differential most favors the Republican, the probability of voting for that party is .76. This effect is striking,

---

[8] The difference is calculated by subtracting the Democratic candidate's personal-quality rating from the Republican candidate's rating in the district. Because all voters are assumed to prefer candidates whose character valence is high over candidates whose character is low, there is no need for voter perceptual data to test the character–valence hypothesis.

since it is independent of party identification, ideology, and incumbency. It is, to our knowledge, the first estimate of a candidate valence differential based on the personal qualities and skills of both candidates estimated in a national survey employing measures of those qualities external to the survey respondents' perceptions. Thus, we have evidence that both policy and valence candidate differentials affect voting choice independently of a number of individual-level variables commonly incorporated in models of voting choice, including perception of choice, familiarity with the candidates, party identification, and presidential approval.

CONCLUSION

Heavy reliance on sample survey methodology combined with dependence on theoretical perspectives borrowed from economics and social psychology has nudged much of the politics out of many studies of citizen behavior. By focusing on the most commonplace questions and hypotheses, we have suggested some limitations associated with studies that do not situate the voter in the political context to which he or she reacts. Decades of research have established that models of the democratic citizen who is highly motivated to become informed about politics are unrealistic. To return to Schattschneider (1975, 138; emphasis in original), "*Democracy is a . . . political system in which competing leaders and organizations define the alternatives of public policy in such a way that the public can participate in the decision-making process.*" In short, it is imperative to take full account of how competition between leaders stimulates citizen response.

Our study of how citizens react to the context facing them must also include theory and evidence about how that context gets defined. Inevitably, this will involve much more work on why and how candidates make the investments they make when they decide whether to run, and why they adopt the positions and emphasize the issue priorities that shape their campaigns. Formal theoretical work on candidate strategic choices, especially with respect to position-taking on the issues, has advanced, but research on many of the other choices that shape the political context is less developed. The implications and meaning of valence in elections, and the links between valence and policy debates, are not well understood. Moreover, as we have noted, the absence of appropriate tests of valence voting along dimensions related to the character and personal quality of candidates in field surveys is a major gap in the empirical literature. Voters care about policy and, given the chance, vote on policy differentials. But voters also care about character and competence in their political leaders. New approaches to supplement laboratory experimentation will have to be adopted to expand our understanding of how politics and the citizen interact if our understanding of citizen behavior is to advance.

REFERENCES

ABRAMOWITZ, A. I. 1981. Choices and Echoes in the 1978 U.S. Senate Elections. *American Journal of Political Science*, 25/1: 112–18.

ADAMS, J. F., MERRILL, S., III, and GROFFMAN, B. 2005. *A Unified theory of Party Competition: A Cross-National Analysis Integrating Spatial and Behavioral Theories*. New York: Cambridge University Press.

ALDRICH, J. H. 1993. Rational Choice and Turnout. *American Journal of Political Science*, 37: 246–78.

ANSOLABEHERE, S. and IYENGAR, S. 1995. *Going Negative: How Political Advertisements Shrink and Demobilize the Electorate*. New York: Free Press.

ARONSON, P. H. and ORDESHOOK, P. C. 1978. Spatial Strategies for Sequential Elections. In *Probability Models of Collective Decision Making*, ed. R. G. Niemi and H. F. Weisberg. Columbus, Ohio: Charles E. Merrill.

BANKS, J. S. and KIEWIET, D. R. 1989. Explaining Patterns of Candidate Competition in Congressional Elections. *American Journal of Politics*, 33: 997–1015.

BARON, D. P. 1994. Electoral Competition with Informed and Uninformed Voters. *American Political Science Review*, 88: 33–47.

BARTELS, L. M. 1988. *Presidential Primaries and the Dynamics of Public Choice*. Princeton, N.J.: Princeton University Press.

—— 2002. Beyond the Running Tally: Partisan Bias in Political Perceptions. *Political Behavior*, 24: 117–50.

BASINGER, S. J. and LAVINE, H. 2005. Ambivalence, Information, and Electoral Choice. *American Political Science Review*, 99/1: 169–84.

BIANCO, W. T. 1994. *Trust: Representatives and Constituents*. Ann Arbor, Mich.: University of Michigan Press.

BLACK, D. 1958. *The Theory of Committees and Elections*. Cambridge: Cambridge University Press.

BLACK, G. S. 1972. A Theory of Political Ambition: Career Choices and the Role of Structural Incentives. *American Political Science Review*, 66: 144–59.

BLAIS, A. 2000. *To Vote or Not to Vote? The Merits and Limits of Rational Choice Theory*. Pittsburgh, Pa.: University of Pittsburgh Press.

BRACE, P. 1984. Progressive Ambition in the House: A Probabilistic Approach. *Journal of Politics*, 46: 556–71.

BRADER, T. 2005. Striking a Responsive Chord: How Political Ads Motivate and Persuade Voters by Appealing to Emotions. *American Journal of Political Science*, 49: 388–405.

BRADY, H. E. and JOHNSTON, R. 2006. *Capturing Campaign Effects*. Ann Arbor, Mich.: University of Michigan Press.

BRODY, R. A. and PAGE, B. I. 1972. Comment: The Assessment of Policy Voting. *American Political Science Review*, 66: 450–8.

BROOKS, D. J. and GEER, J. G. 2007. Beyond Negativity: The Effects of Incivility on the Electorate. *American Journal of Political Science*, 51: 1–16.

BURDEN, B. C. 2004. Candidate Positioning in U.S. Congressional Elections. *British Journal of Political Science*, 88: 211–27.

CAMPBELL, A., CONVERSE, P. E., MILLER, W. E., and STOKES, D. E. 1960. *The American Voter*. New York: John Wiley and Sons.

CLINTON, J. D. and LAPINSKI, J. S. 2004. "Targeted" Advertising and Voter Turnout: An Experimental Study of the 2000 Presidential Election. *Journal of Politics*, 66: 69–96.

CONOVER, P. J. and FELDMAN, S. 1986. The Role of Inference in the Perception of Political Candidates. In *Political Cognition*, ed. R. R. Lau and D. O. Sears. Hillsdale, N.J.: Lawrence Erlbaum.

—— ——. 1989. Candidate Perception in an Ambiguous World: Campaigns, Cues, and Inference Processes. *American Journal of Political Science*, 33: 912–40.

CONVERSE, P. E. 1964. The Nature of Belief Systems in Mass Publics. In *Ideology and Discontent*, ed. D. E. Apter. London: Collier-Macmillan.

COVER, A. D. and BRUMBERG, B. S. 1982. Baby Books and Ballots: the Impact of Congressional Mail on Constituent Opinion. *American Political Science Review*, 76: 347–59.

DELLI CARPINI, M. X. and KEETER, S. 1996. *What Americans Know about Politics and Why It Matters*. New Haven, Conn.: Yale University Press.

DOWNS, A. 1957. *An Economic Theory of Democracy*. New York: Harper.

ENELOW, J. M. and HINICH, M. J. 1984. *The Spatial Theory of Voting*. Cambridge: Cambridge University Press.

EVANS, G. and ANDERSON, R. 2004. Do Issues Decide? Partisan Conditioning and Perceptions of Party Issue Positions Across the Electoral Cycle. *Journal of Elections, Public Opinion, and Parties*, 14: 18–39.

FIORINA, M. P. 1989. *Congress: Keystone of the Washington Establishment*, 2nd edn. New Haven, Conn.: Yale University Press.

FISCHLE, M. 2000. Mass Response to the Lewinsky Scandal: Motivated Reasoning or Bayesian Updating. *Political Psychology*, 21: 135–59.

FRANKLIN, C. H. 1991. Eschewing Obfuscation? Campaigns and the Perception of U.S. Senate Incumbents. *American Political Science Review*, 85: 1193–213.

FREEDMAN, P., WOOD, W., and LAWTON, D. 1999. Do's and Don'ts of Negative Ads: What Voters Say. *Campaigns and Elections*, 20: 20–36.

GEER, J. G. and GEER, J. H. 2003. Remembering Attack Ads: An Experimental Investigation of Radio. *Political Behavior*, 25: 69–95.

GERBER, A. S. and GREEN, D. P. 2000. The Effects of Canvassing, Telephone Calls, and Direct Mail on Voter Turnout: A Field Experiment. *American Political Science Review*, 94/3: 653–63.

GOLDSTEIN, K. and RIDOUT, T. N. 2004. Measuring the Effects of Televized Political Advertising in the United States. *Annual Review of Political Science*, 7: 205–26.

GRONKE, P. 2000. *The Electorate, The Campaign, and the Office: A Unified Approach to Senate and House Election*. Ann Arbor, Mich.: University of Michigan Press.

GROSECLOSE, T. 2001. A Model of Candidate Location When One Candidate Has a Valence Advantage. *American Journal of Political Science*, 45/4: 862–86.

HUCKFELDT, R., JOHNSON, P., and SPRAGUE, J. 2004. *Political Disagreement*. Cambridge: Cambridge University Press.

—— and SPRAGUE, J. 1992. Political Parties and Electoral Mobilization: Political Structure, Social Structure, and the Party Canvass. *American Political Science Review*, 86: 70–86.

—— —— 1995. *Citizens, Politics, and Social Communication: Information and Influence in an Election Campaign*. New York: Cambridge University Press.

JACOBSON, G. C. 1989. Strategic Politicians and the Dynamics of U.S. House Elections, 1946–1986. *American Political Science Review*, 83: 773–93.

—— 2006. Measuring Campaign Spending Effects in U.S. House Elections. In *Capturing Campaign Effects*, ed. H. E. Brady and R. Johnston. Ann Arbor, Mich.: University of Michigan Press.

—— 2009. *The Politics of Congressional Elections*, 7th edn. New York: Longman.

—— and KERNELL, S. 1983. *Strategy and Choice in Congressional Elections*. New Haven, Conn.: Yale University Press.

KAHN, K. F. and GEER, J. G. 1994. Creating Impressions: An Experimental Investigation of Political Advertising on Television. *Political Behavior*, 16: 93–116.

—— and KENNEY, P. 1999. *The Spectacle of U.S. Senate Campaigns*. Princeton, N.J.: Princeton University Press.

KAM, C. D. 2006. Political Campaigns and Open-Minded Thinking. *Journal of Politics*, 68/4: 931–45.

KENNY, C. and McBURNETT, M. 1994. An Individual-Level Multi-Equation Model of Expenditure Effects in Contested House Elections. *American Political Science Review*, 88/3: 699–707.

KUNDA, Z. 1987. Motivation and Inference: Self-Serving Generation and Evaluation of Evidence. *Journal of Personality and Social Psychology*, 53: 636–47.

—— 1990. The Case for Motivated Reasoning. *Psychological Bulletin*, 108: 480.

LACHAT, R. 2007. *The Impact of Party Polarization on Ideological Voting*. Montreal: University of Montreal.

LAU, R. R. and REDLAWSK, D. P. 2006. *How Voters Decide: Information Processing during Election Campaigns*. Cambridge: Cambridge University Press.

LEBO, M. J. and CASSINO, D. 2007. The Aggregated Consequences of Motivated Reasoning and the Dynamics of Partisan Presidential Approval. *Political Psychology*, 28: 719–46.

LEIGHLEY, J. E. 1995. Attitudes, Opportunities and Incentives: A Field Essay on Political Participation. *Political Research Quarterly*, 48/1: 181–209.

—— and NAGLER, J. 1992. Individual and Systemic Influences on Turnout: Who Votes? *Journal of Politics*, 54/3: 718–40.

LEWIS-BECK, M. S. 1990. *Economics and Elections: The Major Western Democracies*. Ann Arbor, Mich.: University of Michigan Press.

LODGE, M. and TABER, C. 2000. Three Steps Toward a Theory of Motivated Political Reasoning. In *Elements of Reason: Cognition, Choice, and the Bounds of Rationality*, ed. A. Lupia, M. D. McCubbins, and S. L. Popkin. New York: Cambridge University Press.

MARKUS, G. B. 1988. The Impact of Personal and National Economic Conditions on the Presidential Vote: A Pooled Cross-Sectional Analysis. *American Journal of Political Science*, 32/1: 137–54.

McCURLEY, C. and MONDAK, J. J. 1995. Inspected by #1184063113: The Influence of Incumbents' Competence and Integrity in U.S. House Elections. *American Journal of Political Science*, 39: 864–85.

McGraw, K. M., Fischle, M., Stenner, K., and Lodge, M. 1996. What's in a Word? Bias in Trait Descriptions of Political Leaders. *Political Behavior*, 18: 263–87.

Miller, A. H. 1990. Public Judgments of Senate and House Candidates. *Legislative Studies Quarterly*, 15/4: 525–42.

Miller, W. E. and Shanks, J. M. 1996. *The New American Voter*. Cambridge, Mass.: Harvard University Press.

Mondak, J. J. 1995. Competence, Integrity, and the Electoral Success of Congressional Incumbents. *Journal of Politics*, 57: 1043–69.

Moon, W. 2004. Party Activists, Campaign Resources and Candidate Position Taking: Theory, Tests, and Applications. *British Journal of Political Science*, 34: 611–33.

Mutz, D. 2002. Cross-cutting Social Networks: Testing Democratic Theory in Practice. *American Political Science Review*, 93: 111–26.

Partin, R. W. 1995. Economic Conditions and Gubernatorial Elections: Is the State Executive Held Accountable? *American Politics Research*, 23/1: 81–95.

Patterson, S. C. and Caldeira, G. A. 1983. Getting Out the Vote: Participation in Gubernatorial Elections. *American Political Science Review*, 77/3: 675–89.

Riker, W. H. and Ordeshook, P. C. 1968. A Theory of the Calculus of Voting. *American Political Science Review*, 62: 25–42.

Rohde, D. W. 1979. Risk-Bearing and Progressive Ambition: The Case of Members of the United States House of Representatives. *American Journal of Political Science*, 23/1: 1–26.

Rosenstone, S. J. and Hansen, J. M. 1993. *Mobilization, Participation and Democracy in America*. New York: Macmillan.

Schattschneider, E. E. 1975. *The Semisovereign People: A Realist's View of Democracy in American*. Hinsdale, Ill.: Dryden Press.

Schultz, C. and Pancer, S. M. 1997. Character Attacks and Their Effect on Perceptions of Male and Female Political Candidates. *Political Psychology*, 18: 93–102.

Sniderman, P. M. 2000. Taking Sides: A Fixed Choice Theory of Political Reasoning. In *Elements of Reason: Cognition, Choice, and the Bounds of Rationality*, ed. A. Lupia, M. D. McCubbins, and S. L. Popkin. Cambridge: Cambridge University Press.

—— and Levendusky, M. S. 2007. An Institutional Theory of Political Choice. In *The Oxford Handbook of Political Behavior*, ed. R. J. Dalton and H.-D. Klingemann. New York: Oxford University Press.

Squire, P. 1995. Candidates, Money, and Voters: Assessing the State of Congressional Elections Research. *Political Research Quarterly*, 48/4: 891–917.

Stokes, D. E. 1963. Spatial Models of Party Competition. *American Political Science Review*, 57/2: 368–77.

—— 1992. Valence Politics. In *Electoral Politics*, ed. D. Kavanaugh. New York: Oxford University Press.

—— and Miller, W. E. 1962. Party Government and the Saliency of Congress. *Public Opinion Quarterly*, 26/4: 531–46.

Stone, W. J. and Maisel, L. S. 2003. The Not-So-Simple Calculus of Winning: Potential House Candidates' Nomination and General Election Prospects. *Journal of Politics*, 65: 951–77.

—— Hadley, N., Peterson, R., Maestas, C. D., and Maisel, L. S. 2008. Candidate Entry, Voter Response and Partisan Tides in the 2002 and 2006 Elections. In *Fault Lines: Why the Republicans Lost Congress*, ed. J. J. Mondak and D.-G. Mitchell. New York: Routledge.

TABER, C. and LODGE, M. 2006. Motivated Skepticism in the Evaluation of Political Beliefs. *American Journal of Political Science*, 50: 755–69.

VERBA, S. and NIE, N. H. 1972. *Participation in America: Political Democracy and Social Equality*. New York: Harper and Row.

—— SCHLOZMAN, K. L., and BRADY, H. E. 1995. *Voice and Equality: Civic Voluntarism in American Politics*. Cambridge, Mass.: Harvard University Press.

WESTLYE, M. C. 1991. *Senate Elections and Campaign Intensity*. Baltimore, Md.: The Johns Hopkins University Press.

WITTMAN, D. 1973. Parties as Utility Maximizers. *American Political Science Review*, 67/2: 490–8.

—— 1983. Candidate Motivation: A Synthesis of Alternatives. *American Political Science Review*, 77/1: 142–57.

WRIGHT, G. C. and BERKMAN, M. B. 1986. Candidates and Policy in United States Senate Elections. *American Political Science Review*, 80: 567–88.

ZALLER, J. R. 1992. *The Nature and Origins of Mass Opinion*. New York: Cambridge University Press.

—— 2004. Floating Voters in U.S. Presidential elections, 1948–2000. In *Studies in Public Opinion*, ed. W. E. Saris and P. M. Sniderman. Princeton, N.J.: Princeton University Press.

CHAPTER 30

....

GETTING UP OFF
THE CANVASS

RETHINKING THE STUDY
OF MOBILIZATION*

....

KENNETH M. GOLDSTEIN
MATTHEW HOLLEQUE

During the 1924 and 1925 elections, Harold Gosnell conducted field experiments in Chicago to determine the impact of non-partisan get-out-the-vote campaigns on stimulating voting (Gosnell 1927). The study is remarkable in many ways. It not only represents one of the first field experiments in modern political science, but its basic findings are consistent with everything we know today about the empirical impact of voter contact. Since Gosnell's pioneering work, eight decades ago, a mountain of research has been conducted to examine the effects of voter contact. Although these studies vary in their theoretical and methodological approaches, virtually all reach the exact same conclusion reached by Gosnell over eighty years ago—namely that voter contact matters at the margin.

To be sure, Gosnell's study is not without its shortcomings and subsequent studies have made meaningful contributions to our understanding of exactly how, when, and why mobilization activities matter. Gosnell's study is bound to a

* The authors would like to thank Barry Burden and Jan Leighley for their helpful comments.

certain place at a certain time, and some have found fault with the design of his experiment (Gerber and Green 2000). Nevertheless, although we certainly know more and are more confident about what we know about mobilization contacts today, the fundamental finding has changed little. Regardless of methodological approach, the vast majority of studies in this literature show that people who are contacted by parties, campaigns, or interest groups are more likely to participate in politics than those who are not. In addition, it has become conventional wisdom among both academics and political operatives that a successful mobilization strategy can play a small, but decisive role in winning elections.

So although effects may vary across contexts and individuals, the effectiveness of political mobilization should no longer be in doubt, and any comprehensive explanation of why citizens participate in politics must incorporate mobilization. So, if we know that voter contact matters at the margin and our understanding of mobilization has changed little over the last eighty years, what is left to discuss in a review essay?

Empirical findings in this area have had unusual penetration into the real world of politics and speak to important normative debates and empirical puzzles in the study of politics. Furthermore, methodological challenges in this debate reverberate well beyond the narrow topic of mobilization and voter turnout. Specifically, we think claims that mobilization is the culprit behind declining levels of aggregate voter turnout since the 1960s have been overstated. And, although problems of endogeneity and self-reporting plague observational studies of mobilization, the recent turn towards randomized field experiments offers no panacea.

That said, the purpose of this chapter is not only to review where we have been in the study of mobilization, but also to suggest where we should be going. In addition to reviewing some of the literature on political mobilization, we also want to expand the field's research agenda beyond the typical canvassing activities. Steven Rosenstone and John Mark Hansen (1993, 25–6) defined political mobilization as the process by which candidates, parties, activists, and groups induce other people to participate, which includes *any* activities that increase the likelihood of someone participating. This definition encompasses a wide range of activities, but most studies employ a far narrower conceptualization of political mobilization, focusing on what we call the canvass, meaning the direct contacts between political organizations and their representatives and citizens (e.g., face-to-face contacts, phone banks, and direct mailings). Concentrating its efforts on the canvass has led political science to focus on the medium of mobilization but not the message of mobilization. Political mobilization is a two-stage process, involving both contacting and message, and we believe that scholars should study both in tandem. Certainly the canvass represents an important aspect of mobilization, and campaigns devote substantial resources to this activity. However, message may just be the best mobilizer, and research on mobilization would benefit by devoting more time to the role of message communication and its ability to motivate potential participants.

The remainder of this chapter proceeds in three parts. We begin by providing a brief review of the literature on political mobilization. Here we discuss the importance of political mobilization for both academics and political professionals. We also discuss our concerns about the study of mobilization, particularly the problems of endogeneity in observational studies and the use of field experiments. Finally, we turn our attention to the future of research on mobilization, arguing that more attention should be paid to how messages mobilize.

WHERE WE HAVE BEEN

Political participation in the United States is a voluntary activity from which many citizens choose to abstain. As Nagel (1987, 3) puts it, "While spontaneous popular action warms the heart of any good democrat, a moment's reflection shows that the people initiate little of what we normally call participation." Many political scientists worry that disparities in political participation translate into unequal democratic representation. It is well known, for example, that those with a higher socioeconomic status are more likely to participate in politics (Verba, Schlozman, and Brady 1995), and this class bias in voter turnout has persisted since at least the 1960s (Leighley and Nagler 1992). Biases such as these potentially lead to certain segments of the public possessing greater political voice, and some believe that this benefits a particular political party (Lijphart 1997; Piven and Cloward 1988).[1] Finally, participatory democrats see political participation as an intrinsic democratic good (Pateman 1970) and advocate for universal turnout rather than simply universal suffrage (Lijphart 1997). Political practitioners, however, have a different set of concerns. They care little about inequality or political voice, seeing mobilization instead as a means of winning elections. The goal of mobilization for these politicians is not to increase overall participation but rather to increase participation among their supporters. But while their perspectives diverge, both scholars and practitioners view mobilization as an important part of the democratic process.

Classic theories of political participation focus on what Riker and Ordeshook (1968) call the "calculus of voting." According to this perspective, citizens decide whether or not to participate based on an individual cost–benefit analysis, weighing the costs of participation against the expected benefits. Since the expected

[1] Others argue, however, that non-voters have preferences similar to voters (Wolfinger and Rosenstone 1980) and that higher levels of participation would not change the outcome of many elections (Citrin, Schickler, and Sides 2003).

benefit of voting rarely exceeds the costs, this theory suggests that "rational" citizens should rarely participate in politics and remain uninformed about public affairs (for a more detailed review, see Aldrich 1993). While this perspective provides some powerful insights into political behavior, it fails to consider the larger context in which political participation occurs, treating each individual in isolation and ignoring the contribution of external political actors. Specifically, the calculus of voting fails to consider the role of political mobilization as a participatory subsidy. Although voter turnout increases in closer elections, this is not necessarily because people decide to vote based on the probability of being decisive. Rather, close elections may give elites incentives to mobilize the electorate, thereby leading to increased participation (Caldeira, Patterson, and Markko 1985; Cox and Munger 1989; Patterson and Caldeira 1983).

Even if people do decide to vote based on a rational cost–benefit analysis, external actors can work to lower the costs of participation. To mobilize the public, campaigns, interest groups, and parties can modify the calculus of voting by underwriting the opportunity cost of participation. As Rosenstone and Hansen (1993, 27) explain:

(P)olitical leaders subsidize the costs of citizen activism. They distribute voter registration forms and absentee ballots. They drive people to the polls on election day. They provide child care to free parents to attend meetings and demonstrations. They supply people with texts for letters to representatives and senators.

Not only can mobilization reduce the opportunity costs of voting, but it can also lower the information costs associated with participation. Since the costs of gathering political information are non-trivial, many scholars argue that mobilization works primarily by reducing the costs of voting by disseminating information to a rationally but woefully ignorant public (Huckfeldt and Sprague 1992; Rosenstone and Hansen 1993; Wiehlhouwer 2003). Through the process of mobilization, political actors subsidize the costs of participation by bringing information directly to potential voters at a substantially reduced cost, though the content of this information is likely geared toward a particular political outcome. Whether it underwrites opportunity or information costs associated with political participation, mobilization can help citizens overcome the problem of rational abstention by making participation cheap enough so that citizens can afford to vote.

On the individual level, the empirical literature finds a preponderance of evidence that mobilization increases the probability of voting (Abramson and Claggett 2001; Blydenburgh 1971; Goldstein and Ridout 2002; Gosnell 1927; Holbrook and McClurg 2005; Huckfeldt and Sprague 1992; Kramer 1970; Rosenstone and Hansen 1993; Wielhouwer and Lockerbie 1994). It seems fairly intuitive that, *ceteris paribus*, people mobilized by campaigns and political parties should be more likely to participate in politics than those not mobilized, and these studies also find that mobilization matters, but it matters at the margins. The effects of political culture, local election laws, and demographics often overshadow the impact of voter contacts. Still, while the positive relationship between mobilization and turnout is generally accepted on the individual level, there is greater disagreement on the macro-level consequences of mobilization for aggregate voter turnout over time. Some scholars have contended that changes in either the quantity or quality of mobilization have been responsible for declining levels of voter turnout over time and reversing these trends could stimulate higher levels of participation.

Many scholars have noted a general decline in aggregate voter turnout starting in the 1960s and continuing through today (Brody 1978; Patterson 2002; Teixeira 1992). Even McDonald and Popkin (2001), who argued that the decline has not been as dramatic as initially suggested, find that voter turnout after 1970 is consistently lower relative to turnout in the 1960s. This downturn occurred despite several important changes that should have increased voter turnout, such as the elimination of practices like the poll tax and literacy tests, changes in registration closing-date laws, and substantial increases in the percentage of the population with a college degree (Highton 2004). All of these changes should have resulted in more people participating in politics, but instead participation rates declined. Indeed, this so-called "puzzle of participation" runs counter to the available theories of voter turnout (Brody 1978).

One plausible explanation for the fall in voter turnout is that either the quantity or quality of mobilization has also declined over time. Rosenstone and Hansen (1993) argued that a decrease in the total amount of mobilizing activity conducted by parties, campaigns, and interest groups has led to the general decline in voter turnout rates. If citizens need an invitation to participate in politics, and if political elites are engaging in less mobilization, then this could account for some of the decline in turnout. Based on a series of simulations, Rosenstone and Hansen claimed that changes in mobilization account for over half the decline in voter participation (1993, 358). The data, however, do not fully support this argument. Data from the American National Election Study (ANES) show that aggregate rates of mobilization have not declined over time (Abramson, Aldrich, and Rohde 2002; Goldstein and Ridout 2002). Therefore, if mobilization is responsible for declining levels of voter turnout, it is not because the quantity of mobilization has decreased.[2]

Mobilization, however, might still be an explanation for the decline in participation, even if the aggregate amount of mobilization activity has remained fairly constant. Since the 1960s, the nature of political mobilization has changed dramatically. Today campaigns depend more heavily on professional mass direct mailings

---

[2] The total amount of mobilization may not have decreased, but it may be more targeted at a smaller number of people today, which would lead to a decline in turnout. Goldstein and Ridout (2002) find, however, that while the amount of targeting has increased, this change can only account for a small fraction of the overall decline in turnout.

and commercial phone banks to contact voters, and less on in-person canvassing (Schier 2000). Robert Putnam (2000) points out that since the 1970s more people have been mobilized by fewer and fewer party workers. As a result, some argue that the effectiveness of mobilization contacts has decreased even while the total number of contacts remained the same or even increased over time. The logic is that these new methods of mobilization are less personal and therefore less effective, because they exert less social pressure on individuals (Putnam 2000; Rosenstone and Hansen 1993). In addition, the early field experiment by Eldersveld (1956) found that personal canvassing was more effective than appeals sent through the mail. Finally, studies outside of political science found that personal canvassing is more effective at soliciting recycling and blood donations compared to alternative methods of mobilization (Jason et al. 1984; Reams and Ray 1993). Regardless of the reason, this explanation is consistent with the empirical findings that the number of contacts may have remained fairly stable over time while the voter turnout rate has fallen.

While changes in mobilization techniques could plausibly lead to changes in political participation, the relationship between these two variables suffers from two serious methodological problems. First, the effect of mobilization on voter turnout is endogenous, because mobilization is a strategic behavior not a public service. Campaigns, interest groups, and parties use political mobilization to accomplish their own political objectives, and they care little about the absolute level of voter turnout independent of their goals. Instead, they only want enough participation by the "right" people so they can win the election, and as a consequence, campaigns generally concentrate their mobilization efforts on those voters who are most likely to participate (Wielhouwer 2003). Studies suggest a number of factors increase the probability of being contacted, including income, education, strength of partisanship, and past participation. The problem arises, because these variables are also strong predictors of voting. For example, campaigns often use voting records to target citizens who have voted in the past. Not surprisingly, voting in the last election is also one of the best predictors of voting in the next one (Gerber, Green, and Shachar 2003; Plutzer 2002). Similar arguments could be made for income, education, and strength of partisanship. Correlational research, therefore, cannot determine whether mobilization is *causing* increased participation or whether some confounding variable is driving both the probability of participating and the probability of being mobilized (Goldstein and Ridout 2002). As Green and Gerber (2002, 812) explain, "If parties direct their appeals disproportionately to committed partisans and frequent voters, those most likely to vote will be most likely to receive political contact, and the apparent link between contact and turnout would be spurious."

The second major problem comes from previous studies' heavy reliance on survey data. These correlational studies hinge on the self-reporting of both whether an individual was contacted during a campaign and whether the respondent voted.

The literature on survey response suggests that people generally tend to over-report voter turnout due largely to either social desirability bias or memory lapses. Burden (2000) finds that for one prominent data source, the American National Election Study, the problem of over-reporting voter turnout has been getting worse over time due to declining response rates. In addition, self-reports of campaign contact may be problematic, because those most interested in politics may also be more likely to remember a campaign contact. Studies based on surveys, therefore, may overestimate the amount of participation but underestimate the amount of mobilization. Furthermore, they may overstate the effectiveness of mobilization, because those most likely to report being mobilized might also be more likely to vote. Both the theoretical and methodological issues raised by the literature on mobilization suggest the need for a study that can compare the effectiveness of different types of mobilization and overcome the methodological issues of endogeneity and self-reporting.

To address these concerns, Alan Gerber and Donald Green (2000) conducted a large-scale, randomized field trial in New Haven, Connecticut. Their study compares the effects of in-person canvassing with telephone canvassing and direct mailings, examining whether the shift toward less effective and less personal mobilization methods could account for the decline in voter turnout over time. The design of their field experiment avoids the two methodological problems that plague correlational studies of mobilization. First, since subjects were randomly assigned to whether or not they would be contacted during the campaign, exposure to mobilization was exogenous to individuals' strength of partisanship or past voting behavior, thereby eliminating any selection bias. Second, the investigators knew which citizens were contacted and by which method, and public records allowed for an independent measure of voter turnout. Both of these features of randomized field experiments rectify some of the problems plaguing past correlational studies and provide additional leverage for making causal statements about the effects of mobilization on participation.

Using field experiments to study the effects of mobilization on voter turnout is of course nothing new to political science. Since the early Gosnell studies, other scholars have employed the method, and several previous experiments have found positive, statistically significant effects of mobilization on voter turnout (Adams and Smith 1980; Eldersveld 1956; Miller, Bositis, and Baer 1981). Gerber and Green (2000) pointed out, however, that many of these experiments lack sufficient statistical power or examine only one mode of mobilization at a time. The lack of statistical power means that the effects these studies found have a high degree of uncertainty, and studies testing only a single type of mobilization are unable to address questions of relative effectiveness. Finally, Gerber and Green noted that some studies incorrectly include non-complying subjects from the treatment group with subjects assigned to the control group (2000, 654). Therefore, while all of these studies find a positive effect of mobilization on voter turnout, their results may be inaccurate. The New Haven Study rectifies these earlier problems by including more participants and implementing multiple treatments.

In their field experiment, Gerber and Green find that, on average, those assigned to the face-to-face canvassing treatment group were roughly 2.4 percentage points more likely to vote than those that did not receive an in-person visit, but this effect size includes those who were assigned to the treatment group but did not actually receive the treatment. However, compliance rates for those assigned to the treatment groups were fairly modest, less than 30 percent for face-to-face canvassing. This non-compliance with the treatments may not be totally random: the citizens who are easier to reach might also be more likely to vote. Certainly not all non-compliance is due to self-selection, but it is plausible that those more likely to vote might also be more likely to listen to a canvasser, either in person or over the phone. To address this concern, they employ a two-stage least squares approach to estimate the effect of personal canvassing while controlling for the higher probability of voting among those easier to contact (Gerber and Green 2000, 657). Since treatment assignment is completely random, it serves as an ideal instrumental variable for exposure to treatment (Angrist, Imbens, and Rubin 1996).[3]

After including their covariates including past participation, their model finds that the effect of being contacted by a canvasser on voter turnout was approximately 9 percentage points. In other words, a participant who was contacted in person was 9 percentage points more likely to vote than one who was not contacted. Telephone contacts appear to have a *negative* but small and statistically insignificant effect on the probability of turning out to vote. Direct mailings also do not have a statistically significant effect on the voter turnout. Gerber and Green conclude that in-person canvassing is more effective than alternative methods of mobilization and that "falling rates of voter turnout reflect a decline in face-to-face political activity" (2000, 661).

But do these results solve the puzzle of participation? Is the decline of political participation caused by the decline in face-to-face canvassing? We remain skeptical for two reasons. First, there is some evidence that, despite conventional wisdom, the effectiveness of mobilization has *not* changed over time (Goldstein and Ridout 2002). Furthermore, although Gerber and Green provide convincing evidence that face-to-face canvassing is more effective than both phone canvassing and direct mailings, this evidence comes from a single cross-sectional study and has a limited ability to speak to broad changes over time. Second, Gerber and Green's findings underscore the point that mobilization matters, but it matters at the margins. In their original analysis, Gerber and Green estimate two models, one with just

---

[3] Imai (2005) has criticized the New Haven Study for incomplete randomization and violating the exclusion restriction. These problems produce bias in their instrumental variable estimates. (For a response see Gerber and Green 2005.)

treatment assignment and one with treatment assignment and other covariates. In both models, we see that the instrumental variable for door-to-door canvassing is positive and statistically significant, but if we look at the adjusted R^2 statistics, we see a striking difference between the two models.[4] The model with covariates explains over a quarter of the variation in people's decision to vote, and that includes controls for past voting behavior. However, in the model without covariates, the instrumental variable alone accounts for less than 1 percent of the variation in the dependent variable. We take this as evidence that while face-to-face canvassing does stimulate voting, it by itself does not explain much of the variation in whether or not one decides to vote. Even if the overall quality of mobilization has declined over time we remain skeptical that this shift is enough to explain the larger trend of declining participation.

THE PROMISE AND PITFALLS OF FIELD EXPERIMENTS

The New Haven Study has opened the way for a new wave of research that uses randomized field experiments to study political mobilization (e.g., Arceneaux 2005; Gerber and Green 2001; Gerber, Green, and Larimer 2008; Green 2004; Green, Gerber, and Nickerson 2003; Nickerson 2008; Nickerson, Friedrichs, and King 2006; Panagopoulous and Green 2008). Across a variety of electoral contexts and treatment conditions, these studies have found that mobilization increases the probability of voting. Field experiments bring many advantages to the study of politics, and experimental research is called the "gold standard" for a reason. Unlike observational research, experiments provide leverage for an investigator to establish clear causality between a treatment and an outcome. Studies relying on observational data often fall prey to the problem of endogeneity, making it difficult to establish a causal relationship between two variables. Random assignment of treatment and control groups prevents systematic differences at the outset of the experiment, and any differences that do arise between the two groups can be attributed to the treatment instead of any preexisting differences (Rubin 1974).

In addition, field experiments avoid criticisms about external validity. Laboratory experiments in the social sciences are often criticized because the setting of these experiments may not emulate the real world, thereby biasing their results.

---

[4] The adjusted R^2 statistic was obtained by replicating Gerber and Green's results using data and STATA code from Donald Green's replication archives: <http://research.yale.edu/vote/replication. html>.

Because they are conducted in a real-world setting, field experiments often have high levels of external validity, while still keeping the power of experimental design. For these reasons, experiments are not just the gold standard but also the only standard in many disciplines.

Clearly experiments have many benefits in political science in general, and in the study of mobilization and turnout in particular. The beauty of field experiments is that they employ random assignment to overcome the problem of endogeneity caused by strategic targeting. Still, in the real world, mobilization contacts are not random. Unlike other disciplines, where field experiments have come into vogue (e.g., educational research), much of what we study in politics is, in fact, strategic behavior. Political mobilization is almost always partisan, and campaigns actively target certain segments of the electorate, focusing their efforts on getting those people to the polls. By using random assignment, Gerber and Green ignore the strategic nature of mobilization and distance themselves from the actual phenomenon under investigation. As the 2008 election vividly illustrates, candidates care not at all about high turnout, they care about differential turnout—high turnout among their partisans.

This disregard for strategy, we believe, biases experimental estimates of mobilization's effect on voting. If the effectiveness of mobilization is different for those who are most likely to be contacted, then the effects produced by a randomized experiment are likely biased, because the treatment group contains both individuals who would have been targeted by campaign mobilization and individuals who would not. A more accurate estimate could be obtained if an experiment first identified which citizens were most likely to be mobilized, and then used random assignment among those people. The literature remains unclear on whether mobilization is more or less effective on those targeted by campaigns. Some scholars have argued that mobilization should have the greatest effect on the least informed and least motivated citizens (Rosenstone and Hansen 1993). Others find that the effect of canvassing is greater among those already intending to vote (Hillygus 2005).

This gives us pause about the spread of field experiments as the method of choice for studying mobilization. This is not to say that field experiments should not be part of our methodological toolkit. The New Haven Study should be applauded for its ingenuity and effort, and experimental research is valuable. That said, field experiments need to resemble more closely the process under investigation, and scholars should be aware of which effects they are actually estimating and what those effects mean substantively. Future field experiments on mobilization should take care to ensure that their treatment and assignment more closely emulate real-life practice. In short, scholars should be cautious about studying the effect of a strategy by removing strategy from the study.

MESSAGE MATTERS

Researchers typically divorce the study of mobilization from the study of political messages or political communication. Yet, as others have pointed out, mobilization can be thought of as a two-stage process, involving both canvassing and communicating. Brady, Schlozman, and Verba (1999) argued that political actors who seek to mobilize the public follow a strategy of rational prospecting. According to this theory, campaigns, parties, and interest groups first identify and target those individuals who are most likely to be receptive to being contacted, and then specific messages are transmitted to these select targets in the hopes that these messages will motivate them to participate. The process of mobilization, therefore, is about getting the "right" message to the "right" people (see also Wielhouwer 2003). This theory is supported by the fact that campaigns utilize extensive databases of voter information to target specific subgroups of the electorate (Leighley and Matsubayashi 2005).

Campaigns often distinguish between fieldwork (the ground war) and a communications strategy, but these two are not independent. Attention should be paid not only to the modes of mobilization, but also to the mobilizing effect of message. In general, studies of mobilization concentrate on whether those contacted by campaigns are more likely to vote than those not contacted or on what kind of contact might matter more (e.g., phone, mail, in person), but rarely does research differentiate between the content of these contacts. Professional political operatives already recognize the importance of message. In a 2007 article for *The Hill*, pollster Mark Mellman argued that while organization and mobilization are important, having an effective message can be equally important. He notes that, "(W)hile organization is vitally important, it is not sufficient . . . When a campaign claims it's going to win on turnout, they will likely lose." The bottom line is that message matters. The empirical research agenda for political science going forward should be less about whether mobilization works and more about why it works, and essential to answering this question is an understanding of the effects of message as a mobilizer.

Consider some initial evidence from the 2008 elections. Although voter turnout nationally was similar to 2004, there was significant variance across states. North Carolina, Georgia, South Carolina, Alabama, and Nevada enjoyed the greatest increases in voter turnout while New Hampshire, Ohio, Utah, Arizona, and Maine saw their turnout rates decrease from 2004 levels. State-level voter turnout also appears to have a low correlation with the amount of voter contact or television advertising in each state. High-turnout states like North Carolina and Nevada had massive GOTV efforts by both parties and large advertising buys, but so did states like New Hampshire, Ohio, and Maine. Furthermore, South Carolina (with only one Obama field office and no advertising) and Alabama (with no Obama offices and no advertising) also saw increases in their turnout rate. Turnout in Alabama, North Carolina, Georgia, and South Carolina appears to have been largely a function of increases in the African American vote, and this suggests to us that voter contact or exposure to advertising alone are not enough. A candidate and a message can have a much greater effect even in the absence of a "ground game." Furthermore, even though turnout as a whole was flat in 2008 as compared to 2004, differential turnout appears to have put Obama over the top in states like North Carolina and Ohio. Ohio is a particularly good example of the importance of message compared to simple voter contact, because, from a nuts-and-bolts perspective, the GOP operation was the same in 2008 as it was in 2004 yet the outcome was not.

Political science has not completely neglected the relationship between mobilization and message. Gerber and Green (2000) do use a variety of messages when encouraging people to vote, varying between messages that highlight an appeal to civic duty, the closeness of the election, and neighborhood solidarity.[5] However, they find that the effectiveness of face-to-face mobilization does not depend on which message was used. While this certainly is a step in the right direction, the problem with this design is how it operationalizes message. There are major qualitative differences between the messages used by the New Haven Study and the messages used by modern electoral campaigns. Message, as we understand it, is aimed at providing its recipient with a reason to vote for or against a particular candidate. Campaign messages are usually partisan and often revolve around candidate qualities or specific issues. In other words, the appeals used in the Gerber and Green study are fundamentally different from what we mean by message. This does not mean that field experiments could not be used to study the mobilizing effects of message. For example, recent studies that look at the effects of radio advertisements (Panagopoulos and Green 2008) could be modified to test the mobilizing effects of different messages.

Another area where the mobilizing effect of message has been extensively studied is in the literature on campaign advertising. Much of this literature centers around the work by Stephen Ansolabehere and his colleagues, who argue that exposure to negative advertising reduces voter turnout rates by as much as 5 percent (Ansolabehere and Iyengar 1995). Although scholars and pundits had bemoaned the damaging effects of what many perceived as a rise in negative campaigning, these studies provided clear supporting evidence. In response to this finding, a flurry of research has looked at the effects of negative campaign advertising on voter turnout. The majority of these studies find that negative campaign advertising has either no effect (Lau et al. 1999) or even a positive effect on voter turnout (Finkel and Geer 1998; Franz et al. 2007; Goldstein and Freedman 2002; Kahn and Kenney 1999; Wattenberg and Brians 1999). Though these studies are based on surveys, even other experiments have been

---

[5] These "messages" are similar to ones used by Gosnell (1927).

unable to replicate the findings of Ansolabehere et al. (Pinkelton 1998). That said, the jury remains out on whether negativity in campaign advertising increases turnout, though it seems clear that it does not demobilize the electorate. The empirical evidence suggests that campaign advertising can have a positive effect on voter turnout, but this effect is neither consistently large nor universal across election years (see Huber and Arceneaux 2007).

Apart from this debate, Sides and Karch (2008) explore whether the issue content of campaign advertising has a mobilizing effect among specific issue publics. They argue that "voters might be more susceptible to campaign messages when those messages focus on the issues personally important to them" (467). To test their theory, they look at whether turnout rates are higher among seniors, veterans, and parents when campaigns air advertising that focuses on issues directly relevant to those groups. Although Sides and Karch find little evidence to support their hypothesis, we do not believe this means that message cannot mobilize. First, message has a broader meaning than simply matching up certain segments of the public with their specific issues. Message is less about whether or not a campaign talks about certain issues and more about how the campaigns talk about the issues. Second, as Sides and Karch acknowledge, the effects of message-based mobilization may be conditional on other factors and have only a marginal effect. The mobilizing effects of message may be mediated by variables such as party identification, demographics, or social context, making message mobilizing for some but not all people.

Beyond this debate, political scientists have explored other mechanisms by which campaign messages mobilize or influence the electorate. Research on emotion suggests that emotional appeals can motivate citizens to participate. Marcus and his colleagues argue that campaigns can influence and motivate citizens through their use of anxiety and enthusiasm, and this in turn can either increase citizens' interest in the campaign and/or heighten their surveillance of the information environment (Marcus and MacKuen 1993; Marcus, Neuman, and MacKuen 2000). Their research suggests that both anxiety and enthusiasm increase interest in politics and the campaign, and both are associated with higher levels of participation in the campaign, though anxiety appears to be more effective than enthusiasm (Marcus, Neuman, and MacKuen 2000). By manipulating the visual cues and music in a series of mock campaign advertisements, Brader (2006) finds that emotional appeals in campaign advertising can increase the intention to participate in politics.

By no means is this a comprehensive review of this literature. Despite this impressive body of scholarship, more still needs to be done to understand the mobilizing power of message. In addition, scholars of mobilization and scholars of message should work together to investigate how these two sides of the campaign field and communications interact with each other. What are the mechanisms by which campaign messages influence voters? Which messages are the most effective and which are the least? How does the effectiveness of campaign messages vary across individuals and contexts? And most importantly, how do we measure message? These questions can be approached from a variety of perspectives and with an array of research methods. The point is that progress in the study of mobilization rests on a better understanding of what motivates citizens to vote.

FINAL THOUGHTS

As is natural in these sorts of essays, we have synthesized and expanded on the concerns of others about some important elements of the mobilization and participation literature. Our concerns have focused on three areas: (1) endogeneity is clearly a challenge for observational studies of voter contact and turnout; (2) mobilization is probably not the main culprit for declines in electoral participation; and (3) the benefits of field experiments, while significant, have probably been overstated. With all that said, what should not be lost in these critiques is the fundamental point that political science has demonstrated beyond a reasonable doubt that voter contact matters. Different studies in different centuries using different research designs have found strikingly similar results. With other factors held constant (no matter how they are held constant), voter contact has a small, but significant effect on the likelihood of a voter turning out to vote. This literature is in many ways a success story for social science.

It is time, however, to move on. It is time to get off the canvas. Whatever the research design that one chooses, it will be crucial to expand the study of how different modes of contact matter. Even more importantly, it will be crucial to look at how the content of the campaign and the content of voter contact influences who votes and who they vote for. Our observations of campaigns and our conversations with professionals who make their living doing election fieldwork strongly suggest that message matters. It is time to put politics and strategy back into the study of a political strategy.

REFERENCES

ABRAMSON, P. R., ALDRICH, J. H., and ROHDE, D. W. 2002. *Change and Continuity in the 2000 Elections.* Washington, D.C.: Congressional Quarterly Press.
—— and CLAGGETT, W. 2001. Recruitment and Political Participation. *Political Research Quarterly,* 54: 905–16.
ADAMS, W. C. and SMITH, D. J. 1980. Effects of Telephone Canvassing on Turnout and Preferences: A Field Experiment. *Public Opinion Quarterly,* 44: 389–95.
ALDRICH, J. H. 1993. Rational Choice and Turnout. *American Journal of Political Science,* 37: 246–78.

ANGRIST, J. D., IMBENS, G. W., and RUBIN, D. B. 1996. Identification of Causal Effects Using Instrumental Variables. *Journal of the American Statistical Association*, 91: 444–55.

ANSOLABEHERE, S. and IYENGAR, S. 1995. *Going Negative: How Political Advertisements Shrink and Polarize the Electorate*. New York: Free Press.

ARCENEAUX, K. 2005. Using Cluster Randomized Field Experiments to Study Voting Behavior. *Annals of the American Academy of Political and Social Science*, 601: 169–79.

—— and NICKERSON, D. W. N.d. Who is Mobilized to Vote? A Re-Analysis of Eleven Randomized Field Experiments. Unpublished working paper.

BLYDENBURGH, J. C. 1971. A Controlled Experiment to Measure the Effects of Personal Contact Campaigning. *Midwest Journal of Political Science*, 15: 365–81.

BRADER, T. 2006. *Campaigning for Hearts and Minds: How Emotional Appeals in Political Ads Work*. Chicago, Ill.: University of Chicago Press.

BRADY, H. E., SCHLOZMAN, K. L., and VERBA, S. 1999. Prospecting for Participants: Rational Expectations and the Recruitment of Political Activists. *American Political Science Review*, 93: 153–68.

BRODY, R. A. 1978. The Puzzle of Political Participation in America. In *The New American Political System*, ed. A. King. Washington, D.C.: American Enterprise Institute.

BURDEN, B. C. 2000. Voter Turnout and the National Election Studies. *Political Analysis*, 8: 389–98.

CALDEIRA, G. A., PATTERSON, S. C., and MARKKO, G. A. 1985. The Mobilization of Voters in Congressional Elections. *Journal of Politics*, 47: 490–509.

CASSEL, C. A. and LUSKIN, R. C. 1988. Simple Explanations of Turnout Decline. *American Political Science Review*, 82: 1321–30.

CITRIN, J., SCHICKLER, E., and SIDES, J. 2003. What if Everyone Voted? Simulating the Impact of Increased Turnout in Senate Elections. *American Journal of Political Science*, 47: 75–90.

COX, G. W. and MUNGER, M. C. 1989. Closeness, Expenditures, and Turnout in the 1982 U.S. House Elections. *American Political Science Review*, 83: 217–31.

DOWNS, A. 1957. *An Economic Theory of Democracy*. New York: Harper and Row.

ELDERSVELD, S. J. 1956. Experimental Propaganda Techniques and Voting Behavior. *American Political Science Review*, 50: 154–65.

FINKEL, S. E. and GEER, J. 1998. Spot Check: Casting Doubt on the Demobilizing Effect of Attack Advertising. *American Journal of Political Science*, 42: 573–95.

FRANZ, M., FREEDMAN, P., GOLDSTEIN, K. M., and RIDOUT, T. N. 2007. *Campaign Advertising and American Democracy*. Philadelphia, Pa.: Temple University Press.

GERBER, A. S. and GREEN, D. P. 2000. The Effects of Canvassing, Telephone Calls, and Direct Mail on Voter Turnout: A Field Experiment. *American Political Science Review*, 94: 653–63.

—— —— 2001. Do Phone Calls Increase Voter Turnout? A Field Experiment. *Public Opinion Quarterly*, 65: 75–85.

—— —— 2005. Correction to Gerber and Green (2000), Replication of Disputed Findings, and Reply to Imai (2005). *American Political Science Review*, 99: 301–13.

—— —— and LARIMER, C. W. 2008. Social Pressure and Voter Turnout: Evidence from a Large-Scale Field Experiment. *American Political Science Review*, 102: 33–48.

—— —— and SHACHAR, R. 2003. Voting May be Habit Forming: Evidence from a Randomized Field Experiment. *American Journal of Political Science*, 47: 540–50.

GOLDSTEIN, K. and FREEDMAN, P. 2002. Campaign Advertising and Voter Turnout: New Evidence for a Stimulation Effect. *Journal of Politics*, 64: 721–40.

—— and RIDOUT, T. N. 2002. The Politics of Participation: Mobilization and Turnout Over Time. *Political Behavior*, 24: 3–29.

GOSNELL, H. F. 1927. *Getting-Out-the-Vote: An Experiment in the Stimulation of Voting*. Chicago, Ill.: University of Chicago Press.

GREEN, D. P. 2004. Mobilizing African-Americans using Direct Mail and Commercial Phone Banks: A Field Experiment. *Political Research Quarterly*, 57/2: 245–55.

GREEN, D. P. and GERBER, A. S. 2002. Reclaiming the Experimental Tradition in Political Science. In *Political Science: State of the Discipline*, ed. I. Katznelson and H. V. Milner. New York: W.W. Norton and Company.

—— —— and NICKERSON, D. W. 2003. Getting Out the Vote in Local Elections: Results from Six Door-to-Door Canvassing Experiments. *Journal of Politics*, 65: 1083–96.

HIGHTON, B. 2004. Voter Registration and Turnout in the United States. *Perspectives on Politics*, 2: 507–15.

HILLYGUS, D. S. 2005. Campaign Effects and the Dynamics of Turnout Intention in Election 2000. *Journal of Politics*, 67: 50–68.

HOLBROOK, T. M. and McCLURG, S. D. 2005. The Mobilization of Core Supporters: Campaigns, Turnout, and Electoral Composition in United States Presidential Elections. *American Journal of Political Science*, 49: 689–703.

HUBER, G. A. and ARCENEAUX, K. 2007. Identifying Persuasive Effects of Presidential Advertising. *American Journal of Political Science*, 51: 957–77.

HUCKFELDT, R. and SPRAGUE, J. 1992. Political Parties and Electoral Mobilization: Political Structure, Social Structure, and the Party Canvass. *American Political Science Review*, 86: 405–23.

IMAI, K. 2005. Do Get-Out-the-Vote Calls Reduce Turnout? The Importance of Statistical Methods for Field Experiment. *American Political Science Review*, 99: 283–300.

JASON, L. A., ROSE, T., FERRARI, J. R., and BARONE, R. 1984. Personal Versus Impersonal Methods for Recruiting Blood Donations. *Journal of Social Psychology*, 123: 139–40.

KAHN, K. F. and KENNEY, P. J. 1999. Do Negative Campaigns Mobilize or Suppress Turnout? Clarifying the Relationship Between Negativity and Participation. *American Political Science Review*, 93: 877–89.

KRAMER, G. 1970. The Effects of Precinct Level Canvassing on Voting Behavior. *Public Opinion Quarterly*, 34: 560–72.

LAU, R. R., SIGELMAN, L., HELDMAN, C., and BABBITT, P. 1999. The Effects of Negative Political Advertisements: A Meta-Analytic Assessment. *American Political Science Review*, 93: 851–75.

LEIGHLEY, J. E. and MATSUBAYASHI, T. 2005. Voter Mobilization. In *Guide to Political Campaigns in America*, ed. P. S. Herrnson. Washington, D.C.: CQ Press.

—— and NAGLER, J. 1992. Socioeconomic Class Bias in Turnout, 1964–1988: The Voters Remain the Same. *American Political Science Review*, 86: 725–36.

LIJPHART, A. 1997. Unequal Participation: Democracy's Unresolved Dilemma. *American Political Science Review*, 91: 1–14.

MARCUS, G. E. and MacKUEN, M. B. 1993. Anxiety, Enthusiasm, and the Vote: The Emotional Underpinnings of Learning and Involvement during Presidential Campaigns. *American Political Science Review*, 87: 672–85.

—— NEUMAN, W. R., and MacKUEN. 2000. *Affective Intelligence and Political Judgment.* Chicago, Ill.: University of Chicago Press.

McDONALD, M. P. and POPKIN, S. L. 2001. The Myth of the Vanishing Voter. *American Political Science Review*, 95: 963–74.

MELLMAN, M. 2007. Myths and Facts in Iowa. *The Hill*, 24 October 2007.

MILLER, R. E., BOSITIS, D. A., and BAER, D. L. 1981. Stimulating Voter Turnout in a Primary: Field Experiment with a Precinct Committeeman. *International Political Science Review*, 2: 445–60.

NAGEL, J. 1987. *Participation.* Englewood Cliffs, N.J.: Prentice Hall.

NICKERSON, D. W. 2008. Is Voting Contagious? Evidence from Two Field Experiments. *American Political Science Review*, 102: 49–57.

—— FRIEDRICHS, R. D., and KING, D. C. 2006. Partisan Mobilization Campaigns in the Field: Results from a Statewide Turnout Experiment in Michigan. *Political Research Quarterly*, 59: 85–97.

PANAGOPOULOS, C. and GREEN, D. P. 2008. Field Experiments Testing the Impact of Radio Advertisements on Electoral Competition. *American Journal of Political Science*, 52: 156–68.

PATEMAN, C. 1970. *Participation and Democratic Theory.* New York: Cambridge University Press.

PATTERSON, S. C. and CALDEIRA, G. A. 1983. Getting Out the Vote: Participation in Gubernatorial Elections. *American Political Science Review*, 77: 675–89.

PATTERSON, T. E. 2002. *The Vanishing Voter: Public Involvement in an Age of Uncertainty.* New York, N.Y.: Vintage.

PINKELTON, B. E. 1998. Effects of Print Comparative Political Advertising on Political Decision-Making and Participation. *Journal of Communication*, 48: 24–36.

PIVEN, F. F. and CLOWARD, R. A. 1988. *Why Americans Don't Vote.* New York: Pantheon Books.

PLUTZER, E. 2002. Becoming a Habitual Voter: Inertia, Resources, and Growth in Young Adulthood. *American Political Science Review*, 96: 41–56.

PUTNAM, R. D. 2000. *Bowling Alone: The Collapse and Revival of American Community.* New York: Simon and Shuster.

REAMS, M. A. and RAY, B. H. 1993. The Effects of Three Prompting Methods on Recycling Participation Rates: A Field Experiment. *Journal of Environmental Systems*, 22: 371–9.

RIKER, W. H. and ORDESHOOK, P. C. 1968. A Theory of the Calculus of Voting. *American Political Science Review*, 62: 25–42.

ROSENSTONE, S. J. and HANSEN, J. M. 1993. *Mobilization, Participation, and Democracy in America.* New York: Longman.

RUBIN, D. B. 1974. Estimating Causal Effects of Treatments in Randomized and Nonrandomized Studies. *Journal of Educational Psychology*, 66: 688–701.

SCHIER, S. E. 2000. *By Invitation Only: The Rise of Exclusive Politics in the United States.* Pittsburgh, Pa.: University of Pittsburgh Press.

SIDES, J. and KARCH, A. 2008. Messages that Mobilize? Issue Publics and the Content of Campaign Advertising. *Journal of Politics*, 70: 466–7.

SIGELMAN, L. and KUGLER, M. 2003. Why Is Research on the Effects of Negative Campaigning So Inconclusive: Understanding Citizens' Perceptions of Negativity. *Journal of Politics*, 65: 142–60.

Teixeira, R. A. 1992. *The Disappearing American Voter.* Washington, D.C.: Brookings Institution Press.

Verba, S., Schlozman, K. L., and Brady, H. E. 1995. *Voice and Equality: Civic Volunteerism in American Politics.* Cambridge, Mass.: Harvard University Press.

Wattenberg, M. P. and Brians, C. L. 1999. Negative Campaign Advertising: Demobilizer or Mobilizer? *American Political Science Review,* 93: 891–9.

Wielhouwer, P. W. 2003. In Search of Lincoln's Perfect List: Targeting in Grassroots Campaigns. *American Politics Research,* 31: 632–69.

—— and Lockerbie, B. 1994. Party Contacting and Political Participation, 1952–90. *American Journal of Political Science,* 38: 211–29.

Wolfinger, R. E. and Rosenstone, S. J. 1980. *Who Votes?* New Haven, Conn.: Yale University Press.

CHAPTER 31

....

PARTIES, ELECTIONS, AND DEMOCRATIC POLITICS

....

JOHN H. ALDRICH

JOHN D. GRIFFIN

DEMOCRATIC politics is the politics of regularized party competition for control of the offices of government. That is our central claim in this chapter. More precisely, our position is that regularized party competition is a necessary condition for viable democratic politics. That is, there must be regularized party competition in elections, or else democracy fails sufficiently as to no longer be worthy of that name.

Our claim that party competition is a necessary precondition for democracy may not strike all readers as particularly innovative. However, some well-known definitions of democracy do not explicitly recognize a role for political parties. For instance, Schumpeter (1962) and Sen (1999) emphasize instead the significance of individual freedom in democracy. Others go further, specifically disavowing the necessity of parties in democracies: "It would be too much to argue that institutionally strong parties are a necessary condition for consolidating democracy or maintaining its vitality" (Diamond and Gunther 2001, x). For example, some have contended that interest groups can perform many of the functions parties do, including interest articulation (Clemens 1997).[1]

Other scholars have observed the coincidence of democracy and political parties. For example, studies have asserted that political parties are "inevitable" (Sartori 1968), "desirable" (Dahl 2003, 30), "critical" and "essential" (Levitsky and Cameron 2003, 1, 5) for, and "endemic" (Stokes 1999, 246) to democracy. Democracy is "unthinkable" (Schattschneider 1942, 1), or perhaps just "unworkable" (Aldrich 1995, 3), without political parties. There is also the view that "parties create[d] democracy" (Schattschneider 1942, 1; see also Aldrich 2007, Levitsky and Cameron 2003).[2]

However, these studies have not followed up their bold proclamations with a rigorous explanation of how, exactly, party competition promotes democratic politics. Instead, the literature contains studies of party competition that are not explicitly tied to democracy, and studies of democracy that are not explicitly tied to competition *among parties*. Studies of the former variety tend to reside in the realm of American Politics, where there is greater variation in competition but less variation in the "level" of democracy. Some have investigated whether political competition stimulates citizens to voice their preferences to governing officials through the electoral process (e.g., Cox and Munger 1989), which may promote accountability. Research has also asked whether electoral competition enhances the responsiveness of policy to public opinion, some studies concluding that it does (Griffin 2006), others that it does not (e.g. Fiorina 1973; Gerber and Lupia 1995).

Studies of the latter variety, where democracy is the primary concern, tend to be cross-national. According to Schmitter and Karl (1991, 76): "Modern political democracy is a system of governance in which rulers are held accountable for their actions in the public realm by citizens, acting indirectly through the competition and cooperation of their elected representatives." Similarly, Powell (1982, 3) argues: "[D]emocratic systems [are] . . . characterized by competitive elections in which most citizens are eligible to participate." Even where there is a

---

[1] For proponents of this view it was no accident that the reforms of the 1880s and 1890s that were intended to limit the role of political parties in elections coincided with an uptick in the creation and activity of interest organizations (Clemens 1997; Wiebe 1967). However, most would agree that while interest groups compete with parties, they do not offer a real alternative to them by fielding candidates for office (Schattschneider 1942). In our view, there may be times when interest groups serve as a substitute for parties, as Hansen (1991) argues, but these are specialized and likely transient instances. So specialized may these be that the interest group in this role differed relatively little in its structures and practices from the party its candidates competed against. More commonly, interest groups combine with parties to help create the conditions for parties to succeed, as the religious right aligned with the Republican Party and the unions and civil rights groups aligned with the Democratic Party.

[2] "[T]he full development of the liberal democratic state in the West required that political criticism and opposition be incarnated in one or more opposition parties" (Hofstadter 1969, xii).

direct linkage drawn from party competition to democracy, as in Przeworski (1991), the mechanism remains underdeveloped.[3]

We contend that democratic politics is created and sustained in the competition that occurs between parties and in the information and incentives that this competition promotes. Perhaps more importantly, absent this organized, repeated competition between or among several political parties, there is no democracy. Politicians may claim to want to be independent of all political parties, abhor partisan "bickering," and seek to "rise above" the partisan fray. Indeed, Washington's warning of the "baneful effects" of political parties was typical of the prevailing views of the Founders. But politicians very quickly discovered that they needed political parties to achieve the desired benefits of a democracy. So, let us take this notion seriously and explore *why* competitive parties are indeed necessary to make democracy effective. We begin, though, by defining what we mean by a political party, by a party system, and by a competitive party system.

WHAT PARTIES ARE

Many groups and organizations can be considered or even call themselves political parties, creating such a diversity of groups that might be expected to be included under a comprehensive definition as to render an inclusive definition nearly meaningless. We are interested in the major political party, a term clear enough in the US, although it may be rather less clear in comparative contexts, particularly in PR systems that generate a large number of often very small parties. A party is or aspires to be a *major political party* when it competes (i.e., offers candidates) for many, even most, electoral offices up for election at any given time, and when it competes (offers candidates) for such offices repeatedly over time, and when a reasonable observer would conclude that these candidates competed strongly (had a reasonably high probability of success) for a substantial number of the offices they contested.

A political system is said to have an associated system of political parties (i.e., *a party system*) when each of the major political parties is at a self-enforcing equilibrium, the nature of which we discuss below. We understand a party system to be denoted primarily by the number of major political parties at this equilibrium. That number could be zero, one, two, or more. That is, we include within

---

[3] Przeworski (1991, 10): "Democracy is a system in which parties lose elections. There are parties: divisions of interest, values and opinions. There is competition, organized by rules. And there are periodic winners and losers."

the definition of a party system at least the logical possibility that there be a no-party system, as Key understood the South to be in the era of Jim Crow, and a one-party system as Key understood the South to be in national politics at that time (Key 1949), as well as the more commonly studied two-party system or multi-party system (where "multi" means anything greater than two). Our definition points to the individual political party as that which is in equilibrium, instead of the entire system. That is, we focus on the party and see the party system as the aggregation of major parties, each of which is in equilibrium. This contrasts with those such as Cox (1997) who derive the number of parties in a system that is in equilibrium, that is, he derives whether a system, in equilibrium, has two or more than two parties. In this view, a system is in equilibrium when all the parties have chosen to compete or not, perhaps when they have chosen spatial positions, and when all individuals agree on the first two points and on the probabilities with which each candidate is expected to win.

While we could spend considerable time outlining what scholars have meant by a "competitive party system," let us simply state it as meaning that there are at least two political parties competing over the full range of elective political offices for lengthy durations. By "competitive" we mean that no one party is given distinct advantage in elections by the laws of the nation and that every party that wins any given election has a realistic opportunity to lose that office to another party or parties in the near future. Under this definition, a party might win, say, the US presidency repeatedly, but it would enter each election with a serious concern about losing.

WHAT PARTIES DO

There are two major sets of actors in a party system, citizens and ambitious politicians (a set which is in turn divided into office-seekers and activists who desire the benefits available from the success of those office-seekers). In this section we discuss how both citizens and politicians benefit from the construction of and adherence to clear party labels in a self-enforcing equilibrium.

Citizens

Many scholars have asked whether and how citizens learn a sufficient amount about the candidates in campaigns to make an informed choice between them (e.g. Delli Carpini and Keeter 1996). Among the sources of information available to citizens are challengers (Arnold 1993; Kingdon 1989), the media (Arnold 2004; Hutchings 1998; Lodge, Steenbergen, and Brau 1995), and cues adopted by the candidates themselves (Erikson 1971; Lupia and McCubbins 1998). This information may be conveyed directly to any particular citizen (who may have, e.g., watched a televised commercial) or indirectly, through the two-step flow of communication, from source through an opinion leader to one or more other citizens (Lazarsfeld, Berelson, and Gaudet 1948). Of the cues available to candidates, none may convey more information to voters than the candidates' party affiliations.

Citizens receive value from a label, including a party label, when it helps them decide how to vote. It helps them decide how to vote when the label has content. We consider two illustrative cases that are particularly prominent in the context of programmatic parties.[4] The party label might stand for ideas, values, or policies, and the voter might therefore choose to support politicians who stand for the same ideas, values, or policies the voter does (e.g., Abramowitz 1988). In this case, the voter is choosing prospectively, in the hopes that those who stand for what the voter desires will be elected and will carry those ideas, values, or policies into practice.

The second case is that in which the party label has content that consists primarily of what prominent politicians of that party have done while in office. That is, parties in government work to advance a policy agenda that is distinct from the competing party's agenda, which helps to improve the clarity of each party's label (Cox and McCubbins 1993). Party organizations contribute to this construction of party labels by working to recruit candidates for office who either hold personal preferences for the direction of policy that are consonant with the mainstream of the party (Gibson et al. 1983), or who are willing to contribute to the development of a meaningful brand or party label by supporting the party line regardless of their own preferences (more on this below). Thus, there may be considerable latitude for candidates and elected members of the party to vote freely on many issues, but not (if the brand name is to convey meaningful information) on those issues that unite the party and distinguish it from its opposition, in equilibrium.

In this second case, the voter is choosing retrospectively, especially in the sense in which "retrospective voting" is used by Downs (1957) and Fiorina (1981). She might be choosing based on outcomes realized while that party held office, and she might use only that evidence as Key's rational god of vengeance or reward. She might, instead, use that evidence as the basis for inference about what current candidates

---

[4] In other electoral systems, parties may be evaluated in other terms. For example, in clientelistic systems, parties may be judged on how effective their local leaders are in distributing goods, services, and jobs to clients/citizens. In ethnically fragmented lineage systems, judgments may be based on effectiveness of tribal or other social organization and its integration into the political system. Of course, distributive and identity politics are a part of the American political system, too.

of that party could be expected to do if in office, in comparison to what candidates of the other party might do.

In either case, a party label's meaning, or clarity, is a product of the cohesiveness of the candidates and associated activists the voter has come across who affiliate with the party. If a voter is aware that the policies espoused by the Democrat running for office in her district are out of step with the policies espoused by another Democratic candidate in a neighboring district or state or region, the voter's certainty about the meaning of the party label declines (Grynaviski forthcoming). Importantly, the meaning of the label declines for all the Democratic candidates the voter encounters, whether it be in this election or the next.

In both cases, the party label is useful to the voter because it carries with it political content. But having content that guides the voter into understanding what the candidates stand for in the election, while necessary, is insufficient for the label to be useful. The party label is useful to the voter only if it conveys political meaning *and* if it is a useful guide to what the candidate would actually do if elected to office, and thus it conveys content about the major outcomes the political system produces. This is a measure of the way in which the party label has both content and accountability built into it, to be effective for the voter and (as we develop below) therefore effective for the candidate running affiliated with a party.

Consider three examples of the failure of the party label, due to the second factor, drawn from the nineteenth century (Woodward 1971 [1951], 237). In the 1890 election, a number of Southern states saw competition that included an Alliance, allying farmers and laborers, strong supporters of the Populists, with some Democrats, those who favored the "wool hats" over those who supported the "silk hats." Tennessee, for one, elected their State Alliance President, John P. Buchanan, governor, as well as numerous Alliance men to the legislature. The radical change called for by the Alliance did not appear, however, because, according to Woodward, Buchanan turned out to be as conservative as the former administration he was elected to replace. Governor John Young Brown, who won election in Kentucky in 1891, said he "went the whole way" with Alliance in that election, but he not only failed to deliver on that promise, he actually reversed a mandate for railroad regulation, supported by the Populists, that a constitutional convention had recently handed down. The Democratic state chairman of Virginia promised the Virginia Alliance a railroad commission in exchange for their support in 1890, but the Democratic assembly defeated it.

The lesson is that the value of the party label may lie in ideas, values, or policies, but it loses all of that value to the voter when politicians are elected on those promises but fail to deliver on them—and especially so when politicians actively choose to oppose them. Thus accountability also requires the ability of the voter to be able to reflect back, even if making prospective choices, on the performance of the candidate or those who affiliate with the candidate's party. That requires, that is, the value of the party label to extend over time, even for the same office. Similarly, Woodward does not say, in his example of the Virginia state party chairman, whether the chairman was unfaithful to his promise or whether he was unable to deliver in the legislature. For the voter, it does not matter which is true. The value of the party label must extend not only over time but across space, across the range of offices necessary to translate those ideas, values, or policies into governmental outcomes.

Politicians

Our perspective argues that the central components of the political party are the activists and the candidates and officeholders who adopt the name of the party (Aldrich 1995), and it is the name of the party—and what meaning that label carries—that makes the party valuable to the voter. That electoral value is always one of the reasons, and it is perhaps the only reason, that a political aspirant, that is the activist and office-seeker/holder, finds affiliation with the party valuable. It is necessary for the party label to be meaningful to the public, and it is necessary for it to have a meaning that is sufficiently positively evaluated by sufficiently large numbers of voters for a political aspirant to imagine winning election under that label.

It might be the case that these are also sufficient reasons for an ambitious politician to affiliate with a party. They are sufficient, for example, if the politician's ambition extends only to the winning of office, which is also to say that the politician herself does not particularly care about the meaning of the label. Such politicians are referred to as pure office-seekers in the theoretical literature (see, for example, Downs 1957). Put in other terms, pure office-seeking politicians, those who find the electoral benefits of adopting a party label both necessary and sufficient for affiliating with the party, are those whose personal ambitions for office entirely override their political concerns as a voter (Strom 1990).

Other ambitious politicians may reap value from affiliation with the party for the same reasons that a voter does—they value what the party stands for (Calvert 1985). Such politicians have multiple motives (Strom 1990). They care about winning office and they care about how those offices are used, what policies they seek to implement, and so on. But they are still ambitious politicians who value office, if for no other reason than that they or those whom they are backing need to win elections to be able to control office. Whether, that is, the office-seeker and those elites who back them are pure office-seekers or have mixed motives, the electoral value of the party label is a necessary condition.[5] Aldrich and Bianco (1992), for example, examine the case of affiliation decisions when both the

---

[5] Politicians who value only what the party stands for, that is, who evaluate the party label just as do the citizenry, are either called lucky politicians, lucky to value what is electorally propitious, or they are called former politicians.

particular political parties and the party system are "out of equilibrium" (both in our sense of the term and in the sense of Cox as described above).

Schlesinger (1966) has long argued that democracy works better when politicians are ambitious in the office-seeking sense and not ambitious in the policy sense: "Ambition lies at the heart of politics. Politicians thrive on the preferments that office brings" (1966, 1). In the former but not necessarily in the latter case, the politician's ambition is harnessed to the wishes of the general public. It has become fashionable to refer to the politician who chooses policies to win votes rather than wins votes to choose policies as one who "panders" to the wishes of the public (see, for example, Canes-Wrone, Herron, and Shotts 2001). If that "pandering" continues into the use of office to do what the public finds valuable, then pandering is precisely what the electoral connection is supposed to achieve—a tie between what the candidate advocates, the voters support, and the governing official enacts (at least in what Riker calls the "populist" view of democracy, 1983). The panderer, most of all, is that politician who is harnessed to the public, by which one can only mean that the panderer-in-office chooses that which he believes he can most effectively run on in the next election. If they pander for election and choose differently when in office, they will lose their support, as assuredly as did the Alliance victors in 1890/91.

We could put this point in the cloak of contemporary game theory. From the voter's perspective, she observes a candidate who has adopted a party affiliation and runs, therefore, as a partisan. That label either has meaning to the voter or it does not. If it has no meaning, then the voter decides on the basis of whatever can be gleaned about the individual candidate, which would be the identity of any groups they fortuitously bring to politics, any policies they demagogically appeal on, or their own record as lone-wolf operator or the friends-and-neighbors effect of appeals within their own little bailiwicks (to paraphrase Key 1949). That they are, let us say, a Democrat is by definition irrelevant, since the label has no meaning.

If, instead, the label has meaning, then that meaning (for good or ill) is part of what enters into the voter's calculations about whom to support. The voter cannot tell from the fact of affiliation whether the candidate values the goals, principles, and policies of the candidate's party, or is merely using the label to seek office for its own sake. If the label has no meaning to the candidate, as seems to be the case with Woodward's accounting of Alliance men, then the voter soon learns that fact, and the label loses value to the voter, as well. Indeed, it was precisely the reversal of promises that (perhaps intentionally on the part of the winning candidates) caused the demise of the Alliance and the end of the populist (and Populist) hopes in the South (and nation). Certainly, we would expect that this might be the case for a politician who desires to hold office for one term and then retire from politics (perhaps seeking to be governor as the capstone of a career). Once elected, there is no longer any electoral sanction that matters, and the politician is freed to do whatever he or she might like. To stand for one thing in the campaign and do another when in office is not a recipe for reelection.

Therefore, it follows that if the label is to have meaning, it must translate into at least some level of guidance of conduct while in office. The voter, even then, cannot distinguish between a candidate who adopts a party affiliation for expediency and one who adopts that label out of belief. It will not distinguish between candidates, for both stand for office affiliated with that party. It will not (greatly) distinguish between officeholders, for the panderer will still pander to the public by being at least modestly faithful to the content of the label that elected him, otherwise the label will lose meaning and not be able to help reelect him, while the true believer will be at least modestly faithful to the content of the label that elected him (and usually more so), otherwise he would be acting against his beliefs *and* putting any reelection hopes at risk as well. This case of a meaningful label that attracts votes because of its meaning to voters and that attracts candidates who desire to win those votes is a type of equilibrium outcome known as "pooling"—one cannot distinguish one type of candidate from the other, one cannot distinguish the pure office-seeker from the candidate who also values policies, ideas, or principles.

There is one exception to the above case. It may be that the purely office-seeking candidate originally wins election in part with the aid of the party label, but once in office is able to develop within the electorate sufficient knowledge of who he is and what he stands for that he can "rise above party" and campaign on the strength of his own personal qualities in his quest for reelection. Given what we know about voter knowledge of candidates, however, this strategy is available only to those who hold among the very highest offices (remember how few can identify their own member of the US House; see, e.g., Mann and Wolfinger 1980), hold it for a long time, and are mostly restricted to those who hold executive offices, except in unusual circumstances. This strategy is most evidently *not* available to those just entering politics, those holding the less visible offices, and those not otherwise able to distinguish themselves in politics or in some high-salience position in an earlier career (or, as Canon 1990 calls them, the "astronauts, actors, and athletes" who turn to elective office). Thus, the value of affiliation with a party, of adopting a party label that is meaningful to the voter, is most valuable to the new entrant to politics, the (usually) young, striving, ambitious newcomer, and those holding the least well known and closely followed offices.

Of course, this exception, which comes to a fair number of US senators, and a few MCs in the US House, also is distinctive to majority electoral systems with single-member districts, and separate elections. That is, only in such institutional circumstances is it possible for a legislator to develop a personal vote (Cain, Ferejohn, and Fiorina 1984). Even in the US, which has the combination of conditions that make candidate-centric politics feasible, it was not until late in the nineteenth century that the first glimmerings of candidate-centered elections emerged in the US Congress (see McGerr 1986), and even then it paled in comparison to that of the 1960s and 1970s, when (at least) a number of MCs developed what we might call a personal constituency rather than a partisan one.

PARTY COMPETITION

As should be evident from our account of the party in equilibrium, a two-party system in which each party is in equilibrium will be a competitive party system. That is, a party is in equilibrium when its label conveys meaning to voters (i.e., the party stands for something), and is sufficiently attractive to enough voters so as to attract ambitious politicians to affiliate with the party label. From the office-seeking, ambitious politician's perspective, "enough" voters is half the electorate. So, the individual party is in equilibrium when it can offer its candidates an even chance of election. In a two-party system, then, each of the parties is in equilibrium when elections are competitive.

Of course, in a one-party system the lone party may be in equilibrium while elections are not competitive. However, this is not a very stable equilibrium in the absence of an opinion consensus among citizens. Indeed, this is precisely the connection that Key drew between the national one-partyism of the Jim Crow South and the local fragmentation and factionalization of that one party in individual Southern states (1949).

In the absence of a competitive party system, some have contended that in-traparty competition among party factions might play the same role. The suggestion is that these factions might serve the same role as parties in tying government policies to citizens' interests. For instance, one assessment of mid-nineteenth-century factionalism in the United States concluded that "factional competition provided another opportunity for the public, and especially active partisans, to influence policy" (Benedict 1985, 386).

However, the politics of faction were to Key thoroughly negative and precisely the opposite of the politics of party (1949, 302–6). Factions were "ill-designed to meet the necessities of self-government" (1949, 310–11). Factions, he claimed, lack continuity in name and in the makeup of their leadership and the political candidates they presented to the public. As a result, factions lack continuity in voter support. The electorate becomes confused because it does not have as clear a set of options, sustained over time, as with parties. Parties, he believed, were able to be held responsible and therefore exercised at least a modicum of responsibility. Factions cannot be held responsible and therefore will not exercise responsibility. With factions, there is no consistent out-group. Such a loyal opposition will search for issues to bring up in their attempt to oust the governing party. Issues are generally not brought up by factions, as he had just demonstrated for the Southern states. They lack "collective spirit," a sense of duty and obligation, and any sense of "joint responsibility" between governor and legislature as well. In sum, factional politics undermines each part of his party triad (i.e., party in the electorate, in government, and as an organization), both in the short term and, more worrisomely, in the long term.

Key is also justly famous for developing a different view of elections, that of retrospective voting based on the successes or failures of the incumbent administration (1966). It might seem that the voter in a one-party, even if factionalized one-party (or, to Key, a "no party"), system could still be a "rational God of vengance or reward." Not so, he argued. At the same time, he extended his argument about how the lack of organized parties also undermines the development of responsible leadership and affects the choices of those ambitiously seeking to enter politics.

American politics is often cynically described as a politics without issues and as a battle between the "ins" and the "outs." In a system of transient factions—in its most extreme form—it is impossible to have even a fight between the "ins" and the "outs." The candidates are new and, in fact, deny any identification with any preceding administration.... Party responsibility is a concept that is greatly overworked, but in a fluid factional system not a semblance of factional responsibility exists. A governor serves his tenure—fixed either by constitution or custom—and the race begins anew. The candidates are, as completely as they can manage it, disassociated from the outgoing administration. The "outs" cannot attack the "ins" because the "ins" do not exist as a group with any collective spirit or any continuity of existence. Moreover, the independence or autonomy of candidates means that legislative candidates are disassociated from the gubernatorial races, and if the electorate wants to reward the "ins" by another term or to throw the rascals out—if electorates behave that way—it has no way of identifying the "ins."

The lack of continuing groups of "ins" and "outs" profoundly influences the nature of political leadership.... Enemies of today may be allies of tomorrow; for the professional and semiprofessional politician no such barrier as party affiliation and identification exists to separate the "ins" from the "outs."... Not only does a disorganized politics make impossible a competition between recognizable groups for power. It probably has a far-reaching influence on the kinds of individual leaders thrown into power and also on the manner in which they utilize their authority once they are in office. Loose factional organizations are poor contrivances for recruiting and sifting out leaders of public affairs. Social structures that develop leadership and bring together like-minded citizens lay the basis for the effectuation of majority will. Loose factions lack the collective spirit of party organization, which at its best imposes a sense of duty and imparts a spirit of responsibility to the inner core of leaders of the organization. While the extent to which two-party systems accomplish these ends are easily exaggerated, politicians working under such systems must, even if for no other reason than a yearning for office, have regard not only for the present campaign but also for the next. In an atomized and individualistic politics it becomes a matter of each leader for himself and often for himself only for the current campaign. (1949, 303–4)

Factional politics was lacking in every positive virtue he felt partisan politics did, or at least could, offer. Most serious among these, however, was its effect on the ability of the public to exercise their sovereignty effectively. For Key, democracy worked from bottom up (his own words) while Southern politics operated from the top down, and it was the creation and maintenance of factional rather than party politics that intentionally destroyed the ability of the public to govern. The solution to the problem of factions was clear—organized and sustained competition. And, if there be organized and sustained competition, then there were political parties, for that is precisely what Key meant by political parties.

The problem Key identified with factional politics was that they did not, that is, stand for any of three things that we might believe partisan contests for control of electoral offices to be about. They did not stand for ideas or policies that would help the voter distinguish one from another in the voting booth.[6] Second, neither did they stand unified with others for control of a large swath of offices, who therefore could be seen as bound together across the legislature, the executive, and whatever other offices were chosen directly, by election, or chosen indirectly, by political appointment by elected officials. Third, they did not typically, in Key's account, stand for control of the same office over time, making the transition from one occupant of that office to the next, and thus stand accountable for conduct while in office.

CONCLUSION

We have contended that a competitive party system is a necessary ingredient of democratic politics. To summarize our view, meaningful party labels allow voters to play a substantial role in selecting the direction of policy and holding politicians accountable; ambitious politicians affiliate with parties that create meaningful and popular labels; a party will be competitive when its label attracts a sufficient number of voters and ambitious candidates; and a competitive party system consists of two or more parties each of which is in equilibrium.

This perspective suggests a number of directions for future research. First, we need more tests of whether voters are attracted to parties with clear and consistent labels (Alvarez 1997). Are voters affected by mixed party messages over time and/or

---

[6] While all stood for a unified South in the national government, to ensure Northern forbearance necessary to maintain the Jim Crow system, that unanimity did not help the voter distinguish one politician from the other.

across space? Is the electoral sanction for failing to follow through on campaign promises severe (Brady, Canes-Wrone, and Cogan 2002)?

Next, we require more study of candidates' affiliation decisions. The candidate emergence studies by Maisel, Stone, and Maestas (e.g., Maestas et al. 2006) have contributed greatly to our knowledge of the factors that affect political aspirants' candidacy decisions. However, we know relatively little about how and when emerging politicians make their party affiliation choices.

Our framework predicts that a party will become competitive by recruiting emerging politicians and luring away prominent politicians from the opposing party who can retain their popularity despite a new party affiliation. This might be tested empirically by mapping the emergence of a competitive party (such as the Southern Republicans or Northern Democrats) at various levels of office. Do parties build systematically from lower offices upward, as our framework suggests will occur, or do parties emerge from the "top down" (Aistrup 1996)?

Finally, we need more investigations of the connection between party competition and democracy. Does party competition lead to greater government responsiveness to public opinion? Does competition encourage citizens to become participants in the democratic process? Do the governments that emerge from competitive elections produce more successful public policies?

In closing, competition between or among political parties in elections, which is to say, in their quest to win political office, leads the parties, once in office, to respect the concerns, needs, and aspirations of the public who elected them. Or, perhaps one might say it leads politicians to respond to the concerns of those who can toss them out of office the next time around.[7] In this way, competitive political parties yield political outcomes that seek to give benefits to all.[8] No other political system can be counted on to reward the mass public consistently.[9] An absence of incentives to reward the full electorate is not only true for all non-democratic systems, but it is also true for putatively democratic systems over which there is no

[7] As V. O. Key put it (1949, 310), "ruling groups have so inveterate a habit of being wrong that the health of a democratic order demands that they be challenged and constantly compelled to prove their case."

[8] Certainly, sometimes it may be one set of voters who are aided more than another set (e.g., Gerber and Lewis 2004), but over time, those losers can become winners. Miller (1983) offers a formal discussion of this and related issues. The major point is that it is the need to seek ways to form majorities of the public that favors competitive democracies over other, non-majoritarian, that is non-democratic, systems.

[9] Bueno de Mesquita and others argue that officeholders respond to the "selectorate," those whose support is needed to attain and retain office. In this view, democracy is distinct in being the particular form of government with the broadest selectorate—the whole electorate, that is, as compared to non-democratic systems that are distinct in having a vastly smaller selectorate and thus being responsive to the few rather than the many. See Bueno de Mesquita et al. (1999). Note that this flows naturally from the argument made by Mancur Olson (1982), that in long-standing democracies, only majority-seeking political parties can be sufficiently encompassing to avoid the policy "sclerosis" that interest groups and small parties support.

genuine competition for office. When there is no competition, the incentive for officeholders to reward the public lessens. It is the desire for office—and more importantly, the consistent risk of losing office—that provides the equally consistent motivation for political elites to pay attention to the public. In this sense, political parties are a device that James Madison would find fitting smoothly with separation of powers and checks and balances in serving to ameliorate the likelihood of tyranny.

References

ABRAMOWITZ, A. I. 1988. Explaining Senate Election Outcomes. *American Political Science Review*, 82/2: 385–403.

AISTRUP, J. A. 1996. *The Southern Strategy Revisited: Republican Top-Down Advancement in the South*. Lexington, Ky.: University of Kentucky Press.

ALDRICH, J. A. 2007. The Study of Party Politics in the Twenty-First Century. *Election Law Journal*, 6/2: 209–19.

ALDRICH, J. H. 1995. *Why Parties?* Chicago, Ill.: University of Chicago Press.

—— and BIANCO, W. T. 1992. A Game-Theoretic Model of Party Affiliation of Candidates and Office Holders. *Mathematical and Computer Modeling*, 16: 103–16.

ALVAREZ, R. M. 1997. *Information and Elections*. Ann Arbor, Mich.: University of Michigan Press.

ARNOLD, R. D. 1993. Can Inattentive Citizens Control their Elected Representatives? In *Congress Reconsidered*, ed. L. Dodd and B. Oppenheimer. Washington, D.C.: CQ Press.

—— 2004. *Congress, the Press, and Political Accountability*. Princeton, N.J.: Princeton University Press.

BENEDICT, M. L. 1985. Factionalism and Representation: Some Insight from the Nineteenth-Century United States. *Social Science History*, 9/4: 361–98.

BRADY, D. W., CANES-WRONE, B., and COGAN, J. F. 2002. Out of Step, Out of Office: Electoral Accountability and House Members' Voting. *American Political Science Review*, 96/1: 127–40.

BUENO DE MESQUITA, B., MORROW, J. D., SIVERSON, R. M., and SMITH, A. 1999. An Institutional Explanation of the Democractic Peace. *American Political Science Review*, 93/4: 791–807.

CAIN, B. E., FEREJOHN, J. A., and FIORINA, M. P. 1984. The Constituency Service Basis of the Personal Vote for U.S. Representatives and British Members of Parliament. *American Political Science Review*, 78/1: 110–25.

CALVERT, R. L. 1985. Robustness of the Multidimensional Voting Model: Candidate Motivations, Uncertainty, and Convergence. *American Journal of Political Science*, 29/1: 69–95.

CANES-WRONE, B., HERRON, M. C., and SHOTTS, K. W. 2001. Leadership and Pandering: A Theory of Executive Policymaking. *American Journal of Political Science*, 45/3: 532–50.

CANON, D. T. 1990. *Actors, Athletes, and Astronauts: Political Amateurs in the United States Congress*. Chicago, Ill.: University of Chicago Press.

CLEMENS, E. 1997. *The People's Lobby: Organizational Innovation and the Rise of Interest Group Politics in the United States, 1890–1925*. Chicago, Ill.: University of Chicago Press.

COX, G. W. 1997. *Making Votes Count*. New York: Cambridge University Press.

—— and MCCUBBINS, M. D. 1993. *Legislative Leviathan: Party Government in the House*. Berkeley, Calif.: University of California Press.

—— and MUNGER, M. C. 1989. Closeness, Expenditures, and Turnout in the 1982 U.S. House Elections. *American Political Science Review*, 83/1: 217–31.

DAHL, R. A. 2003. *How Democratic is the American Constitution?* New Haven, Conn.: Yale University Press.

DELLI CARPINI, M. X. and KEETER, S. 1996. *What Americans Know About Politics and Why It Matters*. New Haven, Conn.: Yale University Press.

DIAMOND, L. and GUNTHER, R. 2001. *Political Parties and Democracy*. Baltimore, Md.: The Johns Hopkins University Press.

DOWNS, A. 1957. *An Economic Theory of Democracy*.

ERIKSON, R. S. 1971. The Incumbency Advantage in Congressional Elections. *Polity*, 3: 395–405.

FIORINA, M. 1973. Electoral Margins, Constituency Influence and Policy Moderation: A Critical Assessment. *American Politics Quarterly*, 1: 479–98.

—— 1981. *Retrospective Voting in American National Elections*. New Haven: Yale University Press.

GERBER, E. R. and LEWIS, J. B. 2004. Beyond the Median: Voter Preferences, District Heterogeneity, and Political Representation. *Journal of Political Economy*, 112: 1364–83.

—— and LUPIA, A. 1995. Campaign Competition and Policy Responsiveness in Direct Legislation Elections. *Political Behavior*, 17/3: 287–306.

GIBSON, J. L., COTTER, C. P., BIBBY, J. F., and HUCKSHORN, R. J. 1983. Assessing Party Organizational Strength. *American Journal of Political Science*, 27/2: 193–222.

GRIFFIN, J. D. 2006. Electoral Competition and Democratic Responsiveness: A Defense of the Marginality Hypothesis. *The Journal of Politics*, 68/4: 909–19.

GRYNAVISKI, J. D. Forthcoming. *Partisan Bonds*. New York: Cambridge University Press.

HANSEN, J. M. 1991. *Gaining Access: Congress and the Farm Lobby, 1919–1981*. Chicago, Ill.: University of Chicago Press.

HOFSTADTER, R. 1969. *The Idea of a Party System: The Rise of Legitimate Opposition in the United States, 1780–1840*. Berkeley: University of California Press.

HUTCHINGS, V. L. 1998. Issue Salience and Support for Civil Rights Legislation among Southern Democrats. *Legislative Studies Quarterly*, 23/4: 521–44.

KEY, V. O. 1949. *Southern Politics in State and Nation*. New York: Knopf.

—— 1966. *The Responsible Electorate: Rationality in Presidential Voting 1936–60*. Cambridge: Belknap Press.

KINGDON, J. W. 1989. *Congressmen's Voting Decisions*. Ann Arbor: University of Michigan Press.

LAZARSFELD, P. F., BERELSON, B., and GAUDET, H. 1948. *The People's Choice*. New York: Columbia University Press.

LEVITSKY, S. and CAMERON, M. A. 2003. Democracy without Parties? Political Parties and Regime Change in Fujimori's Peru. *Latin American Politics and Society*, 45/3: 1–33.

LODGE, M., STEENBERGEN, M. R., and BRAU, S. 1995. The Responsive Voter: Campaign Information and the Dynamics of Candidate Evaluation. *American Political Science Review*, 89/2: 309–26.

LUPIA, A. and MCCUBBINS, M. D. 1998. *The Democratic Dilemma: Can Citizens Learn What They Need to Know?* Cambridge: Cambridge University Press.

MAESTAS, C., FULTON, S. A., MAISEL, L. S., and STONE, W. J. 2006. When to Risk it? Institutions, Ambitions, and the Decision to Run for the U.S. House. *American Political Science Review*, 100/2: 195–208.

MANN, T. E. and WOLFINGER, R. E. 1980. Candidates and Parties in Congressional Elections. *American Political Science Review*, 74/3: 617–32.

McGERR, M. 1986. *The Decline of Popular Politics: The American North, 1865–1928*. Oxford: Oxford University Press.

MILLER, N. 1983. Pluralism and Social Choice. *American Political Science Review*, 77/3: 734–47.

OLSON, M. 1982. *The Rise and Decline of Nations: Economic Growth, Stagflation, and Social Rigidities*. New Haven, Conn.: Yale University Press.

POWELL, Jr., G. B. 1982. *Contemporary Democracies: Participation, Stability, and Violence*. Cambridge: Harvard University Press.

PRZEWORSKI, A. 1991. *Democracy and the Market: Political and Economic Reforms in Eastern Europe and Latin America*. Cambridge: Cambridge University Press.

RIKER, W. 1983. *Liberalism Against Populism: A Confrontation Between the Theory of Democracy and the Theory of Social Choice*. Prospect Heights, Ill.: Waveland Press.

SARTORI, G. 1968. Representational Systems. *International Encyclopedia of the Social Sciences*, 13: 470–5.

SCHATTSCHNEIDER, E. E. 1942. *Party Government*. New York: Farrar and Rinehart, Inc.

SCHLESINGER, J. A. 1966. *Ambition and Politics*. Chicago, Ill.: Rand McNally.

SCHMITTER, P. C. and KARL, T. L. 1991. What Democracy Is . . . and Is Not. *Journal of Democracy*, 2/3: 75–88.

SCHUMPETER, J. 1962. *Capitalism, Socialism and Democracy*. New York: Harper and Row.

SEN, A. 1999. Democracy as a Universal Value. *Journal of Democracy*, 10/3: 3–17.

STOKES, S. 1999. Political Parties and Democracy. *Annual Review of Political Science*, 2: 243–67.

STROM, K. 1990. A Behavioral Theory of Competitive Political Parties. *American Journal of Political Science*, 34/2: 565–98.

WIEBE, R. H. 1967. *The Search for Order, 1877–1920*. New York: Hill and Wang.

WOODWARD, C. V. 1971 [1951]. *Origins of the New South 1877–1913*. Baton Rouge, La.: Louisiana State University Press.

....

CHAPTER 32

ORGANIZED INTERESTS

EVOLUTION AND INFLUENCE*

....

PETER L. FRANCIA

ORGANIZED interests, also known as "interest groups" or "pressure groups," have long played an important and controversial role in American politics and elections. As early as the *Federalist Papers*, James Madison recognized that citizens would pursue their own selfishly motivated interests, leading to what he described as the "mischief of faction." However, Madison understood that government could not prohibit its citizens from pursuing their self-interest without also denying them of their political freedom. Madison's solution to this dilemma was to argue that different groups, with competing needs and concerns, could coexist by checking and balancing one another. The natural diversity of interests, Madison reasoned, would prevent any particular group from dominating society.

As Madison anticipated, organized interests have flourished in the United States. The French aristocrat, Alexis de Tocqueville, observed in the 1830s that the United States is the "one country in the world which, day in, day out, makes use of an unlimited freedom of political association. And, the citizens of this nation, alone in the world, have thought of using the right of association continually in civil life,

* The author thanks Michael Shaw for his research assistance.

and by this means have come to enjoy all of the advantages which civilization can offer" (in Mayer 1969, 520). The principle of association that de Tocqueville mentions is enshrined in the First Amendment of the United States Constitution, which guarantees "the right of the people peaceably to assemble, and to petition the government for a redress of grievances." This founding commitment to the right of freedom of association allowed for the early establishment and eventual explosion of interest groups in the United States.

With the rise of interest groups, more contemporary observers have also wrestled with the problems of the "mischief of faction." David Truman (1951), in *The Governmental Process*, took a benign view of interest groups, arguing that they formed when there was a "disturbance" to the social equilibrium (e.g., an economic downturn might prompt workers to organize into an association to protect their interests), and that based upon how groups came to form, organized interests reflected the distribution of salient interests in society (i.e., pluralism). Years later, E. E. Schattschneider (1960, 34–5) countered this view by famously concluding that the "flaw in the pluralist heaven is that the heavenly chorus sings with a strong upper-class accent." Mancur Olson (1965) noted the inherent difficulties of collective action, and that organized groups did not necessarily reflect the actual distribution of interests in the general population, but rather were heavily weighted in favor of those with the resources to provide the most attractive selective incentives to its membership (see also Walker 1983).

More recent works from a "neo-pluralist" perspective indicate that the collective action problem may not be as serious as Olson suggested, and that the influence of interest groups in American politics, particularly in shaping public policy, is a complex process (see, e.g., Lowery and Gray 2004). Baumgartner and Jones's (1993) punctuated equilibrium analysis, for instance, demonstrates that public policy goes through periods of stability, although with rapid and unpredictable changes that provide advantages to some groups, but not others. Popular accounts, however, suggest that a small subset of "special" interests with the most resources controls public policy at the expense of the public good. Polls indicate, for example, that large percentages of Americans believe elected officials are beholden to groups that contribute large sums of money to their campaigns and that there is widespread corruption in Washington, D.C. (see, e.g., Francia et al. 2003, 6).[1]

Yet, contrary to public opinion, interest groups cannot simply buy an election or an elected official. There is considerably more nuance to understanding the role and impact of organized interests in American politics. As this chapter will demonstrate, interest groups make use of different strategies and have had to adapt to evolving legal and political environments. Borrowing from Jacobson and Kernell's (1981) theory of rational political expectations, interest groups must

---

[1] See also *CBS News/New York Times* Poll, October 27–31, 2006, and *USA Today/Gallup* Poll, April 28–30, 2006, at <http://www.pollingreport.com/politics.htm>.

make frequent adjustments and adaptations to their strategies and allocation of resources based upon changing opportunities and constraints. This has had important consequences for the tactics that interest groups employ and ultimately the political influence they exert.

To be clear from the outset, it is not my intention to review the entire literature on interest groups, nor is it to give equal coverage of every issue. Instead, I offer sharper coverage on the topics related to this volume's emphasis on American elections and voting behavior. As a result, the reader will find that this chapter discusses the "group impact" literature (i.e., what groups do and what effects they have in the electoral and legislative arenas), with a focus on topics such as how interest groups have adapted to various reforms in the campaign finance system, but find comparatively less coverage of the "demand aggregation" literature (e.g., collective action dilemma; how and why groups form; how leaders recruit members).[2]

I begin this chapter by presenting an overview of what interest groups want and the activities that interest groups have pursued historically to achieve their goals. The next section examines the impact of organized interests in American elections, with a specific focus on the effects of financial contributions, voter mobilization efforts, and efforts to set the campaign agenda. Finally, I conclude with a discussion on the state of the academic research on interest groups, and offer some suggestions for researchers to pursue in the future.

INTEREST GROUP GOALS, STRATEGIES, AND TACTICS

There is no generally accepted definition of an interest group. Baumgartner and Leech (1998, 25–30) provide a useful overview of the varieties of definitions that have appeared in the literature over the years. One could simplify the definition of an interest group as an organization whose purpose it is to bring together individuals with shared concerns and to advance their interests in the political process through collective action. Interest groups connect citizens to their government, and serve as "policy maximizers" (Berry and Wilcox 2007, 60–2).

To translate their social and economic interests into public policy, interest groups follow some general strategies (see, e.g., Eismeier and Pollock 1986; Sorauf 1988). Some groups seek access to elected officials who are in positions of power (or

---

[2] For a summary of the demand aggregation literature, see Cigler (1991).

what some refer to as "legislative" strategies). Others have electoral goals in which the purpose is to shape the ideological composition of the legislature (or what some refer to as "ideological" strategies). Some interest groups follow a combined approach, pursuing a mixture of access and electoral strategies.

The course that an interest group decides to follow is often affected by their overriding goals. A group that has taken a firm position on a controversial issue, such as abortion, would be unlikely to follow an access strategy because few legislators are likely to change their position on a high-profile issue in exchange for a contribution, or even after an extensive lobbying campaign (Herrnson 2008, 142). Another factor that can shape group strategies is the political context and environment (Cox and Mager 1999; Grier and Munger 1993; Rudolph 1999). Interest groups may distribute resources differently depending on which political party is in power or which elected officials are in positions of power. They may also react to the tactics of rival organizations or other similarly situated groups. In some cases, there is an arms-race dynamic in which interest groups accumulate resources and spend money in elections in response to the actions of their competitors (Gray and Lowery 1997).

An organization's wealth, structure, office location, and size can affect its strategies as well (Eismeier and Pollock 1984, 1985; Wilcox 1989, 158).[3] Wealthy groups have the advantage of being able to invest in more races, and therefore can afford to gamble on non-incumbents in competitive races more often than groups with fewer financial resources. Federated groups may also behave differently than other groups based upon more demanding constituency concerns, as may those with a central office in Washington, D.C., which often produces more reliable information about which congressional elections are likely to be close (Herrnson 2008, 145–6). Small groups may not have the financial resources to make significant campaign contributions to candidates for political office. Some small groups may not even have a political action committee (PAC). However, consistent with resource mobilization theory, small groups find alternatives, often behaving as social movement organizations, stressing community organizing and protests, as well as legal action (McCarthy and Zald 1977; Schlozman and Tierney 1986, 160).

Tactics and strategies are not only influenced by resources, but by the political environment of different historical periods. During the second half of the nineteenth century, corporate monopolies and related interests exercised their power in American politics in several ways. Big business hired lobbyists (or what some derisively called lobby "barons"), although the most straightforward method of gaining political influence came through large campaign contributions from wealthy industrialists. Charges of vote buying and voter coercion were common, as were allegations of graft. Other scandalous methods included "lurid accounts of

---

[3] For more information about the influence of a group's financial wealth and its likelihood of making a soft money contribution, see Apollonio and La Raja (2004).

the employment of women" to persuade elected officials to support specific policies and legislation (Herring 1929, 36).

With no federal laws at the time to regulate group political activities, corrupt practices dominated the political process until the end of the nineteenth century. Although there were some grassroots organizations from this period, such as the Workingmen's Parties, the Mugwumps, the Greenbackers, the Prohibitionists, and the Populists, wealthy interests with ties to big business typically overwhelmed the political system with their abundance of financial resources. As the situation worsened, investigative journalists, known as "muckrakers," brought corruption to public attention. In response to public outcry from the muckrakers' stories, reformers, known as "progressives," called for new federal laws to limit the power and influence of large corporations and industries. They advocated anti-trust laws as well as restrictions on corporate lobbying and campaign contributions from big business.[4]

The US Congress took its first major steps to reform the nation's campaign finance system in the early 1900s. Led by Senator Ben "Pitchfork" Tillman of South Carolina, Congress pushed for federal legislation to curb the influence of corporations in political campaigns. The Tillman Act, which became law in 1907, banned corporations and interstate banks from contributing directly to federal candidates (Corrado 1997, 36).

Congress went on to pass further regulations on campaign contributions. In 1910, it passed the Publicity Act, which required national political party committees to disclose their expenditures in post-election reports. Congress also imposed spending limits in 1911 (although the US Supreme Court struck down primary election spending limits as unconstitutional in the 1921 case, *Newberry* v. *United States*, on the grounds that the US Congress did not have the authority to regulate elections for party nominations). In 1925, Congress passed a more stringent law, the Federal Corrupt Practices Act, which imposed additional disclosure requirements and limited expenditures in the general election (Corrado 1997, 37–46).

These changes in federal law during the first quarter of the twentieth century altered the activities of organized interests. The overtly corrupt activities of the nineteenth century became less common. Reforms of the period did not completely eliminate corruption; however, the laws did change how groups operated in the system (Reinsch 1907, 231). For starters, reforms weakened party organizations by prohibiting them from receiving corporate contributions. This meant fewer resources for parties to transport supporters to the polls or even to offer bribes to voters, which was not uncommon in the nineteenth and early twentieth centuries. The muckrakers' stories of corruption also discredited many party

---

[4] For an excellent account on the Progressive Era's importance to the development of interest groups, see Tichenor and Harris (2002–2003).

organizations and leaders, further weakening them. Consequently, interest groups began to fill the void left by parties (McCormick 1981, 266).

Interest groups responded to their new role by becoming active disseminators of information in an effort to shape public opinion and discourse in a manner that was favorable to advancing their interests and concerns. During this period, groups relied heavily on pamphlets, press releases, published research, and eventually advertising to spread their message to the public. The American Federation of Labor (AFL), for example, had a publicity service for the daily press known as the *Weekly News Service* (Faulkner and Starr 1949, 296). Organized groups, such as the Farm Bureau, also provided their members with information about the voting records of members of Congress and the bills affecting their interests. In sharing this information with its membership, the Farm Bureau hoped to educate its membership and then mobilize it to elect candidates sympathetic to agricultural issues (Herring 1929, 61).

In general, organized interests grew in number during the twentieth century. This occurred with the growth of the federal government and expanding public services (Walker 1993). Working together, interest groups provided members of Congress with campaign support; members of Congress set the budget for an executive agency; and the executive agency produced outcomes that interest groups desired. This "iron triangle" contributed to the growth of interest groups in the mid-1900s (Heclo 1978).

A separate and unrelated development, but with great significance for interest groups, was the rise of broadcast television advertising as the dominant means of communication. By the second half of the twentieth century, campaign costs grew precipitously, placing increased demands on candidates to raise money. Moreover, the reforms from the early 1900s never created a regulatory agency to monitor and enforce campaign finance rules and restrictions. Instead, the law relied on congressional oversight, which due to partisan pressures proved to be highly ineffective. Early reforms also failed to establish a clear and comprehensive set of penalties for those who violated the law. Consequently, money remained effectively unregulated.

When the Watergate scandal unraveled in the early 1970s, and it became public that Richard Nixon's Committee to Re-Elect the President (CRP or what some referred to as "CREEP") paid "hush money" to silence those with knowledge of the illegal activities of the "plumbers" (a secret investigations unit of Nixon's that plugged news "leaks"), public pressure built to strengthen federal campaign finance laws (Williams 2003, 71). In 1974, the US Congress amended the Federal Election Campaign Act (FECA), and with this legislation, created the Federal Election Commission (FEC), an independent regulatory commission charged with the responsibility of enforcing the law. In addition to the FEC, the new law imposed campaign contribution and spending limits in federal elections.

However, the spending limit restrictions were short-lived. In the 1976 case, *Buckley* v. *Valeo*, the US Supreme Court ruled that campaign expenditures equaled

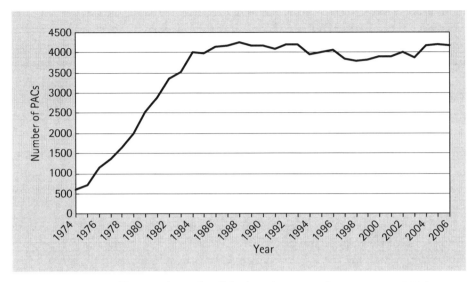

Figure 32.1 The number of political action committees, 1974–2006

Note: All PAC counts reflect year-end totals.
Source: FEC press release, "Number of Federal PACs Decreases," July 10, 2007.

speech, and thus the spending limits authorized in FECA were in violation of the First Amendment (Ortiz 1997, 67–77). The FECA also required that campaigns report contributions and expenditures to the FEC. This provision disclosed campaign finances in the hope it would help expose to the public any potential conflicts of interest between elected officials and their campaign donors (B. Smith 2001, 220).

At least partly in response to the new federal rules, interest groups formed PACs (Epstein 1980, 110; Sorauf 1997, 124). Under FECA, PACs could give up to $5,000 to a candidate in both the primary and the general election. The more significant provision in the law, however, dealt with individual limits, which were set at $1,000 per election to candidates, but went up to $5,000 for individual donations to PACs. The higher limit for PACs made them an attractive option for individuals looking to influence congressional elections. Predictably, the number of PACs rose significantly after FECA went into effect (see Figure 32.1).

PAC contributions also increased. In 1974, PACs gave $12.5 million. More than three decades later, in 2006, PAC contributions totaled roughly $372.1 million (FEC 2007). Additionally, the law allowed for "independent" expenditures (money spent without the candidate's knowledge or consent), and amendments to FECA in 1976 provided an exemption for express advocacy provided that the group disclosed all costs that exceeded $2,000 to the FEC and that it targeted its message to a restricted class. For labor unions, this restricted class includes union members, officials, and their families; for corporations, it includes executive and administrative personnel, stockholders, and their families. The law further allowed an exemption for non-partisan get-out-the-vote and registration drives. These rules encouraged grass-roots activities, which remained an important tactic under FECA.

Additionally, some groups made campaign services, such as polling, issue research, fundraising assistance, and strategic advice, available to candidates. EMILY's List (an acronym for Early Money is Like Yeast) is well-known for popularizing a fundraising technique known as "bundling." Because campaign finance law limits PAC contributions to $5,000 per candidate in each election, EMILY's List requests that its members make individual donations directly to the candidates. EMILY's List collects these checks from its individual members and then physically presents the "bundled" checks to the candidates (Burrell 2003, 75).

A few organizations even have campaign training schools. The AFL-CIO, for example, sponsors the National Labor Political Training Center, which recruits union volunteers for get-out-the-vote activities and political education efforts in competitive congressional districts (Francia 2006). Likewise, the National Federation of Independent Business (NFIB) has a training seminar that provides candidates with educational materials that help them in their presentation of small business issues on the campaign trail (Herrnson 2008, 50; Rozell, Wilcox, and Madland 2006, 41).

Perhaps most significantly, interest groups discovered ways to channel large donations that escaped federal regulations (known as "soft money") into elections. A popular method came about as a result of court rulings that allowed interest groups to use soft money and spend treasury funds for "issue ads" that did not explicitly endorse a candidate (Potter 1997, 229). Advertisements that avoided phrases such as "vote for," "re-elect," "help defeat" escaped federal restrictions even though they often appeared to most viewers to look and sound very similar to most campaign commercials. The law also allowed organizations to hide under ambiguous names, such as "Nevada's Foundation for Responsible Government" (Magleby 2000, 49).

As more money from interest groups poured into political campaigns during the 1990s, arguments against the system once again surfaced. Critics charged that court rulings, advisory opinions, and other developments had rendered FECA obsolete (Corrado and Gouvea 2004, 66–7; Wilcox and Joe 1998). Candidates continued to face intensifying pressure to raise funds, and with money again effectively unregulated and meaningful disclosure all but absent, pressure built for a new round of reforms. Demands to change the campaign finance system grew especially loud following a high-profile financial scandal involving the corporation, Enron. After the company's collapse, reports surfaced that Enron and its executives had used soft-money donations to help the company avoid federal regulations (Nance 2003, 150). By 2002, Congress acted to reform the campaign finance system by passing the Bipartisan Campaign Reform Act (BCRA).

The new BCRA law banned national party committees from raising soft money and from spending funds raised outside of federal limits. BCRA also prohibited candidates from soliciting soft-money funds for interest groups, and redefined what qualified as "electioneering communications" in an effort to close the loophole that had allowed for a surge of issue advocacy advertisements throughout the second half of the 1990s. Under the new definition, interest groups could run broadcast ads that name a federal candidate within thirty days of a primary or sixty days of a general election, but only if they now used funds that were subject to federal limits (PAC funds as opposed to treasury funds) to pay for the advertisements. However, the law still allowed for large contributions to various interest groups that could run issue ads, although there were limits on these ads, as well as new standards for identifying campaign ads. Under the new law, campaign ads included those that mentioned a candidate by name or appeared on television or radio during the period of intense campaigning before the election. PACs could still fund these ads as independent expenditures, but they could only do so with funds raised through hard money contributions.[5]

Although BCRA prohibits political parties from raising unlimited soft-money donations, the law does not ban so-called "527 organizations" from accepting unlimited donations from unions, corporations, or wealthy individuals, or from spending their donations on issue advocacy advertisements and get-out-the-vote efforts. The number "527" comes from the section of the IRS tax code which the organization falls under. A 527 group is defined as a political committee. It is exempt from taxation, although contributions to a 527 group are not tax-deductible.

Since passage of the Bipartisan Campaign Reform Act, many interest groups now rely heavily on these 527 organizations to influence federal elections. During the 2006 election, 527 groups spent $429 million.[6] With a presidential election in 2004, 527 groups spent even more as expenditures reached nearly $612 million.[7] Among the top spenders in 2006 were Republican and conservative 527 groups, which spent more than $65 million, and Democratic and liberal 527 groups, which spent more than $46 million. Labor-affiliated 527s were also extremely active in 2006, spending more than $50 million (see Table 32.1). Some groups also sought cover under section 501(c) of the tax code, which covers non-profit organizations. An early analysis of the 2008 election shows that 501(c) groups spent more money than ever before, and may have surpassed the expenditure totals of 527 groups (Weissman 2009).

---

[5] For information about the BCRA law, see <http://www.cfinst.org/bcra/>.

[6] Information on 527 expenditures comes from the Center for Responsive Politics, see <http://www.opensecrets.org/527s/index.asp>.

[7] Ibid.

Table 32.1 527 receipts and expenditures in 2006

Industry	Total Receipts $	Total Expenditures $
Democratic/Liberal	41,371,160	46,041,219
Republican/Conservative	37,744,180	65,670,045
Miscellaneous Unions	27,288,546	30,337,808
Women's Issues	11,879,743	11,228,642
Building Trade Unions	10,371,049	9,485,049
Industrial Unions	5,739,488	5,761,702
Environment	4,938,315	5,561,115
Miscellaneous Issues	3,651,500	3,250,101
Human Rights	3,555,011	4,790,214
Health Professionals	1,116,019	748,732
Leadership PACs	1,001,504	945,296

Note: Figures include industries that raised at least $1,000,000 in 2006.
Source: The Center for Responsive Politics.

THE EFFECTS OF INTEREST GROUPS
IN AMERICAN POLITICS

What interest groups receive in return for their efforts is at the heart of the controversy surrounding them. Interest groups provide numerous resources to achieve their goals. In the electoral arena, financial resources, such as PAC contributions, are important because they help candidates purchase the services of professionals, such as pollsters, media consultants, and other campaign advisors, needed for them to wage competitive campaigns. These specialists handle advertising, conduct polls, and assemble "PAC kits" to raise money for the campaign (Herrnson 1992, 865).

Political organizations also build political strength by attracting members. A political organization that can claim to represent the interests of millions is more likely to gain the ear of an elected official than one that represents thousands or fewer. Smaller-sized groups, however, can often be as effective as larger groups if they have a committed and energized membership. Some organizations successfully mobilize their members to participate in social movements and other forms of political action. They help do this, in part, by subsidizing the costs of political information (Baumgartner and Walker 1988).

The efforts of group leaders to mobilize their membership are important in bringing individuals into the political process, although some research suggests that there is an unintentional mobilization process in which the reasons for joining a group—solidary, material, and purposive incentives—play a role in explaining mobilization (Knoke 1990; Leighley 1996; Rosenstone and Hansen 1993; Wilson

1973). Verba and Nie (1972), for example, find that active memberships in voluntary organizations and political organizations increase the likelihood that individuals engage in campaign activity and go to the polls to vote. Moreover, participation in organizations is correlated with heightened political efficacy, greater political knowledge, and increased interest in politics (Verba, Schlozman, and Brady 1995). Several studies have found that organizations affiliated with the Christian Right have an especially strong effect on political participation (see e.g., Green, Rozell, and Wilcox 2003). Likewise, other works have shown that labor unions have an especially strong effect on political participation, finding that areas with the highest concentrations of union members have higher rates of voter turnout (Radcliff and Davis 2000, 133).

Interest groups can even have mobilization effects beyond their own members, including the mass public. Political advertisements financed by interest groups can stimulate voter turnout (Freedman and Goldstein 1999; Goldstein 1999, ch. 6; but see also Ansolabehere and Iyengar 1995). Some organized groups provide volunteers to register voters and for get-out-the-vote efforts as well. Labor unions, for example, often assist Democratic Party committees and candidates with phone banks or canvassing patrols, and have worked in alliance with organizations such as the Rainbow Coalition, which serve to stimulate voter turnout beyond the labor movement (Francia 2006).

Organized groups are also a voice for segments of the population that often are the least likely to participate in politics. Labor unions, once again, serve as a good example. Most unions claim to represent middle- and low-income workers. This can have the effect of pushing political parties and candidates to support policies that are favorable to the working class in an effort to win this sizeable bloc of organized voters. As parties and candidates take up issues important to the working class, this can have the effect of stimulating turnout as voters respond rationally by supporting politicians that represent their interests (Radcliff and Davis 2000, 133).

Beyond mobilization, interest groups attempt to set the political agenda. Organizations that are well funded often rely on expensive advertising blitzes to reach a wide audience. Groups that rely more on human resources, by comparison, frequently opt instead for education campaigns, demonstrations, and grassroots lobbying efforts. Mass mobilization campaigns and acts of disruption often attract media coverage, which can bring with it public attention, forcing politicians to pay attention to the group's concerns (Lipsky 1968).

The civil rights campaign of the Southern Christian Leadership Conference (SCLC) in Birmingham, Alabama in 1963 is perhaps one of the best examples of this. The violent actions of Birmingham police chief, Eugene "Bull" Connor, who unleashed police dogs on protestors—many of whom were young school children—and ordered police officers to attack demonstrators, provoked national and international outrage. As the Birmingham campaign continued to generate public anger, racial inequality became a defining political issue in the mid-1960s and beyond (McAdam 1982).

In other instances, organized groups can shape the issue agenda through the work of intellectuals sympathetic to the groups' concerns. Rachel Carson's book *Silent Spring* and Al Gore's film documentary *An Inconvenient Truth* are two examples that brought considerable attention to environmental concerns. Less dramatic working papers and reports from interest groups can also be influential. Elected officials often lack reliable information about their constituents' opinions on certain specific issues. In these instances, elected officials often turn to interest groups to instruct them about constituency preferences (Andrews and Edwards 2004, 495).

Of course, one of the most common ways for interest groups to set the agenda is through advertisements. One memorable advertisement came from the group, Swift Boat Veterans and POWs for Truth, which spent more than $22 million during the 2004 presidential election.[8] Swift Boat Veterans and POWs for Truth drew attention for a series of controversial television advertisements that attacked Democratic presidential nominee John Kerry's Vietnam service record. Only a few small markets televised the advertisements, but the group effectively used its website to spread the ads throughout the nation. The Swift Boat ads dominated coverage of the 2004 presidential election for several weeks, placing the Kerry campaign on the defensive. Some journalists and pundits even credited the Swift Boat Veterans' anti-Kerry ads as a major factor in George W. Bush's reelection in 2004 (Thomas 2004, ch. 6).

While the electoral benefit that candidates can gain from the campaign assistance of PACs and interest groups is clear, the evidence is considerably more mixed about the policy influence of organized interests. As noted earlier, a large number of Americans believe that interest groups use their resources to win favorable policies from the candidates whom they assist. Some of the earliest works in political science seemed to confirm the view of a corruptive relationship between organized groups, particularly big business, and elected officials (Odegard 1928). Research from the 1960s, though, sharply contradicted such conventional wisdom. These studies concluded that interest groups had very limited influence on the decisions of elected officials to support or oppose a bill. Instead, interest groups functioned as little more than "service bureaus" that provided information to legislators (Bauer, Pool, and Dexter 1963, ch. 24). This perspective, however, was also challenged with the publication of such influential works as Grant McConnell's (1966) *Private Power and American Democracy* and Theodore Lowi's (1969)

---

[8] Information on the expenditures of the Swift Boat Veterans and POWs for Truth comes from the Center for Responsive Politics, see <http://www.opensecrets.org/527s/527cmtes.asp?level=C&format=&cycle=2004>.

The End of Liberalism. Both McConnell and Lowi reasserted the importance of organized interests in the political and policy-making process.

Following the passage of FECA, which made public information about PAC contributions and expenditures, scholars attempted to address the influence question with these new data. Yet difficulty lies in unraveling the puzzle of whether legislators support a group's policies because they received campaign contributions, or whether interest groups provide contributions to legislators who are already predisposed to agree with the group's policy positions. Researchers who have attempted to examine this question have produced conflicting results and have arrived at different conclusions.

Some general studies find that PAC contributions do not influence congressional roll-call votes, whereas others have reached the opposite conclusion (for a summary of the literature, see Baumgartner and Leech 1998, 13–17; R. Smith 1995, 91–7; Wright 2003, 136–49). More specific research reports that PAC money can have an effect on legislation before it comes to a vote on the floor of Congress, such as through amendments during committee markups (Conway, Green, and Currinder 2002). Additional research suggests that PAC contributions are most influential in affecting participation in committee deliberations and roll-call votes on non-ideological and non-visible issues (Witko 2006). Another study finds that lobbying has a greater effect than PAC contributions in affecting support from members of Congress on important legislation to the group (Gordon 2001). At minimum, the activities of interest groups provide them with access to elected officials as well as additional time with legislators (Hall and Wayman 1990; Langbein 1986; but see also Brunell 2005).

CONCLUSION: THE FUTURE STUDY OF INTEREST GROUPS

Interest groups, as mentioned at the start of this chapter, have been controversial since the founding of the republic. Despite volumes of research, the debate over interest groups and their effects on American democracy, particularly their role in campaigns and elections, remains unsettled. To some, interest groups continue to influence elections and public policy in a manner that distorts the political process in favor of organizations with the most money and resources. Others credit interest groups for serving as vehicles for citizens to express their concerns to government; for educating their members about political issues; for mobilizing people to participate in the political process; and for serving as agents of social change by playing an important role in the passage of significant legislation. These differing perspectives about interest groups continue to influence the century-long debate about what the rules and laws should be that regulate interest group activities.

As this chapter has made clear, the laws that regulate interest group activities are not a trivial matter. Campaign finance laws, in particular, have played a significant role in affecting the strategies, tactics, and the influence of interest groups in American politics. For this reason, academic research should follow the recent lead of scholar Michael Franz, whose book *Choices and Changes* examines how the political and legal context affects interest group activities. As more elections pass under the laws of the Bipartisan Campaign Reform Act and more data become available, researchers will have an opportunity to compare the effects of different campaign finance regimes on interest group behavior.

The hyper-competitive two-party system that has evolved in recent years also should keep the political environment in flux. The Democrats' sweeping victories in 2006, which followed a disappointing performance in the 2004 election, suggests how tenuous any one party's power may be over the other. This context will force interest groups to make important strategic decisions about where and how to allocate their resources, and to develop new techniques to stay ahead of the competition. Already, some interest groups, such as the Service Employees International Union, have made effective use of innovative methods such as "micro-targeting." The effects of these adaptations are ripe for future research.

In the end, how interest groups ultimately adjust and respond to these ever-changing circumstances will help inform the larger normative debate about the impact of organized interests on American democracy. Indeed, whatever direction future research may take, the study of organized interests remains an important endeavor for political scientists. As Baumgartner and Leech (1998, 188) have appropriately concluded, "Group interests are basic to the practice of politics; interest groups must be basic to the study of politics as well."

REFERENCES

ANDREWS, K. T. and EDWARDS, B. 2004. Advocacy Organizations in the U.S. Political Process. *Annual Review of Sociology*, 30/1: 479–506.

ANSOLABEHERE, S. and IYENGAR, S. 1995. *Going Negative: How Campaign Advertising Shrinks and Polarizes the Electorate.* New York: Free Press.

APOLLONIO, D. E. and LA RAJA, R. J. 2004. Who Gave Soft Money? The Effect of Interest Group Resources on Political Contributions. *Journal of Politics*, 66/4: 1134–54.

BAUER, R., POOL, I. De S., and DEXTER, L. 1963. *American Business and Public Policy: The Politics of Foreign Trade.* New York: Atherton Press.

BAUMGARTNER, F. R. and JONES, B. D. 1993. *Agendas and Instability in American Politics.* Chicago, Ill.: University of Chicago Press.

—— and LEECH, B. L. 1998. *Basic Interests: The Importance of Groups in Politics and in Political Science*. Princeton, N.J.: Princeton University Press.

—— and WALKER, J. L., JR. 1988. Survey Research and Membership in Voluntary Associations. *American Journal of Political Science*, 32/4: 908–28.

BERRY, J. M. and WILCOX, C. 2007. *The Interest Group Society*, 4th edn. New York: Longman.

BRUNELL, T. L. 2005. The Relationship Between Political Parties and Interest Groups: Explaining Patterns of PAC Contributions to Candidates for Congress. *Political Research Quarterly*, 58/4: 681–8.

BURRELL, B. C. 2003. Money and Women's Candidacies for Public Office. In *Women and American Politics: New Questions, New Directions*, ed. S. J. Carroll. New York: Oxford University Press.

CIGLER, A. J. 1991. Interest Groups: A Subfield in Search of an Identity. In *Political Science: Looking to the Future*, ed. W. Crotty. Evanston, Ill.: Northwestern University Press.

CONWAY, M. M., GREEN, J. C., and CURRINDER, M. 2002. Interest Group Money in Elections. In *Interest Group Politics*, 6th edn., ed. A. J. Cigler and B. A. Loomis. Washington, D.C.: CQ Press.

CORRADO, A. 1997. Money and Politics: A History of Federal Campaign Finance Law. In *Campaign Finance Reform: A Sourcebook*, ed. A. Corrado, T. E. Mann, D. R. Ortiz, T. Potter, and F. J. Sorauf. Washington, D.C.: Brookings.

—— and GOUVEA, H. 2004. Financing Presidential Nominations Under the BCRA. In *The Making of Presidential Candidates 2004*, ed. W. G. Mayer. Lanham, Md.: Rowman & Littlefield.

COX, G. W. and MAGER, E. 1999. How Much is Majority Status in the U.S. Congress Worth? *American Political Science Review*, 93/2: 299–309.

EISMEIER, T. J. and POLLOCK, P. H., III. 1984. Political Action Committees: Varieties of Organization and Strategy. In *Money and Politics in the United States: Financing Elections in the 1980s*, ed. M. J. Malbin. Chatham, N.J.: Chatham Press.

—— —— 1985. An Organizational Analysis of Political Action Committees. *Political Behavior*, 7/2: 192–215.

—— —— 1986. Strategy and Choice in Congressional Elections: The Role of Political Action Committees. *American Journal of Political Science*, 30/1: 197–213.

EPSTEIN, E. M. 1980. Business and Labor Under the Federal Election Campaign Act of 1971. In *Parties, Interest Groups, and Campaign Finance Laws*, ed. M. J. Malbin. Washington, D.C.: American Enterprise Institute.

FAULKNER, H. U. and STARR, M. 1949. *Labor in America*. New York: Harper Brothers.

FEC (Federal Election Commission) 2007. PAC Activity Continues to Climb. Press release, October 5.

FRANCIA, P. L. 2006. *The Future of Organized Labor in American Politics*. New York: Columbia University Press.

—— GREEN, J. C., HERRNSON, P. S., POWELL, L. W., and WILCOX, C. 2003. *The Financiers of Congressional Elections*. New York: Columbia University Press.

FRANZ, M. M. 2008. *Choices and Changes: Interest Groups in the Electoral Process*. Philadelphia, Pa.: Temple University Press.

FREEDMAN, P. and GOLDSTEIN, K. 1999. Measuring Media Exposure and the Effects of Negative Campaign Ads. *American Journal of Political Science*, 43/4: 1189–208.

GOLDSTEIN, K. M. 1999. *Interest Groups, Lobbying, and Participation in America.* Cambridge: Cambridge University Press.

GORDON, S. B. 2001. All Votes are Not Created Equal: Campaign Contributions and Critical Votes. *Journal of Politics,* 63/1: 249–69.

GRAY, V. and LOWERY, D. 1997. Re-conceptualizing PAC Formation: It's Not a Collective Action Problem, and It May Be an Arms Race. *American Politics Research,* 25/3: 319–46.

GREEN, J. C., ROZELL, M. J., and WILCOX, C. 2003. *The Christian Right in American Politics: Marching to the Millennium.* Washington, D.C.: Georgetown University Press.

GRIER, K. B. and MUNGER, M. C. 1993. Comparing Interest Group PAC Contributions to House and Senate Incumbents, 1980–1986. *Journal of Politics,* 55/3: 615–43.

HALL, R. L. and WAYMAN, F. W. 1990. Buying Time: Moneyed Interests and the Mobilization of Bias in Congressional Committees. *American Political Science Review,* 84/3: 797–820.

HECLO, H. 1978. Issue Networks and the Executive Establishment. In *The New American Political System,* ed. A. King. Washington, D.C.: American Enterprise Institute.

HERRING, E. P. 1929. *Group Representation Before Congress.* Baltimore, Md.: Johns Hopkins Press.

HERRNSON, P. S. 1992. Campaign Professionalism and Fundraising in Congressional Elections. *Journal of Politics,* 54/3: 859–70.

—— 2008. *Congressional Elections: Campaigning at Home and in Washington,* 5th edn. Washington, D.C.: CQ Press.

JACOBSON, G. C. and KERNELL, S. 1981. *Strategy and Choice in Congressional Elections.* New Haven, Conn.: Yale University Press.

KNOKE, D. 1990. *Organizing for Collective Action: The Political Economies of Associations.* New York: Aldine de Gruyter.

LANGBEIN, L. I. 1986. Money and Access: Some Empirical Evidence. *Journal of Politics,* 48/4: 1052–62.

LEIGHLEY, J. 1996. Group Membership and the Mobilization of Political Participation. *Journal of Politics,* 58/2: 447–63.

LIPSKY, M. 1968. Protest as a Political Resource. *American Political Science Review,* 62/4: 1144–58.

LOWERY, D. and GRAY, V. 2004. A Neopluralist Perspective on Research on Organized Interests. *Political Research Quarterly,* 57/1: 163–75.

LOWI, T. J. 1969. *The End of Liberalism: Ideology, Policy, and the Crisis of Public Authority.* New York: W.W. Norton.

MAGLEBY, D. B. 2000. Interest-Group Election Ads. In *Outside Money: Soft Money and Issue Advocacy in the 1998 Congressional Elections,* ed. D. B. Magleby. Lanham, Md.: Rowman and Littlefield.

MAYER, J. P. (ed.) 1969. *Alexis De Tocqueville's Democracy in America.* New York: Harper-Perennial.

MCADAM, D. 1982. *Political Process and the Development of Black Insurgency, 1930–1970.* Chicago, Ill.: University of Chicago Press.

MCCARTHY, J. and ZALD, M. 1977. Resource Mobilization and Social Movements: A Partial Theory. *American Journal of Sociology,* 82/6: 1212–41.

MCCONNELL, G. 1966. *Private Power and American Democracy.* New York: Alfred A. Knopf.

MCCORMICK, R. L. 1981. The Discovery that Business Corrupts Politics: A Reappraisal of the Origins of Progressivism. *American Historical Review,* 86/2: 247–74.

NANCE, T. 2003. *Gangs of America: The Rise of Corporate Power and the Disabling of Democracy.* San Francisco, Calif.: Berrett-Koehler.

ODEGARD, P. 1928. *Pressure Politics of Equality: The Story of the Anti-Saloon League.* New York: Columbia University Press.

OLSON, M. 1965. *The Logic of Collective Action: Public Goods and the Theory of Groups.* Cambridge, Mass.: Harvard University Press.

ORTIZ, D. R. 1997. The First Amendment at Work: Constitutional Restrictions on Campaign Finance Regulation. In *Campaign Finance Reform: A Sourcebook*, ed. A. Corrado, T. E. Mann, D. R. Ortiz, T. Potter, and F. J. Sorauf. Washington, D.C.: Brookings.

POTTER, T. 1997. Issue Advocacy and Express Advocacy: Introduction. In *Campaign Finance Reform: A Sourcebook*, ed. T. E. Mann, D. R. Ortiz, T. Potter, and F. J. Sorauf. Washington, D.C.: Brookings.

RADCLIFF, B. and DAVIS, P. 2000. Labor Organizations and Electoral Participation in Industrial Democracies. *American Journal of Political Science*, 44/1: 132–41.

REINSCH, P. S. 1907. *American Legislatures and Legislative Methods.* New York: The Century Co.

ROSENSTONE, S. J. and HANSEN, J. M. 1993. *Mobilization, Participation, and Democracy in America.* New York: Macmillan.

ROZELL, M. J., WILCOX, C., and MADLAND, D. 2006. *Interest Groups in American Campaigns: The New Face of Electioneering*, 2nd edn. Washington, D.C.: CQ Press.

RUDOLPH, T. J. 1999. Corporate and Labor PAC Contributions in House Elections: Measuring the Effects of Majority Party Status. *Journal of Politics*, 61/1: 195–206.

SCHATTSCHNEIDER, E. E. 1960. *The Semisovereign People: A Realist's View of Democracy in America.* New York: Harcourt Brace Jovanovich Publishers.

SCHLOZMAN, K. L. and TIERNEY, J. T. 1986. *Organized Interests and American Democracy.* New York: Harper & Row.

SMITH, B. A. 2001. *Unfree Speech: The Folly of Campaign Finance Reform.* Princeton, N.J.: Princeton University Press.

SMITH, R. A. 1995. "Interest Group Influence in the U.S. Congress." *Legislative Studies Quarterly* 20(1): 89–139.

SORAUF, F. J. 1988. *Money in American Elections.* Boston: Scott, Foresman and Company.

—— 1997. Political Action Committees. In *Campaign Finance Reform: A Sourcebook*, ed. A. Corrado, T. E. Mann, D. R. Ortiz, T. Potter, and F. J. Sorauf. Washington, D.C.: Brookings.

THOMAS, E. 2004. *Election 2004: How Bush Won and What You Can Expect in the Future.* New York: PublicAffairs Books.

TICHENOR, D. J. and HARRIS, R. A. 2002–2003. Organized Interests and American Political Development. *Political Science Quarterly*, 117/4: 587–612.

TRUMAN, D. B. 1951. *The Governmental Process: Political Interests and Public Opinion.* New York: Alfred A. Knopf.

VERBA, S. and NIE, N. H. 1972. *Participation in America: Political Democracy and Social Equality.* New York: Harper & Row.

—— SCHLOZMAN, K. L., and BRADY, H. 1995. *Voice and Equality: Civic Voluntarism in American Politics.* Cambridge, Mass.: Harvard University Press.

WALKER, J. L., JR. 1983. The Origins and Maintenance of Interest Groups in America. *American Political Science Review*, 77/2: 390–406.

WALKER, J. L., JR. 1993. *Mobilizing Interest Groups in America: Patrons, Professions, and Social Movements.* Ann Arbor, Mich.: University of Michigan Press.

WEISSMAN, S. 2009. Soft Money Political Spending by 501(c) Nonprofits Tripled in 2008 Election. Campaign Finance Institute [Online]. Accessed September 10, 2009 at: <http://www.cfinst.org/pr/prRelease.aspx?ReleaseID=221>.

WILCOX, C. 1989. Organizational Variables and Contribution Behavior of Large PACs: A Longitudinal Analysis. *Political Behavior,* 11/2: 157–73.

—— and JOE, W. 1998. Dead Law: The Federal Election Finance Regulations, 1974-1996. *PS: Political Science & Politics,* 31/1: 14–17.

WILLIAMS, R. 2003. Political Corruption in the United States. In *Corruption in Contemporary Politics,* ed. M. J. Bull and J. L. Newell. New York: Palgrave Macmillan.

WILSON, J. Q. 1973. *Political Organizations.* New York: Basic Books.

WITKO, C. 2006. PACs, Issue Context, and Congressional Decisionmaking. *Political Research Quarterly,* 59/2: 283–95.

WRIGHT, J. R. 2003. *Interest Groups and Congress: Lobbying, Contributions, and Influence.* New York: Longman.

....

CHAPTER 33

MONEY AND AMERICAN ELECTIONS

....

LYNDA W. POWELL

CLYDE WILCOX

AMERICAN elections are the most expensive in the world. In 2004, candidates, parties, and interest groups spent an estimated $4.27 billion on national elections alone—not counting elections for state and local office (Patterson 2006)—and presidential candidates in 2008 shattered all previous fundraising records. Candidates spend much of their time asking individuals and interest groups to contribute to their campaigns. Interest groups and parties also raise money for electioneering. In closely contested elections voters are often bombarded by appeals from candidates, parties, interest groups, and even individuals.

Issues of money, elections, and policy lie at the heart of many critical questions in the study of American politics. Campaign finance issues involve key values—freedom of speech, controlling corruption, and equality. Donors to political campaigns are demographically unrepresentative of the American citizenry—they are wealthier, older, more white, and male. Does this result in unequal influence in government? Should we and can we reduce this inequality through new laws?

Although political scientists, sociologists, and economists have been studying money in American elections since early in the twentieth century, there is no consensus on the answers to these questions (Overacker and West 1932; Sorauf

1992). Many questions about campaign finance pose challenges in assessing causality. It is difficult enough to measure the money that flows into politics because of the myriad ways that money can be channeled in politics. It is even harder to measure the policy choices that may be affected by donations.

Although a diverse set of approaches has been used to study money and politics, scholars commonly assume that individual donors, candidates, interest groups, and parties are rational actors operating under various constraints. Potential donors have a mixture of motives, and candidates, parties, and interest groups have different assets that they can use to solicit contributions. National, state, and local campaign finance regulations shape and constrain the transactions between donors and recipients, and affect the decisions of these actors to channel money in complicated ways that have changed over time.

CAMPAIGN FINANCE REGULATIONS

Money in American elections is regulated by a complex web of federal, state, and local law. These rules affect the resources that can be mobilized into politics, and the ways that these resources can be used. There are lengthy summaries of the complex and evolving laws that regulate campaign finance (Corrado 2005). Here we briefly note some rules relevant to our discussion. Campaign finance regulations can be categorized as follows:

- *Spending:* The Supreme Court has barred any limits on spending by political candidates, although candidates may agree to spending limits in exchange for public subsidies. Nationally, parties can spend limited amounts in coordination with candidates, and unlimited amounts that are not coordinated. Interest groups can also spend unlimited amounts to advocate the election of a federal candidate, but this money must be raised in contributions of limited size. Groups can also spend unlimited amounts to advocate issues in ways that help candidates, using large contributions and their own treasuries, from some other groups and from individuals.

- *Source prohibitions:* In national and many state and local elections, for example, direct contributions from corporations and labor unions to candidates and to parties' election efforts are prohibited. These restrictions are not absolute: they leave a variety of ways for these entities to make political contributions that indirectly benefit candidates and parties, for example, by contributing to the funding of national conventions or to issue advocacy campaigns.

- *Contribution limits:* In national and many state and local elections, total contributions to candidates by individuals, interest groups, and even political parties are capped during an election cycle. Interest group contributions to federal candidates and parties must be funded through political action committees (PACs), which collect voluntary contributions from individuals which in turn are contributed to candidates. Again, as above, these restrictions are not absolute: these entities may make indirect contributions that benefit candidates' and parties' electoral efforts.

• *Public Funding:* In some national and state elections, the government provides partial or even full funding in exchange for voluntary acceptance of spending limits. In the presidential primary election, small contributions from individuals are matched with government funds. In the general election, nominees of the major parties may receive funding if they agree not to accept private donations. In recent elections, some presidential candidates have refused public funding in both the primary and general elections because they can raise sufficient private contributions to spend more than acceptance of public funds would permit.

• *Disclosure:* Most contributions to candidates and committees involved in national elections must be disclosed to the Federal Election Commission (FEC). Spending that is clearly intended to influence election outcomes must also be disclosed to the FEC. States also require disclosure, although laws vary in coverage and enforcement (Malbin and Gais 1998; Wilcox 2005). A good deal of financial activity related to elections escapes full (and often partial) disclosure. Spending to advocate issues may in some cases be disclosed to the IRS, although these regulations vary by the type of organization. Further, the involvement of individuals and interest groups as intermediaries in fundraising, for example by bundling or by holding a fundraiser at which others contribute, is typically undisclosed or inadequately disclosed.

Individuals and groups adapt to laws over time, finding novel ways to contribute to politics in order to evade limits on their financial involvement in politics. Rules and laws also are modified and evolve over time, although the difficulties of changing rules and laws inevitably slows their response time relative to changes in the behavior of donors and fundraisers. These behavioral and legal changes make longitudinal comparisons difficult. Consider, for example, the contributions from corporate executives. Before the passage of FECA, corporate executives made contributions directly to candidates and parties. After FECA, these contributions were largely channeled through corporate PACs. But in the 1990s many corporations and their executives gave far more "soft money" in large contributions directly to parties than they gave through PACs. In 2004, with soft money banned, some corporate donors made large contributions to 527 committees that were officially advocating issues but in practice clearly involved in elections (Magleby, Monson, and Patterson 2007; Weissman and Hassan 2006). While we have excellent disclosure on corporate PAC donations since the mid-1970s, it would be misleading to study corporate political donations simply by examining PAC contributions since over time these constitute a varying proportion of corporate political donations.

Future research on interest groups in campaign finance might seek to develop more complete data on the various ways that groups spend money in elections. Scholars have only recently begun to explore the way that interest group strategies are networked; instead of treating interest groups as separate units they are frequently part of a broader coalition that coordinates strategy. Finally, most scholarship treats interest group decisions about whether and how to be involved in elections as a standing decision, but in recent years many groups have exhibited sharp change between election cycles. The factors that lead to change in group strategies have been explored, but deserve more attention (Franz 2008).

Research into the impact of national campaign finance rules has typically compared campaign finance activity before and after a new law or regulation, seeking evidence of both intended and unintended consequences. For example, those who drafted the Federal Election Campaign ACT (FECA) did not anticipate the rapid proliferation of PACs which ensued (Malbin 1984). The ban on "soft money" in the Bipartisan Campaign Reform Act (BCRA) appears to have significantly reduced contributions by corporations and corporate executives, but other donors made very large contributions to 527 committees so that the overall flow of large contributions did not decline (Weissman and Hassan 2006).

But it is sometimes difficult to determine the effects of laws which take effect during periods of changing campaign finance practice. The growth of 527 committee spending on voter mobilization in the 2004 election is the continuation of a trend that began in the late 1990s, and may have occurred in the absence of BCRA (Boatright et al. 2006).

While most of the research has focused at the national level, the states provide a richer set of research opportunities. The variety of state campaign finance laws and electoral circumstances provides a large number of case studies and creates opportunities for comparative study among the fifty states (Schultz 2002; Thompson et al. 1998). Studies show complex effects: Powell (2008) reports that "clean election" laws (which provide public funds in exchange for limiting spending) reduce the time that lawmakers who accept the money spend on fundraising for themselves, but they correspondingly increase, although to a lesser extent, the amount of time these legislators spend fundraising for their caucus.

Two problems plague research on the impact of campaign finance laws. First, new regulations are not necessarily exogenous to the political process. We need to model both the adoption of laws and the effects of laws. For example, states that adopted "clean election" laws may have had political systems where money played a smaller role than in states that did not adopt them. Some studies have tried to compare states with similar political systems and cultures, although states differ along many dimensions (Joe et al. 2008).

Second, laws may appear to constrain donating or fundraising more than they actually do because of readily available equivalent alternatives for making contributions. Federal law limited individual contributions to candidates to $2,300 in 2004, but one donor gave more than $20 million to groups that were organized primarily to help elect a presidential candidate. When John McCain accepted public funds for the 2008 general election he agreed to forgo additional fundraising, but party organizations solicited those who might have given directly to McCain and spent money on his behalf. Thus studies that compare the superficial elements of campaign finance laws may miss important differences or similarities in actual campaign finance practice.

Who Gives?

Most of the money in American elections comes from individual donors, who contribute directly to candidates, and who also give to parties and interest groups. Individuals also ask others to give, and can act as middlemen in collecting and bundling contributions.

Donors give for a mixture of motives (Brown, Powell, and Wilcox 1995; Francia et al. 2003). Some individual donors give to candidates who share their policy preferences on issues. These purposive donors care about the overall composition of Congress, and they are therefore more likely to give in close races where their money could make a difference.

Some individuals give for private gain—they may seek government contracts or special treatment on taxes and regulations, as well as policies that benefit their industry. These materially motivated donors give primarily to officeholders with influence over the policy agenda—presidents, congressional party leaders and committee chairs, and other legislative policy entrepreneurs (Herrnson 2008). Their contributions are less concerned with influencing elections than in furthering their lobbying efforts. Others may give for private gain, but not for gain through the political process. They may, for example, wish to maintain a good relationship with a business client who requests a donation for a candidate.

Finally, some give simply because they enjoy politics, and the social connections that it helps to forge. These solidary donors are often friends of the candidate or the individual who solicits them for a donation. And, of course, many contributors have more than one motive for giving.

Surveys show that donors are overwhelmingly white, male, older, well educated, and affluent. Most donors are employed in the business sector, the professions, or politics (Brown, Powell, and Wilcox 1995; Francia et al. 2003; J. Green and Guth

1988; Guth and Green 1991). Although the number of donors has increased dramatically over the past three decades, the demographic composition of donors has remained remarkably constant.

Of all types of individual political participation, contributing is the one that most amplifies the voice of wealthy interests and thus contributes to participatory distortion (Verba, Schlozman, and Brady 1995). Candidates frequently spend considerable portions of their time asking for contributions from wealthy individuals who are already advantaged in the political realm. For this reason, reformers have recently focused on programs to encourage small contributions by the less affluent (Malbin 2008).

Although we know a good deal about individual donors, there remain many important questions. First, how stable is the donor pool? Survey research paints a portrait of a relatively consistent set of donors who give repeatedly over time: almost half of presidential donors surveyed in 1988 said that they give in most elections to presidential candidates (Brown, Powell, and Wilcox 1995). But a recent study that matched the names of donors over time suggests a higher rate of churning of the donor pool. Malbin (2005) found only 30 percent of George W. Bush's donors in 2000 gave to his campaign again in 2004. Do surveys overestimate stability and/or name-matching studies underestimate continuity among donors? Or has the process of fundraising changed so that there is less stability today?

Second, how often do individual donors give in coordination with interest groups? Interest groups can ask individuals to make checks out to specific candidates they support. These checks may then be handed to the candidate or party by the interest group in a "bundle" so that the group is credited by the candidate with raising the money. Groups can ask individuals to buy tickets to political events—a group or PAC can commit to "filling a table," for example, at a dinner. In federal elections and in some states, this allows interest groups to raise more money in support of a candidate than they could give directly. Some studies show a high rate of bundling in individual contributions in state elections (Marshall 1997, 1999), and a somewhat lower rate for national contests (Francia et al. 2003). If many contributions are coordinated with interest groups, then these individual contributions may be better conceived as coming from an interest group than an individual.

Third, how many donors give through multiple channels? Most studies of donors sample donors from one or two types of candidates, but none thus far have traced the multiple paths of influence through national candidates, parties, and PACs, and their state and local equivalent. Individual donors can also give money to other types of interest group organizations such as 527 committees, 501 (c) 3 and (c) 4 committees; in many cases individuals may give far more than is easily visible in disclosure documents.

Fourth, how is the internet changing the nature of soliciting contributions, and the composition of the donor pool? Early studies of internet donors reported that they were younger and somewhat less affluent than older donors, and that they were less likely to fit a consistently liberal or conservative ideology (Powell et al. 2002, 2005). In 2008, the Obama campaign reached many new donors through the internet, and sought to involve them in other ways in his campaign as well (Wilcox 2008). Scholars have begun to consider whether small individual contributions made to candidates, parties, and political groups through the internet might lead to greater interest and participation.[1]

These questions collectively underline the importance of also understanding the contribution decisions of interest groups, which have become increasingly important vehicles for channeling money into politics as direct contributions from individuals to candidates' election campaigns are capped at relatively low levels.

INTEREST GROUPS

Most interest groups are not active in elections, and some that are active do not contribute or spend money (Schlozman and Tierney 1986). The decision to become active may hinge on a policy issue or a change in the political environment, on new leadership, or on other factors (Patterson and Singer 2007). Most research assumes that interest groups have purpose or material motives for their electoral involvement, although solidary motives may be relevant for some small organizations. It is difficult to study empirically which groups are active in elections, because it is difficult to know the universe of existing and latent groups.

There have been many studies of the decision by corporations to form PACs at the national level. This literature has expanded both because it is possible to define the universe of corporations, but also because it is relatively straightforward to posit an economic motive for corporate PACs. Scholars have found that corporations in industries that are regulated or facing regulation are more likely to form PACs (Handler and Mulkern 1992; Hart 2001; Masters and Keim 1985). During the 1990s, corporations and other interest groups also could make large contributions to political parties, and scholars have modeled which groups gave this "soft money" (Appolonio and Raja 2004), reporting that wealthier and more established firms gave larger amounts. Corporate bundling has been less thoroughly studied, in part because of the difficulty in matching donors to their employers.[2]

Because PAC contributions in national elections are transparent and PACs are easily linked to sponsoring interest groups, scholars have also studied the

---

[1] See for example, Institute for Politics, Democracy and the Internet, 2007, "Small Donors and Internet Giving," <http://www.cfinst.org/books_reports/pdf/IPDI_SmallDonors.pdf>.

[2] The Center for Responsive Politics seeks to link individual contributions to employers, although of course not all of these contributions will be coordinated with the company.

contribution decisions of PACs. Business and trade association PACs give primarily to incumbents with agenda power, regardless of their party or ideology, but some corporate PACs have been more aggressive in backing challengers (Evans 1988). Labor unions and ideological groups are more likely to give to candidates who share their ideology and who are in close elections, and they often behave as strategic actors—giving more to vulnerable incumbents in elections when electoral tides are against them, and investing in challengers when the tides run the other way (Francia 2006). PAC decision making is influenced by the nature and structure of the sponsoring organization (Wright 1985), by the changing issue environment (Bedlington 1999), changing resources (Malbin et al. 2002), and the changing nature of congressional politics.

Although most studies have assumed that corporate contributions are rent-seeking, one strand of research has vigorously contested this notion (Ansolabehere, De Figueiredo, and Snyder 2003; Milyo, Primo, and Groseclose 2000). One of the most cited articles argues:

Most of the campaign money does not come from interest group PACs, but rather from individual donors. Most donors give substantially less than the current hard money limits. It doesn't seem accurate to view campaign contributions as a way of investing in political outcomes. Instead, aggregate campaign spending in the United States, we conjecture, mainly reflects the consumption value individuals receive from giving to campaigns.

(Ansolabehere, De Figueiredo, and Snyder 2003, 125.)

These papers are a useful corrective to analyses that assume that all contributions are investments for particularistic policy. Studies have repeatedly shown that many donors give for ideological reasons. Yet many individual contributions, even those below the maximum threshold, are made by those with material motives. In one survey of Congressional donors from 1996 (most of whom gave less than the legal maximum) nearly three-quarters admitted to at least some business motives in contributions, and one-quarter said that business considerations were "always important" in contributing.[3]

Small individual contributions may be investments when bundled by lobbyists, fundraisers, or PACs, so that the aggregate amount given by an individual is not necessarily a signal of motives. Marshall (1997) reported that most individual contributions in one state election were bundled by interest groups. Even when groups do not formally bundle, they may coordinate contributions.

For example, in one election the Association of Trial Lawyers of America (ATLA) asked its members to send contributions to particular candidates in the amount of $212—an unusual amount just above the disclosure threshold, and therefore quite

---

[3] The survey asked donors to rate various reasons for their giving, including "so that my business will be treated fairly," "the candidate is friendly to my industry or work," and "for business or employment reasons."

noticeable to candidates. ATLA asked members to report their giving to ATLA so that contributors could be given honorific designations—information that could allow ATLA to share with legislators the amounts for which ATLA had been responsible.

In addition, individuals and corporations can give much larger contributions to political activities such as funding the national political conventions, supporting inaugural activities, and a range of other activities. They can also make unlimited contributions to various 501 (c) organizations and 527 committees that are active in elections.

Consider, for example, the contributions of the corporate network of Ameriquest, a leader in subprime lending. Ameriquest, its executives, their spouses and business associates donated at least $20.5 million to state and federal candidates, parties, and political groups from 2002 to 2006 (Simpson 2007). Ameriquest used a variety of techniques to raise and contribute to candidates and parties. For example, Arnall, Chairman and founder of Ameriquest, and his family made over $2 million in contributions to federal candidates and party committees in the 2000, 2002, and 2004 election cycles. In addition, Ameriquest and its subsidiaries donated over $1 million to the president's second inaugural committee— corporate contributions can be made directly for a limited number of purposes. The *Washington Post* reported Arnall and his wife were fundraisers, raising over $12.25 million from others for the president since 2002, and his wife contributed $5 million to a 527 organization which spent money in support of Republican candidates (Center for Responsive Politics).

In addition, *The Wall Street Journal* reported that the senior vice president for government affairs at Ameriquest and her husband coordinated much of the subprime industry's lobbying. Her husband ran three subprime industry trade groups which spent over $6 million lobbying on the state level.

Individuals and organizations may view making political contributions and lobbying as two means to achieve the same objective, and a complete understanding of the role of money in politics needs to consider both. Ansolabehere, Snyder, and Tripathi (2002) is among the plentiful studies that report a strong association between lobbying and contributing. Thus the finding that corporations spend more on lobbying than on contributions misses the essential point that in many cases the contribution is in fact merely a part of a larger lobbying effort—and that both are aimed at securing access to and influencing policy-makers.

Of course, individuals, even heads of corporations, may certainly donate for many reasons other than economic benefit to their firm. Some large contributors like to be confidants of politicians, not to influence policy, but to be present when policy is made. Some simply wish to support legislators whom they believe are able and honest. Others may wish a role in public service.

However, if, for example, individuals whose businesses are highly regulated by the government are more likely to give than other equally wealthy individuals, we might expect some proportion of contributions to be related to an *expectation* of financial benefit from influencing government decisions. Gordon, Hafer, and Landa (2007) argue that if corporate executives "expect contributions to yield policies beneficial to company interests, those whose compensation varies directly with corporate earnings should contribute more than those whose compensation comes largely from salary alone." They find a strong relationship between giving and the sensitivity of pay to company performance. Their results are "consistent with instrumental giving but not with alternative, taste-based, accounts."

Of course, contributors' expectations of instrumental gain may not be fulfilled. In the next sections we discuss whether spending influences election outcomes, and whether contributions influence policy making.

THE EFFECTS OF MONEY ON ELECTIONS

Despite a large body of research spanning thirty years, the precise effects of campaign spending on electoral success are still subjects of lively debate. Candidates who spend the most money win most but not all elections. Yet donors are unlikely to contribute to a candidate who is likely to lose, and are more likely to give if their contribution might make a difference in a close race or if their contribution might buy access to a winner. And higher levels of campaign spending in turn increase a candidate's electoral prospects. This reciprocal relationship between spending and success has proven difficult to untangle.

Candidates presumably raise money for their campaigns until the marginal cost of fundraising reaches the marginal benefit of the monies raised. Money is raised and spent because candidates believe the more they spend, the more likely they are to win their election. Incumbents may raise more than they need for a particular election because they believe that the demonstrated ability to raise a large war chest may deter a quality challenger in a future election.

As in any advertising, at some point there is a diminishing return to spending on the current election. Further, large publicly disclosed contributions may suggest to voters that a candidate will make policy decisions in the interests of contributors rather than in those of constituents and have a negative impact on vote margin. A formal literature models these effects of service-induced contributions—those given to purchase future policy decisions adverse to the interests of constituents—on election outcomes. (For a review of this literature, see Ashworth 2006; Stratmann 2005.)

The better an incumbent's electoral prospects, the less the marginal benefit of spending an additional dollar on campaign advertising. Incumbents who represent marginal seats or are involved in scandal raise and spend large sums, whereas safe incumbents raise and spend less. Safe incumbents win overwhelmingly against token opposition, but incumbents who face significant challenges win more narrowly or even lose, despite spending more money than their safer colleagues. Thus for incumbents there is a simple negative correlation between funds spent and votes received. And empirical analyses which do not adequately control for the endogeneity between a candidate's electoral prospects and the candidate's fundraising will underestimate any positive effect of incumbent spending.

The relationship between spending and outcomes is complicated for challengers and open-seat candidates as well. Candidates running against an incumbent weakened by scandal, by the unpopularity of an issue position, or by changing tides of partisanship have the best chances of winning. The better the challenger's electoral prospects, the more easily challengers raise money from contributors. Materially motivated contributors or those seeking to change the partisan composition of congress are both attracted to candidates with reasonable prospects of winning. And some contributors find the same character traits, policy positions, or partisanship that appeals to voters attractive as well. Thus, challenger spending is also endogenous to electoral prospects. Failure to adequately control for endogeneity will result in overestimates of the impact of challenger spending in elections.

Jacobson (1978) developed the first serious model to separate these effects using a two-stage least squares estimation of the effects of campaign spending on US House elections. His work was criticized by D. Green and Krasno (1988) among others for inadequately solving the problem of reciprocal causation. More recently Jacobson (2004) summarized the current debate on the problem of reciprocal causation as follows: "Although theoretically feasible, this turns out to be extremely difficult in practice, and after twenty years of research, the appropriate solution remains elusive." Findings have differed considerably on two issues. First, does challenger spending have equal, greater, or lesser effect on vote margins compared to incumbent spending? Second, does greater spending for either significantly increase vote margin?

Most early studies found challenger spending to have a strong positive effect on the percentage of the vote they received, while incumbent spending had little to no effect (Abramowitz 1988; Jacobson 1985) or even a negative effect (Jacobson 1980). The key question is whether these findings are correct or whether they represent the bias in estimates we would expect from inadequately controlling for endogeneity.

More recent studies have developed a variety of refinements to Jacobson's early model. For US Senate elections, Gerber (1998) uses variation in state population size, candidate wealth, and lagged spending in the election for the other Senate seat in the state to provide leverage to create an instrument for campaign spending. He finds the marginal effect of incumbent spending to be equal to challenger spending and the effect of spending is substantively and statistically significant. Erikson and

Palfrey (2000) develop and test a game-theoretic model deriving the expectation that endogeneity should not bias the results in close races. They too find incumbent spending to be equally as effective as challenger spending and both effects are again significant.

These results contrast with the findings of Levitt (1994), who approaches the problem by modeling first differences on a sample of repeat challengers, assuming this holds constant candidate quality and constituency characteristics. He finds no significant effect for incumbent spending on vote share, and at best a small effect for challengers.

All three studies provide plausible ways to improve our estimation of spending effects and yet yield quite different conclusions about both the relative effects of incumbent versus challenger spending and about the magnitude of effect, if any, of spending itself. In an important sense, the findings of Gerber and of Erikson and Palfrey are more plausible. It seems unlikely that candidates for office would devote enormous time and resources to raising and spending campaign funds if they had no electoral effect. It is precisely because candidates have firm beliefs about the efficacy of spending that spending is so closely tied to electoral prospects, creating the difficulty in measuring separate effects.

Ideally we would like to persuade legislative candidates to participate in an experimental design randomly assigning candidates to various spending levels. Gerber (2004) came close to this ideal experimental design by persuading five candidates (2 congressional, 2 state legislative, and one mayoral) to randomly assign constituents to treatment or control groups with the treatment groups receiving mailings not sent to the control group. Gerber found incumbent mailings to be of little benefit, while those of challengers were quite efficacious. None of the incumbent races were competitive, however, and it is in the competitive races, as Gerber also pointed out, that campaign spending would likely matter for incumbents.

Indeed, the differences in findings across the studies may, at least partly, be due to differences in effect of campaign spending in races of varying competitiveness. This is consistent with the benefit–cost argument that began this section. The marginal return of campaign spending has diminishing returns as the certainty of a win increases, and when incumbents run for reelection, their likelihood of winning almost inevitably places them in the competitive-to-safe range. The Erikson and Palfrey study focuses precisely on competitive races, where campaign spending should, by this argument, matter the most. Senate races are more competitive, on average, than House races, which may also explain the Gerber (1998) findings on the Senate, although by this argument one would expect somewhat less equal effects than he observed. Levitt's sample of rematches, while somewhat peculiar by definition, had a typical predominance of weakly contested races where an incumbent's spending should have little marginal impact.

The answer to the question of the influence of money on elections is likely to be addressed best by considering a more complex model of the effects of campaign spending. Most obviously, the effectiveness of campaign spending is likely to depend on the competitiveness of the race. Further, if constituencies of different population or of varying media costs are being compared (Stratmann 2004), the effectiveness of money should be modeled as dependent on these factors as well. Developing a formal model of the complex benefit–cost considerations outlined here coupled with appropriate empirical tests that build on the three studies cited may be the most promising avenue for future research. Such models may need to consider that contributing and spending occurs throughout a campaign, so that large institutional donors frequently invest more or less late in a campaign, as polls hint at changing dynamics.

It may be that spending influences election outcomes only when the money is spent wisely. A spate of recent studies has explored the various types of spending by politicians and interest groups, including advertisements, mailings, phone calls, and door-to-door contacts. The studies suggest that certain types of activities are more valuable than others, and thus comparing all spending by candidates may obscure the efficacy of certain types of spending (Gerber 2004; Gerber and Green 2000; Imai 2005).

Most studies of campaign spending have focused on spending by candidates, and occasionally by party committees as well. But interest groups frequently engage in substantial spending that is usually not included in these models, including broadcast advertising, mail, phone calls, and direct voter contact (Engstrom and Kenny 2002; Jacobson 1999). Much of this spending is difficult to quantify, but in many races it totals more than the candidates spend, and thus any effort to model the effects of candidate spending must also include interest group and party efforts as well.

THE EFFECTS OF MONEY ON POLICY

Typically studies have looked for the influence of money on policy by examining the relationship between PAC contributions to individual legislators and the votes each legislator casts. Two articles exemplify the differing views of the influence of campaign contributions on the voting behavior of congressional incumbents. Both review and analyze previous work (the same thirty-six studies in both instances) and reference their own research. Ansolabehere, De Figueiredo, and Snyder (2003, 114) find that in the thirty-six studies, "Overall, PAC contributions show relatively few effects on voting behavior." In contrast, Stratmann (2005) finds a significant effect of money on votes in a meta-analysis of the same studies and cites his own work, finding that contributions have a significant effect on the voting decisions of House members.

The relationship between contributions and votes is reciprocal—decisions to contribute are influenced by perceptions of a legislator's likelihood of a favorable vote and the legislator's vote may be influenced by the contribution. Estimating the influence of money on votes absent the influence of votes on money is a difficult statistical problem. Many studies find no effect of money on votes. Those studies that do find an effect are often accused of inadequately modeling the endogeneity of votes and thus overestimating the effect of money.

Some scholars have concluded that campaign contributions have little to no influence on voting decisions of legislators (Abler 1991; Ansolabehere et al. 2003; Bronars and Lott 1997; Grenzke 1989; Wawro 2001). Others find that contributions are influential in special circumstances (Fleisher 1993; Langbein and Lotwis 1990; Stratmann 1991; Witko 2006). And some scholars argue that the measures and research designs in most existing studies are inadequate to capture the effects of campaign contributions.

Studies have focused on the relationship between PAC contributions and roll-call votes because these data are readily available, at least for the US Congress. Yet limiting measures of the independent variable to PAC contributions is problematic, as is limiting the dependent variable to roll-call votes. As we have noted before, interest group electoral activity frequently encompasses far more than PAC contributions. In many cases, the combined contributions by a company's employees can equal or exceed its PAC contributions. Interest groups can spend money in elections in a variety of ways, and any effort to model the impact of money on policy needs to fully account for these alternative pathways.

Moreover, if contributions are intended as investments, they presumably work in concert with lobbying expenditures. Hansen and Mitchell (2000) posit that "corporate political participation includes various dimensions of activity, one dimension of activity is not necessarily a good proxy for all forms, and the different dimensions have differences in the theoretically interesting properties of visibility and instrumentality." In addition to PAC contributions, they add the extent of lobbying representation in Washington, and charitable contributions. By limiting our analysis to the most readily identifiable form of financial effort, PAC contributions, we may seriously misestimate the influence of an organization's total political contribution activity.

In addition, studies that focus only on roll-call voting ignore the more important issue of what gets into the bill in the first place. Minor changes in wording in tax legislation can make a major difference on a company's bottom line. The effort of individual members to introduce, negotiate on markup, and bargain for support of legislation determines the content of legislation.

Notable among the few studies that look beyond votes for the influence of money is the work of Hall and Wayman. They conclude (1990, 814) "While previous research on these same issues provided little evidence that PAC money purchased members' votes, it apparently did buy the marginal time, energy, and legislative resources that committee participation requires." Their study of committee participation clearly suggests that legislative content may be influenced by financial considerations. Evans (1996) further examines the relationship between interest group actions and congressional committee decisions on two bills finding PAC contributions to be important on one of the two bills.

In addition, studies assume the financial linkage is between the individual legislator and his or her contributors and the votes that legislator casts. Increasingly, party leaders, committee chairs, and legislators who aspire to these positions have become fundraisers not just for themselves, but for the caucus. Any influence financial contributions have on leaders' and chairs' efforts to mobilize support for or against legislation in the party caucus will be missed in these models.

In order to determine the influence of money on policy, we need to develop a measure that incorporates all the various ways money may influence the content and passage of legislation. Powell (forthcoming) has implemented one approach using a measure based on a national survey of state legislators that asked them to evaluate the extent to which campaign contributions to legislative candidates and to parties determines the content and passage of bills in their chamber. She used a hierarchical Bayesian model to control for the perceptual biases of individual legislators while testing hypotheses that explain the varying influence of campaign contributions across states and chambers.

The increasing availability of state legislative data makes it possible to develop and test hypotheses about a much greater range of institutional and political variables than we can examine by looking at the federal level. Contribution data is available for state legislative candidates from the National Institute on Money in State Politics (www.FollowTheMoney.org).

Finally, it is also relevant to look beyond elected officials for the influence of contributions on policy. Gordon and Hafer (2005) find, for example, that corporations make political contributions to signal to the bureaucracy their willingness to seek redress from elected politicians. In some circumstances this results in less monitoring from the bureaucracy for these donors.

CONCLUSION

Although political scientists, economists, and sociologists have studied campaign finance for more than thirty years, consensus on many questions remains elusive. Two major barriers confront scholars seeking to ask key questions in this area. First, many questions are plagued with problems of endogeneity which are very complicated to sort out. Candidate fundraising is both a result of and a cause of electoral support, and contributions to candidates are both a result of and a cause of the policy choices that candidates and officeholders make.

Second, measuring campaign contributions is much more difficult than it might initially appear. Disclosure of campaign finance activity varies enormously along fairly complex lines that match court rulings and laws. Contributions from and spending by individuals and PACs to candidates and parties at the national level and in some states is very well documented, but contributions to and spending by other types of organizations are very incomplete. It is thus very difficult if not impossible to get solid estimates of the total contribution activity by specific individuals, organizations, or groups. Ideally we would wish also to include the varied fundraising activities that raise money from others while allowing those monies to be informally "credited" to the fundraiser. Finally, since lobbying and campaign giving are often two means of achieving the same policy goal, measuring and incorporating into analyses the resources directed at lobbying is important as well. These problems are made more difficult by the development of new ways of directing resources into politics in response to changes in campaign finance laws and in technology.

Third, while it is conceptually easy to measure the outcome of an election, it is extremely difficult to measure policy output. While roll-call votes are important, they are insufficient to measure the policy consequences of legislation and its implementation, and other policy-related services that officeholders may provide to donors. Thus the task of modeling the effect of money in influencing policy is inherently more difficult than that in modeling the effect of money in influencing election outcomes.

Solving both measurement and statistical problems is central to understanding questions of influence in both our elections and in our governmental process at both national and state levels. Normatively, evaluating the representational quality of our democracy rests on these understandings.

References

ABLER, D. G. 1991. Campaign Contributions and House Voting on Sugar and Dairy Legislation. *American Journal of Agricultural Economics*, 73/1: 11–7.

ABRAMOWITZ, A. I. 1988. Explaining Senate Election Outcomes. *American Political Science Review*, 82/2: 385–403.

ANSOLABEHERE, S., DE FIGUEIREDO, J. M., and SNYDER, J. M., JR. 2003. Why is There so Little Money in U.S. Politics? *Journal of Economic Perspectives*, 17/1: 105–30.

—— SNYDER, J. M., JR., and TRIPATHI, M. 2002. Are PAC Contributions and Lobbying Linked? New Evidence from the 1995 Lobby Disclosure Act. *Business and Politics*, 4/2: 131–55.

APPOLONIO, D. E. and LA RAJA, R. J. 2004. Who Gave Soft Money? The Effects of Interest Group Resources on Political Contributions. *Journal of Politics*, 66/4: 1134–54.

ASHWORTH, S. 2006. The Economics of Campaign Finance. *The new Palgrave Dictionary of Economics*.

BEDLINGTON, A. H. 1999. The Realtors Political Action Committee: Covering All Contingencies. In *After the Revolution: PACs, Lobbies and the Republican Congress*, ed. R. Biersack, P. S. Herrnson, and C. Wilcox. New York: Allyn & Bacon.

BOATRIGHT, R., MALBIN, M. J., ROZELL, M. J., and WILCOX, C. 2006. Interest Groups and Advocacy Organizations After BCRA. In *The Election After Reform: Money, Politics, and the Bipartisan Campaign Reform Act*, ed. M. J. Malbin. Lanham, Md.: Rowman & Littlefield.

BRONARS, S. G. and LOTT, J. R., JR. 1997. Do Campaign Donations Alter How a Politician Votes? Or, Do Donors Support Candidates Who Value the Same Things That They Do? *Journal of Law and Economics*, 40/2: 317–50.

BROWN, C. W., POWELL, L. W., and WILCOX, C. 1995. *Serious Money: Fundraising and Contributing in Presidential Nomination Campaigns.* New York: Cambridge University Press.

CORRADO, A. 2005. *The New Campaign Finance Sourcebook.* Washington, D.C.: Brookings Institution Press.

ENGSTROM, R. N. and KENNY, C. 2002. The Effects of Independent Expenditures in Senate Elections. *Political Research Quarterly*, 55/4: 885–905.

ERIKSON, R. S. and PALFREY, T. R. 2000. Equilibria in Campaign Spending Games: Theory and Data. *American Political Science Review*, 94/3: 595–609.

EVANS, D. 1988. Oil PACs and Aggressive Contribution Strategies. *The Journal of Politics*, 50/4: 1047–56.

—— 1996. Before the Roll Call: Interest Group Lobbying and Public Policy Outcomes in House Committees. *Political Research Quarterly*, 494/2: 287–304.

FLEISHER, R. 1993. PAC Contributions and Congressional Voting on National Defense. *Legislative Studies Quarterly*, 18/3: 391–409.

FRANCIA, P. L. 2006. *The Future of Organized Labor in American Politics.* New York: Columbia University Press.

—— GREEN, J. C., HERRNSON, P. S., POWELL, L. W., and WILCOX, C. 2003. *The Financiers of Congressional Elections: Investors, Ideologues, and Intimates.* New York: Columbia University Press.

FRANZ, M. M. 2008. *Choices and Changes: Interest Groups in the Electoral Process.* Philadelphia, Pa.: Temple University Press.

GERBER, A. 1998. Estimating the Effect of Campaign Spending on Senate Election Outcomes Using Instrumental Variables. *American Political Science Review*, 92/2: 401–11.

—— 2004. Does Campaign Spending Work?: Field Experiments Provide Evidence and Suggest New Theory. *American Behavioral Scientist*, 47/5: 541.

—— and GREEN, D. P. 2000. The Effects of Canvassing, Telephone Calls, and Direct Mail on Voter Turnout: A Field Experiment. *American Political Science Review*, 94/3: 653–63.

GORDON, S. C. and HAFER, C. 2005. Flexing Muscle: Corporate Political Expenditures as Signals to the Bureaucracy. *American Political Science Review*, 99/2: 245–61.

GORDON, S. C., HAFER, C., and LANDA, D. 2007. Consumption or Investment? On Motivations for Political Giving. *Journal of Politics*, 69/4: 1057–72.

GREEN, D. P. and KRASNO, J. S. 1988. Salvation for the Spendthrift Incumbent: Reestimating the Effects of Campaign Spending in House Elections. *American Journal of Political Science*, 32/4: 884–907.

GREEN, J. C. and GUTH, J. L. 1988. The Christian Right in the Republican Party: The Case of Pat Robertson's Supporters. *The Journal of Politics*, 50/1: 150–65.

GRENZKE, J. M. 1989. PACs and the Congressional Supermarket: The Currency is Complex. *American Journal of Political Science*, 33/1: 1–24.

GUTH, J. L. and GREEN, J. C. 1991. An Ideology of Rights: Support for Civil Liberties among Political Activists. *Political Behavior*, 13/4: 321–44.

HALL, R. L. and WAYMAN, F. W. 1990. Buying Time: Moneyed Interests and the Mobilization of Bias in Congressional Committees. *American Political Science Review*, 84/3: 797–820.

HANDLER, E. and MULKERN, J. R. 1992. *Business in Politics: Strategies of Corporate Political Action Committees.* Lexington, Mass.: Lexington Books.

HANSEN, W. L. and MITCHELL, N. J. 2000. Disaggregating and Explaining Corporate Political Activity: Domestic and Foreign Corporations in National Politics. *American Political Science Review*, 94/4: 891–903.

HART, D. M. 2001. Why Do Some Firms Give? Why Do Some Give a Lot? High-Tech PACs, 1977–1996. *The Journal of Politics*, 63/4: 1230–49.

HERRNSON, P. S. 2008. *Congressional Elections: Campaigning at Home and in Washington*, 5th edn. Washington, D.C.: CQ Press.

IMAI, K. 2005. Do Get-Out-The Vote Calls Reduce Turnout? The Importance of Statistical Methods for Field Experiments. *American Political Science Review*, 99: 283–300.

JACOBSON, G. C. 1978. The Effects of Campaign Spending in Congressional Elections. *American Political Science Review*, 72/2: 469–91.

—— 1980. *Money in Congressional Elections.* New Haven, Conn.: Yale University Press.

—— 1985. Money and Votes Reconsidered: Congressional Elections, 1972–1982. *Public Choice*, 47/1: 7–62.

—— 1999. The Effect of the AFL-CIO's "Voter Education" Campaigns on the 1996 House Elections. *The Journal of Politics*, 61/1: 185–94.

—— 2004. The Politics of Congressional Elections. New York: Pearson/Longman.

JOE, W. Y., MALBIN, M. J., WILCOX, C., BRUSCOE, P., and PIMLOTT, J. 2008. Who Are the Individual Donors to Gubernatorial and State Legislative Elections. Paper presented at the annual meeting of the Midwest Political Science Association. Chicago, Ill.

LANGBEIN, L. I. and LOTWIS, M. A. 1990. The Political Efficacy of Lobbying and Money: Gun Control in the U.S. House, 1986. *Legislative Studies Quarterly*, 15/3: 413–40.

LEVITT, S. D. 1994. Using Repeat Challengers to Estimate the Effect of Campaign Spending on Election Outcomes in the U.S. House. *The Journal of Political Economy*, 102/4: 777–98.

MAGLEBY, D. B., MONSON, J. Q., and PATTERSON, K. D. 2007. The Morning After: The Lingering Effects of a Night Spent Dancing. In *Dancing Without Partners: How Candidates, Parties, and Interest Groups Interact in the Presidential Campaign*, ed. D. B. Magleby, J. Q. Monson, and K. D. Patterson. Lanham, Md.: Rowman & Littlefield.

MALBIN, M. J. 1984. Looking Back at the Future of Campaign Finance Reform: Interest Groups and American Elections. In *Money and Politics in the United States: Financing Elections in the 1980s*, ed. M. J. Malbin. Chatham, N.J.: Chatham House.

—— 2005. A Public Funding System in Jeopardy: Lessons from the Presidential Nomination Contest of 2004. In *The Election After Reform: Money, Politics and the Bipartisan Campaign Reform Act*, ed. M. Malbin. Lanham, Md.: Rowman and Littlefield.

—— 2008. Rethinking the Campaign Finance Agenda. *The Forum*, 6/1: Article 3.

—— and GAIS, T. 1998. *The Day After Reform: Sobering Campaign Finance Lessons from the American States*, 1st edn. Albany, N.Y.: Rockefeller Institute Press. Distributed by the Brookings Institution Press.

—— WILCOX, C., ROZELL, M., and SKINNER, R. 2002. New Interest Group Strategies: A Preview of Post McCain-Feingold Politics? *Election Law Journal*, 1/4: 541–55.

MARSHALL, T. R. 1997. Bundling the Cash: Why do Interest Groups Bundle Donations? *American Review of Politics*, 18: 291–308.

—— 1999. Why PAC, Why Bundle? Patterns of Interest Group Donations. *American Review of Politics*, 20: 245–60.

MASTERS, M. F. and KEIM, G. D. 1985. Determinants of PAC Participation Among Large Corporations. *The Journal of Politics*, 47/4: 1158–73.

MILYO, J., PRIMO, D., and GROSECLOSE, T. 2000. Corporate PAC Campaign Contributions in Perspective. *Business and Politics*, 2/1: 75–88.

OVERACKER, L. and WEST, V. J. 1932. *Money in Elections*. New York: The Macmillan Company.

PATTERSON, K. D. 2006. Spending in the 2004 Election. In *Financing the 2004 Election*, ed. A Corrado, D. B. Magleby, and K. D. Patterson. Brookings Institution Press, Washington, DC.

—— and SINGER, M. M. 2007. Targeting Success: The Enduring Power of the NRA. In *Interest Group Politics*, 7th edn., ed. A. J. Cigler and B. A. Loomis. Washington, D.C.: CQ Press.

POWELL, E. N., POWELL, L. W., THOMAS, R. K., and WILCOX, C. 2002. Casting a Broader Net? Fundraising and Contributing Through the Internet in the 2000 Presidential Election. Paper presented at the Annual Meeting of the American Political Science Association. Chicago, Ill.

—— —— —— —— 2005. Online and Offline Political Contributions: A Preliminary Analysis. Paper presented at the Annual Meeting of the American Political Science Association. Washington, D.C.

POWELL, L. W. 2008. The Time Legislators Spend Fundraising for Themselves and for their Caucuses: Modeling Institutional, Personal and Political Effects in State Legislatures. Paper presented at the annual meeting of the American Political Science Association, Boston, Mass.

POWELL, L. W. 2009. *What Money Buys: The Influence of Campaign Contributions in State Legislatures*. Ann Arbor: University of Michigan Press.

SCHLOZMAN, K. L. and TIERNEY, J. T. 1986. *Organized Interests and American Democracy*. New York: Harper & Row.

SCHULTZ, D. A. 2002. *Money, Politics, and Campaign Finance Reform Law in the States*. Durham, N.C.: Carolina Academic Press.

SIMPSON, G. R. 2007. Lender Lobbying Blitz Abetted Mortgage Mess; Ameriquest Pressed for Changes in Laws; a Battle in New Jersey. *The Wall Street Journal*, December 31.

SORAUF, F. J. 1992. *Inside Campaign Finance: Myths and Realities*. New York: Yale University Press.

STRATMANN, T. 1991. What Do Campaign Contributions Buy? Deciphering Causal Effects of Money and Votes. *Southern Economic Journal*, 57/3: 606–20.

—— 2004. How Prices Matter in Politics: Returns to Campaign Advertising. Unpublished manuscript at <http://harrisschool.uchicago.edu/Academic/workshops/pol_econ_papers/Strat mann.pdf>.

—— 2005. Some Talk: Money in Politics. A (Partial) Review of the Literature. *Public Choice*, 124/1: 135–56.

THOMPSON, J. A., MONCRIEF, G. F., and CONGRESSIONAL QUARTERLY INC. 1998. *Campaign Finance in State Legislative Elections*. Washington, D.C.: Congressional Quarterly Inc.

VERBA, S., SCHLOZMAN, K. L., and BRADY, H. E. 1995. *Voice and Equality: Civic Voluntarism in American Politics*. Cambridge, Mass.: Harvard University Press.

WAWRO, G. 2001. A Panel Probit Analysis of Campaign Contributions and Roll-Call Votes. *American Journal of Political Science*, 45/3: 563–79.

WEISSMAN, S. R. and HASSAN, R. 2006. BCRA and 527 Groups. In *The Election After Reform: Money, Politics, and the Bipartisan Campaign Reform Act*, ed. M. J. Malbin. Lanham, Md.: Rowman & Littlefield.

WILCOX, C. 2005. Designing Campaign Finance Disclosure in the States: Tracing the Tributaries of Campaign Finance. *Election Law Journal*, 4: 371–86.

—— 2008. Internet Fundraising in 2008: A New Model? *The Forum*, 6/1: Article 6.

WITKO, C. 2006. PACs, Issue Context, and Congressional Decisionmaking. *Political Research Quarterly*, 59/2: 283–95.

WRIGHT, J. R. 1985. PACs, Contributions, and Roll Calls: An Organizational Perspective. *American Political Science Review*, 79/2: 400–14.

CHAPTER 34

....

REDISTRICTING

....

BERNARD GROFMAN

THOMAS L. BRUNELL

In modern democracies, virtually all decisions are made by elected representatives rather than by the direct vote of the citizens, although elements of direct democracy such as initiatives, referenda, and town meetings may also be found. But whether we are looking at direct democracy or representative democracy, to conduct an election we must be able to specify the set of voters eligible (or potentially eligible) to vote in that election. Today, almost all democratic elections take place within territorially defined units, with eligible voters some subset of those who "reside" in the constituency. While sometimes such constituencies are coextensive with some single political entity, e.g., a city, a county, a state, a nation, more commonly, when we have a city or county council or a national parliament, constituencies are a partition of that larger-scale political unit divided into a set of pieces that are mutually exclusive and logically exhaustive. In the US, the process of partitioning a given political unit into a pre-specified number of distinct constituencies is called *districting*; in the UK and other English-speaking areas, this process is called *boundary delimitation.*

Districting is a largely ignored component of the electoral process among ordinary citizens. In the US, voters blithely go to the polls and vote, at the same or different times, in elections for the US Senate, the US House of Representatives, State Senator, State Assembly Member, County Supervisor, Community College Trustee, Sewage District Representative, City Council member, etc., without worrying about the exact boundaries of the constituencies to which they have been assigned, or the nature of the overlap among them. Almost always the fight over how to draw constituency boundaries is a fight among political elites that takes place behind closed doors. Only the political elites recognize redistricting choices as having vital political consequences. In the US, the only real exceptions to the public's benign neglect of districting issues arise in situations where boundaries have direct consequences, e.g., parental activism when the issue is whether or not to split or combine school districts in a way that might significantly change the racial or ethnic composition of the schools their children attend.

To understand redistricting processes and consequences we may ask: "Who gets to make decisions about redistricting?"; "What are the types of criteria by which redistricting plans might be evaluated?"; and "Who benefits from a given plan?" We may think of these three questions as dealing with institutions, ideas, and interests, respectively (Schonhardt-Bailey 2006). Our review of these three questions will be restricted to the US, although we will sometimes indicate how districting practices in the US differ from those in other countries.

Except for what is needed to provide necessary context, our focus will be on the question of "Who benefits?" rather than on detailed description of redistricting rules or extended discussion of constitutional issues involving redistricting criteria. Moreover, beyond the specific question of who benefits from a particular plan, we emphasize broader questions about the intended and unintended consequences of redistricting choices by looking at some important outstanding empirical controversies in the political science literature on redistricting, e.g., about the longer-run consequences of the reapportionment revolution and the Voting Rights Act of 1965 for party strengths, the urban–rural balance, minority influence, and public policy choices; about the impact of redistricting practices on party polarization and political competition; and about the nature of tradeoffs among competing criteria.

INSTITUTIONS: "WHO GETS TO MAKE DECISIONS ABOUT REDISTRICTING?"

Technically, we may distinguish *districting* from *apportionment*, where the latter refers to the process of determining how many representatives a given (fixed) political unit is entitled to in the legislature. After the decennial census, the first step in the apportionment process for the US House of Representatives is to give one seat in the House to each of the fifty states; additional seats are allocated on the basis of population, taking into account the seats already allocated. After reapportionment, every state with more than one seat in the House of Representatives must redraw their congressional district lines based on the new population data. Because of state constitutional provisions, decennial redistricting for state legislatures and for most local political bodies is also required. In virtually all instances, there too US Census data is the basis for the redistricting.

There are three main redistricting alternatives in use: (1) having the legislature redistrict itself, (2) having a bipartisan commission, (3) having a non-partisan body (judges or civil servants) do the redistricting. In all of these cases, districting is supposed to conform to formal criteria that constrain the scope of line drawers. But the actual degree of restriction varies with the greatest constraints usually operating when courts draw lines.[1]

In the US, at both the congressional and state level, it is the first two options that initially dominate. For districts in the federal House of Representatives, in thirty-seven states the responsibility defaults to the legislature and the governor. For these states, redistricting is no different than passing a state law. The state legislators pass new maps and rely on the governor to sign them into law. In six states the responsibility falls to a commission, and seven states need not redistrict since they only have one member of the House. For state legislative redistricting, fourteen states have delegated responsibility to a commission while the other thirty-six rely on the governor and state legislature to come to an agreement on new legislative boundaries. In sum, fourteen states use a commission in the initial drafting process for congressional and/or legislative maps: Alaska (legislative), Arkansas (legislative), Arizona (both), Colorado (legislative), Hawaii (both), Idaho (both), Maine (advisory for both), Missouri (legislative), Montana (legislative), New Jersey (both), Ohio (legislative), Pennsylvania (legislative), Vermont (advisory for legislative), and Washington (both). But, in some of the states that do use commissions for redistricting the commissions serve in a strictly advisory capacity. Also, in most of the jurisdictions where a commission is used, the majority of commission members are chosen on a partisan basis.[2]

A common mantra is that modern-day redistricting allows representatives to pick their voters, rather than having voters pick their representatives. In most other democracies, "non-partisan" bureaucrats draw lines (see Handley and Grofman 2008). In the US, sitting legislators largely get to define the districts in which they will run for reelection—subject, however, to possible court challenges.

Since *Baker* v. *Carr* (1962), states can be compelled to redistrict in a timely fashion. Legal challenge to redistricting plans can also result from alleged violations of an equal population standard, or on grounds that the plan violates the minority protection standards of Section 2 of the Voting Rights Act of 1964 as amended in 1982 and 2007, or because the plan is alleged to be an egregious

---

[1] A fourth possibility, advocated by some reformers, is to specify a set of criteria that are so well-defined that a single best plan can be chosen. To reduce the power of the line drawers, advocates of this idea propose allowing any interested parties to submit alternative plans.

[2] For the section above we rely on information from the National Conference of State Legislatures (NCSL) See <http://www.ncsl.org/programs/legismgt/redistrict/com&alter.htm> as well as Bensen (2007).

partisan gerrymander, or because it allegedly makes race the predominant motive in redistricting, or because it violates some state-specific redistricting requirement. Moreover, in sixteen states, plans at all levels of government for all or part of the state are also subject to pre-clearance review by the US Department of Justice (DOJ) under Section 5 of the Voting Rights Act vis-à-vis their racial implications for *retrogression* in minority voting strength or for racially dilutive purpose, and these DOJ decisions can be appealed in federal court. Thus, in the US, to a degree unparalleled anywhere else in the world, the courts are omnipresent in redistricting, with virtually every state generating some litigation during the post-census decade.

IDEAS: "WHAT ARE THE CRITERIA BY WHICH REDISTRICTING IS TO BE JUDGED?"

A useful way to think about redistricting criteria is in terms of a fivefold division of criteria into ones based, respectively, on person (i.e., population), place (i.e., geography and existing political units), race (where we use race in a broad sense, as inclusive of ethnic, linguistic, and religious cleavages), political party, and candidate status (incumbent or not).

Person

The idea of population-based districting may be as American as apple pie, but only relatively recently has it come to be embodied in tough "one person, one vote" standards—albeit standards that differ across levels of government. US House districts must now be equal as is practicable—with plans rejected as unconstitutional whose districts differ by only a few hundred voters from ideal population size. For state legislatures, however, deviations of plus or minus 5 percentage points from ideal will, absent special factors, normally pass constitutional muster; while slightly higher deviations from perfect population equality have been allowed for some local redistrictings.

Place/Geography

Population-based representation is what most of us think of when we think of legislative representation, but it only takes a moment's reflection to realize that there is another principle of equally long standing and substantial contemporary impact, namely the representation of units of political geography, like states. Just as federal apportionment of the House and the districts that it gives rise to does not cross state boundaries, so by analogy, we might wish to preserve existing state subunit boundaries, such as those of cities and counties. Indeed, although population equality by and large is trumps, considerable concern for local subunit boundaries is still apparent in US redistricting case law to the extent it can be reconciled with other criteria. In particular, it is common to report how many "crossings" of subunit boundaries there are in proposed plans, i.e., on the one hand, how many districts in the plan contain population from more than one city or county and, on the other hand, how many different districts any given city or county finds pieces of itself within.

But, arguably, the most important place-related concern in districting is one that we normally give little thought to, since we take it for granted, namely contiguity. The technical definition of *contiguity* is that one can get from any part of the district to any other part of the district without leaving the district. The contiguity requirement is an important one insofar as it puts limits on the creativity of line drawers. Without such a requirement virtually any combination of voters, including the most extreme cases of gerrymandering, would be possible. Moreover, it is hard to imagine having districting based on territory, without imposing a contiguity requirement. Such a requirement is found in most state constitutions for legislative districts in the state (Grofman 1985) and, even when not formally stated, is often taken for granted as an implicit criterion for any viable redistricting plan. Nonetheless, while constituencies are normally based on contiguous territory, occasionally they are not. For example, in the US, because of historical patterns of annexation, some cities contain disconnected pieces. Also, the concept of contiguity may be problematic when the only connections between some parts of a district are by water.

While *contiguity* is perhaps the least controversial redistricting principle, even though there can be arguments about how it is to be operationalized in practice, its frequently twinned companion principle, *compactness*, is both more problematic and more controversial. The idea of compactness is not really a single idea but rather a family of concepts which are not necessarily highly correlated, including areal notions of compactness (districts that can be inscribed in small circles), perimeter notions of compactness (districts that do not have lots of small fingers jutting out), and population-density notions of compactness (districts whose population is concentrated close to the center of the district). Each type of compactness has a variety of different measures (Niemi et al. 1990).

Other place-related concerns include unnecessary crossings of "natural" rather than political boundaries, i.e., rivers or mountains; and concern for the preservation of *communities of interest* such as historic neighborhoods in a city, or coastal areas, or farming areas within a state. Another tack is to argue for preservation of existing boundaries (or as close to them as practicable) on the grounds that voters have, in effect, "grown accustomed to each other's faces" and to associating their representation with a district that has historically embedded and stable boundaries.[3]

Thus, even when we restrict ourselves to place-based concerns, we may find ourselves facing both measurement issues and conflicts among conflicting criteria.

Race

There are two sides to race-related criteria. On the one hand, we have criteria such as those that require us to eschew plans which have either the effect or purpose of being dilutive of minority voting strength or, on the affirmative side, call for race-related districting for benign motives, e.g., to achieve representation for historically underrepresented groups. On the other hand, we have the requirement imposed by the US Supreme Court in *Shaw* v. *Reno* 509 U.S. 630 (1993), and made more specific in subsequent cases, that race not be the predominant motive in districting. A jurisdiction must now thread between the Scylla of avoiding racial vote dilution and the Charybdis of improper reliance on racial consequences. And jurisdictions must weigh up this balance with only remarkably muddy guidance from the Supreme Court to assist it, since the standard for determining whether race is a predominant motive is not, in our view, well defined, and further confusion arises because the legal standards under which claims of vote dilution are tried varies across legal arenas.

In the case of direct constitutional challenges, there is a "totality of the circumstances" standard. For cases brought under Section 2 of the Voting Rights Act, the key standard is a three-pronged test laid down in *Thornburg* v. *Gingles* 478 U.S. 30 (1986). This test requires that voting be racially polarized, that minority candidates regularly lose as a result of a voting history of racial polarization, and that a single-member district remedial plan exists with at least one additional district in which minorities might gain representation wherein the minority is geographically compact. Under Section 5 of the Voting Rights Act, however, the relevant standard involves "retrogression" in minority voting strength, but how to measure retrogression is hotly debated. In *Georgia* v. *Ashcroft* 539 U.S. 461 (2003), the Supreme Court attempted to clarify the Section 5 standard by introducing a new test for minority influence, but this new test has been rejected as not representative of congressional intent in the extension of the Voting Rights Act that passed in 2006.

---

[3] For instance, in a redistricting case in Texas in the 2000 round of redistricting, an attorney was defending a plan that favored the Democrats by arguing that the districts in east Texas were not drawn to favor Democratic candidates but because the map-makers were simply making the districts look like the districts that existed in Texas in the 1950s.

Party

While the Supreme Court reversed earlier precedents to allow for the justiciability of partisan gerrymandering claims in *Bandemer* v. *Davis* 478 U.S. 109 (1986), it has never actually struck down a plan as a partisan gerrymander. On the other hand, in *Gaffney* v. *Cummings* 412 U.S. 735 (1973), the Court upheld the notion that promoting partisan fairness was a valid criterion to use in defending a plan against constitutional challenge.

In general, the Court has treated racial gerrymandering claims much more sympathetically than partisan gerrymandering claims by arguing (a) that the history of racial exclusion requires that the treatment of still stigmatized groups be given special scrutiny, and (b) that the cognizability and "permanence" of racial identities is different from the potential variability of partisan identifications. Moreover, while clear and precise standards have evolved for determining what constitutes a violation of one person, one vote at each of the various levels of government, and some aspects of the Court's test for racial vote dilution are relatively clear (notably the three-pronged test enunciated in *Thornburg* v. *Gingles*), there is no agreement among Supreme Court Justices as to the criteria to be used to determine when something constitutes an unconstitutional partisan gerrymander—and at least two Justices are convinced that no such animal exists.[4]

Candidate Status

Courts often treat protection of sitting incumbents as an acceptable factor in drawing electoral boundaries, especially if it can be argued that doing so creates a plan that provides partisan fairness (see *Gaffney* v. *Cummings*, 1973).

INTERESTS: "WHO BENEFITS?"

Just as we can divide redistricting criteria into those of person, place, party, candidate, and race, we can look at redistricting consequences in similar terms. The two basic mechanisms by which particular intended consequences can be achieved are malapportionment and line drawing, with the two basic gerrymandering mechanisms to cause wasted votes being *cracking* (fragmenting a

---

[4] A criterion that is usually discussed in terms of partisan representation is competitiveness. Brunell (2006, 2008) has advocated partisan homogeneity as a redistricting criterion designed to limit wasted votes and an aid in drawing fair plans.

group's vote), and *packing* (concentrating a group's vote in districts that it wins by very large margins). Another key technique in line drawing is what one of us has previously labeled *kidnapping* (moving district lines so as to place incumbents running for reelection in districts from which some or all of their support base have been excluded).[5] One form of this technique involves putting the home of more than one incumbent of a given party into the same district.

The Impact of Redistricting: Empirical Findings and ongoing Controversies

The Impact of the Reapportionment Revolution

It is hard to imagine any great degree of concern over malapportionment if all districts were random samples of the total population. Malapportionment has historically been the key tool to dilute the influence of urban voters. The reason why political scientists in the 1950s such as Gordon Baker found the failure to reapportion so repugnant was that it led to the dominance of state legislatures by rural interests and the overrepresentation of rural areas in Congress. Moreover, most political scientists of the time expected that changes in redistricting would benefit not just urban areas but also the Democratic party, whose support came disproportionately from big cities. However, this did not happen. We find urban areas and Democrats no better represented today in Congress than they were in 1960. However, there have been substantial gains in urban representation in some state legislatures—especially those, like California, which had state constitutional provisions in place putting a ceiling on the number of representatives to be assigned any given city or county that have now been struck down as violative of one person, one vote.

There is controversy about why, at the congressional level, neither urban areas nor Democrats were much benefited by the reapportionment revolution (Cox and Katz 2002) but a consensus seems to be emerging about the following facts (Brunell and Grofman 2008b). First, in the South and in some other parts of the country, Democrats were doing very well in rural areas, so that the loss of rural seats actually hurt Democrats. Second, population shifts away from rural areas since 1960 have led to suburban (and exurban) growth rather than growth in the big cities. Third,

---

[5] The effects of these mechanisms are, however, potentially strongly affected by choice of electoral rule (e.g., single-seat plurality versus multi-seat plurality versus some form of proportional representation).

during most of the past decades there have been powerful realigning trends away from the Democrats, especially in the South.

How Important is Control of the Line-drawing Process?

One important debate in the redistricting literature is over who should do redistricting.

A fundamental principle of political theory is that no person ought to be judge in his/her own case. Yet, in the US, the process of redrawing congressional and legislative electoral boundaries in the vast bulk of the states is done by elected officials in the state. Those who control redistricting can, in principle, shape its partisan and racial consequences and determine which particular incumbents are most likely to be reelected.

Concern over what is commonly characterized as the primarily partisan nature of the redistricting process in the US has led a number of "good government" reformers to try to take "politics out of redistricting," either (a) by eliminating the power of the legislature (and governor) to control line drawing and switching to a neutral/non-partisan process or (b) by seeking to impose such severe constraints on the process (e.g., based on so-called "neutral" redistricting criteria such as district compactness) that legislative discretion to gerrymander is supposedly severely limited. Issacharoff (2002, 601) has proposed creating a constitutional presumption against *any* redistricting practice entrusted to partisan political officials. And others have proposed a presumption against the lawfulness of any mid-decadal redistricting, a position that the Supreme Court rejected in a Texas congressional case.

At the other end of the continuum, however, are authors who believe that redistricting is best left to the political process, and that court intervention, at least with respect to issues of partisan gerrymandering, is likely to be counterproductive. Moreover, when we look to state-level initiatives designed to change the redistricting process, while proposed redistricting reforms are usually sold to voters as a matter of good government, the truth is that many of the supposed "reformers" (especially those providing the funding to support initiatives) have a covert partisan agenda. In states that are controlled by Democrats it is usually Republicans pushing to take redistricting out of the hands of the legislature; while in states that are controlled by Republicans it is the Democrats who are more likely to be the redistricting "reformers."

While the academic debate over who should control redistricting is substantially normative, at the heart of the debate are disagreements about how much control of the redistricting process matters. While the common perception is that partisan gerrymandering is the most common form of gerrymandering, incumbent protection gerrymanders in some circumstances are even more likely. Similarly, while the common perception is that racial gerrymandering is a recent phenomenon designed to create majority–minority districts that will elect minority candidates, this neglects the earlier history of racial gerrymandering in the South, where minority voters were used as "sandbags" to shore up the reelection chances of white Democrats.

The nature of the differences we expect to get between plans drawn in the political process and those done through commissions or courts depends upon many factors. The likely outcome of any political process for redistricting will depend heavily on whether or not there is unified party control of both the legislature and the governor's office, the absence of unified control making incumbency protection deals more likely. How commissions operate will depend heavily on the membership structure of the commission (especially whether it is simply a disguised form of partisan control) and whether or not supermajorities are required to pass plans. In commissions with partisan majorities and without supermajority requirements we expect to see plans similar to those drawn by legislatures, while supermajoritarian rules foster sweetheart deals to preserve incumbents and the existing party balance. The consequences of court involvement are affected by the nature of the redistricting litigation, with some cases only involving challenges to a few districts so that even taking into account spillover effects as neighboring districts get redrawn, the overall impact of a court's decision is limited.

Racial Representation

A key issue in both the academic and the legal debates about redistricting is over the creation of majority–minority districts. Here we will confine ourselves to the empirical rather than the normative or jurisprudential aspects of this topic. A basic empirical question is whether minority candidates can be elected from districts that are not majority–minority in character. Opponents of majority-minority districts claim that the level of racially polarized voting has now declined to the point that such districts are no longer needed. Although we certainly recognize changes in American racial attitudes—who could be blind to such changes after the election of Barack Obama—we continue to find that virtually all minority officeholders in partisan contests are elected from districts with combined minority populations (Black plus Hispanic plus Native American) sufficient to control the outcome in the Democratic primary, with a limited amount of non-Hispanic white crossover voting then allowing for victory in the general election; and the bulk of minority officeholders are still elected from districts where the majority of the electorate in the general election is itself minority (Grofman, Handley, and Lublin 2001; Handley, Grofman, and Arden 1998; Lublin et al. 2008).

Party Representation

Partisanship overshadows the process of redistricting to such an extent that, in the popular view, partisan gerrymandering has become synonymous with redistricting. The idea that partisan control matters a lot is enhanced by examples such as the congressional re-redistricting in Texas. When they gained unified control of the state, Republicans were able to undo a Democratic-leaning gerrymander from the 1990s. The new plan delivered six additional seats in the House for the Republicans in the 2004 election and the GOP was able to unseat several long-time Democratic lawmakers like Stenholm and Frost.

But there are a number of reasons to be skeptical about the overall importance of partisan gerrymandering. First, in the sometimes 50 percent or so of the cases where we have divided control of the state, partisan gerrymandering is an unlikely outcome.[6] Second, at the national level, partisan gerrymanders in one direction may be largely counterbalanced by partisan gerrymandering by the other party in other states. Third, massive electoral tides (as in 2006) may erode (though not eliminate) the effects of most partisan gerrymandering. Relatedly, if a party gets too greedy they could even draw what Grofman and Brunell (2005) have termed "dummymanders," i.e., plans drawn by one party that actually look like partisan gerrymanders drawn in favor of the other party. Here, victory margins are so thin in so many seats (or election success is too closely tied to the continued stay in office of the present incumbent) that the party suffers in a future election over the course of the decade when vote swings and/or incumbent retirements end up costing the party (most of) those seats and control of the legislature or of a majority of the congressional delegation in the state.

Incumbency Protection Gerrymanders and Political Competition

As we have emphasized, in states that lack unified party control (and there were twenty-eight of these in the 2000 redistricting round), we expect that we will see a sweetheart deal between the parties reflecting bipartisan agreement among incumbents or among risk-averse political leaders of both major parties who see protecting incumbents as a safe bet for perpetuating existing power divisions within a legislature or congressional delegation. Absent such agreements, where there is political control of the districting process, the state will be unable to pass a redistricting plan—leaving matters to the courts to resolve. Remarkably, however,

---

[6] New York, however, did provide us the example of a long-lasting sweetheart deal in which the Republicans were given the right to redistrict the state senate, while Democrats were given the lower chamber to redistrict. Showing the power of redistricting, this resulted in each party having a decades-long lock on its branch of the legislature that was not broken until 2008.

the partisan vote distributions we expect to find in bipartisan gerrymanders look a lot like those we would expect to find in well-crafted partisan gerrymanders. Both types of plans create lots of districts that are very safe (Owen and Grofman 1988).

We expect to see more competitiveness in the districts drawn by courts than in those drawn by legislatures or bipartisan commissions, and there is evidence for House seats that court-drawn plans show a higher level of electoral responsiveness (swing ratio) than plans drawn in other ways (Gelman and King 1994), although one article that examines this relationship for state legislative districts finds no statistically significant differences (Lublin and Mcdonald 2006).

Tradeoffs Among Criteria

Here we will focus on four particularly important tradeoffs.

Population Equality Versus Geography

The tradeoff between population equality and various notions of geographic representation was at the core of the one person, one vote revolution. In Justice Frankfurter's view, choosing between these population-based and other forms of representation (or even assigning a relative weighting of them) was a political decision that courts should keep out of.

The US places far more weight on mathematically exact population equality than any other democracy (Handley 2008; Handley and Grofman 2008). Indeed, especially as it applies to congressional districting, the OPOV doctrine has been pushed to the point of absurdity (cf. Cain and Butler 1992). First, the accuracy of census data is limited, and population equality to within less than 1 percent (or even less than 2 percent) is illusory. Second, the census is only a snapshot and changes in population numbers and distribution continue to take place. Finally, no matter how perfectly we equalize the population within the states (and some states had House districts which differed from one another in total population by at most one *person*, as judged by the 2000 census), due to lumpiness in apportionment, we will never get strict population equality across all districts. In fact, the largest House district has been between 1.5 and 1.7 times more populous than the smallest for several decades. In our view, were the US courts to take a more sensible view of what population equality should mean (or were Congress to legislate its own standards for the House), the conflict between geographic and population-based criteria could be substantially diminished.[7]

---

[7] The one positive aspect of zero population deviations is that it is the only non-arbitrary level of acceptable deviations.

Partisan and Racial Representation versus Geographic Criteria

Districts drawn in tortured shapes inherently raise the suspicions of voters and politicians about gerrymandering motives. Governor Schwarzenegger remarked that some of the California congressional districts drawn in 2002 "looked like they had been drawn by a drunk with an Etch-a-Sketch." Oddly shaped districts also give rise to memorable characterizations: "Bug splat," "Bullwinkle," "Upside-down Chinese Pagoda," "Supine Seahorse," and, of course, Governor Gerry's infamous salamander district immortalized as a "Gerrymander," are all names given to districts that are not regular in shape. Some of the majority-minority districts drawn in the 1990s, including North Carolina's 12th congressional district challenged in *Shaw* v. *Reno*, were downright ugly in shape.

However, the commonly held view that reliance on formal criteria such as compactness (or equal population) can prevent gerrymandering is simply wrong. While lack of compactness may be a critical signal for caution, and may even be undesirable in and of itself under certain circumstances, partisan gerrymandering is fundamentally about the translation of votes into seats, not about shapes *per se*. And perhaps most importantly, compactness may come into conflict with the desire to keep together racial or ethnic communities of interest whose population is not arrayed in a geographically pretty pattern.

Partisan Representation versus Racial Representation

Another debate in the social science literature is about the extent to which majority-minority districts created pursuant to (or in anticipation of) voting rights litigation led to Democratic losses at the congressional and state legislative level in the South. The "bleaching" of neighboring districts by concentrating black (or Hispanic) voters in majority-minority districts can have major consequences for Democratic chances, especially if, as is often the case, the non-Hispanic white voters in these majority-minority districts are heavily Democratic as well, leading to districts in which very large numbers of Democratic votes are being wasted (Grofman and Handley 1998). Nonetheless, in our view, partisan outcomes in most states, both those inside and outside the South, have been affected more by realigning trends than by redistricting.

Also, the conflicts between racial and partisan representation have been exaggerated. First, as it became harder for white Democrats to compete successfully in the non-border South, at the congressional level the black seats became most of the few where Democrats could win. Second, and more generally, once we recognize that it is possible for minority candidates to win if minority voters control the Democratic primary and can win the general election with limited crossover support from non-Hispanic whites, then we can try to craft districts which allow for racial representation without unnecessarily wasting Democrat votes (Grofman, Handley, and Lublin 2001; Lublin et al. 2008).

Racial Representation versus Policy Influence

Opponents of racially motivated districting have argued that creating majority-minority districts ultimately harms black and Hispanic voters because it diminishes their overall influence on policy outcomes, and that minorities would be better off in districts with 20–40 percent minority population, where they could be influential. Our view (see Grofman 2006 and references therein) is that this claim is almost entirely wrong. Minority legislators often offer representation for minority interests that is distinct from what non-minority legislators offer. And one key fact that needs to be taken into account is how likely a given level of minority population is to translate into the election of a legislator sympathetic to minority interests. There is absolutely no reason to believe that a given level of minority population in the district will have the same effect on the policy choices of a Democratic representative as on a Republican representative from that district.

However, we need to be sensitive to tipping-point effects: in general, minority policy influence is enhanced by additional minority representation, but that changes if the spillover effects on neighboring districts of minority representational gains is to tip a legislature into Republican control. But once a legislature is under Republican control, minority influence should still be enhanced by a minority presence in the legislature that is harder to ignore and more likely to be insistent on pursuing issues of special concern to minorities.

Long-Term Redistricting Effects

Political Competition

After a redistricting we expect elections to be, on average, a bit more competitive and for the overall level of responsiveness of the system (i.e., the swing ratio) to go up (Gelman and King 1994; Lublin and McDonald 2006). Despite the number of incumbent protection plans, decennial redistricting does rearrange electoral lines, thus making many incumbents *less* safe because they have new constituents who lack a history of supporting them, or even a less favorable district in terms of overall partisan balance—which makes it more attractive for high-quality challengers to emerge in an attempt to unseat the incumbent. But, due to incumbency advantage effects and name recognition effects, over the course of a decennial redistricting, aggregate-level responsiveness decreases.

Party Polarization

It is common journalistic wisdom that redistricting is an important cause of the extreme ideological polarization between the two parties found in the US House of Representatives and in many state legislatures. The supposed mechanism is that increasingly sophisticated computer-based gerrymandering, whether partisan or bipartisan in nature, tends to create safe seats, and safe seats are allegedly the breeding ground of ideological extremism. Our own work (see especially Brunell and Grofman, 2008a, 2008b), along with that of a number of other scholars, casts doubt on this simplistic story.

First, ideological polarization is found in the Senate, where no redistricting takes place, and not just in the House. Moreover, polarization in the Senate has grown despite the fact that Senate seats have grown only marginally safer, and have not become more politically homogeneous. Second, even though there is evidence supporting the notion that districts are more lopsidedly Democratic or lopsidedly Republican in electoral terms than they once were, when we look at the Poole–Rosenthal DW-NOMINATE scores[8] (first dimension) in the House we find no relationship between the size of the ideological gap between Democratic and Republican House members elected from districts with some identical (near-identical) levels of support for the Democratic presidential nominee and how strong the Democratic presidential vote in that district may have been. In other words, in recent congresses, while both Republican liberalism and Democratic liberalism falls as the district becomes more Republican in its presidential voting patterns, the regression lines for each party have *virtually identical slopes*, and thus the ideological gap between the parties remains roughly constant (and large), even in districts which at the presidential level are highly competitive between the two parties.

FUTURE RESEARCH AVENUES

Because redistricting lies at the intersection of normative and empirical concerns about representation, and because it represents a clash of ideas and of interests, as mediated by institutional choices, despite the development of a growing body of research there are still many interesting questions to study.

Here we identify five areas for future research.

---

[8] These scores are generated by multidimensional scaling of roll call votes in the U.S. Congress.

In the US, social scientists play a key role both in the line-drawing process, and perhaps even more importantly, in the litigation following the decennial line-drawing process. The role of social science (and social scientists) in the redistricting process appears much more vital in the US than in any other country because of the extremely litigious nature of the redistricting process in the US along with the continuing evolution in redistricting case law, because of there being so many different stages in which plans may be amended prior to their actual implementation, and because the line between constitutional law and social science gets blurry indeed when terms of art in the US redistricting case law include one person, one vote, partisan gerrymandering, racial vote dilution, racially polarized voting, geographic compactness, non-retrogression in minority voting strength, minority legislative influence, etc. Nonetheless, with a handful of exceptions, most of which have dealt with the measurement of racially polarized voting, there is little work on the impact of social science research, expert witness testimony, and amici briefs on redistricting and voting rights case law. This seems to us a topic worth studying.

Second, there is a need to demonstrate the reliability of social science tools for demonstrating the presence and level of partisan gerrymandering (Grofman and King 2007). Ideally we would like to see longitudinal studies that seek to predict the durability and magnitude of partisan gerrymanders at the time a plan is put into place, and which then repeat the same analysis after the first election, and then continue to monitor election outcomes to see how well the model demonstrates predictive fit (of an "if, then" sort).

Third, we need more work that looks at redistricting consequences in partisan elections using plurality single-seat districts in contests below the level of the US House: at the state, county, and municipal level.

A fourth area for future research deals with the impact of different redistricting mechanisms on partisan and racial representation and on competitiveness. Not all commissions are equal; not all ostensibly non-partisan arrangements really are such. There is remarkably little empirical work that looks at the more subtle differences among commission forms to try to tease out their implications for the kinds of redistricting choices that will be made (see, however, Bensen 2007).

A fifth issue is an old one, but relatively little recent empirical work on it has been done, namely "How can we estimate the long run impact of post–*Baker* v. *Carr* changes in redistricting rules on policy choices?" (See, however, Ansolabehere, Gerber, and Snyder, 2002; Cox and Katz, 2002.)

If you are not interested in redistricting, you must not be interested in politics, or in democratic theory.

References

Ansolabehere, S., Gerber, A., and Snyder, J. 2002. Equal Votes, Equal Money: Court-Ordered Redistricting and Public Expenditures in the American States. *American Political Science Review*, 96/4: 767–77.

Bensen, C. 2007. Elections . . . Shall Be Described in Each State by the Legislature Thereof: Who Should Draw the Maps: Legislatures or Commissions? Paper Presented at the Annual Meeting of the National Conference of State Legislatures, August 2007.

Brunell, T. L. 2006. Rethinking Redistricting: How Drawing Uncompetitive Districts Eliminates Gerrymanders, Enhances Representation, and Improves Attitudes Toward Congress. *PS: Political Science & Politics*, 39/1: 77–86.

—— 2008. *Redistricting and Representation: Why Competitive Elections are Bad for America*. New York: Routledge.

—— and Grofman, B. 2008a. Evaluating the Impact of Redistricting on District Homogeneity, Political Competition, and Political Extremism in the U.S. House of Representatives, 1962–2002. In *Designing Democratic Government*, ed. M. Levi and J. Johnson. New York: Russell Sage Foundation.

—— —— 2008b. The Partisan Consequences of *Baker v. Carr* and the One Person, One Vote Revolution. In *Redistricting in Comparative Perspective*, ed. L. Handley and B. Grofman. New York and London: Oxford University Press.

Cain, B. and Butler, D. 1992. *Congressional Redistricting: Comparative and Theoretical Perspectives*. New York: Macmillan Publishing Company.

Cox, G. and Katz, J. 2002. *Elbridge Gerry's Salamander: The Electoral Consequences of the Reapportionment Revolution*. Cambridge: Cambridge University Press.

Gelman, A. and King, G. 1994. Enhancing Democracy Through Legislative Redistricting. *American Political Science Review*, 88/3: 541–59.

Grofman, B. 1985. Criteria for Districting: A Social Science Perspective. *UCLA Law Review*, 33/1: 77–184.

—— 2006. Operationalizing the Section 5 Retrogression Standard of the Voting Rights Act in the Light of Georgia v. Ashcroft: Social Science Perspectives on Minority Influence, Opportunity and Control. *Election Law Journal*, 5/3: 250–82.

—— and Brunell, T. L. 2005. The Art of the Dummymander: The Impact of Recent Redistrictings on the Partisan Makeup of Southern House Seats. In *Redistricting in the New Millennium*, ed. P. Galderisi. New York: Lexington Books.

—— and Handley, L. 1998. Estimating the Impact of Voting-Rights-Act-Related Districting on Democratic Strength in the U.S. House of Representatives. In *Race and Redistricting in the 1990s*, ed. B. Grofman. New York: Agathon Press.

—— —— and Lublin, D. 2001. Drawing Effective Minority Districts: A Conceptual Framework and Some Empirical Evidence. *North Carolina Law Review*, 79: 1383–430.

—— and King, G. 2007. Partisan Symmetry and the Test for Gerrymandering Claims after *LULAC v. Perry*. *Election Law Journal*, 6/1: 2–35.

Handley, L. 2008. A Comparative Survey of Structures and Criteria for Boundary Delimitation. In *Redistricting in Comparative Perspective*, L. Handley and B. Grofman. Oxford: Oxford University Press.

—— and Grofman, B. (eds.) 2008. *Redistricting in Comparative Perspective*. Oxford: Oxford University Press.

HANDLEY, L. and ARDEN, W. 1998. Electing Minority-Preferred Candidates to Legislative Office: The Relationship Between Minority Percentages in Districts and the Election of Minority-Preferred Candidates. In *Race and Redistricting in the 1990s*, ed. B. Grofman. New York: Agathon Press.

ISSACHAROFF, S. 2002. Gerrymandering and Political Cartels. *Harvard Law Review*, 116: 593–648.

LUBLIN, D. and McDONALD, M. P. 2006. Is It Time to Draw the Line? The Impact of Redistricting on Competition in State House Elections. *Election Law Journal*, 5/2: 144–57.

—— BRUNELL, T., GROFMAN, B., and HANDLEY, L. 2008. Has the Voting Rights Act Outlived Its Usefulness? In a Word, No! *Legislative Studies Quarterly*, 34/4.

NIEMI, R. G., GROFMAN, B., CARLUCCI, C., and HOFELLER, T. 1990. Measuring Compactness and the Role of a Compactness Standard in a test for Partisan and Racial Gerrymandering. *Journal of Politics*, 52/4: 1155–81.

OWEN, G. and GROFMAN, B. N. 1988. Optimal Partisan Gerrymandering. *Political Geography Quarterly*, 7/1: 5–22.

SCHONHARDT-BAILEY, C. 2006. *From the Corn Laws to Free Trade: Interests, Ideas and Institutions in Historical Perspective*. Cambridge and London: MIT Press.

....

CHAPTER 35

AMERICAN ELECTORAL PRACTICES IN COMPARATIVE PERSPECTIVE

....

MARK N. FRANKLIN
TILL WEBER

NOTWITHSTANDING the important early role of foreign visitors to the US (Alexis de Toqueville, Lord Bryce), modern political science is quintessentially an American discipline. Most of the world's political scientists are Americans and most of them are Americanists—the study of American politics and government has received by far the most scholarly attention. It is thus with some trepidation that we take, in this chapter, a comparative perspective on American elections and voting. This is not so much a chapter about institutions as it is a chapter about how electoral institutions and other relevant rules affect behavior—the word "practices" in the title refers to both types of practice.

We do not attempt to be exhaustive. Rather, we focus on three areas in which American elections have features that are illuminated by voting behavior in countries with somewhat different features. These features are multiple elections, separated powers, and the locality rule. By multiple elections we mean not just the multiplicity of elections (the fact that there are elections in the US every year) but also simultaneous elections for multiple offices. This results in some offices being filled by elections that can be held in very different contextual circumstances from one election to the next (we are thinking especially of elections to the House of Representatives, which are held concurrently with presidential elections and also in the middle of the presidential term of office). By separated powers we mean more than just the separate US executive. As Donald Lutz (2006) has pointed out, it is a mistake to focus on the presidential aspect of the American system of government. A separate executive is not that unusual in comparative perspective, and the American presidency is not that powerful. What is unusual in the American case is the extent and multiplicity of the ways in which sources of political power are split—within as well as between the branches of government. Finally, we bring up the locality rule because it is a feature apparently unique to the American system of elections that we believe to have effects far beyond those generally attributed to it.

Although our focus is on these three areas in which American institutions are distinctively different from those in other countries, we will organize this chapter not according to those features but in terms of the aspects of electoral behavior that we feel to be most affected by them. These are split-ticket voting (and what we believe to be the associated phenomena of party identification and electoral realignments), the cycle of elections (and the associated phenomenon of midterm loss), and low voter turnout. We will start with the last of these.

Low Voter Turnout

The low rate of voter turnout in American elections is a notorious blot on the record of democracy in America. Turnout in presidential elections seldom exceeds 50 percent these days (though recent increases are encouraging), and turnout in congressional elections is always far lower. By contrast, other established democracies (with the exception of present-day Switzerland) see turnout in the 60 to 90 percent range, with a 1945–1999 overall average (including Switzerland and the United States) of 81.4 percent (M. Franklin 2004, 11). Many reasons have been adduced—most frequently the additional costs of voting brought about by registration requirements (which in other countries are generally born by the state), the large number of elections (which might be thought to induce voter fatigue), and the large number of safe (and often unopposed) congressional districts in which the outcome is a foregone conclusion.

None of these proposed reasons for low US voter turnout has been widely accepted as conclusive. Voluntary voter registration is not unique to the United States—it is also a feature of French elections, but turnout there averages more than 25 percentage points higher. Moreover, various attempts to estimate the actual effects of voter registration laws, confirmed by research on the "motor voter" reforms (D. Franklin and Grier 1997), have resulted in estimates between 5 and 8 percent (Mitchell and Wlezien 1995)—far too little. Voter fatigue might play a part, but even if we base our count of voters on those who report "regularly voting," turnout does not rise very much (Verba, Schlozman, and Brady 1995, 72). The role of safe districts is undermined by the fact that any change in turnout that might result from a safe district becoming competitive has never, to the best of our knowledge, been noticed. Indeed, none of these factors has received much attention in the US voter turnout literature, which has focused more on factors that might explain differences between individual voters than on factors that might explain differences between individual US elections. But this focus on "things about voters" led to another set of puzzles, because the factors that have most weight in explaining differences between individuals are education and income, both of which saw considerable increases in the US even while turnout was declining.

The book *Voter Turnout and the Dynamics of Electoral Competition in Established Democracies Since 1945* by M. Franklin (2004) addressed these questions on the basis of a number of theoretical and methodological innovations, of which the most important one was to divide the electorates of established democracies into two groups: a group of older citizens whose voting habits are presumed to be relatively fixed (habitual voters and habitual non-voters) and another group of younger voters whose habits are presumed not to be set. Among citizens of the former type (those mostly set in their ways), the relative size of the habitual voting group (as compared with the group of habitual non-voters) was found to largely determine the turnout level of different countries—the United States and Switzerland have low turnout because many of their citizens are set in the habit of non-voting. Long-term turnout evolution derives from changes in the relative size of this group, brought about by generational replacement (also cf. Flickinger and Studlar 2007). It is citizens of the other type (young adults) who are largely responsible for short-term turnout variations. Among young adults we see considerable responsiveness to factors that change from election to election, particularly factors associated with electoral competition (also cf. Johnston, Matthews, and Bittner 2007). The extent of short-term responsiveness is a joint product of the factors influencing voter turnout and the size of the group that is responding to those factors. So, ultimately, these effects are limited by the number of young adults. Preliminary research has established that this group comprises voters facing one of their first three major electoral contests (presidential elections in the US, parliamentary elections elsewhere)—in other words, citizens between their eighteenth and thirty-fourth birthdays.

Americanists will not find this story completely unfamiliar. Recent US turnout literature has more than once made the point that properly specified models of electoral participation should calculate effects separately for those who are likely to vote and those who are not, and the idea of a habitual basis to the voting act has received increasing attention (Gerber, Green and Shachar 2003; Green and Shachar 2000; Hillygus 2005; Plutzer 2002). It is only a small step from there to an understanding that influences on the relative size of the group of future habitual voters will have long-term consequences for turnout. Such effects are not in fact very special. They can be anything that changes the proportion of voters among young adults—the source from which the pool of future habitual voters is drawn. If the source increases its turnout rate so, in due course, will the pool that it feeds. If turnout among young adults is reduced, and stays consistently lower, eventually the entire electorate will be voting at that lower rate. But these long-term effects require consistent (or at least unreversed) movement in a given direction among young voters. On this logic, the rise in turnout among young adults in the 2000, 2004, and 2008 elections will have long-term consequences for US turnout even if turnout among new voters in 2012 falls again to pre-2000 levels.

Probably the most important implication flowing from this two-stage conception of turnout evolution is that turnout for the electorate as a whole can change only by small degrees, even when turnout among young adults is quite dramatically affected by some change in the electoral context. This provides an explanation for the anomaly noted earlier—that a district can move from uncompetitive to competitive without any noticeable immediate effect on turnout.

This view of voter turnout as having short-term and long-term components brings with it a new way to think about low and (until recently) declining turnout in the United States. M. Franklin (2004, 98–111) argued that low turnout in the US stems from two quite separate sources. First, there is a long-term institutional component deriving from the extreme extent of separated powers (cf. Lutz 2006). This component will have had its effects from the dawn of the Republic by limiting the linkage between election outcomes and policy making. In countries where the complexion of the government directly affects policy, because the government is supported by a majority of seats in a parliament, governments can be held accountable for implementing promised programs, yielding what Powell (2000, 122) called "responsiveness in choosing policymakers." When this institutional factor changes, as happened in Malta and Switzerland in the past fifty years, we see ensuing changes in turnout (M. Franklin 2004, 129–38). We also see US turnout responding to minor changes in the extent of separation of powers, in the guise of divided government (M. Franklin and Hirczy de Mino 1998).

Second, there is a political component which derives from the competitiveness (or lack of it) in US congressional elections. The average margin of victory in congressional races rose between 1892 and 1904, apparently due to the 1896 realignment (Kleppner 1982), and remained consistently high for long enough to engage the motor of long-term turnout change, so that turnout declined progressively until 1920 (M. Franklin 2004, 110). From then until 1960, change in competitiveness of congressional races went into reverse, with districts becoming increasingly competitive, and national turnout rose as short-term changes moved progressively in this new direction, again invoking long-term forces. After 1960 there was a renewed increase in the average margin of victory in Congressional races, associated with the "vanishing marginals" among congressional districts (Fiorina 1977; Mayhew 1974), and turnout in these races fell accordingly (cf. J. Campbell and Jurek 2003). Because these shifts in House margins were progressive and gradual, the initially short-term changes in turnout among younger voters became locked in by repeated reaffirmation and moved progressively into older segments of the electorate with generational replacement.

Because the shifts in each direction lasted so long, almost the entire electorate was replaced during each of the three cycles before the next switch in the evolution of district competition started. This provided virtually perfect translation of short-term into long-term effects. The overall correlation between House margin of victory and turnout during the period from 1840 to 1999 is a spectacular 0.95, and House margin appears to be by far the dominant factor in presidential turnout, too (M. Franklin 2004, 109f.).

Not much can be done about the US separation of powers. It is built into the system and apparently limits the extent of possible US turnout to little above the 80 percent that was regularly seen in nineteenth-century US presidential elections. This level would place US turnout about on a par with average turnout among established democracies. Lack of competition in congressional elections appears uniquely American and is far more troubling. Also unique to the American case is the most popular of proposed solutions—term limits (recently ruled out by Supreme Court decision). This understandable reaction by an irate citizenry to the apparent ability of House members to remain indefinitely in office was quite misguided. It arose from the observation that the only times we see real competition for such races is when there is no incumbent running. But the real problem is the lack of competition in races where incumbents *are* running. In other countries incumbency is no insurance against electoral defeat.[1] If US incumbents had been more readily defeated then there would have been no call for term limits. The natural operations of electoral democracy would yield a selection mechanism that replaced less popular incumbents and ensured a general rise in the level of competence in the legislature, rewarding the best of those experienced with governing. Term limitations only level the playing field by ensuring an equal lack of experience by all—not a recipe for good government. So we need to focus on the

---

[1] Small incumbency effects are documented in Britain and Japan (Cain, Ferejohn, and Fiorina 1987; Hayama 1992; Katz and King 1999). But Gaines (1998) finds virtually no British incumbency effect; nor do such effects appear to be mentioned in the literature on legislative elections elsewhere.

reasons for lack of electoral competition in those House races that are contested by incumbent legislators.

First and foremost, in our opinion, is the locality rule. This rule requiring US congressional candidates to be long-time residents of the districts that they contest appears unexceptionable, and no American political scientist, to the best of our knowledge, has proposed its abolition. Yet we think its consequences are more far-reaching than is generally recognized (cf. Bradshaw and Pring 1982, 88; Burns and Peltason 1960, 421). In the days when Abraham Lincoln was prevented from seeking a second congressional term by the then widespread practice of limiting all congressmen to two years in Washington, the locality rule had only beneficial consequences in ensuring attentiveness to local concerns. But once it became common for congressmen to seek reelection, their monopoly on name recognition and other benefits flowing from incumbency gave sitting congressmen an enormous advantage (e.g., Levitt and Wolfram 1997). In other countries with district-based electoral systems, such as Britain, it is often customary for candidates to undertake to reside in the district if elected—such promises are believed to yield electoral advantages—but the requirement that they already reside there is lacking. This means that an experienced politician can easily find herself in a contest with another politician who gained equivalent experience elsewhere, breaking the monopoly on advantages flowing from incumbency.

There are other reasons for the lack of competition in congressional races, most notably the common practice of drawing congressional boundaries to benefit incumbents, but these other influences would be less potent (and perhaps less frequent) were incumbency itself to be less potent an electoral advantage. The advantages of incumbency, it seems to us, arise almost uniquely from the locality rule, either directly or indirectly. We have done no research on this topic, but it is one that cries out for attention, perhaps taking advantage of the fact that there are areas within the United States (such as New York City) where the locality rule is not enforced. It has no constitutional basis (except for the requirement that members of Congress be residents of the states in which their districts are located) and would be far easier to remove than term limits would be to introduce.

PARTY IDENTIFICATION AND
SPLIT-TICKET VOTING

Party identification is a concept developed to account for the fact that American voters appear to evince a loyalty to party that goes beyond merely voting for it (A. Campbell et al. 1960). This identification appears to serve as a "home base" to which voters return after any temporary defection. More importantly, even those who did not vote generally profess a party identification (or at least a leaning towards a party), making it easier to analyze US partisanship than US voting behavior. However, the concept does not travel well outside the United States. Though Butler and Stokes (1969) did find widespread party identification in Britain, later research over European countries more generally found that far more people reported having voted than reported a party identification (Budge, Crewe, and Farlie 1976)—and that party identification (when reported) was no more stable than party choice. Because party identification is not a very helpful concept outside the United States, comparativists have been led to develop alternative but functionally equivalent concepts. One is the concept of "closeness" to party, which performs better but still leaves us with far more voters than people who report feeling close to any party. If closeness, like party identification, is conceived as a variable antecedent to the vote in causal sequence (as party identification is mostly conceived in studies of US voting behavior), we face a significant anomaly. How can party identification be a cause of something that is observed more frequently than the cause itself? And if party identification (or closeness) cannot be conceived as a cause of voting choice in other countries, why does it serve as such in the United States?

We would like to suggest that an important role is played by the multiplicity of elections. Europeans seldom find themselves voting in more than one election at the same time and thus seldom if ever have the opportunity to cast a ballot for different parties at the same time—to "split their ticket" in American parlance.[2] It seems plausible that if such opportunities were to be introduced and if this were to result in split-ticket voting on the American model, European voters might well start to make more frequent use of a concept like party identification, and failures to respond to the standard party-identification question might decline. However, few comparativists would see such a development as evidence of a newly discovered cause of voting behavior. Rather, many would see it as a simplifying concept used as a guiding principle for voting decisions of lesser salience. Taking the same view in the American case would help to make sense of the somewhat paradoxical fact that willingness to claim a partisanship (or at least to lean in one direction or the other) among American voters is higher among those who split their tickets (almost 89 percent) than among those who vote a straight ticket (only 84 percent).[3]

How can we distinguish between these two possible explanations: party identification as a concept in people's heads which is prior to their voting choice and party identification as a descriptive term used by voters to indicate a habitual preference?

---

[2] Exactly why American voters are prone to vote differently for different offices is not central to our concerns in this chapter, but will be touched upon in the next section.

[3] This highly significant difference varies from year to year. It is the average found, from 1952 to 2004, in the ANES cumulative file.

Evidently this is an empirical question, which could be addressed in a variety of ways; but, to the best of our knowledge, not since the work of Markus and Converse (1979) and C. Franklin and Jackson (1983) have Americanists addressed the question of the direction of causality in regard to party identification and the vote. There are other reasons for supposing that voting for particular parties becomes habitual with the passage of time, as we will see in a later section of this chapter.

The central point, however, is the importance of multiple elections and the opportunity they provide for split-ticket voting. This feature of the American political landscape has implications that go far beyond its possible role in giving rise to party identification separate from actual party choice. Indeed, the phenomenon plays a role in two more topics that will be covered in this chapter—midterm loss and electoral realignments.

MIDTERM LOSS

Midterm congressional elections happen in different contextual circumstances than "on-year" congressional elections. The president's party generally loses votes (and often seats) at such elections, a phenomenon known as "midterm loss." Much work has been done by US political scientists (and some others) on this phenomenon, but it is usually treated as purely American. Standard explanations for midterm loss tailored to the US case such as "surge and decline" (A. Campbell 1960; J. Campbell 1993)[4] or "balancing" (Alesina and Rosenthal 1995; Fiorina 1992)[5] have hardly any place in the literature of comparative elections.

Ignored by most Americanists is the fact that in many countries similar phenomena can be found. To a comparativist's eyes, midterm congressional elections in the US are particular examples of what elsewhere are called second-order elections—a term coined by Reif and Schmitt (1980) to denote elections at which national executive power is not at stake. This term contrasts such elections with first-order elections, which serve to determine the political complexion of the executive. In the US, of course, executive power is technically speaking not at stake at congressional elections, since Congress does not appoint the president as parliaments appoint prime ministers in most established democracies. Still, it seems clear that people vote differently in congressional elections that occur on the

---

[4] The idea that there is a "normal vote" that shows itself in midterm elections, but that a "surge" in support for a presidential candidate will cause deviations from that normal vote at presidential elections.

[5] The idea that voters, being more centrist than the politicians they elect, try to ensure centrist policies by voting at midterm to balance the outcome of the previous presidential election.

same day as presidential elections than they do at midterm congressional elections. Turnout is higher, for one thing (roughly twice as high on average), suggesting a larger electorate with possibly a slightly different complexion. Apparently people are drawn to the polls in a presidential election who would have stayed at home for a merely congressional election—and while they are voting for a president they cast a congressional ballot as well. Moreover, such individuals tend to vote for the same party as the party they vote for in the concurrent presidential election (A. Campbell 1960): there is "spillover" from one electoral arena to the other. So the fact that the ballots for President and Congress are technically separate does not prevent individuals from displaying behavioral patterns that are similar to those found in first-order elections elsewhere.

Various attempts to apply either surge and decline (Marsh 2007) or balancing (Carrubba and Timpone 2005) to second-order elections in parliamentary systems have not succeeded in displacing second-order theory as a preferred explanation for features of these elections. So the question arises whether second-order theory would also do better in explaining midterm loss. First-order behavior is closely linked to national electoral concerns, which are clearly a feature of presidential elections in the United States, distinguishing them from state and local elections and midterm congressional elections as well. This being the case, second-order elections theory should provide a good explanation for midterm loss, leaving no need for a specifically US explanation.

The critical distinction between elections of each order lies in considerations that pertain to where executive office is at stake. Foremost among these is the need to elect a government. In parliamentary regimes this gives rise to strategic incentives that would not exist if executive power were not at stake. In particular, other things being equal, it pays to support a larger party rather than a smaller party, since the larger party is more likely to play a dominant role in government and hence to get its policies enacted into law. This concern has a structuring effect that tends to reduce the votes for small parties (Eijk and Franklin 1996). The importance of strategic influences at first-order elections was shown dramatically when Israel introduced direct elections for the prime minister.

In 1996 a new Israeli electoral system came into effect which gave each voter two votes, one to be cast for a party in the normal way and one to be cast for the person they wanted to be prime minister. The argument by the constitutional lawyers and other members of the Israeli political establishment who pushed this reform through against the vociferous objections of the political science community, was that this would give the Prime Minister more authority. In fact, it allowed Israeli voters to 'split their tickets' just as voters sometimes do in the US, cutting the link between votes for members of parliament and the selection of the prime minister and largely freeing Israeli voters from the strategic considerations normally associated with first-order elections. The result was an explosion in the number of votes for minor parties and a reduction in the size of the largest parties (those that would play a primary role in forming a coalition government) including the prime minister's own party, to the point where this party was no longer the one with the most seats in parliament (Brichta 2001). So the person elected as prime minister found himself leader of a party that was unable to dominate the parliament or even a set of prospective coalition partners. After three elections under this new system, when the Israeli political establishment finally realized what was happening, it changed the system back and Israeli voters in 2003 did them the honor of voting again in a manner that allowed the formation of viable coalitions (Arian and Shamir 2004).

This example demonstrates clearly the structuring influence of first-order concerns in a parliamentary election. These concerns provide whatever order we may see in a national party system. Without them a national party system very quickly moves towards disorder. The progressive movement of the Israeli party system towards disorder when first-order concerns were dramatically reduced provides a test case for second-order theory that is ordinarily lacking. We see less structure in second-order elections than in first-order elections, and the longer the period since the most recent first-order election, the greater the lack of structure (Eijk and Franklin 1996; Weber 2007)—but only up to a point. That point is provided by the approach of the next first-order election, which galvanizes parties and their leaders to make strategic arguments, and motivates voters to focus on national politics in a way that reinstates first-order concerns. Because first-order concerns *are* regularly re-injected we almost never see a party system move more than a short distance towards the disorder that would characterize a party system that never had first-order concerns. The Israeli case is special because it falls outside this usual run of events, providing us with a critical example of what happens when first-order concerns are dramatically reduced for an extended period.

It might be thought that this example and the importance of strategic concerns in parliamentary first-order elections more generally make it clear that first-order elections as such do not exist in the United States, where the separation of the presidential from the congressional vote guarantees a situation similar to the period of the directly elected Israeli prime minister. But first-order / second-order is not a binary split. There are degrees of first-order-ness such that some elections partake more of this phenomenon than others (Eijk, Franklin, and Marsh 1996; Marsh and Mikhaylov, forthcoming). Because of the apparent spillover from presidential to congressional elections in the US, it is clear that on-year congressional elections evince more first-order-ness than midterm congressional elections, as already argued.

The Israeli case also emphasizes another difference between the US situation and the one customarily found in parliamentary first-order elections. There is no strategic incentive in the US to vote for a larger party in order to give one's preferences more chances of being translated into law. The first-order phenomenon in the US is much simpler: just an increased tendency for the president's party to do better in congressional races held in conjunction with presidential races.

But this is enough. Because of spillover, presidential races have a structuring effect on the congressional vote that would be absent if congressional elections were never held in conjunction with presidential elections. A midterm election is a single step closer to the even greater disorder that characterizes elections for state and local offices. No doubt, in the Israeli case, the move towards disorder would not have continued indefinitely. The very existence of direct elections for the prime minister would have provided spillover that injected *some* order into the Israeli party system. But it would have been less than seen when strategic considerations are also at work. In the US, the party system is considerably less structured than in the average parliamentary system—but such structure as *is* seen there, we suggest, is the result of spillover from presidential races (cf. Cox and Kernell 1991, 242).

This view is consistent with the "nationalization of electoral forces" story told by Stokes (1967), but it rather turns surge-and-decline theory on its head. According to second-order elections theory there is no such thing as a "normal vote" (see footnote 4 above), just a vote with more or less order injected into it by national political concerns.

ELECTORAL REALIGNMENTS

In this final section, our focus on electoral realignments is not intended to bring out any difference between American political behavior and political behavior elsewhere—a difference that might be due to different institutional arrangements. Rather, our purpose is to point out the likely similarity of US political behavior to political behavior elsewhere—a similarity actually disguised by differences in institutional arrangements. We believe that institutional peculiarities (especially the rapidity of the congressional electoral cycle) are responsible for what we see as the utter disarray of American political science in terms of understanding the nature and genesis of electoral realignments (cf. Mayhew 2002). A brief recapitulation is perhaps in order.

It has been evident at least since the time of Lord Bryce (1888) that the American party system has moved through a series of "eras" separated by "critical elections" (Key 1955). For example, the so-called "New Deal" era of the 1930s succeeded the so-called "Progressive" era which dated from the late nineteenth century. As early as 1955, V. O. Key Jr. theorized that bonds of party loyalty would have to loosen ("dealignment") as a precursor to the sort of wholesale change in party allegiances that was assumed to be required for a realignment of this classical type. But a journalistic account of the New Deal realignment published only a year later (Lubell 1956) reported that, in interviews of literally hundreds of individuals all across the United States, not a single person had been found who admitted to having changed their party allegiance during the period in question. This extraordinary finding led Anderson (1976) to suggest that the 1930s realignment was based not on changes of partisanship by established voters but on the electoral mobilization of whole new categories of previously non-voting individuals, changing the composition of the electorate rather than the preferences of individuals. Her later *The Creation of a Democratic Majority* (1979) spelled out the mechanisms involved, suggesting that previous realignments had also been based on wholesale enlargements of the politically mobilized US electorate.

The centerpiece of Anderson's work was a reconstruction of the 1930s electorate, based on survey data collected in the 1950s in which respondents had been asked to identify the party that they had supported on the first occasion they had cast a ballot. Of course, recall of past voting behavior is notoriously fallible, and people frequently misreport having voted for the party that they now support. But Anderson (1979, 59) conducted an elaborate validation of her reconstruction using a 1936 Gallup random sample. It seems possible that the accuracy of her reconstruction might be due to the fact that a person's earliest vote is more memorable than other past voting decisions. Some evidence for this has been found in British panel studies (M. Franklin and Ladner 1995).

Anderson's (1979) view of US realignments echoed a wisdom that had by then become conventional among comparativists: that the rise of new parties in European party systems had largely been based on the enfranchisement of new categories of individuals (Lipset and Rokkan 1967). In the European case it is taken for granted that, with the full enfranchisement of all classes of citizens that was completed early in the twentieth century,[6] opportunities for further realignments of the classic type were essentially eliminated.

Despite Anderson's work, however, a similar conventional wisdom did not take hold in the United States. Erikson and Tedin (1981) raised questions about the base from which change was supposed to have taken place, and arcane arguments about whether change between congressional elections in the period of the realignment should count as conversion have left the field with no clear view on the nature of the realignment process. Several attempts to fine-tune Anderson's claims (Brown 1991; Petrocik 1981) appear to have had little impact. A recent book addressing the fundamentals of change in US party support (Stonecash 2006) does not even mention compositional changes. The multiplicity of elections in the United States, with opportunities for temporary defection and split-ticket voting along with

---

[6] With the exception of female enfranchisement which came a little later but did not have the same implication of introducing new political concerns into the electoral arena.

actual conversion at every level, make it especially difficult to pin down the mechanisms that underlie electoral realignments.

Yet Anderson's (1976) reconstruction of the 1930s US electorate is lent weight by the reconstruction conducted by M. Franklin and Ladner (1995) of the 1940s British electorate, in an attempt to explain the last great realignment in British politics which occurred when the Labour Party finally replaced the long-declining Liberal Party at the British General Election of 1945. That reconstruction followed exactly the steps that Anderson had employed, using data collected in Britain ten years later than in the United States, but with the same temporal gap from the realignment concerned (which also happened ten years later than the 1930s US realignment) and asking exactly the same questions about initial partisanship. A feature of the 1945 realignment makes it possible to be more definitive about its nature than in the American case: there had been no General Election in Britain since 1935 (an election that should have been held in 1939 was canceled at the outbreak of the Second World War). There is thus no question in the British case about the base from which change has to be seen as occurring. The British reconstruction showed precisely the same mechanism at work as had been posited in the US by Anderson.

Some might think that the question of how realignments used to occur is moot. Even among comparativists there are few who believe that a contemporary European realignment would follow the same path as the British realignment of 1945. The freezing of party systems that is supposed to have followed that realignment (and similar ones in other European countries) evidently did not continue until the present day, and European countries arguably saw a massive dealignment of party systems during the 1970s and 1980s (M. Franklin et al. 1992 [2009]). Today it is not doubted that large changes in party support can occur without corresponding changes in the composition of the electorate—see for example M. Franklin and Hughes's (1999) analysis of the British electoral landslide of 1997. The unfreezing of party systems has made major change much easier, but at the same time it has disconnected the magnitude of partisan swings from their permanence. An electoral upheaval following an enlargement of European electorates used to inaugurate a new era in electoral politics, very similar to the successive eras that used to typify American electoral politics. Today, such an upheaval has no similar long-term implications. Major change can occur without implying a freezing of the new status quo, so massive electoral change is more readily reversible than used to be the case.

However, these developments do not render the question moot for Americanists. In the first place it matters whether realignments of the old type are still possible in the US. Much energy spent looking for signs of the next great realignment could be saved if it were to be understood that full enfranchisement of all US citizens means that realignments brought about by "critical elections" are no longer possible in the US any more than elsewhere (cf. Jensen 1981). In the second place, even if realignments of the old type are indeed no longer possible, recognizing the role of composition effects in political change can inform research about the nature of political developments (cf. Merrill, Grofman, and Brunell 2008). In the final paragraphs of this chapter we will focus on this last point.

VOTER HETEROGENEITY
AND ELECTORAL CHANGE

That the composition of the electorate changes over time is an important idea that is largely neglected by US scholars who, with no clear recognition of the importance of composition effects in past realignments, generally make the implicit assumption that all voters are equally affected by influences on their electoral decisions. In matters of party choice as in matters of turnout, a single model is supposed to fit all. Even authors such as Miller and Shanks (1996), who give considerable attention to generational effects, still estimate models that do not take account of age-related heterogeneity. To the extent that heterogeneity in electoral behavior is contemplated, the type of heterogeneity that is considered (e.g., by Zaller 1992) is between individuals of different types (better or less well educated, more or less interested in politics, and so forth), not between individuals of different political generations.

Yet it has been clearly shown that a single model does not fit all, in terms of electoral turnout, as discussed earlier, and it makes sense that the same would be true for party choice (cf. Green, Palmquist, and Schickler 2002). Older voters are almost certainly set in their partisanship—capable perhaps of defecting to a different party for an election or two, but not of generating a permanent realignment.[7] Miller and Shanks (1996) have shown us that the political alignments of the 1930s and 1940s are today still evident among the oldest Americans, just as the pre-New Deal alignments were evident among the oldest Americans in the 1950s and 1960s. There is no reason to suppose that in fifty years' time the political alignments of 2010 will not still be evident among the 70-year-olds of 2060. If so, politics in the United States, like politics in other countries, is limited in the extent to which it can register enduring political change from one election to the next. Still, over time considerable change can take place—if it is rooted in compositional shifts.

---

[7] There are clear exceptions to this general proposition when parties disappear (as has not happened in the US within living memory) and possibly when parties change their identity in the eyes of voters—as Miller and Shanks (1996) argue may have happened in the US South in recent years.

Taking composition effects seriously would have two implications for our ability to understand the mainsprings of electoral behavior. In the first place, our models of electoral turnout and decision-making would be elaborated by allowing for different effects on younger members of the electorate than on more established members. Allowing past behavior (perhaps encapsulated in the concept of party identification, as suggested earlier in this chapter) to have more effects on older voters and fewer effects on younger voters requires an interaction of party identification with some version of an age variable. Other variables will almost certainly also be found to have different effects on younger than on older voters. Again interaction terms are called for.

In the second place, distinguishing between voters who are unlikely to shift their allegiances except temporarily and those who are free to acquire new permanent allegiances yields, in matters of party choice as in matters of turnout, a distinction between long-term and short-term forces. Long-term forces create the baseline from which temporary shifts take place. Short-term forces not only create deviations from that baseline but also have the opportunity to shift the baseline itself (cf. C. Franklin and Jackson 1983). These ideas are implicit in Miller and Shanks's (1996) analysis of the realignment of white Southerners in the United States, but are not spelled out in these terms. Our argument is that, by allowing themselves to think about composition effects, American political scientists can greatly advance their understanding of the way realignments have occurred in times past, and continue to occur even in the world of today. In this way, a comparativist perspective on US elections might illuminate the study of realignments in much the same way, as was suggested earlier, as it could help to reshape thinking in such diverse subfields as turnout, party identification, and midterm loss.

REFERENCES

ALESINA, A. and ROSENTHAL, H. 1995. *Partisan Politics, Divided Government and the Economy.* New York: Cambridge University Press.

ANDERSON, K. 1976. Generation, Partisan Shift and Realignment: A Glance Back at the New Deal. In *The Changing American Voter*, ed. N. Nie, S. Verba, and J. Petrocik. Cambridge, Mass.: Harvard University Press.

——— 1979. *The Creation of a Democratic Majority 1928–1936.* Chicago, Ill.: University of Chicago Press.

ARIAN, A. and SHAMIR, M. (eds.) 2004. *The Elections in Israel—2003.* New Brunswick: Transaction Publishers.

BRADSHAW, K. and PRING, D. 1982. *Parliament and Congress.* London: Quartet Books.

BRICHTA, A. 2001. *Political Reform in Israel: The Quest for a Stable and Effective Government.* Eastbourne: Sussex Academic Press.

BROWN, C. 1991. *Ballots of Tumult.* Ann Arbor, Mich.: University of Michigan Press.

BRYCE, J. 1888. *The American Commonwealth.* London: Macmillan.

BUDGE, I., CREWE, I., and FARLIE, D. (eds.) 1976. *Party Identification and Beyond: Representations of Voting and Party Competition.* London: Wiley.

BURNS, J. and PELTASON, J. 1960. *Government by the People.* New York: Prentice Hall.

BUTLER, D. and STOKES, D. 1969. *Political Change in Britain.* London: Macmillan.

CAIN, B., FEREJOHN, J., and FIORINA, M. 1987. *The Personal Vote: Constituency Service and Electoral Independence.* Cambridge, Mass.: Harvard University Press.

CAMPBELL, A. 1960. Surge and Decline: A Study of Electoral Change. *Public Opinion Quarterly,* 24: 397–418.

CAMPBELL, A., CONVERSE, P., MILLER, W., and STOKES, D. 1960. *The American Voter.* New York: Wiley.

CAMPBELL, J. 1993. *The Presidential Pulse of Congressional Elections.* Lexington, Ky.: University Press of Kentucky.

—— and JUREK, S. 2003. The Decline of Competition and Change in Congressional Elections. In *Congress Responds to the Twentieth Century,* ed. S. Ahuja and R. Dewhirst. Columbus, Ohio: Ohio State University Press.

CARRUBBA, C. and TIMPONE, R. 2005. Explaining Vote Switching across First- and Second-Order Elections. Evidence from Europe. *Comparative Political Studies,* 38: 260–81.

COX, G. and KERNELL, S. (eds.) 1991. *The Politics of Divided Government.* Boulder, Colo.: Westview Press.

EIJK, C. VANDER and FRANKLIN, M. (eds.) 1996. *Choosing Europe? The European Electorate and National Politics in the Face of Union.* Ann Arbor, Mich.: University of Michigan Press.

—— —— and MARSH, M. 1996. What Voters Teach Us About Europe-Wide Elections; What Europe-Wide Elections Teach Us About Voters. *Electoral Studies,* 15: 149–66.

ERIKSON, R. and TEDIN, K. 1981. The 1928–1936 Partisan Realignment: The Case for the Conversion Hypothesis. *American Political Science Review,* 75: 951–62.

FIORINA, M. 1977. *Congress: Keystone of the Washington Establishment.* New Haven, Conn.: Yale University Press.

—— 1992. *Divided Government.* New York: Macmillan.

FLICKINGER, R. and STUDLAR, D. 2007. One Europe, Many Elections? Models of Turnout in European Parliamentary Elections After 2004. *Comparative Political Studies,* 40: 383–96.

FRANKLIN, C. and JACKSON, J. 1983. The Dynamics of Party Identification. *American Political Science Review,* 77: 957–73.

FRANKLIN, D. and GRIER, E. 1997. Effects of Motor-Voter Legislation. *American Politics Quarterly,* 25: 104–17.

FRANKLIN, M. 2004. *Voter Turnout and the Dynamics of Electoral Competition in Established Democracies Since 1945.* New York: Cambridge University Press.

—— and HIRCZY DE MINO, W. 1998. Separated Powers, Divided Government, and Turnout in US Presidential Elections. *American Journal of Political Science,* 42: 316–26.

—— and HUGHES, C. 1999. Dynamic Representation in Britain. In *A Critical Election? British Voters and Parties in Long-term Perspective,* ed. P. Norris and G. Evans. Thousand Oaks, Calif.: Sage.

—— and LADNER, M. 1995. The Undoing of Winston Churchill: Mobilization and Conversion in the 1945 Realignment of British Voters. *British Journal of Political Science,* 25: 429–52.

—— MACKIE, T., VALEN, H., et al. 1992. *Electoral Change: Responses to Evolving Social and Attitudinal Structures in Western Countries.* Cambridge: Cambridge University Press. (Re-issued, with updated data, as a "Classic in Political Science" by the ECPR Press, 2009.)

GAINES, B. 1998. The Impersonal Vote? Constituency Service and Incumbency Advantage in British Elections, 1950–92. *Legislative Studies Quarterly,* 23: 167–95.

GERBER, A., GREEN, D., and SCHACHAR, R. 2003. Voting May Be Habit-Forming: Evidence from a Randomized Field Experiment. *American Journal of Political Science,* 47: 540–50.

GREEN, D., PALMQUIST, B., and SCHICKLER, E. 2002. *Partisan Hearts and Minds: Political Parties and the Social Identities of Voters.* New Haven, Conn.: Yale University Press.

—— and SHACHAR, R. 2000. Habit-formation and Political Behavior: Evidence of Consuetude in Voter Turnout. *British Journal of Political Science,* 30: 561–73.

HAYAMA, A. 1992. Incumbency Advantage in Japanese Elections. *Electoral Studies,* 11: 46–57.

HILLYGUS, S. 2005. Campaign Effects and the Dynamics of Turnout Intention in Election 2000. *Journal of Politics* 67: 50–68.

JENSEN, R. 1981. The Last Party System: Decay of Consensus, 1932–1980. In *The Evolution of American Electoral Systems,* ed. P. Kleppner et al. Westport: Greenwood Press.

JOHNSTON, R., MATTHEWS, S., and BITTNER, A. 2007. Turnout and the Party System in Canada, 1988–2004. *Electoral Studies,* 26: 735–45.

KATZ, J. and KING, G. 1999. A Statistical Model for Multiparty Electoral Data. *American Political Science Review,* 93: 15–32.

KEY, V. O., JR. 1955. A Theory of Critical Elections. *Journal of Politics,* 17: 3–18.

KLEPPNER, P. 1982. *Who Voted? The Dynamics of Electoral Turnout 1870–1980.* New York: Praeger.

LEVITT, S. and WOLFRAM, C. 1997. Decomposing the Sources of Incumbency Advantage in the U.S. House. *Legislative Studies Quarterly,* 22: 45–60.

LIPSET, S. and ROKKAN, S. 1967. Cleavage Structures, Party Systems and Voter Alignments: An Introduction. In *Party Systems and Voter Alignments,* ed. S. Lipset and S. Rokkan. New York: Free Press.

LUBELL, S. 1956. *The Future of American Politics.* New York: Harper.

LUTZ, D. 2006. *Principles of Constitutional Design.* New York: Cambridge University Press.

MARKUS, G. and CONVERSE, P. 1979. A Dynamic Simultaneous Equation Model of Electoral Choice. *American Political Science Review,* 73/4: 1055–70.

MARSH, M. 2007. European Parliament Elections and Losses by Governing Parties. In *European Elections and Domestic Politics,* ed. W. van der Brug and C. van der Eijk. South Bend, Ind.: University of Notre Dame Press.

—— and MIKHAYLOV, S. Forthcoming. European Parliament Elections as Second Order National Elections: A Review of the Evidence. CONNEX *Living Reviews.* <http://europeangovernance.livingreviews.org/>.

MAYHEW, D. 1974. Congressional Elections: The Case of the Vanishing Marginals. *Polity* 6: 295–317.

—— 2002. *Electoral Realignments.* New Haven, Conn.: Yale University Press.

MERRILL, S., GROFMAN, B., and BRUNELL, T. 2008. Cycles in American National Electoral Politics, 1854–2006: Statistical Evidence and an Explanatory Model. *American Political Science Review,* 102: 1–17.

MILLER, W. and SHANKS, M. 1996. *The New American Voter.* Cambridge, Mass.: Harvard University Press.

MITCHELL, G. and WLEZIEN, C. 1995. The Impact of Legal Constraints on Voter Registration, Turnout, and the Composition of the American Electorate. *Political Behavior*, 17: 179–202.

PETROCIK, J. 1981. *Party Coalitions: Realignments and the Decline of the New Deal Party System*. Chicago, Ill.: University of Chicago Press.

PLUTZER, E. 2002. Becoming a Habitual Voter: Inertia, Resources, and Growth in Young Adulthood. *American Political Science Review*, 96: 41–56.

POWELL, B. 2000. *Elections as Instruments of Democracy*. New Haven, Conn.: Yale University Press.

REIF, K. and SCHMITT, H. 1980. Nine Second-Order National Elections—A Conceptual Framework for the Analysis of European Election Results. *European Journal of Political Research*, 8: 3–44.

STOKES, D. 1967. Parties and the Nationalization of Electoral Forces. In *The American Party Systems: Stages of Political Development*, ed. W. Chambers and W. Burnham. New York: Oxford University Press.

STONECASH, J. 2006. *Political Parties Matter: Realignment and the Return to Partisan Voting*. Boulder, Colo.: Lynne Rienner.

VERBA, S., SCHLOZMAN, K., and BRADY, H. 1995. *Voice and Equality: Civic Voluntarism in American Politics*. Cambridge, Mass.: Harvard University Press.

WEBER, T. 2007. Campaign Effects and Second-Order Cycles: A Top-Down Approach to European Parliament Elections. *European Union Politics*, 8: 509–36.

ZALLER, J. 1992. *The Nature and Origins of Mass Opinion*. New York: Cambridge University Press.

PART VIII

REFLECTIONS

CHAPTER 36

ON PARTICIPATION

INDIVIDUALS, DYNAMIC CATEGORIES, AND THE CONTEXT OF POWER*

JANE JUNN

THE study of US political participation and electoral behavior in particular has produced more than half a century's worth of systematic research and findings. Models have been proposed, tested, disputed, defended, and revised. Social scientists have innovated new ways to collect data, from the large sample survey to field experiments. Analysts continue to evaluate new evidence on the extent to which ideology, partisanship, and economic conditions influence the political choices of American voters. As the chapters of this volume attest, there is much to consider in the wide swath covered above. In evaluating what all this means for the study of political participation, my approach diverges from an overview of overviews in that I do not offer a summary. Instead, I advance an argument for the consideration of individuals in dynamic relationship to both categories and the context of power in the study of political behavior. Analyzing political participation while taking categories for granted and assuming equal agency among individuals impedes our ability to understand how and why political participation is important in US democracy.

* I thank Jan Leighley and Natalie Masuoka for their input on this chapter.

With insight from areas of inquiry traditionally considered outside of American political behavior, including the fields of race and ethnicity, social movements, and gender and politics, I argue contemporary scholars of US political behavior should consider more carefully two important assumptions when analyzing the relationship between political participation and democracy in the United States. The first is the assumption of individuals as a unit of analysis in stable and meaningful categories. Most analyses of political behavior take categories within variables for granted, particularly those explanatory variables on the right-hand side of an equation representing an inferential model of political behavior. Among the most consequential for conclusions regarding political equality is race and ethnicity, not only because there are long-standing differences in political participation between individuals classified by race, but because the United States has supported racially discriminatory policies and practices throughout its history. Categories of race and ethnicity are much more dynamic than traditional models of political behavior have allowed, and accounting for this dynamism will provide opportunity for more robust interpretation of the meaning of differences in political activism among Americans classified by race. While the general claim to reconsider the assumption of categorical stability in individuals is relevant to other classifications, I concentrate here on race and ethnicity.

A second assumption I suggest holding to greater scrutiny is that of the uniformity of political agency. This assumption is so widely held that it is almost never mentioned, and it is rooted in the notion that Americans have equal ability to influence the US political system. While analysts routinely acknowledge substantial variation among individuals in resources, motivation, and mobilization, the underlying premise is that in the absence of these differences, everyone should want to participate and similarly, that everyone would benefit from participating. Even when analysts acknowledge systematically different effects of education and income on voting, for example among minority voters versus whites, there remains a bias underlying the interpretation of the results that more participation should be better for all who participate.

The link between the assumptions of stable categories and equal agency and their combined influence on the study of political behavior in the United States is simple. Categories inside of independent variables are neither organic nor related monotonically to the dependent variable of political participation. Instead, the categories and the social meaning, economic impact, and political consequences associated with the classification are themselves products of US political and institutional structures. Categories matter for political behavior, not necessarily because individuals in these groups innately share a political agenda, but because the context of politics in the United States creates a structure of unequal advantage for agency in political participation based in group differentiation. Thus, before we can understand the relationship of important independent variables to participation—race, gender, class, and other important distinctions beyond this "holy trinity"—analysts must devote more careful thought to the individual-level conditions theorized to influence political behavior.

LOOKING BACKWARD: INDIVIDUAL-LEVEL ANALYSIS

It is inevitable that a concluding chapter in a volume such as this ask the question of how far we have come in understanding the relationship of political participation to the functioning of American democracy. In Chapter 14 of this volume, and while acknowledging important progress, Larry Bartels makes the assessment that scholars still have a long way to go. "Nevertheless, the aspiration of situating the study of electoral behavior firmly within a more general understanding of American politics seems to me, five decades later, to remain largely unfulfilled." (Bartels, this volume, 255). Moving forward will require not only a closer examination of the assumptions analysts bring to scholarship, but also an expansion in the range of questions that drive research on political participation, as well as a willingness to engage and embrace the sometimes-messy dynamism of social and political life in the United States.

But these are not easy to accomplish, for there is comfort in findings that support the adage that the more things change the more they stay the same. For many observers, it is a relief that party identification still matters and the highly educated reliably participate in politics at a higher rate than Americans with fewer socioeconomic resources. This is so not only because such findings are consistent with long-standing empirical patterns, but also because it is deemed useful for democracy that the relationships remain intact. While there are exceptions, there is a venerable tradition in the study of US political behavior privileging traditional party politics, as well as the normative position that the well-educated are more desirable democratic participants.

At the same time, however, the regularity of empirical findings and the study of continuity in the field of US political behavior stand in contrast with work in allied fields similarly engaged in understanding the dynamics of political participation and social change. These include areas of study classified as social movements and contentious politics; race, ethnicity, and politics; urban politics; and women and politics, in addition to others. These are expansive fields, and while electoral behavior and political participation are not the sole focus of their inquiry, explaining why people do what they do in politics remains an important question.

Consider for example the field of social movements. In contrast to a typical study of US political behavior, social movement scholars study a subset of the universe of political actors, often concentrating on a particular issue or set of political concerns across time rather than taking a sample of everyone at one point in time and analyzing how people react to political events and social conditions. Despite being interested in many of the same questions, the methodologies and analytical techniques utilized by traditional large-N political behavior scholars and students of social movements are often distinct, and sometimes at odds. Chief among these differences is the emphasis on understanding the dynamics of political change instead of stasis, and across time rather than at a single point in time. While this characterization of US political behavior research as the study of continuity in synchronic design is apt for only a subset of scholarship, it is nevertheless the case that this approach remains the most common in research on voting behavior and political participation.

The symbolic fork in the road where traditional US political behavior research took one path and other fields of study took another could very well be the start of the American National Election Studies (ANES), one of the most important systematic data collection efforts in political science. Since the early surveys, most political behavior scholars have continued faithfully along this course, remaining focused on explaining individual actions with individual-level measures of resources, perceptions, and attitudes. In Chapter 16 of this volume, T. K. Ahn et al. deftly argue that the field of political behavior has evolved in this way for a particular set of reasons.

The primary historical model of a voter in the empirical literature is a socially disembodied individual whose decisions, judgments, and voting choices are based on individually held preferences, opinions, beliefs, attitudes, and identifications. This atomistic model is probably best seen as an unintentional by-product of particular observational strategies that have been dominant in political research—most notably randomized sample surveys of large populations that divorce individuals from their social and political environments (Huckfeldt and Sprague 1993, 1995). While relatively few students of politics would advocate an atomistic model on its intellectual merits, traditional methods of data collection have resulted in a *de facto* adherence to a model that separates and isolates one citizen from another in a way that is both theoretically unsatisfying and empirically inadequate. (this volume, 279)

While invaluable in many ways, reliance on the NES and other large-N survey data has also limited the reach of the field by constraining the exercise of explanatory variables to those readily available in the survey data. In contrast, related and emerging fields of study have cast a wider net, highlighting the importance of contextual factors and structural considerations. It is with insight from these areas of inquiry that I argue contemporary scholars of US political behavior should consider more carefully two important assumptions when analyzing the relationship between political participation and democracy in the United States.

A CHANGING POPULATION AND DYNAMIC CATEGORIES

The diverse racial environment of the United States today is a far cry from the relatively homogeneous 1950s and 1960s when data from the first voting studies were being collected from samples of the population. In 1960, nearly 90 percent of the US population was classified as white, with the remaining 10 percent African American and less than 1 percent of some "other" race. During the first two decades of the American National Election Studies, basic civil rights and voting rights were not equally available across the United States, and explicitly denied to blacks in many locales. Groups of American minorities in addition to African Americans were also systematically excluded. For example, not until the passage of the McCarran Walter Act (1953) could Asian Americans become naturalized citizens. Until then, federal law prohibited Asian immigrants from citizenship. Land and property ownership laws in states primarily in the West and South prohibited people classified by race from voting enfranchisement even if they were citizens.

Following the passage of the landmark 1965 Immigration Act, the face of the US population has changed dramatically. The arrival of tens of millions of immigrants to the United States over the last several decades has transformed the demographic landscape of the nation, expanding both the size and diversity of racial minority populations. Nearly half of immigrants are from Latin America, and classified by the government as Hispanic. A quarter of new Americans today are from Asia, and Asian Americans are among the fastest growing groups, increasing from less than a million people in 1960 to roughly 14 million. Indeed, the dramatic growth of the Asian American population has recently earned them the status as a potential swing vote in state elections in California, New York, and Washington. Latinos are today roughly 15 percent of the US population, and while more heavily concentrated in the American West and Southwest, migration patterns both internationally and domestically have placed Latinos in all fifty states in increasing numbers.

Complicating matters further is the rapid growth of the "multi-racial" population in the United States over the last several decades (Foner and Fredrickson 2004; Masuoka 2006; Williams 2006). While being identified as more than one race has always been a reality for Americans, the ability to categorize oneself as such with respect to the federal classification system only became possible with the 2000 census (Prewitt 2004).[1] Now nearly 3 percent of Americans classify themselves as more than one race, and the proportion is expected to grow dramatically.

---

[1] A form of multi-racial classification was used by the US census in the nineteenth century to categorize African American slaves and free persons as, for example, "quadroon" or "octoroon" (Anderson 1988; Nobles 2000). REFS

The malleability of categories of race and ethnicity in the United States is not a new phenomenon. Indeed, the default category of race as white is one that has undergone significant change and incorporation since the founding of the nation. Objection to the foreigner among the earliest settlers of the American republic included a vociferous condemnation of increasing the number of German immigrants by none other than Benjamin Franklin, who famously described the Germans as "swarthy" and "tawny" in contrast to whites. Similarly, when large numbers of Irish, Italian, and Jewish immigrants from Europe arrived in the eastern United States at the turn of the nineteenth century, these groups of newcomers were similarly categorized as less than white, and incorporated into the group only after political struggle and triangulation against American blacks (see Hattam 2007; Ignatiev 2008; Jacobson 1999). African Americans have persistently remained in the racial category furthest away from whites, and racial group consciousness forged of discrimination, exclusion, and necessity for blacks has been among the most consistent findings among this population since the mid-twentieth century.

But the US has now moved, demographically, beyond the black–white binary. The transformation of the mass public from a society clearly divided by color to a diverse and multi-racial environment in the United States presents us with the question of what constitutes the population? With more than a third of the US today considered something other than white, how well do US population surveys do in capturing this diversity? With more than one in ten Americans today foreign-born, how well do English-language surveys do in asking questions of all Americans? How might inferences about the American population and its voting behavior and political activism be biased through a particular measurement strategy?

Beyond the measurement problems, the dynamic population raises a new set of challenges for existing theories of racial group identity. Despite the increasing diversity of the US population, there remains reflexivity in the notion that racial classification implies group consciousness at the individual level and mobilization at the mass level. Making the connection from shared classification in a racial category to group-based political behavior is neither simple nor obvious for minorities whose population growth is attributed to new immigration. It is unclear how new immigrant members will adopt and apply the racial and ethnic categories imposed upon them. In contrast, the shared historical experience of profound structural, economic, and social bias aimed against African Americans coupled with relatively modest immigration of new black immigrants leaves less room for maneuvering (Cohen 1999; Dawson 1994; Rogers 2006).

Group-based consciousness and mobilization to politics have been utilized in social movements to make up for a deficit in material resources. Perhaps the most frequently cited contemporary example is the US Civil Rights movement that nurtured a contentious politics and produced momentous change in American politics. Building on these experiences, scholars of US political behavior have come to expect racial identity to have a strong and predictable relationship to political outcomes, due in large part to Michael Dawson's influential model of "linked fate" among African Americans. In the context of the current population characterized by multiple categories of race and ethnicity beyond black and white, it is no longer clear what should be expected of racial identity in terms of mobilization and political behavior. The new complexity of racial classification and identification suggest that the link from racial and ethnic identification to group-based political mobilization should be treated as a hypothesis rather than a certainty. Analysts should not take as given the notion that racial classification will drive political behavior, and instead, this prior is better understood as an assumption requiring empirical investigation.

INDIVIDUALS, EQUAL AGENCY, AND POLITICAL ACTIVISM

In its most common form, analysis of political action in the mass public is accomplished by aggregating empirical observations taken from individuals. These data are typically quantitative responses to closed questions in surveys from large-N samples. Race at the individual level is taken as given—as exogenously determined—and then aggregated into static and one-dimensional categories. But conventional social science has become increasingly stymied by its reliance on the treatment of racial categories as fixed. Indeed, the current state of knowledge in the literature on political participation and electoral behavior is based in individual-level approaches built on an analytical triumvirate of individual-level synchronic data, the socioeconomic status model, and a mainstream definition of political participation as voluntary legal acts directed at government officials toward policy outcomes.

Undergirding this perspective is the assumption that individuals have equal agency. Inferential models estimated with the data belie this bias: one more year of education or one more mobilization request will increase political participation among people regardless of the particularities of their social and political context. The starting position that makes this assumption defensible is that the system itself—whether political, social, or economic—is neutral, not favoring one or another for any particular characteristic. But if one is suspicious that political responsiveness varies systematically by race, class, gender, or some other category in which individuals exist, we must scrutinize the assumption and devise strategies to test the validity of the starting claim. As Melissa Harris-Lacewell (2003, 244) argues, "The particular racial history of this country requires that researchers be more careful in their assumptions of neutrality. At a minimum, these researchers must engage the historical evidence and offer an alternative account. Ignoring the history of Black people and racialized political ideologies is insufficient."

There is ample evidence within political science and other disciplines to document pervasive inequalities inside the political, economic, and social systems of the United States (see, e.g., Frymer 1999; Marable 1983; Sidanius and Pratto 2004; Smith 1997; Walton and Smith 2000). Yet there is surprisingly little sustained empirical and theoretical effort within the study of US political behavior to illuminate more precisely when and how power and hierarchy structure opportunities and incentives to act in politics. There are certainly exceptions, chief among them John Gaventa's (1982) brilliant study of powerlessness and political quiescence in Appalachia, that serve as a stark reminder that one cannot assume that all individuals have equal ability and desire to influence the political system, and further, that the return on that investment in time and resources will be the same for all who take part.

Instead, agency or individual rights in the liberal democratic vernacular operate in both a social context of power relations as well as a structural context of democratic political institutions where actors deploy accumulated capital in pursuing their interests. Individuals—white, racialized, and otherwise—operate in a political sphere guided by laws and social policy rooted firmly in an order that is anything but neutral. Instead, it is a system designed to maintain the continued monopoly of power and wealth that is based in any number of categorical imperatives, including race, gender, and class. This political context is one that goes well beyond the domain of a single demographic variable, and, rather, strikes to the heart of oppression of multiple varieties. Interpreting political action—or inaction in the face of tremendous power and low odds for success—must therefore take place within the context of this framework. Thus the task is to fashion innovative strategies both to account for complexities in categories populated by individuals and to discern how power structures the opportunities and rewards for political action among individuals.

In Chapter 22 of this volume, Kira Sanbonmatsu argues a similar position with respect to the use of gender as a category of analysis:

We typically assume the existence of two social groups—men and women—and ask whether the two groups behave similarly or differently in politics. This approach regards gender as a characteristic that individuals possess. However, we can view gender as a set of social relationships and practices that are partially created within the political sphere. . . .

Thinking about gender in this way—as a category that can be shaped by politics rather than as a purely social category with consequences for politics—suggests a somewhat different research agenda than that typically pursued by behavior scholars. Scholars can ask whether elections help *create* gender as a category in addition to asking whether the social category of gender is cued in politics.

(Sanbonmatsu, this volume, 417).

The analytical strategy of static categories in individuals as the unit of analysis not only impedes our ability to disentangle the roots of political inequality embedded in race or any other politically salient category, but it also creates other undesirable analytical consequences. Among the most obvious in the field of US political behavior is the "puzzle of participation," the observation of stagnant rates of political activity despite substantial increases in formal educational attainment in the mass public over time. Decade after decade, it is always those who are more advantaged in socioeconomic terms—those with more education and higher incomes—who are the most active in politics. The socioeconomic status model has dominated explanations of individual-level political participation, and when estimating models of participation from voting and campaign work to contacting political officials, indicators of socioeconomic status are always the strongest predictors of activity. The importance of formal education in particular is so ubiquitous that Philip Converse has described it as the "universal solvent." It is impossible to ignore the size and consistency of the coefficient on the education measure, not only because of its replicability across synchronic studies, but because it mirrors the expectations of democratic theorists as diverse as John Stuart Mill, Jean Jacques Rousseau, John Locke, and Thomas Jefferson who identified formal education as the linchpin in the development of otherwise unsuitable ordinary people into democratic citizens.

That education is so consistently documented to have a large and positive coefficient on measures of political participation is not surprising. Education not only helps to transform citizens through skill development and socialization to democratic norms, it also functions as one of the most powerful engines of social stratification, endowing those more highly educated with greater material resources and positions of power relative to those with less education. This other side of the story is well documented by sociologists and political scientists, and is routinely invoked as an explanation for why formal education is such a significant predictor of participation. The most advantaged not only have disproportionate access to governing structures and institutions, they also have important incentives in maintaining a process that benefits their interests, along with the requisite sense of political efficacy to pursue those interests.

Despite the strength and consistency of the finding between education and participation in cross-sectional data, what is unexpected is the inability of substantial increases in formal education in the US mass public over the last several decades to translate into higher levels of participation over the same time period. Dominant political behavior models based on assumptions of static categories and equality of individual agency cannot explain this apparent inconsistency. Stepping away from these assumptions, however, allows both a response to the "puzzle" and a guide to how analysts might refine theories about the relationship of independent variables that have been treated as individual-level attributes (see, e.g., Nie, Junn, and Stehlik-Barry 1996).

Suspending the two assumptions of static categories and equal agency allows one to see that educational attainment—or the categories of any independent variable—can vary in their meaning and relationship to the dependent variable over time as a function of changing context. In the case of education and participation, having a college degree in the early years of the American National Election Study put a person at the top of the socioeconomic ladder. Fifty years later, a college degree is no longer the scarce commodity it once was, with more than a quarter of the adult US population similarly endowed. What matters, then, is not the absolute level of education, but instead, the place an individual occupies in relative terms to those he or she is surrounded by. Considering the meaning of the categories of educational attainment within the context of its "value" to the dependent variable breaks the logjam to understanding how it can be that education can go up in the aggregate in the presence of both stagnant rates of participation as well as a strong, positive, and consistent relationship between education and political activity.

Similarly, widening the lens to consider both disparate constraints as well as unequal rewards for participation allows one to explain how education in real terms can remain important to some forms of political participation and democratic citizenship. In this regard, understanding the context of the dependent variable provides a stronger base for evaluating the contours of US democracy.

GOING FORWARD: THE CONTEXT OF POWER

As the field of US political behavior moves forward to study participation in the diverse racial and ethnic environment of the future, the frailty of models such as the SES model become a liability. In particular, the expectation that education and income ought to positively influence participatory behavior loses traction when the data include significant numbers of minority Americans. Asian Americans in particular have been singled out as anomalous because of their low rates of political participation despite relatively high levels of education and income. The absence of a significant relationship between education and participation among this group of Americans is the reverse of what Verba and Nie (1972) identified as "over-participation" by African Americans, when they documented high levels of political activity despite relatively low socioeconomic status among blacks in the late 1960s. When faced with these inconsistencies, the use of the descriptor "anomalous findings" makes an important statement about what is out of line. Rather than wonder about the applicability and efficacy of the SES model, the burden for explanation falls on why Asian Americans or African Americans are not behaving as the model suggests they should.

These examples suggest a departure from the conventional analytical strategy of assuming static categories and equality of individual agency. Rather than search for consistency in findings among populations using the same model, scholars of political behavior will do well to look beyond standard models for theoretical leverage in explaining political participation among diverse Americans. Minority participation may indeed be "exceptional" when the effect of SES is less weighty or altogether absent compared to its effects for the mainstream population. But these exceptions do not mean that political participation among African Americans, Latinos, and Asian Americans is unpredictable. Rather, it is more likely that we have yet to identify and analyze relevant antecedents to its activation, and the variations in context that structure the incentives and rewards of political partici-pation.

Education and other individual-level resources may work in different ways in influencing political participation among minority populations because individual members of these groups are systematically more likely to occupy a different place in the social structure. For many African Americans and Latinos, this is a lower position, and in this regard, race and socioeconomic resources are endogenous to political participation. Race and social status are not separable; instead, they are inextricably intertwined in the political history of race relations in the United States. For example, the education achievement gap between whites and Asian Americans on the one hand, and African Americans and Latinos on the other, remains significant and persistent. Similarly, whites systematically out-earn their minority counterparts at the same level of educational attainment: a high school, college, or graduate degree provides less income for African Americans, Latinos, and Asian Americans than whites similarly certified. Thus is it not simply the fact that many minority Americans have less resources than whites, it is the interaction of those resources with race and ethnicity that conspire to reduce the significance of individual-level socioeconomic resources for political participation.

Furthermore, if one assumes individuals participate in politics partly as a reflection of their political needs or demands, and these vary across groups due to social and political structures, then the nature of political action is likely to vary across groups. The focus, then, of the field of political behavior on electoral politics at the national level—where racial minorities are just beginning to claim a seat at the table—likewise tends to enhance the privileged position of the SES model despite its lack of fit in a more diverse population. To model political participation among individuals differently situated in the social and political structure of the United States thus requires an evaluation of the costs and benefits of participation to determine when, whether, and what political action is rational, for many of the most politically salient categories closely track distinctions in social status and class, mirroring marginalization based in categorical imperatives. Hierarchies constructed from these distinctions create and re-inscribe structural inequalities in institutions, culture, and the practice of politics, resulting in unjust outcomes.

Justified by the categories themselves, inequalities have become both persistent and pernicious. Without stepping back and considering individuals in dynamic context, we are unable to make progress in identifying the political roots, processes, and consequences of differentiation, stratification, and marginalization based on status and identity.

I have argued that in order for the study of US political behavior to move forward, analysts must reconsider two important assumptions about the durability of categories and the degree of equality of agency among Americans. Treating categories dynamically and considering the context of power has to have a substantive end, and in this case, it is a better understanding of how democracy might work to enhance equality, and on the flip side to exacerbate political inequality. The task at hand is formidable indeed: to reevaluate the utility of prevailing models by taking account of the context of an increasingly diverse population as well as an expanded conceptualization of political voice and participation.

Individual acts such as engaging in protest or working with others in the local community have been counted as political participation among individuals in surveys, but prevailing analytic and measurement strategies are less adept at accounting for behavior within a larger organizational context, as well as over a longer period of time. Few would question the political imperative of Rosa Parks's act of defiance on an Alabama bus, but whether she was interviewed in 1955 or 2005, her violation of a Montgomery city ordinance would not count as political participation as defined by political scientists in the conventional sense. The example is at once absurd and revealing. In retrospect, and particularly for a social movement as significant as the US Civil Rights movement, we recognize Rosa Parks's actions as a legitimate expression of political voice despite the fact that it was illegal for her to ride anywhere but the back of the bus. Political acts and movements that once seemed on the margins challenge conventional definitions, providing opportunities for theoretical innovation. Similarly, populations once on the margins will within the next decade move into the mainstream of the American electorate as millions of newly naturalized voters and their children—foreign and US-born—become eligible to vote. Theories and the methods to study political participation in the US should reflect a similar degree of dynamism to that of democratic politics in the nation.

References

ANDERSON, M. 1988. *The American Census: A Social History.* New Haven, Conn.: Yale University Press.

COHEN, C. 1999. *The Boundaries of Blackness: AIDS and the Breakdown of Black Politics.* Chicago, Ill.: University of Chicago Press.

DAWSON, M. C. 1994. *Behind the Mule: Race and Class in African-American Politics.* Princeton, N.J.: Princeton University Press.

FONER, N. and FREDRICKSON, G. M. (eds.) 2004. *Not Just Black and White: Historical and Contemporary Perspectives on Immigration, Race, and Ethnicity in the United States.* New York: Russell Sage Foundation.

FRYMER, P. 1999. *Uneasy Alliances.* Princeton, N.J.: Princeton University Press.

GAVENTA, J. 1982. *Power and Powerlessness: Quiescence and Rebellion in an Appalachian Valley.* Chicago, Ill.: University of Illinois Press.

HARRIS-LACEWELL, M. 2003. The Heart of the Politics of Race: Centering Black People in the Study of White Racial Attitudes. *Journal of Black Studies,* 34/2: 222–49.

HATTAM, V. 2007. *The Shadow of Race: Jews, Latinos, and Immigrant Politics in the United States.* Chicago, Ill.: University of Chicago Press.

IGNATIEV, N. 2008. *How the Irish Became White.* New York: Routledge.

JACOBSON, M. F. 1999. *Whiteness of a Different Color: European Immigrants and the Alchemy of Race.* Cambridge: Harvard University Press.

MARABLE, M. 1983. *How Capitalism Underdeveloped Black America.* Boston: South End Press.

MASUOKA, N. 2006. Together They Become One: Examining the Predictors of Panethnic Group Consciousness Among Asian Americans and Latinos. *Social Science Quarterly,* 87/5: 993–1011.

NIE, N., JUNN, J., and STEHLIK-BARRY, K. 1996. *Education and Democratic Citizenship in America.* Chicago, Ill.: University of Chicago Press.

NOBLES, M. 2000. *Shades of Citizenship: Race and the Census in Modern Politics.* Stanford, Calif.: Stanford University Press.

PREWITT, K. 2004. The Census Counts, the Census Classifies. In *Not Just Black and White: Historical and Contemporary Perspectives on Immigration, Race, and Ethnicity in the United States,* ed. N. Foner and G. M. Fredrickson. New York: Russell Sage Foundation.

ROGERS, R. 2006. *Afro-Caribbean Immigrants and the Politics of Immigration: Ethnicity, Exception, or Exit.* New York: Cambridge University Press.

SIDANIUS, J. and PRATTO, F. 2004. *Social Dominance.* New York: Cambridge University Press.

SMITH, R. M. 1997. *Civic Ideals.* New Haven, Conn.: Yale University Press.

VERBA, S. and NIE, N. H. 1972. *Participation in America: Political Democracy and Social Equality.* New York: Little Brown.

WALTON, H. JR. and SMITH, R. C. 2000. *American Politics and the African American Quest for Universal Freedom.* New York: Addison-Wesley Longman, Inc.

WILLIAMS, K. 2006. *Mark One or More: Civil Rights in Multiracial America.* Ann Arbor, Mich.: University of Michigan Press.

CHAPTER 37

....

STUDYING AMERICAN ELECTIONS*

....

PAUL R. ABRAMSON

JOHN H. ALDRICH

DAVID W. ROHDE

VOTING behavior research is one of the handful of fields of political science that has advanced as a science since the Second World War. The chapters in this volume provide ample evidence of this advancement. There is a common platform upon which theoretical, substantive, and methodological advances have been built, something approaching a paradigm for the study of public opinion and voting behavior. It can be thought of as a paradigm because, for all the particular differences, research in this area has been dominated by the large-N, random-sample survey design with questionnaires consisting of a large number of topics asked in a mostly closed-ended, or at most open-ended but short-response, format. And voting behavior research has also been dominated by the research traditions established by early voting studies. If the large-N, cross-sectional random sample has been the dominant research design, the National Election Study

* We are grateful to Darren W. Davis, Ada W. Finifter, Matt Grossman, Richard Johnston, Michael S. Lewis-Beck, Diana Mutz, Joseph A. Schlesinger, Brian D. Silver, Paul M. Sniderman, and Herbert F. Weisberg for helpful suggestions. We thank Jan E. Leighley for questions that helped clarify our arguments.

(NES) has set the "gold standard" for the highest-quality application of this design.[1] And, it has been dominated by a tradition of econometric-style statistical estimation with principal considerations being limited dependent variables, measurement error, and non-recursive model estimation (see, for example, Achen 1983, 1992).

In this chapter, we address two topics. First, we summarize what this field, through the NES and similar survey-based analyses of the electorate, has accomplished. What were the major intellectual questions and theoretical debates, and where have they taken us? Second, we assess directions that have spun off from this common core in recent years, and ask where they are likely to lead.

ALTERNATIVE APPROACHES TO THE STUDY OF AMERICAN ELECTIONS

Sociological Approaches

As we have argued since our book on the 1980 elections (Abramson, Aldrich, and Rohde 1982, 73–4), voting decisions can be studied from at least three theoretical perspectives. For the first three decades of the twentieth century, political scientists who wrote about elections were mainly descriptive. The first major studies of voting behavior in the United States analyzed social groups. The vast majority of Americans can be viewed as members of social groups. Americans belong to primary groups of family members and peers; secondary groups such as private clubs, trade unions, and voluntary associations; and broader reference groups such as social classes and ethnic groups.

According to Paul F. Lazarsfeld, Bernard R. Berelson, and their colleagues, understanding these groups is the key to understanding voters. Using a simple "index of political predisposition," they classified voters according to their religion (Catholic or Protestant), socioeconomic level (based upon a fourfold classification of socioeconomic status), and residence (urban or rural) to predict how they would vote in the 1940 presidential election (Lazarsfeld, Berelson, and Gaudet 1944, 174). They argued, "a person thinks, politically, as he is, socially. Social characteristics determine political preference" (27). Many other scholars followed this approach, with two of the major studies conducted by the sociologists Robert R. Alford (1963) and Richard F. Hamilton (1972). Alford's measure of class voting

---

[1] The nomenclature reflects the belief that the most reliable data gathered with procedures of the highest standards of excellence are those used by the NES in its quadrennial pre- and post-, face-to-face interviews.

(which subtracts the percentage of middle-class voters who voted for the Left party from the percentage of working-class voters who voted for the Left party) has been widely used in cross-national studies.[2]

Scholars who use Alford's measure generally conclude that class voting has been declining, not only in the United States but in most industrial societies. Jeff Manza and Clem Brooks (1999), using NES data from 1952 through 1996, challenge this conclusion. They argue that class differences are still important. In many respects, however, their conclusions support our own. They found, for example, that professionals were the most Republican class in the 1950s, but that by the 1996 election they had become the most Democratic. In addition, studies by Larry M. Bartels (2008), Jeffrey M. Stonecash (2000), and by Mark D. Brewer and Stonecash (2007) question the thesis that class differences have declined in the United States. Their basic argument is that class is better defined by differences in income than by occupational differences.[3]

Sociological categories have also guided political scientists who have studied the changing composition of party coalitions. Robert Axelrod (1972) pioneered these analyses by using NES surveys to study the social composition of the Democratic and Republican coalitions between 1952 and 1968. The Democratic coalition, he argued, was composed of the poor; Southerners; blacks (and other non-whites); union members (and members of their families); Catholics and other non-Protestants; and residents of the twelve largest metropolitan areas.[4] John R. Petrocik's (1981) study identified fifteen coalition groups and classified seven of them as predominantly Democratic: blacks; lower-status native Southerners; middle- and upper-status Southerners; Jews; Polish and Irish Catholics; union members; and lower-status border-state whites. He tracks changes in the relationship between social character-istics and party identification between 1952 and 1976.

A more recent analysis by Harold W. Stanley, William T. Bianco, and Richard G. Niemi (1986) analyzed seven pro-Democratic social groups to examine changes in party identification between 1952 and 1984. The pro-Democratic groups were: blacks; Catholics; Jews; women; native white Southerners; members of union households; and the working class. They assess the contribution that group

---

[2] Alford compared the United States, Canada, Britain, and Australia. Seymour Martin Lipset (1981, 505) used Alford's measure to compare the United States, Britain, West Germany, and Sweden. Ronald Inglehart (1997, 255) has compared class voting in the United States, Britain, West Germany, France, and Sweden, and Russell J. Dalton (2008, 148) has used the "Alford Class Voting Index" to compare the United States, Britain, the Federal Republic of Germany, and France. We use Alford's measure of class voting to track change in the United States from 1944 through 2004 (Abramson, Aldrich, and Rohde 2007, 120).

[3] For another study of the effects of income on US voting behavior, see Gelman et al. (2008).

[4] Axelrod (1986) continued to update his analyses through the 1984 election. Using Axelrod's categories, Nelson W. Polsby estimates the social composition of the Democratic and Republican presidential coalition between 1952 and 2004 (Polsby and Wildavsky 2004, 32; Polsby and Wildavsky, with Hopkins 2008, 28).

membership makes toward Democratic loyalties after controls are introduced for membership in other pro-Democratic groups (see also Erikson, Lancaster, and Romero 1989). Through a series of journal articles and book chapters, Stanley and Niemi (2006) expanded and updated their analyses through the 2004 presidential election. Our own analyses focus on race, region, union membership, social class, and religion (Abramson 1975, 11–49; Abramson, Aldrich, and Rohde 2007, 117–31). Chapters in this *Handbook* summarize findings about the voting behavior of Latinos (Garcia, Chapter 21) and of women (Sanbonmatsu, Chapter 22) and John C. Green (Chapter 23) examines the impact of religion.

Social-psychological Approaches

A second approach relies mainly on social-psychological variables to explain the decisions of individual voters. Angus Campbell, Philip E. Converse, Warren E. Miller, and Donald E. Stokes pioneered this tradition, which is most fully developed in their classic study, *The American Voter* (1960; see Jacoby, this volume, Chapter 15). They use data from the 1952 (and even the 1948 and 1958) election studies; however, their main data set was the 1956 NES. Although they acknowledge an intellectual debt to Kurt Lewin for his development of "field theory," they do not rely heavily upon any one social-psychological school. Their "funnel of causality" was a metaphor designed to explain how past forces lead to increasingly proximate forces just prior to the voting decision, although Campbell et al. never illustrated the funnel.[5]

Campbell and his colleagues focused on attitudes most likely to have the greatest effect on the vote just prior to the moment of decision, particularly attitudes toward the candidates, the parties, and the issues. Party identification emerged as a crucial social-psychological variable influencing voting decisions. Whether or not Americans identify (and identify strongly) with a party contributes to whether or not they vote, and even more strongly to how they vote.[6] Although experts in voting behavior agree that the distribution of party loyalties among the American electorate is important to understand elections, the correlates and consequences of party identification have been an ongoing concern among political scientists for the last five decades. There have been controversies about the origins of partisanship, its stability among individuals and electorates, the best way to measure party identification, the extent to which party identification shapes, or is shaped by,

---

[5] The concept was originally developed by Converse as part of a term paper at the University of Michigan (see Converse 2006). For illustrations of the funnel, see Dalton (2008, 171); and Lewis-Beck et al. (2008, 23).

[6] For their discussion of this latter relationship, see Campbell et al. (1960, 120–45).The concept was first introduced in Belknap and Campbell (1951–1952). For an extensive discussion of this concept, see Abramson (1983, 69–131).

policy preferences, and the meaning of partisan independence.[7] Likewise, Campbell and his colleagues drew upon psychological concepts in their analyses of ideology and attitude structure among the electorate. In addition, they discovered that feelings of political effectiveness contributed to political participation, even taking into account that Americans with high feelings of political effectiveness were more likely to have higher levels of education (Campbell et al. 1960, 103–5).[8]

The American Voter's authors also considered sociological measures, including a chapter on social class differences and the voting behavior of farmers. But their main focus was upon individual-level behavior, drawing upon concepts from social psychology.

The social-psychological approach developed by Campbell, Converse, Miller, and Stokes is the most prevalent among political scientists, although many deemphasize its psychological underpinnings. Converse's work provides the best example of this tradition.[9] Warren E. Miller and J. Merrill Shanks's (1996) *The New American Voter* provides another outstanding example of this approach, but even though it reemphasizes the importance of party identification, it also reflects a shift away from the social-psychological orientation employed by Miller and his colleagues in *The American Voter*. Miller and Shanks (1996, 15) explain that their own research "has gradually moved away from explanatory models that rely on voters' explicit evaluations of the candidates and parties by concentrating on the total effect of variables that are presumably located further back in the funnel of causality." In doing so, "we forgo an individual-level description of the psychological processes that connect policy preferences to vote choice." By analyzing political change between 1952 and 1992, Miller and Shanks help explain the long-term processes that transformed the American electorate.

Finally, in *The American Voter Revisited*, Michael S. Lewis-Beck, William G. Jacoby, Helmut Norpoth, and Herbert F. Weisberg (2008) make a valuable contribution to our understanding of American elections by using the 2000 and 2004 NES surveys to attempt to replicate Campbell et al.'s analyses of the 1952 and 1956 elections. Like Campbell and his colleagues, Lewis-Beck and his colleagues do not rely upon any single psychological approach. Like the authors of *The American Voter*, they discuss field theory, but they also discuss reference group theory and the

---

[7] Of these controversies, the most important involves the extent to which party identification responds to events. Fiorina (1981) advanced the most influential "revisionist" critique, arguing that party identification is malleable and represents a "running tally" of past experiences. Erikson, MacKuen, and Stimson (2002) use Gallup data (and the Gallup party affiliation measure) to advance a similar view. For evidence on the stability of party identification over time, see Green, Palmquist, and Schickler (2002).

[8] See also Campbell, Gurin, and Miller (1954, 187–94). For an extensive discussion of this concept, see Abramson (1983, 135–89).

[9] The single most important work by Converse, and one that draws heavily upon the social-psychological perspective, is Converse (1964). For the single best summary of his views on voting behavior, see Converse (1975). For more recent summaries, see Converse (2006, 2007).

functionalist perspective. For the most part, their findings are similar to those reached by Campbell et al. using data collected nearly half a century earlier. In particular, they found that party identification played a key role in explaining voter choice. The main differences they found are higher levels of attitude structure and a stronger relationship between ideological self-placement and partisanship (Lewis-Beck et al. 2008, 210–23).

Like Campbell and his colleagues, Lewis-Beck and his colleagues discuss the role of group membership on voting choices (305–33), as well as an analysis of social class (334–48). But given the shrinking number of farmers, they were unable to include a chapter on agrarian political behavior (see Campbell et al. 1960, 402–40).

Obviously, a study focusing on two elections may wind up choosing atypical contests. Were the elections of 2000 and 2004 more typical than the elections of 1952 and 1956? In all four elections the minority party among the electorate won. Granted America was involved in an unpopular war in 1952, but the incumbent president was not standing for reelection. In 2004, the U.S. was involved in an increasingly unpopular war in Iraq, and the incumbent narrowly prevailed. Analyses of the 2004 NES studies strongly suggest that Bush was narrowly reelected because a majority of voters thought he could deal better with terrorism than John F. Kerry (see Abramson et al. 2007; Norpoth and Sidman 2007; and Weisberg and Christenson 2007). Nonetheless, given the striking differences between the wartime election of 2004 and the peacetime election of 1956, the similarities of the results provide evidence that *The American Voter* approach is robust, at least for the study of American elections.[10]

Rational-choice Approaches

A third approach draws heavily from the work of economists. According to this perspective, citizens weigh the costs against the expected benefits when deciding whether or not to go to the polls. And when deciding how to vote, they calculate which candidate favors policies closest to their policy preferences. Citizens are thus viewed as rational actors who attempt to maximize their expected utility.

Anthony Downs's classic study *An Economic Theory of Democracy* (1957) drew upon an article by Harold Hotelling (1929) that explained why competing firms often chose to locate in close proximity and which observed that political parties often behaved the same way as firms. This led Downs to conceptualize parties as taking positions on policy space along a single continuum, leading to testable

[10] For two excellent summaries of the research on political psychology and political behavior, see Kinder (1998) and Mutz (2007). For alternative approaches, see Sniderman, Brody, and Tetlock et al. (1991). See also Sniderman (1993). For two alternative perspectives, see Zaller (1992) and Lau and Redlawsk (2006).

propositions derived from a spatial theory of voting (114–54). He also developed explanations for why some people voted, even though the cost of voting was very likely to be greater than its benefits (119–20; 260–76). Lastly, Downs explained how citizens could reduce information costs and discussed the role that political parties played in reducing them (36–50).

Propositions developed by Downs have led to research on American elections, much of it using the NES surveys. For example, William H. Riker and Peter C. Ordeshook (1968) tested hypotheses derived from Downs to explain why some citizens vote whereas others do not.[11] The seven-point issue scales, first used by the NES in 1968, have proved especially valuable for testing models of spatial competition, and these models have added to our understanding of the relationship of issue preferences to voting choices (Aldrich and McKelvey 1977). We have been guided by rational choice theory in using these measures to determine whether Americans have the knowledge necessary to vote on the basis of issues as well as to develop measures of apparent issue voting for all nine presidential elections between 1972 and 2004 (Abramson, Aldrich, and Rohde 2007, 143–51). Morris P. Fiorina's (1981) *Retrospective Voting in American National Elections* is the single most important book to study US elections using the rational choice approach. Fiorina elaborates and extends Downs's arguments. In addition to his reformulation of party identification, cited above (note 7), Fiorina analyses the NES surveys of the 1956, 1958, 1960, 1972, 1974, and 1976 elections to determine the extent to which voters use judgments about past performance to make their decisions.[12] There have been several excellent studies that summarize the research literature using this approach.[13] Aldrich and Arthur Lupia (this volume, Chapter 6) discuss in detail the contributions of the rational choice approach to two areas: strategic voting and voter competence and learning.

Comparing These Approaches

Scholars have used NES surveys to test propositions drawn from all of these approaches. In our view, however, none of them provides a comprehensive answer to questions of how voters decide whether to vote and for whom. Although

---

[11] One of their main conclusions is that the expected closeness of an election will increase turnout by increasing the perceived benefits of voting. Two scholars also noted for their contributions to rational choice theory, John A. Ferejohn and Morris P. Fiorina, have challenged this conclusion. See Ferejohn and Fiorina (1974, 1975).

[12] These surveys were chosen because there was a three-wave panel study conducted in 1956–1958–1960 and again in 1972–1974–1976.

[13] For summaries of much of this research, see Hinich and Munger (1997); and Shepsle and Bonchek (1997). For an introduction to voting behavior that draws heavily upon the rational choice literature, see Morton (2006). And for an interesting perspective that combines rational choice and psychological approaches, see Popkin (1991).

individuals belong to groups, they are not always influenced by their group memberships. Moreover, classifying voters by groups does not explain why they are influenced by their group memberships.

Lewis-Beck and his colleagues (2008) are highly critical of focusing on social groups. They argue that the sociological approach focuses on demographic characteristics that can change only gradually over time. But the national vote can change a great deal from election to election, and the changing group composition of the electorate cannot explain short-term shifts. Yet they themselves include two chapters on group characteristics to explain voting behavior in the 2000 and 2004 elections, and acknowledge that changes among social groups can account for partisan realignments (403–4).

Placing too much emphasis on social-psychological factors can lead us away from studying the way political forces shape political behavior. In particular, it may lead to underestimating the extent to which voters rely upon retrospective evaluations. This was V. O. Key's (1966) criticism in his posthumous book, *The Responsible Electorate*, which rejected both the Columbia and Michigan Survey Research Center approaches. These studies, Key argued, painted an overly bleak portrait of the American electorate. Relying upon surveys that asked voters how they had voted in the previous election, Key (1966, 7) argued:

The perverse and unorthodox argument of this little book is that voters are not fools. To be sure, many individual voters act in odd ways indeed; yet in the large the electorate behaves about as rationally and as responsibly as we should expect, given the clarity of the alternatives presented to it and the character of the information available to it.

In his review of *The Responsible Electorate*, Converse (1966) was doubtless constrained both by Key's stature and by the recentness of his death. All the same, he was highly critical of Key's methods, his failure to define rationality adequately, and the lack of clarity of his data presentation. Yet he acknowledged that Key's central thesis that voters usually vote retrospectively was essentially correct. And later, writing about the 1968 election, Converse et al. conclude, "Key's general thesis represented a welcome corrective" (Converse et al. 1969, 1095).

Although we are sympathetic to rational choice analyses, we recognize that this approach is the most likely to be criticized. Lewis-Beck and his colleagues (2008, 28) reveal little sympathy for this perspective. They argue: "When the rational-choice model argues that people vote in their self-interest as they define it, the argument borders on the tautological." And yet, the continued vitality of both theoretical and empirical research in the rational choice tradition suggests that scholars find it an important source of insight. Further, Aldrich and Lupia (this volume, Chapter 6) argue that it has yielded empirical findings in at least selected areas of importance that no other tradition has been able to explain. Thus, we conclude that each theoretical perspective has areas of great strength and thus makes important contributions to understanding electoral politics, while no research tradition has been able to explain all important empirical findings in the literature. Thus, healthy skepticism is in order, but so is careful, eclectic application of each approach necessary for understanding currently observed patterns in the data.

NEWER APPROACHES

The stream of research considered to this point may be thought of as the culmination of a half century of the NES-style paradigm for the assessment of public opinion and voting behavior. As the preponderance of this volume and our own chapter to this point makes clear, this has been—and we are sure will continue to be—a rich generator of insights about the American voter, as well as providing the research platform for the development and comparative assessments of alternative theoretical perspectives. While it seems a natural way to think about electoral behavior, there are other paradigms possible.

Echoing the point made in Aldrich and Lupia (this volume), every approach must make a series of assumptions, and we present these newer developments as they flow from a different set of assumptions. In addition, technological advances (e.g., the internet) have opened new ways of employing different designs.

The "gold standard" set by NES also extends to their openness to revision. This has been especially true in the last few years, as co-PIs (Principal Investigators) Jon A. Krosnick and Arthur Lupia, with support from the National Science Foundation (NSF), have played a leadership role in creating a more open NES. Thus, they sought out perspectives from those who have not been involved deeply in the NES before, particularly from psychologists (see <http://www.ssri.duke.edu/anes/index. html>). They created a more open web-based system for input of ideas and interchanges between scholars (the Online Commons, <http://www.electionstudies.org/onlinecommons.htm>). For the first time in years, they had the resources to be able to run a major pilot study (<http://www.electionstudies.org/studypages/2006pilot/2006pilot.htm>). Reports are on line at <http://www.electionstudies.org/resources/papers/pilotrpt.htm>, and a number will appear in Aldrich and Kathleen McGraw (forthcoming). And, Krosnick and Lupia were able to run a multi-wave internet panel in addition to face-to-face pre- and post-election interviews. They thus had the space to incorporate a large number of new questions and formats in addition to maintaining the core pre- and post-election face-to-face interviews.

Of course, the NES was not a closed operation before this innovation. Panel designs date from 1956/58/60. An intra-campaign panel was conducted in 1980 and a rolling cross-section in 1984, making possible the study of the public's role in nomination politics (e.g., Bartels 1988). Beginning in 1978, in response to the input of congressional scholars, the NES began to collect new data on congressional elections, although the NES did not conduct a survey after the 2006 midterm election (Jacobson 2009, 123). In addition, a three-wave panel geared to the Senate elections was run in 1988/90/92. Pilot studies were designed throughout this period with input from the larger community. Fifty years of common content made projects such as Robert S. Erikson, Michael B. MacKuen, and James A. Stimson's *The Macro Polity* (2002) possible, and generated an interaction between public opinion and voting behavior on the one hand and representation and legislative output on the other, through this pooled cross-section, time-series design.

Both Converse and Stokes took their theoretical insights into comparative contexts (Butler and Stokes 1974, Converse and Dupeux 1962; Converse and Pierce 1986). NES thus became the gold standard for national election studies worldwide. The obvious next step was the development of multi-national projects. Again with support from both the NSF and NES, the Comparative Study of Electoral Systems (CSES) is now well in place and seeking to maintain the academic integrity of the "gold standard" idea in a comparative context. This project (see <http://www.umich.edu/~cses/>) creates a module of questions, based on an open selection process from the world-wide survey research community to be asked exactly the same way worldwide. There are now two such modules online free for analysis. A third module is still being run, and a fourth module is being prepared for use in the future. A special issue of *Electoral Studies* (the March, 2008 issue, Vol. 27, Issue 1) is devoted to research using CSES data. The CSES raises a particular set of statistical challenges and opportunities, particularly multi-level modeling. With the macro-datasets accompanying the surveys, CSES supports four levels of analysis: the respondent, the electoral district, the individual national party, and the national system.

One limitation of the large-N, cross-sectional survey is that the survey is strictly speaking purely a report of what is going on in the heads of respondents (a famous illustration of this point is Zaller and Feldman 1992). The richness of such a large diversity of question responses, however, makes it more difficult to make causal claims. Cross-sectional data typically require the use of statistical procedures, with arbitrary and hard-to-defend assumptions. Two of the most elegant attempts of this type were published side by side, making rather different inferences (Converse and Markus 1979; Page and Jones 1979).

The experiment has a strong advantage over the traditional survey in making defensible claims about causation. Randomized treatment effects imply that if the treatment variable has an effect, that effect is causal, not merely correlational. Paul M. Sniderman championed the embedding of experiments in a survey (Sniderman and Grob 1996). Effective randomization of treatments generates the internal reliability of the experiment, while the random sample yields the external validity of the survey, permitting inferences to the relevant population. Sniderman conducted a large number of such experiments on race and politics (Sniderman and

Carmines 1997). Richard K. Herrmann, Philip E. Tetlock, and Penny S. Visser (1999) also employed experiments to study citizens' reaction to war.

Sniderman offered time freely to the research community on two multi-investigator surveys. These studies led to their current institutionalized form as Time-sharing Experiments for the Social Sciences (TESS, see <http://www.experiment-central.org/>). Scholars submit proposals for experiments that, should they pass peer review, will be run on a national survey at no cost to the researcher. For the most part, TESS interviews are conducted via the internet and Web TV. TESS has made experimentation with externally valid inferences available to many scholars and their students. For an excellent example of using TESS data to study attitudes toward military crises, see Tomz (2007). The Annenberg Surveys, which rely upon rolling cross-sectional surveys, have yielded data for numerous studies of American elections (see, for example, Box-Steffensmeier, Darmofal, and Farrell 2009; Gelman et al. 2008; and Krasno and Green 2008).

Of course, embedding a number of experiments within a survey, including treatments about highly charged topics, raises methodological issues (see Gaines, Kuklinksi, and Quirk 2007; Transue, Lee, and Aldrich 2009). For more on experimentation, the reader can usefully consult Eckel (2004), Fridkin and Kenney (this volume, Chapter 4), Green, Gerber, and Davenport (this volume, Chapter 5), Morton and Williams (2008), and Roth (1995).

NES face-to-face interviewing is the gold standard in the sense that it yields the most reliable data that surveys can provide. It is also very expensive. It is natural that survey researchers explore alternatives to face-to-face interviewing. Originally, telephone surveys became a major alternative (one that was explored by NES in the 2000 election). Yet, the ease of breaking phone connections, screening incoming calls, and, perhaps most of all, the spread of cell phones with numbers that are typically off the list for random sampling, has undermined the reliability of phone surveys and the samples drawn from them. As we have seen above, the rise of the internet has offered a new platform that substantially reduces the costs of surveying. Like other aspects of the internet, it has revolutionary potential for survey research through decentralization. The NES imposes two constraints that external input had to pass: peer review and central decision (PIs and a Board of Overseers). The process also required a considerable commitment by researchers with a good idea, because the complex process of pilot-testing and winning the competition for restricted space on the final questionnaire takes a great deal of time.

This route led to important advances and additions in many areas, but it was an openness that retained centralized quality controls. Compared with the NES, more recent projects have been less centralized. TESS, for example, reduced centralized control while retaining full peer review for experiments. Other internet-based surveys have provided an even more open platform. First the Cooperative Congressional Election Study in 2006 and 2008 (see <http://web.mit.edu/polisci/portl/cces/index. html>) and, for 2008, the Cooperative Campaign Analysis Project (<http://www.

polimetrix.com/news/ccap.html>) make reasonably large blocks of questions in a national sample available at low cost. Thirty universities purchased blocks in 2006. In 2008, several universities purchased such blocks, providing the space free for (competitive) application from their faculty and students. In this sense, the academy has begun to realize the nearly Wiki-like properties of internet surveys. The methodological cost of this easing of constraints is modification of the assumption of randomized selection of respondent. Most internet surveys, at least at this time, recruit respondents who agree to participate in a number of surveys for several years, thus attenuating the idea of random selection. In place of the use of Kish-like formulas (Kish 1965) for confidence intervals, hypothesis tests, and standard errors are various matching techniques (see, for example, Ho et. al. 2007; Sekhon 2008).

In sum, the classical paradigm of the large-N random survey has already taken many new directions. The results are changing the nature of the research problem and it is therefore likely to change the nature of the theoretical structure of the field. It seems likely that new theory will emerge from advances in social psychology and neuroscience. For example, Marcus, Neuman, and MacKuen (2000) and Taber and Lodge (2006) provide examples in the study of emotion as applied to politics. Each new direction raises, in turn, a new set of methodological issues, largely due to the changing set of assumptions that define that approach. The field is thus richer in method as well as substance. How much richer it will prove in theoretical development remains an open question.

References

ABRAMSON, P. R. 1975. *Generational Change in American Politics*. Lexington, Mass.: D.C. Heath.
—— 1983. *Political Attitudes in America: Formation and Change*. San Francisco: W. H. Freeman.
—— ALDRICH, J. H., and ROHDE, D. W. 1982. *Change and Continuity in the 1980 Elections*. Washington, D.C.: CQ Press.
—— —— —— 2007. *Change and Continuity in the 2004 and 2006 Elections*. Washington, D.C.: CQ Press.
—— —— RICKERSHAUSER, J., and ROHDE, D. W. 2007. Fear in the Voting Booth: The 2004 Presidential Election. *Political Behavior*, 29: 197–220.
ACHEN, C. H. 1983. Toward Theories of Data: The State of Political Methodology. In *Political Science: The State of the Discipline*, ed. A. W. Finifter. Washington, D.C.: The American Political Science Association.
—— 1992. Social Psychology, Demographic Variables, and Linear Regression: Breaking the Iron Triangle in Voting Research. *Political Behavior*, 14: 195–211.
ALDRICH, J. H. and McGRAW, K. (ed.). Forthcoming. *The Book of Ideas*.
—— and McKELVEY, R. D. 1977. A Method of Scaling with Applications to the 1968 and 1972 Presidential Elections. *American Political Science Review*, 71: 111–30.

ALFORD, R. R. 1963. *Party and Society: The Anglo-American Democracies*. Chicago, Ill.: Rand McNally.

AXELROD, R. 1972. Where the Votes Come From: An Analysis of Electoral Coalitions, 1952–1968. *American Political Science Review*, 66: 11–20.

—— 1986. Presidential Election Coalitions in 1984. *American Political Science Review*, 80: 281–4.

BARTELS, L. M. 1988. *Presidential Primaries and the Dynamics of Public Choice*. Princeton, N.J.: Princeton University Press.

—— 2008. *Unequal Democracy: The Political Economy of the New Gilded Age*. New York: Russell Sage.

BELKNAP, G. and CAMPBELL, A. 1951–1952. Political Party Identification and Attitudes Toward Foreign Policy. *Public Opinion Quarterly*, 15: 601–23.

BOX-STEFFENSMEIER, J. M., DARMOFAL, D., and FARRELL, C. 2009. The Aggregate Dynamics of Campaigns. *Journal of Politics*, 71: 309–23.

BREWER, M. D. and STONECASH, J. M. 2007. *Split: Class and Cultural Divides in American Politics*. Washington, D.C.: CQ Press.

BUTLER, D. and STOKES, D. 1974. *Political Change in Britain: The Evolution of Electoral Choice*, 2nd edn. New York: St. Martins.

CAMPBELL, A., GURIN, G., and MILLER, W. E. 1954. *The Voter Decides*. Evanston, Ill.: Row, Peterson.

—— CONVERSE, P. E., MILLER, W. E., and STOKES, D. E. 1960. *The American Voter*. New York: Wiley.

CONVERSE, P. E. 1964. The Nature of Belief Systems in Mass Publics. In *Ideology and Discontent*, ed. D. E. Apter. New York: Free Press.

—— 1966. Book Review of *The Responsible Electorate*. *Political Science Quarterly*, 81: 628–33.

—— 1975. Public Opinion and Voting Behavior. In *Handbook of Political Science*, volume 4: *Nongovernmental Politics*, ed. F. I. Greenstein and N. W. Polsby. Reading, Mass.: Addison-Wesley.

—— 2006. Researching Electoral Politics. *American Political Science Review*, 100: 605–12.

—— 2007. Perspectives on Mass Belief Systems and Communication. In *The Oxford Handbook of Political Behavior*, ed. R. J. Dalton and Hans-Dieter Klingemann. New York: Oxford University Press.

—— and DUPEUX, G. 1962. Politicization of the Electorate in France and the United States. *Public Opinion Quarterly*, 26: 1–23.

—— and MARKUS, G. B. 1979. Plus ça change...: The New CPS Election Study Panel. *American Political Science Review*, 73: 32–49.

—— and PIERCE, R. C. 1986. *Political Representation in France*. Cambridge, Mass.: Harvard University Press.

—— MILLER, W. E., RUSK, J. G., and WOLFE, A. C. 1969. Continuity and Change in American Politics: Parties and Issues in the 1968 Election. *American Political Science Review*, 63: 1083–105.

DALTON, R. J. 2008. *Citizen Politics: Public Opinion and Political Parties in Advanced Industrial Democracies*, 5th edn. Washington, D.C.: CQ Press.

DOWNS, A. 1957. *An Economic Theory of Democracy*. New York: Harper and Row.

ECKEL, C. 2004. Vernon Smith: Economics as a Laboratory Science. *Journal of Socio-Economics*, 33: 15–28.

ERIKSON, R. S., LANCASTER, T. D., and ROMERO, D. W. 1989. Group Components of the Presidential Vote, 1952–1984. *Journal of Politics*, 51: 337–46.

—— MacKuen, M. B., and Stimson, J. A. 2002. *The Macro Polity*. Cambridge: Cambridge University Press.

Ferejohn, J. A. and Fiorina, M. P. 1974. The Paradox of Not Voting: A Decision Theoretic Analysis. *American Political Science Review*, 68: 525–36.

—— —— 1975. Closeness Counts Only in Horseshoes And Dancing. *American Political Science Review*, 69: 920–5.

Fiorina, M. P. 1981. *Retrospective Voting in American National Elections*. New Haven, Conn.: Yale University Press.

Gaines, B. J., Kuklinski, J. H., and Quirk, P. J. 2007. The Logic of the Survey Experiment Reexamined. *Political Analysis*, 15/1: 1–20.

Gelman, A., Park, D., Shor, B., Bafumi, J., and Cortina, J. 2008. *Red State, Blue State, Rich State, Poor State: Why Americans Vote the Way They Do*. Princeton, N.J.: Princeton University Press.

Green, D., Palmquist, B., and Schickler, E. 2002. *Partisan Hearts and Minds: Political Parties and the Social Identities of Voters*. New Haven, Conn.: Yale University Press.

Hamilton, R. F. 1972. *Class and Politics in the United States*. New York: Wiley.

Herrmann, R. K., Tetlock, P. E., and Visser, P. S. 1999. Mass Public Decisions on Going to War: A Cognitive-Interactionist Framework. *American Political Science Review*, 93: 553–74.

Hinich, M. J. and Munger, M. C. 1997. *Analytical Politics*. Cambridge: Cambridge University Press.

Ho, D. E., Imai, K., King, G., and Stuart, E. A. 2007. Matching as Nonparametric Preprocessing for Reducing Model Dependence in Parametric Causal Inference. *Political Analysis*, 15: 199–236.

Hotelling, H. 1929. Stability in Competition. *Economic Journal*, 39: 41–57.

Inglehart, R. 1997. *Modernization and Postmodernization: Cultural, Economic, and Political Change in 43 Societies*. Princeton, N.J.: Princeton University Press.

Jacobson, G. C. 2009. *The Politics of Congressional Elections*, 7th edn. New York: Pearson Longman.

Key, V. O., Jr. 1966. *The Responsible Electorate: Rationality in Presidential Voting, 1936–1960*. Cambridge, Mass.: Harvard University Press.

Kinder, D. R. 1998. Opinion and Action in the Realm of Politics. In *The Handbook of Social Psychology*, 4th edn., volume 2, ed. D. T. Gilbert, S. T. Fiske, and G. Lindsey. Boston: McGraw Hill.

Kish, L. 1965. *Survey Sampling*. New York: Wiley.

Krasno, J. S. and Green, D. P. 2008. Do Televised Presidential Ads Increase Turnout? Evidence from a Natural Experiment. *Journal of Politics*, 70: 245–61.

Lau, R. R. and Redlawsk, D. P. 2006. *How Voters Decide: Information Processing during Election Campaigns*. Cambridge: Cambridge University Press.

Lazarsfeld, P. F., Berelson, B., and Gaudet, H. 1944. *The People's Choice: How the Voter Makes Up His Mind in a Presidential Campaign*. New York: Duell, Sloan, and Pearce.

Lewis-Beck, M. S., Jacoby, W. G., Norpoth, H., and Weisberg, H. F. 2008. *The American Voter Revisited*. Ann Arbor, Mich.: University of Michigan Press.

Lipset, S. M. 1981. *Political Man: The Social Bases of Politics*, expanded edn. Baltimore, Md.: Johns Hopkins University Press.

Manza, J. and Brooks, C. 1999. *Social Cleavages and Political Change: Voter Alignments and U.S. Party Coalitions*. New York: Oxford University Press.

MARCUS, G. E., NEUMAN, W. R., and MacKUEN, M. 2000. *Affective Intelligence and Political Judgment*. Chicago, Ill.: University of Chicago Press.

MILLER, W. E. and SHANKS, J. M. 1996. *The New American Voter*. Cambridge, Mass.: Harvard University Press.

MORTON, R. B. 2006. *Analyzing Elections*. New York: Norton.

—— and WILLIAMS, K. C. 2008. Experimentation in Political Science. In *Oxford Handbook of Political Methodology*, ed. J. M. Box-Steffensmeier, H. E. Brady, and D. Collier. New York: Oxford University Press.

MUTZ, D. C. 2007. Political Psychology and Choice. In *The Oxford Handbook of Political Behavior*, ed. R. J. Dalton and H.-D. Klingemann. New York: Oxford University Press.

NORPOTH, H. and SIDMAN, A. H. 2007. Mission Accomplished: The Wartime Election of 2004. *Political Behavior*, 29: 175–95.

PAGE, B. I. and JONES, C. C. 1979. Reciprocal Effects of Policy Preferences, Party Loyalties and the Vote. *American Political Science Review*, 73: 1071–89.

PETROCIK, J. R. 1981. *Party Coalitions: Realignment and the Decline of the New Deal Party System*. Chicago, Ill.: University of Chicago Press.

POLSBY, N. W. and WILDAVSKY, A. 2004. *Presidential Elections: Strategies and Structures in American Politics*, 11th edn. Lanham, Md.: Rowman and Littlefield.

—— —— with D. A. HOPKINS. 2008. *Presidential Elections: Strategies and Structures in American Politics*, 12th edn. Lanham, Md.: Rowman and Littlefield.

POPKIN, S. L. 1991. *The Reasoning Voter: Communications and Persuasion in Presidential Campaigns*. Chicago, Ill.: University of Chicago Press.

RIKER, W. H. and ORDESHOOK, P. C. 1968. A Theory of the Calculus of Voting. *American Political Science Review*, 62: 25–42.

ROTH, A. E. 1995. Introduction to Experimental Economics. In *The Handbook of Experimental Economics*, ed. J. H. Kagel and A. E. Roth. Princeton, N.J.: Princeton University Press.

SEKHON, J. S. 2008. The Neyman–Rubin Model of Causal Inference and Estimation via Matching Methods. In *The Oxford Handbook of Political Methodology*, ed. J. M. Box-Steffensmeier, H. E. Brady, and D. Collier. New York: Oxford University Press.

SHEPSLE, K. A. and BONCHEK, M. S. 1997. *Analyzing Politics: Rationality, Behavior, and Institutions*. New York: Norton.

SNIDERMAN, P. M. 1993. The New Look in Public Opinion Research. In *Political Science: The State of the Discipline II*, ed. A. W. Finifter. Washington, D.C.: American Political Science Association.

—— and CARMINES, E. G. 1997. *Reaching Beyond Race*. Cambridge, Mass.: Harvard University Press.

—— and GROB, D. 1996. Innovations in Experimental Design in General Population Attitude Surveys. *Annual Review of Sociology*, 22: 377–99.

—— BRODY, R. A., and TETLOCK, P. E., et al. 1991. *Reasoning and Choice: Explorations in Political Psychology*. Cambridge: Cambridge University Press.

STANLEY, H. W., BIANCO, W. T., and NIEMI, R. G. 1986. Partisanship and Group Support Over Time: A Multivariate Analysis. *American Political Science Review*, 80: 969–76.

—— and NIEMI, R. G. 2006. Partisanship, Party Coalitions, and Group Support, 1952–2004. *Presidential Studies Quarterly*, 36: 172–88.

STONECASH, J. M. 2000. *Class and Party in American Politics*. Boulder, Colo.: Westview.

TABER, C. S. and LODGE, M. 2006. Motivated Skepticism in the Evaluation of Political Beliefs. *American Journal of Political Science*, 50: 755–69.

TOMZ, M. 2007. Domestic Audience Costs in International Relations: An Experimental Approach. *International Organization*, 61: 821–40.

TRANSUE, J. E., LEE, D. J., and ALDRICH, J. H. 2009. Treatment Spillover Effects Across Survey Experiments. *Political Analysis*, 17: 143–61.

WEISBERG, H. F. and CHRISTENSON, D. P. 2007. Changing Horses in Wartime? The 2004 Presidential Election. *Political Behavior*, 29: 279–304.

ZALLER, J. R. 1992. *The Nature and Origins of Mass Opinion*. Cambridge: Cambridge University Press.

—— and FELDMAN, S. 1992. A Simple Theory of the Survey Response: Answering Questions versus Revealing Preferences. *American Journal of Political Science*, 36: 579–616.

....

IN SEARCH OF REPRESENTATION THEORY

....

PATRICIA A. HURLEY

KIM QUAILE HILL

MANY of the chapters in this volume discuss topics relevant to the quality of political representation. Among these are the character of mass participation and vote choice in elections, the effects of rules and procedures on participation in elections, and various forms of elite behavior that might also shape the process of representation. There is, however, a large body of scholarship that investigates the quality of representation directly and systematically. The latter scholarship will be assessed here to indicate how the concerns of the preceding chapters can be brought into tighter focus for this subject.

Research on representation is distinguished, too. The seminal essay on this topic by Miller and Stokes (1963) is one of the most cited, if not one of the most carefully read, publications in political science. While subsequent research considers many alternative topics and approaches, the focus on dyadic policy representation in Miller and Stokes is the model for much scholarship still today. And abundant scholarship has followed this and various other leads for characterizing the process of political representation.

Much contemporary scholarship on this topic, however, proceeds with at best mixed understanding of the corpus of research findings created since the publication of Miller and Stokes's essay. Established findings are at times ignored. Key concepts are confused in some contemporary research. Empirical data that are ready to hand and therefore widely employed fail to match the theoretical concepts that some authors claim to study. Some authors do not recognize the implications of their research for well established general conceptions of the process of representation.

For the preceding reasons the bulk of this chapter will review what we consider the central concepts for and most critical research challenges that characterize the systematic study of representation. We also seek to identify the frontier of our knowledge and the most notable gaps in that frontier—based on what is known from both classic and contemporary research. We recognize that the topic of democratic representation leads to many topical questions of interest to both scholars and the general public. Yet our intention is to encourage research that would advance the creation of basic-science general theory.

CONCEPTUALIZING REPRESENTATION

Most scientific research relies on Hannah Pitkin's normative definition of representation. The most frequently quoted line from that work is that representation "means acting in the interest of the represented, in a manner responsive to them" (Pitkin 1967, 209). Eulau and Karps (1977) have identified four forms of representational responsiveness: policy, allocation, service, and symbolic. Typically, Pitkin's definition is used to apply to policy responsiveness, but allocation, service, and symbolic representation all have responsiveness components. We begin, however, with policy representation, because this is at the core of theories of representative democracy.

Policy responsiveness is generally construed to mean that elected representatives follow the bidding of their constituencies. The standard "demand-input" model, which dominates the study of representation, posits members of legislative bodies as instructed delegates (Wahlke 1971). Constituencies signal policy preferences to their respective legislators, who then respond. Constituency preferences therefore inform policy making. Presumably, the net result is that public policy is congruent with public preferences.

In the real world of representation, things are not so simple. A number of factors complicate this model of representation. The first complication is imbedded in Pitkin's definition, although it is frequently ignored by researchers. Responsiveness suggests that constituency preferences motivate legislator action. Indeed, this is the definition of the instructed delegate model. But Pitkin also makes reference to interests, and these do not necessarily coincide with preferences. One's preference may be for lower taxes, but one's interest may be better served by the policies financed by higher tax rates (e.g., a more expensive education system may deliver higher-quality education, a lower federal deficit may produce a more favorable economic environment).

The tension between responding to interests or preferences is resolved in a trustee model of policy representation. The trustee represents constituency interests, regardless of preferences, giving his or her constituents what is good for them, even if it is not necessarily what the constituents want. The trustee is not unfettered by constituency: Pitkin (1967, 209–10) maintains that the representative "must not be found persistently at odds with the wishes of the represented without good reason in terms of their interest, without a good explanation of why their wishes are not in accord with their interest." The possibility of electoral sanction forces representatives to earn their constituents' trust if they wish to stay in office while representing interests over preferences.

Trust is the core of symbolic representation, as well. Fenno (1978) documents how the "homestyle" adopted by legislators can forge bonds of trust with constituents that buy them the leeway needed to represent interests over preferences. Trust also allows representatives to educate constituents about their interests, which can bring preferences and interests into alignment (see also Bianco 1994). The notion of symbolic representation lays the groundwork for a complex model of representation that moves beyond simple constituency control. Such a complex model allows the flow of influence in the representative process to run from legislator to constituency (the reverse of the classic responsiveness model), to exist simultaneously in both directions, or on some occasions, to allow a representative to act without any reference to constituency opinions. The insight that representational linkages should be conceptualized in these complex terms is long standing (e.g., Eulau and Karps 1977, 236–7; Kuklinski and Segura 1995; Wahlke 1971). Yet the majority of contemporary students of representation cling to the demand-input conceptualization.

Trust may also be created when an elected representative shares descriptive characteristics with constituents. Mansbridge (1999) discusses the normative advantages of descriptive representation, giving contingent approval to the idea that certain subsets of the population are best represented by "one of their own." In this conceptualization, women are best represented by women, African Americans by African Americans, Latinos by Latinos, and so on. There is a growing body of empirical scholarship that examines the substantive implications of such minority representation.

Note that representation conceptualized this way implies that certain subsets of a geographic constituency might be better represented than others. Unless district preferences or interests are completely homogeneous, an elected representative can only represent some portion of the constituency. That portion may be conceptualized in a variety of ways, some of which overlap. A legislator may represent members of his or her political party, those constituents who voted for him in the last election, those constituents who may vote for her in the next election, or some central tendency of opinion within a district. How we conceptualize and measure constituency interests or preferences has a powerful impact on the empirical assessment of the extent of representation. Yet there is no common resolution for these concerns in existing research on dyadic representation. Some scholars even fail to recognize how the empirical measures they employ may not be valid indicators of the conceptual attribute of the constituency in their theory.

The idea of sub-constituencies suggests that certain groups in a legislative district go unrepresented on policy matters by their official representative. But such groups go without representation only if the process is perceived as purely dyadic—one geographic constituency with one officially elected representative. But members of the minority party in a district, women in a district represented by a male legislator, African Americans or Latinos in a district represented by a white legislator can be represented by legislators who share their characteristics but who are sent to the legislature from other districts. The model of representation is then collective rather than dyadic.

Weissberg's (1978) evidence shows that collective representation of general public preferences almost always outperforms dyadic representation in bringing about correspondence between public opinion and legislative voting, although Hurley (1982) has demonstrated that dyadic can exceed collective representation when national minority preferences become public policy.

Mechanisms for Achieving Representation

Elections are the mechanism for achieving representation through constituency control. The demand-input delegate model works like this: constituencies choose a representative on election day. That representative is expected to be aware of constituency policy preferences (or interests) and should respond to them as he or she goes about legislative business. Failure to do so will lead to defeat at the next election. A good record of responsiveness will result in reelection. Thus elections tether legislators to their constituencies. Yet this gross overview of the process masks important distinctions about how and to what portion of the constituency a legislator should respond.

The most prominent characterization of the process is the median-voter model. In this model the median voter casts the decisive vote in any election. To win, the legislator must appeal to the median voter. When running for his or her first term, the candidate appeals to the policy preferences of the median voter. So does the opponent. Whichever candidate is closer to that median wins the seat. When running for reelection, the representative must have a record of legislative voting that reflects the preferences of the median voter. Failure to compile such a record can be exploited by an electoral opponent, who will claim to be more faithful to the constituency median if elected. If the incumbent has strayed too far from the median, the opponent will be victorious. Thus legislators have an electoral incentive to provide representation to the constituency median.

Note that the median-voter model of elections implies that the differences between the candidates on policy are minimal. Both candidates will position themselves near the preferences of the median voter. Elections matter for achieving representation, but outcomes do not. If there are few differences between the candidates on policy matters, either will represent the constituency equally well on this dimension. Policy differences between candidates arise only if incumbents shirk (i.e., compile a voting record that strays from the opinions of the median voter). Note as well that a median-voter model always conceptualizes policy representation as dyadic.

In contrast, a responsible-parties model of representation assigns importance to both elections and their outcomes. Candidates compete before the electorate by offering alternative sets of policies that are in line with national party positions. Choosing a Republican will get the constituency a different voting record than choosing a Democrat. Reelection will depend on whether a representative remains faithful to the party *and* whether the party policies turn out to be pleasing to voters within and across districts.

Common to both the median voter and the responsible parties models is the notion that elections are the mechanisms of constituency control. These are active models of control, assigning a key role to voters. Thus, the extent of voter participation in elections as well as the foundations of voter choice will shape the character and quality of responsiveness.

But representation may also be achieved in passive ways that place less importance on the role of elections. The process of belief sharing can produce roll-call voting that reflects the predominant view in the constituency when representation is considered dyadically. The elected representative is a product of the constituency and is shaped by its political culture. Thus, when representatives act on their own attitudes, constituencies are represented even though no overt pressure is placed on the representatives. Collectively, female legislators might represent women in general (or black legislators represent blacks, and so on) because their shared life experiences and common reference points give rise to a shared set of policy concerns. Such passive representation underlies much of the discussion of symbolic representation. Activities by legislators designed to create trust advance the possibility of passive representation. Fenno (1978) observes that a legislator's homestyle promotes the view that he or she is of the constituency—the message of a successful homestyle is "I am one of you." In this view, competitive elections do not foster policy representation. In fact, the trust that underlies symbolic representation may decrease the competitiveness of elections and is thought by some scholars to be a fundamental basis of the incumbency advantage. How the incumbency advantage promotes or inhibits policy representation will be discussed later in this chapter.

Empirical Problems in Assessing Representation

What we know about the extent of representation is dependent on how we measure constituency preferences or interests, legislative actions, and the techniques used to relate the two. The most challenging problem in studying representation dyadically is the measurement of constituency preferences. Few national (or state) surveys of public opinion are designed to measure preferences at the district level, although there are some famous and frequently used exceptions (the American Representation Study of 1958, the American National Election Study for 1978, and the Senate Election Study of 1988, 1990, and 1992—all archived with the Inter-University Consortium for Political and Social Research). Even these have a relatively low number of respondents per district, so constituency preference data are especially prone to measurement error. An alternative is to use election outcomes as an indicator of constituency preferences. Some studies have employed referenda results, but the opportunities to do so are limited to only a small number of states. These are specific with reference to policy, but low turnout in such elections means that measurement error is still a problem.

An alternative is to use presidential election outcomes at the district or state level to indicate the overall liberalism/conservatism of the constituency. This practice too can be contaminated with notable measurement error. Presidential vote choices may be made on factors other than ideology or policy agreement with the candidates, and some presidential elections do not reflect such agreement in data aggregated to the level of constituencies (LeoGrande and Jeydel 1997). The problem of using opinion data to measure sub-constituency preferences is even more acute. Measuring policy opinions to study collective representation is easier—national surveys serve this purpose well, and are still representative when broken down by party identification or other relevant groups.

Perhaps because the measurement of preferences is so difficult, many analysts have turned to demographic data instead. Profiles of districts with respect to racial make-up, income levels, education levels, concentration in urban areas or different sectors of the economy, and so on, are readily obtained from census data. Demographic indicators are often treated as proxies for preferences, but opinions are not solely the product of social determinism. Such indicators are better conceptualized as proxies for interests, and some research indicates they are quite limited proxies (e.g., Erikson, McIver, and Wright 1987, 798–804). Further, some scholars are careless about the theoretical implications of the failure to distinguish interests from preferences, frequently drawing erroneous normative conclusions or arguing in favor of propositions that have not been properly tested because their measured data do not fit their theoretical concepts.

Measuring legislator action is not immune from challenges, but data are more readily available. Roll-call voting records in the US Congress are easy to obtain. The harder decision is which roll calls to use and whether and how to aggregate them. Interest-group ratings based on subsets of roll calls in particular policy areas or a general set of votes indicating an ideological orientation are often employed. Poole and Rosenthal's (2007) composite indicators of ideology, which are available in a form that is comparable over time, are appropriate for some purposes. Clinton, Jackman, and Rivers's (2004) ideal point estimation methodology is an alternative with a number of posited theory-testing advantages, although few data using this method have to date been derived for any legislative body.

The challenge in the selection of roll calls is to overcome the equivalence problem—that is, of selecting roll-call data that are equivalent, as appropriate to one's theoretical expectations, with one's measures of constituency preferences or interest. Yet surmounting this challenge is essential to any test of the delegate model of representation. Both Stone (1979) and Weissberg (1979) identify this as critical. Stone (1979, 625) argues that "if independent measures of constituency opinion and representative behavior are employed, the problem of indicator equivalence is pervasive to all designs." The problem, however, is more theoretical than analytic. Stone elaborates: "[o]ur concept of representation builds in nonequivalence of the sort attacked when survey items do not 'match' roll call indicators. . . . Our concept of representation, in short, includes an institutional framework that is designed to translate mass interests (as generalized opinion about the proper direction of public policy) into policy" (1979, 625). *What this means is that many studies that purport to test an instructed-delegate model in fact cannot distinguish it from a trustee model of representation.* Democracy that is representative rather than direct dictates that legislators must function simultaneously as delegates and trustees.

Even with satisfactory measures for the key variables of constituency and legislator position, analytic challenges exist. How best to relate the two? Early work (e.g., Miller and Stokes 1963) relied on correlation coefficients. Achen (1977) discredited this approach because correlations are not comparable across samples or even across issues within samples and because the magnitude of the correlation is affected by within-constituency variances. Weissberg and Stone demonstrated that the equivalence problem means that perfect correlations can arise from situations that are instances of fundamental misrepresentation.

Alternatives to correlations advocated by Achen include proximity scores (the distance between the constituency and legislator position) and unstandardized regression coefficients. The later are generally viewed as indicators of responsiveness, with larger coefficients indicating greater responsiveness. Unstandardized regression coefficients (or the alternative from analytic techniques such as logit) have become the conventional standard for assessing representational linkages. Yet the use of proximity scores merits exploration, although they require policy-position measures for representatives and their constituents on equivalent measures that only rarely exist in datasets presently available for secondary analysis.

The most commonly used measures and analytic techniques assume a demand-driven process of representation. Constituency preferences are exogenous and fixed. They are the independent variable of interest for predicting legislator action. Statistically significant coefficients are interpreted to mean that legislators respond to constituency demands. There are few efforts to test for alternative flows of influence between these variables or to predict in advance how influence flows might vary across issues.

The remainder of this chapter will review what the empirical literature on representation tells us about how the process works. In particular, we will focus on how elections affect representation, examining the influence of turnout, candidate choice, competition, electoral frequency, and electoral change on the extent of policy representation. We will briefly review as well work on the representation of minorities. We conclude with a discussion of complex models of representation that move beyond the basic assumptions of most empirical work on the subject, and note how they can resolve a number of contradictory empirical results.

ELECTIONS AND REPRESENTATION

Elections provide one of the most important institutional venues for influencing the character and quality of representation, as discussed in general terms above. Yet particular aspects of the election process merit further discussion, either because they directly shape the character of representation or they function as mediating factors that do so. Five attributes of elections are discussed here because of their particular importance in these respects.

Turnout and Representation

A number of chapters in this volume explore the causes of individual-level and aggregate electoral turnout. One implicit assumption of such work is that levels of turnout matter for the quality of the democratic process, and hence the representational process. Empirical democratic theory also assumes that the level of electoral participation of the mass public in elections is central to the quality of representation, whether of the mass public generally or of groups that might once have endured especially poor representation (e.g., Dahl 1971, 17–32). Yet conventional research on mass political behavior rarely explores directly this expected connection. Unfortunately, the same must be said for research intended to advance general theory about the representation process.

Considerable evidence indicates that those individuals or groups in the mass public who participate more in elections also benefit more from the activities of their elected representatives. Evidence of one kind or another for this conclusion arises in studies of local government representation (e.g., Verba and Nie 1972, 265–344), the American states (e.g., Hill and Leighley 1992) and for various analyses of members of the US Congress and their constituents (e.g., Griffin and Newman 2005; Martin 2003).

Yet findings of the latter sort have not been systematically integrated with efforts to develop general theory about the representational process. Consider the classic Miller–Stokes model of dyadic policy representation and the variations on it that populate subsequent research studies. For such models the level of participation of the eligible electorate should constitute an attribute of individual constituencies that moderates the degree of representational linkage. This expectation might be elaborated in various ways, such as how higher turnout might mean that the median voter better represents the median constituent, the active electorate better reflects the partisan and policy preferences of the constituency for responsible party models, or the active electorate better reflects various sub-constituency interests or preferences. Again, however, no research has explored these possibilities.

Candidate Choice and Representation

Constituencies can influence policy representation by choosing the candidate who is closer to district preferences. Yet the evidence for *prospective* issue voting, where voters make choices among candidates based on their positions on current or expected future policy concerns, suggests that it is minimal. Stokes and Miller's (1966) analysis of the 1958 election revealed that few citizens met the basic criteria for issue voting: awareness of issues, having a position on issues, and being able to distinguish the candidates on the issues. Hurley and Hill's (1980) analysis of the 1978 congressional election revealed that little had changed—only 17 percent of survey respondents met the criteria twenty years later. Delli Carpini and Keeter's (1996, 105–34) general assessment of changes in political knowledge over the second half of the twentieth century suggests that a contemporary assessment would not deviate from those specific, earlier characterizations.

There is considerably greater evidence in favor of *retrospective* issue voting, with a number of studies providing evidence that voters punish candidates of the president's party when the president's popularity or the economy—or both—suffer (as representative examples see Hibbing and Alford 1981, Kinder and Kiewiet 1979, Tufte 1975). Both prospective and retrospective issue voting contain elements of the responsible-parties model of representation.

An alternative way to test for issue voting is to determine whether the candidate who was positioned closer to the median voter wins the election. Both Achen (1978) and Erikson (1978) have reanalyzed the Miller–Stokes data (introducing corrections for error in the measurement of constituency opinion) and come to opposite conclusions. Erikson finds constituency opinion more highly correlated with the positions of winners than losers, while Achen finds losers located closer to constituency than winners on his measures of proximity and centrism, although winners performed better on his measure of responsiveness. Ansolabehere, Snyder, and Stewart (2001) cite strong evidence over a lengthy time period for divergent positioning by congressional candidates that is largely influenced by the national positions of the two major parties (with greater responsiveness to districts in the 1940s to 1970s period). They find evidence of generalized ideological voting, concluding that "the strong correlation between incumbents' and districts' ideologies arises almost entirely because voters are presented with largely partisan choices and select the candidate whose party more closely resembles them" (152).

In sum, the literature on issue voting yields contradictory and inconclusive evidence regarding its utility for achieving representation. Overall, however, there is more evidence for representation achieved through the agency of party than through the Downsian spatial model.

Electoral Proximity and Representation

The staggered character and longer terms served by senators in states and the US Congress allow scholars to test whether electoral proximity induces senators to attend more closely to constituent preferences. Kuklinski (1978) demonstrated that California senators exhibited roll-call voting patterns that correlated more highly with constituent opinion on contemporary liberalism in reelection years than in the first three years of their term. In contrast, California assembly members' roll-call voting patterns showed a constant (and generally higher) level of correlation with constituency opinion. Elling (1982) and Thomas (1985) examined shifts in roll-call voting patterns by US senators over the course of their six-year terms, controlling for party and region. In general, both found that most groups of senators exhibited changes in their roll-call behavior, for the most part becoming more moderate. Neither analysis has a clear measure of constituency preference, but Elling interprets observed moderation as a shift toward the median voter while Thomas interprets it as a shift toward the position of likely electoral opponents.

Ahuja (1994) improves on Elling and Thomas by testing the proximity hypothesis with a survey-based measure of constituency opinion. Using data from the 1988 and 1990 Senate Election Study, he finds that senators facing reelection are more responsive to mean constituency preferences than those who are not. Differential responsiveness to voters by those senators standing for reelection is also confirmed in Griffin and Newman's (2005) analysis of senatorial responsiveness to voters and non-voters, covering the 101st through 107th senates.

The twin findings of senatorial moderation of voting behavior and greater responsiveness to the mean constituency (or voter) position in election years indicate episodic support for a median-voter model of representation. But what sort of representation is achieved in the earlier portion of a senatorial term? There is a good deal of evidence that a partisan model is operative then.

The fact that each state has two senators allows for tests of the "two constituencies" thesis—that is, that senators are responding to different portions of the full state. Various scholars have shown that senators from mixed-party delegations exhibit quite different patterns of roll-call voting while representing the same state. Some contend that they are responding to reelection constituencies (e.g., Bullock and Brady 1983; Markus 1974) while others (e.g., Wright 1989) argue that the responsiveness is to state party elites. In either case, this supports a partisan model of representation.

Yet, if dyadic partisan representation arises from senator responsiveness to the reelection constituency, one might legitimately wonder whether roll-call vote shifting in an election year is necessary. Presumably responsiveness to the reelection constituency would be enough to insure reelection. Shapiro et al. (1990) offer a variation on the two-constituencies thesis that accounts for selective election-year shifts. Comparing the effects of co-partisan, opposition partisan, and independent constituents on roll-call voting, they find that senators in states where their own party is dominant are responsive to their own partisans rather than to other constituency groups, and the result holds regardless of whether these senators are running for reelection. In contrast, those senators representing states not dominated by their own party do show differential patterns of responsiveness in election years, with independents (the ranks of which likely contain the median voter) as election-year beneficiaries. Thus the relative size of the partisan groupings within the state can affect how senators respond to constituency preferences (see also Bishin 2000). Clinton's (2006) findings for the 106th House may be interpreted as partially corroborating evidence: minority-party Democrats were more responsive to weighted non-same-party ideology than they were to Democratic identifiers' ideology, while majority-party Republican House members showed greater responsiveness to the ideology of Republican constituents.

Competition and Representation

A different approach to the role of elections is to focus on the impact of electoral competition on representation. The most basic version of the "marginality hypothesis" is that legislators from highly competitive districts will be more responsive to median constituency preferences than will legislators from non-competitive or safe districts. A related, and sometimes confused, hypothesis is that legislators from marginal districts will be less loyal to their party leadership in roll-call voting than those from safe districts. This is sometimes presented as the hypothesis that members from marginal districts will display moderate voting patterns while safe members are more likely to be extremists.

Numerous scholars have tested variants of the marginality hypothesis, with varying results (not all of which can be reviewed here). Fiorina (1973) offers a compelling critique of early work on the topic that applies equally well to much that was done later. The core of the critique is that a proper test of the impact of marginality on representation requires a measure of constituency attitude and within-district rather than across-district comparisons of legislator responsiveness. Fiorina accomplishes this by comparing the legislative voting behavior of switched-seat congressmen (a phenomenon produced by electoral competition) and shows that Democrats who unseated Republicans (and vice versa) vote differently while representing the same geographic constituency. Fiorina contends, like Miller (1970) and Huntington (1950) before him, that marginal members do not represent the median voter. In contrast, Griffin (2006) examines the period 1972–2000 and finds that greater competition in presidential races in House districts heightens House members' responsiveness to mean constituency ideology, particularly after 1992 (although competition in presidential races is not strictly faithful to the marginality hypothesis, which concerns the marginality of legislators *per se*).

A close reading of the literature on the subject leads to the firm conclusion that the marginality hypothesis is wrong, except for when it is right. What has been given less systematic attention is the interesting question of why such a pattern of results is observed. To begin to understand why, we must return to the basic assumption of the hypothesis.

The underlying logic of the marginality hypothesis in its purest form is that competition forces legislators to respond to the preferences of the median voter of the full constituency. Failure to do so will allow an opponent to position at the median and defeat the incumbent who strays from that point. Safe incumbents can ignore the median voter in favor of voting their own or their party leadership's preferences without fear of electoral retribution. Researchers often fail to account for the fact that marginal districts are most likely heterogeneous with respect to demographic factors and the distribution of party identification while safe districts are likely to be more homogeneous in this regard. Focusing on the location of the full constituency median ignores the possibility that both safe and marginal members represent their partisan or reelection constituencies.

The nature of the district determines how extensive a portion of the full constituency the electoral constituency is. In homogeneous districts the medians of the full and electoral constituencies will be closer together than their respective locations in diverse districts. This is particularly important in interpreting the results of those studies that show that safe members exhibit higher levels of party loyalty than marginal members—for the former group, party and (full) constituency are not countervailing forces. For marginal members, the full constituency and the electoral constituency medians will be further apart, leading to greater cross-pressures for these representatives. Deckard (1976) recognizes this with her introduction of controls for district "typicality" (i.e., the extent to which a district is demographically typical of one for the party of its representative). She finds that both the competitiveness of a district and the party loyalty of its representative are a function of the nature of the district, although the relationship is much clearer for the majority party. Deckard also argues that the original statement of the marginality hypothesis may have the causality wrong—electoral safety may derive from responsiveness rather than the reverse.

Kuklinski's findings (1977) on the effects of competition for responsiveness in the domain of "contemporary liberalism" echo Deckard's, despite his disavowal of her inclusion of district typicality. While representatives from competitive districts exhibited greater party disloyalty on this domain than those from safe districts, this disloyalty did not make the marginal members more responsive to constituency than their safer colleagues. Constituency mean positions in safe versus competitive districts were located such that safe members could simultaneously be responsive to constituency and remain loyal to their party positions on roll-call votes, while marginal members had to defect from the party position to respond.

The fundamental importance of the nature of the district for responsiveness is further supported by Bailey and Brady's work (1998) on free-trade votes in the US Senate. They offer evidence that the impact of constituency characteristics on trade votes is conditional on heterogeneity within the state, with constituency playing a clear role in homogeneous states, as well as evidence that senators of different parties respond to constituency factors that are typical of their party's broad electoral coalition.

The overall pattern of results of tests of the marginality hypothesis is more consistent with a responsible-parties model of representation than with a median-voter model of representation. Yet Kuklinski's 1977 work demonstrates that the effects of electoral competition vary across issue domains, suggesting that for some issue types, the median-voter model is operative. On the issue of taxation—a salient issue that was not clearly related to typical party positions—competition raised responsiveness to the mean constituency position. What is needed to reconcile the contradictions in this literature is a theory of representation that allows the effects of competition to vary and predicts the circumstances under which it should matter. We offer such a theory later in this chapter.

The Rise of the Incumbency Advantage

Regardless of the role of competition, there is ample evidence that the number of competitive seats in the US House declined during the 1960s. Tufte (1973) and Mayhew (1974a) offered evidence that incumbent members of the House began winning by larger margins in the late 1960s, and thus were more insulated than they had been from the probability of electoral sanction (but see Jacobson 1987 for a contrary point of view). These observations resulted in the proliferation of congressional elections research as scholars sought to identify the causes and consequences of the incumbency advantage.

The causes have been assigned to a variety of mutually reinforcing factors, including a decline in the impact of party identification that coincided with the rise in electoral margins (and has since been reversed), the cultivation of a personal vote through advertising, credit claiming, and attention to homestyle, and the growth of federal programs that allows House members to run interference with a bloated bureaucracy on behalf of constituents who then reward them electorally (see Burden and Wichowsky in this volume, Chapter 24, for citations to particular works on these points).

More important for the present chapter are the consequences of this change for representation. Most accounts contend that dyadic representation has not suffered from an increased incumbency advantage. Indeed, allocation and service responsiveness by House members are better than ever, and these benefits are delivered to constituents regardless of partisanship. Position taking by House members creates an illusion of policy responsiveness to constituency as members introduce, co-sponsor, or vote for bills that they know will never become law or pander to constituents by supporting popular but flawed policies. Mayhew (1974b), Fenno (1978), and Fiorina (1989) offer extended treatments of these subjects.

The wide margins incumbents enjoy make it difficult for national partisan tides to alter the partisan composition of Congress, especially the House. At the collective level, then, representation suffers as a consequence of limited partisan accountability—individual legislators are not held accountable for the collective actions of their party, and even when a party is punished at the polls the vote loss suffered by incumbents is not sufficient to unseat them. By the early 1990s, researchers were claiming that the House was nearly immune to electoral tides, and that only an unusual confluence of partisan tide and open seats persisting across several congressional elections could alter the House majority (Ansolabehere, Brady, and

Fiorina 1992). Ironically, that is precisely what allowed the 1994 Republican take-over.

Despite laments about the decline of collective accountability there have been few attempts to provide systematic evidence for its disappearance. Sweeping policy changes that follow electoral realignments are sometimes held up as evidence of party responsibility and accountability. In these critical election years, the victorious party promised and delivered change. The persistent new electoral alignments that followed are evidence of retrospective voter approval. During realignments, the responsible-party model of linkage is operative (Brady 1988; Clubb, Flanigan, and Zingale 1980).

There is an unacknowledged assumption in such accounts that the policies ushered in by realignments were good ones. The same assumption in reverse characterizes the work of those who lament the incumbency advantage—somehow it is allowing bad policy to triumph over good, allowing national interests to be superseded by local ones. But no scientific scholarship has yet defined the national interest separate from normative preferences.

The thesis of declining accountability receives some support when contrasting representation in the late 1950s and 1970s if we take that to mean representation of partisan or public preferences aggregated nationally. Partisan representation was lower within the Democratic party in the 1970s than in the 1950s, but it improved within the Republican party between the two time periods. Collective representation was lower in the latter time period (Hurley 1989a). Yet by the 1980s partisan representation had improved considerably within the Democratic party (Hurley 1989b), suggesting that the incumbency advantage alone is not responsible for declining partisan or collective representation.

"Minority" Representation

Considerable research explores normatively or empirically the representation of one or another American ethnic or racial minority group. Some research has also assessed the representation of gay and lesbian political interests (Haider-Markel 1999) and the implications of the voting participation of disabled Americans for their political representation (Schur et al. 2002). How might we identify the universe of minority groups for which such research is of interest? Many argue that such consideration is appropriate for traditionally underrepresented groups (e.g., Mansbridge 1999). By this criterion women are also often judged to be appropriate subjects for such research. But is this criterion sufficient? Why are not the political interests of other demographic or "special interest" groups of equal interest? And might we really understand the representation of traditionally underrepresented groups if we only study a select few of those, *or* if we fail to execute comparable analyses for a wide range of other categorical groups?

Another concern about research on underrepresented groups is with the scientific goals of such scholarship. There are *particular* questions about African American and Latino and women's representation that have notable factual, normative, or public-policy implications. Research on these questions by political scientists may help answer these questions. Some of this work also has legal relevance, as when it assesses the effectiveness of institutional remedies intended to enhance representation *or* the implications for representation of conventional political rules, such as those for the creation of electoral constituencies (e.g., Cameron, Epstein, and O'halloran 1996; Canon 1999).

Yet extant research on the representation of ethnic minorities, women, and other underrepresented groups is not well integrated with the general theoretical concerns that motivate traditional scholarship on representation and that are outlined in the first portion of this chapter. One avenue for such integration is suggested by an often-ignored parallel discussed in traditional representation research. It has long been recognized that *partisan minorities* in electoral constituencies typically enjoy little representation, and various empirical studies have documented the degree to which this is the case. Yet partisan-minority underrepresentation can be accounted for theoretically when party is an integral part of one's theory about mass–elite linkages and, perhaps, when other factors that condition the representational linkage like constituency homogeneity, candidate marginality, and the like are also considered. This example may also suggest an approach, and a series of causal forces, that might produce a theoretically informed explanation for variations in the representation of underrepresented groups generally.

A second possible approach for developing stronger theory on this topic is suggested by Weissberg (1978, 542–3), who discusses how in principle any minority interest might be advantaged by collective as opposed to dyadic representation. He and Hurley (1982) illustrate alternative assumptions and empirical approaches for assessing levels of collective vs. dyadic representation. Yet little research on ethnic-minority or women's representation has recognized explicitly the theoretical potential of a collective representation approach. Among the few exceptions, Hero and Tolbert (1995) offer some exploration of dyadic and collective representation of Latinos in Congress. Reingold (1992) explored the attitudes of women legislators in two states and found evidence of their commitment to represent women as a group, and Berkman and O'Connor's (1993) work on state legislatures suggests that women may have a policy impact only after their numbers reach some critical mass in an institution.

The prospects for dyadic representation of underrepresented groups are, of course, limited precisely because of their minority status. Despite the existence of some "majority-minority" districts, no national electoral district or state represented by an African American includes only African American residents. No district or state represented by a woman includes only female residents. Thus efforts to assess the conditions under which dyadic representation of minorities is enhanced have been especially constrained by this "structural" limitation. Yet research such as that of Hero and Tolbert (1995), Hutchings, McClerking, and Charles (2004), and Overby and Cosgrove (1996) explores ethnic-minority representation under varying levels of minority constituency size as imposed by this constraint.

Other notable research on minority representation in national political institutions has considered how descriptive representation might lead to policy representation. Early work and debate on this question were considerably divided. Recent work like that of Griffin and Newman (2007), Hero and Tolbert (1995), and Kerr and Miller (1997), however, finds evidence of independent, positive policy consequences of descriptive representation along with policy representation based on the party of the legislator.

Scholarship on minority representation is likely most advanced in the study of local and state venues, where there are relatively larger numbers of elected officials of color and who are women (as recent examples, see Meier et al. 2005; Preuhs 2006). The causes of descriptive, allocational, and policy representation have all been studied in such locales. Yet the complexity of the possible causal forces—such as how the size of the minority population varies in individual districts, the method of election employed in a particular local or state political system, the varying size and powers of the possible legislative bodies that might be examined, the competitiveness of elections for and electoral success of minority candidates, and the relevance of broader representational forces such as those based on political party, along with varying foci in terms of the particular form of representation under study—mean that there is little theoretical consensus in the findings of such research.

Further, research that examines whether legislators of color or female legislators act on behalf of minorities or women generally employs a trustee model of representation. That is, such research seeks the causes for responsiveness to constituency interests that the researcher *assumes* based on minority social or economic position, shared fate, or the like, rather than on measured group preferences. This focus is typically dictated because of the rarity of having survey data on the literal preferences of the group. Yet the implications of such research for some forms of representation are highly circumscribed.

In sum, even the most advanced research in this area has not produced a general, or generally accepted, assessment of the conditions which account for representational outcomes. The challenge, then, in terms of scientific goals is to move beyond particular questions to general explanations and theory.

COMPLEX MODELS OF REPRESENTATION

The work discussed so far in this chapter is based on the simple demand-input model of representation: constituency opinion is the independent variable and legislators' attitudes and actions are the dependent variables. But various scholars have proposed and tested models that posit a more complex set of relationships than the demand-input one, in line with Kuklinski and Segura's (1995) call for consideration of endogeneity, exogeneity, space, and time.

The most basic of this class of models tests for the effects of changes in public opinion on changes in public policy. Page and Shapiro (1983) examine numerous instances of specific opinion and policy changes and conclude that opinion change leads to alterations in policy, especially when the shift in public opinion is substantial and stable. Hartley and Russett (1992) look for the effects of variation in the proportion of the public stating military expenditures are too high (or too low) on total obligational authority for military spending over a twenty-five-year period, and find that opinion change affects policy. Both sets of researchers probe the possibility that changes in policy lead to changes in opinion. Although these tests do not completely rule out that possibility, both indicate public opinion has an exogenous role in this dynamic process. Note that these models are highly aggregated (that is, collective) and offer little insight into the specific linkage process.

Stimson, MacKuen, and Erikson (1995) offer a more refined look at the process, testing for the direct effects of general opinion changes (i.e., "policy mood") on policy makers' behaviors, the effects of opinion change on the composition of policy-making institutions (i.e., electoral effects), and the effects of opinion change on policy, controlled for electoral effects. Electoral effects are the indirect effects of opinion on policy (changing policy by changing the policy makers). But if independent effects of opinion on policy persist with electoral effects controlled, then politicians are responding to changing public tastes directly as well as indirectly. Their tests reveal both direct and indirect effects on opinion change on policy, and the direct effects of opinion are particularly pronounced for the President and the House of Representatives. Note that the finding that direct effects of opinion persist even with electoral effects controlled still assigns a highly important role to elections. Stimson et al. argue that politicians respond to opinion precisely because they anticipate an electoral sanction if they do not and therefore act to ward it off. Public opinion plays a primary causal role in this model.

Gerber and Jackson (1993) question the assumption that public preferences are exogenous to institutions. They demonstrate that preferences of Democratic and Republican identifiers changed in response to changes in the positions of the two parties as organizations on the issues of civil rights and the Vietnam War. Such a finding raises the possibility of congruence between public opinion and attitudes or actions of public officials arising from elite influence rather than public demand. Relatedly, Hill and Hinton-Andersson (1995) provide evidence that public policy making in the American states is driven by a reciprocal-influence, opinion-sharing process between the mass public and the political elite. The findings of both these studies suggest that the fundamental assumption of the demand-input model is incorrect.

Wlezien (1995) also allows public opinion to be endogenous to the representative process. He posits a negative feedback model that allows opinion to move policy, but in turn policy moves opinion. Using time-series data on preferences for more or less spending on various government programs, he finds evidence for reciprocal relationships in the area of defense spending, and to a lesser extent in the area of social welfare.

Hurley and Hill (2003) have proposed a theory of representational linkages that predicts that the nature of linkages between constituencies and representatives will vary depending on two aspects of the nature of issues: their complexity as perceived by the public and the nature of the cleavage between the two parties. Issues that are simultaneously uncomplicated and cross-cutting should conform to the standard demand-input or delegate model of representation. If issues are easy for the public to follow, legislators have an incentive to attend to constituency preferences. Failure to do so will allow an electoral opponent to exploit such an issue, and such electoral challenges will be credible if the issue cross-cuts party positions. In contrast, the public is unlikely to exercise influence on complex issues that cross-cut the lines of party cleavage. The difficulty of such issues renders them problematic as campaign themes to be exploited by challengers seeking to unseat incumbents. Therefore little in the way of systematic linkages between constituencies and representatives should be observed for such issues.

Simple issues that define the fundamental ideological positions of the respective parties should exhibit reciprocal linkages between constituents and representatives, and these linkages should be especially strong between a legislator and his or her co-partisan constituents. Members of a party may owe their electoral success to their party's—and their own—position on such an issue. A general election opponent will have difficulty exploiting such an issue because the incumbent's party owns it. Partisan constituents demand continuation of policies they like and expect from a party, and elected members of that party reinforce the demand through continued emphasis of the party's commitment on the issue.

Complex party-defining issues result when party elites develop clear and opposing positions on difficult issues that had been cross-cutting or when new dimensions of a party-defining simple issue arise that make it complicated. Partisan elites adopt an educational role in these circumstances, working to influence the public on these issues. Consequently, the flow of influence should be from elites to mass but not the reverse. New positions adopted by party elites may both alienate and attract citizens, potentially altering the nature of a party's electoral coalition. For this reason, complex party-defining issues may precipitate realignments, but by the time one is solidified the issue is likely to have been simplified in the public understanding and a demand link should develop.

This latter point underscores the fact that issues evolve over time. Issues that cross-cut party lines in one year may define the line of cleavage a decade later. Issues that were once complex can come to be understood as simple, or new considerations may arise to complicate what was once an easy matter. Thus predicting the nature of representational linkages requires attention to the historical context of issues.

In tests of the theory, Hill and Hurley (1999) demonstrated that the demand-input model operated for civil rights in the late 1950s, at which time it was a simple, cross-cutting issue, and that no linkages existed between constituents and representatives on complex cross-cutting matters of foreign policy. Social welfare exhibits reciprocal linkages in the 1950s, at which time it is fairly characterized as a simple, party-defining issue. A variety of factors complicated social welfare as a partisan issue by the late 1970s and 1980s, and empirical tests with data from 1978 and 1988 show only one-way links from elected legislators to constituents for these years, as anticipated by the theory (Hurley and Hill 2003).

Many of the standard findings in the representation literature are compatible with this issue-based theory of representation. Equally important, many of the contradictions in the literature can be reconciled by it. In general, legislators represent full constituencies on cross-cutting issues but represent their co-partisans on party-defining issues. Marginality should matter for representation on cross-cutting issues but not on party-defining issues. Analyses of the same general issue at different points in time may yield different results because the issue has evolved with respect to complexity or cleavage or both.

CONCLUSION

We have summarized the most fundamental concepts, assumptions, and findings in research on representation in the American political system. Limitations of space have forced us to deal summarily with some bodies of scholarship and to ignore others, like most of that on subnational governments, almost entirely. Yet the most prominent and the best replicated work in this field is considered in some detail. This scholarship has produced a significant body of well-established research findings, too, although notable puzzles remain along with differences of opinion about the optimal directions for future research.

We have argued, drawing on our own work but also that of many others, that an accurate, systematic characterization of the process of representation must adopt the assumptions behind the "complex models" outlined in the preceding section of this chapter. This is, then, the direction for future research that we judge to be essential and profitable. If that direction is our future, it is wise to remember that it is part of our past, as well. Miller and Stokes (1963, 56) observed of the findings of their seminal investigation of Congressional representation, that "[t]he American system is a mixture, to which the Burkean, instructed-delegate, and responsible-party models all can be said to have contributed elements. Moreover, variations in the representative relation are most likely to occur as we move from one policy domain to another." Moving forward with the research program we recommend, then, is in the spirit of perhaps the most remarkable single research report in this field.

Yet moving forward will enrich our knowledge and our theory, just as an abundant body of scholarship after Miller and Stokes has already done. Our theory might eventually be more rigorous, and more broadly applicable across time, levels of American government, and perhaps across additional nations. It might also— and should in our view—incorporate more than policy representation, as much scholarship we have summarized urges.

References

ACHEN, C. 1977. Measuring Representation: Pitfalls of the Correlation Coefficient. *American Journal of Political Science*, 21: 805–15.
—— 1978. Measuring Representation. *American Journal of Political Science*, 22: 475–510.
AHUJA, S. 1994. Electoral Status and Representation in the United State Senate: Does Temporal Proximity to Election Matter? *American Politics Quarterly*, 22: 104–18.
ANSOLABEHERE, S., BRADY, D., and FIORINA, M. 1992. The Vanishing Marginals and Electoral Responsiveness. *British Journal of Political Science*, 22: 21–38.
—— SNYDER, J. M. JR., and STEWART, C. III. 2001. Candidate Positioning in U.S. House Elections. *American Journal of Political Science*, 45: 136–59.
BAILEY, M. and BRADY, D. W. 1998. Heterogeneity and Representation: The Senate and Free Trade. *American Journal of Political Science*, 42: 524–44.
BERKMAN, M. B. and OCONNOR, R. E. 1993. Do Women Legislators Matter? Female Legislators and State Abortion Policy. *American Politics Quarterly*, 21: 102–24.
BIANCO, W. T. 1994. *Trust: Representatives and Constituents*. Ann Arbor, Mich.: The University of Michigan Press.
BISHIN, B. 2000. Constituency Influence in Congress: Does Subconstituency Matter? *Legislative Studies Quarterly*, 25: 389–415.
BRADY, D. W. 1988. *Critical Elections and Congressional Policymaking*. Stanford, Calif.: Stanford University Press.

BULLOCK, C. S. III and BRADY, D. W. 1983. Party, Constituency, and Roll Call Voting in the U.S. Senate. *Legislative Studies Quarterly*, 8: 29–43.

CAMERON, C., EPSTEIN, D., and OHALLORAN, S. 1996. Do Majority-Minority Districts Maximize Substantive Black Representation in Congress? *American Political Science Review*, 90: 794–812.

CANON, D. T. 1999. *Race, Redistricting, and Representation.* Chicago: University of Chicago Press.

CLINTON, J. 2006. Representation in Congress: Constituents and Roll Calls in the 106th House. *Journal of Politics*, 68: 397–409.

—— JACKMAN, S., and RIVERS, D. 2004. The Statistical Analysis of Roll Call Data. *American Political Science Review*, 98: 355–70.

CLUBB, J., FLANIGAN, W., and ZINGALE, N. 1980. *Partisan Realignment: Voters, Parties and Government in American History.* Beverly Hills, Calif.: Sage.

DAHL, R. A. 1971. *Polyarchy.* New Haven, Conn.: Yale University Press.

DECKARD, B. S. 1976. Electoral Marginality and Party Loyalty in House Roll Call Voting. *American Journal of Political Science*, 20: 469–82.

DELLI CARPINI, M. X. and KEETER, S. 1996. *What Americans Know about Politics and Why It Matters.* New Haven, Conn.: Yale University Press.

ELLING, R. C. 1982. Ideological Change in the United States Senate: Time and Electoral Responsiveness. *Legislative Studies Quarterly*, 7: 75–92.

ERIKSON, R. S. 1978. Constituency Opinion and Congressional Behavior: A Reexamination of the Miller-Stokes Data. *American Journal of Political Science*, 22: 511–35.

—— McIVER, J. P., and WRIGHT, G. C. JR. 1987. State Political Culture and Pubic Opinion. *American Political Science Review*, 81: 797–813.

EULAU, H. and KARPS, P. 1977. The Puzzle of Representation: Specifying Components of Responsiveness. *Legislative Studies Quarterly*, 2: 233–54.

FENNO, R. F. JR. 1978. *Home Style.* Boston: Little Brown.

FIORINA, M. 1973. Electoral Margins, Constituency Influence, and Policy Moderation: A Critical Assessment. *American Politics Quarterly*, 1: 479–98.

—— 1989. *Congress: Keystone of the Washington* Establishment, 2nd edn. New Haven, Conn.: Yale University Press.

GERBER, E. R. and JACKSON, J. E. 1993. Endogeneous Preferences and the Study of Institutions. *American Political Science Review*, 87: 639–56.

GRIFFIN, J. D. 2006. Electoral Competition and Democratic Responsiveness: A Defense of the Marginality Hypothesis. *Journal of Politics*, 68: 911–21.

—— and NEWMAN, B. 2005. Are Voters Better Represented? *Journal of Politics*, 67: 1206–27.

—— —— 2007. The Unequal Representation of Latinos and Whites. *Journal of Politics*, 69: 1032–46.

HAIDER-MARKEL, D. P. 1999. Morality Policy and Individual-Level Political Behavior: The Case of Legislative Voting on Lesbian and Gay Issues. *Policy Studies Journal*, 27/4: 735–49.

HARTLEY, T. and RUSSETT, B. 1992. Public Opinion and the Common Defense: Who Governs Military Spending in the United States? *American Political Science Review*, 86: 905–15.

HERO, R. E. and TOLBERT, C. J. 1995. Latinos and Substantive Representation in the U.S. House of Representatives: Direct, Indirect, or Nonexistent? *American Journal of Political Science*, 39: 640–52.

HIBBING, J. and ALFORD, J. 1981. The Electoral Impact of Economic Conditions: Who is Held Responsible? *American Journal of Political Science*, 25: 423–39.

HILL, K. Q. and HINTON-ANDERSSON, A. 1995. Pathways of Representation: A Causal Analysis of Public Opinion-Public Policy Linkages. *American Journal of Political Science*, 39, 924–35.

—— and HURLEY, P. A. 1999. Dyadic Representation Reappraised. *American Journal of Political Science*, 43: 109–37.

—— and LEIGHLEY, J. E. 1992. The Policy Consequences of Class Bias in American State Electorates. *American Journal of Political Science*, 36: 351–65.

HUNTINGTON, S. 1950. A Revised Theory of American Party Politics. *American Political Science Review*, 44: 669–77.

HURLEY, P. A. 1982. Collective Representation Reappraised. *Legislative Studies Quarterly*, 7: 119–36.

—— 1989a. Party Dealignment and Policy Representation in the House of Representatives: Comparing Opinion-Policy Congruence in the 1950s and 1970s. *Congress and the Presidency*, 16: 37–55.

—— 1989b. Partisan Representation and the Failure of Realignment in the 1980s. *American Journal of Political Science*, 33: 240–61.

—— and HILL, K. Q. 1980. The Prospects for Issue Voting in Contemporary Congressional Elections: An Assessment of Citizen Awareness and Representation. *American Politics Quarterly*, 8: 425–48.

—— —— 2003. Beyond the Demand-Input Model: A Theory of Representational Linkages. *Journal of Politics*, 65: 304–26.

HUTCHINGS, V. L, McCLERKING, H. K., and CHARLES, G.-U. 2004. Congressional Representation of Black Interests: Recognizing the Importance of Stability. *Journal of Politics*, 66: 450–68.

JACOBSON, G. C. 1987. The Marginals Never Vanished: Incumbency and Competition in Elections to the U.S. House of Representatives 1852–1982. *American Journal of Political Science*, 31: 126–41.

KERR, B. and MILLER, W. 1997. Latino Representation: It's Direct and Indirect. *American Journal of Political Science*, 41: 1066–71.

KINDER, D. and KIEWEIT, R. 1979. Economic Grievances and Political Behavior: The Role of Personal Discontents and Collective Judgments in Congressional Voting. *American Journal of Political Science*, 23: 495–527.

KUKLINSKI, J. H. 1977. District Competitiveness and Legislative Roll Call Behavior: A Reassessment of the Marginality Hypothesis. *American Journal of Political Science*, 21: 627–38.

—— 1978. Representativeness and Elections: A Policy Analysis. *American Political Science Review*, 72: 165–77.

—— and SEGURA, G. M. 1995. Endogeneity, Exogeneity, Time, and Space in Political Representation. *Legislative Studies Quarterly*, 20: 3–21.

LEOGRANDE, W. M. and JEYDEL, A. S. 1997. Using Presidential Election Returns to Measure Constituency Ideology. *American Politics Quarterly*, 25: 3–18.

MANSBRIDGE, J. 1999. Should Blacks Represent Blacks and Women Represent Women? A Contingent "Yes." *Journal of Politics*, 61: 628–57.

Markus, G. B. 1974. Electoral Coalitions and Senate Roll Call Behavior. *American Journal of Political Science*, 18: 595–607.

Martin, P. S. 2003. Voting's Rewards: Voter Turnout, Attentive Publics, and Congressional Allocation of Federal Money. *American Journal of Political Science*, 47: 110–27.

Mayhew, D. R. 1974a. Congressional Elections: The Case of the Vanishing Marginals. *Polity*, 6: 295–317.

—— 1974b. *Congress: The Electoral Connection*. New Haven, Conn.: Yale University Press.

Meier, K. J., Juenke, E. G., Wrinkle, R. D., and Polinard, J. L. 2005. Structural Choices and Representational Biases: The Post-Election Color of Representation. *American Journal of Political Science*, 49: 758–68.

Miller, W. E. 1970. Majority Rule and the Representative Systems of Government. In *Mass Politics*, ed. E. Allardt and S. Rokkan. New York: Free Press.

—— and Stokes, D. 1963. Constituency Influence in Congress. *American Political Science Review*, 57: 45–56.

Overby, L. M. and Cosgrove, K. M. 1996. Unintended Consequences? Racial Redistricting and the Representation of Minority Interests. *Journal of Politics*, 58: 540–50.

Page, B. and Shapiro, R. 1983. Effects of Public Opinion on Policy. *American Political Science Review*, 77: 175–90.

Pitkin, H. 1967. *The Concept of Representation*. Berkeley, Calif.: University of California Press.

Poole, K. T. and Rosenthal, H. 2007. *Ideology and Congress*. New Brunswick, N.J.: Transaction Publishers.

Preuhs, R. R. 2006. The Conditional Effects of Minority Descriptive Representation: Black Legislators and Policy Influence in the American States. *Journal of Politics*, 68: 585–99.

Reingold, B. 1992. Concepts of Representation Among Male and Female State Legislators. *Legislative Studies Quarterly*, 4: 509–37.

Schur, L., Shields, T., Kruse, D., and Schriner, K. 2002. Enabling Democracy: Disability and Voter Turnout. *Political Research Quarterly*, 55: 167–90.

Shapiro, C., Brady, D., Brody, R., and Ferejohn, J. 1990. Linking Constituency Opinion and Senate Voting Scores: A Hybrid Explanation. *Legislative Studies Quarterly*, 15: 599–622.

Stimson, J. A., MacKuen, M. B., and Erickson, R. S. 1995. Dynamic Representation. *American Political Science Review*, 89: 543–65.

Stokes, D. E. and Miller, W. E. 1966. Party Government and the Saliency of Congress. In *Elections and the Political Order*, ed. A. Campbell, P. Converse, W. Miller, and D. Stokes. New York: John Wiley.

Stone, W. 1979. Measuring Constituency-Representative Linkages: Problems and Prospects. *Legislative Studies Quarterly*, 4: 623–39.

Thomas, M. 1985. Election Proximity and Senatorial Roll Call Voting. *American Journal of Political Science*, 29: 96–111.

Tufte, E. 1973. The Relationship between Seats and Votes in Two-Party Systems. *American Political Science Review*, 67: 540–54.

—— 1975. Determining the Outcomes of Midterm Congressional Elections. *American Political Science Review*, 69: 812–26.

Verba, S. and Nie, N. H. 1972. *Participation in America*. New York: Harper & Row.

Wahlke, J. 1971. Policy Demands and System Support: The Role of the Represented. *British Journal of Political Science*, 1: 271–90.

WEISSBERG, R. 1978. Collective v. Dyadic Representation in Congress. *American Political Science Review*, 72: 535–47.

—— 1979. Assessing Legislator-Constituency Policy Agreement. *Legislative Studies Quarterly*, 4: 605–22.

WLEZIEN, C. 1995. The Public as Thermostat: Dynamics of Preferences for Spending. *American Journal of Political Science*, 39: 981–1000.

WRIGHT, G. C. 1989. Policy Voting in the U.S. Senate: Who is Represented? *Legislative Studies Quarterly*, 14: 465–86.

Name Index

Note: Includes all referenced authors.

Subject Index